THE AGE OF

SİNAN

ARCHITECTURAL CULTURE IN THE OTTOMAN EMPIRE

THE AGE OF

SİNAN

ARCHITECTURAL CULTURE IN THE OTTOMAN EMPIRE

GÜLRU NECIPOĞLU

Architectural drawings and photographs of Sinan's works
by Arben N. Arapi and Reha Günay

REAKTION BOOKS

To Cemal

Published by Reaktion Books Ltd
33 Great Sutton Street
London EC1V 0DX
www.reaktionbooks.co.uk

First published 2005
Reprinted with corrections 2011

Published with the assistance of the Getty Grant Program

Additional contributions have been made by The Aga Khan Program of Islamic Architecture at Harvard University and the Massachusetts Institute of Technology, The Aga Khan Trust for Culture, Geneva, and The Institute of Turkish Studies Grant Program

Printed and bound in Hong Kong

British Library Cataloguing in Publication Data

Necipoglu, Gulru
The age of Sinan : architectural culture in the Ottoman Empire
1.Sinan, Mimar, 1489 or 90-1588 2.Mosques – Turkey – Design and construction – History – 16th century 3.Architecture, Ottoman
I.Title
726.2'092

ISBN 978 1 86189 253 9

Contents

Acknowledgements

I began to conceptualize this book a decade ago during a sabbatical leave from Harvard University in 1993–94, when the bulk of my fieldwork and research in archives and manuscript libraries was completed. This was followed by fragmented periods of research over the summers and trips to sites graced with Sinan's monuments. After an unforseen interruption of nearly two years due to health problems, the thematic chapters of the book were written during another sabbatical in 1998–99. It was only after writing those chapters, which were to be followed by a brief appendix of monuments, that I realized my initial outline had to be modified.

I decided to treat the monuments much more extensively than originally planned because their analysis in existing publications focused primarily on formal aspects. I felt the need to integrate unpublished sources collected over the years with my own readings of the monuments, combining contextual and formal analyses. The decision to add interpretative chapters on individual monuments doubled the length of the book, which consequently took many more years to complete.

I am grateful to Michael Leaman, the General Editor at Reaktion Books, for his steadfast interest in this book since we first met in 1998, and his readiness to accommodate subsequent changes in scope. I am particularly thankful for his generosity with the number of pages and illustrations that allowed me to explore my project in depth, avoiding the pitfalls of surveys and introductory texts. I deeply appreciate his unwavering faith in my effort to create a comprehensive book evoking the cultural moment of intense creativity embodied in Sinan's architecture, a book accessible to general readers and, hopefully, provocative to specialists.

Such an undertaking could not have been realized without the help of many institutions and individuals. My initial research during the academic year 1993–94 was supported by a National Endowment for the Humanities Fellowship awarded by the American Research Institute in Turkey. All the remaining funding for research, travel and illustrations came together with a publication subvention from the generous endowment of the Aga Khan Program for Islamic Architecture at Harvard University and the Massachusetts Institute of Technology. I am very grateful to the Aga Khan Trust for Culture and the Getty Center for the History of Art and the Humanities for additional publication grants awarded to Reaktion Books for this project.

Institutions that invited me to give lectures on the subject offered the priceless opportunity to try out some of my ideas: The Center for Near Eastern Studies, New York University (The Hagop Kevorkian Lecture in Near Eastern Art and Civilization); the Departments of Art History and Middle East Studies, University of Michigan, Ann Arbor; the Department of Art and Archaeology, Princeton University (The James F. Haley Memorial Lecture Series); the Istituto Universitario di Architettura di Venezia; the Graduate School of Design, Harvard University; The Metropolitan Museum of Art; and The Institute of Ismaili Studies, London. For facilitating my research, I especially appreciate the help of Filiz Çağman and Ülkü Altındağ at the Topkapı Palace Museum, Istanbul; Sadi Bayram at the Directorate of Waqfs in Ankara; and Maria Pia Pedani at the Archivio di Stato, Venice. The extensive group of photographs from the Topkapı Palace Museum library and archives were taken by Hadiye Cangökçe, and John Cook photographed images from books in the Harvard University libraries.

I consider it a privilege that Reha Günay agreed to photograph Sinan's monuments for this book, bringing into the process his profound knowledge on the subject. The plans, elevations and axonometric drawings of Sinan's works (primarily based on those of Ali Saim Ülgen, Aptullah Kuran and Wolfgang Müller-Wiener) were prepared by Arben N. Arapi, with whom it was a pleasure to collaborate. I thank him for the time and sensitive draughting skills that went into their execution. I am also indebted to Zeynep Yürekli, who prepared architectural drawings for monuments by other architects. Under the generous supervision of their professor, Zeynep Ahunbay, students of the Istanbul Technical University (Turabi Ağdalı and Nisa Semiz) measured and made drawings of some buildings for which no previous plans and elevations existed. Ahmet Ersoy prepared the maps, drawn by Nurcihan Doğmuş Kadıoğlu and revised by Zeynep Yürekli. I am deeply grateful for the help of my resourceful research assistants, who contributed in numerous ways to this book: Diana Abouali, Ladan Akbarnia, Çiğdem Kafescioğlu, Ruth MacQuiddy, Oya Pancaroğlu, Michael Pregill, Barry Wood and Zeynep Yürekli. I would also like to express my appreciation for the expert assistance of Erdem Çıpa in scanning and editing the illustrations and Kutalmış Görkay in performing magic with Photoshop.

Parallel projects that complement the book include a website on Sinan's mosques and mosque complexes put together by Leslie Schick for ArchNet, an online digital library of texts and images on Islamic architecture funded by the Aga Khan Development Network and administered through MIT's School of Architecture (http://archnet.org.). Another affiliated project is Howard Crane's critical edition and English translation of autobiographical texts Sinan dictated to the poet-painter Mustafa Sai. I am thankful that he accepted to collaborate on the preparation of this much-needed sourcebook for the publications of the Aga Khan Program of Islamic Architecture at Harvard and MIT, which I edit (*Studies and Sources in Islamic Art and Architecture: Supplements to Muqarnas*).

My deepest gratitude goes to Cemal Kafadar, who was my travel companion to all sites and my intellectual companion at all times. He fortified me with his nurturing support, patiently listened to my embryonic thoughts, helped me refine them with his wise criticisms, and made invaluable suggestions on the finished manuscript. Some of the ideas explored in chapters addressing cross-cultural exchanges with Italy germinated in two classes taught with Howard Burns at Harvard University on the architectural history of the eastern Mediterranean basin during the early modern period. I extend my very special thanks to him, Cornell Fleischer, and Julian Raby for inspiring me in many different ways and for their precious comments on some chapters as well as the conceptual framework of the book.

I warmly acknowledge memorable discussions with friends and colleagues, many of whom provided personal support, comments, references, offprints, and illustrations, or accompanied me to some monuments to decipher irksome inscriptions: Zeynep Ahunbay, Nurhan Atasoy, Serpil Bağcı, Sibel Bozdoğan, Peter Brown, Filiz Çağman, Maurice Cerasi, Joseph Connors, Slobodan Ćurčić, Walter Denny, Necdet Ertuğ, Zeynep Ertuğ, Emine Fetvacı, Oleg Grabar, Reha Günay, Robert Hillenbrand, Deborah Howard, Halil İnalcık, Alice Jarrard, Baber Johansen, Çiğdem Kafescioğlu, Nuha Khoury, Machiel Kiel, Klaus Kreiser, Doğan Kuban, Neil Levine, Nevra Necipoğlu, Victor Ostapchuk, Robert Ousterhout, Peter Parsons, Günsel Renda, Andras Riedlmayer, David Roxburgh, the late John Shearman, Jeffrey Spurr, Zeren Tanındı, Baha Tanman, Wheeler Thackston Jr., Nicolas Vatin, Heghnar Watenpaugh, Steven Wolf, Stéphane Yerasimos, Aydın Yüksel, and Zeynep Yürekli. My parents Ülkü and Hikmet Necipoğlu were a constant source of support with their genuine interest in my work.

I would like to express my debt to graduate students with whom we exchanged ideas in three seminars on Sinan, taught at various stages of my research. It was their infectious enthusiasm that sustained my faith in this project during moments of despair. Julia Bailey generously offered me her much appreciated incisive comments, often imbued with a delightful sense of humour, on an early draft of the manuscript, which she improved with her editorial expertise.

I am grateful for the prizes awarded to this book since it was first published: the bi-annual 'Fuat Köprülü Book Prize', awarded by the Turkish Studies Association (TSA) in 2006, and the 'Albert Hourani Book Award' Honorable Mention, awarded by the Middle East Studies Association (MESA) in 2005.

Abbreviations Used in References

AE	Ali Emiri
ASV	Archivio di Stato di Venezia, Venice
BA	Başbakanlık Osmanlı Arşivi, Istanbul
BL	British Library, London
BN	Paris, Bibliothèque nationale de France
CB	Chester Beatty Library, Dublin
DBI	*Dizionario Biografico degli Italiani*, Rome, 1960–
EI(1)	*Encyclopedia of Islam*, 1st edition, Leiden, 1913–38
EI(2)	*Encyclopedia of Islam*, 2nd edition, Leiden, 1954–
IA	*Islam Ansiklopedisi*, Istanbul, 1965–86
ISTA	*Dünden Bugüne Istanbul Ansiklopedisi*, Istanbul, 1993–95
IÜ	Istanbul University Library, Istanbul
KK	Kamil Kepeci
MAD	Maliyeden Müdevver Defterler
MD	Mühimme Defterleri
ÖNB	Vienna, Österreichische Nationalbibliothek
TB	Tezkiretül-bünyān
TIEM	Türk ve Islam Sanatları Müzesi, Istanbul
TE	Tezkiretül-ebniye
TM	Tuḥfetü'l-miʿmārīn
TSA	Topkapı Sarayı Müzesi Arşivi, Istanbul
TSK	Topkapı Sarayı Müzesi Kütüphanesi, Istanbul
VIA	Türkiye Diyanet Vakfı Islam Ansiklopedisi, Istanbul
VGM	Vakıflar Genel Müdürlüğü Arşivi, Ankara

ABBREVIATIONS FOR MONTHS OF THE *HICRI* CALENDAR

M	Muharrem
S	Safer
Ra	Rebi'ül-evvel
R	Rebiü'l-ahir
B	Receb
Ş	Şaban
N	Ramazan
L	Şevval
Za	Zilkade
Z	Zilhicce

CONTEXTUALIZING SİNAN

The name of Sinan has become synonymous with the so-called classical style of Ottoman architecture codified during his tenure as chief royal architect between 1539 and 1588. Istanbul consummated the zenith of its urban form with his stunning monumental accents, and his distinctive architectural idiom left its imprint over the terrains of a vast empire extending from the Danube to the Tigris. The global fame of Sinan, the most celebrated architect of the premodern Islamic lands, is bolstered by the affinity between his centrally planned domed mosques and Italian Renaissance churches: an affinity rooted in the shared Romano-Byzantine architectural heritage of the eastern Mediterranean basin that was concurrently being revived in Istanbul and Italy.

Nevertheless, Sinan's legacy falls between the cracks of the traditional divide between 'Islamic' and 'Western' architectural history. The unique manner in which it bridges building traditions defies standard classifications. With the exception of Spiro Kostof's history of world architecture, which offers a compelling juxtaposition of Italian and Ottoman monuments from the fifteenth and sixteenth centuries, general surveys include Sinan's works only as derivative variations of Hagia Sophia (transformed into the premier imperial mosque of Istanbul in 1453).[1]

The ingenious experimentation of Sinan with centralized domed baldachins that push the boundaries of structure, space, and light is rarely integrated into the Eurocentric narratives of art history whose exclusions are only recently being criticized. The critique of Eurocentrism has generated a new interest in exploring the extensive global interaction of Italian visual culture with the Islamic East and the New World in the early modern period.[2] However the current trend to reframe the Italian Renaissance in a more inclusive multicultural paradigm, which acknowledges its hybridity and heterogeneity, has had little impact on the conceptual framing of Ottoman architecture. A cross-cultural comparative perspective has not yet emerged, even though some scholars have voiced the need for a 'fresh narrative' negotiating the alterity of Sinan's architecture through a reassessment of its departures from what is traditionally considered Islamic, its 'classical allegiance', and its 'analogies with the Renaissance in Italy.'[3]

Sinan's works have been doubly marginalized by the nineteenth-century orientalist legacy, with its stereotyped definitions of Islamic architecture. Primarily attracted to the 'otherness' of non-European visual cultures (whether Islamic, Chinese, or Indian), orientalists privileged the early 'golden ages' of foreign artistic traditions supposedly encompassing timeless characteristics and essences. Sinan's architecture tends to be considered less original as an 'Islamic' tradition, not only because it is a later post-medieval development, but also because of its assertive dialogue with the Mediterranean classical tradition which ironically is hailed as a central component of early Islamic architecture. The crystalline and prismatic forms of Sinan's externally articulated domed mosques are often regarded as somewhat untypical regional offshoots of 'truly Islamic' architecture, which tends to be essentialized in terms of the prevalence of decorative surface values over architectonic ones, and the preference for stressing the interior at the expense of the exterior.

Interpretations of Sinan's architecture have been coloured by the 'universal' and 'national' paradigms of orientalism that utterly fail to historicize his works. If universalist notions of what constitutes 'typical' Islamic architecture is one side of the orientalist legacy, its other side exhibits an equally problematic tendency to read monuments of 'later Islamic' cultures as confined to distinct ethnic regions. Rooted in the racial cultural theories of the nineteenth century, this anachronistic reading of architectural traditions in terms of ethnic/linguistic categories – Arabic, Persian, Turkish – subtly permeates even the most recent surveys of Islamic architecture which continue to use such categories or substitute them with dynastic/regional labels carrying implicit national connotations (e.g., 'Ottoman Turks', 'Ottoman Turkey'). National paradigms have also been enthusiastically reclaimed by the modern nation states that supplanted former Islamic empires characterized by complex multiethnic, multilinguistic, and multiconfessional identities. In the case of Sinan (a Christian convert recruited for imperial service from the Karaman region in Anatolia), this has given rise to tedious polemical debates concerning his Greek, Armenian, or Turko-Christian identity:

debates that overlook the multicultural character of the Ottoman empire in which it was common practice to exploit the talents of diverse subjects from eastern Europe, the Balkans, Anatolia, and the Arab lands.

Acclaimed as a national hero in modern Turkey, Sinan has been designated the 'Turkish Michelangelo' ever since the early twentieth century, when a number of German publications called attention to the striking kinship between his works and those of celebrated Italian Renaissance architects.[4] These were specialized publications, which did not have an impact on the Eurocentric narratives of mainstream architectural history. For instance, Cornelius Gurlitt wrote in his monograph *Die Baukunst Konstantinopels* (Berlin, 1907–12) that just as 'Roman forms were revived during the Renaissance with a totally new notion and vigor, an original architecture of the same magnitude was born in Istanbul with the inspiration taken from Hagia Sophia.'[5] A few years later, the orientalist historian Franz Babinger promoted Sinan as the grand master of the 'Turkish Renaissance,' inviting historians and art historians to cooperate in bringing his works universal recognition.[6] For this urgent task, he compiled a short biography and a preliminary list of monuments derived from various versions of the autobiography that Sinan dictated to the poet-painter Mustafa Sai, the only examples of their kind in the premodern Islamic world.[7]

Among the earliest studies on Sinan were those written by the architecture professors of the Academy of Fine Arts in Istanbul, founded in 1883. These European professors contributed to the still prevalent interpretation of Sinan's architecture through the lens of modernism, with its emphasis on rational form and function. One of them was the Vienna-trained Swiss architect Ernst Egli, who wrote the first monograph to be published in Europe, *Sinan: Der Baumeister Osmanischer Glanzzeit* (Zurich, 1954). His book traces Sinan's style to the Seljuk heritage of Anatolia without dismissing the influence of Hagia Sophia, 'which came less as a revelation than as an incentive to further effort'. Egli stresses the universal values of the chief architect's works that echo the precepts of modernism:

> His greatness lay in the complete harmony in his work between form and content; his uniqueness lay in his ability to transform the strictly individual aspects of the commissions given to him into something of enduring and universal value. That is why his work is today as alive as ever. It preserves the immortal features of the past.[8]

The simultaneously national and universal formal values Egli identified in the chief architect's style turned it into a valid source of inspiration for modern Turkish architects. Sinan's architecture was even more explicitly inscribed into a modernist narrative in an influential textbook written by the German architect Bruno Taut, Egli's successor at the Academy in Istanbul. Published for the students of that institution in 1938 and subsequently translated into Japanese (1948) and German (1977), Taut's *Mimari Bilgisi* (Knowledge of Architecture) presents a functionalist interpretation of historical styles, seen, like costumes, as reflections of national character.[9] Grouped together with the Gothic style under the category of 'Constructive Architecture', Sinan's style epitomizes the ideal harmony between rational construction technique and proportion (a notion originating in nineteenth-century publications on Ottoman architecture).[10] Engineering technique is aestheticized both internally and externally in the domed monuments of this style. Taut regards Roman and Byzantine builders as mere engineers in comparison to Sinan and his students. The imperial domes of the Pantheon and Hagia Sophia 'leave one cold' as engineering feats meant to 'show off'. Hagia Sophia, visually improved by the addition of minarets, is only a 'prelude' to the style of Sinan, who perfects its proportions in his mosques where decoration, subordinated to structure, has been 'respectfully stepped aside'. Sinan, under whom domed construction reaches its highest degree of development and flexibility in world history, is a genius of the art of proportion, of beauty born from rational construction.[11]

Taut's emphasis on structural rationalism once again turned Sinan into a legitimate role model for modern Turkish architects. Sedad Hakkı Eldem, one of the pioneering architects of the 'Second National Movement' (1940–50), acknowledged that the balance between form and function observed in the classical Ottoman style made it a particularly appropriate exemplar for modernism.[12] He judged Ottoman architecture as more modern than the European Renaissance building tradition that privileged the façade and ornament over functional form.'[13] The striking convergence of Sinan scholarship with the discourse of modernist architecture is also reflected in such architectural journals as *Arkitekt*, *Yapı*, *Mimar*, and *Mimarlık*, which promoted the 'Second National Movement'. These journals regularly commemorated the death anniversaries of the chief architect, glorifying him as the symbol of a newborn nation's artistic creativity that was inherited by the 'children of Sinan, bearing the blood and genius of the Master.'[14]

The cult of Sinan was no doubt nurtured by his autobiographies, written according to his own words to leave an imprint of his 'name and reputation on the pages of Time' (illus. 1).[15] The chief architect, who lived more than a hundred years and claimed authorship for hundreds of monuments, was nicknamed 'Koca Mimar' (Great Old Architect) soon after he passed away.[16] His autobiographies compare him to the sage Lokman with his God-given wisdom and to the saintly figure of Hızır (Khidr), the legendary discoverer of the fountain of life who allegedly revealed the divinely inspired plan of Hagia Sophia to its architect.[17] Sinan was subsequently transformed by folklore into a hero with superhuman powers, including the ability to fly from one construction site to the next like Hızır and Daedalus (a feat demonstrated by footprints at some sites believed to be those of the chief architect)[18]

Sinan's self-mythologizing autobiographies played a pivotal role in shaping his future reputation and in directing the focus of monographic studies on his creative genius to the exclusion of other factors. The 'Turkish Michelangelo' is often imagined as a Renaissance prodigy driven by an insatiable urge for artistic experimentation, a perception not so far removed from the self-image constructed in his autobiographies (illus. 2).[19] Sinan's oeuvre is therefore interpreted chronologically, as a trace of evolving personal creativity during the early, middle, and late stages of his career.[20] His works are generally analysed as a self-referential corpus representing formal evolution along a linear historical model: a single-minded search for perfectly centralized, unified domed spaces filled with light. Buildings that do not fit this model are ignored or judged as aberrations triggered by the occasional mediation of patrons 'who generally did not intervene in his artistic decisions'.[21]

Sinan's architecture is injected with precisely the same modernist aesthetic values that permeate Rudolf Wittkower's paradigm of Renaissance architecture: the ahistorical emphasis on the structural rationalism of design to the near exclusion of ornament; the abstract clarity of geometric schemes; and the centralized conception of space.[22] To rescue Sinan's work from 'the cliches of orientalist theories and to set it into a more universal historical perspective', Doğan Kuban, for example, stresses the chief architect's concept of centralized spatial unity, the structural rationalism of his flexible domed baldachins in which ornament is subordinated to functional form, and his unparalleled contribution to domical construction in world architecture. Arguing that 'decoration had absolutely no influence on the architectural design' of Sinan's mosques, which represent a 'Turkish-Anatolian' synthesis with a Mediterranean spirit, Kuban observes in them 'a purism that is not to be seen in Europe until the twentieth century'[23]

The preoccupation with Sinan's modernist sensibility and the universal values of his style has, however, hindered an understanding of his architecture in its own terms. Ottomanist architectural historians, generally trained as architects, have imagined that the international appeal of Sinan's works might be compromised through a culturally specific, contextual reading that replaces external global comparisons with less accessible internal meanings. Their tacit assumption is that a non-European building tradition is doomed to become marginalized and lose its relevance for mainstream architectural history if its historical specificity is foregrounded. This unfounded assumption implies that attempts at cross-cultural comparison are bound to remain superficial, limited to formal analyses ignorant of the contextual factors that informed the production of meaning.

With a few exceptions, the secular narratives of most Turkish architectural historians play down the religious, socio-political, and cultural contexts in which Sinan's works came into being.[24] Likewise, the international scholarship on the chief architect is dominated by stylistic analysis and ahistorical frameworks.[25] When considered as part of an Islamic visual

1 Sinan *c.* 1579 holding a wooden measuring stick and overseeing the construction of Sultan Süleyman's mausoleum (detail of illus. 118).

2 Münif Fehim, a modern portrait of Sinan in his office with the Selimiye mosque in the background, 1938.

tradition, Sinan's architecture is once again admired for its inventively varied domed spaces transcending the specificities of meaning engendered in particular contexts, whether interpreted from a secular perspective or as a timeless spiritual expression of God's oneness (*tawhid*).[26] The abstraction of the chief architect's works into an autonomous evolution of formal types, then, lends itself equally well to diverse visions of universalism.

The mosques of Sinan are generally classified in terms of a spatial typology of domes resting on square, hexagonal, and octagonal support systems – a classification initiated by Cornelius Gurlitt, further elaborated by Albert-Louis Gabriel, and embraced by later architectural historians (illus. 3–5).[27] The reductionist comparative agenda of typological classifications irons out differences in favour of an abstract space conception reflected on a two-dimensional ground plan. The mosque of the grand vizier Rüstem Pasha in Istanbul and that of Sultan Selim II in Edirne (Selimiye), for example, end up being grouped together because they share central domed baldachins with octagonal support systems. This classification, however, marginalizes other differentiating formal components such as smaller domes, porticoes, galleries, fenestration, and façades.[28] Moreover, it overlooks differences in scale, elevation, siting, patronage level, functional programme, decoration, epigraphy, and iconography that engender distinctive design solutions with nuanced contextual meanings. The individuality of each mosque is undermined as it turns into an anonymous road station within a typological series, devoid of the complex cultural and personal considerations that went into its making. Furthermore, the focus of scholarship on monumental mosques with more innovative domed baldachins, structures concentrated in Istanbul and Edirne, distorts the pluralism of architectural production across different social strata and geographical regions, leaving out Sinan's numerous mosques with domes raised on simple cubes and his even more rudimentary domeless mosques covered by hipped roofs. Because these humble works are dismissed as too simple for his genius, they tend to be excluded from most monographs, even though the chief architect chose to list them in his autobiographies as monuments supervised by his office.[29]

The dynamically varied designs of Sinan's mosques defy being reduced to examples of spatial typology or to benchmarks in a unilinear scheme of stylistic evolution. These mosques certainly display typological schemes and stylistic progression over time, but their formal characteristics were not shaped in a cultural vacuum. Their degree of individualization increased in proportion to the prominence of the patron and the proximity of the site to the capital Istanbul. That is why formally innovative and conservative mosques were simultaneously created at the same moments in Sinan's career. For example, the ambitious mosque of Sultan Süleyman I (Süleymaniye) built in the 1550s on an elevated hilltop inside the walled city of Istanbul is clearly more innovative than that of the grand admiral Sinan Pasha, erected at about the same time along the waterfront of the marginal suburb of Beşiktaş (illus. 3 [3], 4 [1]). Süleyman's mosque complex in Istanbul and the smaller one he commissioned in Damascus during the 1550s exhibit similar stylistic disparities. The latter complex is grouped around a relatively generic mosque designed as a basic domed cube whose decorative vocabulary integrates distinctive regional elements.

Style was not just a matter of chronology, for it varied according to a given project's patron and location. The question of style is further complicated by the fact that many mosques for which Sinan claims authorship in his autobiographies were designed by him but executed by other royal architects who worked with different teams of builders and decorators. The chief architect's oeuvre, then, was essentially a collective corpus stamped by his controlling vision, and only the most important projects in or near Istanbul were fully supervised by him. As such, his works constituted a shared cultural product of the centralized corps of royal architects which he headed. Sinan was undeniably an architectural genius, but a genius whose style had to negotiate the tension between his identity as an individual artist and the head of an institution. The unresolved negotiation of that tension is felt in his autobiographies, which capture his 'authorship anxiety' by listing hundreds of monuments as his own works.

The formalist paradigms in which Sinan's works are generally

3 Square baldachin system:

1. Şehzade Mehmed, Istanbul (1543–48)
2. Mihrümah Sultan, Üsküdar (1543/44–1548)
3. Süleymaniye, Istanbul (1548–59)
4. Mihrümah Sultan, Edirnekapı (c. 1563–70)
5. Shahsultan and Zal Mahmud Pasha, Eyüp (1577–90)

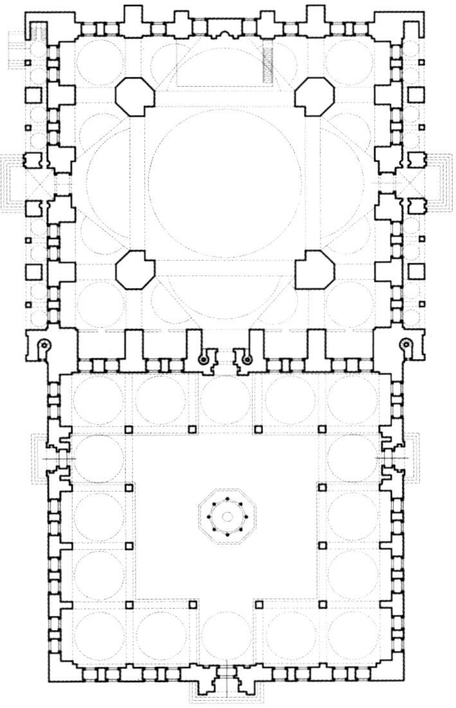

1

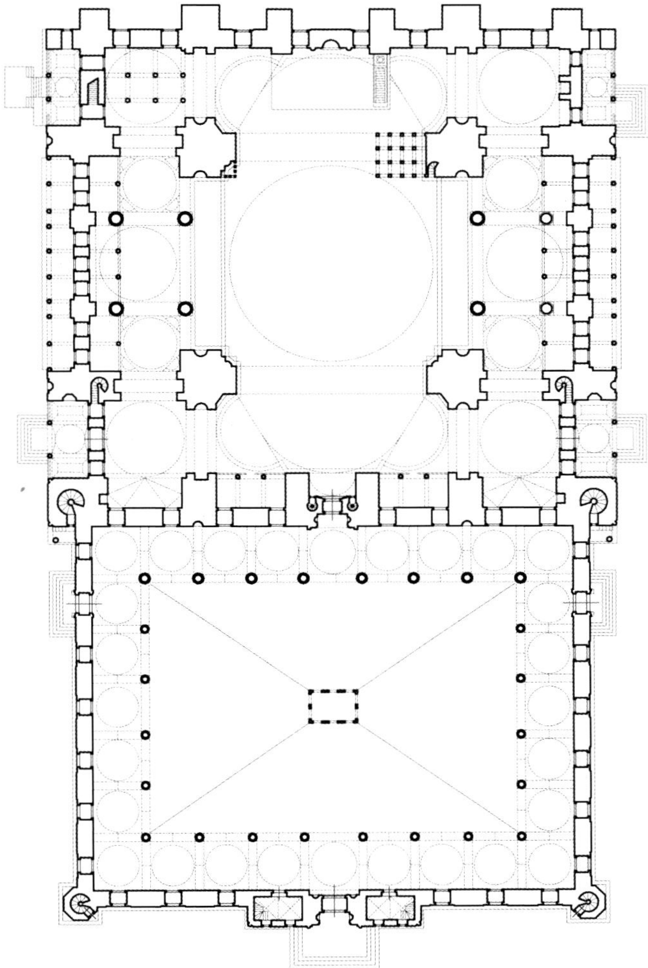

3

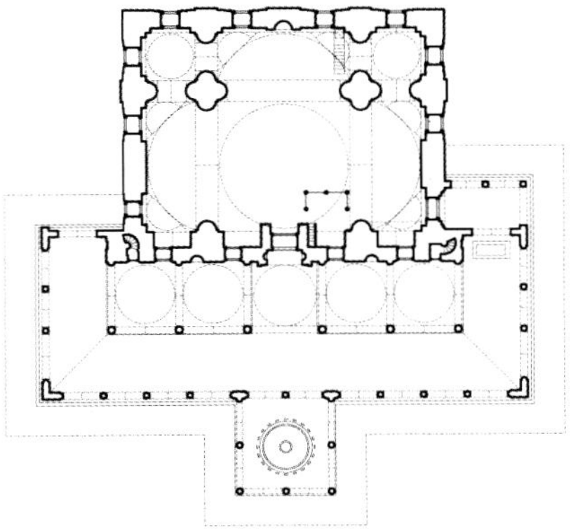

2

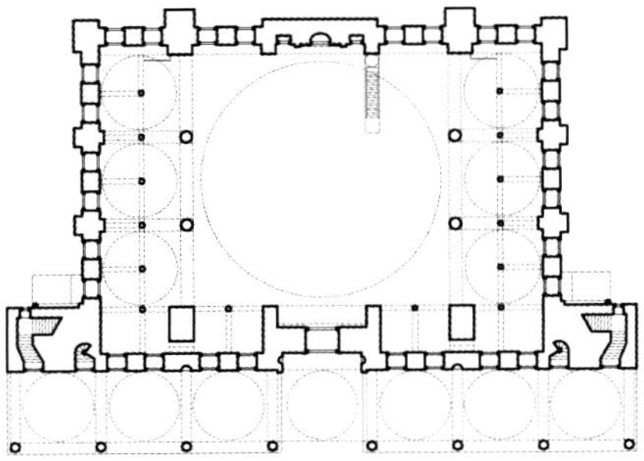

4

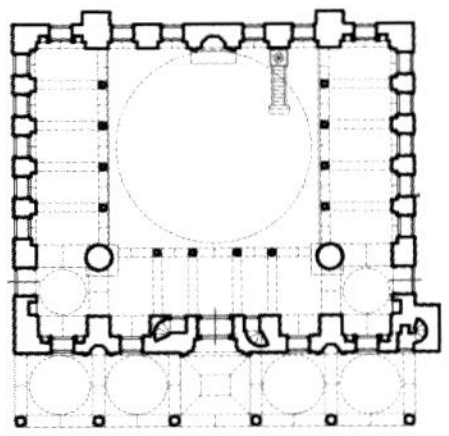

5

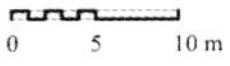

4 Hexagonal baldachin system:

1. Sinan Pasha, Beşiktaş (1554–1555/56)
2. Kara Ahmed Pasha, Topkapı (1555, 1565–71/72)
3. Ismihan Sultan and Sokollu Mehmed Pasha, Kadırgalimanı (c. 1567/68–71/72)
4. Nurbanu Sultan, Üsküdar (1571–86)
5. Semiz Ali Pasha, Babaeski (c. 1569-75, 1585–86)
6. Molla Çelebi, Fındıklı (1570–84)
7. Kazasker Ivaz Efendi, Egırikapı (1586)
8. Cerrah Mehmed Pasha, Avratpazarı (1593–94)

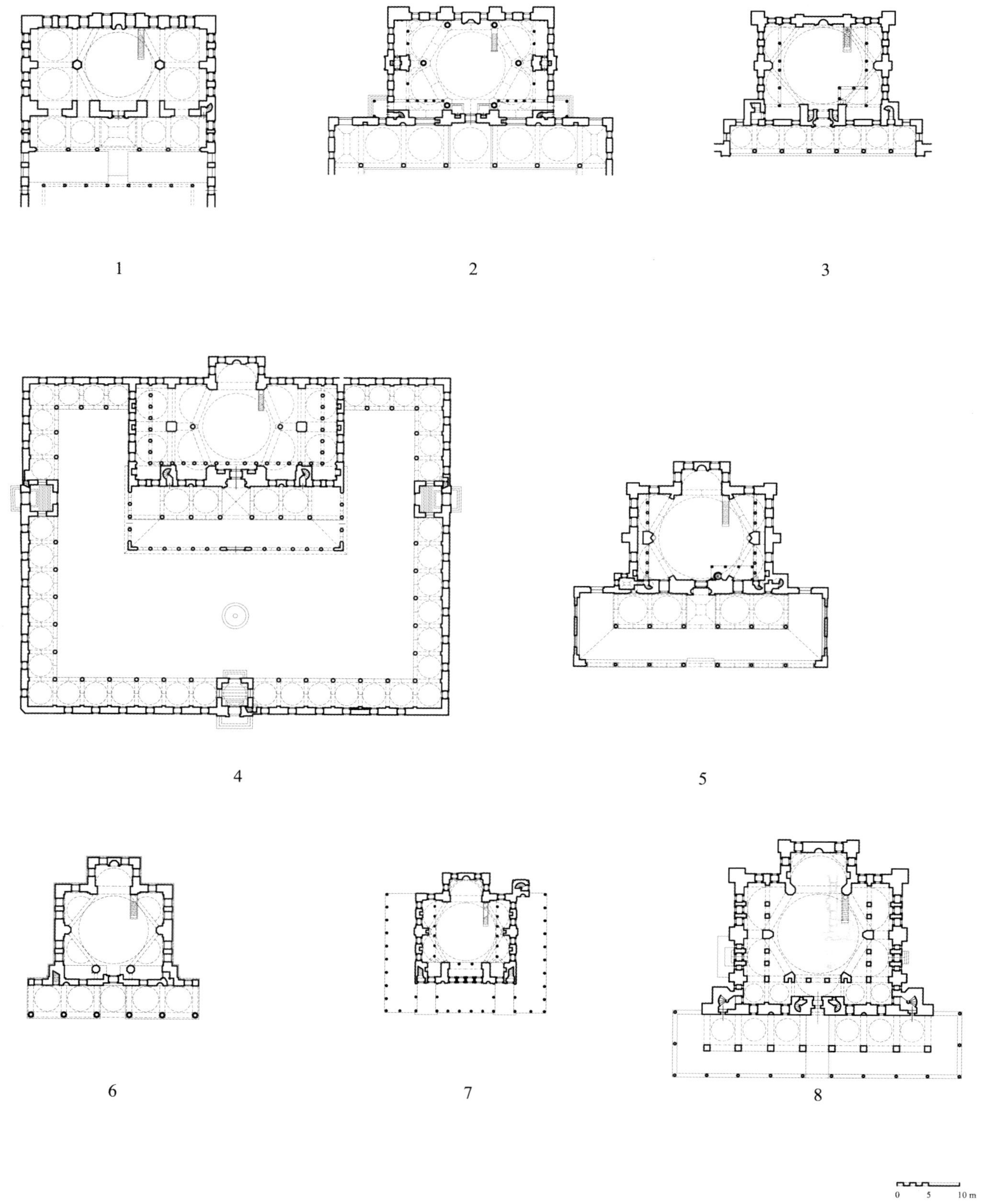

5 Octagonal baldachin system:

1. Rüstem Pasha, Tahtakale (*c.* 1561–63)
2. Selimiye, Edirne (1568–74)
3. Sokollu Mehmed Pasha, Azapkapı (*c.* 1573–1577/78)
4. Mehmed Agha, Çarşamba (1584–85)
5. Mesih Mehmed Pasha, Yenibahçe (1584–1585/86)
6. Nişancı Mehmed Pasha, Karagümrük (1584/85–1588/89)

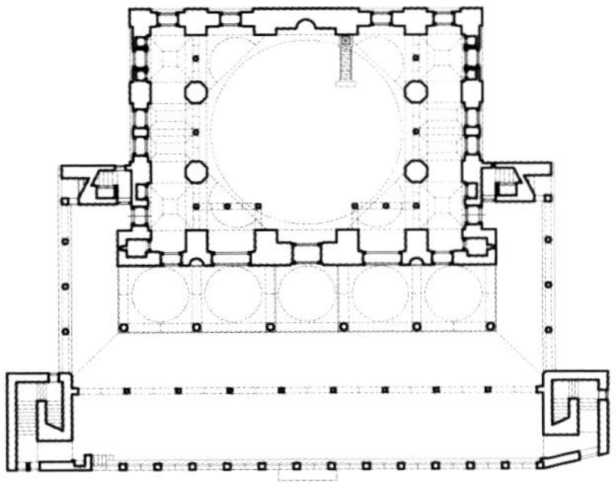

1

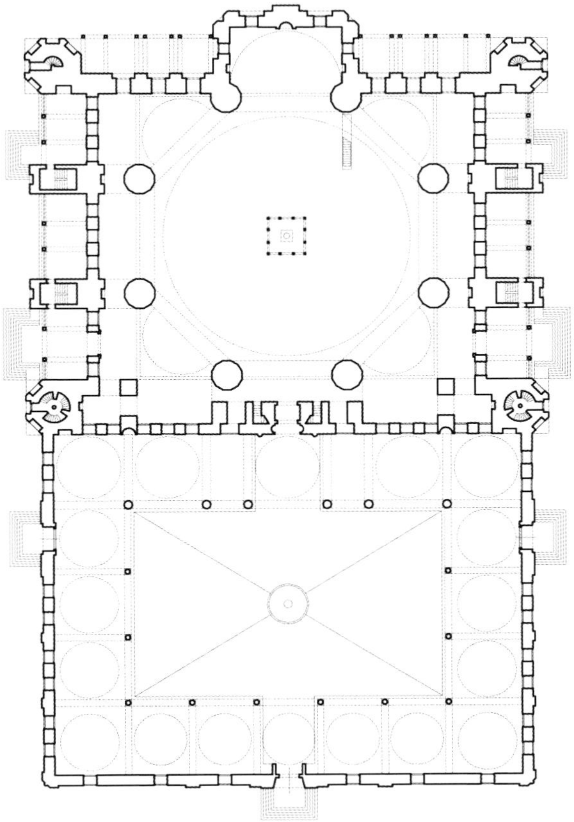

2

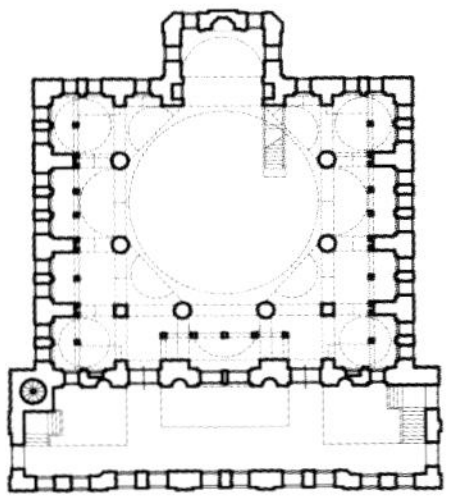

3

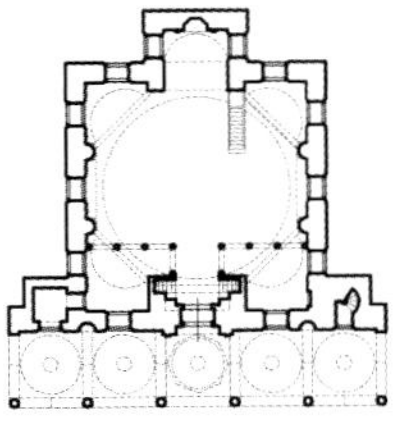

4

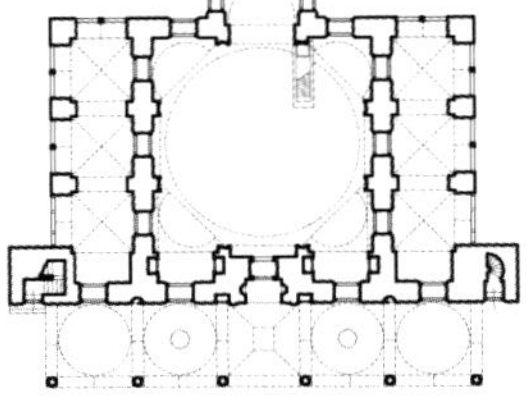

5

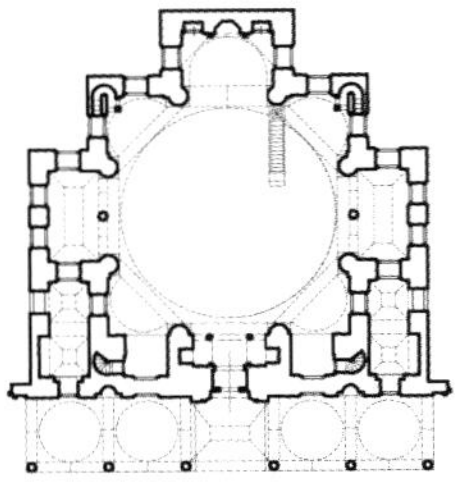

6

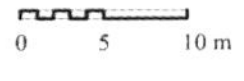

analysed underestimate the contextual processes that informed their design, production, and reception. Primarily concerned with formal evolution and typology, most monographs on the chief architect treat the contextual settings of his architecture merely as an appendix. The cooperation Babinger envisioned long ago between historians and architectural historians has not materialized in interdisciplinary studies that integrate textual sources with visual analyses of the buildings themselves to understand how and why the built environment took the shape it did.[30]

It was this shortcoming that prompted me to write a formally grounded, contextual study of Sinan's oeuvre framed by the architectural culture of his age. The emphasis on architectural culture shifts the conceptualization of architecture as an autonomous, self-referential field concerned primarily with forms to a wider arena of institutional, political, social, economic, cultural, and aesthetic practices that inform the meaning of monuments. It is not my aim to replace formalist readings with an all-encompassing, deterministic framework reducing Sinan's creative genius to the contexts of architectural patronage.[31] Nor do I claim that the 'correct' interpretation of his monuments is restricted to the original settings in which they were produced and consumed, for they transcend historical confinement and occupy a timeless present. His masterpieces are certainly available to endless reinterpretation because they hold within them inexhaustible reservoirs of 'ontological possibility'. I simply aim to present a more nuanced, context-sensitive reading of Sinan's works that crosses the boundaries between architectural and cultural history, with the hope of opening up the field to new directions of research.[32] Thanks to the invaluable groundwork laid by earlier studies that have extensively documented his monuments and sharpened our understanding of their formal characteristics, we can now begin to address different kinds of questions in a field so rich with possibilities that it has aptly been compared to 'a vast ocean, on the shores of which we have just arrived'.[33]

This book draws on years of fieldwork and documentation compiled in various manuscript libraries and archives. Besides the buildings themselves, its primary sources include contemporary texts and images, both European and Ottoman. The richness of the written sources, unparalleled in other fields of Islamic architecture, allows an unusual level of specificity in the exploration of contextual questions. I focus on Sinan's Friday mosques, for which he is mainly renowned and which he himself ranks above all other building types in his autobiographies, whether neighbourhood masjids, madrasas, hadith colleges, schools for Koran recitation, elementary schools, hospitals, hospices, caravansarays, mausoleums, palaces, garden pavilions, bath-houses, storehouses, aqueducts, or bridges.[34] I only consider examples of these building types in conjunction with the mosque complexes to which they belonged as dependencies or were endowed as sources of income.

The book is based on the premise that, far from constituting an entirely autonomous realm, the domain of architecture intersected with a wide range of interconnected representational practices in which Sinan, his patrons, and his audiences were embedded. The chief architect's works were not merely artistic expressions of his penchant for restless formal experimentation, freed of all social constraints except the occasional interference of a capricious patron.[35] Their programmes were negotiated with his patrons, who intervened not only in the early stages of planning when he presented them with various design options, but also through written communications or visits to building sites during the construction process. These monuments were not only shaped by the personal visions of Sinan and his patrons, but also by culturally defined notions of identity, memory, and decorum.

My interpretation of Sinan's mosques is based on the argument that he developed a stratified system of architectural representation, which relied on a standardized vocabulary of repetitive canonical forms to express the status hierarchies of his patrons and the cultural prestige of the empire's centre over its provinces. Codifying mosque types according to the gradations of social and territorial rank, he created a richly varied typology responsive to culturally defined expectations of propriety. The historian Mustafa Āli's late-sixteenth-century book on etiquette elaborates the concept of decorum with respect to such status symbols as clothing and residential architecture, classifying the intricate gradations of house types appropriate for different social ranks.[36] Just as clothes and residences distinguished the hierarchically ranked members of the Ottoman ruling elite, so too were mosque types stratified according to various levels of patronage. This is recognized in Ottoman texts that invariably rank monumental 'royal' (*selāṭīn*) mosques above non-royal ones.[37]

The concept of decorum revolved around the restricted use of visual signs of 'distinction', to use a term coined by Pierre Bourdieu.[38] These signs reinforced the corporate group identities of the ruling elite and at the same time articulated its nuanced gradations of status, without daring to challenge the sultan's overarching supremacy. Status signs reserved for sultanic mosque complexes in the capital cities of Istanbul and Edirne included siting on commanding hilltops, innovative ground plans, monumental scale, grand domes, quadruple minarets with multiple galleries, and marble-paved forecourts surrounded by domical arcades. Unlike other mosques, those of the sultans entered into an iconographically meaningful visual dialogue with Hagia Sophia (Ayasofya), the ultimate symbol of imperial magnificence embodying the grandeur of the state and religion.[39] The exclusiveness of this dialogue, limited to sultanic mosques, challenges the looming presence of Hagia Sophia in ideologically motivated debates concerning the 'origin' and 'originality' of Ottoman architecture.[40]

The smaller domed mosques commissioned by male and female members of the imperial family used only some prestigious visual signs, such as double minarets signifying royal status. Non-royal mosques with single minarets were further stratified according to relative rank, starting with the highest patronage level of the grand viziers and viziers, and moving down the social ladder. Lower ranks were represented by modest domeless structures crowned by hipped roofs and fronted by wooden-pillared porticoes instead of domed marble colonnades. Codes of decorum only set an 'upper limit' on the use of prestige signs; patrons of high standing often built modest functional mosques as well as monumental ones. However, their monumental prestige mosques were invariably shaped by the 'upper limit' rules negotiated between the chief architect, his patrons, and society at large.

The differing programmes of Sinan's mosque complexes inside and outside Istanbul accentuated the dichotomy between the centre and periphery of the empire. The simpler designs of provincial mosques generally consisted of domed cubes of average size. These generic mosques projected a hegemonic imperial identity that could comfortably accommodate regional voices. With their relatively homogeneous lead-covered hemispherical domes and pointed cylindrical minarets, they were built in an immediately recognizable Ottoman idiom, mixed with local dialects. Confined exclusively to the boundaries of the empire, these iconic mosques functioned as territory markers that visually unified diverse regions.

The generic uniformity of provincial mosques contrasted with the elaborately variegated plans and domical superstructures of the prestige mosques densely concentrated in Istanbul. The landmark quality of these mosques was foregrounded above and beyond their functional character. Sinan designed them as showpieces to be displayed within the showcase of the capital. Their highly articulated exteriors entered into a dialogue with the urban setting within which meaning was produced, a characteristic that has been regarded as a 'triumphant reversal of the standard Islamic preference of mosque architecture for stressing the interior.'[41] Generally sited on hilltops or along the shoreline, Sinan's mosques were almost never perceived alone, but in juxtaposition with other mosques. They invited comparison with one another, both within and across various patronage levels, as well as between the antiquated past and the innovative present. Comparisons between mosques, and by extension between their patrons, accentuated the status gradations of a ruling elite from diverse ethnic origins that sought to construct its collective urban identity in the empire's symbolic centre. Architectural descriptions by sixteenth- and seventeenth-century Ottoman writers such as Mehmed Aşık and Evliya Çelebi tacitly acknowledge this intertextual dimension of decorum by assessing mosques in a comparative framework, frequently drawing attention to their similarities and differences.

Far from being an inflexible straightjacket, decorum allowed a series of meaningful inversions and manipulations through which official norms could be conflated with private ambitions. Unwritten codes of decorum constituted a fragile social contract. Neither monolithic nor entirely consistent, they provided ample room for manoeuvring and self-expression. Architectural patronage was not simply a means of confirming, but also of bestowing social rank as a mark of aspiration for higher status. It could, therefore, potentially turn into a site of contestation involving the intervention of community members in cases of dispute. Sinan's mosque complexes had the capacity to affirm, negotiate, and even contest hegemonic concepts of power by testing the limits of permissibility. Decorum restricted unrestrained architectural imagination through the pressure of social conventions, yet it could also empower by offering the possibility of reconstituting the order of things. The empire's urban landscape simply was not the same after it had been reconfigured with hundreds of socio-religious monuments put up by Sinan during his half-century-long career: it came to embody a new visual order with a particular set of urban institutions and ritual practices.

The first two thematically organized sections of the book analyse the contexts of architectural patronage and production. The longer third section interprets Sinan's individual mosques, with or without complexes, grouped in terms of patronage level rather than stylistic chronology. The epilogue evaluates the chief architect's legacy after his demise, when patronage patterns were transformed along with shifting notions of decorum within the emerging context of the post-classical imperial regime.

The first section of the book outlines the hierarchical organization of the empire's territories and social structure, with a new emphasis on centralization during the reign of Sultan Süleyman, as a backdrop for patterns of architectural patronage. Chapter 1 considers the ideological bases of dynastic legitimacy that informed sultanic monuments and the ascendance of an oligarchic ruling elite. It sketches how the governing body increasingly became dominated by converts into Islam who, like Sinan himself, were conscripted from the empire's ethnically diverse Christian population as *kul*s (slave-servants). The rise to prominence of an oligarchy of elite patrons paralleled the consolidation of a pyramidal social structure occupied at the top by the sultan, the royal family, and royal sons-in-law of *kul* origin appointed as grand viziers and viziers.

The patrons of Sinan's Friday mosques primarily belonged to the upper strata of the social pyramid, unlike the sponsors of more modest building types such as masjids, madrasas, or elementary schools that were commissioned by a wider group of patrons including the ulema and the urban middle classes. The majority of mosque patrons – including the mothers and wives of the sultans who originated from such diverse places as Venice,

Poland, or Albania – had been recruited from the empire's Christian subjects or captured as slaves from non-Ottoman territories (Appendix 1). I address the ways in which the Ottoman ruling elite's supra ethnic collective identity, unified by religious affiliation to Sunni Islam, shaped the notions of decorum in architecture that occupied a prominent place in its consumption patterns and in its public self-representation.

Chapter 2 analyses the legal and memorial dimensions of architectural patronage together with the religious orientations of the sixteenth century, which were marked by an ethos of fervently orthodox piety. I use legal texts and fatwas to outline the juridical parameters of mosque construction, dictated by the shariʿa (religious law). Friday mosques, in which the sultan's claims to sovereignty were broadcast and re-broadcast each week with the khutba (sermon delivered before the midday service on Fridays), stood out as a building type closely tied to the ruler's legitimacy. Their construction was strictly a royal prerogative, requiring special written permission from the sultan himself, unlike other building types. This meant that all mosques in the empire were built as an emanation of the sultan's caliphal authority to maintain control over where and by whom the Friday prayer could be performed.

The chapter correlates the unprecedented boom in mosque construction with the official enforcement of the daily congregational and Friday prayers during the age of Sinan, when the state increasingly defined its identity as the defender of the shariʿa and of Sunni Islam. The patronage of Friday mosques helped consolidate the empire's centralized dynastic regime dominated by the *kul* system, playing a major role in the construction of collective and individual identities. I also address the modes in which memory was objectified in mosque complexes through various strategies that turned them into potent sites of remembrance.[42] Carrying the names of his patrons, Sinan's mosques were not just places of worship, but also embodied personal, familial, and communal memories that have largely fallen into oblivion through erasure or reinterpretation. Constituting 'architectural portraits' of their patrons, these mosques were individualized by specific memory markers such as inscriptions, mausoleums, and sites associated with the identity of patrons. Waqfiyyas (endowment deeds) institutionalized memory by stipulating particular types of charity and rituals for the perpetual remembrance of mosque founders and their families. I analyse the role rituals and various forms of commemoration played in articulating the contextual meanings of mosques, together with the ways in which the institution of pious endowments (waqf) encouraged their construction.

Chapter 3 focuses on architectural culture and concepts of decorum. It starts with an overview of Ottoman imperial policies of urban development that motivated the construction of mosque complexes, strictly limited to cities by the Hanefi legal system. This is followed by a brief survey of early Ottoman architecture as a background for the evolution of Sinan's distinctive mosque-centred complexes and his contribution to the urban image of Istanbul. I interpret the development of Ottoman socio-religious architecture from the fourteenth through the sixteenth centuries within the comparative framework of eastern Islamic and Italian Renaissance architectural developments to highlight parallels and differences. I link Ottoman architecture, which is often analysed in isolation from architecture in the rest of the Islamic world, with Mongol Ilkhanid, Timurid, and Mamluk prototypes. I also reconsider analogies between the Ottoman and Italian Renaissance architectural cultures by drawing attention to their mutual Roman heritage and to modes of cross-cultural exchange. This is followed by a discussion of the chronological development of Sinan's style in order to counterbalance the book's third section, where his individual mosques are ordered in terms of patronage level. The chapter ends with an analysis of contemporary texts alluding to Ottoman concepts of decorum in various spheres of visual culture, along with a consideration of codes that shaped architectural propriety during Sinan's tenure.

The second section of the book turns from patronage to architectural production, focusing on Sinan both as an individual and as the head of a centralized corps of royal architects. Using his autobiographies, his endowment deed, and archival documents, I revisit in Chapter 4 the biographical details of the chief architect's life and career in order to revise some prevalent misconceptions. I interpret Sinan's autobiographies as vehicles for self-representation through which he participated in the Italian Renaissance discourse on artistic genius and the evolutionary progress of architecture by means of invention. Speculating that he may have been inspired by the biographies of artists and architects that were being written in Italy, I argue that his autobiographies reflect a comparable self-consciousness and a proud sense of individualism.

Chapter 5 traces the rise of an architectural profession with the development of the corps of royal architects between the fifteenth and seventeenth centuries. It evaluates Sinan's contribution to the increased centralization and expanded scope of that institution, parallel to the budding provincial organization of city architects. I consider the chief architect's responsibilities as an administrator and designer, along with the role of plans and models in architectural practice. The chapter ends with observations on the administrative mechanisms of the centralized Ottoman construction industry that contributed to the creation and dissemination of Sinan's 'classical' idiom. The building process was an essential part of the context of architecture, with its integrative power signifying economic and political control over material resources and labour throughout the empire. The potency and magnificence of Sinan's grand mosques resided as much in their theatrical creation process, which turned Istanbul into a perpetual construction site, as in their finished state.[43]

In the third section of the book I present my own interpretations of the mosques and mosque complexes that Sinan's autobiographies identify as his works. I read these monuments as concrete expressions of the concepts of identity, memory, and decorum discussed in earlier thematic chapters, assessing the ways in which they embody the aspirations of Sinan and his patrons. I analyse not only individualized mosques, but also generic ones that are often excluded from studies on the chief architect. The latter works are treated here as an integral part of Sinan's variegated corpus, regardless of his degree of involvement in their construction.

I reconstruct as much as possible the urban settings of mosque complexes to understand why they were built on particular sites and to elucidate modes of vision and visuality embodied in their composition. I also consider decorative and epigraphic programmes that tend to be ignored in studies on Sinan,[44] and quote contemporary architectural descriptions that mirror the aesthetic categories through which his works were perceived.[45] In this book, the colourful biographical details of individual patrons (the rich and famous of Ottoman high society) serve to offset the dominant focus on rulers in surveys of Islamic architecture, which generally marginalize the agency and subjectivity of other patrons. I integrate the patronage of royal women, which specialized feminist studies treat separately, with that of men in order to map out the role of gender in architectural constructions of identity.[46]

In addition to archival documents, I extensively use unpublished waqfiyyas that shed light on the functional programmes of mosque complexes and hint at the personal motivations of their patrons. Waqfiyyas also situate the prestige mosques patrons commissioned to Sinan within a larger group of monuments they endowed. Endowment deeds unveil a hitherto unnoted but evidently quite widespread phenomenon: mosques willed by dying patrons and posthumously built by the executors of last wills under the supervision of endowment administrators (*mütevelli*) and overseers (*nazır*). This phenomenon necessitates a revision of accepted dates for several mosques that lack foundation inscriptions, and are usually assumed to have been built during the lifetime of their patrons (Appendix 1).

The epilogue considers Sinan's legacy during the seventeenth century and later centuries, when mosque-centred complexes no longer constituted the primary focus of the ruling elite's architectural patronage. The chief architect's stratified mosque typology was not impervious to change, since Ottoman architectural culture constituted an ongoing process of identity formation rather than a static entity. That is why the codes of decorum formulated during Sinan's unusually long career had already started to erode towards the end of his life, when the classical Ottoman regime was being supplanted by a relatively decentralized system of government in which new types of architectural patrons, building programmes, and tastes emerged. Although the legacy of Sinan's distinctive style survived for many generations, perpetuated by his students who succeeded him as chief architects, the hierarchy of mosque types he codified enjoyed only a short life. Not immune to transgression and contestation, its codes of decorum were subverted as soon as they appeared to acquire canonical status.

PART I

ARCHITECTURAL PATRONAGE IN THE CLASSICAL PERIOD

Chapter 1

IMPERIAL TERRITORY, SOCIAL HIERARCHY, AND IDENTITY

I. SULTANS AND THE BASES OF DYNASTIC LEGITIMACY
II. THE ASCENDANCE OF AN OLIGARCHIC ELITE

I. SULTANS AND THE BASES OF DYNASTIC LEGITIMACY

Sinan served as chief architect for nearly half a century during the apogee of centralized imperial power under three sultans: Süleyman I (r. 1520–66), Selim II (r. 1566–74), and Murad III (r. 1574–95). By the sixteenth century the Ottoman state had evolved into an autocratic centralist regime that preserved some aspects of its earlier ghazi (warrior on behalf of Islam) frontier identity; namely, 'its dynamic conquest policy, its basic military structure, and the predominance of the military class within an empire that successfully accommodated disparate religious, cultural, and ethnic elements.'[1]

Originating in northwestern Anatolia at the turn of the fourteenth century as a tiny frontier principality caught between two worlds, the House of Osman had grown into a grand dynastic empire that regarded itself as the heir of Turkic, Islamic, and Eastern Roman imperial traditions.[2] After the conquest of Constantinople in 1453 Sultan Mehmed II created a territorially unified early modern empire by annexing rival principalities in the Balkans and Anatolia, and bringing the Crimean Khanate under Ottoman suzerainty. After defeating the Safavids of Iran in 1514, Selim I officially adopted the ancient royal title of 'Shah' that complemented his Turkic titles of 'Khan' and 'Khaqan'. Subsequently eliminating the Mamluk sultanate of Syria and Egypt in 1516–17, he terminated the line of Abbasid pseudo-caliphs based in Cairo, from whom his ancestor Bayezid I had procured the title 'Sultan of Rum' in 1394.[3] Bringing the Hijaz under Ottoman protection allowed Selim I to assume an additional title, the modesty of which only served to emphasize its prestige: 'Servant of the Two Noble Harams' (Mecca and Medina).[4]

Contrary to the legend that al-Mutawakkil, the last Abbasid pseudo-caliph of Mamluk Cairo, handed over his rights as universal caliph to Selim I in an official investiture ceremony, the sultan did not consider the caliphate necessary for legitimizing his rule. According to a daily record of his sojourn in the former Mamluk capital, he held a council meeting with the leading religious scholars of Cairo, who declared that the authorization of al-Mutawakkil was not imperative for the confirmation of his authority. Like many other Muslim rulers of the post-Mongol era, the Ottomans had adopted the title of caliph for rhetorical effect since the fifteenth century. Selim I perpetuated that practice by calling himself 'the caliph of God on earth.'[5]

The extension of Ottoman rule over the three principal sanctuaries of Sunni Islam in Mecca, Medina, and Jerusalem inspired Süleyman I to claim symbolic leadership over the Islamic world. He began to style himself 'the caliph of the whole world', and 'the caliph of all Muslims in the world' following the prestigious conquest of Baghdad (1534), the ancient capital of the Sunni Abbasid caliphs. Upon 'rescuing' that city from the Twelver Shiʿi Safavids, who had desecrated its religious monuments, the sultan had the 'khutba of the caliphate' pronounced in its resuscitated Friday mosques.[6] Sinan was one of the janissary architects (foot soldier chosen from the periodic levy of Christian children, or *devşirme*) who renovated Baghdad's despoiled mosque-cum-convent complexes.[7]

During Süleyman's reign, the doubled Ottoman territories were expanded to include Hungary in the west; Azerbayjan, western Iran, and Iraq in the east; and the North African coast (with the exception of Morocco) in the south, resulting in a formidable world empire that dominated the eastern Mediterranean basin. The claim for universal sovereignty was visually expressed by seven flags of different colours, representing Ottoman rule over the 'seven climes' of the world, and by four horse-tail standards (*tuğ*) symbolizing dominion over the 'four corners of the earth'.[8] Süleyman competed with his Hapsburg rival Charles V, the Holy Roman Emperor, by adding to his titulature the title of 'master of the lands of the Roman Caesars and Alexander the Great'. This competition was advertised in Europe by his Venetian-made helmet featuring four superimposed crowns that represented his universal rulership over the 'four quarters' of the world. The spectacular bejewelled golden helmet, iconographically associated with Alexander the Great, was paraded with other imperial insignia during the sultan's theatrical march to Vienna in 1532 (illus. 6).[9]

Süleyman was the first Ottoman sultan to claim the office of the caliphate 'with its implications of universal sovereignty'. His chief spokesman in formulating that claim was the shaykh al-Islam Ebussuud Efendi (grand mufti between 1545 and 1574), who publicized the sultan's titles in monumental inscriptions, dedicatory prefaces, and legal documents.[10] Such medieval scholars as Mawardi and Ghazali had differentiated the sacred office of caliph from the secular post of sultan, the latter holding office by delegation from the former: a custom perpetuated after the Mongol sack of Baghdad in 1258 by the pseudo-Abbasid caliphs of Cairo (1261–1517). Ebussuud combined both forms of sovereignty in the person of Süleyman, who held not only temporal but also spiritual authority as the possessor of the 'Great Imamate' and the 'Grand Caliphate' that God had bestowed on him as a hereditary office. By implication, Süleyman and his descendants became the modern heirs of the early Islamic caliphs, who once personified the sultanate and the caliphate.[11]

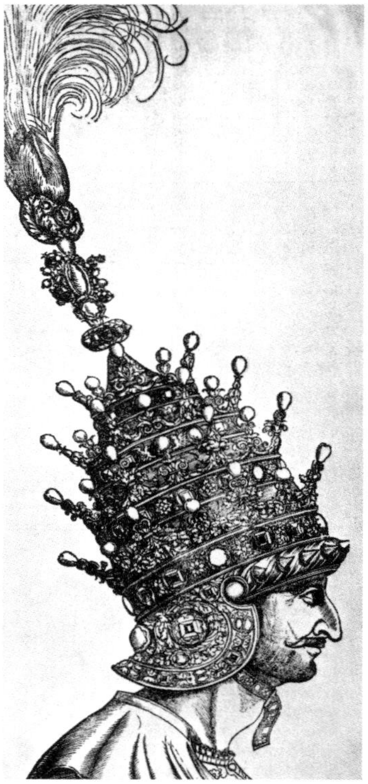

6 *Sultan Süleyman*, 1532, Venetian woodcut.

In mainstream Sunni doctrine, a necessary qualification for the caliphate was descent from the Prophet's tribe of Quraish, a requirement that theoretically excluded the Turkic Ottoman sultans from that office. To overcome this hurdle, Süleyman's Albanian-born retired grand vizier, Lutfi Pasha (g.v. 1539–41), composed a treatise on the 'Ottoman Caliphate' in 1554. It argued that descent from the Quraish tribe or appointment by a descendant of the Abbasid caliphs were no longer legal requirements for a sultan to adopt the title of 'Imam' and 'Caliph'. According to the Hanefi ulema of modern times, one of the four legal schools of Sunni Islam to which the Ottomans adhered, the only requirements for that title were 'conquering power and power of compulsion'. As the maintainer of the religious law and the reformer of the secular sultanic laws, Süleyman was unquestionably 'the Imam of the Age' and the defender of the shariʿa. So were his deputies, his amirs, and the ulema who served him.[12]

The claim to the universal caliphate enhanced the authority of the 'Sultan of the Arabs, Persians, and Ottomans [*Rūmī*, lit. Romans]' over his Muslim subjects belonging to diverse ethnic groups. It also proclaimed Süleyman's supremacy over other Islamic rulers as the divinely chosen vindicator and interpreter of the 'luminous shariʿa,' and as the 'shadow of God' on all nations. This exalted function was fulfilled by the sultan's incessant wars against the 'heretical' Twelver Shiʿi Safavids in the east and the 'infidel' Hapsburgs in the west. The formulation of Süleyman's image as an orthodox universal caliph brought with it an unprecedented emphasis on the shariʿa, with which Ebussuud harmonized the Ottoman dynastic laws. Süleyman, later on nicknamed Kanuni (the Lawgiver), is portrayed in the chronicles of his reign as a just ruler who 'entered the path of the Prophet's sacred shariʿa from which he never allowed any departure', and who never lost a moment in conducting holy warfare.[13] The early-seventeenth-century historian Hasanbeyzade describes the aged monarch, whose piety rose to puritanical proportions during the grand vizierate of his Croatian-born son-in-law, Rüstem Pasha (g.v. 1545–53, 1555–61), as follows (illus. 7):

> In his old age he completely gave up listening to the harp and stringed instruments and wearing silk robes. By adopting the use of wool and cotton cloths he strengthened the edifice of his righteousness. Removing gold and silver wares from his table, he began to eat from china and ceramic plates, in each instance distinguishing what was canonically allowed and forbidden. He took away the dervish convents of such rebellious heterodox groups as the Kalenders, giving them to Sunni Muslims belonging to the Hanefi legal school. He had faith in the pure shariʿa to such a degree that he is believed to have said to the army judges: 'If my hand has to be cut according to the religious law do not hesitate to do so!' He continually used to eradicate mischief plotters, depraved atheists, heretics, and the schismatic Shiʿis.[14]

Süleyman's successors, Selim II and Murad III, no longer adhered to such a strict interpretation of Sunni orthodoxy (illus. 8, 9). Nor did they personally conduct any military campaigns, preferring instead to delegate that function to their viziers. These two sultans, under whom Sinan continued to serve as chief architect, perpetuated the imperial legacy of the Süleymanic age, adding some islands in the Mediterranean (e.g. Cyprus) and strongholds at the Hapsburg and Safavid frontiers (including Tabriz, Erivan, and Shirvan) to an already overgrown empire that

7 Melchior Lorichs, *Sultan Süleyman*, etching based on a drawing made in 1559, *c.* 1562.

8 (top right) and 9 (right) Circle of Veronese, *Sultan Selim II* and *Sultan Murad III*, *c.* 1579, oil on canvas.

was proving hard to manage. Nicknamed 'the Sot' because of his unbridled passion for wine, Selim II could hardly be expected to follow his father's rigidly austere path. Among the sufi orders that flourished in his reign, the Halvetis came to occupy a particularly privileged position with a wide following among the ruling elite. The resurgence of sufi orders during the second half of the sixteenth century, especially during the reign of the mystically-inclined Murad III brought about a reconciliation of moderate sufism with the shariʿa, giving rise to a softened brand of orthodoxy formulated by Ebussuud during the grand vizierate of the Serbian-born Sokollu Mehmed Pasha (g.v. 1565–79).

The assassination of Sokollu (d. 1579), who like Sinan served under three sultans, is generally regarded as a turning point that marked the end of the empire's 'classical age'. A combination of factors paved the way for the crises of the late sixteenth and early seventeenth centuries when the centralized autocratic regime – governed in the sultan's name by the cabinet of the grand vizier who headed the imperial council – became challenged by factionalism and decentralizing forces. The discourse of decline, developed at that time by disenchanted Ottoman writers, interpreted troubling transformations as a corruption of the idealized Süleymanic order, which they desired to revive against the tide of changing times.[15] Despite this perception of decline, however, the empire was still a formidable entity and the dynasty's overall legitimacy remained unchallenged.

In 1593–94 the court historian Talikizade identified twenty qualities bolstering the legitimacy of the Ottoman dynasty that assured its supremacy over all preceding and contemporary Islamic dynasties. The superior qualities he attributes to the House of Osman reflect an inflated insider's view of sultanic identity. Before commenting on the implications of some of these qualities for architectural patronage, let me give a complete list that provides insights into the idealized self-image of the Ottoman sultans:[16]

1. Their unwavering adherence to Sunni Islam and the Hanefi legal school.
2. The inclusion of Mecca and Medina in their empire, which justified their title 'Protector of the Two Noble Harams' and required all Muslims on earth to obey their rule.
3. Their continual dynastic growth through the 'progression of son over father' in an unbroken line of patrimonial succession, with each sultan adding a land to inherited domains.
4. Their title 'Sultan of the Land and the Sea', especially bolstered by conquests in the Mediterranean that transformed their state into a seaborne empire.
5. Their emphasis on maintaining a strong standing army; no other contemporary dynasty in the Islamic east or in Europe had 80,000 *kul*s paid full-time by the state treasury, in addition to provincial fief (*timar*) holders.
6. The unequalled prestige of Istanbul as their 'exalted sultanic capital'; no other city could claim its fame and its location at the 'confluence of the two seas [Black Sea and Mediterranean]' where ships from the east and west continually loaded and unloaded merchandise.
7. The territorial extent of their empire encompassing the 'seven climes' in each of which the Ottoman khutba was pronounced in Friday mosques: Yemen in the first clime, Mecca in the second, followed by Cairo (third), Aleppo (fourth), Istanbul (fifth), Caffa (sixth), and Buda (seventh).
8. 'The prosperity of lands and the riches of subjects' in their imperial domains; no other Muslim state possessed such a fertile country with uninterrupted prosperous lands and 'an abundance of pious foundations'.
9. The diverse 'collection of communities' living peacefully under their multiconfessional empire; no other sultanate possessed a capital assembling such a variety of religions and races.
10. Their bravery.
11. Their poetic talent.
12. Their not having sought refuge in the court of another ruler.
13. Their moral purity.
14. Their miraculous immunity from the plague or other illnesses of the common people.
15. Their 'noble ancestry' going back to the Turkic ruler Oğuz Khan, with 'each Khan being the son of a Khan' unlike some earlier dynasties that 'appeared lowly in the eyes of notables' because they could not boast a distinguished lineage (such as the medieval sultanates tributary to the Abbasids and the Timurids).
16. Their adherence to the 'noble shariʿa'; in no other Islamic dynasty had the 'luminous shariʿa' been honoured to such a degree along with the respect paid to the ulema after Mehmed II's establishment of a centralized system of state-sponsored madrasas.
17. Their unmatched breeding and 'dignified gravity' (*edeb-ü-vakār*), as well as their resistance to oppressing subjects.
18. Their maintenance of a full treasury, unlike the example of the Safavid ruler Shah Ismaʿil, who merely left behind 60,000 aspers when he died.
19. Their absolute power and ability to enforce imperial laws even in remote areas simply by sending written decrees bearing their monogram, in contast to the Safavid shahs and the doges of Venice who were subject to the control of prominent patricians.
20. Their 'respect for individual property' and the right of even a simple villager in the Ottoman lands to accumulate money without any interference, unlike the domains of the Safavid shahs who greedily and unjustly appropriated the income of their subjects.

As official court panegyrist, Talikizade was no doubt expected to eulogize the sultans, whose idealized image he constructed against the foil of their Safavid rivals. The first and foremost characteristic of the Ottoman sultans he highlights, their Sunni-Hanefi identity, explains why Sinan's imperial patrons focused their architectural patronage on charitable complexes centred around Friday mosques: 'the Islamic building *par excellence*' and the traditional setting for the only universally recognized form of canonic ritual in Sunni Islam.[17] The second characteristic of the sultans, their title as protectors of the 'Two Noble Harams', was actively cultivated by the three rulers under whom Sinan served as chief architect. It found architectural expression in the successive remodelling projects of the holy shrines in Mecca and Medina which Sinan steered from the capital.[18]

Talikizade contrasts the third characteristic, the dynastic continuity of thirteen uninterrupted generations of Ottoman sultans, with the brevity of other Muslim dynasties characterized by only one famous ruler who conquered lands often dispersed in the next generation among competing male descendants. The House of Osman with its father-to-son succession principle (reinforced in Mehmed II's law code by the rule of fratricide) boasted a three-century-long pedigree unlike any other contemporary Muslim dynasty: by comparison, the Safavids and Mughals, whose states had recently emerged in the early sixteenth century, were mere upstarts. The principle of dynastic continuity was architecturally expressed through funerary socio-religious complexes that successive sultans commissioned in the capital cities of Bursa and Istanbul as personal victory memorials supported by pious endowments comprising the revenues of conquered lands. Accompanied by mausoleums built by the ruling sons of deceased sultans, these commemorative complexes named after individual rulers concretized the dynasty's uninterrupted patrilineal genealogy.[19]

The sixth quality of the sultans had even more obvious implications for their architectural patronage. The distinction of Istanbul as the empire's capital was architecturally articulated by the prestige mosques Sinan built for the upper echelons of the ruling elite, who resided there together with the royal family. It was he who reconfigured the imperial image of the capital with its famous skyline, one of the most recognizable icons of the Islamic lands. The primacy of Istanbul was enunciated through the differing programmes of mosque complexes sited in the empire's centre and periphery. This dichotomy materialized the spatial conceptualization of the empire in terms of an inner core (*iç-il*, inner domain), with the capital forming its nucleus, and an outer extension of provinces (*taşra*, exterior). The inner core incorporating Bursa, Istanbul, and Edirne was architecturally the most Ottomanized part of the empire, conceptualized as a series of cities radiating outward from the capital. During the 'classical age', the frontier zone (*uc*, border, extremity) constituted an ever-expanding fluid boundary, extended by newly conquered cities whose iconic Friday mosques symbolically functioned as territory markers. Sinan's provincial mosques were an architectural manifestation of the centralized reorganization of the Ottoman territories with the establishment of new provinces under Süleyman and his immediate successors.

The seventh dynastic quality closely related to this development was the territorial extent of the empire. Congregational mosques built by Sinan and local architects in each of the seven climes were an extension of the sultans' jurisdiction over the Friday prayers that provided legitimacy to their imperial dominion. The eighth quality, the prosperity of lands and the abundance of pious foundations, once again had important implications for architectural patronage and urban development. Talikizade criticizes the sparseness of urban settlements in the Safavid lands, noting that the Ottoman territories from Yanik (Györ, near Vienna) to Tabriz formed a continuously developed area traversed in four months:

> By contrast, the land of Iran is not cultivated and prosperous (*ābādān-u-ʿumrān*) unlike this country; most of its lands are deserts filled with the ghoul of wilderness. Sometimes a long distance of a week or two weeks is uninhabited and empty, due to which one has to carry water and bread while travelling. Between Qazvin and Khorasan is a twenty-five-day road where there is nothing but thorny plants. It is for this reason that the khans Sultan Alaüddin [the thirteenth-century Rum Seljuk ruler] built in Anatolia do not have next to them any villages or towns. According to the Iranian manner (*üslūb-ı ʿAcem*) there is no need for a khan at an inhabited region; they say khans are required only in empty places of wilderness. They do not have village after village as in our lands. It is recounted that when an Iranian gazed from the mountain of Bozdağ toward the plain of Birgi [in western Anatolia] he exclaimed: 'What a beautiful city, but alas, its neighbourhoods are separated from one another!' He imagined that the contiguous villages constituted a single city.[20]

Talikizade's pride in the cultivation of Ottoman lands dotted with many pious foundations was the outcome of a consistent imperial policy of endowing socio-religious complexes forming the nuclei of new settlements to promote Islam and to facilitate travel conditions for merchants and hajj pilgrims. These mosque-centred charitable pious foundations built by the sultans and their foremost *kul*s contributed to the urbanization of the Ottoman lands, unlike the free-standing caravansarays of Seljuk Anatolia and Safavid Iran sited in the midst of wilderness with no accompanying urban institutions.

Talikizade once again conceptualizes imperial territories in terms of road-like traversed distances, measured in units of time, in another historical work. He contrasts urban development in the Ottoman empire with the desolation of the Iranian world through an imagined conversation between the Safavid ruler Shah Tahmasp I (r. 1524–76) and his courtiers. The shah asks whether the domains of Mahmud of Ghazna (extending from Iran to India over a six-month distance) or of the Ottoman sultan (a three- to four-month distance stretching from Hungary to Van) are more prestigious. The courtiers judge the Ghaznavid territories superior, but the shah corrects them by explaining the superiority of the Ottoman domains. The latter, he says, is built up with contiguous villages and no empty spaces; whereas half of the Ghaznavid lands (a three-month distance) consisted of deserts, with inhabited places often separated by ninety days of travel. Even in built-up regions, it was rare to find a village or two within a day-long distance. By contrast, the Ottoman sultans possessed within a single day's distance fifty to sixty villages, excluding those lying beyond the road traversed. According to this calculation, their domains constituted a year-long distance as opposed to the two-and-a-half-month-long distance of inhabited lands within the Ghaznavid territories.[21]

Talikizade's passage brings to mind the main highway of the Ottoman empire, connecting the Balkans to the Hijaz, on which the majority of provincial mosque complexes designed by Sinan are distributed (Map 1). Beyond Istanbul, the chief architect's imperial style was primarily displayed along this continuously built up diagonal highway traversing the whole empire. Sinan's other provincial mosque complexes often fall on the trajectory of secondary routes linking the empire's centre to its eastern and western borders. Each halting station (*menzil*) along those routes was regularly recorded in *menzilnāme*s, diaries of military campaigns cataloguing the army's camping places. Illustrated versions of such manuscripts are painted with topographic images of cities lined up along military routes, the only examples of their kind in Islamic art. One of the famous illustrated versions, Matrakçı Nasuh's *Mecmūʿ-i Menāzil* (Compendium of Halting Stations, 1537–38), depicts the capital Istanbul along with cityscapes encountered during Süleyman's campaign of the 'Two Iraqs' (Arab and Persian) in which Sinan participated as a member of the janissary corps (illus. 34, 51, 102, 489).[22] This manuscript's representations of urban landscapes capture the progressively diminishing Ottoman architectural character of 'exotic' places in the east as Süleyman's army moves away from Istanbul. But these images also visually appropriate newly conquered towns through real or imagined details that add Ottomanizing touches to their architectural monuments. The illustrated *menzilnāme*s, then, can be seen as a visual counterpart to the territorial conceptualization of the empire as a collection of flourishing cities and ports lined up along major routes.

The architectural corollary of the ninth dynastic quality, the multiculturalism of the empire (composed of Gregorian Armenians, Orthodox Greeks, Jews, and Muslims) was the coexistence of churches, synagogues, and mosques conforming to differentiated codes of decorum that are discussed in Chapters 2 and 3. This exemplified a 'strategy of simultaneously welcoming non-Muslims into the Ottoman polity and denying equality to them' to underscore the privileged position of the dominant religion.[23] The unsurpassed status of the Ottoman sultans as the masters of their *kul*s, mostly recent converts into Islam recruited by the levy of Christian children or captured as slaves, found architectural expression in sultanic mosque complexes whose monumentality overshadowed all others. Smaller mosques built exclusively with the sultan's permission embodied the shared corporate identity of *kul*s who owed their social standing to their master. These mosques stamped by Sinan's distinctive 'classical' idiom were the products of an imperial regime in which the sultan and his family commanded the highest prestige at the apex of a pyramidal social order, defined by the *kul* system.

The Ottomans had created the first standing army in Europe with the janissary corps which buttressed their centralized imperial power, increasingly dominated during the sixteenth century by the *kul* system (the fifth dynastic characteristic highlighted by Talikizade). The stratified mosque typology codified by Sinan, himself a former janissary, both reflected and contributed to the consolidation of that system. The preference for an absolute monarchy (the nineteenth dynastic quality) over an oligarchic republican regime is captured in a fascinating passage by Talikizade which contrasts the authority of Ottoman sultans with the weakness of Venetian rulers:

> In Europe the doges (*doj begler*) do not have liberty, for in Venice there are 2800 patricians (*beg*) who are not allowed to own anything without permission from one another. And they do not have an income from any place. Their only revenue is trade. As the head of all patricians, the doge receives a wage of ten gold pieces per day; without their approval he cannot even move a mustard seed. Whatever he does, he does with the approval of all the 2800 patricians. He only has the power to appoint or dismiss the brokers of the city.[24]

This passage expresses the primacy of politics over trade in the Ottoman conception of sovereignty. Although the ruling elite increasingly came to resemble an oligarchy starting with Süleyman's reign, the absolute power of the sultan who mediated the religious and secular laws reigned supreme. It was this faith in centralized autocracy that contributed to the emergence of a decline discourse in late-sixteenth-century Ottoman historiography that lamented the decentralization of the imperial order.

The fifteenth quality of the sultans, their noble dynastic lineage, accentuated their master-slave relationship with *kul*s or manumitted *kul*s, whose social mobility did not depend on aristocratic origin but on merit. The Hapsburg ambassador to Süleyman's court, Ogier Ghiselin de Busbecq, observed in 1555 that no value was attached to 'nobility of birth' in the sultan's empire where 'personal merit' counted more: 'The House of Osman is the sole exception to this rule, being the only family in which birth confers rank.'[25] Prince Dimitrie Cantemir, the voivode of Moldavia who lived in Istanbul between 1688 and 1710, made a similar observation in his early-eighteenth-century history of the Ottoman empire:

The Turks do not measure nobility from a series of illustrious ancestors, as well because all Othomans in their opinion are equally noble, as because they think honours are to be conferred not on those who are nobly descended, but on those who are prudent, and by long experience have acquired by the culture of virtues, a nobleness of mind. The offspring of the Emperor therefore excepted, no man has any right to claim a precedency or a distinction on account of his ancestors.[26]

In this 'meritocracy' the *kul*s primarily owed their position to the person of the sultan whose noble dynastic lineage assured the perpetuation of the empire, a revered lineage that induced a popular cult of the emperor. During his stay in Istanbul (1589–91), the Moroccan ambassador al-Tamgrouti was struck by how greatly the sultan was venerated by his grandees and common subjects. 'The destitute, the most miserable people, who have never even seen him, pray for him at the end of all their meals and ask God to preserve him for them and to let him live and prosper', he wrote; 'It is the same for all the people in this country, where they pray for the sultan in the marketplace and the mosque alike.'[27]

Unlike its Ottoman counterpart, the Mamluk sultanate, which was based on a comparable system of slave soldiers recruited from the pagan Turks and Circassians of the Caucasus, did not develop into a dynasty where the sultan ruled by hereditary right. Ottoman *kul*s had no chance of rising to the sultanate; the highest post they could hope to attain in the state hierarchy was the grand vizierate. By contrast, in the Mamluk regime, any powerful slave soldier could theoretically become a sultan, a position that required the legitimizing approval of the Abbasid pseudo-caliphs housed in Cairo. The late-sixteenth-century Ottoman historian Hoca Sadeddin articulated this notable difference by pointing out that every Mamluk qualified to become a sultan, 'for neither did they care about the rights of lineage nor about the natural talents conferred by noble descent'.[28]

The increased pomp and gravity of court ceremonies during the Süleymanic age stressed the secluded sultan's majesty to such a degree that a coded sign language was invented in the palace to avoid speaking the ordinary language of the people in his presence.[29] The 'dignified gravity' (*vakār*) Talikizade attributes to the sultans (their seventeenth quality) is also recommended to the grand viziers in the *Āsāfnāme* (Book of Asaph, King Solomon's vizier), a book of advice written by the retired Lutfi Pasha.[30] It was during Süleyman's reign that the ceremonial representation of imperial grandeur increasingly became elaborated in public parades. These parades distinguished the sultan's hierarchically ranked *kul*s, wearing different types of costumes, from his ordinary subjects (illus. 10). When Süleyman rode into Bursa with his retinue in 1539, he was not at all pleased because the city's people came to greet him on their horses. Since this did not agree with his 'noble temperament', the sultan ordered that the people of Bursa should no longer ride on horses, except when they belonged to the fiefholding cavalry (*sipahi*). Later that year, Süleyman commanded his royal cavalry troops (*bölük halkı*) to ride from then on with pomp in front of him during ceremonial

10 Pieter Coecke van Aelst, *Friday Procession of Sultan Süleyman through the Hippodrome*, c. 1553, from a series of woodcuts published in 1553.

parades, carrying swords and fully armed.[31] The sultan raised the number of janissary guardsmen (*solak*) accompanying him in parades from eighty to a hundred because his augmented magnificence required more of them to stride in front of him to Friday mosques and other places.[32] The Frenchman Philippe du Fresne-Canaye (1573) notes that Selim II was less scrupulous about attending the Friday prayers than was his father Süleyman, who used to ride to a mosque each week. The 'grave and slow' pace of the sultan's horse 'befitting the majesty of such a grand monarch' was induced by suspending it in mid-air without any food the night and morning before the parade.[33]

The ranks of imperial officers subordinate to the grand vizier (the sultan's alter-ego) were reclassified during Süleyman's reign, parallel to the recodification of the ranks of provinces. The legendary magnificence of the sultan's court was further augmented by his costume reforms; it was during his reign that a red-capped tall white turban (*mücevveze*) was invented to distinguish the ruling elite from ordinary people. According to Mustafa Āli, by the end of Süleyman's reign, shops selling this type of turban rapidly multiplied 'as the slave soldiers and imperial council members began to wear it in a manner that affirmed their awesome grandeur (*ihtişām*) and majestic gravity (*mehābet*).'[34]

The architectural idiom codified by Sinan during the Süleymanic age was yet another expression of the aura of solemn magnificence. This is precisely the quality that a treatise commissioned by Sultan Abdülaziz for the international exhibition of Vienna in 1873 (*ʿUsūl-i Miʿmārī-yi ʿOsmānī*, Principles of Ottoman Architecture) singles out as the dynastic 'character' of the architectural style perfected by Sinan: a style whose 'majestic gravity' (*mehīb*) is complemented by 'grace' (*leṭāfet*).[35]

Talikizade specifically links the eighteenth dynastic quality, the maintenance of a full treasury, with architectural patronage. He explains that the builder of Hagia Sophia, who ran out of money, had to discover a treasure to complete its construction, while the Umayyad caliph who commissioned the Great Mosque of Damascus financed it with only four hundred chests of gold. By contrast, Süleyman's treasury remained full even after he spent huge sums for construction projects in addition to paying the wages of all his *kul*s. He paid 30,060,960 aspers for the Kağıdhane water channels in Istanbul, 54,697,560 aspers for his Friday mosque in the same city (Süleymaniye), and more than that sum for the great bridge of Büyükçekmece en-route to Edirne.[36] This boastful statement demonstrates the perception of Süleyman's grand architectural projects, all of them supervised by Sinan, as testimonials to the sultan's economic power (Appendix 2).[37]

The sixteenth quality of the Ottoman sultans highlighted by Talikizade is their adherence to the shariʿa. He explains that each country where the 'pure shariʿa' is adhered to becomes prosperous, which in turn leads to an accumulation of the state treasury, which in turn enables the state to support victorious soldiers.[38] This nuanced reformulation of the ancient Persian concept of the 'cycle of equity', substitutes the shariʿa for the royal category of justice. Such a claim could only be made after Ebussuud had harmonized the secular sultanic laws with the religious precepts of the shariʿa. Talikizade's passage indirectly implies that the sparseness of urban development and pious foundations in the Safavid domains mentioned earlier was a corollary of the shahs' failure to observe the rules of the shariʿa. Hadidi, a chronicler from the early part of Süleyman's reign, explicitly connects the high degree of urbanization in the Ottoman empire with the triumph of religious orthodoxy and royal justice, expressed by the unprecedented multitude of mosques:

> Today among the inhabited quarters of the world famous is
> The kingdom of Rum for being prosperous and well-built.
>
> Thanks to its just Imam and Sunni congregations,
> Its mosques overflow with worshippers.[39]

Another author writing around that time, Mevlana Isa, also draws attention to the proliferation of mosques in the empire's flourishing cities during the reign of Süleyman. He interprets this as a sign indicating that the sultan was the long awaited messiah, the prophesied 'renewer of religion' in the tenth century of the Islamic era: 'You know the open space around a mosque is [traditionally] a mile, / At this time one mile has ten mosques.'[40]

One of the main polemical criticisms Ottoman jurists directed against the Safavids, whom they on occasion declared 'heretics' worse than non-Muslim 'infidels', was their resistance to observe the canonically obligatory congregational and Friday prayers.[41] Talikizade's chronicle on the Ottoman conquest of Tabriz in 1585 remarks how 'the voices of wandering minstrels [chanting dervishes of the Safavid sufi order] became replaced with the sound of the call to prayer' at the abandoned congregational mosque of the Akkoyunlu ruler Uzun Hasan in that city.[42]

In Safavid Iran, the question of the legality of the Friday prayer service during the absence of the hidden Imam (who according to Twelver Shiʿi theology had disappeared and would reappear only on the Day of Judgment) was a highly debated subject revolving around three options. Some scholars argued that the Friday prayer was 'forbidden' during the occultation of the Imam. Others held that it was either an 'essential' (*takhyiri*) or 'optional' (*ʿayni*) duty. Proponents of the former position contended that the presence of the Imam or his deputy was required to lead the prayers, while the advocates of the latter position did not consider their presence necessary for undertaking the prayers. During the reign of Shah Tahmasp, official attempts to establish the Friday prayer as an 'essential' duty by Shaykh ʿAli al-Karaki, a cleric closely associated with the

Safavid court, proved unsuccessful and Friday services were discontinued after his death in 1534. The same position was more effectively promoted under Shah ʿAbbas (r. 1588–1629) by the shaykh al-Islam of the new capital Isfahan, Shaykh Baha'i (d. 1620–21).[43] Another scholar, Mulla Sadra, attempted to synthesize sufism with the shariʿa in this new context. Criticizing sufi assemblies characterized by 'gorging on stew (*āsh*), mystical concerts (*samāʿ*), clapping and stamping', he asserted that one must be 'worshipping in accordance to the shariʿa without which spiritual exercises are confusing and confused.'[44]

The architectural patronage of the shahs did not include monumental mosques until the early seventeenth century, when Shah ʿAbbas built in Isfahan the first and only Safavid example of a grand Friday mosque flanked by two theological madrasas. His new capital became the centre of a budding autocratic regime partly inspired by the Ottoman model, bolstered by the codification of Shiʿi orthodoxy and the institution of slave servants (*ghulam*) recalling the sultan's *kul*s. But continuing disagreement within the community only permitted limited attempts to establish the Friday prayer, and thus lend legitimacy to the Safavid identification with the faith.[45]

We shall see in Chapter 3 that Sinan's centralized Friday mosques with unified spaces supplanted former multifunctional T-type convent-mosques housing sufi rituals not unlike those of the Safavid order. It was during the reign of Süleyman that centrally-planned Friday mosques became the pre-eminent mode of architectural patronage for the sultans, their family, and their foremost *kul*s. The boom in the construction of Friday mosques throughout the Ottoman domains under Süleyman and his immediate successors closely revolved around the question of the ruler's legitimacy as an Imam, on which the legitimacy of the Friday prayers depended.[46]

The fourteenth-century Maghribi scholar Ibn Khaldun singles out the administration of Friday mosques and the delegation of the leadership of prayer as the most important function of the caliphate, higher than royal authority:

> It should be known that city mosques are of two kinds, great spacious ones which are prepared for holiday prayers, and other, minor ones which are restricted to one section of the population or one quarter of the city and which are not for the generally attended prayers. Care of the great mosques rests with the caliph or with those authorities, wazirs, or judges, to whom he delegates it ... The administration of mosques that are restricted to one section of the population or to one quarter of the city rests with those who live nearby. These mosques do not require the supervision of a caliph or ruler.[47]

Mustafa Āli regards the khutba, exclusively pronounced in Friday mosques, as the ultimate symbol of sultanic and caliphal legitimacy:

> The mighty sovereigns have been given two divine gifts, one being the noble *khutba* and the other one [the privilege to strike] the illustrious coins [in their names]. Of course, in the sublime *khutba* the idea of the greatness of the royal prestige and of the glory of the immaculate person of the ruler is expressed, it teaches high and low to obey their leaders and instructs the just and the righteous to follow the caliph of the time.[48]

Ebussuud's reforms discussed in Chapter 2 required the construction of masjids in every village and Friday mosques in cities where they were lacking, along with the compulsory observance of congregational prayers. As Halil İnalcık observes, this trend was 'the beginning of a more conservative, shariʿa-minded Ottoman state' bitterly resented by the Turkmen tribes of Anatolia, many of whom were ardent devotees of the Safavid sufi order.[49] Lutfi Pasha's treatise on the 'Ottoman Caliphate' refers to Süleyman as the 'Imam of the Age who stands in the place of the Apostle of God' in maintaining the congregational prayers and the religious festivals.[50] It was the inextricable link between the destinies of the caliph-sultan and his grandees, whose personal interests were intimately bound with those of the dynasty, that ensured dynastic legitimacy:

> For the majority of the people of his age are his freedmen (*ʿutaqa*) and the freedmen of his fathers and ancestors, and it is not possible ... to agree upon becoming subject to other than him; since there is no possibility of banding together for the support of any other than the ʿOthmānī, because the ʿOthmānī[s] are blameless in respect of maintenance of the Faith and Equity and the Jihād.[51]

II. THE ASCENDANCE OF AN OLIGARCHIC ELITE

In the classical Ottoman regime the population was divided into two main groups. The first group (*askeri*), exempted from all forms of taxation, comprised the military and administrative ruling class, including the ulema, which performed various public functions as delegates of the sultan. The tax exempt Ottoman officialdom had separate career paths, each with its prescribed 'ladder' of titular ranks: the ulema, the various military corps, the palace service, and the bureaucracy. A certain solidarity or fellow-feeling bound together the members of each career as a group, and the ruling elite shared a corporate identity that marked it off from the sultan's ordinary subjects. The second group (*reaya*, literally 'the flock'), included the merchants, artisans, and peasants who pursued productive activities and paid taxes. The sultan's protected non-Muslim subjects (*dhimmi*), organized as semi-autonomous religious communities who were free to practice their own religion, albeit subordinate in status, had to pay an extra poll-tax. Between the two groups was an intermediary group (*muaf ve müsellem*) exempt from extraordinary taxes in return for special services, such as

1

2

5

6

guarding mountain passes and repairing bridges, roads, or castles. Although a certain degree of mobility existed between these groups, it was considered more appropriate for individuals to 'remain in their own status group so that equilibrium in the state and society could be maintained.'[52]

After the conquest of Constantinople, the sultans increasingly began to rely on *kul*s to consolidate the centralized administration of the state. The *kul* system, an institution partly inspired by slave soldiers used by such Islamic states as the Abbasids and the Mamluks, augmented the dynasty's autocratic regime by curbing the rise of rival aristocratic families. The levy of Christian children (*devşirme*) enabled non-Muslim subjects converted into Islam to attain the highest positions in the military and bureaucracy, ordinarily denied to those born as Muslims. Besides the fiefholding cavalry (*tımarlı sipahi*), by far the most common career paths open to Muslim-born subjects were the religious bureaucracy and the scribal ranks.

It was during Süleyman's reign that palace-educated pages – captured slaves or novice boys recruited by the *devşirme* system – infiltrated the upper ranks of the ruling elite to an unprecedented degree. Trusted *kul*s with whom the sultan had developed a personal relationship in his palace tied together the imperial system at multiple levels. Mustafa Āli notes how Süleyman exclusively promoted former servants of his private inner palace (*enderun*) to the empire's highest posts: 'Making the viziers his sons-in-law and selecting the majority of the grandees among the fortunate ones exiting from his inner palace was his innovation; in his reign no other [type of] accomplished and judicious person was given the vizierate.'[53] From the twenty-three viziers of Süleyman's reign (nine grand viziers and fourteen viziers), only four were born as Muslims; the remaining nineteen were converts who had served as pages or white eunuchs at the sultan's inner palace.[54]

Āli observes that the viziers were increasingly integrated into the royal family through marriage to Süleyman's sisters, daughter, and granddaughters. After the late fifteenth century, princesses were no longer wedded to the descendants of prominent Turkish families or of neighbouring dynasties to forge political alliances. Instead, they married the sultan's *kul*s as part of a dynastic policy of centralization. Selim I's sons-in-law tended

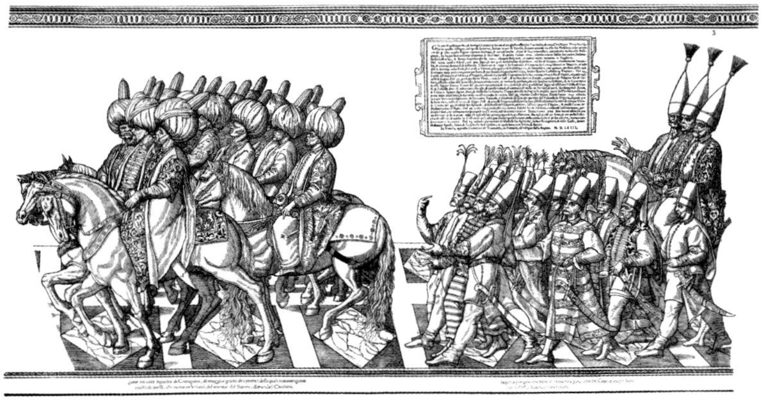

3

4

7

8

11 Domenico de' Franceschi, *Friday Procession of Sultan Süleyman*, a series of nine wood engravings published in Venice in 1563:

1. Cavalry soldiers (*sipahioğlanı*) and policemen (*ases*)
2. Chief policeman (*subaşı*) and chiefs of janis sary regiments (*bülükbaşı, yayabaşı*)
3. Court tasters, janissaries and their captains
4. Agha of janissaries, grand admiral, and chief of stables
5. Chief gatekeepers and finance ministers
6. Army judges, and footmen attending the sultan in processions (*solak*)
7. Court messengers (*çavuş*) and their chiefs (*çavuşbaşı*), two young viziers, two older viziers
8. Grand vizier, *çavus*es who clear the sultan's path, and running footmen (*peyk*)
9. Sultan Süleyman 'the Turkish Emperor', with two pages carrying his cushion and saddle

9

to be viziers or statesmen who eventually rose to the vizierate. Süleyman I continued his father's policy but almost exclusively selected his grand viziers and viziers from royal sons-in-law.[55] The ancient dynastic policy of keeping royal bridegrooms from rising above the rank of provincial governor had been instituted to prevent them from interfering with politics at the capital. That policy was abandoned during Süleyman's reign, when vizierial posts at the imperial council increasingly became the preserve of sons-in-law married to princesses.

The growing centralization of the royal family inside the capital contributed to the emergence of an oligarchic elite with hitherto uncustomary privileges and a more luxurious lifestyle. The early-seventeenth-century reformist writer Koçi Beg complains about this transformation:

> [Sultan Selim I] used to marry his noble daughters either to individuals with an aristocratic lineage or to talented men

brought up at their venerable inner palace; the royal sons-in-law did not stay at the capital but were sent away as a precaution against meddling with the affairs of the state. Appointed for the duration of their lifetime to a sanjak, they became powerful and mighty there and contributed to the prosperity of those places, demonstrating many talents in the victorious frontiers of the empire.[56]

Koçi Beg traces the growing magnificence of *kul*s, who became preoccupied with reputation and conspicuous consumption, to the reign of Süleyman (illus. 11[1–9]):

> His Highness the late Sultan [Süleyman], seeing the power of the *kul*s and the abundance of the treasury, augmented his splendour and fame, and the viziers imitated his example according to the saying: 'The people follow the religion of their ruler.' All the people thus became preoccupied with magnificence and reputation, to such an extent that eventually the income of office holders and the wages of the *kul*s did not even suffice for their bread money; consequently they had to resort to aggression and injustice.[57]

Declaring that the introduction of magnificence was Süleyman's most harmful innovation, Koçi Beg observes how in his own time office holders preferred spending their income on 'houses and gardens and kiosks and sable furs and other luxuries, such that in wartime they cannot even raise two soldiers'.[58]

Another innovation of Süleyman was the nearly autonomous power he delegated to his grand viziers. As the deputy of the secluded sultan, the grand vizier became the empire's *de facto* ruler, at the head of a centralized bureaucracy governed by his cabinet, which met four times a week at the imperial council of the Topkapı Palace (illus. 12). The Venetian diplomat Bernardo Navagero (1553) observes how Süleyman, unlike his predecessors, entrusted the government to his grand viziers. Daniele Barbarigo (1564) says the grand vizier was now all-powerful, contrary to the custom of earlier sultans, who encouraged the viziers to consult with each other.[59]

The deposed grand vizier Lutfi Pasha's mid-sixteenth-century book of advice affirms that 'there is no rank higher than the grand vizierate'. The holder of this office, who gave extra public and private audiences in his own palace, is urged to regularly consult with the shaykh al-Islam, the head of the salaried ulema, who did not belong to the imperial council.[60] The post of shaykh al-Islam (grand mufti) gained new prominence with the unparalleled prestige and power of Ebussuud, who held that office from 1545 until his death in 1574.[61] Such powerful grand viziers as Rüstem Pasha and Sokollu Mehmed Pasha formed strong alliances with Ebussuud, whose fatwas provided religious legitimation for the policies of their cabinets. Lutfi Pasha's book of advice outlines in minute detail the relative position of each officer's rank in order to clarify who should be superseded by whom during state ceremonies and who should visit the palace of whom. The Moroccan ambassador Abu'l Hasan al-Tamgrouti (1589–91) could not help but be astonished by the Ottoman ruling elite's excessive concern with relative rank: 'Never should any one of them deal on an equal basis with his superior, be it in marching in the same row, in wearing a turban or clothes of the same quality, or in sitting on a similar seat; I have never seen men observe marks of precedence more scrupulously.'[62]

Prior to Süleyman's time, the administration of the state had been a relatively ad hoc affair. The tripled size of the bureaucracy in the early part of his reign necessitated the rationalization of administrative structures, along with the hierarchical re-classification and professionalization of ranks in terms of function and salary. Cornell Fleischer observes that the late 1530s and 1540s saw the 'energetic compilation, codification, and

12 Sokollu Mehmed Pasha presiding over the imperial council with Selim II over-looking from a window above him as the chancellor records the proceedings at the lower left: at the grand vizier's left sit five viziers with the two army judges and three finance ministers at the right; *c.* 1581, watercolour on paper from, Lokman, *Shāhnāma-i Salīm Khān*.

modification of imperial ordinance, its regularization, universalization, and reconciliation with the dictates of the Holy Law, and also the rapid expansion and deepening of the machinery of government based on newly articulated principles of hierarchy, order, meritocracy, regularity, and replicability of basic structures based on function rather than on persons'.[63]

Steps were taken to reorganize the provincial administration through the classification of ranked provinces (entrusted to governor-generals, *beglerbegi*), which in turn were subdivided into sanjaks (sub-provinces commanded by *begs*). The harmonization of dynastic law codes (*kanun*) with the shariʿa, the zealous reinforcement of religious orthodoxy, the formulation of a new diplomatic language of empire in the bureaucracy, and urban renewal were different facets of the Süleymanic programme of universal imperial dominion.[64] Fleischer observes that by the 1540s Süleyman and his lieutenants had built 'a new cadre of servitors educated wholly within his palace and acculturated under his regime'. These men raised in the new ethos of order and hierarchy were 'committed to the dynastic cause by the promise of regular reward for the performance of specified, depersonalized, bureaucratized functions'. The emergence of a 'self-aware, corporatized elite conscious of its prerogatives guaranteed by imperial law' became the bearer of a coherent dynastic culture not consolidated until the 1550s.[65]

The shift to a new universe of precision, with clearer articulations of hierarchical structure across space and society, became deeply ingrained in classical conceptions of empire. The chancellor Mustafa Celalzade, one of the architects of the new order and the codifier of forms of titulature used for government officials in imperial decrees, was also the architect of a new historiography that glorified the Süleymanic age.[66] The dual system of classification used in ranking provinces and offices forms the very basis of Celalzade's history covering Süleyman's reign until the year 1557, as its title, *Ṭabaḳātü'l-Memālik ve Derecātü'l-Mesālik* (The Ranks of Imperial Dominions and the Grades of Government Officials), implies. Working closely with Ebussuud, its author had composed Süleyman the Lawgiver's secular law codes while he served as chief chancellor of the imperial council for twenty-three years (1534–57). No wonder, then, that this 'mufti of the law codes' (*müftī-i ḳānūn*) wrote a historical work conceptualizing the Ottoman empire in terms of an overlapping hierarchy of territories and bureaucratic posts emanating from the central core of the capital and speading outwards to the provinces.[67]

This hierarchical conception of empire found its counterpart in the nuanced gradation of mosque types codified by Sinan, who brought architecture in line with the rank-conscious mentality of the classical age. The emergence of a new architectural paradigm, different from the loosely ordered system that preceded it, was not simply the reflection of a zeitgeist. The corps of royal architects belonged to the machinery of the state, with its chief occupying an administrative position as one of the aghas of the sultan's extended household of *kul*s. Sinan had personally witnessed the codification of ranks at the imperial council, under whose portico he sat whenever he attended the grand vizier's cabinet meetings (he incidentally built a Friday mosque for Celalzade in the capital's suburb of Eyüp). Placed under the grand vizier's jurisdiction, the chief architect was a salaried officer from the ranks of the ruling elite whose mentalities he shared.[68] Sinan's autobiographies and the endowment deed of his pious foundations, analysed in Chapter 4, show how integrally his own sense of being was bound up with the corporate identity of the ruling elite to which he belonged.

The Ottoman state's emphasis on religious affiliation rather than ethnic identity as the critical factor of cultural distinction made the Friday mosque the monument of choice to express imperial hegemony during the classical age. The strong sense of belonging to a hierarchically ranked corporate group did not necessitate the complete erasure of childhood memories or ethnic affiliations; in fact, *kul*s holding official posts often endowed charitable monuments in their place of birth (as Sinan did at Ağırnas in Kayseri). This resulted in a colourful mixture of multicultural identities among the ruling elite, identities misunderstood or suppressed in nationalist historiography. The frequently used modern label 'Ottoman Turks' would have been flatly dismissed as an anachronism by an intellectual like Mustafa Āli, who regarded the amalgamation of different ethnicities as the very basis of the Ottoman elite's distinctive identity:

> Those varied peoples and different types of Rumis (Romans) living in the glorious days of the Ottoman dynasty, who are not [generically] separate from those tribes of Turks and Tatars . . . are a select community and pure, pleasing people who, just as they are distinguished in the origins of their state, are singled out for piety, cleanliness, and faith. Apart from this, most of the inhabitants of Rum are of confused ethnic origins. Among its notables there are few whose lineage does not go back to a convert to Islam ... either on their father or mother's side, the genealogy is traced to a filthy infidel. It is as if two different species of fruitbearing tree mingled and mated, with leaves and fruits; and the fruit of this union was large and filled with liquid, like a princely pearl. The best qualities of the progenitors were then manifested and gave distinction, either in physical beauty, or in spiritual wisdom.[69]

Nor could the royal family itself claim ethnic purity by the sixteenth century. Even though the dynasty's founders were Turkish in origin, the sultans had intermarried during the fourteenth and early fifteenth centuries with the daughters of allied Muslim and non-Muslim rulers from Anatolia, Byzantium, and the Balkans. After the consolidation of the *kul* system in the second half of the fifteenth century, they began to bear children exclusively with non-Turkish concubines of slave origin, a practice that further diluted the dynasty's original ethnic identity.[70]

The Austrian Hapsburg traveller Hans Dernschwam observed in the 1550s that Süleyman preferred not to promote Turks to important positions; it was converted Christians from a *devşirme* or slave origin who became viziers and pashas. These converts became angry when they were called Turks, preferring instead to be called Muslims. They regarded themselves superior to Anatolian Muslims, because converts commanded higher respect; but they were also embarrassed to talk in their native tongues with their countrymen. Nevertheless, all languages were spoken in Istanbul, which resembled ancient Babylon in its linguistic diversity.[71] Prince Cantemir wrote in the early eighteenth century that the ruling elite preferred to identify itself as 'Ottoman', an identity connoting refinement and elegance, rather than 'Turkish', which was associated with roughness and crudeness (Turks in the empire were generally nomadic tribal groups with 'heterodox' religious leanings).[72] Ottoman-ness was the culturally constructed identity of a refined, literate, and sedentary ruling elite characterized by its multiethnic orientation. This fabricated identity became largely unified through religious affiliation to Sunni Islam objectified in Friday mosques, through the Ottoman-Turkish court language (a flowery composite of Turkish, Persian, and Arabic), and through a distinctive visual culture in which architecture reigned supreme.

As Eric Hobsbawm has argued, a powerful combination of representations – visible symbols of collective practices – give palpable reality to an otherwise imaginary community.[73] The Topkapı Palace became the nucleus from which visual signs, with a two-fold function of homogenization and distinction, were disseminated. Its architectural layout with multiple courtyards, its staff of household servants wearing different types of uniforms, its codes of behaviour, and its modes of conspicuous consumption were replicated on a smaller scale in the palaces of the grandees (illus. 13 [1-4]).[74] Acculturated in the sultan's palace as royal pages, top-ranking dignitaries shared a court culture they continued to cultivate after being married to princesses or concubines brought up in the imperial harem.

Ottoman visual politics played an important role in the construction of a cohesive communal identity. Much like the Roman empire, the Ottoman world, with its public rituals, buildings, and industrial arts (renowned especially for İznik tiles, textiles, and carpets), was an intensely visual culture. Besides the gradation at all levels of society of such signs of status as costumes and headgear, the messes of the janissary corps were classified by pictorial emblems (illus. 14). Unlike abstract Mamluk blazons, these emblems placed over the doors of janissary dormitories and paraded in processions, featured more concrete representational imagery. Ever present in the public arena, such emblematic signs were also displayed at the entrances of coffee shops frequented by specific janissary messes and on military tents, standards, tattoos, and tombstones.

The politics of space and vision not only conferred a sense of cultural unity to diverse imperial territories, but also played a role in the construction of identity. Uniforms corresponding to a graduated scale of salaries began to define the corporate identity of *kul*s from the moment they were recruited as novices (*acemi oğlan*). A miniature painting from the 1550s in the *Süleymānnāme* (History of Süleyman) depicts the levying of Christian children in a Balkan town to underscore the role of the *kul* system as the backbone of the autocratic sultan's centralized regime (illus. 15). As the selected youngsters are lined up in their new red uniforms, a janissary officer records in a register their name, physical description, place of origin, and regiment number. The miniature shows parents and the local priest witnessing this emotionally-charged procedure that evoked mixed reactions. Although the compulsory levy gave a chance for upward mobility to Christian children from rural areas, the primary source of recruits, obviously not every family was willing to give away its offspring. According to Dernschwam, fortunes were made by those who helped eligible boys hide from levy officers, and Āli admits that some officers were prone to bribery.[75]

This understandable parental reluctance is illustrated in an anonymous biography of the grand vizier Sokollu Mehmed Pasha and his nephew Sokollu Mustafa Pasha (both of them patrons of Friday mosques designed by Sinan).[76] We learn from this source that a recruitment officer sent by Sultan Süleyman to find appropriate boys to serve as pages in his palace spotted the future grand vizier at the Bosnian village of Sokolovići (Hawk's Nest). From his looks, the officer immediately knew the child was destined for greatness. As he began to research the identity of the boy's parents, an uncle, who was a rich and influential monk at the Mileševa monastery, offered a bribe to dissuade him, but to no avail. The parents, too, tried to keep their child, but the officer gave them the following advice:

> Don't you know that your son will be honoured with the sultan's service and after he rises to a high post all of you will enjoy happiness and riches? You should not reject the bird of fortune that has perched on your head; without leaving your desolate homeland how can this boy attain an influential position at the court?

Promising that one day their son would come back to take care of them in old age, the officer managed to persuade the parents, and he 'took the baby hawk from its nest'.[77]

Sokollu did not forget his roots: he eventually searched for his parents and brothers, convincing most of them along with other relatives to convert into Islam, and he established a pious endowment in his hometown. He was married to Süleyman's

1

2

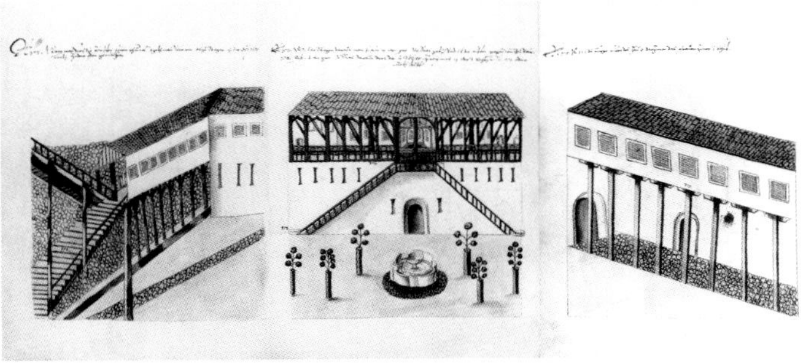

13 Anonymous Austrian artist, Şokollu Mehmed Pasha's palace in Istanbul, *c.* 1570s, watercolour on paper. 1. Gatehouse. 2. Courtyard of the public audience hall. 3. Public audience hall. 4. Private audience hall.

grandaughter (İsmihan Sultan) and he rose to the highest post in the empire as grand vizier (illus. 16). In addition to promoting converted family members to high offices, he backed the distinguished ecclesiastical vocations of those relatives who chose to remain Christian. The trajectory of his career, which I discuss more fully in relation to his architectural patronage, was not uncommon.[78] The majority of patrons who commissioned Sinan to build Friday mosques were converts to Islam who came from a *devşirme* background, like the chief architect himself (Appendix 1).

Although Christian children were recruited to ensure loyalty to the sultan through a complete severance of family ties,

3

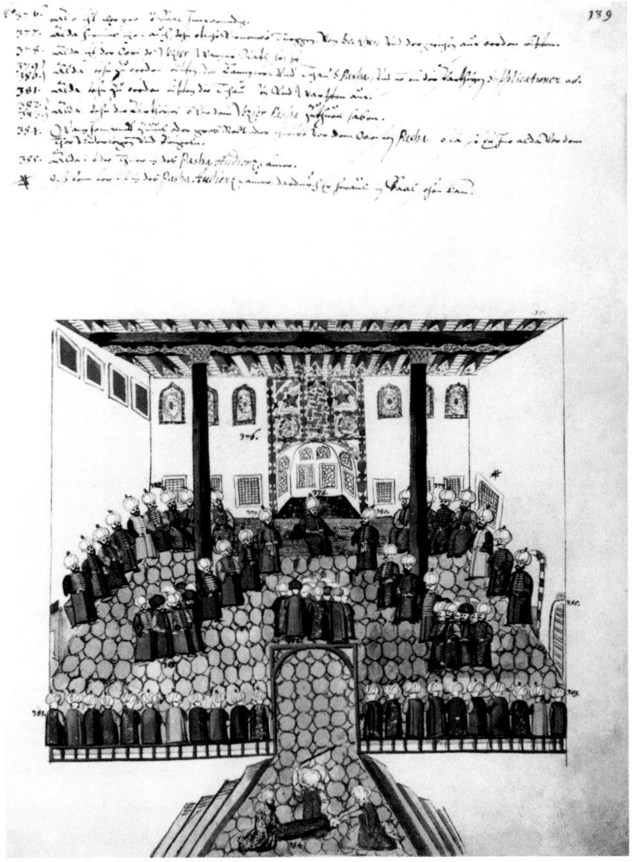

4

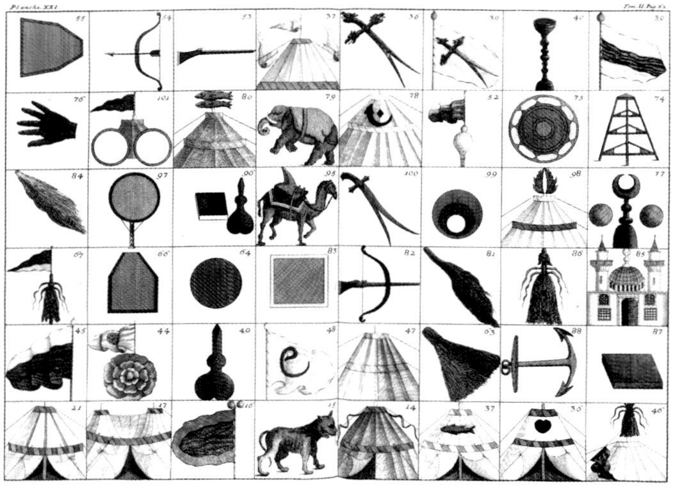

14 Emblems of some janissary messes.

the biographies of mosque patrons considered in Part 3 confirm how many of them reestablished contact with their families, traceable through levy registers and childhood memories. Individuals who had been captured as slaves by raiders on land or at sea also contacted distant relatives beyond the empire.[79] One of them was the queen Nurbanu Sultan (wife of Selim II and mother of Murad III), who vividly remembered being born to a Venetian aristocratic family before she was taken as a slave by corsairs. Her official identity as an Ottoman queen, who commissioned Sinan to build a monumental mosque complex in the capital, did not deter her from actively searching out her relatives in Venice and Corfu through intermediaries and letters.[80]

An early-seventeenth-century source entitled the 'Customs of the Janissaries' testifies to the importance attached to noble descent and signs of good character in the recruitment of Christian children. Written by an elderly janissary at a time when the *devşirme* system had started to disintegrate, this source makes the following recommendation to levy officers:

> And in levying the children of infidels they should recruit the sons of notables, such as preachers and those with a noble lineage. They should only take one of two sons and not both of them, choosing the one who is preferable. And they should avoid taking single sons who are needed to help their father in agriculture, so as not to reduce the taxes collected by the provincial fiefholders. They should not levy nameless children who are bound to be greedy and uncouth, the sons of village representatives who are the basest among villagers, or the sons of shepherds who are also uncouth due to having grown up in the mountains (except when the latter is the son of a notable who has impersonated a shepherd from fear of being recruited).[81]

The author points out that it was uncommon to levy boys from the borderlands of Bulgaria and Hungary because they did not generally become good Muslims, being inclined to reconvert to Christianity at the first chance and to escape back to their homelands. Nor was it a custom to take children from eastern Anatolia because they were 'ethnically mixed with Turkmens, Kurds and Georgians.'[82]

The author lists preferred physiognomic traits that should be sought among the recruits, and highlights the special privilege enjoyed by Bosnians, many of whom rose to high positions after being selected for service in the sultan's palace and its gardens. The importance attached to physical beauty is confirmed by Mustafa Āli, who explains how experts in the science of physiognomy presided over the process of selecting the most handsome boys for the sultan's inner palace, boys whose face and demeanour showed signs of 'goodness and fairness'.[83] The janissary author also explains why the levy officers should avoid recruiting Turks or non-Muslim children who spoke Turkish:

> The reason for not levying Turkish children is that most of them are without pity and lack religiosity. Should they

15 The recruitment of novices from a Balkan village, 1558, watercolour on paper from Arifi, *Süleymānnāme*.

> become servitors of the sultan, their relatives would imagine themselves as *kul*s, harming the sultan's subjects living in their province, in addition to refusing to pay taxes and causing disorder in the countryside by pretending to be janissaries. The value of recruiting the children of infidels is that upon conversion their religious zeal turns them into enemies of their own relatives and people.

In other words, Turks would bond with the native populations with which they shared familial, ethnic, and religious ties; whereas converts would bond with their masters by developing new identities after cutting ties with their own people. The author adds that converts proved to be more heroic in war and more effective in collecting taxes from their relatives who remained infidels.[84]

This observation is confirmed by many European travellers. For instance, Dernschwam asserts that converts to Islam turned out to be worse enemies of Christians in Europe than native Turks. They forgot their parents during long years of servitude in which they formed a stronger bond with their masters, whose favour brought them to positions of power. He reports that eight- to twelve-year-old boys were systematically recruited in three-year intervals, with the most handsome ones selected to serve in the sultan's palaces and gardens as the future grandees. The Christian citizens of Istanbul, Edirne, and Bursa were excluded from the levy together with Jews, Turks, and Muslims.[85] European writers also note the presence among the Ottoman ruling elite of numerous renegades (including Hungarians, Italians, Germans, and occasionally Frenchmen) who had become Muslims either through voluntary conversion due to prospects for advancement or through compulsion. For instance, a Franciscan friar who visited the Holy Land in 1565, became friendly with the police chief of Damascus, who had been captured in Hungary in a raid when he was twelve. This man remembered meeting Martin Luther as a small boy and asked what had happened to him, not knowing that Luther had died many years ago. Now he had two attractive wives and children he was very fond of.[86]

Mustafa Āli notes the kinship Ottoman dignitaries felt towards their own ethnic group, which did not necessarily conflict with their official identity:

> And whenever a grand vizier or vizier is Bosnian, it is for certain that the prestige of imperial council members belonging to that group will daily increase through advancement and promotion to higher posts. If he is Albanian, his own group becomes fortunate, for he is likely to promote his relatives and siblings, appointing to reputable positions those from his own city and hometown.

Āli adds that no grand vizier failed to 'fully incline towards his own people.'[87]

16 Sokollu Mehmed Pasha, in an engraving published in Innsbruck in 1601.

Another intriguing facet of the identity of viziers and grand viziers is their marriage to princesses who figure prominently among Sinan's patrons. Such conjugal unions confounded ordinary gender relations to such a degree that European observers were astonished by the subordination of viziers and pashas to their royal wives. The Venetian diplomat Costantino Garzoni (1573), for example, comments on the power of Rüstem Pasha's super-rich widow Mihrümah Sultan, the only daughter of Süleyman, who commissioned Sinan to build two superb mosques carrying her name in the capital, in addition to overseeing the construction of her late husband's posthumous mosque in Tahtakale. Remarking that Mihrümah's son-in-law (Güzelce Ahmed Pasha) held the vizierate thanks to having married her daughter, Garzoni notes the authority of royal women over their husbands: 'These sultanas are considered by their husbands not as wives, but as masters, since there is no comparison whatsoever between the former's royal blood and that of the pashas, who are all slaves; therefore, they revere [their wives] with great submission.'[88] Marrying into the royal family required giving up some basic rights. As Gerlach pointed out in the 1570s, when a pasha married a sultana he had to divorce his former wife even if they had conceived children. These pashas were more or less 'ruled' by their royal wives who would every now and then remind their husbands: 'You were once my father's slave!' Royal sons-in-law had to obey their wives, who carried a dagger as a token of authority over them.[89]

It is reported that Sokollu, who virtually ruled the whole empire, was afraid only of his young royal wife, İsmihan Sultan, who frequently insulted him as a boorish bumpkin (this daughter of Selim II and the Venetian queen Nurbanu was the founder of a spectacular mosque that Sinan built in the capital at Kadırgalimanı).[90] Should Sokollu fail to please her, he risked deposition. Such was the case of the Albanian-born Lutfi Pasha (d. 1563), dismissed from the grand vizierate in 1541 because his royal wife, Shahsultan (a sister of Süleyman and one of Sinan's patrons), chose to divorce him after a quarrel in which he stubbornly defended the cruel punishment of circumcision he inflicted on a female prostitute. Spending the rest of his days in retirement, he remarked in the preface of his *Āsafnāme* that leisurely seclusion at his farm in Didymóthichon was preferable to being subject to subordination by women.[91]

European visitors to Istanbul commented on the public visibility of the sultanas (princesses and queens) who, accompanied by female attendants and eunuchs, moved about the city in textile-covered baldachins or wagons during wedding processions or on visits to relatives (illus. 17, 18). The Albanian-born chief consort of Murad III, Safiye Sultan, passed several times in front of the Austrian Hapsburg embassy (near the Column of Constantine) with her two sons, inside a carriage covered by red fabric from which she could observe the streets without being seen.[92] Reading the diary of Gerlach, the chaplain of that embassy, provides a truly vivid picture of daily life in the Ottoman capital between 1573 and 1578, capturing the heightened visibility of the oligarchy of aristocratic families in public festivities. The parades of Selim II and Murad III to imperial mosques or hunting expeditions were outnumbered by the processions of grandees that marked such familial occasions as the weddings and circumcisions of their children, or funerals (illus. 19).[93] These rituals enhanced the group solidarity of the ruling elite, whose most prominent members shared family ties either through marriage within the dynasty or intermarriage with one another's relatives.[94]

The demilitarized lifestyle of Sultan Süleyman's two successors, who no longer accompanied military campaigns, played a role in promoting a luxury-oriented existence in the capital. The Venetian diplomat Lorenzo Bernardo (1592) noted that the cream of the Ottoman upper class had become corrupted by the delights of luxurious living, such as drinking wine, residing in beautiful residences, and wearing extremely valuable robes of gold-and-silver cloth lined with fur. Daily embracing more flamboyant luxuries, the grandees voluntarily followed the example of their ruler, who preferred staying in his palace, where he could enjoy all types of pleasure, to military glory resulting from personal participation in wars. Bernardo's observation recalls the criticism voiced above by Koçi Beg, who traced the roots of this transformation to Süleyman's reign:

> Imitating their ruler's example, all the magnificent pashas, governor-generals, sanjak governors, and soldiers desire to stay home in order to satisfy their own pleasures, escaping whenever they can from going to war with its dangers and incommodity. To this end, the magnificent pashas use as intermediaries their wives, who are relatives of the *Grand Signore* and ready to do anything in their power to keep their husbands at home. They do this not only to satisfy their spouses, but also because they know that by staying home their husbands will acquire more influence with the *Grand Signore* through serving his person in the capital; whereas by going away on a war their likeliness of being deposed and the danger of losing the *Grand Signore's* favour would increase. Behind the footsteps of the grandees follow the lesser officials and soldiers, all of them preferring to enjoy the commodities of their own houses.[95]

Along the same lines, Mustafa Āli remarks that the members of the imperial council, preoccupied with real estate and money, were lamentably no longer administering justice but rather enjoying the pleasures of their luxurious urban palaces and suburban garden villas, when they could have been 'the architects of world-conquering plans.'[96] Āli was voicing a widely shared criticism of architectural construction as a rival to warlike pursuits at a time when military values were rapidly

17 Anonymous Austrian artist, The queen's wagon, from an album, c. 1570s, watercolour on paper.

18 Lambert de Vos, detail from an album illustration of the wedding procession of a princess, 1574, watercolour on paper.

19 Zacharias Wehme, The Friday Procession of Sultan Selim II to the Süleymaniye mosque, detail from an album, 1582, watercolour on paper.

becoming eroded. The competition between the war and construction industries did not deter the oligarchy of aristocratic families from the patronage of grand palaces and mosque complexes, a form of conspicuous consumption that assumed a pivotal role in public self-representation during the tenure of Sinan. The concentration of the ruling elite's pre-eminent members in Istanbul, where they were continually on view to one another, fuelled a competitive spirit in architectural patronage that turned the capital into a continual construction site. Writing in 1586–87, just before the chief architect's demise, Āli regarded the concentration of building efforts in Istanbul as a wasteful extravagance triggered by prestige value rather than piety and need:

> To build masjids and mosques in the well-developed and prosperous seat of government and likewise to construct convents and madrasas in a famous capital city are not pious deeds performed to acquire merit in God's sight. Every wise and intelligent man knows that these are pious deeds performed in order to accomplish being a leader and to make a good reputation. There are thousands of towns whose inhabitants are in need of masjids and convents . . . Yet, those who wish to perform pious deeds for ostentation and display obviously wish to be renowned in cities that are seats of the throne.[97]

Architecture became the principle means by which patrons staked out their claims to piety and magnificence. Gianfrancesco Morosini (1585) observed that the sultan's *kul*s, constituting a 'republic of slaves', built mosque complexes whose endowments provided an income to their sons serving as waqf administrators. They regularly performed the daily prayers in public to court the reputation and high esteem attached to being 'zealous in their religion'.[98] Mosque complexes exalted not merely the stature of pious patrons wishing for a place in paradise, but also of their families and dependents. Many of these complexes were endowed with no longer extant neighbouring or distant palaces, some of them designed by Sinan himself. This recalls the Byzantine practice of endowing palaces to churches, thereby turning them into 'foundations' with a religious status, a process through which Constantinople acquired its multiplicity of churches.[99] The endowment deeds of Sinan's patrons often stipulated that their palaces should initially be inhabited by themselves and then by their descendants until their lineage ceased, thereafter passing to manumitted slaves until they too had no more descendants. It was only then that these palaces would be rented out, sold, or replaced with commercial structures to bring additional income to the endowment. Such sprawling palaces, built with an eye to the future, gave architectural expression in the cityscape to the founders' families and extended households.

The endowment of mosque complexes with landed and commercial properties, the surplus of which could be used by the founder during his or her lifetime, enabled patrons to leave behind a substantial income to their progeny and dependents. The relatively flexible rules for establishing pious endowments in Ottoman Hanefi law provided a convenient legal framework to bypass confiscation and laws of inheritance that favoured the subdivision of family estates among inheritors. Pious endowments reflected a sharpened dynastic concern for the perpetuation of aristocratic families across the generations, enhancing their prestige and enlarging their patronage networks. The end of the sixteenth century saw the consolidation of prominent aristocratic families whose sons were appointed to influential provincial posts; in many instances, their descendants continued to administer inherited waqfs well into the early twentieth century.

The late-sixteenth-century historian Selaniki refers to such aristocratic families that emerged during Süleyman's reign as 'old dynasties' (*ḫānedān-i ḳadīm*). He clearly preferred these families to 'upstarts' (*nev-devlet*) because they upheld 'old traditions' (*ḳānūn-i ḳadīm*) of magnificence that were fast disappearing in his time.[100] In 1591 he described an impressive military parade staged in accordance to 'old traditions' by the late grand vizier Sokollu's son Hasan Pasha (the governor-general of Rumelia), the majesty of which had not been seen in recent years. 'Because he belonged to an old dynasty and was noble, venerable, and a renowned lord,' the people of Istanbul enthusiastically greeted that parade with laudations and prayers.[101] Both Āli and Selaniki were among the authors who initiated the discourse of decline that would gain momentum during the seventeenth century, with reformist treatises seeking to revive the idealized law and order of the old days.

After Sokollu's death in 1579, the centralized state governed in the sultan's name by the grand vizier's cabinet gave way to a more decentralized regime. The clearcut pyramidal social hierarchy of the classical age, with the sultan and grand vizier occupying its summit, evolved into a fluid structure with competing factions dominated by royal women and palace eunuchs. Just as former status hierarchies were being challenged, the traditional relationship between the centre and periphery of the empire was altered by the growing independence of provinces triggered by the Celali rebellions and the emergence of such provincial cities as Izmir that rivalled Istanbul.[102] Members of the imperial harem and royal favourites began to compete with grand viziers and viziers in the patronage of ambitious mosque complexes during the last decade of Sinan's tenure. Thereafter, these offices changed from being relatively stable posts occupied for long periods by the same individuals into unstable positions that did not favour patronage on a large scale.

A complex combination of factors – including short terms in office, economic problems triggered by inflation, diminished territorial expansion, abandonment of the *devşirme* system, reduced prominence of *kul*s, and changing identities of the dynasty and ruling elite – ushered in a new architectural paradigm at the turn of the seventeenth century, when, as I explain in the Epilogue, mosque-centred complexes were ousted by smaller madrasa-centred compounds. Times had changed, and change brought with it the demise of Sinan's canon of elaborately stratified mosque types corresponding to gradations of social and territorial rank no longer relevant in the post-classical period.

Like Sokollu and Sinan, most members of the 'old guard' ruling elite enjoyed long terms in office. Leading dignitaries dominated the notoriously gerontocratic centralized government for many years, still holding positions of power over the age of seventy. Sokollu, for example, was nearly sixty years old in 1562, when as a vizier he married his much younger royal wife. Having served in several provincial posts that prepared him for the vizierate, he was already an old man when he reached the apex of the administrative hierachy in 1565, a post he occupied for fourteen years before he died in his late seventies. Sinan himself broke a record by holding the life-long post of chief architect under three sultans, and passing away at an age of nearly one hundred years. The longevity and stability of his and his patrons' careers were vital aspects of the setting in which a rank-conscious architecture celebrating the grandeur of the Ottoman state, its religion, and the fame of its intensely pious ruling elite flourished.

Chapter 2

THE LEGAL APPARATUS AND MEMORY

I. RELIGIO-LEGAL CONTEXTS OF MOSQUE CONSTRUCTION
II. PIOUS ENDOWMENTS AS MEMORIALS TO VICTORY AND FAME

I. RELIGIO-LEGAL CONTEXTS OF MOSQUE CONSTRUCTION

In three versions of his autobiography, the number of Friday mosques (*cāmiʿ*) Sinan claims to have built ranges from eighty to over a hundred.[1] Eliminating those he created before he became chief architect, the ones he renovated, and the ones he converted from masjids, leaves seventy-seven Friday mosques, of which thirty-nine were located in Istanbul (Appendix 1; Maps 1, 2). These were mainly commissioned by the sultans, the royal family and the highest ranking grandees, the majority of whom were converts into Islam. The ulema and urban middle classes were represented by only three patrons – one grand mufti and two merchants. The mosques of the sultans, grand viziers, and viziers were located both inside and outside the capital, while those of governor-generals were primarily concentrated in provincial capitals. Royal women, grand admirals, members of the imperial council, aghas of the imperial palace, the grand mufti, and the two merchants commissioned their mosques almost exclusively in Istanbul, where they resided.

The autobiography entitled *Teẕkiretü'l-bünyān* (Biographical Memoir of Constructions) and the epitaph of Sinan's tomb mention eighty Friday mosques and 'more than four hundred' masjids among his works.[2] The masjids must have been built throughout the empire, for only forty-six to fifty-two, all in Istanbul, are enumerated in the autobiographies.[3] Compared to Friday mosques, neighbourhood masjids without dependencies were commissioned by a wider spectrum of patrons. Among those that Sinan claimed to be his own works, none were named after sultans or members of the royal family, and only a few were built for high-ranking grandees. The majority of masjid patrons were minor officers of the imperial council and the military establishment, members of the ulema, wives and daughters of grandees, servants and aghas of the imperial palace (including the chief architect himself), and chiefs of craft guilds. Sinan also rebuilt a number of pre-existing masjids (dilapidated or ruined in fires), which are listed under their old names, and created others named after royal workshops.[4]

Unlike Friday mosques, for which the sultan's permission had to be obtained, the construction of masjids did not require royal approval because the Friday prayers were not held in them. Masjids were relatively cheap, modest neighbourhood affairs with small waqfs. Since early Islamic times, residents of city quarters had held corporate rights with regard to their maintenance and administration.[5] Their endowments were often augmented by additional waqfs made by pious community members. By the early sixteenth century, an administrative system had developed in Istanbul that divided the city into neighbourhoods (*mahalle*), each predominantly Muslim neighbourhood having its own masjid whose imam represented the community in its dealings with the state. The neighbourhood constituted a semi-autonomous nuclear administrative unit, with the imam and muezzin of its masjid appointed by a royal diploma upon the recommendation of kadis. Candidates for these positions, paid from the waqfs of masjids, were usually chosen according to the petitions of neighbourhood dwellers who could play a role in self administration.[6]

A register surveying Istanbul's waqfs in 1546 shows that its 219 neighbourhoods were largely named after the persons who had built masjids in them (although several carried the names of famous landmarks and non-Muslim neighbourhoods mostly distributed along the city walls were designated by gate names).[7] In fifteenth-century documents, nearly half of the neighborhoods bore non-religious names; therefore, the survey of 1546 signals a transformation in urban administration that accorded a more prominent role to masjids in the lives of neighbourhood inhabitants.[8] Masjids were evenly spread, about 150 to 200 metres apart, in the city's quarters and were often accompanied by independent elementary schools and dervish convents. Late-sixteenth-century surveys dating from the reigns of Murad III and Mehmed III indicate that this administrative structure had not changed significantly, except in its details, after Sinan built many additional Friday mosques and masjids.[9] These new monuments were integrated into a pre-existing administrative framework in which neighbourhoods had been grouped under thirteen large districts (*nahiye*) named after Friday mosque complexes built by the sultans and viziers between the second half of the fifteenth and first quarter of the sixteenth century. Some of them were sited in the three townships (Eyüp, Galata [Pera], Üsküdar) and their newly developing suburban extensions (Map 2).

Sinan's masjids in the capital responded to the state's growing emphasis on the compulsory performance of the five daily congregational prayers, which reinforced the communal bonds of neighbourhood residents. New masjids for artisanal workshops reflected the increasing importance of congregational prayers in the context of craft guilds that were administratively brought under the state's control for revenue collection. A fatwa pronounced by the shaykh al-Islam Ebussuud poses the following question testifying to the official enforcement of religious orthodoxy in artisanal workshops: 'If the steward of a crafts guild (*ehl-i ḥiref ketḫüdāsı*) asks someone belonging to his group to perform the congregational prayers, and the latter continues to abandon them, can he legally say, "You cannot be part of our craft?" The emphatic answer is: "Yes, may he enjoy long life and prosperity!"'[10] This ruling throws light on why so many masjids built by Sinan are named after chief craftsmen.

During the first half of the sixteenth century the enforcement of Sunni orthodoxy became an official policy of the Ottoman state, which increasingly defined its identity as the defender of the shariʿa against 'infidels' and 'heretics'. Under Süleyman this policy involved the support of every separatist movement in Europe against the Pope and the Hapsburg Emperor, who claimed to be the head of a unified Christian Europe (particularly those led by the French king and the Protestant princes). In the east, an important turning point was the emergence in 1501 of the Safavid state, which adopted Twelver Shiʿism as its official religion. Its first ruler, Shah Ismaʿil I, was the charismatic leader of a sufi order (Safaviyya) that commanded a wide following among Turkmen tribes with ʿAlid leanings who were settled throughout the Ottoman domains. After Selim I temporarily averted the Safavid threat by defeating Shah Ismaʿil in 1514, the Ottoman state began to systematically purge Shiʿism and rebellious 'heterodox' dervishes in its own territories. This policy gained momentum during the reign of Süleyman I, who conducted three military campaigns against the Safavids, legitimized by fatwas, obtained from such jurists as Kemalpaşazade and his student Ebussuud, that declared the Safavids 'infidels' against whom it was appropriate to wage holy war. These fatwas asserted the Caliph's (Süleyman's) obligation to restore the shariʿa and eradicate 'heresy', giving the whole operation the semblance of a jihad.[11]

I have already discussed in Chapter 1 that criticisms raised against the Safavids included their abandonment of the Friday prayers due to the absence of a legitimate Imam. This 'offence' was compounded by their ritual cursing of the Prophet's wife ʿA'isha along with the first three Sunni caliphs (Abu Bakr, ʿUmar, and ʿUthman), and their alleged lack of reverence for the Koran, over which they preferred hadith of 'questionable origin' concerning the Prophet's appointment of ʿAli as his successor.[12] Under Süleyman, who claimed to be a universal caliph, the performance of the congregational prayers came to be enforced throughout the Ottoman territories. An undated fatwa issued by Ebussuud poses the following question: 'If there are no masjids in some Muslim villages, and if their inhabitants do not perform the congregational prayers, when the judge of the holy shariʿa forces them to build a masjid, is it necessary to punish those who continue not to perform the prayers?' The answer is yes, because 'in order to force the construction of masjids in such villages for the regular performance of the congregational prayers, the governor-generals of the empire's protected domains had been sent a noble decree in 944 (1537–38), which is still valid'.[13] That order, issued one year before Sinan's appointment as chief architect, accounts for the subsequent boom in the construction of masjids as well as Friday mosques.

The resistance to Süleyman's imperial decree is captured in an order addressed in 1546 to the kadi of Vize in Thrace, commanding him to investigate in the shariʿa court a certain village under his jurisdiction and others like it, whose abandoned masjids had become dilapidated because their congregations stopped performing the prayers in them. The kadi is advised to warn these communities and urge them to observe the compulsory congregational prayers five times a day, punishing those who are stubborn. He is ordered to make the endowment administrators of ruined masjids repair them with waqf funds, and to replace incompetent imams unable to correctly recite the Koran with capable ones, reporting the names of new appointees to the sultan. We learn from this decree that 'in the past when similar situations arose, the kadis used to appoint an official prayer enforcer (*namazcı*)'. Given the tyranny of such officers, the kadi is asked not to appoint one this time, but instead to personally take care of the problem in a just manner, without harming the villagers.[14]

Ebussuud pronounced several fatwas authorizing the punishment of those who failed to attend the daily prayers in masjids.[15] In one of them, where he is asked what measure should be taken if the people of a village abandon their prayers as a group, he says they must renew their profession of faith and their marriage contracts, implying that they would become apostates if they insisted. In another fatwa he declares that such Muslims have to be vigorously punished and thereafter executed. This harsh ruling is repeated in another fatwa where Ebussuud defines those who deny

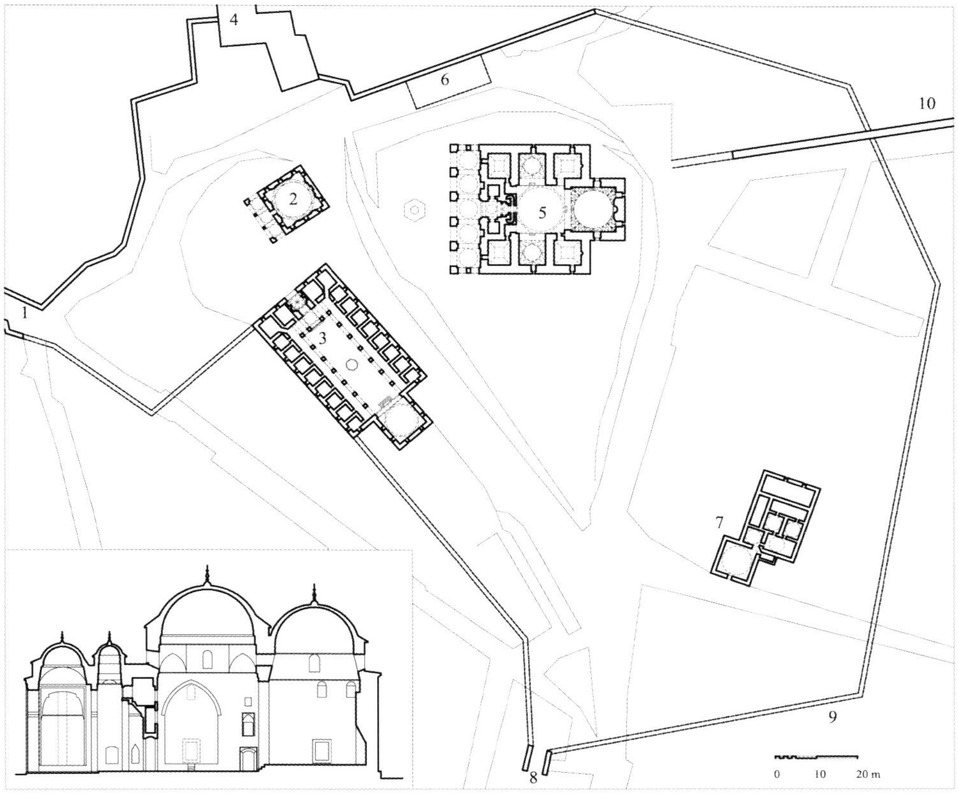

20 Plan of the Bayezid I complex, Bursa, and cross-section of its convent-masjid:

1. Gate
2. Mausoleum
3. Madrasa
4. Site of royal garden palace
5. Convent-masjid
6. Hospice
7. Bathhouse
8. Gate
9. Reconstruction of precinct wall
10. Aqueduct

the necessity of performing the communal prayers as infidels deserving execution.[16] According to one of Ebussuud's fatwas, not performing the communal prayers in one's own neighbourhood masjid is an act disapproved of but not forbidden by religious law.[17] This legal opinion discouraging the attendance of masjids in neighbourhoods other than one's own reflects a desire to control the mobility of neighbourhood residents so as to more closely monitor their conduct. Besides pronouncing fatwas that enforced communal prayers on a micro-scale in masjids, in both villages and nuclear city neighbourhoods, Ottoman jurists also promoted the Friday prayers on a macro-scale, in cities and towns. Let us briefly review previous religious orientations in the empire, before we return to the sixteenth-century fatwas.

In the formative period of the Ottoman principality, when the majority of its Muslim subjects were Turkmen tribesmen with 'heterodox' leanings or newly converted populations, Islamization had been encouraged through socio-religious complexes centred around T-shaped convent-masjids. These multifunctional buildings are identified in their foundation inscriptions and endowment deeds as hospices or convents (*ʿimāret, zāviye, ḫānḳah, tekke, buḳʿa*). Entrusted to colonizer shaykhs, the convent-masjids provided free food and lodging to travellers for up to three days. Their shaykhs won the hearts of the heterogenous masses with a relatively flexible brand of popular religion dominated by mysticism, quite different from the rigid

21 Complex of Bayezid I, Bursa.

22 Complex of Bayezid I, Bursa, from the north.

rules of Sunni orthodoxy that would be enforced during the sixteenth century.[18]

Until the conquest of Constantinople, each Ottoman sultan had built one or more of these socio-religious complexes in the capital cities of İznik (Nicea), Bursa (Prussa) and Edirne (Adrianople). Less monumental versions founded by non-royal patrons such as viziers and the ghazis were spread throughout Anatolia and Rumelia. According to the late-fifteenth-century chronicler Neşri, Orhan I (r. 1324–60) had built two '*ʿimārets*' in Bursa and İznik, in addition to endowing smaller 'convents' (*zāviye*) for sufi shaykhs he was particularly attached to. The chronicler adds: 'He was fond of urbanizing desolate and uninhabited places, where he settled Muslims. For example, the *ʿimāret* he built in Bursa was located in such an uninhabited area that one used to be scared to go there later than the afternoon prayer.'[19] A Turkish copy of Orhan's endowment deed, dated 1360, identifies his pious endowment in Bursa as 'a convent (*zāviye*) known as the hospice (*ʿimāret*)'. The T-shaped convent-masjid's extant Arabic inscription identifies it as a 'hospice' (*al-ʿimāra*).[20] These interchangeable terms hint at the derivation of the T-type plan from dervish convents where resident shaykhs similarly took care of travellers and guests. It was the incorporation of a masjid that differentiated the larger versions of this building type, oriented towards Mecca, from smaller convents which did not always include masjids.

The complex of Bayezid I (r. 1389–1401), perched on a hilltop at Bursa, is similarly identified in its Arabic endowment deed, dated 1400, as 'the noble convent (*al-zāwiya*) and charming hospice (*al-ʿimāra*)' (illus. 20–22). The complex, asymmetrically following the irregular contours of the sloping terrain, was originally accompanied by a hospice (comprising a kitchen, storeroom, and stables), a hospital, a double madrasa, residences for personnel, a bath-house, and a public fountain to which water was conducted by an aqueduct.[21] The sultan's posthumously built domed mausoleum was added to these dependencies by his son and successor, stamping the complex with a funerary character linked to the memory of its founder. The royal versions of T-shaped convent-masjids, generally fronted by five-domed porticos and oriented towards the qibla, comprised two axially aligned large domed halls at the centre and lower domed corner chambers provided with fireplaces and built-in cupboards that served as 'guest-rooms' (*tābḫāne*, literally a warm room heated by a fireplace).[22] The first of the central domed spaces (often crowned by a higher dome with a lantern) was an assembly hall furnished with a fountain. It was flanked by a raised iwan on each side and communicated through doors with guest-rooms tucked in the corners. The second domed area, raised from the first one by a few steps and featuring a mihrab, functioned as a masjid for communal prayers.

Bayezid I's waqfiyya stipulates that fifteen young boys should serve food twice a day to guests and staff. More elaborate food was to be prepared on Fridays, during the month of Ramadan, for the two religious festivals, and on holy feast nights. The convent-masjid was entrusted to a shaykh whose duty it was to be a spiritual guide and host to guests lodged and fed there for up to three days free of charge. The shaykh received the highest wage among the religious staff, which consisted of an imam, two muezzins, and thirty Koran reciters. The absence of a preacher (*khatib*) responsible for delivering the Friday sermon (khutba) confirms that hospitality was the *raison d'être* of such convent-masjids. The endowment deed of the Bayezid I complex specifies that the guests should not be 'infidels' or 'those subscribing to one of the six sins', a stipulation reflecting this particular convent-masjid's function as the centre of a new Muslim quarter on the outskirts of Bursa.[23] It was common practice, however, to accept non-Muslim travellers into the hospices of socio-religious complexes located on major routes. In any case, endowment deeds generally lack specifications concerning the exclusion of non-Muslims from the guest-rooms of such charitable complexes.

The Friday noon prayers, originally not a function of convent-masjids, were instead performed in the Great Mosques (*Ulu Cami*) of Ottoman cities, either converted from cathedral churches or, like the one Bayezid I founded in Bursa's densely populated market centre, built anew (illus. 23, 24). Unlike the Great Mosques, comparable to cathedral churches, socio-religious complexes with convent-masjids akin to monasteries were situated at the uninhabited peripheries of towns, where they formed the nuclei of new Muslim neighbourhoods, or in rural settings where they constituted the embryo of new towns populated by tax-exempt settlers. In the early Ottoman period, Great Mosques were solitary monuments without charitable dependencies, exclusively built by the sultans and associated with the collective identity of cities. Characterized by a wider patronage base and surrounded with dependencies that often included the patron's mausoleum, the convent-masjid was a commemorative monument intimately connected to the memory of its founder, after whom it was named.

We shall see in Chapter 3 that socio-religious complexes commissioned by the sultans following the conquest of Constantinople began to incorporate Friday mosques named after successive rulers. Mehmed II was the first sultan to combine a Friday mosque with a grand complex that included his own mausoleum, which was added after his death by his son and successor. The Friday mosque did not feature attached guest-rooms; instead, it had a freestanding *tabhane* with a courtyard of its own, inside a walled enclosure comprising a caravansaray with stables and a hospice (*imaret*) that functioned as a soup kitchen (illus. 59, 60). In contrast, the complexes of his two successors, Bayezid II and Selim I, reintroduced into the fabric of their Friday mosques flanking guest-rooms that were associated with the frontier culture of the ghazis (illus. 66, 78, 80). This modification acknowledged the continuing importance of the ghazi ethos that challenged Mehmed

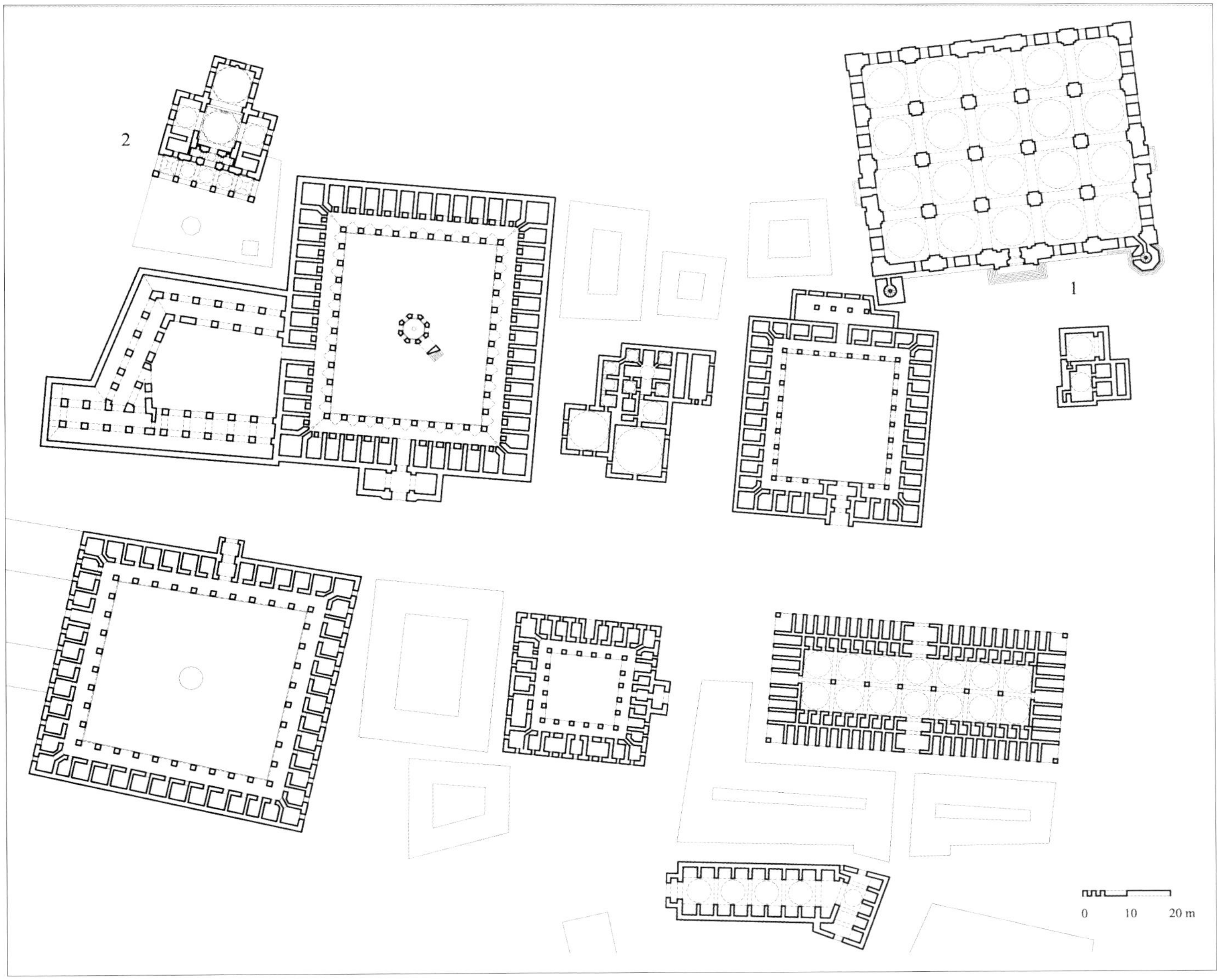

23 Plan of the Bursa marketplace with caravansarays and baths: 1. Great Mosque of Bayezid I. 2. Convent-masjid of Orhan I, built in 1339.

24 Great Mosque of Bayezid I, Bursa, from the southeast.

II's uncompromising imperial vision, a vision that would be consolidated under Süleyman I. With the growing emphasis on religious orthodoxy, T-shaped convent-masjids and Friday mosques with flanking guest-rooms fell out of favour. Chapter 3 shows that their last examples were built in the first quarter of the sixteenth century, just before Sinan became chief court architect. Most of the multifunctional convent-masjids were eventually transformed into Friday mosques with the addition of a minbar (pulpit for the Friday sermon, or khutba, delivered by a preacher).

During Sinan's tenure, complexes grouped around Friday mosques with centralized ground plans, no longer featuring attached guest-houses, became the norm (with a few exceptions in Diyarbakır, Syria, and the Arab provinces conquered under Selim I, where old traditions of 'colonization' prevailed). Detached from the body of masjids and Friday mosques with unified inner spaces, guest-houses were now built as free-standing dependencies either incorporated into or accompanied by hospices (*imaret*) functioning as soup kitchens.[24] The detachment of guest-rooms from the body of mosques was paralleled by their spatial segregation behind walled enclosures. An imperial decree sent in 1573 to the kadi of Çorlu, on the road between Istanbul and Edirne, reveals that the presence of non-Muslim travellers in non-segregated guest-rooms that surrounded the forecourt of Süleyman's Friday mosque in that city – a simple domed cube with a single minaret dated by its inscription to 928 (1521–22) – was now being resented:

> You have sent me a letter reporting that the madrasa professor and the Muslims of Çorlu have come to you, complaining about ambassadors being lodged in the guest-rooms (*tābḫāneler*) adjacent to their noble Friday mosque, a practice that fills the porticos and courtyard of that Friday mosque with infidels engaged in vice and debauchery. You say that they request this practice be abolished, since it has led them to abandon using that Friday mosque. From now on I order non-Muslims, whether they are ambassadors or else, not to be lodged there but in a distant caravansaray. When this order arrives, tell the court messengers (*çavuş*) assigned to accompany ambassadors that they should no longer be lodged next to the noble Friday mosque but in distant caravansarays, so that mosques and masjids do not become empty in the manner described; let nobody disobey my order and do not use this as an excuse to infringe on the rights of ambassadors.[25]

No wonder, then, that the hospices and guest-houses Sinan built as the dependencies of Friday mosques are segregated structures often accompanied by caravansarays also functioning as stables (illus. 25, 26).[26]

The fall from favour of Friday mosques and masjids with appended guest-rooms in the age of Sinan responded to fatwas that condemned sufi rituals practised in these multifunctional edifices as unorthodox forms of worship, too similar to the rites of the Safavid order centred on eating, chanting, and dancing. With their unified interior spaces, Sinan's new masjids and Friday mosques were primarily destined for the performance of the congregational prayers.[27] The types of ritual performed in T-shaped convent-masjids can be deduced from the travelogue of the mid-fourteenth-century Maghribi traveller Ibn Battuta (d. 1369) who stayed during his journey through Anatolia at the hospitable convents of sufi dervishes and akhi brotherhoods in various Turkmen principalities. In these multifunctional buildings, where Ibn Battuta was served free food and found a warm place with a fireplace to sleep in, brotherhood members gathered for communal meals after which they danced and chanted Turkish hymns. He singles out Orhan I, based in Bursa, as the peripatetic ruler of the most powerful Anatolian principality at that time. Within the Ottoman territories, Ibn Battuta lodged at a dervish convent between Geyve and Mudurnu where the villagers gathered on a Thursday night to recite litanies (*dhikr*) until the next morning, eating the food they brought along.[28]

25, 26 Exterior and interior of a caravansaray, watercolour paintings from a mid-seventeenth-century album.

The *Ḥulviyāt-i Şāhī* (Royal Sweetmeats), a late-fifteenth-century compendium of orthodox religious practice in Turkish, includes a fatwa forbidding the 'common people to form circles in Friday mosques and recite battle epics or stories (*cengnāmeler ve kıṣṣalar*)'. Sinan endowed to his own masjid in Istanbul a copy of this popular work, compiled by the ruler of the İsfendiyaroğlu dynasty of Kastamonu (İsmail Beg, d. 1479) subjugated by Mehmed II.[29] Ebussuud's fatwas similarly renounce the performance of such rituals in convent-masjids and Friday mosques.[30] One of them poses the following question:

> In the masjid of a convent (*zāviye*) if gathered boys distort the monotheistic formula with numerous melodies, crying out 'my soul, my heart' and uttering such invocations as, 'You are a great sultan, oh soul of souls, for I saw you become manifest from the door of hiddenness!' or 'You can give paradise to those who desire a houri, what I need is only you but you!' [a couplet by the immensely popular Anatolian Turkish mystic poet Yunus Emre (d. 1320–21)] while beating their breasts and making strange gestures, what happens if the inhabitants of that neighbourhood ask the shaykh why he allows such behaviour and he answers: 'What more is needed anyhow?'

Ebussuud declares the shaykh to be an infidel for regarding such rituals as acceptable forms of worship. If the shaykh and his disciples refuse to give up their habits, they should be executed.[31] In addition to rejecting the recitation of mystical Turkish poetry, the grand mufti opposes ecstatic dancing and chanting in mosques. In one of his fatwas the following question is posed: 'If the sufis recite litanies praising God by forming circles in Friday mosques and start whirling out of ecstasy, now falling and now stepping forward, while exclaiming 'hay-huy', and reciting verses and poems, and melodically uttering the monotheistic formula, what happens if the Muslims advise them to give up these strange practices that have been denounced by the muftis of the age as inappropriate for Islam and for noble Friday mosques, and they do not obey this advice?' The answer is that they have to repent.[32]

Several other fatwas of Ebussuud advise kadis and governor-generals to forbid such rituals in mosques.[33] If sufis reject the outer forms of canonical worship required by the shariʿa as incompatible with the inner forms of esoteric devotion favoured by sufism, and denounce the necessity of performing the daily congregational prayers, then they certainly deserve being killed. Likewise, if a sufi Friday mosque preacher publicly preaches that the ulema subscribing to outer forms of worship are unable to fathom the inner mysteries of mystical devotion, he is a 'heretic' who has to be executed.[34]

The official policy of imposing the shariʿa on all Muslims within the Ottoman empire placed dervish convents under close scrutiny; those found suspect were inspected by imperial command and often converted into madrasas. The purging of 'heterodoxy' also gave rise to the inquisition of some shaykhs with a large following who were officially denounced as heretics and executed. One of them, İsmail Maşuki, nicknamed Oğlan Şeyhi (Boy Shaykh) because he was only nineteen years old, belonged to the Melamiye branch of the Bayramiye order. He used to make fun of fatwas enforcing religious orthodoxy as he preached in Friday mosques, arguing that sufis who had attained a high degree of spirituality were not bound by the shariʿa and that canonical lawfulness or unlawfulness did not apply to them. Becoming a threat to the state's authority because of his large following among the court's cavalry soldiers and the artisans of Istanbul, he was publicly tried by a committee of the ulema that included Ebussuud (a madrasa professor at that time). The shaykh was executed with his twelve disciples in 1528–29 by a fatwa of Kemalpaşazade that condemned him as a heretic.[35]

Another executed heretic was Shaykh Muhyiddin Karamani of the Gülşeni order. Süleyman's vizier Çoban Mustafa Pasha had appointed this shaykh to the dervish convent he built as a dependency of his Friday mosque complex in Gebze, where Ebussuud (a madrasa professor at the same complex in 1525) developed an enmity towards him (illus. 27). At that convent, Karamani was teaching his own panthestic interpretation of monotheism (*waḥdat al-wujūd*, or the unity of existence) that equated God with nature and the universe. The shaykh then moved to Istanbul and subsequently to Edirne, where the ulema complained about him to authorities in the capital. He was publicly tried by a committee of ulema at the mosque of Bayezid II in Edirne and hanged in 1550 by ordeal with a fatwa of Ebussuud (now shaykh al-Islam), which declared him to be a heretic.[36]

Dervish convents subscribing to acceptable forms of orthodox sufism, compatible with the shariʿa, not only continued to exist but indeed flourished throughout the sixteenth century. The Halveti order, with whose support Bayezid II had ascended the throne, was one of these. We shall see in Part 3 that many Friday preachers appointed to Sinan's mosques were chosen from among the shaykhs of the Halveti order which came to enjoy a wide following among the ruling elite. With its emphasis on a static and silent form of *dhikr* unaccompanied by music, the Nakshbandi order, institutionalized in Istanbul during Bayezid II's reign by the Central Asian shaykh Emir Ahmed Bukhari, also prospered along with the Mevlevi order.

Even the staunchly orthodox Sultan Süleyman had sufi sympathies, since there is nothing inherently objectionable in sufi piety as such from an orthodox point of view. As a prince, he became attached to the Halveti-Sünbüli Shaykh Merkez Efendi in Manisa, where that shaykh delivered moving sermons in his mother Hafsa Sultan's mosque and convent complex (illus. 28). Subsequently chosen as the 'army shaykh' of the Corfu campaign in 1537, Merkez Efendi had a wide following at the capital, including Süleyman's sister Shahsultan, who commissioned Sinan to create two mosques with convents for the shaykh and his disciples.[37] Süleyman also developed a fondness for the Nakshbandi order. At the capital he endowed a convent with a masjid at Fildamı

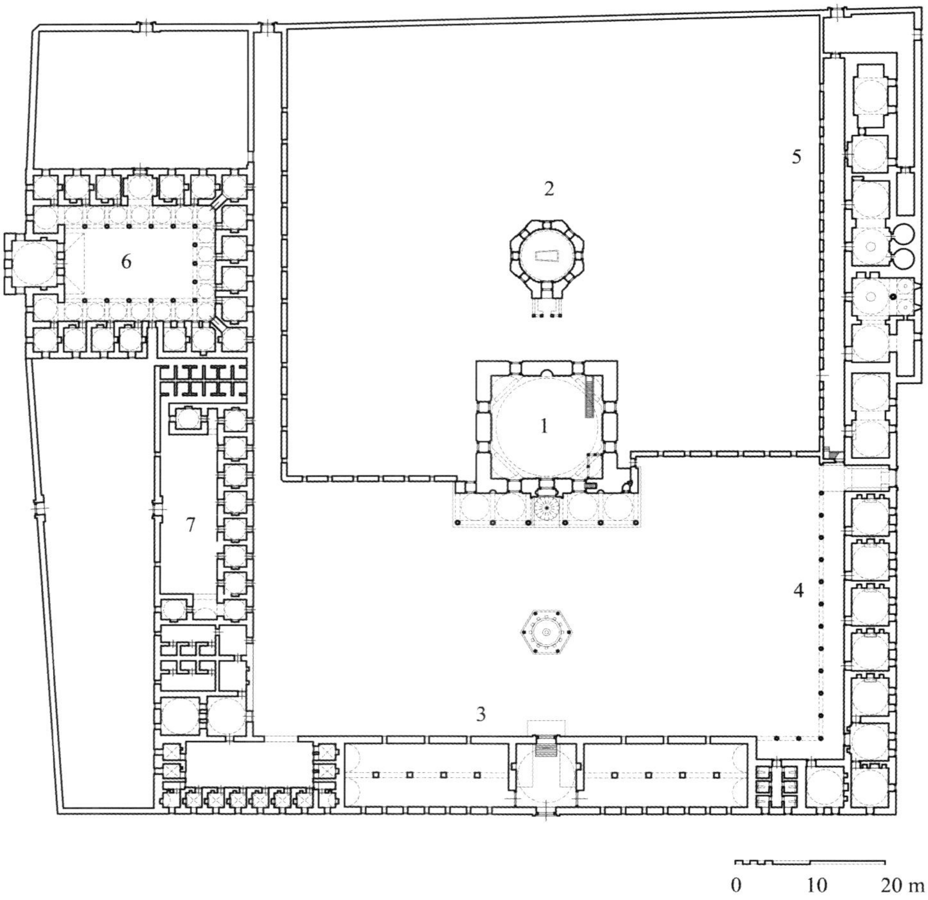

27 Plan of the Çoban Mustafa Pasha complex, Gebze:

1. Mosque
2. Mausoleum
3. Double caravansaray
4. Guest-rooms
5. Hospice
6. Madrasa
7. Convent

28 Plan of the Hafsa Sultan complex, Manisa:

1. Mosque
2. Madrasa
3. Hospice
4. Elementary school
5. Double bath
6. Hospital

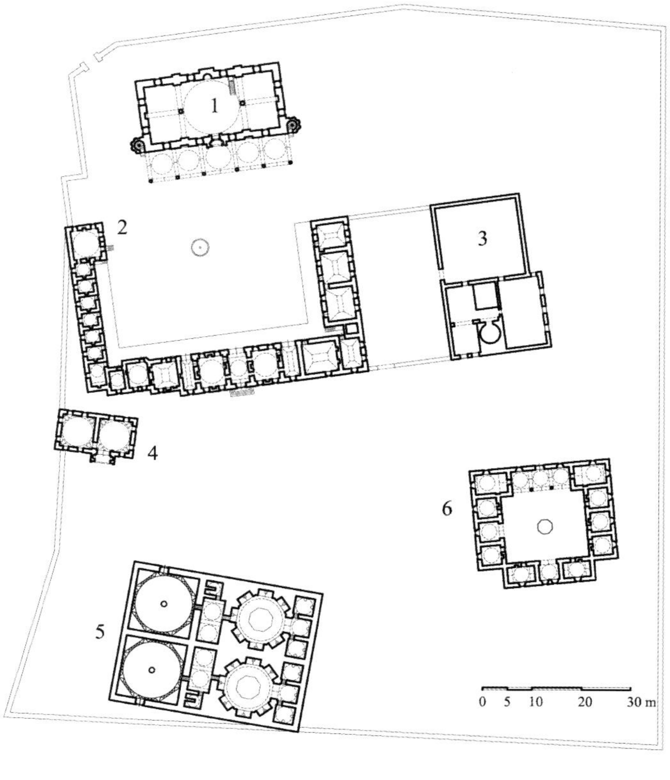

(Koska) for the Nakshbandi shaykh nicknamed Hekim Çelebi (d. 1566–67), a physician learned in the science of medicine, whose devotees included the grand vizier Rüstem Pasha.[38] Later in his life, Süleyman would become devoted to the Halveti shaykh Nureddinzade Efendi, who used to frequent the Topkapı Palace for spiritual conversations. This shaykh is said to have incited the elderly ruler to undertake his last victorious campaign to Szigetvár in 1565–66 by recounting a dream in which the Prophet charged him to ask the sultan why he had abandoned the sacred obligation of the jihad (illus. 29). During that campaign, masterminded by the grand vizier Sokollu, Nureddinzade served as 'army shaykh'.[39]

Despite Süleyman's sufi inclinations, the construction of dervish convents was downplayed during his reign, coloured by the zeal of three theologically motivated wars fought against the Safavids. The Amasya peace treaty signed in 1555 (effective until the Persian war of 1578–90) ushered in a more tolerant atmosphere that encouraged the spread of sufism during the reign of Selim II. This sultan was an ardent disciple of the Halveti Shaykh Süleyman Efendi, nicknamed the 'Sultan's Shaykh'.[40] In his reign, the shaykh al-Islam Ebussuud (d. 1574) formulated a more flexible version of Sunni orthodoxy characterized by the reconciliation between moderate sufism and the shariʿa. Under Murad III sufism would flourish even more vigorously.

Sinan's autobiographies mention only a few sufi convents (*tekye*), monumentally built in the manner of madrasas, among the dependencies of Friday mosques created during the reigns of Selim II and Murad III. They include the Halveti convent (*c.* 1574) of the mosque complex at Kadırgalimanı, jointly endowed by İsmihan Sultan and Sokollu; and that of the queen mother Nurbanu Sultan in Üsküdar (*c.* 1583). In these two mosque complexes, each featuring a madrasa, dervishes of the Halveti order practised their sufi rituals in the segregated domed assembly halls of their convents, which resembled madrasa classrooms. They were required to regularly perform the congregational prayers inside the Friday mosque of each complex, where their shaykh preached on Fridays, as a corollary of the integration of orthodox sufism with the shariʿa.[41] A modus vivendi had been established between sufism and orthopraxy towards the end of Sinan's tenure as chief architect. With its unified interior space, the new type of Friday mosque codified by the chief architect emphasized the centrality of the obligatory congregational prayers with which palatable forms of mystical behaviour were allowed to coexist, albeit subordinately. Eventually sufis from various branches of the Halveti order came to dominate the preacher positions in Istanbul's Friday mosques to such a degree that a conservative backlash, namely the Kadızadeli movement discussed in the Epilogue, emerged in the seventeenth century.

The policy of rigid orthodoxy under Süleyman materialized through the close cooperation of the shaykh al-Islam Ebussuud with the grand vizier Rüstem Pasha. Mustafa Āli criticized the impeccable jurist Ebussuud for the distance he kept from the sufi orders, 'his only shortcoming became manifest in his lack of adherence to the path of the sufis'.[42] The comfortable rapprochement with sufism during the reign of Selim II was shaped by a coalition between Sokollu, Ebussuud, and the Halveti shaykh Nureddinzade, a champion of Sunni orthodoxy celebrated for his expertise in interpreting the Koran and the Prophet's traditions (hadith). The grand vizier was an enthusiastic disciple of that shaykh, for whom he commissioned Sinan to build the convent at the mosque complex in Kadırgalimanı.[43]

The change in atmosphere was foreshadowed by the public festivities held in Istanbul after Selim II's enthronement in 1566 to celebrate the recent conquest of Szigetvár, where Süleyman had expired. Sokollu was initially reluctant to authorize a carnival that would likely be disapproved by the ulema. In 1560 a ban on wine-drinking had publicly been announced along with an ultimatum for the compulsory performance of the five daily congregational prayers. It was Sokollu's intimate advisor Feridun Ahmed Beg (later promoted chief chancellor) who convinced him to change his mind with the following advice: 'The temperament of the world cannot tolerate being continually constipated; it sometimes needs to be intoxicated!'[44] The chronogram composed for the new sultan's accession date, 'inebriated day and night', marked the end of his venerable father's puritanical regime (illus. 30).[45]

29 Nigari (Haydar Reis), the elderly Sultan Süleyman accompanied by pages, *c.* 1560–65, watercolour on paper.

Let us now turn back to the hardheaded enforcement of the five daily congregational prayers and the Friday prayers during the reign of Süleyman, with its obvious implication for the boom in Friday mosque construction. The *Multaḳa al-abḥur* (Junction of the Seas), the most widely used compendium on Hanefi jurisprudence in the Ottoman world (written by the jurist İbrahim b. Muhammad al-Halabi, d. 1549), categorically asserts that the necessity of the Friday prayer is fixed by the Koran, the Prophet's traditions, and by the consensus of the Muslim community: the one who denies this becomes an infidel, and whoever misses three consecutive Friday prayers has abandoned being a Muslim. According to this authoritative source, the Friday prayer is required of all Muslims residing in a city or a place equivalent to a city, with the exception of travellers, slaves, children, invalids, the physically disabled, and women, who were exempt from this requirement because traditionally they stayed at home.[46]

Unlike masjids addressing the congregational needs of small-scale communities, Friday mosques were limited to towns (*kasaba*) and cities (*şehr*). Conversely, Hanefi jurists in the Ottoman period came to define cities and towns (together with their outskirts from which the muezzin's call to prayer was audible) as 'places where the Friday prayers are performed and markets are held'.

30 Nigari (Haydar Reis), double-page composition: (left) Selim II drinking wine; (right) boon companions and musicians accompanying the sultan, c. 1560–61, watercolour on paper.

In addition to their generally (but not always) larger size, Friday mosques differed from masjids by the inclusion of a minbar. Every town having a minbar and a kadi to enforce the shariʿa was legally defined as a place whose inhabitants were obliged to perform the Friday prayer, which was not allowed in villages.[47]

According to Hanefi jurists of the classical Ottoman period, Friday worship was valid only with written permission from the sultan or his delegate.[48] For instance, in 1552 Süleyman allowed the governor-general of Baghdad to build a Friday mosque in the Medina of Algiers for which he had requested a permit.[49] A similar decree sent by Selim II in 1570 to the governor-general of Algiers orders him to allow the construction of Friday mosques to volunteering individuals with their own money in recently conquered North African cities. The governor is asked to report how many Friday mosques have been built, so that written 'imperial permits' (*icāzet-i hümāyūn*) for the performance of the Friday prayers can be dispatched accordingly.[50] We learn from the account book of a Friday mosque built in Sarajevo (1559–61) for the deceased governor-general Ali Pasha that the fee paid for filing a petition to the imperial court, which requested authorization for the construction of that mosque, was 32 aspers. Obtaining a written imperial permit, in turn, cost 38 aspers.[51]

Hanefi jurists' definition of a town by the presence of a Friday mosque opened the way to the recognition as towns of larger villages with their own markets, provided that the sultan approved the performance of the Friday prayer in them. This politico-juridical understanding of the town made it lawful for the sultan to grant or deny urban status to borderline settlements.[52] During the age of Sinan, this facilitated the creation of Friday mosques in sparsely inhabited sites along trade or pilgrimage routes that were expected to form the nuclei of new towns populated by settlers exempt from taxes.

Unlike their peers of the Shafiʿi legal school, which coexisted with the Hanefi school in Ottoman Syria and Egypt, Hanefi lawyers did not consider city walls as the borders of towns. This made the definition of town outskirts a matter of juristic dispute, accelerating the construction of suburban Friday mosques in the many large Ottoman cities that expanded beyond their walls. Hanefi jurists no longer required that a town or city have only a single Friday mosque to unify urban congregations, an old tradition still upheld by their Shafiʿi colleagues.[53] This legitimized the construction of multiple Friday mosques in major cities of the Ottoman empire; in Istanbul, for example, each of the thirteen districts (*nahiye*), corresponding in scale to small towns, had one Friday mosque by the time Sinan became chief architect. At the end of his career, many of these administrative regions had acquired more than one Friday mosque, and these were accompanied by others in the three townships and outlying suburbs.

The general population growth in the sixteenth-century Mediterranean world and the concomitant process of urbanization seem to have been among the factors that contributed to the rising demand for Friday mosques during the age of Sinan. In Istanbul, for instance, the population had grown from about 100,000 people at the end of the fifteenth century to over 500,000 in the 1590s. Even though Mustafa Āli found the presence of so many Friday mosques in the capital unnecessary, they had been created at the request of community members who presented petitions to the court of the kadi, who in turn sought written permission from the sultan.[54] The two most common criteria used in communal petitions to justify the construction of a new Friday mosque were the increased size of a congregation and the inconvenience caused by the distance of the nearest existing Friday mosque. It also became general practice to convert a sufficiently large masjid into a Friday mosque simply by the addition of a minbar, so long as the sultan accepted this change of status.

One such example was the masjid Sinan built in Eyüp for Süleyman's sister Shahsultan; this was transformed into a Friday mosque with a royal permit obtained in 1555. Addressed to the kadi of Istanbul, the permit acknowledges that the kadi had sent a petition informing the sultan of four residents from Eyüp who, as witnesses at the sharʿia court, made the following appeal: 'During the winter and on other days with foul weather we suffer extreme difficulty and hardship in going to the Great Mosque (*cāmiʿ-i kebīr*) because our neighbourhood is far; the above-mentioned masjid is capable of becoming a Friday mosque and we request it to become one.' Süleyman's permit ends with the statement: 'I give permission and sanction with my imperial decree and order that in the said masjid the Friday prayers be performed, the khutba be pronounced, and prayers be offered for the acceptance of her [Shahsultan's] charity and for the continuation of my imperial reign.'[55] Another order sent to the kadi of Istanbul in 1574 gives permission for the transformation of the masjid of the chief white eunuch, Mahmud Agha, in the Nahlbend quarter (Ahırkapı) into a Friday mosque. Once again, neighbourhood residents had confirmed that this masjid built by Sinan could be converted into a Friday mosque, which they urgently needed.[56]

The large number of Friday mosques the chief architect built in Istanbul must have blurred their difference from masjids, turning them into monuments associated with specific neighbourhoods. This is implied in one of Ebussuud's fatwas, which asserts that the residents of a neighbourhood with a Friday mosque should not attend mosques elsewhere. The fatwa poses the following question: 'If Zayd's quarter has a noble Friday mosque and without a reason justifiable by the shariʿa he does not perform the Friday prayer in that mosque but in another one, does this constitute a sin?' Ebussuud considers it a sin if Zayd was motivated by the desire to listen to that mosque's preacher or its Koran chanters.[57] His response not only shows that neighbourhood inhabitants were discouraged from freely wandering beyond their nuclear settlements, but also signals an attempt to stabilize the congregations of Friday mosques in cities with multiple mosques.

It was deemed necessary to build Friday mosques with legitimately earned funds on justly acquired sites, since resorting to injustice would cancel the value of building them as good deeds. Clearing up large enough spaces for the construction of mosque complexes in Istanbul became increasingly problematic during the age of Sinan, given the dense urban fabric of the capital. This gave rise to an intense competition for premium real estate among mosque patrons. With royal permission, several Friday mosques built by Sinan supplanted masjids or churches. A permit obtained from the sultan in 1584 allowed the Friday mosque of the vizier Mesih Mehmed Pasha in the Yenibahçe quarter, for example, to replace a masjid.[58] The Friday mosques the chief architect designed for the grand vizier Rüstem Pasha in Tahtakale and for his brother Sinan Pasha in Beşiktaş also replaced masjids. In all three cases, a surrogate masjid was constructed in the relatively empty area along the land walls of Istanbul, in exchange (*bedel*) for the demolished masjids.[59]

Churches and monasteries continued to be transformed into Muslim sanctuaries long after the conquest of Constantinople, particularly during the reigns of Bayezid II and Selim I. The popular demand to appropriate churches for the creation of mosques, either through conversion or rebuilding, is reflected in a fatwa by Ebussuud that poses the following question: 'Did sultan Mehmed II conquer Istanbul and the villages surrounding it by force?' The answer is:

> The sultan's conquest by force is well known, but the preservation of old churches signifies conquest by peace. In the year 944 (1538–39) this situation was investigated and two aged individuals, one-hundred-and-thirty and one-hundred-and-seventeen years old respectively, were found. They testified in front of the investigator that Jews and Christians who had secretly formed an alliance with Mehmed were permitted to remain in the city. With this testimony old churches were allowed to remain as they are today.[60]

This investigation, which took place during the year Sinan became chief architect, testifies to an ongoing process of Islamization that authorities tried to keep in check by inventing the tradition that parts of the capital had peacefully surrendered.[61] Such a legitimizing story was required because the shariʿa restricted the number of non-Muslim sanctuaries in forcibly conquered places.

Like mosques, non-Muslim sanctuaries within the empire were subject to legal supervision and codes of decorum that are discussed in the next chapter. According to the shariʿa, no new church or synagogue could be built in a Muslim town; only those that already existed were to be repaired in accordance to their old form.[62] A church or synagogue demolished for the construction of a mosque, on the other hand, had to be replaced by a new one built elsewhere if there was no legal justification for its seizure. In general the arbitary expropriation of non-Muslim places of worship was discouraged. Moreover, in non-Muslim villages where new sanctuaries were permissible, a veritable boom in church building followed the re-establishment of the Serbian patriarchate in 1557, after which a number of important medieval churches in the Balkans underwent extensive restoration.[63]

Ebussuud's fatwa referring to the investigation in 1538–39 implies continued attempts to seize non-Muslim sanctuaries in Istanbul. This is confirmed by the jointly endowed mosque complex Sinan built in Kadırgalimanı for the couple İsmihan Sultan and Sokollu; its foundation inscription, dated 1571–72, celebrates the 'Muhammedan conquest' attained by demolishing a church formerly on its site.[64] Ebussuud approves the conversion of a church into a mosque, even if its non-Muslim users possessed a waqfiyya, provided that Muslim congregations had previously prayed in it. One of his fatwas regards testimony by aged witnesses that a church in Istanbul had been used as a masjid after the city's conquest as evidence sufficient to justify its conversion into a Friday mosque. This was especially appropriate if it had become surrounded by Muslim houses requiring a congregational mosque and if the Muslims residing there were disturbed by the taverns of 'infidels'.[65] The same type of reasoning was also used in 1587–88 to justify the conversion of the monastery church of Teotokos Pammakaristos, functioning as the Greek Orthodox patriarchate, into a Friday mosque because the call to prayer had been performed there during the day of the city's conquest (illus. 31).[66] The patriarchate was transferred to another church in Istanbul and the appropriated building was proudly renamed 'Fethiye' (Monument of Conquest) to commemorate Murad III's recent military victories in Georgia.[67]

Gerlach reports that Selim II had already contemplated appropriating the patriarchate's church, but changed his mind.[68] It was during his reign that Ottoman authorities decided to confiscate and sell the endowed estates of churches and monasteries in the Balkans. Between 1567 and 1571 several imperial decrees informed sanjak governors in Rumelia that it was no longer legally possible to renew the title deeds (*berat* or *hüccet*) that Selim II's

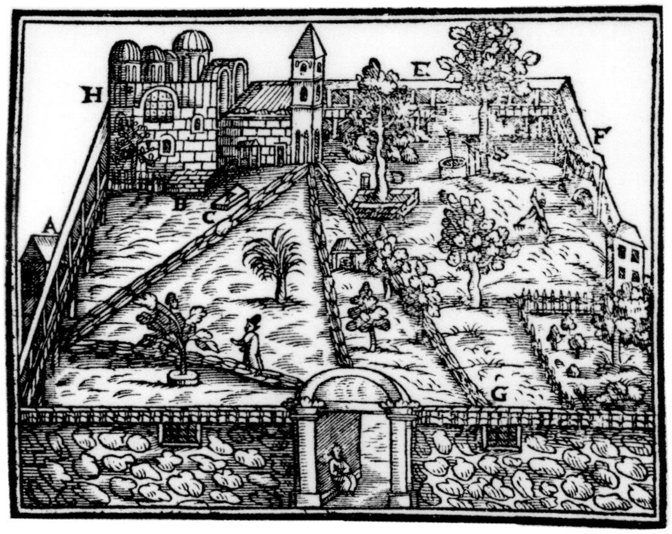

31 The Greek Orthodox Patriarchate at the Pammakaristos church in Istanbul, woodcut based on a drawing of *c.* 1578–81.

non-Muslim subjects had sent for renewal upon his accession to the throne. Ebussuud issued a fatwa declaring that it was illegal for non-Muslim subjects to bequeath as endowments to churches and monasteries lands belonging to the state, or such properties as vineyards, mills, gardens, houses, shops, and cattle. Endowed lands in Rumelia would be confiscated and sold in return for a deed (*tapu*); churches and monasteries were allowed to buy back their lands with such a deed, provided that they agreed to pay a tithe and other taxes. Lands of inactive endowments would revert to the public treasury.[69]

This revenue-increasing measure has been attributed to Ebussuud's systematization of lands in the empire, classified in accordance to the shariʿa as 'tithable' (*ʿöşrī*), 'tribute-paying' (*ḫaracī*), and 'state property' (*mīrī*).[70] Some abandoned sanctuaries provided space for new charitable buildings commissioned by Muslim patrons, such as the caravansaray and covered bazaar (*bedesten*) complex the grand vizier Sokollu created in Belgrade on the site of a synagogue and three deserted churches unable to pay taxes.[71] These transactions continued during Murad III's reign, when the grand vizier Koca Sinan Pasha bought the church of St George in Thessaloniki, a sixth-century rotunda sumptuously decorated with gold mosaics, which he converted into a Friday mosque.[72]

The late-sixteenth-century traveller Mehmed Aşık, who had previously visited that beautiful church several times as an excursion site, provides a firsthand account of how its conversion came about: 'Whenever this author went for an outing (*teferrüc*) to that church with several acquaintances from the people of Selanik, we would wish it to become a sanctuary of Islam (*maʿbed-i islām*). With the help of God, after a short while ... our wish was granted.' At the urging of a local sufi shaykh, the grand vizier Koca Sinan Pasha passing through Thessaloniki appropriated the church as a

32 A miraculous apparition over the Piyale Pasha mosque, and the oldest church of Istanbul (La Madonna) converted into a mosque, 1571, Venetian woodcut.

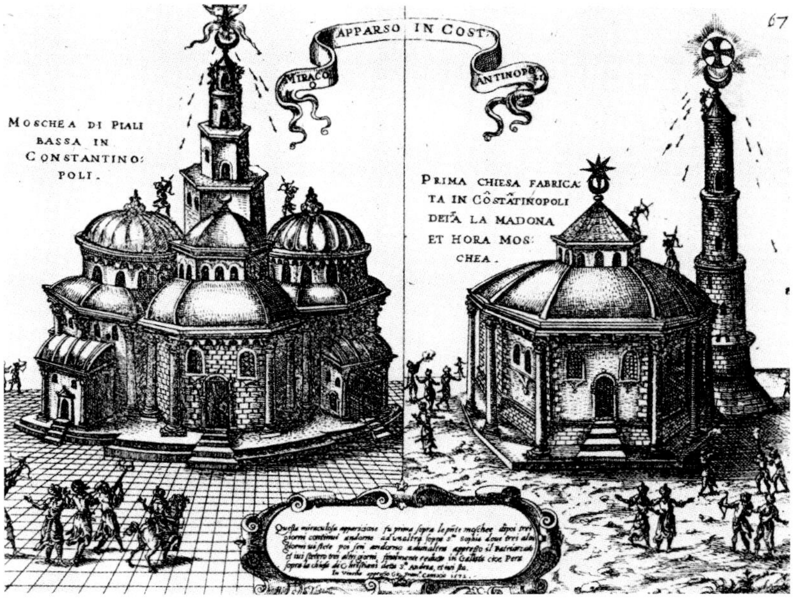

'conquest' from the Christians by means of a sultanic decree, adding to it a minbar, mihrab, muezzins' tribune, and minaret:

> When this author was in Selanik a second time at the end of 1595 that shaykh was diligently engaged in the completion of the minaret, courtyard, and gates of this exhilarating Friday mosque. As he asked for a suitable foundation inscription to be written on its gate, I composed the following chronogram: 'Sinan Pasha passed from this elevated place with his desire accomplished after destroying the monument of the wrong faith; / For its conquest Shaykh Khurtacı (?) exerted diligence and devotion. / In the path of God, he directed [the construction] by helping as its building supervisor. / It was taken from the people of Jesus when the sultanic decree arrived; / The flock of Muhammad became a follower of that shaykh in its conquest. / When the prayers were conducted in it, Aşık pronounced its date: 'This old monastery without doubt became a sanctuary for the people of Islam', 998 (1589–90).[73]

This eyewitness account captures the religious enthusiasm evoked by the conversion of the monastic church into a Friday mosque, regarded as a conquest on behalf of Islam.[74] A firman sent to the governor and kadi of Aleppo in 1587 shows that the conversion of another church in Istanbul (most likely Fethiye) had created repercussions throughout the empire; the firman (copies of which were sent to the kadis and governor-generals of Damascus, Van, Diyarbakır, Tripoli, Nikopolis, and Ahyolu) forbade the transformation of churches into Friday mosques in those cities, ordering that churches retained by the Christians at the time of each city's conquest be left untouched.[75]

After the demoralizing defeat of the Ottoman navy at Lepanto in 1571, the well-established practice of transforming cathedral churches into Friday mosques in newly conquered territories seems to have given way to the conversion of some churches within the imperial domains: a token of the victory of Islam at a time of diminished military expansion. A print published in Venice that year testifies to the comparable Christian fantasy of reclaiming Istanbul's churches along with the new mosque Sinan designed outside the walls of Galata for the grand admiral and vizier Piyale Pasha, who had recently conquered Cyprus from the Venetians in 1570 (illus. 32). We learn from the inscription on the print that the miraculous apparition of a cross first lingered in the skies over the mosque of Piyale Pasha and the Church of the Madonna (believed to be the first church built in Constantinople but now functioning as a mosque). After three days, the apparition moved to Hagia Sophia for three days, then to the Patriarchate for another three days, and finally returned to Galata, where it stopped over the church of St Andrea. Stereotyped Ottomans with turbans frantically shoot arrows and guns at the luminous apparition to forestall its dreadful prophesy of the defeat of Islam. From the seventeenth century onwards, the loss of Ottoman territories in Hungary and thereafter in the Balkans would partly fulfill this prognostication. Captured Muslim sanctuaries were either Christianized or demolished for the construction of monumental domed churches with prominent belltowers, which had been banned under Ottoman rule.[76]

II. PIOUS ENDOWMENTS AS MEMORIALS TO VICTORY AND FAME

European and Ottoman observers identify sultanic mosque complexes as victory memorials, legitimately built with war booties by rulers who had personally commanded successful military campaigns in Christian lands. This had a precedent in early Islamic times. The people of Cordoba, for instance, refused to pray in the costly enlargement the tenth-century Umayyad caliph al-Hakam II made to the city's Great Mosque until the qadi swore that it had been financed with the ruler's legal one-fifth share of war booties. The second justification made for the mosque's luxurious expansion was necessity, a justification also common in the Ottoman context: the congregation had grown so large that many fainted and perished from the press of the crowds.[77]

In his book of advice dedicated to Murad III, Mustafa Āli declares that the sultans should only finance charitable socio-religious monuments with the spoils of holy war, because the shari'a neither permitted the public treasury to be used for that purpose, nor did it allow the foundation of unnecessary mosques or madrasas:

> As long as the glorious sultans, the Alexander-like kings, have not enriched themselves with the spoils of Holy War and have not become owners of lands through gains of campaigns of the Faith, it is not appropriate that they undertake to build soup kitchens for the poor and hospitals or to repair libraries and higher *medreses* or, in general, to construct establishments of charity, and it is seriously not right to spend or waste the means of the public treasury on unnecessary projects. For, the Divine Laws do not permit the building of charitable establishments with the means of the public treasury, neither do they allow the foundation of mosques and *medreses* that are not needed.[78]

One of the European travellers who acknowledged the victory symbolism of sultanic mosque complexes built on Istanbul's hilltops was Reinhold Lubenau (1587–88), an apothecary attached to the Austrian Hapsburg embassy (illus. 33[1–8]):

> In addition to Hagia Sophia, there are in this city four other imperial mosques [those of Mehmed II, Bayezid II, Selim I, and Süleyman I] all of which are sited on elevated hilltops. These resemble monasteries with their hospices, madrasas, schools, gardens, fountains, guest-houses, and bath-houses ... They have a custom that only allows a sultan, who with his own hand has conquered a place from the Christians, to build a mosque in the city as a memorial. All of these mosques are built very grandly with beautiful marbles and quarried stones artistically joined together in such a way that one does not even notice their joints. The Turks do not spend anything on their residences so long as they are protected from the rain, but they spend with great magnificence on their mosques, schools, hospices and bath-houses.[79]

Andreas von Steinach (1583) similarly notes that 'no Turkish sultan is allowed to build a mosque if he has not personally led a campaign two to three days of travel from Istanbul'.[80]

The Venetian diplomat Domenico Trevisano (1554) lists several examples of sultanic mosques in Istanbul that were endowed with the land tax paid by non-Muslims in conquered territories:

> Revenues from the *caraz* [*harac*, tribute] have mostly been assigned by former emperors to their mosques, depending on the territories they conquered; as in the mosque of Mehmed II, to which are assigned the tribute of Constantinople, Pera (Galata), Caffa, Negroponte and other islands; or that of Bayezid II receiving the tribute of Corone, Modone, Lepanto, and Durazzo. To the mosque of Selim I no tribute was assigned, but rather possessions and lands, since this *Grand Signore* had not conquered any place from the Christians. They say that for this reason his mosque was not built with the same grandeur and magnificence as others, because they believe the principal goal of each Ottoman emperor should be the ruin of Christians and not of Muslims.

Selim I had, indeed, focused his military energies on the conquest of Muslim territories in Syria, Egypt, and Iran. Trevisano adds: 'To the mosque of the presently reigning emperor Süleyman, for the construction of which more than a million gold coins will be spent, as [the grand vizier] Rüstem Pasha has informed me, numerous tribute revenues will similarly be assigned.'[81]

Ottoman sources link the construction of earlier sultanic mosques in Bursa and Edirne with military victories in Christian lands. The Great Mosque (Ulu Cami) of Bursa, for example, was built by Bayezid I with the booty of a crushing victory over crusading forces at Nikopolis in 1396.[82] The Old Mosque (Eski Cami) in Edirne, initially financed with the war booties of Bayezid I's two rival sons (Süleyman and Musa), was completed by their reigning brother Mehmed I according to its foundation inscription dated 1411.[83] The construction of the Üç Şerefeli (Triple Galleried) mosque in Edirne, on the other hand, fulfilled a vow made by Murad II before a military campaign to Hungary. The sultan left for his destination after having laid the foundation of this 'New Mosque' (Yeni Cami) with his own hands in 1437–38 as a pledge to be fulfilled in return for awaited triumph. Built with war booties and completed in 1447–48, its endowments included revenues from lands in Rumelia 'conquered by the sultan's own sword'.[84] In similar fashion, Bayezid II, in anticipation of victory, laid the foundations of his mosque complex in Edirne before leaving in 1484 for a campaign at Kili and Akkirman in Rumania. Part of the money taken from the treasuries of these two conquered cities was used to finance the sultan's votive mosque complex.[85]

As Trevisano notes above, the mosque complex of Selim I in Istanbul is not particularly monumental; it was built as a posthumous memorial by his reigning son Süleyman (1520/21–1526/27).[86] The monuments Selim I erected during his lifetime commemorated his victories in Syria and Egypt. One of these was the prophet David's shrine in Marjdabik, the battlefield north of Aleppo where Selim I defeated the last Mamluk sultan in 1516 (illus. 34). This victory was attributed to the spiritual aid of David, next to whose tomb the sultan had pitched his imperial tent after praying there.[87] The Friday mosque and hospice the same sultan built in 1518 adjacent to the burial place of the sufi shaykh Ibn Arabi in Salihiyya, a suburb of Damascus, was another thanks-offering. The shaykh, who had miraculously predicted Selim I's victory in his writings, became honoured with a domed mausoleum. During the first Friday prayer performed at the adjoining mosque in the sultan's presence, thanks were offered to God for the conquest of Syria.[88] For the Halveti shaykh İbrahim Gülşeni (d. 1534), who forecast Selim I's next victory over the Mamluks in Cairo, the sultan ordered the construction of a dervish convent in 1519–20 next to the mosque of the Mamluk ruler

33 Melchior Lorichs, details from a *Prospect of Istanbul*, a series of 21 sheets drawn in 1559 and reworked in c. 1561–62, ink and colour on paper:

1. (Sheet 6) Hagia Sophia
2. (Sheet 8) Constantine's Column with the mosques of Mahmud Pasha and Atik Ali Pasha
3. (Sheet 9) complex of Bayezid II

1

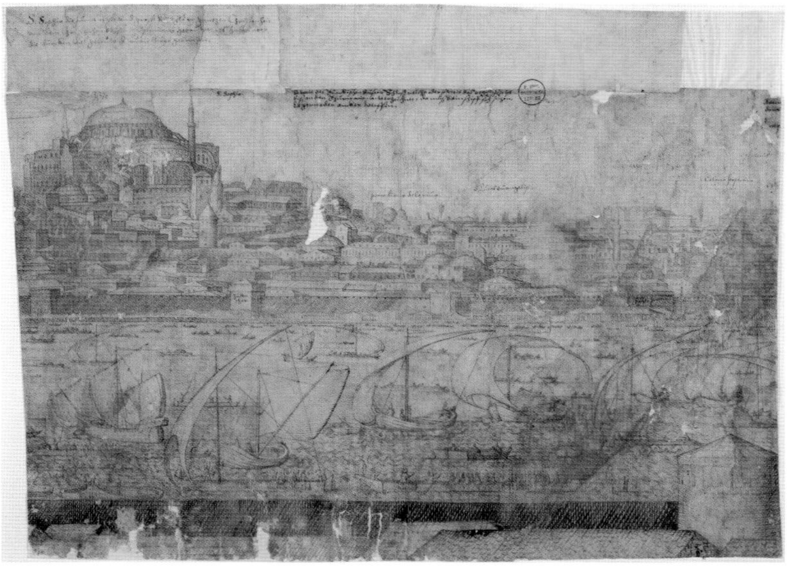

2

3

4

5

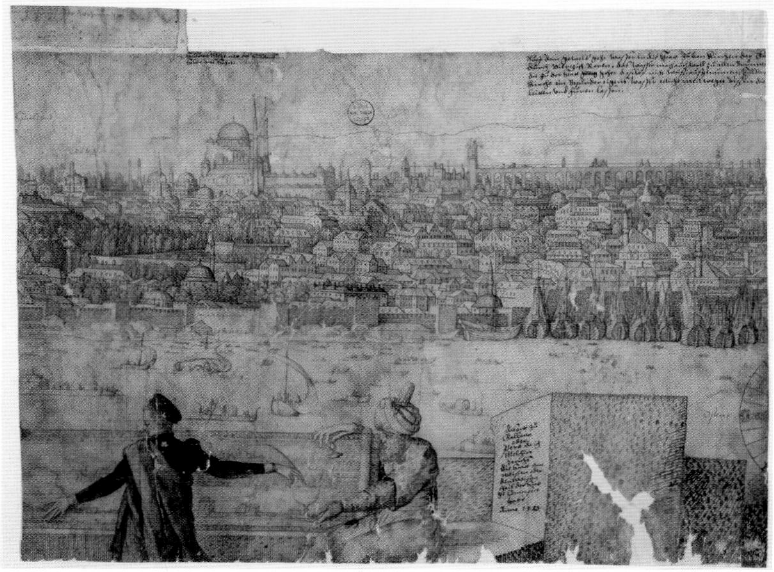

6

4. (Sheet 10) Süleymaniye complex with the Old Palace to its left and the janissary agha's place to its right
5. (Sheet 11) Şehzade Mehmed complex and the Valens aqueduct with a self-portrait of Lorichs and his Ottoman assistant in the foreground
6. (Sheet 12) Column of Arcadius at Avratpazarı and the Yedikule fortress

7. (Sheet 13) Complex of Mehmed II.

8. (Sheet 14) Complex of Selim I.

Muayyad; it was completed in 1524–25.[89] The grand mufti Çivizade was dismissed by Sultan Süleyman in 1542 because he pronounced fatwas against the teachings of such sufi shaykhs as Ibn Arabi, İbrahim Gülşeni, and Mevlana Celalüddin Rumi (the founder of the Mevlevi order).[90] Later on, Ebussuud's fatwas confirmed the orthodoxy of these sufi shaykhs and recommended the punishment of those who claimed to find passages out of line with the shariʿa in their written works.[91]

Like his father, Süleyman also created several victory memorials in the east. The two Friday mosques with adjoining hospices and convents that he commissioned in Baghdad, after taking that city from the Safavids in 1534, announced the inauguration of Sunni Ottoman rule in the former capital of the Abbasid caliphs (illus. 35). These mosque-cum-convent complexes were built next to two resuscitated domed mausoleums that had been desecrated by the Safavids: those of the legal scholar Abu Hanifa (d. 767, the eponym of the Hanefi school), and the sufi shaykh ʿAbd al-Kadir al-Gilani (d. 1166, who gave his name to the Kadiriyya order). As a janissary Sinan, who accompanied Süleyman's victorious campaign, participated in the construction of these two monuments, which are mentioned in only one of his autobiographies.[92] Abu Hanifa's complex, protected from the 'heretics' by a fortified enclosure, symbolically confronted the Shiʿi shrine of al-Kazimayn on the other side of the Euphrates.[93] Now under Ottoman control, that shrine contained the tombs of the seventh Imam (Musa al-Kazim, to whom the Safavid shahs traced their holy descent) and the ninth Imam.

Another memorial monument commissioned by Süleyman is his Friday mosque in Konya, next to the funerary shrine of Mevlana Celalüddin Rumi (illus. 36–38). According to Mustafa Āli, the sultan first had a domed masjid built adjacent to the shaykh's 'illumined tomb'. Later in 1559–60 he added another domed hall for the whirling ritual (*semāḫāne*) next to the tomb tower and a free-standing 'double-minaret Friday mosque of matchless elegance'.[94] The construction of the mosque (not cited among Sinan's works in his autobiographies) must have been initiated soon after the battle of succession fought between Süleyman's two sons (Bayezid and Selim) outside the walls of Konya in 1559.

Mustafa Āli attributes prince Selim's victory to the military support he received from his father and to the spiritual aid of Celalüddin Rumi. Bayezid, on the other hand, had been punished for rebelling against his father and 'not hesitating to defile with the corpses of rebels the pure soil of Konya filled with saintly tombs.'[95] Another source describes how prince Selim obtained permission from his father to visit the tombs of Konya's saints to gain their spiritual sanction prior to the battle, especially that of Rumi. His troops, commanded by his tutor Lala Mustafa Pasha, and the imperial forces sent by his father pitched their tents in a garden in front of Rumi's *extra-muros* funerary complex, where the war of princes took place.[96] A chronicle attributes Bayezid's defeat to a miracle: 'A dust cloud suddenly emerged on top of [the tomb tower of] His Highness Mevlana Hüdavendigar, rose to the sky, and after whirling for a while descended upon prince Bayezid and his soldiers.' Engulfed by the blinding dust, his soldiers either fled or were put to the sword.[97] Forced to retreat, Beyazid sought refuge at the court of Shah Tahmasp, giving rise to a dynastic crisis that was not resolved until the shah agreed to have the prince and his sons strangled in 1562.

The war of princes, which determined the empire's future ruler, was a major event commemorated not only by Süleyman's sultanic mosque in Konya, but also by the princely mosque of his victorious son Selim in the nearby town of Karapınar (illus. 203–8).[98] The sultanic mosque in Konya preserved the memory of the encampment site of Selim's victorious army. Commissioned and endowed by Süleyman, its construction was likely overseen by the crown prince while he resided in Konya between 1559 and 1562. Associated with both Süleyman and Selim, the mosque celebrated the mutual military triumph of father and son against prince Bayezid, who was declared a rebel by a fatwa of Ebussuud and posed a threat to dynastic stability until his elimination at Qazvin in 1562.[99] The intimate connection of the mosque with Celalüddin Rumi, who sanctioned the victory of Selim, is visually expressed by the blue-painted marble hood of its unique minbar, which replicates the fluted conical superstructure of the saint's neighbouring tomb tower clad with blue glazed tiles (illus. 37, 39). The Friday preacher and staff of the sultanic mosque were selected among Rumi's descendants who administered the neighbouring shrine complex.[100]

The shrine of Mevlana Celalüddin Rumi (whom the shaykh al-Islam Çivizade had declared an 'unbeliever') became a popular visitation site along a strategic junction of the Anatolian hajj route and the eastern avenue leading to Iran. Selim's former tutor Lala Mustafa Pasha visited it on his way to a campaign against the Safavids

34 (left) Matrakçı Nasuh, shrine of the Prophet David in Marjdabik, *c.* 1537, watercolour on paper, from *Beyān-i Menāzil-i Sefer-i ʿIrāḳeyn*.

35 (above) View of Baghdad with the shrine complexes of ʿAbd al-Kadir al-Gilani at the upper left within the city walls and of Abu Hanifa in an *extramuros*, fortified enclosure at the lower right, 1587–88, watercolour on paper, from Seyyid Lokman, *Hünernāme*.

in 1578, which he commanded as a vizier. There he listened to mystical music in a trance and had a prognostication made from a page of Rumi's *Mathnawī* regarding the outcome of the Persian campaign (illus. 40). Süleyman's building activities at the shaykh's shrine were followed up by Selim II's construction of a hospice there and by Murad III's creation of a dervish convent dated by its inscription to 992 (1584–85), but only the 'renovation of the hospice' is attributed to Sinan in one of his autobiographies. The pious endowments of these three sultans contributed to the development of an extensive shrine complex exemplifying the dynasty's support of sufi orders compatible with the shariʿa.[101]

Süleyman's magnificent mosque complex in Istanbul (1548–59) was an architectural expression of the triumph of Sunni Islam under the 'sultan of the ghazis', who perpetually

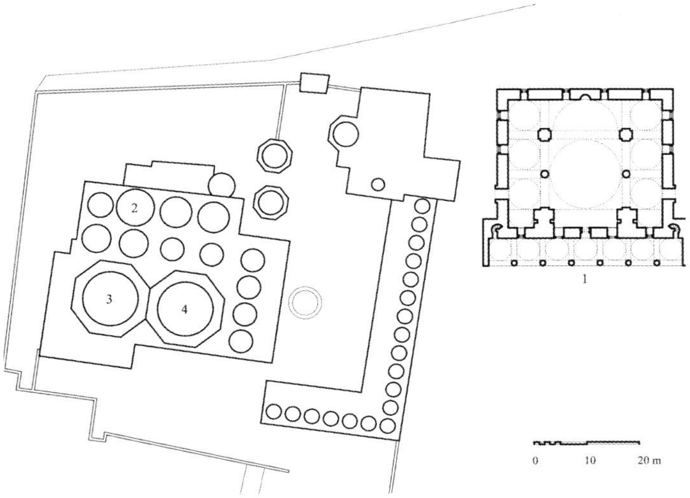

36 Plan of the Sultan Süleyman mosque, Konya, next to the shrine complex of Mevlana Celalüddin Rumi, 1. Friday mosque. 2. Rumi's tomb tower. 3. Ritual hall of convent. 4. Masjid.

37 Mosque of Süleyman, Konya, with the shrine complex of Rumi in the background (the domed library adjoining the mosque is a later addition).

38 Mosque of Süleyman from the north.

39 Minbar of Süleyman's mosque.

waged wars against enemies of the faith in the eastern and western frontiers of his empire. Its foundations were laid in 1548, just before Süleyman left the capital with the refugee Safavid prince Elkas Mirza to fight a holy war against the prince's brother, Shah Tahmasp.[102] The two Persian campaigns that Süleyman undertook during the construction of his mosque complex yielded a victory that was ideological rather than military. With the peace treaty signed at Amasya in 1555, Tahmasp agreed to abolish the ritual cursing of the orthodox caliphs, and to protect the shariʿa in his domains.

Selim II's mosque complex in Edirne, the Selimiye (1568–74), was conceived as a victory monument proclaming the triumph of Islam over Christianity at a time when peaceful relations prevailed with Safavid Iran. Its foundations, laid in 1569, just before the campaign of Cyprus (1570–71), embodied a vow that would be fulfilled in gratitude for divinely bestowed victory.[103] European visitors report that tribute money from Cyprus, captured from the Venetians by the sultan's generals, was used for the mosque's construction and endowment.[104] According to Evliya Çelebi, Selim had a dream in which he pledged to the Prophet Muhammed: 'If I become the conqueror of the island of Cyprus, I will build a Friday mosque from the spoils of holy war.' Evliya recounts that the sultan ordered his general Lala Mustafa Pasha, who conquered Cyprus for him, to bring the booty of Famagusta

40 Lala Mustafa Pasha (holding a manuscript, top right) and his secretary Mustafa ʿĀli (top left) visiting the shrine of Rumi in 1578, watercolour on paper, from Mustafa ʿĀli, *Nuṣretnāme*, c. 1584.

for the construction of his mosque to Edirne, a frontier city celebrated as the 'rampart of Islam'.[105]

The fact that Selim II did not conquer Cyprus with his own sword seems to have been one of the reasons why the Selimiye was built in Edirne rather than in Istanbul. Under his son Murad III, no European territory whatsoever was conquered, therefore, as the French pilgrim Jean Palerne (1581–83) observed, this sultan did not build a mosque in the capital 'because their Mufti or Pope does not allow any other funds to be used for that purpose except for revenues gained from the Christians.'[106] Instead, the sultan simply converted the Greek Orthodox patriarchate's church in Istanbul into a memorial mosque named Fethiye (Monument of Conquest) to celebrate the relatively minor victory of his generals in Georgia.

Funerary mosque complexes named after successive sultans accentuated the celebrated skyline of Istanbul as dynastic victory memorials. Meant to be read serially, these sultanic landmarks distinguished the superior status of the walled city, where they were exclusively concentrated, over the three subordinate townships. They were linked together by courtly processions held on highly charged state occasions, when sultans visited one by one the royal tombs of ancestors. During these sequential ritual visits the cityscape became charged with a collective message of dynastic continuity punctuated by a string of victories. The posthumous mausoleums of the sultans, erected by their reigning sons, expressed the uninterrupted chain of dynastic succession identified by Talikizade as one of the bases of Ottoman legitimacy. The consecutive visitation of ancestral tombs, together with the sanctified tomb of the city's patron saint, Abu Ayyub al-Ansari (a martyred companion of the Prophet Muhammad), symbolically linked the present with a dynastic and mythical Islamic past. These rituals, practised after each royal accession (at least beginning with Selim II), legitimized the reign of the deceased sultan's successor by stressing his glorious lineage that turned the whole empire into the inherited legacy of a single family. Visiting ancestral tombs in sequence, after having obtained the blessing of the martyred warrior Ayyub (Turkish: Eyüp), the Ottoman sultans gathered the collective *baraka* of their royal forebears. The repetition of these rituals before departing on military campaigns served as a potent reminder of past victories.[107]

The collective message of sultanic mosque complexes was also animated through prayers offered for the success of Ottoman armies during military campaigns. According to Dernschwam, when Süleyman was away from the capital during the Safavid campaign of 1553, prayers begging for victory had been held twice a week on Mondays and Thursdays in successive sultanic mosques. Dernschwam describes how the grand mufti Ebussuud led a parade of three to four hundred religious officials, who received their wages from pious endowments, to the designated sultanic mosque.[108] The kadi of Istanbul was ordered in 1566, during Süleyman's last campaign to Szigetvár, to have special prayers performed twice a week in sultanic mosques under his jurisdiction where congregations including the ulema, shaykhs, madrasa students, and Koran reciters would plead for the victory of Islam. The first large congregation was to be gathered at the mosque of Ayyub's shrine on a Thursday. This would be followed by smaller congregations assembled on Mondays and Thursdays in each sultanic mosque, comprising the salaried employees of those mosques and others in their neighbourhood. Copies of this order were sent to the kadis of Bursa and Edirne.[109]

Another imperial decree, of 1578, ordered the kadi of Istanbul to enlist the city's ulema and shaykhs to pray for the victory of Islam and the defeat of the 'heretics' in the Persian campaign commanded by the vizier Lala Mustafa Pasha. Congregations would meet in the mosques of the capital, reciting the Cattle sura (al-Anʿam) on Wednesdays and the Victory sura (al-Fath) on Fridays. Related orders sent to the kadis of Bursa, Edirne, and Aleppo specified that these prayers should be held on Mondays and Thursdays. The kadis

41 Nocturnal mosque illumination, woodcut based on a drawing of c. 1578–81.

of Cairo and Damascus, on the other hand, were instructed to hold them on Sundays and Wednesdays, while Saturdays and Tuesdays were the days reserved for the kadi of Diyarbakır.[110] During his Hungarian campaign of 1596, Mehmed III asked the grand mufti to organize congregational prayers in successive sultanic mosques: Hagia Sophia, followed by the mosques of Mehmed II, Bayezid II, Selim I, Süleyman I, and Abu al-Ayyub.[111]

The religious personnel of sultanic mosques, then, constituted an army of supplicants ready to offer prayers for military victory on behalf of Islam. Another common practice was the melodic chanting of the call to prayer at minarets by a rich chorus of muezzins, who performed special chants on Fridays and on other festive occasions, both religious and profane, including the births of princes and the deaths and accessions of sultans. It became customary during the reign of Murad III to illuminate the galleries of the multiple minarets in royal mosques throughout the month of Ramadan, on the two religious festivals and the four holy nights, and during victory celebrations.

On such festive occasions, oil lamps were suspended on cords between the minarets of royal mosques to form illuminated pictures and words that sometimes spelled out the name of the reigning sultan together with the conquests he had won. Visually enticing polychromatic effects were produced by pouring coloured water under the layer of oil.[112] Murad III's Jewish physician wrote the following about illuminations that decorated the Süleymaniye's four minarets (*campanili*): 'At the time of their greatest feast of the year, they extend cords from one tower to another, to which are attached rows of covered and lighted lamps, by which a most beautiful vista is produced of the moon and the sun and various other things of theirs, for eight consecutive days.'[113] Written around the same time, Schweigger's travelogue includes a woodcut of such minaret illuminations that 'marvellously' depicted 'now a full moon, then a crescent, and other forms' (illus. 41).[114]

The sultanic mosques of Istanbul were proudly displayed to foreign dignitaries on special tours. Such an excursion was organized in 1546 for the Safavid prince Elkas Mirza, who viewed the city on horseback 'in the company of the pillars of the state and the grandees'.[115] The inauguration ceremony of the Süleymaniye mosque in 1557 was attended by religious scholars, court officials, and foreign diplomats, including Shah Tahmasp's ambassador, specially sent for the occasion with gifts.[116] The shah's letter of congratulation to the sultan humbly offered to have custom-made large carpets, unavailable in the Ottoman lands, prepared for the mosque: 'The appointment of befitting carpets is a cause of ornament and perhaps a necessity for that mosque, and in that country there are no carpets as large as that mosque.' The ambassador was knowledgeable in matters of 'design' (*naḳḳāşī*) and the shah's letter continued, if written dimensions and specifications for those carpets were given to him they could be prepared 'all at once'. The shah would be blessed with the fortune of contributing to the ornamentation of the mosque, but this depended on the identification of the number of carpets needed, their length and width, and the colour of their centre and borders.[117] Süleyman curtly responded that his fully-furnished mosque did not need any additional ornaments:

> Before the construction of the noble Friday mosque and illustrious sanctuary was commenced, for the provision and preparation of its needs we sent worldwide-obeyed orders to all regions of our well-protected imperial domains, in such a way that the amount of carpets, oil lamps, lanterns, and other needs of decoration and customs of adornment were designated in advance, and before the commencement of the congregational prayers all the requisites had fully been prepared and completed, for no object was delayed little or much.[118]

What appeared in the guise of a humble gift offer was in actuality nothing but a reminder of Safavid artistic superiority, a subtext certainly not lost on Süleyman. The sultan's proud response ended with the bottom line assurance that his mosque had been built to win the favour of the 'Seal of the Prophets' and the intercession of the 'Four Pillars of the Illustrious Shariʿa' on the Day of Judgment. Thereupon, Tahmasp was warned that the continuation of the peace treaty signed in 1555 depended on his respect toward orthodox religion: 'So long as the noble shariʿa becomes an object of respectful treatment and protection in the lands subject to your rule, the possibility of harming the foundations of peace is null and the customs of friendly alliance eternal.'[119]

When the Safavid ambassador Shahkulı arrived in 1567–68 with a huge retinue and impressive presents to congratulate Selim II on his accession to the throne, he was given a guided tour of mosques by the lieutenant of Istanbul, Piyale Pasha, while the sultan's court was wintering in Edirne. Among the 'paradise-like noble Friday mosques of sultans from the House of Osman, he was especially shown the great Ayasofya', along with those of Selim I and Süleyman I, before he left for Edirne.[120] After being received with pomp and circumstance by the sultan in the royal palace of Edirne, the ambassador was kept waiting there until the end of Ramadan, when all mosques in that city were decorated with lights to impress him.[121] The members of another Safavid embassy sent to the court of Murad III in 1576, just before the declaration of a protracted Persian war (1578–90), were subjected to yet another propagandistic tour of Istanbul's sultanic mosques, where they observed Ottoman-style prayers and chants extolling the Prophet's companions.[122] These official excursions organized for Safavid dignitaries expressed an unabashed pride in the spectacle value of Istanbul, designed as a showcase for sultanic mosque complexes built as victory memorials.

Outside the capital cities of Bursa, Edirne, and Istanbul, many single-minaret state mosques had been created in the name of the sultans in newly conquered territories, generally using the capitation tax (*cizye*) collected from the non-Muslims. The function of such generic frontier mosques as inalienable territory markers is noted in several dispatches that the Austrian Hapsburg diplomat Johann Maria Malvezzi sent to king Ferdinand I. On 9 May 1550 he wrote:

> We have discovered in diverse ways until now that the Turks create difficulties when it comes to giving up those places where they have their mosques, and they say that their law neither tolerates nor permits this.[123]

He later reported that the grand vizier Rüstem Pasha and the second vizier Kara Ahmed Pasha held the same inflexible position regarding the inalienability of lands in Hungary where mosques had already been built.[124] After the conclusion of the post-Lepanto peace treaty in 1573, the Venetian diplomat Marcantonio Barbaro informed the Senate about the same religious prohibition that banned giving back conquered territories featuring mosques.[125]

Evliya Çelebi cites many examples of non-sultanic mosques financed with war booties, but only some mosque complexes Sinan designed for grandees celebrated military feats. Those he built in the capital for the grand admirals Piyale Pasha and Kılıç Ali Pasha, for instance, commemorated their personal contributions to naval conquests by displaying mementos of victory: a model of Chios hung from the mausoleum dome of Piyale Pasha, who had conquered it, and cannons Kılıç Ali Pasha captured during the conquest of Goletta in Tunisia were exhibited in front of his mosque along the seashore of the cannon foundry in Tophane.[126] Mosques named after grandees were often individualized through such memory markers, which have since disappeared along with the collective memory of the circumstances that occasioned their construction. Patrons utilized various strategies to leave their individual mark on the public sphere, such as manipulating well-known plan types within the limits of decorum, devising personalized inscription programmes with specific messages, and selecting sites associated with their person (residential neighbourhood, birthplace, or seat of office). Waqfiyyas stipulated the types of ritual that would perpetuate the remembrance of patrons in their mosque complexes, often accompanied by mausoleums enshrining personal memorabilia.

Gilded finials decorating the pinnacles of domes and the conical caps of minarets sometimes functioned as visual emblems of their patrons' identity. Some mosques attributed to Sinan were once decorated with such emblematic finials. One of them is the masjid of the finance minister Defterdar Mahmud Efendi (1541) along the shore of Eyüp. The no-longer-extant finial of its minaret was in the shape of an inkpot and pen, symbolizing the scribal profession of its patron, a skilled calligrapher.[127] Another example is the Friday mosque of the royal companion Şemsi Ahmed Pasha in Üsküdar (1580–81), whose dome finial was in the shape of a sun disk, alluding to its founder's penname (*şemsī*, pertaining to the sun).[128] The foundation inscription of the vizier Nişancı Mehmed Pasha's Friday mosque in the capital, built in the 1580s, bears an imperial monogram (*tughra*) of the reigning sultan Murad III, denoting the patron's celebrated career as a chief chancellor in charge of inscribing the sultan's monogram on imperial documents (illus. 415).[129]

Trevisano interprets non-royal mosques as pious deeds functioning as personal memorials:

> The institution of building mosques assigned with revenues has not only been practised by the emperors but also by many individuals who spend such revenues to build mosques in cities and towns. These edifices appear to have been built because of the desire everyone has to leave behind a memorial of themselves and to accomplish a good deed beneficial for one's soul.[130]

While mosques built for lower ranking patrons were generally endowed with cash, real estate, and commercial properties, the waqfs of prominent grandees also included state lands – exempted from all taxes except for tribute (*harac*) – which were donated as freehold estates with a patent by the sultan (*temlik*).[131]

The donation of state lands to individuals had been practised on a limited scale until the reign of Süleyman, who was the first sultan to bestow *temlik*s on an unprecedented scale to relatives and grandees as an impetus for the creation of pious endowments contributing to urban development.[132] Koçi Beg regards Süleyman's donation of lands to favourites as a harmful innovation that weakened the state treasury. He particularly criticizes the lands this sultan bequeathed to his daughter Mihrümah Sultan after marrying her to Rüstem Pasha, whom he then raised to the rank of grand vizier: 'because of his great affection for her, he donated to her as *temlik*s so many villages from the domains conquered at the time of his forebears that they would suffice as the treasury of a minor king.' Unlike previous sultanas, whose fiefs reverted to the state when they died, Mihrümah used hers to create pious endowments for the benefit of her offspring. Other sultanas followed her model and 'against the shariʿa, royal fiefs belonging to the public treasury of the Muslims thus vanished and perished'. Süleyman had thereby 'committed a sin while believing he was meriting God's reward for a pious act.'[133]

Koçi Beg argues that the shariʿa only justifies the donation of villages and meadows belonging to the public treasury to the ghazis, in return for the lands they conquered. He says the sultans of the past used to reward the ghazi *beg*s and *beglerbegi*s by donating as *temlik*s some of the lands vanquished by them, with which these valorous individuals had endowed mosques, hospices, and dervish convents. He regards the donation of state lands by later sultans to their favourites, who had not even added a single village to the Ottoman domains, as illegal, just as he considers waqfs established with the revenues of such donations as unlawful pretexts for providing an income to one's progeny.[134]

Mosque complexes, so vital for the socio-economic life of cities, appeared to be private undertakings funded by the personal wealth of the patrons whose names they carried, but in reality many of them were partly sustained by state subsidies.[135] Pious endowments are generally grouped in two categories, 'charitable' (*khayrī*) and 'familial' (*ahlī, dhurrī*), but in non-sultanic waqfs both categories were inextricably intermingled. The Hanefi legal school, much like the Hanbeli school, allowed the donors of waqfs and their descendants to benefit from the surplus income of pious endowments. By contrast, the Shafiʿi and Maliki legal rites prohibited pious endowments benefiting the founder as the first beneficiary and subsequently other named beneficiaries. The flexibility of Hanefi law encouraged the Ottoman ruling elite to endow mosque complexes with properties whose surplus could be used by the donor in his or her lifetime and then by named descendants or manumitted slave servants.

The founder of a waqf could simultaneously satisfy both worldly and otherworldly benefits. In addition to promising a reward in the afterlife, pious endowments ensured a good name and social standing during one's lifetime. Stipulations made for the recitation of prayers on behalf of the souls of founders and their family members perpetuated their memory in the public spaces of mosque complexes over the generations. Besides being a type of insurance that safeguarded family funds from confiscation, endowments allowed the bypassing of Islamic inheritance laws by naming chosen beneficiaries to preserve large estates from fragmentation. It was also common practice to give priority to relatives, household servants, and freed slaves in selecting the staff of mosque complexes. The endowment deeds of complexes attributed to Sinan, which I discuss in Part 3, often include specifications that turned them into welfare institutions for the descendants and dependents of their founders, who maintained large households with *kul*s. Another widespread practice was to name the successors of the founder's official post as endowment overseers, a practice testifying to the ruling elite's strong sense of corporate identity. Royal women, on the other hand, tended to extend favours to their own gender, including daughters, household servants, and needy women.

The tendency to attribute mosque complexes, which we know from waqfiyyas to have been built and endowed by royal women, to their husbands or fathers reflects the widespread perception of women as daughters or wives in a man's world. The grafting of a woman's identity onto that of her male relatives could therefore muffle her own voice in the public arena of architecture. For example, Selim II's daughters, İsmihan Sultan and Shahsultan, were overshadowed as patrons of architecture by their husbands (Sokollu Mehmed Pasha and Zal Mahmud Pasha), with whom they jointly built and endowed their mosque complexes as couples. Even Sinan's autobiographies list these mutual monuments under the names of their husbands.[136] However, powerful matrons like Haseki Hürrem Sultan (Süleyman's legal wife), and such esteemed widows as Shahsultan (his sister), Mihrümah Sultan (his daughter), and Nurbanu Sultan (the mother of Murad III) managed to play a highly visible and less ambiguous role as patrons of architecture.

Fatwas that discourage women from frequenting mosques raise the question of whether these sultanas, who were among the foremost patrons of Sinan's Friday mosques, attended congregational prayers in their own foundations. The most widely used compendium of Hanefi jurisprudence in the Ottoman world states that attending the congregational prayers is actually disapproved for women; nevertheless those who are old may participate in the morning, evening, and nighttime prayers, since troublemakers are prone to attend the noon, afternoon, and Friday prayers (being occupied with eating in the evening and sleeping in the morning). According to a 'less reliable' tradition, old women could attend all prayers because they were not physically attractive. Women who did go to Friday mosques had to stay at the back, or behind a curtain.[137] The exclusion of younger women from the Friday prayers is also revealed in a fatwa of Ebussuud, which asks: 'In some towns, if women go to mosques to perform the Friday prayers, is it necessary to forbid them according to the shariʿa?' The answer is that the young ones should be forbidden from doing so.[138]

According to sixteenth-century European travellers, Ottoman women were only rarely seen in Friday mosques. In the 1550s Dernschwam says that they prayed at home rather than publicly in mosques.[139] Around the same time, a Spanish slave attached to the household of the grand admiral Sinan Pasha noted that unmarried young women were legally excluded from mosques, but that widows were allowed entry five months after the death of their husbands. The few women who did go to mosques prayed unseen in a separate space because their visibility could distract men.[140] The French traveller Pierre Lescalopier (1574) observes that women prayed in spaces reserved for them at the back of mosques.[141] Philippe Du Fresne-Canaye (1573) wrote: 'Women never go to mosques to perform their prayers, but remain at home because the law does not permit them to enter paradise, but to stay at its gate.'[142] This observation is repeated by Gerlach: 'The wives of Turks do not come into any mosque, because women are believed to enter into a different [part of] paradise; they may, however, pray alone in their houses'.[143]

These eyewitness reports confirm the general exclusion of women from the predominantly male space of Friday mosques. None of the sixteenth-century travelogues describe ceremonial processions to mosques by royal women, whereas they abound in descriptions and images of sultans parading to mosques with their all-male retinues. If Sinan's female patrons did not frequent the Friday mosques they founded (perhaps with the exception of inauguration ceremonies and special rituals like the annual recitations of the Prophet's Nativity Poem), their patronage of this building type takes on a special significance. By commissioning ambitious Friday mosques, royal women could claim their access to a status symbol associated with the architectural patronage of the male ruling elite. Their mosques advertised their ability to finance the most expensive and prestigious building type available, visually negotiating within the public arena their increasing prominence in the world of men who often preferred to relegate them to the private sphere. The gendered codes of decorum observed in these monuments reflected nuanced differences of rank among queen mothers, mothers of princes, and princesses married to grandees. Royal women not only used the same architectural language as did men, but also took advantage of the institution of pious endowments that provided a public arena for the cultivation of patronage networks.

Sultanas could exercise an influence on the design process of their mosques through male intermediaries acting as their agents or by personally visiting construction sites in covered carriages (illus. 17, 18). We know, for instance, that Hürrem Sultan paid at least one visit to the site of her mosque complex in Avratpazarı, where she rewarded novices (*acemi oğlan*) with a donation of five aspers per month.[144] A different source connects the same event with a visit Hürrem paid to the construction site of the Şehzade Mehmed mosque in Istanbul, built to commemorate her oldest son, who had passed away in his youth.[145] Some widows like Mihrümah played an active role in overseeing the construction of their late husbands' mosques. The queen mother Nurbanu, on the other hand, was selected by her dying daughter Shahsultan to oversee the construction of a posthumous mosque complex built for her and her late husband (Zal Mahmud Pasha) as a joint memorial in Eyüp.[146]

Some of Sinan's elite patrons left behind wills for the posthumous construction of mosque complexes under the supervision of former household stewards (*kethüda*), appointed as endowment administrators. In these cases, only one-third of the founder's financial resources could legally be used.[147] The posthumous mosque complexes of such grand viziers and viziers as Kara Ahmed Pasha, Rüstem Pasha, Semiz Ali Pasha, and Pertev Mehmed Pasha were built with bequeathed funds. The waqfiyyas of the grand admiral Sinan Pasha in Beşiktaş and of the couple Shahsultan and Zal Mahmud Pasha in Eyüp itemize in detail how the funds designated in their wills were allotted to construction costs by their endowment administrators (Appendix 2).

Çivizade (shaykh al-Islam between 1539 and 1542) issued several legal decisions that forbade cash waqfs and funds endowed for Koran readers. His fatwas, however, were countered by the refutations of Ebussuud (at that time still an army judge) and others, who forcefully argued that abolishing the peculiarly Ottoman custom of the cash waqf would only harm the large number of individuals and institutions deriving benefit from it. Eventually, the more flexible party of Ebussuud won, and endowment practices rejected as unlawful by Çivizade became firmly established in the Ottoman imperial domains.[148]

Pious endowments were periodically subject to inspection by kadis and royal land grants had to be renewed by an imperial patent upon the accession of each new ruler, a requirement that interfered with the semi-autonomous legal status of waqfs. One of Ebussuud's fatwas announces that in 1537–38 pious endowments administered by the progeny of waqf founders had been ordered to be inspected by judges. To the question of who was responsible for preparing the annual expense reports of waqfs, he replied: 'Acting according to the stipulations of endowment founders has been annulled in 944 (1537–38) and replaced by the ruling of the judge.'[149] The date of this ruling coincides with others cited earlier, concerning the enforced construction of masjids and the protection of Istanbul churches from conversion to mosques. These decisions testify to a coordinated systematization of state policies regarding religious monuments and pious endowments on the eve of Sinan's appointment as chief architect.

Chapter 3

CULTURE OF ARCHITECTURE AND DECORUM

I. POLICIES OF URBAN DEVELOPMENT
II. ARCHITECTURE IN THE ISLAMIC EAST AND RENAISSANCE ITALY
III. THE NEW AESTHETIC OF MOSQUES AND SİNAN'S ISTANBUL
IV. CODES OF DECORUM

I. POLICIES OF URBAN DEVELOPMENT

One of the bases of Ottoman dynastic legitimacy enumerated by Talikizade was the density of settlements and pious foundations in the empire. An early example of the imperial policy of urban development in uninhabited passes (*derbend*) is the new settlement that Murad II created at both ends of an unusually long bridge he commissioned to cross the Ergene river at a strategic pass en route to Edirne (illus. 42). The site chosen for this protracted project (1427–28 to 1443–44) was 'a marshland serving as a lair for bandits and a sinkhole for the loads of merchants.' The towns at each end of the bridge were settled with inhabitants exempt from taxes, and a complex with a convent-masjid and hospice (*ʿimāret*) was built on one side to provide food and lodging to travellers. The day before the inauguration ceremony of the complex, the sultan himself, humbly wearing an apron, prepared food for the poor as a gesture of generosity.[1]

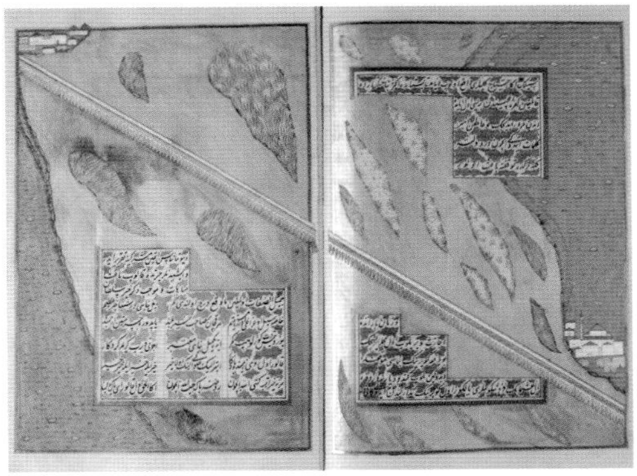

42 Bridge and complex of Murad II at the Ergene river, 1584–85, watercolour on paper from Lokman, *Hünernāme*.

The colonization of space through settlement (*temeddün*, from the Arabic *tamaddun*, 'becoming civilized') played a central role in Ottoman architectural culture. The Turkish term *ʿimāret* is generally used in inscriptions and written sources for early Ottoman socio-religious complexes, grouped around T-shaped convent-masjids and hospices. Derived from the Arabic *ʿimāra*, the term semantically embodies the concept of improvement by cultivating, building, inhabiting, populating and civilizing. The term *ʿumrān*, derived from the same Arabic triliteral root (*ʿ-m-r*), not only denotes inhabitedness, populousness, and prosperity, but the very concept of 'civilization' (*m-d-n*, to settle). During the age of Sinan the term *ʿimāret* generally came to denote a hospice (soup kitchen) built as the free-standing dependency of a Friday mosque complex (Appendix 3). This linguistic transformation paralleled the displacement of early Ottoman complexes, grouped around multifunctional T-type convent-masjids, by compounds whose focal point became 'unifunctional' Friday mosques with undivided interior spaces. Imperial decrees issued for the construction of the Süleymaniye, however, continue to use the term *ʿimāret* with reference to the Friday mosque and its complex as a whole, sometimes identifying the compound as 'the *ʿimāret* and noble Friday mosque'.[2] The Selimiye complex in Edirne is also referred to in decrees as an *ʿimāret*, even though its dependencies lack a soup kitchen. The modern term *külliye* (complex), which I prefer not to use in this book, was invented in the early twentieth century.[3]

Sinan's socio-religious complexes with Friday mosques that no longer feature attached guest-rooms (*tabhane*) are generally classified by architectural historians under three categories: urban complexes with or without lodging facilities for travellers, and roadside complexes designed as halting stations (*menzil*) on major routes. The latter were primarily located on the empire's main highway connecting the Balkans to the Hijaz – Sofia, Svilengrad, Havsa, Babaeski, Lüleburgaz, Üsküdar, İzmit, Karapınar, Belen (Bakras), Payas (near Aleppo), Damascus – and most densely concentrated along the Istanbul–Edirne route frequently traversed by the imperial court during its seasonal visits to the secondary capital (Map 1).[4]

Dernschwam (1553–55) had encountered the remains of the

43 Bridge and complex of Sultan Süleyman at Büyükçekmece, c. 1581, watercolour on paper, from Seyyid Lokman, *Shāhnāma-i Salīm Khān*.

ancient Roman road extending between Nish and Istanbul, but its pavements were not well preserved and its bridges needed repair. Commenting on the absence of clock towers, he observes that the distance between halting stations was conceptualized in terms of time (length of travel on horse or foot) rather than in miles: an observation confirmed by Talikizade's remarks on the territorial extent of the Ottoman empire.[5] The section of the Roman road between Istanbul and Edirne was considerably improved between the 1560s and 1570s; muddy places were repaved and stone bridges, including Sinan's masterpiece in Büyükçekmece (1565–67/68) were erected. New mosque complexes punctuated halting stations separated by a day's trip. The small complex that Sinan created at one end of the Büyükçekmece bridge is composed of a caravansaray for travellers and a public fountain commissioned by Süleyman, complemented by a masjid added by Sokollu after the sultan's demise in Szigetvár (illus. 43). On the same highway, the grand vizier would later commission from Sinan two larger mosque complexes in Lüleburgaz and Havsa, the first for himself and the second for his deceased son Kasım Pasha (Map 1). The Istanbul–Edirne highway, which had previously caused major difficulties to travellers, thus became an impressive grand entry for European ambassadors and tourist on their way to the capital.

Sinan's roadside complexes formed the nuclei of towns that were also provided with various religious, educational, social, and economic facilities and with running water, often brought to public fountains from a considerable distance. These complexes were accompanied by such income-producing structures as bath-houses and markets where travellers could buy goods. The distribution of tax-free lands nearby provided an incentive for new settlers to build houses.[6] On the road from Sofia to Europe and from Damascus to the Hijaz, the number of mosque complexes dropped sharply and gave way to caravansarays, which were also more common along secondary routes. Pierre Lescalopier (1574), with some exaggeration, observed that in the empire's western borderlands only caravansarays were allowed to be built (illus. 25, 26). To hinder slaves and *kuls* from escaping to Europe, innkeepers were required to ask the identity and travel plans of each customer, who had to pay upfront for the goods they bought to avoid delaying departure the next morning. Standing at the caravansaray's gate, the 'carvaceratgis' (*kervansarayci*) greeted their guests each morning, wishing them a good day. 'It is a marvel,' wrote Lescalopier, 'that in the same caravansaray arrive all sorts of people from different backgrounds – Arabs, Turks, Greeks, Jews, Armenians, and Franks (the name they give to Latin Christians) – each of them stays there cordially and no one complains about the other.'[7]

The monumental desert caravansarays beyond Damascus are listed in Sinan's autobiographies as 'the caravansarays, fortified castles, and reservoirs built for Sultan Süleyman along the noble hajj route.'[8] The late-sixteenth-century court historian Lokman's *Hünernāme* (Book of Skills) describes the sultan's pious foundations for pilgrims:

> On the road from Rumelia to Damascus and from there until Mecca he built and organized many needed stone bridges, khans, and caravansarays, while in the desert at dangerous halting stations he created lofty castles and reservoirs for the collection of rainwater. The following is a list of his charities along that road: At the Dil pass between İzmit and Gebze he endowed a few ships free of charge for the pilgrims, stipulating that in their honour others wanting to cross the sea should also be taken along. And he also built an elevated Friday mosque at Konya on the burial site of the sufi saint Mevlana Celalüddin Rumi. Also at the mountain pass (*derbend*) of Bakras [Belen], a frightful halting station on the road from Edirne to Aleppo and Damascus, he built two solidly-constructed monumental khans facing one another, creating there a large village resembling a town. It was made prosperous with a bath-house, Friday mosque, bazaar, and a dervish convent (*zāviye*) providing soup for travellers. It thus became a safe haven protected from the harm of bandits.[9]

The miniature painting accompanying this description depicts Süleyman's complex in Bakras (Belen) with its surrounding settlement in a mountain pass between Iskenderun and Aleppo (illus. 44, 45). One of Sinan's autobiographies refers to this complex as 'the caravansaray and dervish convent built in the Bakras mountain pass on the road to Aleppo'.[10] The painting shows a caravan with camels crossing the high mountain pass and entering the picture plane vertically from the upper-right corner. In the foreground are two caravansarays with horses and grooms at their gates, and in the background is the village with a mosque, convent, and hospice where cooks are preparing bread and soup for travellers. The roofs of the complex are shown covered with lead, a distinctive sign of high-status architectural patronage.

What remains of the royal complex in Belen today is the partially ruined double caravansaray, the bath-house, and a small single-minaret mosque whose central domed space is extended on three sides with cross-vaulted projections and fronted by a spacious walled-in vestibule and a lateral extension added later. This roadside complex, spatially dominated by the double caravansaray, is still bisected by the historical hajj route. The Arabic inscription on the remaining part of the caravansaray refers to Süleyman as the 'servant of the two Noble Harams'.[11] The village was settled between 1550 and 1553 with 250 persons, who were given tax exemptions as mountain pass guards (*derbendci*) expected to feed couriers and their horses. The duties of *derbendci*s included policing the safety of strategic roads and passes, protecting and repairing roads or bridges, and populating uninhabited places.[12] After several years, sixty-five more families were settled there, and surrounding state lands within an hour's distance were distributed tax free to encourage urban development.[13]

The creation of such new settlements is referred to in the trilingual dictionary of an early-seventeenth-century Ottoman architectural treatise by words that mean 'to make prosperous and flourishing' (*ʿimārat* in Arabic, *ābādān kardan* in Persian, and *şen itmek* or *maʿmūr itmek* in Turkish).[14] Among Sinan's roadside mosque complexes, those in Svilengrad, Lüleburgaz, Karapınar, and Payas were each sited in *derbend*s provided with new markets and populated with settlers exempted from taxes (Map 1). The waqfs of these mosque complexes were enriched with lands donated by the sultan with diplomas (*temlik*) to their founders: Hürrem Sultan, the crown prince Selim, and Sokollu Mehmed Pasha.

Lokman's *Hünernāme* goes on to describe the fortified castles with reservoirs that Süleyman built or restored along the hajj route beyond Damascus, a city in which Sinan designed for him a mosque complex for pilgrims (1554–58/59). The desert castles were protected from bedouin bandits by guards appointed from the janissaries of Damascus. A painting in Lokman's manuscript depicts one of Süleyman's big reservoirs in front of a desert castle featuring a lead-domed mosque with a muezzin on its single minaret. At the upper-right corner is a caravan arriving from Damascus (illus. 46). Another painting depicts a castle, well, and reservoir created by the sultan in a halting station for pilgrims arriving from Egypt (illus. 47). Along a winding road in the desert is a single-minaret mosque within a fortified settlement guarded by janissaries. In front of this settlement is a rectangular reservoir and a nearby well operated by a camel, with some Arab nomads camped in black felt tents. Pointing out that similar measures were taken for pilgrims arriving from Yemen, Lokman concludes: 'Such great charities had not even been imagined by rulers of the past.'[15]

Süleyman's charities were not, however, entirely unprecedented. A series of fortified halting stations provided with water tanks and caravansarays with praying facilities for pilgrims had been built in the ninth century by the Abbasid caliph Harun al-Rashid's pious wife, Zubayda, along the hajj route between Kufa

44 Complex of Sultan Süleyman in Belen (Bakras), 1587–88, watercolour on paper, from Seyyid Lokman, *Hünernāme*.

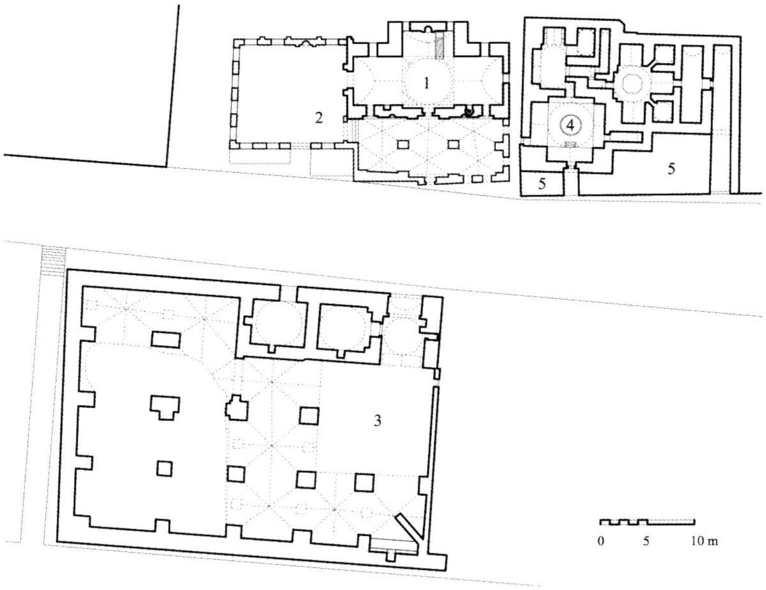

45 Plan of the Sultan Süleyman complex in Belen:

1. Mosque
2. Later extension of mosque
3. Remains of the double caravansaray
4. Bathhouse
5. Shops

46 A castle and watertank built by Sultan Süleyman for hajj pilgrims from Syria, 1587–88, watercolour on paper, from Lokman, *Hünernāme*.

47 Another castle and watertank built by Sultan Süleyman for hajj pilgrims, this time from Egypt, 1587–88, watercolour on paper, from Lokman, *Hünernāme*.

and Mecca, which was hence known as 'Darb Zubayda'. The queen also had constructed an aqueduct (ʿAyn Zubayda) that carried water from the spring of Hunain to Mecca some twelve miles away. Her charities, familiar in the Ottoman context from translated Abbasid histories, were emulated by the queen Hürrem Sultan who started to rebuild ʿAyn Zubayda, a project completed by her daughter Mihrümah Sultan.[16]

Hürrem's building projects in Mecca, Medina, and Jerusalem complemented those of her husband, Süleyman, who renovated the Harams of these three Holy Cities. We shall see under the patronage of Süleyman, Selim II and Murad III that each of these sultans funded extensive renovation projects at the Kaʿba, mentioned in Sinan's autobiographies. Vizirial foundations along the pilgrimage route included fortified caravansarays provided with Friday mosques, guest-rooms, hospices, stables, bath-houses, and water tanks: like those built for Lala Mustafa Pasha (Qunaytara) and Koca Sinan Pasha (Ktaifa and Saʿsaʿa) who had served as governor-generals in Syria. Omitted from Sinan's autobiographies, these fortified complexes were created by local architects, just as the majority of mosque complexes in Bosnia and Herzegovina were built by masons imported from Dubrovnik.[17]

The grand vizier Sokollu's nephew, Mustafa Pasha, who commissioned Sinan to design a Friday mosque in Buda, was one of the governor-generals who played an active role in the urban development of Bosnia and the newly established province of Hungary at the western frontier of the empire.[18] Fortified cities created along the eastern Safavid border during the age of Sinan include Gulanbar (Shahrizor) in Iraq (illus. 48). One of the chief architect's autobiographies lists a Friday mosque built there for Süleyman, an entry that was later crossed out, perhaps because of his minimal contribution to this project.[19] The construction of Gulanbar is described by Lokman, who participated in its foundation ceremony. We learn from him that a royal architect had been sent from Istanbul for the two-year-long project (1563–65) triggered by a petition from the governor-general of Shahrizor to the sultan's court. The petition explained the desolate condition of that province, which only had one district (*nahiye*) with a bazaar, and no flourishing town where soldiers could reside. Lokman

48 Construction of the Gulanbar castle overseen by the governor-general of Shahrizor under a tent, also supervised by a royal architect holding a wooden measuring stick at the left, 1579, watercolour on paper, from Lokman, *Tārikh-i Sulṭān Sulaymān*.

narrates how the construction of the new town was carried out in Gulanbar, using the troops of governors stationed nearby:[20]

> This is a land famous for its foul weather, yet it is three days distant from Hemedan, and five halting stations away from Qazvin. The governor-general suggested that a joyful city be built in that dangerous pass (*derbend*) at the border with the enemy. Its construction would make the nobles of Kurdistan and Luristan in that region obey the Ottomans. Therefore, the construction of a city was ordered by an imperial decree, and a fiefholder in Birecik called Sinan Beg was appointed its building supervisor (*emīn*). He brought 100,000 ducats from the Aleppo treasury, and held a meeting with the governor-general of Shahrizor and with an architect-engineer (*miʿmār-ı mühendis*) sent from Istanbul. The construction was to be carried out by sanjak governors, army commanders, and their troops. The architect-engineer found the site of a small castle with a suburb at its foot (*varoş*), previously built on the hill of Gulanbar by Hızır Pasha, the most suitable place for the construction of an upper castle (*ḳalʿa*) and a lower city (*şehr*) facing the direction of Baghdad. The timber was prepared, and the site dug and cleared before the laying of the foundations. At that time, this servant [Lokman], having been appointed to compose a *Shāhnāma* (Book of Kings] while serving as the kadi of Harir, was present there. In mid-Zilkade (July 1563), an auspicious hour was selected for laying the foundations; together with the above-mentioned governor-general, I laid a pleasant foundation by pronouncing the basmala. With many prayers and *tekbirs* [God is most Great], the battle cry of the janissaries was uttered (*gülbang-i Muḥammedī*) and sacrificial animals were slaughtered with the gove rnor-general's own hands. The construction was completed in two years, after which the lofty castle and well-fortified city became prosperous (*maʿmūr*), a phenomenon unprecedented in those lands. Because of surrounding districts and villages it became rich. In that city, a Friday mosque, khan, market (*çārsu*), covered bazaar (*bezzāzistān*), bath-house, mill, governor's palace, residences for grandees and aghas, quarters for inhabitants, and barracks for janissaries and novice boys were all perfectly and elegantly built. The water and air improved by the day and inhabitants gradually got used to it. Much money was spent on those constructions, but they were indispensable. It is hoped that from this *derbend* castle the lands of Dergüzin, Hemedan, Qazvin, and Isfahan, and perhaps the land of Khorasan, may be conquered.[21]

The construction process of Kars in eastern Anatolia, another fortified city along the Safavid border, provides additional information about how such large-scale urban projects were carried out. This project, not listed in the autobiographies, was overseen by the vizier Lala Mustafa Pasha during the Persian campaign he commanded in 1578–79 and executed by royal architects Sinan appointed to accompany the army (*ordu mimarları*).[22] A letter sent to the pasha by Murad III personally addresses the troops, inciting them to work hard in building the castle of Kars as a religious duty, like the holy war they were fighting against the Safavids. Several decrees dated 1579 inquire about the ongoing construction of the castle, ordering the pasha to build it with materials and masons gathered from neighbouring places in Georgia since sending them from distant provinces would prove difficult. The pasha is also instructed to populate the completed castle and its environs up to the Safavid border with tribal chiefs from Diyarbakır and Van. The settlers would be given fiefs there in order to speed up the urbanization of this frontier region.[23]

Mustafa Āli provides an eyewitness account of the city's construction in his history of the Safavid campaign, the *Nuṣretnāme* (Book of Victory), dedicated to Lala Mustafa Pasha, whom he served as a secretary and chronicler. He explains that each of the castle's seven towers was built by groups of soldiers and builders under the supervision of the janissary agha and provincial governor-generals participating in the campaign. The competing groups of builders were spurred on by the energizing military music of drums and pipes, each group trying to outdo the others.[24] Āli recounts how a 'strange secret' was revealed just before the completion of building activities. An old man appeared in a dream to a soldier and said: 'I am Abu'l-Hasan Kharraqani, my burial is here, and its sign is a well at the tip of my feet.' After revealing the location of his tomb, the saint requested its renovation. When the soldier reported his dream to Lala Mustafa Pasha, the well was discovered and the pasha created a shrine at the saint's tomb.[25] This parallels the renovation of other saints' or martyrs' tombs next to which charitable complexes were built to sanction Ottoman rule in newly conquered cities: Abu Ayyub al-Ansari (Eyüp) in Constantinople, Ibn Arabi in the Salihiyya suburb of Damascus, Abu Hanifa and ʿAbd al-Kadir al-Gilani in Baghdad.

Two paintings in different *Nuṣretnāme* manuscripts depict the construction of Kars (illus. 49, 50). They show the janissaries and masons supervised by staff-holding pashas wearing long caftans. The text and captions identify the names of the building supervisors and the monuments they created within a year in 1578–79: the governor-general's palace with a pyramidal roof at the centre of the outer castle, a Friday mosque commissioned by 'the sultan of the ghazis' (Murad III) at its right side together with the convent of Abu'l Hasan al-Kharraqani at its left, a second mosque sponsored by Lala Mustafa Pasha at the inner castle, a third mosque founded by the governor-general of Diyarbakır, a fourth built for the governor-general of Rum, and a fifth named after the agha of janissaries. The text also mentions dormitories constructed for the janissary guards, houses for the grandees and notables, shops, two bridges, three city gates, a bath-house, and a water channel that brought water from nearby mountains.[26]

Rebuilding the castle of Kars not only fulfilled military and strategic functions, but also announced the inauguration of Sunni orthodoxy with its multiple Friday mosques. The mosques in eastern Anatolia, designed by Sinan for governor-generals who personified the state and its official religion along the Safavid frontier, fulfilled the same function. Whether located in pre-existing cities or in newly created urban settlements, mosque complexes built throughout the imperial domains in the age of Sinan boosted not only the observance of religion but also economic and social life (Map 1). These mosque-centred complexes articulated the transformation of the Ottoman state from a heterogenous frontier principality into a relatively homogenous world empire with an officially cultivated Sunni identity.

49, 50 Two paintings of the construction of Kars castle, *c.* 1584, watercolour on paper, from Mustafa Āli, *Nuṣretnāme*.

II. ARCHITECTURE IN THE ISLAMIC EAST AND RENAISSANCE ITALY

The Friday mosque, which the Maghribi scholar Ibn Khaldun (d. 1406) identified as a fundamental symbol of the caliphate, had ceased to be the primary form of religious architecture after the Islamic lands splintered into regional principalities during the eleventh century. Under the Seljuk rulers and their successors, madrasa and convent complexes incorporating founders' mausoleums emerged as viable alternatives to Friday mosques in the eastern Islamic lands.[27] With the demise of the Abbasid caliphate in Baghdad (1258), multifunctional funerary complexes became even more widespread in the post-Mongol period.[28]

A new concept of monumentality, underscored by texts commenting on the size and cost of ambitious building projects, emerged in the early fourteenth century with the rise of two major dynasties: the Mongol Ilkhanids in Iran and Central Asia, and the Mamluks in Syria and Egypt. The competitive spirit that characterized the architectural patronage of the early Islamic caliphates was first manifested in such monuments as the Dome of the Rock and the Great Mosque of Damascus, built by the Umayyad caliphs to vie with the splendour of churches in Syria-Palestine. Subsequently, the petty dynasties that ruled the fragmented medieval Islamic world between the eleventh and thirteenth centuries commissioned relatively modest structures. The re-emergence of architectural monumentality in the fourteenth century paralleled the ascent of powerful late medieval dynasties with hegemonic claims.[29]

The Ottomans, who were at that time a relatively modest frontier principality, had to wait until the reign of Mehmed II to compete in terms of architectural monumentality with their Muslim neighbours. Mehmed was the first to build in his new capital, Istanbul, a monumental funerary mosque complex (1463–70) surpassing in grandeur the funerary madrasa-cum-convent complexes of contemporary rulers in Mamluk Cairo and Timurid Herat, but his competitive urge was fuelled from yet another direction as well. Centuries after the Umayyads, the Ottomans inherited the magnificent churches of Constantinople, an encounter that engendered a similar dialogue with the Romano-Byzantine classical heritage of the eastern Mediterranean basin.

It was not the modest tradition of late-Byzantine architecture, but the grandiose monuments of the 'golden age' of Byzantium that inspired the Ottomans to redefine their concept of imperial architecture in the early modern age. Monumental domed constructions like Hagia Sophia had become a thing of the past and the late-antique architectural tradition was no longer alive, as it had been in the Umayyad period: it was revived by the Ottomans at a time when Italian Renaissance architects were involved in a similar enterprise. Before turning to Istanbul's sultanic mosques that aspired to match in magnificence Justinian's great sixth-century cathedral church of Hagia Sophia – the supreme achievement of early-Byzantine architecture hailed as the last grand monument of the Roman imperial tradition – I will provide a brief survey of post-Mongol religious architecture in the eastern Islamic lands as a framework for comparison.

MONUMENTAL ISLAMIC ARCHITECTURE IN THE EAST AFTER THE MONGOLS

Recent converts to Islam, the Mongol Ilkhanids particularly favoured the construction of convents for communal mystical devotion (*khanaqah, zawiya*), colleges for the teaching of law and theology (*madrasa*), and shrines for the veneration of saints (*turba, mashhad*). The gigantic but now lost funerary complex commissioned by Ghazan Khan (r. 1295–1304) in a suburb of the Ilkhanid capital, Tabriz, comprised his monumental dodecagonal domed mausoleum, a Friday mosque, two madrasas for the Shafiʿis and Hanefis, a khanaqah, a hospice for Sayyids descending from the Prophet (*dār al-siyāda*), a hospital, a library, a house of law (*bait al-qānūn*), a residence for the overseer, a bath-house, and a fountain. The vizier Rashid al-Din describes it as follows:

> It was founded in the west of Tabriz at the place called Shanb; he [Ghazan Khan] himself drew the plan. At this time it has been in the course of construction for several years. It was built to be more magnificent than the tomb of Sultan Sanjar in Marv, which he [Ghazan] had seen, and which is the most magnificent building in the world.[30]

This passage exemplifies the competitive streak of Ilkhanid monumental architecture.

Ghazan Khan's successor, Uljaytu (r. 1304–1317), had a comparable funerary complex built in his new capital, Sultaniya, from which only his enormous domed octagonal mausoleum survives. As in the memorial monument of his brother in Tabriz, the mausoleum was the focal point of a surrounding socio-religious complex, which Sinan saw during Süleyman's campaign of the Two Iraqs in 1534 (illus. 51). With its 25-metre-wide and 50-metre-high dome, this was the largest mausoleum in the Islamic world, once accompanied by a madrasa, a dervish convent, a hospice for Sayyids, and a hospital.[31] The Friday mosque of Sultaniya, with its twin minarets, four-iwan courtyard, and domed prayer hall, was removed at a distance, as in the early Ottoman capitals of Bursa and Edirne, where a Great Mosque sited at the city center was complemented by outlying suburban socio-religious complexes (illus. 20–24). The funerary sultanic complexes of Bursa, grouped around a T-type convent-masjid and accompanied by subsidiary structures, were smaller versions of their grandiose counterparts in the Ilkhanid capitals of Tabriz and Sultaniya. The focal point of these Ottoman complexes was their convent-masjids, to which the posthumously built domed mausoleums of sultans were humbly subordinated in scale.

51 Matrakçı Nasuh, Map of Sultaniya, *c.* 1537, watercolour on paper, from *Beyān-i Menāzil-i Şefer-i ʿIrāḳeyn*.

Fourteenth-century complexes in the eastern Islamic lands brought together the diverse sectors of heterogenous societies through the mediation of varied institutions of piety. During the fifteenth century, the Timurids continued to commission royal complexes combining several pious institutions and dominated by monumental domed mausoleums. Known as the Gur-i Amir (*c.* 1400–4), that of Timur in his new capital, Samarqand, included a madrasa and a sufi convent grouped inside a courtyard with its corners marked by four minarets. This complex was complemented at a distance by the ruler's colossal Friday mosque (1398–1405), popularly named after his wife, Bibi Khanum, who endowed a funerary madrasa across from it. The mosque based on a four-iwan plan featured a lofty domed sanctuary and eight minarets, one in each corner, and pairs flanking the entrance portal and sanctuary iwan.[32]

Timur's defeat of Bayezid I in the battle of Ankara (1402) plunged the Ottoman realms into a fratricidal civil war, brought to an end by Mehmed I (r. 1413–21), who reunited the dynasty under his rule. This triggered the emulation of Timurid architectural models in the Ottoman world, a trend perpetuated well into the first quarter of the sixteenth century. Mehmed I's funerary complex in Bursa (*c.* 1419/20–24), composed of a T-type convent-masjid, hospice, madrasa, and bath-house, initiated the fashion with its Persianate painted decorations and *cuerda seca* tiles signed by 'the masters of Tabriz'. Its decorative programme was coordinated by an Ottoman painter who had been captured by Timur and trained at his court in Samarqand. The sultan's posthumously completed domed mausoleum, lofty and untypically sited on a hilltop higher than the rest of his complex, alluded to Timurid royal mausoleums with the external turquoise tile revetments that once covered its bulbous dome.[33]

With its fabulous collection of funerary complexes characterized by a proliferation of domes and minarets, the late-Timurid capital Herat continued to be a source of inspiration for the Ottomans. Now in ruins, the Friday mosque (1417–37/38) and madrasa (1432) complex of Shahrukh's wife, Gawharshad, was one of these. Its madrasa, entered by a portal flanked by two minarets, preserves its domed chamber where the queen lies buried with her descendants. A hundred metres distant stood her grand Friday mosque, featuring a lofty domed sanctuary and four minarets in the corners of its four-iwan courtyard. It is said to have been even more magnificent than her mosque in Mashhad (still extant), inserted into the shrine of Imam Riza, which she restored between 1416 and 1418. Herat's now-lost ensembles included Sultan Husayn Bayqara's (r. 1470–1506) four-minaret madrasa and convent complex (1492–93), comprising his domed mausoleum, where food was served each morning to the poor at the khanaqah.[34]

The Mamluk sultanate was yet another source of inspiration for early Ottoman architecture. Using materials stripped from the Crusader fortress at Jaffa seized from the Franks in 1268, its founder al-Malik al-Zahir Baybars I (r. 1260–77), a former Turkish slave of the last Ayyubid sultan of Egypt, had inaugurated his rule with a domed Great Mosque in Cairo (1266–69): a monument intended to represent 'Sunni Islam militant and triumphant'. With a few exceptions, however, his successors preferred to commission multifunctional funerary madrasa and convent complexes whose lofty ashlar masonry façades were dominated by mausoleum domes, tall portals, and one or two minarets with multiple galleries.[35] The visual focus of the monumental madrasa complex of Sultan Hasan in Cairo (1356–61), for instance, is his huge domed mausoleum located behind the qibla iwan of the four-iwan madrasa. Its monumentality was no doubt inspired by such Ilkhanid models as Uljaytu's mausoleum in Sultaniya. According to the Mamluk author Khalil al-Zahiri, the madrasa's qibla iwan was meant to be larger than the Sasanian

Iwan-i Kisra in Ctesiphon: 'Sultan Hasan ... asked the architects which is the highest building in the world? He was told: Iwan Kisra. So he ordered it should be measured and recorded exactly and that his madrasa should be 10 cubits higher.'[36]

The smaller early-fourteenth-century funerary complexes of Orhan I and Murad I in Bursa, grouped around T-type convent-masjids, had adopted local late Byzantine construction techniques, such as hemispherical brick domes covered with moulded terracotta tiles, and composite masonry with alternating courses of stone and brick.[37] Bayezid I's preference for more ambitious royal monuments in ashlar masonry reflected his inflated sultanic claims; he had his title 'Sultan of Rum' authorized by the pseudo-Abbasid caliph residing in Cairo. The sultan's Great Mosque (Ulu Cami) with twin minarets and twenty domed bays (1396–1400) and his T-type funerary complex (1390s), both in Bursa, are built of cut stone (illus. 20–24). This prompted a new demand for Mamluk stone masons imported from Syria, who left their distinctive imprint on the decorative details of Bayezid's Great Mosque in Bursa and that of his son in Didymóthichon.[38]

Architects from Syria who signed monuments commissioned by the post-Seljuk Anatolian principalities include ʿAli b. Mushaymash al-Dimashqi, who built the Friday mosque (1374–75) of the Aydınid ruler İsa Beg in Selçuk (Ayasluk, near Ephesus). The domed mosque reinterpreted the plan of the Umayyad Great Mosque in Damascus, including its atrium-like forecourt unprecedented in Anatolia. The nephew of this Damascene architect, Abu Bakr b. Muhammad b. Hamza b. Mushaymash al-Dimashqi, signed the T-type convent-masjid of the Ottoman vizier Bayezid Pasha in Amasya (1414–19).[39] The latter's son, on the other hand, left his signature on the T-type convent mosque of the Ottoman governor-general Karacabey at Ankara (1427–28).[40]

The late fourteenth and early fifteenth century, then, was a dynamic period of cross-fertilization in which the post-Seljuk architectural heritage of the Anatolian principalities was inseminated with new elements imported from the Mamluk and Timurid domains. This process, which is overlooked by architectural historians who tend to treat Anatolia in isolation from the rest of the Islamic world, continued well into the reign of Murad II (d. 1451). This sultan was the last ruler to commission sultanic complexes grouped around T-type convent-masjids, one in Bursa and another in Edirne. The latter complex, initially planned as a convent-masjid for Mevlevi dervishes, was converted by him into a Friday mosque after a skirmish not specified in the sources.[41] This initiated the transformation with the addition of a minbar of many other convent-masjids into Friday mosques during the late fifteenth and sixteenth centuries. In accordance to his last will, Murad II was buried in a mausoleum added to his complex in Bursa by his son and successor Mehmed II. Until that point, each of the sultans had been interred in domed mausoleums accompanying their convent-masjids in Bursa. Thereafter, the focus of patronage would shift to the new capital, Istanbul, which became the collective burial site of Mehmed II and his successors until the demise of the Ottoman dynasty.[42]

The Üç Şerefeli (Triple Galleried) mosque of Murad II, built between 1437 and 1448 in the market centre of Edirne, has aptly been regarded as the culmination of early Ottoman experiments with domed spaces (illus. 52, 53). Originally called the New Mosque in contrast with its predecessor, the Old Mosque (Eski Cami), it was eventually named after one of its four variegated minarets – the tallest minaret (67.65 metres) in Ottoman architecture until that time, distinguished by three galleries reached from three separate spiral staircases. Like the Ulu Cami of Bursa, the Old Mosque in Edirne (*c.* 1402–14) combined domed bays of equal size, nine in all, fronted by a five-bay portico with twin minarets at each end (illus. 53). The Üç Şerefeli mosque introduced two innovations that would become standard features in later sultanic mosques: a large central dome (24.10 metres wide and 27 metres high) to which other domes are subordinated, and a marble-paved forecourt with a central ablution fountain surrounded by domical arcades. A third innovation (not repeated until Sinan built the Süleymaniye and Selimiye mosques) was the use of four minarets with multiple galleries, likely inspired by their Timurid counterparts, such as the recently inaugurated mosque of Gawhar Shad in Herat (1437–38).

Murad II's assertive Friday mosque in Edirne announced his augmented sultanic claims. The inspiration for the monumental dome and atrium-like forecourt must have come from the Umayyad Great Mosque of Damascus, variants of whose plan had recently been introduced into southwestern Anatolia by Mamluk architects imported from Syria: the mosques of the Aydınid ruler İsa Beg in Selçuk (1374–75) and the Saruhanid ruler İshak Beg (1367) in Manisa.[43] Unlike these mosques, however, the Üç Şerefeli expands the small dome of its Damascene model to cover the whole central space of the prayer hall.

The fascination with Timurid models is manifested in the decorative programme of the Üç Şerefeli, which juxtaposes Persianate paintings with underglaze tiles combining two blues, purple, white, and black.[44] Murad II's convent-masjids in Bursa and Edirne also feature Timurid-flavoured painted decorations, along with underglaze, *cuerda seca*, and monochrome tiles.[45] The few extant examples of painted domes and tilework lunettes in the forecourt of the Üç Şerefeli combine minutely interlaced abstract patterns with intricate inscriptions that superimpose cursive and Kufic scripts. Constituting a regional variant of the international Timurid decorative vocabulary, these ornaments and inscriptions favour visual complexity over legibility. Evliya Çelebi, who attributes the 'exemplary chameleon-like variegated painted designs' using many thousand colours to a Persian painter, says that the 'connoisseurs of the arts who observe these with a scrutinizing gaze (*imʿān-ı naẓar*) bite their fingers in awe and become amazed, dumbfounded, and bewildered.' He also notes the convolution of foundation inscriptions on the gates of the

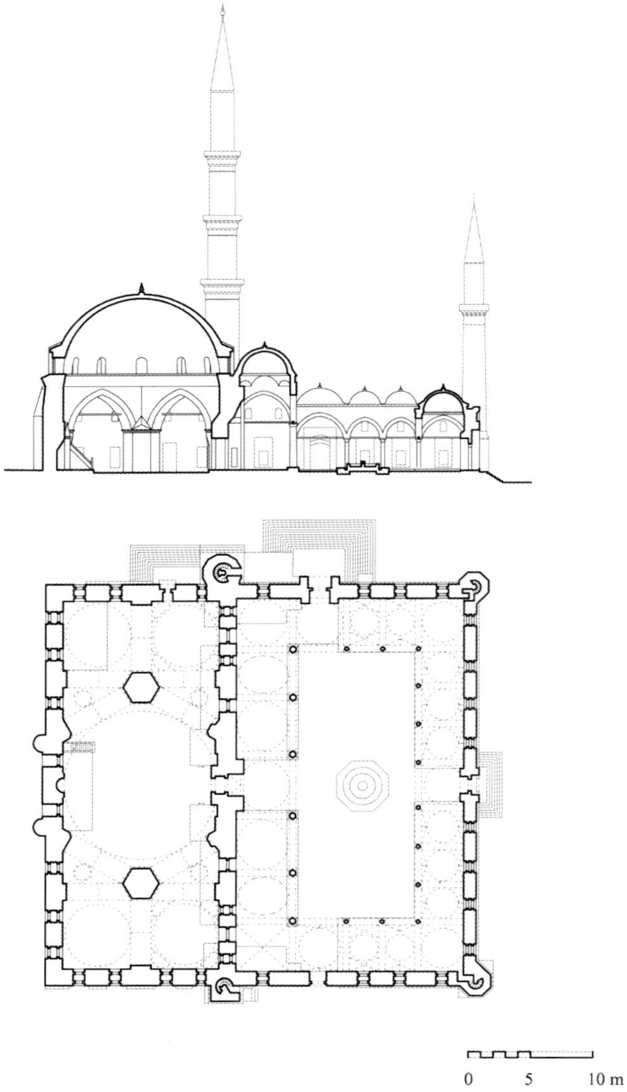

52 Plan and cross-section of the Üç Şerefeli mosque, Edirne.

53 Aerial view of the Üç Şerefeli mosque at Edirne, with the Old Mosque seen in the background.

forecourt: 'Above each gate are Arabic chronograms with dates written in old-style monumental scripts, but their writing is extremely entangled and complex.'[46]

The late antique Mediterranean imperial iconography of the Umayyad Great Mosque, with its combination of royal dome and atrium, would find an uncanny parallel in Hagia Sophia, which Mehmed II converted into the premier Friday mosque of his new capital (illus. 54–57). Sultanic mosques henceforth perpetuated the compounded memories of two imperial traditions, Islamic and late-Roman/early-Byzantine, filtered through the lens of the Ottoman dynastic architectural idiom that had been evolving since the fourteenth century. Starting with Mehmed II, each sultan up to Selim II commissioned a grand funerary Friday mosque complex in Istanbul. Like their smaller precedents in Bursa, these hilltop complexes represented an uninterrupted chain of dynastic succession from father to son, permanently inscribed on the cityscape.[47]

Neither the Safavids nor the Mughals, younger dynasties that emerged in the early sixteenth century, would place such a premium on the construction of Friday mosque complexes. The early Safavid rulers preferred to focus their architectural patronage on shrine complexes, into which they inserted royal mausoleums as an affirmation of their holy lineage: Shah Isma'il I was buried at the ancestral shrine in Ardebil founded by Shaykh Safi, and Tahmasp I at the shrine of Imam Riza in Mashhad, which he renovated. As we have seen in Chapter 1, the only monumental Friday mosque built under Safavid rule was the Masjid-i Shah (1611–38) in Isfahan, where a growing emphasis was placed on the performance of the congregational and Friday prayers. Commissioned by 'Abbas I, the four-iwan plan of this mosque which reinterprets Timurid prototypes incorporates twin madrasas for the juridical elaboration of Twelver Shi'i orthodoxy.[48]

Nor did the Mughal emperors stress the construction of grand Friday mosques until the reigns of Shah Jahan (r. 1628–57) and Aurangzeb (r. 1658–1707), characterized by a growing concern for religious orthodoxy. Their forebear Akbar (r. 1556–1605), for instance, had commissioned mosque-cum-shrine complexes in Fatehpur Sikri and Ajmer, which incorporated the venerated tombs of Chishti shaykhs, a sufi order that bolstered Mughal legitimacy with its openness to both Muslim and non-Muslim disciples. The Mughals showed a special proclivity for sponsoring mausoleum-centred royal complexes where the death anniversaries of deceased emperors were commemorated. These charitable complexes within vast formal gardens brought together the Muslim and non-Muslim members of the multiconfessional Mughal ruling elite for the symbolic affirmation of dynastic allegiance.[49]

Dominated by grandiose mausoleums like those built for their Timurid forebears, the funerary complexes of the Mughal emperors differed from their mosque-centred Ottoman counterparts

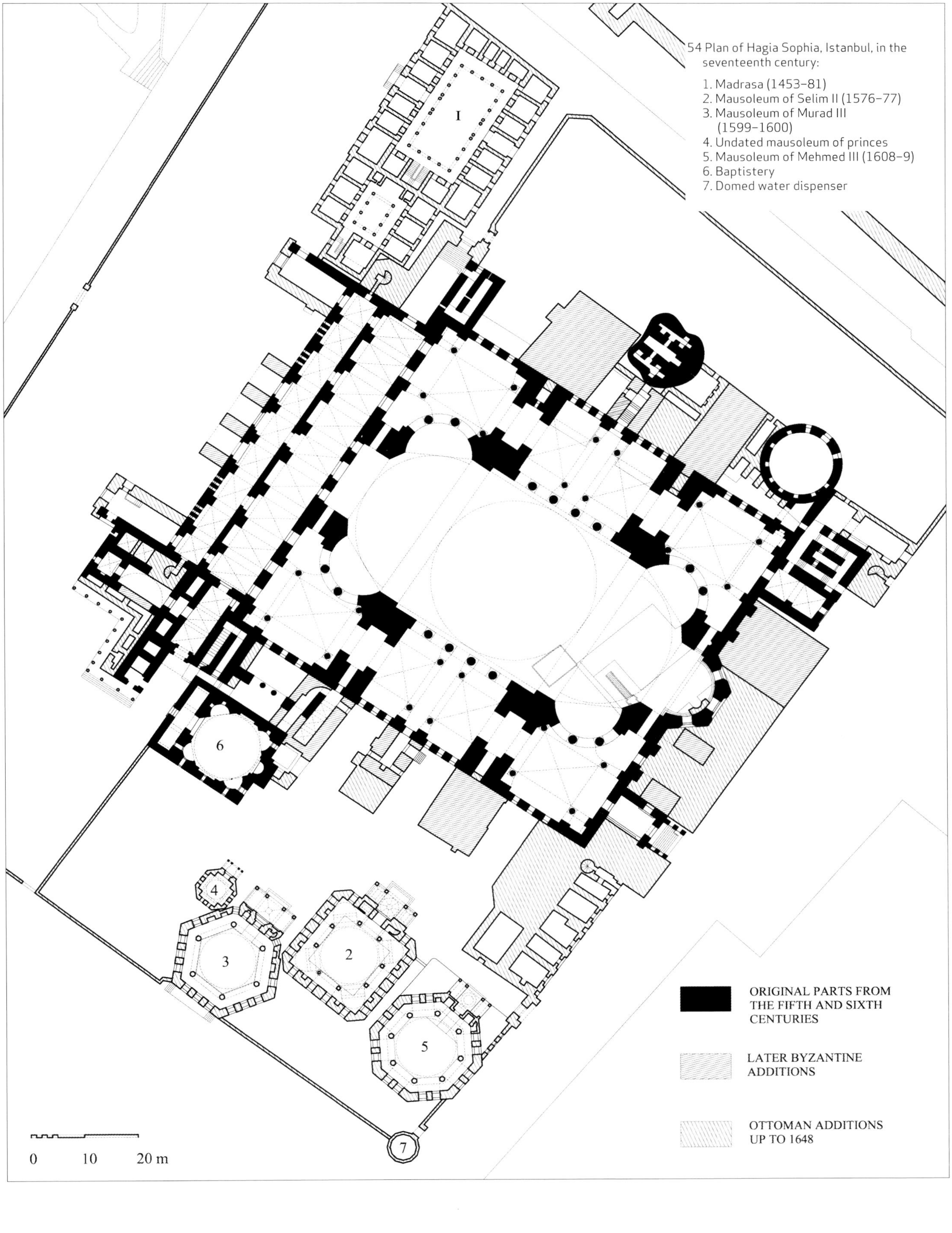

54 Plan of Hagia Sophia, Istanbul, in the seventeenth century:

1. Madrasa (1453–81)
2. Mausoleum of Selim II (1576–77)
3. Mausoleum of Murad III (1599–1600)
4. Undated mausoleum of princes
5. Mausoleum of Mehmed III (1608–9)
6. Baptistery
7. Domed water dispenser

55 Cross-section of Hagia Sophia, Istanbul.

56 Aerial view of Hagia Sophia with imperial mausoleums and the neighbouring bath-house of Hürrem Sultan at the lower-left corner.

57 Interior of Hagia Sophia.

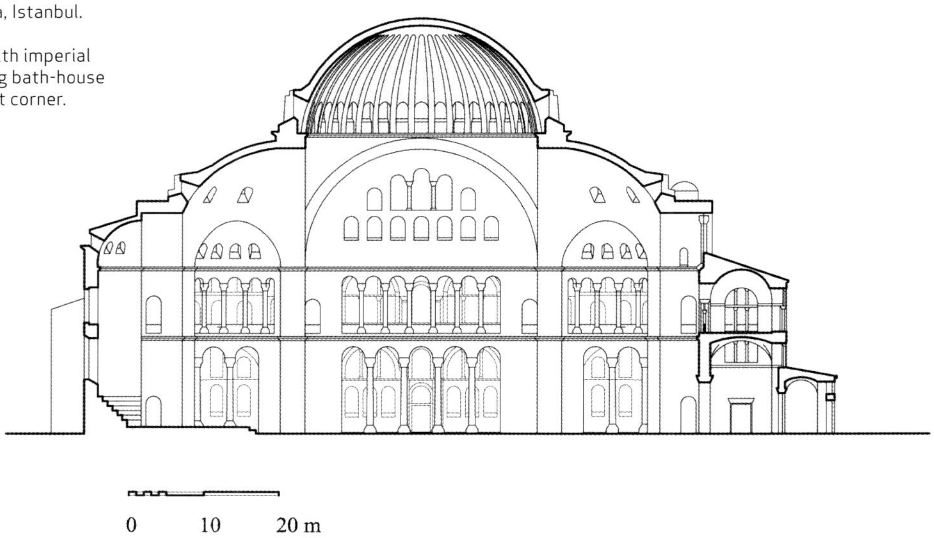

whose sultanic tombs were modest in scale. The seventeenth-century Great Mosques of Agra, Delhi, Lahore, and Isfahan were not complemented by extensive complexes, nor were they supplemented by numerous smaller Friday mosques commissioned by leading members of the ruling elite. The nuanced stratification of mosque types codified during the age of Sinan constituted a unique phenomenon, unparalleled in the history of Islamic architecture. The origins of that phenomenon can be traced to the new emphasis on funerary complexes centring on Friday mosques after the conquest of Constantinople in 1453.

DOMED CENTRAL-PLAN SANCTUARIES IN THE OTTOMAN EMPIRE AND RENAISSANCE ITALY

The transfer of the Ottoman capital to Istanbul (Kostantiniyye) engendered a new imperial vision: the dream of reviving the ancient glory of the Roman empire. The utopian project of reuniting Constantinople with Rome, particularly upheld by Mehmed II and the young Süleyman, would trigger a special receptiveness to artistic developments in Renaissance Italy. Until that project was abandoned around the time Sinan became chief architect, the sultans actively sponsored Italian artists and architects to promote a visual culture befitting their multicultural world empire.[50] The so-called classical idiom of Sinan crystallized in the 1550s after a century of experimentation in the making of the Ottoman imperial image. It proclaimed a distinctive dynastic identity that materialized with the hardening boundaries of the empire, which had reached the territorial limits of expansion. The codification of the classical idiom at a time when foreign artists and architects were no longer invited to the Ottoman court coincided with the consolidation of the corps of royal architects, corresponding to the empire's centralized administrative system.[51]

Parallels between Italian Renaissance churches and Ottoman mosques with domed centralized plans have largely been obscured by the contemporary written discourses of these building tradi-

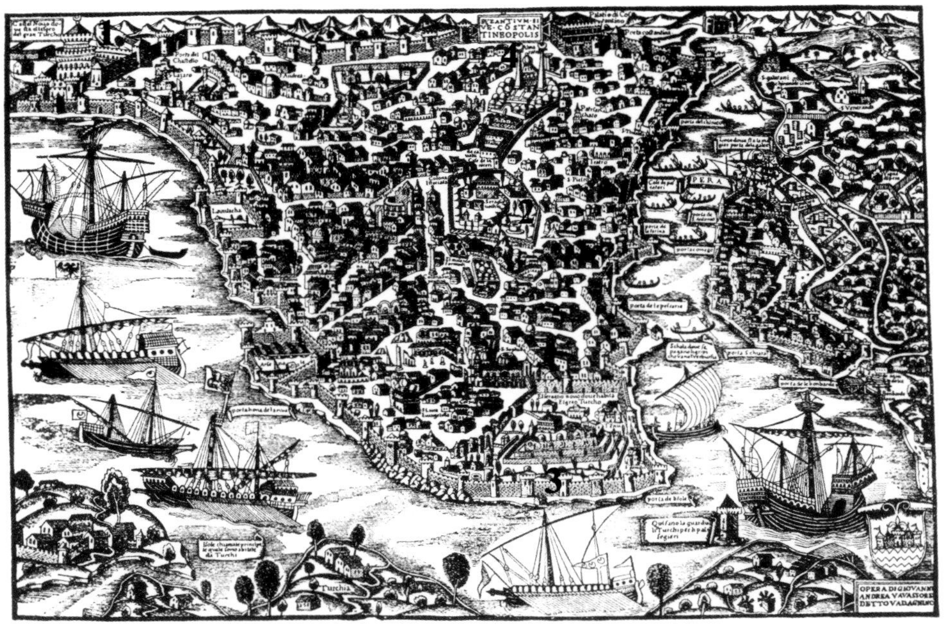

58 Giovanni Andrea Vavassore, *Map of Istanbul*, woodcut printed in Venice *c.* 1520 on the basis of a lost drawing of *c.* 1479.

tions, each stressing an origin in a different historical past. The Italian humanist preoccupation with a pure classical pedigree and the Ottoman emphasis on an Islamic dynastic heritage gave rise to exclusivist discourses on architecture that contain little hint of shared early modern sensibilities and cross-cultural exchanges. The discourse of humanism particularly accentuated this cultural divide. The monuments themselves, however, suggest a more connected universe of architectural culture in the eastern Mediterranean world during the fifteenth and sixteenth centuries.

The simultaneous emergence of centrally planned domed sanctuaries in Italy and the Ottoman empire can partly be attributed to the concurrent revival of a mutual Romano-Byzantine architectural heritage. But the knowledge each culture had of the 'other' should not be underestimated as a factor contributing to the appearance of similar plan types. The Ottoman receptiveness to Italian architectural innovations is more readily recognized because of documented invitations to architects from Italy, but imagining the possibility of a more fluid, two-way traffic in architectural concepts is doubly hindered by the lack of written evidence and by the great divide in scholarship between 'Islamic' and 'Western' architecture.

The remodelling of Constantinople and Rome by the sultans and popes during the fifteenth and sixteenth centuries brought about intriguing parallels: the rehabilitation of ancient water systems and bridges, the creation of new urban axes to link major landmarks, and the selective preservation or demolition of ancient monuments, with which modern edifices attempted to compete in magnificence. In both cities, religious monuments commissioned by the sultans and popes shared an aspiration to merge the grandeur of the faith with the monumentality of the imperial past. They combined references to unsurpassed antique prototypes (such as the Pantheon or Hagia Sophia) with allusions to recently built admired examplars (Florence Cathedral or the Üç Şerefeli mosque). The new St Peter's in Rome, designed by Donato Bramante, served as the premier training ground for major architects and the primary locus of architectural innovations under the patronage of successive popes over more than a century. A series of mosques commissioned during the same period by individual sultans, on the other hand, represented steps in the development of architectural ideals that culminated with the Selimiye in Edirne. By interweaving the evolution of sultanic mosques with the protracted construction history of St Peter's here, I hope to highlight some overlooked parallels and veiled cross-cultural dialogues.

Mehmed II's aspiration to revive the fame of Constantinople, as it had been in the age of Constantine and Justinian, is a well documented project that roughly coincided with the renewal of Rome between the papacies of Nicholas V (1447–55) and Sixtus IV (1471–84). According to his Greek historian Kritovoulos, it was the sultan's plan 'to make the city in every way the best supplied and strongest city as it used to be long ago, in power, and wealth, and glory.' To this end, 'he was constructing great edifices, which were to be worth seeing and should in every respect vie with the greatest and best of the past' (illus. 58).[52] The technological groundwork for the construction of monumental sultanic mosques in Istanbul had to a certain degree been laid by early Ottoman experiments with domed spaces. It was not, however, until the tenure of Sinan as chief architect that a mature architectural idiom combining engineering feats with aesthetic refinement could be realized.

Following the city's conquest, Mehmed II built a complex combining a hospice and T-type Friday mosque with two minarets next to the miraculously discovered tomb of the Arab martyr Abu

Ayyub al-Ansari.[53] This *extramuros* monument along the Golden Horn, evoking the memories of an early Islamic past, perpetuated the tradition of founding charitable complexes at the peripheries of Ottoman capitals; a flourishing new Muslim settlement (Eyüp) and holy necropolis grew up around it. The continuity with the Byzantine imperial past, on the other hand, was underscored by the conversion of Hagia Sophia (Ayasofya) to the city's first and foremost sultanic mosque, endowed with a special sanctity that was believed to increase the value of prayers performed in it. Subsequent sultanic mosques in the capital would engage in a pointed formal dialogue with Hagia Sophia to stress a shared genealogy and imperial iconography.[54]

The building that initiated the dialogue was the mosque complex that Mehmed II commissioned as part of a broader campaign to revive the former splendour of Constantinople, a campaign in which his viziers were ordered to participate by building smaller mosque complexes at their own expense. Kritovoulos says the sultan's new imperial mosque (1463–70) was meant to rival the city's most famous temples (illus. 33[7], 59, 60): 'The sultan himself selected the best site in the middle of the city and commanded them to erect a mosque which in height, beauty and size should compete with the largest and finest temples already existing there.'[55] This grandiose complex, which would eventually contain the sultan's posthumously built domed mausoleum, replaced the celebrated church of the Holy Apostles, with its adjoining mausoleum enshrining the bodies of the city's founder, Constantine (d. 337), and his successors. The memory of that church, remodelled by Justinian in the sixth century, is preserved by St Mark's in Venice which, like it, features a centralized plan: a Greek cross with five domes.

The church of the Holy Apostles, which Mehmed II had initially donated to the Orthodox Patriarchate, marked the outermost limits of the city's inhabited section at that time.[56] Unlike the complexes of former sultans in Bursa and Edirne, that of Mehmed II had a unique layout, axially aligned and symmetrical, with a novel combination of two distinct building types: a Great Mosque (Ulu Cami) and a funerary socio-religious complex with an unusually large number of dependencies, including a guest-house (*tabhane*) not attached to the mosque.[57] The Great Mosque, named after the sultan, differed from its predecessors, which had neither accompanying complexes nor imperial mausoleums. Its unprecedented royal tribune (*hünkar mahfili*), raised on columns at the left corner of the qibla wall and entered from a private gate, denoted the sultan's secluded imperial image; such tribunes became a standard feature of later sultanic mosques (illus. 61).[58]

Mehmed II's complex integrated selected elements from the Romano-Byzantine and Italian Renaissance building traditions with an Ottoman architectural vocabulary to fabricate a new imperial idiom. The contemporary historian Tursun Beg regarded its style as a 'modern' synthesis:

> And he [Mehmed II] built a Great Mosque based on the design of Ayasofya, which not only encompassed all the arts of Ayasofya, but in addition incorporated modern features constituting a fresh new idiom unequalled in beauty.[59]

This passage recalls Giorgio Vasari's description of Bramante (1444–1514) as an architect who translated the Roman architectural heritage into a modern idiom through new inventions: 'While the Greeks invented architecture and the Romans imitated them, Bramante not only added new inventions, but greatly increased the beauty and difficulty of the art, to an extent we now perceive.'[60]

The innovative plan of Mehmed II's ashlar masonry mosque with twin minarets closely followed that of his father's Üç Şerefeli mosque in Edirne, to which it added a half-dome over the mihrab. Structural elements quoted from Hagia Sophia were limited to a few elements, including the half-dome and tympanum arches perforated with windows, on which the main dome (26 metres wide) could now be raised to an unprecedented height (44 metres). The mosque's central domed baldachin, supported by a free standing pier and a colossal red granite column on each side, was spatially unified with the side aisles covered by three small domes. Contemporary written sources emphasize the heavenly symbolism of Mehmed's mosque and its madrasas alluding to the eight gates of paradise. Another paradisiac feature, inspired by Hagia Sophia, was the planting of four cypresses around the ablution fountain of the forecourt, a motif repeated in the early-sixteenth-century mosques of Istanbul. The cypress trees in the atrium of the church are depicted in an elevation drawing attributed to Cyriac of Ancona and copied in the sketchbook of Giuliano da Sangallo (illus. 70).[61]

A project plan for Mehmed II's mosque, drawn on Italian paper datable by its watermark to the second half of the fifteenth century, proposes an alternative design with a central dome resting on two lateral piers and surrounded by three half-domes (illus. 62).[62] That this inventive plan was meant for Mehmed's mosque (rebuilt in a quatrefoil scheme after collapsing in an earthquake in 1766) can be deduced from its forecourt with domical arcades, an exclusive feature of sultanic mosques, which is depicted with stairs on each side as in the still extant original courtyard. This plan testifies to an early experimentation with centralized schemes that would subsequently be elaborated by Sinan.

Compared to the dimly lit Üç Şerefeli mosque, covered by a squat central dome that rests directly on walls without the transitional zone of window-pierced tympanum arches, Mehmed's light-filled mosque was much loftier. Nevertheless, according to an anonymous chronicle, which states that the two granite columns carrying the lateral tympana were cut too short and consequently diminished the height of the dome, the sultan remained dissatisfied with the result.[63] The ambition to compete with the dome of Hagia Sophia was clearly beyond the

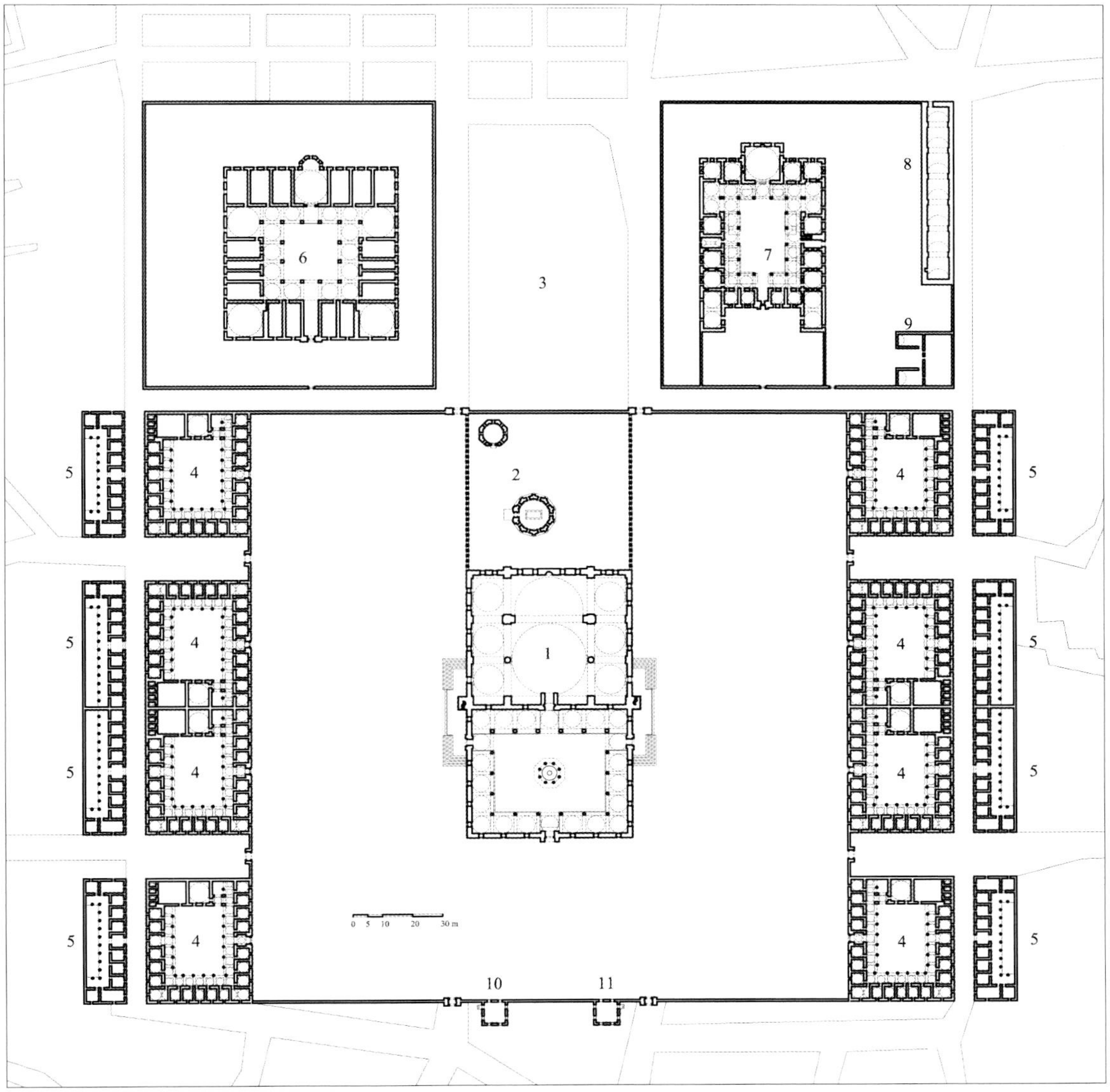

59 Reconstruction plan of the complex of Mehmed II, Istanbul:

1. Mosque
2. Mausoleums of Mehmed II and his wife Gülbahar Sultan
3. Formal garden
4. Madrasas
5. Preparatory madrasas
6. Hospital
7. Guesthouse
8. Caravansaray
9. Hospice
10. Elementary school
11. Library

60 Hypothetical cross-section of the mosque of Mehmed II.

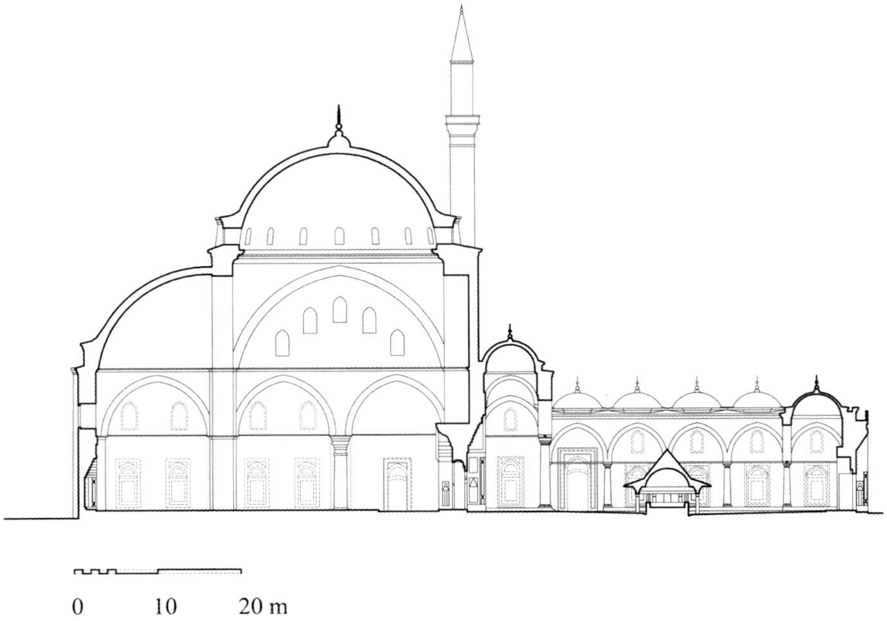

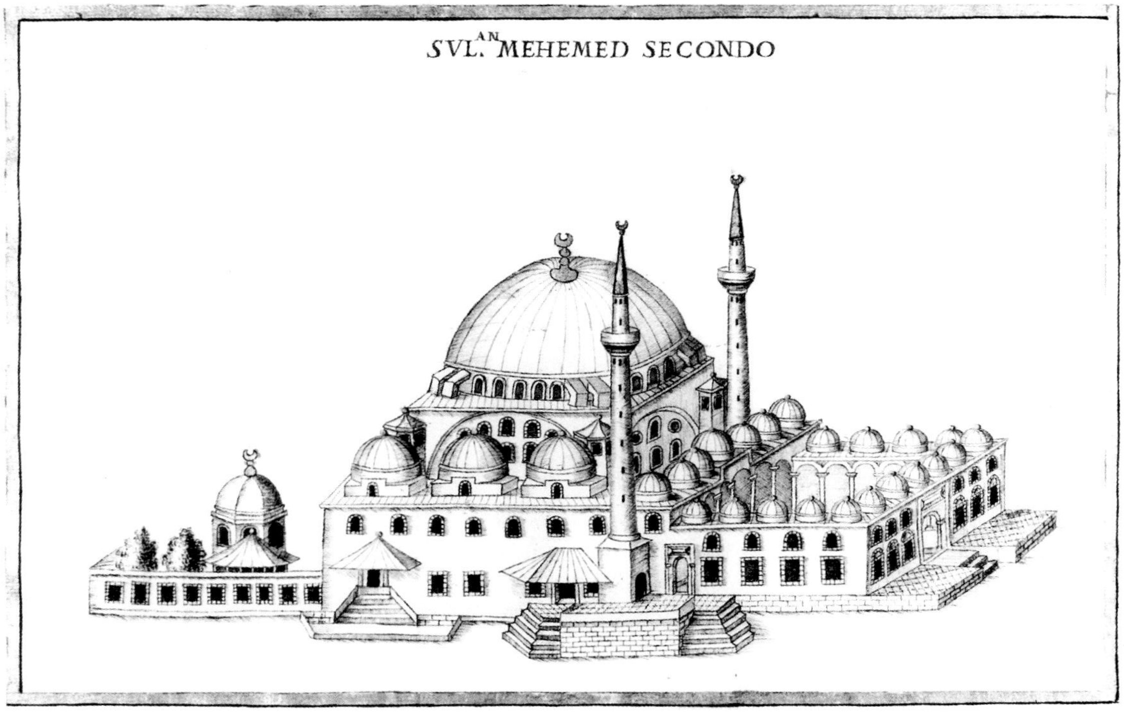

61 Francesco Scarella, mosque of Mehmed II, Istanbul, 1686, ink drawing.

technical skills of Mehmed's architect, Atik Sinan (d. 1471–72). Even with the shortened columns, the dome proved to be unstable: having suffered serious damages in earlier earthquakes, it eventually collapsed.

The Ottoman formal repertory of the mosque produced a stark contrast between cubic walls and hemispherical lead-covered domes that lacked the harmonious proportional subtleties developed later on by Sinan. Its decorative vocabulary represented a regional variant of the international Timurid mode, as revealed by the two surviving polychrome tile lunettes of the forecourt (illus. 63). They copy *cuerda seca* tiles in the underglaze technique, expanding the palette of the Üç Şerefeli tiles with the addition of yellow. Once again, they combine vegetal scrolls and abstract floral motifs with superimposed cursive and Kufic scripts.

Mehmed's complex was unprecedented in its large number of dependencies: eight madrasas with eight preparatory schools, an elementary school, a library, a hospital, a hospice, a guest-house, a caravansaray, and a bath-house. Inside the formal garden behind the mosque, surrounded by a window-pierced precinct wall, Bayezid II added the domed mausolea of his father and mother. The foundation inscription, carved on three panels above the main gate of the mosque, emphasizes the restoration of 'knowledge and learning' by the great sultan who took with his sword the unmatched city that former Muslim rulers had tried in vain to conquer (illus. 64). A small panel on the side is inscribed with a hadith foreshadowing the conquest of Constantinople: 'They will conquer Kostantiniyya; hail to the prince and army to whom this is given!'[64]

The eight madrasas, which integrated the ulema into the administrative hierarchy of the centralized state and subordinated them to the sultan's absolute authority, may partly have been inspired by the memory of the Byzantine patriarchal college that once accompanied the church of the Holy Apostles, sited in the middle of a huge plaza laid out to hold large crowds of pilgrims. With its colleges and preparatory schools dedicated to the study of the trivium and quadrivium, this was the foremost educational institution in Constantinople.[65]

The bilaterally symmetrical, axial layout of Mehmed's complex, built on a vast platform raised on vaulted substructures, seems to have been inspired by Italian Renaissance concepts of ideal planning. Its composition has been compared to the plan of the Ospedale Maggiore in Milan, which is included in the architectural treatise of the Florentine architect Antonio Averlino, known as Filarete (illus. 65). Filarete's intent to visit Istanbul in 1465 is recorded in a letter his humanist friend Francesco Filelfo, wrote in order to ask the help of George Amirutzes, a Greek scholar attached to the sultan's court.[66] The architect combined experiences in Florence in the circle of Filippo Brunelleschi, who completed the double-shell dome of Florence Cathedral (1423–38) just before the construction of the Üç Şerefeli mosque, with a knowledge of antique monuments in Rome. Filarete's activities at the court of Francesco Sforza in Milan during the 1450s and early 1460s played an important role in the diffusion of centralized domed plans for churches throughout northern Italy. These plans based on the Greek cross inscribed in a square were subsequently elaborated by Bramante and Leonardo, who, like Filarete, entered the service of the court in Milan. There they were inspired by the late antique church of S. Lorenzo (*c.*

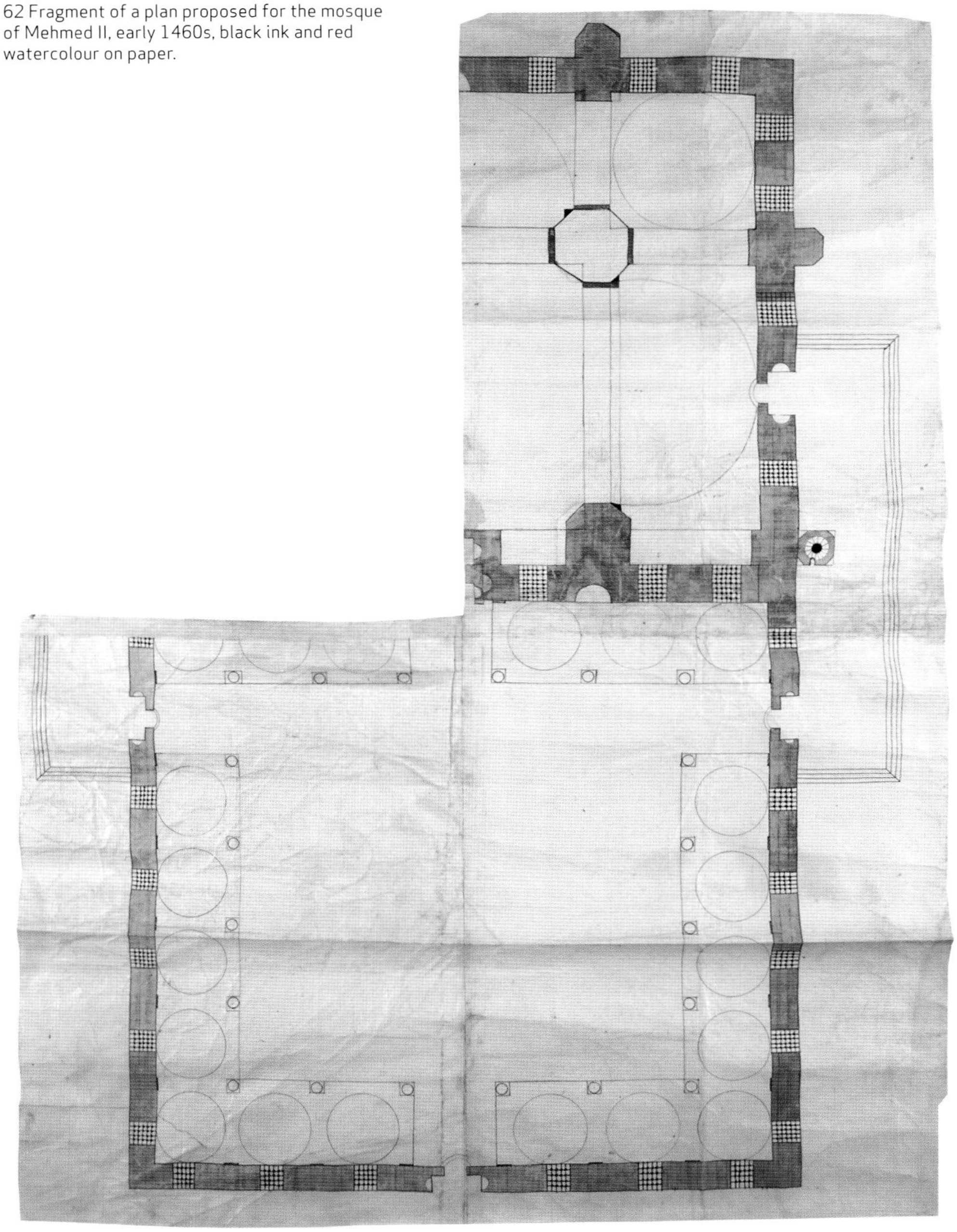

62 Fragment of a plan proposed for the mosque of Mehmed II, early 1460s, black ink and red watercolour on paper.

352–375), with its quatrefoil plan featuring four corner towers and an atrium.[67]

Whether Filarete's visit to Istanbul materialized or not (sources are silent about him after 1465), Mehmed II's architects must have had access to Italian architectural treatises and drawings. The treatise of Filarete (*c.* 1460–64) did reach the court of the sultan's Hungarian rival Matthias Corvinus, who invited the Bolognese architect-engineer Aristotele Fioravanti to Buda in 1467. The same architect was invited to the sultan's court before he left for Russia in 1475.[68] These bits of evidence point to an Italian connection in the symmetrical layout of Mehmed's complex and the experimentation with centralized plan types, which were mediated by Romano-Byzantine models both in Istanbul and Italy. Leon Battista Alberti, whose architectural treatise (*c.* 1452) demanded that the principal temple of a city should be centralized in plan, isolated in the centre of an ample square, and raised on a podium to elevate its dignity, would have approved the design.[69] In its sheer scale, Mehmed's complex outstripped the funerary madrasa-cum-convent complexes of contemporary Mamluk and Timurid rulers: that of Qa'itbay in Cairo (1472–74) and Husayn Bayqara in Herat (1492–93). As Spiro Kostof observes, the immense complex trumpeted Mehmed's 'modernism' by embracing the 'authority of ancient Rome':

63 Underglaze tile lunette at the forecourt of the mosque of Mehmed II, Istanbul.

64 Tripartite foundation inscription on the north gate of the mosque of Mehmed II.

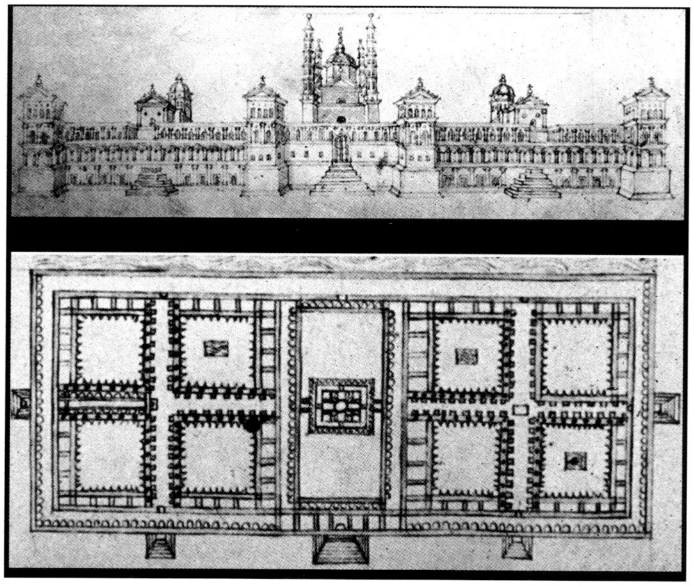

65 Detail of plan and elevation of the Ospedale Maggiore in Milan, from Antonio Averlino, called 'Filarete', *Trattato di architettura* (c. 1461–64).

> Nothing so early in the Western renaissance has this grandeur. We have to remember that Constantinople was originally created as the New Rome. In her the Conqueror inherited the one city that safeguarded the Classical tradition in the eastern half of the Christian world as authentically as Rome did in the West. After the fall of Constantinople, the Turks were well placed to stage their own renaissance.[70]

The sultan's interest in Italian architectural innovations, also exemplified by his request for a master builder from Venice in 1480, did not entirely vanish during the relatively conservative reign of his son, who succeeded him in 1481.[71] Bayezid II sought the help of Michelangelo and Leonardo for the construction of a bridge spanning the Golden Horn; the sketch for that project in Leonardo's notebook (*c.* 1502–3) is complemented by the surviving Turkish translation of a letter that the artist addressed to the sultan, in which he boastfully promotes his design for the bridge along with other proposed projects (including a moveable bridge across the Bosphorus).[72] A marginal note in Ascanio Condivi's life of Michelangelo (1553) confirms Michelangelo's involvement in designing the same bridge: 'He told me that this is true and that he had made a model [for it].'[73]

This must have happened around 1506, when Michelangelo abandoned Rome, to which he had been invited for the construction of Pope Julius II's tomb at the new St Peter's. When the pope insisted on his return, the artist contemplated leaving for Constantinople:

> Then Michelangelo, seeing that it had come to this and fearing the wrath of the pope, thought of going away to the Levant, chiefly as the Turk sought after him with the most generous promises through the intermediary of certain Franciscan friars, because he wanted to employ him in building a bridge from Constantinople to Pera and in other works. But, when the *gonfaloniere* heard of this, he sent for him and dissuaded him from this idea, saying that he should prefer to die going to the pope than to live going to the Turk.[74]

The projected bridge was never built, but Bayezid II's attempt to procure the services of two leading Renaissance artists for its construction shows his global outlook and his willingness to mobilize international networks. Pera (Galata), populated by a bustling Frankish community to which the above-mentioned Franciscan friars belonged, must have continued to be a source of information about new architectural developments in Italy throughout the sixteenth century.

Bayezid II's two-minaret mosque in Istanbul, built between 1501 and 1505, just before Julius II's architects started to prepare projects for the new St Peter's, made an even more direct allusion to Hagia Sophia's superstructure than did the mosque

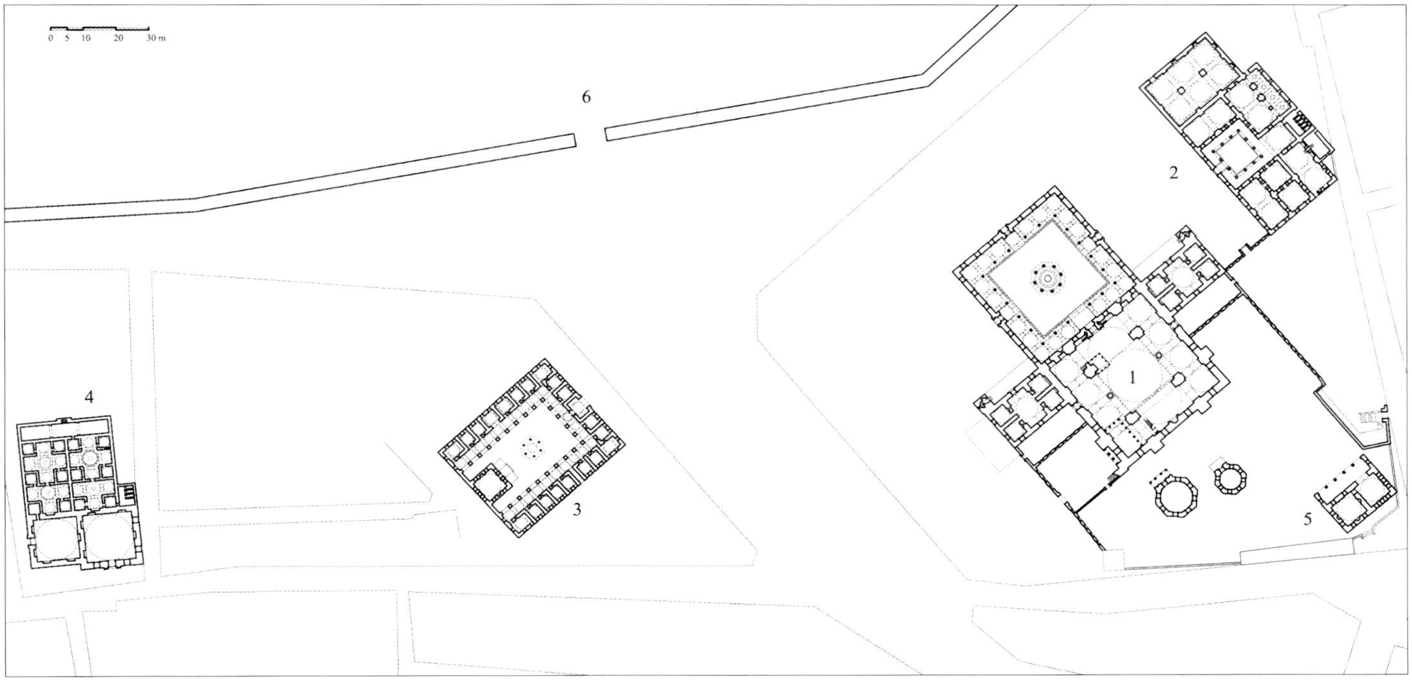

66 Plan of the complex of Bayezid II, Istanbul: 1. Mosque with mausoleums of Bayezid II and his daughter Selçuk Hatun. 2. Hospice and caravansaray. 3. Madrasa 4. Double bath. 5. Elementary school. 6. Old Palace.

of his father (illus. 33[3], 66, 67). Its smaller hemispherical dome (16.8 metres wide, 44 metres high) is flanked by two half-domes along the north–south axis, with four small domes covering each of the side aisles. The central baldachin, which rests on two piers and a red granite column on each side, is spatially integrated with the lateral aisles. But reintroduced *tabhanes*, appended to the mosque's rectangular body, conflict with spatial unity and represent a backward step.

The hybrid plan of Bayezid II's mosque can be interpreted as a conciliatory tribute to the egalitarian frontier culture of the ghazis and dervishes with whose help he ascended the throne. His reign was characterized by concessions made to these groups, who resented Mehmed's centralizing imperial project. Departing from the strict axial symmetry of his father's complex, a visual metaphor for the centralized autocratic state, Bayezid II's scaled down complex reverted to the asymmetrical layout of earlier royal foundations. Despite its concession to ghazi traditions, however, its T-type mosque with a Friday preacher (*khatib*) was far from modest. It readily perpetuated the new imperial image of Istanbul's sultanic mosques by paraphrasing the superstructure of Hagia Sophia.

More than any of his predecessors, it was Bayezid II's contemporary Julius II (r. 1503–13) who left his personal stamp on Rome. The pope's radical decision to demolish the old basilica of Constantine to make room for the new St Peter's, intended as the site of his own tomb, resonates with the precedent set by

67 Mosque of Bayezid II, Istanbul, from the north.

Mehmed II's funerary mosque complex, which required the demolition of another early Christian church founded by Constantine. The sultan's complex, designed as a grand centre of learning, had announced the foundation of a cultured Islamic empire and promoted his image as the emperor of New Rome. In a similar vein, the new St Peter's would express the achievements of the papacy under Julius II, who sought to emulate the imperial grandeur of ancient Rome, with his own tomb occupying a principal place in the rejuvenated centre of Christendom. It was the first grand cathedral church of Italy designed according to a centralized plan, a cross in a square, covered by a large dome surrounded by four

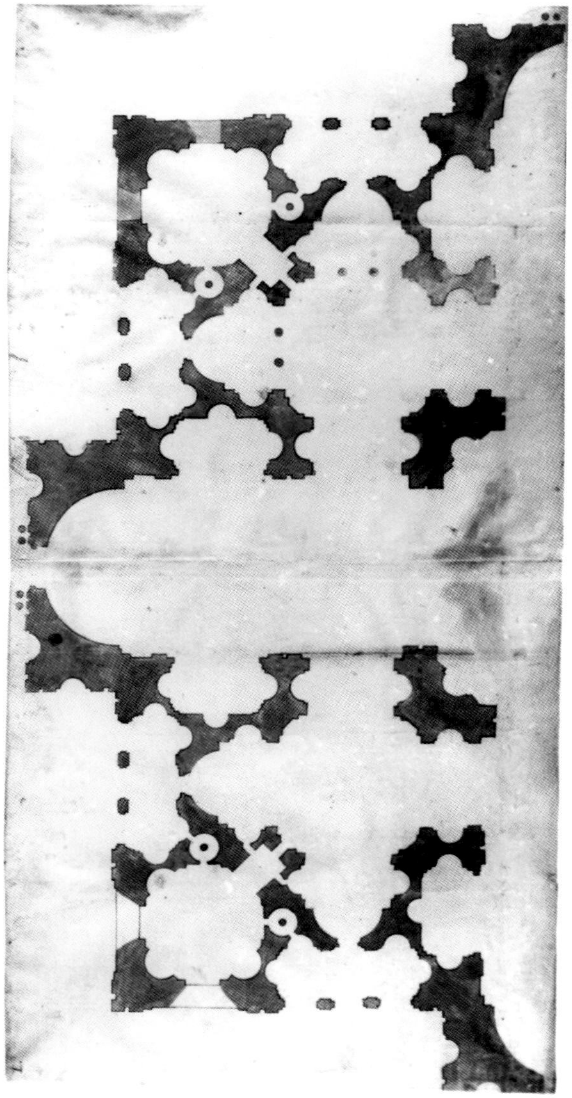

68 Donato Bramante, half-plan of St Peter's, 1505 (?), dark-brown ink and red watercolour on parchment.

69 Cristoforo Foppa, called 'Caradosso', bronze foundation medal of St Peter's, Milan, 1505 (?).

smaller ones. The half-domed apses projecting from the arms of the Greek cross may have been inspired by the late antique church of S. Lorenzo in Milan, whose quatrefoil plan is sketched on one of Bramante's drawings for St Peter's.[75]

The centralized design of Bramante for the church, intended to surpass in magnificence all others in Christendom, is well known from his fragmentary presentation plan and Caradosso's foundation medal depicting its elevation (both of them probably dating from the summer of 1505, illus. 68, 69).[76] The resemblance of the elevation, with hemispherical domes and two minaret-like towers, to the double-minaret sultanic mosques of Istanbul (Hagia Sophia, Mehmed II, and Bayezid II) is too striking to ignore. It has been suggested that the models of Bramante's great domed church may have included Hagia Sophia.[77] A letter of 1411 written by the Byzantine scholar Manuel Chrysolaras and entitled 'Comparison of Old and New Rome' had, years before, promoted Hagia Sophia as the ultimate paragon by declaring that 'nothing like it ever was, or ever would be, built by man.'[78] Addressed to the Byzantine emperor Manuel II, this letter which was written in Rome after Chrysoloras joined the entourage of the pope, was widely disseminated among Italian humanists. It stressed the common cultural heritage of Old and New Rome but clearly favoured the latter city, whose superiority was justified by arguments of cultural and natural progress.[79]

The post-Byzantine fame of Hagia Sophia was enhanced by such panegyrical texts, familiar both in the Italian and Ottoman courts. A manuscript of the ninth- or tenth-century *Diegesis peri tes Hagias Sofias* (Narrative concerning Hagia Sophia), copied in 1474 and preserved in the Topkapı Palace library, attests to Mehmed II's interest in legends about the construction of the church. Unable to comprehend how Justinian's monument (built by Anthemius and Isidore) could have been created without divine intervention, these Byzantine legends attribute it to a mythical architect called Ignatius and ascribe its plan to an angel who appeared in a dream to the emperor.[80] Turkish and Persian translations of this semi-mythical text, made for Mehmed II in 1479–80, indicate his desire to appropriate the imperial prestige of Hagia Sophia, which he renovated as the legitimate successor of Justinian.[81]

The ongoing Italian interest in Hagia Sophia after the fall of Constantinople is exemplified by copies of the humanist Cyriac of Ancona's early-fifteenth-century plan, section, and elevations of the church in Giuliano da Sangallo's (1445–1515) sketchbook (illus. 70, 71).[82] Hagia Sophia had already been declared the paragon for the Duomo of Pavia: a letter asking permission for the demolition of the basilica and baptistery in 1487 specified that Pavia's new cathedral was to be comparable to the best edifices in Rome and particularly the principal temple of Constantinople.[83] Bramante is thought to have played a role in designing the cathedral of Pavia, to which he was summoned from nearby Milan in 1488. Though never completed, this was the most important example of Renaissance cathedral design before St Peter's itself, with its composite plan combining a basilica and a centralized octagonal crossing. It is not surprising, then, that the new St Peter's as represented on Caradosso's medal is so similar to the Hagia Sophia and the imperial mosques of Istanbul. It is hard to imagine that Julius II was unaware of Hagia Sophia's conversion to a Muslim sanctuary and its emulation in the new mosques of the sultans. By appropriating the imperial iconography of both Hagia Sophia and the Pantheon (whose hemispherical single-shell dome with a stepped profile is mimicked in the medal), the pope may have aspired to reclaim the combined architectural heritage of Old and New Rome. The allusion to Hagia Sophia, an early Christian sanctuary associated with the Temple of Solomon and the 'New Jerusalem', reinforced the ecumenical claims of the papacy.[84]

The reference to Hagia Sophia implies a denial of its new identity as a sultanic mosque. This denial brings to mind post-conquest copies of Cristoforo Buondelmonti's early fifteenth-century map of Constantinople, which symbolically attempt to reappropriate the contested city for Christianity by ignoring its architectural transformation under Ottoman rule. Ian Manners has argued that these maps of the antiquities of Constantinople, which continue to depict Hagia Sophia without minarets, contest the capture of the city by emphasizing its Christian heritage, 'in effect privileging all those elements in the urban landscape that were part of the iconography that had been constructed in the image of a New Rome.' A late-fifteenth-century Ottoman version of the same map, datable to the beginning of Bayezid II's reign, not only adds minarets to Hagia Sophia but also inserts new mosques into the cityscape reconfigured as an Islamic capital (illus. 72).[85]

In the context of this cartographic contest, Julius II's inclusion of Hagia Sophia among the illustrious models of St Peter's – as if it had never been lost to Christianity – can be read as a competitive response to the challenge posed by Istanbul's sultanic mosques.[86] The Buondelmonti maps represent Hagia Sophia with two tower-like buttresses and sometimes a lanterned hemispherical dome, not unlike the image of St Peter's on the Caradosso medal.[87] The centralized plan that Bramante initially proposed was soon translated into a Latin-cross plan, perhaps because it was deemed more appropriate for Christian devotion in terms of liturgy. This contributed to the well-known vaccilation between centralized Greek-cross and longitudinal Latin-cross plans proposed by successive architects throughout the construction of the new St Peter's, which was resolved in the end in favour of Michelangelo's central plan (illus. 73–76).[88]

When he was conceptualizing the hemispherical dome he designed for the church (for which a model was made in

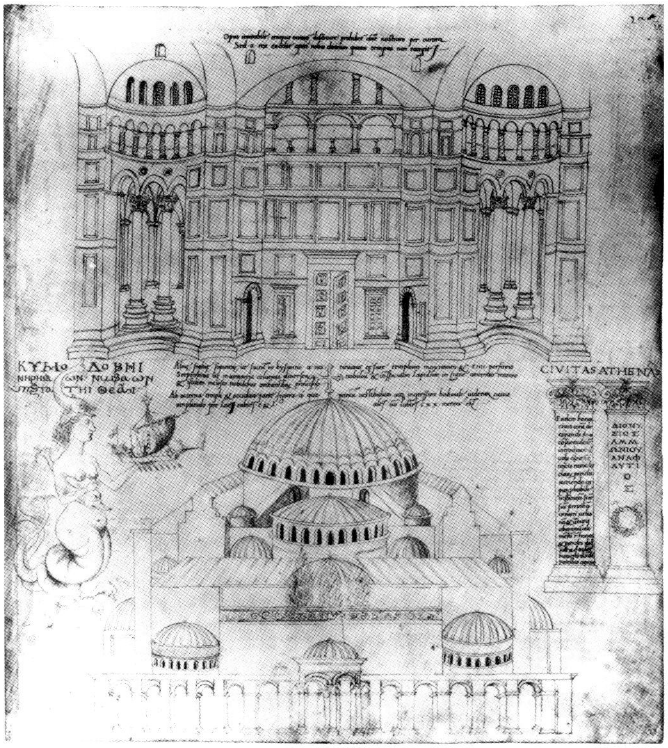

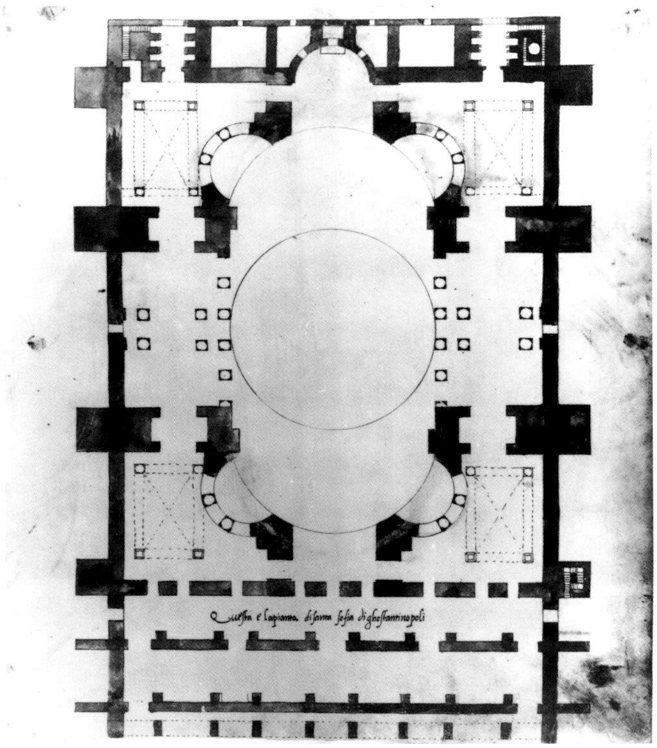

70, 71 Giuliano da Sangallo, cross-section, elevation and plan of Hagia Sophia in Constantinople, late fifteenth or early sixteenth century (after Cyriac of Ancona), ink drawings.

72 Cristoforo Buondelmonti, map of Constantinople, c. 1481, ink drawing.

1558–61), Michelangelo is known to have studied the domes of Florence Cathedral, the Pantheon, and most likely Hagia Sophia.[89] The artist, who once contemplated entering the service of the Ottoman court, may also have collected practical information about the current technology of dome construction in Sinan's sultanic mosques, particularly the Süleymaniye (1548–57) built around that time (the base of Michelangelo's dome was completed in 1552 and its drum in 1564). Differing from the circular drums with continuous colonnades Bramante and Antonio da Sangallo proposed for the single-shell dome of St Peter's, the double-shell dome of Michelangelo has spur-like buttresses (fronted by paired columns) that alternate with windows, not unlike the drums of Hagia Sophia and the contemporary mosques of Sinan (illus. 77).[90]

The initially intended resemblance of the new St Peter's to Hagia Sophia was eventually downplayed by the elimination of its twin towers and the simplification of its subsidiary domes. After Michelangelo's death in 1564, the lanterned hemispherical dome he designed was modified with a steep profile like that of Florence Cathedral because Giacomo della Porta, who completed the dome (1588–93), 'judged that it would be more beautiful as well as stronger'.[91] Michelangelo's centralized plan, on the other hand, was transformed with a nave added by Carlo Maderno following a competition held in 1607. Even after these substantial modifications, however, the learned Roman traveller Pietro della Valle, who visited Istanbul in 1614, was struck by the likeness between the city's sultanic mosques 'which are truly beautiful to look at' and Michelangelo's new church of St Peter's:

> That which is noteworthy are the mosques, in particular four or five of them built by the Turkish emperors, all of them situated on the highest hilltops in such a way that they almost form a row, visible from one end of the sea to the other and equally distributed along the whole length of the city. They are well built in marble and differ little in architecture from one another, being in the form of a temple composed of a domed square, like the design of St Peter's in Rome by Michelangelo; and I believe they have taken as their model Hagia Sophia which they encountered there.[92]

On his return to Rome, Della Valle promised to bring back paintings of Hagia Sophia and imperial mosques, along with a panorama of Constantinople, that he hoped modern Italian architects would emulate.[93]

As Joseph Connors has shown, Borromini did in fact make a drawing of Hagia Sophia while he was designing S. Ivo alla Sapienza in 1642, for which he probably consulted Della Valle in Rome.[94] This is not the only known instance of 'a great architect indulging in a moment of historical research before embarking on a commission in which historical sources were left behind or profoundly transformed.'[95] Sir Christopher Wren explains in his second tract on architecture (1680s) that for the vaulting of St Paul's Cathedral he followed the dome-building technique used at Hagia Sophia, and which is 'yet found in the present Seraglio [the Topkapı Saray].'[96] Discovered in the 1980s, measured drawings of Hagia Sophia associated with Wren (possibly in Hawksmoor's hand) are thought to have been based not only on Grelot's illustrated travelogue published in 1683, but also on unpublished drawings brought to England by his patron John Chardin. It is also known that Wren consulted merchant friends about modern dome construction methods used in Istanbul and Smyrna, including their technique of lead-sheathing.[97] These examples allow us to speculate on the likelihood of similar cross-cultural exchanges in the age of Sinan. Such veiled exchanges would necessarily have remained unrecorded in the written sources because both the Ottoman and Italian courts had established by that time their distinctive architectural idioms and discourses.

IMAGINING CROSS-CULTURAL ARCHITECTURAL DIALOGUES IN THE AGE OF SİNAN

The last sultanic example of a T-type mosque in Istanbul is attributed to Sinan's predecessor, the chief architect Alaüddin,

73

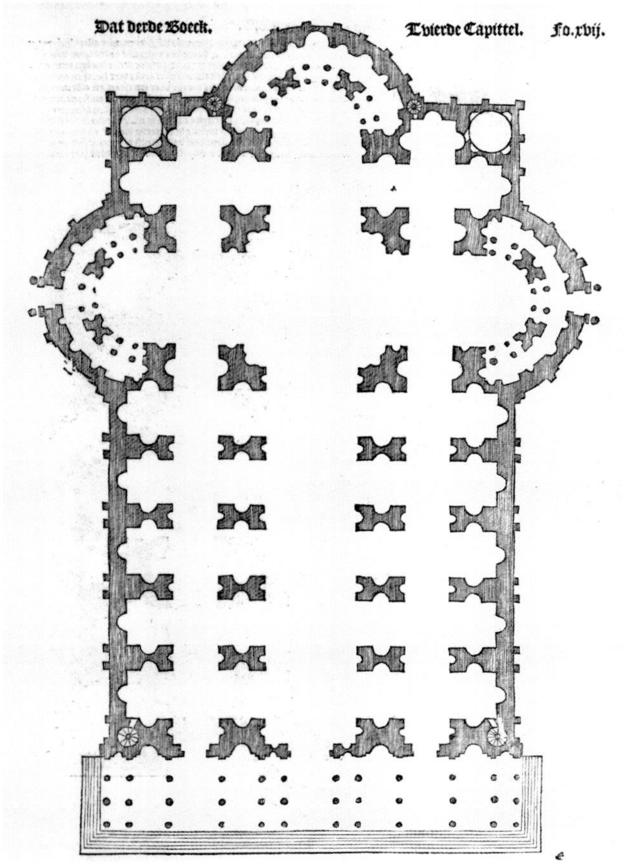

74

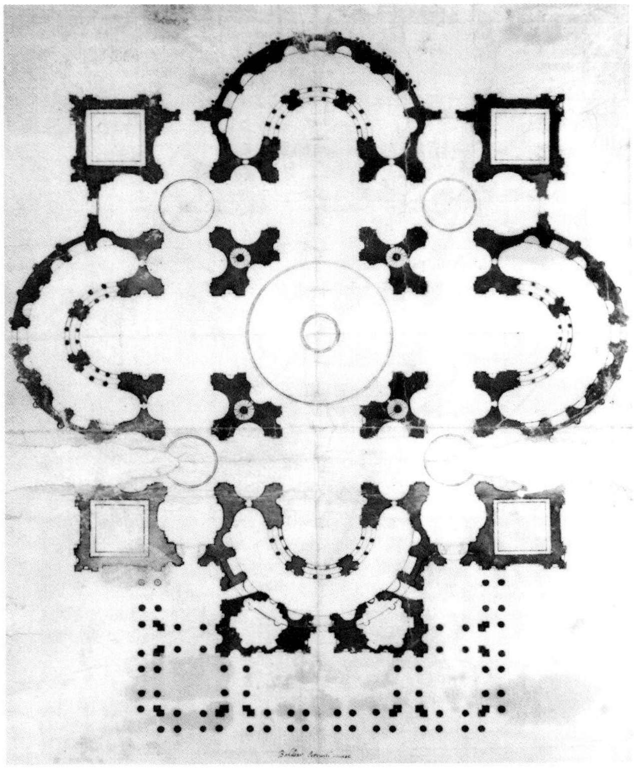

73 Raphael, plan of St Peter's in a woodcut from Sebastiano Serlio, *Libro d'architettura*, III, 1546.

74 Baldassare Peruzzi, plan for St Peter's, 1535, pen and ink on paper.

75 Antonio da Sangallo (the Younger), plan of the model of St Peter's in an engraving by Antonio Salamanca, 1549.

75

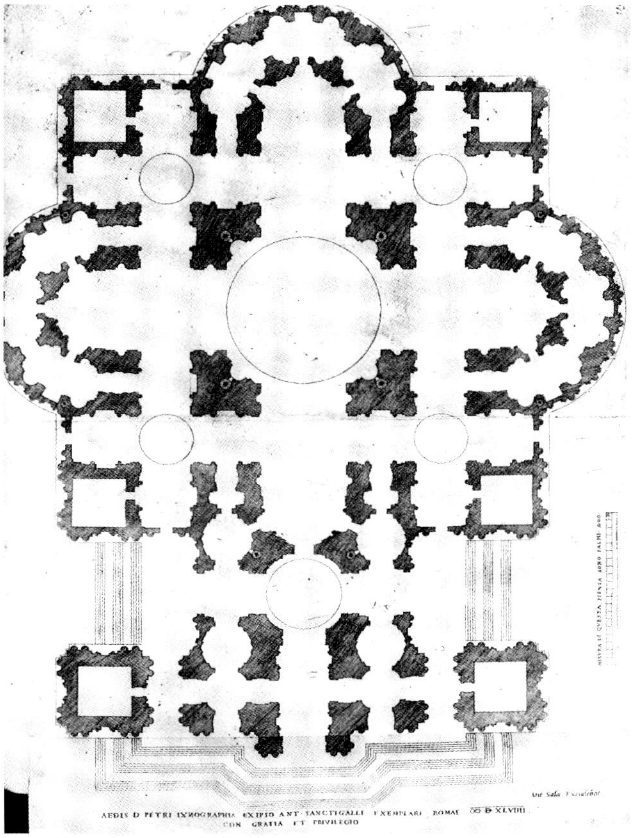

76 Michelangelo, Plan for St Peter's in an engraving by Etienne Dupérac, 1569.

77 Michelangelo, Elevation of the exterior of St Peter's in an engraving by Etienne Dupérac, 1569.

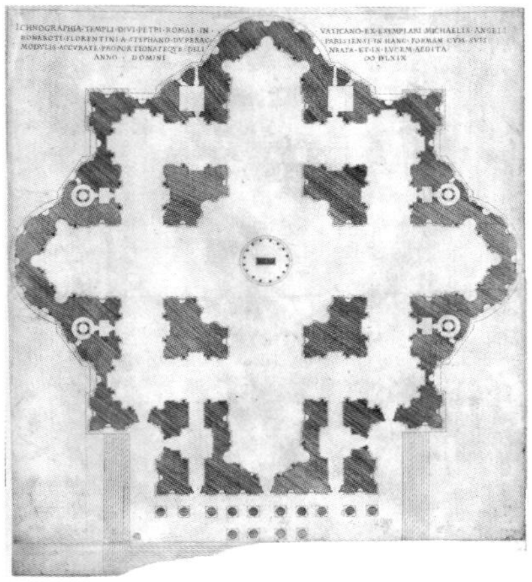

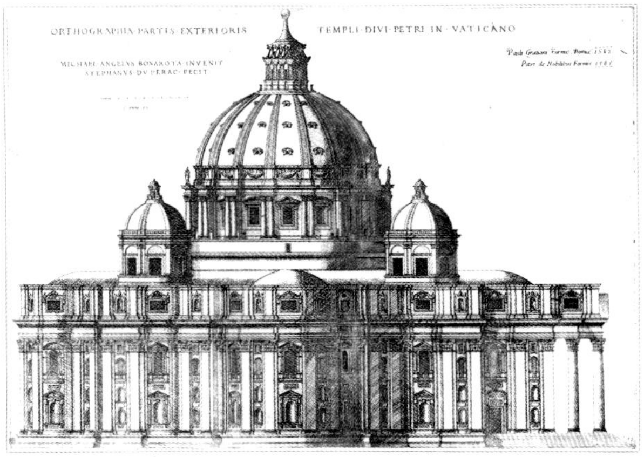

nicknamed Acem Alisi (illus. 78, 79). Built by Sultan Süleyman to commemorate his late father, Selim I (1520/21–1527/28), it paraphrases the plan of Bayezid II's mosque in Edirne (1484–88) with a larger dome (illus. 80, 81). The departure in the smaller complexes of Bayezid II and Selim I from the majestic scale and axial geometric composition of Mehmed II's complex, with its detached *tabhane*, reflects the unresolved tension between the Conqueror's centralizing imperial vision and the lingering egalitarian ethos of the frontier polity. Mehmed II's pioneering complex, which dwarfed the smaller mosque complexes of his viziers, visually expressed the gulf between the absolute monarch and his *kuls*. It signalled the commencement of a contested imperial regime that would firmly be consolidated under Süleyman I.[98]

The complexes of Mehmed's viziers in Istanbul, grouped around Friday mosques with T-type plans, acknowledged the continuing efficacy of the earlier ghazi ethos. The most monumental example is the funerary mosque complex of the grand vizier Mahmud Pasha that adjoined his residence near the Topkapı Palace. Accompanied by its founder's domed mausoleum, the complex contributed to the urban development of the new capital with its ashlar masonry Friday mosque, hospice, madrasa, elementary school, and bath-house. Its single-minaret mosque (1462–63), fronted by a five-bay portico, is composed of two domed halls aligned along the mihrab axis and separated by a U-shaped corridor from smaller domed spaces on each side (illus. 82, 83). The central twin domes no longer cover separate spaces with different floor levels, as in former convent-masjids where only the space under the second dome, with a raised floor,

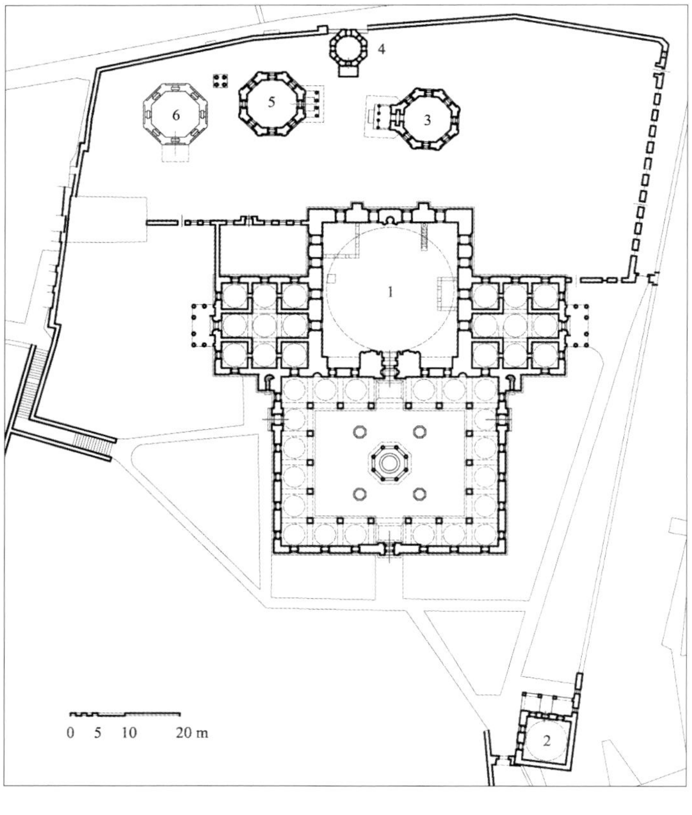

78 (left) Plan of the complex of Selim I, Istanbul: 1. Mosque. 2. Elementary school. 3. Mausoleum of Selim I. 4. Mausoleum of Hafsa Sultan (demolished). 5. Mausoleum of Sultan Süleyman's children. 6. Mausoleum of Sultan Abdülmecid (1861).

79 (above) Mosque of Selim I from the west.

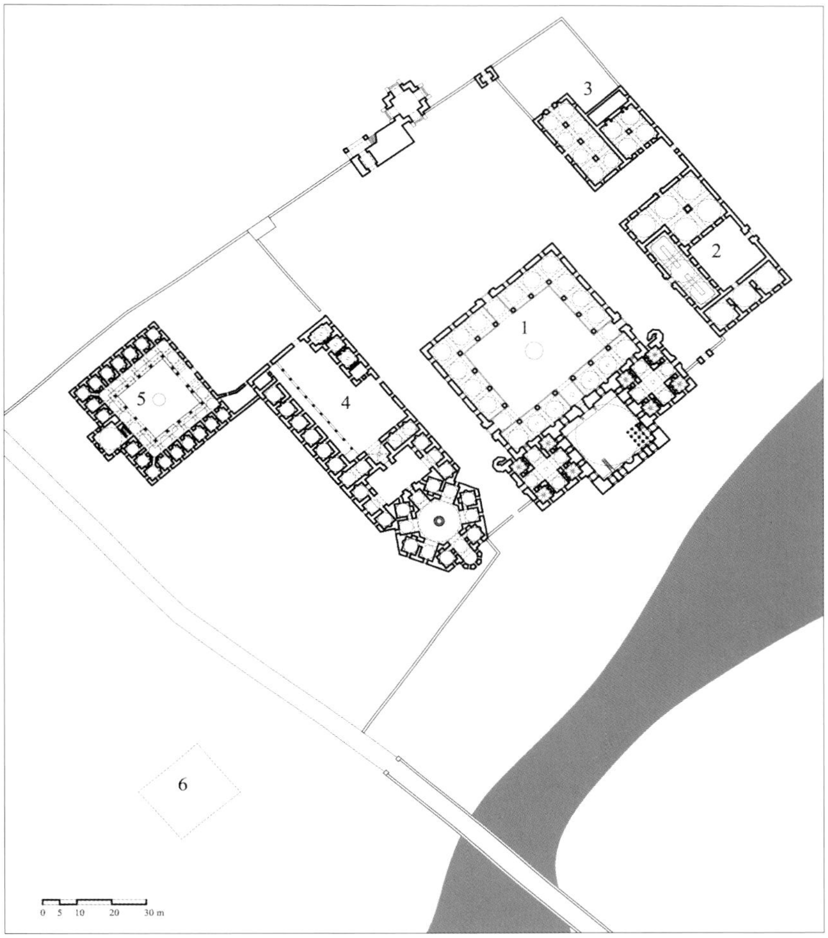

80 Plan of the complex of Bayezid II along the Tunca river, Edirne: 1. Mosque. 2. Hospice. 3. Caravansaray. 4. Hospital. 5. Madrasa. 6. Site of bath-house.

was designated for prayers (illus. 20). Now both domed halls define a unified space functioning as a Friday mosque appointed with a *khatib*, while the subsidiary lateral spaces are identifiable as the guest-rooms of a convent.[99]

The grand vizier Rum (Greek) Mehmed Pasha's complex in Üsküdar, centred around another variant of the T-type plan, was accompanied by a madrasa, hospice, and domed mausoleum (illus. 84). Dated by an inscription to 1471–72, the Friday mosque of composite striped masonry, crowned by a Byzantinizing dome, is fronted by a five-domed portico. Its central domed prayer hall with a semi-dome over the mihrab is flanked by pairs of square guest-rooms on each side. With their attached guest-rooms and dependent hospices, the multifunctional T-plan Friday mosques built by Mehmed II's grand viziers and viziers exemplified the charitable emphasis on food and shelter in the newly colonized capital. These transitional buildings paved the way to the stratified mosque types codified for a wider range of elite patrons during Sinan's tenure, when attached guest-rooms were altogether eliminated.

T-plan Friday mosques continued to be created until the early part of Süleyman's reign. A non-sultanic example near the capital is that of the grand vizier Piri Mehmed Pasha (1530–31) in Silivri (illus. 85). An unusual provincial variant of this building type is the Friday mosque built by Bıyıklı Mehmed Pasha in Diyarbakır (1516-20) after he conquered the city from the Safavids for Selim I and became its first governor-general (illus. 86). The pasha's mosque with a central dome (9 metres wide) surrounded by four half-domes is a provincial descendant of imperial mosques in Istanbul, erected with the sultan's order to announce the inauguration of Ottoman rule in the capital of a newly established province.[100] With two lateral *tabhane* halls appended to it, the single-minaret mosque is fronted by a wide seven-domed portico instead of an imperial forecourt surrounded by domical arcades. Its fully centralized plan adds two lateral half-domes to the layout of Bayezid II's mosque in Istanbul. These lateral half-domes are anticipated in the discarded plan prepared earlier for Mehmed II's mosque, which featured three half-domes around a central dome (illus. 62).

81 Mosque of Bayezid II, Edirne, from the south with a partial view of the hospital.

The centralized quatrefoil plan type was repeated at the nearby Great Mosque (Ulu Cami) of Elbistan (*c.* 1515–22), commissioned by the Dulkadirid prince Şehsuvaroğlu Ali Beg, who had just conquered that city as Selim I's vassal. In 1515, after defeating the rival Dulkadirid ruler Alaüddevle, an ally of

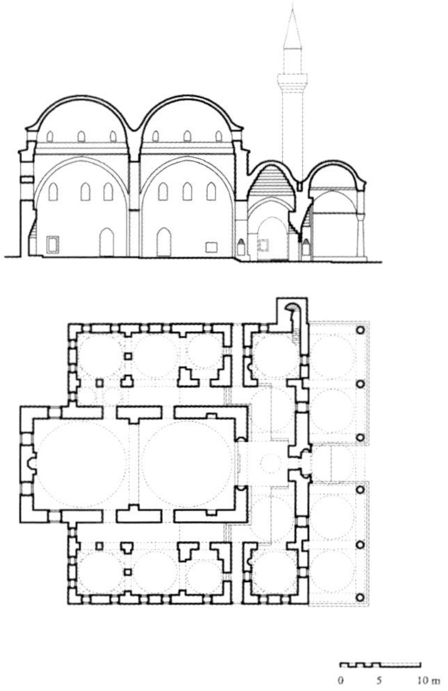

82 (above left) Plan and cross-section-of the Mahmud Pasha mosque, Istanbul.

83 (above) Mahmud Pasha mosque from the west.

84 Mosque of Rum Mehmed Pasha, Üsküdar, on a hilltop above the waterfront complex of Şemsi Ahmed Pasha designed by Sinan; in the background is the eighteenth-century Ayazma mosque.

the Mamluk sultan, he became the first governor-general of this newly established province. His single-minaret mosque with a modest three-bay portico and a central dome 8 metres wide is, like its companion in Diyarbakır, another miniaturized version of Istanbul's imperial mosques.[101] These perfectly centralized mosque plans with four half-domes recall Bramante's design for St Peter's and its smaller offshoots, such as S. Maria della Consolazione in Todi (modified during its lengthy construction between 1508 and 1607).[102] Their sudden appearance in southeastern Anatolia must have been triggered by the recent conquest of that region where stationed Ottoman troops were likely accompanied by royal architects.

A related provincial mosque featuring three half-domes is that of Hadım Süleyman Pasha (1528) inside the citadel of Cairo (illus. 87). The mosque of this governor-general, who replaced his rebellious predecessor in the former Mamluk capital between 1524 and 1534, affirmed Ottoman control in Egypt, a province regulated with a new law code promulgated in 1525. Dominating the hilltop of the Cairene citadel, which also contained the governor's palace and the janissary barracks, this mosque has a free-standing double-galleried minaret (a royal sign denoting its special status) and a small marble-paved forecourt incorporating the shrine of a local saint: Sidi Sariya, a companion of the Prophet.[103]

Sinan's provincial mosques – simple domed cubes without half-domes – departed from the elaborate designs of the three mosques in Diyarbakır, Elbistan, and Cairo, built to announce the consolidation of Ottoman rule in major cities conquered by Selim I. The chief architect's single domed cubical mosques in provincial cities come closer to those built in the early sixteenth century along the hajj route, such as that of Çoban Mustafa Pasha in Gebze, dating from the 1520s (illus. 27). Their generic plans fronted by three, five, or seven domed porches (sometimes doubled in two rows) sharpened the dichotomy between mosques at the centre and the periphery of the empire. With the exception of the Selimiye mosque in Edirne (the secondary capital), and the Muradiye mosque in Manisa (governed by crown princes), Sinan's

85 Plan of the Piri Mehmed Pasha mosque, Silivri.

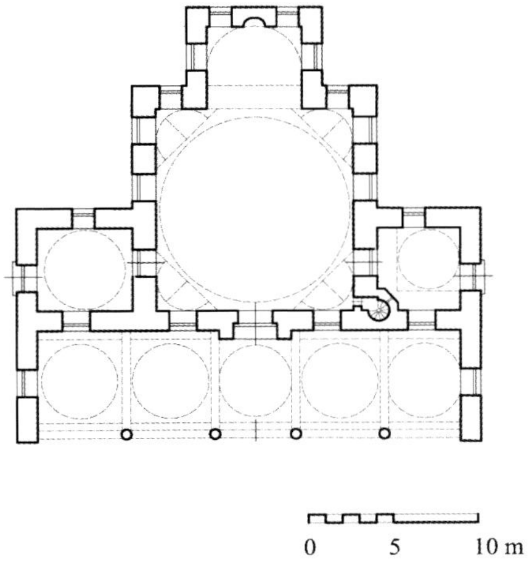

86 Plan of the Bıyıklı [Fatih] Mehmed Pasha mosque, Diyarbakır.

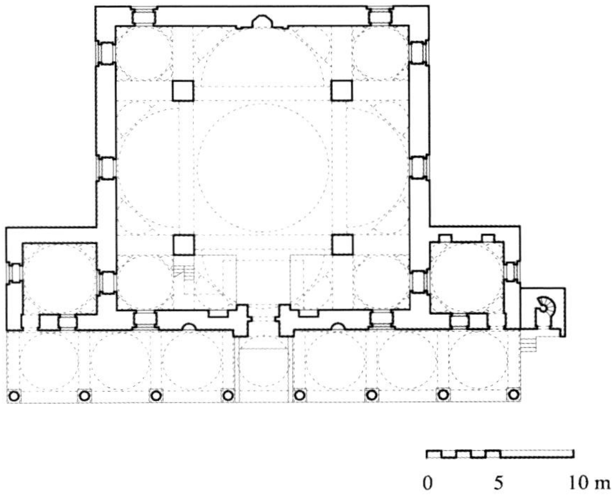

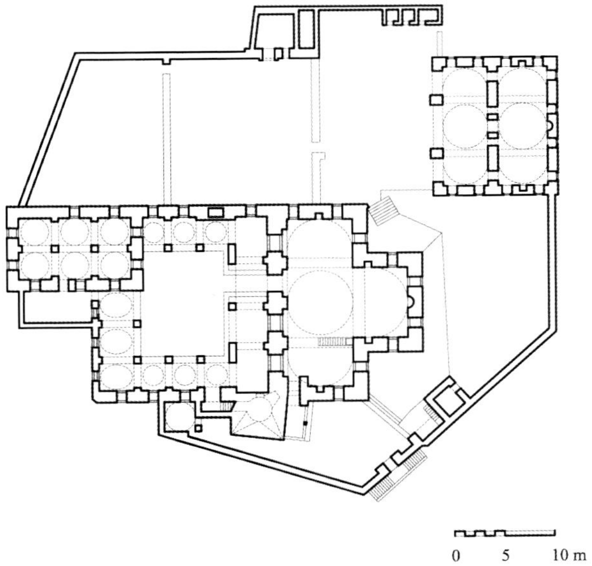

87 Plan of the Hadım Süleyman Pasha complex, Cairo citadel, with the funerary shrine of Sidi Sariya at the northeast corner of the mosque forecourt and an elementary school in the lower platform.

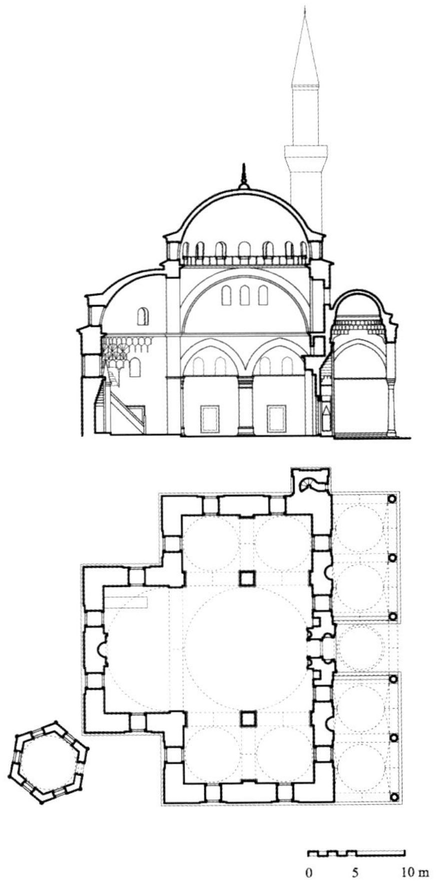

88 Plan and cross-section of the mosque and mausoleum of Atik Ali Pasha, Istanbul.

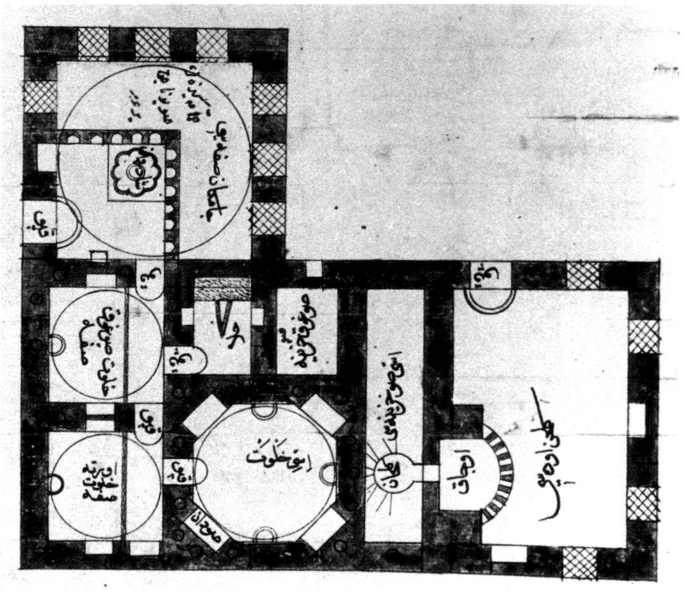

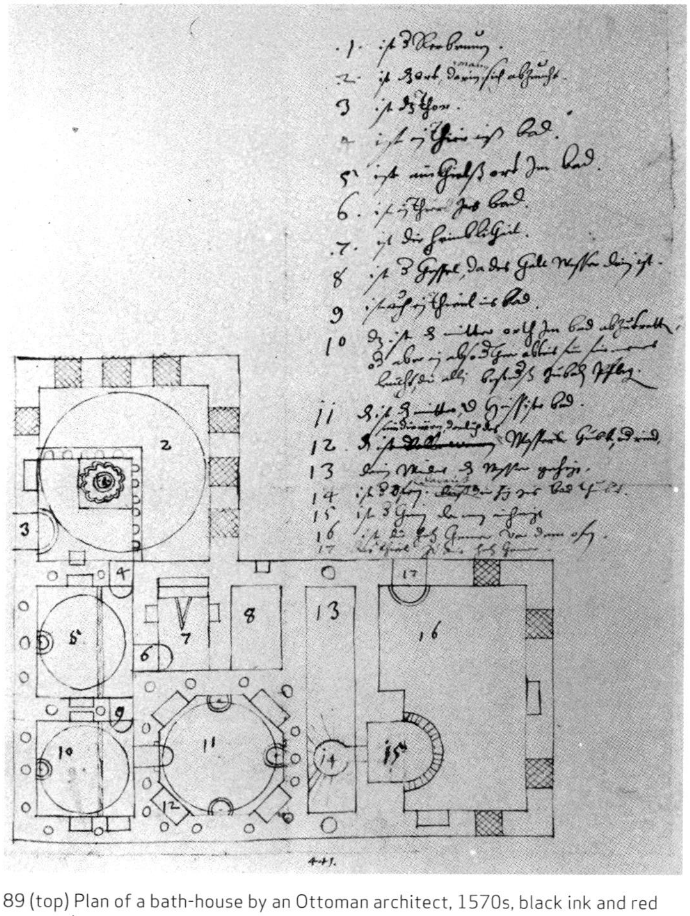

89 (top) Plan of a bath-house by an Ottoman architect, 1570s, black ink and red watercolour on paper.

90 (above) Austrian copy of the Ottoman bath plan, c. 1570s, black ink on paper.

mosques outside Istanbul were usually domed cubes with relatively simple decorative and epigraphic programmes comfortably accommodating regional voices.[104] Only a few exceptions in Diyarbakır and Aleppo still feature attached guest-rooms: Hüsrev Pasha in Aleppo, Çerkes İskender Pasha in Diyarbakır, and Sokollu Mehmed Pasha in Payas near Aleppo. Otherwise, the T-plan with flanking *tabhane*s was abandoned in Sinan's mosques, and centralized plans with unified interior spaces became the rule.[105]

The unified interiors of non-sultanic domed mosques Sinan designed in Istanbul are foreshadowed to a certain degree by that of the grand vizier Atik Ali Pasha (1496–97), which eliminates attached guest-rooms while still clinging to a T-plan (illus. 88). For high ranking patrons, Sinan developed a richly varied typology of rectangular mosques spatially unified under domed canopies resting on four, six, or eight supports (illus. 3–5). Often featuring handsome internal galleries with precious marble columns entirely missing in earlier mosques, their lateral façades, freed from appended guest-rooms, are more refined. His simplest mosques in the capital were variants of the domed cube, or even more basic masjid-like structures without domes.

Before turning to Sinan's famous sultanic mosques, I shall take a brief detour to consider the channels through which the cross-cultural exchange of architectural ideas might have taken place during his tenure. Knowledge in Europe about Ottoman architecture was spread by oral and written travel accounts, as well as by drawings and prints of monuments made by artists who accompanied embassies. In his prospect of Istanbul the Danish artist Melchior Lorichs, who was attached around 1555–59 to an Austrian Hapsburg embassy led by the Flemish humanist Busbecq, depicted himself with his turbaned Ottoman assistant, probably a *çavuş* appointed as his official escort (illus. 33[5]). That foreign artists did, on occasion, get in contact with Ottoman architects is indicated by a picture album compiled in Istanbul during another Austrian Hapsburg embassy in the 1570s. It includes two bath plans executed by an anonymous Ottoman architect, likely belonging to Sinan's office, together with the copy of one of those plans featuring German translations of Turkish annotations (illus. 89, 90).[106]

91 Lamberto Sustris, *Marcantonio Barbaro*, c. 1568–73, oil on canvas.

92 Woodcut of 'Il volo del Turco' showing Ottoman acrobats in Piazzetta San Marco, Venice.

93 Georg Hoefnagel, Ottomans strolling in Piazza San Marco, Venice, c. 1578, engraving.

Besides artists who accompanied embassies to Istanbul, some learned diplomats must also have played a role in the transmission of architectural knowledge. Their descriptions of Ottoman monuments are often filled with enthusiasm and recognize the kinship between Hagia Sophia and sultanic mosques.[107] One such diplomat, endowed with a special artistic sensibility as a sculptor and amateur architect, was the Venetian *bailo* Marcantonio Barbaro who resided in the Ottoman capital between 1568 and 1570 (returning there again in 1573 to negotiate a peace treaty with the grand vizier Sokollu Mehmed Pasha). His brother Daniele Barbaro had written a commentary on the architectural treatise of Vitruvius, published in 1556 with illustrations by the architect Andrea Palladio (1508–80). As a token of friendship, Marcantonio Barbaro gave his own portrait (depicted against a background view of Istanbul) to Sokollu, dedicating it to him with the following inscription: 'Illusistrissimo Domino Mahomet Pacha Musulmanorum Visiario amico optimo' (illus. 91).

Marcantonio's official correspondence with Venice contains several references to mosque complexes being built by Sinan, which he enthusiastically praised as '*superbissime fabriche*' without mentioning their architect; he noted in particular those of Sokollu in Lüleburgaz and Kadırgalimanı, and the Selimiye in Edirne.[108] It is likely that Palladio was informed about Sinan's central-plan domed mosques through conversations with his patron Marcantonio. During the design phase of Palladio's church of Redentore in Venice, Marcantonio is known to have unsuccessfully campaigned for a centralized plan. Howard Burns and Deborah Howard have suggested that the two thin *campanili* of that church (1576–80) could have been inspired by the minarets of Sinan mosques that the Venetian diplomat had so keenly admired.[109] Considering the close diplomatic, cultural and mercantile relations with Venice at that time, nor is it unlikely that Palladio's architectural treatise (first published in 1570) was available to Sinan (illus. 92, 93). Marcantonio may even have presented a personal copy to his friend Sokollu, given their mutual passion for architecture. The architectural drawings of the treatise include not only the Villa Barbaro in Maser, but also a winding staircase designed by 'the Clarissimo signor Marc'Antonio Barbaro, a Venetian gentleman of fine genius'.[110]

94 Matteo Pagan, Procession of the Doge of Venice with turbanned Ottoman spectators watching from the upper-right windows of the Procuratorie, Venice, *c.* 1555–60, detail from a woodcut.

95 Parade of European galley slaves during a circumcision festival at the Hippodrome with Venetian diplomats watching from the lower-left booth (in the right-hand image), *c.* 1582, watercolour on paper from İntizami, *Sūrnāme-i Hümāyûn*.

Regardless of whether or not Palladio and Sinan knew about each other's works, the affinity between their approaches to architectural design is often noted. Trained as a stone cutter, Palladio not only lived around the same time as Sinan (who started out as a carpenter), but also created a flexible typology of buildings adapted to the social hierarchies of the Venetian ruling elite. Like Sinan's palaces and mosques in Istanbul, his villas and churches, concentrated around Venice and Vicenza, embody a strong sense of place. Both architects derived practical lessons from the study of antique ruins, in Rome and Constantinople respectively. Their design practice was anchored in the variation of versatile building types guided by decorum, and they shared similar concerns: the importance of laying firm foundations and constructing solid buildings with an appearance of strength, the blending of beauty with effective engineering, the sensitivity to siting, the aesthetic value attached to distant views, the visual impact of the silhouette, the treatment of buildings as organic wholes, the concern with crisp geometric clarity, and the emphasis on creamy white interiors flooded with light.[111]

These parallels were surely informed by the common Byzantine architectural heritage of Venice and Istanbul, with their similar topographies inseparable from water; nevertheless shared early modern sensibilities may also have played a role. The Ottoman and Venetian ruling elites, who had closely observed one another during more than a century of diplomatic and trade relations, came to develop remarkably kindred tastes (illus. 94, 95). With Palladio and Sinan, the two cities invented their own Renaissances – pragmatic, flexible, and full of radiance and lightheartedness. They reached the zenith of their urban form in the second half of the sixteenth century with the prominent landmarks of these architects, which transformed the skyline of each city and established new visual links with outlying areas.[112]

After Sinan codified the classical Ottoman style in the 1550s, the earlier receptivity to Italian architectural innovations diminished considerably. Nonetheless, the chief architect's intense preoccupation with global fame and his penchant for experimentation may have induced him to follow contemporary developments in the Italian architectural scene through his acquaintance with Ottoman merchants and diplomats – such as the court translator Dragoman Yunus Beg, who was sent to Venice on several diplomatic missions and for whom Sinan built a mosque in the capital.[113] It is important to note that ambassadors dispatched to Europe were often imperial messengers (*çavuş*), a profession whose ranks included architects such as Sinan's two successors, Davud Çavuş and Dalgıç Ahmed Çavuş.[114]

The chief architect was probably well informed about the ongoing construction of St Peter's in Rome, both from oral reports by Ottoman travellers and from architectural prints. Howard Burns has discovered an intriguing reference in Francesco de Marchi's treatise on military architecture, which describes the excursion of a group of unidentified Ottomans to the construction site of St Peter's in Rome sometime in the late 1530s or 1540s:

> The temple of S. Pietro in Rome is the most magnificent in all Christendom, and when it is built according to the design and model none other like it will be found anywhere … and certainly all men on earth desire that this temple should be completed and seek to aid and favor its completion, even including the Turks, enemies of the true faith. I spoke with some of them in Rome, who desired that this Church may be finished according to its beautiful and marvellous beginnings.[115]

These Ottoman travellers had apparently seen the church before Michelangelo took over its construction in 1547 from Antonio da Sangallo the Younger (d. 1546). Burns speculates that Antonio Salamanca's set of engravings of Sangallo's wooden model of St Peter's (1546–49) may have been available to Sinan. He hypothesizes that the striking difference between the four simple polygonal piers of the Şehzade Mehmed mosque (1543–48) and the considerably more complex piers of the Süleymaniye (1548–57) may have resulted from a cross-cultural exchange of ideas through the medium of architectural prints: the Süleymaniye piers reinterpret those of Hagia Sophia, but are cut at an angle to form an octagon under the central dome, like the piers designed by Sangallo (illus. 3 [1,3], 54, 74).[116]

The lost archive of the office of royal architects at Vefa in Istanbul, where Sinan's architectural drawings were once kept, in all likelihood included European architectural prints and treatises, in addition to Islamic manuscripts on the mathematical sciences

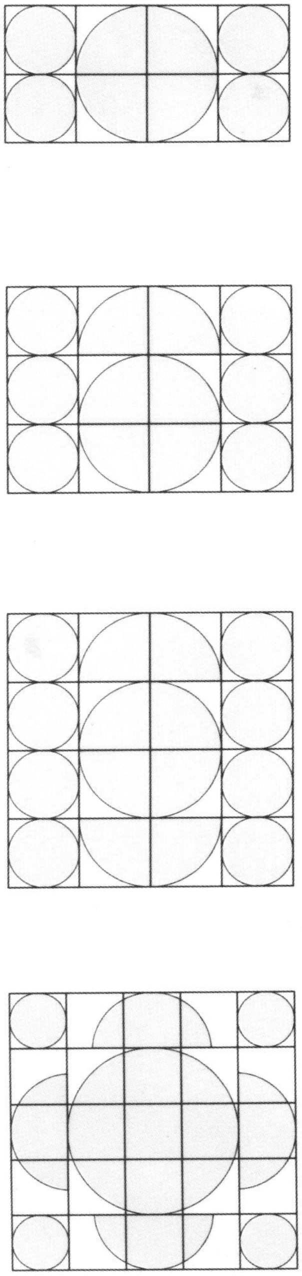

96 Modular spatial evolution of sultanic mosque plans: Üç Şerefeli, Mehmed II, Bayezid II, Şehzade Mehmed.

and engineering (rooted in the same classical Greek sources as their counterparts in Europe).[117] The Frenchman Jean-Claude Flachat reports in the middle of the eighteenth century that Sultan Mahmud I's chief architect owned 'an ample collection of plans and prints'. Moreover, 'he had the finest treatises of architecture translated for himself' and 'arduously applied himself to the study of mathematics'.[118] Although deducing sixteenth-century practices from those of the eighteenth century is problematic, it is not unreasonable to imagine that Sinan had access to current architectural publications. After all, he was the chief architect of an empire whose territories extended up to the gates of Vienna and included formerly Italian-ruled islands such as Cyprus and Chios.

We know, for instance, that the copy of a Latin manuscript of Vitruvius' *De architectura*, sent by the Duke of Milan to Matthias Corvinus had entered Sultan Süleyman's imperial library after the conquest of Buda in 1526.[119] Widely circulating illustrated editions of Vitruvius' treatise and others provided with woodcut illustrations – such as the treatise of the Bolognese architect Sebastiano Serlio (1475–1554), six of whose seven books were published separately in 1537, 1540, 1545, 1547, 1551, 1575 – could easily have been available in the workshop of royal architects. It was Serlio's treatise that initiated the idea of making architectural works more widely known through illustrations; its third book on Roman antiquities (first published in Venice in 1540) contained contemporary designs for St Peter's by Bramante, Raphael, and Peruzzi.[120] European renegades employed as architects in the Ottoman court or as naval engineers in the imperial arsenal must have constituted yet another source for the transmission of architectural knowledge. For example, a Portuguese sea captain was enrolled among the corps of royal architects in the late 1530s, and during the 1570s a renegade architect employed in the household of the Calabrian grand admiral Kılıç Ali Pasha drew the 'European style' plan of an Italianate castle built at the strategic Mediterranean port of Navarino (Pylos).[121]

Let us now turn to Sinan's three major sultanic mosques to sum up the evolution of centralized domed plans. His first royal mosque in Istanbul, commissioned by Sultan Süleyman to commemorate the deceased crown prince Şehzade Mehmed (1543–48), turned away once and for all from the antiquated T-plans of Friday mosques built for Bayezid II and Selim I (illus. 3 [1]). The persistence of this spatially fragmented, archaic plan type well into the early part of Süleyman's reign had hindered the development of centralized interior spaces. Its fall from favour during Sinan's tenure coincided with Süleyman's policy of a state-imposed religious orthodoxy that no longer tolerated such rituals as the whirling and chanting formerly practiced inside multifunctional mosques. Sinan's experimentation with spatially unified centralized plans, then, was not merely an aesthetic preference but also a corollary of liturgical transformation at a time when unifunctional Friday mosques devoted exclusively to the congregational prayers became strictly enforced. The grand sultanic mosques of Sinan were not the natural culmination of an uninterrupted linear evolution (illus. 96), but the forceful reiteration of an imperial ideal launched by Mehmed II's mosque without attached *tabhane*s.

The double-minaret mosque of Şehzade Mehmed has a quatrefoil plan, composed of a central dome surrounded by four half-domes and four small domes in each corner. It perfects the provincial versions of this plan type that emerged in southeastern Anatolia in the early sixteenth century and comes close to the 'ideal Renaissance temple' plans designed by Bramante for St Peter's and smaller churches.[122] The Şehzade mosque refines the archaic style of Istanbul's previous imperial mosques with its pyramidally massed superstructure and harmonious proportions. Freed from projecting *tabhane*s, its lateral façades are more elaborately composed with unprecedented external domical arcades and complex window arrangements (illus 154–55).[123]

Sinan's next two major sultanic mosques, the Süleymaniye in Istanbul (1548–59) and the Selimiye in Edirne (1568–74), boast four multi-galleried minarets and further cultivate the iconographically potent dialogue with Hagia Sophia. The Süleymaniye complex reinterprets the unrivalled symmetrical layout of Mehmed II's complex with its large number of dependencies, outranking the former's madrasas with new ones institutionally classified as the highest in the empire (illus. 167–68). Its mosque revises a scheme adopted earlier in Bayezid II's mosque with its central dome flanked by two half-domes, using two colossal granite columns on each side of the central baldachin supported on four piers. The Süleymaniye realizes Mehmed II's unfulfilled ambition to create an Ottoman style mosque matching Hagia Sophia in magnificence with its refined proportions, its harmonious pyramidal cascade of varied domes and half-domes, its internal galleries resting on precious arched colonnades, and its lateral façades embellished with lavish superimposed arcades.

The Selimiye in Edirne sets out to rival Hagia Sophia without paraphrasing its layout, using an original design concept with a centralized octagonal baldachin that departs from the square baldachins of earlier sultanic mosques featuring red granite columns (Mehmed II, Bayezid II, Süleyman I). Breaking free from dynastic tradition, Sinan creates a world-class monument that apparently responded to an international competition voiced by the critique of European architects. His preoccupation with a global reputation is implied in the *Teẕkiretü'l-bünyān*, analysed in Chapter 4, which mentions the 'so-called architects of the infidels' who had troubled his heart by claiming that Hagia Sophia's inimitable dome could not possibly be equalled in size by Muslim architects. According to the same source, Sinan disproves that claim by building the Selimiye mosque, a matchless monument that is 'deserving to be seen by the people of the world'.[124] His preoccupation with size, not unlike examples cited above from the post-Mongol Islamic world, also found a parallel in St Peter's, whose dome vies in its dimensions with those of the Pantheon and Florence Cathedral.

Dominated by a large dome slightly surpassing in diameter that of Hagia Sophia, the Selimiye mosque abandons the pyramidal cascade of domes and half-domes that became a trademark of Sinan's classical idiom (illus. 209–10). With a novel sculptural dynamism and plasticity, its lofty lateral façades that counterbalance layered horizontal tiers by vertical continuities inaugurate a new chapter in Sinan's mosque design, characterized by transgressions of the classical code.[125] One wonders whether the chief architect's revised concept of the façade may not have been another response to 'infidel' architects, perhaps inspired by Etienne Dupérac's recently published engravings of St Peter's (1569) based on designs by Michelangelo (illus. 77). Primarily intended for export, these prints, made for an audience of specialists curious to know what was being planned for St Peter's, could have reached Sinan around the time he was preparing designs for the Selimiye, whose foundations were laid in 1569.

Spurred on to outdo himself by the real or imagined critique of his European colleagues, the chief architect may have familiarized himself with the project for St Peter's: the most ambitious of all cathedral churches in the Christian West. None of this should, of course, diminish the significance of early Islamic and Ottoman architectural traditions within which Sinan self-consciously situated himself. As I argue in Chapter 6, his veiled examplars possibly included such famous eastern precedents as the imperial mausoleum of Uljaytu in Sultaniya, which he had seen in 1534: its double-shell octagonal dome surrounded by eight turrets was the largest ever built in the Islamic lands (illus. 51). Whatever models he may have used, Sinan's breakthrough in centralized mosque design profoundly transformed and concealed his sources of inspiration by unrecognizably filtering them through the lens of canonical Ottoman architectural forms.

III. THE NEW AESTHETIC OF MOSQUES AND SİNAN'S ISTANBUL

The monumental domed mosques and churches of the eastern Medditterranean world expressed the conviction that public places of worship represented the pinnacle of architectural values. This conviction, articulated in Vitruvius's treatise, is reiterated by Alberti: 'There does not exist any work which requires greater talent, care, skill and diligence than that needed for building and decorating the temple. Needless to say, a well-tended and ornate temple is without doubt the foremost and primary ornament of the city.'[126] The same idea is stressed in Palladio's treatise and in Sinan's autobiographies, which rank the Friday mosque as the premier building type, on which he lavished most of his attention (Appendix 3).[127]

The chief architect's mosques combined a limited repertoire of canonical forms already in use since the late fifteenth century. His autobiographies (discussed in Chapter 4) elucidate his ambition to improve upon celebrated examplars from the past, such as the Hagia Sophia, the Üç Şerefeli, and the sultanic mosques of Istanbul built prior to his time. They disclose his concern with finding elegant solutions to structural problems and with refining the proportional system of the dynastic architectural idiom he inherited. His mosques achieve that goal through the harmonious integration of varied support systems and modulated domical superstructures.

While his Italian contemporaries focused much of their creative energy on the classical orders and on pedimented façades with classicizing sculptural details, Sinan adopted an elastic approach to architectural design. He enveloped spatial volumes with domical shells and rectilinear walls embellished by inner and outer arcades and innovative window compositions. His emphasis on laying strong foundations, attested to in his autobiographies, was informed by texts narrating the collapse of Hagia Sophia's unstable dome and by the collective memory of Istanbul's notorious earthquakes. According to the early-sixteenth-century historian Ruhi, the earthquake of 1509 (dubbed the 'small doomsday') not only cracked the dome of Mehmed II's mosque, bringing down many domes of its dependencies, but also caused the dome of Bayezid II's mosque 'to fall and break into many pieces, cracking its outer domes and arches' and toppling one of its minarets.[128]

Sinan erected his light-filled mosques, featuring seemingly weightless domed baldachins, with a substantial margin of safety. Using heavy wall masses to construct organically unified edifices, he came closer than did his Italian contemporaries to emulating the structural techniques of Roman and Byzantine architects. His steadfast devotion to the geometry of hemispherical domes also brought him closer to the Roman tradition than Renaissance architects, who were equally attracted to domes with elevated profiles like that of Florence Cathedral. Unhampered by the Renaissance compromise between the theoretical perfection of central plans and the dictates of liturgical space (more suited to the Latin cross), Sinan was in many ways freer to experiment with centralized domed structures. Unlike his Italian colleagues who left behind many unrealized projects and sketches for domed churches with central plans, he was able to realize his innovative design concepts in mosques built for a wide range of patrons. Nevertheless, for the accommodation of rows of worshippers parallel to the qibla wall, Sinan remained bound by the traditional rectangular format of the mosque. He never used curved forms in his ground plans, focusing instead on the variation of domed superstructures. His main concern in mosque design was the coordination of infrastructure and superstructure, characterized by a marked duality: the former defined entirely by straight lines and windows with pointed Islamic arches descending all the way to the ground level, the latter composed of semicircular Roman arches and hemispherical domes evoking cosmic analogies.

The evolution of Sinan's new aesthetic in mosque architecture can best be traced in monuments sponsored at the highest levels of patronage and located inside or near Istanbul. Since distant provincial mosques were hardly ever executed by him, they have been assessed in this book as a collective corpus stamped by his unifying vision, communicated through plans drawn on paper and models, as well as through written and oral instructions. Sinan's style can roughly be divided into three stages: his formative period, from 1539 to 1548 marked by the completion of the Şehzade Mehmed complex; his mature period, from 1549 to 1568, encompassing the 'classical' style perfected in the Süleymaniye complex; and his post-classical period, from 1569 to 1588, propelled by innovations introduced in the Selimiye mosque.[129]

The last period includes highly experimental mosques in Istanbul designed after the completion of the Selimiye in 1574, mosques with 'manneristic' departures from the classical concordance between interiors and exteriors articulated through the pyramidal massing of domes and half-domes. The taller façades of post-classical mosques become more vertical and planar, as their domed baldachins gained increasing autonomy from walls perforated with dynamically variegated windows.[130] It is not entirely clear whether these monuments reflect Sinan's unquenchable quest for innovation in old age or the explorations of his aspiring assistants, but they were projects he approved and listed as his own. The less experimental mosques of his immediate successors, which are analysed in the Epilogue, attest to Sinan's ongoing contribution to mosque design until his demise at nearly one hundred years old. Breaking the rules he himself established, he remained 'the master to the end' and 'managed to keep under control the conflicting aspirations for change during the 1580s'.[131]

Sinan's mosques are characterized by a relatively restrained use of ornament to accentuate architectonic elements, but exceptions to the rule demonstrate his versatility in meeting the demands of individualized programmes. It is often assumed that he was primarily concerned with structural rationalism, to which ornament and epigraphy were subordinated as an insignificant appendage. This is at best an anachronism that injects modernist aesthetic values into his architecture. Sinan's autobiographies reveal that he regarded decoration and calligraphy as integral components of mosque architecture.[132] He was instrumental in the formulation of a novel decorative idiom since artisanal workshops and the İznik tile industry came under his jurisdiction.[133]

The Süleymaniye built in the 1550s constitutes an important turning point in the codification of Sinan's new decorative idiom. It was in this mosque that underglaze-painted İznik tiles – based on an unprecedented palette of white, blue, turquoise, and tomato red (expanded with green in the 1560s) – were used for the first time. Thereafter shiny white-ground tiles (sometimes featuring imitation marble patterns), replaced the matte-surfaced Persianate *cuerda seca* tiles used in Sinan's early mosque complexes, as they more effectively matched the colour of sandstone walls with white marble revetments. Another, less often noticed innovation was the epigraphy of the Süleymaniye (designed by the court calligrapher Hasan Karahisari), which gave precedence to a single mode of writing: monumental *thuluth*.[134]

Sinan's active involvement in the decorative and epigraphic programme of the Selimiye mosque is confirmed by an imperial decree handed over in 1572 to the 'superintendent of tilework' (*kāşī emīni*). It informs the chief architect that the calligrapher he had requested, Hasan Karahisari (Molla Hasan), had been appointed to design the inscriptions of the mosque. He is ordered to show the calligrapher the places to be decorated with inscriptions on tilework and with painted 'plain calligraphy' (*sāde ḫaṭṭ*). Once these inscriptions were prepared according to the manner Sinan saw 'fitting and appropriate' (*vecih ve münāsib*), the tilework superintendent presumably took the relevant cartoons to the İznik ateliers. A related imperial decree also dating from 1572 responds to Sinan's written progress report, in which he asked whether the projecting mihrab of the Selimiye should be 'decorated' (*müzeyyen*) or 'plain' (*sāde*). The sultan chooses the first alternative and declares it 'necessary to have tiles up to the level of windows and the Fatiha sura written on tiles over the windows,' according to the manner the chief architect sees 'fitting and appropriate' (*vecih ve münāsib*).[135] This shows that the content of inscriptions was controlled from the capital, whereas aesthetic choices concerning their placement and medium were left to Sinan's own sense of decorum.

The prestige of tile revetments largely depended on the privileged access of the sultan and the ruling elite to the İznik workshops, which were otherwise geared to the mass production of tablewares for the open market. Local animosity towards the tilework superintendent is captured in a decree sent to the kadi of İznik in 1572, which orders a court trial of Musli and his friends who in a night attack wounded Mehmed, the person 'in charge of the service of having tiles made for the state'.[136] Whatever the reason for this hostile behaviour, it foreshadowed future problems in İznik, which suffered from internal unrest and crime in the wake of the Celali rebellions. After the catastrophic devaluations of 1585–86, orders sent to İznik attempted to enforce the production of tiles ordered for state constructions at officially-fixed prices that lagged behind those paid by merchants for more lucrative tablewares. The marked decline in the quality of İznik tiles towards the end of the sixteenth century would culminate in the early seventeenth century with the disappearance from the İznik ceramic palette of red and pure white.

The brief but glorious lifespan of 'classical' İznik tiles overlapped Sinan's tenure; such tiles were among the trademarks of his prestige mosques. Except for the royal mosques of Selim II and Murad III in Edirne and Manisa respectively, provincial mosques designed by Sinan feature simpler painted decorations. Those in eastern Anatolia and Syria-Palestine, on the other hand, are distinguished by imitations of İznik tiles produced by local workshops. Unlike modular tiles with repeat patterns, custom-made ones conforming to the outlines of arched panels, lunettes,

97 Interior of the mausoleum of princes Mahmud and Cem, Muradiye complex, Bursa.

98, 99 Paintings on the transition zone of the mausoleum dome, and in the dome itself.

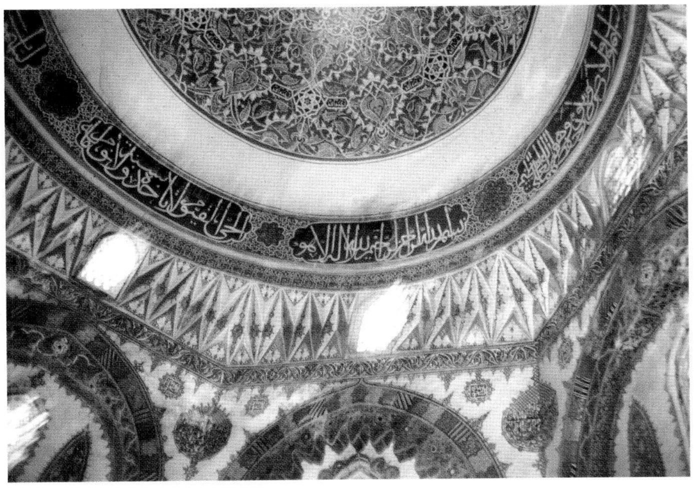

and spandrels had to be prepared on the basis of measured drawings on paper. In a later instance, tile revetments ordered from İznik for a shore kiosk at the Topkapı Palace, built by Sinan's successor Davud, were based on designs on paper drawn by Bali, a non-Muslim designer of patterned silk brocades, which were sent to İznik together with forty-nine stencils for inscriptions made by the 'designer' (*ressām*) Mehmed Çelebi.[137]

The predominantly floral patterns of İznik tiles, echoing those on textiles, were often complemented by legible inscriptions in cursive scripts, among which monumental *thuluth* reigned supreme. During the age of Sinan, both calligraphy and ornamental patterns assumed a new formal clarity and precision, an aesthetic preference in keeping with the overall impact of his harmoniously proportioned architectural forms. Fashionable semi-naturalistic floral designs occupied the places of honour, relegating the abstract vegetal scrolls and geometric interlaces of the international Timurid mode to marginal positions. The decorative vocabulary of earlier Ottoman mosques (discussed in Chapter 3) had privileged complexity over legibility, a taste that characterizes the unusually well-preserved painted decorations of a mausoleum built in Bursa in 1479 for Mehmed II's son Mustafa and popularly named after prince Cem, who was buried there next to his brother in 1499.[138] The interior of the mausoleum is ornamented with calligraphy in diverse scripts, ranging from *thuluth* and varieties of kufic to superimposed, overlapping, mirror-reverse, and bilaterally symmetrical mirror-image compositions (illus. 97–99). The walls are surrounded by particularly complex red-ground inscriptions in rectangular frames that combine three colour-coded layers of script: a line of monumental *thuluth* in white, superimposed with the same script in green mirror-reverse letters, and an angular kufic superscript in black. The kufic medallions at the centre of the dome and its zone of transition are so tiny and lost among abstract decorative motifs that they require binoculars to decipher.

The wall surfaces are treated as if samples of calligraphy in varied scripts are being displayed on an illuminated album page. Examples of Timurid albums preserved in the Topkapı Palace library capture the taste for virtuoso performance in diverse scripts, a taste that affirmed the superiority of form over meaning declared by a saying attributed to the sixteenth-century Persian calligrapher Mir ʿAli of Herat: 'O calligrapher! As long as thy pen continues to work miracles, / It is fitting if Form proclaims superiority over Meaning!' This 'formalist' aesthetic stance becomes supplanted in the epigraphy of Sinan's monuments by one that stresses the clarity of writing as a medium for a message.

The importance attached to legibility is exemplified by an imperial decree sent to Mecca in 1576, upon completion of new domical arcades around the Kaʿba, supervised from a distance by Sinan. The decree informs the kadi of Mecca (the building overseer), the governor of Jidda (the building supervisor), and Mehmed Çavuş (the royal architect, sent from Istanbul) that the text of a foundation inscription has been dispatched from the capital, along with an order to the governor-general of Egypt that he send a competent marble cutter to carve the inscription. The recipients of the decree are to have the inscription copied by a scribe with 'beautiful writing (*hūb ḫaṭṭ*) so that onlookers should experience no hesitation in reading it.'[139] This is one of the few statements where the beauty of writing is explicitly linked with legibility and the unambiguous communication of content.

The combination of Koranic inscriptions with hadith and Persian poetry in early Ottoman mosques gave way in the age of Sinan to a preponderance of Koranic passages, with occasional quotations of hadith.[140] This new emphasis exalted the Koran as the ultimate source of religious truth, superior to other texts as the authoritative Word of God. The consecration of the Divine Word in monumental *thuluth* script accentuated its sacred character, thereby raising it to iconic status. Primarily Koranic inscriptions underscored the unifunctional character of Sinan's Friday mosques, whose sanctified space was mainly devoted to the worship and glorification of God.

Referring to the Koranic inscriptions on the domes of the Süleymaniye mosque, composed of roundels with radiating letters in gold, Evliya Çelebi explains that 'each *alif*, *lam*, and *kaf* was made ten cubits tall in order to be easily read'.[141] This suggests that the legibility, and by implication, the content of the written word mattered as much as its visual impact. That monumental epigraphy was meant to be read is implied by the description of a party Sokollu Mehmed Pasha hosted to celebrate the inauguration of a pavilion in his palace, decorated with poetic inscriptions. After giving his guests a tour of the pavilion, he tests them by asking who could recite from memory the inscribed poems. Only Ebussuud's son succeeds in this exercise, which instantaneously wins him the admiration of those present.[142] Although this episode concerns poetic inscriptions in a palatial context, it also has implications for the Koranic epigraphy of mosques, whose learned users included the resident professors and students of dependent madrasas. Groups of visitors staying at the hospices of mosque complexes may also have read inscriptions, with imams and staff acting as tourist guides. One can imagine inscriptions being pointed out during the propagandistic tours of sultanic mosques to Safavid ambassadors to highlight topics of theological dispute.

The predominantly Koranic epigraphy of Sinan's mosques must have been intelligible to a large percentage of the urban population, particularly in Istanbul. The upper echelons of the Ottoman elite, generally educated in the imperial palace or in madrasas, were literate and trilingual. Most of them could read Turkish, Arabic, and Persian. All three languages appear in the historical foundation inscriptions of Sinan's mosques, which from the second half of the sixteenth century onward increasingly use

Turkish, the spoken language. The relatively high degree of basic literacy among the urban masses can be deduced from the large number of public elementary schools, where children were taught to read, write, and memorize the Koran for use in daily prayers. According to a census prepared in 1577–78, Istanbul had a record number of 1,653 elementary schools.[143] A Spanish slave commented in the 1550s on the countless schools of the capital for teaching the Koran, and observed that 'people who know how to read and write are by far more numerous' there than in Spain.[144]

Semi-literate males receiving even a minimal elementary school education learned enough Arabic for 'contextual literacy'. Anyone sufficiently familiar with the Koran could decipher at least a few words and deduce the rest from having memorized the most frequently quoted popular verses, repeated in different combinations in Sinan's mosques to highlight specific themes.[145] The new concern with legibility was paralleled by a marked reduction in the number of inscriptions that enabled their overall thematic content to be more easily grasped. The multivalent Koranic verses of Sinan's mosques were often accompanied by invocations of the ninety-nine beautiful names of God and eight iconic names inscribed around the transition zones of domes as sectarian emblems: Allah, Muhammad, the four Sunni caliphs, Hasan and Husayn. The varied combination of familiar Koranic verses and occasional departures from the norm yielded messages that were simultaneously context-specific and general, open to several levels of reading.

Only a few fragments of painted decorations survive in Sinan's mosques, most of which were overpainted with baroque and rococo designs. Since calligraphy was generally repainted, more of it has survived, complemented by writing on tiles, stone, and woodwork. İznik lamps and spherical pendants, Murano-glass oil lamps and windows, mirror globes, painted ostrich eggs, and illuminated Korans displayed on lecterns were among the coveted ornaments of Sinan's mosques, whose floors were covered with precious carpets. Unfortunately none of his mosques preserve their original lighting fixtures and decorative pendants, a major aesthetic handicap when coupled with the nearly wholesale disappearance of authentic painted decorations. Among the surviving examples of painted ostrich eggs with silk tassles are those in Sultan Süleyman's mausoleum; that of his wife also preserves its mirror globes (*top-ı āyine*) resembling spherical Christmas-tree ornaments (illus. 186–87).[146]

Inside the Selimiye, Reinhold Lubenau (1587–88) saw five thousand oil lamps and 'spherical mirrors resembling globes of damaschined iron' in addition to ostrich eggs hanging from large iron rings. He wrote: 'When the lamps burnt, their dazzling reflection on those mirrors made the whole mosque appear as if it were on fire!'[147] Gerlach (1578) says the lamps hung in three superimposed tiers, an arrangement described in some detail by Wratislaw von Mitrowitz (1591–96):[148]

> There are three galleries ... round which are iron rings, at the bottom of which hang 326 handsome lamps. Higher over these is a second set of rings, from which ostrich eggs and balls of looking-glass are suspended by silken straps. Over this, again, is a second gallery, all round which is a set of rings with lamps, and above it a second set of rings with ostrich-eggs and balls of looking-glass. On the third and highest gallery is a set of iron rings, and lamps suspended all around. Highest of all, in the midst, hangs a gilt ball.[149]

A similar gilt ball hung from the central dome of the Süleymaniye mosque, where Evliya Çelebi saw a less elaborate, two-tiered arrangement of oil lamps and pendants, as in the mosque of Şehzade Mehmed.[150] Such multilayered light fixtures are often praised in waqfiyyas and architectural descriptions as recalling the strata of the heavens. Superimposed tiers of windows framing patches of light on the surface of white stone walls constituted the foremost ornaments of Sinan's mosques, whose light-filled spaces differ from the dim interiors of their early Ottoman counterparts and the even darker Byzantine churches converted into mosques. No wonder that in 1568, just before he was commissioned to build the sparkling Selimiye, the chief architect was ordered to add windows to the Old Mosque in Edirne.[151]

Another prized ornament was carpeting. For the Süleymaniye, for instance, ten 'large top quality carpets' were commissioned through the governor-general of Cairo in 1551.[152] Two years later, the kadi of Küre (in the sanjak of Aydın near Birgi) was informed that the neighbouring kadi of Tire had been sent an imperial decree with a 'sample register' (*nümūne defter*) ordering him to have carpets woven for the Süleymaniye. The kadi of Küre was asked to oversee 'day and night' the production of these custom-made carpets in Tire, making sure they matched without any deviation the dispatched design samples that probably indicated size and pattern type.[153] The waqfiyyas of several mosques discussed in Part 3 list the types of carpets endowed by their founders.

In Sinan's mosques, architecture and decoration worked in complement to create harmonious ensembles permeated with a sense of proportion. The standardization of canonical forms in architecture also extended to decorative patterns and calligraphy, often appearing similar yet rarely identical. Through a narrow repertoire of recognizable forms and colours that departed from the Persianate aesthetic that had been cultivated ever since the early fifteenth century, the decoration of Sinan's mosques enunciated a hegemonic visual identity exclusively confined to the Ottoman territories. The creation of a territorially bound new aesthetic canon is always too complex a phenomenon to explain. As important as the role of visual identity politics and changing religious orientations was that of aesthetic preferences, signalling the emergence of an early modern sensibility that moved away from the late medieval fascination with visual complexity and

100 Anonymous Austrian artist, Panoramic views of Istanbul, watercolour on paper, c. 1590:
1. Walled city of Istanbul
2. Pera (Galata) showing the seashore mosque of Kılıç Ali Pasha and the hilltop mosque of prince Cihangir at the right
3. Üsküdar and Chalcedon, watercolour on paper

variety. The new aesthetic criteria in architectural ornament and epigraphy were unity, clarity, and refined simplicity.

SİNAN'S CONTRIBUTIONS TO THE URBAN IMAGE OF ISTANBUL

The mosque complexes of Sinan enhanced the spectacular image of Istanbul by elaborating already established urban patterns (Map 2). It was the imperial vision of Mehmed II that shaped the structural framework for transforming the triangular promontory of the Byzantine walled city (Istanbul proper) into an Islamic megapolis, complemented by three townships and suburbs (illus. 58, 72). Separated by stretches of water, each developed its own distinctive character by the end of the sixteenth century. Mehmed II's mosque complex and New Palace (the Topkapı Palace, which replaced the Old Palace in the centre of the city) were linked together by a branch of the Byzantine ceremonial avenue known as the Mese. This became the Divanyolu, on which four times a week dignitaries paraded to imperial council meetings at the Topkapı Palace. Connecting the public square of the Hippodrome (Atmeydanı) to the Edirne gate (Edirnekapı) on the city's land walls, this branch of the Mese would subsequently be lined with sultanic mosque complexes sited on elevated hilltops. The second branch of the avenue leading to the Golden Gate (now blocked by Mehmed II's seven-towered citadel, the Yedikule) lost its former prominence as the main axis along which the Justinianic city had developed parallel to the shores of the Marmara. By contrast, the Ottoman city developed its distinctive silhouette facing the Golden Horn, a turn of direction heralded by the siting of Mehmed II's mosque complex and the Topkapı Palace.

Sinan crowned the remaining hilltops of the walled city with impressive mosque complexes built for Süleyman and his two favourite children, Şehzade Mehmed and Mihrümah Sultan. The Süleymaniye, sited at a distance from the Mese on a view-com-

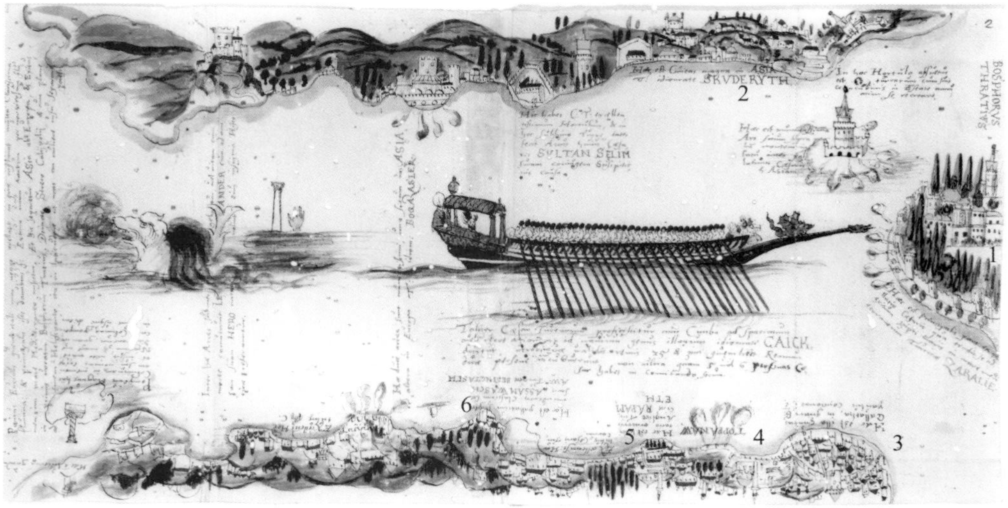

101 Panoramic view of the Bosphorus with the sultan's red galley, 1588, watercolour on paper: 1. Topkapı Palace. 2. Üsküdar with Nurbanu Sultan's hilltop mosque. 3. Galata. 4. Tophane with the Kılıç Ali Pasha mosque and cannons along the waterfront. 5. Tophane-Fındıklı with the hilltop mosque of prince Cihangir and the shore mansion of Arap Ahmed Pasha used as the English embassy. 6. Shore palace of the grand-admiral Hasan Pasha in Beşiktaş.

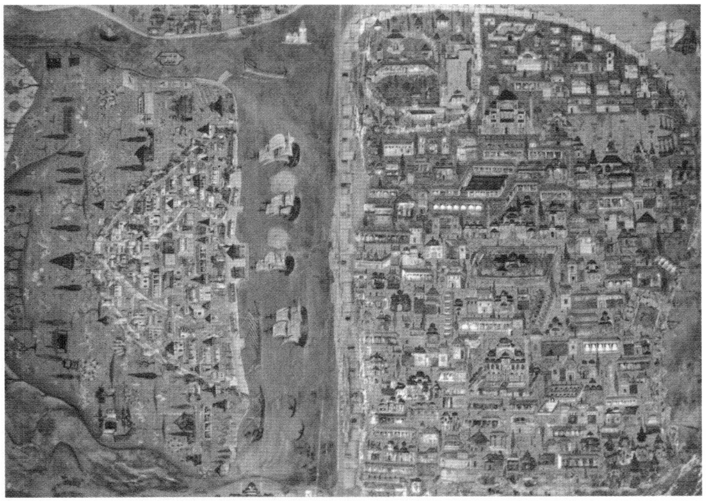

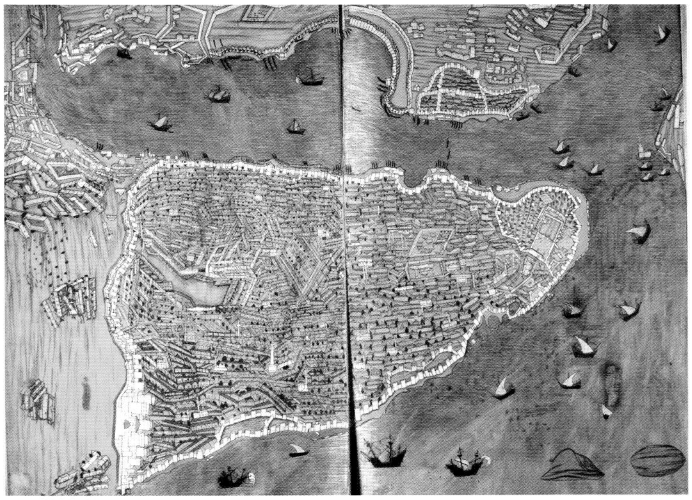

102 (left) Matrakçı Nasuh, map of Istanbul, *c.* 1537, watercolour on paper, from *Beyān-i Menāzil-i Sefer-i ʿIraḳeyn.*

103 (right) Anonymous, map of Istanbul, *c.* 1584–85, watercolour on paper, from Seyyid Lokman, *Hünernāme.*

manding plot borrowed from the Old Palace, reconfigured the cityscape facing the Golden Horn with a grand landmark. Sinan's mosques were generally concentrated in the margins of the densely inhabited walled city, particularly along the land walls in Yenibahçe and inside the bustling city gates.[154] His other mosques were distributed in the three townships and in new suburbs that emerged along the shores of the Golden Horn and the Bosphorus. The preferred siting of mosques on hilltops and along the waterfront enhanced their visibility, contributing to the adornment of the capital (illus. 100[1–3], 101). Inserted into cityscapes separated by bodies of water, Sinan's mosques actively interact with the topography of Istanbul. They are almost never perceived alone but rather in juxtaposition with others, both contemporary and old (illus. 84, 364, 519). Their structured relationship as *genus loci* in the city fabric played a part in the production of meaning. The homogenous urban texture of the walled city, defined by uniform multicoloured houses with low brick-covered roofs, provided a neutral backdrop against which monumental domed public edifices were enchantingly displayed.

Comparing the city map of Matrakçı Nasuh, depicting Istanbul around 1537 just before Sinan became chief architect, with the *Hünernāme* map of 1584–85 reveals the increased density of the continuous urban fabric within the walled city (illus. 102, 103). The later map documents the expansion around the Golden Horn, in both Eyüp and the new suburb of Kasımpaşa, whose shoreline is taken up with the amplified shipyards of the imperial arsenal. The growth of Galata beyond its walls with the new suburbs of Tophane, Fındıklı, and Beşiktaş is also depicted, together with the extension of Üsküdar. By the 1580s the cityscape reshaped by Sinan became increasingly oriented towards the water, a transformation captured in the *Hünernāme* map, where buildings turn their faces in multiple directions towards the silver-coloured sea. Later versions of the Piri Reis map (*c.* 1670–1700) represent a composite megapolis straddling two continents (illus. 104). They emphasize the panoramic view along the Golden Horn, first recorded in Melchior Lorich's prospect (illus. 33[1–8]) and in many later European images representing the viewpoint of Galata's cosmopolitan residents. The Frenchman Guillaume-Joseph Grelot describes (1683) the 'enchanted' amphitheatre-like cityscape seen from the harbour 'in the midst of three great Arms of the Sea':

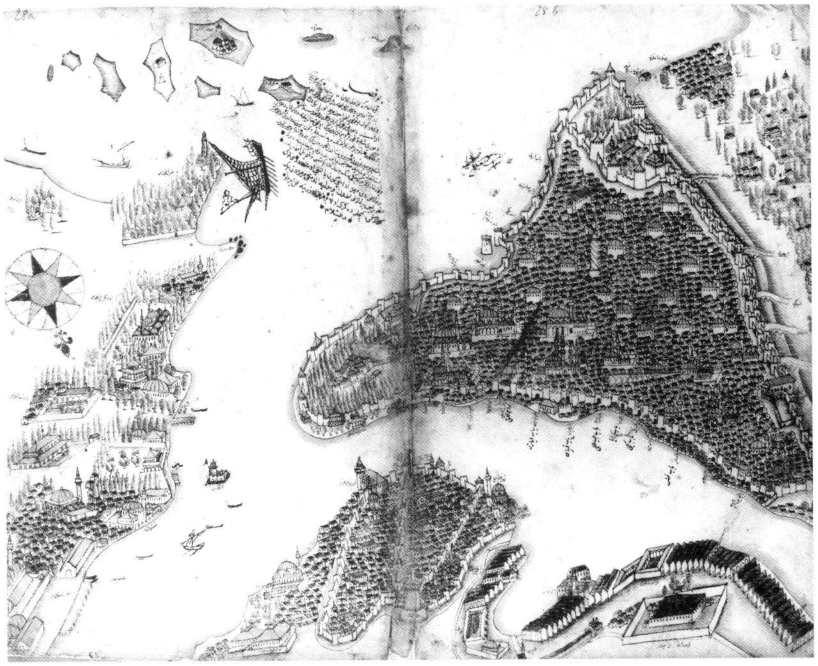

104 Map of Istanbul, *c.* 1670–1700, watercolour on paper, from *Piri Reis, Kitāb-ı Bahriye.*

105 Melchior Lorichs, View over the roofs of houses in Istanbul with the mosque of Atik Ali Pasha in the background, *c.* 1559, pen and ink on paper.

izing, and entertainment.[157] These self-centred complexes were designed as urban spaces whose crisp geometric regularities expand radially from their centre toward their organically modulated peripheries, blending with vernacular architecture and pre-existing street networks (illus. 105). Their molecular nodules were not part of a larger concept of urban totality and the sense of visual unity externally projected by the skyline was lost to pedestrians inside the congested city fabric.

One of the chief architect's talents was his ingenuity in inserting mosque complexes into their urban settings, creating proper viewing conditions and ideal perspectives that acknowledged the subjectivity of the viewer-user. Compared to Mehmed II's rigidly symmetrical mosque complex (illus. 59), the equally vast Süleymaniye is less static (illus. 167–68). Sinan exploits its terraced hilltop site by manipulating changes of level, establishing more dynamic links with the surrounding neighbourhood, and creating diagonal streets to relieve the monotony of the grand rectilinear composition. Open spaces inserted into its southwest and northeast corners function as ideal viewing places at the entrances from major streets. As in many smaller complexes, these ideal viewpoints stage oblique prospects of the mosque, de-emphasizing its central axis in favour of diagonal vistas.

> This is certainly that part of the Universe above all others, where the eye most deliciously feeds itself with a prospect every way delightful ... In the midst of those houses, variously painted, appears an incredible number of Domo's, Cupola's, Steeples and Towers, much higher than the ordinary Buildings. All those Domo's are cover'd with Lead, and also the Steeples, the Spires of which are Gilded: And the verdure of the Cypress and other Trees, abounding in a prodigious number of Gardens, contribute infinitely to the pleasing confusion of various colours that charm the eyes of all that approach near to the City ... And the vast number of *Kaicks*, Gondola's and little Boats, which is said to amount to above Sixteen Thousand, which are continually in motion from all parts, some under Sail, some Row'd with Oars, for the convenience of the Inhabitants, seem to represent to the Spectators of so lovely an Amphitheater, the continual divertisement of a Naval Combat.[155]

This distinctive urban image was gradually constructed in the course of the sixteenth century through the articulation of the natural topography with stunning architectural accents. The outward-looking cityscape sculpted by Sinan exemplifies a type of incremental town planning in which nodal points, marked by domed mosque complexes, shaped the skyline and spatial orientation of the city, conceived as a collection of nuclear units. European observers remarked on the absence of street names, and the function of major Friday mosques as the principal points of reference in defining directions.[156] The mosques and their dependencies were not only forums for major religious, political, and judicial affairs, but also for trading, social-

106 Melchior Lorichs, Eyüp shrine with double minaret mosque and necropolis, detail of illus. 33, sheet 20.

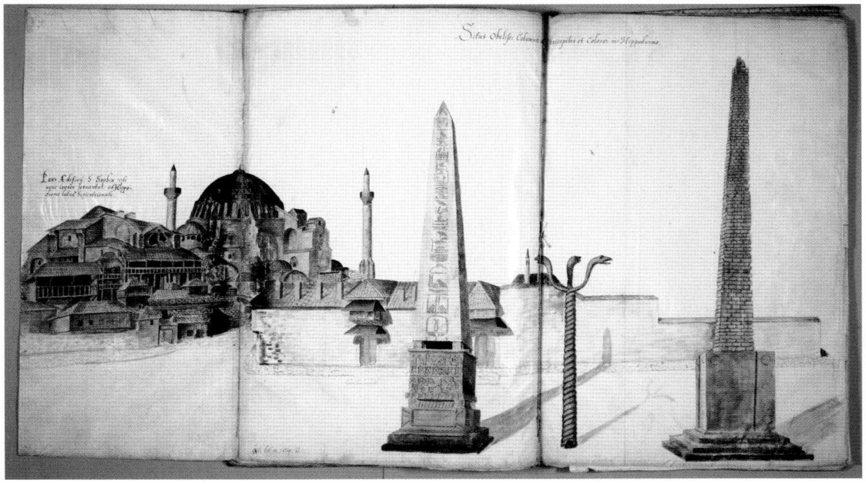
107 Anonymous Austrian artist, Hagia Sophia and the Hippodrome, Istanbul, c. 1574, watercolour on paper.

Sinan privileged the experiential dimension of architecture over the absolute order of static single-point perspective, creating multiple view-points adapted to the vision of a moving viewer-user. His concern with visual subjectivity finds a parallel in the representational conventions of sixteenth-century topographic miniature painting, a uniquely Ottoman genre. Not merely a naive version of Western perspective drawing, such painting, with its 'cubist' explosion of architectural space and form, embodies a subjective visual order that collapses multiple perspectives into a single composition. Architecture is represented as if the moving subject is positioned within rather than outside the picture plane. The importance Sinan accorded to the experiential quality of architecture, and hence to the body of the viewer turned his buildings into 'lived performances' by humanizing their monumental urban scale through intimate details, transparencies and surprises.[158]

The sites of Sinan's mosques often command panoramic vistas framed by porticoes and windows looking out onto gardens and distant prospects. Contemporary texts describe their outer courts as pleasurable excursion spots and their lighthearted interiors as 'joy-increasing' spaces. The spacious precincts with window-pierced walls that surround Sinan's sultanic mosques functioned as public promenades. For smaller complexes, the resourceful chief architect devised asymmetrical enclosures responding to the constraints of urban space, inventing dynamic multi-leveled compositions towards the end of his career. Their irregular precincts were carved out from the densely built-up city as spatio-visual frames enhancing the iconicity of his mosques. In contrast, Sinan's provincial mosque complexes, in road stations with available land, are characterized by more symmetrical layouts. During the 1560s and 1570s he developed innovative axial compositions for these roadside complexes, which were functionally dominated by service buildings for travellers (notable examples include those of Prince Selim in Karapınar and of Sokollu in Lüleburgaz, Havsa and Payas).

In comparison to the complexes commissioned earlier by Mehmed II's viziers to urbanize the newly conquered city, the programmes of Sinan's non-royal mosque complexes in Istanbul were more restricted. Their dependencies lacked guest-houses and hospices, now reserved for the mosque complexes of the royal family. Hospitals, exclusively associated with royal patronage, are only featured in three exceptionally grand complexes: Süleymaniye, Hürrem Sultan and Nurbanu Sultan. The construction of founders' mausoleums adjoining non-royal mosque complexes became a restricted privilege during the second half of the sixteenth century, requiring special written permission from the sultans.[159] *Intramuros* mausoleums were permitted only in marginal districts along the city's land walls, in the three town-ships, and their outlying suburbs.

This policy gave rise to the proliferation of monumental domed mausoleums in the sanctified necropolis of Eyüp (illus. 106, Map 3). Gerlach and the Maghribi traveller Tamgrouti both observed that grandees were paying great sums to be buried near the tomb of Ayyub al-Ansari.[160] Sinan built prominent mausoleums there for viziers and grand viziers, functioning as chapels for their extended families (illus. 319, 364). With a few exceptions, princesses were not buried next to their husbands and children in these mausoleums, but in the mausoleums of sultanic mosques. The tombs in Eyüp were lined up beyond the main ceremonial route, the Divanyolu, along which Gerlach observed numerous funeral processions attended by the members of the ruling elite. Imperial mausoleums, on the other hand, were exclusively concentrated within the walled city, in the funerary gardens of sultanic mosques. This pattern would change in the last quarter of the sixteenth century, when rulers stopped commissioning mosque complexes in the capital. At that time, Sinan remodelled the Hagia Sophia to accommodate Selim II's posthumously built mausoleum. Murad III and Mehmed III, would eventually be buried there as well, each in his own domed mausoleum (illus. 54, 56).[161]

The renovation of Hagia Sophia is a significant project omitted from Sinan's autobiographies, even though he supervised it from a distance while he was busy completing the Selimiye in Edirne (illus. 107).[162] The urbanistic principles followed in this remodelling project testify to the chief architect's concern with visually displaying public monuments by clearing spaces around them. The project was initiated after Mimar Ahmed, the repair-architect belonging to the permanent staff of Hagia Sophia, filed a report in 1572 of damages caused by residential structures encroaching upon the walls of the mosque. The damages were

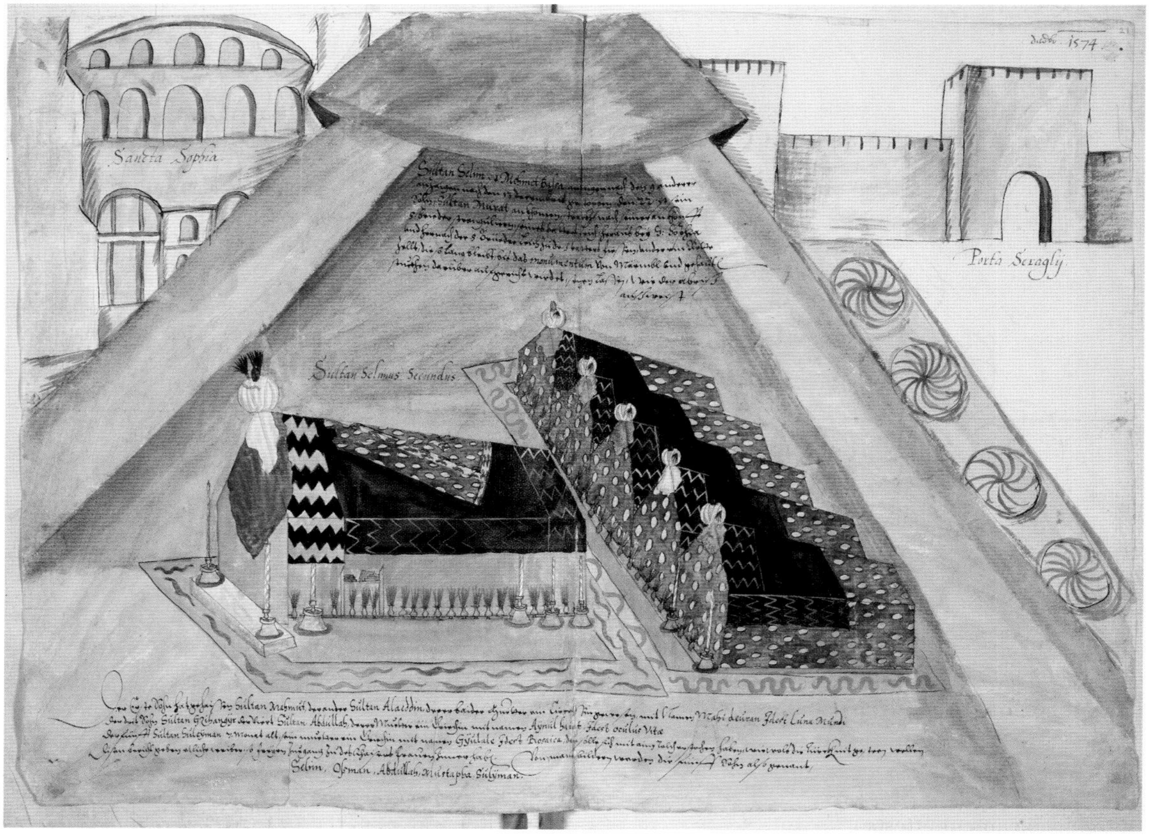

108 Anonymous Austrian artist, Burial tent of Selim II and his sons at Hagia Sophia, c. 1574, watercolour on paper.

confirmed when the kadi of Istanbul had the monument inspected by a committee that included his regent, the mosque's imam, and architectural experts (*ehl-i vuḳūf*).[163] The sultan then ordered the kadi to oversee the demolition of adjacent houses after personally confirming that they were indeed causing harm to the structure of the mosque.[164] Related imperial decrees addressed in 1573 to the endowment administrator of Hagia Sophia and to the royal architect, Mimar Usta Mehmed, approve the repair of buttresses, along with the construction of the base of a new minaret in brick that would replace a dilapidated one in wood.[165]

A few months later, the endowment administrator and the kadi of Istanbul were ordered to undertake more extensive repairs recommended by the chief architect Sinan after he and a committee of architectural experts had personally inspected the threatened building in the sultan's presence. We learn from the historian Selaniki that Selim II was accompanied by viziers, grandees, and religious scholars during his inspection of Hagia Sophia, which, leaning to one side by one-and-a-half cubits faced imminent collapse. On that occasion the sultan 'personally commissioned Koca Mimar Sinan Agha with his blessed words: Build strong buttresses in necessary places and clear the surroundings for the purpose of consolidation; it is my wish to renovate the noble Friday mosque as my own imperial monument.' After bestowing a robe of honour on the chief architect, he ordered that houses abutting the mosque be demolished and their owners be compensated for a 'lower value'.[166] Dated 1573, Selim II's imperial decree provides detailed information about the scope of the renovations recommended by a committee of experts headed by Sinan:

> This is an order to the kadi of Istanbul and the endowment administrator of Ayasofya: Given that the repair of masjids and sanctuaries is the order of God, the unique creator, when it was reported that some parts of the Great Mosque of Ayasofya located in front of my imperial palace needed to be repaired, it was personally inspected by me with prosperity and felicity together with the chief of my royal architects – who is the leader of grandees and nobles, may God increase his grandeur – and the architectural experts who had gathered there. They estimated and determined the following requirements: leaving a thirty-five-cubit-wide open space along the right and left sides of the Great Mosque, leaving a three-cubit-wide street next to the madrasa, demolishing and removing the state's storehouse, removing the [wooden] minaret on top of the half-dome and constructing a minaret above the buttress located in front of it, building buttresses and water channels in the thirty-five-cubit-wide open space, repairing and cleaning all necessary places at the interior and exterior of the mentioned mosque, demolishing superfluous buildings within its boundary and

> reusing their stones and bricks for the repair of required places, and covering places that need a roof with lead.[167]

The decree goes on to explain that a fatwa was obtained from the grand mufti concerning the need to 'partially compensate with indemnities' those who had damaged the mosque with illegal tenements. He then was asked how mischief-makers who might oppose this ruling by declaring Hagia Sophia an 'infidel's building' should be treated:

> In the process of being removed [from the mosque's grounds] in accordance with the requirements of the noble shariʿa, if some of the said individuals should persist by saying, 'This is an injustice to us, we will not leave!'; and if others support those obstinate persons by arguing, 'This is an infidel's building, it is bound to collapse, so what if it collapses?', he [the mufti] made the following judgment: 'They are infidels, it is permissible to execute them.' Therefore, enforce whatever is required by the straight shariʿa and have the above-mentioned superfluous buildings completely removed ... Without losing a moment, assiduously and diligently oversee the repair and renovation according to the manner the chief architect deems decorous (*münāsib*).

This document attests to the role played by inspection committees, composed of legal and architectural experts, in negotiating the parameters of decorum. The chief kadi of Istanbul (the three townships had their own kadis) played a crucial role, not only in mediating between the urban community and the government, but also in supervising all urban matters.[168] That is why construction-related orders were often sent to both the kadi of Istanbul and Sinan. The extensive renovation of Hagia Sophia was completed after Selim II's demise. Besides the specifications made in the decree quoted above, it involved the addition of two single-galleried minarets that raised the total of minarets to four, and the creation of a funerary garden containing the sultan's domed mausoleum (completed in 1576–77), with a domical water dispenser appended to its fenestrated precinct wall (illus. 108–9).[169] The opening of a wide space around Hagia Sophia transformed it into a veritable funerary sultanic complex.

In 1573 the area around two other Byzantine monuments belonging to the endowment of Hagia Sophia was similarly cleared of tenements. An imperial order addressed to the kadi of Istanbul and to Sinan shows that the congregations of the Zeyrek mosque (Pantokrator) and the convent-masjid known as Eski İmaret (Kalenderhane) had applied to the kadi's court for the inspection and removal of abutting houses. When the kadi's regent and the royal architect Mimar Mustafa went with other experts to inspect these two ancient monuments, they confirmed that houses with chicken coops and stables had been built on the grounds of the endowment, causing harm to the sanctuaries and blocking their windows and gates. The sultan's subsequent order instructing the kadi of Istanbul and Sinan to inspect the Zeyrek, Kalenderhane and Hagia Sophia mosques in order to report damages in writing confirms that these three projects were interconnected. Selim commands them to demolish houses around the Zeyrek and Kalenderhane mosques according to the requirements of the shariʿa and to create a five-cubit-wide open space around each monument.[170]

109 Anonymous Austrian artist, domed mausoleum of Selim II and princes at the renovated Hagia Sophia mosque, c. 1570s, watercolour on paper.

A comparable urban intervention characterized the extensive renovations carried out by Sinan's assistants at the Meccan Haram, where houses and latrines abutting the sacred precinct of the Kaʿba were demolished by imperial decree in 1574 in order to create a six-cubit-space around it.[171] In each instance, the encroaching structures were removed not only to save threatened ancient monuments but also as urbanistic measures masterminded by Sinan to increase their architectural visibility, improve circulation around them, and eliminate potential fire hazards. The periodic repetition of citywide demolition campaigns in Istanbul represented attempts to keep in check the squatter phenomenon caused by a flood of migrations to the capital. Istanbul's overgrown population had caused the grand vizier Semiz Ali Pasha (g.v. 1561–65) to oppose Sultan Süleyman's costly project of renewing the city's Byzantine water distribution network, lest it attract more migrants.[172] However, the sultan chose to go ahead with his charitable enterprise, to the joy of Sinan, who renovated the Kırkçeşme system of channels and aqueducts, increasing their

110 Mağlova aqueduct outside Istanbul.

capacity with newly discovered sources of water (illus. 110).[173]

The chief architect's contributions to improving the sense of order in Istanbul's congested urban fabric can be deduced from imperial decrees that record his interventions. The periodic demolition of houses and shops built adjacent to the city walls, on top of water channels, or projecting into streets was paralleled by the removal of structures encroaching on the walls of aqueducts and public monuments. In 1559 imperial decrees were sent to the vizier Ferhad Pasha, the chief architect, and the kadi of Istanbul, ordering them to jointly oversee the demolition of houses and shops that abutted the city walls internally and externally. After eliminating these unauthorized fire hazards, the three had to supervise the creation of a four-cubit-wide public street along the city walls.[174] In 1575 the kadi of Istanbul was ordered to cooperate with Sinan and the water channel superintendent Davud in demolishing the houses, barracks, and latrines that squatters had built adjacent to the Valens aqueduct and within its arcades. The agha of janissaries was appointed to oversee the process of demolition, initiated by a joint petition sent by Sinan and Davud to the kadi, who then reported the situation to the sultan. On this occasion, the owners of demolished structures were compensated with money, but this would not be so in the future.[175]

Documents confirm the close cooperation of the chief architect with water channel superintendents (*suyolu nazırı*) in the maintenance of water channels and aqueducts. Imperial decrees addressed to water channel superintendents and kadis ordered them to demolish illegal constructions and gardens on top of water channels, leaving a three-cubit-wide open space on both sides (a total of seven cubits).[176] Public streets were periodically repaved by the corps of pavers (*kaldırımcı*) under the direction of the chief architect, who appointed experienced royal architects such as Mimar Mehmed (in 1573) and Davud (in 1584) as supervisors.[177] Sinan's precautions against fires, which repeatedly devastated the capital, are also documented. In 1552, after a fire that had spread rapidly because of contiguous wooden structures, the kadi of Edirne was ordered to enforce the construction of masonry shops and the royal architect Ali was sent to Edirne to instruct shop owners how to rebuild their shops in the manner of 'those now being built in Istanbul, with bricks and roof tiles bordered by saw-tooth (*kirpi*, hedgehog) fringes'.[178]

In 1559 the kadi and police superintendent of Istanbul were commanded to enforce the housing codes previously established in 1539–40 (soon after Sinan's appointment as chief architect), which were particularly violated by the Jewish patrons of high houses with roof terraces. Codes stipulated that houses should only be two storeys high and built without projecting bay windows along public streets four mason's-cubits in width. The officers were ordered to enforce the construction of 'two-storey houses, built without projections in such a way that their lower and upper walls are continuous, and without projecting eaves, using saw-tooth brick fringes in accordance with the law'. Shops fronted by wooden benches and porches were also forbidden.[179] The kadi of Galata likewise received an order that year to prohibit the construction of houses with eaves; instead they had to be built with brick-tile roofs, again featuring saw-tooth fringes.[180] In 1568 an imperial decree requested by the chief architect himself required the kadi of Istanbul to demolish with Sinan's help the constructions of those who appropriated the space of public streets by building projecting bay windows and shops.[181]

Despite these precautions, in September 1569, a devastating fire swept through a section of the city, extending from the outer walls of the Topkapı Palace all the way to the Süleymaniye and Rüstem Pasha mosques. Selaniki reports that the pillaging janissaries refused to extinguish the flames in the absence of their agha, who was sick in bed, and that only the masonry (*kargir*) houses of the Jewish population remained unaffected by this catastrophe.[182] The *bailo* Marcantonio Barbaro blames the grand vizier Sokollu, the janissary agha's father-in-law, who could have prevented the fire by increasing the pay of janissaries. He reports to the Venetian Senate that the conflagration had rapidly spread over a three-to-four-mile area (which he marked on a now-lost map sent to Venice), because nearly all the city had been built of wood and unbaked bricks, with the exception of mosques, baths, and some viziral palaces.[183] He adds that, since the affected area constituted 'the most densely populated and richest part of the city, one can say that in truth more than half of Constantinople had burnt down', and that, in the section completely consumed by flames, a 'new city was being rebuilt' in accordance with building codes ordered by the sultan.[184]

These codes were no doubt established by Sinan. The fire created an opportunity to reshape the urban fabric of Istanbul according to more rational principles. Barbaro reports: 'They have expressly commanded that in building up that burnt space everyone should enlarge streets by half a cubit on each side, and that no building higher than two storeys should be erected (each storey only eight cubits tall) because the janissaries have said that they cannot demolish higher houses while trying to extinguish fires.'[185] The building codes mentioned by Barbaro are recorded in some imperial decrees. One example addressed to the kadi of Istanbul in 1570 reads: 'In the protected metropolis of Istanbul, houses that are going to be built at previously burnt down places must be ten cubits high if they are constructed with saw-tooth roofs and only eight cubits high if they are constructed without saw-tooth roofs.'[186]

An imperial decree sent to Sinan in 1572 shows that the chief architect had complained to the sultan about low-quality constructions erected in Istanbul during this rebuilding flurry:

> You have sent a petition to my threshold of felicity, reporting that some individuals have been coming from Rumelia and other places, and without knowledge of carpentry and the science of construction, they have been taking the yardstick (cubit measure) into their hands and practising architecture without your information; since you have reported that the furnaces of the houses built by these unqualified persons often catch fire and burn, when my decree arrives I order you to be firm in this matter and to forbid such individuals who, without training in the sciences of construction and carpentry, take the yardstick into their hands and practice architecture in that manner; do not allow such unqualified persons to practice architecture without your knowledge.[187]

Sinan's indignation concerning inexpert builders holding the yardstick, an emblem of the professional architect trained in the mathematical sciences, confirms that architects were not supposed to practice in the capital without obtaining his certificate of approval. Just as public monuments designed by Sinan reconfigured the urban image of Istanbul, the city itself was redesigned as a suitable frame for the monuments themselves.

IV. CODES OF DECORUM

Unlike codes regulating the height of houses and the width of streets, the notions of decorum that shaped Sinan's mosques are not recorded in writing. A revealing passage by Mustafa Āli, however, confirms that there were certain expectations of propriety relative to the rank of mosque patrons. Puzzled by the sultanic features of the mosque commissioned by Süleyman in memory of his late son, Şehzade Mehmed, Āli observes: 'That noble Friday mosque has not been built according to the type of plan proper for princes; instead, it is constructed with a pair of double-galleried minarets and a spaciousness characteristic of mosques built in the past for the magnificent Ottoman sultans.' Āli perceptively attributes this transgression of decorum to the privileged status of Şehzade Mehmed (d. 1543), the beloved heir apparent.[188]

Not trusting contemporary historians like Āli and Celalzade Mustafa, who identify the mosque as a commemorative monument built for the prince, the seventeenth-century historian Peçevi provides another explanation: he claims to have heard from old informants that its foundations had originally been laid as a sultanic mosque intended for Süleyman himself, and that it was named for the prince only after he was buried in a domed mausoleum behind its qibla wall.[189] The rumour reported by Peçevi was no doubt invented to rationalize the unusual features of the Şehzade mosque, whose foundations in actuality were laid after the completion of the prince's mausoleum according to documents discussed in Chapter 6.

The mosque deliberately conflates signs of sultanic and princely status to commemorate Şehzade Mehmed's unfulfilled destiny as ruler. This ambiguity was not lost on Āli and Peçevi. Their puzzled reactions demonstrate how the codes of decorum that Sinan was simultaneously formulating and manipulating could challenge expectations of propriety. In the absence of written regulations, decorum turned into a fragile form of social contract open to negotiation between the chief architect, his patrons, and society at large. It was not uncommon for community members to be involved in this negotiation process, particularly when their collective interests were at stake.

The principles of decorum in residential architecture are articulated in Āli's late-sixteenth-century book of etiquette, in which he discusses the luxury and status symbols of Ottoman gentlemen. Distinctive headgear, lavish costumes, gem-studded weapons, costly horses with extravagant trappings, handsome servants in luxurious attire, rare house furnishings, and sumptuous residences are, according to Āli, exclusively the privilege of the ruling elite, 'of those glorious ones at the highest peak, the viziers and generals of wide fame.'[190] Given the importance of preserving the existing social hierarchy, the adoption of status symbols reserved to a group higher than one's own deserves rejection by peers and superiors as dangerous, foolish, and 'perhaps downright subversive'. If men of lower status have the audacity to use symbols restricted to higher social rank, 'sharp-tongued critics will lash them and will punish them severely by their abuse'.[191] If they dare to exceed the upper limit of decorum; namely, what is considered 'appropriate and proper' (*vecih ve münāsib, muvāfıḳ, lāyıḳ*) for their social standing, 'men of sense should censure them and fine them in the currency of slander and ill talk'.[192]

Āli lists three levels of status among the members of the ruling elite: the highest (sultans and princes), the high (viziers, governors, and amirs), and the middle stratum (*evsāṭ-ı nās*, middling notables and fiefholders).[193] As members of the royal family, the sultanas, whom he omits from the ruling class, clearly belonged to the 'highest' level. He excludes the rest of the population, the fourth social stratum of 'the lowly ones' (*edāni* or *erāzil*), who comprise the sultan's ordinary subjects, including merchants and artisans, from access to status symbols. Āli deeply regrets that these four groups are not subject to stricter rules of decorum regulated by legal codes:

> Would that it were seen fit that the clothes of these four categories, the harnesses of their horses, and the style and fashion of their weapons were distinct and fixed by statute arranged in four degrees![194]

He believes that status symbols appropriate for each of these groups should be more rigidly codified so that members dare not 'overstep the limits of their assigned station' (*ḥaddini bilmek*).

Āli's yearning for firmer codification fixed by written law codes reflects his desire to control attempts at social climbing that obfuscate his idealized conception of a four-part Ottoman social order, an order then rapidly changing. He notes the intense competition for rank and laments the 'inordinate appetite' for increased status as a departure from 'old customs':

> When their reins are loosened, the steed of their demands does not stop at the [lower] ranks ... the glances of judges are fixed on the *emir* (*sancak begi*) positions, the *emir*s are focusing on the job of the *beglerbegi* and of the governor, and on the other hand the *beglerbegi*s look full of expectation at the seat of the vezir. After having reached that office each one of them concentrates his unceasing efforts on the happiness-covered seat that is the privilege of the grand vezirate. Thus each one covets what is higher than him, and daily he is led by greed and ambition to come up with several new desires.[195]

The aspiration for higher prestige manifested itself in attempts to push the limits of decorum in conspicuous consumption. The hierarchy-conscious mentality of the ruling elite, however, ensured to a certain degree the jealous guarding of its perquisites, and the drive for upward mobility, which could potentially endanger the observance of decorum, was largely kept in check by peer pressure. Consciousness of rank, which strengthened the sense of corporate identity within each social stratum, brought with it the vigilant guarding of subtle distinctions in signs of prestige.

The final category of status symbols that Āli discusses, residential architecture, is particularly relevant to the typology of Sinan's mosques. The chapter 'On building one's residence in accordance with [the number of one's] servants and on building lofty palaces in harmony with [one's] means', recalls discussions of decorum in contemporary Italian Renaissance architectural treatises.[196] Āli argues that the size of a residence and the quality of its furnishings should be consonant with one's social status:[197]

> This again will be obvious and clear as daylight to all understanding and cultured contemporaries, namely that everybody's living quarters must be consistent with his status, that his house and residence must fit his taste and rank, so that he stays within his limits, not overstepping his appropriate measure ... For instance, the janissaries and the marines, the *sipāhi*s that belong to the palace cavalry, the scribes of the charitable institutions, the assistant professors, the apprentices serving in government offices, and similar educated men should afford only a single room, which should have the furnishings and items fitting their status. Above these the honorable *zāʿīms* [large-scale fiefholders], the secretaries of the *dīvān* [imperial council], the palace officers, the palace butlers, the members of the special guard, the supervisors of charitable foundations, the judges in provincial towns with a salary of up to 150 aspers [a day], the professors in madrasas with up to 50 aspers [a day], and all others of equal status should have two proper rooms ... Likewise, the sons of governors, the registrars of military fiefs, the stewards, the *agha*s of the imperial palace, the great and glorious generals, and the honourable experts up to the madrasa professors with a salary of 60 aspers [a day] should have at least three rooms of first quality ... Beyond these, the finance directors of the imperial treasury, the great thinkers serving as judges of the capital, the independent magistrates entrusted with the registration of the provinces, the governors of the lands that have the title of *beglerbegi*, and, of course, the glorious mullahs of angelic qualities, the army judges and His Highness, the *sheikh'-ül-islām*, should occupy at least five rooms in perfect condition ... Outside of these [five rooms], there should definitely be many storerooms, and the entire structures and dwellings should definitely be divided threefold by walls and courtyards into exterior and interior sections ... The great viziers, finally, stand out high: each one can pride himself of twice the set-up of a *beglerbegi*; and in their living quarters and life style they can pursue their wishes like the kings of earlier times.[198]

The most lavish residences appropriate for the viziers and grand viziers, then, comprised up to ten state rooms accompanied by others organized around three courtyards (as in the palace of Sokollu Mehmed Pasha, illus. 13 [1–4]). Next came residences with five state rooms, also arranged around three courtyards for the members of the grand vizier's cabinet at the imperial council – the army judges (*kazasker*) and finance ministers (*defterdar*) – along with the grand mufti, the kadis of Istanbul, and the provincial governor-generals (*beglerbegi*). Among this group, only the representatives of the ulema who were not included in the imperial council refrained from commissioning mosque complexes from Sinan. Residences with three state rooms, arranged around fewer courtyards, were reserved for middle-ranking dignitaries, some of whom were among Friday mosque patrons: the aghas of the imperial palace, notables (*ümera-i kübera*), and stewards (*kethüda*). Fief holders (*zaim*) and court messengers (*çavuş*) deserving two rooms also commissioned a few Friday mosques from Sinan, unlike the lowest ranking members of the ruling elite having access to only one room.

The concept of decorum in residential and public architecture, inherited from Vitruvius, was theorized in Italian Renaissance architectural treatises. Vitruvius' *De architectura*, a manuscript copy of which is known to have existed in the Topkapı Palace library, defines decorum as a form of social contract that must be respected.[199] It guides the coherence of form, content and purpose in the architecture of temples. Decorum also regulates the architect's aesthetic judgments and assumes the presence of an audience whose expectations must be acknowledged. It relates to every aspect of architectural propriety: site, plan type, ornament, function and the client's status. Its socio-economic implications become particularly apparent in Vitruvius' typology of Roman houses dependent on the rank of their patrons and their location in the city or countryside. In Vitruvius' treatise architecture represents social structure and the town/country opposition through built form. The 'representational' and 'narrative' function of architectural decorum is further elaborated by Renaissance writers.[200]

In his mid-fifteenth-century treatise (published in Florence in 1486), Alberti argues that a patron should take into account his social standing in commissioning an 'appropriate' building, for 'it is the sign of a well-informed judicious mind to plan the whole undertaking in accordance with one's position in society and the requirements of use.' He adds: 'That which we should praise first in an architect is the ability to judge what is appropriate.'[201] Serlio writes in the *Terzo Libro* (1537) of his treatise that 'the architect must proceed with great modesty and reserve, especially in public buildings and those of *gravità*, where it is always praiseworthy to respect decorum'. In this case, decorum involves the use of artistic judgment and the curbing of unbridled licence (*licentia*) in the selection of ornaments for solemn public monuments. It allows the socio-economic position and profession of patrons to find appropriate visual representation in architecture.[202] In his *I quattro libri dell'architettura* (1570), Palladio includes a chapter on decorum, concerning buildings that are suitable to the different ranks of men, depending on whether they are located in the city or countryside.[203] The concept of decorum induced both Palladio and Serlio to think in terms of types (*generi*) much like Sinan.

Āli's social hierarchy of Ottoman gentlemen is no doubt sketchy, but it captures the keen sense of decorum that regulated the typology of residential architecture. Elsewhere he notes that the palace of Süleyman's grand vizier İbrahim Pasha (d. 1536) overlooking the Hippodrome exceeded appropriate bounds of decorum with the sultan's permission:

> Until that time, it was not customary to cover the roofs of vizierial palaces with lead, the law (*ḳānūn*) being that only the private pavilions of royal women in the palaces of viziers who had married into the dynasty could be covered with lead; yet it was deemed proper for İbrahim Pasha to build [his residence] in the manner of the sultan's imperial palace.[204]

Codes of decorum were also applied to the houses of non-Muslim subjects. After Mehmed II's death in 1481, for instance, two royal architects were ordered to inspect the unusually sumptuous mansion of a Jewish scribe named Simo because it had transgressed norms of appropriateness. It made use 'of hexagonal tiles befitting my sultan's assembly hall, of all sorts of walnut doors and window shutters, and variegated inlaid woodwork ceilings suitable (*lāyıḳ*) to the rank of sanjak governors.'[205] Favoured courtiers like İbrahim Pasha were sometimes given special licence by the sultan to overstep norms of propriety. For example, Süleyman had also allowed his chief physician, Moses Hamon, to build a masonry house three to four storeys high in the Jewish quarter of Istanbul.[206]

The learned early-eighteenth-century Armenian author Mouradgea D'Ohsson observes that one of the reasons for limiting the height of houses in Istanbul was to enhance the visual prominence of mosques in the cityscape:

> The height of houses is fixed by regulations; it is twelve *pics* for Muslim houses and ten for those of non-Muslims ... The motive for these regulations is to diminish the danger of fires, to facilitate the means of extinguishing them, to let air circulate freely in the relatively narrow streets, and to more effectively bring out public monuments, especially mosques, which by nature of their destination must always dominate over other edifices in the city.[207]

The sight of mosques and the sound of the muezzin's call to prayer from their minarets made Islam visible and audible. Imperial mosques in particular had to rise above the city, dominating its most elevated points to be seen from far away. This criterion is hinted in Celalzade Mustafa's description of the site chosen for Selim I's posthumous mosque complex in Istanbul as 'one of the hills called Mirza Sarayı, a lofty and exalted site higher than all the houses of the Muslims.'[208] Elsewhere he refers to the same site as 'a stately place called Mirza Sarayı, which is a high and elevated joy-giving spot towering over the sea'.[209]

Alberti's instructions about siting major public monuments on elevated places would not have been unfamiliar in the Ottoman context: 'Let the site have a dignified and agreeable appearance, and a location neither lowly nor sunk in a hollow, but elevated and commanding, where the air is pleasant and forever enlivened by some breath of wind.'[210] The Ottomans were making use of a well-established method in the history of urban planning by regulating not only the relative heights of sultanic and non-sultanic mosques, but also of non-Muslim sanctuaries which had to be visually subordinate to mosques in terms of both site and scale. An imperial decree dated 1565 orders the kadi of Istanbul to demolish the upper section of a recently erected tall church outside the Balat gate, bringing its height down to the level of surrounding houses: 'Since it has been reported that underneath the said church there was previously a house on top of which the unbelievers built a church elevated above surrounding houses, I order it to be brought down to the level of the houses around it.' The kadi is instructed to forbid the Christians from using that house as a church and from raising its height contrary to the stipulations of the noble shariʿa.[211]

In 1560 the kadis of Nevrekop and Drama in Greece were asked to investigate a complaint to the sultan's court about a church under their jurisdiction that was situated 'on an elevated site from which it dominates mosques and masjids'.[212] In 1579 the governor-general of Egypt and the kadis of Mina and Ashmouin were instructed to stop the repair of old churches under their jurisdiction without an official permit. They were to forbid the renovation of churches with walls higher than masjids and bells that disturbed Muslim prayers.[213] We have already seen in Chapter 2 how the shariʿa forbade the construction of new churches and synagogues in Muslim towns, also subjecting their restoration to strict control. A non-Muslim sanctuary rebuilt after a fire or an earthquake was to maintain its previous form. New sanctuaries could be constructed only in exceptional cases, such as when a church or synagogue, displaced by a mosque, was rebuilt elsewhere.[214]

Mehmed II's 1453 treaty with the Genoese inhabitants of Galata, who had peacefully surrendered during the conquest of Constantinople, affirms the protected status of their churches:

> I impose upon them the Islamic poll tax (*kharādj*), which they pay each year as other non-Muslims do, and in return I will give my attention [and protection] as I do to those in other parts of my dominion, that they keep their churches and perform their customary rites in them with the exception of ringing their church bells and rattle (*nāḳūs*); that I do not take away from them their present churches and turn them into mosques, but that they also do not attempt to build new churches.[215]

These laws had been established in the early days of Islam, when the seventh-century caliph ʿUmar forbade the Christians and Jews to wear costumes, headgear, and shoes resembling those of the Muslims. Such codes articulated the marginal status of non-Muslims within multiconfessional empires in which Islam enjoyed a privileged position. Thankfully, the everyday lives and interactions of ordinary people softened somewhat the barriers between religions.

Slobodan Ćurčić, who has analysed how official regulations and restrictions affected church design in the Balkans under Ottoman rule, regards the relatively modest scale of monastic and parish churches as a 'correct gauge of the general status enjoyed by Christianity within the Ottoman empire' and of the economic power of their patrons, 'a modest Christian middle class and generally small monastic communities'. Sometimes large churches were also built, but these were invariably monastic and removed from Muslim urban centres. Church construction under Ottoman rule in the Balkans (dubbed *Byzance après Byzance*) revived familiar medieval prototypes in the late-Byzantine style, but deprived of certain crucial formal components.[216] Although monumental domed churches were not uncommon in semi-autonomous rural monastic centres, Muslim towns featured a 'predominance of domeless, mostly basilican churches' without bell towers.[217]

In accordance with the shariʿa, the ringing of church bells, permitted only in semi-autonomous non-Muslim centres (such as Mt Athos and the vassal principalites of Moldavia and Vallachia), was strictly prohibited in Muslim towns. The Ottomans perpetuated the early Islamic custom of demolishing bell towers in forcibly conquered places or converting them into minarets. Ćurčić observes that 'during the veritable church building boom following the re-establishment of the Serbian patriarchate in 1557, a number of important medieval churches underwent extensive necessary restorations, but none of them regained their lost belfries.'[218] Dernschwam noted in the 1550s the conspicuous absence of church bells and belfries in the Ottoman domains, where minarets had substituted the chime of bells with the call to prayer by a muezzin, who 'shouts like a madman as if he were in a virgin forest.'[219]

The Islamic tradition of using captured church bells as symbols of victory continued under Ottoman rule. In 997 the Spanish Umayyad caliph al-Mansur had sacked the shrine at Santiago de Compostela, bringing its bells to Cordoba, where they served as lamps in the Great Mosque. When Ferdinand III conquered Cordoba for the Christians in 1236, he returned the bells to Santiago on the backs of Muslim prisoners. Many of the lamps in the Qarawiyyin mosque in Fez were likewise made from the silenced bells of churches, captured in battle and carried to the mosque as trophies.[220] In Edirne, the late-fifteenth-century pilgrim Arnold von Harff had seen the recasting into cannons of church bells captured from conquered Christian lands. He was told that 'each Turk, when he crosses a mountain or the sea to conquer a country, must bring back a piece of a bell', a custom that gave rise in the Balkans to the Christian practice of burying bells.[221] Evliya Çelebi reports that the bronze window grilles of the mosque built by Sinan outside Galata for the grand admiral Piyale Pasha had been cast from church bells collected during the pasha's conquests of such Mediterranean islands as Jerba and Chios.[222]

Decorum not only differentiated non-Muslim religious monuments from their Muslim counterparts, but also shaped the hierarchies of status among Friday mosques. The implicit hierarchy of mosques in the Ottoman mental universe – headed by the three major sanctuaries in Mecca, Medina, and Jerusalem – is reflected in classifications that differentiate 'royal' from 'non-royal' mosques.[223] The description of Istanbul's secular and religious monuments, which the mid-sixteenth-century historian Celalzade Mustafa planned to write, would have been based on such a classification explained in the introduction of his unrealized work. It ranks the Hagia Sophia mosque at the head of religious monuments, followed by the royal mosque complexes of Mehmed II, Bayezid II, Selim I, Şehzade Mehmed, and Süleyman I. Shorter accounts of other mosques, masjids, and dervish convents in the walled city were to be supplemented by descriptions of landmarks in the three townships (Eyüp, Galata, Üsküdar) and their suburban extensions. This catalogue of the capital's monuments, in turn, was to be accompanied by an inventory of each province ranked hierarchically.[224]

The hierarchy of Istanbul's Friday mosques becomes also apparent in the late-sixteenth and mid-seventeenth-century travelogues of Mehmed Aşık and Evliya Çelebi, where detailed descriptions of royal mosque complexes are followed by laconic references to a selected sample of non-royal ones. Evliya's account of Istanbul starts with a description of sultanic mosques headed by Hagia Sophia and moves on to mosques built by members of the royal family, followed by those of viziers and grandees. The primacy of Hagia Sophia in this hierarchy is captured by Evliya's description of the Great Mosque (Ulu Cami) of Bursa, the largest congregational mosque in that city: 'It is as if it were the Ayasofya of the city of Bursa.'[225] Evliya first describes monuments within the walled city of Istanbul, subsequently turning to its townships and suburbs. Thereafter his multi-volume travelogue, whose first volume covers Istanbul, moves on to descriptions of provincial cities that catalogue their famous mosques and landmarks.

Sinan's autobiographies follow the same organization principle in their lists of monuments, which are grouped by function. The *Tuḥfetü'l-miʿmārīn*'s list of mosques (an incomplete draft, full of revisions) is roughly ordered according to the status of their patrons.[226] It begins with mosques commissioned by the sultans and the royal family in a mixed order, also including the mosque of the vassal Khan of Crimea. The list then moves on to the mosques of the highest ranking grandees (grand viziers and viziers) grouped under the heading: 'Addendum of the buildings of Friday mosques by viziers and grandees.'[227] These are followed by the mosques of other officials: 'Addendum of mosques by grandees.'[228]

These section headings disappear in the *Teẕkiretü'l-ebniye*, where mosques are no longer ordered according to the status of their patrons, but in terms of their geographical location. Those mentioned first are mosques sited within the walled city of Istanbul, followed by mosques in the townships of Eyüp, Galata (including its suburbs of Sütlüce, Kasımpaşa, Tophane, Beşiktaş, Ortaköy), and Üsküdar up to Kanlıca along the Bosphorus (Map 2). Then come provincial mosques in Anatolia and in the Arab lands. Mosques in the Rumelian provinces, starting with the secondary capital Edirne and moving further west, complete the lists (Map 1). Only a few exceptions deviate from this otherwise consistent ordering principle.

The conceptual structure of lists of mosques in Sinan's autobiographies confirms his acute awareness of two overlapping systems of hierarchy, social and territorial, that shaped his graduated mosque typology. The intersection of these two axes of hierarchy defined a consensual field of 'appropriateness' within which the patron and chief architect negotiated decorous mosque programmes. The same ordering principle structured Hüseyin Ayvansarayi's late-eighteenth-century monumental catalogue of Istanbul's mosques: it begins with a description of Hagia Sophia and other imperial foundations, followed by monuments inside the walled city and then its outlying areas.[229]

The concept of decorum in Sinan's mosque typology relied on the restriction of status signs: monumental domes, multiple minarets with several galleries, marble forecourts surrounded by domical arcades, and porticoed façades with differing numbers of domes (three, five, seven, or nine) resting on single or double rows of marble columns. Such factors as siting, the use of precious materials (lead, stone, marble revetments, columns, and İznik tiles), and the elaborateness of ornament also conformed to notions of appropriateness. While provincial mosques retained relatively generic plans (with a few royal exceptions sited in Edirne and Manisa), an intricately stratified hierarchy of mosque types made its appearance in Istanbul.

A trademark of prestige mosques in the capital was their inclusion of domed baldachins resting on four, six, or eight supports. Domes on four supports, abutted by two, three, or four half-domes – or used independently without half-domes – were primarily reserved for royal patrons (illus. 3).[230] Sinan used hexagonal and octagonal domed baldachins surrounded by exedral half-domes for some royal patrons, grand viziers, and viziers (illus. 4, 5). The innovative plans of these mosques stood out from the simpler plans of mosques he designed for the middle to lower echelons of the ruling elite, using either domed or domeless cubical structures.

Sinan's varied treatment of mosque façades was another means of encoding hierarchies of status. The only mosques honoured with marble-paved forecourts surrounded by domical arcades – an imperial prerogative introduced with the Üç Şerefeli mosque in Edirne – are the Şehzade Mehmed, Süleymaniye, and Selimiye. Miniature versions of the arcaded forecourt had been used in some non-sultanic provincial mosques before Sinan became chief architect.[231] The stricter codes of decorum observed in his mosques reserved arcaded forecourts paved with marble exclusively for the sultanic level of patronage. To enhance their prestige, he embellished the façades of some mosques with lavish porticoes featuring two rows of columns. Simpler façades with a single row of columns were complemented by more modest ones without domical porticoes. Generally fronted by wooden pillars protected by overhanging eaves, these were mosques with hipped roofs. In some prestige mosques, Sinan subtly mimicked the fountained forecourts of sultanic prototypes by means of U-shaped madrasas. The forecourts of sultanic mosques were more blatantly paraphrased in several late mosques dating from the 1580s, whose courtyards do not resort to the subterfuge of the U-shaped madrasa: mosques of the queen mother Nurbanu Sultan in Üsküdar, and of the viziers Nişancı Mehmed Pasha and Mesih Mehmed Pasha in Yenibahçe. These monuments signalled the erosion of classical codes of decorum towards the end of Sinan's career.

The chief architect's graduated mosque typology can roughly be correlated with Āli's tripartite classification of the Ottoman ruling elite, excluding the fourth group of tax-paying subjects. The 'highest' level corresponds to mosques sponsored by sultans, crown princes, and royal women. Then come the ranks of non-royal mosques: the 'high' level built for pre-eminent grandees (grand viziers, viziers, grand admirals, governor-generals), followed by the 'medium' to 'low' level for the middling ranks. In the absence of written codes with clear-cut rules, notions of decorum paralleled the three-tiered ranking system encountered in various spheres of Ottoman visual culture. Such a system of classification was common, for instance, in the hierarchy of textiles and standardized timbers used in construction, grouped as first grade (*aʿlā*, superior), second grade (*evsāṭ*, medium), and third grade (*ednā*, ordinary or low).[232] Robes of honour donated by the sultans were similarly ranked: according to Prince Cantemir, the first quality, reserved for the highest ranked ambassadors and pashas, was the 'sumptuous royal robe' (*ḫilʿat-ı fāḫire*); the second quality, or 'superior' (*aʿlā*) robe, was destined for other pashas and ambassadors; and the third quality, appropriate for lower ranks was the 'medium' (*evsāṭ*) or 'ordinary' (*ednā*) robe.[233] The wages of royal architects were also classified in three grades corresponding to relative skill: high, medium, and ordinary or low.[234]

These examples signal a ubiquitous habit of ranking, also observed in architectural culture. An imperial decree Selim II sent in 1568 to the kadi of Bursa and the superintendent of the royal purse orders them to oversee the construction of a mausoleum with a medium-sized dome for his half-brother prince Mustafa, who had been executed in 1553. The dome of that mausoleum – intended for a rival prince from a different mother who had been denied burial at the imperial capital – was to be 'neither excessively large nor small, but scaled in accordance with moderation.'[235] In like fashion, an order addressed to the kadi of Rhodes in 1559 orders him to have an estimate prepared for a compact masjid built on the shore where it was needed, 'in accordance with limited scale'.[236]

The selection of large, medium, or small domes for a mosque depended on the status of its patron and its location (Appendix 1). Dome size was not a major consideration in Sinan's relatively standardized provincial mosques. His sultanic mosques in the capital cities of Istanbul and Edirne are distinguished by the largest domes, surpassing others in diameter and height. A collection of imperial decrees (1549–53) related to the construction of the Süleymaniye complex includes a note comparing Istanbul's sultanic mosques in terms of their dome diameters and the dimensions of their rectangular ground plans. These comparative dimensions, in cubits, testify to the importance of size:[237]

The mosque of Sultan Mehmed [II] Khan:
Length 126, *width* 75, *dome* 32.
The mosque of Sultan Bayezid [II] Khan:
Length 122, *width* 56, *dome* 22.
The mosque of Sultan Selim [I] Khan:
Length 85, *width* 39, *dome* 33.
The mosque of the late Şehzade Sultan Mehmed Khan, may he rest in peace:
Length 112, *width* 63, *dome* 25.
The new sultanic mosque [Süleymaniye]:
Length 136, *width* 86, *dome* 36.

Istanbul's previous sultanic mosques, then, were taken as points of departure in establishing appropriate dimensions for the Şehzade Mehmed and Süleymaniye mosques. The Şehzade mosque, built for a deceased crown prince, slightly exceeds in its measurements those of Bayezid II and Selim I (whose dome is larger), but it does not dare to outrank the mosque of Mehmed II. That honour is decorously reserved for the mosque of the sultan himself: the Süleymaniye, designed to surpass the largest sultanic mosque complex in the capital. The omission from this comparative list of Hagia Sophia, privileged as the capital's premier sultanic mosque, shows that competing with its dimensions was not yet a consideration in the design of the two royal mosques Süleyman commissioned from Sinan. But according to the *Teẕkiretü'l-bünyān*, 'infidel architects' who boasted that such a large dome had not been built by the Muslims, challenged the chief architect to build the dome of the Selimiye mosque bigger than that of Hagia Sophia.[238] With its 31.22 metre dome roughly equalling the uneven diameter of Hagia Sophia's elliptical dome (30.9 metres to 31.8 metres), the Selimiye mosque became the proud possessor of the largest dome in the Islamic world after the Süleymaniye (26.5 metres).

Although there were no written codes regulating the dome sizes of Sinan's mosques, comparing their diameters discloses certain patterns (Appendix 1). The largest diameters over 20 metres (26.5 and 31.22 metres) were reserved for the leading sultanic mosques of Istanbul and Edirne; the domes of provincial mosques built for sultans in Damascus and Manisa were considerably smaller (10 and 11 metres respectively). Next came the prestige mosques of some royal patrons in Istanbul, distinguished by domes with diameters exceeding 15 metres: Şehzade Mehmed (19 metres) and Mihrümah at Edirnekapı (20.25 metres). Medium to small domes ranging between 10 and 15 metres were used in mosques built for the royal family, grand viziers, viziers, and governor-generals inside or outside Istanbul. The mosques of governor-generals in the provinces were roughly comparable in scale to those of viziers and grand viziers in the capital, from which they differed with their simpler plans based on the domed cube.

Grand admirals who commanded the imperial fleet stood out as a distinctive new group of patrons; their unusual mosques were sited outside the walls of Galata. Stéphane Yerasimos has convincingly argued that these atypical mosques with relatively small dome diameters (ranging from 8.90 to 12.70 metres) share a common characteristic: they all adopt 'archaic solutions'. He writes: 'Unable to increase the size of the dome because of institutional constraints, they were obliged to adopt old models.'[239] Mosques with small domes (ranging between 8.20 and 11.80 metres) or mosques with hipped roofs characterized the relatively modest foundations of imperial council bureaucrats, aghas of the royal palace, stewards of grand viziers, the grand mufti, and tradesmen. There was no clear-cut boundary between these small mosques and neighbourhood masjids; the latter were often converted into Friday mosques simply by the addition of a minbar.

In the sixteenth-century Ottoman context, the use of more than one minaret, or of a minaret with multiple galleries, had become a prerogative restricted to royal mosques, whether sultanic or built for patrons with royal blood. Transgressing the unwritten minaret code was a serious offense: Evliya Çelebi explains that the founder of the Double Galleried mosque (*İki Şerefeli Cami*) in Thessaloniki, a certain Gariki Efendi, 'was executed because he had its minaret built with two galleries'.[240] Imperial decrees dispatched to provincial cities about the construction of new Friday mosques or the conversion of cathedral churches into mosques are careful to specify the number of minarets permitted. For example, in 1577 the governor-general of Buda, Sokollu Mustafa Pasha, was authorized to add two minarets to the local cathedral, which Sultan Süleyman had converted into a mosque:

> You have sent a letter to my court reporting that the people of Buda have come to you, requesting the repair of the Great Mosque of the late Sultan Süleyman in that city, the superstructure of which had previously been covered by brick according to an imperial order. You propose that it would be decorous (*münāsib*) to build two new minarets in that mosque, which is comparable to Ayasofya but has an infidel's bell tower functioning as a minaret.

The governor-general's proposal, triggered by the request of the mosque's congregation, justifies the replacement of the belfry with a pair of minarets as a matter of decorum. He is ordered to add two single-galleried minarets and replace the mosque's roof tiles with lead.[241]

Following the conquest of Cyprus, its governor-general and finance officer had inquired in 1572 about the number of minarets they should build in two recently converted Gothic churches, the 'small Ayasofya' in Famagusta and the 'large Ayasofya' in Nicosia.[242] Taking into account the relative status of each sultanic mosque, the imperial decree of Selim II, for whom the Hagia Sophia in Istanbul was remodelled around the same time, responds:

> You have reported that the Friday mosques in the castles of Famagusta and Nicosia do not have minarets and ask how many should be built; I order two minarets be constructed in the noble Friday mosque of Nicosia, and only one in the mosque of Famagusta: build those minarets once the repair of those castles is completed.[243]

With four multi-galleried minarets each, the imperial mosques built by Sinan in Istanbul and Edirne stood out from their provincial counterparts, which featured only one or two minarets with single galleries. As we have seen, Sinan also articulated the sultanic status of the Hagia Sophia mosque in Istanbul by increasing its minarets from two to four, thereby accentuating its iconographic link with his two masterpieces. The only mosques in the Ottoman domains featuring more than four minarets were the Prophet's mosque in Medina, with five, and the Haram al-Sharif in Mecca, honoured with six (and a seventh marking Sultan Süleyman's adjoining madrasa).

Among mosques built by Sinan, the use of two minarets with single galleries was restricted to the vassal Khan of Crimea and to a few patrons of royal blood (the crown prince Selim in Karapınar, Mihrümah Sultan, and Nurbanu Sultan in Üsküdar). The only non-sultanic mosque boasting twin minarets with double galleries is that of Şehzade Mehmed, built in the manner of a sultanic mosque. The small number of mosques featuring two minarets reflects the restraint exercised by sultans in granting this privilege to the members of the royal family. Even the powerful legal wife of Süleyman, Haseki Hürrem Sultan (d. 1558), was allotted only one single-galleried minaret in the mosque complex Sinan built for her at Avratpazarı in Istanbul. The queen's posthumously constructed mosque at the head of the bridge of Çoban Mustafa Pasha near Edirne (now Svilengrad in Bulgaria), was built according to its initially dispatched plan, with an important change in detail specified by an imperial decree addressed to the kadi of Edirne in 1559: 'but in that plan (*resim*) two minarets have been indicated, reduce them to one.'[244] Had Hürrem lived to see her son reign, she would certainly have been eligible to use two minarets, but her status as Süleyman's wife was considerably lower than that of a queen mother, distinguished by royal blood. Hürrem's successor Nurbanu, who outlived her husband, Selim II, and completed her mosque in Üsküdar during her son's reign, did use a pair of single-galleried minarets. It was Nurbanu's blood tie to her reigning son, Murad III, that provided her with a retroactive dynastic lineage.

Comparing the relative costs of mosque complexes dating from Sinan's time sheds light on the economic dimension of decorum. The costs of only a small number of mosque complexes attributed to the chief architect can be tabulated, given the scarcity of documentation, but these examples enable us to correlate buildings with budgets (Appendix 2). Chapter 5 shows that estimates of various design options with differing price tags were often presented to patrons before the selection of a decorous plan. This custom not only confirms the active role patrons played in the negotiation of decorum, but also draws attention to the importance of financial considerations.

The cost of the Süleymaniye complex (54,096,000 aspers), about three and a half times as much as that of Şehzade Mehmed (15,000,000 aspers), is in keeping with the relative status of father and son. The somewhat low budget of Selim I's earlier mosque complex (12,000,000 aspers), built by Sinan's predecessor, reflects the relatively modest programme Süleyman chose for his deceased father, who had not conquered any lands in Christendom. Another posthumous complex commissioned by Süleyman in memory of his youngest son, Şehzade Cihangir, is far cheaper (733,851 aspers) than that of his brother Şehzade Mehmed. The hunchbacked Cihangir's single-minareted mosque with a hipped roof, situated on a hilltop in Tophane, a suburb of Galata, was so humble because of his inconsequential status as a minor prince. Living with his parents as an unviable successor to the throne, he had not even been sent away to a sanjak while his brother governed Manisa as heir apparent.[245]

The disparity between the costs of the Süleymaniye and Selimiye (at about 21,930,000 aspers, less than half the price of the Süleymaniye) initially comes as a surprise. What seems to have contributed to the costliness of the former complex was its large number of marble columns, transported from distant places, and its numerous dependencies (illus. 167–68). Because the Selimiye's dome rests on eight colossal piers, no monumental columns like those of Süleymaniye, 'equal in value to the treasury of Egypt', were required to support it (illus. 209-10). Only two madrasas and an elementary school were built as dependencies of the Selimiye mosque, whereas the Süleymaniye features an elementary school and has four extra madrasas (a total of six), a school for Koran recitation (*darülkura*), a hospital, a guest-house (*tabhane*), a hospice (*imaret*), a caravansaray, and Hürrem Sultan's mausoleum (not counting the posthumously built mausoleum of Süleyman himself). While it took over a decade to build the Süleymaniye complex (1548–59), the Selimiye was finished in less than six years (1568–74). Consequently, wages paid to the labour force were considerably reduced.[246]

Barkan has published a resumé of expenses, covering about forty-nine percent of the total cost incurred for the Süleymaniye between 1553 and 1559.[247] This amounted to 26,251,938 aspers, largely paid by the sultan's personal treasury (25,802,000 aspers), from which lump sums were taken out at regular intervals as a personal charity.[248] An unpublished document which records sums paid from Selim II's private treasury for the construction of the Selimiye complex confirms that it, too, was primarily financed with the sultan's personal funds (the annual income of the sultan amounted to 31,466,314 aspers according to a budget compiled in 1567–68).[249] The periodic payment of money from the Topkapı Palace's 'inner private treasury' (*iç ḫazīne*) to the 'outer public treasury' (*taşra hazīne*), or to the building supervisor in Edirne, started on 13 April 1568 and ended with the last payment made on 2 November 1574 – approximately a month before Selim II's death.[250] The mosque complex was inaugurated that year, before the completion of its outer courtyard and commercial dependencies, which were largely financed from the surplus income generated by its endowment.[251] Additional expenses may have raised the costs of the Selimiye to about 25,000,000 aspers. This amount is far less than the sum paid for the Süleymaniye complex, whose mosque alone cost 30,000,000 aspers. Yet the Selimiye was unmatched in its aesthetic value, eulogized not only in the *Teẕkiretül'l-bünyān* but also in contemporary texts and in Selim II's posthumous endowment deed discussed in Chapter 6.

The expense of Sinan's engineering feats explains why they are praised as much as imperial mosques in his *Teẕkires*. At about 12,000,000 aspers, the Büyükçekmece bridge was roughly equal in value to Selim I's mosque. The Kırkçeşme water system in the capital, which cost over 50,000,000 aspers, rivalled the Süleymaniye complex in value (Appendix 2). Comparing the costs of non-royal mosque complexes is equally revealing. For instance, the relatively modest cost of the governor Ali Pasha's posthumous mosque in Sarajevo, built by a royal architect, befits its medium-sized, generic plan composed of a domed cube with a three-bay portico. This mosque of rough-cut stone masonry was financed with an initial sum of 366,297 aspers, increased to 432,997 aspers after being loaned out at interest.[252] The money spent in the mid-1550s on the grand admiral Sinan Pasha's posthumous mosque complex in Beşiktaş (3,273,800 aspers) was less than half the amount expended on the joint complex in Eyüp of the princess Shahsultan and the vizier Zal Mahmud Pasha (7,828,382 aspers), erected after their death between 1577 and 1590. This proportion is in keeping with the ranks of the patrons and the rising costs of construction following the inflation of the mid-1580s. These two mosque complexes designed by Sinan were built with alternating courses of stone and brick; hence, their costs must have been exceeded by mosques constructed with more expensive ashlar masonry for prominent patrons in the capital.

The surge in mosque construction during the age of Sinan can be correlated with the rising income of royal women and grandees under Sultan Süleyman, who additionally showered his favourites with land donations to encourage the creation of waqfs. The assignment of 1,200,000 aspers to grand viziers by Mehmed II's law code continued to be in effect until the early part of Süleyman's reign, when that sultan awarded İbrahim Pasha a fief worth 1,800,000 aspers. By the second half of the sixteenth century, the fiefs of grand viziers had doubled in value (the value of the asper did not change much in the meantime). An account book from 1560–61 shows that Semiz Ali Pasha's yearly income consisted of 3,529,139 aspers, of which 2,577,918 came from the revenues of his fief, 73,021 from his farms, 324,991 from miscellaneous income, and 169,320 from loaning out money at an interest.[253]

According to Gerlach, when the pasha passed away in 1565, he had left behind an inheritance of eight million gold coins (about 480,000,000 aspers). He reports that the next grand vizier, Sokollu Mehmed Pasha, was considerably richer than his predecessor.[254] His yearly income of 4,000,000 aspers from the sultan was far exceeded by annual gifts amounting to a million ducats (60,000,000 aspers). The historian Peçevi, whose source was Sokollu's steward and treasurer, confirms Gerlach's report that the grand vizier's annual income from his fief was at least 4,000,000 aspers, but the gifts he received were worth many times more.[255] Gerlach and Peçevi also concur that the pasha largely financed his architectural monuments with income from gifts, employing his own galley slaves as labourers.[256] Gerlach observes that the viziers had a lower annual income of about 20,000 ducats (1,200,000 aspers) from their fiefs, a sum doubled by gifts and other sources of income.[257]

Given the high cost of prestige mosques relative to masjids and dervish convents (Appendix 2), it is not surprising that their patrons belonged to the upper echelons of the ruling elite whose income level was high enough to permit such extravagant generosity. Nevertheless, the upper-limit rules of decorum constrained unusually rich patrons like Rüstem Pasha and Sokollu, who certainly could afford to build monumental mosques approaching those of the sultans, to cautiously spread their resources to multiple medium-sized projects. Likewise, Rüstem Pasha's widow, Mihrümah Sultan, who is said to have been even richer than her reigning brother, Selim II, was circumspect in the design of her mosque complex at Edirnekapı, using her remaining funds to finance a costly water channel in Mecca around the same time. The upper limit of decorum, then, was correlated not with what patrons could afford, but with what they were allowed to build.

The tiered ranks of Sinan's mosque typology represented the individuality of patrons under their corporate group identity. This premodern concept of identity, which amalgamated the group and the individual, also characterized Ottoman costume albums, a pictorial genre that emerged in the late sixteenth century. In these albums individuals are classified in terms of their social rank and occupation, with each profession and social group metonymically represented as an unindividualized type, identified by distinctive costume and headgear. Late-sixteenth-century miniature-painted portraits of the Ottoman sultans represent them as more individualized types. Despite their physiognomic realism, however, these portraits also depict the sultans' attributes of royal status. As such, they occupy an ambiguous space at the interstices of individualized and generic portraiture, collapsing each sultan's persona with the office of the sultanate.[258]

Ottoman texts from the sixteenth century abound in comparable verbal classifications of social rank, primarily defining individuals in terms of their public office. The preoccupation with social typecasting informed the typology of Sinan's mosques, which can be interpreted as architectural portraits representing patrons as relatively generic or individualized types. The degree of individualization increased the higher up a patron was on the social ladder, particularly in prestige mosques sited in the capital. The contextual meanings of Sinan's mosques revolved around their similarity to and difference from the type to which they belonged, a flexible framework allowing infinite formal variation and transformation.

Aldo Rossi has likened the architectural type, a repository of collective memory enabling legibility, to the concept of deep structure in language.[259] Recent interest in architectural theory with the concept of the type has been attributed to the postmodern search for meaning: whereas the modernist movement rejected imitation in favour of innovation, typology is now seen in a more favourable light as an instrument of cultural memory and a condition of architectural meaning coded with multiple layers of signification. Governed by certain inherent structural and functional similarities, the type ostensibly rules out individuality. However, the typological design process – a method of creative transformation – can be seen as a way of bringing the elements of a type into the precise state that characterizes the single work.

Sinan's mosques simultaneously constitute typological series and single works charged with specific contextual meanings which have largely been erased over time. These mosques established a hegemonic regime of legibility, a convincing semblance of consensus with regard to decorum. Yet the negotiation of decorum, a fragile social contract, was not immune to resistance, contestation, and a process of change that resisted homogenization. Inspection committees made up of royal architects, building supervisors, waqf administrators, kadis, muftis, and prominent members of the community played a significant role in the calibration of decorum in cases of dispute. The building history of the Muradiye mosque in Manisa (discussed in Chapter 6), which replaced a smaller princely mosque Murad III had built while he was governing that city, demonstrates how community members could intervene in the selection of appropriate designs. The mosque's present form is the end product of a complex bargaining process that involved the royal patron, the chief architect Sinan, the sultan's waqf administrator, the kadi and governor of Manisa, and the users of the original princely mosque.

The intervention of external parties was not uncommon, particularly in the refurbishment of endowed monuments involving the legal rights of the Muslim community. Renovation projects undertaken in the holy sanctuaries of Mecca and Medina required especially delicate negotiations with local authorities to reach consensus about architectural decorum. As vassals of the Ottoman sultans who enjoyed a degree of autonomy, the Sharifs of Mecca did not readily approve the construction projects of their suzerains. Given the absence of a governor-general in the Hijaz, the sanjak governors of Jidda and the governor-generals of Egypt represented the Ottoman state *vis à vis* the Sharifs as the supervisors of royal building projects in Mecca and Medina.[260] The importance of obtaining public approval is captured in an imperial decree sent in 1577 to the kadi of Mecca, who was instructed to have the floors under the newly completed domical arcades of the Haram (a project overseen from a distance by Sinan) paved in an appropriate manner after holding a 'consultation' (*istişāre*) with local notables.[261] When Sinan was sent by Murad III to Mecca in 1584 to prepare an estimate for renovating the leaning walls of the Kaʿba, his proposal to the sultan was rejected because the ulema judged the repairs to be unlawful.[262]

Murad III's subsequent addition of domical arcades to the Haram in Medina was another project that faced opposition. The royal architect İlyas, appointed by Sinan's successor, Davud, to execute that project in 1589, was sent from Istanbul to Medina with a team of builders. His two letters to the sultan and the chief architect complain about delays in construction caused by public resistance, confirming the necessity of negotiating communal consensus.[263] His longer letter to the sultan requests that the present building supervisor – a retired finance minister sent from the capital – be replaced with someone more experienced in architectural matters and negotiating skills:

> And if the building affairs are inquired about, most people of Medina do not want the building to be rebuilt; they say it should just be repaired. However, repairing it is not possible. More than half of its north side has become dilapidated; if it is repaired it will inevitably collapse within a few years. How can it be appropriate to delay [the rebuilding project] if it is bound to collapse in our sultan's felicitous reign? We say, let us rebuild it before it collapses. Nobody listens. Meanwhile, our carefree building supervisor has no expertise in matters of construction. Old age has won him over. Most of the time his bodily constitution is unhealthy. He is incapable of initiating the construction simply by asserting: 'I have come to renovate the building with the sultan's decree, and rebuilding it is necessary, and in accordance with the firman I will rebuild those parts that need to be rebuilt and repair those parts that need to be repaired!' We say the following: 'They sent us here to build three hundred domes, and this is needed.' But having heard more moderate words from our supervisor, nobody listens to us. In short, more than half of the building, perhaps two-thirds of it, needs to be demolished and rebuilt, but they oppose its rebuilding. Only some persons agree that it needs to be rebuilt, but our supervisor does not flatter them ... Moreover, he is not informed about the laws of construction and of the masters (*bināya ve ustalar ḳānūnına vuḳūfı yoḳ*) ... And Mustafa Efendi, the ex-finance minister of Buda, who then became Shaykh al-Haram of Mecca, in addition to having supervised many buildings, is an expert in the science of construction (*binā ʿilminden vuḳūfı var*). Since he is in every regard a diligent and eager person, who in addition is said to be well-known to our sultan, please favour us by appointing him as our supervisor. The noble building cannot reach completion without freedom from disgrace in the absence of a person like him, or someone like him who is an expert in construction. Let this be known to your majesty, to whom we have humbly petitioned the response needed by this servant of yours, so that later on we can preempt the question: 'Why did you not make this known?' The remaining order and firman is yours, my felicitious sultan. Your lowly servant İlyas, the architect of the construction in Medina the Illuminated.

Mimar İlyas's letters reveal the importance of competent building supervisors with architectural, financial, and diplomatic expertise. They also exemplify the type of long-distance communication between architects and the court. The comparable written correspondence between Sinan and Selim II during the building process of the Selimiye in Edirne demonstrates how issues of decorum raised in the course of construction were resolved through periodic progress reports. Building projects in the capital gave patrons the option of visits to construction sites, where they could personally communicate with Sinan; the chief architect's autobiographies proudly record several encounters and 'consultations' (*meşveret*) with his royal patron Süleyman.[264]

Decorum in religious architecture was negotiated through the mediation of government officers within the institutional mechanisms of the centralized corps of royal architects. The next two chapters elucidate the institutionalized practices of the corps of architects and Sinan's role in that corps, reorganized under his leadership as a centralized department of the state, in which he operated both as an individual and as the head of a government office in the codification of decorum.

PART II

THE CHIEF ARCHITECT AS AN INDIVIDUAL AND INSTITUTION

Chapter 4

PORTRAIT OF THE DIVINE MAESTRO

I. SİNAN'S FORMATIVE YEARS IN HIS AUTOBIOGRAPHIES
II. SİNAN'S SELF-IMAGE AND THE BIOGRAPHIES OF ITALIAN ARTISTS
III. SİNAN'S PERSONA IN HIS ENDOWMENT DEED

I. SİNAN'S FORMATIVE YEARS IN HIS AUTOBIOGRAPHIES

In the last years of his life, Sinan decided to dictate autobiographical notes to Mustafa Sai, a visually sensitive poet-painter who also composed the epitaph of the chief architect's tomb adjoining the Süleymaniye complex. Embellished with Sai's literary interpolations, the autobiographies have come down to us in five versions. Three of them are drafts preserved in the Topkapı Palace archives: a text without a title (the so-called *Adsız Risāle* or Untitled Treatise), the *Risāletü'l-miʿmāriyye* (Treatise on Architecture), and the *Tuḥfetü'l-miʿmārīn* (Gift of the Architects). Unlike these sketchy drafts that never reached the public eye, two edited versions of Sinan's autobiography circulated widely in many copies: a longer edition titled *Teẕkiretü'l-bünyān* (Biographical Memoir of Construction) and an abridged variant *Teẕkiretü'l-ebniye* (Biographical Memoir of Buildings).[1]

With their sketchy format, full of crossed lines and insertions that testify to an extensive editing process, the *Tuḥfe* and its two preliminary drafts represent an early stage in the collaboration between Sinan and Sai.[2] It is difficult to imagine that these drafts could have been composed after the *Teẕkires*, which are highly polished texts combining prose and verse. The first two drafts culminated in the longer *Tuḥfe* and all three belonged to Sinan's personal papers. They are bound together with documents related to him, an account book of the 'waqf of Sinan Agha' dated 1540, and the construction expenses of a bath-house built in 1565 for İskender Pasha at Kanlıca along the Bosphorus.[3] The latter is stamped with the only known imprint of Sinan's seal as it was created 'by the expertise of (*be-maʿrifet-i*) the leader of the illustrious and the generous, Sinan Agha, the chief of royal architects (*ser-miʿmārān-ı ḫāṣṣa*)' (illus. 111).[4] The signature above the seal reads: 'the humble Sinan, the chief of royal architects.'[5] The central part of the almond-shaped seal is incribed, 'the humble and lowly Sinan'. Its border reads, 'the poor, meek, pitiful servant, the humble chief of royal architects'.[6] Such expressions of humility are repeatedly used in Sinan's autobiographies to counterbalance his hubris.

111 Sinan's seal, 1565.

The autobiographies reflect Sinan's desire to leave a personal mark on history and collective memory through self-fashioning. The preface of the *Teẕkiretü'l-bünyān*, dedicated to Murad III, the crown prince Mehmed, and the grand vizier Siyavuş Pasha (g.v. 1582–84, 1586–89, 1592–93), explains why the aged chief architect commissioned this work from Sai who presented it to him as a gift while he was still alive:

> The reason for writing this beautiful book, which resembles a perfumed veil adorning the beloved's face, is that one day our felicitous sultan's chief architect Sinan, the son of Abdülmennan, having become a frail old man, desired to have me record his conversations in prose and verse in order to leave his fame and reputation on the pages of Time so that he may be remembered with well-wishing prayers. And I, Sai, God's broken-hearted, meek, impoverished and humble servant realized his wish by writing down this work to the best of my ability as a pitiful gift with which I entered

into his happiness-causing presence. I named it *Tez̲kiretü'l-bünyān* and humbly beg friends who read this epic to veil my shortcomings as much as possible with forgiveness, and not to turn this humble servant into a target of criticism with the saying 'The higher you reach, the harder you fall!'[7]

The *Tez̲kiretü'l-ebniye*'s preface likewise refers to Sinan as still alive. It touchingly announces the grand master's continuing artistic creativity under Murad III, despite the decrepitude of old age that filled him with maudlin thoughts of mortality:

In his reign countless buildings have I made,
Scores of mosques and palaces.

Thanks be to God that this servant realized his art
In the service of [building] many a House of God.

This apprentice of Habib-i Pir-i Neccar [patron saint of carpenters]
Your servant Mimar Yusuf b. Abdullah,

Becoming the saint (*pīr*) of this dervish convent [the world]
Lived through the reigns of four sultans.

After having seen the world with the eyes of wisdom,
Its impermanence I fully understood.

To the body of many a building have I laid foundations,
Yet Adam's body is mortal and unlasting.

The palace of my body nearly turned into ruin,
Causing me much suffering under its fetter.

My beard turned white from the signs of age
And my skin shivered from the fear of God.

Do not think my bent back is an arch,
For it is a bridge that leads to sadness and grief.

In order to travel on the road to the next world,
Have I bent my head [in obedience] to the vaulted palace of heaven.

Thanks be to God that I am still an upright man,
When it comes to my art in which completely upright and solid I remain.

It is my wish from the possessors of skill (*ehl-i hüner*)
That after reading these verses,

They pray to the pillar of religion,
That supports the palace of this world.

And remember me with their well-wishing prayers,
So as to give joy to my dejected heart.[8]

The absence of such phrases as 'the late' or 'may God grant him mercy' with regard to Sinan, in the five undated autobiographical texts implies that he was alive at the time they were written. The *Tez̲kiretü'l-bünyān* and its shorter version seem to have been completed during the second grand vizierate of Siyavuş Pasha (1586–89) since they list mosques built around that time.[9] The three unicum drafts were probably composed shortly before the two *Tez̲kire*s, sometime in the mid 1580s.[10] Each of the autobiographies includes a brief biographical section outlining Sinan's recruitment, his initial training, and his early career in the army. They subsequently discuss his achievements as chief architect and group the monuments built under his tenure according to various building types (Appendix 3). Before turning to Sinan's career as chief architect, I will focus here on his formative years.

Sinan's autobiographies, which narrate his extraordinary accomplishments from an assertive, first-person point of view, testify to his acute sense of individualism. The growing esteem for architecture in Ottoman court culture nourished a new self-consciousness and 'that proud sense of individuality that we associate with the Renaissance idea of the artist.'[11] Yet Sinan's self-description is largely confined to a laconic overview of his career and discloses relatively little about his personality. His life is summed up as a sequence of promotions from one office to the next, until he finally accepts the lifelong post of chief architect: 'In sum, becoming progressively promoted to higher ranks / I held many official posts'.[12] He appears to have fully internalized the hierarchy-conscious mentality of the sultan's *kul*s, but his public identity as a member of the Ottoman ruling elite did not erase ties to his place of origin and family. The shortest version of Sinan's biography, repeated with minor variations in each text, is in the 'Untitled Treatise':

This sinful and humble servant, being an Abdullah's son [a patronymic used for converts], came [to Istanbul] as a *devşirme*, became a janissary, went on the campaigns of Rhodes [1522] and Belgrade [1521] as a janissary, and then as an *atlusekbān* [mounted keeper of hounds] attended the Mohacz [1526] campaign, and then became an *ʿacemīoġlānlar yayabaşısı* [commander of a unit of novice boys], and after a long while became a *ḳapu yayabaşısı* [or *yeniçeri yayabaşısı*, commander of a unit of janissaries], and after some time became a *zenberekçibaşı* [commander of the janissary regiment in charge of catapults], and went on the German campaign [1532] and after that to the Baghdad campaign [1534–37]. Subsequently becoming a *ḫāṣeki* [member of the sultan's elite guard], he participated in the campaigns of Corfu and Puglia [1537], and upon returning from the Moldavia campaign [1538] he was appointed to the post of chief architect (*miʿmārbaşılıḳ*). From the above mentioned date to this day he has remained in the service of [chief] architect (*miʿmārlıḳ*).[13]

This mini-biography, which reads more like a promotion list, reflects a premodern concept of the individual as the sum total of his public posts. The same information is repeated in the *Risāle* and *Tuḥfe*, which provide additional details identifying the chief architect's name and place of origin:

> This lowly servant Sinan b. Abdülmennan [another patronymic used for converts], known as the humble chief architect (*miʿmārbaşı*), being in truth an Abdullah's son, came to the Imperial Porte in past times according to the illustrious Ottoman laws and customs together with the *devşirme* boys of the province of Karaman and the land of 'Ionia' (*bilād-ı yunān*).[14]

The *Tezkiretü'l-bünyān*, which is the most lengthy autobiographical text, specifies: 'This humble servant was a *devşirme* of sultan Selim [I] Khan's rose-garden-like sultanate; since the conscription of boys from the sanjak of Kayseri [in the province of Karaman] had been initiated at that time, I was among the first youths to be conscripted from there.'[15]

A seventeenth-century treatise entitled 'Customs of Janissaries' confirms that it was Selim I who introduced the practice of recruiting novice boys from Karaman and Trebizond in Anatolia to counterbalance the insolent power of those from Rumelia.[16] Even though the Anatolian recruits initially behaved well, eventually 'seditious boys of Turkish origin' came to infiltrate their ranks, causing Mehmed III (r. 1595–1603) to discontinue this practice. In a passage I quoted in Chapter 1, the author of the 'Customs' categorically asserts that Turks and Turkish-speaking Christians (a group particularly widespread in Karaman) should at all cost be excluded from the levy of conscripted boys. A saying attributed to Sultan Süleyman also excludes Turks as a group from the *devşirme*: 'God forbid taking the children of Ukranian, Iranian, Gypsy, and Turkish subjects, or the children of Harputians, Diyarbakırians, and Malatians!'[17] According to the Koçi Beg, in the classical age the *devşirme* levy was applied only to Albanians, Bosnians, Greeks, Bulgarians and Armenians.[18]

The evidence of Sinan's autobiographies about his *devşirme* origin from Kayseri has been questioned on the basis of an endowment deed dated 1563. This is not the chief architect's waqfiyya, however, but rather that of his namesake, who served as the second building superviser of the Süleymaniye mosque.[19] The confusion has resulted in errors repeated in many publications. One of them is Sinan's alleged slave origin as a war captive, since the waqfiyya refers to the endower as a freed slave of the grand vizier İbrahim Pasha (d. 1536).[20] In an attempt to reconcile this reference with the information provided in Sinan's autobiographies, some scholars have mistakenly proposed that the chief architect may have been conscripted from Kayseri after being freed by his former master,[21] or have linked him to names of relatives mentioned in the waqfiyya of his namesake.[22]

Dismissing this irrelevant document eliminates doubts concerning the chief architect's *devşirme* origin from Karaman. It is generally agreed that he was conscripted from Ağırnas, a village of Kayseri where he would later request from Selim II the donation of a field as his freehold property. An imperial decree of 19 April 1571 addressed to the sanjak governor and the kadi of Kayseri orders them to investigate whether this field had been appropriated by some individuals after its owners passed away without descendants, as reported by 'the chief architect Sinan'.[23] The decree was handed over to 'the steward of the chief architect's son', who is believed to have served as a sanjak governor in central Anatolia.[24] According to Mustafa Āli, thanks to Sinan's accomplishments, Sultan Süleyman had awarded his son 'distinguished sanjaks' and 'high-ranking offices'.[25] The chief architect's own undated waqfiyya, in which his late son Mehmed Beg is referred to as a martyr, shows that he endowed for his pious foundation a piece of land in Ağırnas along with a fountain. Donated to him with a sultanic patent, this land was most likely the property he had requested in 1571.[26]

An often-cited imperial decree dated 1573 refers to Ağırnas as the town where Sinan once lived. It mentions his Christian relatives still residing there and in neighbouring villages, whom he saved from being resettled in newly conquered Cyprus. The lack of consensus over Sinan's ethnic origin revolves around this crucial document, which was handed over at the imperial council to one of his assistants, Mehmed Usta. Addressed to the kadi of Akdağ and to the officer of coerced migration, it reads:

> Presently the chief of my architects (*miʿmārlarım başı*) has sent a letter requesting that among the subjects of Kayseri, whose resettlement in Cyprus has been ordered, the people of the village of Ağırnas where he himself resided (*kendü sākin olduġı ḳarye ḫalḳı*) and his non-Muslim relatives residing in other villages [namely] Sarıoğlu Düvenci living in Kiçibürüngüz and Ülise and Kudanshah living in the village of Üsküvi [Üskübü] be forgiven from coerced migration to Cyprus; therefore I have exempted from migrating to Cyprus the non-Muslims in the village where he himself resided and his named relatives, and when my order arrives have the inhabitants of the village where he once lived (*sābıḳā sākin olduġı*) and the said non-Muslims among his relatives be removed from the register if they have been recorded among the non-Muslims chosen for being sent to Cyprus.[27]

Some have argued that Sinan's named relatives were Armenian, while others believe that they must have been Greek or Christian Turks.[28] The controversy is complicated by the fact that the Christians of Karaman included Gregorian Armenians, Orthodox Greeks, and non-Muslim Turks affiliated with both of these churches. The latter are thought to have been turcophone Greeks (known as Karamanlı) or 'Armeno Turks'. The prevalent use of Turkish names among Christians in that region has been used as evidence for their Turkic origin, but the same names were adopted by other ethno-religious groups as well. The names Kudanshah and Sarı (Sarıoğlu), mentioned in the decree quoted above, are encountered among the seventy-six Christian inhabitants of Ağırnas in a land survey from Bayezid II's reign that cites only three Muslims.[29] A later survey from 1584 lists five Muslims and 189 Christians, many of whom had Turkish names, including nine individuals called Düvenci (whose paternal names were Koço, Ormişe, Karyağdı, Yani, Çakır, Hurşudi, Yahşi, Yanakon, Viton) and others whose names end with the suffix 'shah' (as in Kudanshah).[30]

The use of Turkish names is documented among some Armenian architects. For example, an account book recording the renovation expenses of the castle of Kili in 1489–90 identifies its builder as 'Yakubshah the Armenian architect'.[31] This was no doubt the architect who later built Bayezid II's mosque complex in Istanbul, Yakubshah b. Sultanshah.[32] The account book of an unidentified construction, dated 1568–69, cites among Armenian stonecutters (*ermeniyān-i sengtrāşān*) Kudanshah (the same name used by one of Sinan's relatives), along with Armenian sewer-diggers with Turkish names originating from Karaman.[33] The account books of the Süleymaniye published by Barkan frequently refer to Christians with Turkish names, often identifying them as Armenians: Sinan Ermeni, Murad Ermeni, Hüdaverdi Ermeni, Yakub Ermeni.[34] Stéphane Yerasimos observes that the *cizye* registers of Istanbul (dated 1540 and 1545), which record taxes paid by non-Muslims, group Christians with Turkish names under the 'community of Armenians'. He concludes that stonecutters and sewer-diggers with such names, who are listed in the Süleymaniye account books, were Armenians mostly originating from Cappadocia (Kayseri, Ürgüp, Niğde) and the Karaman quarter of Istanbul.[35] However, the fact that Turkish names were also adopted by turcophone Greeks from the Karaman region makes it difficult to conclusively identify Sinan's ethno-religious origin.

A number of scholars have also claimed a Greek origin for Sinan, following the lead of Ahmed Cevdet. The latter's influential preface to the *Tezkiretü'l-bünyān* (1897) fabricates an imaginary biography of Sinan based on an alleged Arabic source (*Ḳuyudāt-ı Mühimme*, Historical Records). This source, which not surprisingly has disappeared, allows the author to invent childhood details missing from Sinan's autobiographies, such as his exact birthday (15 April 1490) and the name of his father: a Greek from Kayseri called Hristo.[36] Ahmed Cevdet asserts that the chief architect, recruited from Kayseri at the age of twenty-three, had learned carpentry there as a child; then he allegedly continued his training as a carpenter at the school of novices in the İbrahim Pasha Palace (a palace built in the Hippodrome during the mid-1520s, many years after Sinan's arrival in Istanbul!).[37] Rifat Osman 'discovered' another highly questionable source mentioned in an article published in 1927, which happened to have a marginal note 'proving' Sinan's Turkish origin. This was a copy of Örfi Mahmud Agha's (d. 1778) *Tārīḫ-i Edirne* (History of Edirne):

> Sinan Agha b. Abdülmennan, the builder of the Selimiye mosque in Edirne, was a pious old man who lived more than a hundred years. Whenever he used to come to Edirne he would stay in the Mirmiran quarter, at the house of my grandfather Abdullah Agha, who was the Kethüda (Steward) of the Old Palace. One night he had drawn up the plans and calculations of the noble mosque [of Sokollu] in Lüleburgaz. Master Sinan used to recount to my grandfather that his grandfather, Togan Yusuf Agha, was a master carpenter from whose workshop he received the tools of his trade in his youth.[38]

Although several historians have demonstrated the unreliability of this marginal note, apparently a forgery, others have accepted its 'evidence'.[39]

It has been reported that before the Greeks of Ağırnas left for Greece in the population exchange of the 1920s, sixty Greek families lived in that village, which is said to have had two Orthodox churches and no Armenians at that time. A family of Greek masons, known by the name Taşcıoğulları (Masons' Sons), claimed to be the descendants of Sinan, whose house they could still identify.[40] It is difficult to assess the accuracy of this report, just as it is methodologically problematic to deduce the sixteenth-century population of Ağırnas from modern times. We simply do not have sufficient information to resolve the debate on Sinan's ethnic origin, even though an Armenian (or perhaps a Greek origin) seems more plausible in light of *devşirme* practices that generally excluded Turks and Turkish-speaking non-Muslims. Future research on the complex socio-ethnic composition of the Karaman region and new documents may provide additional clues.

The preoccupation with ethnic identity is largely a misguided and anachronistic exercise, given the racial pluralism of the empire's ruling elite during the age of Sinan. The chief architect's self-representation in his autobiographies implies that ethnic origin mattered less to him than his identity as a convert belonging to the Ottoman ruling class. His waqfiyya, discussed at the end of this chapter, shows how he motivated the two sons of his Christian brother in Kayseri to become Muslims, so that they could join the military ranks in Istanbul. Sinan may well have developed an inclination towards architecture in his youth, since Kayseri is a region rich with Seljuk and post-Seljuk ashlar stone monuments. Moreover, in an almanac dated 1900, Ağırnas is recorded as having a gypsum quarry.[41] The autobiographies, however, mention only his training in carpentry as a novice in Istanbul and omit any reference to his childhood.

The epitaph Sai composed for the chief architect's tomb adjoining the Süleymaniye complex indicates that he died in 1588 at over a hundred years of age (over ninety-seven years in the solar calendar). This implies that he was born sometime between 1489 and 1491.[42] The *Tezkiretü'l-bünyān*'s statement that he attended Selim I's (r. 1512–20) campaigns in Iran (1514) and Egypt (1516–18) as a novice, after an initial period of apprenticeship as a carpenter, suggests that he must have been conscripted sometime before 1514.[43] If so, Sinan was over twenty years old when he left his home town, an age rather advanced for novices, who were generally recruited between the ages of eight and twenty, preferably as teenagers (illus. 15, 112).[44]

Whatever Sinan's childhood experiences may have been, it was the rigorous training he underwent during his military career, first as a novice and then as a janissary, that moulded his artistic development. We learn some details about his years as a novice (*c.* 1512–21) from his autobiographies. The *Tuḥfe* says, 'I arrived at the capital and was used for a while in some outer services until I completed the rank of novice and became promoted to the rank of a janissary.'[45] According to the *Tezkiretü'l-ebniye*, as a novice he was 'honoured with the glory of the faith of Islam and the service of grandees and important people'.[46] The *Tezkiretü'l-bünyān* explains that it was his natural aptitude that made Sinan incline towards the craft of carpentry, taught to novices by a master carpenter:

> Among the [specializations] of novices I became desirous [to join] the quarter of carpentry (*neccārlıḳ semti*), given the straight-edge of my straight-lined natural disposition. In the master's (*üstād*) service I remained fixed like a compass, keeping an eye on centre and orbit. Then, just as a compass draws an arc, so I desired to tour countries. For a while, in the sultan's [Selim I] service I wandered in the Arab and Persian lands, deriving my sustenance from the pinnacle of each iwan, and my lodging from the corner of each ruin. Upon my return to the city of Istanbul, I was occupied with the service of the grandees of the age, and became a janissary.[47]

This shows that Sinan was apprenticed at the workshop of carpenters before he attended Selim I's Safavid and Mamluk campaigns, thereafter serving in the households of grandees until he participated in the Belgrade campaign (1521) as a janissary. Novices served in the palaces of grandees, in ships used for transporting building materials, in stone quarries, and in buildings commissioned by the sultan or grandees.[48] Placed under the jurisdiction of the agha of Istanbul (Istanbul Ağası), the corps of novices was lodged in thirty-one dormitories forming two parallel rows near the janissary dormitories known as the Old Chambers (Eski Odalar), next to which Sinan would later build the mosque of Şehzade Mehmed (illus. 157[4]). In each of these dormitories, eighty to a hundred novices, who received daily wages ranging from one to seven-and-a-half aspers, lived under the supervision of a *yayabaşı* (or *subaşı*, a post later held by Sinan).[49] Certain novices were apprenticed to master craftsmen

112 Nicolas de Nicolay, Novice ('Azamoglan', Acemioğlan), woodcut, from his *Les Navigations* (Antwerp, 1576).

at workshops (*kārḫāne*), including that of carpenters, some of which were located in their dormitory complex and others inside the janissary agha's palace (*aġa ḳapusı*) situated between the Old and New Chambers of the janissaries – next to the sultan's Old Palace where Sinan built the Süleymaniye complex, (illus. 33[4]).[50]

In the *Tezkiretü'l-bünyān* Sinan expresses gratitude to the unnamed master carpenter who taught him his craft (art): 'Talent is a special favour granted by God / With diligent effort did I perfect my art (*sān'at*).// May God give joy to his soul, / By granting a place in the uppermost paradise, // To my master (*üstādım*) whom I applaud with a bravo! / For making me a master in carpentry (*neccārlıḳ*).'[51] In a poem quoted above, Sinan is identified as Mimar Yusuf b. Abdullah, the apprentice of Habib-i Pir-i Neccar (the patron saint of carpenters). This is the name used in the only monument he ever signed, the Büyükçekmece bridge en route to Edirne: 'The work of Yusuf b. Abdullah' (illus. 113). The chief architect's full name must have been Yusuf Sinan

113 Sinan's signature at the Büyükçekmece bridge.

[or Yusuf Sinanüddin], followed by varying patronymics, typical for converts, that are used interchangeably in his autobiographies and waqfiyya: Abdullah, Abdülmennan, Abdurrahman, and Abdülkerim.[52]

The training method used in the workshop in which Sinan was enrolled can be deduced from an early-seventeenth-century biography of his student Mimar Mehmed Agha (the chief architect who built the Sultan Ahmed mosque), written by Cafer Efendi. The author explains how novices were educated in another carpentry workshop, located in the imperial garden of the Topkapı Palace (its trainees were generally promoted to the corps of royal architects).[53] Mimar Mehmed Agha decided to study in that workshop after listening to a youth who was holding a book on the science of 'geometry and architecture' and reading it aloud.[54] As he read each section, he would 'narrate and explain it' to his audience, stressing the importance of geometry to his pupils: 'As long as a person does not understand this rare and agreeable science, he is not capable of the finest working in mother-of-pearl, nor can he be expert and skilled in the art of architecture.'[55]

When the Albanian-born novice Mehmed expresses his wish to study in that workshop, he is asked to prove his talent by hitting a marked spot on a plank with an adze. Succeeding admirably in this initiation ceremony, he is greeted by workshop members as if he were joining a brotherhood:

> May your hand and arm be strong! God, whose name be exalted, bless you with long life! It is your right to be a master of the arts of architecture (*miʿmārlıḳ*) and the working of mother-of-pearl (*sedefkārlıḳ*). The appropriate thing is this, from now on you enter our brotherhood and learn and grow in this art.[56]

Then the young man who read the book says: 'If this boy turns towards this art with his skill, let me also teach him the science of geometry, and transcribe and present him with a copy of the book in my hand so that so long as he lives he will have in his hands a token from me.'[57] This reveals that applied geometry was regarded as the common theoretical basis of architecture and inlaid mother-of-pearl carpentry, which was based on interlocking geometric figures (and like architecture relied on the art of proportion).[58]

Sinan's training in geometry was complemented by practical lessons derived from the study of monuments. Accompanying Selim I's campaigns in Iran and Egypt in his early twenties provided him with his first opportunity to examine historical buildings and ancient ruins. During Süleyman's reign, he travelled between 1521 and 1538 more extensively as a janissary to the Balkans, eastern Europe, Corfu, Puglia in southern Italy, Anatolia, Azerbayjan, Iran, Iraq, and Syria (illus. 114). He recounts the difficulty of those long and arduous marches: 'Becoming a janissary I endured much suffering / Attending as I did many a ghaza as a foot soldier.'[59] Military campaigns during which janissaries were employed in the construction of fortifications, bridges, and mosques provided him with his earliest building experiences (illus. 49–50, 115–17). His years as a commander of novices and janissary regiments (*yayabaşı or subaşı*) developed his administrative skills which he would marshal later on in the disciplined organization of labour at construction sites.

Sinan's army training gave him a solid grounding in engineering, not unlike that of Roman military architects and some of his contemporaries in Italy who designed warships, bridges, fortresses, pile-drivers, and machines for lifting and moving construction materials or columns. Ottoman military technology was based not only on a knowledge of medieval Islamic treatises of applied engineering, rooted in Greco-Roman sources, but also on contemporary European ones: the Topkapı Palace library, for instance, preserves an illustrated printed copy of Roberto Valturio's *De re militari* (a manuscript copy of this treatise, which was sent in 1461 to Mehmed II by Sigismondo Malatesta of Rimini, had been confiscated by the suspicious Venetians).[60] Sinan's skill in military engineering can be inferred from his appointment to the post of *zenberekcibaşı*, chief of the 82nd janissary regiment in charge of catapults and mechanical devices (whose emblem was a crossbow, illus. 14 [82]). He was serving in that capacity during the Baghdad campaign of 1534–37, when he participated in the construction of two mosque-cum-convent complexes adjoining the tombs of Abu Hanifa and ʿAbd al-Kadir al-Gilani (illus. 35). It was then that the vizier Lutfi Pasha ordered him to build warships to cross Lake Van and obtain military intelligence about Safavid troops stationed on the other side:

> To this end he summoned me and ordered me to diligently attend to the construction of ships. With God's help, even though conditions were not suitable there due to the campaign, I and my fellow janissaries (*yoldāşlarım*, comrades) worked hard and within a short time we built three galleys, obtained sails, anchor-chains, and oars, and equipped them with war weapons, cannons, and guns. His Excellency the pasha then ordered, 'You be their captain!' and in accordance with his noble wish, my fellow soldiers and I set sail and gathered thorough knowledge about the Kızılbaş (Safavid) soldiers. He was extremely pleased and honoured this humble servant with his favour.[61]

This episode not only testifies to Sinan's skills as a *mechanicus* (architect-engineer), but also as a commander and intelligence officer. The latter role parallels the assignment of Mimar Mehmed Agha (who was appointed royal gatekeeper after his apprenticeship in carpentry at the palace gardens) to collect 'news of the infidels' plans' by secretly inspecting fortresses along the Rumelian borders (Austria, Hungary, Croatia, Italy, France, Spain and Malta) of the empire.[62]

After the Baghdad campaign, Sinan was promoted to the sultan's elite guard. During the Moldavian campaign of 1538 he was once again favoured by Lutfi Pasha, who recommended him for the construction of a bridge on the Pruth river for the passage of the army. When others proved incapable of constructing the bridge on marshland, the vizier made the following suggestion to Sultan Süleyman:

> My felicitous sultan, the construction of this bridge can only be realized through the mastery and expertise of your *kul* known as Sinan Subaşı [synonym for *yayabaşı*]. He serves as one of your personal elite guards (*ḫāṣeki*). Order him to attend to that task with his fellow soldiers. He is a world-famous master (*üstād*) and a skilled architect (*miʿmār*).[63]

Sinan completed the bridge in ten days. After the army passed over it, Lutfi Pasha proposed to prevent its destruction by the enemy by adding a watchtower staffed with janissary guards. When the grand vizier Ayas Pasha (g.v. 1536–39) and the governor-general of Rumelia (Sofu Mehmed Pasha, who later commissioned a mosque in Sofia) consulted Sinan's opinion, however, he suggested demolishing the bridge, since it could easily be rebuilt again. Following the victory in Moldavia, Sinan felt 'extremely afflicted with anxiety' for having contradicted the opinion of his benefactor Lutfi Pasha, in whose household he may well have been employed as a novice. Little did he know that the forgiving pasha would soon become grand vizier (g.v. 1539–41) and in 1539 offer him the job of chief architect:

114 Nicolas de Nicolay, 'Janissary', woodcut, from his *Les Navigations*.

> I was worrying that perhaps some harm might befall me, but with God's wisdom Mimar Acem Alisi happened to die and the post of [chief] architect (*miʿmārlıḳ*) became vacant. In those days the late grand vizier Ayas Pasha [d. 1539] also passed away, and the grandees of the age made the following observation about the construction of his tomb: 'There is no qualified architect who is a perfect master in that science (*fenn*)'. Lutfi Pasha replied: 'Sinan Subaşı, who is the sultan's bodyguard, must become [chief] architect (*miʿmār*); there is nobody capable of that service other than him.' They inquired: 'Would he accept this and abandon his career path?'[64]

It was the opportunity to build monumental Friday mosques that tempted Sinan to accept the grand vizier's offer, which was communicated to him via the janissary agha:

115 (top left) Construction of the Areş castle with a red awning over the scaffolding and supervisors holding staffs: showing masons, stonecutters, stone carriers, lime mixers, and iron smiths, 1584, watercolour on paper, from Mustafa Āli, *Nuṣretnāme*.

116 (left) Construction of the Erivan castle overseen by the commander Ferhad Pasha with supervisors holding staffs as janissary builders and masons erect the walls, 1592, watercolour on paper, from Lokman, *Shahanshāhnāmā*.

117 (above) Construction of the Tomanis castle overseen by the commander Ferhad Pasha, 1592, watercolour on paper, from Lokman, *Shahanshāhnāmā*.

This humble servant actually felt sorrow at the thought of abandoning my career path, but in the final analysis I accepted the proposal after considering that this would be a pretext to build many mosques through which my wishes in this world and in the next would be granted.[65]

This explanation is followed by a poem expressing Sinan's aspiration for global artistic fame:

I resolved to become [chief] architect
To leave monuments in this world with my perfection.

I used to say, may God see me worthy
Of building a soaring sanctuary for Him.

Granted was my prayer by His Divine Wisdom
That brought me to the sultan's attention.

Sinan offers thanks to God 'who brought us to Islam, for if He had not shown us the true path, we would not have found it'. He expresses gratitude for the acceptance of his prayers through the construction of 'many soaring paradise-like mosques' for the sultans with whose conversation he was honoured.[66] Sinan also enjoyed close personal relations with the rich and powerful of the Ottoman court: patrons whose public image became increasingly bound up with building in the new style that the chief architect codified and who came to regard him as an unrivalled professional with intellectual respectability, distinguished in status from a mere craftsman. Had Sinan declined the grand vizier's job offer, he could have been promoted to higher-income posts, but artistic ambitions, so vividly expressed in his autobiography, lured him to accept the lifelong office of chief architect: 'With my art and service, it was my lot in life to become a skilful architect and to become famous in all regions.'[67]

II. SİNAN'S SELF-IMAGE AND THE BIOGRAPHIES OF ITALIAN ARTISTS

Architecture gained intellectual respectability as the least manual of the crafts not only in Renaissance Italy but also in the Ottoman empire, where elite patrons developed a vital interest in architectural patronage as part of their public image. The only known portrait of Sinan is a painting that shows him overseeing the construction of Sultan Süleyman's mausoleum behind the Süleymaniye mosque (illus. 1, 118). Wearing a caftan and a large, bulbous turban (*mücevveze*), the chief architect, who is in his late seventies, holds a wooden cubit measure – an emblem signifying the intellectual basis of his profession in the mathematical sciences, particularly applied geometry.[68] By setting him apart from manual labourers, master masons, and the foreman holding a staff, the painting expresses Sinan's dignified social stature as an agha of the imperial court. It brings to mind pictorial representations of contemporary Italian architects shown with compasses, drawing instruments, and plans that highlight the intellectual status of their profession. The exalted self-image projected in Sinan's autobiographies echoes the *Lives* of Italian artists and architects, with their notion of the artwork as a material trace of its maker's mental powers of invention. The term 'divine' (*divino*), used for Brunelleschi and Michelangelo, is also applied to Sinan by his biographer, who is intent on advertising the chief architect's God-given genius: 'divine maestro' (*ʿazīz-i kārdān*), 'divine architect' (*miʿmār-ı mübārek*).

Prior to the establishment of the corps of royal architects around the second half of the fifteenth century, Ottoman buildings often included inscriptions specifying the names of their architects and decorators.[69] The lack of architects' signatures on late-fifteenth and sixteenth-century monuments (with a few exceptions) not only underscores the primacy of the patrons named in foundation inscriptions, but also implies a collaborative notion of authorship for buildings created under the supervision of chief architects. Hence, the *Tuḥfe*'s assertion that all buildings erected in the course of Sinan's tenure as chief architect came into being under his 'supervision' (*mübāşeret*).[70] In his autobiographies the chief architect claims authorship of an overwhelming number of projects as if to compensate for the absence of his signature on monuments he considered his own. Sinan's personal contribution to these monuments varied according to the relative importance of their patrons and their proximity to the capital, which he rarely left. By claiming authorship of essentially collaborative works, realized with the mediation of royal architects based in Istanbul or stationed in provincial cities, he stressed his role in conceptualizing their design. This is not unlike the Italian Renaissance notion of *disegno* as a cerebral pursuit rooted in the power of judgment and transcending the execution of a building: a mental abstraction relatively separate from its material manifestation. The reliance of architecture on drawings confirmed the authority of the architect and the conception of the discipline as an intellectual activity.

The *Teẕkiretü'l-bünyān* highlights Sinan's role in drawing the plans of a vast number of projects (698) commissioned by distinguished patrons whose company he relished:

> In short, for the sultans, viziers, and grandees of the age this humble servant drew plans (*resm*) for and built noble Friday

118 Süleymaniye mosque and a domed burial tent erected in its funerary garden next to Hürrem Sultan's mausoleum: Sinan oversees the construction of Süleyman's mausoleum while the funeral cortège in the foreground carries a royal coffin, 1579, watercolour on paper, from Lokman, *Tārīkh-i Sulṭān Sulaymān*.

> mosques in eighty places, more than four hundred masjids, sixty madrasas, thirty-two palaces, nineteen mausoleums, seven schools for Koran recitation, seventeen hospices, three hospitals, seven bridges, fifteen aqueducts, six store-houses, nineteen khans, and thirty-three bath-houses.[71]

The epitaph composed by Sai for Sinan's tomb also mentions eighty Friday mosques and more than four hundred masjids, numbers that vary in differing lists appended to the autobiographies. The masjids must have been built throughout the empire, for those enumerated (ranging between forty-six and fifty-two) are concentrated in Istanbul. If we disregard the unnamed masjids outside the capital, the number of monuments is reduced to around 350, coming close to those enumerated in the *Tezkiretü'l-ebniye*. The count is higher in the *Tuḥfe* (over 400).[72] Kuran attributes this numerical discrepancy to the growth of Sinan's corpus over time and dates the three autobiographies accordingly: the *Tezkiretü'l-bünyān* to about 1583-84, the *Tezkiretü'l-ebniye* to about 1586-87, and the *Tuḥfe* to the 1590s.[73]

There are compelling reasons to argue that the *Tuḥfe*'s longer list preceded rather than followed that of the *Tezkiretül-ebniye*, which seems to have been formed by a process of elimination and condensation. Clues to how the latter list was distilled from a larger pool are preserved in the *Tuḥfe* and its two unicum drafts. The preface of the 'Untitled Treatise' mentions buildings grouped in terms of eleven 'types' (*nev*ʿ), but includes only a list of bath-houses with many items and repetitions crossed out, and others added in the margins or between the lines. For instance, the bath of İskender Pasha in Kanlıca, mentioned twice, is crossed out, even though the account book of that bath, stamped with Sinan's seal, confirms his role in supervising its construction.[74] Executed by the architect Üstad Manol and his two 'assistants' (*şāgird, ḳalfa*) Yorgi and Yani, this bath was apparently judged too insignificant to be included in Sinan's corpus; hence it disappears from the subsequently compiled lists of the *Tuḥfe,* and the *Tezkiretü'l-ebniye* (only some late copies of the *Tezkiretü'l-bünyān* feature such lists).[75]

Comparison of the list of Friday mosques in the *Tuḥfe* and the *Tezkiretü'l-ebniye* suggests that the latter was derived from the longer catalogue of the former (Appendix 1).[76] Mosques named on the more comprehensive list of the *Tuḥfe*, but omitted from the *Tezkiretü'l-ebniye*, seem to have been works that Sinan in the final analysis decided to exclude from his corpus. Most of these are distant provincial mosques, renovations, or projects completed before his appointment as chief architect. For example, the mosque of Selim I in Istanbul, which the *Tuḥfe* counts among Sinan's works, but identifies as a building executed 'under the supervision (*mübāşeret*) of another architect', is notably absent from the *Tezkiretü'l-ebniye*.[77] Some late mosques built in Istanbul after the mid-1580s, and listed in the *Tuḥfe*, are likewise deleted from the *Tezkiretü'l-ebniye*, perhaps because they were largely created by Sinan's assistants with his stamp of approval.[78]

The *Tezkiretü'l-ebniye*, then, seems to reflect a consensus about the chief architect's corpus reached after reconsideration of longer lists compiled earlier from archival documents, like the account book of the Kanlıca bath which bears Sinan's seal. Monuments cited in both the *Tuḥfe* and the *Tezkiretü'l-ebniye* are stronger candidates for Sinan's authorship, but his contribution to those mentioned only once cannot automatically be dismissed. Moreover, the varying lists are by no means exhaustive catalogues of all monuments designed or approved by the chief architect, but rather a sizeable sample that he apparently considered significant enough to be identified as his own works. Some projects we know he was involved in, such as the renovation of Hagia Sophia, are not even mentioned.

Sinan's autobiographies overtly emphasize Friday mosques, always listed first among building types to elevate the prestige of his profession. The differing classifications of building types (ranging from eleven to thirteen) once again reflects a continuous process of revision culminating in the final redaction of the *Tezkire*s (Appendix 3). These building types do not exhaust Sinan's repertoire, as they exclude less monumental structures like fountains, water dispensers, elementary schools, and dervish convents.[79] The *Tuḥfe* enumerates the components of complexes in its list of Friday mosques, including the mausoleums of founders and other dependencies such as otherwise excluded elementary schools and dervish convents. The grouping of dependencies together with Friday mosques, no matter how sketchy and unsystematic, confirms their conceptualization as units belonging to complexes. This is no longer apparent in the *Tezkiretü'l-ebniye*, where dependencies are not listed with Friday mosques but separately: schools and dervish convents are omitted altogether, and mausoleums are either classified as a separate building type or grouped together with Koran recitation schools. It is therefore somewhat futile to try to pinpoint Sinan's contributions to the smaller components of mosque complexes.

The chief architect's autobiographies have long shaped the inordinate focus of scholarship on his person, and by extension on his style. Much like Giorgio Vasari's *Lives* of Italian artists and architects (1550, 1568), Sinan's autobiographies, in an exaggerated celebration of his individualism, foreground his artistic genius to the exclusion of other factors. Their reductive discourse suppresses the contributions of other architects who executed his designs and exclusively focuses on the grandest sultanic projects. Nor do the autobiographies attempt to outline in the manner of a treatise the theoretical bases of architectural design.

Sinan may well have been familiar with, and inspired by, the biographies of Filippo Brunelleschi (d. 1446) and Michelangelo (d. 1564), penned by their associates Antonio di Tuccio Manetti (1480s) and Ascanio Condivi (1553) respectively. The Italian genre of the *vita* condensed an artist's career to a series of key anecdotes: a recurrent theme is the topos of the misunderstood genius-protagonist, who is constantly undermined by the slanders of envious rivals but ultimately vindicated by his own professional expertise. In Condivi's life of Michelangelo, this theme is exemplified by the envy of Bramante, who deprives Michelangelo of Pope Julius II's favour, and by the accusations of the deputies of works at St Peter's, who try to restrict his authority [between 1551 and 1553]. Yet Michelangelo is vindicated in the end by Pope Julius III, who confirms the artist's authority in directing the construction of St Peter's, where he ingeniously corrects the mistakes of his predecessors.[80]

The *Teẕkiretü'l-bünyān*'s narrative structure is propelled by similar episodes displaying Sinan's cunning ability to overcome obstacles that cast doubt on his professional competence. Much like Michelangelo's pupil Condivi, who drew information 'from the oracle of his [master's] speech', Sai based his text on Sinan's 'blessed words' reflecting 'the divine wisdom of the sage Lokman'.[81] Dedicated to Pope Julius III, Condivi's biography of Michelangelo may in certain respects be considered an autobiography. The biographer writes that his aim is 'to contribute as best as I can to the fame of my master', and to prove to the world 'how great are his powers of invention and how many beautiful ideas spring from that divine spirit.'[82] Both Condivi and Sai record those attributes by which their subjects most wanted to be remembered, particularly their creative genius that won the reverence of powerful rulers and the envy of rivals.

The literary genre of autobiography is a rarity in the late-sixteenth-century Ottoman world, and there is no precedent anywhere in the Islamic lands for an architect's biography. Sai drew upon the existing genres of the biographical memoir (*teẕkire*), the treatise (*risāle*), and the book of deeds or the vitae of saintly figures (*menāḳıbnāme*). Sinan's autobiographies, so unusual in their use of the first-person point of view, differ from short entries found in the biographical memoirs of poets, calligraphers, and painters. Nevertheless with their conception of Sinan's works as mementoes of divinely bestowed creative power they rely on authorship paradigms formulated for artists. In addition, their narratives particularly recall books of deeds recounting the miraculous exploits of sufi saints and ghazis.[83] It is therefore not a coincidence that they enumerate the many campaigns he participated in as a ghazi and liken him to a sufi saint, often comparing him to the sage Lokman and the miracle-working saint Hızır (Khidr).

Cafer Efendi, Mimar Mehmed Agha's biographer, explains that he wrote the *Risāle-i miʿmāriyye* (Treatise on Architecture) in 1614-15 because it had become customary to compose 'books of deeds' (*menāḳıbnāme*) for some chief architects.[84] In addition to Sinan's autobiographies, he must have been thinking of semi-mythical texts on the construction of Hagia Sophia that relate stories about Justinian's legendary architect, Ignatius (İgnadyus), and the architect of Mehmed II's mosque complex, Atik Sinan. These popular texts, to which Sinan's autobiographies allude several times, left a deep imprint on Ottoman architectural culture. We have seen that their earliest versions (based on the *Diegesi peri tes Hagias Sofias*, Narrative concerning Hagia Sophia), which were translated from Greek into Persian and Turkish for Mehmed II, emphasized the regal symbolism of the church built for Justinian. They narrate the emperor's construction of the church for the glory of Christianity after the pagan Nika Riot of 532, using precious marbles and columns collected from the provinces of his empire by governors, who were instructed to remove them from pagan temples.[85] Critical versions of this text, revised during Bayezid II's reign and inserted into anonymous chronicles, idealize the construction process of Hagia Sophia to underscore Mehmed II's oppression (*ẓulm*) during the erection of his mosque complex in Istanbul.[86]

The anonymous author of one resentful chronicle, which particularly opposes the sultan's imperial policies, contrasts the rewards received by Justinian's architect with the sultan's unjust treatment of the architect of his mosque, Atik Sinan, who was beaten to death in prison.[87] He explains that the ill-fated royal architect was accused of overspending by the inspection committee sent by the sultan to investigate the high cost of his mosque complex:

> They subject the building supervisor (*emīn*) and his scribe to various kinds of inspection and call him to account, with the intention of discovering a mistake and finding a pretext for taking back the money spent for that building. If they cannot manage to find any mistake, then they let the architect fall into disfavour, holding him in contempt and looking down upon him, saying: 'He spent too much money from lack of knowledge!'[88]

Another reason Atik Sinan allegedly fell from favour was his shortening of the mosque's two red granite columns that supported the lateral arches of its central dome: 'Seeing them today, some masters say, 'Those columns should have been left longer, they have been cut too short.'[89]

Critical texts in which Hagia Sophia's looming presence overshadows Ottoman attempts at building monumental mosques informed Sinan's autobiographies, in which his artistic competition with Ignatius's masterpiece and with early Ottoman sultanic mosques is a recurrent theme. The self-centred narratives of the autobiographies have been endlessly mined as a repository of 'facts' to reconstruct the chief architect's career and corpus, but their conceptual implications have largely been overlooked. As the products of an intimate collaboration between Sai and Sinan, they provide invaluable insights about architectural culture and practice, with some fascinating glimpses of aesthetic theory. I will therefore take a closer look at the autobiographies, often dismissed as simplistic narratives, starting first with the *Tuḥfe* and then turning to the two *Teẕkire*s.

Dedicated to Murad III, the *Tuḥfe*'s preface wills that the sultan commission great works in the capital: 'Let his works in Istanbul be lofty and sun-like! / And his gifts and honours to the possessors of skill (*erbāb-ı hüner*) be beyond limit!'[90] This is followed by the chief architect's brief biography and a poem eulogizing him as a 'wise architect' and a 'learned engineer, pious, and mature', who has perfected his mastery in the science of architecture with the Süleymaniye mosque. The purpose of the text is summarized as follows:

> The reason this treatise was caused to be written was in order that the monumental buildings, which were completed and finished under our supervision, would remain as an exemplar and souvenir on the pages of Time; it has been named *Tuḥfetü'l-miʿmārīn*, and its blessed contents are organized in terms of an introduction, twelve [building] types, and an epilogue, so that it may be the occasion for prayers of blessing. And success comes from God![91]

The epilogue describing 'this servant's artistic accomplishments (*taṣarrufāt*)' exclusively deals with innovations that Sinan introduced in the Süleymaniye mosque. The omission of any reference to the Selimiye, presented as the culmination of Sinan's mastery in the *Teẕkire*s, is striking. But the preface inviting Murad III to commission major works in Istanbul hints why the *Tuḥfe* focuses on the Süleymaniye, the capital's most impressive mosque complex: the sultan had never laid eyes on the Selimiye in Edirne. Perhaps it was for the same reason that royal architects chose to display a model of the Süleymaniye to Murad III in 1582, during the circumcision festivities of the crown prince Mehmed.[92]

The *Tuḥfe* seems to have been conceived as a tract emphasizing the evolutionary progress of mosque architecture in Istanbul, brought to perfection in the Süleymaniye. The introduction and epilogue of this work were entirely eliminated in the redaction of the *Teẕkire*s, whose titles emphasize buildings (*bünyān, ebniye*), just as their contents focus on a range of selected masterpieces from Sinan's corpus. By contrast, the *Tuḥfetü'l-miʿmārīn* and its draft, called *Risāletü'l-miʿmāriyye*, concentrate on architects and on the profession of architecture. Sinan's view of architecture as a history of the progress of civilization is summarized in the *Tuḥfe*'s introduction, which briefly outlines the principles of construction and the necessity of laying strong foundations:

> It is obvious and proven to men of intelligence and wisdom and persons of understanding and vision that building with water and clay, being an auspicious art, the Children of Adam felt an aversion to mountains and caves and from the beginning were inclined to build cities and villages. And because of the civilized nature of human beings, many types of buildings were invented, day by day, and refinement (*nezāket*) increased and not a moment was lost by those striving to leave a memorial. In fact, a building such as Ayasofya, which is without equal in the world, was built in fourteen years through the efforts of the architect named İgnadyus. But a few years after the completion of its design (*ṭarḥ*), its flat dome (*yassu ḳubbe*) collapsed. And it is recorded in histories that it was rebuilt by the above-mentioned architect-engineer (*miʿmār mühendis*) with various apologies. In like manner, your servant, Sinan of Kayseri has also suffered many troubles during the completion of each building. No doubt, with the help of God, all these [buildings] came into existence due to the auspicious government and lofty patronage of the kingdom-conquering Ottoman dynasty and the bountiful sincerity of our own heart. In short, there is no art more difficult than architecture; and whosoever is engaged in this honourable service must, first of all, be righteous and pious. He should not begin to lay foundations if the building ground is not firm, and when he sets out to lay the foundations, he should pay great attention to their strength, so that his work should be free from defect. And, in proportion to the abundance or paucity of piers, columns, and buttresses, he should wrap up the domes and half-domes on top of them, and bind the arches together in an agreeable (*ḫoşca*) manner without carelessness. And he should not hurry in important matters, but bear his burden according to the saying 'Patience brings victory to man!' in order that, with God's help, he may find divine guidance for the immortality of his work. And in this there is no doubt![93]

This passage indirectly alludes to legendary accounts of Hagia Sophia's construction, which attribute the collapse of Ignatius's dome to the hasty removal of its wooden centering because of Justinian's impatience, and to damage to its foundations caused by timbers carelessly thrown down to the floor.[94] Sinan's reference to primitive architecture built of mud recalls Pliny's account (repeated in Alberti's treatise) that humans first lived in caves before inventing mud huts.[95] The notion of historical progress recalls Vitruvius' definition of architecture as a transition from a primitive mode of life to 'civilization and refinement' through the emergence of differentiated building types.[96] The idea of progress is also enunciated in Manuel Chrysoloras's essay 'Comparison of Old and New Rome' (1411) that proves the superiority of Hagia Sophia to monuments in Rome through arguments of biological and cultural advancement. Whereas Rome did not derive its form from a model, Constantinople, using Rome as an archetype, 'brought many things to greater perfection and splendour', for 'the works of men competing with others can progress toward greater beauty'.[97]

According to Chrysoloras, the inimitable grand dome of Hagia Sophia merited admiration not only for its unsurpassed size, but also for the inventiveness of the architects who had mentally conceived it without precedent.[98] Along the same lines, Alberti wrote that the merit of Brunelleschi's dome in Florence lay both in its size and its absolute novelty.[99] He associated the Florentine dome with the concept of historical progress, measured by the architect's capacity for invention through the divine power of *ingenio*: a mysterious creative force akin to genius.[100] Yet Alberti's treatise argues that invention must not be *ex novo*, because admired exemplars from the past lend distinguished pedigree to new proposals: 'Inspired by their example, we should strive to produce our own inventions, to rival, or, if possible, to surpass the glory of theirs.'[101]

Sinan's autobiographies participate in the Renaissance discourse on the history of artistic progress by eulogizing his own inventions that surpass admired monuments built in the past, thanks to his creative genius and piety. From the primitive hut to Hagia Sophia, the evolution of architecture toward variegated building types and greater aesthetic refinement eventually culminates in his own superior works, which feature stabler domes built in a shorter time, and simultaneously reflect the triumph of Islam, the grandeur of the Ottoman dynasty, and his God-given talent.[102] Sinan is the 'agent' on whom depends the architectural glorification of God and His shadow on earth, the sultan. The skilled architect must be pious in order to overcome the difficulties of his profession. The cultural value attached to piety also becomes apparent in Cafer Efendi's treatise, which stresses the devoutness of 'Koca Mimar Sinan Agha', who spent most of his life 'on ghazas and jihads and on buildings and edifices for the sake of God'.[103] The biographer likewise praises the piety of his own patron, Mimar Mehmed Agha, who was another convert of *devşirme* origin:

> And the Agha is here like a shaykh, for he both orders the masters incessantly, saying 'Work!', and moreover, taking his rosary in his hand, is busy with devotions and prayers. This is a fortunate circumstance for His Majesty the felicitous Padishah, that he should have such a devout master architect, and that such a devout agha should build his noble mosque accompanied by prayers and devotions.[104]

Sinan's autobiographies attribute his ability to overcome professional difficulties to unceasing prayers and the help of God, the divine source of his talent. By reminding his readers of Hagia Sophia's notoriously unstable dome, he indirectly praises the sounder construction of his own domes. His preoccupation with structural stability is tempered by an aesthetic concern with agreeable solutions, based on the harmonious correspondence between domical superstructures and a solid infrastructure of supports resting on firm foundations. The epilogue of the *Tuḥfe* which focuses on Sinan's innovations in the Süleymaniye, once again takes up the theme of structural elegance achieved through the skilful balancing of domes and half-domes atop columns and piers. Read together, the introduction and epilogue turn into an extended eulogy of the Süleymaniye, which reformulates Hagia Sophia's plan and elevation without attempting to surpass its monumentality. The epilogue describes the Şehzade Mehmed and Süleymaniye mosques as the pioneers of a more refined Ottoman aesthetic that perfects the Hagia Sophia-inspired style of earlier sultanic mosques:

> It is manifest and apparent to the engineers of the age and the overseers of auspicious monuments that although [formerly] buildings constructed in the style of Ayasofya (*Ayaṣofya ṭarzında*) did not possess refinement (*nezāket*), this servant of yours perfected the honored Friday mosque of Şehzade Sultan Mehmed – may God illuminate his tomb – which became the model for the noble mosque of His Majesty Sultan Süleyman Khan – may he rest in peace. Subsequently, in this lofty edifice various beautiful works of art came into being, each of which was designed with refinement (*nezāketle*).[105]

Among his artistic inventions, Sinan singles out the central fountain of the forecourt, unique in the downpour of water from the top of its ceiling; the unprecedented ablution spouts placed along the mosque's lateral façades; the unmatched style of the mihrab and minbar; the marble pulpits attached to the four piers; the four colossal red granite columns erected between the great piers along with internal and external colonnades, according to the science of statics; the construction of domes and half-domes in which 'demons' gave a helping hand to humans; and the subterranean conduits built by 'water channel experts in our corps'. Another innovation is the number of galleries in the four minarets, corresponding to the Solomon-like patron's position as the tenth victorious ruler of the Ottoman dynasty. Sinan also draws attention to 'doors opened from the minarets around the noble dome, and several small, upper domes provided for the [scrutiny] of experts (*erbāb-ı te'līf*), an artifice not previously accomplished by any master.' This implies that the mosque's elaborate superstructure with lateral domes alternating in size is a novelty displayed for the gaze of connoisseurs from its roof terrace. Sinan provided access to this viewing terrace, surrounded by unprecedented stone balustrades, from the doorways of the southern pair of minarets and from the doors of the unique 'small, upper domes' that crown the mosque's lateral stepped buttresses as belvedere chambers provided with windows (illus. 174–75).[106]

The *Tuḥfe*'s introduction and epilogue, then, stress the difficulty of erecting stable edifices with strong foundations whose varied support systems carry equally complex domical superstructures. In the chief architect's own words, the Şehzade and Süleymaniye mosques exemplify his refinement of the 'Hagia Sophian' aesthetic of Istanbul's previous sultanic mosques. He perfects this well-established dynastic idiom rather than directly

119 Map of the Kırkçeşme water distribution system outside the walls of Istanbul, 1579, watercolour on paper, from Lokman, *Tārikh-i Sulṭān Sulaymān*.

competing with Hagia Sophia, an unmatched masterpiece 'without equal in the world'. Sinan translates the layout of Hagia Sophia into the Ottoman architectural idiom, which he critically revises, distills, and refines. The Süleymaniye not only rationalizes the plan of its unsurpassed model with a more centralized spatial conception, but also improves on the unrefined style of Istanbul's earlier sultanic mosques.

The *Tezkiretü'l-bünyān*, a more general account of skills displayed in various imperial projects, shows the importance that Sinan attached to engineering and hydraulics. Starting with the mosque of Şehzade Mehmed, this text eulogizes the capital's Kırkçeşme water distribution system, the Süleymaniye, a well and water wheel at one of Sultan Süleyman's royal gardens, the Büyükçekmece bridge, and finally the Selimiye mosque, which is presented as the culmination of his artistic genius. Five of these six works were commissioned by Sinan's greatest patron, Sultan Süleyman, who is again idealized as the 'Solomon of the age', whose grand building projects are realized by 'demons' and 'jinns'. Each of the six royal projects involves Sinan's hidden contest with the architectural heritage of 'infidel' times. The Romano-Byzantine building tradition is associated with a non-Muslim past that lacks the connotations it held in the humanist context, with its cult of antique revival. Nevertheless, much like his Italian colleagues who intently study the ancient ruins of Rome, Sinan eagerly examines and sets out to improve the classical antiquities he encounters in and near Constantinople.

Let us first consider works of civic engineering in which Sinan revives ancient technologies. Prior to the construction of the Büyükçekmece bridge, Süleyman asks his chief architect to prepare a report about how the collapsed Roman bridge on that site was constructed in 'infidel' times, and why it fell into ruin (illus. 43). After some archaeological fieldwork, Sinan presents a written report emphasizing the importance of strong foundations laid on firm ground:

> My sultan, the old bridge was destroyed because they built it with thrift in mind and chose a site far from the sea, placing its foundations in a marshy area by the shore that could not withstand the load. Consquently, it collapsed and fell into ruin. For this reason, we should build it within the sea where the water is shallow and the ground is firm.

Süleyman promptly gives his royal approval for the proposed plan (*resm*) which corrects the mistakes of the old bridge.[107]

The construction technique used by Sinan comes close to the ancient method of bridge construction described in Vitruvius' treatise, where the use of watertight wooden boxes (*batardo*) is recommended for the digging of foundations:

> With the sultan's order, many hundreds of carpenters and stone masons were gathered, and a galleon-like coffer was made for each of the supports of the bridge. Solomon's demons emptied out the seawater with pumps and large skin bags, and fine strong wooden stakes equal to the height of two or three men were driven into the foundations with a pile-driver. On top of these [stakes] cubit-sized stone blocks (*arşun taşları*) were joined together by strong iron clamps with molten lead poured in between them to form one solid mass.[108]

In this way, Sinan creates several artificial islands on top of which the bridge is raised, once again using stones joined by iron clamps filled with molten lead (a Roman construction technique).[109]

This technique is described in detail in Eyyubi's history on the construction of the Kırkçeşme aqueducts, a project that again requires Sinan to study antique ruins (illus. 119).[110] After ordering grandees to investigate the history of the ancient waterworks of Istanbul, Süleyman holds a 'consultation' (*müşāvere*) with his chief architect to discuss the rehabilitation of their ruins.[111] The *Tezkiretü'l-bünyān* describes how Sinan then proceeds to survey the ruins, using an astrolabe to calculate the available amount of water:

> This humble servant, placing myself in God's hands, measured the heights and depths of valleys with a surveying instrument (*havāyī terāzū*, literally aerial scale or astrolabe) and investigated the [ruins of] ancient waterways from all angles ... The conduits of the stream flowing from the rocky mountains had crumbled away, leaving the waters run to waste and trickle through the grass into the valley. Catching the stream at its source above, I dammed the waters that flowed from the mountaintop into the valley by digging a ditch. Then, according to the science of geometry (*'ilm-i hendese*) I placed water measures (*lüle*) on top of planks and calculated their quantity. On that comparative basis I then estimated the other streams by judging the growth of plants with the eye of geometry (*'ayn-i hendese*) and wrote down their approximate value, which I subsequently reported to His Majesty, the ruler of the world.[112]

The sultan holds another consultation with Sinan, who proposes two renovation options, using either forced or paid labour. Süleyman, intending to create a charitable work, selects the second choice.[113]

The *Tezkiretü'l-bünyān* narrates how rivals try to undermine Sinan's credibility through baseless accusations; even the viziers hope to persuade the sultan to abandon this costly project. We learn from Selaniki that the architect Kiriz Nikola was imprisoned by the grand vizier Semiz Ali Pasha (g.v. 1561–65) for tempting the sultan with the expensive project, which he accomplished by being always present at the site of the springs where the sultan went hunting.[114] The survey estimating water sources for the Kırkçeşme project, then, must have been jointly prepared by Sinan and his assistant Nikola. According to Selaniki, the two also collaborated during Süleyman's reign in 'surveying' (*mesāḥā*) 20,000 cubits of land to prepare an estimate for digging a canal between Lake Sapanca and the bay of İzmit; this ambitious and costly project failed to materialize.[115]

Sinan's autobiography recounts how the designated building supervisor, the chief of janissaries Müezzinzade Ali Agha, in collaboration with those opposed to the Kırkçeşme project, urges the sultan not to trust Sinan's estimate of underground water sources, which he dismisses as a mere dream and mirage: 'It would be unwise to take the word of an architect and spend so much labour and treasury funds!' He cynically asks, 'Is this architect so knowledgeable in the occult sciences as to be able to determine how many measures of water exist under the ground?'[116] The disappointed sultan rushes in all haste to personally confront Sinan, who, unaware of these calumnies, is busy damming the streams and measuring their quantity.[117] Unceasingly praying for the help of God, he improves Süleyman's foul mood by showing the collected water flowing from measuring spouts. In the end, he not only rehabilitates the ruined waterworks by uncovering 'large masonry basins and ornamented marble conduits' from 'infidel times' (*kāfirī*), but also discovers additional water sources with which he considerably increases the city's ancient water supply.[118]

Sinan vindicates himself by successfully completing this grand project, for which the sultan amply rewards him with a robe of honour and royal gifts. Sai's panegyrical account omits reference not only to the assistance of Kiriz Nikola, but also to the great flood that destroyed some of the aqueducts rebuilt between 1563 and 1565. The poet compares Sinan to the legendary sculptor and architect Farhad who out of his love for the 'Shirin-like sovereign' carves a canal through Mount Bisutun.[119] Sai also equates Sinan with the miracle-working saint Hızır (Khidr), the discoverer of the fountain of life.[120]

The chief architect once again merits being compared to Hızır in his miraculous discovery of an underground water source and the ruins of an ancient well from 'infidel times' (*kāfir zamānından*) during the construction of a water wheel at one of the imperial gardens in Istanbul.[121] This time he is faced with a life-threatening challenge by the sultan, whom he contradicts in a conversation. The spot in his garden that Süleyman chooses for the water wheel is declared unsuitable by Sinan, who responds it should be at the garden's highest point, so that water will flow to all its parts. He then teaches the sultan a lesson in hydraulics, explaining why most springs are on hilltops: 'Water upon the earth's surface runs from high to low,/ Water beneath the ground, though, runs from low to high.'[122] With hurt pride, the sultan says: 'If water is not found in that place, then we will talk again with the architect!' Sinan is saved when novices digging up the ground in the spot he has recommended uncover the ruins of an ancient well with drops of water between its crumbling stones. The sultan rewards Sinan with a robe of honour, and his saintliness is acknowledged by the chief of the privy chamber (Odabaşı Behruz Agha, for whom the chief architect later on built a mosque at the capital): 'My felicitous sultan, your servant the agha of architects is not a vacuous person; he seems to possess amazing spiritual qualities (*'acīb ḥālet*) as if he had saintly powers (*velāyet*)'.[123] Sai's accompanying poem declares the 'radiant-faced old man' Sinan the 'Hızır of the age', who has found the water of life for the sultan. Süleyman himself praises the chief architect's miraculous skill: 'This outwardly appears to be an art, / But in terms of inward meaning it essentially is a miracle (*kerāmet*). // If a person reaches mastery in his art, / The gate of happiness opens up for him. // Thanks be to the all-forgiving God that, / He has given us such a perfect man (*kāmil insān*)'.[124] This episode once again proves Sinan's ability to vindicate himself through professional skill, even against the opinion of the all-powerful sultan who eventually acknowledges the chief architect's status as 'perfect man', the highest spiritual station attainable by humans in sufi parlance.[125]

The three royal mosques singled out in the *Tez̠kiretü'l-bünyān* as milestones in Sinan's career engage with the ancient past by means of a structural and aesthetic criticism of Hagia Sophia and early Ottoman mosques. These mosques, too embody ancient techniques, such as the insertion of clay jugs into the fabric of brick domes to improve acoustics.[126] The 'paradise-like' mosque of Şehzade Mehmed wins the chief architect the favour of Sultan Süleyman, who then commissions his own mosque. Sinan and his patron hold a 'consultation' (*meşveret*) during which the plan of the building (*resm-i binā*) and its site are selected.[127] The collection of rare columns and marbles from antique ruins emphasized in the text echoes Justinian's appropriation for Hagia Sophia of antique spolia from pagan temples all over his empire with decrees sent to provincial governors.

According to the *Diegesis* and its translations, spolia – removed from pagan temples in Rome, Ephesus, Cyzicus (Aydıncık, where Solomon built a palace), the Cyclades, the Troad, Baalbek, Palmyra and Egypt – more valuable than their weight in gold, had been used in the construction of Hagia Sophia. The church was not just a magnificent monument, but the product of an imperial building process exemplifying Justinian's orchestration of manpower and material resources across the territories of his vast empire. The comparable transportation of columns and marbles for Süleyman's mosque complex represents a deliberate reenactment of building practices from antiquity. The *Tez̠kiretü'l-bünyān* draws attention to the value of spoliated marbles brought from various imperial provinces for the Süleymaniye:

> Each of its coloured marbles, which arouse admiration in men of perception, came from a different land as a keepsake. According to historians, most of them originated from the palace Solomon had built for the Queen of Sheba. The white marbles were quarried in the Marmara island (Proconnesus) and the green ones came from the Arab lands, while the incomparable porphyry roundels and panels were priceless treasures.[128]

The reference to marbles originating from Solomon's palace is confirmed by the daily account books of the Süleymaniye, which record marbles brought from Aydıncık (Cyzicus), the legendary site of the palace of Süleyman's namesake. The *Tez̠kiretü'l-bünyān* also describes how the Maiden's Column (Kıztaşı) in Istanbul, one of the four colossal red granite columns supporting the lateral arches of the Süleymaniye's domed baldachin, was removed with ropes and pulleys using yet another ancient technique:

> Erecting timbers tall like ship's masts with the world-protecting sultan's order, we created a multi-layered strong scaffolding. Then we collected massive ship cables in one place and passed mooring ropes thick as a man's body through iron pulleys, reinforcing the column all around with ship masts. In two places those ship cables thick as a man's body were attached to steel pulleys, and in many places strong windlasses and gigantic treadmills rotating like the wheel of heaven were set up. Thousands of novice boys entered into the treadmills and numerous Christian galley slaves resembling the demons of Solomon shouted in unison 'Heave ho!'. Then an additional tow-rope was attached to the above mentioned strong cable. With cries of 'Allah! Allah!' as soon as they uprooted from the ground the column resembling the axle of the wheel of heaven, sparks streamed forth from the pulleys like a thunderbolt. And the colossal cable, unable to bear the strain, cracked like a cannon. Fibres flew far and wide like cotton from the cotton-fluffer's bow. Immediately it was reinforced with additional tow-ropes, and to the cries of 'Allah! Allah!' the column was lowered to the ground with ease during the sultan's rule. Sacrificial lambs were slaughtered and gifts distributed to the poor. Then the demons of Solomon placed the column on a slipway and brought it to the construction site.[129]

A similar technique is illustrated in low-relief on the base of the Egyptian obelisk at the Hippodrome in Istanbul, which depicts the erection of the obelisk itself along with imperial games presided over by Theodosius I (379–95). The spectacle value of such engineering feats was also prized in Renaissance Italy. A celebrated example is the architect Domenico Fontana's (1586) moving of the Vatican obelisk in St Peter's square to its present location. Fontana proudly records the process as a testament to Sixtus V's triumph over paganism.[130] Precious building materials laboriously transported from great distances were likewise valued in Italy: Alberti says valuable columns and stones are what makes a monument impressive 'especially if the stone comes from abroad and has been conveyed along a difficult route.'[131] It is no surprise, then, that the *Tezkiretü'l-bünyān* proudly identifies the origin of three other red granite columns in the Süleymaniye:

> With His Majesty's permission its [Maiden's Column] excess was cut and brought to the same height with the other columns. One of these columns was brought from Alexandria on a barge. Another one had been carried [on a slipway] from Baalbek up to the coast from which it was loaded onto a barge; and the remaining column was found ready [in the royal storehouse] at the imperial palace.[132]

Seeking to avoid the tragic fate of Mehmed II's royal architect, Sinan is careful to indicate that the Maiden's Column was shortened with the sultan's permission. In fact, Süleyman, when he comes to find out why the completion of his mosque is delayed, threateningly reminds him about the execution of his namesake, Atik Sinan:

> When the felicitous sultan was in Edirne, the palace of Ferhad Pasha was built (1557). At that time various gossips, who wished to sow the seeds of discord and who were filled with hatred and loathing, wrote scurrilously that the building superviser and scribes had been repairing their own houses while pretending to work in the construction [of the mosque] and that all the houses built at that time used embezzled materials belonging to the noble mosque. Because of this the mosque could not be completed on time, they claimed. These questions should in fact have been addressed to the building superviser (*emīn-i binā*), but this menial servant was also accused by some idiots who said: 'He is incapable of removing the wooden centering (*ḳaraçav*) of the building for fear that his fault may become self evident! It is not certain that the dome will stand. The fellow is infatuated with it; he spends the whole day gazing at it, unable to find a solution. Obsessed with it, he has lost his sanity!'[133]

The dome centering of the Süleymaniye, which served as scaffolding for the decorators, must have been structurally much more elaborate than the type of rotating centering used for smaller domes (described by W. Eton in 1799).[134] The reference to Sinan's fear of removing the wooden centering of his dome is yet another allusion to Hagia Sophia myths, which attribute the collapse of its dome to the impatience of Justinian which triggered the untimely removal of its carelessly dismantled centering. Anxious to see the completion of his mosque, the furious sultan finds Sinan busy at the construction site, designing the decorative details of the mihrab and minbar himself:

> While his humble servant, quite unaware of this situation, was at the place where the workshop of marble-workers (*mermerciler kārḫānesi*) is located, occupying myself with the plan (*ṭarḥ*) and elevation (*taḳsīm*) of the noble mihrab and the high minbar, our felicitous sultan suddenly arrived. Politely greeting him, I stood waiting in his presence. Our late sultan, who has been granted peace and forgiveness by God, wrathfully asked this pitifully weak subject about the circumstances of those [other] buildings and said, 'Why don't you restrict your attention to my mosque and not waste time with unimportant things? Isn't the example of my ancestor sultan Mehmed Khan's architect enough for you? When will this building reach completion? Tell me at once or you know what the consequences will be!'[135]

In response, Sinan promises to finish the mosque in two months and the sultan says, 'Well, architect, if this building is not completed at the end of two months, then we will talk again!' Suspecting that the chief architect is incapacitated with fear for his head, the sultan asks his palace aghas to interrogate him. Süleyman revisits the construction site a week later and asks, 'Well, architect, do you still think you can keep your word?'[136] Sinan confirms his pledge, which he then fulfills against all odds with his superior management skills:

> This humble servant instructed all available builders, unemployed stone-cutters, and the [workless] rabble, and appointed capable foremen, and corner by corner delegated piece work that could be subcontracted on a lump sum basis to capable masters for a flat rate. To supervise each of them, I appointed teams of trustworthy and hard-working men. Holding an iron staff in my hand, I continually kept rotating around the centre and circumference of the dome like a compass, day and night, without resting for a single moment.[137]

The Süleymaniye's daily account books reveal that just before its completion in 1557, workers were employed overtime, not even taking weekend breaks.[138] During the mosque's inauguration ceremony, Sinan is greatly honoured by the sultan, who hands over to him the gilded key to its door, following the recommendation of the chief of the privy chamber: 'Your Majesty, your servant the agha of architects is a saintly old man (*pīr-i ʿazīz*); he is a veteran who has laboured on this gate with the wisdom of the sage Lokman.'[139] This is followed by a poem in which Sinan is characterized as the 'blessed architect' and the 'saint of the dervish convent of the world'.[140]

The Süleymaniye's opening ceremony not only vindicates Sinan against his enemies, but also proves his superiority to his predecessor and namesake. At the same time, the ceremony reveals the justice of Süleyman as a generous patron. This is recognized by Mustafa Āli, who contrasts the just sultan's donation

120 Selimiye mosque, c. 1581, watercolour on paper, from Lokman, *Shahnāma-i Salīm Khān*.

of a sanjak to Sinan's son, with the dire fates suffered by Ignatius and Atik Sinan: the former was imprisoned when the dome of Hagia Sophia collapsed and the latter was executed by Mehmed II.[141] Sai once again compares Sinan's relationship with his royal patron to that of Farhad and Shirin. It is out of his love for the sultan and for his own art that Sinan carves the mountainlike Süleymaniye: 'He approaches his task with Shirin's love, / Behold the mountain and stones hewn by that Farhad. // Art's soldier he is, ready to give up his life for it, / Whenever with a challenging task he finds himself enlisted.'[142]

The last major challenge recorded in the *Teẕkiretü'l-bünyān* comes from Sinan's professional rivals in Europe, the 'so-called architects of the infidels', who claim (presumably after the Süleymaniye's completion) that a dome as large as that of Hagia Sophia could not possibly be built by the Muslims. The chief architect builds the Selimiye to contradict them (illus. 120). In a famous passage, he announces the competitive programme of the mosque, which challenges two previously unsurpassed feats of construction: the dome of Hagia Sophia and the unique triple-galleried minaret of the Üç Şerefeli mosque featuring three helicoidal staircases:

> After [Selim II] ascended the imperial throne with felicity, having an excessive regard and affection for the city of Edirne, he ordered [there] the construction of a mosque that would be matchless in the world. Therefore, this humble servant drew up a plan (*resm*) for a monumental mosque in Edirne worth being seen by the people of the world. Its four minarets have been placed on the four sides of the dome, each having three galleries. Two of them feature three independent staircases forming separate passages [to the galleries]. The minaret of the Üç Şerefeli, built in the old days, is like a tower, being excessively thick. The difficulty of making the minarets of this [Selimiye] both refined (*nāzik*) and with three separate staircases is quite apparent to the judicious. Because a dome as large as that of Ayasofya had not been built during the Muslim era – a thing that people all over the world regarded as impossible – the so-called architects of the infidels used to say 'We have surpassed the Muslims!'. Their invalid presumption was: 'To build such a [big] dome is extremely difficult; if it had been possible to match it (*naẓīre mümkin olsa*), they would have done so.' This had stuck as a sore point and remained fixed in the heart of your humble servant. Working hard on the construction of this mosque, with the help of God – the King, the Conqueror – and under the rule of Sultan Selim Khan, I demonstrated my mastery by making the height (*ḳadd*) of this dome 6 cubits [4.5 metres] and its circuit (*devr*) 4 cubits [3 metres] larger [than that of Ayasofya.][143]

The elegantly proportioned tall minarets of the Selimiye eclipsed that of the neighbouring Üç Şerefeli, until then the highest minaret in the Ottoman domains. Built so near their paragon, they proclaim by their synthesis of engineering skill and aesthetic refinement Sinan's triumph over early Ottoman architecture.[144] The competition with Hagia Sophia focuses on the unsurpassed size of its dome. The chief architect boasts: 'The world used to bet that no other dome / Like Ayasofya could ever be made // This soaring dome exceeds it / I know not the rest, for God alone knows the best!'[145]

Sinan's claim to have surpassed the dimensions of Hagia Sophia's dome has long puzzled architectural historians, because the diameter of Selimiye's dome (31.22 metres) is slightly wider than that of its elliptical counterpart (30.9 metres to 31.8 metres), while its height is lower (42.5 metres as opposed to 55.6 metres). His assertion that the Selimiye's dome is both wider and higher is therefore dismissed as a vain boast or an error of Sai.[146] However, instead of contending that he had surpassed the diameter (*ḳutr or çāp*) of Hagia Sophia's dome, Sinan may have been referring to the curvature of its profile.[147] If the height of the dome is measured not from ground level, but from its base, as if it were an autonomous shell, Selimiye's rounder dome with its taller apex is in fact higher than the flatter, saucerlike dome of Hagia Sophia. On these grounds Sinan could rhetorically claim that he had not only succeeded in building 'a dome *as large as* that of Hagia Sophia' – a feat considered impossible – but also in surpassing it (surely he knew the greater difficulty of stabilizing a dome with a lower profile). Evliya Çelebi's comparison between the domes of the Süleymaniye and Hagia Sophia suggests that computing a dome's apex from its base rather than from the ground level was common practice. He recognizes that the height of Hagia Sophia from 'its floor to the finial on its dome is more elevated than the domes of all mosques, but it is flatter (*yaṣṣıca*)'.[148] Nevertheless, he asserts: 'The elevated summit of this [Süleymaniye] mosque's dome is rounder than that of Ayasofya and seven cubits higher from it.'[149]

Having reached the peak of his career, Sinan steered away from paraphrasing the layout of Hagia Sophia in the Selimiye mosque, where he freely explored his own imagination. The *Tezkiretü'l-bünyān* declares the mosque his masterpiece: 'Both in terms of utmost refinement (*nezāket-i diḳḳat*) and overall design (*resm-i heyyet*), / It is the ultimate realization of art.'[150] The Selimiye proves Sinan's capacity for invention, setting up a new standard of its own as an inimitable paragon. Just like the 'response poems' (*naẓīre*) of poets that emulated admired exemplars judged inimitable by critics, the Selimiye's dome was intended as an architectural *naẓīre* responding to the challenge of Hagia Sophia's unsurpassed dome. Once completed, the Selimiye dome itself became the new paragon according to the *Tezkiretü'l-bünyān*: 'No dome like it has been built or can ever be built on earth; / It is a non-pareil equalled only by the sky!'[151] This proud assertion is repeated in the *Tezkiretü'l-ebniye*: 'The people of the world used to say, / "A dome like that of Ayasofya can never be built." // This dome is indeed larger, / God knows best that it is a non-pareil (*naẓīre yoḳdurur*). // It was His favour that served as my guide in this building, / Whose completion was granted with divine blessing.'[152]

Sinan's autobiographies deliberately announce his references to admired monuments from the past to underline his originality in updating and refining his models. By calling the reader's attention to the intertextuality of his mosques, he affirms his historical consciousness and the superiority of the more eloquent present. His Hızır-like saintly status is evoked once again in a poem eulogizing the Selimiye:

> His highness the agha of architects, that patron saint of
> masters (*pīr-i üstādān*)
> Is acknowledged by the whole world for creating his works
> with saintliness (*velāyetle*).
>
> He has wondrously cultivated such a high level of artistic
> mastery,
> That it is not at all among things describable in words.
>
> They say the plan (*resm*) of Ayasofya was designed by
> the saint Hızır,
> This human Hızır accomplished this building [Selimiye],
> do not think of him as a mere builder![153]

The tradition that Hagia Sophia had been designed with the help of Hızır goes back to Persian and Turkish versions of the *Diegesis*. The Greek original attributes the divinely inspired plan to an angel who appears to Justinian in a dream. In some translations Hızır is substituted for the angel, who reveals the same plan to both the emperor and his architect.[154] Unlike Ignatius, Sinan does not need the assistance of Hızır in designing the Selimiye, thanks to his own miracle-working powers.

Even though the *Tezkiretü'l-bünyān* presents the Selimiye as the apogee of the chief architect's career, there is no suggestion in its narrative to lend support to a saying of Sinan that Evliya Çelebi claims to have heard from his father: 'The Şehzade is my apprenticeship work, the Süleymaniye my work as a journeyman, and the Selimiye my work as a master.'[155] Instead, the autobiography refers to the Süleymaniye as a masterpiece in its own right, which 'brought to completion' and 'sealed' Sinan's skill in architecture: 'The possessors of skill know from beginning to end / The many arts that have become manifest in it';[156] and 'The masters of the arts know how rare it is, / In both nimbleness and elegance as well as matchlessness.'[157]

The *Tezkiretü'l-bünyān* abruptly ends with the completion of the Selimiye, the glowing culmination of Sinan's artistry. But the brusque ending of the text implies the unfortunate fate of the building: Selim II passed away before seeing the chief architect's masterpiece and Murad III never laid eyes on it. The absence of an epilogue hints at the sudden interruption of royal patronage with Selim's death, after which no imperial mosque of the same calibre is commissioned by Murad III. The complaint in some critical histories of Hagia Sophia about the lack of appreciation for the 'possessors of skill' during Mehmed II's reign is echoed in the preface of *Tezkiretü'l-bünyān*.[158] Sai's poem entitled 'Complaint about these Times' laments the present devaluation of talent: 'Ignorant and uncouth men are accorded respect, / While the possessors of wisdom have no value. // Nobody pays attention anymore to those whose inner world is rich, / To tell the truth, skill is now regarded as a fault.'[159] Although the poet's complaint primarily refers to his own field, one wonders whether it also insinuates Sinan's disappointment about diminished royal patronage, which he hoped to bring to the attention of the reigning sultan and grand vizier, evoked in the preface. If so, the *Tezkiretü'l-bünyān* can be considered a hitherto unnoted example of the decline discourse that emerged in Ottoman historiography during the last quarter of the sixteenth century.

The abbreviated *Tezkiretü'l-ebniye* focuses on the same royal works. Containing no reference to a grand vizier nor any plea for patronage, this abridged text may have been intended for a more general audience. Its preface expresses the hope that the 'brethren of purity' (*ḫullān-i ṣafā*) who read it over the generations may judge it with fairness and express their remembrance of Sinan with well-wishing prayers. These readers – addressed in the *Tezkiretü'l-bünyān* as 'companions' (*dost*) – are no doubt fellow architects and connoisseurs capable of recognizing the chief architect's innovations with their special powers of discrimination.

Cafer Efendi's architectural treatise and Evliya Çelebi's travelogue (which is filled with attributions of buildings to Sinan) confirm that enthusiasts of architecture read the autobiographies. Evliya does, in fact, claim to be a connoisseur 'acquainted a little with the science of architecture and the works of engineering' thanks to which he examined noteworthy monuments 'with the eye of scrutiny'.[160] Dayezade Mustafa Efendi, the author of an eighteenth-century panegyrical essay on the Selimiye, notes that he consulted a copy of the *Tezkiretü'l-bünyān* at the Revan Kiosk library in the Topkapı Palace.[161] One of the surviving *Tezkiretü'l-ebniye* manuscripts bears the ownership seal of the late-seventeenth-century chief architect Hafiz İbrahim, and copies of both *Tezkire*s travelled as far as Cairo. One of the Cairo manuscripts belonged to Hafiz Hüseyin Ayvansarayi (d. 1786–87) who wrote a description of the mosques of Istanbul.[162]

Sinan's autobiographies are replete with references to architectural experts, referred to as the possessors of skill, perception, understanding, and vision.[163] The prefaces of these works reflect a 'humanist' ethos in their exaltation of humankind as a mirror of God's perfection and their reference to special powers of perception divinely bestowed on select individuals. They describe the creation by the 'Divine Architect' of the multi-tiered heavens without the aid of masons or drafting instruments, along with 'the palace of man's body' fashioned from water and clay and raised above all creatures in terms of nobility of heart and soul. The preface of Sinan's endowment deed similarly narrates the creation of Adam's body as an embodiment of the Divine Artist's wisdom, which raises some men above others by endowing them with special talents.[164] Sinan is clearly one of these favoured men whom Sai compares to Lokman and Hızır.[165] These comparisons are not mere topoi; they reflect the cultural esteem of artistic creativity as a form of God-given inspiration.[166]

There is an implied parallelism between the Divine Architect and His human counterpart and 'agent' Sinan, whose domed mosques are described as microcosmic representations of the universe. The cosmic metaphor perpetuates a theme ubiquitous in the ekphrases of Byzantine church architecture.[167] In the texts of Sai, both prose and verse are packed with natural imagery to undescore the 'mimetic' quality of Sinan's mosques which echo the divine creation, filled with signs of God's wisdom: columns and minarets like cypresses, marbles with wavy patterns like oceans, arches with alternating voussoirs soaring to the heavens in the manner of rainbows, bubble-like domes on the surface of the sea of pleasure, great domes like mountains carved out from the earth, cupolas suspended in the manner of heavenly spheres, interior spaces and fountain courtyards like paradisaical gardens. Sai's poetic images (repeated in Cafer Efendi's treatise) find numerous parallels in descriptions of architecture by Ottoman poets, historians, travellers, and waqfiyya writers (quoted in Part 3), which testify to a widely shared discourse. Such descriptions mirror the aesthetic perceptions that framed the reception of Sinan's works, with their direct sensuous appeal and intensely pleasurable achievements: joy-giving, heart-captivating, and glittering with light.

Encomiums of Sinan were not limited to the texts he commissioned from Sai. The respect he commanded as the agha of royal architects is evident in the honourable titles with which he is addressed in imperial decrees, and in the admiring descriptions of him in contemporary texts. Eyyubi's history of Sultan Süleyman's building projects, written around 1563 prior to Sai's autobiographies, attributes saintly powers to the chief architect: 'God has given him the power of sanctity manifested in miracles (*kerāmet*),/ Endowing his soul with rare spiritual states (*özge ḥālāt*).' The same author praises the 'agha of architects' as 'the philosopher of the age' to whom 'many an Aristotle would willingly become a disciple'.[168]

Mustafa Āli also draws attention to the wisdom manifested in Sinan's works: 'The mighty architect of the noble mosque of Sultan Süleyman Khan, may he be blessed, who was an exemplar of skill and whose works displayed wisdom and insight in their rarity, came to be infinitely favoured, and his dependents were generously rewarded.'[169] Celalzade Mustafa praises the chief architect in glowing terms in his description of the Süleymaniye as 'Üstad Sinan, who is excellent and perfect in the science of architecture, and a superior engineer in the laying of foundations, and an expert in building Friday mosques and masjids that serve to strengthen the perpetuity of merit, the perfect architect with blessed fingertips and wisdom in august matters, the first among the chiefs of expert and famous builders, incomparable in this age in terms of intelligence, who is unique and rare among his peers in all times and ages.'[170]

Despite the enthusiasm for architecture and the centrality of architectural patronage in the modes of conspicuous consumption by the ruling elite, Ottoman high culture did not develop a written discourse on the theory of architecture. We have seen that Vitruvius' *De architectura*, which inspired theoretical treatises written in Renaissance Italy, was not unknown in the Ottoman world. Beyond the orbit of European humanist culture, however, its resonance remained limited: Ottoman 'humanism' was not steeped in homage to the Greco-Roman literary tradition; in the realm of literature, the preferred models were Turco-Persian and Arabic 'classics'. The absence of treatises addressed to learned patrons or fellow architects does not justify the conclusion that Sinan's architecture lacked a theoretical basis and was entirely based on an empirical approach to design.[171] Such a conclusion underestimates the importance of orality in the transmission of knowledge in Ottoman architectural culture and the estimation of architecture as a 'science' in contemporary texts. The theoretical dimensions of Ottoman architectural practice were not articulated in treatises because the transmission of professional knowledge remained largely confined to workshop training within the corps of royal architects headed by Sinan.

Nor does the lack of theoretical treatises warrant the inference that the Ottoman ruling elite was architecturally illiterate, an assumption contradicted by the extensive involvement of the *askeri* class at all levels of the construction industry, to which I shall turn in the next chapter. Sinan's patrons certainly possessed a sophisticated knowledge of architecture and refined tastes that informed the projects they commissioned. It is incorrectly presumed that the chief architect enjoyed nearly complete control over the design process in a 'theoretical vacuum' that gave free reign to his 'artistic will'.[172] This presumption takes at face value the self-centred image constructed in his autobiographies, proving their ultimate success in shaping the memory of his legacy.

III. SİNAN'S PERSONA IN HIS ENDOWMENT DEED

The epitaph Sai composed for the chief architect's tomb summarizes the divine maestro's achievements. Facing the street above an iron-grilled prayer window on the stone precinct wall of the tomb garden, the Turkish inscription asks passers-by to offer prayers of blessing for Sinan's soul (illus. 121):[173]

> O you, who settle for a day or two in life's palace,
> The world is not a place of repose for man.
>
> Becoming the architect of Süleyman Khan, this distinguished man
> Built him a Friday mosque that is a sign of the highest paradise.
>
> With the sultan's orders he exerted great effort on water channels,
> Like Hızır, he made the water of life flow to the people.
>
> At the [Büyük] Çekmece bridge such a lofty arch did he raise that
> Identical it is to the form of the Milky Way in the mirror of Time.
>
> He built more than four hundred lofty masjids,
> Creating Friday mosques in eighty places, this divine maestro.
>
> He lived more than a hundred years and finally passed away;
> May God make his resting place the garden of paradise.

121 Inscription over the iron-grilled prayer window of Sinan's tomb, Istanbul.

> Sai the well-wisher said the date of his departure: 'Passed away from the world at this time, Sinan,
> the patron saint of architects, 996 [1587–88],'
> May old and young offer the Fatiha [Opening sura] for his soul.

The chief architect established a waqf to perpetuate his memory through monuments carrying his own name and endowed with a staff to offer continual prayers for the salvation of his soul. His undated endowment deed eulogizes 'Sinan Agha the son of Abdurrahman' as 'the eye of the notables of engineers, the ornament of the pillars of foundation-layers, the master of the masters of the age, the chief of the epoch's ingenious men, the Euclid of the century and all times, the architect of the sultanate and the imperial master architect.'[174] It lists the pious foundations and income-producing properties that Sinan endowed towards the end of his life. Signed by the army judge of Rumelia, Kazasker İvaz Efendi, who held that post twice (in 1583 and 1585), the waqfiyya seems to have been recorded around 1583–85, close to Sinan's trip to Mecca.[175] His pious foundations comprised a masjid and elementary school with a public fountain in the Yenibahçe quarter of Istanbul, another elementary school built next to his mausoleum adjoining the Süleymaniye complex, a public fountain and arable field donated by an imperial patent in his home town, Ağırnas, and two more public fountains at the villages of Urgaz (in Vize) and Soğanlı (in Haslar beyond Eyüp).

For the upkeep and staff of these monuments Sinan endowed 300,000 aspers that would be loaned at interest and real estate properties in Istanbul. The properties comprised thirty-three residences, fifteen shops, a boathouse, and a large garden in Yenibahçe. He also endowed four mills at the village of Gergeme in Kayseri, each with a tax exemption of thirty aspers donated for his waqf with an imperial patent (*temliknāme*). The chief architect reserved the right to use the surplus income of his endowment while he was alive. After his death, ten thousand aspers from the surplus were to be sealed in a bag kept as a

122 Sinan's masjid in Yenibahçe, Istanbul.

reserve fund for repairs. The remaining surplus was to be divided equally among Sinan's children, grandchildren, and descendants over the generations. When his progeny became extinct, this money would be spent on creating stone-paved sidewalks for pedestrians (*piyāde ḳaldırımı*) one cubit and six fingers wide in Istanbul wherever they were needed, an urban charity particularly suitable for Sinan, who spent most of his life shaping that city.[176]

The chief architect appoints himself the administrator and overseer of his waqf. After his demise the chief architects who succeeded him would oversee his endowment, a testimony to Sinan's sense of corporate identity. So long as capable individuals existed among his children and grandchildren and his freed slaves, and their children, the waqf administrators would not be chosen from 'outsiders'.[177] The endowment's secondary overseers would be the congregation of Sinan's masjid in Yenibahçe, its imam and muezzin, the staff of his endowment, his descendants, and freed slaves (illus. 122).[178] The ten architects who signed the endowment deed as witnesses must have been Sinan's close associates. The list is headed by his favourite, Mehmed Subaşı, whom he had selected as his lieutenant before leaving for Mecca in 1584 and was likely regarding as his successor. Others on the list are Mahmud Halife (d. 1586), İsmail b. Abdullah, Ahmed b. Abdullah, Hızır b. Abdullah, Ferruh b. Abdullah, Mustafa b. Abdullah (d. 1586), Mehmed b. Abdullah, Süleyman b. Abdullah, and Mehmed b. Veys (Appendix 4.4). The absence of Davud, who succeeded Sinan in 1588, from this list is striking (Appendix 4.4, 4.5). I argue in the epilogue that he owed his position to the patronage ties he cultivated with the powerful harem faction.[179]

At least two of the three fountains endowed by the chief architect as personal memorials in the villages of Ağırnas (Kayseri), Urgaz (Vize), and Soğanlı (Haslar near Eyüp) were connected to landed properties associated with his memory. The one in his home town must have been the piece of land he requested from Selim II in 1571. We learn from an imperial decree dated 1576 that he also had a fief (*arpalıḳ*) in Vize.[180] The nature of his connection with Soğanlı, possibly an estate he owned, has yet to be established.[181] The fountain in Ağırnas, like his effort to save Christian relatives residing there and in nearby villages from being resettled at Cyprus in 1573, is a touching testament to Sinan's emotional attachment to his birthplace.

The waqfiyya provides additional details about the chief architect's family. For the souls of his deceased wife Mihri bint-i Mahmud, and his martyred son Mehmed Beg, he designated two individuals to recite a thirtieth section of the Koran daily.[182] For Mehmed's 'fine soul' Sinan also endowed four aspers a day so that pavements would be created wherever they were needed.[183] The chief architect's grandson Derviş Çelebi attended the law court that approved his waqfiyya.[184] Sinan's two daughters, Ümmihan and Neslihan, were assigned a stipend of three aspers a day.[185] Together with their dead brother's daughter Fahri, they received an additional daily income of eleven aspers each. The waqfiyya also allocates funds to Sinan's three grand-nieces born to the two sons of his Christian brother residing in Kayseri: 'to Raziye and Kerime, who are the daughters of his brother's son whom he brought from Kayseri and made a Muslim, and to Ayşe, who is the daughter of Süleyman, the [late] son of his brother who became a Muslim and a *sekbān* [keeper of hounds in the janissary corps], he assigned a daily stipend of five aspers each.'[186]

The endowment deed allocates three contiguous houses to these grand-nieces who are asked to pray for Sinan every moment. The houses belonged to the chief architect's estate at Yenibahçe, which was a meadow near the land walls where janissary houndsmen grazed hounds as had the chief architect. After his grand-nieces passed away, their houses would be given to Sinan's needy descendants until his lineage became extinct and would thereafter be rented out. Sinan assigned 'eleven newly built rooms' in his mansion to the most deserving among his freed slaves on condition that they regularly offer prayers of gratitude for him. Once their descendants ceased to exist these rooms, too, would be rented out. Known as the 'Shahnama-writer's house' (Şehnameci evi), Sinan's mansion featured six second-storey rooms, four halls, three ground-storey rooms, a stable, two wells, and two toilets. It was endowed along with a neighbouring garden adjacent to his masjid and elementary school in Yenibahçe. This was 'a large garden (*bostān*) with fruit-bearing and non-fruit-bearing trees, an open shed, three pools, running water, a tap, and on top of a raised terrace a kiosk (*köşk*) built in the middle.' With a sultanic permit, surplus water conducted from the water wheel of Ali Pasha's bath flowed into the tap of the garden. In addition, bitter water channelled with a 'royal order' from a water distribution cistern located 'near his own endowed house' was carried to a fountain near Sinan's masjid and to his endowed garden.[187]

Sinan endowed a water channel to conduct some of this bitter water 'for the ablutions of the Muslims' to the neighbouring

123 The astronomer Takiyüddin and his colleagues working at the Galata observatory, 1581, watercolour on paper, from Lokman, *Shahanshāhnāma*.

'Friday mosque built by Hüma Hatun'; his autobiographies list the mosque, popularly named after her husband Bali Pasha, among his corpus.[188] An additional endowment to this mosque in 1592 by Hızır b. Abdullah (the captain of royal water channel experts, *ḫāṣṣa ṣuyolcı bölükbaşı*) implies that the residents of the neighbourhood included some of the royal architects who had signed Sinan's waqfiyya.[189] Among them, Mehmed b. Veys is identified as an 'inhabitant of that quarter.'[190]

Sinan's large residence known as 'Şehnameci evi' was in all likelihood the one formerly owned by the court historian Şehnameci Arifi Fethullah Çelebi (d. 1561–62), who in the 1550s added rooms for calligraphers employed in the production of a multi-volume illustrated world history commissioned by Sultan Süleyman.[191] Sinan's friendship with the poet-painter Mustafa Sai may well have developed in the artistic milieu of Yenibahçe. The new quarter created around his masjid and school came to be known as Mimar Sinan Mahallesi; the waqfiyya refers to it as 'the quarter associated with himself'. A legal document dated 1566, which records the sale of a large house to Sinan at the 'chief architect's quarter near the site known as Yenibahçe', reveals that this neighbourhood where he owned properties was already associated with him at that date.[192] The waqfiyya lists the houses and shops he endowed there: three adjacent residences contiguous to the elementary school, seven residences adjacent to the masjid (two of them endowed for the imam and muezzin), and seven residences with shops across the masjid.[193]

Sinan's personal attachment to the neighbourhood is captured by a clause in his waqfiyya which requires the endowment administrator to set aside one asper a day and hand it over to the imam of the masjid. With this the latter would pay extraordinary taxes (*avarız*) imposed on the neighbourhood people, and cover other communal needs in consultation with them.[194] The pious imam had to lead the five daily congregational prayers in Sinan's masjid, reciting on behalf of the endower the Ya-Sin sura after each morning prayer. It was also the imam's duty to be the teacher of the elementary school and to read a thirtieth section of the Koran for Sinan. The muezzin would recite for the endower's benefit the al-Mulk sura after each night-time prayer and would serve as assistant teacher in the elementary school and as janitor in the masjid.[195]

An imperial decree addressed to the kadi of Istanbul in 1578 shows that the imam and muezzin possessed a valuable collection of mathematical manuscripts, once owned by the scholar Molla Lutfi (d. 1495), that are ordered to be given to the royal observatory in Galata (illus. 123):

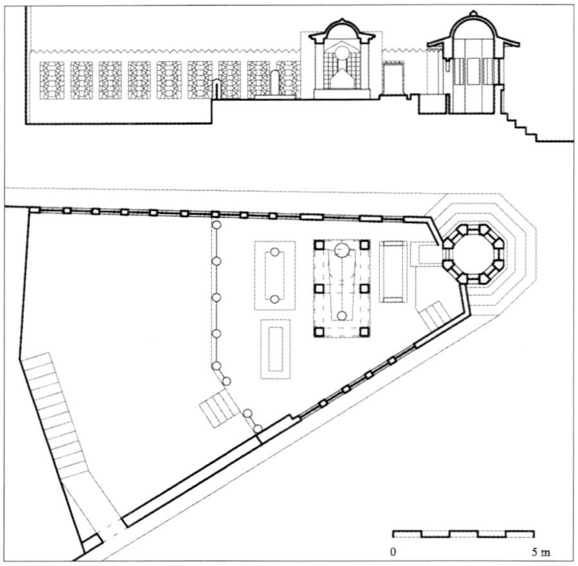

124 Plan and cross-section of Sinan's tomb enclosure, Istanbul, with a baldachin over his sarcophagus on a raised prayer platform and an octagonal domed water dispenser at the corner.

125 Sinan's tomb by the Süleymaniye complex, with a domed water dispenser.

> Since it has been reported that the late Lutfullah's [Molla Lutfi] books for astronomers are in the possession of the imam and muezzin of the quarter of Mimar Sinan in the above-mentioned protected city [Istanbul], I order them to be taken and given to the imperial observatory [in Galata]. When my royal order arrives, without delay find whoever has the books of the deceased, dealing with the science of astronomy and geometry, whether they are in the hands of those individuals or others, and give all of them to the pride of astronomers, Mevlana Takiyüddin, may his virtue continue, who is now fulfilling the service of astronomical observation, without allowing anybody to dispute and contend this order.[196]

The fact that rare manuscripts on the mathematical sciences were kept by the imam and muezzin of Sinan's masjid testifies to the learned milieu of the neighbourhood named after him. These manuscripts would have been relevant for architectural practice, since geometrical surveying techniques used by royal architects involved the use of the quadrant, a simplified form of the astrolabe principally made for astronomical observation. We have seen above how Sinan used such an instrument, much like his colleagues in Europe did, to survey Istanbul's water sources.[197] It is not surprising, then, that an astronomer called Molla Fütuh was included in a survey committee Sinan headed in 1582 to prepare an estimate for a canal connecting Lake Sapanca to the Bay of İzmit.[198]

The chief architect's endowment deed emphasizes the performance of the obligatory daily prayers, Sunni practices, and canonically approved rituals in his masjid for which he endowed a copy of a popular Turkish manual on orthodox religious practice: 'The elegant book called *Ḥulviyyāt* [*Ḥulviyyāt-ı Şāhī*, Royal Sweetmeats] for the needy in search of pleasing God.'[199] Only the kiosk-type stone minaret of the modest masjid, which was covered by a hipped roof and built of alternating courses of stone and brick, is now preserved. The rest of the building, damaged during a fire in 1918, was entirely rebuilt in 1976 on the basis of a sketch by Gurlitt and the archaeological remains.[200]

The site of Sinan's second elementary school and tomb is a plot adjacent to his main residence at the edge of the Süleymaniye complex, described in the waqfiyya (illus. 124, 125, 167):

> His own residence near the sultanic complex, may God protect it from calamities, containing three walled courtyards – one interior, one middle, and one exterior – the interior [courtyard] consisting of ten second-storey rooms, two ground-storey rooms, a bakery, two bath-houses, a kitchen, a storage depot, and five toilets; the middle [courtyard] consisting of two second-storey rooms with a roof loggia and a hall in between and a garden in front; six stables and a room in front of the stables featuring a storehouse above and a water well; and the outer [courtyard] consisting of four contiguous chambers, the south side of the whole [residence] being adjacent to the noble madrasa of the late Sultan Süleyman Khan and the other three sides surrounded by public streets.[201]

This residence was endowed along with twenty shops adjacent to its façade, 'an upper storey elementary school', and a walled enclosure surrounded by 'a most beautifully constructed geometric lattice of stone' (*aḥcār-i müşebbeke*)' The enclosure prepared as the site of Sinan's tomb was adjacent to the north side of his residence. The chief architect reserved the right to reside there as long as he lived, after which his descendants would live in it until their lineage became extinct; thereafter it would be rented out.[202]

Anonymous petitions sent to Murad III in 1577 complained about the lavish bath-houses and water installations of Sinan's residence, accusing him of illegally diverting water from the Süleymaniye complex. An imperial decree ordered the kadi of Istanbul to investigate these compaints, but we do not know the results of the ensuing inspection.[203] Whatever its basis was, the accusation is a telling example of the biting envy of rivals against which Sinan had to struggle on other occasions narrated by his autobiography. He must have obtained royal permission for the site of his tomb, since burial inside the walled city was an exceptional privilege granted by the sultans. Sai's epitaph identifies Sinan as the architect of the neighbouring paradise-like Süleymaniye mosque. Through the grilled window below the inscription one can view the interior of the ornate domed baldachin over his sarcophagus, which features a headstone sculpted in the shape of a bulbous coiled turban (*mücevveze*) (illus. 126). The visual integration of Sinan's endowed residence, shops, elementary school, and funerary garden into the Süleymaniye complex inscribed the chief architect's signature on his architectural masterpiece (illus. 167–68). The small triangular piazza in front of his tomb enclosure – framed by a domed water dispenser, the guest-house of the Süleymaniye complex, and the janissary agha's palace – provides an ideal oblique perspective of the sultanic mosque.[204]

126 Sculpted turban of Sinan's sarcophagus and its domed baldachin seen from the street through an iron-grilled prayer window.

The water dispenser, which was financed with surplus funds from Süleyman's endowment and added to the corner of Sinan's tomb enclosure in 1587, ambiguously blurs the boundaries of the sultan's and the chief architect's waqfs. Its construction shortly before Sinan passed away was authorized with an imperial decree addressed to the endowment administrator of the Süleymaniye:

> Presently the chief architect, Sinan Agha, may his glory be increased, has sent a petition reporting that a large group of individuals living around the late Sultan Süleyman's noble mosque in the protected city of Istanbul came to request the construction of a water dispenser (*sebīlḫāne*) for the soul of Sultan Süleyman Khan at the prayer platform (*muṣalla yiri*) near the janissary agha's residence, which is a public place of passage at the intersection of three streets distant from the [neighbourhood] fountain. Since the construction of a water dispenser on that site has been judged decorous, he asks for a decree to be sent to the endowment administrator for its construction with that mosque's endowment funds.[205]

The fact that this document does not mention Sinan's projected tomb (now standing above the open-air prayer platform) implies a deliberate omission in the chief architect's petition, lest his request be seen as a self-serving pretext to monumentalize his own tomb enclosure, whose plan has been compared to an open compass.[206] The widespread misidentification of the domed water dispenser as a personal charity of Sinan hints at a calculated ambiguity he must surely have been aware of.

The chief architect's endowment deed specifies that the teacher and assistant teacher of 'the elementary school located on the site reserved for his own tomb' were each required to recite a thirtieth section of the Koran for him daily.[207] The inextricable link of his waqf with the Süleymaniye complex is underlined by the following clause: 'At the tribune (*kursi*) placed inside the noble mosque of the late Sultan Süleyman Khan, everyday at noon-time a pious chanter should beautifully recite a tenth portion of the holy Koran and dedicate its merit to the endower [Sinan].' Moreover, the thirty litany chanters of the mosque were allocated half an asper each to gather at Sinan's tomb daily to recite for him the Ikhlas sura three times and the Fatiha once.[208]

The fusion of his waqf with the sultanic complex was also expressed by an endowment of eighteen aspers, earmarked for madrasa graduates residing in eighteen chambers tucked under the retaining walls of the twin madrasas adjacent to his residence.[209] Everyday these madrasa graduates, waiting to be appointed to the ranks of the ulema, had to recite a thirtieth section of the Koran for the souls of all prophets, the Prophet Muhammad, and the chief architect.[210] Three individuals, who each day at any time or place recited a thirtieth section of the Koran for Sinan were to gather in his endowed residence annually on the tenth day of Muharram. Following a charitable banquet for the poor, these individuals had to read the whole Koran on behalf of the endower, after which alms would be distributed to those present.[211] The account books of the endowment of the Süleymaniye mention the costs of food and bread periodically donated for 'the feast of the *miʿmār aġa*'. This implies that Sultan Süleyman had rewarded his chief architect by assigning for his charitable feasts a special allowance of food cooked in the hospice kitchens.[212] Given Sinan's intimate connection with the Süleymaniye complex, it is not surprising that one of his household members was appointed its endowment administrator in 1596. According to Selaniki, 'the late Koca Mimar Sinan Agha's protégé, Kabil Çavuş' was assigned that position because of his expertise in financial administration.[213]

The plot of land for Sinan's residence must have been donated with a sultanic patent to facilitate the architect's supervision of the Süleymaniye complex during its decade-long construction. We know that Atik Sinan (d. 1471) was given a piece of land near the complex of Mehmed II while he was in charge of its construction. On that plot, he, too, endowed for himself and his heirs a residence that featured many small and large rooms on two floors.[214] A privilege unique to Sinan, however, was the insertion of his impressive tomb with a domed baldachin into the grounds of the Süleymaniye complex. The simpler burial places of his predecessors, adjoining the hipped-roof mosques and masjids they endowed, were marked by domeless sarcophagi featuring flat stones at their head and feet.

Atik Sinan (Sinanüddin Yusuf b. Abdullah), a manumitted slave, had two waqfiyyas drawn up in 1465 and 1468. He endowed a funerary complex consisting of a masjid and an elementary school on a plot of land donated to him by Mehmed II at the quarter of Kıztaşı (Maiden's Column), to the west of the sultan's mosque complex. The extant masjid, known today as Kumrulu Mescid, features a tomb garden where the executed royal architect is buried.[215] He also endowed a residence that functioned as a dervish convent (*zāviye*) in the quarter of Baba Saltuk, adjacent to the masjid of Aşıkpaşa, and dedicated it to the shaykh Yahyaoğlu Derviş Ahmed (the historian Aşıkpaşazade) and his descendants. For his pious foundation, the architect endowed a number of houses and shops in the city.[216]

In 1523–24 near Yenikapı Sinan's predecessor, the chief architect nicknamed Acem Alisi (Alaüddin Ali Beg b. Abdülkerim; Alaüddin Ali Beg b. Abdülvehhab), built a masjid-like Friday mosque with a hipped roof, accompanied by an elementary school and a Halveti convent (*zāviye*). The convent, sited across from the mosque, functioned as a residence for dervishes whose food expenses were covered by endowed funds. The chief architect's sarcophagus is behind the mihrab of the mosque, known as Mimar Acem Camii.[217] To support this funerary complex, Acem Alisi endowed fewer properties than Sinan did: 15,000 aspers, twenty-seven shops, and nineteen houses in the capital, most of which had shops underneath. We learn from his two waqfiyyas of 1525 and 1537 that he also endowed his residence at the Oruçgazi quarter in Aksaray for his own use. Following his death, this residence, consisting of 'many ground-storey and second-storey rooms, a kitchen, a bath-house, bakeries, two stables, a roof loggia, a hall, two chambers, and toilets' would be inhabited by his descendants until they became extinct.[218] The house seems to have been less monumental than that of Sinan next to the Süleymaniye complex, which was complemented by a second residence at Yenibahçe with a garden featuring pools and a kiosk. Nor is there any mention of household slaves among the beneficiaries of the waqf of Acem Alisi.

Unlike Atik Sinan and Acem Alisi, Sinan did not endow a dervish convent: a preference that may be rooted in the rigid orthodoxy of Süleyman's reign during which he matured.[219] The assumption that he was affiliated with the Bektashi order of dervishes because of his janissary background is not supported by his waqfiyya, in which he endows a manual for orthodox worship. Likewise, the *Teẕkire*s simply refer to the symbolic initiation of the janissary corps into the Bektashi order, rather than announce Sinan's personal affiliation with that order: 'With my trade, my art, and my service / As well as my perseverance among peers / I laboured since my childhood days / And matured in the hearth of Hacı Bektaş Veli (the janissary corps).' By the sixteenth century, it is difficult to discern more than a nominal link between the janissaries and the saint Hacı Bektaş Veli, whose sufi order had assumed a Shiʿi identity incompatible with the state's Sunni orthodoxy.[220]

Sinan's endowment deed bears testimony not just to his intense piety but also to a civic consciousness expressed by the creation of several public fountains and sidewalks for pedestrians. Far from being the misunderstood genius of architectural rationalism, out of sync with the rest of a society caught in medieval irrationalism, he fully assimilated the mentalities of the context in which his identity was forged and his artistic orientations were formed.[221] The chief architect perpetuated his remembrance by means of his endowments and autobiographies that claimed authorship for an impressive corpus of monuments. The collective aspect of the corpus, created with the mediation of the corps of royal architects discussed in the next chapter, came to be almost completely overshadowed by the unabashed self-aggrandizement through which Sinan successfully controlled the shaping of memory over the generations.

Chapter 5

INSTITUTIONAL FRAMEWORKS OF ARCHITECTURAL PRACTICE

I. THE CORPS OF ROYAL ARCHITECTS
II. THE CHIEF ARCHITECT AS ADMINISTRATOR AND DESIGNER
III. THE CONSTRUCTION INDUSTRY

I. THE CORPS OF ROYAL ARCHITECTS

The earliest known references to the 'corps of royal architects' (*miʿmārān-ı ḫāṣṣa, ḫāṣṣa miʿmārları*) date from the reign of Bayezid II (1481–1512), even though its kernel seems to have emerged during the flurry of building activity triggered by the conquest of Constantinople.[1] During Sinan's tenure the corps was bureaucratically consolidated as an administrative branch of the centralized state to cope with the upsurge of construction enterprises coordinated from the capital. The emergence of the chief architect's innovative style coincided with the total revamping of the depleted corps, injected with new blood. The membership of the corps of royal architects before Sinan's tenure had manifested a remarkable continuity from the late fifteenth century to the early part of Süleyman's reign. The break in continuity during the 1540s paralleled the flowering of Sinan's 'classical' idiom, which was disseminated throughout the empire by royal architects dispatched from Istanbul and by city architects stationed in major provincial capitals.

In 1844 Charles White compared the Ottoman chief architect to the minister of a board of public works, who commanded a council of architects created by Bayezid II:

> Although police regulations relative to the cleansing and good keeping of public thoroughfares are much neglected, the laws concerning the construction of houses are imperative and nicely defined. In order to ensure direct compliance, and to preserve some degree of regularity in the construction of houses and the laying out of new streets, Bajazet II established a council of architecture, and placed at its head a Mimar Agha, or President of Board of Works.[2]

Before architects were organized as a corps under Bayezid II, they were loosely grouped within the ranks of 'distinguished royal servants' (*müteferriḳa*). Angiolello, an Italian page attached to Mehmed II's court, reports that the members of this motley group receiving monthly wages included the sons of nobles and defeated monarchs, physicians, astrologers, architects, engineers, painters, goldsmiths, jewellers, and other artisans.[3] One of the earliest surviving registers of royal servants with 'monthly wages' (*müşāhereḫorān*) datable to Bayezid II's reign (1490s) mentions the 'corps of architects, carpenters, lathe turners, and their assistants': in all, twenty-one individuals.[4] Most of the court artists were paid tri-monthly wages recorded in the registers of 'craftsmen' (*ehl-i ḥiref*). By contrast, architects are listed in monthly wage registers along with the privileged sons of grandees and vassals, palace aghas, physicians, court messengers (*çavuş*), scribes, musicians, poets, royal companions, astrologers, and distinguished royal servants.

A book of royal donations (1503–12) lists some members of the 'corps of architects' (*cemāʿat-i miʿmārān*) rewarded by Bayezid II for their services in specific building projects (Appendix 4.1).[5] These architects were complemented by others enrolled in the 'corps of royal water channels' (*cemāʿat-ı rāh-i āb-ı ḫāṣṣa*) headed by Mimar Hayrüddin.[6] The book of royal donations also lists architect-restorers of the palace and royal mosques, along with such specialists as lead sheet makers, glaziers, marble cutters, bricklayers, and carpenters employed at the construction-related workshops of the Topkapı Palace's imperial garden.[7] Sixteenth-century documents indicate that some trainees of these workshops, grouped near the 'royal storehouse' (*anbār-ı ḫāṣṣa*) at the left side of the palace's first court, were promoted to the corps of royal architects. The storehouse had a staff of its own, including a storekeeper, a scribe, novices, and artisans including architect-restorers, carpenters, marble cutters, lime-burners, whitewashers, water-channel experts, water-wheel keepers, blacksmiths, glaziers, painters, lead sheet makers, locksmiths, bucket-makers, porters, and labourers.[8]

In Sinan's time the storehouse was provided with two official 'seats' (*nişīmen*), one for the city prefect (*şehremīni*) and one for the chief architect (*miʿmārbaşı*).[9] The city prefect, an officer of the imperial council's finance department, was in charge of payments for state constructions in the capital and for palace repairs. The royal storehouse where building materials were kept together with assorted supplies consumed in the palace came under his jurisdiction.[10] Chief architects frequented the construction-related workshops subordinate to the royal storehouse to supervise the training of novices employed at the palace garden. We learn from the seventeenth-century biography of the chief architect Mimar Mehmed Agha that Sinan periodically visited the workshop of carpenters, where a master called Üstad Mehmed and his assistants were responsible for training the novices:

> From the date 1569–70, when the aforementioned [Mehmed] Agha took up the arts of architecture and the working of mother-of-pearl, until the year 1588, [that is] until the death of the warrior renowned as the Great Architect [*ḳoca miʿmār*], the late Sinan Agha, who was the chief of the world's engineers [*ser-i mühendisān-ı cihān*] and famed in the two horizons and throughout the ages, he studied under Üstad Mehmed, the assistant masters [*ḫalīfe*] of the [Imperial] Garden, and the above-mentioned Sinan Agha. And each time the late Great Architect came to the Imperial Gardens, he [the Agha] studied the science of geometry and the art of architecture with him and others. And each time that he executed some artistically fashioned work of art, he showed it to the above-mentioned deceased Sinan Agha. And Sinan Agha said now and then, 'Bravo, apprentice! You have created a work without equal.'[11]

The apprentice Mehmed then studied under Sinan's successors, Davud Agha and Dalgıç Ahmed Agha. Working in public buildings created under the latter, he eventually became chief architect after holding the post of water channel supervisor (Appendix 4.5).[12]

Sixteenth-century renovation expenses of the royal storehouse name its dependent workshops. Between the years 1527 and 1531, its repaired dependencies included the 'workshop of carpenters' (*kārḫane-i neccārān*) and the 'rooms of water channel experts' (*odahā-i rāh-ı ābīyān*).[13] The corps of royal carpenters is listed separately from architects in the tri-monthly wage registers of court artisans (*ehl-i ḥiref*). Other groups affiliated with the storehouse are generally cited in monthly wage registers under the categories of distinguished royal servants (*müteferriḳa*) and court messengers (*çavuş*).

A monthly register from around 1523 mentions the 'corps of royal water channel servants' (*cemāʿat-i ḫademe-i rāh-ı āb-ı ḫāṣṣa*) staffed with twenty-two members, the 'corps of lead sheet makers and glaziers' (*cemāʿat-i sürbger maʿa camger*) consisting of four individuals, two restorer-architects of the imperial palace and its garden, and a 'marble cutter' (*mermerī*) called Hızır who subsequently joined the corps of royal architects in the mid-1520s (Appendix 4.2).[14] A later monthly register (1527–31) shows that the corps of royal water channel servants headed by Mimar Mustafa Beg had a staff of thirty. Other specialists affiliated with the royal storehouse included five members of the corps of lead sheet makers and glaziers, two restorer-architects of the imperial palace and garden (Rüstem, Nasuh), and the marble cutter Hayrüddin. The names of Rüstem and Hayrüddin are later encountered among the corps of royal architects (Appendix 4.2, 4.3).[15]

Sinan eventually added new warehouses to expand the capacity of the royal storehouse, whose dependencies in the imperial garden extended from the left side of the first court down to the seashore.[16] The nineteenth-century historian Ata reports that the 'team of the storehouse for repairs' formed an architectural council that regularly met at the Shore Kiosk and the Kiosk of Basketmakers along the seashore of the palace gardens. In descending order he lists the members of this committee as the city prefect (*şehremīni*), the chief architect (*miʿmār aġa*), the superintendent of water channels (*şu nāẓırı*), the agha of Istanbul [the commander of novices], the chief limeburner (*kireççibaşı*), the storehouse director (*anbār müdīri*), the chief storehouse scribe (*anbār birinci kātibi*), the first architect (*ser-miʿmār*), the second architect (*miʿmār-ı s̱ānī*), and the director of repairs (*taʿmīrāt müdīri*).[17]

This organization reflects the nineteenth-century rationalization of a system that emerged in the late fifteenth century and matured under Sinan. The organization of the corps of royal architects had two foci: the royal storehouse at the Topkapı Palace and the chief architect's office at Vefa, near the Old Palace. These two centres may have originated during Mehmed II's reign, when both palaces were built. The chief architect's office at Vefa was located near the dormitories of novices (commanded by the agha of Istanbul) where Sinan himself had received his initial training as a carpenter and the Old Chambers of janissaries employed as construction workers.

Bayezid II's book of royal donations (1503–12) names rewarded architects without specifying their chief (Appendix 4.1). The contemporary chronicler Ruhi Edrenevi, however, identifies Mimar Murad 'who was most learned and unequalled in his art' as the 'chief' (*re'īs*) of Bayezid's architects.[18] Also known as Murad Halife, he had graduated to that post after serving for twenty-eight years as an 'assistant architect' (*ḫalīfe*) under Mehmed II.[19] This must be Mimar Murad b. Abdullah, who established a pious foundation at the capital with a waqfiyya dated 1500.[20] He seems to have passed away around that time, because he is not mentioned in Bayezid II's book of royal donations, which names his son Mimar Hızır Bali b. Murad Halife among the corps of royal architects. According to the chronicler

Ruhi, his other son, Mimar Hayrüddin b. Mimar Murad, had repaired the walls of Galata after the earthquake of 1509.[21] The book of royal donations lists Mimar Hayrüddin as the chief of the corps of water channels in 1511.[22]

Some nineteeth-century sources maintain that Hayrüddin had built Bayezid II's mosque complex in Istanbul (1501–5).[23] The sultan's book of royal donations, however, shows that its architect was Yakubshah b. Sultanshah, who was assisted by two masters (*ḫalīfe*): Ali b. Abdullah and Yusuf bin Papas.[24] He is referred to simply as 'architect' (*miʿmār*), but his annual perks from the royal treasury (which supplemented his monthly wages) imply his status as chief architect: 3,000 aspers, a robe of honour, and a sable-skin fur coat.[25] Later on, the chief architect Sinan had the same annual bonus.[26]

I have argued in Chapter 4 that the architect of Bayezid II's mosque complex must be the same person as 'Yakubshah, the Armenian architect', who is mentioned in an account book recording the renovation expenses of the castle of Kili in 1489–90.[27] He seems to have originated from Amasya, where Bayezid II had governed as a prince. This is implied by the royal donation that his nephew, who resided in Amasya, received from the sultan in 1506 for bringing apples from that city.[28] It is unclear whether Yakubshah converted to Islam before he succeeded the chief architect Mimar Murad sometime after 1500, because he does not seem to have established a waqf.[29] His son Hüdaverdi (a name commonly adopted by Armenians) is listed among the corps of architects in Bayezid II's book of royal donations (Appendix 4.1).

The next chief architect, nicknamed Acem Alisi (Ali of Persia), succeeded Yakubshah, whose name disappears from the book of royal donations after 1509.[30] He is assumed to have been brought to Istanbul from Tabriz along with other Persian artists following Selim I's victory over the Safavids in 1514. This assumption and the claim that he was an Azeri Turk are not supported by any documentary evidence.[31] Persian architects are known to have been employed at the Ottoman court long before Selim I's reign. One of them was Abdülali b. Puladshah, nicknamed Abdülali Mimar-ı Acem, who built a khan for Bayezid II in Bursa in 1490.[32]

The seamless continuity in architectural style between the reigns of Bayezid II and Selim I makes one wonder how Acem Alisi could so quickly have mastered the Ottoman building tradition if he was, indeed, a foreign architect imported from Tabriz in 1514. With its central domed cube flanked by lower *tabḫane* wings, the mosque of Selim I in Istanbul (1520/21–1527/28), which is attributed to him, closely paraphrases that of Bayezid II in Edirne (1484–88) (illus. 78–81). It is therefore tempting to conjecture that the chief architect Acem Alisi was none other than Yakubshah's main assistant, Ali b. Abdullah (also referred to as Alaüddin Halife, Appendix 4.1).[33] Ali was appointed to major building projects as the highest paid royal architect after 1509, when Yakubshah's name disappears from Bayezid II's book of royal donations.[34]

The differing paternal names of the chief architect Acem Alisi, used in his 1525 and 1537 waqfiyyas, strongly suggest his Christian origin: Alaüddin Ali Beg b. Abdülkerim, Ali Beg b. Abdülvehhab. Both waqfiyyas refer to him as 'chief architect' (*ra'īs al-miʿmārīn*), praising him as 'the learned and perfect master,' 'the talented and great engineer', and 'the most learned of all engineers'.[35] The 1537 waqfiyya mentions his son, Hamza Çelebi; in the book of royal donations, Yakubshah's leading assistant, Ali b. Abdullah, is listed among the corps of royal architects together with his son Hamza in 1511 (Appendix 4.1).[36]

Monthly wage registers dating from the 1520s up to 1537 regularly mention Acem Alisi as 'Alaüddin, the chief architect' and indicate that his salary was increased from forty-five to fifty-five aspers in 1534 (Appendix 4.2).[37] The names of several architects previously cited in Bayezid II's book of royal donations appear in registers from the early part of Süleyman's reign (1523–28) among the team of Acem Alisi: Hızır Bali, the son of Murad Halife; Hüdaverdi, the son of Yakubshah; Mahmud, Derviş Ali, and Şeyhi. This testifies to an uninterrupted continuity in architectural tradition, extending from Mehmed II's reign into Süleyman's (Appendix 4.1, 4.2).[38] It also reflects a familial continuity in the architectural profession, which would disappear with the bureaucratization of the corps under Sinan.

Between 1525–26 and 1534 the majority of the highest paid royal architects inherited from Bayezid II's reign had disappeared. An even more drastic depletion of corps members occured between 1534 and 1537, just before Sinan was appointed chief architect. Several new architects were recruited into the corps during the 1530s, three of them carrying Christian names for the first time. Among these three the Portuguese captain Francesco, who seems to have been a naval architect, received the highest pay. His initial wage of fifty aspers was raised to sixty aspers in 1536, a salary exceeding even that of the chief architect Alaüddin. The number of royal architects was reduced from seventeen in 1525–26, to thirteen in 1534, and to seven or eight in 1536–37 (Appendix 4.2). No wonder, then, that the grand vizier Lutfi Pasha found nobody among them worthy to succeed Acem Alisi in 1539. He thus appointed as chief architect the janissary officer Sinan Subaşı, an outsider not enrolled in the corps of royal architects.[39]

A monthly wage register from the year 1548–49 demonstrates the radical break with past tradition during the first decade of Sinan's tenure, when only two of the architects (Anton and Hayrüddin) who had joined the corps in 1536 were still active (Appendix 4.3). Before his promotion to the corps, the marble cutter Hayrüddin Mermeri was enrolled among distinguished palace servants (*müteferriḳa*) at the imperial garden, as was Rüstem, the restorer-architect of the palace who subsequently joined Sinan's team of royal architects. The 1548–49 register lists a crew of eight architects (five Muslims and three non-Muslims) with whom Sinan built his early monuments in the capital. From an imperial decree we learn the name of another non-Muslim architect: Mimar Yani, who received a daily wage of fifteen aspers, was sent to the port of İnoz (Enez in Thrace) during 1544 to quarry sandstones for the Şehzade Mehmed mosque and he may have passed away by 1548–49.[40] The royal mosque complexes that Sinan constructed in the capital with his new team include those of Şehzade Mehmed and Mihrümah Sultan (Üsküdar), which initiated the refined 'classical' style he perfected in the Süleymaniye complex during the 1550s.

On a comparative scale Sinan earned a relatively modest daily salary (fifty-five aspers in 1548–49), about one-tenth the wage of the janissary agha, who received five hundred aspers a day as the highest ranked agha of the imperial court. Nevertheless, the chief architect, who is grouped with the 'aghas of royal artisans' (*aġayān-i ehl-i ḥiref*), was the best paid member of his cohort: the chief court painter, for instance, received only twenty-five aspers a day. By 1553 Sinan's daily salary had been raised to sixty-five aspers.[41] This stipend was complemented by the income of his fief (*arpalık*) in Vize, an annual allotment of 3,000 aspers with a robe of honour and a fur coat, as well as robes and gifts donated by the sultans in compensation for major projects. Sinan must have received additional fees and gifts for monuments commissioned by members of the ruling elite.[42]

The city prefect and chief architect, who had official seats at the royal storehouse of the first court in the Topkapı Palace, also attended imperial council meetings in the second court. According to a seventeenth-century source, they both sat under the portico of the imperial council: 'Outside, in between the two domes is the place of the chief scribe (*re'īsü'l-küttāb*) and his scribes. And the prefects (*ümenā,* sing. *emīn*) sit lined up on a bench: the prefects of the kitchen, the city, the arsenal, the customs house, and the sheep, and the [chief] architect (*miʿmār*)'.[43] It was through the chief architect's petitions to the chief scribe of the imperial council that new members were appointed to the corps of royal architects and current members received raises with the grand vizier's approval.[44]

One such petition was written by Sinan in 1556 (Appendix 4.3):

> The aforementioned [Sinan] has sent a letter petitioning that since Rüstem, who had been appointed military campaign architect (*sefer miʿmārı*) with a daily salary of ten aspers, has died, his vacant post is appropriate for the person called Mustafa b. Abdullah, who is presently in the service of marble cutting (*mermercilik*) with three aspers. [Marginal note: He was subsequently appointed with ten aspers].[45]

When the marble cutter Kasım (Appendix 4.3) died in 1560–61, Sinan recommended an eight-asper salary raise for the same Mustafa:

> The chief architect has sent a letter reporting that Kasım b. Abdullah, a royal architect with a daily salary of ten aspers has died; his request that eight aspers of that post be given to Mermerci Mustafa, whose vacant place [in turn] be given to Murad b. Ali, with the remaining two aspers added on to the seven-asper salary of the royal architect Ferhad b. Abdullah, has been petitioned by the finance minister for acceptance as requested; it thus has been recorded.[46]

In 1586, when two royal architects – Mustafa (with a salary of twelve aspers) and Mahmud (receiving eight aspers) – passed away, the chief architect recommended in their place the architects Mehmed, Hüseyin, Dede, and Bali (five aspers each) on condition that they attend the ongoing Safavid campaign.[47] During the same year, Çerkes Ahmed, one of the ten royal architects appointed to that campaign, passed away, and his salary of thirteen aspers was subdivided among five architects on the basis of a similar petition by Sinan.[48]

Unfortunately monthly wage registers from the second half of the sixteenth century are lost. Therefore, it is not possible to identify the membership of the corps of royal architects during the peak of Sinan's career. Some of the architects who worked under him are mentioned in documents related to the construction of the Süleymaniye complex between 1550 and 1553. Many of them were sent to collect antique marbles and columns for the complex: Mimar Bali (Alexandria), Mimar Hacı Hüseyin Halife (d. 1553, Alexandria, Baalbek, Anatolia), Mimar Ali (Alanya, Baalbek), Mimar Hızır (Silifke), Mimar Veli (Thessaloniki, Sidhirókastron), and Mimar Hacı Mustafa (Nicea, Mitilini, Miletos). These architects scouted antique ruins throughout the empire, and wherever they could locate suitable marbles and columns they marked them with a 'sign' (*nişān*), and together with provincial administrators (governor-generals, sanjak governors, and kadis) prepared detailed catalogues containing stone 'samples' (*nümūne*) chipped from the ruins, and specifying number, dimensions, and estimated transportation costs including the construction of landing stations in nearby ports.[49]

This systematic search for marbles and columns amounted to an archaeological survey of major classical sites and quarries within the imperial domains, most of which are mentioned in the semi-legendary construction histories of Hagia Sophia. Although such search operations were later mounted for the Selimiye and other major mosque complexes, none equalled in comprehensiveness the chain of interlinked expeditions precipitated by the Süleymaniye. In those years royal architects were also sent to quarries to oversee the cutting of stones according to Sinan's specifications. Sandstone (*küfeki*) quarries in the suburbs of Istanbul were supplemented with others in archaeological sites. For example, Mimar Hacı Mustafa headed an operation to quarry foundation stones from Yalakabad (now Yalova), where he was assisted by one of the Süleymaniye foremen and by Musa Subaşı, the captain of a group of novices sent from the capital.[50] Another stone quarry in İzmit (ancient Nikomedia) was initially overseen by the architect Mimar İbrahim Halife and then by Kiriz Nikola.[51] Architects appointed to supervise stonecutting in the quarries of Kavak İskelesi (Karamürsel) and Aydıncık (ancient Cyzicus) included Hüsam b. Ali Karamani Halife, Hacı Hüseyin Halife, Mimar Kasım, and Üstad Murad.[52] The names of the ten royal architects who signed Sinan's endowment deed (*c.* 1583–85) and some others employed in various constructions are listed in Appendix 4.4.

Compiling a comprehensive roster of royal architects who worked under Sinan is complicated by the fact that some of them were enrolled in the corps of water channels or in the staff of architect-restorers attached to the endowments of sultanic mosques. For instance Mimar Dimitri, one of the architects who worked on the Süleymaniye complex, was appointed the architect-restorer of the recently finished mosque after converting to Islam in 1556 and adopting the name Mehmed.[53] The post of 'water channel superintendent' (*ṣuyolı nāẓırı*) came into being in 1566, soon after the completion of the Kırkçeşme water distribution system.[54] The appointment document of Mehmed Çavuş to that post in 1577 outlines his duties: inspecting and repairing the water channels of the royal palace, its garden, other royal gardens, imperial mosque complexes, and the Kağıdhane water channels, and reporting with petitions those who in transgression of the shariʿa caused harm to the water conduits.[55] Prior to the creation of the post of water channel superintendant, the 'head of water channels' (*ser-rāh-ı āb*) belonged to the corps of distinguished palace servants (*müteferriḳa*). Holders of the upgraded post often belonged to the same corps or to the ranks of imperial messengers (*çavuş*). Sinan must have been instrumental in the genesis of the new post which became a stepping stone to his own position. His immediate successors Davud, Dalgıç Ahmed, and Mehmed all served as water channel superintendents before their promotions (Appendix 4.5).

Monthly wage registers recording the names of royal architects reappear during the early seventeenth century, after a half-century gap. The number of architects fluctuates between thirty-nine and forty-four, an increase that reflects the expanded organization of the corps during Sinan's tenure. Ayn Ali Efendi's (1609) treatise on the structure of the Ottoman state explains that 'the corps of royal architects consists of forty-four persons who receive their wages once every month.'[56] Eyyubi's mid-seventeenth-century law code specifies that 'the royal architects are forty persons.'[57]

A wage register from 1604–5 lists thirty-nine corps members (twenty-three Muslims and sixteen non-Muslims) working under the chief architect Dalgıç Ahmed Çavuş, each group headed by its own steward (*ketḫüdā*) and master (*ḫalīfe*).[58] During the seventeenth century, which witnessed several devaluations, the daily salary of the chief architect rose to 120 aspers.[59] In 1691 the expulsion of twenty-three architects from the corps, after an inspection by the chief architect, reduced its membership to between eleven and thirteen until the end of the century.[60] Parallel to this change, the wage of the chief architect (illus. 127) was lowered to 80 aspers in 1697, a change in keeping with the diminished scope of building projects that seems to have reduced the importance of the corps.[61] Its fall from prestige is implied in Evliya Çelebi's report that the chief architect, who used to precede the chief musician during official parades, followed him during a guild procession in Murad IV's reign (r. 1623–40).[62]

As the literary historian Ahmet Hamdi Tanpınar perceptively observed, 'towards the end of the seventeenth century, the main form of creativity [in Ottoman cultural life] had shifted from architecture to music.'[63] One of the great experts of Ottoman music, Prince Demetrius Cantemir (1673–1723), observes that patrons of monumental architecture no longer approached the chief architect, but turned instead to talented Greek or Armenian architects, who came to dominate the architectural profession (illus. 128).[64] He says the 'Mimar Agha' appointed masters (*ḫalīfe, ḳalfa*) to inspect all new houses in the capital to ensure their conformity with codes, but building codes could often be bypassed by bribing the chief architect. The post had become so lucrative that grand viziers often gave it to their favourites who lacked architectural knowledge (illus. 129). The corps of royal architects would eventually become modernized with the establishment of an imperial school of military engineering in 1795, followed by other reforms in the nineteenth century.

CITY ARCHITECTS STATIONED IN PROVINCIAL CAPITALS

The expansion of the corps of royal architects in Istanbul during the second half of the sixteenth century was paralleled by the development of the institution of provincial city architects. Contrary to the assumption that the institution of city architects was not established until the seventeenth century, the capitals of major provinces began to acquire their own chief architects in the age of Sinan.[65] The earliest known references to architects stationed in the border regions of the empire suggests that they were initially appointed for military constructions. The 1516 lawcode of the province of Bosnia, for example, stipulates the appointment of an architect with a fief (*timar*) in charge of building castles there.[66] An imperial decree addressed to the kadi of Skopje in 1568 reveals that the chief architect (*miʿmārbaşı*) of that provincial capital was Hayrüddin, whose assistants included Üstad Memi and Yusuf. Based on their recommendation, the kadi

127 Chief architect, watercolour on paper, from a mid-seventeenth-century costume album.

128 Jean-Baptiste Vanmour, Armenian architect holding a measuring stick with a hammer and axe and saw attached to his belt, c. 1707–8, engraving.

requested a decree requiring all carpenters and masons enlisted for imperial constructions in Edirne and Istanbul, whether outsiders or locals, to find a 'guarantor' (*kefīl*) who would reimburse to the state the travel stipends of those builders who escaped. This implies that the chief architect of Skopje was in charge of recruiting masons and architects for Sinan's major building projects, some of them against their will.[67] Buda also had a chief architect (*Budun mi*ʿ*mārı*) who in 1572 prepared an estimate for renovating Sultan Süleyman's Great Mosque in that city, which had been converted from a cathedral.[68]

Soon after the provinces of Erzurum and Van were created along the Safavid border in 1548, we hear of official architects being appointed in that frontier region. Until an architect was assigned to Erzurum in 1556, constructions were carried out there by the architect of Diyarbakır, whose post must have been established sometime after 1517 when that city became the capital of a new province.[69] The governor-general of Van sent a petition to the sultan's court in 1556, requesting that the fifteen-asper salary of the non-Muslim chief architect Selman, who was 'talented in architecture and a possessor of sagacity', be raised to twenty aspers for his services in state constructions. Since this was the fee his predecessor had received, he clearly was not the first architect in Van to hold that post.[70]

The institution of city architects – appointed by the chief architect from Istanbul and subordinate to the kadis of provinces – flourished during the seventeenth century, but its kernel was already in place during Sinan's time. Appointment documents from the seventeenth century reveal that the chiefs of provincial city architects had to be experts in the 'art of architecture' (*ṣan*ʿ*at-ı mi*ʿ*māriyye*), 'the science of geometry' (ʿ*ilm-i hendese*), 'construction methods' (*emr-i binā*), and 'surveying techniques' (*mesāḥa*). Like the chief architect of Istanbul, they were responsible for inspecting the products of construction-related artisanal guilds and for settling disputes among guild members. No new buildings or water channels were allowed without their certification. For the appointment of a regional chief architect, the kadi of that province had to send a petition to the capital, on the basis of which the chief architect of the empire

129 Circumcision ceremony parade of the chief architect and the agha of *nahıls* (artificial trees) with models of two trees towering above kiosks and fountains; both turbaned aghas wearing white robes walk holding staffs, c. 1720, watercolour on paper, from Vehbi, *Sūrnāme-i Vehbī*.

recommended an appropriate candidate to the chief secretary of the imperial council.[71]

An imperial decree of 1579 identifies the 'chief architect' (*miʿmārbaşı*) of Damascus as the fiefholder Zaim Davud. The decree handed over to him, at his own request, at the imperial council in Istanbul authorizes him to repair the lead roofs of the Dome of the Rock and the Aqsa mosque in Jerusalem, which he had promised to renovate for only two hundred gold coins (a repair previously estimated to cost six thousand florins). His presence in Istanbul shows that provincial chief architects maintained direct contact with Sinan, and that there was two-way traffic between the capital and provinces.[72] Another order sent in 1579 to the governor of Tripoli commands him to deliver to their destination the amount of lead dispatched for renovations at the Umayyad Great mosque in Damascus and at the Dome of the Rock and Aqsa mosque, which were to be carried out by the chief architect of Damascus, Zaim Davud.[73]

Sinan's personal involvement in the appointment of provincial chief architects is confirmed by an entry in a 1588 waqf register of Damascus: 'The chief architect Sinan Agha has sent a letter recommending that in Damascus the Noble the vacant position of the deceased Davud, who was an architect with a large fief (*zeʿāmet*) and an expert (*ehl-i ḫibre*) serving as a lead specialist (*ḳurşuncı*) and water channel expert (*ṣuyolcı*) in the Umayyad mosque, is appropriate for Nakkaşoğlu (Painter's Son) İshak who resides in Damascus.' İshak, 'an expert and an architect', was appointed to the vacant post through an official memorandum from the chief secretary of the imperial council. The same document refers to the appointment of two other royal architects in Damascus, Mimar Mehmed b. Mansur, and Yusuf b. Kadir, who was 'an architect of masjids and madrasas and Friday mosques and other buildings in Damascus the Noble.'[74]

The Jerusalem shariʿa court records show that during the sixteenth and seventeenth centuries, since the first reference to a *miʿmārbaşı* in 1532, the post of chief architect there was virtually the preserve of the Nammar (al-Nammari) family.[75] Nevertheless, the kadi of Jerusalem and the building supervisor in charge of extensive renovations at the Dome of the Rock and the Aqsa mosque informed the sultan in 1586 that there were no masons, stone cutters, carpenters, or architectural experts capable of carrying out the repairs. Hence construction experts were sent there from Damascus, under the jurisdiction of which Jerusalem was placed.[76]

Aleppo was another Syrian city with its own corps of architects, frequently appointed to imperial projects in Jerusalem, Mecca, and Medina. One of these Aleppine architects, Mimar Cemalüddin, was ordered in 1560 to construct Prince Selim's mosque complex in Karapınar, near Konya, which Sinan himself designed.[77] In 1566 the governor-generals of Damascus and Aleppo were asked to send stone masons for the renovation of the ʿArafat water channel in Mecca upon the request of the Egyptian governor-general in charge of overseeing that project. Nasrüddin, the father of Mimar Abdülkadir, was appointed the chief of the Aleppine masons sent for that project.[78] Another architect from Aleppo, Mimar Abdülnebi, was selected in 1577 to complete the construction of a moat around the castle of nearby Payas, where Sinan had designed a mosque complex for the grand vizier Sokollu Mehmed Pasha. The enterprising Abdülnebi had visited the capital to offer his services, promising that he would complete the moat quickly and cheaply if ten persons were assigned for the job from the castle of Aleppo, together with 'master masons' (*üstādlar*) of his own choice.[79]

Cairo also possessed its own chief architect, usually appointed from the city's *müteferriḳa* corps; his function was to collect taxes from artisans and to supervise all public works.[80] According to the *Tuhfe*, repairs in Mecca overseen by the governor-general of Egypt in 1551 were executed by the chief architect (*miʿmārbaşı*) of Cairo, Kara Mustafa, who replaced the golden rain spout of the Kaʿba and repaired its damaged wooden ceilings.[81] For the renovation of the ʿArafat water channel in Mecca, initiated during Süleyman's reign, the governor-general of Egypt was ordered in 1568 to send the 'Arab architect Mimar Yahya', skilled in the 'science of construction' and enrolled there in the *müteferriḳa* corps.[82] In 1572 the water channel expert Mehmed, belonging to the same corps, received an imperial order appointing him to work in Mecca because of his knowledge 'in the science of geometry and hydrostatic balances'.[83] In 1574 the Sharif of Mecca requested the promotion of İbrahim b. Abdullah (a *çavuş* from Egypt), who from the very beginning had served as an architect in the water channel project.[84]

The rebuilding of porticoes around the Kaʿba's precinct during Selim II's reign, completed under Murad III, was supervised by Sinan from the capital. In 1572 Memi Muhyiddin was appointed from Egypt as the architect of this project.[85] Selaniki refers to him as 'the architect and engineer of the age, Horos Memi [Mehmed the Hen], who was among the officers guarding Egypt.'[86] The remodelling of the Kaʿba also required the presence of royal architects from the capital, including Mimar Mehmed Çavuş (1573–77) and the chief architect himself (1584).[87]

Cairene architects were sometimes appointed to building projects in other cities of the Hijaz. For example, the governor-general of Egypt was asked in 1573 to send 'a fairly good architect together with sufficient masons and carpenters' to repair the castle of Jidda.[88] That year the Cairene architect Kara Mustafa (who had restored the Kaʿba in the 1550s) surveyed with a group of thirty experts the feasibility of constructing a water channel from Mecca to Jidda in accordance with Sultan Süleyman's last will. On the basis of that survey, Selim II judged the project impractical; in its stead, he ordered the same committee to determine appropriate places for several cisterns and prepare a correct estimate of their expenses.[89] In 1579 the governor-general of Egypt was asked to dispatch marbles and the Cairene architect Mimar Zeynizade to Medina for the creation of a new minbar at the Prophet's Mosque, since the old one was about to collapse.[90]

Sinan may have met the architects of Syria and Egypt on his way to Mecca in 1584. His concern with improving the quality of architectural practice in Cairo is captured by an imperial decree that Murad III addressed to the kadi of that city in 1585:

> Sinan, who is presently the chief of my architects at my threshold of felicity, has sent a letter reporting that Mahmud b. Mehmed, an imperial messenger (*çavuş*) in that city [Cairo], who is an architect (*miʿmār*) and an expert (*ehl-i ḫibre*) receiving a wage of twelve aspers, had been performing his duties there as [chief] architect when some unqualified persons took upon themselves the responsibility of building the houses of many people without any knowledge in the science of construction (*ʿilm-i binā*), which resulted in the emergence of all kinds of defects. When Mahmud Çavuş told them that these were harmful to the Muslims, they did not heed his words and did not stop for a moment. Since you have requested a noble decree to punish those who do not recognize and obey Mahmud Çavuş as [chief] architect, I order you to forbid them and not to employ those who are unqualified. When my [decree] arrives, I command you to be attentive to this matter and not to allow those without expertise or skill to interfere with the constructions of the Muslims, but do not permit anybody to be treated unjustly and oppressively. Forbid those who do not obey him [Mahmud Çavuş] and punish those who remain disobedient.[91]

The creation of auxiliary branches of the corps of royal architects in major provincial cities during Sinan's tenure paralleled the increasing centralization of the empire. Through his administrative acumen, the corps in Istanbul became an empire-wide network with tentacles reaching out into distant provinces. The emergence of many more local architectural bureaus during the seventeenth century eventually reduced the frequency with which royal architects were sent from the capital for building projects in the provinces. The growing autonomy and independence of city architects at that time echoed the decentralizing trends of the post-classical age.

II. THE CHIEF ARCHITECT AS ADMINISTRATOR AND DESIGNER

Sinan's responsibilities as chief architect were centred in Istanbul and to a lesser degree in the secondary capital Edirne. Yet he was also in charge of state constructions in distant places, which he coordinated by appointing either royal architects from the capital or city architects stationed in provincial centres. Building projects in the provinces were generally triggered by petitions of need sent to the imperial court by governor-generals or regional administrators. Sinan maintained control over such remote projects through plans and possibly models, accompanied by written communications. Just as royal architects were sent with drawings to the provinces, architects based in other cities occasionally came to Istanbul to have their project proposals approved. The two-way traffic of architects and designs was channelled through the nerve centre of the empire, the imperial council.

Much like provincial city architects, Sinan in the capital was in charge of approving new constructions and inspecting the products of building crafts. His tasks included establishing urban codes for Istanbul houses and streets, codifying the dimensions and costs of building materials, determining the wages of royal architects and construction workers, recommending hard-working novices for promotion to the janissary corps, selecting royal architects to accompany military campaigns, proposing replacements for deceased royal architects in the capital and in other cities, surveying construction sites with committees of experts, preparing cost estimates and plans, as well as supervising major buildings commissioned by the sultans and grandees.

MUNICIPAL DUTES AND THE SUPERVISION OF BUILDING CRAFTS

Sinan's codification of norms that fixed the height of houses and the width of streets in Istanbul was discussed in Chapter 3. In addition to municipal functions, the chief architect had jurisdiction over the building crafts. A book of officially fixed market prices dating from 1640 declares that ever since the conquest of Istanbul, workshops related to the construction industry had been subject to the chief architect's (*miʿmārbaşı*) control. These included the workshops of timberjacks, adze makers, brick makers, lime burners, box makers, İznik tile makers, carpenters, glaziers, lead sheet makers, water channel makers, stone cutters, marble cutters, plasterers, paint makers, painters, locksmiths, pavement makers, labourers, and porters.[92] Construction-related workshops attached to the royal storehouse of the Topkapı Palace were, not surprisingly, staffed with artisans specializing in most of these crafts.

Evliya Çelebi's detailed description of a guild procession in Istanbul during the reign of Murad IV lists the crafts falling under the chief architect's jurisdiction. He groups them under two broad categories: carpenters' guilds and masons' guilds.[93] At their head marched 'architectural carpenters' (*neccārān-ı miʿmārān*), whose workshop was located near Vefa, in the vicinity of the chief architect's office.[94] Evliya explains that the chief carpenter regularly held audiences with a council of elders in his own residence. Each of his masters (*ḫalīfe*) was 'capable of building a castle like Istanbul, or a mosque like Ayasofya and Süleymaniye.' Accompanied by their stewards (*ketḫüdā*) and court messengers (*çavuş*), these masters constantly toured the capital to demolish houses that transgressed the boundaries of public streets or looked into other houses. It was also their duty to punish builders responsible for illegal constructions.[95] Evliya goes on to describe how carpenters with adzes and other tools in their hands or tucked in their belts passed in front of the sultan on a cart where they proceeded to buils a house, exclaiming 'Oh! ah! pass the wood, pass the nails!'[96] They were followed by masons (*bennā*) who constructed a wall as they rode on their cart, shouting 'bring the stones! bring mud! bring wood!'.[97] Evliya counts numerous other dependent guilds behind which paraded the chief architect with his assistants enrolled in the corps of royal architects:

> Accompanied by their shaykhs and prayer reciters, the master architects (*miʿmār ḫalīfeleri*) paraded fully armed on purebread Arab horses; behind them passed the chief architect (*miʿmar aġa*) armed in full splendour together with all his household pages to the beating of drums; the chief architect's subordinates consisted of forty-four guilds.[98]

During an earlier procession staged at the Hippodrome for the circumcision festivities of 1582, Sinan had paraded with three-dimensional models (*resm*) of the Kaʿba and the Prophet's mosque in Medina, which had recently been renovated under Murad III.[99] One day earlier, a colourfully painted and richly gilded model (*resm ü timṣāl*) of the Süleymaniye mosque had been displayed during the parade of one of the masters belonging to the corps of royal architects.[100] A miniature painting in the *Sūrnāme* (Book of Festivities) represents this procession, showing six young royal architects, wearing long kaftans and bulbous white turbans, walking in pairs, each holding an axe in his hand (illus. 130). Several men carry the Süleymaniye model, which was large enough to accommodate an individual who from the interior sang loud praises of God, the Prophet Muhammad, the four orthodox caliphs, and the Ottoman dynasty.[101]

Then came the stone cutters (*taşcı*), wearing long caftans and elegantly-wrapped turbans and holding hammers and chisels (illus. 131). They carried examples of their work as they

130 Circumcision ceremony parade of royal architects at the Hippodrome with a model of the Süleymaniye, *c.* 1582, watercolour on paper, from İntizami, *Sūrnāme*.

obediently walked behind their staff-holding masters.[102] Empty-handed masons (*bennā*) wore white turbans and elegantly fitted brand-new caftans of brocaded silk and gold brocade (illus. 132). Their masters, used to giving firman-like orders to construction workers, walked in front, some of them never having driven a nail with their own hands. None of the master masons were 'manual labourers,' nor would they take orders 'even if these were drilled into their ears!' Behind them followed pairs of ordinary masons, who stayed by their work as if nailed to it.[103] The glaziers (*cāmcı*) displayed samples of their work on a cart, where they fashioned plaster window frames fitted with colored glass cut in the shape of carnations, roses, and cypresses (illus. 133). Other parading craftsmen included sawyers, who cut large timbers, sundried brick makers, lime-burners, Khorasan mortar mixers, and gardeners (illus. 134–36).[104]

The circumcision festival of 1582 presented a spectacular display of the crafts under Sinan's control. The chief architect had at his disposal the industrial and human resources of an empire still enjoying economic strength and stability, just before the catastrophic devaluation of 1584–85 triggered a monetary crisis. Thereafter, chief architects were afflicted with a decline of quality standards and a sharp rise in prices and wages in nearly all sectors. In the last years of his life, Sinan had to struggle with the repercussions of this devaluation which dealt a blow to the centralized construction industry. It was he who negotiated with the sultan the readjustment of wages for dissatisfied masons and carpenters, after a transitional period during which the state had resisted raising their pay fixed by 'ancient laws'.

The wages of builders had not substantially changed since the days of Selim I whose law code stipulates that 'for ten aspers covering food expenses, masons and carpenters should work all day long, arriving at sunrise and not leaving before sunset; those masons and carpenters asking for more money should be punished.'[105] In his memoirs, a Spanish galley slave who uses the penname Pedro describes a typical workday at the construction site of the grand admiral Sinan Pasha's palace in the Hippodrome, built within six months in the early 1550s and listed in the chief architect's autobiographies.[106] Each day 1,500 skilled masters

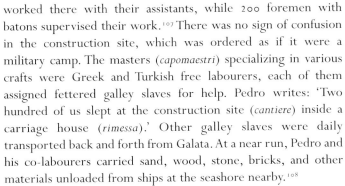

131 (top) Parade of stone cutters with their chief walking in the front holding a wooden measuring stick; watercolour illustrations from Intizami's *Sūrnāme*.

132 (above) Parade of masons, from the same source.

133 Parade of glaziers, from the same source, fol. 402r.

worked there with their assistants, while 200 foremen with batons supervised their work.[107] There was no sign of confusion in the construction site, which was ordered as if it were a military camp. The masters (*capomaestri*) specializing in various crafts were Greek and Turkish free labourers, each of them assigned fettered galley slaves for help. Pedro writes: 'Two hundred of us slept at the construction site (*cantiere*) inside a carriage house (*rimessa*).' Other galley slaves were daily transported back and forth from Galata. At a near run, Pedro and his co-labourers carried sand, wood, stone, bricks, and other materials unloaded from ships at the seashore nearby.[108]

Early each morning, day labourers with professions were separated from unskilled labourers called 'ergates' (*ırgad*) and the building supervisor (*capocantiere*) assigned them to where they were needed. At noon a trumpet announced a short break (*faitos*), when everyone received free bread; water was supplied from a nearby fountain. Pedro says unskilled labourers like him were paid one asper to cover their soup expenses at night, after a long workday that ended when stars appeared in the sky. Those who carried heavier loads were rewarded with bonuses as an incentive.[109] Among the master masons, whoever built the largest wall area each day was rewarded with brocades or other bonuses to speed up the construction.[110]

An imperial decree sent to the kadi of Istanbul in 1585 reveals that masons and carpenters who were paid fixed wages in state constructions (*mīrī binālar*) in accordance with ancient customs were abandoning them for higher wages offered on the free market for private buildings. The sultan orders the kadi to forbid builders from deserting state constructions and patrons from paying more than twelve aspers between spring and autumn, and ten aspers in the intervening wintry season.[111] Sinan's negotiations to increase the pay of construction workers are recorded in several decrees, reflecting the extent to which he was involved in administrative tasks. An imperial decree addressed to him in 1587 shows that masons and carpenters had been granted a pay raise with his recommendation, but the sultan could not comprehend why they continued to demand higher wages:

134 Parade of sawyers, from Intizami's *Sūrnāme*.

135 Parade of makers of sundried bricks, from the same source.

> You had previously sent me a letter recommending that the insufficient daily salary of twelve aspers received by masons (*bennā*), carpenters (*neccār*), and stone cutters (*sengtrāş*) should be raised to sixteen aspers. Having agreed to increase their salaries to sixteen aspers, I had ordered them not to be paid any higher. Now it has been reported that in the noble Friday mosque being built at my threshold of felicity by [Nişancı] Mehmed Pasha, those who are paid sixteen aspers according to my order are disputing and contending their wages, refusing to work there unless they are paid more money. It is necessary to punish those who disobey my command. I order you to warn as required the carpenters, stone cutters, and their masters (*ḫalīfe*) working in the above-mentioned construction so that they accept the sixteen asper salary I have ordered without any dispute or quarrel. Have those who against my decree desert their work and continue to complain caught wherever they are by their masters, and scold them with a severe chastisement. If their masters show any negligence in this matter and fail to catch those who complain and disobey my order, inform them that their post (*gedik*) will be given to someone else. And from now on, do not employ those persons who disobey my orders![112]

A related decree issued that year jointly commands the chief architect and the kadi of Istanbul to enforce the sixteen-asper wage of master masons and carpenters, and the eight-asper wage of unskilled labourers who traditionally received half the pay of masters:

> It has been heard that in some constructions more money is given and taken. You who are [chief] architect had requested and received my imperial decree. If it is true that the above-mentioned groups are being paid more, do not delay enforcing my decree. I order you that when my noble decree arrives act as required in this matter, advising the patrons of ongoing constructions together with their appointed architects (*miʿmār*) and masters (*ḫalīfe*) not to allow one extra asper to be paid to and received by the groups concerned.

136 Parade of gardeners, from Intizami's *Sūrnāme*.

The sultan's decree ends with the following warning: 'If work against my order is carried out in any construction, you will be held responsible and your excuse will not be accepted!'[113]

Sinan's jurisdiction over the building crafts is confirmed by several decrees, which also testify to the monopoly of the state over construction materials. Sinan and the kadi of Istanbul were ordered in 1577 to close down newly created lime shops in the capital because they caused a 'shortage of lime needed by the state'.[114] Later in 1584, lime workshops were commanded to improve the quality of their impure products, which they illegally mixed with stones and earth. Yahşi Çavuş was appointed the overseer (*nāẓır*) of the capital's lime makers (*kireççiler*) and stone quarriers (*taşçılar*) in order to check the quality of lime and forbid the sale of hewn stones to Christians and Jews, who caused a stone shortage in state constructions by using them in their tombs.[115]

It was Sinan who determined, after some negotiation, the costs and sizes of such building materials as stones, timbers, and bricks, setting new standards during the construction of the Süleymaniye complex. A document dated 1551 records the officially fixed prices of 'bevelled stones' (*seng-i pehlu*) established by the chief architect, specifying their length, width, and thickness in cubits.[116] In 1550 Sinan took special measures for the production of high quality dome bricks for the Süleymaniye by drawing up the following contract with brickmakers for piece-work at an agreed price:

> Previously for the dome of the noble mosque the brick-makers of Hasköy (along the Golden Horn) had agreed to take it upon themselves to make each piece of dome brick for one asper and a hundred pieces of half bricks for forty-seven aspers. Presently, in accordance with the chief architect's approval, they have voluntarily agreed to take upon themselves the production of top quality dome bricks by sifting the earth from sieves, using clay composed of very fine dust, and baking that type of clay, charging for each brick 1.3 aspers, and for half bricks (previously valued at forty-seven aspers) an additional asper (each hundred pieces costing forty-eight aspers); their agreement was thus recorded.[117]

During the same year, the kadi of Gelibolu was ordered to have bricks made for the Süleymaniye domes according to an 'examplar' (*nümūne*) sent with the architect Kosta Halife, using the same furnaces where bricks had previously been prepared for the mosque of Şehzade Mehmed. If the bricks failed to conform to specifications, they would not be bought.[118] In 1552, the kadi of Gelibolu was asked to send master brickmakers for the new brick kilns needed in Istanbul, together with the brick moulds (*tuğla ḳalıbları*) kept by the local warden.[119] Sinan seems to have decided to increase the capacity of brick kilns at the capital, thereby reducing his reliance on distant production centres.

At the chief architect's prompting an order was sent to the kadi of Istanbul in 1568 for the standardization in cubits of timber pillars and beams, wooden planks, and roof shingles in accordance with their previous measurements. This decree, handed over to the chief architect himself, concludes: 'Since it has been reported that timbers are no longer cut for buildings in accordance with old customs, but in smaller sizes that cause harm to constructions, they should be cut again in the old manner.'[120] In 1573 the sultan sent decrees to the kadis of all places where timbers were cut, informing them that timbers did not conform to measurements determined by old customs. A memorandum prepared by the chief architect, which lists different types of timber in terms of length and width, is appended to the decree. The kadis had to warn sawyers that timbers cut shorter and narrower would be confiscated by the state.[121] Despite such threats, an order addressed to Sinan and the kadi of Istanbul in 1582 reveals that timbers and wood used in construction work continued to be cut in smaller sizes. This order, handed over to the chief architect's protégé, Kabil Çavuş, once again includes a list of codified dimensions that the kadi is asked to enforce.[122]

Standardization reduced the reliance on custom-made construction materials, allowing Sinan to cope more easily with the large number of monuments commissioned by the ruling elite. His mosque complexes in the capital relied heavily on standardized components, complemented by piecework contracted to skilled masters specializing in various media. Fixed dimensions and prices were also crucial for preparing cost estimates for building projects, one of Sinan's primary duties in addition to designing plans and models.

COST ESTIMATES, PLANS AND MODELS

With committees of experts Sinan often surveyed the sites of major building and renovation projects. I have described in Chapter 3 how he surveyed the Hagia Sophia in 1573 with a group attended by the sultan, before its renovation was undertaken on the basis of an estimate (*taḫmīn*) that he prepared, with measurements indicated in cubits. In 1562 Sinan also surveyed the site of Rüstem Pasha's posthumous mosque at Tahtakale to oversee the clearing of the urban space required for its construction. We learn from the title deed, which specifies in cubits the amount of land acquired with the consent of various endowment administrators, that 'the mentioned place was visited with the present chief architect Sinan Agha, who is the pride of the great nobles and grandees, and with a multitude of other experts (*ehl-i vuḳūf*).'[123]

The preparation of site surveys relied on the 'science of mensuration' (*ʿilm-i mesāḥa*), defined in Cafer Efendi's early seventeenth-century treatise as the measuring of a place in cubits.[124] Imperial decrees frequently asked Sinan to prepare cost estimates of labour and materials required for construction projects. For instance, in 1552 he was ordered to personally visit the mosque complex of Mehmed II to prepare 'an overall correct estimate' for renovations and their cost, and to send other experts for assessing minor repairs.[125] As we have seen in Chapter 4, during Süleyman's reign 'Koca Mimar Sinan Agha and the non-Muslim known as Kiriz Nikola had made an accurate estimate' for digging a canal between Lake Sapanca and the bay of İzmit by surveying (*mesāḥa*) twenty thousand cubits of land, an expensive project that failed to materialize. The project was taken up again in 1582 during the grand vizierate of Koca Sinan Pasha, when the chief architect prepared another fruitless survey with a committee that included the royal architects Mimar Mehmed, Mimar Davud, Mimar Çavuş, and Mimar Süleyman, the water channel experts Yusuf and Ali, as well as the astronomer Molla Fütuh (Appendix 4.4).[126]

Written estimates were often accompanied by plans drawn on paper. According to Prince Cantemir, whenever a sultan donated a house to someone at the capital, he would send a decree to the city prefect and the chief architect to draw a survey plan estimating its value. It was customary to keep such drawings with the sultan's decree at the city prefect's archive.[127] Estimates had to be made both before a building project began and after its completion, because payments were considered credit against the settlement of accounts at the end of construction. Hence assessors were appointed to measure in cubits what construction work had been done and to assess its value. For instance, Sinan was asked to calculate how many measures (*lüle*) of water had been conducted to the Süleymaniye complex once its water channel was finished in 1559.[128] Similarly, the former water channel superintendent Davud Çavuş was ordered in 1585 to appraise with a committee of expert water channel builders the water conduits of the Süleymaniye, after they had been repaired by its endowment administrator. Carefully inspecting the repaired places, Davud had to determine in his 'accurate estimate' (*taḫmīn-i ṣaḥīḥ*) 'how many cubits they measure and for how many aspers they can be repaired.'[129]

The custom of preparing estimates before and after costruction work is amply documented for castles built in the provinces. Upon the completion of a moat at the Payas castle in 1580, the governor-general and finance officer of Aleppo reported that the local architect there was unable to calculate a correct estimate of its costs over a period of four years, since stones and other materials had been bought for different prices and some walls were built stronger than others. Therefore, an architect was sent from Istanbul to prepare a written appraisal of the costs of building materials and labour.[130] Such reports calculated construction work in cubits, since masons were generally paid per cubit (except for piecework) and building materials were standardized by cubit measures.

Decrees related to several fortresses in Morea, repaired on the basis of estimates prepared by the royal architect Mimar Kasım, who had trained as a marble cutter, confirm the importance of accurate assessments (Appendix 4.3 and 4.4). One of them, addressed in 1544 to the sanjak governor of Morea, the kadi of Kalavrita, and the architect Kasım (who had just been sent to repair a castle near Balyabadra), indicates that the first two officials had petitioned the sultan's court about the need for repairs at the castle of Kalavrita. They are ordered to go to that castle with the named architect and to have him make an accurate estimate (*taḫmīn-i ṣaḥīḥ*) of repairs, specifying how many cubits of wall, towers, cisterns, and underground storerooms were in need of repair, in addition to describing renovations required in the mosque of the castle and its warden's residence. The written estimate sent to the imperial court had to be made so precisely that it should not be any different from the final appraisal of the completed castle, which was to be made by another expert sent from the capital.[131]

Several months later that year, Mimar Kasım was ordered to estimate the cost of repairs at the castle of Navarino (Pylos) in Morea upon the request of its kadi and warden. Since Kasım had returned to the capital before the sultan's decree reached him, he had to travel again to Morea.[132] Another decree dated 1545 informs the kadi and warden of the castle of İzdin in Morea that Mimar Kasım was sent with a building supervisor (*emīn*) and secretary (*kātib*) to renovate their castle. Upon its completion the castle would be assessed by another architect arriving from the capital. Should any difference in cost emerge with respect to the original assessment, the warden, kadi, building supervisor, and secretary would be held responsible.[133]

Architectural drawings used in the construction of castles are frequently mentioned in the sources. After the conquest of Cyprus in 1570, its conqueror Lala Mustafa Pasha sent to the capital a design (*resm*) for renovations proposed at the castle of Baf (Páphos) and another one for the Friday mosque that was going to be built there with the sultan's permission.[134] In 1573 the governor-general and finance officer of Cyprus were ordered to have a master (*üstād*) prepare another design (*resm*) for that castle and send its copy to Istanbul together with a reassessment of costs.[135] The construction had not yet commenced in 1578 when yet another design (*resm*), proposing a castle half the size of the previous one, was dispatched to Istanbul to cut costs; the sultan approved the building of the castle in accordance with the new design.[136]

In 1573 the sanjak governor of Morea was instructed to supervise the construction with state funds of a new fortress at the strategic port of Navarino (Pylos) according to a design (*resm*) previously dispatched by Hızır Çavuş. Mimar Şaban, an architect already in Navarino, was to be assisted by another architect accompanying the grand admiral Kılıç Ali Pasha when the latter arrived there with the imperial fleet. A related decree, addressed to the grand admiral as the building overseer, commands him to have his own architect, who made the design (*resm*) of that castle 'in the European manner' (*frenk üslūbunda*), build it in cooperation with Mimar Şaban (Appendix 4.4).[137] The extant fortress of Navarino with its hexagonal bastion does indeed have an Italianate plan.[138] The unnamed architect who designed it was likely an Italian renegade like the pasha himself, who originated from Calabria.[139]

The governor-general of Buda was ordered in 1573 to have an appropriate design (*resm*) made for the citadel of Szigetvár and to send it to the sultan's court for approval.[140] During the same year the court messenger Hüsrev Çavuş returned to Istanbul to report that renovations ordered at the castle of Thessaloniki had already started. He brought back with him the design (*resm*) of a barbican that had to be built around a newly constructed tower. The sultan commanded the kadi of Thessaloniki to have the barbican built 'in accordance with that design' upon the messenger's return.[141] Designs of castles, then, were sent back and forth between Istanbul and provincial centres. That some of these may have been three-dimensional models is suggested by an account book recording an earlier renovation at the castle of Thessaloniki between 1538 and 1539 by Mimar Kosta. It mentions lining, size, glue, and cardboard for the 'tower model' (*nümūne-i ḳulle*) that cost 277 aspers.[142]

Written estimates of projected buildings often presented three options with differing price tags, offering patrons a choice in the negotiation of decorum. One such example is mentioned in a decree sent in 1573 to the kadi and the chief gardener of Edirne, who were overseeing the renovation of a kiosk built by Bayezid II in the royal palace of that city. Sinan, who was then building the Selimiye, estimated the cost for repairing that kiosk, but when it suddenly collapsed, his assistant Mimar İstemad prepared a revised estimate with three options:

> You had sent a petition reporting that for the repair of the imperial palace in Edirne its site had been visited with the chief architect and estimated (*taḫmīn*) to cost 36,000 aspers. In the imperial garden a poplar tree had fallen on the kiosk of the late sultan Bayezid Khan and some of its places needed to be repaired according to the above-mentioned estimate … on the twelfth night of this month, the kiosk having collapsed completely, the chief gardener sent a message and [the site] was revisited with the architect İstemad, who estimated it with an accurate estimate (*taḫmīn-i ṣaḥīḥ*). If, in accordance with the previous estimate, the roof is made with inscriptions, floral decorations, and lapis lazuli, and the walls are made in ashlar masonry it has been estimated to cost 200,000 aspers; whereas making a plain roof with ashlar masonry walls [will cost] 80,000 aspers, and a plain roof with a timber frame wall filled with bricks [will cost] 70,000 aspers.[143]

Choosing the middle option, the sultan sent 80,000 aspers and ordered the chief gardener to supervise the construction of the kiosk. Upon its completion, the overseeing kadi had to sign and dispatch its account book to the imperial court.

A petition sent to Selim II by the governor-general of Egypt, Koca Sinan Pasha, about the need to renovate the precinct of the Kaʿba similarly proposed three alternative estimates. On 11 August 1571 the sultan responded by selecting the cheapest option (40,000 ducats), repairing the holy precinct 'according to its old form' with wooden shed roofs for which planks and timbers would be sent from the capital.[144] On 7 December 1571 he changed his mind in favour of the most expensive option (100,000 ducats): namely, domical arcades built with locally available stones and lime. This shift was not provoked by an impulsive outburst of generosity, but by a shortage of the wooden planks and timbers required for rebuilding the fleet (recently decimated in Lepanto) for an upcoming jihad:

> Your letter has arrived at my sublime porte in which you report that wooden planks, lead, nails, and timbers need to be sent from here for repairing the roofs that have fallen into ruin around the Haram of Mecca the Honoured,

> and you have indicated that an additional 40,000 to 50,000 ducats are needed in cash. Whatever you have said at length has come to my noble attention. Now, when you previously petitioned about the estimated repairs of the venerable precinct in terms of three alternative options, you had reported the possibility of having it repaired for 40,000 ducats according to its old form by importing some timber from the Ottoman lands in the north. I had thus ordered you to start its repair according to its old form. However, wooden planks and materials required from the Ottoman domains have to be taken from the imperial arsenal, and now the construction of ships has started in my imperial arsenal to be sent with God's permission to the jihad planned at the beginning of this coming auspicious spring. Hence timber is being used for that purpose and it is no longer possible to send timber there. But since it is not deemed decorous to delay the repair of the venerable precinct, the first estimate of 100,000 ducats you petitioned has been approved, according to which stones and lime available in that land must be used.[145]

The sultan's written correspondence with successive governor-generals of Egypt, who served as the overseers (*nāẓır*) of this project, and with the sanjak governor Ahmed Beg of Jidda, who was appointed building supervisor (*emīn*), exemplifies the control of distant projects through detailed progress reports.[146] We learn from an imperial decree sent on 18 September 1573 to the governor-general and finance minister of Egypt that the building supervisor Ahmed Beg had personally inspected the dilapidated roofs of the Haram and already started construction work by demolishing the most ruined areas. Since the old foundations were incapable of bearing the load of stone domes, new foundations were laid (150 mason's cubits long and 4 to 6 cubits deep). As the existing white marble columns were not strong enough, they had to be supplemented with new pillars carved of stone (one cubit and eight fingers wide) – one between every three marble columns. Thus far, thirty-two domes had been built for 14,000 gold coins (840,000 aspers). Because seven hundred domes had been estimated, the remaining six hundred and sixty-eight domes would cost 336,000 gold coins (20,160,000 aspers).[147]

This alarming new estimate was more than three times the original assessment (100,000 gold coins equalling 6,000,000 aspers). No wonder, then, that at that point the sultan decided to intervene by sending the royal architect Mimar Mehmed Çavuş from Istanbul (Appendix 4.4). Upon the architect's arrival, the sanjak governor of Jidda and the shaykh al-haram of Mecca were to have him execute the ordered constructions as it was deemed 'appropriate and fitting' (*vecih ve münāsib*), not allowing unqualified outsiders to interfere with his work and making sure that the structures were strongly built without overspending.[148] On 25 September 1573, Mimar Mehmed Çavuş left the capital with twenty-five masons (*bennā*) and building materials (200 iron tie-beams and chests full of other supplies) to execute the renovations in Mecca, for which plans were likely designed by Sinan.[149] Mehmed Çavuş served as the supervisor (*mübāşir*) of both the domical arcades and the ʿArafat water channel in Mecca. Under his supervision a local architect sent from Egypt, Horos Memi (Memi Muhyiddin), executed the three hundred and sixty domes built around the Kaʿba's precinct (illus. 137, 138).[150]

Sinan's autobiographies list both projects – the domical arcades completed early in Murad III's reign (1576–77) and the ʿArafat water channel – because they were coordinated through his office.[151] Even before the construction of arcades was undertaken, he directed from a distance the repaving with white marble of the Haram's ruined black stone pavement, based on an estimate that Selim II ordered the governor-general of Egypt to have prepared by experts in 1567.[152] Evliya Çelebi says the pavements were completed in 1571-72. An archival document, which records the payment made to the 'chief architect Sinan Agha' in 1569 'for marbles required in the noble Haram of Mecca the Honoured', confirms his involvement in the renewal from the very beginning.[153]

Thanks to the timely intervention of the royal architect Mehmed Çavuş, the number of estimated domes was reduced by half and the money spent on them came close to the original estimate of 100,000 ducats. From an undated petition, sent to Murad III by the shaykh al-haram of Mecca and the sanjak governor of Jidda, we learn that 105,000 gold coins (6,300,000 aspers) had been expended for the pavements and for approximately four hundred domes at the Meccan Haram. On the basis of that sum they proposed a new estimate for renovating the Prophet's mosque at Medina: repairing its cracked pavements and building three hundred new domes around its Haram would cost 35,000 gold coins (2,100,000 aspers), a sum they requested sent with the chief court painter Lutfi (Lutfullah).[154]

The stone domes around the precinct of the Kaʿba have slightly pointed conical profiles differing from typically Ottoman hemispherical brick domes (illus. 138). Despite a provincial flavor attributable to masons imported from Damascus, Aleppo, and Cairo, these domical arcades visually Ottomanized the Haram, appended with Sultan Süleyman's madrasa, built in 1564–65. The conical capped minaret of that madrasa was complemented by three other Ottoman-style minarets renewed by Süleyman and Selim II at the Haram; the remaining three had been built by the Mamluk sultans.[155]

Written estimates presenting three price options find a visual counterpart in a plan datable to the early sixteenth century (illus. 139, 140). Identified by its annotations as a working drawing (*kārnāme*), it presents three design alternatives for the domed mausoleum of the Bektaşi dervish Abdal Ata in Çorum. The plan is drawn in black ink on paper with no watermark, the surface of

137 Renovation of the Kaʿba, Mecca, with stone cutters and sacrificed animals in the foreground: the two figures praying with raised hands at the upper-right are the kadi and Sharif of Mecca who oversaw the project; the two conversing figures at the left are the building supervisor holding a staff and the architect who holds a wooden measuring stick, c. 1581, watercolour on paper, from Lokman, *Shāhnāma-i Salīm Khan*.

138 Old photograph of the Kaʿba showing Ottoman minarets with pointed caps and domical arcades around the Haram.

which is incised with a grid of uneven squares. Three plans are superimposed on the grid, with the thickness of their walls filled in red watercolour. Four sarcophagi, identified as those of Abdal Ata, Emir Seyyid, Receb Dede, and Burhan Dede, are indicated. Other annotations specify cubit measures and cost estimates. Those on the cheapest single-unit structure at the bottom-right read: 'This is a single dome and its estimated value is 50,000 aspers'; 'its length and width is ten cubits'; 'the upper part of this dome is hexagonal'.[156] The second variant features two square domed halls of the same dimensions, the second identified as a guesthouse (*tābḫāne*). It has the following scribbled note: 'This consists of two domes, it is approximately 70,000 aspers.'[157] On the most elabourate plan with four domed halls of equal size, the function of each hall is specified: 'the dome of the sarcophagi (*ḳubbe-i maḳābīr*)', 'the dome of the guestroom (*ḳubbe-i tābḫāne*)', 'the dome of the intervening space (*ḳubbe-i miyān-serā*)', and 'the dome of the anteroom (*ḳubbe-i ṣoffa*)'. This last project is annotated: 'The working drawing (*kārnāme*) seen here, when its value is calculated, is approximately 120,000 aspers.' Another note shows that this is the preferred choice: 'And in fact, the layout of the dervish convent (*tekye*) is this, and they [presumably its keepers] also request this; it consists of four domes.'[158]

This third inscription shows that a pre-existing structure was being remodelled, a conclusion supported by the presence of four sarcophagi and the survival of an endowment deed for Abdal Ata's 'dervish convent' (*zāviye*) dating from 1419.[159] The preservation of this plan in the Topkapı Palace archives suggests that it was presented to a sultan. A likely recipient is Bayezid II, during whose reign convents suppressed by his father flourished with new donations. Perhaps the renovation of Abdal Ata's funerary convent was triggered by the earthquake of 1509, when many buildings were destroyed in Çorum.[160] Its two extant ashlar masonry domed halls (the burial chamber with four sarcophagi and the guesthouse with a mihrab) are stylistically datable to the

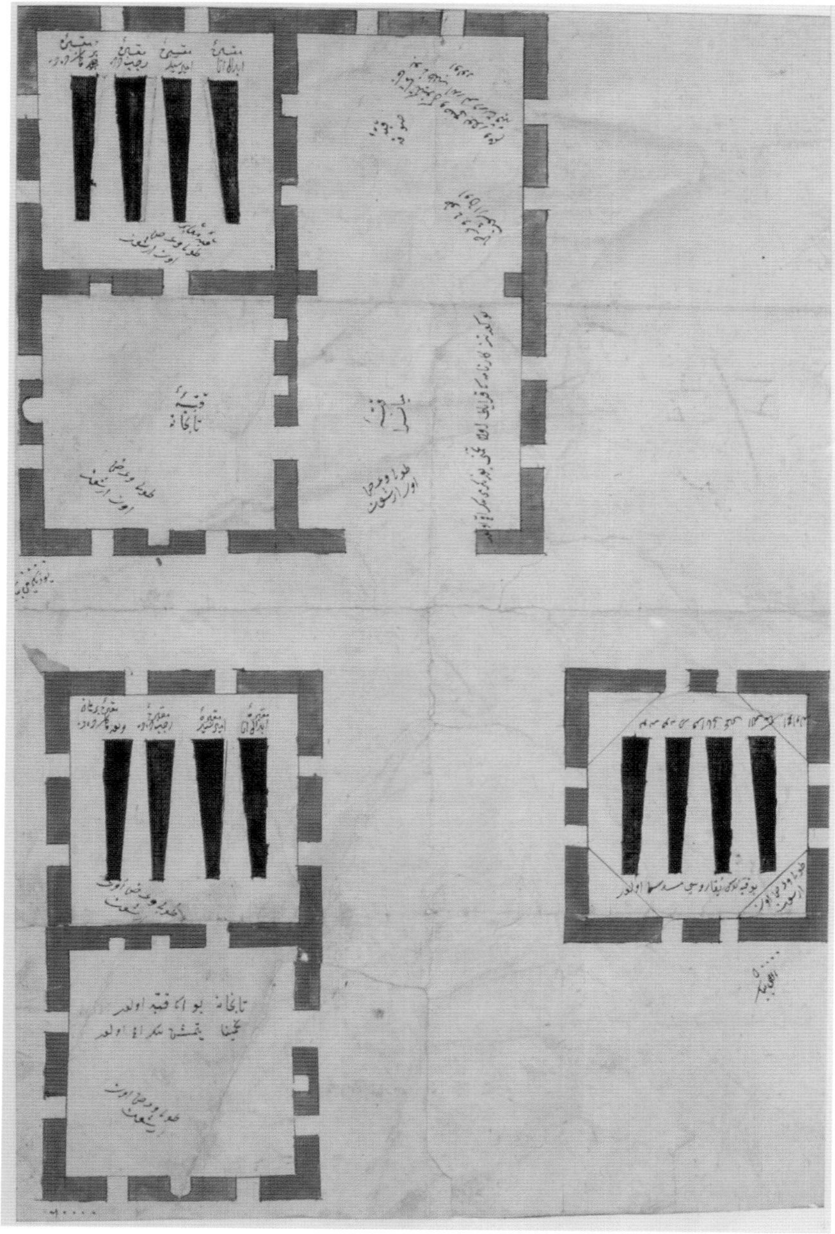

139 Plan of the Abdal Ata convent in Çorum presenting three options, early sixteenth century, black ink and red watercolour on paper.

early sixteenth century (illus. 141). With an appended minaret, they are fronted today by a wooden vestibule that roughly corresponds to the area on the plan of the remaining two domed halls. The sultan, then, had apparently chosen the middle, two-domed option.

On the plan, the interior spaces, measuring ten by ten cubits, are indicated by ten squares on each side (twelve, including wall thickness). Given the standardized sizes of building materials and the custom of paying masons per square cubit of wall, it must have been relatively easy to calculate approximate amounts of materials and labour costs simply by counting the squares inside the thickness of walls and deducting the openings. Adding expenses for piecework (such as stone frames for windows and gates) could yield a highly reliable estimate. The modular grid system must also have facilitated tracing the outlines of plans on the ground by means of a grid marked out with stakes and ropes.[161]

The tradition of presenting royal patrons with alternate plans implies that Ottoman sultans were sufficiently familiar with design conventions to read them. The historian Celalzade Mustafa says that Sultan Süleyman had selected the plan of the Şehzade Mehmed mosque from several 'designs and plans' (*resmler ve ṭarḥlar*) petitioned as options. From these drawings, the one that was found to be most 'agreeable and well-proportioned in style was selected.'[162] We have seen that the *Tezkiretü'l-bünyān* mentions a meeting to which Sinan was invited by his royal patron for the selection of the plan (*resm-i binā*) and site of the Süleymaniye complex.[163] Celalzade writes that Sinan 'prepared the plan and design (*resm ve ṭarḥ*) of the exalted mosque according to an esteemed and agreeable manner.' He then traced the plan with stakes and ropes on the levelled ground in the presence of the sultan, after which engineers skilled in geometry dug the foundations. The sultan paid a second official visit with his whole court and religious dignitaries at an auspicious time determined by astrologers; animals were sacrificed and alms distributed, and the grand mufti Ebussuud placed the corner stone of the mihrab 'with his blessed hands'.[164]

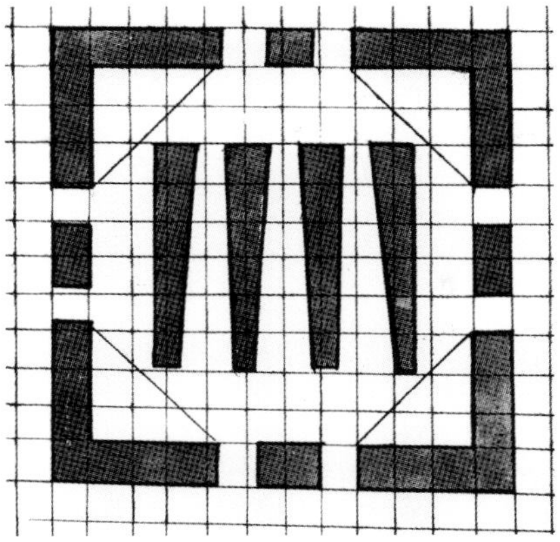

140 Copy of uninked grid incised on the plan of the Abdal Ata convent shown opposite.

Written estimates and plans providing several design options to patrons indicate that the chief architect was not alone in decision making. Progress reports that Sinan periodically submitted to Selim II during the construction of the Selimiye in Edirne testify to the sultan's continuing input into decision-making even after the selection of an appropriate plan. The pivotal role of plans in the negotiation of decorum is demonstrated by a design (*resm*) Mimar Hüseyin Çavuş prepared in the late 1580s for the ongoing construction of income-producing dependencies at the Selimiye after Sinan's death (Appendix 4.4). The kadi of Edirne who was overseeing construction work suggested in a petition that the costs of the projected commercial buildings should be estimated in the sultan's presence by the architect Hüseyin and his master Davud Agha, on the basis of the plan dispatched to Istanbul that depicted the mosque together with existing and newly planned structures around it.[165]

141 Abdal Ata convent, Çorum, from the southwest.

Only a few fifteenth- and sixteenth-century plans drawn on paper have been discovered thus far, and no architectural models from Sinan's time are known to have survived. This can be attributed to the wholesale disappearance of the architectural workshops and their archives in Vefa and in the palace gardens. The rare plans that have survived from this period are some of the presentation drawings and rejected proposals stored at the inner treasury of the Topkapı Palace.[166] In the absence of plans and models, we can only speculate about Sinan's working methods and design techniques. This is a major shortcoming: just imagine writing the history of Italian Renaissance architecture without any surviving drawings and models. The few plans from the second half of the sixteenth century, identified by their annotations as 'working drawings' (*kārnāme*), include an estimate for the Kırkçeşme water system (the only extant design attributable to Sinan), and a scroll plan of Istanbul's water channels drawn by their former superintendent, Davud, in 1584. Both are technical drawings annotated with explanatory notes.

The sketchy Kırkçeşme plan is a black ink drawing on burnished paper with an inscription on the reverse (illus. 142): 'According to the calculation of the working drawing (*kārnāme*) of Mimar Sinan Agha, in accordance with the survey (*mesāḥa*): in total water pipes 26,475 cubits, big arches 205,400 cubits, small arches 1,800 cubits, curtain walls 1,900 cubits.'[167] Other annotations indicate the approximate length of pipes and the dimensions (length, height, and width) of aqueducts in cubits, and of curtain walls measured in squared cubits – referred to as the 'calculation of masons' (*ḥisāb-ı bennā*) or the 'chess-board' (*ṣaṭranc*) method. The fifty-five measures (*lüle*) of water estimated in this drawing is considerably less than the amount obtained – in excess of 100 measures – after the Kırkçeşme water system was completed. This suggests that the plan represents a more conservative preliminary estimate or an estimate made for rebuilding some of the damaged aqueducts after the flood of 1563.[168] A note added later to Davud's 1584 scroll plan explains why it was made (illus. 143): 'When the late sultan Murad strongly reprimanded the former water channel superintendent Üstad Davud, asking him "Where do you divert my water?", he quickly created this *kārnāme*, may God bless both of them.' The drawing, which indicates the amount of water flowing to various places, may have been made in response to accusations of illegal water distribution (already made in 1577) that seem to have caused Davud's dismissal from his post in 1582 (Appendix 4.4, 4.5).[169]

The three *kārnāme*s we have considered thus far are all

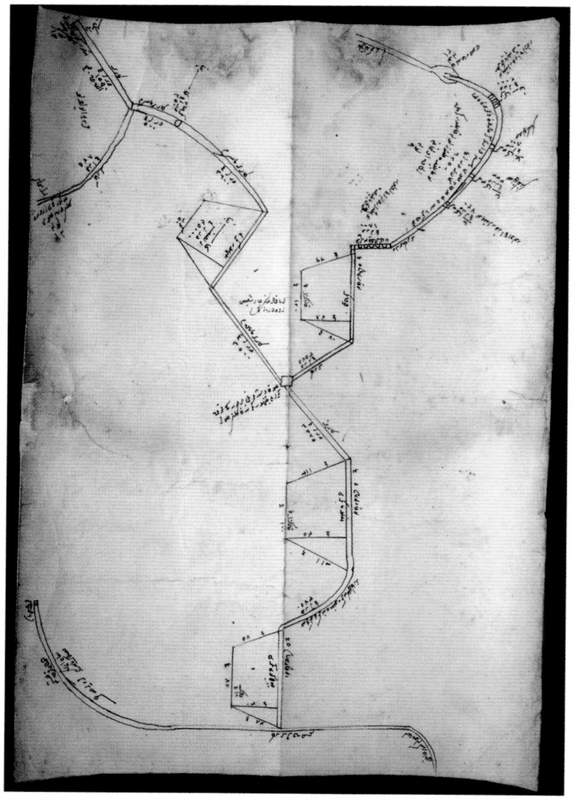

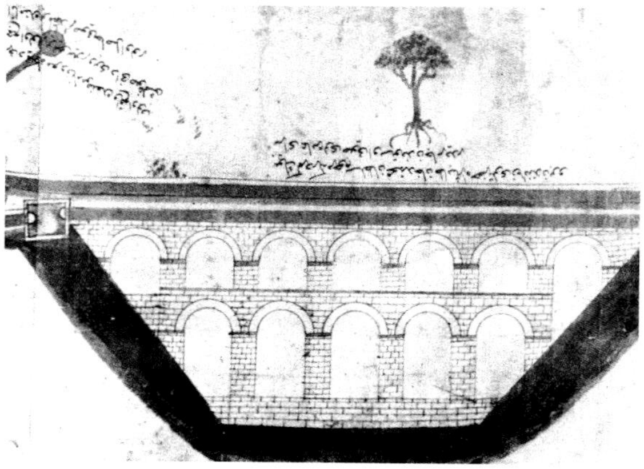

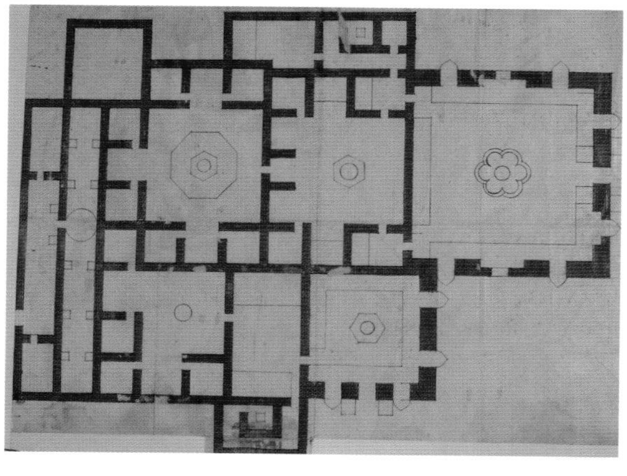

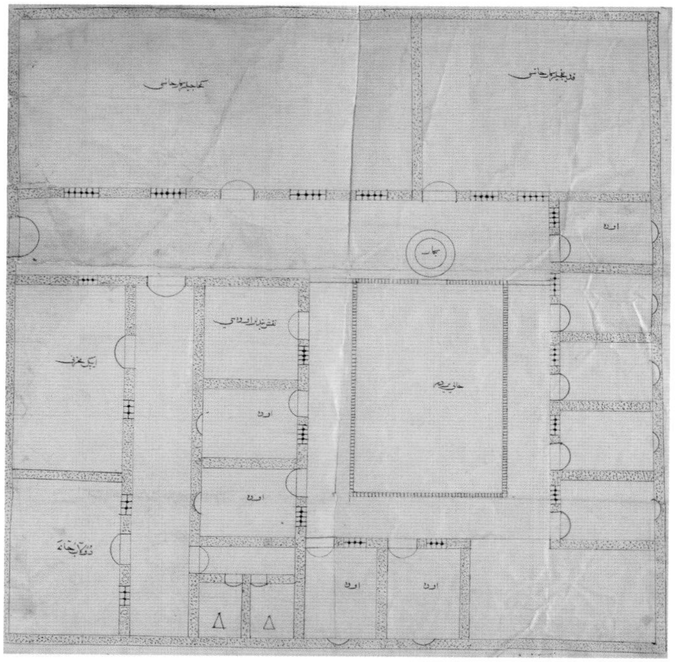

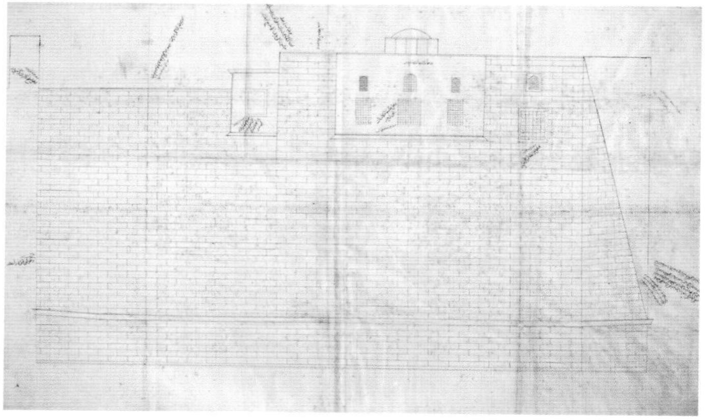

142 (top left) Sinan's survey drawing for the Kırkçeşme water distribution system, Istanbul, early 1560s, black ink on paper.

143 (middle left) Elevation of the Valens aqueduct, detail from a scroll plan of Istanbul's water channels drawn by the water channel superintendant Davud, 1584.

144 (bottom left) Plan of a double bath, second half of the fifteenth century, black and red ink on paper.

145 (top) Plan of the royal textile workshop in Istanbul with stippled walls, early sixteenth century, black ink on paper.

146 (above) Elevation of a buttress built in front of the royal bath and inner treasury of the Topkapı Palace, Istanbul, *c.* 1509–11, black ink on paper.

drawings annotated with written explanations. Therefore, the term '*kārnāme*', derived from the Persian root *kār* (work) seems to refer to a working drawing annotated with dimensions, a pictorial counterpart to a written survey based on cubit measures. Imperial decrees occasionally mention such designs sent from Istanbul for provincial mosques attributed to Sinan. A working drawing (*kārnāme*) was dispatched in 1559 for Hürrem Sultan's posthumous mosque complex at the bridge of Çoban Mustafa Pasha near Edirne (now Svilengrad). We have already seen how Sultan Süleyman ordered the kadi of Edirne to build the mosque 'according to the dispatched design (*resm*),' reducing its two minarets to one. The plan in question must have been drawn by Sinan since the mosque is listed among his works in the two *Teẕkiretü'l-ebniye*.[170] In 1583 the royal architect Mahmud was sent to Manisa with a *kārnāme* of the Muradiye mosque, also drawn by Sinan. The overseeing kadi and building supervisor were ordered to have the mosque built in accordance with the plan and without intervention from other parties.[171]

When Sinan was sent by Murad III to Mecca in 1584 to survey the Kaʿba and prepare an estimate for its renovation, he returned to Istanbul with a set of drawings. Cafer Efendi's treatise explains that these designs (*rusūm* sing. *resm*), which had been 'sealed and protected' by the chief architect Mimar Mehmed Agha, were consulted when Ahmed I decided to take up the unrealized renovation of the Kaʿba, a project previously rejected as unlawful by the ulema. Mehmed Agha only had to refer to Sinan's designs, most likely annotated with dimensions, to know the Kaʿba's 'width, height and length'.[172]

What Sinan's architectural drawings looked like is hard to infer from the few surviving examples. Extant plans from the fifteenth and sixteenth centuries, like the multiple-choice plan of Abdal Ata's renovated funerary convent, are all drawn in black ink over uninked squared grids incised on the paper surface, with the thickness of walls indicated in colour (usually red, sometimes yellow) or stippling (illus. 62, 89, 144, 145). Relative to the funerary convent plan, however, plans presenting new projects use more sophisticated design conventions combining European and Islamic traditions. Among the conventions Ottoman plans share with their Italian Renaissance counterparts, which on occasion feature grids, include compass-drawn circles and half circles to indicate domes and half-domes, circles inscribed in squares to represent columns, and coloured walls. The use of squared grids and coloured walls is also common convention in Iranian and Central Asian ground plans, on which domical superstructures are not indicated. Distinctive Ottoman conventions include the indication of iron-grilled windows by cross-hatching, arched doors shown in elevation, and latrines marked by triangles.[173]

Only one elevation drawing has survived among early plans kept at the Topkapı Palace archives. It is identified as a '*kārnāme*' and concerns the construction of a buttress on the garden façade of the royal bath and inner treasury at Topkapı Palace after the 1509 earthquake. A note explains that for this 'buttress (*ṭayama*), a sum total of 1,234,557 aspers has been spent' (illus. 146). We learn from Bayezid II's book of royal donations that the building supervisors Solak Ali and Mehmed b. Kemal were rewarded for serving in the construction of 'the buttress (*ṭayama*) of the wall of the imperial palace' upon its completion in 1511.[174] As in other *kārnāmes*, annotations on the elevation drawing give the cubit measures of the length, width, and thickness of the buttress. The position of the buttress is clarified by notes that identify the buildings in front of which it was constructed: 'this place is the curtain wall at the edge of the kitchen'; 'behind this wall is the bath'; 'this place is the windows of the undressing chamber of the bath'; and 'this place is the windows of the imperial treasury'.[175]

At the far right side of the buttress, on which individual stones are meticulously drawn in black ink, appears a triangular cross-section. The note scribbled next to it reads, 'This [diagonal] line is the [buttress] wall, and the inner [vertical] line represents how it leans against the treasury wall.'[176] The elevation drawing, then, represents the buttress both frontally and in cross-section, a convention also used in Sinan's sketchy Kırkçeşme plan (where each of the four main aqueducts features a triangular cross-section indicating the slant of arched walls). The domed bath hall with three double-tiered windows is not drawn to scale, because the renovation project mainly concerned the buttress.

Sinan's elevations for major new buildings were probably orthogonal projections drawn to scale. The perspectival impulse of Ottoman miniature painters, expressed in architectural representations that depict receding and projecting planes, must have been suppressed in technical designs projected onto the plane according to a fixed measure. When the chief architect Mehmed Agha's biographer saw the 'forms (*eşkāl*) drawn for the design (*resm*)' of the Sultan Ahmed mosque, he was so inspired by them that he composed a panegyrical poem describing the incomplete mosque in detail. He says that one who wishes to understand the layout of the mosque in its 'illustrated designs and estimated numbers' should first become greatly skilled in the science of geometry and then ponder its forms 'for many days and months and years.'[177]

The prestige mosques that Sinan designed for prominent patrons in the capital must have been built on the basis of ground plans, elevation drawings, and in some cases three-dimensional models. The account books of the Süleymaniye complex covering the years between 1553 and 1559 mention the costs of paper used for architectural drawings: 120 folios of 'Istanbul paper' had been used for the 'drawings of dome inscriptions and working drawings' (*resm-i ḫaṭṭ-ı ḳubbehā ve ḳārnāme*) during this six-year period.[178] These designs, prepared during the later stages of construction work (account books covering the years 1549–53 are lost), concerned the decorative programme of the mosque and some of its dependencies. Nine of the folios were for 'inscriptions of the noble mosque and a *kārnāme*', five for another *kārnāme*, three for an 'architectural design' (*resm-i binā*), three for the 'working drawing of a madrasa' (*kārnāme-i medrese*), and fourteen for the 'design of inscriptions and the architect's working drawing' (*resm-i ḫaṭṭve ḳārnāme-i miʿmār*).[179]

The dimensions of the Süleymaniye mosque, from the height of its columns to the exact size of its window shutters, were determined at the very beginning. This is confirmed by a decree sent to the governor-general of Egypt on 12 September 1550, about three months after the mosque's foundations were laid. It specifies the dimensions of required columns and the size of two windows for which deluxe shutters were ordered from Cairo:

> In Alexandria there are supposed to be four pieces of red sparrow's eye (*ḳızıl serçe gözi*) columns seventeen cubits long and two cubits wide. Since it is necessary to bring these columns here, I order you to immediately report where the aforementioned columns are, and how much their transportation will cost, and what type of ship they need to be loaded on, after fully informing yourself about the truth of the matter in detail. And besides the aforementioned columns, send as many esteemed verdantique and porphyry columns five to six cubits [long] as you can, and the best marbles suitable for revetments ... And since it is necessary to have two of the windows – that is four shutters – of the noble mosque presently being built artistically fashioned there by masters with tightly fitted pieces, all of their required materials have been sent together with the measurements of their length and width.[180]

We have seen that according to the *Teẕkiretü'l-bünyān* only one of the four colossal red granite columns from Alexandria was used in the mosque.[181] The two deluxe shutters must have been intended for the pair of windows flanking the sultan's private mihrab at the royal tribune; these windows are distinguished from others in the mosque with their verdantique frames, gilt brass grills and wooden shutters luxuriously inlaid with ivory and mother-of-pearl.[182] The shutter dimensions could not have been determined without detailed elevation drawings or a three-dimensional model.

Generic mosques would have only required ground plans and perhaps simpler elevation drawings with some basic dimensions shown on them. While grid-based ground plans could mechanically be reproduced, elevations were more open to regional and personal readings. Most provincial mosques attributed to Sinan are typically Ottoman in their ground plan, but their elevations, executed by teams of local masons, exhibit a strong regional flavour. The architect's role was not just the execution of a plan designed by Sinan, but one involving a certain degree of interpretation and improvisation. Standard mosques of the domed-cube type did not require elaborate drawings, as their elevations could be generated from their ground plans.

More generic buildings did not even require plans drawn on paper. For instance, a bathhouse commissioned in 1575 by the vizier Koca Sinan Pasha from local architects residing at the central Anatolian city of Larende was not built on the basis of a plan but from a verbal description recorded in a legal document. Contracted for a lump sum, this unindividualized building was modelled on the familiar typology of Istanbul's monumental fifteenth-century double baths:

> Copy of the voucher (*ḥüccet*) for the bathhouse that is being built by contract (*götürü*) in the town of Larende, whose total cost has been handed over to the architects in the year 1575 during his vizierate: sum of money 220,000 [aspers]. The reason for writing this document is that the persons named Üstad Pirli b. Osman, Sinan b. Hamza, Derviş b. Hüseyin, Mehmed b. Ali, the other Mehmed b. Sevindik, Resul b. Hüdaverdi, Mustafa Dede b. Ali, and Kadri b. Ramazan, who reside at the quarter of Siyahser among the quarters of Larende, assembled at the court of the noble shariʿa and declared the following: 'Inside Larende the double bath that is going to be built at the Hatib quarter in the manner (*üslūb*) of the bathhouse of Mahmud Pasha [1467] in Istanbul and of bathhouses along the route of the imperial council and near Tahtakale, will consist of an outer dressing hall at the men's bathhouse measuring fifteen cubits in mason's cubits, with the distance between its raised basin platforms flanking the central shaving space measuring nine cubits (each having a length of nine cubits and a width of four cubits); and it will feature an inner dressing hall measuring eleven cubits between the supports of its main dome with eight arches, under which each of the four private rooms measure four by four cubits; the men's bathhouse having two fountains, with its inner and outer halls and all basins being made of marble, with no stone other than marble used in it. The women's bathhouse is to be built according to custom (*ʿādet üzre*) with basins of Kozviran stone and floors of İspendik stone, its sewer pipes reaching the poplar tree near the house of ... At the bathhouses characterized by the description above, the costs of their plot, their boiler, water channels, stones, lime, and all materials required for their completion until they are fully functioning are incumbent upon us (*ʿuhdemiz*), and we are guarantors of each other's losses, and it is hoped that, Godwilling, the said bathhouses will reach completion in August of 1581, and will be rented out without taking a single [additional] asper from its owner.' For the completion of the above-mentioned two bathhouses in accordance with their description, they agreed to become contractors (*müteʿahhid*) for 220,000 aspers of current value, with the previously mentioned Pirli b. Osman acting as the leader and architect (*reʾīs ve miʿmār*).

147, 148 Two views of an eighteenth-century wooden model of the Xeropotamou Monastery Catholikon, Mount Athos, 1762.

What they accepted was written down in detail and its copy was made so that, when needed, it should act as a reminder of the state of affairs and as a record of the actual state of the case; written on the twentieth of the month of R. in the year 983 (29 July 1575).[183]

The main dimensions of this generic building were fixed by the written contract. Koca Sinan Pasha's bathhouse was not alone in referring to older monuments as familiar prototypes. A fortified square tower built in 1577 along the coast of Payas, about a kilometre away from the main castle (based on a plan sent from Istanbul in 1568), was similarly commissioned with reference to a well-known type. The governor and kadi of Uzeyr and Mustafa Çavuş received an order to build this 'strong tower in the manner of (*üslūb*) the Maiden's Tower (Kızkulesi) across from the imperial palace in Istanbul' on a site they deemed 'decorous and appropriate' (*vecih ve münāsib*).[184]

For some prestige mosques in Istanbul and Edirne Sinan likely prepared models. The lavishly painted and gilded models of the Süleymaniye mosque and of the recently renovated sanctuaries in Mecca and Medina that were paraded during the circumcision festivities of 1582 seem to have been ceremonial models prepared for that occasion, rather than working models used during the construction process. Commemorative models of the sanctuaries in Mecca and Medina were also kept inside the mausoleum of Sultan Süleyman, who had renovated the holy sites.[185] Just as Antonio da Sangallo the Younger and Michelangelo had models of St Peter's made to guide workmen, Sinan probably prepared models for major projects like the Süleymaniye and Selimiye mosques to guide construc-tion work, in addition to full-scale models and templates of details.[186]

Judging from eighteenth-century Ottoman architectural practice, models prepared for important projects were made out of wood. An account book recording the expenses for rebuilding the mosque of Mehmed II in Istanbul after the earthquake of 1766 shows that its wooden model (*resm*) cost 7,021 aspers.[187] A surviving model of wood, covered with papier-mâché and resting on a wooden board with a squared grid providing its scale, was sent from Istanbul around that time for the construction of the Catholikon of the Xeropotamou monastery in Mount Athos (illus. 147, 148). This scale model, made of paper-covered wooden pieces with removable elevations that provide a view of the interior, was signed on 13 April 1762 by the royal architect Constantinos. The extant Catholikon shows that the design of the model was slightly altered by the master mason Chatziconstantis during the construction process between 1762 and 1764.[188]

It is hard to imagine that the expertise in preparing ceremonial and commemorative models was not channelled into functional uses in architectural practice during the age of Sinan, or that ceremonial models were not an outgrowth of functional ones. Texts frequently mention glass globes containing small wooden or ivory mosque models, hung from domes along with oil lamps and ostrich eggs. A model of the Süleymaniye mosque inside a glass globe was prepared in 1593 under the supervision of the chief architect Davud for the dome of Koca Sinan Pasha's mausoleum at Divanyolu.[189] In 1665 the Frenchman Thevenot saw at the Sultan Ahmed mosque 'a large quantity of lamps and small gallantries inside glass balls'; one of them was 'a wooden design of that mosque'. Antoine Galland (1672–73) noticed a similar miniature model suspended among oil lamps and ostrich eggs at the Yeni Valide mosque in Eminönü: 'Among all that, one sees an ivory design of the mosque made in the round, which is

149 (below) A seventeenth-century ivory model of the Sultan Ahmed mosque, Istanbul, inside a glass casket.

150 (bottom) A seventeenth-century wooden model of the Yeni Valide mosque, Eminönü.

enclosed within a glass case.'[190] One extant example of a commemorative model, contained in a glass lantern, is a gilded ivory representation of the Sultan Ahmed mosque (illus. 149). Another is a gilded and colourfully painted wood-and-papier-mâché model of the Yeni Valide mosque in Eminönü, resting on a board (illus. 150).

In an unillustrated, short version of the *Sūrnāme*, the models of Mecca and Medina with which Sinan paraded in 1582 are attributed to 'the chief architect, who is unique and incomparable in his time, unequalled in talent and art, sagacious, wise, and prudent.'[191] The longer, illustrated version of the *Sūrnāme* eulogizes an unnamed but 'Euclid-like' designer of plans (*ṭarḥ*), elevations (*taḳsīm*), and models (*timṣāl*) who paraded with the model of the Süleymaniye mosque that he had fashioned for the occasion (illus. 130):

> His intellect was endowed with power in geometry,
> His cultivated mind was an architect for all types of work.
>
> When he drew the universe on the tablet of his wisdom,
> He would turn it into a working drawing (*kārnāme*).
>
> When he lacked a compass, his fist
> Would suffice to him with two fingers.[192]

Ceremonial models continued to be displayed in later festivities. During the 1675 circumcision festivities held in Edirne, the chief architect paraded with the models of two gardens and two large trees.[193] His gift to the sultan was the 'skilfully fashioned' model of a large kiosk inside a garden with a pool. The gift of the carpenters 'designed with the supervision of the chief royal architect, Ahmed Agha' was another model of a garden kiosk.[194] The *Sūrnāme* of Vehbi (*c.* 1720) depicts cheerful models of gardens with kiosks and pools displayed in yet another circumcision festival in Istanbul during the reign of Ahmed III, when the agha of architects (*mi'mār aġa*) paraded wearing an elegant white silk caftan and a tall headdress (*mücevveze*), holding a staff in his hand (illus. 129, 151, 152). The emphasis had clearly shifted from religious to secular architecture in the ceremonial self-representation of chief architects, a change corresponding to post-classical patterns of patronage, in which mosques lost their former prominence.

III. THE CONSTRUCTION INDUSTRY

Bayezid II's book of royal donations discussed earlier indicates that the custom of appointing a building overseer (*binā nāẓırı*), a building supervisor (*binā emīni*), and a secretary (*binā kātibi*) for the financial management of major construction enterprises had become standard practice by the early sixteenth century.[195] The fact that the architect of Mehmed II's mosque complex was punished for overspending, after account books kept by the building supervisor and scribe were inspected, implies a certain overlap in responsibilities. Sinan, too complains that he was held

151 Models of gardens with pavilions, pools, and fountains paraded during a royal circumcision ceremony, c. 1720, watercolour on paper, illustration from Vehbi, *Sūrnāme-i Vehbī*.

152 Models of gardens with pavilions, pools, and fountains, from Vehbi, *Sūrnāme-i Vehbī*.

under suspicion around 1557, when gossips informed the sultan that the Süleymaniye mosque could not be completed on time because its custodians and scribes were busy building their own houses with materials embezzled from the complex. 'These questions should in fact have been addressed to the building supervisor,' he retorts indignantly.[196]

The final resumé of expenses for the Süleymaniye, covering the years 1553 to 1559 and recorded by the scribe (*kātib*) Halil, was jointly prepared by the madrasa professor Mevlana Mehmed b. Mehmed acting as overseer (*nāẓır*), the supervisor (*emīn*) Sinan Beg, and the 'architect Sinan, the chief of the architects of the Sublime Porte.' Although it was the supervisor's responsibility to supply building materials and to be in charge of financial matters, errors in the resumé of accounts could potentially implicate each individual who signed it.[197] The resumé lists left-over materials ordered in advance that were either sold on the market or transferred to other royal constructions, thereby generating a series of satellite projects.[198] According to Gerlach, the custom of preparing in advance three times the quantity of building materials required gave rise to a rampant black market of stolen supplies.[199]

In the age of Sinan, building overseers were usually selected from the ranks of such pre-eminent grandees as the janissary agha, the grand admiral, madrasa professors, kadis, governor-generals, or viziers in charge of commanding military campaigns. After the flood of 1563, when Sultan Süleyman went with his grandees to inspect the ruined Kırkçeşme aqueducts, he assigned the chief of the janissaries, Müezzinzade Ali Agha, and the grand admiral, Piyale Pasha, to oversee the rebuilding of the Mağlova and Uzunkemer aqueducts respectively, employing their own teams of construction workers. Eyyubi's eyewitness account explains that the admiral's labourers, consisting of ship captains, marine soldiers, and fettered galley slaves, did not work as efficiently as the novices, janissaries, and janissary captains, who 'fought heavily' with the building, their lifted skirts tucked in their belts. During a visit to the building site, the disappointed sultan reassigned Uzunkemer to Ali Agha, remarking that 'these [marines] are useless on dry land'.[200] Upon the completion of each aqueduct, an inauguration ceremony was held during which the sultan inspected the finished work, with the janissary agha and the chief architect walking in front of him. Royal donations were distributed and hardworking janissaries promoted into the ranks of *solak*, *sekban*, *yayabaşı*, and *çavuş*.[201]

Even though Eyyubi is critical of Piyale Pasha's team, admirals frequently oversaw constructions in the capital, using galley slaves of the imperial arsenal at Kasımpaşa along the Golden Horn. In 1569 Marcantonio Barbaro wrote that the grand admiral Müezzinzade Ali Pasha (the former janissary agha mentioned above) was responsible not only for building galleys, but also for overseeing the buildings of the sultan and grandees. When Barbaro went to visit Sokollu Mehmed Pasha's palace at Kadırgalimanı that summer, he encountered the admiral at the construction site of the neighbouring mosque complex commissioned from Sinan by Sokollu and his royal wife. He was holding a baton 'as if he were a foreman or solicitor of construction workers'.[202] The imperial arsenal under the jurisdiction of grand admirals had its own staff of caulkers, rope-twisters, blacksmiths, painters, carpenters, ship-designing architect-engineers, and chief architect.[203] These experts, well-versed in European shipbuilding techniques, included many renegades, such as the Ragusan galley artisan Marcus, who adopted the name İbrahim after converting to Islam during the 1570s.[204]

The technical similarities of wood-frame ship building and house construction allowed the grand admiral Kılıç Ali Pasha's team of 'galley-slave carpenters' *(forşa dülgerleri)* to build in a single day temporary wooden galleries at the Hippodrome, where European ambassadors sat during the circumcision festivities of 1582.[205] The 'infidel galley slaves' *(forşa keferesi)* of the same pasha, who under Murad III oversaw the construction of several buildings at the Topkapı Palace, paraded on that occasion carrying the model of a pastoral landscape populated with animals, farmers, and pipe-playing shepherds performing Karacaoğlan folksongs. To everyone's surprise, it suddenly exploded in fireworks (illus. 95). This curious spectacle was accompanied by another entertaining show, staged by the late Sokollu Mehmed Pasha's galley slaves whom his son had inherited.[206] The late grand vizier, like Kılıç Ali Pasha, had employed his slaves as construction workers.[207]

Grand admirals also served royal construction projects by transporting columns and marbles from various ports. The memoirs of the grand admiral Barbarossa (d. 1546) relate how Sultan Süleyman had ordered him to pick up marbles from the antique ruin known as Temaşalık (Aydıncık, ancient Cyzicus) with a 'light galley' (*ḳırlanġıç*).[208] In the 1550s the Spanish galley slave Pedro accompanied his master, the grand admiral Sinan Pasha, who was commanded to take ten galleys to İzmit to transport marbles for the Süleymaniye.[209] For the sultan's own use, Kılıç Ali Pasha was likewise instructed in 1574 to carry fifteen marble columns found at the Aegean island of Bozcaada (Tenedos) 'when the navy goes to those parts'.[210]

Building supervisors were chosen from trustworthy administrators with financial expertise and preferably some experience in construction work: retired finance ministers, keepers of the royal purse, endowment administrators, household stewards, sanjak governors, fiefholders, court messengers, distinguished royal servants, and court painters. Painters employed in the decoration of monuments were frequently appointed building supervisors because of their combined expertise in administrative and aesthetic matters. The Jerusalem court records mention 'Muhammad Çelebi al-Naqqāsh' who in the course of the late 1530s or early 1540s collected the sultan's taxes and supervised building projects that included the city walls, water channels, and the tomb of the prophet Moses.[211] A decree addressed to the governor of Alexandria in 1585 informs him that the chief court painter Mustafa had been dispatched to Egypt with some money and timbers for a building project in Mecca.[212] Between 1586 and 1589 another chief court painter, Lutfullah (Lutfi), was appointed building supervisor at the Haram in Medina.[213]

Supervisors were also chosen from court messengers experienced in construction work, who were often used in procuring building materials and delivering architectural plans. A striking example is Mustafa Çavuş, the building supervisor of the Azak (Azov) castle in Crimea, who was such an experienced architect that he replaced the inefficient, elderly royal architect sent from Istanbul for that construction in 1577. The sanjak governor of Azak, who served as the building overseer, received the following order when he requested a new architect from the capital:

> Because timber beams and other needed materials are not found there, [you report that] the building supervisor Mustafa Çavuş has been sent in the direction of Caffa, and that the construction will start once he reaches the district of Sudak and the timber arrives. You indicate that since the architect who has been sent there is old, he does not have the strength required for some services, and that another architect needs to be sent in his place. Now, since the said Mustafa Çavuş is a master architect (*üstād miʿmār*), another architect has not been sent from here. I command you to have the castle's repairs carried out according to the previous order … by using the above-mentioned Mustafa Çavuş as its architect, having him renovate it strongly in accordance with the manner he sees fitting and appropriate (*veciḥ ve münāsib*), using all your diligence and effort in avoiding wasteful expenditure.[214]

Hüseyin Beg of the *müteferrika* corps, who successively served as building supervisor in the Şehzade Mehmed and Süleymaniye complexes, was a financial expert experienced in architecture. His continuous employment in these two sultanic mosque complexes must have ensured the transfer of administrative expertise from one construction to the next. The construction sites of sultanic complexes constituted immense labouratories of technological and managerial expertise. Imperial decrees issued in the years 1554–55 for construction of the Şehzade mosque confirm the close cooperation between the chief architect Sinan and Hüseyin Beg, paving the way for their teamwork in the more monumental Süleymaniye complex.[215] The latter's appointment to the Süleymaniye in 1549 is recorded by the historian Celalzade Mustafa: 'The service of the building was assigned to Hüseyin Çelebi, from the servants of the sovereign's court, who was famous among those of praiseworthy endeavour as a possessor of wisdom and sagacity in all the customs and regulations of supervising; the affairs of the building and its expenses were handed over to his discerning judgment and he was commanded to collect and acquire whichever supplies and materials were needed.'[216] The extent of Hüseyin Beg's authority in collecting building materials is documented in an imperial decree sent to all kadis of Anatolia in 1552:

> In the imperial complex that is presently being built in the metropolis of Istanbul timbers and other materials are daily required. I order those of you to whom the building supervisor Hüseyin, the leader of the eminent and the notables, sends a letter requesting materials to act in accordance with his wish. If the said supervisor sends a letter to any of you about materials needed for my imperial complex, do not kill a moment in providing whatever he requests. But I certainly do not authorize anybody to be treated unjustly and oppressively with this pretext. Buy [those materials] with their price and pay their costs without harming any individual. When the supervisor's letter arrives, if any of you shows negligence or causes delay, there is no possibility that your excuse be accepted. Be on the alert not to provoke the said supervisor to petition me against you![217]

Ömer Lutfi Barkan's monumental book on the Süleymaniye complex – based on a collection of imperial decrees issued during Hüseyin Beg's term as building supervisor (1549–53) and on the account books kept by his successor, Sinan Beg (1553–60) – provides a fascinating day-to-day picture of the workings of a vast construction site. This unsurpassed publication, which illustrates the ability of the Ottoman central administration to coordinate complex operations on a grand imperial scale, documents the sequence of construction, the collection of building materials and builders, and the composition of the labour force.[218] Nothing as detailed as the documents published by Barkan survives for any other mosque complex, before the early-seventeenth-century account books of the Sultan Ahmed mosque.[219] Not surprisingly, the building supervisor of the Sultan Ahmed mosque found it expedient to turn back to the Süleymaniye registers as a model for administrative procedures. To that end, he compiled a model-book of imperial decrees related to construction work, a kind of 'specimen anthology of orders'. Its three hundred and eleven decrees, dating between 1549 and 1553, provide an overview of the complex coordination of long-distance operations for the supply of workers and materials.[220] These geographically widespread operations constituted a metaphor for Süleyman's ability to command the manpower and resources of his empire, turning the building process of his complex into a potent site of meaning. Communications with the provinces triggered by this project and others reinforced large-scale patterns of political integration.

We have already seen how royal architects were sent all over the empire to collect antique spolia and to cut stones in various quarries for the Süleymaniye. Decrees also help us identify the origin of such building materials as bricks (made in Hasköy along the Golden Horn and in Gallipoli), timbers (cut in Thrace, the southern coast of the Marmara Sea, and the Black Sea), iron (mined in Samokov in Bulgaria), and lead (brought from Macedonia and Bulgaria). The discovery in 1579 of a new lead mine in Cyprus is recorded in a decree addressed to the governor and finance minister of the island, which orders them to help Ömer Çavuş, who has been sent from the capital because of his knowledge in 'matters of mining.'[221] Perhaps it was this new source that increased the availability of lead, which towards the end of Sinan's career is used more extensively in Istanbul mosques, completely covering their domical superstructures including drums and buttresses. The accessibility of lead also increased thanks to English merchants who sold to the Ottomans the bells and picture frames stolen from churches during the Reformation. In 1582 the Spanish ambassador in London informed Philip II that the English were profiting from the sale, prohibited by the Pope, of lead and other metals to the Ottomans:

> Two years ago the English opened up the trade, which they still continue, to the Levant, which is extremely profitable to them, as they take great quantities of tin and lead thither, which the Turk buys of them almost for its weight in gold, the tin being vitally necessary for the casting of guns and the lead for purposes of war. It is of double importance to the Turk now, in consequence of the excommunication pronounced *ipso facto* by the Pope upon any person who sells to infidels such materials as these.[222]

While it was the building supervisor's responsibility to procure materials for the Süleymaniye, enlisting skilled builders largely fell to Sinan. In 1550 all the kadis and sanjak governors of Rumelia received the following order:

> Presently, since masons and carpenters are required for the needs of the imperial complex that is being built in Istanbul, if the chief of my architects Sinan, may his glory increase, appoints and requests with a memorandum masons and carpenters under your jurisdiction, hand them over to the man who arrives and send them to Istanbul; in case they show resistance, give them an escort of capable men so that they are delivered here.[223]

This order, anticipating resistance, shows that master craftsmen were given no choice but to accept work for fixed wages in the sultan's complex. The copy of a memorandum written in 1550 by the chief architect requests an imperial decree for enlisting several Christian carpenters working at that time in building a house in Aydos.[224] An order sent to the kadis of Edirne, Bursa, Amasya, Kastamonu, and Larende in 1551 enjoins them to dispatch the stone cutters and lead specialists listed in a register to the building site with capable escorts. The kadis are asked to prepare a register of other masters not included on that list and to assign a guarantor to those who might escape.[225] One such list prepared by the kadi of Bursa names ten masons, four stone cutters, and nine carpenters along with the quarters they resided in.[226] The kadi of Edirne was asked in 1553 to send the skilled marble cutters listed in a register compiled by the chief architect to the Süleymaniye complex with their tools.[227]

Similar decrees issued for later building projects, both royal and non-royal, indicate that the conscription of named masters selected from catalogue-like registers had turned into standard practice. Recording the empire's skilled labour resources, these registers complemented catalogues of marbles and columns, with attached samples, that were prepared during the early 1550s. Much like lists of builders compiled by provincial kadis, inventories of worked and unworked marbles throughout the empire must have been consulted and updated during subsequent building projects. A decree addressed to the kadi of Aydıncık (Cyzicus) in 1568, and given to one of Sinan's men during the construction of the Selimiye, forbids cutting marbles there without an imperial permit, so as to offset the scarcity of marbles needed for the sultan's project.[228] The vigilant guarding of precious marbles and columns, accessible only to the royal family and prominent grandees, is also made explicit in a decree sent in 1577 to various administrators in Greece (the sanjak governor of Negroponte and the kadis of Athens, Livadia, and İstife). They are ordered to forbid the sale of antique marbles to Europeans, who coveted them as much as did Ottoman patrons of architecture:

> It has been reported by a petition presented to my threshold of felicity that some carved marble columns and porphyry marbles found in your districts have been taken and used in the construction of churches by Christian subjects and sold by them to infidel enemies and to others; I order that when [this decree] arrives hold onto such columns and porphyry marbles in appropriate places at your district and do not allow their sale to unbelievers.[229]

In addition to listing the costs of building materials and labour, the building accounts of the Süleymaniye include samples of piecework contracts. These pledges confirm Sinan's role as a large-scale contractor in projects he personally supervised. I have already quoted the description in the *Tezkiretü'l-bünyān* of how the chief architect subcontracted much of the remaining work at the Süleymaniye mosque two months before its completion to able masters at lump sum rates.[230] An early example of such a contract with two stone cutters, drawn up in 1550 according to 'the chief architect's approval', specifies the costs of coarse sandstone cut by novices at the Kavak quarry: 'The mentioned rough cut stones should not be neglected, and in no way should they be crooked or faulty, so as to be acceptable to the chief architect.' Unfinished stones quarried on the basis of a large mould (*ḳalıb*, 2.5 by 1.5 cubits with varying thickness) would cost sixty aspers, while others based on a small mould (1.5 by 1 cubits) would be bought for twenty aspers. The two masters who took it upon themselves to oversee their preparation were paid twice that year in lump sums that did not cover the expenses of iron and steel tools repaired by a blacksmith posted at the quarry.[231]

A year later in 1551, another contract was drawn up with a master and his partners who 'agreed to faultlessly cut with a clean finish the rough quarried coarse sandstones from the Kavak quarry, according to the calculation of twenty aspers per piece of large-mould stone.'[232] More complicated custom-made marbles were cut under the supervision of royal architects assigned to various quarries with accompanying novices. For example, the copy of a memorandum written by Sinan in 1550 indicates that Mimar Kasım was appointed to supervise the cutting of sixty window frames, sixty sills, two hundred and fifty large voussoirs and six hundred small voussoirs at the Aydıncık quarry.[233] A detailed contract from the same year concerns the domed portal with a ramp that still connects the outer courtyard of the Süleymaniye to the lower street of madrasas overlooking the Golden Horn. In the presence of the chief architect and the building supervisor, it was witnessed and signed by carpenters holding military rank, Hasan Subaşı, Sinan Subaşı, Hüseyin Çavuş, and Ali Zağarcı (janissary houndsman):

> Contracted to Köse Mustafa from the stone masons (*taşcı-yān*) of Istanbul: In the presence of the below-mentioned carpenters, and the chief architect, and the building supervisor, the above-mentioned [Mustafa] has agreed to receive two thousand aspers for the two marble columns of the dome surmounting the gate at the head of the

> staircase that descends from the courtyard to the madrasa, along with the column bases and capitals, and the floor pavements, and the sections up to the brick [dome level] consisting of slate (*taş taḫtası*) and capping stones (*ḳafa taḫtası*) and consoles (*ḳoltuḳlar*), constructing with a clean finish and smoothly and perfectly all of the stone structure, with the exception of the dome, which is going to be made of brick; and this has been recorded in the presence of the aforementioned individuals, on 21 Zilhicce 957 (31 December 1550).[234]

The *Teẕkiretü'l-bünyān* indicates that it was Sinan who in 1557, at the workshop of marble cutters located on the construction site, drew the plans and elevations of the Süleymaniye mihrab and minbar.[235] Account books published by Barkan show that this workshop was headed by Muhiddin Halife.[236] Other details singled out by the *Tuhfe* as innovative features of the mosque may also have been designed by Sinan, whose sense of what was 'appropriate and fitting' extended from custom-made architectonic elements to the decorative programme.[237] We learn from an imperial decree addressed in 1585 to the kadi of Istanbul and the water channel superintendent that Sinan had personally installed with his 'own hands' one measure (*lüle*) of water at the Şehzade Mehmed complex when it was being built in the 1540s.[238]

The imperial mosque complexes that established the chief architect's fame were those in which he was employed virtually full-time. Nevertheless, trustworthy assistant architects who executed his designs and building supervisors who took charge of financial matters released him from direct responsibility for managing construction work in all its details, enabling him to be involved in several building projects simultaneously, much as were Italian Renaissance architects. For instance, Brunelleschi was consulted by numerous patrons for whose projects he travelled to many places. According to his biographer Manetti, he had to make plans and models for them, but mistakes inevitably occurred in execution because he could not possibly supervise all of these projects.[239] Condivi similarly points out that Michelangelo's time was torn between several projects.[240]

Howard Burns explains that Palladio's role in designing and in setting up constructional and costing procedures was more important than his subsequent supervision of the building operation. His function was not unlike the traditional role of the Venetian proto, outlined in a document dated 1546: 'The custom and usage of the protos when they undertake to make a building and have made a model or design is to take it to the building site, and the bricklayers (*murari*), stone masons, and carpenters proceed to work according to the model and instructions which the proto gives from time to time, and the proto commands everyone and is obeyed; and the protos always have the task of commanding, measuring and assigning everything which is necessary on a building site and providing dimensions, template drawings (*sagome*), etc.' Much like Sinan, Palladio checked prices and the quality of work, advising on craftsmen to employ and the terms of their employment. He moved ceaselessly between a large number of sites, in town and in the country, ensuring adherence to his designs (including structural details) and providing a general control of quality. Both architects educated a generation of craftsmen capable of interpreting their designs and of repeating their style in more modest works, to which Sinan and Palladio contributed as consultants.[241]

As in the Süleymaniye, a hierarchical delineation of authority characterized the construction site of St Peter's in Rome, where the architect was no longer a manager but 'a kind of technical adviser, albeit one with comprehensive authority to intervene at any point in order to assure the full realization of his intentions.' Richard Goldthwaite observes that the architect was freed 'from direct responsibility for management of the construction enterprise and provided with the means to communicate his ideas at least in a general way through drawings, plans, and models'. He could thus 'hope to take on more projects, thereby expanding his creative output'. Although he was employed on a large project, it was 'no problem for him to design other buildings and check in occasionally at their sites'.[242]

This description perfectly fits Sinan's architectural practice, but the lack of documentation hinders an assessment of the degree of his involvement in smaller, non-sultanic projects. Nor is it clear how he was compensated for these constructions, for which he must have submitted plans. It is likely that rather than working full-time on them, he acted more as a consultant who showed up on occasion to monitor progress. The fact that the sultan scolded Sinan in 1557 for delaying the completion of the Süleymaniye mosque by diverting his attention to other constructions implies that the chief architect was expected to focus primarily on imperial projects.[243]

The continuous chronology of the buildings singled out in the *Teẕkire*s as the chief architect's major works shows that he was employed nearly nonstop in grand sultanic constructions: Şehzade Mehmed (1543–48), Süleymaniye (1548–59), Kırkçeşme waterworks (1561–65), Büyükçekmece bridge (1565–67), and Selimiye (1568–74). While he was busy with these projects he could hardly travel to distant provincial cities, but he must have been able to supervise nearby monuments on a part-time basis, particularly in the 1560s, when engineering projects did not require his full presence. The cessation of sultanic patronage in the capital under Murad III meant that he was relatively freer between 1574 and 1588 to supervise mosque complexes commissioned by prominent patrons in the capital, projects built under his supervision but because of his old age largely entrusted to other royal architects (Appendix 1).

In this abstract conception of architecture, the design of a building existed separately from its execution. This separation, which enabled Sinan to simultaneously supervise several projects, is also implied in the biography of his student Mimar Mehmed Agha. During a visit to the construction site of the Sultan Ahmed mosque, the biographer asks the chief architect why he looks so dejected. The overworked Mehmed Agha replies:

> O, Caʿfer Efendi, why should our nature not be much downcast and weary? Observe how the heavy burden of a noble building like this bears down upon me! If it were only this, persisting with my devotions and prayers, distress would not be suffered. But in addition to this noble building, there are other buildings scattered in many places. It is necessary to pay attention to each one. They cannot be neglected. Now this is the reason for the uneasiness and dejection which you have observed in our spirit. [For] I am also anxious about those other scattered buildings.[244]

The biographer describes how the chief architect, who had a 'room of his own inside the noble building', was supervising construction work as he sat on a small carpet spread before the fountain of the mosque: 'In his right hand he held a rosary and in his left hand a measuring stick (*arşun*) … Now and then, looking around, he would shout to negligent masters, "Work!", and would point with the measuring stick in his left hand.' Several foremen ceaselessly walked around the building, enjoining the craftsmen to work.[245]

Religious monuments built with private funds generally employed wage labourers. By contrast, it was common practice to use soldiers and subjects owing services in lieu of tax payment (*yaya, müsellem, yörük*) in military constructions financed by the state treasury: castles, city walls, arsenals, cannon foundries, roads, and bridges. For the Süleymaniye, conscription of the labour force was part of an imperial policy that deemed forced-but-paid labour more palatable than the corvee or unpaid military service incumbent upon tax-exempt groups. Barkan explains that the conscription of paid masters, working for government-fixed salaries and conducted to building sites under close supervision by foremen (who kept a register of their names), was typical in a construction industry not based on principles of economic and political liberalism.[246] Decrees that permit members of the ruling elite to conscript paid workers, to buy state-controlled materials for officially fixed prices, and to transport them with forcefully rented carts abound in the archives. These documents, cited extensively in Part 3, confirm the degree to which the dirigist mechanisms of the centralized state were mobilized for pious constructions sponsored by royal and distinguished non-royal patrons.

The majority of the workforce at the Süleymaniye complex consisted of free labourers who had been conscripted by imperial decrees. The additional use of novices and galley slaves, who were paid minimal daily allowances, lowered labour costs in building projects of sultans, the royal family, and grandees.[247] Barkan attributes the absence of unpaid compulsory labour in the Süleymaniye account books to the belief that such labour reduced the merit of pious constructions.[248] Chroniclers had strongly criticized Mehmed II for levying taxes and coercively recruiting construction workers from the provinces for his building projects in Istanbul. The sultan had thus committed a sin rather than acquiring merit in God's eyes, they claimed.[249]

A supplication letter that Hüseyin Beg submitted to Sultan Süleyman after being dismissed from the post of building supervisor repeatedly underlines the special care he took not to harm any employee of the Süleymaniye complex, which was built as a charitable deed and meant to assure its patron a secure place in paradise. The author of this long letter explains how he was unjustly dismissed and imprisoned by inspectors who examined the mosque's daily account books kept by his two scribes. The letter not only provides an intimate glimpse of the duties fulfilled by building supervisors, but also shows the unprecedented difficulties faced in record-keeping. Although innovative ad hoc measures were improvised along the way to increase the efficiency of accounting procedures, two scribes simply could not cope with such an immense enterprise:[250]

> This petition to the exalted throne of His Highness, the felicitous and fortunate sultan, who is the refuge of the universe, is as follows: The daily account books kept by Hüseyin and Ali, who were appointed scribes by a noble order issued at the beginning of this servant's tenure as supervisor until its end, have been examined. During those six years [beginning of 1548 until the end of 1553], the expenses of the complex (*ʿimāret*) in Hüseyin's daily account book add up to eight thousand aspers. When the scribe Ali was sick or hindered, the scribe Hüseyin would record in the daily account book the names of labourers who received wages so as to avoid delaying the payment of their fees and not to hurt anyone in such a charitable deed. And in the scribe Ali's daily account book, the expenses of the building complex within six years add up to twenty-three thousand aspers. When the scribe Hüseyin could not come because of an impediment or hindrance, he [Ali] used to record in the daily account book those who were paid in order to avoid delaying the payment of fees to labourers and to stop them from cursing. Within six years, whenever one scribe was present and the other one absent, the fees of labourers were regularly paid and recorded in a daily account book. In the registers presently sent to the felicitous threshold, the materials bought have been fully recorded. Because your above-mentioned scribe servants were unable to keep up with the abundance of work when the foundations of the noble mosque were commenced in the year seven [957/1550] and difficulties were faced, among the ten

scribes appointed by a noble order, Mehmed recorded the registers of labourers (*ırġād defterleri*). When money was paid on Thurdays, the register of those who received wages was immediately copied by the scribe Hüseyin and kept in his possession. Because of the abundance of work, some were written by him and some by his assistant; during some weeks he was unable make full copies, and in other weeks he only copied half a register, unable to record the other half.

Hüseyin Beg explains how difficulties in record-keeping resulted in an innovation: alphabetically organized registers. Yet the scribes still could not find enough time to make full copies of each register:

> And the registers of labourers have been written in alphabetical order. Names connected to the letter *elif* are separate, and names connected to the letter *bā* are separate, all the way until the end. Ahmeds, and Mahmuds, and Mehmeds, and Cafers, and Hasans, and Hüseyins, and Alis are each under a different letter. There were about one hundred to one hundred and fifty labourers. They have been written and recorded in the registers in this manner. [Sometimes] eight to nine hundred labourers were working in the building complex. When written in mixed order, many difficulties were faced in searching and finding the name of a paid individual [to make a check mark next to his name]; consequently work was delayed. Later on, the alphabetical system of ordering was adopted. When a person pronounced his name, it was found under the corresponding letter, and his money was immediately paid without causing delay. When the assistant of the scribe Hüseyin or he himself copied the register, he did not fully copy all the Ahmeds, Mahmuds, and Mehmeds from some registers. The mentioned scribe admitted to the inspectors that he had made errors in copying and in some weeks was unable to make full copies from lack of time. Consequently, the inspectors wrote commentaries with their own writing on those registers, recording separate commentaries on each register.

Hüseyin Beg complains about the building overseer who inspected the account books, the Süleymaniye madrasa professor Kadızade Şemsüddin Ahmed Efendi (d. 1580). His commentaries on the disparity of registers did not sufficiently clarify the building supervisor's innocence:

> In some registers, Kadızade has written commentaries with his own hand. When he petitioned the disparity between the labourer registers, he did not clearly report what had transpired. He told this servant: 'Giving an explanation to the court is not our responsibility; in accordance with the noble shariʿa you are not found guilty of anything and since we have not made a legal judgment, it is preferable to give a short answer. It is sufficient for the felicitous sultan to know that no judicial decision has been pronounced against you', and he thus sent the petition. In this servant's time, when the abundance of work was at its peak, the scribes faced difficulties and were unable to make [full] copies. At the time of the present supervisor, Sinan Beg, even though the abundance of work is not at such a high level and there is more leisure, a different scribe records labourers and the scribe Halil copies it. This is confirmed by our present inspector, Kadızade, who is the overseer (*nāẓır*) of the building complex, and it is so in actuality. The aim is for the sultan's wealth not to be wasted, and for expenditures to be recorded in registers. From all the accounts, a seventy-three-thousand asper deficit emerged and they recorded this difference. That amount was missing from the [miscounted] money bags when they were taken out of the imperial treasury. And in the building complex, when the aspers were distributed each week to three thousand labourers (*rençber*) and masters (*üstād*), the money was counted in four or five places and then distributed. Time and again, when the pay [of someone] had missing aspers, it was repaid. From the error and mistake of those who counted the money, a surplus or deficit occurred. God forbid, that in the felicitous reign of His Highness, the sultan who is the refuge of the universe, should the money set aside for charity be treacherously swallowed and embezzled. Presently, when the supervisor Sinan Beg takes aspers in money bags from the imperial treasury, certainly there are missing aspers. And when other trustworthy servants of yours who serve in the sultanic affairs receive money, bags with missing aspers are unavoidable. If at the time of distribution, complete caution had not been exercised, there would have been an endless deficit.

The building supervisor explains that he was accused by resentful individuals to whom he refused to give free building materials for their own use:

> For the sake of His Highness, the felicitous sultan who is the refuge of the universe, I gave my heart and soul in such a way that the thought of treachery would not even enter my mind. In this desire-bestowing court, I was a friendless loner. Those men to whom I did not give marble, lime, and other materials they asked for found a pretext and secretly incited the person called Muzaffer to present a petition to the throne of the sultanate, making many kinds of allegations concerning my treachery against His Highness the sultan's good deed for the other world. None of that being true, it was the fortune of the sultan, who is God's shadow on earth, that despite the alliance of so many people to betray the charitable work that is being built for his

> hereafter, they did not succeed [in embezzling materials]. Nevertheless, they brought about a degree of injustice and oppression on this servant such that it has not been experienced by anybody else in this age of justice.

Hüseyin Beg goes on to explain that on the basis of Muzaffer's unfounded accusations, he was imprisoned for six months 'at the residence of the imperial messenger', during which time his house was looted and his mother and son died. He was not granted permission to attend their funerals: 'Having had to part from them in longing and grief, I was not even allowed to perform my last filial duty towards my mother!' In the meantime, when it became apparent that Muzaffer owed a large sum of money to the sultan's private purse, he ran away and disappeared. Even though the building supervisor's innocence finally became apparent, this was not reported to the sultan. So he decided to take the matter into his own hands by writing a personal petition:

> God forbid, that anybody should harm the good deed destined for the hereafter of His Highness, the felicitous sultan who is the refuge of the universe, and that a person hurting so many needy labourers should prosper in this desire-bestowing court! They have complained that this servant did not pay the fees of masons and carpenters working in the building complex and of labourers and persons who brought materials to it. During the one year and two month period in which they have been inspecting my accounts, not even one person has filed a legal suit about not being paid according to the shariʿa in the building complex. And while I was supervisor, those persons who used to bring materials to the noble building complex, whether they were stone cutters, brick makers, lime burners, blacksmiths, or others, were paid their aspers in advance by me from the funds of the noble building complex, so that no shortage of materials would be experienced. The needs of the building complex being many, endless materials were required. In order for the labourers to give their blessings for the lack of shortage when they requested materials, they were treated with complete respect. Moreover, because paying aspers in advance is a law (*ḳanūn*), I acted in accordance with old customs. When this servant was dismissed, the inspectors took the prepaid money possessed by the labourers and deposited it in the imperial treasury. Thank God, it became apparent that the felicitous sultan's money was in the hands of labourers and that none of them were owed money from the noble building complex, which confirmed this servant's good services at the exalted court.

Hüseyin Beg claims that the inspectors were reluctant to report his innocence because they had accused him unjustly:

> When the inspectors had first begun their inspection, without even having looked at the registers, this servant was presumed guilty. Not fearing God, Glory be to Him, some judicial matters were recorded and sent to the court, omnipotent as heaven. I cried out many times saying, 'Gentlemen! you send the register of judicial matters without having examined anything according to the shariʿa; even if you do not care to protect yourself, do not harm the good deed of the building complex; the end of this will not fare well for you because the answers of those judicial matters are recorded in the daily account books and registers sealed with your own seal! Do not act rashly!' However, not heeding my words, they went ahead and sent the register. Later on, the answers of the judicial matters written in the register they had sent were indeed found in detail in the daily account books. Because it became apparent that they had sent the previous register against the noble shariʿa, they are now reluctant to write their findings and petition the court... Since the fact that they have perpetrated great injustice and oppression in the previously sent register has become evident from the new commentaries they have presently written, they are under incredible distress. It is requested from the court of His Highness, who is the refuge of the universe, that a noble firman be issued [to the inspectors], acknowledging that previously they had sent a register about the circumstances of the dismissed building supervisor and presently they have prepared another sealed register answering the previous one. Please request that the throne of the sultanate be petitioned with the latter [register]!

Hüseyin Beg's touching letter mentions approximately three thousand labourers and masters. The average number of a hundred to a hundred and fifty unskilled labourers rose to eight or nine hundred when the mosque's foundations were being laid in 1550. Barkan has calculated that the daily workforce under the second supervisor Sinan Beg reached 2,500 to 3,000 during spring, summer, and fall.[251] It was thanks to the employment of such an enormous construction gang that a monumental complex like the Süleymaniye could reach completion within a decade; according to its foundation inscription of 1557, the mosque itself was finished in eight years. Medieval cathedral workshops, which rarely employed more than a hundred men, took centuries to complete. Despite its large administrative staff that included an architect, co-architect, general manager, paymaster, three measurers and assessors, two treasurers, a secretary, five to ten supervisors and their assistants, as well as the foremen of crews, the construction of St Peter's in Rome took nearly two centuries and outlasted several popes and architects.[252]

The unpublished building accounts of a mosque posthumously built for the governor-general Ali Pasha in Sarajevo

(1559–61), a generic domed cube fronted by a triple-domed portico, gives us a sense of the much smaller crews employed in medium-sized mosques. A register recording the wages of masons (*bennāyān*) headed by the royal architect Mimar Ferhad and of unskilled labourers (*ırġadān*) during a four-month period in 1559 shows that the team of skilled masons ranged between eleven to forty-seven, while the number of labourers varied from three to twenty-four. Mimar Ferhad, who received twelve aspers a day, was assisted by master masons who were paid ten aspers each, while the wages of apprentices ranged from two to eight aspers.[253]

Barkan has calculated that between 1553 and 1559, only a small fraction (5.23%) of the Süleymaniye's work-force consisted of galley slaves, the remainder being novices (39.93%) and wage labourers (54.85%).[254] The most qualified masons and stone cutters received ten to twelve aspers a day, while apprentices were paid between one and nine aspers.[255] A larger proportion of galley slaves and novice boys may have been used during the earlier stages of construction work under the first supervisor Hüseyin Beg, whose account books are now lost. In the stages involving the quarrying of stones, transportation of building materials by land and sea, and laying of foundations, more numerous unskilled labourers must have been required. Some novices, like the young Sinan himself, were specialized craftsmen: stone cutters, carpenters, Khorasan mortar mixers, canal-diggers, lead sheet makers, and blacksmiths.[256] They were paid higher stipends than unskilled novices, who received one asper a day, while strong novices employed as porters were given two aspers.[257] Fettered galley slaves also had a minimal daily stipend; unspecialized ones were paid one asper and those specializing in crafts received two aspers.[258]

The expected reward for novices working at low-level subsistence allowances was promotion within the military hierarchy. In 1559–60, twenty-six novices and their captains were promoted to janissary rank for their service in the recently completed water channels of the Süleymaniye complex.[259] Sinan and the building supervisor of the Selimiye complex (the ex-finance minister Hasan Çelebi) were ordered in 1572 to send a register listing the names of fifty veteran novices, who were old and faithful servants, to their agha for promotion to janissary troops.[260] Later in 1573, Sinan recommended for advancement seven more novices who specialized as blacksmiths and had just completed the iron window grilles of the mosque.[261]

Hard-working galley slaves used in royal and non-royal constructions were often rewarded with freedom. According to the Austrian diplomat Betzek (1564–65), upon the completion of the Süleymaniye, four hundred prisoners who had worked in its construction were set free.[262] The employment and freeing of galley slaves is well attested at the construction site of the Selimiye.[263] The French ambassador François Noailles tried to free some of them by negotiating their ransom with the grand vizier Sokollu in 1574, the year the mosque was inaugurated. During the same year, the kadi of Edirne was ordered to send to Istanbul half of the 'infidel state slaves' working at the sultan's complex, together with their guardians and twenty to thirty foremen from the royal cavalry troops, for the renovation of the burnt kitchens at the Topkapı Palace. The rest stayed in Edirne with the chief guardian to work in the incomplete dependencies of the mosque complex.[264]

According to Barkan, 47% of the skilled masters specializing in different branches at the Süleymaniye complex were Muslims.[265] The percentage of Muslim to non-Muslim differed in each branch of specialization. For example, 83% of the masons (*bennā*) were non-Muslims; whereas non-Muslims constituted only 11% of the stone cutters (*sengtrāş*).[266] Muslims constituted the majority of carpenters (77.4%), painters (87.3%), glaziers (93.7%), and lead specialists (90%); while non-Muslims predominated among blacksmiths (63.4%) and sewer diggers (92%).[267]

The largest group of Christian masters consisted of masons, employed in structural work such as the construction of walls, piers, domes, and minarets. For instance, the mosque's four free-standing monumental piers, built between 1553 and 1554, were constructed by teams of a dozen to two dozen masons, each team directed by a leader (*bölükbaşı*): three Christians and one Muslim.[268] When the arches of the main dome were completed in 1555, the same masters distributed bonuses to masons.[269] The four minarets were erected between 1554 and 1556 by mixed teams of Christian and Muslim masons, who were later joined by stone cutters responsible for carving decorative mouldings, railings, and muqarnased galleries.[270] Dominated by Muslims, stone cutters worked not only in the mosque's minarets, but also in the preparation of its columns, capitals, door and window frames, lunettes, mouldings, and decorative stonework. Teams of Muslim stone cutters carved the marble arches, gates, fountains, pulpits, mihrabs, and minbar. While the predominantly Christian masons put the building together structurally, then, it was the largely Muslim stone cutters and decorators who shaped its stylistic markers.

The Süleymaniye accounts specify only about 44% of the skilled masters in terms of their place of origin. Among those with known origin, the majority came from Istanbul (1018 masters: 607 non-Muslim and 411 Muslim). The second-largest group was recruited from Rumelia, Crimea, and the islands (491 masters: 300 non-Muslim and 191 Muslim), followed by a slightly smaller group from Anatolia (464 masters: 153 non-Muslim and 311 Muslim). Most of the non-Muslim masters from Rumelia, Crimea, and the islands were masons (coming from Thessaloniki, Morea, Gallipoli, Mytilene, Rhodes, and Caffa), whereas Muslims (from Edirne, Skopje, Seres, Bosnia, and Thessaloniki) were primarily stone cutters.[271] The greater part of Anatolian masons (67 non-Muslim and 64 Muslim), came – like

Sinan – from Kayseri, followed by others from Amasya, and Bursa.[272] The biggest group of non-Muslim masons originated from Kayseri (20 masters). Most Anatolian stone cutters (210 Muslim and 32 non-Muslim) came from Amasya, which was followed in importance by Kayseri, Konya, and Bursa.[273] Regardless of religious affiliation, the biggest crew of Anatolian masters in different branches of specialization originated from Kayseri (187 masters), followed by those recruited from Amasya (85), Bursa (38), and Konya (21).[274]

The account books of the Süleymaniye complex help us imagine the mechanisms of the centralized construction industry that were mobilized in varying degrees for each of Sinan's mosque complexes. The written correspondence triggered by these projects testifies to the existence of a widely shared culture of architecture that facilitated communication between patrons, architects, and administrators. The immersion of the imperial bureaucracy and army in the workings of the construction industry engendered an unusual sensitivity to architectural decorum, accompanied by a passion for building.

The frequent involvement of grandees as building overseers meant that they could hardly remain ignorant about practical matters of construction, which inevitably involved aesthetic judgments. A sizeable sector of the ruling elite possessed firsthand knowledge of architecture that did not find expression in the traditional genres of written culture. Many of Sinan's high-ranking patrons had in the earlier stages of their careers participated in the construction and administration of imperial building projects. The sophisticated tastes they developed from those experiences were channelled to a large number of mosque complexes they eventually commissioned from Sinan. Instead of generating a literary tradition of theoretical treatises, the enthusiasm for architecture sparked a demand for impressive public monuments shaped by the collaboration of the chief architect with his discerning patrons.

PART III

INTERPRETING MOSQUES AND MOSQUE COMPLEXES ATTRIBUTED TO SİNAN

Chapter 6

SULTANS, PRINCES AND VASSALS

I. SULTAN SÜLEYMAN I

ŞEHZADE MEHMED, ISTANBUL (1543–48)

SÜLEYMANİYE, ISTANBUL (1548–59)

TAKİYYA AL-SULAYMANİYYA, DAMASCUS (1554–58/59, 1566–67)

II. SULTAN SELİM II

SULTANİYE, KARAPINAR (1560–63/64, 1569–70)

SELİMİYE, EDİRNE (1568–74)

III. SULTAN MURAD III

MURADİYE, MANİSA (1583–86/87, 1590)

IV. DEVLET GİRAY KHAN I

TATAR KHAN MOSQUE, CRIMEA, GÖZLEVE (NOW YEVPATORIA, *c.* 1552)

I. SULTAN SÜLEYMAN I

The elderly Süleyman's near puritanical austerity ran counter to the extravagant passions of his youth, which had been coloured by messianic hopes and a taste for luxury that won him the epithet 'Magnificent' in the West. By the late 1540s the sultan's health was deteriorating, his dream of creating a world empire encompassing Rome no longer seemed feasible, and he was increasingly preoccupied with internal succession struggles between his sons. As imperial enterprise turned inward, the changing nature of dynastic ideology found expression in Süleyman's uncompromising image of 'sobriety and legalistic rectitude'.[1]

European diplomats were quick to note how the sultan grew more scrupulous about religious correctness in his late fifties. Abandoning his youthful preoccupation with imperial magnificence, he now wore humble robes of cotton and wool, gave up drinking wine and listening to music, and replaced gold and silver table wares with Chinese porcelain (illus. 6, 7, 29).[2] Bernardo Navagero reports in 1551 that the sultan had just ordered all musical instruments in his palace burnt and jewel-encrusted gold- and silver-plated wall decorations stripped off. Preoccupied with thoughts of his own mortality, he inquired about the location of his future burial during a visit to the Süleymaniye complex that was then being built as an investment for his salvation in the other world: 'Show it to me, for I know well death is common to all and that I am old.'[3]

A letter addressed to Ferdinand I in 1551 predicts that Süleyman only had a short life ahead of him, not more than 'three to four years, because his infirmity cruelly molests him and he fears death in the months of February and March when his illness reaches a climax.'[4] The sultan would, however, live on for another fifteen years. By the time the Süleymaniye complex reached completion in 1559, he was a 'blessed old man' in his mid-sixties, suffering terribly from gout and emotionally worn out by personal tragedies. In 1558 his beloved legal spouse, Haseki Hürrem Sultan – whose figure dominates his divan of poems composed under the pseudonym Muhibbi (he who loves with affection) – had passed away.

The distraught sultan would live on to see a bitter war of succession fought at Konya in 1559 between his two surviving sons from Hürrem, Selim and Bayezid. The couple's oldest son, Şehzade Mehmed, died in 1543, followed by the demise of their youngest son, the hunchbacked Cihangir, who expired from grief in 1553 soon after the execution of his half-brother Mustafa (born to another woman). The dynastic crisis that emerged when the defeated prince Bayezid sought refuge in the Safavid court would not be resolved until Shah Tahmasp agreed to have him and his sons strangled in 1562, thus securing the throne for Selim. A few years later in 1566, Süleyman passed away as a ghazi-martyr during his last victorious campaign in Szigetvár. When the funeral cortège led by the Halveti army shaykh Nureddinzade arrived in Istanbul, his coffin was carried by a great crowd of janissaries and novices to the site of his grave, which was temporarily marked by a domed imperial tent where Sinan had begun to lay the foundations of his mausoleum.[5] The miniature that depicts this mournful event shows the procession led by Ebussuud, who performed the funeral prayers (illus. 118). The recitation of a poignant elegy composed by the famous poet Baki caused much lamentation among the grieving populace.[6]

Süleyman's profile as a patron of architecture displays an

153 Melchior Lorichs, Sultan Süleyman with the Süleymaniye complex seen from an arched portal of the Old Palace, 1559, engraving.

empire-wide architectural vision that diverged from the relatively narrow geographical scope of monuments commissioned by his forebears. His premier prestige monument, the Süleymaniye complex in Istanbul, affirmed the primacy of the imperial capital from which his architectural benevolence radiated outwards to major provincial capitals to enhance his public image as a generous ruler and protector of orthodox Islam (illus. 153).[7] The court historian Lokman equates Süleyman with the legendary builder-king Solomon, a leitmotif we have already encountered in Sinan's autobiographies, where miracle-working builders employed in the sultan's projects are likened to the jinns and demons commanded by his namesake Solomon.[8]

Among Süleyman's countless monuments, Lokman enumerates the many cathedral churches converted into mosques in recently conquered European cities, along with new Friday mosques built in Rhodes, Algiers, Yemen, Ta'if, Basra, Baghdad, Erzurum, Van, Lahsa, Abyssynia, and Shahrizor (Gulanbar).[9] In the capital he mentions the mosque complexes commissioned by Süleyman in memory of his late father, Selim I (illus. 78-79), and his two deceased sons, Şehzade Mehmed and Cihangir; the Süleymaniye complex; and the Kırkçeşme water supply system (illus. 119).[10] As we have seen in Chapter 3, Lokman also draws attention to the sultan's improvement of the hajj route extending from Rumelia to Syria, followed by fortified desert caravansarays with reservoirs built for pilgrims departing from Damascus and Cairo (illus. 46–47).[11]

Along the hajj route Lokman cites the Büyükçekmece bridge and the nearby lodging facilities for travellers (illus. 43), the Friday mosque in Konya adjoining Mevlana Celalüddin Rumi's shrine (illus. 36-38), the new settlement in the uninhabited pass of Belen (Bakras) near Aleppo (illus. 44–45), and the sultan's mosque complex outside the walls of Damascus. Among Süleyman's renovations at the holy sanctuaries of Mecca, Medina, and Jerusalem, he particularly emphasizes the repair of the Kaʿba, the construction of a madrasa for the muftis of the four Sunni legal schools abutting the Meccan Haram, and the renewal of the ʿArafat water channel, completed after the sultan's reign. Mustafa Āli's account of Süleyman's architectural patronage adds to these monuments a water channel in Edirne, and the two mosque-cum-convent complexes built next to the tombs of Abu Hanifa and ʿAbd al-Kadir al-Gilani in Baghdad (illus. 35).[12] Sinan's autobiographies omit the churches converted into mosques, generic state mosques in provincial towns, the Friday mosque in Konya, and renovations at the holy sanctuaries in Medina and Jerusalem. Selim I's mosque complex in Istanbul (1520s) and the two complexes in Baghdad (1534–35) are only cited in the *Tuḥfe*, perhaps as works in which Sinan was employed as a janissary (Appendix 1). The chief architect's autobiographies claim authorship for the remaining monuments mentioned by Lokman.

Public monuments sponsored by the sultan were dominated by Friday mosques, often accompanied by complexes with charitable hospices and madrasas for Sunni legal studies. Another focus of Süleyman's patronage was the construction of water channels, a caliphal prerogative alluding to his image as the second Solomon: his namesake not only commanded the jinns and animals, but also the winds and water. The development of the hajj route was complemented by the sultan's renovations at the holy sanctuaries in Mecca, Medina, and Jerusalem that spanned his whole reign. Fortified city walls built around these three Holy Cities literally and metaphorically took them into his custody.[13] Süleyman and his wife Hürrem jointly sponsored the renewal of water channels in each of these cities, following the precedent set by the Abbasid caliph Harun al-Rashid and his consort Zubayda. The Ottoman queen's three charitable hospices complemented her husband's refurbishment of the sacred Harams.[14] In 1556–57 the royal couple added a new water channel in Edirne, together with public fountains, some of which bear inscriptions referring to the sultan as the second Solomon and to his wife as the Queen of Sheba.[15] Following the conquest of Baghdad in 1534, Süleyman took under his protection the shrines of the Shiʿi Imams ʿAli, in Najaf, and Husayn, in Karbala, also revered by the Sunnis, unlike the Safavids who had desecrated Iraqi monuments associated with the memory of the orthodox caliphs. His renovation of a silted irrigation canal extending from the Euphrates to Karbala provided tax-free water to the custodians of Imam Husayn's shrine.[16]

The Kırkçeşme water supply system that Süleyman renovated as a personal charity remedied the shortage of water in Istanbul. According to its endowment deed of 1565, it brought 'the water of life that Alexander the Great had sought in vain to the fountains of the sultan of the seven climes.'[17] The waqfiyya refers to Süleyman as the 'second Solomon' and compares the new water distribution system to the miraculous creations of Solomon's jinns, praising Istanbul as 'the seat of the throne of the great sultanate, the orbit of sublime glory, the rising point of the sun of the state, the congregation place of the scholars of the shariʿa, the well-protected Kostantiniyya, may it continue to be dotted with the most exalted and glorious mosques.'[18] The endowment deed includes among Süleyman's proud titles 'the possessor of the Greatest Imamate and the inheritor of the Greatest Caliphate'. He is referred to as 'the ruler of the two continents and the two seas, the servant of the Two Noble Harams (Mecca and Medina), the possessor of the Arabian and Persian lands, the overseer of the regulations of the Two Mashhads (Najaf and Karbala), the pilgrim of the tomb of the Greatest Imam (Abu Hanifa in Baghdad), the developer of the lands of the Muslims with charitable hospices, the provider of flowing water in such Muslim cities as the sacred Jerusalem and the well-protected Kostantiniyya, the restorer of religion with a fresh new vigour in the beginning of the tenth century (of the Hegira) by the confirmation of divine support, the tenth and greatest of the sultans descending from the exalted Ottoman family.'[19]

The tenth and foremost ruler of the House of Osman thus claims to be the divinely appointed renewer of religion in the tenth century of the Muslim era, the long-awaited Millenium that would mark the universal glory of Islam.[20] Süleyman's lifelong architectural patronage strove to legitimize each of the titles listed in his last waqfiyya, that is, the one for the Kırkçeşme water supply system, registered a year before his demise. His building activities in Mecca and Medina advertised his role as the servant of the Two Noble Harams. His protection of Sunni and Shiʿi shrines in Iraq broadcast his ecumenical vision of Islam. His renovations in Jerusalem, the third Haram associated with the memory of Solomon, reinforced his image as the second Solomon, announced by the inscriptions of public fountains he added to that city.[21] His waterworks in Istanbul, dotted with glorious mosques constructed throughout his reign, extended his benevolence to the inhabitants of the capital: the centre of the 'Great Sultanate' and the 'Great Caliphate'.

The three mosque complexes that Süleyman commissioned from Sinan in Istanbul and Damascus – one of them named after the deceased crown prince Şehzade Mehmed and the other two built for the sultan himself – conformed to differing codes of decorum calibrated according to specific building programmes. As we have seen in Chapter 3, the complex commemorating Şehzade Mehmed deliberately blurred the boundaries of sultanic and princely status to articulate his identity as heir apparent at a time when the issue of dynastic succession was a major preoccupation for Süleyman and his wife. The sultan's own mosque complex at the administrative centre of the empire memorialized his imperial image as a divinely sanctioned universal caliph who reconciled the shariʿa with dynastic codes of law. The smaller mosque complex outside Damascus was shaped by codes of decorum suitable for provincial foundations; it exemplified Süleyman's policy of developing the hajj route along with the three Holy Cities at the symbolic centre of the Islamic world. While the two mosques in Istanbul represent stages in the evolution of Sinan's 'classical' style, the one in Damascus embodies a hybrid regional idiom.

THE COMPLEX OF ŞEHZADE MEHMED

The funerary mosque complex Süleyman commissioned Sinan to build in the name of his beloved son Şehzade Mehmed (d. 1543), who passed away in his youth, is a memorial monument of great sorrow built to defeat grief (illus. 154, 155). Born in 1520–21, prince Mehmed was the eldest of Süleyman and Haseki Hürrem's four sons (Selim, b. 1524; Bayezid, b. 1525; Cihangir, b. 1530–31). He was overshadowed in popularity by a half-brother born in 1515, prince Mustafa, whom the populace and particularly the janissaries championed as their future ruler. In 1533 Mustafa had been sent to Manisa, where he spent eight years as sanjak governor. By 1534 Süleyman had legally married his consort Hürrem, breaking from a dynastic custom that favoured the concubine status of royal mothers. Mustafa and his mother were transferred in 1541 to the distant sanjak of Amasya. The following year, the royal couple sent their own son Mehmed as sanjak governor to Manisa, the princely seat closest to the capital, with the hope of increasing his chances of seizing the throne.

Süleyman's marriage to Hürrem further enhanced the legitimacy of prince Mehmed as a contender to the throne. The queen was allowed to stay at the capital with her husband, unlike prince Mustafa's concubine mother who had been sent to her son's provincial post in accordance with old dynastic customs. Mustafa Āli and Peçevi concur that Şehzade Mehmed had been chosen heir apparent (*velīʿahd*) by his loving parents. Āli attributes this uncustomary privilege to the popularity the prince enjoyed in the imperial court. Being the 'darling of his glorious father, the favourite of his fortunate mother, and the pupil of the eyes of the notables and grandees', all his wishes were granted by Süleyman.[22]

When the sultan learned of his cherished son's demise in 1543, on the way back from a victorious campaign in Hungary, he was grief-stricken and composed the following chronogram

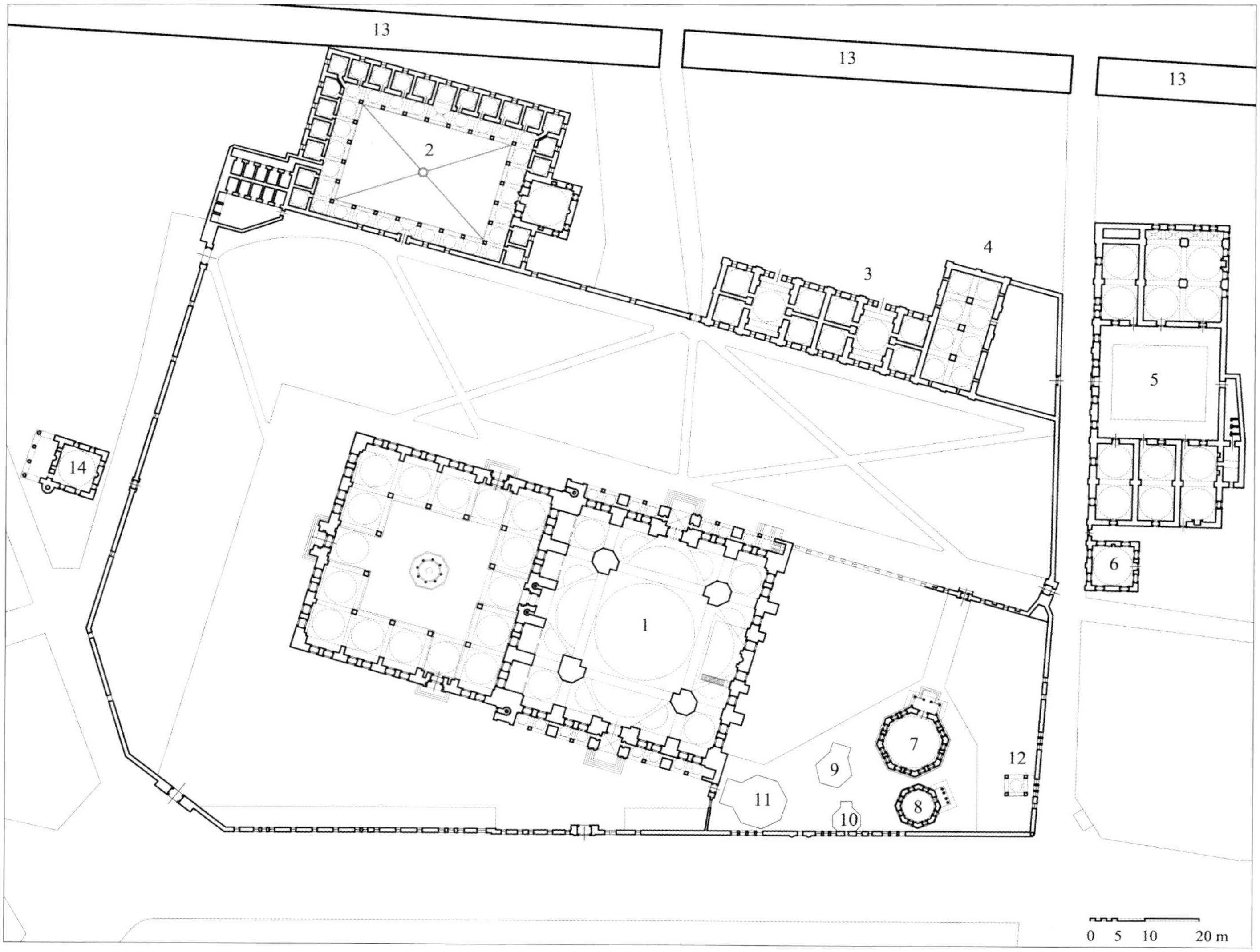

154 Plan of the Şehzade Mehmed complex, Istanbul: 1. Mosque. 2. Madrasa. 3. Guest-rooms. 4. Caravansaray with stables. 5. Hospice. 6. Elementary school. 7. Mausoleum of Şehzade Mehmed. 8. Mausoleum of Rüstem Pasha (1561–62). 9. Mausoleum of Şehzade Mahmud (d. 1603). 10. Mausoleum of Şeyhülislam. Bostanzade Mehmed (d. 1598). 11. Mausoleum of İbrahim Pasha (1603). 12. Baldachin tomb of Şehzade Mehmed's granddaughter, Fatma Sultan (1588–89). 13. Foundations of the Valens aqueduct. 14. Pre-existing Burmalı Minare masjid (1497).

for the apple of his eye: 'The most distinguished among the princes, my Sultan Mehmed.'[23] Historians narrate how a great crowd of courtiers and grandees, clad in black mourning attire, gathered in Üsküdar when the prince's body arrived there from Manisa. Accompanied by sufis who loudly chanted litanies affirming the unity of God, the dignitaries transported the coffin across the sea to Istanbul, whose gathered masses resembled a tumultous scene from the Last Judgment. The solemn cortège carried the prince's coffin to the mosque of Bayezid II, where funeral services were performed in the sultan's presence and alms were distributed to the poor. Free food was given out at sultanic hospices during the three days of mourning when all shops were closed and throughout the empire commemorative prayers were held.[24]

From the mosque of Bayezid II the coffin was taken to the prince's designated burial site, referred to by Āli as 'a place appointed and cleared in the middle of the Old Chambers of the janissaries inside the city.'[25] Celalzade identifies the site as 'a pleasant place and a purified abode inside the Old Chambers in the middle of the city'.[26] Talikizade recounts how Süleyman wept for two and a half hours, embracing the prince's coffin and not allowing anyone to bury it; he would never again mourn so much for anyone. 'Madly distracted and tormented by grief', the sultan attended prayers at his son's grave for forty days, personally distributing alms to the poor. It was only after this period of mourning that grandees were allowed to wear their ceremonial robes.[27] Talikizade explains that several city quarters at the rear side of the Old Chambers were bought with the deceased prince's inheritance (*muḫallefāt*) for the mosque complex built 'for the repose of his soul'. The fountained forecourt of the mosque, for instance, once housed the library of the 'fountain-head of knowledge', the shaykh al-Islam Kemalpaşazade (illus. 156, 157).[28] A reduced group of janissaries continued to reside in the Old Chambers, situated near the dormitories of novices where Sinan had once been trained as a carpenter. The rest moved to the New Chambers at Aksaray.

The posthumous waqfiyya of Şehzade Mehmed explains that the sultan commissioned a 'flourishing complex' (*ʿimāret-i ʿāmire*) next to the prince's mausoleum, which was a centre for the forgiveness of sins, in order to bless his son's soul.[29] Like the waqfiyya, the *Tezkiretü'l-bünyān* implies that the mausoleum had already been built at the time Sinan laid the foundations of the mosque, his first sultanic commission:

> One day Sultan Süleyman Khan ... ordered that the construction of a lofty Friday mosque be started in Istanbul near the Old Chambers for the blessed soul of the cherished and honoured Şehzade Sultan Mehmed Khan, who was dear to his heart, at the site of the latter's mau-soleum. As soon as His Majesty's noble order reached me, I gathered together masons and stone cutters and the foundations of the building were laid at an auspicious hour.[30]

As we shall see below, the Persian foundation inscription of the mausoleum is dated to 1543–44 and that of the mosque gives the dates 1544–48.[31] According to Ramazanzade Mehmed's chronicle, the construction of the complex, comprising 'an exalted Friday mosque, a lofty madrasa, a prosperous hospice, a guest-house, and an elementary school for teaching the Koran' began in 1544–55.[32] During its foundation ceremony, alms and the meat of sacrificed animals were distributed to the poor residents of all Muslim quarters in Istanbul, Eyüp, Galata, and Üsküdar, grouped around 236 masjids and 38 Friday mosques.[33] Celalzade explains that the prince's mausoleum was built 'within a short time', after which the construction of the mosque complex began.[34] He quotes the poet Kandi's Persian chronogram, which gives the completion date of 1548–49 for the complex commissioned by the sultan for his son's 'pure soul'.[35]

The untimely death of Süleyman's and Hürrem's first-born child gave rise to a crisis of dynastic succession. During the summer of 1544, soon after the foundations of the prince's funerary mosque were laid, the sultan went to hunt in Bursa, inviting his older son Selim, then the sanjak governor of Karaman (Konya). Süleyman's retinue included his wife Hürrem, his son Bayezid, his daughter Mihrümah, his son-in-law Rüstem Pasha (then ranked as second vizier), and the grand vizier Hadım Süleyman

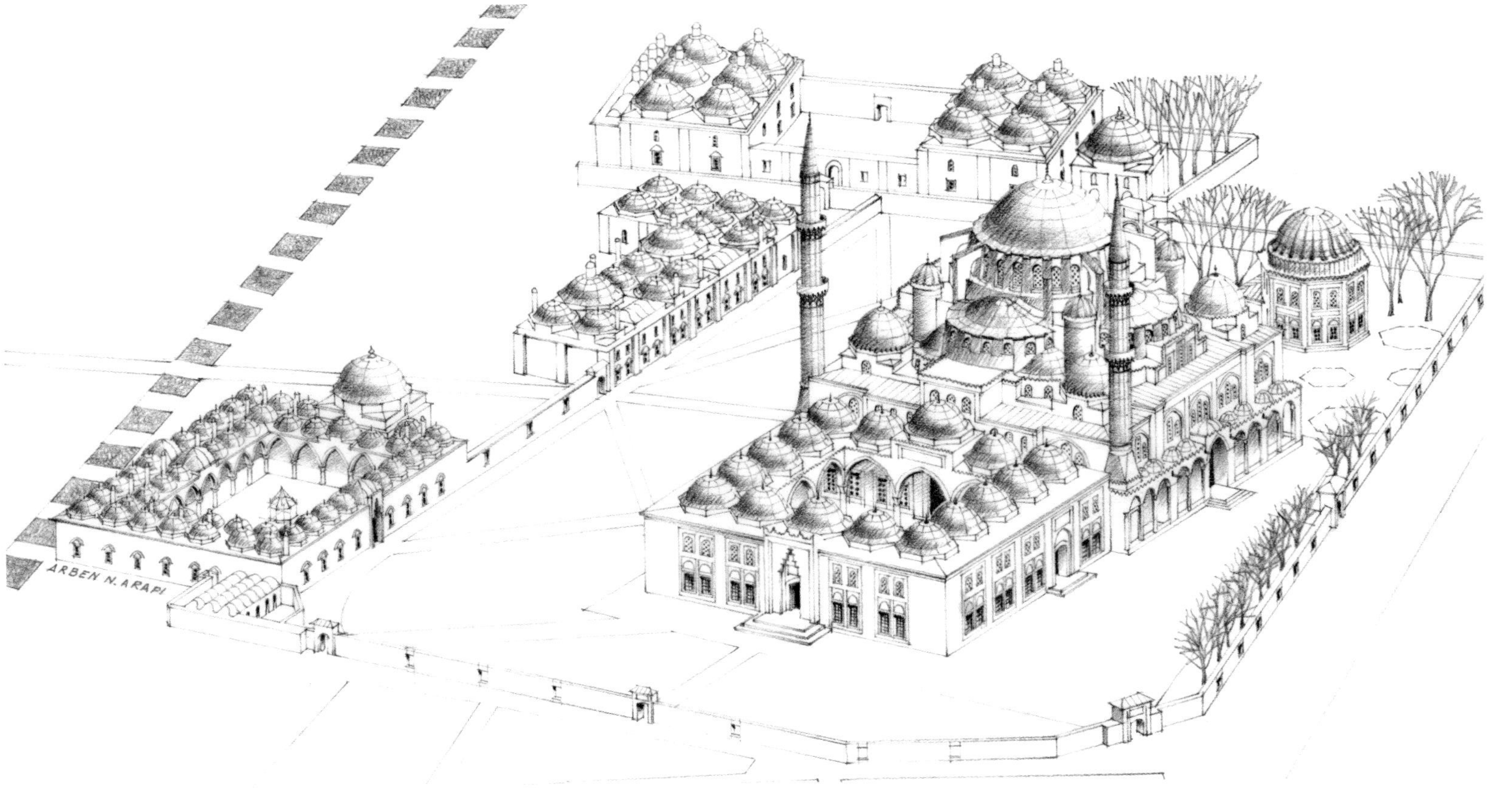

155 Axonometric projection of the Şehzade Mehmed complex, Istanbul.

156 Mosque of Şehzade Mehmed, Istanbul, seen from Divanyolu.

Pasha. The frail and hunchbacked younger prince, Cihangir, did not come to Bursa, probably because he was not considered a viable candidate for the throne. After 'many days passed in friendly conversation, assemblies, and hunting', the sultan and his escort returned to the capital.[36] The subsequent transfer of prince Selim, Hürrem's oldest remaining son, to Manisa implies that while in Bursa he had emerged as the new heir apparent.[37]

Throughout the construction of the Şehzade mosque, prince Selim's candidacy for the throne was sanctioned by the sultan, his queen, and her two loyal allies, Mihrümah and the new grand vizier Rüstem Pasha. The prince was temporarily appointed to guard the western border of the empire as lieutenant governor of Edirne in 1548, the year the mosque complex reached completion and Süleyman led a campaign against the Safavids. Selim held a hunting party in nearby Yanbolu, where he met with his mother, 'the Queen of Sheba of the age, whom the people of Edirne did not fail to eagerly serve'. The Austrian Hapsburg secretary Johann Maria Malvezzi reports that both Hürrem and Rüstem Pasha at that time supported Selim's claim to the throne, whereas the people preferred Mustafa.[38] After the latter's execution in 1553, the notorious trio (Hürrem, Rüstem, and Mihrümah) threw their support behind prince Bayezid.[39] However, the sultan continued to favour his eldest son, who won the battle of Konya in 1559 thanks to the aid of Süleyman's imperial troops.

The construction of the Şehzade mosque, however, preceded the resolution of the conflict among Mehmed's surviving brothers and thus overlapped with a crisis of dynastic succession during which prince Mustafa was still alive and strongly championed by the janissaries. The selection of the site for the funerary mosque inside the Old Chambers, the core of the corps until then, can therefore be interpreted as a political gesture (illus. 157). The foundation inscriptions of the mosque and mausoleum, to which I shall return, simultaneously mourn the blessed prince's death and pray for the continuation of the benevolent reign of the world emperor 'Shah Süleyman Khan'. The preamble of the posthumous waqfiyya likewise exalts the reigning sultan, listing his pompous titles.[40] Celalzade points out that inside the mosque, illuminated manuscripts of the Koran displayed on reading stands were read day and night both for the continuation of the sultan's sovereignty and for the salvation of the late prince's soul.[41]

The congregation of the mosque must have been dominated by the janissaries. Through its construction the sultan may have hoped to win their support not only for the succession of his oldest remaining son by Hürrem, but also for himself, since he was in no small danger of being deposed by Mustafa's faction. The removal in 1511–12 of the elderly Bayezid II by Selim I, Süleyman's grandfather and father respectively, was not a distant memory. While it was being built between 1543 and 1548, Şehzade Mehmed's unusually monumental mosque complex also touted the privileged status of his mother, the sultan's legal wife, whose second-oldest son was now being endorsed by the royal couple as the next ruler. Hürrem seems to have played a central role in the construction of her favourite son's funerary complex, a role hitherto overlooked by architectural historians. Āli recognizes her contribution to the mosque's uncustomary layout, more decorous for a sultanic than a princely foundation, which he attributes to the excessive love the deceased prince's 'fortunate mother and illustrious father felt for him in their hearts'.[42] The Venetian diplomats Navagero (1553) and Trevisano (1554) credit the queen as much as the sultan in the creation of this lavish memorial for prince Mehmed, 'who was a very gracious youth loved by his mother and father and by all others who knew him, not only on account of his beauty but also his habits, being by nature humane and liberal.' That is why the sultan and his wife honoured their son's mausoleum 'with a most beautiful and extremely sumptuous' mosque named after him.[43]

Hürrem's active participation in the construction process of her son's memorial is confirmed by the 'Customs of Janissaries', written in the early seventeenth century by an old janissary. According to this source, during a visit to the building site, 'Her Highness Haseki Sultan' was so moved by the plight of novices carrying building materials with 'bare head and feet' that she requested the sultan to augment their monthly wages by five aspers. This raise, assigned to cover the haircut and shoe expenses of novices, was financed by the queen herself as a pious charity for which she sold all her gold, jewellery, and pearls. After her death, the raise she initiated was legally fixed by the sultan.[44] Through this charitable display of maternal compassion, the unpopular Hürrem, accused of bewitching the innocent sultan with her charms, may have hoped to win over the support of the janissaries (former novices) for herself and her candidate to the throne.

Imperial decrees issued in 1544 and 1545 by the grand vizier Rüstem Pasha's cabinet for the construction of the mosque complex show that the agha of janissaries, Pertev Mehmed Agha, was ingeniously coopted into the building process. These documents disclose the close cooperation between the chief architect Sinan, the agha of janissaries who served as the building overseer, and the building supervisor, Hüseyin Çelebi, who would hold the same job during the early years of the Süleymaniye's construction. Pertev Agha's involvement with the construction of the Şehzade mosque seems to have been prompted not only by its site at the centre of the janissary barracks, but also by his personal connection with the deceased prince's family. Married to the widow of Şehzade Mehmed, he was the stepfather of the late prince's royal children.[45]

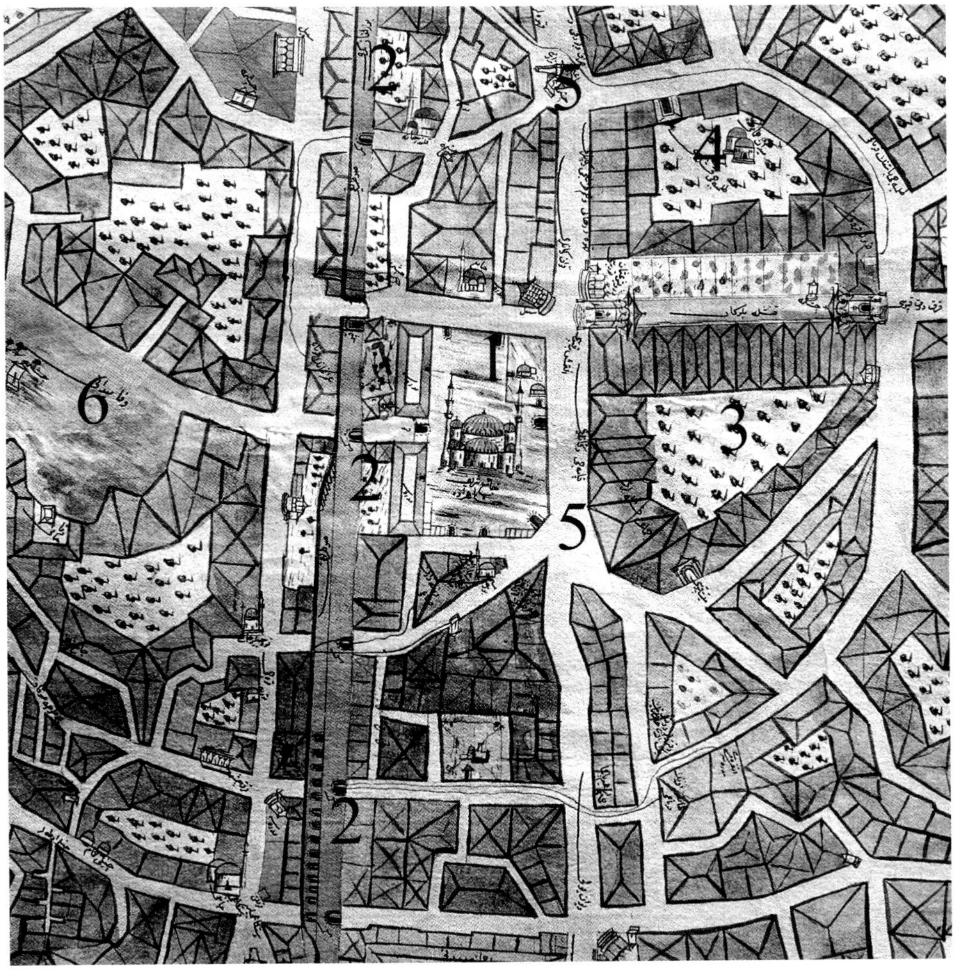

157 Şehzade Mehmed complex, Istanbul, site plan, detail from a map of the Bayezid II water supply system, 1815–17: 1. Mosque precinct, 2. Valens aqueduct and its water channel, 3. Old Chambers of the janissaries, 4. Dormitory block of novices, 5.Divanyolu lined with shops, 6. Public square of Vefa Meydanı.

Surviving decrees from 1544–45 are largely concerned with the preparation of building materials. In an order of 20 December 1544, jointly addressed to the janissary agha, the building supervisor, and the chief architect, the sultan (who was wintering in Edirne) acknowledges having received Pertev Agha's progress report indicating that 'the stones that have arrived until this point at the complex (*'imāret*) are five thousand cubits, and that the foundations of the building have been dug, and that its upper parts will be built when the construction season starts.'[46] The sultan accepts the agha's recommendation favouring the quarrying of stones by novices from the Azadlu river bed outside the city walls over the option of dismantling a ruined Byzantine tower (*yaruḳ burġaz*) that would yield only one thousand cubits of ashlar stone and be more expensive to transport.[47] The trio is instructed not to waste a moment in matters concerning the rapid completion of the complex.

Another decree sent on 7 January 1545 from Edirne asks the same trio to report in writing how much timber, stone, and other building materials have been prepared for the complex and what stage the construction of the noble mausoleum's gates have reached.[48] Other imperial orders from those years concern the quarrying of marbles in Aydıncık and the burning of lime in Üsküdar and Rumelia, tasks for which tax exempt unpaid labourers (*müsellem* and *yaya*) were enlisted by the janissary agha from Thrace, Bursa, Sultanönü, Aydın, Bolu, Biga, Hüdavendigar, Teke, Hamidili, Kütahya, Saruhan, and Ankara.[49] Decrees were also issued for the importation of iron from the Samokov mines in Bulgaria,[50] and for the assignment by the kadi of Haslar (Eyüp) of two hundred rented carts used in state fields for the transportation of building materials.[51]

A book of royal donations records bonuses given at significant turning points in the construction. Usta Ahmed received twenty florins (1,200 aspers) on 8 August 1545, and an unnamed architect was given fifteen florins (900 aspers) on 9 September 1546. When the 'dome arches of Sultan Mehmed's mosque were locked together' on 21 June 1547, the bringers of good news were rewarded with twenty florins.[52] According to the foundation inscription above its main gate, facing the marble-paved forecourt, the mosque was completed a year later. The seven Persian couplets carved in paired cartouches inside a quadrangular panel, flanked by two panels inscribed with the Sunni profession of faith, identify 'Shah Süleyman Khan, the sovereign of the face of the earth' as the patron of the Friday mosque built 'for the soul of the prince', a 'joy-giving and illuminated building' resembling the 'Garden of Eden and the uppermost level of paradise' which was started in May–June 1544 and completed in August–September 1548. The inscription ends with a chronogram that dedicates the mosque to the congregation of the Prophet Muḥammad: 'The sanctuary of the community of the manifest Prophet, the year 955 (1548–49).'[53]

The complex is sandwiched between the main ceremonial avenue, known as Divanyolu, and the Roman-period Valens (Bozdoğan) aqueduct. The aqueduct stops abruptly at the north side of the complex and is believed to have been transformed by Sinan into an inverted syphon at that point in order to free the sight of the Şehzade mosque on the Istanbul skyline (illus. 33[5], 100[1], 165).[54] To further enhance its visibility, Sinan moved the mosque and its funerary garden to the edge of Divanyolu, from which they are separated by a transparent wall pierced with iron-grilled windows. The less visible dependencies tucked in the back are loosely grouped along the south and east sides of the irregular precinct wall. A hospice and elementary school are located across the street at the south, and a madrasa and guest-house-cum-stable are adjacent to the precinct's east wall.[55] The diagonally cut, bevelled northwest corner of the outer enclosure provides an ideal oblique perspective of the mosque at the juncture of Divanyolu with several arteries. The asymmetrical composition of the complex, then, maximizes the visibility of the mausoleum and the elaborately articulated west façade of the mosque from the public avenue. The funerary garden would later on be transformed into a cemetery containing the mausolea of prince Mehmed's descendants and relatives, including grand viziers married into the royal family such as his brother-in-law Rüstem Pasha (d. 1561).[56]

The modular plan of the Şehzade mosque is composed of two squares roughly equal in size – a marble-paved forecourt and a sanctuary linked by a pair of double galleried minarets. As we have seen in Chapter 3, the mosque is celebrated for its perfectly centralized domed baldachin, raised on four polygonal piers and surrounded by four half-domes, a scheme often compared to that of central-plan Italian Renaissance churches. The mosque reinterprets the quatrefoil plan type introduced earlier in Bıyıklı Mehmed Pasha's mosque in Diyarbakır (1516–20), from which it eliminates the appended lateral guest-rooms (illus. 86).[57] It is hailed as the rational culmination of previous sultanic mosques built by Mehmed II and Bayezid II in the capital, mosques whose domes resting on four piers and lateral granite columns are flanked by half-domes. The elimination of the lateral granite columns and guest-houses reinforces spatial centralization, freeing the side façades of the mosque for a more complex treatment. Its elaborately fenestrated lateral façades are enlivened with unprecedented single-storey domical arcades that conceal the projecting buttresses and minaret bases (illus. 158).

The configuration of inner space is fully reflected by the exterior of the mosque, with its four weight turrets capped by fluted domes that rise above the inner piers and firmly anchor the central dome and the four half-domes, accompanied by exedras never before used in Ottoman architecture (illus. 159). The pyramidal massing of the innovative domical superstructure softens with curvilinear forms the rigidly cubical dome bases of Mehmed II's and Bayezid II's mosques, which mimic that of Hagia Sophia (illus. 56, 61, 67). The proportional harmony between the pyramidal silhouette and the integrated minarets is another innovation. As the Ottoman geographer Mehmed Aşık notes in the 1590s, the dome of Bayezid II's mosque is too distant from its minarets attached to the lateral guest-rooms, 'as if the minarets did not belong to the mosque'.[58] Sinan's predecessor tried to remedy this perceptive criticism in Selim I's mosque by placing its two minarets closer to the dome, in between the body of the mosque and the projecting guest-houses (illus. 67, 78, 79). The mosque of Şehzade Mehmed, on the other hand, revived the plan of Mehmed II's mosque with its detached *tabhane*. Noting the typological similarity between these two mosques, Mehmed Aşık recognizes the originality of Sinan's style:

> This noble mosque's two minarets, and the plan and design (*ṭarḥ ve resmi*) of its layout, are close to the characteristics of Sultan Mehmed Khan Ghazi's mosque, but the architectural refinement (*nezāket-i bināsı*) of this mosque is astonishing and wonderful; its minarets are graceful and well-proportioned, each having two galleries.[59]

Evliya Çelebi is particularly impressed by the minarets that 'bewilder the minds of onlookers' with their intricately carved motifs: 'These are such exemplary decorated minarets that their like has not been built in Istanbul, Bursa, and Edirne; the great architect [Sinan] has displayed his artistic power in architecture in these minarets and this mosque.'[60] The twin minarets with double galleries, which represent Şehzade Mehmed's privileged status as heir apparent, are unique in their decorative profusion, carved as they are with vertical rows of crescents, stars, rosettes, and knot motifs, accompanied by oil lamps inlaid in red sandstone beneath their muqarnased galleries (illus. 160). Crested cornices that articulate the layered façades and the dome bases are another example of ornamental exuberance. The accentuation of the arch voussoirs and frames of windows in red sandstone creates a rich polychromatic effect. Such lavishness, deemed decorous for a mosque built in memory of a handsome

158 Şehzade Mehmed mosque, Istanbul, from the east.

159 Şehzade Mehmed mosque from the north.

160 Aerial view of the Şehzade Mehmed mosque, Istanbul, with the Süleymaniye in the background.

young prince, would be abandoned in the austere aesthetic of the Süleymaniye, representing the sultan's own image of dignified imperial majesty.

The unified interior space of the Şehzade mosque epitomizes the concept of centralization with its harmonious orchestration of half-domes and exedras fluidly descending from the central dome to meet the four walls (illus. 161, 162). The interior, brightened with multiple tiers of windows, is divided into five distinctly articulated zones separated by painted mouldings. Above the lowermost zone of walls faced with cut stones rises a second zone, which constitutes an elastic transitional belt beneath the domical superstructure, composed of muqarnased squinches and fenestrated arches. The upper levels of the four central piers are fluted to give the impression of a weightlessly suspended superstructure. The third zone, reaching up to the half-domes, is composed of exedras and tympanum arches perforated with windows. The fourth zone of semi-domes, also lined with a row of windows, culminates with the fifth zone of the central dome encircled by its own corona of windows.

The qibla wall is differentiated by the use of painted inscriptions on blind-arched window lunettes, and stained glass upper windows. Ground-level windows on the north, east, and west walls feature arch-shaped lunettes with openwork grills resembling those of Bayezid II's mosque.[61] Above the lunettes are placed hollow acoustic resonators hidden behind unique stone roundels, each covered with a hexagonal openwork grill. Buttresses abutting the north wall of the prayer hall create private loggias on the ground floor, with three prominent balconies raised above them. The perception of spatial unity is somewhat undermined by the four bulky piers (simpler than their counterparts in the Süleymaniye) and the white marble muezzin's tribune attached to the northwest pier. Raised on twelve Bursa arches, three on each side, it is a forerunner of the tribune marking the centre of the domed baldachin in the Selimiye.

The prince's octagonal mausoleum, representing the timeless realm of paradise, embodies an unrestrained ornamental approach (illus. 163, 164). Preceded by a triple-arched portico and crowned by a Timurid-flavoured fluted dome recalling that of Selim I's mausoleum, it has an elaborate drum of fluted ribs and crested friezes that encircle the base of the dome and the muqarnas cornice running above the façades. Framed by engaged cylindrical pilasters, the exterior walls are encrusted with red sandstone and coloured marble. Between their two tiers of windows extend rectangular bands with paired inscription cartouches of green-and-white inlaid marble.

The decorative programmes of the mosque and mausoleum represent the culmination of an era. Their inscriptions combine *thuluth* and *muḥaḳḳaḳ* scripts which differ from those of the Süleymaniye and Selimiye, unified by a single script: Hasan Karahisari's boldly magnified monumental *thuluth*. The same two scripts are used together with *naskh* in a celebrated Koran manuscript written by Hasan's master in 1546–47, just before the inauguration of the Şehzade mosque. It is therefore tempting to attribute the calligraphy of the mosque and mausoleum to the leading court calligrapher of

161 (top) Şehzade Mehmed mosque, Istanbul, interior view of the domical superstructure.

162 (above) Şehzade Mehmed mosque interior.

the time, Ahmed Karahisari (d. 1556).[62]

The pointed-arch window lunettes of the forecourt, with painted plasterwork abstract vegetal scrolls and geometric interlaces, show no trace of the semi-naturalistic floral style that would emerge in the 1550s. Faced with exquisite tiles, unlike the mosque, the mausoleum is the *raison d'être* of the funerary complex. Its *cuerda seca* tiles represent the glorious culmination of a Persianate ceramic technique and colour scheme (green, blue, turquoise, yellow, purple, and white) that would be abandoned in the Süleymaniye.[63] The tile revetments, dominated by green, begin at the portico with two crested panels in arched frames that flank the gate. The remarkably serene interior is panelled up to the dome level with *cuerda seca* tiles featuring abstract floral designs composed of rosettes, palmettes, and *saz* leaves. The band of paired inscription cartouches that encircles the inner walls between the two tiers of windows echoes the composition of the external façades. Arched motifs that frame the inscribed window lunettes delineate an illusionistic arcade around the interior space, 'through' which one sees a heavenly green meadow, visually continuous with the real garden outside the windows. The innovative integration of tilework with architectural design can be attributed to Sinan's artistic vision.

Kuban describes the mausoleum as 'an edifice of love, in which Süleyman's feelings were reflected by the hand of Sinan.'[64] Goodwin writes, 'the unprecedented beauty of this sepulchre must have been a consolation to Süleyman when he came, in a kaftan of black watered silk, into this room of the applegreen colour of youth.'[65] Hürrem was no doubt another mournful visitor to the mausoleum, where another of her sons is also buried. Its four sarcophagi are those of prince Mehmed, his youngest brother Cihangir (d. 1553), his daughter Humashah (Huma) Sultan, and an unidentified person. A prominent wooden throne above Şehzade Mehmed's sarcophagus represents his status as heir apparent.[66]

The Persian inscription carved on a rectangular marble panel above the mausoleum gate wishes the prince eternal rest in paradise, a vision of which is provided by the mausoleum itself. Composed of four couplets contained in paired cartouches, it reads:

> In the end, no one from high to low shall remain in the palace of the world, because of the words, 'Say: He is Allah, the One! (112:1).'
>
> The prince with pure faith passed from this transitory realm to the permanence of eternity, may God the eternal have mercy on him.
>
> Inasmuch as he has gone to rest in the next world by God's command, may the days of the sultan's [Süleyman] life be filled with endless eminence.
>
> Its date was inspired by God the timeless: 'May the resting place of Sultan Mehmed become eternal paradise, the year 950 (1543–44).'[67]

The gate is flanked by rectangular frames containing two carved Koranic inscriptions that greet those who enter the Garden of Eden (13:24, 39:73). The inlaid inscription cartouches that encircle the seven external façades spell out Koranic verses in *thuluth* script (102:1–8, 112:1–4), followed by some of the ninety-nine beautiful names of God. The first sura contains a warning against 'rivalry in worldly increase' punishable with hell-fire on doomsday. The next sura affirms the oneness of God, and lists His divine epithets.

Each tilework panel flanking the mausoleum gate has an epigraphic cartouche; read continuously, they profess the monotheistic formula: 'There is no God but God, the Just Sovereign, the Manifest / Muhammad is the Prophet of God, the Faithful Keeper of Promises, the Trustworthy.' The interior of the gate is flanked by a pair of tilework panels with squared kufic calligraphy repeating the name 'Muhammad'. This device draws an implicit parallel between the Prophet and his namesake Mehmed (whose name is spelled and vocalized as 'Muḥammad' in his waqfiyya, instead of the Turkified 'Meḥemmed'). The

163 Şehzade Mehmed mausoleum, Istanbul, from the west.

parallel is a leitmotif that unifies the epigraphic programmes of the prince's mosque and mausoleum. The tilework window lunettes of the mausoleum, inscribed in monumental *thuluth*, quote the Throne verse (2:255) affirming the absolute sovereignty of God, the arbitrator of the Last Judgment. The paired tilework cartouches in *muḥaḳḳaḳ* script cite verses (59:22–24) that list God's beautiful names. The divine names also appear in eight small rectangles between each lower window frame and inside eight octagonal rosettes placed between the stained glass upper windows.

The exclusively Koranic epigraphy of the funerary mosque, which is dedicated by its foundation inscription to the Prophet's community as a place of divine forgiveness resembling paradise, emphasizes the role of the Prophet Muhammad in transmitting the revelation of God. Koranic verses, grouped in four distinct zones descending from the apex of the dome, request divine mercy for pious believers, and by implication for the deceased prince. They glorify God from whom every being originates and to whom all returns.[68] The uppermost zone of the central dome has two concentric inscription bands in *thuluth* and *muḥaḳḳaḳ* scripts, which clarify the nature of the relationship between God

164 Şehzade Mehmed mausoleum interior.

and His Prophet Muhammad. The outer band quotes verses from the Isra' sura, alluding to the Prophet's vision of being carried by night from Mecca to Jerusalem, where he ascended through the seven heavens to the presence of God (17:1–2). The verses quoted here exalt 'the Hearer, the Seer', who is the believer's only guide to salvation through scriptures divinely revealed to the prophets. The centre of the dome is inscribed with the Fatiha sura (1:1–7), considered the gist of the Koran. It begs the 'Beneficent' and 'Merciful' God, who is the 'Owner of the Day of Judgment', to reveal the 'straight path' to favoured ones.

The painted calligraphic roundels on the four pendentives thematically complement the central dome. Each roundel contains an eight-pointed star around which are inscribed rotated divine epithets that highlight the mercifulness of God as the ultimate referee during the Last Judgment: 'O! The All-Bounteous! O! The Most Passionate!'; 'O! The Supreme Judge! O! The Merciful Pardoner!'; 'O! The Opener of All Ways!'; 'O! The Most Holy!' The four half-domes quote verses from the Baqara sura (2:144–45), starting at the qibla side and moving in a counter-clockwise direction. They exhort the congregation to turn in prayer toward the divinely revealed qibla. Believers to whom the holy scriptures are disclosed through the Prophet Muḥammad's mediation are asked to follow the qibla revealed by him and to reject the qibla of others.

The eight small exedras constituting a lower zone are inscribed with supplicatory prayers soliciting God's forgiveness. The four exedras on the qibla side continuously quote a verse from the Baqara sura (2:285) in which the Prophet and the community of believers who obey God's scriptures plead for divine mercy:

> The messenger believeth in that which hath been revealed
> unto him from His Lord and (so do) the believers.
> Each one believeth in Allah and His Angels and His
> Scriptures and His messengers – We make no distinction
> between any of His messengers – and they say: We hear,
> and we obey. (Grant us) Thy forgiveness, our Lord!
> Unto Thee is the journeying.

The allusion to a journey toward God resonates with the Prophet's Night Journey mentioned on the central dome, and with prince Mehmed's hoped-for journey to paradise. The four exedras on the anti-qibla side quote the next verse of the same sura (2:286), containing more pleas for God's mercy.

The lowest zone of inscriptions appears on the four piers, the qibla wall, and the royal tribune. The middle of each pier features a carved rectangular panel facing the central space. The two qibla-side panels are inscribed 'Allah' and 'Muhammad;' the remaining two bear the paired names of the four Sunni caliphs: 'Abu Bakr and ʿUmar'; 'ʿUthman and ʿAli'. These names are much less prominent than their counterparts in the Süleymaniye and in most later mosques built by Sinan, which feature eight names in roundels, including those of Hasan and Husayn (hereafter referrred to as the revered names). The main entrance at the north is flanked by two panels of squared kufic calligraphy repeating the phrase 'Praise be to God'. Axially aligned with that gate, the muqarnas-hooded stone mihrab surmounted by a triangular crested pediment resembles a gate, an analogy reinforced by its inscription which quotes part of a verse with the word mihrab (3:37): 'whenever Zachariah went into the sanctuary [mihrab] where she [Mary] was.' Commonly used in most of Sinan's mosques, I shall henceforth refer to it as the standard mihrab verse.

The painted window lunettes of the qibla wall cite verses from the Fath sura (48:1–4), which confirm that God will guide His Prophet 'on a right path' and end with a pledge made to the congregation following Muhammad's path: 'He it is Who sent down peace of reassurance into the hearts of the believers that they might add faith unto their faith. Allah's are the hosts of the heavens and the earth, and Allah is ever Knower, Wise.' The lunettes of the royal tribune quote the Throne verse (2:255) testifying to the absolute sovereignty of God, the source of the sultan's divinely sanctioned authority.

The presence of a royal tribune inside the late prince's mosque announced to the public that the reigning sultan was very much alive and still in power.[69] The inscriptions of the mosque imply that one can attain salvation in the other world only by obeying the scriptures God revealed to Muhammad. The reassurance that the pious prince is destined to dwell in paradise helps dispel the tragic sadness of his untimely death. Celalzade remarks that the beauty of the 'paradise-like' mosque fills one's heart with joy and makes one forget sorrow. He praises the abundance of light pouring in from its windows and its construction in a 'pleasing manner' (*ṭavr-ı marġūb*) with a heavenly dome and smaller 'celestial domes' around it.[70]

Şehzade Mehmed's posthumous waqfiyya likewise depicts the prayer hall as 'delightful and comfort-giving'. This was an 'illuminated mosque that encompassed all adornment and embellishment, and whose arches and porticoes were like the vaults of the universe.' Its forecourt and outer precinct were paradise-like, and 'those with perceptive vision' (*ehl-i naẓar*) considered it 'matchless' in the world and a 'novelty of the age' encompassing the most beautiful of all charms.[71] The *Teẕkiretü'l-bünyān* refers to the Şehzade mosque as having 'joy-giving porticoes, each of which resembled delight-increasing excursion spots.'[72] The mosque's intimate relationship with the Divanyolu is also stressed: 'And its venerable precinct (*ḥarem*) became like a road of pleasure (*rāh-i ṣafā*) along the edge of the highway.'[73] When the foundations of the mosque were laid, the 'edifice slowly rose from the ground, and its domes began to emerge like bubbles on the surface of the sea of elegance, with its many-hued arches soaring skywards like the rainbow.' Sai's description ends with a eulogy:

> How lofty is this paradise-like building,
> Whose air is soul-reviving and its waters purified.
>
> Becoming esteemed by the whole world,
> It was deemed excellent by the person of His Majesty.
>
> In laying its foundations I concentrated my full attention,
> For its completion I exerted a thousand endeavours
> and efforts.
>
> How many days I laboured through the grace of God,
> With whose blessing its completion was facilitated.
>
> The Shah complimented me with commendations,
> Bestowing on me many unhoped-for gifts.[74]

Lokman praises the 'exhilarating' marble-paved forecourt of the mosque, its 'two exquisite double-galleried minarets', and its 'lofty domes raised on four great piers'. He adds that the prince's 'illuminated' mausoleum inside a garden planted with fruit trees and flowers was built 'in the sultanic manner' (*resm-i selāṭīn üzre*).[75] As we have seen in Chapter 3, Mustafa Āli was puzzled by the sultanic features of the Şehzade mosque: 'its pair of double-galleried minarets and its spaciousness characteristic of mosques built in the past for the magnificent Ottoman sultans.'[76] He speculates that codes of decorum suitable for a princely foundation had been bypassed to express Şehzade Mehmed's privileged status as a crown prince:

> In terms of its elaborate plan, its exaltation with two minarets featuring multiple galleries, and the high rank accorded to its madrasa professor, it equalled in rank the mosques built by previous Ottoman sultans whose names had appeared on coins and had been mentioned in khutbas. The style and manner (*üslūb ve āyīn*) observed in the pious foundations of other princes were not conformed to in the good work of the late prince, who had attained God's mercy. Likewise its endowments were incomparably augmented and made strong. It became clear and manifest to all that the reason for these unprecedented privileges was the late prince's great popularity and the excessive love his fortunate mother and illustrious father felt for him in their hearts.[77]

The seventeenth-century historian Peçevi provides a different justification for these anomalous features; he claims to have heard

165 Skyline of Istanbul showing the Şehzade Mehmed and Süleymaniye mosques, with the Valens aqueduct at the far right and the Old Palace at the far left, c. 1590, detail of illus. 100 (1).

from old informants that the mosque had originally been intended as a sultanic monument for Süleyman himself and was subsequently named after the prince once he was buried behind its qibla wall.[78] Since earlier written sources leave no doubt that the mausoleum was built first, this rumour must have been invented later on to rationalize the mosque's unusual sultanic features: its marble-paved forecourt surrounded by domical arcades, its pair of double-galleried minarets, its monumental domed baldachin, and its royal tribune.[79]

The Şehzade mosque competes with Istanbul's first three sultanic mosques in stylistic novelty. Its twin minarets are more assertive than their single-galleried counterparts in earlier sultanic mosques. Nevertheless, its dome (19 metres), comparable to that of Bayezid II (17.5 metres), is smaller than those of Mehmed II (26 metres) and Selim I (24.5 metres).[80] Moreover, the prince's mosque lacks the prestigious red granite columns that add distinction to the domed baldachins of Mehmed II's and Bayezid II's mosques and that of his father Süleyman. The sultan's exalted self-image as the tenth and greatest ruler of the dynasty certainly required a more ambitious monument than that of his son, surpassing in size and magnificence all previous sultanic mosques in the capital (illus. 167–68). The lower status of the Şehzade mosque was clearly articulated by the codes of decorum Sinan later established in the Süleymaniye and Selimiye, both of which boast four multi-galleried minarets along with bigger and taller domed baldachins. The subordinate rank of the Şehzade mosque is also revealed by the panoramic silhouette of Istanbul, which is dominated by the much larger Süleymaniye, built on a hilltop closer to the Golden Horn. Against the skyline of the capital, the prince's mosque appears comparatively small in its recessed inland position, a contrast that effectively conveys the relative status of father and son (illus. 165).

When Āli noted the deviation of Şehzade Mehmed's mosque from princely prototypes, he must have been thinking of monuments built for later princes. After the mid-fourteenth century, princes had lost the prerogative of sponsoring mosques as a sign of subordination to their reigning fathers.[81] Prior to the construction of Şehzade Mehmed's mosque complex, it was common practice for the mothers of princes to commission mosques of their own in sanjaks governed by their sons. This practice was abandoned after Hürrem Sultan set an example for future *haseki*s by staying in Istanbul with her royal husband. The mosque complex built for her son Şehzade Mehmed was the first example of its kind in the capital. Trevisano points out that the prince's mausoleum, honoured with a lavish mosque by his loving parents, broke away from dynastic tradition, 'a thing not done before, as all the sons of emperors had always been buried in Bursa.'[82] Actually, the prince's mausoleum was preceded by the one that Süleyman built at his father's complex in Istanbul for his three sons who died as infants in the early 1520s.[83] But a mausoleum with a mosque complex of its own, created to commemorate a single prince, was indeed an innovation.

When Şehzade Cihangir passed away at Aleppo in 1553, during his father's last Safavid campaign, his body was transported to Istanbul by imperial decree and buried in Mehmed's mausoleum. It is noteworthy that Cihangir was not interred at the site of his own mosque complex, built by his parents in a suburb of Galata after his death: a decision in keeping with the dynastic custom of burying the members of the royal family inside the walled city. Illegitimate princes who had rebelled did not enjoy this privilege; Süleyman's executed sons Mustafa (d. 1553) and Bayezid

166 View of Tophane (Cannon Foundry) outside Galata, with the hilltop mosque of Şehzade Cihangir (1) and the Kılıç Ali Pasha mosque along the shore lined with cannons (2), 1588, detail of illus. 101.

(d. 1562) are buried in Bursa and Sivas respectively. The striking contrast between the mosque complexes of Şehzade Mehmed and Şehzade Cihangir, both of them Sinan's works, shows how codes of decorum differentiated the status of an heir apparent from a physically disabled younger prince not even seen fit to govern a sanjak.[84]

Sited outside the walls of Galata, Cihangir's mosque was a much simpler structure with a hipped roof and a single-galleried minaret suited to his humble stature (illus. 100[2], 166). Despite its prominent position on a hilltop, its suburban site expressed Cihangir's lower rank in comparison to his brother. Evliya Çelebi apologetically attributes the simple form of the view-commanding mosque to the difficulty of constructing a monumental dome on a steep hill:

> Sited on a high hill, it has a lead covered four-hipped vault (*ḫarpuşte*) raised on four walls because building a monumental construction on such a soaring site is impossible. It has one minaret, a dervish convent, a hospice [kitchen], and a courtyard decorated with tall plane trees. Following the afternoon prayers, its whole congregation and pleasure-loving companions [dervishes] gather there to watch the ships cruising the sea; it is indeed a world-viewing mosque. On its walls the artistic power of Koca Mimar Sinan's hands are manifest and evident.[85]

According to Ayvansarayi, the site was once a suburban garden estate where prince Cihangir had erected a belvedere pavilion. Whenever he frequented that garden for pleasurable excursions, he would express his ardent wish 'to build an elegant mosque on this pleasant site'. Upon his death, his mother Hürrem reminded Süleyman of that wish, which prompted the sultan to commission a mosque complex for the soul of their son.[86] Cihangir's memorial mosque, then, was created at the initiative of his mother, who had also played a decisive role in the construction of Şehzade Mehmed's complex. The account books of the Süleymaniye show that building materials and lead were supplied from it for the 'noble Friday mosque of Cihangir, may he rest in peace, at Tophane', completed around 1559–60.[87]

An undated account book of 'the noble Friday mosque located at the Tophane garden' mentions among its dependencies an elementary school and rooms for the imams. The cost of the complex was in keeping with the modesty of its programme: 722,240 aspers, of which 527,240 aspers came from the sale of properties owned by the prince and 150,000 aspers from the sultan's inner treasury (Appendix 2).[88] Prince Cihangir's complex included an elementary school and a convent on one side of its courtyard for Halveti dervishes who served as imams in the mosque.[89] Nothing remains of these structures, and the present ashlar masonry mosque, entirely rebuilt in 1889–90, is a domed cube honoured with two single-galleried royal minarets.[90] Lokman says two elementary schools were endowed in connection with the mosque complex of Şehzade Mehmed because of the two princes buried in its mausoleum; one school was located within the mosque complex itself and the other one near the dervish convent (*zāviye*) that the sultan endowed for Hekim Çelebi (d. 1566–67) at Fildamı (Koska). The latter was a Nakshbandi shaykh-cum-physician whose disciples included the ailing Süleyman and his son-in-law, Rüstem Pasha.[91] An undated appendix of Şehzade Mehmed's waqfiyya documents the endowment of the elementary school at Fildamı.[92]

Late-sixteenth-century mosques built by crown princes in the sanjaks they governed were not as modest as that of prince Cihangir, but they certainly failed to measure up to the grandeur of Şehzade Mehmed's complex. That of his brother prince Selim (II) in Karapınar, near Konya, is a basic domed cube with a five-domed double portico flanked by two single-galleried minarets (illus. 203).[93] Because prince Murad's (III) no-longer-extant princely mosque in Manisa proved too small for its congregation, it was replaced during his sultanate by the more monumental Muradiye featuring a five-domed portico and two single-galleried minarets (illus. 236).[94]

The plan type of Şehzade Mehmed's mosque complex in Istanbul was never repeated for a crown prince. This unique complex deliberately conflated sultanic and princely status to proclaim Mehmed's unfulfilled destiny as future ruler. Its design, comparable to earlier sultanic mosques of the capital, implied that the heir apparent was equal in status to Süleyman's venerable forebears. The *Tuḥfe* proudly asserts that the Şehzade mosque aesthetically surpassed previous sultanic mosques built 'in the manner of Hagia Sophia'.[95] Even foreign observers were able to distinguish its stylistic superiority to former sultanic mosques. The secretary of the French ambassador Gabriel d'Aramont (1546–55) noted the 'marvellous beauty, magnificence, and sumptuousness' of the mosques built for Mehmed II, Bayezid II, and Selim I, but he judged the one recently constructed by Süleyman 'more beautiful and distinct' than the others.[96] The fact that Süleyman could build a mosque for his son that rivalled

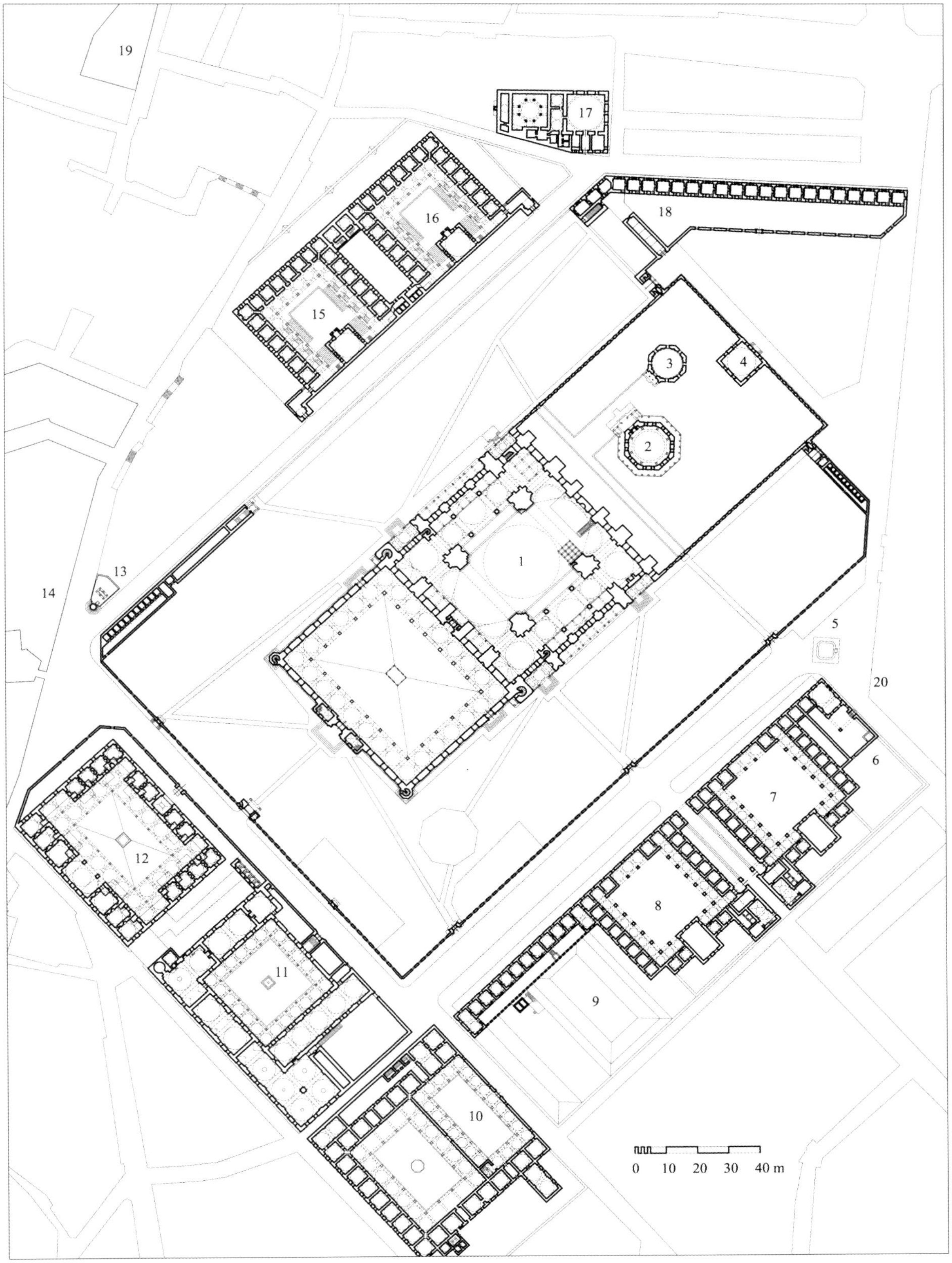

167 Plan of the Süleymaniye complex, Istanbul: 1. Mosque. 2. Mausoleum of Süleyman. 3. Mausoleum of Hürrem. 4. Koran recitation school, also known as the hall of mausoleum keepers (Türbedar Odası). 5. Public fountain,.6. Elementary school. 7. First (Evvel) madrasa. 8. Second (Sani) madrasa. 9. Remains of medical school. 10. Hospital, 11. Hospice. 12. Guest-house. 13 .Sinan's tomb with domed water dispenser and the empty plot of his endowed school and residence. 14. The janissary agha's residence, 15. Third (Salis) madrasa. 16. Fourth (Rabi) madrasa. 17. Bathhouse. 18. Hadith college. 19. Madrasa near the palace of Fatma Sultan and Siyavuş Pasha, 20. Old Palace.

those of former sultans doubly amplified his own unmatched rank within the dynasty. The intentional ambiguity between princely and sultanic status in Şehzade Mehmed's mosque also accentuated the prestige of his mother. The context-specific memories it embodied, concerning the legitimacy of Süleyman's sons from Hürrem as heirs to the throne, seem to have been forgotten once the crisis of dynastic succession was resolved with Selim II's accession.

The equivocal identity of the Şehzade mosque contributed to its classification as a sultanic monument, included in the itineraries of sultans whenever they ceremonially toured the mausoleums of their forebears.[97] Evliya Çelebi identifies the Şehzade as the sixth sultanic mosque of Istanbul, ranked after the mosques of Hagia Sophia, Mehmed II, Bayezid II, Selim I, and Süleyman I. He assesses it as a synthesis of elements inspired by former sultanic prototypes in the capital: 'It has been built by borrowing an elegant and pristine feature from each mosque.'[98] This astute observation is in keeping with Sinan's own stated goal of refining the style of earlier sultanic mosques in the synthetic architectural idiom of the Şehzade mosque.

The chief architect's budding new idiom bridged the past and the future. It not only perfected elements distilled from early Ottoman architecture, but also sowed seeds of novelty that would be cultivated further in the 1550s. Soon after the inauguration of the Şehzade mosque, imperial orders were issued in 1548 to collect building materials for Sultan Süleyman's own imperial mosque. The close cooperation between Sinan and the building supervisor Hüseyin Çelebi in both projects would ensure an unbroken continuity of architectural and administrative expertise. No wonder then, that the mosque of Şehzade Mehmed is presented in the *Tuḥfe* as a preparatory exercise for the Süleymaniye, where its embryonic innovations would culminate in the formulation of a mature 'classical' synthesis.[99] It was more than two decades after the completion of the Şehzade mosque that its pioneering conception of centralized space would be consummated in the

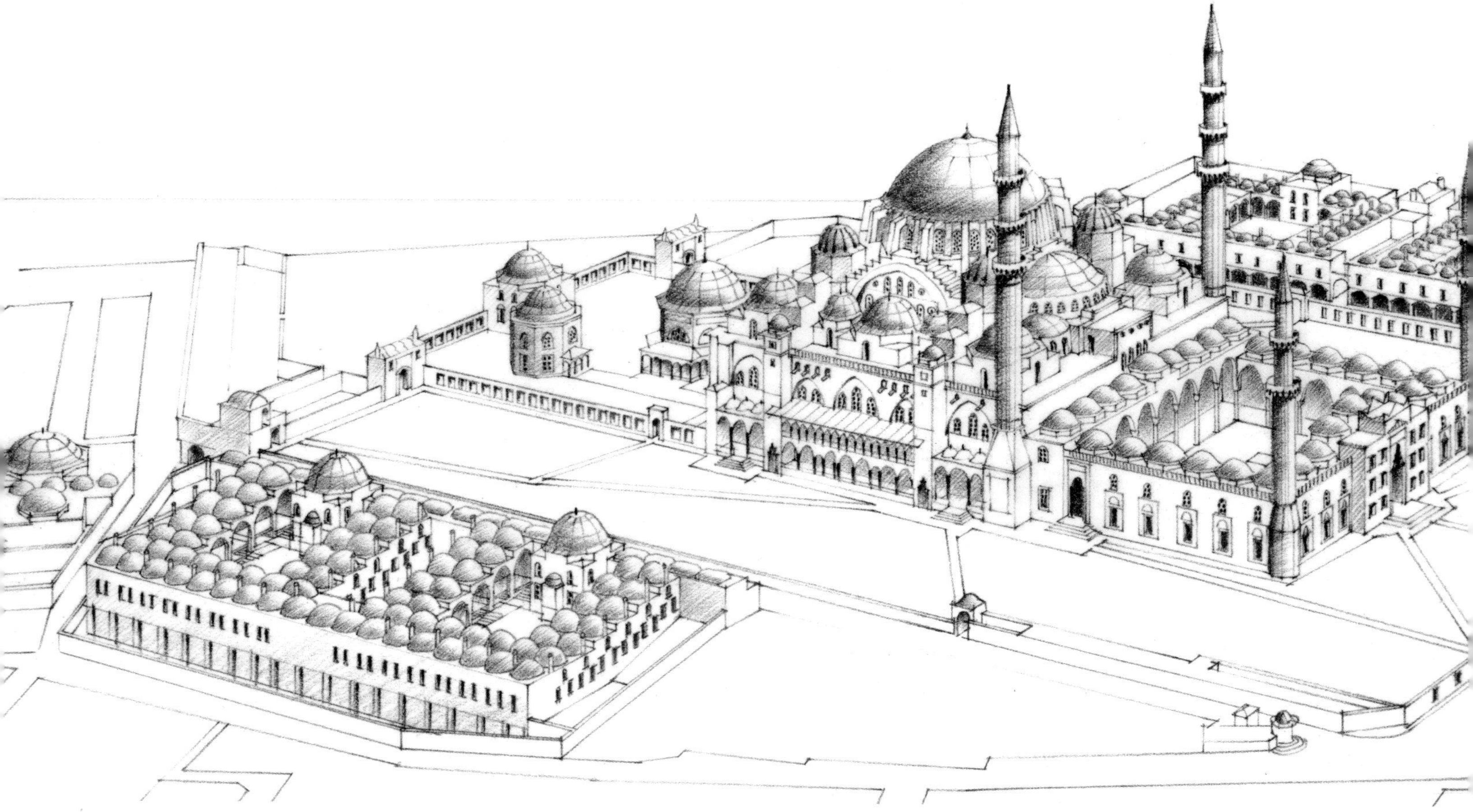

168 Axonometric projection of the Süleymaniye complex, Istanbul.

169 Süleymaniye mosque, Istanbul, (left) tripartite foundation inscription of the north portal, (right) detail of engaged colonette with 'hourglass' motif.

Selimiye, where Sinan fully unleashed his poetic imagination from the shackles of archaism.

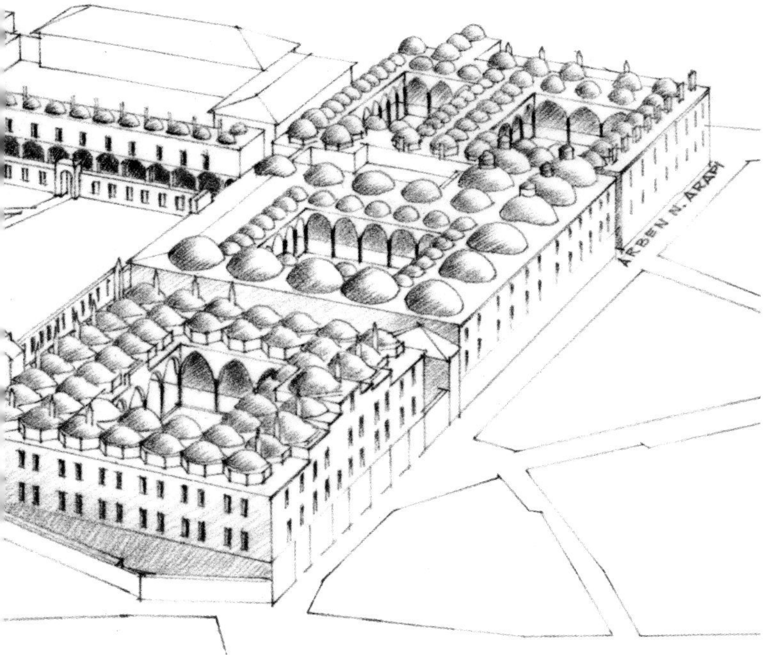

THE SÜLEYMANIYE COMPLEX

With its layout modelled on Hagia Sophia, the Süleymaniye mosque proclaimed the perfect concordance of state and religion in the person of the sultan (illus. 167, 168). At the time it was planned, Süleyman had just signed a 1547 treaty with the Holy Roman Emperor, Charles v of Spain, and Ferdinand I of Austria, granting peace in Hungary in return for tribute. The sultan, who considered himself to have wrested the Roman imperial title from his Hapsburg rivals, was now ready to confront his main rival in the east, Shah Tahmasp. The construction of the Süleymaniye overlapped two Ottoman military campaigns against the Safavids. An anonymous chronicle explains that the sultan decided to build his mosque complex in March 1548, at the time he sent Tahmasp's refugee brother Elkas Mirza on a holy campaign to the east as the governor of Tabriz and Shirvan and the future 'monarch of Iran':

> At that time, his highness the world-ruling sultan realized the impermanence of the base world, destined to come to an end, and the necessity to leave behind a monument so as to be commemorated till the end of time and to rejoice with the grateful remembrance of pious deeds. Following the devout path of former sultans, he ordered the construction of a matchless mosque complex for his own noble self.

170 Süleymaniye complex, Istanbul, from the northwest with the Golden Horn in the background.

> From pure gold and tablewares, the melting of which raised no suspicion or doubt [of canonical unlawfulness], 150,000 gold pieces (9,000,000 aspers) were minted and handed over [as an advance] to the building supervisor for the preparation of materials and other needs.[100]

When the Elkas Mirza adventure failed, Süleyman mounted a second campaign against the Safavids, which resulted in the signing of the Amasya peace treaty in 1555. Although he had not won a pitched battle against his rival, he had scored an ideological triumph by forcing Tahmasp to abolish the ritual cursing of the Sunni caliphs and other practices diverging from the shariʿa. In 1557 the submissive Safavid monarch's ambassador brought gifts for the inauguration of the noble mosque, 'peerless and unique on the face of the earth'.[101] Its Arabic foundation inscription encapsulates Süleyman's claim to the universal sultanate and caliphate by both secular and divine right (illus. 169). Composed by the shaykh al-Islam Ebussuud and signed by the calligrapher Hasan b. Ahmed al-Karahisari, the monumental *thuluth* inscription, carved on three marble panels above the north portal of the mosque, refers to Süleyman as God's slave, 'made mighty with divine power, the caliph resplendent with divine glory who performs the command of the hidden book [the celestial prototype of the Koran] and executes its decrees in [all] regions of the inhabited quarter, the conqueror of the lands of the Orient and the Occident with the help of almighty God and his victorious army, the possessor of the kingdoms of the world, the shadow of God over all peoples, the sultan of the sultans of the Arabs and the Persians, the promulgator of the sultanic law codes, and the tenth of the Ottoman sultans.'[102]

The inscription provides a foundation date of 1550 and an inauguration date of 1557, but building activities started before and continued after those dates.[103] Some components of the complex – Hürrem Sultan's (d. 1558) mausoleum, two of the madrasas, and the water channels – were not finished until 1559, the year the final resumé of expenses was drawn up.[104] The undated waqfyya of the Süleymaniye complex must have been registered around the same time. The resumé excludes the sultan's own mausoleum, which was built by his son between 1566 and 1568.[105] Handed over to 'the man of the chief architect' in 1568, a decree of Selim II addressed to the kadis of Bursa, Amasya, Kastamonu, and Merzifon urgently orders skilled masons capable of marblework to be sent with their tools for his late father's mausoleum.[106]

The Süleymaniye complex was designed as a grand centre of higher learning dominated by five madrasas primarily dedicated to theological studies that would bolster the shariʿa, the backbone of the imperial legal system (illus. 170). Four of these were theological seminaries, while the fifth and highest one (earmarked for retired ulema equalling muftis in rank) functioned as a hadith college specializing in the Prophet's traditions and in commentaries on the Koran.[107] The endowment deed of the

171 Anonymous Austrian artist, Süleymaniye complex, Istanbul, from the east, c. 1590, watercolour on paper.

Süleymaniye explains that these madrasas were built to exalt the religious sciences as a means of 'strengthening the mechanisms of worldly dominion and of reaching happiness in the next world.' They contributed 'to strengthening the right religion and the upright shariʿa, which is the main requisite of the house of the caliphate and the main support of the mansion of the sutanate.'[108] The geographer Mehmed Aşık compares the madrasas to 'the five pillars of the Islamic religion'.[109] The professorship of the sixth madrasa, a medical school, was reserved for the chief royal physician.[110] Ranked higher than Mehmed II's eight madrasas, those of Süleyman underlined the growing emphasis on theology. The new complex eclipsed that of the Conqueror as the largest and programmatically most comprehensive sultanic foundation in the capital for nearly a century after its construction in 1463–70.

The intention to surpass, in both beauty and size, all mosques built by former sultans was proudly announced to the *bailo* Bernardo Navagero in 1550 by the grand vizier Rüstem Pasha.[111] This ambition is recognized by the ambassador Catharin Zen (1550), who after describing the sultanic mosques of Mehmed II, Bayezid II, and Selim I, makes the following observation:

> And there is another mosque of Mehmed, the son of this *Signore*, who died, and presently they have started to lay the foundations of the mosque of Sultan Süleyman, who lives and rules today, for which they have taken away a large piece of the Old Palace from one end of the hill to the other, and they want to make it larger, more beautiful, and better ornamented than all others that have been built, for which it is said they will spend so much that if I tell you, I will not be believed![112]

The desire to create an unmatched edifice is confirmed by Dernschwam, who was told in 1554–55 that the Süleymaniye would be larger and more beautiful than previously built sultanic mosques, with its dependencies covering an area bigger than the city of Pressburg (Bratislava) in Hungary and approaching the size of Belgrade. Dernschwam explains that the site on which the mosque complex was being built consisted of a large piazza extending in front of the walled enclosure of the Old Palace (illus. 33[4], 165). He witnessed marble panels being removed from the steps of the Hippodrome and spolia brought from the ancient ruins of İzmit (Nicomedia) for the complex that was estimated to reach completion within three years, an estimate which turned out to be accurate.[113] The antiquarian Pierre Gilles (1549–51), who saw the removal of seventeen white marble columns from the Hippodrome, mentions the precious marble being collected from imperial ruins all over the sultan's domains:

> The present Emperor Süleyman has taken up residence in the middle of this precinct, where he is laying a foundation for a caravansaray and his future sepulchre. These are now building with the most elegant marble, brought from several parts of the Turkish dominions, so that you may see infinite

172 Süleymaniye complex, Istanbul, stepped madrasa domes with vistas of the Yeni Valide mosque and the Topkapı Palace.

173 Süleymaniye complex, stepped madrasa courtyard with its pavilion-like classroom featuring a projecting alcove over a fountain.

> varieties of it lying about the building, not lately dug out of the quarry, but ones that for many ages have been used in the palaces of several princes and emperors, not only in Byzantium but in Greece and in Egypt.[114]

Lokman explains that the Old Palace was selected in March 1548 as an appropriate site for the mosque complex destined to become the sultan's future burial place:[115]

> A plot of land with some extra space was taken over from the Old Palace, so that in addition to the required buildings several quarters and palaces for viziers and grandees could be built around it ... First, a great courtyard and garden were prepared around which several maydans were laid out on all sides and corners; near them were built a bathhouse, shops, and laundry rooms [for construction workers].[116]

Like the grand complex of Mehmed II, that of Süleyman is surrounded by a spacious esplanade flanked by two rows of madrasas and an elementary school along the longer sides, with social service buildings (a hospice, guest-house, and hospital) grouped along the third side. The lack of rigid symmetry was partly the result of open-ended planning. For instance, an imperial decree dated 1552 commands the chief architect and building supervisor to acquire new land for the recently ordered hospital.[117] Another decree issued that year indicates that the position of the hadith college, apparently another afterthought, had not yet been determined. Addressed to the building supervisor, it acknowledges having received his report that the college had to be fitted into the empty space remaining between the Old Palace and rooms built at the back side of the mihrab, without damaging pre-existing foundations.[118] This explains the unusual diagonal plan of the hadith college, which deviates from standard madrasa typologies.

The bevelled back corners of the hospital, guesthouse, and pair of madrasas facing the Golden Horn adapt themselves to pre-existing street networks. Sinan inserted shops and rental rooms under the retaining walls of the madrasas, the northern block (featuring a caravansaray underneath), and the eastern edge of the esplanade. Fronted by twenty shops endowed by himself, the chief architect's elementary school and mausoleum complex, which occupied a triangular plot next to his own residence, constituted a signature of authorship (illus. 124–26). It is unclear whether the janissary agha's palace (identified on Melchior Lorich's panorama, illus. 33[4]) existed before the construction of the mosque complex or was one of the newly built neighbourhood palaces mentioned above by Lokman. Sinan positioned the outer walls of the janissary agha's palace and the Old Palace across opposite corners of the outer courtyard, as parallel diagonals echoed by the bevelled corners of the window-pierced precinct wall. The shops and rental rooms encouraged a symbiotic relationship of commerce, religion, and education within the aristocratic neighbourhood of the Old Palace that still housed part of Süleyman's harem.

The mosque is surrounded by an ample outer courtyard criss-crossed by diagonal paths leading to various gates. The three sides of this courtyard are enclosed by stone walls perforated with rectangular, iron-grilled windows, providing the general public with inviting vistas of the sanctuary and its funerary garden. Raised on vaulted substructures, the fourth side commands panoramic views. In Evliya Çelebi's words, no wall was built there so that the mosque's congregation could watch the cityscape and seascape from the 'world-viewing courtyard'.[119] An Austrian album painting from the 1590s depicts individuals leaning over a tree-lined parapet to enjoy the vistas (illus. 171). It also shows the funerary garden, with its geometrically designed parterres and its arched pergola extending between two gates. The sand-covered outer courtyard, with a few grass plots and a still extant raised octagonal platform,

174 Süleymaniye mosque, Istanbul, seen from the twin madrasas at the west.

175 Süleymaniye mosque from the southwest.

176 Süleymaniye mosque, detail of west façade.

177 Süleymaniye mosque, Istanbul, monumental north portal of the forecourt.

is shown traversed by pedestrians and horseback riders. In the foreground appear the red brick roofs of Sinan's residence adjacent to the leaded domes of the madrasas and bathhouse.

Trying not to obstruct the exquisite view from the eastern esplanade, Sinan ingeniously adjusted the height of the stepped twin madrasas along the Golden Horn (illus. 172, 173). He reshaped the sloping terrain with terracing and retaining walls in such a way that the mosque complex seems to grow organically from the third hill of the city. Raised on the pedestal of its levelled podium, the mosque visually dominates both the cityscape and its surrounding complex. Unlike Mehmed II's two-dimensionally planned complex, evenly spread on a single raised platform, the Süleymaniye is sculpted in three dimensions upon layered terraces to enhance its mountainlike pyramidal silhouette. Manipulating changes of level and approach, Sinan created a dynamic interplay with the surrounding neighbourhood and with distant prospects.

The fenestrated precinct wall of the Süleymaniye is encircled by a public avenue forming a continuous belt around it. No such wall separates Mehmed II's mosque from its dependencies which are too far apart for visual integration. The semi-transparent precinct wall iconically defines the Süleymaniye mosque and its funerary garden as a hallowed inner sanctum separate from the outlying dependencies, conceived as 'exterior' spaces. This allows Sinan to shift their axes with respect to the central mosque in a more flexible design. The dependencies with inward-looking courtyards are no longer orthogonally aligned with the mosque as in Mehmed's complex, whose outer precinct constitutes an 'interior' space cut off from its urban context. The Conqueror's complex, aligned with the city's main ceremonial avenue, which passes through its precinct, was designed as a forum-like enclosed space traversed by a major road. By contrast, the Süleymaniye, removed from the Mese and sited in dramatic proximity to the Golden Horn, is surrounded by a network of roads that circulate around it without encroaching on the privacy of its residential neighbourhood. These streets approach the diagonal corners of the complex that are its main points of entry.

The outer beltway acts as a spatio-visual frame interacting with the mosque through street-connected ideal perspectives that exemplify Sinan's sensitivity to ocular effects. Through selective visual prioritizing, the chief architect scenographically presents his masterpiece from multiple primary and secondary viewpoints. The L-shaped western and northern dependencies block a full view of the mosque, thereby heightening the dramatic effect of visual anticipation and surprise (illus. 174). Two triangular viewing stations inserted into the bevelled northeast and southwest corners of the complex frame oblique vistas that present a gestalt of the mosque. Conceiving the visually more elaborate lateral sides of the mosque as its main façades, Sinan accentuates diagonal perspectives over frontal views (illus. 175, 176).

The visitor encounters one of the triangular viewing stations in front of the domed water dispenser adjoining Sinan's tomb by climbing the steep street that runs between the guest-house and the janissary agha's palace.[120] Another triangular space, reached from a street extending between the Old Palace and the elementary school, is marked by a free-standing fountain at its centre. Popularly known as the Account Fountain (Hesap Çeşmesi) or Tent Fountain (Çadır Çeşmesi), it carries the memory of the tent under which payments are believed to have been made to construction workers.[121] A larger triangular piazza tucked between the walls of the Old Palace and the funerary garden exposes the two mausoleums and the buttressed qibla wall of the mosque. The domed hall reached by a double flight of stairs from the piazza was staffed by two mausoleum keepers and numerous Koran reciters, who prayed for the continuation of the sultan's reign during his lifetime and for the salvation of his soul after his death.[122] According to Lokman, some of the gatehouses on the precinct wall had 'exhilarating rooms for distinguished brethren among the literati and calligraphers, provided with endowed books entrusted to a librarian'. Evliya Çelebi says the timekeeper, gatekeepers, and janitors resided in the rooms of the monumental three-storey northern gatehouse of the marble forecourt (illus. 177).[123]

The Süleymaniye recognizably refers to the most celebrated sultanic mosques of Istanbul and Edirne, which it aims to surpass. While its overall design comes close to the complex of Mehmed II, its mosque (crowned by a central dome flanked by two half-domes) invites direct comparison with the Bayezid II and Hagia Sophia mosques. Its four slender minarets improve on those of the Üç Şerefeli in Edirne, which are both thicker and disparate in shape. Skilfully integrating the minarets into the four corners of the marble-paved forecourt, Sinan accentuates the north–south axial movement and pyramidal mass of the Süleymaniye by varying the size of each matching pair: the shorter ones with two galleries at the north, and the higher triple-galleried pair at the south.

178 Süleymaniye mosque, Istanbul, north façade from the forecourt with a central fountain.

The layered domical superstructure of the Süleymaniye, demarcated from the lower zone of walls by unprecedented stone balustrades, dissolves the rigidly cubical base of the Hagia Sophia's dome through harmoniously integrated curvilinear forms. Unlike the dominant lateral buttresses of Hagia Sophia, those of the Süleymaniye are partly concealed within the walls and given a stepped profile rhythmically in tune with the layering of domes. The stepped buttresses feature domed belvedere chambers with view-commanding windows and doors that communicate with the roof terrace, protected by balustrades: an innovation singled out in the epilogue of the *Tuhfe* discussed in Chapter 4 (illus. 175). Four weight turrets capped with fluted domes are firmly anchored above the inner piers, and the grand fenestrated tympanum arches with stepped extradoes are fronted by five domes of alternating size over the side aisles. With their five window-framing arches, the lateral façades visually echo the domical superstructure. Buttresses divide these façades into three sections, fitted in the middle with stately two-storey porticoes boasting porphyry roundels and alternating marble voussoirs. At each end are triple-domed porticoes reached by steps, which provide access to side entrances and the royal tribune at the southeast corner. The alternating rhythm of the nine-arched lower portico, created with columns of differing height bearing muqarnas capitals, is echoed in the composition of windows above. The upper porticoes, featuring dainty columns with lozenge capitals, are covered by a colourfully painted, slanting wooden roof that shelters the ablution fountains with seats at ground level (another innovation highlighted in the *Tuhfe*, illus. 176).[124]

This innovation allowed Sinan to design the rectangular central fountain of the forecourt, no longer needed for ablutions, as a decorative drinking fountain that once sprayed water from its

179 Süleymaniye mosque, Istanbul, interior toward the qibla wall.

180 Süleymaniye mosque interior toward the east, with the royal tribune at the right corner.

181 Süleymaniye mosque, Istanbul, interior view of the domical superstructure.

ceiling (illus. 178). The Frenchman Du Fresne Canaye (1573) was so impressed by this fountain, where 'thanks to a cunning artifice water falls like rain into a square basin of marble', that he judged it 'dignified enough to be compared with the most famous grottoes of Naples'. It is yet another artistic invention mentioned in the *Tuḥfe*, where it is likened to the pool of paradise.[125]

The structure of interior space is perfectly legible from the exterior of the mosque (illus. 170). The 'triumphal' triple arches of the central domed baldachin, defined by pairs of colossal red granite columns on each side, are reflected on the mosque's lateral façades in the form of three fenestrated arches topped by domes (illus. 179, 180). One of the novelties in the prayer hall is its arcaded inner galleries raised on precious columns at the east and west sides, complemented by private loggias inserted between the north buttresses. The spatial continuity between interior and exterior is particularly strong in the tripartite qibla wall. Its floral İznik tiles and stained glass windows create an illusion of transparency, as if the funerary garden visible from the ground-level windows is continuous with the mosque interior. According to Evliya, the odours of flowers filled the prayer hall from these open windows, 'perfuming the minds' of the congregation as if they had entered heaven.[126] The longitudinal axis that begins at the monumental north portal of the forecourt and passes through the main gate culminates at the mihrab with an earthly vision of paradise. The white marble mihrab, with its muqarnas hood evoking a gate, invites the congregation to enter into the promised eternal garden represented by the actual garden containing the mausolea of Süleyman and Hürrem.

The visual continuity between interior and exterior creates a feeling of unboundedness inside the mosque. Lokman poetically describes this spatial effect: 'All four sides are opened up with pleasure-increasing windows on multiple layers, from which Space and Time is exposed.'[127] Eyyubi exclaims that inside the mosque 'the garden of paradise becomes visible to the mystically inclined' (*ehl-i ḥal*).[128] The interior space of the Süleymaniye, evenly lit by 249 windows in multiple tiers, 'is overwhelming but not mysterious'.[129] The central theme of the mosque has been defined as a 'structural criticism' and 'rationalization' of Hagia Sophia's scheme by means of a more centralized spatial conception (illus. 181).[130] In contrast to the dim, mysteriously lit interior of Hagia Sophia, covered with glittering gold mosaics that hide its structure (illus. 74), the white stone interior of the Süleymaniye is characterized by a rigorous geometrization and articulation of architectonic forms to express structural strength.

182 Süleymaniye mosque, Istanbul, the qibla wall, from a nineteenth-century photograph.

Inside the prayer hall, only the qibla wall features stained-glass windows and İznik tile revetments (illus. 182, 183). The remaining tiles are concentrated on the north façade facing the forecourt (illus. 184), and at the two mausoleums. The costs of these tiles, and of paper given to Hasan Karahisari (Hasan Katib) for designing the inscriptions of the mosque and those of Hürrem Sultan's mausoleum, are listed in the Süleymaniye's account books together with painters' wages and materials, which included lapis lazuli and gold leaf.[131] Karahisari's painted calligraphy on the domes is more legible than its counterparts in the Şehzade mosque. The latter's concentric circular inscription bands are substituted here by roundels with radiating letters in gold that resemble rays of light emanating from heavenly bodies (illus. 161, 181).[132] The original dome paintings, no longer extant, are described by Ramazanzade Mehmed as replete with dazzling 'sun-like disks' and medallions composed of gold and silver designs.[133]

At the Süleymaniye mosque Sinan formulated what would become his 'classical' idiom of architecture, clad by a novel decorative skin of underglaze-painted İznik tiles that banished to oblivion the Persianate aesthetic of *cuerda seca* tiles. Borrowed from chancery illumination, the ornamental patterns of the qibla wall tiles (*c.* 1556–57) are too minute to be visible from a distance. This shortcoming was remedied in Hürrem Sultan's mausoleum (*c.* 1558–59), where tile patterns are magnified to make an impact from afar. The emergence of a new repertoire of semi-naturalistic floral motifs is paralleled by the stylistic unification of calligraphy in a single preferred mode of writing, monumental *thuluth*. The *Tezkiretü'l-bünyān* praises the inscriptions of the mosque:

> The late Hasan Karahisari, the qibla of scribes, inscribed in the *müsennā* script (lit. script doubled in size) the Koranic verse 'God keepeth the heavens and the earth' from beginning to end on the sky-like dome, and he eagerly volunteered [to compose] appropriate inscriptions for each paradise-like door, designing many a heart-attracting written line, which stonecutters and painters drew on the pages of Time, attaining fame and repute by carving them in marble.

A poem eulogizes the calligrapher, who seems to have been a personal favourite of Sinan: 'Some say that in *thuluth* and *naskh* Hasan / Is unquestionably better than [Ahmed Kara]Hisari; // Some say that in *müsennā* Hasan / Has become the world's second Yakut [al-Mustaʿsimi]'.[134] This declaration of Hasan Karahisari's superiority to former masters, including his teacher Ahmed Karahisari, explains why the chief architect later on requested Hasan to design the inscriptions of the Selimiye.

The interior of the Süleymaniye is relatively sombre in comparison to the interiors of the Şehzade and Selimiye mosques because its lateral porticoes, protected by overhanging eaves, limit the amount of light that filters into it. This heightens the atmosphere of sober dignity and gravity that is present inside the sanctuary. Decorative restraint characterizes the predominantly white interior and exterior walls, which omit the red sandstone accents used in the façades of the Şehzade and Selimiye mosques. The waqfiyya indicates that gilding and jewel-encrusted decorations were deliberately downplayed in conformity with the Prophet's traditions that oppose luxurious ornament in mosques:

> If decorating masjids and beautifying sanctuaries with silver, gold, and jewels had been a requirement of the religion of Islam and approved by the shariʿa of the Prophet Muhammad, gilding the foundations and structure of the above-mentioned noble mosque and gracious sanctuary with silver and gold, as well as encrusting its gates and walls with rubies and pearls, would certainly have been planned to glorify this place of worship for God and to present thanks for His benevolent favours. It was stripped bare from gold and bejewelled ornamentation because they paid attention to its correctness (*iḥkām*) and lawfulness (*ibrām*).[135]

The reference here to jewel-encrusted, gilded decorations can be read as a response to written descriptions of the Hagia Sophia, which present the church as Justinian's competition with the Temple of Solomon not only in its monumentality but also its

183 Süleymaniye mosque, Istanbul, İznik tile calligraphic roundel flanking the mihrab.

184 Süleymaniye mosque, İznik tile window lunette on the north façade.

glittering bejewelled decorations.[136] The decision to downplay ornament at the Süleymaniye mosque is in keeping with the elderly sultan's newly adopted austerity. Although the interior of the mosque exhibits the finest samples of the decorative arts, which are praised in the *Tezkiretü'l-bünyān*, it favours dignified solemnity over lavish display and excess. The result is a severe magnificence that inspires awe and reverence like the persona of its patron.

The epigraphic programme of the Süleymaniye can be interpreted as a manifesto of the sultan's official policy of religious orthodoxy, a theme missing from the inscriptions of the Şehzade mosque that emphasized the role of the Prophet as a guide to the scriptures revealed by God. The programme was formulated at a time of wars against the Safavids, who agreed in 1555 to implement the requirements of the shariʿa in their domains. The Süleymaniye inscriptions resonate with Ebussuud's fatwas, discussed in Chapter 2, that enforced the compulsory performance of the five daily communal prayers and the Friday noon prayers. The Arabic foundation inscription composed by him identifies the mosque as a place for those who dedicate themselves to congregational prayers and divine worship. Celalzade notes that the epigraphic programme was exclusively Koranic. In all likelihood, it was masterminded by Ebussuud himself, who was then writing his famous commentary on the Koran for Sultan Süleyman. Reminding the congregation about the religious duties incumbent on orthodox Muslims, the inscriptions liken the mosque to the paradise promised to obedient worshippers.[137]

The paradise metaphor is expressed by Koranic passages carved in stone above the lateral gates of the mosque and its forecourt, which invite the congregation into the garden of paradise (39:73, 16:32, 13:24). The Sunni profession of faith is prominently inscribed above the muqarnas hood of the north portal providing access into the forecourt (illus. 177). The Koranic passage over the arch of the gate reminds the congregation of its communal ritual duties: 'Worship at fixed hours hath been enjoined on the believers' (4:103). The same theme is repeated inside the courtyard, in rectangular panels carved above the central north and south arcades (illus. 178): 'And those who are attentive at their worship, these will dwell in gardens honoured' (70:34–35); 'Be guardians of your prayers, and the midmost [Friday noon] prayer, and stand up in devotion to Allah' (2:238). The rectangular İznik tile lunettes on the right side of the north façade quote the Throne verse (2:255) which affirms the absolute sovereignty of the all-knowing God. The lunettes on the left cite the last verse of the Fath sura (48:29), which promises God's 'forgiveness and immense reward' to those followers of the

185 Süleymaniye mosque interior, Istanbul, lateral triple arcade with two monolithic red granite columns and two white columns composed of cylindrical drums.

186 (below) Hürrem Sultan mausoleum: (left) interior view, (right) detail of İznik tiles with blossoming trees.

Prophet who bow and prostrate themselves in worship, seeking bounty from God.

The themes of worship and divine forgiveness are further elaborated inside the prayer hall (illus. 181). The north half-dome reads: 'O ye who believe! Bow down and prostrate thyself, and worship thy Lord and do good and haply ye may prosper' (22:77). The exedral half-domes flanking it quote thematically related verses: 'Recite that which hath been revealed to thee of the Scripture, and perform worship. Lo! Worship preserveth from lewdness and iniquity' (39:45). Inscriptions on the south half-dome above the mihrab (6:79) and the exedras that flank it direct the congregation to turn toward God in worship (7:29, 2:115). The north–south mihrab axis intersects with the vertical axis of the central domed baldachin, whose cosmic symbolism is reinforced by Koranic roundels professing God's supreme power over the cosmos and human destiny. The verse quoted on the central dome implies a parallel between the cosmos held steadily in balance by the Divine Creator and the heavenly dome of the mosque, firmly supported on piers: 'Lo! Allah graspeth the Heavens and the Earth so that they deviate not, and if they were to deviate, there is not one that can grasp them after him. Lo! He is clement, forgiving' (34:41). The four calligraphic roundels on the pendentives once again stress the absolute power of the merciful God, who needs no

intermediaries to judge the conduct of his subjects (11:88, 13:16, 17:84, 6:102).

The four colossal piers are decorated with roundels that bear the names of the first four caliphs, representing the pillars of Sunni theology, and the Fatiha sura (1:1–7) repeated on the qibla wall.[138] Two roundels, inscribed 'Muhammad' and 'Allah', are placed higher up on the pendentives of the half-dome over the mihrab. Another pair of roundels, inscribed 'Hasan' and 'Husayn', appears on the piers of the anti-qibla wall. Missing in the Şehzade mosque, these two additional names (commonly used in Sinan's later mosques) exemplify the ecumenism of the Sunni orthodoxy formulated by Ebussuud. The four rectangular marble plaques over the lateral arches of the central dome, supported by the four colossal red granite columns, sequentially cite a verse promising everlasting felicity in paradise to the believer who follows the path of orthodoxy (9:112). The roundels on those arches display invocations that rotate the divine epithets (illus. 185).

The two rectangular inscription panels above the west and east gates sequentially quote a verse ensuring those who leave the prayer hall that the merciful God forgives all sins (39:53). Panels over the upper gallery windows surrounding the central space on three sides invoke the ninety-nine beautiful names of God, some of which are repeated in the stained glass windows of the qibla wall (illus. 182, 185). The window above the mihrab quotes the profession of faith along with the names of Allah, Muhammad, and the four Sunni caliphs; the light verse is intricately inscribed in cartouches along its border (24:35). The *shahāda* is repeated on two rectangular marble panels that flank the mihrab, whose muqarnas hood is topped by a panel quoting the standard mihrab verse (3:37). The two İznik tile calligraphic roundels cite the Fatiha sura (1:1–7), which begs God, the 'Owner of the Last Judgment', to show the 'straight path' to favoured believers. The tilework window lunette next to the minbar, with its star-studded conical cap, enjoins the congregation to worship the one and only God (72:18). The corresponding lunette next to the royal tribune advises believers to wear beautiful apparel in places of worship (7:31). The sultan's muqarnas-hooded private mihrab is inscribed with another verse using the word 'mihrab' (3:39), which appears on the mihrabs of some late mosques attributed to Sinan: 'And the angels called to him [Zachariah] as he stood praying in the sanctuary [*mihrab*].' The royal mihrab is flanked by a pair of windows whose lunettes quote the only hadith cited in the mosque, which alludes to Sultan Süleyman's justice: it announces that those who act with justice are raised above minbars of light in the sight of God.

187 Interior of Süleyman's mausoleum, Istanbul.

The two mausoleums behind the qibla wall elaborate the paradise theme, common in other funerary structures. With its innovative floral İznik tiles, Hürrem Sultan's octagonal mausoleum evokes the lavish pavilions promised to believers in the gardens of paradise (illus. 186). Süleyman's waqfiyya explains that the sultan built it to commemmorate his beloved late queen, the Zubayda (Harun al-Rashid's wife) of the age, who is destined to dwell in paradise with the Prophet's daughter Fatima, his wives 'A'isha and Hadija, and the Basran female mystic Rabiʿa (d. 801). The mausoleum which is said to amaze 'those with perceptive vision' (*erbāb-ı naẓar*)[139] is compared to the Garden of Eden and the 'dome of paradise'. The exterior of its cylindrical stone drum is carved with a monumental *thuluth* inscription that quotes the Throne verse (2:255), followed by several related verses believed to protect the deceased during the Day of Judgment (3:18-19, 26).

Flanking the gate of the mausoleum, illusionistic pictorial panels composed of blue-ground İznik tiles represent eternal spring gardens, each with a blossoming tree amidst tulips and carnations. Set above imitation-marble skirting tiles, these panels prepare the visitor for the dazzling sixteen-sided interior of the mausoleum, sheathed with İznik tiles up to the second tier of stained-glass windows. The interior tiles depict perpetually blossoming trees, semi-naturalistic flowers, peonies, and palmettes, accompanied by inscriptions consisting of supplications in Arabic for God's protection in the other world.[140] The seven rectangular window frames, surmounted by arched İznik tile lunettes and epigraphic panels, alternate with eight mihrab-like muqarnas-hooded niches. The light-filled, cheerful mausoleum personifies the queen, whose name means 'smiling, joyful, fresh, and blooming'. Süleyman addressed her in a love poem as, 'my spring, my joy, my glittering day, my exquisite one who smiles on and on.'[141] These emotions are captured in Hürrem's mausoleum, in which Du Fresne-Canaye saw 'porcelain vases, the most beautiful ones in the world, filled with fragrant flowers', and the queen's cenotaph, decorated with 'many extremely rich embroideries' and a 'very precious headdress featuring an aigrette of rubies and turquoises'.[142]

The maintenance expenses of the Süleymaniye complex in the 1580s list ceramic vases for decorating its mausoleums with flowers cut from the cemetery garden (the oversupply of flowers and fruits was sold for the benefit of the waqf).[143] Süleyman's more monumental octagonal mausoleum, aligned with the mihrab axis, is crowned by a double dome and surrounded by an outer and inner arcade with precious columns (illus. 187). Its plan distantly recalls the layout of the Dome of the Rock in Jerusalem, associated with Solomon, which the sultan renovated. The Venetian diplomat Marcantonio Pigafetta (1567–68) reports that marble plaques removed from Hagia Sophia in 1567, because Ebussuud and the ulema blamed their presence for a recent earthquake, were reused in the mausoleum pavement. Their Greek inscriptions recorded the decrees of a Byzantine church council held at Constantinople in 1166.[144] The sanctity of Süleyman's mausoleum is enhanced by a piece of the black stone from the Kaʿba set into the keystone of the tympanum arch above its entrance. The sepulchre once contained architectural models of the sanctuaries in Mecca and Medina, which Süleyman had restored.[145] Du Fresne Canaye says that the mausoleum, where prayers were continually chanted, was considered a 'very sacred place'. He reports that the cenotaph, covered by a green textile, displayed the black-plumed white turban and the kaftan that the sultan wore during his last victorious campaign.[146] Wratislaw von Mitrowitz (1591–96) saw displayed inside the mausoleum Süleyman's bow and arrows, commemorating his identity as a ghazi warrior.[147]

The mausoleum gate is flanked by two İznik tile panels and a Koranic inscription affirming the unity of God, the eternal judge (28:88). The epigraphic band around the İznik-tile clad interior quotes the Throne verse, particularly popular in funerary architecture, and the two verses that follow it (2:255–58).[148] The painted decorations of the dome are studded with glittering rock crystals and gems that create a bejewelled effect deemed indecorous for the mosque. Unlike Hürrem's cheerful mausoleum, however, that of Süleyman is sombre, in accord with the sultan's majestic persona. Light filters into its dim interior from the portico eaves and upper stained-glass windows, decorated with 'seal of Solomon' motifs. Its İznik tile revetments feature abstract floral designs rather than the naturalistic blossoming trees that so conspicuously decorate the queen's mausoleum.

Despite the originality that Sinan displays in the dependencies of the Süleymaniye complex, contemporary descriptions generally focus on the mosque. The *Tuhfe* attributes numerical symbolism to the minaret galleries representing the patron's title, 'tenth of the Ottoman sultans', which appears on the foundation inscription.[149] Their dynastic message is recognized by several authors, including Lokman, who compares the ten galleries to 'necklaces indicating that the sultan's person is the tenth sovereign of this caliphal dynasty'.[150] Celalzade assigns them religious significance as 'signs and symbols of the Prophet Muhammad's ten companions'.[151] Both Celalzade and Sai interpret the dome and four minarets of the Süleymaniye as iconic representations of the Prophet, who is the 'Dome of Islam', and his 'four friends', the Sunni caliphs.[152] The four piers and four red granite columns supporting the central dome are likewise compared to the Sunni caliphs in one of Sai's poems:

> This well-proportioned mosque became the Kaʿba,
> Its four columns became the Prophet's four friends.
>
> This house of Islam supported by four pillars,
> Became firm with the Prophet's four friends.[153]

As we have seen in Chapter 4, the *Tuhfe* emphasizes the difficulty of hoisting in place the four colossal granite columns, accompanied by inner and outer colonnades on both sides of the mosque, and balancing on top of them the five lateral domes according to the science of statics. European and Ottoman observers did not fail to be impressed by the rich marble collection of the Süleymaniye and its four granite columns, each worth a fortune.[154] The elaborate search for columns and precious marble panels, discussed in Chapters 4 and 5, augmented the imperial prestige of the mosque and its paradisiac allusions. The waqfiyya, which refers to the patron of the mosque as 'the second Solomon and the Alexander of the age', compares it to the legendary Iram (an ancient columnar garden palace built by the

188 Melchior Lorichs, Mosque complex of Sultan Süleyman, 1570, woodcut.

emperor Shaddad to imitate paradise on earth, the columns of which were reused by Alexander).[155] The appropriation of marbles associated with Solomon (from Cyzicus and Baalbek), with Alexander (from Alexandria), and with the Byzantine emperors (from Constantinople) echoed Justinian's use of spolia in the Hagia Sophia.

The hunt for oversize columns all over the empire was necessitated by Sinan's elaborate design for the Süleymaniye, structurally more complex than the Şehzade, whose interior lacks columns. The design required eight enormous columns to support the lateral arches of the central baldachin and the five domes of varying size atop the side aisles. The four monolithic red granite columns (9.1 metres tall, 1.26 metres wide) originated from Alexandria, Baalbek and Constantinople, according to the *Tezkiretü'l-bünyān*. These are complemented by four others of the same size composed of superimposed white marble drums (illus. 185). Judging from the documents published by Barkan, it seems likely that each of these eight columns was planned to be of red granite: four were ordered from Alexandria, two from Baalbek, and two already existed in Constantinople (the Maiden's Column was removed in 1551 and the other column was available at the warehouse of the Topkapı Palace). The original plan did not materialize, probably because two of the columns from Alexandria sank in a ship, according to al-Tamgrouti (1589–91), whose source of information was an eyewitness who saw the four columns hauled through a hole opened in the city walls.[156]

The columnar supports of Süleymaniye, which increased the structural complexity of the mosque, called attention to Sinan's engineering skills and to Süleyman's imperial glory. Claiming that the chief architect was single-mindedly striving towards an ideal of spatial centralization, some scholars have negatively judged the longitudinal plan of the Süleymaniye as a 'retrogression' in the chief architect's stylistic evolution, brought about by his royal patron's intervention.[157] This assessment finds no support in Sinan's autobiographies, which proudly proclaim the Süleymaniye the feat that certified his artistic mastery and achieved the aim of surpassing all mosques built by former sultans. Āli maintains that the Süleymaniye came to be recognized throughout the world as a 'rarity of the ages and all times'.[158] Indeed, such European travellers as Fynes Moryson (1576) and John Sanderson (1594) judged it a masterpiece that matched the seven wonders of the world (illus. 188).[159] Costantino Garzoni (1573) states that the Süleymaniye was esteemed as much as Hagia Sophia with its 'lofty and beautiful structure', being inferior to it 'neither in grandeur nor in architecture'.[160]

Evliya Çelebi asserts that 'in the Ottoman empire, one of the world-famous mosques is the Süleymaniye and the other one is the Selimiye.'[161] He extols the former's unparalleled structural solidity:

> In the lands of Islam no monument stronger and more
> solid than the Süleymaniye mosque has been built;
> all engineers agree that in this world no monument
> as firm as the Süleymaniye and no dome like its heavenly
> dome exists. The strength of its foundations, the elegance
> embodied in each of its corners, and the perfect con-
> clusion of all the magical arts characterize both the
> interior and exterior of this mosque![162]

The Süleymaniye is imagined as an unshakeable mountain by Evliya, who puts the following words into Sinan's mouth: 'My Emperor, I have built for you such a mosque that it will remain on the face of the earth until the Day of Judgment, and when Hallaj Mansur comes to shake Mount Damavand from its foundations, he will be able to shatter that mountain, but not this dome!'

Foreign travellers frequently compare the Süleymaniye with Hagia Sophia, though not always with the same verdict. Even the most favourable comparisons comment on the smaller size of the sultan's mosque. For instance, Carlier de Pinon (1579) writes that Süleyman's mosque, which 'does not at all cede Hagia Sophia in beauty and magnificence', was nevertheless estimated to be two cubits smaller.[163] This criticism seems to have provoked Sinan to build a dome competing in size with that of Hagia Sophia in his next imperial mosque, the Selimiye in Edirne.

Evliya Çelebi describes the visit of a committee of ten European architectural experts, who kept biting their fingers in astonishment as they toured the Süleymaniye, accompanied by its gatekeepers and janitors. Upon examining the dome they removed their hats as a sign of homage, exclaiming 'Maria! Maria!' When Evliya asks what they think of the mosque, one of them answers:

> Every creature and every building is beautiful either within or without, but never do these two kinds of beauty coexist. However, both the interior and exterior of this mosque have been built in a charming manner (*şīrīnkārlıḳ*). In the whole of Frangistan (Europe) we have never seen such an exemplary building so perfect in the science of geometry.

Evliya then asks him to compare the Süleymaniye with Hagia Sophia, and the expert answers:

> True, the latter is an ancient work in brick, built larger than this mosque. It is an immense building of ancient times, artistic in terms of solidity, but in terms of pleasantness (*leṭāfet*), elegance (*zerāfet*), purity (*neẓāfet*), and charm (*şīrīnkārlıḳ*), this [Süleymaniye] is a more artistic, exemplary building. Regarding costs, more money has been spent on this mosque than on Ayasofya.[164]

In this comparison, which certainly reflects Evliya's own aesthetic evaluation, the Süleymaniye is judged superior in its refined elegance and its costly stone masonry.[165] The monumentality of Hagia Sophia is admired yet perceived as representing an antiquated taste, different from the 'modern' Ottoman aesthetic.

In terms of decorum, Justinian's Hagia Sophia, designed as the *templum novum Solomonis*, was a perfect model for the mosque of Süleyman, the second Solomon. Widely circulating mythical histories which describe the inauguration ceremony during which Justinian declared, 'Solomon, I have surpassed you!' made the Solomonic associations of Hagia Sophia apparent to Ottoman audiences. Its potent cultural associations in the Ottoman collective memory rendered the Süleymaniye's imperial iconography transparent. The mosque complex translated into architectural terms the image of Süleyman, 'the quintessence of the House of Osman',[166] who personified the universal sultanate and caliphate. As a stronghold of Sunni orthodoxy, the Süleymaniye simultaneously glorified God, the divinely appointed sultan, and Sinan's artistic mastery. Its restrained magnificence reconciled imperial majesty with the austerity of orthodox religion upheld by Süleyman, who is hailed in a chronogram composed for his mosque as 'Patron of Friday prayer, Sunni Shah, Solomon of the Age!'[167]

THE TAKİYYAL-SULAYMANİYYAA, DAMASCUS

The first Ottoman sultan to build a Friday mosque and hospice complex in Damascus was Selim I, who victoriously entered the city in 1516 after having defeated the Mamluks outside Aleppo. He settled with his encampment at the Ablaq Palace, also known as the Sultan's Mastaba, built by the Mamluk ruler al-Zahir Baybars at an *extra-muros* hippodrome to the west of the city (Gök Meydan or Maydan al-Akhdar, Sky Blue or Green Hippodrome). Returning to Damascus after his victory in Egypt, Selim I stayed at the Ablaq Palace for four months during the winter of 1517–18.[168] On that site his son Süleyman would later build a Friday mosque and hospice complex overlooking the verdant banks of the Barada river (illus. 189–91). Named after its alternating courses of black basalt and ochre-white limestone that were reused in Süleyman's complex, the Ablaq Palace was a symbolically charged site because the defeated Mamluk sultans had held their councils of justice there, and the maydan extending in front had been the former polo field of Mamluk cavalry soldiers.

Historical sources report that Selim spent the winter of 1517–18 hunting, carousing, and administering justice there. It was then that he commissioned a mosque complex next to the tomb of Ibn al-ʿArabi (d. 1240), in the suburb of Salihiyya.[169] Aimed to consecrate the newly established Ottoman regime,

189 William Henry Bartlett, *View of the Barada River in Damascus and the Takiyya al-Sulaymaniyya, with tents of Hajj Pilgrims*, c. 1836, engraving.

this memorial monument was a thanks-offering to the sufi shaykh Ibn al-ʿArabi whose esoteric works allegedly predicted Selim's conquest of Syria. An endowment deed drawn up in 1518 explains how the shaykh's debris-covered grave had been left to ruin by 'bigoted fanatics' who viewed his teachings as heretical. Selim honoured his burial place overlooking a lush garden with a domed mausoleum, accompanied by a Friday mosque and a hospice (*ʿimāret*) across the street.[170] The Arabic foundation inscription on the courtyard gate of the hypostyle mosque cites its date as 923–24 (1517–18). It was rapidly constructed by a team of local masons under the supervision of the Damascene chief architect, Shihab al-Din Ahmad b. al-ʿAttar, who must have served the Mamluks earlier.[171]

Functioning as a charitable convent (referred to variously as a *tekye*, *takiyya*, *zāviye*, and *ʿimāret*), the hospice was built after the sultan left Damascus in 1518, following the ceremonial inauguration of his mosque.[172] It was the novelty of this characteristically Ottoman building type, uncommon in the Mamluk period, that gave the complex its popular name: Takiyya al-Salimiyya.[173] Writing in the 1590s, the geographer Mehmed Aşık was nevertheless quick to recognize the Mamluk-flavoured style of Selim I's complex, which he perceptively attributes to Damascene architects:

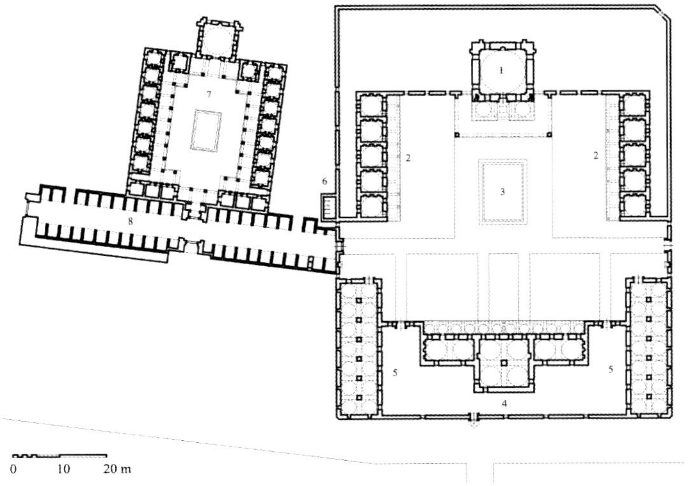

190 Plan of Takiyya al-Sulaymaniyya, Damascus:

1. Mosque
2. Guest-rooms
3. Ablution pool
4. Hospice
5. Caravansarays with stables
6. Latrines
7. Madrasa
8. *Arasta*

191 Axonometric projection of Takiyya al-Sulaymaniyya.

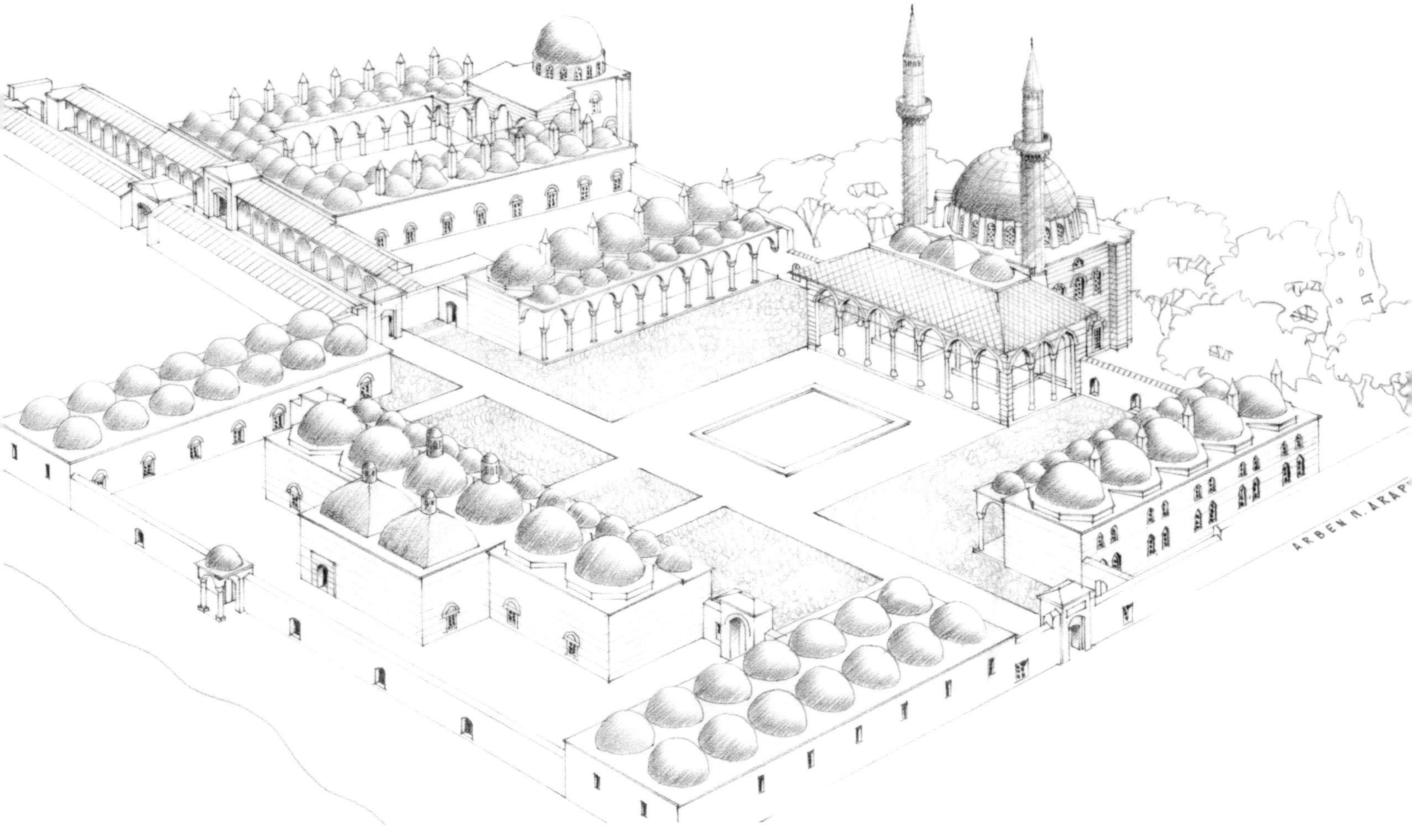

194 Takiyya al-Sulaymaniyya, guest-rooms with bulbous domes at the mosque courtyard, with ablution pool.

192 (top) Takiyya al-Sulaymaniyya mosque, Damascus, from the north.

193 (above) Takiyya al-Sulaymaniyya mosque from the south.

Besides reviving and repairing the illuminated mausoleum, on its west side he built a lofty and exalted Friday mosque in the plan and style of Friday mosques in the Arab lands. And to honour the soul of that shaykh, at the north of the Friday mosque, across from a public avenue, he built a lofty hospice (*ʿimāret*) comprising a pantry, bakery, kitchen, and other dependencies to benefit the needy residents of the Salihiyya quarter. One descends by ten stone steps to the shaykh's mausoleum from the east side of the courtyard of the noble Friday mosque, and it is in an exhilarating location. And the minaret of this mosque, too, is designed after the minarets of the Arab lands. The mosque, its minaret, and other elements conform to the design and plan of architects from the Arab lands because in the days of the conquest of Damascus it was probably not deemed suitable to wait for the arrival of masons from the Ottoman lands (*diyār-i Rūm*).[174]

The stylistic continuity of Selim's complex with Mamluk precedents paralleled the sultan's non-intrusive policy in the newly conquered province, whose first two governors were former Mamluk officers: the ex-governor of Aleppo, Khayrbak, replaced in 1518 by the ex-governor of Damascus, Janbirdi al-Ghazali. Perceived as the symbolic locus of Ottoman-Hanefi rule in Syria, the sultan's complex was closed down by al-Ghazali when he rebelled after Selim I's death.[175] The seditious governor's head was cut off in 1521 by Sultan Süleyman's janissary troops under the command of one of his viziers, following a military confrontation outside the city walls near the Sultan's Mastaba. The Takiyya al-Sulaymaniyya built three decades later on that site was the first Ottoman-style monument erected in Damascus, which became the capital of a new province established in the beginning of Süleyman's reign by dividing Syria-Palestine into two regions governed from Damascus and Aleppo.

The complex visually affirmed the consolidation of the new political regime in Damascus, more fully integrated into the Ottoman domains by non-native governor-generals appointed from Istanbul (illus. 190, 191). Its foundations seem to have been laid during Süleyman's last Persian campaign, while he stayed in Aleppo between 8 November 1553 and 3 April 1554, following the tragic deaths of princes Mustafa and Cihangir. According to the local historian ʿAbd al-Basit b. Musa al-ʿAlmawi (d. 1573), the complex was created soon after Süleyman ordered his son Mustafa's execution.[176] The guilt-ridden and distraught sultan may have felt that an additional charitable foundation, complementing the one that was being built for him in Istanbul, might increase his chances for salvation in the other world. During his stay in Aleppo, he spent most of his time hunting and administering justice, particularly reorganizing the waqfs of Aleppo and Damascus that had been 'unjustly' managed under Mamluk rule.[177]

Doctors had prescribed hunting as a remedy for the phlegmatic temperament caused by Süleyman's inconsolable grief over the loss of his sons. In thanks for his companionship during

195 Takiyya al-Sulaymaniyya, Damascus, underglaze tile lunette from the hospice façade.

196 Takiyya al-Sulaymaniyya, mosque portal.

those hunts outside Aleppo, the sultan promoted Şemsi Ahmed (at that time the agha of cavalry soldiers) to the governor-generalship of Damascus, a post he occupied in the mid-1550s.[178] Şemsi Pasha (who later commissioned Sinan to build a mosque in Üsküdar) seems to have overseen the construction of the sultan's complex during his term there. Historians date the foundation of the mosque complex to 962 (1554–55) and its completion to 966 (1558–59). The pasha, a renowned poet, composed the Turkish inscription carved above the gate of the mosque. Its chronogram yields the completion date of 966 (1558–59) for the main core of the complex, which comprised a Friday mosque and hospice (*ʿimāret*).[179] A madrasa, added later, was not part of the original plan.

The construction of the charitable complex overlapped with Süleyman's renovations during the 1550s at the Harams in Mecca, Medina, and Jerusalem where his wife founded three hospices. The endowment deed of the Damascus complex (written soon after the inauguration of the Süleymaniye mosque in Istanbul) was registered on 14 May 1557, close to the completion date of its main core in 1558–59. It only refers to the Friday mosque and hospice.[180] The added madrasa, funded by the surplus of endowed revenues, reached completion at the beginning of Selim II's reign in 974 (1566–67). With its professorship assigned to the Hanefi mufti of Damascus, the madrasa complemented the one built for Süleyman next to the Meccan Haram in 1564–65, whose four professors, representing the Sunni legal schools, also drew their salaries from the waqf revenues of the sultan's complex in Damascus.[181]

According to al-ʿAlmawi, the construction of the madrasa in Damascus was initiated under the Persian endowment administrator and overseer Mawlana Molla Agha al-ʿAjami, who acted as the first building supervisor. The first Arabic-speaking Hanefi professor arrived from Istanbul prior to its completion. This reference has led some scholars to misattribute the construction of the madrasa to a Persian architect. Agha al-ʿAjami was temporarily replaced by another building supervisor called Mustafa. When he was reinstated, he enlarged the complex and changed the original endowment stipulations accordingly.[182]

An imperial decree sent to the governor-general of Damascus in 1567, soon after the completion of the madrasa, inquires about plans to add a dervish convent (*ḫānḳāh*) to the complex. The proposed site was an incomplete barrack for janissaries at Gök Meydan, whose construction had been abandoned because they might indulge in mischief at a place so far removed from the walled city.[183] The new endowment administrator appointed to the complex in 1568 asked for a copy of the sultan's previous order approving the construction of a convent with twenty rooms.[184] Another decree sent to the kadi and endowment administrator in 1573 reveals that the convent had not yet been built. Its recipients are asked to check whether 'the rooms constructed on top of shops in between the madrasa built on my father's behalf and the large caravansaray located across from it are usable by dervishes.' After investigating whom that caravansaray belonged to, they were to convert these upper rooms into a convent, if deemed appropriate.[185] A follow-up order addressed to the governor-general of Damascus in 1576 indicates that the earlier option of transforming the incomplete janissary barracks into a convent was preferable, because the rooms above the shops did not provide enough seclusion to the dervishes:

> You have sent a letter to my court of felicity reporting that previously when an order was received about the construction of a convent (*zāviye*) for shaykhs and sufis with the surplus of the endowment, in addition to the imperial hospice, madrasa, noble Friday mosque, and caravansaray that had already been built in Damascus for my forebear, the late Sultan Süleyman, the endowment administrator had in his possession a noble decree ordering him that the already built rooms near the madrasa should be assigned to the dervishes if these were deemed suitable for a convent. When the site was inspected together with many Muslims, it was seen that the aforementioned rooms, located above the courtyard wall of the madrasa, had each been built spaciously in masonry, but that they were not made in the manner (*üslūb*) of a convent. Therefore, the present shayk Nasuh did not consent to their use as a convent, since the group of sufis would come into contact with the people in the shops underneath. But at Gök Meydan, near some other buildings, the construction of a strong building had been started previously as a dormitory for janissaries. Using quarried stones, four high walls had been built, but given that site's location outside the city its construction was abandoned due to the possibility that the janissaries may cause mischief there. Since you have reported that it would cost little to buy that structure for the endowment and build a convent inside it, I order that when [this decree] arrives, in accordance with your petition have twenty rooms built in that place and demolish the rest. Reusing the [old] timber during the construction of those rooms, take care not to overspend.[186]

These decrees show the involvement of local government officers, kadis, and members of the Muslim community in the negotiation of decorum during the protracted planning process of the convent. An account book of Süleyman's endowment in Damascus from the year 1596, which lists the wages of two alternating convent shaykhs and twenty dervishes, indicates that the convent had finally been built (it is no longer extant). This account book, which reflects changes in personnel brought about by posthumous contructions, lists the components of Süleyman's complex: a Friday mosque, madrasa, dervish convent (*ḫānḳāh*), guestrooms (*tābḫāne*), and hospice (*ʿimāret*) composed of a kitchen (*maṭbaḫ*), bakery (*furun*), pantry (*kilar*), refectory (*ma'kel*), and a charitable double caravansaray (*ḫān-ı sebīl*) whose two long hypostyle halls flank the hospice on both sides.[187]

The account books of the Süleymaniye complex in Istanbul document the amount of lead sent for the superstructure of the mosque at Damascus in 1558–59, when its original core was close to completion: 'Since lead is necessary for the needs of the noble Friday mosque that is being built in the protected city of Damascus the Noble, in accordance with the sultan's order, six thousand qintars of lead was given [for it] from the noble [Süleymaniye] mosque.'[188] The name of a royal architect sent to Damascus is also recorded in the Süleymaniye's account books, which cover expenses between November and December 1553. One of the entries reads: 'Paid to Müslihüddin Halife, who arrived from Damascus, for his own salary, with the mediation of Sinan Agha, the chief of architects: 300 [aspers].'[189] Müslihüddin, one of Sinan's assistants who headed a team of novices employed at the construction site of the Süleymaniye in Istanbul, may have been sent to Damascus with plans drawn by the chief architect (Appendix 4.4).[190]

Busy with the sultan's monument in the capital, Sinan seems to have designed its smaller provincial counterpart without going to Damascus. This direction from afar was facilitated by the unhindered openness of the site, which allowed him to create a symmetrical complex, unlike the Şehzade Mehmed or the Süleymaniye in densely urban Istanbul. Sinan probably remembered the Damascus site, since he had camped there with Selim I's troops. Müslihüddin Halife apparently stayed in Damascus for over a month (300 aspers corresponds to a daily wage of 10 aspers for thirty work-days) and may have been accompanied by royal architects and masons escorting the sultan's army in Aleppo. The architect put in charge of construction work was Mimar Todoros. On 17 June 1560, after a letter sent by the governor-general of Damascus to the capital reported the completion of the 'flourishing hospice', the 'non-Muslim called Todoros who had been appointed as its architect with a decree' received a promotion.[191] We do not know whether Damascus had a chief architect at the time, but a group of Damascene masons and decorators was almost certainly employed in the sultan's construction. The availability of skilled local architects is implied by the omission from Sinan's autobiographies of the mosque complexes built in Damascus for such governor-generals as Şemsi Ahmed Pasha and Lala Mustafa Pasha during the 1550s and 1560s.[192]

The madrasa, linked by a shopping artery (*arasta*) to the symmetrical core of the original complex designed by Sinan, was, like the now lost dervish convent an afterthought: it is only mentioned in the *Tuḥfe* and the convent is omitted altogether from the autobiographies.[193] Like the waqfiyya, the *Teẕkiretü'l-ebniye* refers only to the components of the original core of the complex situated at the east side of the hippodrome: the Friday mosque at 'Gök Meydan on the site known as Kasr-ı Ablak' and the 'hospice' (*ʿimāret*).[194] The bi-focal complex designed by Sinan is composed of U-shaped edifices at both ends of a rectangular walled enclosure bisected by a passageway. The passageway connecting the lateral gates of the walled precinct separates the mosque, fronted by rows of six guest-rooms on each side, from the hospice flanked by two caravansarays. The passageway along the east–west axis defined the flow of traffic between the oblique shopping arcade (linked to the walled city further east) and the hippodrome at the west. The central north–south axis on which the mosque and hospice are aligned is less accentuated than is the lateral axis because access is blocked from the north side by the Barada river.

The Takiyya al-Sulaymaniyya has aptly been compared to the vizier Çoban Mustafa Pasha's earlier complex in Gebze, which is listed in Sinan's autobiographies even though it was built under the supervision of his predecessor in the 1520s (illus. 27).[195] Sinan, who may have participated in its construction as a janissary, borrows from it such elements as the two long hypostyle caravansarays bisected by piers, the row of domed guest-rooms for privileged travellers, and the hospice (composed of a kitchen, bakery, refectory, and pantry). The madrasa and dervish convent included in Çoban Mustafa Pasha's semi-urban funerary mosque complex on the hajj route are notably absent in the first phase of Süleyman's complex in Damascus.

Executed by local builders, the typically Ottoman plan of the madrasa (perhaps designed by Sinan) differs from the iwan-type madrasas of Damascus, but it has a strong local flavour unlike the mosque. The dome of its classroom, raised on a simple polygonal drum, has a bulbous profile characteristic of Damascene domes from Ayyubid and Mamluk times. By contrast, the mosque, which was overseen by a royal architect, is crowned by a Sinanesque hemispherical dome raised on a window-pierced drum with engaged pilaster-shaped tapering buttresses and a pair of flying buttresses at each corner (illus. 192, 193). It is a simple domed cube, constructed with alternating courses of black and white stone on its exterior, but its interior is faced with white stone. Its royal status is articulated by conical-capped twin minarets with muqarnas-friezed single galleries. The wide double portico that conceals the small size of the mosque is a trademark of Sinan. The three-bay first portico has columns with muqarnas capitals that carry a central cradle vault flanked by two domes. The second portico with a slanting roof supported on smaller columns with lozenge capitals defines a handsome façade with seven pointed arches, echoed by those around the courtyard with its bulbous domes (illus. 194). Three arches on each side of the mosque portico are connected to a window-pierced garden wall. The arch-shaped iron-grilled windows that flank the north façade provide pleasant vistas from the shady portico into the garden at the back, as in several other mosques designed by Sinan.

Arched lunettes with underglaze-painted tile revetments decorating the porticoes of the guest-houses and the hospice visually unify the central courtyard (illus. 195). The white marble mosque portal, framed by a frieze with polychrome geometric designs in the local manner, has a typically Ottoman triangular muqarnas hood that differs from its conch-shaped Ayyubid and Mamluk counterparts (illus. 196). The portal is flanked by windows and a pair of mihrabs with raised prayer platforms. The interior of the mosque, with its plain dome raised on four pendentives, no longer preserves any of the original painted decorations and inscriptions (illus. 197). Compared to its elaborate Arabic counterpart in the Süleymaniye, the laconic Turkish foundation inscription cited below by Mehmed Aşık hints at the simple epigraphic programme of the mosque. The polychrome marble dadoes between each window are composed of pink and white vertical strips inset with white roundels framed in black squares. The muqarnas-hooded mihrab featuring polychrome geometric inlays is inscribed with the standard Koranic verse (3:37) seen in most Ottoman mihrabs. The minbar of white, pink, and black marble has a Mamluk-type domical cap. A marble muezzin's tribune, raised on columns with pointed arches, occupies the right side of the entrance. The window lunettes are decorated with underglaze-painted tiles of uniform design in white, sage green, cobalt blue, turquoise, and a pale red that tries in vain to approximate the intense tomato red of İznik. Lacking naturalistic flowers, the designs are dominated by palmettes, rosettes, and *saz* leaves. The local workshop that produced them in the late 1550s seems to have been associated with Süleyman's renovation of the Dome of the Rock in Jerusalem with tile revetments. According to Mustafa Āli and the signature of a Persian tilemaker, ʿAbdullah Tabrizi, the renovation project was completed in 1551–52. Perhaps the potters moved to Damascus after the conclusion of work at the Haram (briefly resumed in 1561–62), establishing a local industry that catered to the needs of late-sixteenth-century Ottoman monuments in the city.[196]

In terms of their colour scheme and patterns, the locally produced tiles of the Takiyya al-Sulaymaniyya are less innovative than those made in İznik for the sultan's mosque complex at the capital. They nevertheless introduced to Damascus a novel mode of decoration associated with Ottoman visual culture. The regional Damascene elements of Süleyman's complex, such as striped masonry and polychrome marble panelling, are largely ornamental. These localisms could have been avoided if the goal had been to impose an entirely foreign architectural style without indigenous affiliations. The preference for a hybrid approach resulted in a distinctive regional idiom: a fitting visual metaphor for the inclusive colonizing policies of the Ottoman regime which often allowed local traditions to coexist with new ones imported from the capital.

The large rectangular ablution pool in the courtyard of the mosque is a case in point. Featuring a central *jet d'eau* and spouts in the middle of each side, it represents a compromise catering to both Hanefi and Shafiʿi congregations. Provided that they were ten by ten square cubits in surface area and deep enough, water

197 Takiyya al-Sulaymaniyya, Damascus, mosque interior.

tanks (preferred by the adherents of the Shafiʿi legal school) were considered equivalent to running water by the Hanefis, who regarded flowing water as the cleanest source for ablutions.[197] The ablution pool of Süleyman's mosque simultaneously accommodates the Hanefi preference for running water and the Shafiʿi custom of performing ablutions from pools.

Minarets with conical caps and a profusion of lead-covered hemispherical domes must have been quite a novel sight in Damascus when the complex was first built. The symmetrical distribution of free-standing dependencies, sensitively merging with the landscape, was another novelty. Pre-Ottoman complexes differ from the Takiyya al-Sulaymaniyya in their organically integrated blocks tightly fitted into the urban fabric. The local scholar al-ʿAlmawi noticed the unfamiliar Ottoman elements of Süleyman's mosque, such as the absence of a northern minaret punctuating the mihrab axis. He curiously attributes the placement of the two minarets along the east-west axis to the fact that its architects were mostly recent converts to Islam.[198] He nevertheless appreciates the new architectural style of the complex:

> This mosque combines materials, stones, clear and coloured marble worked artistically, and lead-covered domes that awe the spectator and give joy to the soul; and it contains rooms and private cells, each of them featuring a dome and a chimney and windows overlooking the mosque, a kitchen, and a refectory built with extreme solidity, and two minarets on the east and west sides ... The artistic work of the dome, minbar, and mihrab is mind-boggling; and the pool at the courtyard of the mosque is among its charming features, and at the qibla side of the mosque is an enclosed garden replete with all kinds of fruit trees and flowers.[199]

The Ottoman visual identity of Süleyman's mosque complex was obvious to the geographer Mehmed Aşık, who notes its difference from Selim I's earlier 'Arab style' complex. He singles out four *extra-muros* mosque complexes as representatives of the 'Ottoman style' in Damascus, among which that of Süleyman was the earliest. The rest were commissioned by governor-generals whose names they still carry: Murad Pasha (1568/69–1575/76), Derviş Pasha (1574–75), and Koca Sinan Pasha (1586–91). Mehmed Aşık observes that 'these four mosques built during the reign of the Ottoman sultans do not display the style and plan of mosques in the Arab lands; in terms of their building style and plan they conform to mosques in the [northern] Ottoman domains (Anatolia and Rumelia).'[200] It is worth quoting his detailed description of Süleyman's complex:

> Of these four mosques one was built by the late Sultan Süleyman, may he rest in peace, at the eastern end of the wide arena called Gök Meydan, which is a gathering place for the high and low. Attached to its east and west walls are two well-proportioned minarets and between these two minarets is a joy-giving and exhilarating stone-masonry mosque with a single small dome covered by lead. And the mihrab of this mosque is built completely with ochre stone on which inscriptions and decorative mouldings are carved. In its [foundation] inscription, the saying 'He who builds masjids for Allah' is inscribed, and it is placed in the middle of the north wall across the mihrab. And in this inscription the following date is given for the construction of the mosque by a poem of Şemsi Pasha: 'Sultan Süleyman, son of Selim, built such a hospice that / Meals in Damascus became submerged in benefaction. // Şemsi briefly said

its date, / The Friday mosque of the Sultan of Rum gave new life to Damascus.' And on both sides of the gate of the mosque are two raised platforms under small domes.[201]

The geographer then describes the courtyard flanked by guest-rooms and the pergola that once covered the passageway extending between the east and west gates, like the one at the Süleymaniye's funerary garden (illus. 171):

> And in front of these platforms is a spacious courtyard. And the courtyard is paved with black and white stones resembling marble. On the east and west sides of this courtyard are elegant and clean verdant meadows five mason's cubits wide along the east–west axis, and fifteen mason's cubits long along the south–north axis. And next to these two meadows is the banquet house for guests (*ziyāfetḫāne-i misāfir*) which consists of chambers under lead-covered domes. They are adjacent to one another and extend along the south–north axis. And these chambers of the banquet house for guests extending on both sides are twelve wide rooms, six on each side. And in front of these rooms, which overlook the courtyard of the mosque, are twelve small, lead-covered domes on each side resting on twelve marble columns, that is, a total of twenty-four small domes. And in the middle of this courtyard is a quadrangular pool whose north–south side is longer than its east–west side. In the middle of this pool is a fountain (*şādırvān*) of solid marble from which water flows nonstop. At the centre of each of the four sides of this pool is a brass spout from which water flows continually. This enclosed courtyard is bounded on its north side by a wooden fence which in the Turkish language is called railing (*ṭrabzon*). And across this railing, separated from it by one-and-a-half mason's cubits to the north, is another railing, and between these two railings is a public street. And the top of these two railings is covered with [a pergola of] grapevines. Beyond the two railings, on the north side, is an elongated small garden, its length extending along the east-west axis and its width along the south–north.

The description finally turns to the hospice and madrasa:

> At the north end of this garden is a lofty hospice (*ʿimāret*) consisting of a pantry, kitchen, bakery, and other dependencies. Behind the banquet house for guests at the east side of the mosque courtyard is built a lofty madrasa containing eighteen rooms surmounted by lead-covered masonry domes. Its professor receives a daily wage of sixty Ottoman aspers and has the duty of pronouncing fatwas according to the Hanefi rite in Damascus. Its students, who study the sciences there daily, receive two aspers and food twice a day from the aforementioned hospice. And from the kitchen, food is also provided to those who arrive at the banquet house for guests located in the courtyard of the mosque. May God comfort the soul of its builder.

Mehmed Aşık devotes only a few sentences to the simple mosque, focusing instead on the symmetrical layout of the complex, which modern scholars also regard as its most notable feature.[202] For him the dome and minaret constitute the primary signifiers of the provincial Ottoman style in Damascus. For instance, Murad Pasha's mosque has a single dome in the Ottoman manner, but its minaret is 'in the style of minarets in the Arab lands'.[203] Derviş Pasha's mosque has a pleasant dome 'in the style of domes in the Ottoman lands' even though it is covered with Khorasan mortar instead of lead. Its stone minaret, too, is 'in the manner of minarets in the Ottoman lands'.[204] Koca Sinan Pasha's mosque, crowned by a lead-covered single dome, has a composite minaret faced with green-glazed tiles and is built 'in the Ottoman manner', but it features a shade above its gallery like the 'minarets of Arab lands'.[205] This stylistic dissection of hybrid provincial mosques built by governor-generals signals an intense preoccupation with visual identity markers.

Evliya Çelebi also recognizes the 'Ottoman style' (*Rūm ṭarzı*) of Süleyman's complex in Damascus, which he attributes to Sinan.[206] Likening the complex to a resort-like, pleasurable countryside retreat, he describes Gök Meydan as a popular place for evening promenades and fishing.[207] Intended as the final halting station in settled territory on the hajj route (before the pilgrim reached the desert which was dotted with Süleyman's fortified caravansarays), the Takiyya complex was surrounded by meadows and gardens along the river where pilgrims could pitch their tents. Along with Cairo, Damascus was one of the two main centres from which official pilgrimage caravans departed to the Holy Cities under the leadership of high-ranking Ottoman officials. Damascus became the annual meeting place of twenty to thirty thousand pilgrims arriving from the north of the empire and from Iran. The departure and return of the hajj caravan constituted a major ceremonial event, accompanied by an ostentatious procession that included the governor, local notables, and the army. During 1558–59, the year the Takiyya complex was completed, the Damascus caravan was escorted by 150 janissaries and a hundred cavalrymen, who probably assembled in Gök Meydan before leaving for the Hijaz.[208]

Although it was economically and demographically surpassed by Aleppo, Damascus enjoyed higher symbolic status in Ottoman imperial geography since it was the former capital of Syria and carried the architectural memories of several Sunni dynasties. Translations of popular medieval texts dealing with the early Muslim history and 'virtues' of Damascus attest to Ottoman interest in appropriating its prestigious royal legacy.[209] That is why Damascus is one of the few Arab cities honoured with the sultanic mosque complexes of both Selim I and Süleyman I, the

198 Nigari (Haydar Reis), *Prince Selim Practising Archery*, c. 1561–62, watercolour on paper.

only other exceptions being Baghdad and the three Holy Cities.

Situated on sites chosen for their symbolic significance, the royal foundations of Selim I and his son represented the two stages in which the new Ottoman regime was introduced to Damascus. The non-royal counterparts of these complexes, commissioned by governor-generals, have been interpreted by Kafescioğlu as 'acts of mediation between the central authority and the local population'. For instance, the appointment of a Hanefi and a Shafi'i professor in the madrasa of Derviş Pasha's funerary mosque complex signals an attempt to intermingle with Damascene local culture. Unlike Süleyman's imperial complex, which only employed Hanefis as its preacher, imams, and professor, that of Koca Sinan Pasha made these positions open to either Shafi'i or Hanefi candidates.[210]

Late-sixteenth-century mosque complexes sponsored by governor-generals in Damascus (none of them listed in Sinan's autobiographies) contributed to the development of an increasingly hybrid indigenous style. The Takiyya al-Sulaymaniyya remained the most typically Ottoman complex ever built in that city, for its design had been monitored by Sinan through architects sent from the capital. The relative independence of architectural practice in Damascus can be attributed to the consolidation of a regional office of city architects after the construction of Süleyman's complex. The three non-royal complexes mentioned by Mehmed Aşık must have been built under the supervision of the chief architect of Damascus, Zaim Davud (d. 1588), who was succeeded by Nakkaşoğlu İshak, appointed with Sinan's recommendation.[211]

With its striped ablaq masonry walls that reused stones from the dismantled Mamluk palace once occupying the same site, Süleyman's distinctive mosque complex in Damascus was a potent memory marker. It carried reminiscences of the former Mamluk regime, and of victorious Ottoman encampments pitched at Gök Meydan. It not only enshrined memories, but was also concerned with shaping the future. The Takiyya al-Sulaymaniyya articulated the new visual identity of Ottoman Damascus. Linked to a chain of roadside complexes along the hajj route extending from the Balkans all the way to Mecca, it architecturally expressed the invisible connection between Damascus and the distant capital Istanbul, where Sinan had recently inaugurated his 'classical' idiom with the mosque complexes of Şehzade Mehmed and Süleymaniye, also commissioned by Sultan Süleyman.

II. SULTAN SELİM II

Unlike his father, whose lengthy reign lasted nearly half a century, Selim II ruled for only eight years, between 1566 and 1574 (illus. 7, 30). He was already forty-two years old when he ascended the throne, having spent most of his youth as a governor in various sanjaks ([Karaman] Konya 1542–44, [Saruhan] Manisa 1544–58, Konya 1558–62, and Kütahya 1562–66). He secured his position as sole heir to the throne after his victory at Konya (1559) over prince Bayezid, who was executed at the court of Shah Tahmasp in 1562 (illus. 198).[212] The crown prince's three daughters from Haseki Nurbanu Sultan were married to prominent statesmen in 1562 to consolidate his future regime: İsmihan Sultan to Sokollu Mehmed Pasha, Gevherhan Sultan to Piyale Pasha, and Shahsultan to Hasan Pasha (she later married Zal Mahmud Pasha).[213] It was not until 1571 that Selim legally married his Venetian-born chief consort, Nurbanu, whose son Murad had been singled out as heir apparent from younger sons born from other women.[214]

The Venetian diplomat Marcantonio Donini described prince Selim in 1562 as a drunkard with an 'overly lascivious appetite'.[215] Marino Cavalli, the ambassador sent from Venice to congratulate his accession to the throne in 1567, noted the unpopular lifestyle of the new sultan, noting that he was unlikely to lead a military campaign because, 'besides eating and inordinate drinking, he is preoccupied with every kind of

L A M E N T O
ET VLTIMA
DISPERATIONE
DI SELIM GRAN TVRCO
per la perdita della sua Armata, il qual
dolendosi di Occhiali, & di se
stesso & d'altri,

R A C C O N T A   C O S E   D E G N E
d'esser intese. Con vn Dialogo di Ca-
ronte, & Caracosa, & altre com-
positioni piaceuolissime nel
medesimo genere.

STAMPATA IN VENETIA,

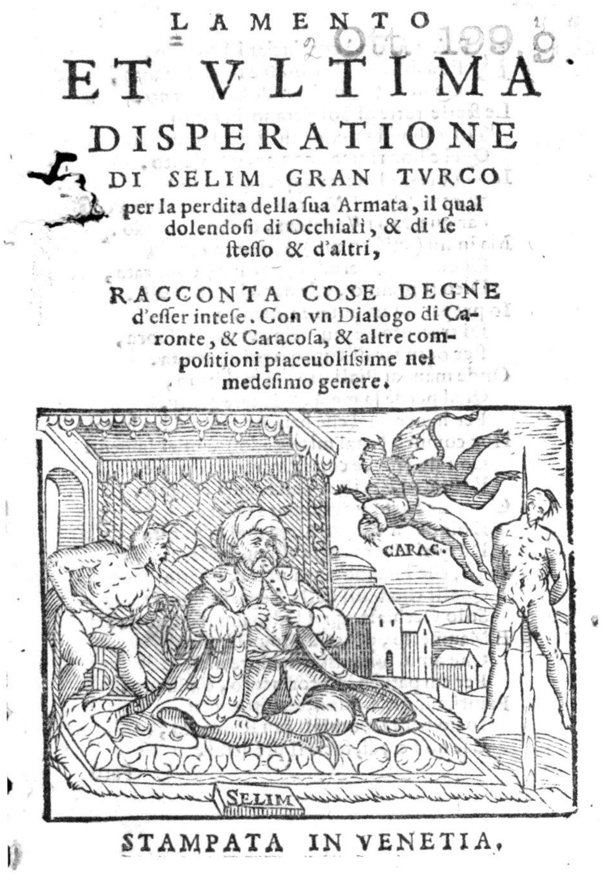

199 Selim II grieving after Lepanto, woodcut frontispiece from an undated Venetian pamphlet, *Lamento et ultima disperatione di Selim Gran Turco*.

voluptuousness one can possibly imagine, not wanting to be bothered with anything else.' Cavalli comments on the *bon vivant* sultan's extravagant tastes, his penchant for lavish costumes with multi-plumed turbans, and his days spent in leisure:

> He is fat and always very red in the face, which is a sign of the great amounts of liquor he consumes. He acts with an extreme gravity and affected manners, such as staying for an hour with downcast eyes, without ever moving, talking, or making a sign or gesture. He takes pleasure in dressing extravagantly, with jewels, perfumes, and plumes… In a boat he often goes to gardens where he entertains himself by drinking more than he can support. He has four to six companions whom he calls *Musaipi* (*musahib*).[216]

Selim II was fond of sumptuous robes of silk and brocade, unlike his father who in old age came to prefer humble robes of camlet or wool. According to Lokman, he tinged his eyes with kohl, wore a *mücevveze* type turban more voluminous than that of his father, and wanted to inspire awe with his opulent attire: 'In exhibiting pomp he did not show any deficiency whatsoever, for he used to appear in front of his enemies in full splendour.'[217] His notorious garden outings lasted several days and nights and were spent in feasting, drinking, and witty conversation in the company of poets, musicians, and boon companions. An accomplished poet with the pen-name Selimi, the sultan was also skilled in archery and particularly devoted to hunting in the woods of Edirne (illus. 198). He was a generous patron of the ulema and shaykhs on whom he is said to have showered donations.[218]

The sultan entrusted most affairs of state to his son-in-law, the grand vizier Sokollu. As he no longer participated in military campaigns, that task was delegated to his viziers. Relations with Safavid Iran remained cordial because of Selim's indebtedness to Shah Tahmasp for the elimination of his rival. An eight-year treaty signed with the Austrian Hapsburgs in 1568 also ensured peaceful relations at the western front of the empire. His reign was dominated by naval battles in the Mediterranean: he issued orders for the campaign of Cyprus as early as 1568, having sworn during his princehood to seize it from the Venetians, who had appropriated his personal goods sent by sea from Egypt.[219]

The shaykh al-Islam Ebussuud issued a fatwa that justified breaking the Ottoman-Venetian peace treaty with the argument that if a land had once been ruled by Muslims and its masjids became dilapidated after being conquered by Christians, an existing pact could be abolished.[220] A contemporary chronicler explains that the campaign of Cyprus was undertaken 'to renew the customs of Muhammad's religion' and 'to fulfil the requirements of the shariʿa'.[221] The island was conquered under the command of the sultan's former tutor, the vizier Lala Mustafa Pasha, in 1570–71. Its cathedrals, where the vestiges of early Islamic mihrabs are said to have been discovered, were converted to Friday mosques.[222]

European powers responded to the conquest of Cyprus swiftly and effectively. With the ensuing naval battle of Lepanto, the Ottoman fleet experienced its first major defeat by the allied Papal-Venetian-Spanish forces in October 1571 (illus. 199). The chief of the Prophet's descendants (Nakibüleşraf) from whom the grieving sultan sought consolation resorted to a time-honoured interpretation of this debacle as divine punishment inflicted by God for the unapproved actions and sins of the Muslims. He recommended that the 'monarch of Islam' should rebuild his decimated fleet to show the unbelievers the 'majesty and grandeur of the manifest religion', and to reconfront them with 'God's sword of power and the mighty upper arm of Islam'.[223] The widespread psychology of 'sinful times' is also voiced by Selaniki in a chapter of his chronicle entitled 'Complaint about the Circumstances of the Age'. He criticizes the weakened morals of the 'soldiers of Islam', who are now motivated not by 'the honour of the manifest religion,' but by worldly gains, and he blames rampant bribery in the sale of offices. This is surely 'a sign of the Last Judgment!'[224]

The fleet was rapidly rebuilt and Venice recognized Ottoman

200 Restored Hagia Sophia mosque, Istanbul, c. 1581, watercolour on paper, from Lokman, *Shāhnāma-i Salīm Khān*.

201 Mausoleum of Selim II at Hagia Sophia, Istanbul.

202 Interior of the mausoleum of Selim II at the Hagia Sophia, Istanbul.

supremacy in 1573 by agreeing to pay a war indemnity of 300,000 ducats. The success of the sultan's naval forces was affirmed with the conquest of Goletta in Tunis just before his death, which sealed Ottoman control of the North African littoral up to Morocco. The Mediterranean orientation of Selim II's campaigns ushered in an anti-Catholic ethos fuelled by the crusader mentality of the European Holy League, with its exaggerated celebratory propaganda after Lepanto (illus. 199). The ideological confrontation between Islam and the Latin Church helped dilute the Ottoman theological rivalry with the Safavids, and the puritanism of Süleyman's reign was tempered by the rising prominence of sufi orders compatible with Sunni orthodoxy.

Given his unbridled passion for wine and his hedonistic lifestyle, Selim II could hardly be expected to follow his father's rigidly austere path. Lokman characterizes Selim as having a 'dervishlike disposition'; among the sufi orders that flourished during his reign, the Halvetis came to occupy a particularly privileged position.[225] Just before his death, the repentant sultan is said to have summoned his confidant, the Halveti Shaykh Süleyman Efendi (nicknamed the 'Sultan's Shaykh'), to a last meeting at which the ruler 'sought penance with tearful eyes, begged for God's forgiveness, and made his last wishes', vowing to give up 'jollity and drinking' and 'music and parties'.[226] Abstention from drinking increased his frailty, yet he stubbornly refused to follow the advice of doctors who prescribed him wine as medication. Repenting for his sins when he realized the imminence of his death, Selim II is also said to have sought the company of his boon companion Şemsi Ahmed Pasha. During their final meeting at the arsenal garden along the Golden Horn, the penitent sultan once again wept continually from remorse. Passing away shortly thereafter at the age of fifty, he was buried at Hagia Sophia, where Sinan built his posthumous mausoleum (illus. 201, 202).[227]

Ottoman historians attribute the following architectural projects to Selim II: the completion of his father's Büyükçekmece bridge (1567–68); the Selimiye complex in Edirne (1568–74); the renovation of the black stone precinct of the Kaʿba with white marble pavements and domical arcades, a project completed under Murad III (1567–77); the extension of the ʿArafat water channel in Mecca with a new pipeline (1572–74); the conversion of two cathedral churches in Nicosia and Famagusta to mosques called Selimiye (1570–71); and the renovation of Hagia Sophia (1573–74).[228] Historians do not list among the sultan's architectural monuments the mosque complex that Sinan designed for him in Karapınar while he was a prince, which is mentioned in all three autobiographes of the chief architect. Nor do historians refer to relatively minor princehood projects near Manisa, which are included in his endowment deeds, such as a school for Koran recitation (*darülkurra*) and a dervish convent in Tire, another dervish convent in İzmir that was later converted to a madrasa, and an elementary school at Sardis.[229]

The renovation of the Meccan Haram and the ʿArafat water channel, discussed in Chapter 5, were projects intimately connected to the Cyprus campaign (illus. 137–38). The sultan's posthumous waqfiyya of 1579 boasts about the conquest of the island, which was aimed at securing overseas travel for hajj pilgrims and merchants, and its again being filled with religious monuments as in the ancient days of Islam. The waqfiyya explains that the renovation of the Hagia Sophia mosque was completed by Murad III, who built and endowed his father's mausoleum there (illus. 54, 56, 107–9, 200).[230] As we have seen in Chapter 3, the renovation began towards the completion of the Selimiye in Edirne. It transformed Hagia Sophia into a funerary sultanic mosque with its four minarets and imperial mausoleum, but the originally planned twin madrasas were omitted when the sultan passed away.[231] Like the four minarets surrounding the dome, the madrasas would have enhanced the long-distance dialogue between Hagia Sophia and the Selimiye complex, which features two madrasas. The intended connection between these imperial monuments is also suggested by an Italian source from 1575, which reports that 'Santo Sofia is now called Selimiye after the name of Sultan Selim'.[232]

An imperial tent was temporarily erected on the burial site, where vases with flowers lined the cenotaphs of Selim and his five sons executed in accordance with the law of fratricide to ensure dynastic stability (illus. 108–9).[233] Decked with splendid İznik tiles, the mausoleum designed by Sinan in 1574 was completed in 984 (1576–77) according to its Turkish foundation inscription, which likens it to 'the sublime garden of paradise', and gives its chronogram: 'the mausoleum of Sultan Selim of pure faith (*pāk dīn*)' (illus. 201, 202).[234] Like Süleyman's mausoleum, it is crowned by a double dome and has an inner arcade of eight columns, but its layered façades articulated by cornices and horizontal mouldings are not surrounded by an outer arcade (illus. 54[2]). With its more complicated spatial configuration and elaborate superstructure, the mausoleum inaugurates Sinan's post-Selimiye 'mannerism'. The 'tunnel-vault' windows cut into the lead-covered surfaces of the dome and exedras are a diagnostic feature of the chief architect's late style (seen in the mosques of Nurbanu Sultan, Kılıç Ali Pasha, and Molla Çelebi). The subdivision of the façades into two zones by a stringcourse moulding – in this case a unique classicizing torus moulding carved with bay leaf garlands – is another characteristic of the new style (continuous mouldings appear on the façades of mosques built in the capital for Sokollu (Azapkapı), Kılıç Ali Pasha, and Mesih Mehmed Pasha, and in Manisa at the Muradiye). The interior of the mausoleum introduces subsidiary flat-roofed vaults lined with contiguous strips of windows, a distinctive feature of royal mosques designed in the late 1570s and 1580s (the Muradiye, and the mosque of İsmihan Sultan and Zal Mahmud in Eyüp). The convergence of these innovations in Selim II's mausoleum, a project Sinan could not have delegated to an assistant, proves his personal contribution to the so-called manneristic style.

Compared to his father's empire-wide architectural patronage, Selim II's role as a patron of architecture remained relatively limited. With the exception of his princely mosque in Karapınar, his architectural enterprises largely involved renovation projects. In that respect, the world-renowned Selimiye complex in Edirne was not only Sinan's *tour de force*, but also the sultan's main claim to fame as a sponsor of monumental architecture. The princely mosque in Karapınar, ambitiously named Imperial (Sultaniye), paved the way for the grand sultanic mosque carrying Selim's name: Selimiye.

THE SULTANİYE COMPLEX IN KARAPINAR

Unlike the mosque complexes of Selim's late brothers, Şehzade Mehmed and Cihangir, posthumously built in the capital by their reigning father, his complex in Karapınar (ninety kilometres east of Konya) was commissioned by himself (illus. 203, 204). Since the mid-fourteenth century, Ottoman princes serving as sanjak governors had been denied the privilege of sponsoring public monuments. Prince Selim's license to build a mosque complex while he governed the sanjak of Karaman from its capital Konya (1558–62) was a breach of dynastic custom to which his father consented.

We learn from two decrees issued by Sultan Süleyman in 1560 that prince Selim had asked permission to build a masjid, khan, and bathhouse in a 'ruined village' between Konya and Ereğli, where he requested 120 tax-exempt households be settled. The sultan authorized the prince's construction project

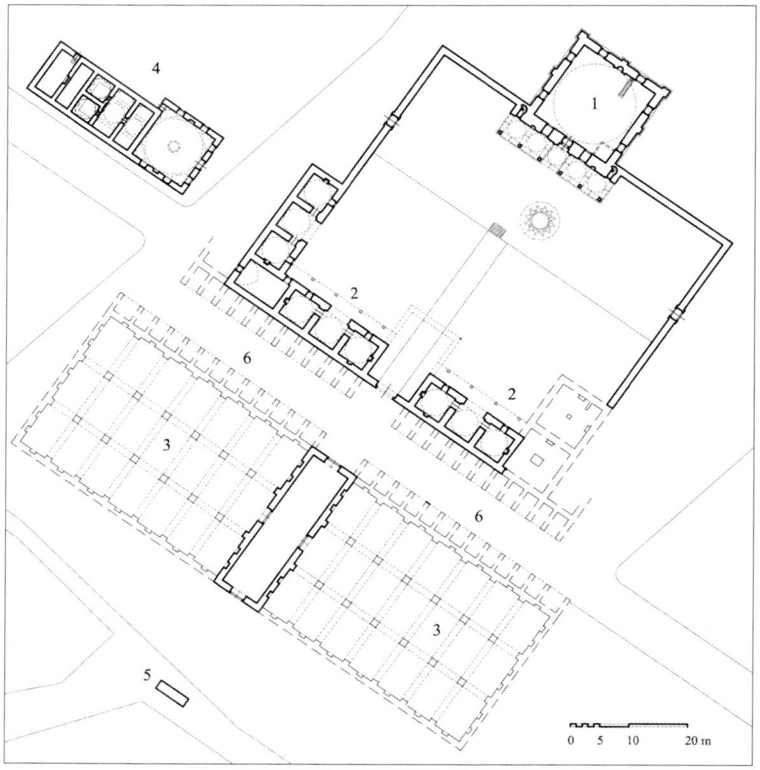

203 Plan of the Sultaniya complex, Karapınar: 1. Mosque. 2. Excavated remains of guest-rooms and hospice. 3. Double caravansaray (hypothetical reconstruction). 4. Bathhouse. 5. Public fountain. 6. *Arasta* with excavated shop foundations.

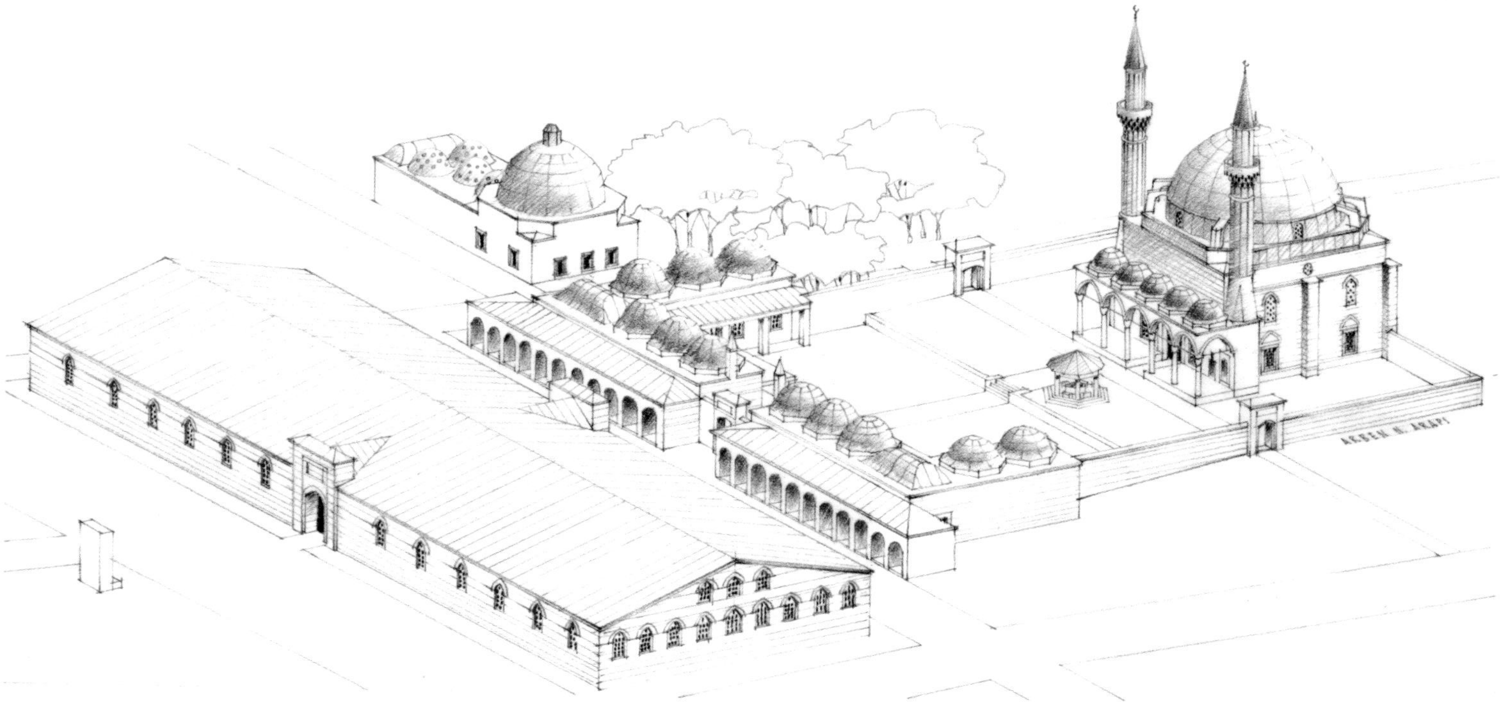

204 Axonometric projection of the Sultaniya complex, Karapınar.

205 Mosque of prince Selim, Karapınar, framed by the arched passage of the double caravansaray.

206 Mosque of prince Selim, Karapınar, interior.

207, 208 Mosque of prince Selim, Karapınar, from the north (top) and south (above).

in the uninhabited pass (*derbend*) known as Karapınar and ordered the requested settlement.[235] Three of Süleyman's surviving decrees related to this project date from 14 May 1560.[236] One of them appoints the kadi of Niğde as building supervisor, according to the prince's request.[237] The second commands the kadis of Karaman to dispatch builders and carpenters with their provisions to the construction site.[238] The third decree, sent to the kadi of Aleppo, announces the name of the architect designated for the prince's building project: 'As an architect is needed for the masjid, caravansaray, and bathhouse that my estimable son Şehzade Selim wants to build in the place called Karapınar, bringing the architect called Cemalüddin from the city of Aleppo has been decreed; I order you to send him without delay with the needed provisions, so that he arrives to work there as desired.'[239]

Yet another decree, issued in October 1563, commands neighbouring kadis to send provisions for the pantry of the 'hospice' (*ʿimāret*) in the 'place called Sultaniye' (Imperial).[240] The foundation inscription of the mosque, to which I shall return, gives the completion date of 971 (1563–64). The complex was composed of a Friday mosque with two minarets, a hospice, a double caravansaray, an elementary school, a bathhouse, a public fountain, and thirty-nine shops.[241] Lokman explains that it was created after prince Selim, together with his adviser Sokollu, pursued his defeated brother Bayezid from Konya to Diyarbakır and Aleppo, returning to Konya (December 1559) when his rival sought refuge at the Safavid court. On his way from Aleppo to Konya, Selim camped with his army 'in the desert called Karapınar, located between Ereğli and Ilgın'. Observing that this barren halting station lacked any sign of architecture and agriculture, he ordered the construction of a city and a charitable complex for which he appointed a 'building supervisor (*emīn*) and an architect (*miʿmār*)'. Lokman reports that the prince entrusted a considerable amount of gold to the building supervisor for the construction of an excellent mosque and hospice complex around which tax-exempt populations were settled to encourage development (*şenlik*), and that the site became a 'joy-increasing' city called Sultaniye, which had 'no equal in the west and the east'.[242]

The mosque complex, which changed the legal status of Karapınar from a forsaken village into a town, was built during the critical period when Selim and his father were negotiating with Shah Tahmasp for the execution of Bayezid. Its construction chronology coincided with that of Süleyman's mosque in Konya, whose foundations were laid in 1559–60 next to the *extra muros* shrine of Mevlana Celalüddin Rumi, on the site where prince Selim had pitched his tent during the war of princes (illus. 36–39). I have argued in Chapter 2 that the sultan's memorial mosque, supervised by prince Selim during his governorship of Konya (1558–62), was a victory monument commemorating the military triumph that Süleyman's candidate to the throne had won with the help of imperial troops, thanks to the sufi saint Rumi's spiritual support. Granted in 1560, the sultan's permission for the construction of the Sultaniye complex publicly affirmed his endorsement of prince Selim's legitimacy as heir apparent while Bayezid was still alive and a potential liability. Completed soon after the dynastic succession crisis was resolved in 1562, the Sultaniye complex along the much-traversed hajj route announced with its name the identity of the empire's next ruler.[243] Süleyman donated eighty-four villages and arable fields as the prince's freehold property for the endowment of the 'Sultaniye hospice and mosque' in 1562. These were supplemented with additional revenues in 1566, just before the sultan passed away.[244]

Several decrees issued by Selim II in 1568 show that he continued to develop the new town which grew around the nucleus of his complex. They document the construction of a water channel and fifty houses for the tax-free settlement of additional households; among the previously appointed 260 households, only forty-two had arrived.[245] The water channel that resuscitated the barren town was completed in 1569. It is described by Lokman:

> The site lacked water like the desert of Kerbela;
> to receive the grateful prayers of the thirsty and for
> the love of God, in addition to the expenses of several
> municipal constructions, more than three million aspers
> were spent from the private imperial treasury for a water
> channel. Water was brought from a distance of three days,
> from the high plateau of Ovacık in Karacadağ whose
> 360 springs were gathered at several collecting reservoirs.
> Thus water began to flow into the city like the Tigris river;
> thereafter its gardens bloomed with trees and flowers
> and its baths and mills started to function.[246]

The generosity of the sultan is commemorated in a Turkish inscription composed by the poet Meşami of Konya. It is carved above the pointed arch of the public fountain, sited across a street in front of the complex, and refers to four other fountains distributed throughout the city:[247]

> The Shah of the world's Shahs, the builder of Sultaniye,
> That is, the prosperity-spreading Shah Selim Khan
>
> Gave an order and pure water began to flow
> So that those burning with thirst could drink it with joy.
>
> These five fountains began to flow like the Prophet's
> fingers,
> It is as if that Shah performed miracles.
>
> When Meşami saw the gushing of those fountains,
> He said their date: 'The springs of Kauthar have flown.'
>
> O God! O Muhammad! The year 977 (1569–70).

The off-centre ablution fountain in front of the mosque (rebuilt in 1784) bears a repair inscription dated 1596, which once again refers to Selim II, who caused its water to flow.[248] Two decrees sent by the sultan in 1571 to the kadi of Sultaniye and the endowment administrator of his complex mention additional posts not listed in the waqfiyya (now lost) that increased the personnel of the Friday mosque, hospice, and elementary school.[249] Decrees issued during Murad III's reign reveal that absenteeism plagued the town, whose tax-exempt settlers only showed up there during official inspections. It was only after the enforcement of stricter measures by the state that the town gradually flourished and its population rose to over 900 households by the late sixteenth century.[250]

Sited in a valley, the Sultaniye complex has a symmetrical layout, with the public fountain and the mosque punctuating the ends of its north–south axis, which bisects the double caravansaray (now in ruins) and the dilapidated hospice-cum-guest-house.[251] Three arched gates mark the central passageway on that axis, which frames a perspective of the mosque to those approaching it from the street of the fountain (illus. 205). Two smaller gates mark the ends of the east–west axis, which is defined by a shopping arcade (*arasta*) whose shops are no longer extant.[252] The U-shaped guest-house and hospice form a garden courtyard in front of the mosque. The bathhouse, which produced income to support the complex, is asymmetrically located at the east side, and the elementary school has disappeared.[253]

The cross-axial layout of the ensemble, where the central qibla axis intersects with the secondary commercial axis of the shopping artery, is an innovation further developed by Sinan in Sokollu's complexes at Lüleburgaz, Havsa, and Payas of the late 1560s and 1570s. The chief architect, who camped at Karapınar during the campaign of the Two Iraqs in 1534, may have remembered the uninhabited rural site. The availability of space permitted the creation of a symmetrically designed complex, which the Aleppine architect Cemalüddin must have executed on the basis of a plan sent from the capital.[254] Cemalüddin was selected either by Sinan (who designed a mosque complex in Aleppo for Hüsrev Pasha, *c.* 1546–47) or by prince Selim and his adviser Sokollu (the latter wintered in that city in 1559–60 to monitor the moves of the refugee prince Bayezid).[255] A recently discovered archival document shows that a royal architect called Mimar Mehmed had served in the 'noble Friday mosque of the prince built in the place called Sultaniye' from its foundation until its completion.[256] Hence his income from a fief (*timar*) yielding 6,000 aspers was raised to 15,000 aspers on 20 December 1563. This was probably a royal architect sent from Istanbul to oversee the construction, entrusted to Mimar Cemalüddin; he may have been either Mimar Mehmed Subaşı or Mimar Mehmed Çavuş (Appendix 4:4).[257]

The Sultaniye complex was once dominated by its dependencies, which are built of rubble masonry, unlike the ashlar masonry mosque and monumental gateways. The beige sandstone mosque is a domed cube preceded by a portico with five domes raised on columns featuring muqarnas capitals (illus. 207, 208). The portico is flanked by two elegantly proportioned minarets with muqarnased single galleries. An old photograph shows that there was once a second outer portico with a slanting wooden roof.[258] The dome is raised on a curved cylindrical drum with four windows and pairs of flying buttresses at each corner. The drum lacks the typically Sinanesque pilaster-shaped, engaged buttresses seen in Süleyman's mosque at Damascus (1554–58/59). The layered walls of the Sultaniye mosque are composed of three receding zones. The east, west, and south walls, cautiously reinforced with buttresses at the corners and in the middle, have pairs of two-tiered windows. The sparsely fenestrated façades signal the provincial character of the harmoniously proportioned mosque, whose marble gate has a classicizing conch shell instead of a muqarnas hood.[259]

The simple interior is dominated by a dome raised on four pendentives that descend close to the floor level (illus. 206). The muqarnas-hooded marble mihrab, the minbar, and the muezzin's tribune at the northwest corner are carved in a plain manner. Kuran notes the 'tasteful simplicity' of the interior space, which clashes with the brash red, blue, and green of renovated paintings.[260] He has shown that the system of proportion used for the elevations was generated by basic modular dimensions of the ground plan: half the diameter of the dome and one side of the square walls. As Goodwin observes, the mosque 'depends entirely on exactitude of proportion' for aesthetic effect.[261]

The purpose of prince Selim's mosque is announced in the Arabic foundation inscription carved in two lines of *thuluth* script contained within six cartouches above its gate:

> Our God, accept this building from us,
> And generously endorse our repentance and guide us in the right direction.
>
> When this noble Friday mosque is completed,
> May our God, the Most High, accept it!
>
> The invisible speaker said its date:
> 'Indeed this is a place of worship which was founded upon duty [to Allah] (9:108).'[262]

The inscription, framed as an address to God, simulates the voice of prince Selim, whose name is decorously omitted as a humble gesture of deference to his reigning father.[263] The chronogram yielding the completion date of 971 (1563–64) partly quotes a verse from the Tauba or Repentance sura, which emphasizes the foundation of the mosque on piety. The full verse promises divine mercy to repentant believers: 'A place of worship which was founded upon duty [to Allah] from the first day is more worthy for thee to stand [pray] in, wherein are men who love to purify themselves. Allah loveth the purifiers.'[264] The penitent prince presents the mosque as a pious offering to God, humbly begging for divine mercy and guidance towards the right path. The reference to repentance can perhaps be read as a vow of the prince to change his debauched lifestyle, or as an expression of sorrow over the fact that he had just fought his brother and undoubtedly killed many Ottoman soldiers. It addresses not only God, but also the users of the mosque and the people of Karaman, whose loyalty the unpopular prince was trying to win with his charitable foundation. The support of cities had been instrumental in the success or failure of many a prince competing with his brothers.

Compared to the Selimiye in Edirne, the epigraphic and decorative programme of the provincial princely mosque in Karapınar is notably simple. Inside the prayer hall a non-standard Koranic verse from the Shuʿara' sura (26:89), painted in red-on-white above the mihrab, can be interpreted as another reference to the patron. Selected because it includes the word *salīm* (whole, pure), a pun on Selim's name, this verse begs for God's forgiveness on the Day of Judgment: '[The day when wealth and sons avail not (any man) (26:88)] / Save him who bringeth unto Allah a whole [pure] heart (*qalb salīm*) (26:89).' The man with a 'pure' heart is the prince himself, known for his leanings toward sufism with its emphasis on the heart's inward purification. The reference to purity resonates with the foundation inscription, which affirms God's love of those who purify themselves. It is no coincidence that the same verse from the Shuʿara' sura appears on the private mihrab of the royal tribune at the Selimiye mosque in Edirne and at the vestibule of Selim II's mausoleum, which alludes to the sultan's 'pure faith'. The muqarnas hood of the Sultaniye mihrab is flanked by two painted roundels inscribed with invocations of divine epithets: 'O, the Clement one!'; 'O, the Omniscient one!'. Roundels of the eight revered names are painted above the mihrab and gate and on the pendentives. The only other extant inscription roundel is at the centre of the dome; it quotes a popular verse from the Fatir sura that exalts the absolute power of the clement and forgiving divine creator over the cosmos (35:41).[265]

The circumstances that triggered the construction of the Sultaniye complex did not leave a lasting imprint on the Ottoman collective memory. In 1648 Evliya Çelebi referred to it as the 'lead-covered monumental mosque of Sultan Süleyman inside the market-place, built by Mimar Sinan, which has a flourishing hospice with a refectory.' His misattribution of the complex can be explained by its anonymous foundation inscription and its imperial name: Sultaniye.[266] As the very first example of a provincial complex built by a crown prince in his seat of government, this was a monument for which no prototype existed. Single-galleried twin minarets announced the royal status of this relatively unindividualized provincial mosque, built to broadcast the crown prince's identity as future sultan.[267]

Executed by skilled local masons imported from the Karaman region, the Sultaniye mosque comes closer to Sinan's 'classsical' idiom than the heavily proportioned mosque of Sultan Süleyman in Konya, mention of which is omitted from the chief architect's autobiographies. The latter copies in reduced scale the archaic design of Mehmed II's mosque, omitting its marble-paved forecourt reserved for sultanic mosques in Istanbul and Edirne (illus. 36–39).[268] Based on an imperial prototype, its plan asserts Süleyman's authority, contested by the disobedient prince Bayezid and his supporters. By contrast, the sultan's smaller mosque along the hajj route in Damascus conforms to codes of decorum applied to roadside complexes like that of his son: featuring two single-gallery minarets, it is a simple cube crowned by a 10-metre dome and fronted by a three-bay double portico (illus. 190–91). Compared to Süleyman's complex in Damascus, that of his son on the same route is larger with its 14.80-metre dome and its five-bay double portico.

Lokman notes the unprecedented imperial prerogatives that prince Selim enjoyed after defeating his brother and becoming the 'acting representative and lieutenant of the sultanate (*ḳāymaḳām-ı salṭanat*)', excluding only permission to mint coins and to have the khutba read in his name.[269] His being allowed to build the Sultaniye complex during his father's reign was one of these royal privileges. Another prince who founded a mosque complex of his own in the sanjak he governed is Selim's son Murad, thanks again to his special status as heir apparent.[270] It was only after his accession that Selim II could commission Sinan to build a truly monumental mosque complex in Edirne with a uniquely individualized plan shaped by sultanic codes of decorum.

THE SELİMİYE COMPLEX

Le Corbusier compares the Selimiye, which dominates Edirne from its highest hilltop, to a crown: 'Adrianople is like a swelling on this vast plateau, culminating in a magnificent dome ... Sultan Selim gives the city a tiara of great splendour.'[271] The *Teẕkiretü'l-bünyān* portrays Sinan's incomparable masterpiece in similar terms (illus. 209, 210).

> This lofty domed mosque is the crown of the city of Edirne,
> Whose face is honoured by the Tunca river.
>
> You did such a favour to the inhabitants of Edirne, O Shah!
> That their hearts burst from their bodies with pleasure.[272]

In another passage, the sultan's gift to Edirne is declared an unrivalled monument of world architecture:

> After [Selim II] ascended the imperial throne with felicity,
> having an excessive regard and affection for the city
> of Edirne, he ordered [there] the construction of a mosque
> that would be matchless in the world. Therefore, this

humble servant drew up a plan (*resm*) for a monumental mosque in Edirne worthy of being seen by the people of the world.[273]

The Selimiye was the first grand sultanic mosque that travellers from Europe and the Balkans encountered on their way to Istanbul, and the last one they saw on their way back.[274] Its mountainlike silhouette concludes the triumphal axis of the imperial highway from Istanbul, along which the court travelled in peacetime and armies marched to Europe in wartime.

The Selimiye announced its patron's affection for Edirne, whose inhabitants had loyally supported his candidacy for the throne while he was posted there between 1548 and 1550 as lieutenant governor in charge of protecting the western frontier of the empire.[275] It was then that the prince developed a lifelong passion for the city, which he would continue to frequent for hunting and diversion throughout his sultanate. He spent the first year of his reign there, receiving the many ambassadors who came to congratulate him on his accession.[276] The lack of a light-filled 'modern' sultanic mosque in Edirne prompted him on 6 March 1568 to summon Sinan to add windows to the Old Mosque (Eski Cami).[277]

The Selimiye seems to have been planned at that time. A hitherto unnoted register recording periodic payments from the sultan's inner treasury for its construction shows that the first payment was made on 13 April 1568 and the last on 2 November 1574, about a month before the sultan's death (Appendix 2).[278] Decrees addressed in June 1568 to the building supervisor Halil Çelebi (the keeper of the royal purse in Edirne, who was later replaced by the ex-finance minister Hasan Çelebi), concern the collection of materials and timbers for the 'noble Friday mosque' and a kiosk at the New Palace along the Tunca river where the sultan was clearly planning to spend more time.[279] In August 1568 the overseer of the Samokov mines, who had just dispatched an order of iron for 'the noble Friday mosque and flourishing hospice that is going to be built in Edirne', was asked to send nails to the imperial arsenal at the capital, where ships were being constructed for the impending naval campaign of Cyprus.[280] The collection of building materials coincided with campaign preparations in 1568 and 1569. The Genoese diplomat Battisto Ferraro reported on 15 October 1569 that several galleys loaded with 'large columns' in Alexandria were going to drop off their load at Rodosto (Rodoscuk, now Tekirdağ) for the sultan's 'New Mosque' in Edirne.[281]

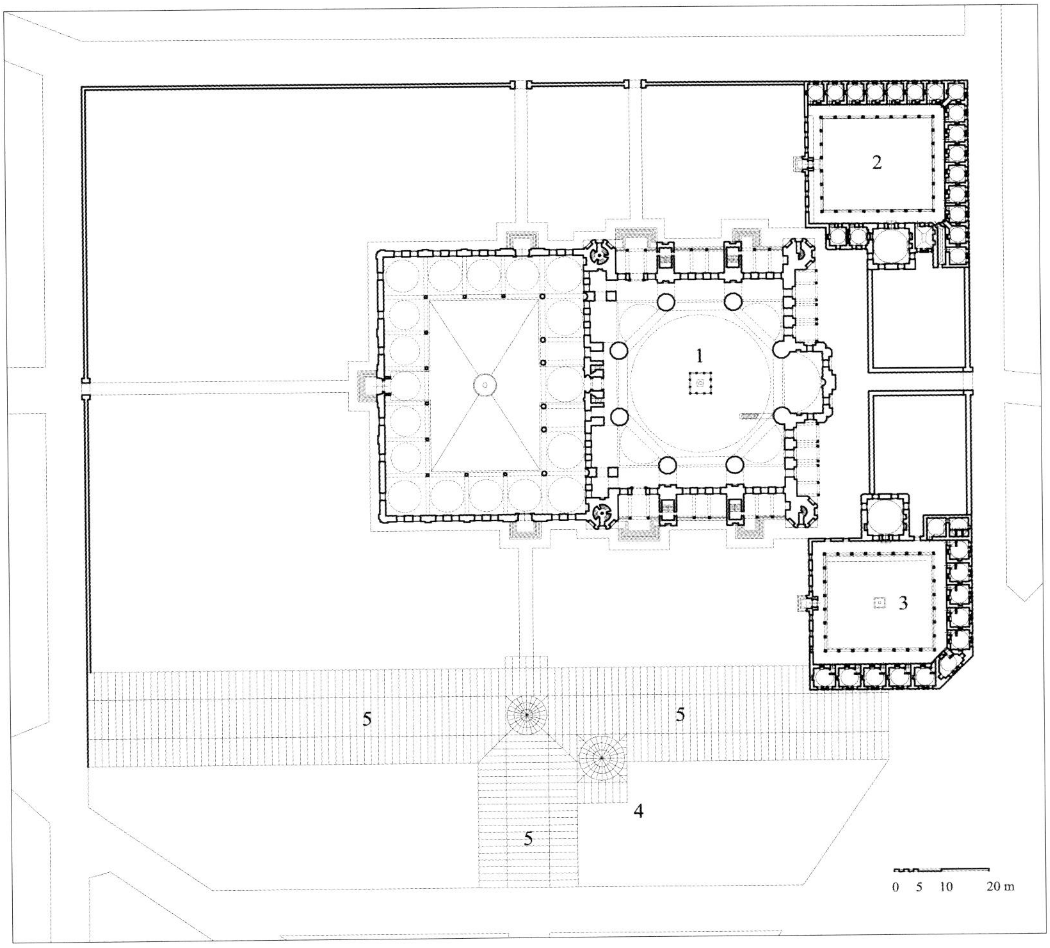

209 Plan of the Selimiye complex, Edirne:

1. Mosque
2. Madrasa (hadith college)
3. Madrasa (Koran recitation school)
4. Elementary school
5. *Arasta*

The *bailo* Marcantonio Barbaro informed the Venetian Senate on 30 April 1569 that Selim II was planning to spend the following winter in Edirne because he adored the city and was having a '*superbissima Moschea*' built there:

> His majesty has sent men to diverse parts of the Levant in order to search for antique edifices, to make use of their columns and marble panels for the mosque that is being built in Andrinopoli, which in reality is going to be a thing most noble (*nobilissima*), both in its size and in the excellence of its columns, marble revetments, and rare stones.[282]

Barbaro reports that the kadi of Edirne discouraged the sultan from revisiting the city because carts needed to haul the construction materials would have to be redirected to provisioning the court. Not heeding the kadi's warning that the arrival of the whole court might cause shortages and famine, the sultan ordered him to find additional carts.[283]

An archival register records the gold-and-silver brocade robe of honour awarded to Sinan on 12 April 1569, after the foundation ceremony.[284] Lokman says that the foundations of the 'New Mosque', on the site of the Old Palace of Edirne, were laid in 976 (1568–69) at an auspicious time determined by astrologers, reaching completion 'within six years'.[285] The foundation inscription discussed below confirms that it was built between 976 (1568–69) and 982 (1574–75). As we have seen in Chapter 2, it was common practice for sultans to lay the foundations of a mosque before embarking on a military campaign, with the hope that the spoils of victory would be dedicated to its construction and its endowments. The assertively monumental layout of the Selimiye, designed just before the conquest of Cyprus, reflects Selim's self-confidence and sense of certainty in imminent triumph: Nicosia was taken in July 1570, and Famagusta surrendered in August 1571.

European and Ottoman writers concur that the mosque was financed with the sultan's legal share of booty from Cyprus, revenues of which were assigned to its waqf.[286] The buoyant victory was followed by the Lepanto disaster in October 1571, about which the sultan learned on the day he arrived in Edirne with his whole court. The chief of the Prophet's descendants (Nakibüleşraf), who interpreted the defeat as a divine punishment inflicted on the sinful Muslim community, urged the ruler to undertake a jihad as the protector of Islam.[287] Hence, the final stages of construction were infused with a pensive mood and

210 Axonometric projection of the Selimiye complex, Edirne.

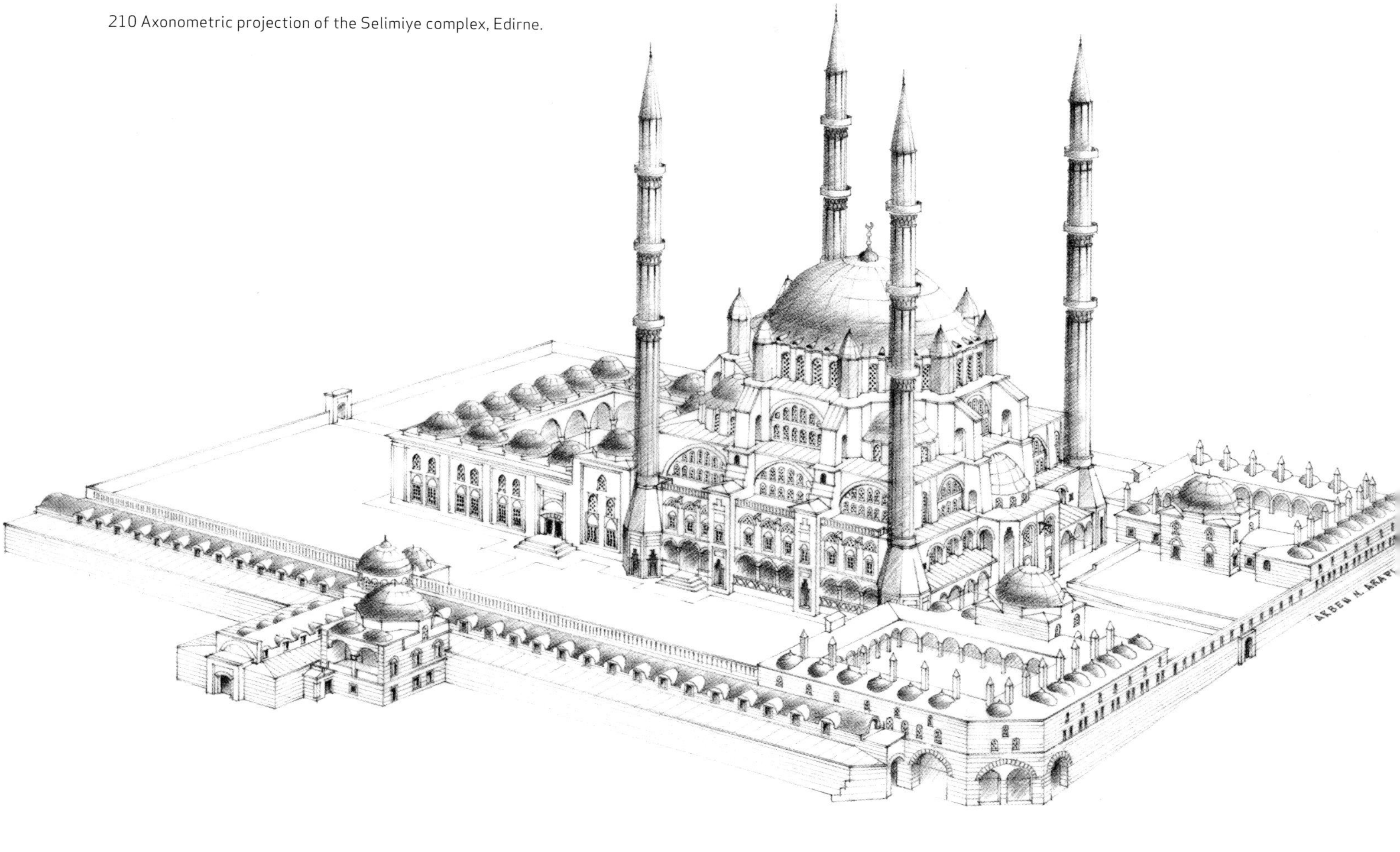

a defensive anti-Catholic ethos.

Evliya Çelebi explains Selim II's decision to build the Selimiye in Edirne, instead of Istanbul, with a vow he made to the Prophet Muhammad who appeared to him in a dream. The sultan promises: 'If I become the conqueror of the island of Cyprus, I will build a mosque from the war booty.' He then summons Lala Mustafa Pasha, the conqueror of Cyprus, to bring his royal share of the island's booty along with Venetian tribute money inherited from his father, for 'the construction of a mosque in my beloved Edirne, the bastion of Islam, protected by myself.'[288] The sultan's imagined words allude to the traditional image of Edirne as the abode of the ghazis and the bulwark of Islam at the edge of Christendom.[289] A late-fifteenth-century mythical history of Edirne, 'the hearth of the ghazis', likewise attributes the construction of the Old Mosque there to a dream in which the Prophet appears to Amir Süleyman (son of Bayezid I) and requests a mosque for his followers. Built with booty from 'two ghazas', this hallowed mosque completed by Murad II becomes 'the Kaʿba of Rum' with two pieces of the venerated black stone installed at the right side of its mihrab.[290]

Evliya, who conflates the construction myths of the Old Mosque and Hagia Sophia, says it was the Prophet himself who selected the Selimiye's site at Kavak Meydanı (a public square extending in front of the Old Palace) and revealed its plan, distinguished by the most perfectly oriented mihrab of the city.[291] The eighteenth-century writer Dayezade repeats the popular tradition that the Prophet indicated the site to the sultan in a dream, and that a rock equal in length and width to the dimensions of the Selimiye miraculously appeared upon digging its foundations.[292] These myths were no doubt inspired by mythical texts on Hagia Sophia, which attribute its divinely inspired plan to an angel who appeared to Justinian in a dream (in some versions the plan is revealed to both the emperor and his architect by the saint Hızır).[293]

Evliya Çelebi links the Selimiye with Hagia Sophia through another myth derived from the same texts, which deeply coloured the Ottoman architectural imagination. Among the holy memorial sites (*maḳām*) of Edirne, he mentions the spot under the spherical pendant hanging from the centre of the Selimiye dome, where lime mortar mixed with the Prophet Muhammad's saliva and Meccan earth was used: 'a powerful site of vision (*naẓargāh*) frequented by those cognizant of mysteries.' Sinan allegedly removed that miraculous mortar from the dome of Hagia Sophia (presumably during its renovation in 1573–74), which had been rebuilt with the sanction of Muhammad after it collapsed at the time of his birth.[294] The 'cross-fertilization' of the two domes not only consecrates the Selimiye as a holy sanctuary but also underscores its formal and semantic affiliation with Hagia Sophia, which was renovated as the funerary mosque of Selim II.

Mythical explanations aside, why such a magnificent imperial mosque was built in Edirne and not in Istanbul has always been

211 The Selimiye complex and the Old Mosque of Edirne, with the covered bazaar Sinan designed for Semiz Ali Pasha in the foreground.

212 Aerial view of the Selimiye complex, Edirne, from the southeast with the Üç Şerefeli mosque seen in a distance.

a matter of debate (illus. 211, 212). Evliya's account suggests that Selim II selected Edirne on the eve of the Cyprus campaign as a locus associated with holy warfare. Another reason for the choice of site seems to have been the sultan's failure to fulfil the requirement of the shari'a for building a sultanic mosque in the capital: he had not personally commanded a victorious army against the Christians.[295] In addition to his affection for Edirne, yet another consideration may have been the lack of an available hilltop site in Istanbul, and the fact that building a sultanic mosque there would have required the appropriation of a large number of properties. According to the English traveller Sanderson, the 'somptiouse' Selimiye was built in Edirne precisely for the 'waunt of place' in Istanbul.[296] It is difficult to gauge which of these reasons weighed most heavily; probably a combination of factors proved decisive. Like the Süleymaniye, built on a plot taken over from the Old Palace of Istanbul, Selim II's mosque bypassed the need for expropriation, since its site was carved from the Old Palace of Edirne. To the remaining core of that palace, which continued to house the dormitories of novices, Sinan added a new bath and bakery in 1570–71.[297]

The construction chronology of the Selimiye complex can be traced from imperial decrees. The periodic written progress reports that Sinan sent to his royal patron in Istanbul in order to negotiate decorum show the chief architect in charge of all matters of construction and decoration, in which the sultan clearly took a personal interest. Decrees issued between 1568 and 1571 concern the appointment of construction workers,[298] and document the transportation of columns and the quarrying of marble in Kavala,[299] Feres,[300] Kırklareli,[301] Tokat,[302] İnecik,[303] Aydıncık,[304] and at the Marmara Island (Proconessus).[305] During the construction of the dome in 1572 and 1573, just around the time the sultan ordered the renovation of Hagia Sophia, large amounts of lead were imported from Greece and Bulgaria.[306]

Documents also indicate when the channel that carried water from the neighbouring village of Kaya was dug (1572–74), when the calligrapher Hasan Karahisari came to Edirne at Sinan's request (May 1572), and when four of the eight arches supporting the dome were locked in place (July 1572).[307] At that time Sinan asked the sultan whether the mosque should be decorated lavishly or in a plain manner; his patron chose the former option and instructed him to use tile revetments inscribed with the Fatiha sura around the projecting mihrab (*ṣāhnişīn*). At the imperial council, the superintendent of tiles was handed a decree ordering the chief architect to show the calligrapher which places would be decorated with tilework and which with painted plain inscriptions (he must have taken the relevant cartoons to İznik in the summer of 1572).[308] On 28 December 1572 manuscripts prepared for the recitation of the Koran inside the Selimiye were sent to Edirne on carts loaded with chests.[309] In February 1573 five Greek painters identified by name were imported from the island of Chios to decorate the mosque.[310] Sinan sent a progress report in April 1573 mentioning the construction of the dome, the forecourt, and income-producing structures proposed for developing the uninhabited neighbourhood. The sultan responded:

> You have sent a letter reporting that the noble mosque under construction in Edirne has presently reached dome level and that it is deemed appropriate (*münāsib*) to use marble [pavements] around the fountain of the noble courtyard, on the floors of the courtyard gates on four sides, and on the landings of the staircases, whereas coarse sandstone

213 Selimiye complex, Edirne, from the west.

214 Selimiye mosque, Edirne, west façade.

is considered suitable for the pavement of the raised porticoes. And in order that the surroundings of the mosque become inhabited (*maᶜmūr*), experts have deemed it appropriate to build a wholesale fruit market and ten houses on the empty plot at the side of the Old Palace measuring 160 by 30 cubits. Since you have petitioned these matters, I order you to have all of them built according to the manner you have reported and to see to their completion without any probability of overspending; and to have the houses required for the wholesale market bought for their value by the state and have it built as you deem appropriate (*münāsib*).[311]

Upon the completion of the dome, the sultan impatiently inquired on 25 August 1573 when his mosque would be finished:

You have presently sent a letter to my felicitous threshold reporting that the dome of the noble mosque has been joined together with God's help, and when the dervish who came with your letter was interrogated about when the noble mosque would reach completion and when it would be possible to perform the prayers in it, he answered, not before the Sacrificial Feast. Now, since my being fully informed about the circumstances of the mosque is extremely important, when this [decree] arrives, report what the remaining construction of the noble mosque entails from now on, and if it is carefully built without harm in the winter, whether it is possible to perform the prayers in it by the Sacrificial Feast or not. Without leaving anything unclear, write in detail and petition it to my felicitous threshold.[312]

Details such as gilding the metal dome finials and installing the window grilles were completed in April 1574.[313] An imperial decree dated 15 October 1574 reveals that serious provision shortages reported by the kadi of Edirne would deter the court from wintering there.[314] The sultan ordered the kadi to inaugurate the Friday prayers on 28 October in his absence 'so that supplications are made for the continuation of my reign, and the stability of my glory and my sustenance.'[315] Selim II died shortly thereafter, in December 1574, without having seen his mosque in its final glory.

The sultan's posthumous waqfiyya of 1579 indicates that Murad III finalized the endowments of the Selimiye after completing its dependencies, his father's mausoleum, and the renovation of Hagia Sophia.[316] A decree dated 16 March 1576 reveals that the outer courtyard of the Selimiye remained unfinished, 'surrounded on each side by a wooden enclosure without doors.' It orders the kadi of Edirne to build a gate in an appropriate place to remedy the difficulties experienced by the congregation.[317] As this document does not mention Sinan, he must have returned to the capital after Selim II's demise. Another decree, which was sent to the kadi of Edirne on 18 May 1578, orders that an empty stable near the mosque, which had become a den of mischievous scoundrels, be replaced with a wholesale flour market.[318] On 19 August 1578, the kadi and endowment administrator were asked to build instead of the flour market a wholesale fruit market when the royal architect Hüseyin Çavuş arrived from the capital. Financed by the waqf's inadequate surplus funds, this cheaper option would increase the meagre congregation of the mosque, which was surrounded by abandoned properties previously bought for its endowment.[319]

In 1584 Sinan was ordered to go to Edirne to prepare an estimate for repairs resulting from the fall of a minaret that had been struck by lightning, damaging some parts of the mosque.[320] That year the architect Hüseyin Çavuş was appointed to repair the damages, employing 150 galley slaves.[321] The same architect was appointed in 1588, during Mimar Davud Agha's tenure as chief architect, to finally build the projected fruit market; it was completed in 1590–91.[322] At that time the kadi of Edirne and the building supervisor were instructed to construct other income-producing structures approved by Davud Agha in an empty plot which extended in front of the recently finished fruit market (demolished in 1937).[323]

Nothing remains of the urban fabric that once surrounded the Selimiye complex, now fronted by a park that sets it apart from the bustling commercial centre occupied by two sultanic mosques: the Old Mosque and the Üç Şerefeli (illus. 211–13). The twin madrasas, one of them functioning as a hadith college, were completed before Sinan left Edirne.[324] The T-shaped covered market (*arasta*), with its central dome raised on an attractive latticed drum, is attributed to Mimar Davud. But it must have been planned by Sinan, because it buttresses the western terrace of the mosque raised on vaulted substructures and provides access to it by a staircase.[325] The domed upper-storey school for Koran recitation, mentioned in the waqfiyya of 1579, is attached to the *arasta*. The absence of a hospice may have been the outcome of the patron's untimely death. Nevertheless, the few dependencies that were built imply that the Selimiye was conceived as a non-funerary sultanic mosque without a grand complex. The outer walls of its dependencies, economically built with alternating courses of stone and brick, accentuate the primacy of the ashlar masonry mosque. There is no such hierarchy of materials in Sinan's earlier royal complexes with ashlar masonry dependencies (Hürrem Sultan in Avratpazarı, Mihrümah Sultan in Üsküdar, Şehzade Mehmed, and Süleymaniye). Only in princess Mihrümah's smaller mosque and madrasa complex in Edirnekapı, constructed in the 1560s, has the chief architect introduced comparable dependencies with a contrasting wall fabric.

Referring to the site of the Selimiye at the centre of the town, Kuban finds it 'difficult to comprehend why three imperial mosques were concentrated at this point.'[326] The conspicuous juxtaposition of old and new can be interpreted as a strategy meant to draw attention to Sinan's innovations. The modernity of the Selimiye could best be appreciated against the contrasting

215 Selimiye mosque, Edirne, north portal of the forecourt.

216 Selimiye mosque, Edirne, north façade from the forecourt.

217 Sedat Çetintaş, elevation of the north façade of the Selimiye mosque, Edirne, 1934.

backdrop of the ancient Friday mosques of Edirne (illus. 211–12). We have witnessed in Chapter 4 how the *Teẕkiretü'l-bünyān* announces the chief architect's ambition to outdo the tower-like triple-galleried minaret of the nearby Üç Şerefeli and his long-distance competition with the dome of Hagia Sophia. His departure from the traditional placement of different sized minarets at each corner of the marble forecourt (as in the Üç Şerefeli and Süleymaniye mosques) focuses attention on the central dome, framed by four identical triple-galleried minarets. The dialogue with Hagia Sophia (renamed Selimiye) was enhanced by adding two extra minarets around its dome.

Sinan strove to build a dome as large as that of Hagia Sophia without alluding to its plan and elevation, which he had already reworked in the Süleymaniye. The claim of 'infidel' architects that the Muslims were incapable of matching the dome of the ancient church had induced him to fight his own artistic battle. The titanic dome of Selimiye transmuted the spoils of Cyprus into an architectural statement of the triumph of Islam over Christianity. The *Teẕkiretü'l-bünyān* applauds Sinan's personal victory in this artistic ghaza, achieved with divine help and the sultan's generous patronage.

The interior configuration of the Selimiye is reflected in its exterior, where no structural element contests the dictatorship of the domineering dome. The pyramidal cascade of smaller domes and half-domes used earlier in the Şehzade Mehmed and Süleymaniye mosques is abandoned to accentuate the crescendo of the gigantic single-shell dome. The vertical massing of the Selimiye is further emphasized by eight hexagonal weight turrets with pointed lead caps that surround its dome and mark the tops of its internal piers. The four vertically fluted symmetrical minarets amplify the upward thrust, shooting towards the sky like rockets from each corner of the mosque.[327] Below dome level, the elaborately fenestrated tall façades are covered with simple shed roofs articulated by cornice mouldings. The lateral façades are subdivided into three sections by pairs of stepped buttresses descending from the weight turrets. Their horizontal layering in several tiers is counterbalanced by pronounced vertical continuities. The lower zone, topped by a stone balustrade as in the Süleymaniye, is composed of triple-arched porticoes raised above rows of ablution fountains (illus. 214). Unlike the two-storey lateral porticoes of Süleyman's mosque, which boast precious columns and porphyry roundels, the single-storey arcades of the Selimiye support flat façades with two tiers of windows. Those of the upper tier, with their lunette-shaped openwork geometrical grills, become a trademark of Sinan's late mosques infused with increasing amounts of light. The second and third zones of the lateral façades have fenestrated tympanum arches that echo in form the four corner exedras. The octagonal third zone, visually continuous with the lead-covered circular drum above it, can be read as a tall masonry drum like those of ancient Islamic domes.

I have speculated in Chapter 3 that the unprecedented lofty façades of the Selimiye may have been yet another response to 'infidel' architects, perhaps inspired by Etienne Dupérac's engravings of St Peter's published in 1569 (illus. 77). As the largest cathedral church of Latin Christendom, St Peter's would have been a worthy counterpart to Hagia Sophia. Sinan's veiled models, transmuted into canonic Ottoman forms, may also have included celebrated Islamic exemplars. As Kuban observes, the dome on eight squinches was an old scheme in the rich monumental heritage of Islamic architecture, just as the use of eight turrets around a dome belonged to a 'design tradition stretching from Iran to Sind'. He convincingly speculates that the early-fourteenth-century mausoleum of Uljaytu in Sultaniya, which Sinan had seen in 1534, must have been 'imprinted as a provoking image in his mind' (illus. 51).[328] Since the octagonal dome of the Ilkhanid imperial mausoleum, once surrounded by eight turrets, was the largest in the Muslim lands (25 metres wide), it constitutes a proper Islamic complement to the Romano-Byzantine dome of Hagia Sophia, which is emulated in the 31.22-metre-wide Selimiye dome.

With its octagonal domed baldachin the Selimiye comes close to funerary and commemorative architecture. It is there-

218 Selimiye mosque, Edirne, interior view of the domical superstructure.

fore not surprising that Sinan's biographer likens it to the Dome of the Rock (Masjid-i Aqsa) in Jerusalem, an octagonal commemorative structure marking the sacred rock where God's throne would descend during the Last Judgment according to a widely held belief.[329] Besides the octagonal scheme of the Selimiye, its Koranic passages (discussed below) underscore its conceptual affinity with the Dome of the Rock by stressing the absolute unity of the one and only God and by alluding to the Last Judgment.

The polychromy of the Selimiye's external walls, recalling that of the Şehzade Mehmed mosque, contrasts with the sternly monochrome greyish-white sandstone façades of the Süleymaniye. The difference in mood, also manifested in the exuberant interior decoration of Selim's mosque, is the outcome of differing aesthetic goals: dignified gravity versus graceful magnificence. The austere severity of the Süleymaniye, decorously befitting its patron's persona, is further softened in the Selimiye by the warmer hue of its honey-coloured sandstone façades with their palatial quality. Unlike the heavily buttressed qibla wall of the Süleymaniye, that of the Selimiye is enveloped by columnar porticoes with slanting eaves flanking the pavilion-like projection of the mihrab, fronted by two garden terraces (illus. 212).

The dramatic approach to the north façade of the mosque is staged by the axially aligned gates of its outer precinct wall and forecourt, designed to expose the great dome from afar. The north gate of the forecourt lacks a muqarnas hood and is remarkably modest in scale compared to its three-tiered counterpart in the Süleymaniye (illus. 215). Its arch optically frames the dome of the Selimiye, whose majesty is additionally enhanced by the elimination of the customary canopy above the ablution fountain (illus. 216).[330] The arcade fronting the north façade of the mosque is proportionally adjusted to the vast dimensions of the dome and its buttressing system (illus. 217). The arches of this arcade are considerably higher and wider in span than those of the Süleymaniye, whose lower courtyard façade has two tiers of windows rather than three (illus. 178). The north façade of the Selimiye mosque can be read as a lofty triumphal arch framing the entry into the prayer hall. Its three monumental arches, alternating with two smaller ones aligned with the buttresses above, visually echo the transition zone of the dome and the structure of the inner space (illus. 216–17).

The eight piers supporting the Selimiye dome, which is raised on 'Islamic' muqarnas-corbelled squinches instead of 'Byzantino-Roman' spherical pendentives, depart from the customary square baldachin layout of former sultanic mosques in Istanbul (illus. 218). The smoother transition from octagon to circle not only creates a structurally more stable support system, but also enhances the monumental effect of the dome crowning a perfectly unified space. Sinan had recently experimented with smaller domed structures featuring eight supports, such as Rüstem Pasha's posthumously built memorial mosque in Tahtakale (*c.* 1561–63) and Süleyman's mausoleum (1566–68). Before designing the Selimiye, he may have studied the centralized octagonal scheme of the sixth-century church of SS. Sergius and Bacchus in Istanbul, with its eight free-standing piers and projecting apse: converted to a mosque during the early sixteenth century, it was known as Küçük Ayasofya (Small Hagia Sophia).[331] Sinan's fascination with the illusion of a weightlessly suspended single dome, crowning a light-filled space with transparent curtain walls, had already manifested itself in the pioneering mosque he built for Selim II's sister, princess Mihrümah, in Edirnekapı (*c.* 1563–70).

The exhilarating spatial unity inside the Selimiye is achieved by Sinan's skilful subordination of all architectural features to the grandiose dome (illus. 219, 220). The continuous U-shaped upper gallery arcade that surrounds the prayer hall on three sides is an innovation inspired by Hagia Sophia, as is the apse-like projecting mihrab.[332] The placement of the muezzin's tribune, punctuating the centre of the domed baldachin in the manner of a church altar or ambo, is yet another innovation. Such a striking departure from the norm could not have been merely a design 'lapse'; it was a purposeful transgression never repeated in any later mosque by Sinan.[333]

The square tribune, with three foliate ogee arches on each side, is raised on stone supports and has a pier-shaped staircase

219 Selimiye mosque, Edirne, interior toward the qibla wall.

220 Selimiye mosque, interior toward the east.

221 Selimiye mosque, Edirne, muezzin's tribune.

222 Selimiye mosque, painted decorations of the muezzin's tribune.

223 Selimiye mosque, interior upper gallery from the northeast.

224 Selimiye mosque, mihrab recess with half-dome.

225 (top left) Selimiye mosque, Edirne, detail of mihrab recess with İznik tile panels.

226 (top right) Selimiye mosque, royal tribune with gate and partial view of mihrab on the qibla wall.

227 (above left) Selimiye mosque, royal tribune with painted ceilings and stained-glass windows.

228 (right) Selimiye mosque, mihrab of the royal tribune.

229 Selimiye mosque, Edirne, minbar and preacher's lectern.

230 Selimiye mosque, arched İznik tile panel on the minbar canopy depicting a blossoming tree.

protruding from one corner (illus. 221, 222). Its wooden arches preserve gilded polychrome paintings – composed of palmettes with *saz* leaves and Chinese cloud bands against a red background – that would have harmonized with the original carpets.[334] The tribune is set above a shallow marble pool in the form of an octagon inscribed in a square, with a central fountain providing drinking water. On the wooden ceiling a square panel, equal in size to the pool below it, is decorated with a whorled circle emblematically representing the wheel of heaven. The superimposition of square, octagon, and circle echoes the geometrical scheme of the microcosmic mosque. To accentuate spatial centralization, the muezzin's tribune marks the *axis mundi* at the 'navel' of the prayer hall, as does the rock at the centre of the Dome of the Rock in Jerusalem (thought to mark the omphalos, or navel of the earth). Obstructing the horizontal, axial view towards the mihrab from the north gate, the central tribune gives optical and symbolic precedence to the vertical axis of the heavenly dome.[335]

At ground level, the nearly square walls of the prayer hall are positioned close to the bases of the eight piers to optimize the centralized spatial effect. Sinan conceals the eight buttresses by adopting a double diaphragm wall system. The buttresses of the qibla wall are hidden by the protruding mihrab flanked by external porticoes. The lateral buttresses are concealed on the ground floor by an internal diaphragm and external porticoes, complemented on the upper floor by an external diaphragm and internal galleries.[336] Undesirable areas of interior space are thus transformed into external porticoes that support the luminous arcaded upper galleries inside. The dynamic manipulation of wall surfaces, causing a reversal of interior and exterior, is likened by Kuban to a 'palpitation'.[337]

Above the brilliantly illuminated belt of the upper galleries is a transparent zone of tympanum arches perforated with windows. Reaching up to the next zone, the piers carry eight squinches whose arches frame four window-pierced tympana and four exedras. The dome balustrade, lined by a circular band of windows, constitutes the uppermost zone of light. The archaic

231 Selimiye mosque, Edirne, İznik tile revetment with blossoming tree and tulips on an arch spandrel of the anti-qibla wall.

muqarnas-corbelled squinches reinforce the illusion of a weightlessly suspended dome hovering above the light-filled central space. Sinan's miraculously floating 'Islamic' dome not only challenges that of Hagia Sophia, but also those of famous Muslim religious monuments. Its dematerialized transition zone rests on eight fluted piers surmounted by muqarnas 'capitals' from which the arches of the dome grow organically.

Sai's eulogy of the dome strikingly recalls Procopius's sixth-century ekphrasis of Hagia Sophia, which praises the heavenly dome of the church 'suspended in mid-air', as if it had no masonry supports. The Selimiye is described in similar terms: 'Under the dome [of the sky] without columnar supports, / Its dome became a suspended globe. // Imagine that its dome is hung by the Milky Way to the mosque of the sphere of heaven, / Like a mirror globe within which the earth is visible.' Sai then compares the pendant mirror globes (*ṭop-ı āyine*) hanging with silk straps from the Selimiye dome together with glittering oil lamps to the 'world-adorning sun and moon', likening the polychrome arches to rainbows.[338]

The exquisite decorative skin of the Selimiye, befitting its patron's taste for extravagance, introduced to Edirne the innovative ornamental vocabulary developed in Istanbul from the 1550s onward. Sai's eulogy praises the ornaments of the mosque as resembling the 'garden of paradise' with 'spring blossoms' and '*ḫaṭāyi*, *rūmi*, *islīmī*' motifs. It then extols Hasan Karahisari's calligraphy, especially the Fatiha verse of the projecting mihrab, whose rhythmically flowing letters are likened in fluidity to the 'river of paradise': 'Katib Hasan' has displayed the 'canonic laws of beautiful writing' in these 'peerless' inscriptions (illus. 224, 225).[339] Evliya Çelebi concurs that the calligrapher has reached the 'epitome of his mature skill' in the Selimiye, where he has 'demonstrated his power in the science of design (*ʿilm-i resm*)'.[340]

The mihrab recess creates an illusion of transparency with its white-ground İznik tile panels delineating pointed arches. Its kiosk-like space forms a self-contained visual focus set apart from the central baldachin. Stained glass is used only on the upper level windows of the projecting mihrab and the qibla wall, which according to Evliya Çelebi were once inscribed with the Light verse.[341] Like the mihrab recess, the royal tribune at the southeast corner of the qibla wall is densely decorated with impeccable İznik tile panels combining floral designs and boldly magnified calligraphy. Its arched upper window lunettes are fitted with stained glass, and its ceilings are lavishly painted (illus. 226–28). Tiles with spring blossoms and naturalistic flowers also decorate the canopy of the marble minbar with lacelike openwork geometric patterns (illus. 229, 230), and the arch spandrels of the anti-qibla wall (illus. 231). Geometric interlaces in painted plasterwork on the east, west, and north window lunettes of the prayer hall and the forecourt are relegated to a subordinate position, dominated by more fashionable floral designs.

The epigraphic programme of the Selimiye, conceived in 1572, soon after the Lepanto debacle, differs from that of the Süleymaniye which emphasizes the ritual duties of orthodox Muslims awaiting reward in paradise. It focuses instead on the central tenet that differentiates Islam from Christianity: the indivisible unity of God glorified by divine epithets, and the subordinate status of the Prophet Muhammad as His messenger and thus merely a human, no matter how exalted. Its Koranic passages are complemented by some hadith (omitted in the Süleymaniye) to emphasize the role of the Prophet as an intercessor and reliable messenger. The Last Judgment theme constitutes another focus which is missing in the Süleymaniye.

The absence of a foundation inscription on the superbly sculpted muqarnas-hooded gate of the Selimiye, featuring three empty panels, can be explained by the untimely death of its patron (illus. 232, 233). The gilded Arabic inscription with eight cartouches, carved at the north gate of the forecourt, is considerably more modest in content than the one Ebussuud composed for the Süleymaniye (illus. 234):

> This chosen place (*maḳām*) was built by the munificent commander, the sultan of mankind,
>
> Namely, the Sultan of Sultans King Selim – his abode of peace [in paradise] will be built similarly.
>
> May God (exalted is He) bless his good work and multiply

232, 233 Selimiye mosque, Edirne, north portal featuring blank inscription panels, and detail of engaged colonette with 'hourglass' motif.

his reward on the day of Resurrection.

'The Grace of God' came to be the date/chronogram of the foundation. The year 976 (1568–69).

'The grace of the Good Lord' was the date/chronogram of the completion. The year 982 (1574–75).[342]

The inscription alludes to a popular saying of the Prophet: 'Whoever builds for God a place of worship, for him God builds a dwelling in paradise.' The identification of the sultan's pious work as a *maḳām* accentuates its character as a holy place where one offers prayers for the fulfilment of wishes, recalling Evliya Çelebi's reference to the *maḳām* underneath its dome. The foundation inscription turns the supplicatory Koranic verses inscribed on the qibla wall and mihrab recess of the mosque into pleas for the patron's reward for his 'good work' on the Day of Judgment.

With their paired invocations of God and Muhammad, the inscriptions of the forecourt form a prelude to those of the prayer hall. The arched İznik tile window lunettes on the north façade repeat the same verses used in the Süleymaniye: the Throne verse (2:255) affirming God's absolute sovereignty and a verse from the Fath sura (48:29) referring to Muhammad, whose followers oppose disbelievers and seek bounty from Allah, who promises 'forgiveness and immense reward' to those who worship and do good works. The two rectangular panels carved above the middle arch of the north portico cite the monotheistic formula (illus. 217): 'There is no God but God, the Just Sovereign, the Manifest. / Muhammad is the Prophet of God, the Faithful Keeper of Promises, the Trustworthy.' These panels are flanked by two carved roundels that in rotating script emphasize God's attributes as a merciful and prudent judge: 'the Most Compassionate, the All-Bounteous'; 'the Assembler on the Day of Judgment, the Vigilant Guardian.'

The painted inscriptions inside the mosque were extensively

234 Selimiye mosque, detail of north courtyard portal with foundation inscription.

reworked and signed by nineteenth- and twentieth-century calligraphers, but they preserve their overall thematic coherence. God's unity is powerfully expressed by the calligraphic roundel at the centre of the dome, which quotes the Ikhlas sura also known as 'al-Tawhid' (112:1–4). This sura, which is the most explicit disavowal of the Christian doctrine of the Holy Trinity, affirms the indivisible oneness of the eternal God, who neither gives birth nor was born. It is surrounded by eight medallions inscribed with rhyming exhortations that proclaim some of the divine epithets (illus. 218): 'O, the Light of Lights!; O, the Omniscient one who knows what is in all hearts!; O, the Resuscitator of the lifeless among the seas!; O, the Eternal one who remains despite the rush forward of ages!; O, the one who is All-Sufficing for everything!; O, the Healer of all hearts!; O, the Clement one who does not make haste!; O, the Generous one who does not stint!'. The four exedras under the dome are inscribed with verses from the Jumʿa sura (62:9–10), starting at the right side of the mihrab and proceeding counter-clockwise. They recommend the canonically prescribed Friday prayers alongside the 'remembrance of Allah'. The half-dome above the mihrab quotes a verse which reminds the 'rightly guided' congregation facing the qibla of its basic religious duties and introduces the Last Judgment theme that unifies the qibla wall and the projecting mihrab (9:18).

The arch spandrels above the colossal piers bear roundels with the eight revered names. Below them, the ninety-nine beautiful names of God, sometimes preceded by the formula 'Praise be to God!', are inscribed above the lateral upper gallery arcades (illus. 220). Painted white-on-blue and blue-on-white inside cartouches, their rectangular frames form a continuous horizontal band on each side.[343] The beautiful names inscribed on window lunettes at the Süleymaniye galleries are much less prominent than their counterparts directly overlooking the central baldachin of the Selimiye. Complemented by the invocations on the dome, the boldly calligraphed divine names recall oral recitations (*dhikr*) glorifying God that were particularly favoured by the sufis. They function as a form of visual recitation that confers a mystical overtone to the group of inscriptions concentrated on and around the central baldachin, an overtone in keeping with the rising esteem of sufi orders under Selim II. Above the balcony of the north gate are inscribed the attributes of Muhammad – the Witness, the Messenger, the Admonisher, the Bearer of Good News, the Missionary of Allah – that supplement the beautiful names of God.

While the qibla wall presents the gist of the divine revelation disclosed in the first three chapters of the Koran, the anti-qibla wall is inscribed with the Prophet's hadith concerning the canonical requirement of congregational prayers and the superiority of the Friday noon prayer. This arrangement spatially expresses the hierarchy between the Words of God and those of His Prophet. The mihrab recess is inscribed, according to the sultan's wish, with the Fatiha sura (1:1–7), considered the essence of the Koran (illus. 224, 225). Written in cartouches on İznik tiles above the ground-level windows, it affirms the merciful God's role as the supreme arbiter during the Day of Judgment and begs Him to show the congregation the 'straight path' of favoured ones. The triangular pediment of the muqarnas-hooded mihrab is carved with the standard verse, which includes the word 'mihrab' (3:37). The profession of faith is inscribed in a rectangular frame beneath it. The band of İznik tile inscriptions above the window lunettes cites verses from the Baqara sura (2:285–86), regarded as a commentary explaining the Fatiha sura. It concludes with a prayer for the forgiveness of shortcomings and victory over disbelieving folk.

The tilework window lunettes of the qibla wall, which flank the mihrab recess, quote other passages from the Baqara sura (2:101, 201) and the next sura (3:8–9, 16) (illus. 219).[344] These supplications, directly addressed to God, ask for divine guidance and for protection from hellfire during the Last Judgment.[345] They can perhaps be interpreted as communal pleas by the congregation, chastised for its sins in Lepanto. One may even detect in them the voice of the repentant sultan, who built the Selimiye for the salvation of his soul, according to its foundation inscription.

The inscriptions of the royal tribune contain even more personalized references to the patron. The gilded lunette above the sultan's private muqarnas-hooded mihrab, fitted with a window featuring mother-of-pearl-inlaid wooden shutters, quotes the same non-standard Koranic verse from the Shuʿara' sura (26:89), used earlier above the public mihrab of Selim's princehood mosque at Karapınar (illus. 228). Chosen as a pun on the patron's name, it asks forgiveness on the Day of Judgment for 'him who bringeth unto Allah a whole [pure] heart (*qalb salīm*)'. Once again, the man with a 'pure' heart is none other than the sultan himself. The chronogram of a Turkish poem commemorating the completion of the Selimiye similarly refers to the sultan's pure heart: 'The mosque of the Shah with a pure heart (*selīmü'l ḳalb*), the Imam who is the embodiment of religion.'[346]

Above the sultan's mihrab, two İznik tile cartouches quote other verses from the same sura: 'My Lord! Vouchsafe me wisdom and unite me to the righteous (26:83)'; 'And place me among the inheritors of the Garden of Delight (26:85).' This can be read as an invocation by the sultan himself, seeking the inner spiritual wisdom particularly valued by the sufis and acceptance into paradise, which is pictorially represented by İznik tile panels on the mihrab wall that depict blossoming trees in semi-naturalistic flower gardens. The wish to enter the 'Garden of Delight' turns the mihrab, which overlooks the garden below, into a window providing a preview of Eden.

The L-shaped royal tribune is composed of the sultan's prayer space at the west, separated by an arcade from an anteroom at the east (illus. 226–28). The luxurious anteroom, where the ruler may have relaxed and conversed with companions, anticipates the tile-covered imperial pavilions that would be attached to the royal tribunes of the Sultan Ahmed and Yeni Valide mosques during the seventeenth century[347]. A dark rectangular space with a tiny window, reached from a door on the qibla wall of the anteroom, has been identified as a cell for seclusion, a form of spiritual exercise that was the hallmark of the Halveti order to which the sultan subscribed.[348] The mihrab-like door of the cell, crowned by a magnificent palmette crest, visually and metaphorically complements the larger mihrab on the same wall. The door is flanked by two tilework cartouches citing the monotheistic formula.[349]

The tiled window lunettes of the anteroom quote fragments of Koranic verses invoking the divine epithets (59:22–23) in an order echoing the mystical recitations of the Halvetis.[350] The lunettes are thematically related to the beautiful names of God written on İznik tile cartouches above the arcade of the royal tribune, which overlooks the sultan's prayer space and the mosque's interior. These tilework cartouches are visually continuous with the ninety-nine beautiful names painted above the upper galleries of the prayer hall (illus. 219, 220). The mystical tone of the epigraphic programme, missing in the Süleymaniye, shows that the carefully selected inscriptions of both mosques resonated with the differing religious climates of their patrons' reigns.

The *Tezkiretü'l-bünyān* interprets the combination of a large dome and four minarets at the Selimiye as a metaphor for the dome of Islam illuminated with the 'light of the Prophet' and supported by the pillars of the four Sunni caliphs:

> Its four minarets, like the [Prophet's] four companions, are
> the glory of the world;
> That dome is an allusion to the light of the Prophet's religion.
>
> A house of Islam with four pillars,
> That dome between four minarets is a wise spiritual guide.[351]

A leitmotif in Ottoman written sources is the unique aesthetic quality of the Selimiye mosque, which according to the *Tezkiretü'l-bünyān* came to be acknowledged as peerless by the possessors of 'perceptive vision' (*erbāb-ı nazar*).[352] As we have seen in Chapter 4, the same source eulogizes the mosque as the climax of Sinan's artistic mastery in its 'utmost refinement'.[353]

The sultan's waqfiyya praises the Selimiye as the most superior sultanic mosque ever created:

> He [Selim II] built a paradise-like and graceful mosque which in addition to being most beautiful, artistic, and novel, is unanimously judged by those who observe its four cypress-like minarets reaching the sky and its matchless dome as superior and preferable to the pious works of his virtuous and powerful ancestors, according to the saying: 'How much the former was surpassed by the latter.'[354]

Selaniki considers the Selimiye 'a rarity of the ages' built in a 'desirable manner and agreeable style' by the world-admired architect and engineer Sinan Agha: 'a monument the likes of which did not fall to the lot of any previous sultan'.[355] The geographer Mehmed Aşık describes the mosque as an unrivalled monument with which its patron has 'honoured and greatly dignified' the city of Edirne:

> Sultan Selim II built on an elevated site in Edirne an unrivalled mosque and paradise-like sanctuary with four minarets, the refined architectural qualities (*evṣāf-ı nezāket-i bināsı*) of which cannot be expressed by the written language of the pen. Nor can the characteristics of its plan and layout (*ṭarḥ ve resmi*) be orally described with words; it is subject to be seen. The four minarets on the four sides of the mosque have taken into their midst the dome, each of them with three galleries and equal in size, so identical that from a distance of one parasang (3 miles), whichever direction one looks from, these minarets do not appear to be four but two. Only when one looks at them not from a central but from an off-centre position do these four minarets become visible.[356]

This optical illusion is mentioned with astonishment by such authors as Evliya Çelebi, Dayezade, and Dimitri Cantemir, and still holds true upon entering Edirne from the Istanbul highway.[357]

In 1636–37 the local historian of Edirne, Abdurrahman Hibri, hailed the Selimiye as the most distinguished sultanic mosque of the city, whose like no traveller had seen in the world:

> Among them the best and largest, and in terms of architecture the most beautiful, is the elegant mosque built by Sultan Selim II, which without exaggeration has not been equalled until now on the face of the earth. The reason for this is that the great old architect, who lived over a hundred years and built an unprecedented number of monuments, including the mosques of Şehzade Mehmed and Sultan Süleyman, applied all the arts and novelties he developed in those buildings to this mosque, inventing in it such an original manner distinct from the style of noble mosques constructed in earlier times that it perplexes the minds of the engineers of the age.[358]

Hibri then turns to the mosque's interior, perceptively noting its spatial unity achieved by the closeness of its piers to the enveloping walls:

> Inside its four walls are eight piers on which the dome rests. Since those piers are close to the walls, unlike the piers of other mosques, someone who first enters it does not notice them without a scrutinizing gaze (*imʿān-ı naẓar*).

> Because of this, the muezzin's tribune is built exactly in the middle of the noble mosque and has been transformed into a joy-giving pavilion in the midst of a flower garden.[359]

Evliya Çelebi astutely compares the octagonal baldachin of the Selimiye to that of Rüstem Pasha's smaller mosque in the capital.[360] Drawing attention to the unique dome with four minarets and other innovations, he asserts that the Selimiye is 'beyond imitation'.[361] Singling out the Süleymaniye and the Selimiye as the two world-famous mosques of the Ottoman empire, Evliya adds: 'But the like of the latter does not exist in the world's inhabited regions; human beings are impotent and deficient in describing its layout ... and the beauty of its elegance (*ḥüsn-i leṭāfeti*) and its graceful works (*kār-i zerāfeti*) are beyond description and discourse.'[362]

The Selimiye mosque evoked such a sense of admiration that myths evolved about its construction.[363] Its wondrous forms prompted prolonged visual contemplation and meditation. Dayezade, for example, attributes symbolic significance to each of its distinctive features because of the Prophet's contribution to its design. He ponders the forms of the Selimiye as a kind of spiritual revelation, engaging in an interpretative exercise of unrestrained freedom. He reports that the city's kadi Nevizade was so enamoured of the mosque that he had one of its muezzins measure and record in a notebook the auspicious dimensions of its minarets and dome for interested visitors. Likewise, a painter called Nakkaş Ahmed Çelebi had fallen so in love with the Selimiye that he dedicated all his spare time to gazing at its amazing design, in which he daily discovered new artistic marvels that he would report to his friends each evening.[364]

Intended as an unmatched exemplar 'worthy of being seen by the people of the world', the multivalent Selimiye transcended the limits of the Ottoman architectural tradition.[365] By boldly reclaiming the Romano-Byzantine and Islamic roots of that tradition, and perhaps even making an indirect reference to contemporary Italian Renaissance architecture, the elderly chief architect in his eighties created a timeless testament to his creative genius. The Selimiye was also a decorous memorial to the person and reign of its royal patron. On a personal level it expressed the pure-hearted, remorseful sultan's hope for salvation much as did his simpler princehood mosque in Karapınar. On a public level it proclaimed the image of the monarch, less popular than his father, as the protector in troubled times of the state and the glory of Islam.

III. SULTAN MURAD III

Prince Murad was born and circumcised in Manisa (1546 and 1557), and governed there for twelve years (1562–74) before he became sultan (illus. 9, 235). The Muradiye complex, designed by Sinan during his sultanate, replaced a smaller princely mosque he had built in Manisa as heir apparent. Travellers concur that

235 *Portrait of Murad III*, oil on paper, 1570s.

the sultan refrained from commissioning a mosque complex in Istanbul because he could not take credit for a victorious campaign in the West againt unbelievers.[366] Murad's reign was dominated by a protracted war (1578–90) against the Safavids, commanded by his viziers, during which parts of Azerbayjan, Armenia, and Georgia came under Ottoman control. To commemorate his relatively minor forays in the Christian kingdom of Georgia, the sultan converted the Orthodox patriarchate in Istanbul into an imperial mosque named Fethiye or Conquest. The subsequent Hungarian campaign of 1593 (not concluded until 1606) was defensive rather than offensive, triggered by the revolt of vassal kingdoms in Wallachia, Moldavia, and Transylvania, who joined forces with the Austrian Hapsburg emperor to attack Ottoman frontier castles. It resulted in the capture of only minor fortresses long after the demise of Murad III in 1595.

Selaniki regards the lack of major conquests as a symptom of weakness: 'Everywhere the adversaries of the manifest religion have started to attack the community of Islam; may God the exalted and blessed save us from worse and forgive our disgrace!'[367] The glorious victories of Süleyman's reign now seemed a distant memory to the successor generation of Ottomans, whose collective psychology was coloured by premonitions of the approaching millennium (1000/1591–92), with its portents of impending doom. A consciousness of decline is first articulated in this era by some intellectuals, prompted by a combination of changes in the military regime, the monetary system, and the status hierarchies of the centralized state. Widespread bribery in the sale of offices, a budgetary deficit arising from the increased number of soldiers, and currency inflation that reduced the scope of architectural ambitions were the order of the day. Sultanas and eunuchs gained an upper hand in politics, and factionalism in the imperial palace meant that grand viziers and viziers did not last long in office.[368]

The uncharismatic monarch never left Istanbul because of his 'falling sickness'. The Venetian-born queen mother Nurbanu Sultan, who took it upon herself to look after her fragile son, thus gained unprecedented power.[369] Another woman with some influence over Murad was his Albanian-born chief consort Safiye Sultan, the mother of his oldest son and successor Mehmed. The sultan initially remained loyal to Safiye, but his mother and sister İsmihan (Sokollu's wife) attempted to diversify his erotic appetite by offering him irresistible concubines. The initially reluctant Murad finally fell for two alluring slave girls presented by İsmihan, thereafter becoming addicted to an inordinate number of concubines, to the chagrin of his chief consort, whom he never married.[370]

At the time of his death in 1595, the promiscuous ruler left behind more than forty *haseki*s (consorts), seven of them pregnant, and forty-nine children. Among his sons only the oldest prince, Mehmed, singled out as heir apparent, left the imperial palace to govern Manisa,[371] and his popularity is said to have provoked the sultan's jealousy and fear.[372] Prince Mehmed was appointed sanjak governor during his extravagant circumcision festival (29 May – 24 July 1582), which lasted nearly two months and abruptly ended with a street fight between the janissaries and royal cavalry troops (illus. 130–36).[373] He was kept on hold in the capital until the death of the queen mother, Nurbanu, whose intense rivalry with his own mother, Safiye, preoccupied her throughout Murad's reign. On her deathbed, the queen mother's last advice to her reigning son was threefold: to be just to his subjects, to restrain his natural avidity for money, and above all to keep an eye on the conduct of his son.[374] Prince Mehmed left Istanbul on 17 December 1583, about ten days after Nurbanu's death, arriving at Manisa in mid-January 1584 while his father's Muradiye mosque was being built.[375]

Renowned for his sufi orientation, Murad III composed mystical poetry under the pen-name 'Murādī'. Hasanbeyzade reports that the sultan 'preferred the masters of esoteric knowledge to experts in the external precepts of religion, expressing clearly the gravitation of his natural disposition toward the possessors of spiritual wisdom.' Shayhks were treated with increased royal favour in the capital because the ruler communicated with them in writing or face-to-face about the interpretation of his dreams and sufi topics.[376]

The sultan's affection for dervishes found architectural expression in the construction of several convents, although the primary focus of his architectural patronage was the remodelling of the two sacred Harams in Mecca and Medina. These projects, which lasted throughout his reign, exemplify the notable shift in sultanic patronage away from the capital. Sinan's addition to the Meccan Haram of new domical arcades, initiated under Selim II, was completed in 1576–77.[377] The monuments Murad III endowed in Mecca included a madrasa, mention of which is omitted from the autobiographies of the chief architect, who was sent to the Holy City in 1584 to prepare a survey of the leaning structure of the Kaʿba,[378] but whose proposed renovation failed to materialize due to resistance from local notables and the ulema.[379]

The remodelling of the Prophet's mosque in Medina began in 1576 and continued after the death of the sultan (d. 1595), whose endowments were recorded in a posthumous waqfiyya drawn up in 1598.[380] His building activities in Medina, completed during the tenure of Davud Agha as chief architect, are also excluded from Sinan's autobiographies. As we have seen in Chapter 5, the royal architect İlyas was sent there from Istanbul with a team of builders in 1589 to add domical arcades around the Haram, a project that once again faced local resistance but was eventually realized.[381] The sultan's pious endowments in Medina included a madrasa, a hospice, a water dispenser surmounted by an elementary school, and a convent (*ribaṭ*) functioning as a guest-house (*tābḫāne*) for dervishes and the poor.[382]

Murad III commissioned a similar convent (*ribāṭ, zāviye-i ṣūfīyye*) next to the masjid of Quba near Medina, where the Prophet is said to have built the first mosque. It was endowed for resident sufis who would perform *dhikr* rituals and litanies glorifying God.[383] The sultan also sponsored the construction of a convent adjoining the tomb of Shaykh Abu al-Hasan al-Kharraqani, which had been miraculously discovered during the creation of the castle of Kars. The convent commemorating that shaykh was built in 1579, together with a Friday mosque and elementary school that the sultan endowed in 1591 (illus. 49, 50).[384] Another convent with dormitory cells for Mevlevi dervishes and an assembly hall was constructed for Murad III in 1584–85 as a dependency of Mevlana Celalüddin Rumi's shrine in Konya.[385] The Muradiye complex in Manisa (1583–90), which included yet another dervish convent, is the only major monument the sultan commissioned from Sinan, and not without some reluctance.[386]

THE MURADİYE COMPLEX

Imperial decrees record the protracted construction of the Muradiye complex along with the negotiation of decorum that involved an unusually complicated set of interested parties: the

236 Plan of the Muradiye complex, Manisa:

1. Mosque
2. Madrasa
3. Hospice and guest-house (hypothetical reconstruction)
4. Library (1812)
5. Latrines

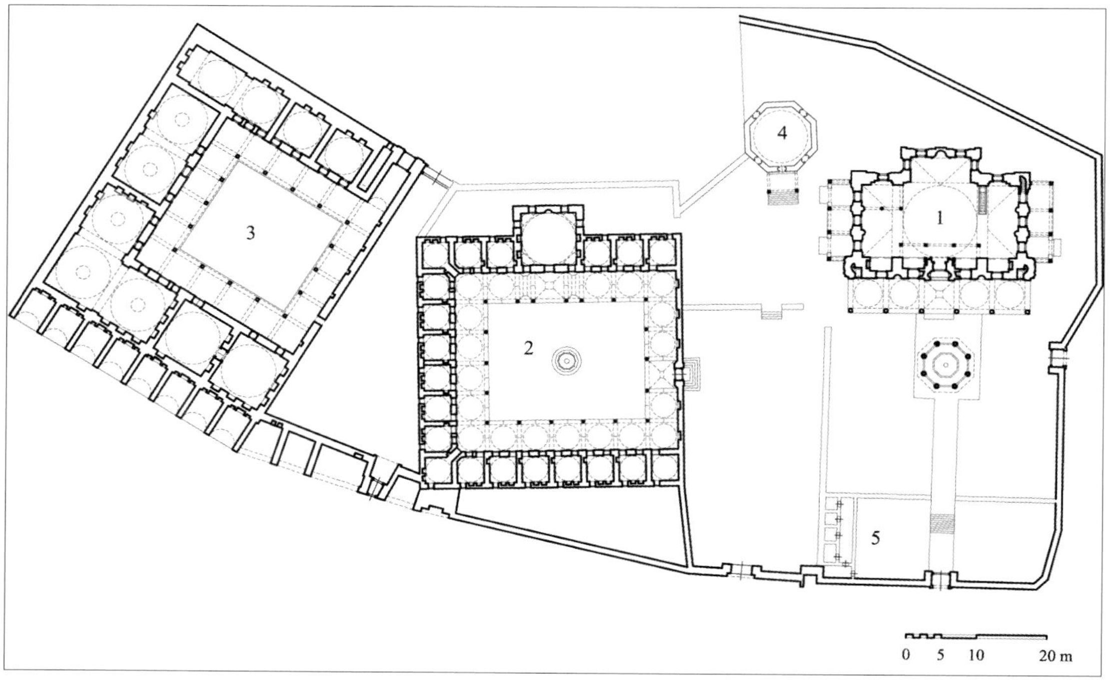

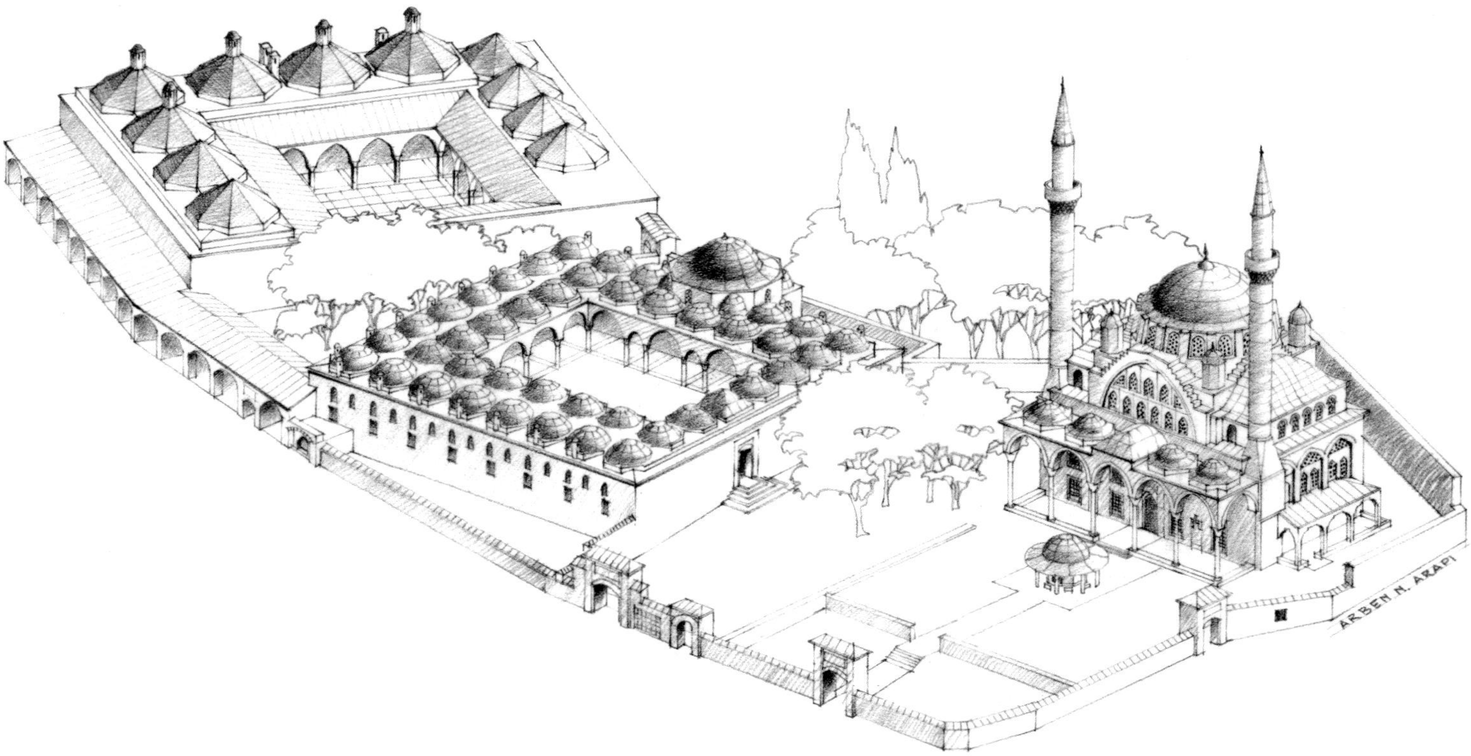

237 Axonometric projection of the Muradiye complex.

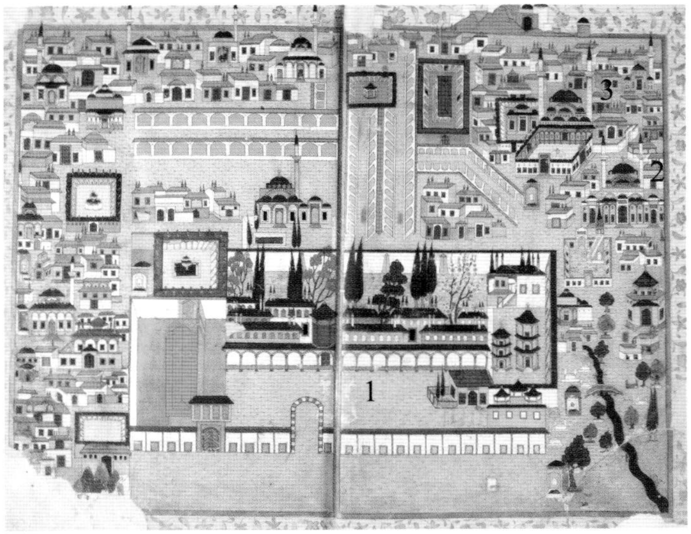

238 Map of Manisa (1. Palace of princes, 2. Hafsa Sultan mosque, 3. Muradiye), *c.* 1595, watercolour on paper, from Talikizade, *Shāhnāme-i Āl-i ʿOṣmān*.

royal patron, his endowment administrators, provincial officials, the users of the mosque, its architect, and the chief architect Sinan. The construction process can be subdivided into three distinct stages corresponding to the building and endowment of the small princely mosque (*c.* 1571–74), attempts at enlarging it without demolition (1577–82), and finally its replacement by a new sultanic mosque designed by Sinan (1583–86). The foundation inscription of the mosque, to which I shall return, only records this last stage: it gives the dates January–February 1583 and November–December 1586. The dependencies of the complex were not completed until 1590 (illus. 236, 237).[387]

The princely mosque seems to have been built shortly after prince Murad obtained permission in 1570 for the construction of a bath-house in Manisa. A likely date is 1571, the year his father married his mother. That year Nurbanu Sultan celebrated her upgraded status by laying the foundations of her own mosque complex in Üsküdar, designed by Sinan, who was then busy building the Selimiye in Edirne for her husband. Her son's provincial mosque must have been completed by 26 May 1572, when he requested a salary increase for the royal architect Nikola, who had served well in its construction.[388] Villages were endowed for the crown prince's pious foundation in February and November 1574, just before Selim II passed away in December, and an endowment deed was drawn up that year.[389] An auxiliary waqfiyya, dated 1576, lists additional villages endowed during the sultanate of Murad III and appoints Hacı Lüftullah as endowment administrator.[390]

The second stage of construction (1577–82) was precipitated by a decree issued on 31 May 1577, which responds positively to the endowment administrator Lütfullah's petition requesting the expansion of the mosque for the accommodation of its too large congregation. The sultan's response approves the enlargement of

239 (top) Muradiye mosque, Manisa, from the south with the Hafsa Sultan mosque in the background.

240 Muradiye mosque from the north.

241 [top] Muradiye mosque, Manisa, from the west.

242 [above] Muradiye mosque from the southwest.

the mosque on three sides (north, east, and west): 'I order it to be enlarged with vaulted extensions (*ṭurre*) above the gate and its two sides.'[391] We learn from a decree addressed to the kadi of Manisa on 23 March 1578 and handed over to Muhyiddin Halife (perhaps the architect in charge of the construction) that the endowment administrator had sent a letter explaining the lack of sufficient space at the west and north sides of the mosque. Extending its north portico would overlap with the ablution fountain (*şādırvān*), making it impossible to pray outdoors in the courtyard (*ḫarem*) in summertime.[392] Buying neighbouring 'endowed rooms' and adding some of their space to the mosque would allow not only its expansion with domes (*ḳubbe*), but also the construction of a much-needed elementary school in addition to a garden. The sultan approves the annexation of those rooms for the enlargement of his mosque 'with vaulted extensions (*ṭurre*) as previously ordered' and authorizes the school to be built in an 'appropriate' (*münāsib*) place, asking the kadi to start construction and send a written report of expenses.[393]

An auxiliary waqfiyya dated 1580 records new villages added to the endowment, most likely to increase the surplus income with which the remodelling project would be financed.[394] The endowment was further amplified during 1581 and 1582.[395] On 27 June 1582 the sultan ordered the sanjak governor of Saruhan, residing in its capital Manisa, to inspect the mosque together with the city's kadi and an imperial gatekeeper sent from the capital. They had to check whether the endowment was sufficient to cover renovation costs, since the waqf administrator had recently visited Istanbul to report the inadequacy of surplus funds. They are also asked to investigate the trustworthiness of the endowment's administrator and overseer. Moreover they had to report whether the proposal to replace with a madrasa the neighbouring convent (*zāviye*), whose dervishes were alleged to indulge in wine-drinking, was justifiable.[396] On 12 October 1582 the sultan asked the governor and the kadi to determine whether the mosque should be enlarged with 'vaults (*şundurma*) or domes (*ḳubbe*)', without harming its original core. They are urged to rapidly complete its construction and send a written report of expenses.[397]

Murad's instructions were clear: the mosque was to be enlarged but not demolished. That year the sultan dispatched an advance of 600,000 aspers to speed up its expansion.[398] A decree sent on 28 January 1583 to the neighbouring kadis of İzmir, Pergamum, Sardis, and Biga for the provision of carts to carry stone in return for a fee shows that the long-delayed remodelling project had finally started.[399] This date agrees with the foundation inscription, according to which the construction was commenced in January–February 1583. Another decree sent to the kadi of Manisa on 10 July 1583 acknowledges the sultan's receipt from the endowment administrator of a letter that reported the 'erection of scaffoldings inside the noble mosque, the demolition of its lateral domes, the laying of new foundations on its four sides, and the digging of the foundation

243 (right) Muradiye mosque, Manisa, interior with the royal tribune at the southeast corner.

244 (bottom) Muradiye mosque interior toward the west.

of a portico (*ṣoffa*) at its front.' This implies that the princely mosque had domed side aisles and that its preserved central dome was now being extended on all four sides (rather than just three, as previously ordered).[400]

The third stage of construction (1583–86) begins with a furious decree addressed on the same day to the kadi of İzmir, the former finance officer of Temesvár, and the kadi and the mufti of Manisa. They are asked to investigate why the princely mosque had been demolished against the sultan's explicit order:

> Despite my earlier imperial decree commanding the enlargement of the mosque as far as possible with wide wings on both sides (*ṭarafeynde vāsiʿ ṣoffalar*), it has been torn down, and new foundations have been laid, and a new construction has been initiated that is not large enough, and perhaps even smaller than its predecessor. Although it would have been feasible to build at a smaller cost a noble mosque in the manner of (*miṣāl*) the Mahmud Pasha and [Atik] Ali Pasha mosques in Istanbul, presently the construction of a smaller building has been commenced at a greater cost and expense. The copy of a petition and round robin, which explains the unseemly squandering of my wealth besides the many circumstances perpetrated against the noble shariʿa and the exalted decree, has been appended to this imperial decree and sent to you for the preparation of a report after examining the matter in question.[401]

The recipients of the decree are asked to explain in writing what had transpired, after inspecting the site and interrogating the individuals who signed the round robin. Another decree sent a week later, on 17 July 1583, to the kadi of Manisa and the building supervisor indicates that Manisans had formed various discordant but vocal factions supporting differing remodelling projects. As the users of the princely mosque, endowed to the Muslim community, they must have regarded it their legal right to interfere in its construction. At that point, the sultan asked his chief architect Sinan to settle disputes by drawing a new plan. The royal architect Mahmud Halife was sent from the capital to build the new mosque in accordance with that plan, approved by the sultan, without the interference of outsiders (Appendix 4.4):

> Presently, despite their lack of knowledge in matters of construction, the people of that town have come to disagree about the building and enlargement of my noble mosque in accordance with the manner seen appropriate (*münāsib*) by the architect. They have divided into many groups, each group urging it to be built differently. Consequently, the chief architect Sinan has drawn the plan (*kārnāme*) of the above-mentioned mosque and sent it to the foot of my imperial throne. After considering it with my imperial gaze I have given it my noble approval; when the royal architect Mahmud arrives there, I order you to have the above-mentioned mosque built according to the chief architect's plan, without allowing any outsider to dispute [it] or to intervene against my imperial order.[402]

What precipitated the unauthorized demolition of the princely mosque remains unknown. The tight-fisted sultan regarded the late-fifteenth-century grand vizirial mosques of Mahmud Pasha and Atik Ali Pasha in Istanbul as decorous exemplars for his generic remodelling project without ambitious pretensions (illus. 82–83, 88). Fronted by five-domed porticoes, each of those mosques has a projecting mihrab and subsidiary lateral spaces. In the end, the discrepancy between the sultan's notion of decorum and that of factional Manisans precipitated the construction of a more ambitious new mosque. Extra money was provided from Istanbul that year, along with stonemasons and porters called in from Bursa.[403]

After prince Mehmed's arrival at Manisa in 1584, his tutor Lala Pasha received several orders to oversee construction activities together with the building supervisor, Mustafa Çavuş. On 3 October 1585, close to the completion of the mosque, the court painter Üstad Mehmed Halife was sent from Istanbul to decorate it with his team of twelve royal painters.[404] A hundred and fifty custom-made Murano oil lamps, based on a design drawn on paper, were ordered for the sultan on 12 October 1584. Most likely destined for his mosque, whose profuse Murano lamps are praised by Evliya Çelebi, they were shipped from Venice at the end of December.[405] The prince's tutor was notified on 31 January 1586 that the royal architect Mehmed had been appointed with Sinan's recommendation to succeed his deceased predecessor, Mahmud Halife (Appendix 4.4). The tutor is asked to help the new architect complete the mosque without allowing the interference of outsiders:

> Sinan, who is presently the chief of my royal architects, has sent a letter reporting that Mahmud, the architect of my noble mosque that is being built in Manisa, has died and that Mehmed has been appointed with a decree as the architect in charge of finishing its incomplete construction with a daily wage of thirty aspers. Since he [Sinan] requests from me an imperial decree against the interference of any outsider, I order you that when the architect arrives, you employ him in all architecture-related matters for the remaining construction of that mosque, without allowing anyone to interfere, and that you oversee the completion of the ordered building according to the manner he deems appropriate (*münāsib*).[406]

The dependencies of the mosque took longer to build according to Mehmed Aşık, who stayed in Manisa for a year and a half in 1585–86 as the council scribe of prince Mehmed. The mosque had been inaugurated while he was still there, but when he left the city, the foundations of the madrasa were just being laid, and a site had been selected for the hospice. Later on, he heard from people who visited Manisa that both buildings had been completed. Writing in the late 1590s, he enumerates the components of the complex:[407]

> This unique city certainly is the most pleasant and beautiful of all towns in those parts. Especially after the completion of the double-minaret (*ẕū'l-mināreteyn*) mosque, the madrasa, and the hospice with a banqueting house for guests, built by the late Sultan Murad III – may he rest in peace – there is no question that Manisa became a paradise-like abode.

On 16 September 1590, prince Mehmed's finance officer was ordered to inspect the completed mosque, madrasa, and hospice in order to prepare an account book recording their construction costs from beginning to end.[408] Details of the complex were not finished until 1593, when the chief architect Davud sent from Istanbul the mason İstemad to lay pavements around it.[409] The first professor of the madrasa was appointed in the summer of 1592.[410] The hospice apparently replaced a smaller structure with a kitchen and pantry entrusted to a shaykh, which is mentioned in the waqfiyya dated 1576.[411] This pre-existing building may have been the dervish convent (*zāviye*) referred to above in a decree dated 1582, which asks whether or not it should be replaced by a madrasa. It seems to have been supplanted by the present hospice-cum-guest-house, where the 'shaykhs of the convent' (*ḫānḳāh şeyḫleri*), listed in a document drawn up in 1596–97, were based.[412] An undated Arabic waqfiyya of the Muradiye complex lists the madrasa, elementary school, and 'guest-house (*al-tābkhāna*) and hospice (*al-ʿimārat*)'. The latter, also referred to as a convent (*ṣawmaʿa*), was entrusted to a shaykh and twelve resident sufis.[413] Sinan's autobiographies mention only the mosque and hospice, omitting the madrasa, whose foundations were laid in 1586. An old photograph shows that the mixed masonry hospice once had modest vaults covered with red brick tiles, which have now been replaced by lead-covered domes.[414] The elementary school has disappeared, and the irregular composition of the complex testifies to its additive development with no preconceived master plan.[415]

The Muradiye is located at the southern end of Manisa, at a considerable distance from the no-longer-extant palace of princes depicted in a late-sixteenth-century miniature (illus. 238).[416] It is close to the mosque complex of Süleyman's mother Hafsa Sultan, built during the 1520s on the site of an outlying suburban garden estate (illus. 28, 239, 240).[417] The architectural novelty of the Muradiye mosque, with its layered polychromatic façades and elaborate fenestration, was accentuated by its proximity to the queen mother's archaic foundation. The stark cubical massing and heavy proportions of Hafsa Sultan's double-minaret mosque sharply contrasts with the graduated profile and lightness of the Muradiye, the only other mosque in Manisa featuring two single-galleried minarets.

The new mosque introduced to the 'City of Princes' not only the innovative architectural idiom of Sinan but also classical İznik tiles and up-to-date painted decorations. Its plan is a modern variant of the Atik Ali Pasha mosque, regarded as a decorous model in one of the sultan's decrees cited above (illus. 88). Fronted by a five-domed portico, the Muradiye features a small central dome (10.6 metres) extended on three sides with rectangular wings covered by cradle vaults. Its Bursa-arched lateral porticoes, supported on square pillars covered with slanting shed roofs, are simpler versions of their counterparts in the Şehzade Mehmed, Süleymaniye, and Selimiye mosques. Stringcourse mouldings and cornices articulate the layered composition of the east, west, and south façades, whose multi-tiered window arches are accentuated with alternating voussoirs of white and rose-coloured sandstone (illus. 241, 242). A prominent corkscrew moulding divides the walls into two horizontal zones, separating the ground-level windows from the paired upper ones which are framed by arches featuring lunettes with openwork grills. The rectangular, fenestrated bases of the cradle vaults constitute a third zone beneath the lofty central dome. The twin windows corresponding to the two lateral gates, and the royal tribune at the southeast corner (reached from its own gate on the east façade) are oddly differentiated from others by their blind-arch lunettes with internal İznik tile revetments. Another incongruity, attributable to the royal architects who executed Sinan's plan, is the lack of correspondence between the north façade and its five-bay portico.

The Muradiye comes close in conception to the royal mosques with square baldachins that Sinan designed for princesses in the capital: decorous models for a provincial sultanic mosque in the 'City of Princes'. It particularly recalls princess Mihrümah's mosque at Edirnekapı (*c.* 1563–70), with which it shares a stepped north tympanum arch perforated by windows and four dome-capped weight turrets punctuating the corners of the central dome, raised on a cubical base (illus. 286–87).[418] Its three cradle-vaulted projections, on the other hand, are reminiscent of the scheme of Mihrümah's mosque in Üsküdar (1543/44–48), whose central dome is surrounded by three half-domes (illus. 279–80). The corner domes of the Üsküdar mosque are eliminated in the Muradiye to create a projecting mihrab, typical of Sinan's post-Selimiye mosques.[419]

The Muradiye also resembles the mosque of the sultan's sister Shahsultan and her husband, Zal Mahmud Pasha, in Eyüp (1577–90), which was built under the supervision of the queen mother Nurbanu in accordance with her daughter's will (illus. 361–62).[420] Like the Muradiye, it has a square domed baldachin externally articulated by four dome-capped weight turrets. The extension of its central dome on the east, west, and north sides by means of vaulted wings conceptually resonates with the renovation project for the princely mosque initially proposed in 1577. Despite their differing ground plans, the two mosques share tall polychromatic façades with multiple tiers of windows accentuated by alternating voussoirs (illus. 365). Their windows, featuring pointed-arched lunettes with openwork grills, are a typical feature of Sinan's late mosques, whose innovative façade compositions no longer correspond to the configuration of inner space.

The luxurious decoration of the Muradiye compensates for its lack of monumentality (illus. 243, 244). İznik tile revetments combining floral designs with cursive inscriptions add to its prestige, given the omission of tilework from Sinan's other mosques in western and central Anatolia. Original painted decorations are preserved on the stone minbar and mihrab, and the wooden ceilings of the royal tribune and the muezzin's tribune along the north wall of the prayer hall. Europeanizing paintings added to the domical superstructure have been replaced with classical medallions and inscription roundels.[421]

The tapering dome on pendentives, which is too high to be seen upon entering the prayer hall, directs one's attention to the mihrab recess lavishly decorated with tiles and stained glass upper windows. The splendidly lit interior takes one by surprise, as do the continuous strips of windows lining the bases of the three curved cradle vaults, which lean inward at a marked angle. The sultanic status of the mosque is announced by its royal tribune (missing from prince Selim's mosque in Karapınar) and the foundation inscription carved on the three sides of its muqarnas-hooded portal. The central panel, in Arabic, gives the dates of construction and asks for the continuation of the reign of the sultan, who by building this elevated Friday mosque came nearer to God.[422] Accompanying Turkish inscriptions at the right and left above the lateral portal niches read:

> The possessor of the abundance of the sea of munificence,
> The Shah of the dominions of the Hijaz and Rum and Iraq,
> Who is the embodiment of all perfection,
>
> Built a mosque lofty as the horizons.
> A man of perception came for its visit,
> And recited its chronogram: 'The Kaʿba of Lovers'
> (*Kaʿbetü'l-ʿuşşāḳ*), the year 994 (1586).[423]

The reference to the Hijaz resonates with Murad's renovations in Mecca and Medina, while Iraq refers to newly conquered Persian territories. There are also unmistakeable allusions to the sultan's mystical orientation: his image as the 'perfect man' and the identification of his mosque as the 'Kaʿba of Lovers', that is, of enraptured sufis. A reference by Evliya Çelebi to the lecturing pulpits of shaykhs implies that the resident sufis of the complex actively participated in the mosque rituals.[424]

The epigraphic programme of the Muradiye glorifies God and invites the congregation to worship before it is too late. The beautiful names of God, prominently inscribed on İznik tile lunettes above some of the upper-level windows, resonate with oral litanies particularly favoured by the sufis. Goodwin compares the painted mihrab to that of Mevlana Celalüddin Rumi's shrine in Konya.[425] Popularly known as the 'Kaʿba of Lovers' (*Kaʿbetü'l-ʿuşşāḳ*), the shrine was provided with a new convent by Murad III in 1584–85. The white marble mihrab of the Muradiye has gilt inscriptions over red and green; the roundels that flank its muqarnas hood are inscribed with the Ikhlas sura (112:1-4), the names of Muhammad and the four caliphs, and the phrase 'What (wonders) God has willed!' Two rectangular İznik tile panels above the muqarnas hood cite the profession of faith and the standard mihrab verse (3:37). Another inscription panel above the mihrab partially quotes a verse from the Anʿam sura (6:54): 'Peace be unto you! Your Lord hath prescribed for Himself mercy.' The cartouches of the rectangular İznik tile window lunettes in the mihrab recess cite the Ikhlas sura affirming God's indivisible oneness; the same sura is repeated on the central roundel of the dome, accompanied by painted roundels with the revered names. The continuous tilework inscription band above the lunettes of the mihrab recess is inscribed with the Throne verse (2:255) declaring the absolute sovereignty of God over the heavens and the earth.

The rectangular tile panels above the ground-level windows that surround the prayer hall repeat the same verse, starting under the royal tribune and proceeding counter-clockwise up to the window at the right of the minbar, ending with the first two words from the next verse of the Baqara sura (2:256). The remaining part of that verse is inscribed outside the mosque, on four rectangular tile panels above the windows of the north portico: 'There is no compulsion in religion. The right direction is henceforth distinct from error. And he who rejecteth false deities and believeth in Allah hath grasped a firm handhold which will never break. Allah is Hearer, Knower.' On top of the pair of stone mihrabs on the same wall are carved the two lines of a hadith that extend invitations for worship and repentance: 'Hasten to prayer before passing away'; 'Hasten to repentance before death.' The inscriptions outside are not self-sufficient but follow those inside. In turn, the exhortative external inscriptions point toward the interior, by enticing repenting believers to enter and turn toward the 'right direction' inside the sanctuary, where God's oneness, sovereignty, and mercy are proclaimed together with the exaltation of His beautiful names.

Among the few early descriptions of the Muradiye complex is that of Hasanbeyzade:

> In the protected city of Manisa, which had been his seat of government as a prince, he [Murad III] built an ornate mosque with two minarets and a madrasa of unequalled foundations next to it, assigning seventy aspers to its professor, which made it the highest ranking of all madrasas. So much so that during his sultanate and caliphate some virtuous professors of the age came from the Süleymaniye, to this madrasa where they were appointed posts. And near that madrasa he also built a hospice-cum-convent (*ʿimāret ü ribāṭ*).[426]

Evliya Çelebi draws attention to the similarity between the Muradiye and the mosque of the couple Shahsultan and Zal Mahmud Pasha, which he calls the mosque of Zal Pasha:

> The mosque of sultan Murad III is so light-filled that it is as if its like were the mosque of Zal Pasha near Eyüp in Istanbul. In reality the said mosque of Zal Pasha is built in the same manner as this mosque, like an exact replica. But since this is a royal (*selāṭīn*) mosque it is more spacious and more ornate.[427]

Evliya's claim that the Muradiye was an exact replica of the 'Zal Pasha' mosque seems somewhat exaggerated, but he perceptively recognized their common gestalt. He may have been struck by the similar feel of their tall window-tiered façades and he particularly underlines the affinity of their light-filled interior spaces: both mosques feature vaulted side wings lined with continuous strips of upper windows (illus. 365, 367–69).

The Muradiye is not only the most innovative mosque of Manisa, but also of all provincial royal mosques attributed to Sinan. With its more elaborate plan, elevations, superstructure, and decorative programme, it stands out from the generic domed cubes of such roadside mosques as those of Sultan Süleyman in Damascus and of prince Selim in Karapınar. Neither Murad III nor Sinan visited Manisa to see the completed mosque. After its inauguration in 1586, it was mainly used by the princely court of the future ruler Mehmed, who like his father spent nearly twelve years in Manisa (1584–95). The administrators of Mehmed's court were actively engaged by imperial decrees to oversee the ongoing construction of the Muradiye. It is difficult to gauge whether the sultanic mosque was perceived as a status sign legitimizing the heir apparent's rule, or whether it robbed Mehmed of the option to build a princely mosque of his own. Given the sultan's jealousy of the popular crown prince, it seems likely that the Muradiye was meant to reinforce the subordination of son to father.

This conjecture is further supported by the building

chronology. To speed the delayed remodelling project, the sultan had sent decrees to the governor and kadi of Manisa in 1582 just around the time of his son's circumcision ceremony. The original mosque had been demolished by 10 July 1583, and the new Muradiye was designed within a week. One wonders whether Nurbanu Sultan might have seized this opportunity to stamp her own son's sultanic seal on the appanage of her archrival's son Mehmed.

The queen mother was experienced in matters of architectural decorum. She had overseen the construction of two of Sinan's royal mosque complexes that partially filled the vacuum of Murad's sultanic patronage in the capital: that of her own in Üsküdar (1571–86) and that of Shahsultan and Zal Mahmud in Eyüp (1577–90). Nurbanu's double-minaret mosque was enlarged after her death between 1584 and 1586. Overseen by Murad III, this posthumous remodelling project had been initiated by the ambitious queen mother herself, just before she passed away at the height of her power. Its implementation coincided with the construction of the new Muradiye in Manisa (1583–86).[428]

Can we perhaps see Nurbanu's imprint on the Muradiye's final design, through which she was seeking to create a noticeable familial resemblance between the mosques of her daughter and her son (a resemblance recognized by Evliya Çelebi)? Could she have incited the sultan to build a more impressive monument than the one he had initially conceived? Given the modesty of Murad's original remodelling project and his inability to withstand pressure from local factions, it is likely that the driving force behind the much more assertive third phase of construction was not the sultan but his formidable mother. The queen mother's desire to see her son's imperial authority projected more strongly in Manisa may explain the sudden change in tone that characterizes the new construction. Nurbanu had spent fourteen years (1544–58) in Manisa, during which she gave birth to prince Selim's three daughters and son Murad. The precedent of mosques built in that city by the mothers of governor-princes (Hüsnişah Sultan in 1490, and Hafsa Sultan in the 1520s) could have given her an extra incentive to get involved with the final construction phase of her own son's mosque.

In addition to creating a mosque complex of unprecedented monumentality for herself inside the capital, Nurbanu may have wished to leave her personal mark on her son's provincial foundation, following the example of former queens. The timing of the new Muradiye allows us to speculate on her ultimate goal: trumping Safiye and her son prince Mehmed. With its sultanic identity embodying a higher status level than its demolished predecessor, the Muradiye commemorated the former presence of the reigning monarch in Manisa during his days as a crown prince. Like the Selimiye, recognized by contemporaries as Selim II's gift to Edirne, where he had once governed during his princehood, the Muradiye became a permanent memory marker associated with its royal patron's initially reluctant munificence toward Manisans.

IV. DEVLET GİRAY KHAN I

The funerary mosque of Devlet Giray I (r. 1551–77) alongside the port of Gözleve is the only example of its kind in the Crimea (illus. 245, 246). It was built soon after its patron assumed the title of khan in 1551, upon eliminating his reigning uncle Sahib Giray in a bloody coup staged with the help of Sultan Süleyman. After the khanate of Crimea had become a vassal of the Ottoman state during Mehmed II's reign in 1475, the Giray dynasty, boasting Chingizid descent, enjoyed sole rights of succession.[429] A faction headed by the grand vizier Rüstem Pasha convinced Süleyman to replace Sahib Giray with his nephew, who had been kept hostage in Istanbul according to dynastic custom. Factors contributing to the reigning khan's fall from favour included bypassing the grand vizier in his written correspondence with the sultan, his growing political autonomy, and his audacity in requesting for himself the customs of the Gözleve port, which the sultan granted with considerable resentment.[430]

Sahib Giray was ordered to lead a campaign against the Georgians so that his nephew could seize the throne in his absence. Before his departure from Istanbul with soldiers and a treasury, the new candidate to the khanate ceremonially kissed the hand of the sultan, who reminded him not to forget this favour. Accompanied by 300 janissaries and 400 newly recruited *kuls*, Devlet Giray embarked on a ship at Akkirman that landed in Gözleve on 28 September 1551. With horses supplied by the port's garrison and its people, who were the first to offer him their allegiance, he headed to the capital, Bahçesaray. He declared himself khan on 2 October after confiscating the palace treasures there, and ordered his uncle, who was returning from the Caucasus, killed along with all male descendants.[431]

The plan of the funerary mosque in Gözleve, referred to in Sinan's autobiographies as the mosque and mausoleum of 'Tatar Khan', may have been designed by the chief architect and approved by the sultan just before Devlet Giray left Istanbul.[432] The chief architect, who was then fully preoccupied with the Süleymaniye, could not have left the capital. The date of construction, recorded by a modern Turkish inscription on the mosque portal, is 1552.[433] The mosque was probably built under the supervision of a royal architect sent from Istanbul, with the help of janissaries and local masons, perhaps imported from nearby Caffa, which supplied builders for the Süleymaniye.

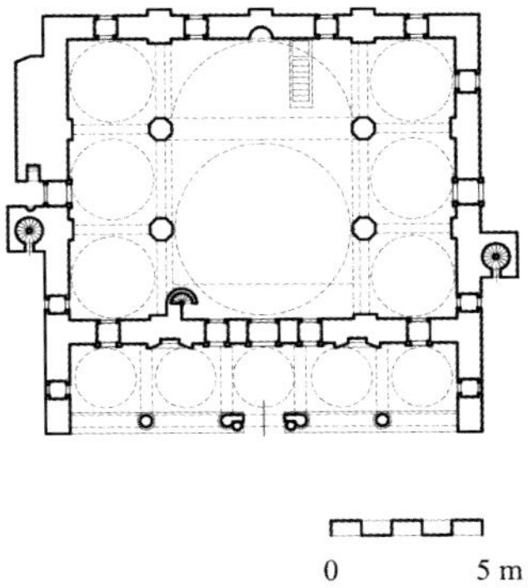

245 Plan of the Tatar Khan mosque, Gözleve (now Yevpatoria).

246 Sketch with Spanish legends displayed at the Tatar Khan mosque, showing its missing minarets and neighbourhood, 1892.

The renovated mosque dominates the port of Gözleve, whose customs were collected by Devlet Giray and his successors (illus. 247, 248).[434] It can be interpreted as a victory monument commemorating the successful coup by its patron. To articulate Devlet Giray's newly won status as khan, it paraphrases in miniature scale the plan of Mehmed II's sultanic mosque in Istanbul. Decorum was maintained by omitting the forecourt of its model, exclusive to sultanic mosques in Istanbul and Edirne, in favour of a five-domed portico carried on columns with muqarnas capitals. The six-metre-wide central dome is considerably smaller than that of Mehmed II's mosque, which was crowned by a twenty-six-metre dome and flanked by lateral domes seven metres wide (illus. 59–61).[435] Devlet Giray's sovereign status is communicated by single-galleried twin minarets that asymmetrically protrude from the lateral walls of the mosque and an internal royal tribune at the southeast corner, reached from the staircase of a projecting tower-like annex.

A variant of the same antiquated plan was used in Sultan Süleyman's provincial mosque adjoining Mevlana Celalüddin Rumi's shrine in Konya, another victory monument built around 1559–60 to commemorate prince Selim's triumph during the war of the princes. The more monumental mosque in Konya, omitted from Sinan's autobiographies, must have been the work of a local architect. It is covered by a twelve-metre dome and fronted by a seven-domed portico appended with two single-galleried minarets (illus. 36–38). The dome of the Gözleve mosque is raised on pendentives above a layered cubical base carrying a Sinanesque window-pierced drum with engaged buttresses. Its central space is flanked by upper galleries resting on round arches above two piers on each side, with a wooden gallery extending along the anti-qibla wall (illus. 249). The whitewashed prayer hall exhibiting a provincial flavour has completely lost its original paintings and inscriptions. Its quaint muqarnas-hooded mihrab is accompanied by a modern minbar of wood.

The layout of the mosque decorously expressed the status of the khans of Crimea, outlined in a mid-seventeenth-century Ottoman law code. They had the right to strike their own coins, but it was not until 1584–85 that their name began to be mentioned in the khutba after the sultan's:[436]

> As descendants of Chingis Khan, the Crimean khans, who are among Islamic monarchs with the right to have the khutba recited and coins struck in their own name, have accepted obedience and submission to the Ottoman dynasty. Their deposition and accession, or their replacement and appointment, have been the prerogative of the mighty sultans. Nevertheless, in letters and various circumstances they enjoy precedence over other rulers in magnificence and honour. The sons of khans have priority of status over the viziers; during religious festivities they are the first to kiss the sultan's hand.[437]

In terms of protocol, then, the khans ranked higher than other monarchs, while their sons, held hostage in Istanbul, ceremonially superseded the viziers. With its prestigious Chingizid lineage, the Giray family descended from an older and, in certain parts of Eurasia, better-known dynasty than the House of Osman. Hence Ottoman establishment of political supremacy over the Crimean Tatars was no trivial matter.

Decorum dictated that the mosque of Devlet Giray I, once sited next to the fortress of Gözleve, should befit his privileged royal status without surpassing the rank of the sultan. Evliya Çelebi describes it as the most impressive among the city's twelve congregational mosques, mentioning its dynastic mausoleum (no longer extant), where the khan and his descendants were buried:

> The tallest, most elaborate, and most excellent of all is the mosque of Bahadır Giray Khan [*sic*], whose length and width from its main gate to its mihrab is 150 feet. On the left side of this mosque is an artistic [royal] tribune where the great khans perform their prayers, and it has two tall minarets. But one of them has collapsed during an earthquake, while the other one at the right side is extant. This humble one climbed it to observe and scrutinize the monuments of the city and its pentagonal shape. On my way down I counted 105 steps. In reality this tall minaret is artistic because it is the work of the great architect Mimar Sinan Agha b.

247 (top) Tatar Khan mosque, Yevpatoria, from the north.

248 Tatar Khan mosque from the seaside, with the projecting entrance to the royal tribune near the southeast corner.

249 Tatar Khan mosque interior, detail of east gallery with the door of the royal tribune.

> Abdülmennan, who built Sultan Süleyman's mosque in Istanbul. Indeed it is an agreeable, cheerful, and joy-increasing, beautiful sanctuary, but its forecourt is too small for this mosque, which is located in the crowded market-place of the city. It is an exhilarating royal (*selāṭīn*) mosque with a large congregation. In fact, this city has no other light-filled and ornate mosque covered with indigo-coloured lead. The lead on its domes sparkles from a distance of one parasang. In front of its mihrab the lords and khans are buried. Across the street from its forecourt is an elegant and graceful bathhouse only rivalled by the Defterdar and Sinaniye baths in Damascus... Again across the street, at the left side of the forecourt of the mosque, is the inner citadel of the city... At the east side of this citadel is a great and beautiful fortress with big cannons facing the port. Every Friday its warden raises flags and banners from the crenellations and after the prayers are over they close the fortress gates.[438]

The imperial iconography of the 'Tatar Khan' mosque raised its rank above the generic domed cubes that Sinan designed for governor-generals in the provinces of the empire. The royal mosque proclaimed the sovereign status of Devlet Giray I, whose cultural identity had been forged during his formative years in Istanbul, while at the same time announcing the growing intrusiveness of Ottoman suzerainty in the Crimea. That is why the uneasy khan gave little help in 1569 to Sokollu's project of connecting with a canal the Volga and the Don in order to counter the threat of Muscovy, to establish a base for campaigns against the Safavids, and to encourage trade relations with Central Asia: he feared that by stationing troops there the Sublime Porte might further tighten its clutch on the Crimea.[439] The victory mosque built to celebrate the successful coup of the understandably cautious khan also expressed the limits of his subservient royal authority, circumscribed by that of his overlord.

Chapter 7

QUEENS: WIVES AND MOTHERS OF SULTANS

I. HÜRREM SULTAN (HASEKİ SULTAN)
ISTANBUL, AVRATPAZARI (1538/39–1540, 1550–51)
JERUSALEM (*c.* 1550–57)
MUSTAFA PASHA BRIDGE NEAR EDİRNE
(NOW SVİLENGRAD, 1559–60)

II. NURBANU SULTAN (ATİK VALİDE)
ISTANBUL, ÜSKÜDAR (1571–86)

I. HÜRREM SULTAN (HASEKİ SULTAN)

Süleyman's wife, Haseki Hürrem Sultan, stamped her architectural imprint on the principal urban centres of the empire: its two capitals and three Holy Cities (illus. 250). Her pious foundations were part of a consistent building programme through which she must have hoped to construct her public persona as a philanthropic queen devoted to the welfare of Ottoman subjects, travellers, and pilgrims. Bearing her official title, 'Haseki Sultan', each of her foundations was provided with a hospice and water channel, forms of charity reserved for the highest level of patronage. It was Hürrem's special status that fuelled her aspiration to launch a legacy of charitable foundations unmatched by that of any former Ottoman queen.

The unique stature of Hürrem stemmed from Süleyman's transgression of three dynastic principles on her behalf in allowing her to bear more than one son, taking her as his legal wife, and keeping her by his side at the capital.[1] Unable to tolerate these innovations, certain segments of the populace blamed her for bewitching the sultan with her charms. Luigi Bassano wrote in the 1530s that Hürrem was called '*Ziadi*, which means witch', and noted with some exaggeration her unpopularity: 'The janissaries and the entire court hate her and her children likewise, but because the sultan loves her, no one dares to speak; I have always heard everyone speak ill of her and of her children, and well of the firstborn and his mother, who has been repudiated'.[2]

250 *Haseki Hürrem Sultan* (La Rossa), c. 1550, woodcut published by Matteo Pagan in Venice.

The mother of Süleyman's oldest son Mustafa, born in 1515, fell from favour when Hürrem gave birth to six children in rapid succession: Mehmed (1521), Mihrümah (*c.* 1522), Abdullah (1522–23; he died shortly after birth), Selim (1524), Bayezid (1525), and Cihangir (1531). Believed to have been captured as a slave during a Tatar raid in Ruthenia, Hürrem seems to have originated from Rogatin in the 'Little Russia' of Poland, now in the western Ukraine. Polish tradition identifies her as Aleksandra Lisowska, the daughter of a Ruthenian Catholic priest. According to some sources, she was first raised in the household of one of Süleyman's sisters and then given to his mother, who in turn presented her as a gift to her son. She was nicknamed Hürrem (cheerful, smiling, blooming), but Europeans called her Roxelana (a Polish term for 'Ruthenian maiden') or La Rossa (a reference to her 'Russian' origin).[3] The Venetian diplomat Pietro Zen commented in 1524 that Süleyman was now faithful to a single woman, an observation repeated in 1526 by Pietro Bragadin who characterizes Hürrem as 'young, not beautiful, but graceful and petite.'[4] After becoming monogamously devoted to her, the sultan married off nearly all the eligible concubines of his harem.[5]

With his mother, Mustafa was sent away to govern Manisa in 1533 and Hürrem began to reign supreme at the imperial harem after her mother-in-law passed away in March 1534. Süleyman married her in a lavish wedding held at the Hippodrome sometime around June 1534.[6] Through this radical breach of dynastic tradition, Hürrem became the first slave concubine freed to become a sultan's legal wife. Süleyman's boundless passion for her is immortalized in his poems, just as the private letters she penned to him during his frequent absence in campaigns are filled with yearning and the anguish of separation: 'I swear by God I am burning day and night by the fire of your longing; my only wish in this world is you!' They also reflect her special maternal devotion to her two senior children, Şehzade Mehmed and Mihrümah, who are singled out in a letter explaining how much the absent sultan was missed: 'When your noble letters are read, your servant and son Mir Mehmed and your slave and daughter Mihrümah weep and wail from missing you. Their weeping has driven me mad ... my sultan, your son Mir Mehmed and your daughter Mihrümah and Selim Khan and Abdullah send you many greetings and rub their faces on the dust at your feet.' The queen's letters additionally bear witness to her influence as the sultan's intimate political confidante.[7] Among her diplomatic letters, those addressed to the kings of Poland document her role in preserving peaceful relations with her native country.[8]

Promoting her sons as legitimate heirs to the throne was Hürrem's lifelong preoccupation. According to Hans Dernschwam (1553–55), Süleyman had married her after making her a freedwoman so that her sons would inherit the throne 'and not Mustafa, born from a slave and bondswoman.' Busbecq observes that Hürrem tried to 'counteract Mustafa's merits and his rights as the eldest son by asserting her authority as a wife.'[9] She was instrumental in the execution of the grand viziers İbrahim Pasha (d. 1536) and Kara Ahmed Pasha (d. 1555) because they both favoured prince Mustafa, and she formed a notorious alliance with her son-in-law Rüstem Pasha, who was promoted to grand vizier soon after marrying her only daughter Mihrümah in 1539. The trio's scheming was crowned with success in 1553 with prince Mustafa's elimination, but the queen did not live long enough to see the outcome of the bitter struggle for succession between her own sons Selim and Bayezid.[10] She passed away as Haseki Sultan (mother of princes), unable to relish the higher status of Valide Sultan (queen mother) that would have retroactively conferred on her a royal lineage.

The Meccan Sharif's envoy, who was in Istanbul when Hürrem passed away in 1558 from 'malaria and colic', applauds her pious foundations in Mecca, Medina, Jerusalem, and other places. He says the heart of the sultan, who was 'madly in love', was shattered by her death, which 'filled with grief the whole population of Istanbul.' Her coffin was carried on the shoulders of grandees to the mosque of Bayezid II, where the shaykh al-Islam Ebussuud performed her funeral service. He buried her with his own hands behind the Süleymaniye mosque where Sinan began to build her mausoleum (illus. 186).[11] Surely not everyone mourned the demise of Hürrem, who was amply hated for her unsavoury 'meddling' in politics. Some late-sixteenth-century historians stigmatized her as the conniving instigator of harem intrigues, perceived as a leading cause of Ottoman 'decline'. The much-maligned queen's elusive persona lies somewhere between the bad press she received and her own attempts at self-representation, dominated by the palpable record of her architectural memorials.

Hürrem publicized her benevolence through a multitude of charitable foundations, formally modest yet functionally magnanimous. Shaped by codes of decorum befitting her official title, her mosques did not boast such royal status markers as twin minarets. The use of two minarets, previously limited to sultanic patronage, had been permitted for the first time during Süleyman's reign in mosques built for his closest blood relatives: his mother Hafsa Sultan (Manisa, 1520s), his daughter Mihrümah Sultan (Üsküdar, 1543/44–48), and the crown princes Mehmed (Istanbul, 1543–48) and Selim (Karapınar, 1560–63/64). During the late fifteenth and early sixteenth centuries, the mothers of princes generally built mosque complexes in provincial cities where they resided with their only son. Hürrem, the mother of several princes, was the first queen to stay in the imperial palace with her husband and to build a mosque complex of her own inside the capital. Nevertheless, the simple domed-cube plan of her mosque in Avratpazarı discreetly conformed to norms of propriety observed in the single-minaret mosques of former royal consorts.[12]

Codes of decorum constrained Hürrem to negotiate her contested status in the public sphere through visually restrained monuments. It was neither their monumentality nor their stylistic originality that made them distinctive, but rather their unprecedented quantity and the richly endowed charitable services they provided. Through these pious foundations, Hürrem not only aspired to acquire merit in God's eyes, but also to rectify her negative public image. That the queen's project to redeem herself, and by extension her children, through a 'public relations' strategy centred on architectural patronage was not lost on some Ottoman historians. An anonymous chronicle written for Rüstem Pasha, for instance, portrays the 'late Haseki Sultan' in an unusually positive light as 'such a generous patroness of charitable foundations and good works that no noble site remained where she had not expended her largess and favours.'[13] In the 1590s Talikizade eulogized Hürrem as a sturdy 'pillar' of her husband's sultanate, comparing her innumerable public works with those of the celebrated Abbasid queen Zubayda:

> One of the firm pillars supporting the sultanate of his noble highness was his illustrious, canonically lawful wife's world-nourishing, potent magnanimity and the flourishing harvest of her benevolence. In the Abbasid state the glorious wife of Harun al-Rashid, Zubayda Hatun, had shown an affinity and inclination for the sciences, helped the ulema, strengthened the soldiers, who are the protectors of the

nation's borders, and comforted the peasants, who are the supports of the state's dominions. Books of history are filled with that great lady's glory and generosity. Similarly, wherever there was a pious shaykh deserving veneration, Haseki Sultan made him happy with good works, and wherever she found out about the existence of a place in need of assistance, she ordered her fortune to be spent on it, building many Friday mosques and convents for shaykhs and constructing numerous madrasas for the ulema. Wherever there was a dilapidated masjid she would have it repaired, and she built countless neighbourhood masjids, Friday mosques, bath-houses, shops, convents for the poor dervishes, waterworks, and bridges. She endowed weapons and horses for the ghazis of the frontiers; and in halting stations on the way to Holy Mecca she built reservoirs and castles. For hajj pilgrims and their caravans she provided travelling provisions, including medicines for the sick, saddled beasts, horses, and resting places. She also endowed funds for janissaries whose baggage had been destroyed during imperial campaigns. And she had scribes with calligraphic talent write books of excellence distributed to students throughout the empire's protected domains, making a gift for the pure soul of the Prophet of 1,200 *Muḥammediye*s [written by Yazıcıoğlu Mehmed in 1449]. And in whichever country she heard of a rare curiosity, she was in the habit of taking great pains to have it brought to Istanbul. For instance, she imported a golden goblet from the island of İstanköy, multi-layered velvets from Europe, and from Egypt a thousand pairs of Yusufi turtledoves, which are still used as mail pigeons in the lofty imperial council. In this exalted and fortunate state she left behind numerous and countless praiseworthy memorials. The Lady of Time has not seen such an abundantly benevolent dame![14]

This remarkably favourable passage, also testifying to Hürrem's passion for rarities, conveys the kindness she showered on various groups such as the ulema, shaykhs, students, pilgrims, travellers, ghazis, and the janissaries, who detested her for scheming against prince Mustafa. To maximize the visibility of her charitable endevours, the vilified queen not only built new structures but also renovated old ones to which she assigned additional endowments. The 'populist' dimension of her charitable works, targeting various sectors of society, suggests that she recognized the mediating role of architectural patronage in the construction of favourable public opinion.

Since Hürrem was widely identified with Zubayda – Süleyman's waqfiyya and a title deed dated 1560 refer to her as 'the Zubayda of the age' – it is not surprising that she consciously cultivated this association by undertaking the renovation of charitable works named after the Abbasid queen: castles with reservoirs along the hajj route (Darb Zubayda) and a conduit carrying water to the Kaʿba from Mount ʿArafat (ʿAyn Zubayda).[15] After his wife's demise, the sultan continued the renovation of the ʿArafat water channel, which was completed by their daughter Mihrümah in 1572 and further expanded by their son Selim II (1572–74).[16] Through their combined munificence in Mecca, Süleyman and Hürrem strove to be perceived as a royal couple worthy of succeeding the great caliphs, sultans, and queens of the past.[17] Most Ottoman writers, however, silence Hürrem's voice in these jointly sponsored Meccan projects, which Sinan supervised from the capital, by ascibing them exclusively to Süleyman.[18] This prejudice of patriarchal male authors is exemplified by Ramazanzade Mehmed's chronicle from the early 1560s, which enumerates the queen's monuments under her husband's patronage, thereby denying her agency in architectural enterprises:

> For the late mother of princes, Haseki Sultan, a decorated Friday mosque, an excellent madrasa, a generous hospice, and a hospital for patients was built near the [Arcadius] column in the year 932 (1525–26) [*sic*]. Again for the late Haseki Sultan, a magnanimous hospice was erected at the Great Kaʿba and another grandiose hospice was constructed in Medina the Illuminated, where each day the poor of Mecca and Medina are liberally feasted. And in the city of Edirne a kauthar-like water channel bestowing life to the gardens of hope was created, along with many fountains flowing day and night with water. And on the river of Meriç [Maritza, near Edirne], at the head of the bridge of [Çoban] Mustafa Pasha, a Friday mosque, a hospice, and caravansarays were constructed.[19]

Among these monuments, all actually commissioned and endowed by the queen herself, only the last one was built by her husband as a posthumous memorial on her behalf. Ramazanzade's list is also incomplete: it omits Hürrem's hospice complex in Jerusalem and other charities recorded in her waqfiyyas. The deeds to crown lands that Süleyman donated as her freehold property indicate that her endowments were made possible by his generosity, just as his imperial decrees expedited her construction projects, but that is true for almost all monuments built by grandees. Moreover, it was Hürrem's own vision and personal wealth that sustained her nearly full-time career as a patroness of architecture, empowering her to erect a widespread network of monuments far surpassing the limited undertakings of her predecessors. The sultan awarded his bride with a substantial dowry of 100,000 ducats (6,000,000 aspers) when he married her.[20] In the 1550s her daily stipend rose to 2,000 aspers, a record sum much greater than the salary of previous mothers of princes. Süleyman's own mother, for example, had received only 200 aspers a day during his time as a prince, and the stipend of *haseki*s dropped to 1,000 aspers later in the sixteenth century. The sum granted to Hürrem underlines the exceptional nature of the sultan's treatment of his one and only queen, who had borne him so many children.[21]

Her two waqfiyyas, dated 1540 and 1551, record the endowments of her mosque complex at Avratpazarı in Istanbul.[22] Its waqfs supported various other monuments with endowed funds: a now-lost Friday mosque in Ankara named after the queen;[23] a mosque at Kağıthane in Istanbul, built by the nurse of her son Şehzade Mehmed;[24] Shaykh Toklu Dede's convent-masjid at the Ayvansaray quarter of the capital;[25] the convent of Shaykh Hasan Dede at Aksaray (Istanbul); another convent in the village of Acı Pınar (Karapınar) at Aksaray (Anatolia); the convent-mosque built by the Halveti shaykh Mevlana Muslihüddin (Merkez Efendi, d. 1552) in his birthplace at Sarı Mahmudlu in Denizli, and the convent of his son Shaykh Ahmed b. Mevlana Muslihüddin (d. 1562–63) in Uşak. A convent, endowed in 1549 by Hürrem near Edirnekapı, was transformed later on into a madrasa because of the unorthodox behaviour of its dervishes.[26] Known as the Kariye (or Kahriyye) madrasa, and listed in Sinan's autobiographies, it can be identified as the Toklu Dede convent.[27] Hürrem's sponsorship of dervish convents, which were downplayed in her husband's architectural patronage, displayed her personal sufi piety and her desire to enhance her reputation among the populace as a supporter of popular religion. The three monuments that Sinan designed for her in Istanbul, Jerusalem, and near Edirne were Friday mosque-cum-hospice complexes.

THE COMPLEX IN AVRATPAZARI

Hürrem's complex at Avratpazarı comprises a Friday mosque, a hospice, a madrasa, an elementary school, and hospital (illus. 251, 252). This paratactical complex, bisected by a narrow cobbled street lined on both sides with window-pierced walls and gates, was Sinan's earliest royal project. Built shortly after Hürrem's marriage to the sultan in 1534, and probably financed by her dowry, it can be interpreted as an architectural celebration of her newly enhanced status. According to Dernschwam, its construction marked Hürrem's graduation from a slave concubine into a freedwoman married to the sultan:

> Before his Russian wife was freed by the sultan, she wanted to build and endow a masjid for which she petitioned the clerics. This was not allowed and approved by the mufti, who is the Turkish Pope, until she was manumitted by the sultan. Thereupon she had a mosque built at her own expense, together with a bath-house in the Jewish quarter [Eminönü] that brings yearly rents to that mosque.[28]

In the *Tuhfe* the complex is identified as the 'noble Friday mosque of Haseki Sultan in Avratpazarı; madrasa, 1; hospital, 1; elementary school, 1'; but the hospice is curiously omitted.[29] Hürrem's waqfiyya of 1540 mentions the madrasa constructed across from her Friday mosque, the adjacent elementary school for teaching the Koran to poor children, and the adjoining 'flourishing hospice' composed of a kitchen, refectory, pantry, firewood cellar, and latrines. The hospital 'behind the madrasa' is only included in the queen's second waqfiyya dated 1551, as it was added to her complex during the construction of the Süleymaniye.[30] Ayvansarayi quotes the now-lost chronogram on its gate: 'A hospital beneficial to the people of the world, 957 (1550–51).'[31]

The single domed mosque was completed in 945 (1538-39) according to a Turkish foundation inscription added above its portal in 1612–13, which explains that the 'late sultana's' building was expanded with a second dome by its endowment administrator to accommodate its larger congregation.[32] The lunette-shaped Turkish inscription panel in *cuerda seca* tilework formerly on the portal of the madrasa shows that it was finished in 946 (1539–40), a year after the mosque.[33] The arched lunette of the street gate of the hospice bears a carved stone inscription in Turkish whose chronogram yields the completion date of 947 (1540): 'May the kitchen (*maṭbaḫ*) always be prosperous.'[34]

A hitherto unknown account book of Hürrem's hospice confirms that it was built in 1540, soon after the madrasa.[35] This document is identified on its title-page as:

> The account of expenses for the construction of the kitchen (*maṭbaḫ*), and pantry (*kilār*), and bakery (*furun*), and storage cellar (*anbar*), and refectory (*ma'akil*), and raised platform (*sedd*), and water conduit (*kehrīz*), and pavement (*ḳaldırım*), and water channel (*rāh-ı āb*), and spout (*muṣluḳ*), and the trough of the spout (*dibek-i muṣluḳ*) near the noble Friday mosque by the order of Her Highness the mother of Sultan Mehmed – long may she live – with the mediation of Mehmed Beg, the *müteferriḳa* of the imperial court, and by the pen of the poor scribe Katib Halil, from the beginning of the month of Zilkade in the year of 946 until the month of Receb 947 [March to November/December 1540].[36]

We learn from this preamble that the hospice lacked a guest-house, probably because it was sited in a residential quarter served by the neighbouring hospice-cum-guest-house of Davud Pasha's mosque complex built in the late fifteenth century. The hospice commissioned by the 'mother of prince Mehmed' was constructed by her building supervisor Müteferrika Mehmed Beg. The account book later identifies him as the administrator of the queen's endowment, overseen by Ahmed (probably a eunuch).[37] Hürrem's waqfiyyas list the same Mehmed Beg b. Abdurrahman as her endowment administrator, and the chief white eunuch of the imperial palace as its overseer.[38] The grand total of expenses for the hospice (1,579,085 aspers) was covered by money periodically given out from the imperial palace, supplemented by funds left over from the madrasa and the surplus accruing from the waqf (Appendix 2).[39]

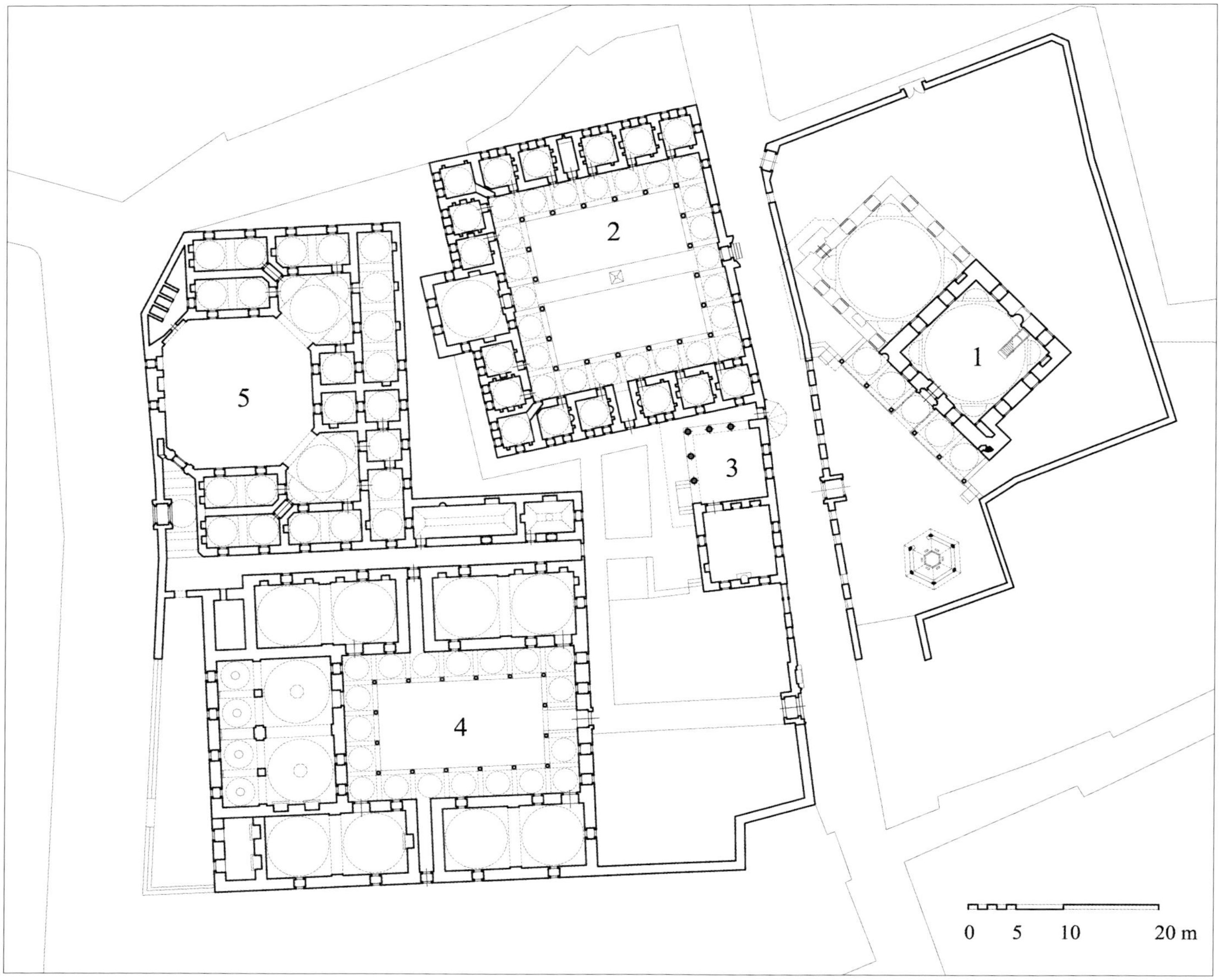

251 Plan of the Hürrem Sultan complex, Avratpazarı: 1. Mosque with extension added in 1612. 2. Madrasa. 3. Elementary school. 4 Hospice. 5 Hospital.

The purchase in 1540 of the plot of land for this building confirms the lack of a master plan for the complex, which developed by accretion.[40] A paved street with a water channel connected to the bazaar of Aksaray supplied water to the hospice and the arched public fountain adjacent to its street gate.[41] The account book shows that the hospice once had tilework lunettes over its inner courtyard gate and the six windows flanking it.[42]

The timing of the deeds of villages Süleyman donated as Hürrem's freehold property in 1539 and 1540 coincided with the first stage of construction, marked by the initial waqfiyya of 1540.[43] The second waqfiyya, registered in 1551 after the completion of the hospital, includes additional endowments. Hürrem also bequeathed real estate properties in the capital, including shops and rental rooms for families near her complex and a double bath designed by Sinan in the Jewish quarter in Bahçekapı (Eminönü).[44] She reserved the right to administer and alter the stipulations of her endowment during her lifetime, using its surplus income as she pleased. After her death it would be monitored by her proxy, the ruling sultan.

The queen's maternal compassion is captured by the unusually considerate specifications of her waqfiyyas: the elementary school teacher had to be affectionate like a father, and the cheerful shaykh of the hospice had to greet needy visitors with sweet words, refraining from breaking their hearts with derogatory treatment. The two congenial physicians of the hospital had to converse with patients like affectionate friends, avoiding 'unkind words that can be a heavier burden than the worst kind of affliction to invalids', to whom tender words are 'sweeter than the fountain of paradise'.[45] Such humane requirements are missing in the hospital section of Süleyman's waqfiyya, which stresses

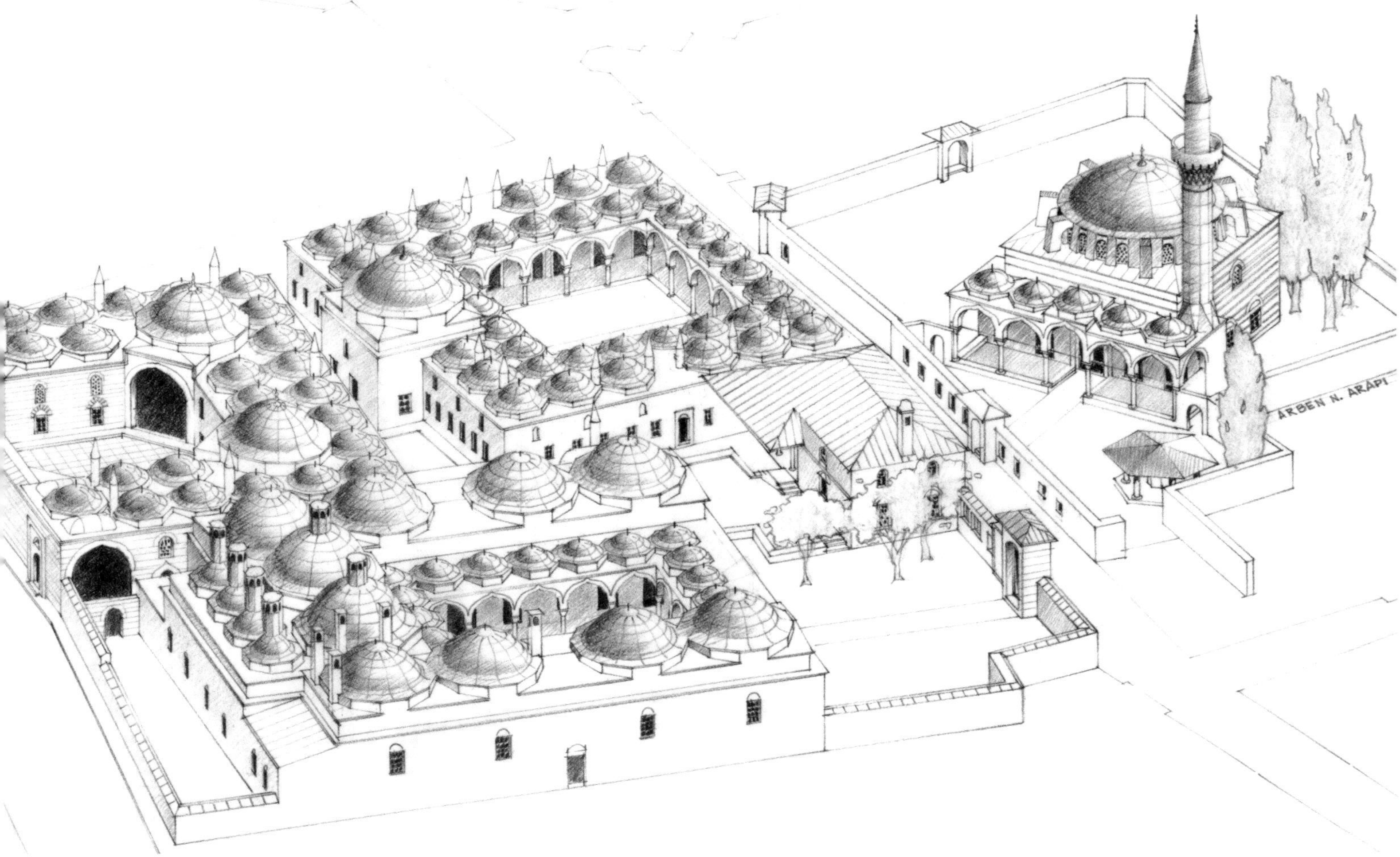

252 Axonometric projection of the Hürrem Sultan complex, Avratpazarı.

competence in the science of medicine.[46] The queen's concern with patient psychology was perhaps a corollary of her own nurturing qualities, stemming from her personal experiences with her frail, hunchbacked son Cihangir and her gout-stricken, ailing husband. Part of the surplus of her endowment was earmarked to free slaves, an indication that she never forgot her slave origin.[47] Touched by the plight of novices (janissary cadets) employed in the construction of her mosque, Hürrem is said to have sold her jewellery to increase their monthly wage with a perpetual endowment so that they could afford haircuts and shoes. This tradition (alternatively reported with reference to the complex of her son Şehzade Mehmed), not only shows that she inspected these building sites but also demonstrates her maternal empathy.[48]

Hürrem's mosque complex was sited at the north side of Avratpazarı, the imperial forum of Arcadius, featuring at its centre a historiated triumphal column known as the Maiden's or Woman's column (Kıztaşı or Avrattaşı) (illus. 253). The arcaded forum, which once extended beyond the walled garden behind the qibla wall of the mosque, is shown intact in late-fifteenth-century city maps (illus. 72).[49] Annual account books of the queen's waqf list the income generated from selling fruits and flowers grown in the gardens of her complex.[50] An employee of the waqf was a gardener in charge of 'the gardens in front of the mosque and along its sides', and of 'the garden fronting the hospice'.[51]

Dernschwam says the public square known as 'Awrat Pazar, or Women's Market' was surrounded on three sides by cheap wooden stalls and huts bringing income to various pious endowments. Only its fourth side preserved the remains of the forum arcade. Dernschwam saw seeds, plants, vegetables, and kitchen basics (*Fratschlerei*) sold at the weekly market held there on Sundays. He says the public square functioned as a 'whore-market' on other days. In the 1630s Bayram Pasha endowed there a khan for the sale of slaves, bringing income to the madrasa complex he built adjacent to that of the queen.[52] Avratpazarı was,

253 Avratpazarı and the column of Arcadius, *c.* 1610, woodcut.

indeed, a generic term used for markets where both male and female slaves were sold.[53] However, some sources attribute the name of the public square in Avratpazarı to its weekly market catering to women. A Spanish slave who lived in Istanbul during the 1550s refers to flower shops at 'Abratbazar' where 'each week some women reunite themselves at a market which has a very tall and large column, historiated in the Roman manner.'[54] John Sanderson (1594) describes the site as 'the markett place of women, for thether they come to sell thier wourks and wares'.[55] A seventeenth-century album painting shows that the buyers and sellers included both men and women (illus. 254).

Whatever the source of its name, we can imagine the produce of gardens from Hürrem's neighbouring complex being sold at Avratpazarı, and its slaves being freed with the surplus funds of her endowment. The queen's clemency toward slaves was echoed by the bequest of her waqf administrator Mehmed Beg, who established a charity of his own in that neighbourhood. He endowed the interest of 3,000 aspers to buy shoes and slippers for needy male and female slaves, and to renew the jugs with which slaves and children carried water from the public fountain of the queen's complex.[56]

The gendered character of Avratpazarı made it a particularly decorous place for her mosque complex. Despite the growing architectural presence of royal women in the capital during Süleyman's reign, their foundations were located either in the suburbs (Eyüp and Üsküdar) or in relatively marginal districts of the walled city (particularly along the Marmara Sea and the land walls). Hürrem's complex on the Marmara axis of the Mese was also removed from the city's central core, even though its site boasted Byzantine imperial associations. The quarters in that area featured several small mosques and masjids commissioned by women, including princesses and the female relatives of grandees.[57] One of the women who left her mark in the neighbourhood of Hürrem's complex was her concubine Nevbahar: with materials left over from the queen's construction, she renovated an old masjid that was renamed after her.[58]

Hürrem's mosque complex, a massive welfare project noteworthy for the variety of public services its dependencies provided to the poor and needy, was the most monumental foundation established by a woman in that area. Nevertheless, the modest plan of its mosque matched the marginal location of its site (illus. 255). The stark and simple mosque is a domed cube with a single-galleried minaret and a five-domed portico, fronted by an off-centre octagonal ablution fountain. It is generally compared with the mosque of the vizier Çoban Mustafa Pasha in Gebze (1522–23), attributed to Sinan's predecessor Acem Alisi, but it is considerably smaller in size (illus. 27).[59] Constructed with alternating courses of stone and brick like the pasha's mosque, it has a simpler brick portico supported on six marble columns with unassuming lozenge capitals. Its archaic-looking massive stone portal has a scalloped muqarnas hood, flanked by two niches on top of which squared kufic inscription panels spell out the profession of faith and the repeated name of the Prophet (illus. 256). The small dome (11.3 metres) rests on a cylindrical drum with pairs of heavy flying buttresses at each corner; the drum lacks the engaged pilaster-shaped buttresses typical of Sinan's works. Internally surrounded by a crested muqarnas frieze along its base, the dome has an octagonal zone of transition with four squinches in the form of scalloped conches (illus. 257).

The painted decorations inside the prayer hall, restored in the 1960s, no longer preserve their original character and inscription programme.[60] Unlike the madrasa and hospice, the mosque lacks *cuerda seca* tiles. The Persianate tilework of Hürrem's complex, characterized by attenuated cursive calligraphy mixing monumental *muḥaḳḳaḳ* and *thuluth* scripts, perpetuates a decorative vocabulary rooted in late-fifteenth- and early-sixteenth-century

254 Weekly market at Avratpazarı, painting from a mid-seventeenth-century album.

models. In comparison to its sophisticated counterparts built just a few years later for Hürrem's senior children, Şehzade Mehmed and Mihrümah Sultan, the queen's mosque completed in 1538–39 (the year Sinan became chief architect) is strikingly conservative in structure. One therefore wonders whether it may not have been designed by Sinan's predecessor. It is also unclear whether Sinan contributed to the hospice, which visually dominates the complex with its monumental domes. Featuring an octagonal courtyard, the hospital is the only ashlar masonry structure in the complex and its most original building; it embodies Sinan's 'classical' style.[61] Surprised by the smallness of the queen's mosque, Evliya Çelebi notes the abundance of its dependencies and the decorousness of its site, which he assumes was selected as a thoughtful gesture by the sultan:

> This is a noble and invaluable mosque in Avratpazarı, but unlike other mosques it is not large. It is an agreeable mosque with one single-galleried minaret and a flourishing complex with its hospice, hospital, madrasa, and elementary

255 Hürrem Sultan mosque, Avratpazarı, from the north.

256 Hürrem Sultan mosque portal.

257 Hürrem Sultan mosque, view of the domical superstructure, Avratpazarı.

school for teaching the alphabet. And it was the delicate character of the prudent Süleyman Khan that made him build the mosque of Haseki Sultan in Avratpazarı.[62]

The tactful subordination of formal ostentation to functional utility foregrounded the 'fecundity' of Haseki Sultan's 'flourishing harvest of benevolence' eulogized by Talikizade. The mosque complex publicized her ascendancy as Süleyman's legal wife and negotiated her contested status on the capital's public stage. The inauguration of the mosque in 1538–39 marked a significant turning point in the *vita* of the queen, who was then in her early thirties: her rank had recently been raised through marriage, and her firstborn son Mehmed was approaching his political coming-of-age. In 1539 her daughter Mihrümah was married to Rüstem Pasha during the public circumcision festivities of her youngest sons, Bayezid and Cihangir. The complex was finished and endowed in 1540, two years before the prince and heir apparent Mehmed left the capital for Manisa, from which his rival Mustafa had been transferred to the more distant sanjak of Amasya.

Everything seemed to be perfectly in order until the untimely death of crown prince Mehmed in 1543, a devastating tragedy for the royal couple. After the construction between 1543 and 1548 of Şehzade Mehmed's memorial mosque complex in the capital, the queen embarked on her own building projects in the three Holy Cities. Designed by Sinan, her hospices with water channels in each of these cities spread the message of her munificence to pilgrims arriving from all parts of the empire and the Muslim world. Built between 1549 and 1552 (prior to the execution of prince Mustafa), the first two hospices in Mecca and Medina were complemented by the third one in Jerusalem (*c.* 1550–57): they enhanced the visibility of the queen's prestige as Süleyman's lawfully wedded wife and the mother of his rightful heirs.

THE COMPLEX IN JERUSALEM

Hürrem's waqfiyya for her hospice complex in Jerusalem eulogizes her spiritual qualities manifested through her charitable foundation, which is construed as a public act of 'unveiling':

> The Creator of the Universe – exalted be His favours and honoured be His most comely Names – has from the very beginning distinguished her Majesty for sublime favours, and created and formed her for admirable deeds, implanted in her a high moral disposition and endowed her with excellent qualities, thus enabling her to bring forth later on the hidden virtues from behind a veiled canopy, in order that they may be publicly known ... Yea, Allah ordained that she should be brought up in the shadow of the magnificent sultanate and in the harem of the resplendent caliphate, thus bestowing upon her all kinds of graces, both apparent and hidden, as well as bounteous blessings and gifts, so much so that the pavilion of her grandeur and felicity reaches with her crowned head to the stars [Ursae minoris], and her glorious majesty touches the highest sky.[63]

The two versions of the waqfiyya were registered on 24 May 1552 and 13 June 1557.[64] Like the sultan's construction-related decrees issued on her behalf, these waqfiyyas identify the queen as the 'mother of prince Mehmed', her firstborn son, long after he had passed away.[65] Perhaps these public documents refrain from naming Hürrem's oldest living son Selim in order to avoid privileging him over his younger brother Bayezid, who was also a contender to the throne.[66]

The complex in Jerusalem is cited only in the *Tuhfe*, without mentioning the name of its patron: 'The noble Friday mosque and madrasa and hospice in Jerusalem the Holy' (illus. 258, 259).[67] The queen's madrasa in Jerusalem and her two hospices in Mecca and Medina (designed by Sinan and executed by local builders under the supervision of Hürrem's agents) have disappeared.[68] Two decrees dated 1549 ask the sanjak governor of Jidda and the governor-general of Egypt to help in every possible way Selman Agha, the chief eunuch of the Old Palace, who had been sent from Istanbul by the 'mother of prince Mehmed' to supervise the construction of her hospices in Mecca and Medina.[69] These hospices were built just around the time the

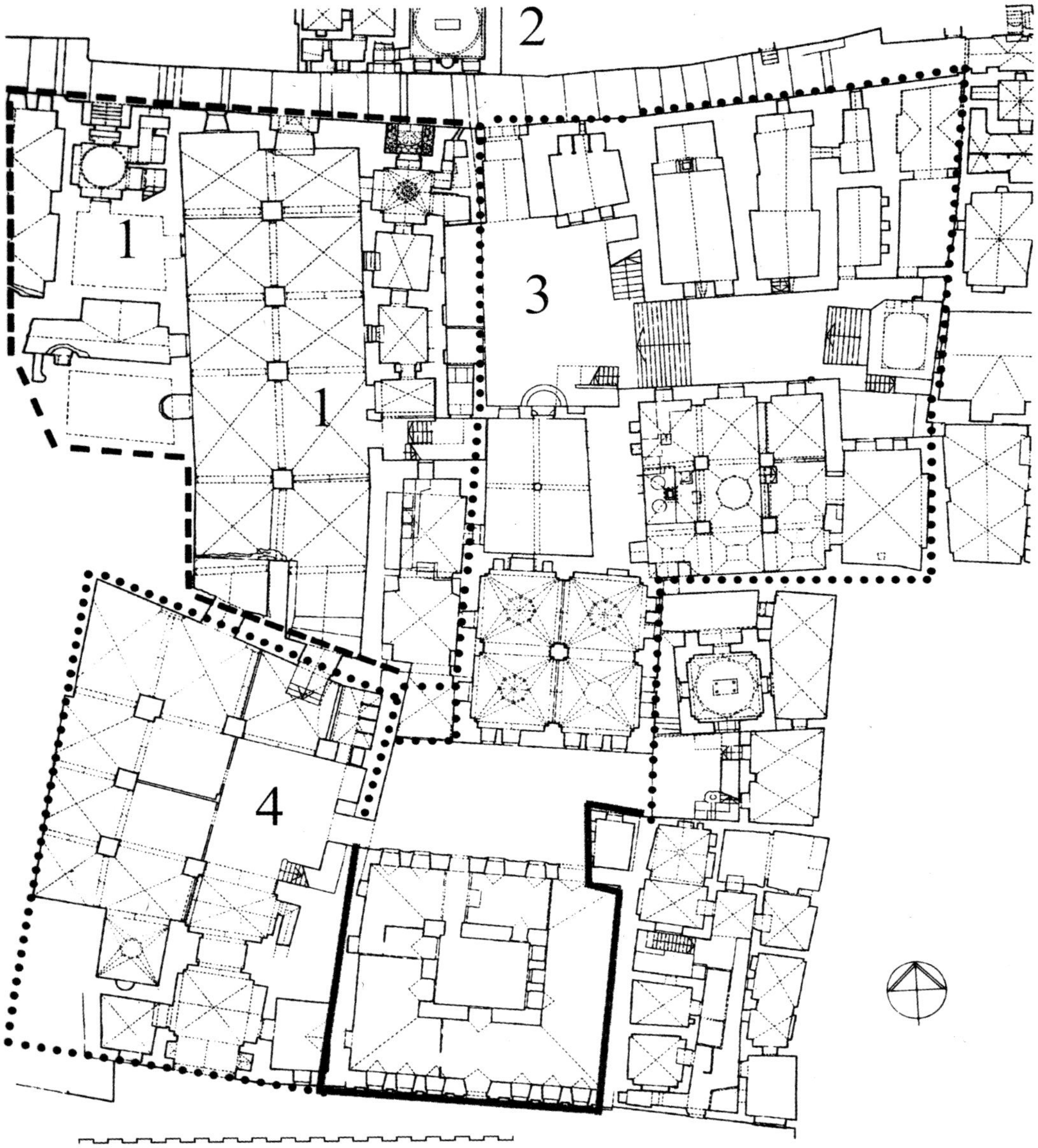

•••••••• Original parts of al-'Imara al-'Amira (Khassaki Sultan)

– – – – Dar Sitt Tunshuq, integrated into Khassaki Sultan

▬▬▬ Reconstructed later, but originally belonging to Khassaki Sultan

258 Plan of the Takiyya complex of Hürrem Sultan, Jerusalem:

1. Mamluk palace.
2. Mamluk mausoleum.
3. Hospice courtyard.
4. Caravansaray with a small masjid (The Friday mosque is either lost or unidentifiable).

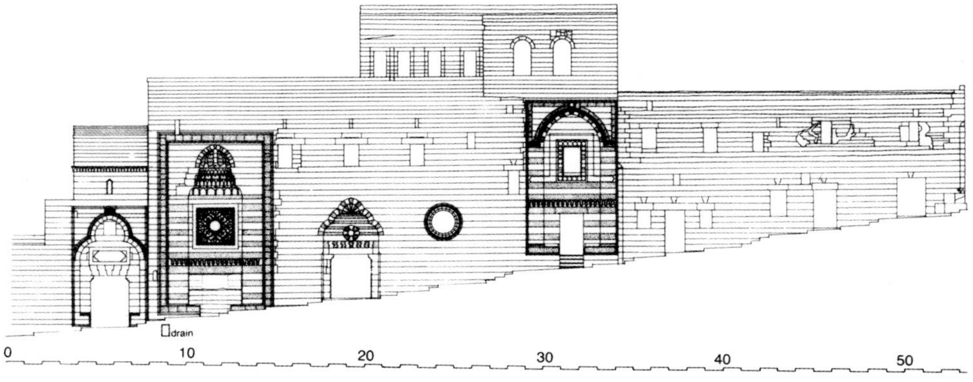

259 Takiyya complex of Hürrem Sultan, Jerusalem, north façade.

Ka'ba was being renovated (1551–52) for Süleyman by the chief architect of Cairo, Kara Mustafa.[70] In the summer of 1552 the sultan gave the eunuchs Yakub Agha and Sünbül Agha full charge of managing the completed hospices in Medina and Mecca respectively.[71]

The construction of the queen's hospice complex in Jerusalem took longer to complete. Revenues were paid to its waqf starting in late 1549, and its kitchen already served food by September–October 1551, before its initial waqfiyya was drawn up in 1552.[72] The first endowment administrator of the queen's complex in Jerusalem, the steward Haydar Kethüda, was also in charge of managing imperial waqfs there: the Dome of the Rock, the Holy Sepulchre, the mosque of Hebron, and the tombs of Abraham, Isaac, Jacob, and Moses.[73] A decree sent to the governor-general and kadi of Damascus on 24 June 1552 identifies 'Emin Haydar Kethüda' as the building supervisor of the 'flourishing hospice presently being built in Jerusalem the Noble' who was overseeing the construction of its new water channel. Since the water channel restored earlier for the sultan by the building supervisor Nakkaş Mehmed proved insufficient for the needs of the hospice, Süleyman orders its amplification with an additional water source.[74]

Another decree dated 15 July 1552 instructs the governor-general of Damascus, who had jurisdiction over Jerusalem, to assist the construction of the hospice of 'the mother of my son Mehmed'. He is ordered to send 'in addition to masons and carpenters, whatever needs the waqf administrator requests' without unjustly harming anybody. The imperial emissary Abdülkerim, who visited Jerusalem on his way to Istanbul from Cairo to transport tax revenues, saw the hospice functioning in 1555 and reported that its double bath was still under construction. Sited at a distance from the hospice, the bath-house was built between June 1554 and April 1556 to generate income.[75]

Hürrem's complex must have been completed by the summer of 1557, when its second waqfiyya was recorded. Its construction complemented her husband's building activities in Jerusalem, which spanned his whole career.[76] Her complex is situated about 160 metres west of the Haram, on a high point at the western slope of the central valley of Jerusalem, from which it commands a view of the Dome of the Rock. Its waqfiyyas refer to the site as the 'Lady's quarter' (*maḥallat al-Sitt*).[77] Suitably removed from the Haram, the site of her husband's renovations, Hürrem's complex near the Holy Sepulchre occupies a 'gendered' locus of memory associated with women, both Christian and Muslim. One of these women was the Byzantine emperor Constantine's mother, Queen Helena, who had built a hospice for pilgrims on that site. The other was Lady Tunshuq al-Muzaffariyya (d. 1398), a slave convert to Islam, who as a devoted religious pilgrim resided in her Mamluk-style palace on the same site and is buried in a domed mausoleum across the street from it.[78]

Lady Tunshuq's sumptuous palace (dār al-Sitt Tunshuq) was incorporated into Hürrem's complex and appended with new constructions adjoining its east and south sides.[79] The queen's waqfiyya identifies the components of her complex, which was grouped around two courtyards extending between two streets: a masjid with a Hanefi imam and a magnificent guest-house with fifty-five rooms for pious 'devotees who dwell in the holy precinct' and follow the 'orthodox practice' of the sacred law by assiduously attending the devotional prayers; a hospice with a spacious courtyard (comprising a kitchen, refectory, bakery, pantry, storeroom, woodshed, and latrines) that served food twice a day to resident devotees, staff, and 400 needy persons; and a spacious caravansaray functioning as a stable for the accommodation of travellers.[80]

Having transformed the palatial residence of Lady Tunshuq into a 'magnificent guest-house' for sufis and devotees, the Ottoman queen added to it a mosque, hospice, and caravansaray constructed in the regional Mamluk manner. Probably built by masons imported from Syria under the supervision of the chief architect of Jerusalem, the irregular complex, constrained by the dense urban setting, has little to do with Sinan's 'classical' style.[81] Its Ottomanness was not embodied in its forms, but rather in its institutional functions, which combined orthodox Hanefi rituals with free lodging and food.

Charitable complexes with hospices (*'imāret*) and guest-houses (*tābḫāne*) – locally called Takiyya (*tekye*, dervish convent) – were novel Ottoman institutions unknown in Syria-Palestine during the Mamluk period. Introduced into the empire's Arab provinces with Selim I's Takiyya al-Salimiyya in Damascus, such complexes were an integral component of the Ottoman imperial project of colonization, urban development, and legitimization.[82] Hürrem's complex, popularly called the 'Takiyya Khassaki Sultan', was a counterpart to her husband's more monumental Ottoman-style Takiyya al-Sulaymaniyya along the hajj route of Damascus (1554–58/59).[83] Her posthumous mosque complex on the same route near Edirne (1559–60) was a conceptually related monument announcing her status as the mother of the next sultan.

THE COMPLEX NEAR THE BRIDGE OF MUSTAFA PASHA

Hürrem's mosque complex, 30 kilometres west of Edirne next to the bridge of the vizier Çoban Mustafa Pasha, has disappeared without trace (illus. 260). The bridge, still extant, is dated by an inscription to 935 (1528–29); it is cited in Sinan's autobiographies, perhaps because he renovated it or participated in its construction as a janissary. Before the creation of Hürrem's complex at the head of the bridge, Dernschwam described the site as surrounded by vineyards without houses and connected to a paved avenue lined with a long market of wooden huts and shops, a bath-house, and a caravansaray for horses and travellers, all of them belonging to the waqf of Mustafa Pasha.[84] The *Tezkiretü'l-ebniye* (but not the *Tuhfe*) mentions the 'Haseki Sultan' mosque 'in Edirne at the head of the bridge of Mustafa Pasha on the Meriç river.' It also lists her hospice, but omits her elementary school.[85]

The complex may have been planned while the queen spent the winter of 1557–58 in Edirne with her husband, just before her death in Istanbul on 15 April 1558. The *bailo* Antonio Barbarigo (1558) tells us that Hürrem, 'who is the absolute master of the life of the sultan by whom she is exceedingly loved', refused to allow him out of her sight for fear of his imminent death.[86] Doctors had recommended that the sickly Süleyman winter each year in Edirne, and this seems to have provided the impetus for the queen's building activities in and near that city, where she created a water channel and fountains in 1556–57.[87]

Several decrees sent by Süleyman to the kadi of Edirne in 1559 and 1560 document his vigilant control from afar of his deceased wife's mosque complex. It must have been financed by the surplus income of her ever-expanding waqfs, increased in 1556–57 with a double bath built by Sinan near Hagia Sophia, which was accompanied by numerous rental rooms and shops (illus. 56, 544).[88] The late queen's endowment administrator may have supervised the construction near Edirne under the guidance of the overseers of her waqf, the chief white eunuch and the sultan. A decree addressed to the kadi of Edirne on 17 July 1559 shows that the hospice was built before the Friday mosque (ambiguously referred to as a masjid):

> Previously the plan (*kārnāme*) of the masjid, which is going to be built near the hospice whose construction had been ordered at the bridge of Mustafa Pasha, was dispatched. I order you to start building the masjid according to that plan (*resim üzre*), if a sufficient number of builders is available. If not, begin and finish its construction after the completion of the hospice. But the plan (*resim*) shows two minarets; reduce them to one.[89]

The reason for this radical modification is not stated. The plan with two minarets, previously approved by the sultan, was likely designed before the queen's demise. She was now, after all, virtually queen mother whichever of her two remaining sons should succeed his father.

The sultan's decree retracting his prior permission for twin minarets in his wife's mosque was issued at a critical juncture. Its timing followed the conclusion of the war of the princes that broke out in Konya soon after Hürrem's death. Although prince Selim had won the battle with his father's military support in June 1559, his status as heir apparent would not be confirmed until Bayezid's execution in 1562. The intervening limbo constituted a veritable dynastic crisis.[90] As we have seen, Süleyman in 1560 granted Selim the unprecedented permission to build a double-minaret mosque at Karapınar near Konya, dubbed Sultaniya (Imperial) to announce his identity as future sultan. During 1559–60 he commissioned his own sultanic mosque with two minarets adjacent to the shrine of Mevlana Celalüddin Rumi

260 Hürrem Sultan mosque at the Çoban Mustafa Pasha bridge near Edirne (now Svilengrad), in a nineteenth-century photograph.

in Konya to commemorate the victory granted by that saint to his heir.[91] Süleyman's reluctance to honour his late wife's mosque with twin minarets during this critical context is understandable. In the last years of her life, the queen with her political allies Mihrümah and Rüstem Pasha had championed Bayezid's candidacy to the throne. The double-minaret plan for her mosque could now be perceived as potentially subversive, given that she had supported the 'rebel' Bayezid, who was still alive. The plan may also have been revised to appease prince Selim, whose strong aversion towards his conspiring mother, sister, and brother-in-law was noted by a Venetian secretary in 1562.[92]

Süleyman apparently deemed it more decorous for his wife's posthumous mosque to commemorate her status as Haseki Sultan, rather than as prospective queen mother. His next imperial decree to the kadi of Edirne, on 22 February 1560, concerns the water supply of the queen's hospice. The chief of water channel builders (*şuyolcılar başı*), Bali, had previously been ordered to estimate the comparative costs of a conduit carrying water from two villages and of a water wheel on the Meriç river. After inspecting both villages with a committee of experts, the kadi reported the opposition of the people and of the administrator of another waqf, who claimed water rights. Due to the lack of consent, the sultan ordered the construction of a cheaper water wheel.[93] The kadi was interrogated on 13 May 1560 about tax-exempt lands required for new settlers willing to build their houses around the 'Friday mosque' and its hospice. Since this was opposed by local notables, who had bought those plots for agricultural purposes, the sultan asks how much land would be required for the settlers.[94]

Another decree addressed to the kadi on 28 May 1560 indicates the ongoing confusion concerning the status of the mosque: 'You have sent a letter asking whether a Friday mosque or a masjid is to be built near the bridge of Mustafa Pasha, reporting that its construction has been postponed because this question has not yet been clarified by an imperial order; I order you to have it built in the manner of a Friday mosque.'[95] The construction had been delayed because of the ambiguity of imperial decrees that referred to it variously as a 'masjid' (*mescid*) and a 'Friday mosque' (*cāmi*ʿ). It was no doubt intended as a Friday mosque, judging by its initial plan featuring two minarets, but the overly cautious kadi felt obliged to make sure that this was indeed the case. A decree dated 23 June 1560 commands him to have a 'smallish elementary school' built nearby.[96] One last decree, issued on 9 September 1560, accepts his recommendation to substitute for the previously ordered water wheel a channel conducting two measures (*lüle*) of water from a newly discovered source at a distance of 1,400 cubits. The water channel had already been initiated to avoid 'killing time', and the sultan orders its completion before the arrival of winter.[97]

Süleyman's written correspondence with the kadi of Edirne once again demonstrates how codes of decorum were established through a process of negotiation that tested the acceptable limits of propriety. Sinan's plan for Hürrem's mosque was probably executed by a royal architect sent from Istanbul or Edirne. Old photographs indicate that the queen's ashlar masonry mosque was covered by a hipped roof and fronted by a five-bay double portico (illus. 260).[98] The mosque complex complemented the shops, caravansaray, and bath-house that Mustafa Pasha had created earlier along his bridge by providing additional services to travellers with its hospice-cum-caravansaray. Its elementary school addressed the educational needs of the new Muslim community settled nearby to encourage urban development.

The complex is described by several European diplomats and travellers who either stayed in its hospice or saw it on their way to and from the capital. Jacob von Betzek (1564–65) mentions the market, the bath, the 'new mosque', two caravansarays, and a hospice. He imagines all of these lead-covered structures were built and endowed by the sultan's favourite 'Russian' wife.[99] Du Fresne-Canaye (1573) also identifies 'La Rossa' as the founder of the mosque, hospice, and large caravansaray built of stone and covered with lead. He says Muslims and non-Muslims alike could stay for three days in the hospice, where they were served free bulghur, four loaves of bread, and boiled meat.[100]

Jacopo Soranzo (1575) thinks it was Selim II's wife (rather than his mother) who built and endowed the mosque, caravansaray, and hospice 'where the ambassador stayed to escape the stench and heat of the caravansaray'.[101] Because of the bridge, many European travellers misattribute the queen's complex to Mustafa Pasha.[102] Evliya Çelebi, the only Ottoman writer to give a detailed description of the prosperous town that grew around it, does not identify its patron even though he cites the Koranic verse quoted in the foundation inscription of the mosque. The same verse (9:108), referring to the mosque as a 'masjid' built on the foundations of piety, appears in the inscription of prince Selim's provincial mosque in Karapınar (1560–63/64):

> The town at the bridge of Mustafa Pasha belongs to the sanjak of Çirmen. Situated along the Meriç river, it is a flourishing settlement with gardens and vineyards and seven hundred brick-roofed houses. It has seven mihrabs. But the mosque of [empty] at the head of the great bridge is a luminous structure built in the manner of a royal mosque (*selāṭīn miṣāl*). It has a decorated foundation inscription on its high courtyard portal facing the road, calligraphed by the magical script of Karahisari Hasan Çelebi on white marble: 'A place of worship which has been founded upon duty (to Allah), in the year [empty] [9:108].' The mosque has a hospice, an elementary school, a caravansaray, a bath-house, and a market, all covered with pure lead and constructed by Koca Mimar Sinan during the reign of Süleyman. The minaret and mosque are very artistic. In the refectory of the hospice plenty of food is served to travellers.[103]

The programme of Hürrem Sultan's complex mirrors her insistent policy of addressing the needs of travellers and pilgrims. Even though she was not recognized by all as its patroness, it increased her renown along the main highway of the empire near the secondary capital Edirne and complemented her hospices in Istanbul, Jerusalem, Mecca, and Medina. These monuments, built to 'unveil' the pious queen's divinely bestowed inner virtues, were architectural expressions of her motherly compassion on an empire-wide scale. They embodied a user-oriented rather than a design-oriented approach to architecture, emphasizing her humanitarian dispensation of charity to enhance the reputation of the royal family and contribute to the greater glory of Süleyman's reign. Whether or not they succeeded in countering Hürrem's unpopular public image, they effectively broadcast her unprecedented ascendancy as Süleyman's lawful wife who had given birth to his royal offspring and the next ruler of the dynasty.

II. NURBANU SULTAN [ATİK VALİDE]

Haseki Nurbanu Sultan was the only slave concubine other than her mother-in-law Hürrem to lawfully wed a sultan during the classical age. Having outlived her husband Selim II, she also became the first queen mother honoured with the official title of Valide Sultan. The foundations of her extensive mosque complex, perched on a hilltop in Üsküdar, were laid in 1571, the year she became the sultan's legal bride with a dowry of 110,000 ducats (illus. 261, 262).[104] Completed during the reign of her son Murad III, its incremental growth over a period of fifteen years paralleled her graduation from the rank of Haseki Sultan to Valide Sultan.

The origins of Nurbanu (Lady of Light), popularly known as the Venetian Sultana, are veiled in uncertainty. She is generally believed to have been Cecilia Venier-Baffo, the illegitimate daughter of the Venetian patrician Nicolo Venier, lord of the island of Paros, and of Violante Baffo. In 1559 the Senate informed the secret emissary through which Nurbanu had enquired about the identity of her Venetian parents that her nearest living relative was her cousin, Zuan Francesco Venier, the castellan of Corfu.[105] The ambassador Marino Cavalli concluded in 1567 that it was not possible to establish whether the sultana, a descendant of the Venier family, had originated from Corfu or Paros (both of them Venetian territory).[106] According to Gianfrancesco Morosini (1585), the queen herself believed that as a twelve-year-old girl she had been enslaved by the grand admiral Barbarossa in Corfu, where her Venetian father was appointed governor.[107] Whatever her ancestry was, Nurbanu flaunted her pedigree as a '*gentiledonna veneziana*'. During the last years of her life she even claimed to remember the house her family owned on the Grand Canal.[108]

The French ambassador complained in 1583 about Nurbanu's partiality to the Venetian lords 'as much because it is said that she is from their country as because of the grand and frequent presents they give her'. Indeed, shortly before her death during that year, the queen mother was awarded 2,000 sequins for her services to the Senate, which included her prevention of a possible invasion of Crete.[109] Nurbanu's letters to the *bailo*, the Doge, and the Senate speak of the fond memories she had of her homeland and capture her love of luxury. The baubles she requested as 'gifts' included bales of silk, robes of silk damask and gold cloth, and in one instance small lap-dogs of the kind so fashionable among Venetian aristocratic ladies.[110] Annoyed by two large dogs not to her liking, she sent the following imperious note to the *bailo* in June 1583: 'Thus let it be known to the Bāliyūs! You have sent two lap-dogs. Now, lap-dogs like that are not required, and they are big, also long-haired. Thus shall you know! Let them be white and let them be little!'[111]

Joining prince Selim's harem around 1542, Nurbanu gave birth to his oldest son Murad in 1546 after having delivered three daughters in rapid succession in 1544 and 1545 (İsmihan Sultan, Gevherhan Sultan, Shahsultan). Her youngest daughter Fatma Sultan was born in 1560–61.[112] All of these princesses were married off to favoured statesmen who rose to become viziers and grand viziers, and prince Murad was singled out as heir apparent and sent to govern Manisa (1562–74). When Nurbanu moved to Istanbul as the head of the imperial harem during her husband's accession in 1566, the Venetian ambassador Jacopo Soranzo commented that she was said to be 'extremely well loved and honoured by His Majesty both for her great beauty and for being unusually intelligent.'[113] The affections of her 'lustful' husband, however, extended to several concubines who gave birth to other children, and it was not until her son's reign eight years later that Nurbanu's power reached its zenith. The queen mother's financial resources included income from crown lands granted to her as 'slipper money' (*paşmaklık*), a daily stipend of 3,000 aspers (she received only 1000 aspers as Selim II's wife), and countless gifts.[114]

The increased leverage of harem factions was criticized by Ottoman and European observers alike. Soranzo observed in 1581 that it was Murad's mother and his Albanian-born chief consort Safiye (mother of the heir apparent Mehmed) who controlled 'posts or favours at the Porte'.[115] The *bailo* Paolo Contarini (1583) says the viziers had now turned into puppets of the sultanas:

> This empire is largely governed by the sultanas,
> the magnificent viziers being no more than executors
> of orders coming from the harem rather than independent counsellors; and in order to conserve their positions
> they seek to please the sultanas without ever opposing
> anything requested by them, presenting them with
> gifts to obtain favours, knowing that the most important
> posts are given to those who are favoured by these
> women who are all-powerful.[116]

The queen mother had more influence than any other person on Murad III, who trusted her loyal advice and revered her 'rare qualities and many virtues'. Next in authority came Safiye. Noting Nurbanu's intense rivalry with her, Contarini attributes the dismissal in 1582 of Safiye's compatriot, the Albanian-born grand vizier Koca Sinan Pasha, to the queen mother. She wanted to 'avenge herself for the words that [Koca] Sinan had dared to speak, that empires are not governed with the counsel of women, and moreover that authority did not rest with her [Nurbanu], even though she might try to make it seem so, but rather with the sultan's consort [Safiye].'[117]

Contarini's successor observes that the queen mother's demise in 1583 evoked mixed reactions:

> Some are saddened by this lady's death and others
> consoled, each according to his or her own interests,
> for just as she provided enormous benefits to many as
> a result of the great authority she enjoyed with her son,
> so conversely did she deprive others of hopes of obtaining
> what they desired. But all universally admit that she was
> a woman of the utmost goodness, courage, and wisdom.[118]

A miniature painting depicts black eunuchs carrying Nurbanu's coffin out of her palace in Yenikapı, with the sultan walking in front, as grandees and subjects gathered at the palace gates pray with uplifted hands (illus. 263).[119] Selaniki's description of the stately funeral procession to Selim II's mausoleum at Hagia Sophia, where she was buried next to her husband, unlike former queens, captures her enormous prestige:

> On Wednesday, 7 December 1583, the mother of his
> highness the caliphate-protecting sultan, may God exalt
> his victories and strengthen his sultanate, who was a

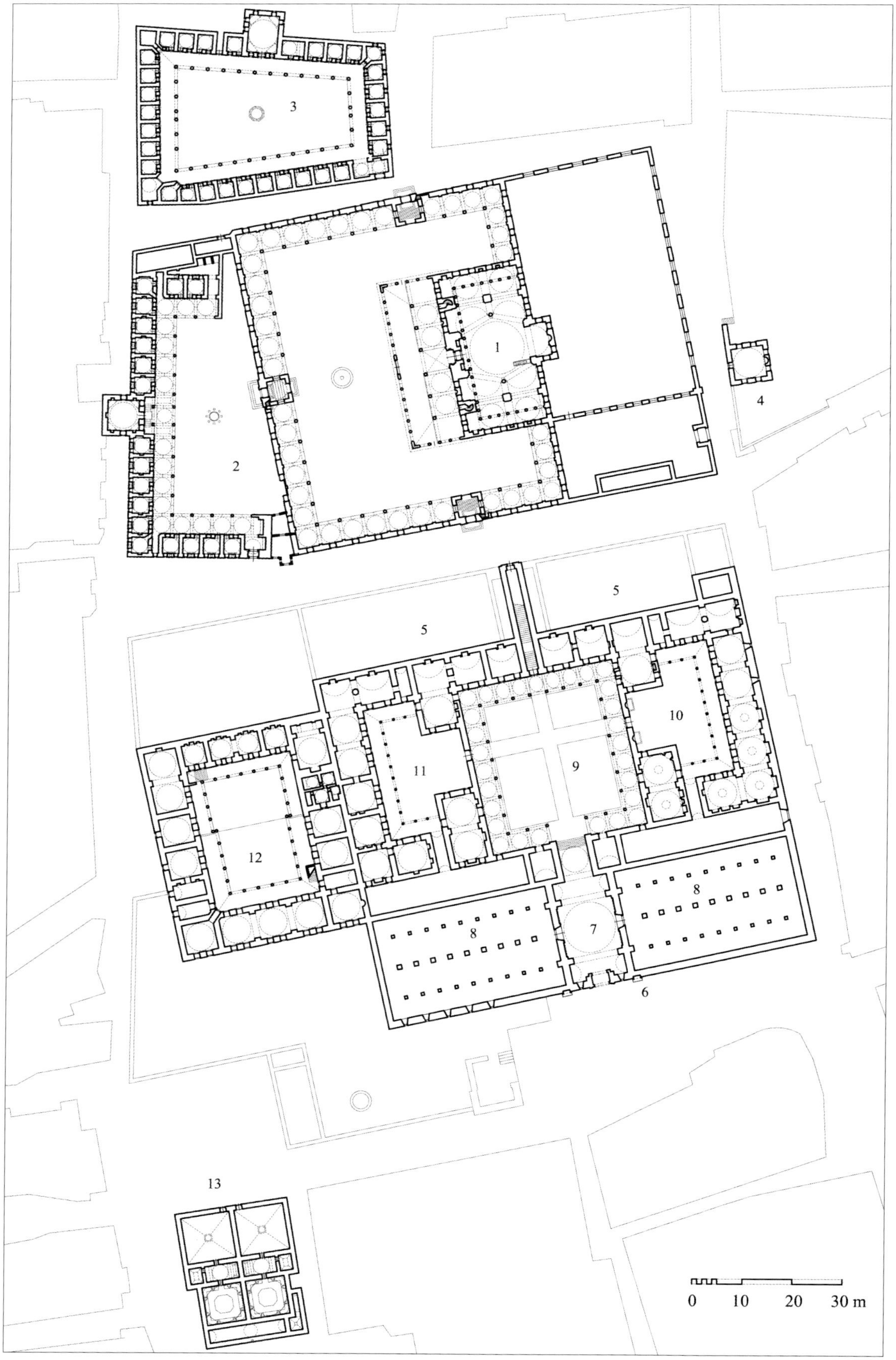

261 Plan of the Nurbanu Sultan complex, Üsküdar, with a hypothetical reconstruction of its hospice-caravansaray-hospital block:

1. Mosque
2. Madrasa
3. Convent
4. Elementary school
5. Hadith college and Koran recitation school
6. Fountain of Hasan Çavuş
7. Vestibule
8. Double caravansaray with stables
9. Hospice courtyard
10. Hospice kitchens
11. Guest-rooms
12. Hospital
13. Double bath

> patroness of pious foundations, passed away from this transitory world to the palace of eternity by the will of God in her garden palace at the Yenikapı quarter. All the great ulema, the honourable shaykhs, and the pillars of the state walked alongside her coffin, while his highness the world-protecting sultan followed on foot behind them with tearful eyes, wearing a robe of mourning, up to the noble mosque of Sultan Mehmed II, may he rest in peace, where the common people had gathered. After the funeral prayers were performed, his highness the religion-protecting sultan returned to the imperial palace. The pillars of the state, together with the ulema and the pious shaykhs, buried the coffin inside the noble mausoleum of Sultan Selim Khan, may he rest in peace, near Ayasofya. For a forty-day period, the great viziers and the honorable chief judges did not fail to attend her burial place day and night. The Koran was recited from beginning to end, litanies in praise of God were sung, and large sums of money and food were distributed as alms to the poor and needy.[120]

During this period of mourning, the sultan ordered kadis throughout the empire to have commemorative prayers performed for his mother's soul after the Friday prayers.[121]

Nurbanu's ambitions as a patroness of architecture are recorded in her waqfiyya, drafted in April 1582, but not registered until after her death by her reigning son, who had inherited her properties.[122] It lists her two pious foundations, one in the capital and the other in Lapseki, across the straits from Gallipoli. The modest provincial complex, now lost, was composed of a masjid, an elementary school, a dervish convent, and a hospice. The grand complex in the 'new quarter' of Üsküdar included a Friday mosque, a madrasa, a hadith college, a school for Koran recitation, an elementary school, a dervish convent, a hospital, and a hospice (comprising a kitchen, a pantry, a guest-house, and a double caravansaray). The presence of a convent (*ribāṭ, ḫānḳāh*) in both complexes hints at the personal attachment to sufism that Nurbanu shared with other royal women. This is not surprising, given the mystical orientations of her husband and son. The first shaykh appointed to her convent in Üsküdar was Vişne Mehmed Efendi (d. 1584) of the Halveti order. Like the earlier Halveti convent (*c.* 1574) of the mosque complex jointly sponsored by her daughter İsmihan and the grand vizier Sokollu in Kadırgalimanı, that of Nurbanu is one of the few monumental examples of its kind attributed to Sinan.[123] The queen mother's waqfiyya

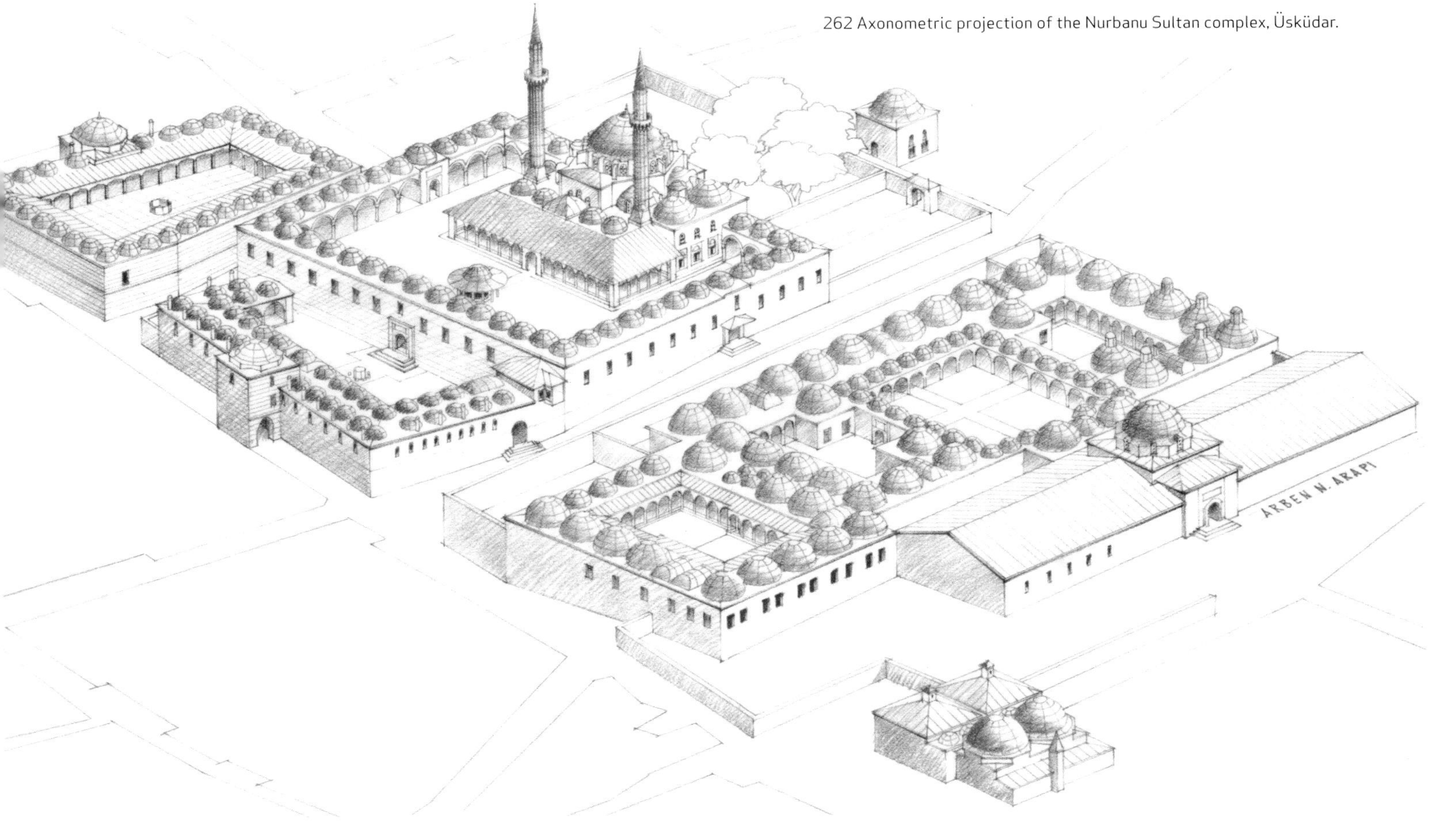

262 Axonometric projection of the Nurbanu Sultan complex, Üsküdar.

263 Funeral procession of Nurbanu Sultan, 1592, watercolour on paper, from Lokman, *Shahanshāhnāma*.

stipulates that her convent in Üsküdar would be entrusted to a righteous shaykh who should not transgress the bounds of the shariʿa and who, in addition to providing spiritual guidance to resident dervishes, would preach inside her Friday mosque.[124]

The mosque complex came to be known as Atik Valide Sultan (Old Queen Mother) after two others were built in Üsküdar for later queen mothers. The details of its construction can be traced from imperial decrees. The earliest one, issued by Selim II, is dated 16 February 1571. It orders the kadis of Sapanca and İzmit to help the men sent by the endowment administrator and by Mustafa, the building supervisor of 'the mosque that is being built in Üsküdar for the mother of my son Murad', in their search for marble. Their assistance was also required in buying and transporting with rented carts timber, lime, and other building materials.[125] Two days later, the kadi of Üsküdar was ordered to help the endowment administrator's man purchase stone, lime, and various materials for the queen's mosque.[126]

In May and June 1571, the kadis of İzmit and Gallipoli were asked to provide their assistance in having 500 cubits of slate (*ḳayḳān taşı*) quarried at officially fixed prices.[127] Another decree sent by Selim II on 19 March 1572 to the kadis of Üsküdar and İzmit orders their help in buying timber required for 'the shops that are being built in Üsküdar by the mother of my son Murad.'[128] The kadis of Sapanca and İzmit received a directive on 13 May 1573 to facilitate the purchase of timber for the mosque in the 'new quarter' of Üsküdar.[129] For the bath-house of his wife in the same quarter, the sultan dispatched an order on 24 July 1574 to the kadis of ports in the Black Sea and the Mediterranean: they are instructed to allow the sale of timber at officially fixed prices when state ships arrive there, ignoring the opposition of local sanjak administrators.[130]

These imperial orders, issued by Haseki Nurbanu Sultan's reigning husband advertised her status as the mother of the heir apparent. After 1574, the construction-related decrees of Murad III refer to her as queen mother. In late July 1576, the kadi of Marmara was asked to have stone prepared for the ongoing construction of the queen's 'noble mosque in Üsküdar.' He is instructed to have the quarried stone carried to the shore of the Marmara Island and to load it onto ships that had been sent there.[131] On 22 April 1577 the sultan commanded the kadi of the port of Ahyolu in Bulgaria to provide timber for the 'buildings' (*binālar*) of 'my mother' without anybody's interference. One of these structures was an endowed slaughterhouse for which Istanbul butchers were obligated to give six oxen each.[132]

Murad III's donation of villages for his mother's waqf in 1578 must have marked the completion of her mosque, depicted on a map painted in 1581 (illus. 264).[133] The geographer Aşık Mehmed confirms that the double-minaret mosque was built in 985 (1577–8),[134] and Schweigger and Gerlach saw it in 1578.[135] The kadi of Üsküdar was informed on 21 September 1578 that from now on the queen mother's endowment administrator would collect the capitation tax from Christians, Jews, and Gypsies settled around her mosque and from new settlers. The sultan also donated to his mother's waqf a neighbouring plot of land used as a horse market.[136] An order that he issued a week later concerns the donation of additional crown lands for her waqf at Yeni-il in Anatolia.[137] That the noble mosque of 'Her Highness the Valide Sultan' was completed before 1579 is also indicated by the fiefs awarded during that year to those who had served in its construction.[138]

The construction of dependencies continued after that date. On 30 March 1580 the kadi of Vize was ordered to buy long pieces of timber for 'the hospice (ʿ *imāret*) of the Valide Sultan'.[139] This is in keeping with the date (1579–80) inscribed on a public fountain attached to the façade of the hospice, created by the new building supervisor Hasan Çavuş. Its Turkish inscription refers to the 'mosque, caravansaray, and hospice' of the 'Valide Sultan who is the pearl of the crown and the most charitable of all women.'[140] This inscription does not refer to other buildings such as the adjacent hospital, madrasa, and dervish convent, which seem to have been completed later. On 25 June 1581, the kadi of Istanbul was informed that the queen mother had asked her son's permission that her endowed rental rooms at Ayakapı (a city gate along the Golden Horn) be replaced with an income-generating bath-house, using the water of a sacred spring (*ayazma*) on that site.[141]

The dates and costs of construction activities after the queen's death in 1583 (supervised by her endowment administrator Pir Ali b. Mustafa and overseen by the chief black eunuch of the imperial harem, Mehmed Agha) are detailed in a decree issued on 13 March 1589. It certifies a petition presented by Mehmed Agha to Murad III, requesting the final approval of completed constructions that had previously been authorized by an imperial decree. We learn that the mosque was enlarged by order of the sultan between January 1584 and March 1586, with the addition of domes on its two sides, the construction of internal upper galleries (*fevḳāniyyeler*), and the creation of a courtyard (*ḥarīm*). At that time, additional water was brought to the complex from the neighbouring village of Bulgurlu. Between January 1586 and November 1588 the water wheel and water channel of a new bath-house in Istanbul (Çemberlitaş) was built, and another bath-house was constructed near the Üsküdar waterfront.[142]

This hitherto unnoted important document shows that Nurbanu's mosque was posthumously remodelled between 1584 and 1586, while the construction of additional income-producing structures continued until the end of 1588.[143] A decree dated 31 October 1583 provides conclusive evidence that the ambitious remodelling project was initiated before the queen mother's death later in December. It orders the grand admiral Kılıç Ali Pasha to transport on the ships of the imperial fleet the marble quarried at the Marmara Island for 'my mother's noble mosque.' The marble ready for transportation consisted of 560 window frames (*pencere sövesi*), 200 cubits of slabs for steps (*ḳademe*), and 2,640 cubits of slabs for pavements (*döşeme*).[144] The numerous window frames must have been intended not only for the enlargement of the mosque (which features a total of 114 windows) and the window-pierced wall of its forecourt, but also for new commercial structures. Some of the slabs for pavements and steps would have been required for the domical arcades of the forecourt and the staircases of its three gates.

Decrees issued in 1585 and 1586 concern the water channel for the new bath-house at Dikilitaş (Çemberlitaş), whose foundation inscription is dated 1584–85,[145] and the construction of the bath-house in Üsküdar, for which the chief architect Sinan enlisted masons and carpenters.[146] These posthumously built bath-houses (included in the autobiographies) are mentioned in Nurbanu's waqfiyya along with the numerous income-producing structures created in the 'new quarter' of her complex: the still extant double bath near the complex mentioned in Selim II's decree of 1574, a commercial caravansaray, stables, shops, rental rooms, slaughterhouses, and tanneries.[147] Pervitich's cadastral map of 1930 shows the horse market at the foot of the hill, whose grounds belonged to Nurbanu's endowment, and the square of tanners (Tabaklar Meydanı), around which her

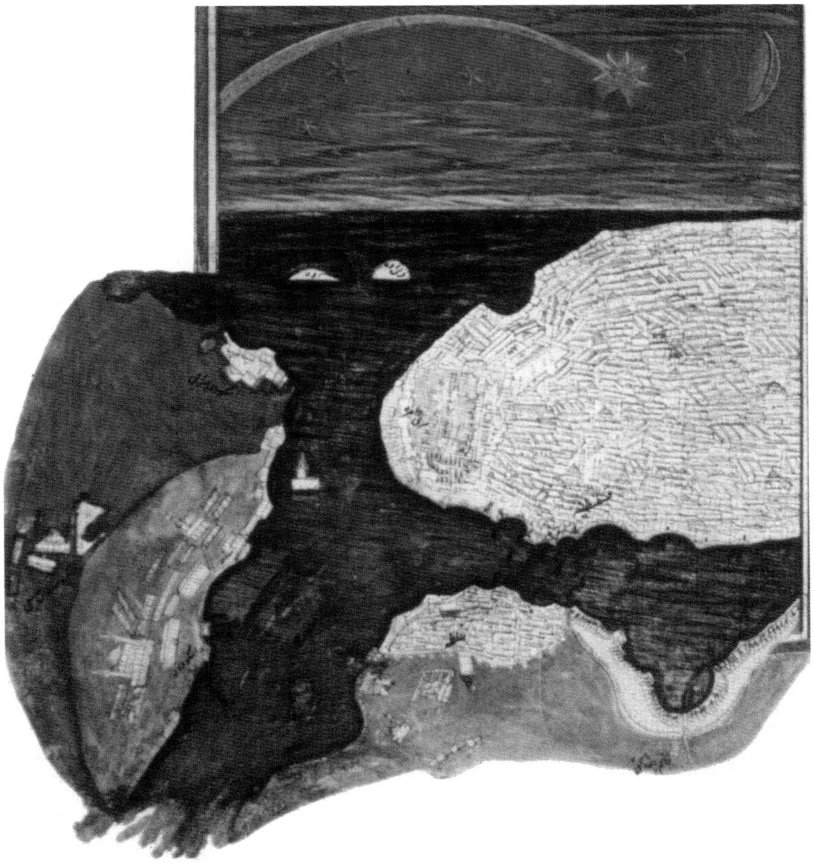

264 Map of Istanbul with a comet seen in 1577: detail of Üsküdar showing the double-minaret mosque and complex of Nurbanu ('Valide Sultan Camii'), the complex of Mihrümah Sultan along the waterfront, and the mosque of Rum Mehmed Pasha, 1581, watercolour on paper, from Lokman, *Shahanshāhnāma*.

tanneries must have been grouped. Animal hides from various slaughterhouses in the capital were endowed for the use of tanners settled near her complex in the outskirts of Üsküdar, a site ideal for tanneries, which are traditionally banished to the outer edges of towns.[148]

The construction of Nurbanu's mosque can be divided into three stages (illus. 265). The first stage, between 1571 and 1574, celebrating her newly earned status as Selim II's legal wife, overlapped with the construction of the princely mosque built by her son in Manisa (1571–74). The queen's mosque was designed by Sinan but executed by another royal architect in the course of Sinan's extended absence in Edirne, where he was busy building the Selimiye (1568–74). The second stage, between 1574 and 1577–78, when Sinan had returned to Istanbul, corresponded to Nurbanu's augmented status as queen mother. The initial plan of the mosque must have been modified at that time with the addition of a second single-galleried minaret and the extension of its five-bay portico with an outer portico. The central dome (12.7 metres), resting on an hexagonal support system with two free-standing brownish porphyry columns, was surrounded by four exedral half-domes and a half-domed projecting mihrab: a typical feature of Sinan's post-Selimiye mosques in the capital.

With the exception of its twin minarets, Nurbanu's ashlar masonry mosque resembled royal and grand vizierial mosques with hexagonal baldachins built during the late 1560s and early 1570s: İsmihan and Sokollu in Kadırgalimanı with its 13 metre dome, and Kara Ahmed Pasha in Topkapı with its 12 metre dome (illus. 4). Among the mosques that Sinan created for royal women in Istanbul, that of the queen mother was surpassed in dome size by those of her daughter in Kadırgalimanı and of her sister-in-law, princess Mihrümah, in Edirnekapı (20.25 metres). Had she not commenced the construction of her mosque as the wife of Selim II, the formidable Nurbanu would almost certainly have commissioned a more monumental structure.[149]

It was precisely this shortcoming that the third stage of construction between 1584 and 1586 attempted to remedy. Laterally expanded by two domes on each side of its hexagonal baldachin, Nurbanu's mosque was now provided with a U-shaped inner gallery raised on white marble columns with lozenge capitals and a forecourt surrounded by domical arcades. The remodelling of her mosque coincided with the construction of the new Muradiye in Manisa (1583–86/87), which replaced the illegally demolished princely mosque of her son, the enlargement of which had been ordered in 1577. I have argued earlier that the more impressive new mosque designed by Sinan for Murad III may carry the imprint of his mother's vision. Asserting the sultan's challenged authority in the capital of his former sanjak, it was planned just before the more popular son of Nurbanu's archrival, Safiye, went to govern Manisa as heir apparent.[150]

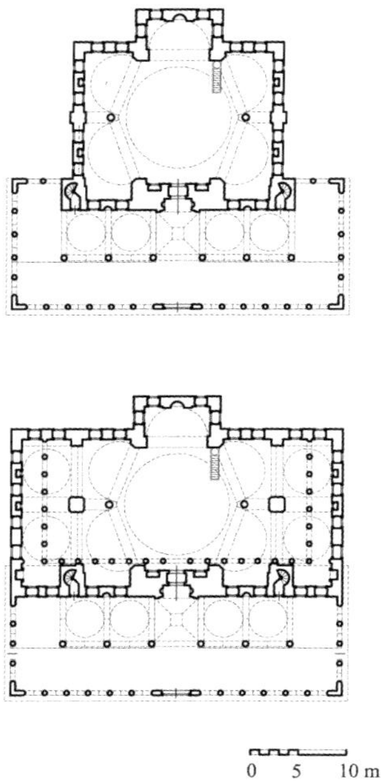

265 Mosque of Nurbanu Sultan, Üsküdar, showing the second and third stages of construction.

The addition of side wings awkwardly embedded the twin minarets of the queen mother's mosque in the midst of its north façade, to which the pre-existing double portico was reconnected. With its final form mimicking the sultanic model of the Üç Şerefeli in Edirne, Nurbanu's mosque expressed her aggrandized self-image in her last years (illus. 266). The domical arcades of its courtyard are unprecedented in the oeuvre of Sinan, who generally framed the forecourts of non-sultanic mosques with madrasa cells. Although the forecourt is planted with trees, it comes close in conception to the marble-paved courtyards of sultanic mosques in Edirne and Istanbul. The appropriation of this exclusive imperial prerogative bore testimony to Nurbanu's unparalleled position.[151]

The expansion of Nurbanu's mosque, planned before Sinan's trip to Mecca in 1584, is thought to have been carried out by the architect Davud between 1582 and 1583, but the textual evidence I have discussed above proves that this happened after the queen's death.[152] A chronogram inscribed on an impermanent wooden panel hanging above the muqarnas-hooded white marble gate of the double portico has contributed to the inaccurate assumption that the remodelling project was completed by 1583 (illus. 267). Its Turkish inscription in *ta'lik* script reads:

> Nurbanu (Lady of Light), that person full of purity,
> Resolved to perform charitable works.
>
> She built this charming place of worship.
> Wonderful sight, most beautiful and charming!
>
> This peerless work of charity is her personal foundation;
> Its date was 'Excellent, sublime paradise!' 991 (1583–84).[153]

This seems to refer to either the queen's demise or the inauguration of the complex in 1583, when the first Friday preacher of the mosque was appointed, rather than to the subsequently finished remodelling project.[154]

The attribution of the expansion of the mosque to Davud is not unreasonable because this architect was a protégé of the chief black eunuch Mehmed Agha, who directed the remodelling

266 Mosque of Nurbanu Sultan, Üsküdar, from the north with rebuilt modern fountain.

of the mosque as the overseer of its waqf. Davud may also have been the architect responsible for executing Sinan's initial plan, since his connection with Mehmed Agha extended back to the 1570s.[155] The names of other architects who contributed to Nurbanu's complex are linked to smaller mosques that they endowed in its vicinity, built with leftover building materials from her construction.[156]

The queen mother's roadside complex addressed the needs of pilgrims and merchants on their way to and from Asia, along the main highway of the empire. In 1582 the French pilgrim Jean Palerne wrote that it had been created as a place of assembly for caravans passing from Asia to Europe and departing from Üsküdar to Aleppo and Damascus:

> For this purpose the sultana, who is the mother of the Grand Seigneur, has had a caravansaray built, with a mosque and a hospice (Amarath), which is the most superb and magnificent caravansaray I have seen in the Levant, and to which she has donated great revenues, both for the service of the mosque and for the subvention of passengers who are fed there for three days, themselves and their horses, whatever nation they may belong to. There are two long stables, in each of which one can lodge 200 horses, with a pretty courtyard featuring a marble fountain in the middle, enclosed by four beautiful wings of buildings subdivided into 200 small rooms, their elegant galleries supported by pillars and arcades. In addition, there are two other separate buildings in the back that overlook the pretty mosque above, entirely built of marble with open courtyards, baths, and chambers to lodge the priests, all of them cubes covered with lead, and so well ordered that in this caravansaray the passengers, the women, and the poor each have their own separate compartments.[157]

The novel combination of a double caravansaray with a hospice-cum-guest-house grouped around several courtyards, including female quarters, was first introduced in Sokollu's roadside complex in Lüleburgaz (1565–69/70). Nurbanu's special concern for women is captured in her waqfiyya, which assigns daily stipends to some of her freed female slaves and to needy widows who had served her husband and herself: the latter were to be given food from her hospice day and night.[158]

Palerne praises the pleasant suburban site surrounded by gardens planted with beautiful cypresses and tall trees. One of these housed the queen's summer palace, next to which she chose to build her mosque complex as a personal memorial much like princess Mihrümah, whose complex at the Üsküdar boat landing (1543/44–48) was also sited near her garden palace. The queen mother's palace is mentioned by Schweigger (1578): 'In Üsküdar

267 Mosque of Nurbanu Sultan double portico.

is also a dwelling where enslaved Christians reside, which belongs to the sultan's mother; the same sultana built in that place a pretty residence for herself and a beautiful temple.'[159] Another garden nearby was owned by the chief black eunuch Mehmed Agha, the head of the queen's harem faction, who established waqfs of his own in that quarter. Surrounded by the residences of her extended household, including her steward, after whom a neighbouring street is still named Valide Kahyası Sokağı, the mosque complex was closely associated with Nurbanu's memory.[160]

The asymmetrical complex is aligned on a horizontal axis over a terraced hill, with the mosque perched on the highest terrace (illus. 268, 269). The central block, comprising both the mosque and the madrasa on a lower terrace to the north, is separated from other buildings by streets. The largest block, at the west, was transformed during the nineteenth century by the addition of upper storeys, following its conversion into a military hospital and state prison. With its hospital and hospice-cum-guest-house linked to the domed vestibule of the double caravansaray on a lower level, it combines several functions.[161] This western block also incorporated the school for Koran recitation and the hadith college, facing the central block of the mosque. The elementary school is located across the street behind the cemetery of the mosque, and the dervish convent is situated at the east side of the madrasa. The mosque and its main dependencies are constructed of ashlar stone masonry. In keeping with their lesser status, the elementary school, the school for Koran recitation, and the double caravansaray with stables are built of alternating courses of stone and brick. The commercial character of the double bath is reflected by its masonry of cheaper rubble mixed with broken pieces of brick.

The complex is a sophisticated example of the organic urban design concept developed by Sinan during the last decade of his career, when he softened the geometric rigidity of earlier compositions with informality and lyricism. The terracing of the gently sloping hillside merges the architecture with the landscape, while at the same time articulating the hierarchical order among the components of the complex. The lowest level is occupied by the bath-house and double caravansaray, above which rises the hospice and hospital block surmounted by educational facilities. The primacy of the mosque is visually expressed by its dominant position on the uppermost level, with its garden courtyard surrounded by domical arcades whose iron-grilled windows command delectable vistas.

As there was no shortage of land, the first structures of the complex, built during the 1570s, consist of regular blocks unhampered by neighbouring structures: the central block of the mosque and the compact western block, whose hospice is dated by its public fountain to 1579–80. The trapezoidal courtyards of the madrasa and the dervish convent were apparently planned after the creation of streets, once the new neighbourhood had been parcelled out to settlers. The U-shaped madrasa is set askew because of the lane behind it, over which its domed classroom is raised on arches forming a bridge. Although its first professor was appointed in 1579, its construction may have continued beyond that date.[162] The Halveti shaykh of the convent, who served as the mosque's first Friday preacher, was not designated until 1583. Resembling a madrasa, the ashlar masonry convent has an irregular courtyard surrounded by ogee arches. It is provided with a domed hall for sufi rituals and its nearly blind outer walls express the Halveti devotional practice of seclusion (*ḫalvet*, retirement).[163] The street ascending from the horse market below, which runs between the western block and the madrasa, frames an impressive oblique perspective of the mosque. The lower end of that street, which the skewed layout of the madrasa allows to be widened, constitutes an ideal viewing spot. The parallel street separating the madrasa from the convent is similarly wider at its lower end due to the bevelled façade of the latter. These subtle adjustments, which stage the perspective of the mosque to those approaching it from the north, exemplify the priority that Sinan gave to experiential vision over symmetric regularity.

The hybridity of Nurbanu's mosque is particularly noticeable on its qibla wall, where the differing masonry of its extended side wings could not be concealed (illus. 270). On that wall the tripartite windows of the lateral wings do not match the pre-existing windows. The unclassical new windows resemble those of the Mesih Mehmed Pasha mosque in Yenibahçe, also built between 1584 and 1585–86 (illus. 407).[164] The drumless exedras and half-domes surrounding the central dome are punctured with ungainly round-arched 'tunnel vault' windows cut into their curved surfaces. This is another unclassical feature seen in the mausoleum of Selim II (1574–76/77) and in some of Sinan's post-Selimiye mosques (Kılıç Ali Pasha and Molla Çelebi).

The expansion of Nurbanu's mosque diminished the unity of its interior space (illus. 271, 272). The U-shaped gallery adds to the crowded feeling of the prayer hall. The central dome, raised on six arches, sits on four piers embedded into the north and south walls, and a porphyry column on each side. The short colums with muqarnas capitals, awkwardly lengthened by an impost block featuring a second muqarnas capital, are connected with an arch to the piers of the spatially unintegrated lateral wings. A stately balcony with a five-arched colonnade is inserted between the north piers, above the muezzin's tribune that sits directly over the gate (illus. 272, 273). The balcony with a flat vault is externally expressed on the north façade of the mosque as a triple-windowed rectangular projection of ashlar masonry, prominently rising above the lead-covered double portico. Could this have been intended as the private prayer space of Nurbanu? Hanefi law discouraged young women from attending congregational prayers, but made an exception for widows like the queen mother.[165]

268 (Top) Louis-François Cassas, Sketch of the Nurbanu Sultan complex in Üsküdar ('Escki Validé, vieille mère à Scutari'), c. 1786, pencil on paper.

269 Another sketch by Cassas, with a fountain in the foreground.

270 Mosque of Nurbanu Sultan, Üsküdar, from the south.

The muqarnas-hooded white marble mihrab is inscribed with a relatively uncommon verse containing the word 'mihrab' (3:39) which appears in some late mosques attributed to Sinan. The intricately carved lacelike minbar is of high quality, as are the inlaid woodwork window shutters and the splendid İznik tiles of the qibla wall and mihrab recess. Particularly alluring are a pair of matching arched panels on the lateral walls flanking the mihrab, which depict spring gardens with blossoming trees and central floral medallions springing from a red vase. With their exuberantly colourful bouquets of tulips, carnations, and roses amidst blooming branches, these panels can be seen as an evocation of the 'sublime paradise' mentioned in the wooden inscription panel. The internal tile revetments are confined to the original central core of the prayer hall and do not extend to its added lateral wings. The unusual arrangement of the ten rectangular calligraphic lunettes on the porticoed north façade implies that the pair at each end, corresponding to the new side wings, was added around 1584–86. These four panels at both ends quote two continuous Koranic verses (48:3–4). The six lunettes between them cite another verse (39:53) and are datable, like the İznik tiles inside the mosque, to around 1577/78–83.[166]

Although the painted decorations of the prayer hall are mostly restored, the flat wooden ceilings under the upper galleries retain their original scheme. The gilt paintings over a dark red background consist of interlocking hexagons and six-pointed stars that frame floral designs. The inscriptions in monumental *thuluth* are attributed to the calligrapher Hasan Üsküdari (d. 1614).[167] Painted and tilework inscriptions from the Koran, concentrated around the original central core of the mosque, glorify the omnipotent creator of the universe, who is merciful and forgiving of sins. Their emphasis on the promise of redemption for unbelievers who turn to the 'right path' of Islam may have been the Venetian Sultana's own choice.

271 Mosque of Nurbanu Sultan interior toward the qibla wall.

272 Mosque of Nurbanu Sultan interior with the anti-qibla wall and west gallery.

273 Mosque of Nurbanu Sultan, Üsküdar, interior view of the domical superstructure.

The central calligraphic roundel of the main dome quotes the popular Fatir sura affirming the absolute power of the clement God who maintains the order of the universe by holding the heavens and the earth in place (35:41). Starting with the half dome over the mihrab and moving in a counter-clockwise direction, the exedral half-domes cite two verses from the Anʿam sura (6:79–80), explaining how the Prophet, unlike the 'idolaters', turned his face towards the creator of the heavens and the earth. The six pendentives have painted roundels with the revered names. Yet the placement of those bearing the names of Hasan and Husayn on the pendentives of the mihrab recess is highly unusual, as these names are generally relegated to anti-qibla walls. This deviation from the norm can perhaps be attributed to the connection of the mosque with a Halveti convent whose shaykh was its Friday preacher. Roundels with the names of Hasan and Husayn are painted in a similar position above the mihrab-like ritual niche of the Halveti convent at the mosque complex in Kadırgalimanı.[168]

The inscriptions on İznik tile at the mihrab recess quote the Throne verse (2:255) declaring God's absolute sovereignty over the heavens and the earth. The rectangular tilework window lunettes of the qibla wall flanking both sides of the mihrab recess are inscribed with the first two verses of the Fath sura (48:1–2): 'Lo! We have given thee (O Muhammad) a signal victory (1), that Allah may forgive thee of thy sin that which is past and that which is to come, and may perfect His favour unto thee, and may guide thee on a right path (2).' The next two verses of the same sura appear outside the mosque on the lunettes at both ends of the north façade (48:3–4). They reassure the congregation that the all-knowing creator will help to inspire faith in the hearts of believers by 'adding faith to their faith'. The façade tiles feature another verse (39:53) that repeats the theme of divine mercy towards sinners and encourages them not to despair. The two smaller rectangular tile panels above the minaret gates, which provide access to the internal upper galleries, quote the monotheistic formula. The inscriptions of the north façade invite sinful believers into the mosque by assuring them of divine mercy and guidance, a theme picked up again on the qibla wall. This brings the inside-to-outside direction of the inscription programme full circle, as in the Muradiye mosque at Manisa, completed around the same time.

The final form of Nurbanu's mosque, approximating the plan of the Üç Şerefeli, aspires to a sultanic aura. The previous mosque commissioned by a queen mother, that of Hafsa Sultan in Manisa (1520s), had also paraphrased the layout of Üç Şerefeli (a plan type widely recycled in that city) but had humbly omitted its sultanic courtyard. Honoured with two single-galleried minarets and boasting an unusually large number of dependencies (hospice, dervish convent, madrasa, elementary school, and hospital), Hafsa Sultan's mosque signalled the rising status of queen mothers during Süleyman's reign. Nurbanu, who lived in Manisa for many years with her husband (1544–58), was well acquainted with this mosque complex, next to which her son built the Muradiye (illus. 28, 239). The earlier queen mother's mosque, with its antiquated style and its stark dome raised on a rigidly cubical base, gives way in Nurbanu's 'modern' mosque to the layered massing of a hexagonal baldachin and a lavish decorative programme with classical İznik tiles. The mosque in Üsküdar also eclipses its provincial predecessor with dependencies both more numerous and more monumental.

In the 1590s Aşık Mehmed notes the contribution of the queen mother's vast complex to the urban development of Üsküdar beyond its former boundaries (illus. 264):

> On an elevated site at the southern limits of Üsküdar, the mother of Sultan Murad Khan the Third – may she rest in peace – built in the year 985 (1577–78) a decorated, well-ordered, joy-giving, and pleasure-increasing mosque with two artistic minarets and an agreeable dome. And she built at the east side of this mosque an elegant dervish convent (*ṣavmaʿa*) encompassing many rooms for pious Muslims and at the north side of the mosque a lofty madrasa for the study of the sciences, and at the west side of the mosque a kitchen-cum-refectory for guests with two lofty stables [caravansaray]. Before the above-mentioned lady established these charitable buildings, their site and environs had been vacant plots. With the construction of new housing, they attracted around them a large population, and they augmented Üsküdar's inhabited region by at least one-third.[169]

Evliya Çelebi, who likewise dates the light-filled mosque of Nurbanu (Lady of Light) to 1577–78, says it was built for Murad III's mother:

> Situated on a slope, it is like a dome of light. On its three sides are upper galleries for the congregation and multi-tiered oil lamps; it also has stained glass windows. The mosque features lateral domes and its big central dome is especially lofty. Plane trees and linden trees have been planted in its courtyard. On its right and left sides are two well-proportioned minarets with single galleries. All the buildings are completely covered with resplendent blue lead; they are strongly built monumental structures created by Mimar Sinan.[170]

In terms of its large number of dependencies, Nurbanu's complex was only rivalled by the sultanic foundations of Mehmed II and Süleyman I in Istanbul. The identification of its sponsor by Ottoman and European observers alike as the mother of Murad III implies its association with the sultan himself. Like former rulers who had overseen the posthumous construction of their mothers' mosque complexes in the provincial sanjaks they once governed as princes, the sultan contributed to Nurbanu's pious foundation in the capital (the first of its kind) during and after her lifetime.[171] His imperial decrees facilitated its construction and the crown lands that he donated enriched its endowments.

Legally constrained from building a mosque complex of his own in Istanbul, Murad III indirectly boosted the public image of the dynasty by supporting his mother's efforts in creating an unsurpassed architectural memorial for herself. The gap in imperial patronage at the capital since Selim II's reign was partly filled by the increasing architectural visibility of royal women. The mosque complexes of Nurbanu and her daughters İsmihan and Shahsultan (jointly sponsored by their husbands) helped reclaim the sovereign image of the dynasty. The posthumous complex of the royal couple Shahsultan and Zal Mahmud Pasha was created under the supervision of the queen mother herself. The familial architectural presence in the capital was extended to the provinces with the Muradiye in Manisa. The late Nurbanu's mosque, remodelled with her son's permission, commemorated her status at the top of the imperial harem hierarchy: a position resented by rival factions and those critical of the 'reign of women'. It was her blood tie to her reigning son that provided her with a retroactive noble lineage that legitimized her access to imperial visual signs. Her unrivalled prestige was rooted in a mutually beneficial mother-and-son relationship that could strengthen rather than threaten the dynastic image of the empire, so long as it was not perceived as an undecorous infringement of sultanic authority.

PRINCESSES AND THEIR HUSBANDS

I. SHAHSULTAN

Süleyman's half-sister Shahsultan, a prolific patroness of pious foundations and the arts of the book, married the Albanian-born Lutfi Pasha sometime before 1523.[1] It was he who appointed Sinan to the post of chief architect, soon after he became grand vizier in 1539. The couple initially spent some time in Ioannina (Yanya) where the pasha was posted as sanjak governor. There the princess became a disciple of Shaykh Yakub from the Sünbüli branch of the Halveti order. When her husband was summoned back to the capital as a vizier in 1534–35, Shahsultan with her former shaykh's recommendation joined the Halveti-Sünbüli circle of Merkez Efendi (Shaykh Muslihüddin Merkez Musa b. Mustafa). Her subsequent architectural patronage in Istanbul was entirely shaped by her fervent devotion to her shaykh.

Merkez Efendi was a sufi healer-physician who is said to have invented the still celebrated Dionysiac paste of Mesir Macunu during his tenure at the mosque and convent complex of Hafsa Sultan in Manisa. As the governor of that city, prince Süleyman developed a fondness for the shaykh, whose majlises and moving Friday sermons made him cry.[2] When his master Sünbül Sinan died in 1529, Merkez Efendi succeeded him as the head of the convent of Koca Mustafa Pasha in Istanbul: the headquarters of the Halveti-Sünbüli order. He held office there for twenty-three years until his death in 1552 at over ninety. His funeral prayer was performed at the mosque of Mehmed II by the shaykh al-Islam Ebussuud Efendi, who composed a chronogram for his death; he lies buried in a mausoleum at his convent complex outside Yenikapı.[3]

Merkez Efendi's following in the capital included such royal women as Haseki Hürrem Sultan, who endowed funds for the mosque-cum-convent complexes of the shaykh at the Sarı Mahmudlu village in Denizli (his birthplace), and of his son Ahmed in Uşak.[4] Thanks to his esteem at the imperial court, Merkez Efendi was appointed 'army shaykh' during the military campaign of Corfu in 1537, commanded by the second vizier Lutfi Pasha and attended by Sinan.[5] Shahsultan accompanied that campaign in the retinue of her royal brother, Süleyman, camping on the coast of Albania near Ioannina and returning to Istanbul in the fall of 1537. On her way back, the princess was attacked by bandits, who were driven away by the miraculous apparition of Merkez Efendi. After experiencing this miracle Shahsultan became an even more ardent disciple of the shaykh, remaining attached to his circle for the rest of her life.[6]

Lutfi Pasha was dismissed from the grand vizierate within

two years, following a violent quarrel with his royal wife in which he stubbornly defended the cruel punishment of circumcision he had inflicted on a female prostitute. The sultan promptly granted his sister's request for a divorce, putting an end to the pasha's career in 1541.[7] A title deed dated 28 May 1541, witnessed by the chief architect Sinan among others, states that the princess renounced her rights to a widowhood dowry and support (terms that often accompany divorce initiated by women). In return, Lutfi Pasha handed over to her some of his properties in Istanbul.[8]

Shahsultan chose not to marry again, preferring instead to devote herself to her cherished shaykh Merkez Efendi. Her endowment deed, registered in January 1570, lists her three pious foundations in Istanbul, each featuring a Halveti-Sünbüli convent and a mosque. These sufi institutions were supported by revenues from villages near Didymótichon, donated to Shahsultan by her royal brother, and from real estate in the capital.[9] She selected her influential niece Mihrümah Sultan as the executor of her last will, according to which one third of her inheritance (170,000 aspers) was added to her waqf upon her death (*c.* 1577).[10] She appointed herself as the overseer of her endowment and her great-grandson as its administrator. She also assigned daily stipends to several women, including herself, her only daughter İsmihan Sultan, her freed slave Belkıs, her father Selim I's freed slave Nazperi Hatun, and the daughter and granddaughter of her deceased shaykh, Merkez Efendi.[11]

Shahsultan's three pious foundations at the capital are sited in Davudpaşa, Eyüp, and outside the Yenikapı gate along the land walls. Sinan's autobiographies list only the Friday mosques of the latter two complexes and the convent in Eyüp. Created first, the complex at Davudpaşa was located next to the palace where she lived with her husband. Its masjid, built in 1528, was supplemented around 1534–35 with a convent to which she invited her old shaykh Yakub Efendi from Ioannina. When he left to succeed the late Merkez Efendi's son at the Koca Mustafa Pasha convent in 1552, the princess was so offended that she transformed her convent into a madrasa.[12] She upgraded the masjid to a Friday mosque with an imperial permit obtained from her brother in 1562.[13] The madrasa no longer exists, and the extensively rebuilt Friday mosque is a domeless structure with a single-galleried minaret.[14] Shahsultan's two other complexes were also humble structures, sited in the suburbs of the capital.

THE COMPLEX IN EYÜP

The princess's second masjid and convent complex, created in 1537 on a plot of land removed from her garden palace along the waterfront of Eyüp, was a token of gratitude for Shaykh Merkez Efendi's miracle that rescued her from the clutch of bandits (illus. 274, 275). The *Tuḥfe* lists both her Friday mosque and convent (*tekye*) in Eyüp among Sinan's works.[15] Because the shaykh declined the position he was offered in Shahsultan's convent, his favourite disciple (Gömleksiz Mehmed Efendi, d. 1544) was appointed in his stead.[16] The complex seems to be an early work of Sinan before he became appointed chief architect as a protégé of Lutfi Pasha, with whom he collaborated in several military campaigns. Its masjid, built before the princess divorced her husband, was converted to a Friday mosque with a permit she obtained from her brother in 1555.[17] The Turkish inscription on the mosque door celebrates Shahsultan's dedication to the path of God and ends with a chronogram that yields the date 963 (1555–56), the year the masjid became a Friday mosque:

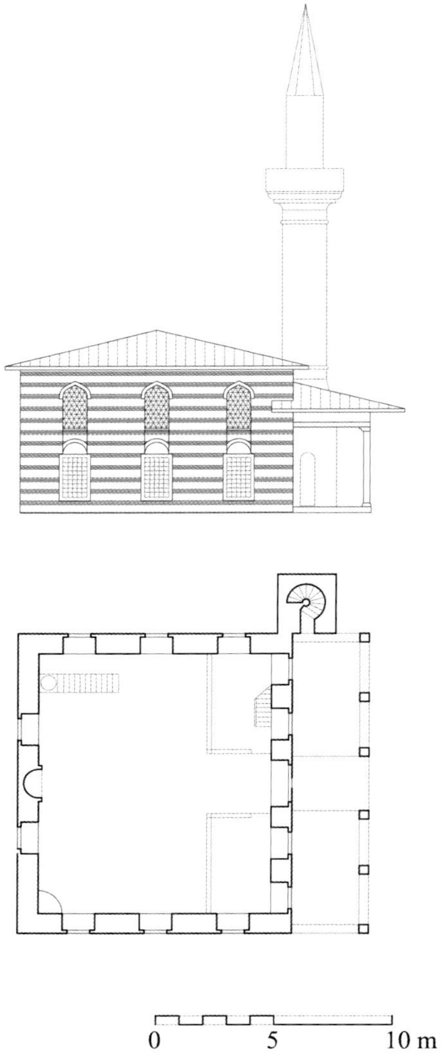

274 Plan and elevation of the Shahsultan mosque, Eyüp.

She discovered the Way to God,
And set out directly for God.

Shah the daughter of Selim Shah,
Erected this building; may it be accepted!

275 Shahsultan mosque, Eyüp, from the west.

The voice expressed a date for it:
'And good indeed is what belongs to God!'[18]

Evliya Çelebi identifies the single-minaret mosque, built of alternating courses of stone and brick, as a work of Sinan. Surrounded by a lush garden, its quadrangular walls were crowned by a 'four-hipped roof covered with deep blue lead'. Restored several times during the eighteenth and nineteenth centuries, the complex lost many of its original features when it was remodelled in 1953. The mosque now has a hipped roof covered with terracotta tiles and is fronted by a wooden-pillared portico built in 1971.[19]

The courtyard portal was once surmounted by an elementary school, originally a wood kiosk whose function was transformed after Shahsultan's death according to the stipulations of her waqfiyya.[20] The now lost convent (*zāviye*) with rooms for fifteen dervishes was located along the shore, together with a house endowed for the shaykh where food was cooked and served daily to the dervishes in a refectory. The imam, muezzin, and caretaker of the mosque were assigned individual rooms, like the schoolteacher and his assistant. Another room was reserved for the masseur of the neighbouring income-producing bath-house.[21] The princess endowed her seashore palace for her own use as long as she lived. After the cessation of her lineage, it was to be dismantled and its grounds distributed to deserving Muslims for the construction of houses.[22]

The complex also featured a mausoleum overlooking the main road to Eyüp, which grew dilapidated and was demolished in 1953. Shahsultan's waqfiyya stipulates that sections from the Koran were to be recited in it daily for her own soul, and the souls of her late mother (a concubine of Selim I) and granddaughter (who died from the plague in 1556).[23] Shahsultan was eventually buried there with several other female relatives whose tombstones survive in the graveyard.[24] The princess's complex in Eyüp was intimately associated with her person through her convent, her neighbouring shore palace, her private kiosk transformed into an elementary school, and her mausoleum.[25] Deprived of its dependencies and its surrounding suburban fabric, her decontextualized mosque stands lonesome today along the shoreline of the Golden Horn.

THE COMPLEX OF MERKEZ EFENDI OUTSIDE YENİKAPI

Shahsultan's waqfiyya refers to the main components of her third pious foundation outside the Yenikapı gate as 'the noble Friday mosque she built near the tomb of the late Shaykh Merkez Efendi, which is a centre for God's mercy', and 'the convent (*zāviye*) located near that mosque' (illus. 276).[26] The *Tezkiretü'l-ebniye* lists among Sinan's works 'the mosque of Merkez Efendi outside the Yenikapı gate,' but the *Tuhfe* refers to it as 'the mosque of Shahsultan outside Yenikapı, for the soul of Shaykh Merkez Efendi.' Mention of the convent is omitted.[27] The construction history of the *extramuros* complex is shrouded in myth. Ayvansarayi says it was built by the shaykh himself before he became the head of the convent of Koca Mustafa Pasha in 1529, a post he occupied until his death in 1552. During this period he is said to have frequented his own convent outside Yenikapı, where he would seclude himself in his personal retirement chamber.[28]

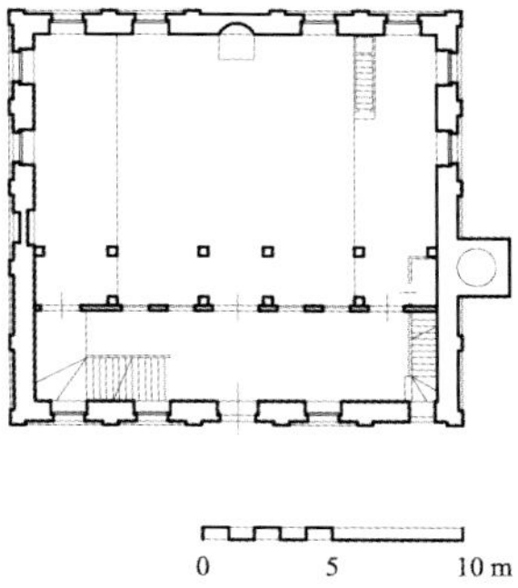

276 Plan of the Shahsultan mosque (Merkez Efendi), Istanbul, outside Yenikapı.

According to hagiographic tradition, Merkez Efendi had built a masjid and convent at Yenikapı with his own hands, aided by his dervishes. The site was selected after the shaykh miraculously heard the sound of running water under its grounds. When his dervishes dug there, a well and a holy spring with curative properties were discovered. Merkez Efendi immediately recognized this as a sanctified site associated with ancient saints. The extant pool-shaped Byzantine sacred spring (*ayazma*), to which one descends by steps, contains the shaykh's cave-like subterranean retirement chamber, which after his death became a place of pilgrimage, especially popular among women. A well in the garden, into which women still throw stones to make wishes, is connected by a tunnel to the shaykh's chamber.[29] The neighbouring double bath for men and women, which Merkez Efendi endowed in 1552, became popular among invalids because of its curative waters.[30]

The princess seems to have commissioned Sinan to build the Friday mosque as a posthumous memorial for her beloved shaykh soon after his death in 1552. The humble structures erected by Merkez Efendi himself were in all likelihood remodelled by her.[31] The convent with rooms for fifteen dervishes was accompanied by a house endowed for its shaykh, where food was cooked and served to the dervishes.[32] Three other houses were assigned to the mosque's imam, muezzin, and caretaker.[33] Shahsultan's waqfiyya stipulates the daily recitation of sections from the Koran in the shaykh's mausoleum for the souls of the Prophet Muhammad, Merkez Efendi, and deceased Halveti shaykhs.[34] It requires that the shaykhs of her two convents in Eyüp and Yenikapı, each of them housing fifteen dervishes, should be selected from the disciples of 'His Highness the late Shaykh Merkez Efendi', and from the disciples of his disciples. If nobody fitting that qualification could be found, the shaykhs were to be chosen from the Halveti order.[35]

Today, the entirely rebuilt complex includes a Friday mosque, the *ayazma* containing the shaykh's retirement chamber, a fountain, a well, a bath-house, a mausoleum, dervish rooms, the shaykh's residence, a kitchen, a refectory, and other dependencies. An inscription over the courtyard portal records the renovations of Mahmud II in 1837–38. The only element remaining from Sinan's mosque, completely rebuilt at that time, might be the base of its minaret. Raised on an elevated platform at the entrance of the courtyard, it is a domeless rectangular structure of rubble stone and bricks, with a walled-in portico. Crowned by a hipped roof covered with red terracotta tiles, it has a single-galleried brick minaret. None of the present buildings in the complex preserve their sixteenth-century character.

The architectural simplicity of Shahsultan's three complexes at the outskirts of the capital befitted her status as a relatively minor princess, the reigning sultan's half-sister, born from a different mother. Her pious foundations conformed to codes of decorum observed in the domeless, single-minaret mosques that Sinan designed for other princesses who did not belong to Süleyman's nuclear family. One of these was a now-lost mosque and madrasa complex built at Aksaray in 1543 for Süleyman's late sister Hanım Sultan, by her son, Osmanshah.[36] Another mosque, which has disappeared with no trace, is referred to in Sinan's autobiographies as that 'of Sultan Bayezid's daughter in Yenibahçe'.[37] The unassuming architecture of these mosques contrasted sharply with princess Mihrümah's domed prestige mosques in Üsküdar and Edirnekapı which proclaimed her special status as the only daughter of Süleyman.

The formal modesty of Shahsultan's complexes, then, was not a factor of gender but of social stature: an index of her relatively minor rank within the hierarchy of royal women. The widow princess memorialized her ascetic mystical devotion through humble foundations, comprising domeless Friday mosques indistinguishable from neighbourhood masjids and convents undifferentiated from vernacular residential architecture. She thus left her distinctively personal imprint on the urban landscape of Istanbul as a devout patroness of pious foundations, who is likened in her waqfiyya to the renowned female mystic Rabiʿa of Basra (d. 801).'[38]

277 Portrait of Mihrümah Sultan, 1541, oil on canvas.

II. MİHRÜMAH SULTAN AND THE GRAND VIZIER RÜSTEM PASHA

1. MİHRÜMAH SULTAN

Sinan created two outstanding mosque complexes for Mihrümah (Sun and Moon), who as the only daughter of Süleyman and Hürrem basked in privileges granted to no other Ottoman princess (illus. 277).[39] Her first complex near the landing station of Üsküdar was built while she was in her twenties, around the time her husband Rüstem Pasha rose to the grand vizierate. She was a wealthy widow in her forties when she commissioned her second complex, whose construction inside the Edirne gate (Edirnekapı) began towards the end of her father's reign and was completed during her brother's sultanate. The differing codes of decorum applied to each monument negotiated her status in the public domain: first as the cherished daughter of her reigning father, then as the not-so-beloved sister of Selim II.

Mihrümah's hand was given in marriage to the Croatian-born third vizier Rüstem Pasha in 1539, during the circumcision ceremony of her youngest brothers, Bayezid and Cihangir, when she was about seventeen. The Bosnian pasha and his younger brother Sinan (who died as grand admiral in 1554) are believed to have been recruited as swineherds from a village near Sarajevo. While he was a page in the imperial palace, Rüstem first attracted Süleyman's attention by dauntlessly jumping from a window to retrieve an object that fell from his master's hand, thereby outshining other pages who simply ran down the stairs to fetch it.[40] According to Mustafa Āli, the sultan was thoroughly impressed by the 'superior intelligence and mind' of Rüstem, who was not particularly handsome. The monarch deemed his loyalty, politeness, piety, and sobriety ideal qualities for a son-in-law destined for the grand vizierate.[41]

Hürrem Sultan, who preferred to marry her daughter to the more handsome governor-general of Cairo, is believed to have incited the chief court physician to spread the rumour that Rüstem Pasha (then the governor-general of Diyarbakır) had contracted leprosy.[42] When a medical expert disproved that allegation by spotting a louse on his body, the so-called 'louse of good fortune' helped bring about the pasha's serendipitous union with Mihrümah,[43] thus assuring his swift promotion to the rank of second vizier in 1541 and to grand vizier in 1544. Rüstem evidently bore no grudge; the couple formed an infamous triumvirate with Haseki Hürrem Sultan to enable one of her sons to succeed the throne. Blamed for the execution of the rival prince, Mustafa, Rüstem Pasha spent two years in retirement between 1553 and 1555. But as European diplomats predicted, he was quickly reinstated with the intervention of his mother-in-law and his royal wife, 'whom the sultan loves beyond measure'.[44] Thereafter he held the grand vizierate until his death in 1561.

The well-educated Mihrümah, whose literacy is apparent in the intimate letters she penned to her father, matched her husband in intelligence, ambition, and piety.[45] The letters she wrote in 1548 as 'Hanım Sultan' together with her mother 'Haseki Sultan' to congratulate King Sigismund II of Poland on his accession display her active involvement in diplomacy; both mother and daughter promised to mediate the king's political affairs with their husbands.[46] The *bailo* Bernardo Navagero reported in 1553 that Rüstem Pasha's wife, 'greatly favoured by her father and mother', frequently visited the private quarters of the Topkapı Palace, which remained off limits to her husband. He urged the Venetian Senate to periodically send gifts not only to the pasha, but also to his wife 'who is likewise most prudent'.[47] Recognizing her influence, the Meccan Sharif's envoy gave some of the presents intended for 'Haseki Sultan' to the grand vizier's wife, 'Hanım Sultan', in 1557.[48]

A Spanish slave physician attached to the household of Rüstem Pasha's brother, the grand admiral Sinan Pasha, observed after curing the sick princess in the 1550s that the two brothers 'would be reduced to nothing' if she were to die.[49] Mihrümah outlived her mother (d. 1558), her husband (d. 1561), and her father (d. 1566) as an incomparably rich widow who passed away in 1578, in her mid-fifties.[50] To fulfil her mother's last wish, she supported the candidacy of prince Bayezid during the 1559 war of succession at Konya that catapulted her older brother Selim to victory as heir apparent.[51] The princess is said to have mourned more for the execution of Bayezid in 1562 than for her husband's demise.[52] Her undisguised partisanship would forever sour her relationship with the prospective ruler Selim. A Venetian secretary speculated in 1562 that the crown prince might avenge himself in the future, not only because of his disdain for Mihrümah's machinations, but also because of 'the great riches of that sultana'.[53]

The princess sought reconciliation with her resentful brother by subsidizing the wedding ceremony of his three daughters in 1562.[54] On that occasion, the *bailo* Daniele Barbarigo reported that Mihrümah had just proposed marriage to her late husband's successor, the grand vizier Ali Pasha, nicknamed 'the Fat' (Semiz). The pasha refused her proposition, announcing he had no intention ever to get married.[55] It was surely ambition and perhaps a sense of social decorum that motivated Mihrümah to contemplate marriage with the new grand vizier, too fat even to ride a horse. A month later, the *bailo* informed the Senate that prince Selim had attempted to antagonize his sister, whom he 'mortally hates', by asking the sultan to donate the late Rüstem Pasha's palace 'now belonging to that sultana' to the grand admiral Piyale Pasha (the prince's son-in-law). Süleyman curtly denied his request, urging him to leave his sister in peace.[56] In the meantime, Mihrümah had given up the idea of getting remarried, resolving to spend the rest of her days as a widow in the Old Palace, replacing her mother as the sultan's chief counsellor.[57] It was she who urged Süleyman to undertake the siege of Malta in 1565 (for which she offered to outfit 400 ships at her own expense) and his last campaign to Szigetvár, where he passed away in 1566.[58]

Mihrümah was the first to congratulate Selim II on his accession, with 'woeful tears pouring from her eyes'. Not allowing him to touch the palace treasury, she offered him a substantial loan of 50,000 gold coins before he left for his official enthronement ceremony in Belgrade.[59] The affluent princess continued to exercise power during her brother's reign through such political allies as her son-in-law, the vizier Ahmed Pasha, nicknamed 'the Handsome' (Güzelce), whom she had hand-picked to marry her only daughter, Humashah Ayşe Sultan, in 1561, while he was still the agha of janissaries. The agha partly owed this honour to having helped the new grand vizier prevent the sack of the late Rüstem Pasha's palace.[60] He further won the widow princess's confidence by offering tearful prayers each night at the grave where her husband lay buried next to their only son, who had just expired from the plague.[61] Following the concurrent deaths of her husband and son, Mihrümah must have felt the urgent

278 Detail from the Piri Reis map (illus. 104): 1. Mihrümah Sultan complex at the Üsküdar landing station. 2. Şemsi Ahmed Pasha complex. 3. Rum Mehmed Pasha complex. 4. Terraced garden palace of Mihrümah (?). 5. Salacak landing station. 6. Kavak landing station. 7. Ayazma garden palace (now the royal Ayazma mosque, 1757–60). 8. Imperial garden palace of Üsküdar. 9. Topkapı Palace. 10 Kılıç Ali Pasha mosque. 11. Tophane cannon foundry.

need to add a loyal and politically promising man to her family. Güzelce Ahmed Pasha became second vizier in the last years of Süleyman's reign, but was deposed after the accession of Selim II, who appointed his own son-in-law Piyale Pasha to that post. Thanks to the intercession of his mother-in-law, Ahmed was reinstated as third vizier within a month. A year after her death in 1578, he succeeded Sokollu as grand vizier, only to pass away in 1580.[62]

Mihrümah owed her influence not only to her connections, but also to her enormous wealth that was doubled by her inheritance from her husband, a penny-pinching financial wizard. Her revenues from crown lands were supplemented during her retirement at the Old Palace with a daily stipend of 600 aspers, the highest sum awarded to any princess in the classical age.[63] According to Marcantonio Barbaro (1573), Rüstem Pasha had left behind properties worth fifteen million gold coins, from which his widow derived an annual income of at least half a million sequins (30,000,000 aspers) even by the most conservative estimate.[64] Costantino Garzoni (1573) declared that with her daily revenue of 2,500 gold coins (150,000 aspers) Mihrümah was richer than all the pashas and even her reigning brother. He says the princess, who had recently created a costly aqueduct in Mecca, displayed an uninhibited appetite for luxury goods: 'In addition to the large quantity of jewels she already owns, she buys almost everything that is sold in the city.'[65] When she passed away, her astonishing treasury of gold objects and jewels was sold at the covered bazaar. Once it was converted to cash, her reigning nephew Murad III inherited two-thirds, and the remaining third went to her daughter, Ayşe Sultan.[66]

Mihrümah was honoured with burial inside her father's mausoleum at the Süleymaniye; the Koran reciters who prayed there for her soul were paid from her own waqf.[67] The domed mausoleum and water dispenser that she built in 1562 for Rüstem Pasha at the funerary garden of her brother Şehzade Mehmed's complex was also supported by her waqf. The memory of the princess and her husband was perpetuated through their separately registered yet interconnected pious endowments, initially administered and overseen by their daughter Ayşe Sultan.[68] Unlike Rüstem Pasha's waqf, dominated by numerous commercial properties spread throughout the empire, that of the princess boasted countless villages and agricultural estates. The early-seventeenth-century reformist writer Koçi Beg criticized Sultan

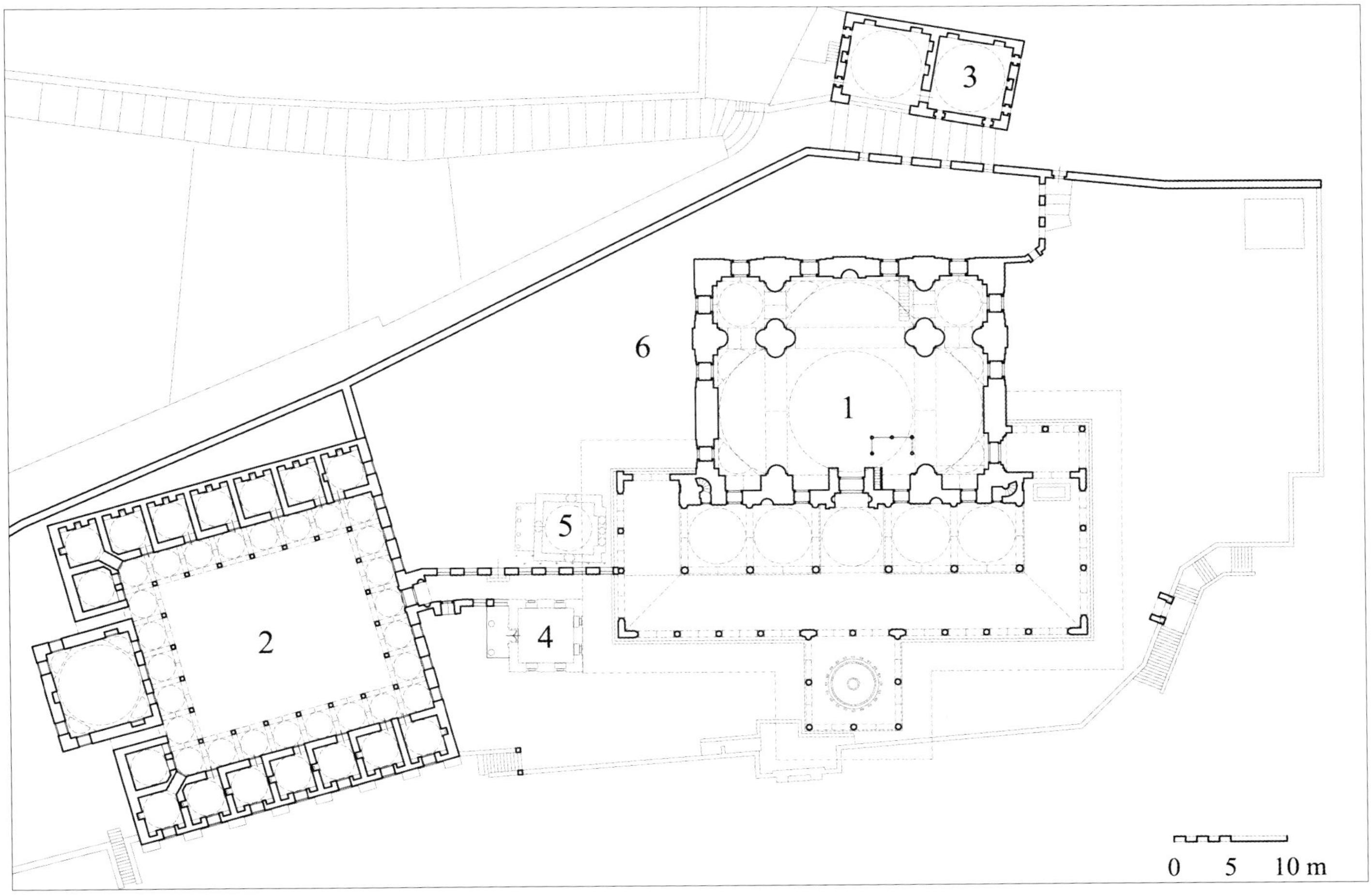

279 Plan of the Mihrümah Sultan complex, Üsküdar: 1. Mosque. 2. Madrasa. 3. Elementary school. 4. Mausoleum of Cigalazade Sinan Pasha (d. 1605). 5. Mausoleum of Edhem Pasha (1892–93). 6. Cemetery garden.

280 Axonometric projection of the Mihrümah Sultan complex, Üsküdar.

Süleyman for having donated as *temlik*s so many crown lands to his daughter 'that they would suffice for the treasury of a minor king'. With these properties she had created pious foundations yielding her offspring an annual income of ten million aspers.[69]

The auspicious combination of wealth and widowhood empowered Mihrümah with unrestrained freedom as a patroness of pious foundations: she spent the later part of her life as a full-time builder. Hasanbeyzade enumerates her major public works:

> In Üsküdar, at the edge of the waterfront, she commissioned a noble mosque, a madrasa, a hospice, an elementary school, and caravansarays on two sides for lodging guests. And for the soul of her husband, Rüstem Pasha, she built an artistic and elegant mosque with a madrasa [*sic*] at Tahtakale. She sold her golden crown to bring water to Mecca the Revered, and spent endless sums on numerous charitable deeds. The noble mosque with an elegant madrasa at Edirnekapı is also this sultana's work; she assigned fifty aspers to its professor.[70]

Rüstem Pasha's madrasa, built during his lifetime by Sinan (1550–51), is located not next to his posthumous mosque in Tahtakale but in the neighbourhood of his winter palace at Mahmudpaşa (Cağaloğlu).[71] Ayşe Sultan inherited the palace together with three others that the chief architect had created for her parents in the capital: a winter palace at the Hippodrome, and two suburban summer palaces (outside the city walls and in Üsküdar).[72]

Mihrümah's first mosque complex was built next to her garden palace at Üsküdar, a vast hilltop estate descending in stepped platforms to the boat landing at Salacak (illus. 278). Her husband's posthumous mosque at Tahtakale (*c.* 1561–63), constructed under her supervision, was financed by his own money in accordance with his last will. Its construction overlapped with Mihrümah's own widowhood projects initiated in 1562–63: her second mosque complex at Edirnekapı and her water channel in Mecca. The Edirnekapı complex was completed around 1570, the year its endowment deed and that of the Tahtakale mosque were registered. Mihrümah's representatives at the law court that approved her reconfigured waqfs included her husband's former steward Mehmed Kethüda (the building supervisor of the mosques in Tahtakale and Edirnekapı) and her own steward, Behram Kethüda.[73]

The conduit conducting water from Mount ʿArafat to the Kaʿba, a project commenced by Mihrümah's royal parents, took nine years (from 1562–63 to 1572) to build.[74] Selaniki and Atai attribute its completion to the princess, who spent 500,000 gold coins (30,000,000 aspers) on its construction.[75] The *bailo*

281 Louis-François Cassas, Mihrümah Sultan mosque, Üsküdar, c. 1786, pencil on paper.

Marcantonio Barbaro's dispatches to the Venetian Senate in 1569 report that she had already expended half a million gold coins on this grand project.[76] That year, she repeatedly requested permission to buy steel for tools needed to cut through the mountainous terrain. Her insistent pleas were refused, however, because of the Pope's prohibition on the sale of metals used in manufacturing weapons.[77] Before turning to the architectural patronage of Rüstem Pasha, let us consider the two mosque complexes built by Sinan for the princess, who is identified in his autobiographies as 'Rüstem Pasha's Sultana' or 'Mihrümah Sultan'.

THE COMPLEX AT ÜSKÜDAR

Built between 1543–44 and 1548, Mihrümah's first mosque complex in Üsküdar broadcast the special status accorded to the sultan's only daughter by his esteemed legal wife (illus. 279, 280). Boasting twin minarets and a dome surrounded by three half-domes, it stood out from the single-minaret mosques with hipped roofs that Sinan designed in the capital for other princesses who were Süleyman's sisters.[78] Ottoman princesses had been relatively minor patrons of architecture during the fifteenth and early sixteenth centuries, when they were assigned more modest incomes; hence one of the grander Friday mosques built for a princess before the age of Sinan, that of Sultan Mehmed I's daughter Ayşe Hatun (1468) in Edirne, features only a domed cube with a single minaret, fronted by an unassuming wooden portico.[79]

Mihrümah was the first princess to commission a monumental mosque complex at the capital, albeit on a suburban site. It celebrated the escalating prestige and wealth of her family marked by her husband's promotion to the grand vizierate in 1544. The chronological overlap of its construction with that of the mosque complex of her late brother Şehzade Mehmed (1543–48), commissioned by the sultan himself, must have facilitated the provision of builders and materials. Construction-related decrees issued by Rüstem Pasha's cabinet for the prince's funerary mosque complex were likely complemented by others expediting Mihrümah's concurrent project.

The grand vizier's active involvement in the construction of his wife's complex may explain why some thought he had built it for himself. For instance, Dernschwam (1553–55) imagined that the complex, sited near the garden palace where the deposed pasha was residing during his retirement, had been built by him as his designated burial place.[80] The Spanish slave of Rüstem Pasha's brother, the grand admiral Sinan Pasha (d. 1554), who witnessed his master's burial at the cemetery behind the mosque, also believed that it had been constructed by Rüstem Pasha.[81] The grand admiral must have been buried there because his own mosque complex in Beşiktaş, designed by Sinan, had not yet been built. In accordance with the late pasha's last will designating his sister-in-law Mihrümah Sultan as his proxy, the complex in Beşiktaş was posthumously erected under Rüstem Pasha's supervision (1554–55/56).[82] When the Meccan Sharif's envoy stayed at the princess's hospice at Üsküdar in 1557, he fancied that it

282 Mihrümah Sultan mosque, Üsküdar, double portico with projecting ablution fountain.

had been founded by the grand admiral who was buried there.[83]

The apparent confusion about the builder nevertheless reveals the association of the complex with Mihrümah's family. It became a potent site of familial memory, with the graves of her relatives from the bloodlines of Rüstem Pasha and Cigalazade Sinan Pasha (d. 1605), who successively married two of her granddaughters from Ayşe Sultan. The latter vizier, from the Genoese house of Cigala, lies buried there in a domed mausoleum he built for himself and his offspring.[84] Ayşe Sultan's nearby mausoleum is incorporated into the mosque-cum-convent complex of her beloved shaykh Aziz Mahmud Hüdayi, the founder of the Halveti-Celveti order, who preached in her mother's mosque. She contributed to the construction of the shaykh's shrine complex by donating a piece of land and water from the garden palace she inherited from her mother, endowing in 1595 a convent there for the shaykh, whose influential devotees included Cigalazade Sinan Pasha.[85]

The endowments Ayşe Sultan made for the shrine of Mahmud Hüdai further enriched the familial associations of Mihrümah's neighbouring mosque complex. Its waqfiyya, registered in 1550, refers to her as the sultan's favoured daughter 'Mihrümah Sultan Hanım', a 'Fatima in innocence, a Khadija in chastity, an ʿA'isha in intelligence, a Bilqis (Queen of Sheba) in natural disposition' and the 'Rabiʿa of the epoch'.[86] Mihrümah harboured sufi sympathies like her mother Hürrem and her aunt Shahsultan, who were both compared in their waqfiyyas to the Basran mystic Rabiʿa (d. 801). Mihrümah is known to have developed an attachment in the 1560s to the Halveti shaykh Nureddinzade, who served as 'army shaykh' in her father's last campaign to Szigetvár.[87] Without specifying a particular sufi order, her waqfiyya stipulates that the Friday preacher of her mosque should be an upright shaykh who will conclude his sermon with prayers to the souls of the prophets and saints, especially to the Prophet's daughter Fatima, and to the Ottoman sultans.[88]

Mihrümah's waqfiyya identifies the dependencies of her Friday mosque: a madrasa, a guest-house (*misāfirḫāne*) composed of eight magnificent rooms worthy of lodging kings, a caravansaray (*ḫān*) functioning as a stable, and a hospice (*ʿimāret*) comprising a kitchen, pantry, and storage cellar. The complex near Üsküdar's boat landing was conceived as a charitable foundation for travellers at the convergence point of routes to and from Asia. An updated version of the waqfiyya drawn up in 1558 endows additional income-producing properties along with two elementary schools, one of them incorporated into the complex in Üsküdar and the other in Yenibahçe. It names Rüstem Pasha as the princess's proxy (*vekīl*) and assigns daily stipends to their daughter, Ayşe Sultan and her children. Upon Mihrümah's death, the surplus funds of her endowment were to be collected by her daughter's descendants who over the generations would serve as waqf administrators and overseers. When their lineage ceased, these funds had to be used in the construction of pavements and fountains along imperial highways.[89]

283 Mihrümah Sultan mosque from the south.

The Arabic foundation inscription, carved in five lines of *naskh* above the muqarnas-hooded marble gate of the mosque, identifies its patroness as follows:

> The foundation was laid for the construction of this strong-pillared Friday mosque by the patroness of pious foundations and good deeds, the pearl of the crown of the sultanate, the greatly renowned honour of the state and the world and the faith, Hanım Sultan – may God, the Exalted, distinguish her with the utmost beneficence – the daughter of the sovereign of sovereigns of the East and West, the sultan of sultans of the Orient and Occident, the cultivator of the inhabited world with justice and benevolence, the founder of the edifice of safety and security for the people of the faith, the Sultan, son of the Sultan, Sultan Süleyman Khan b. Sultan Selim Khan – may his caliphate be eternal! It was completed by the grace of God in the sacred month of Zilhicce in the year 954 (January–February 1548).[90]

Sinan's autobiographies mention only the mosque, madrasa, and hospice of the complex, whose linear composition conforms to the narrow site between the seashore and the steep slope behind it.[91] The mosque and madrasa, raised on an elevated stone terrace with two staircases, are separated by a narrow street from the elementary school to the south. Hospice, guesthouse, and caravansaray have disappeared.

284 (top) Mihrümah Sultan mosque, Üsküdar, interior view of the domical superstructure.

285 Mihrümah Sultan mosque interior toward the qibla wall.

Prints and drawings depict rows of wooden shops with slanting shed roofs lining the raised platform of the mosque with its central arched fountain (illus. 281).[92] They capture the bustling traffic of the jetty, after which Mihrümah's mosque, originally much closer to the shoreline, is known today as the Jetty Mosque (İskele Camii). The weekly market held there on Fridays increased the congregation of the mosque, whose immediate commercial setting was surrounded by a pastoral landscape and garden palaces.[93] With the broad eaves of its double portico, which is fronted by a kiosk-like projecting square belvedere containing an ablution fountain surrounded by stone seats, Mihrümah's mosque resembles a shore pavilion (illus. 282). The five-domed first portico, supported by tall columns with muqarnas capitals, is enclosed on three sides by a second portico of smaller columns with lozenge capitals. The north façade of the mosque has unusual semicircular engaged pilasters with capitals at each side of the central portal and at both ends. They visually complement their counterparts inside the prayer hall: two freestanding clover-shaped composite piers with engaged pilasters topped by muqarnas capitals and semicircular buttresses with matching capitals abutting the internal walls. The attractive double portico is an innovation, the earliest known example of its kind built by Sinan in the capital. Mihrümah's two mosques and those of Rüstem Pasha at Tahtakale and Rodoscuk (Tekirdağ) are visually unified by such double porticoes that add a palatial touch to their façades.

The main block of the İskele Mosque, crowned by a central dome surrounded by three half-domes, rises from behind its imposing double portico (illus. 280–81, 283). Two single-galleried minarets frame the starkly cubical superstructure with its prominent, window-pierced tympanum arch. Kuran observes that the plans of the concurrently built mosques of Mihrümah and Şehzade Mehmed alluded to older sultanic prototypes in the capital: the three-petal plan of the former a 'direct descendant' of Mehmed II's mosque, and the four-leaf clover plan of the latter exhibiting a kinship with the mosque of Bayezid II (illus. 59–61, 66–67). Kuran notes, however, that 'Sinan's mosques emulate the older ones with one significant difference: their two-domed side units flanking the central domed space are surmounted by half-domes.'[94] We have seen that one of the discarded plans proposed for Mehmed II's mosque had three half-domes, a plan implemented in Hadım Süleyman Pasha's mosque at the citadel of Cairo, built in 1528–29 while he served as the governor-general of Egypt (illus. 62, 87). He later rose to the grand vizierate but was deposed in 1544 to make way for Rüstem Pasha. The same plan is reinterpreted by Sinan in Mihrümah's mosque, commissioned just around the time her husband ousted his predecessor.

Compared to the innovative pyramidal superstructure of Şehzade Mehmed's mosque, which blends the no-longer-cubical base of its central dome with curved forms and weight turrets, that of Mihrümah's mosque is relatively archaic (illus. 159, 283). Kuran attributes this difference to stylistic chronology, speculating that the construction of the princess's mosque may have started a year earlier, while her brother's mausoleum was being built.[95] However, the discrepancy in style was more likely a corollary of the lower priority accorded to Mihrümah's smaller suburban mosque. While he was supervising the Şehzade complex, Sinan must have delegated the execution of his simpler plan for the princess's monument to a trustworthy assistant, periodically checking its progress himself.

The three half-domes of Mihrümah's mosque amplify the dramatic impact of the central dome, directly encountered upon entering the prayer hall (illus. 284, 285). This lofty dome rests on four pendentives supported by composite clover-shaped columnar piers with muqarnas capitals. It dominates the lower half-domes, which are flanked by exedras lined with muqarnas corbels. The muezzin's tribune is raised on columns at the west side of the north portal, which is surmounted by a high balcony with loggias on both sides. Since young women were not encouraged to attend congregational prayers, the absent patroness of the mosque must have been represented there by her husband and his retinue of household servants (though later on, she may occasionally have frequented it in person as a widow). The lateral door at the northwest corner of the prayer hall must have been a ceremonial entrance, as it faces the direction of the couple's garden palace located further west.

The muqarnas-hooded white marble mihrab and lacelike minbar are elegantly carved, but the original painted decorations have been completely replaced by modern ones.[96] Besides roundels with the revered names, the few painted inscriptions concentrated on the domes invoke the beautiful names of God in the manner of sufi litanies. The mihrab is inscribed with the typical verse (3:39), and the centre of its first muqarnas tier is carved with a pious exclamation: 'Allah, May His Glory be exalted!' The absence of tile revetments and the use of arched lunettes with openwork grills above the ground-level windows find a parallel in Şehzade Mehmed's mosque. Unlike the latter's qibla wall, featuring windows with blind-arched lunettes bearing painted inscriptions, that of Mihrümah's mosque has stained glass lunettes with ornate openwork grills and distinctive bullseye windows above them. This unique scheme is repeated on the lateral walls of the mosque.

The light-filled mosque, distinguished by its striking fenestration, can be interpreted as a visual evocation of Mihrümah's luminous name: Sun and Moon. Her endowment deed, which is suffused with light imagery, describes the complex, on a 'soul-reviving' and 'charming' site along the seashore, as having 'elevated buildings constructed in a simple sultanic manner (*ber vaż*ʿ*-i sāde-i sulṭānī*)'. The mosque is portrayed as 'an embodiment of beautiful honours and graceful decorations, with its lofty dome resembling in light and luminosity the roof of the Kaʿba's celestial prototype and its illuminated surface bright like the heavenly spheres'. The waqfiyya praises the lofty dome that recalls the celestial bodies, the mihrab, the radiant minbar, 'the novel design of the porticoes and belvederes that amaze skilled masters with perceptive vision', the minarets resembling the tree of paradise, and the *Kauthar*-like ablution fountain.[97]

Ramazanzade Mehmed's chronicle describes the ornate mosque and its dependencies in the early 1560s:

> Her Highness, the foundress of pious foundations and the bestower of good works, the daughter of His Highness the world-protecting sultan – may God make their lives eternal and everlasting – built in Üsküdar as an expression of her pure intentions a Friday mosque encompassing all beautiful characteristics and every adornment, an embellished mosque that is a gathering place for piety and worship, a madrasa, a generous hospice, an unequalled elementary school to which a teacher was appointed to instruct children with the recitation and chanting of the Koran, and several independent chambers and rooms where distinguished and poor guests are given abundant food in banquets day and night, treated respectfully so that they might enjoy repose, tranquillity, and pleasure. In the year 950 (1543–44).[98]

Mehmed Aşık's more detailed description from the 1590s suggests that the hospice, guest-house, and caravansaray were independent structures like their counterparts at Şehzade Mehmed's complex, rather than an integrated block as in Nurbanu's later complex on a hilltop of Üsküdar:

> The daughter of Sultan Süleyman, the late Mihrümah Sultan, built along the seashore of Üsküdar a lofty mosque with an agreeable dome and two well-proportioned minarets, and an elevated madrasa for the study of the sciences at the east side of this mosque, and a hospice kitchen (*maṭbah-ı ḫaʿām*) near the madrasa, and a multi-chambered banqueting house (*dārü'z-ziyāfe*) for guests at the west side of the mosque, as well as two lofty caravansarays (*ribāṭ*, stable) for travellers at its north side.[99]

Also mentioned in Hasanbeyzade's description, cited earlier, and by Evliya Çelebi, the two caravansarays that flanked the mosque on both sides along the waterfront are depicted on a copy of Piri Reis's Istanbul map (illus. 278).[100] The guest-house at the west side of the mosque must have visually balanced the hospice kitchen and madrasa to the east.[101]

Several seventeenth-century authors have misattributed Mihrümah's complex to her father. Peçevi writes: 'For her daughter of exalted fortune, Mihrümah Sultan, two caravansarays, a madrasa, an elementary school, a mosque, and a hospice located at the seashore of Üsküdar were entirely created on account of that high-ranked sovereign's charity; all of these were built with his own noble order, and most of their expenses and needs were taken care of from his side.'[102] Although the complex could not have been constructed and endowed without the sultan's support, it certainly was not intended as his own pious foundation. Evliya Çelebi likewise asserts that 'the royal mosque (*cāmiʿ-i selāṭīn*) of Mihrümah Sultan at the head of the Üsküdar boat landing' was built by Süleyman as a charity on behalf of his late daughter in 1547–48 (Evliya wrongly assumes Mihrümah died before her father). His description of the mosque draws attention to its innovative stone-paved forecourt raised on a terrace and planted with trees on both sides of its ablution fountain:

> Its courtyard situated at the edge of the sea is reached by climbing stone staircases on two sides. The centre of this courtyard is decorated with an ablution fountain and plane trees; it has lofty domes raised on tall columns above external prayer platforms and features two minarets, each with a single gallery.[103]

Louis-François Cassas' eighteenth-century sketch, which depicts the trees that once flanked the kiosk-like projecting fountain, shows that the belvedere terrace was designed as a hanging garden (illus. 281).

The misattribution of Mihrümah's mosque to her father can perhaps be explained by its twin minarets, which distinguish it from the single-minaret mosque she built in Edirnekapı and from the mosques designed by Sinan for later princesses. The simultaneous construction at the capital of two mosque complexes with royal signs for the favourite children of Süleyman and Hürrem acclaimed the heightened magnificence of the nuclear dynastic family. The modesty of the queen's own mosque complex at Avratpazarı was amply compensated for by the assertive monumentality of those built for her firstborn son and her daughter who was married to the grand vizier. Doubtless, it was Süleyman who permitted the mosques of their children to be honoured with marks of status associated with the foundations of former sultans in the capital.

The difference in rank between sister and brother was articulated by the relative dome sizes of their mosques: that of Mihrümah is only 11.4 metres wide and 24.2 metres high, whereas the 19-metre-wide and 37-metre-high dome of Şehzade Mehmed's mosque approaches sultanic proportions. The princess's stylistically more conservative mosque, with its three half-domes, is a truncated version of the fully centralized quatrefoil design of her brother's more innovative mosque. The removal of one half-dome on its entrance axis and the substitution of a double portico for Şehzade Mehmed's sultanic forecourt were manifestations of decorum, as was the reduction of minaret galleries from two to one. These decorous cutbacks marked not only the relatively lower status of the princess with respect to her brother, but also the suburban rank of Üsküdar with respect to the centre of the capital. Despite the subtractive strategies employed in arriving at its design, nothing like the İskele Mosque had ever been built for any Ottoman princess. Designed in a 'simple sultanic manner', it proclaimed the unique prerogatives granted to Mihrümah as the object of her parents' boundless affection and as her mother's firm ally.

THE COMPLEX IN EDİRNEKAPI

Eminently sited on a hilltop marking one end of Divanyolu, Mihrümah's complex at Edirnekapı eclipsed her more extensive suburban foundation with the innovative structure and aesthetic refinement of its monumental mosque (illus. 286, 287). It expressed her image as a mighty widow to whom her father Sultan Süleyman turned for intimate advice during the last years of his life. With her mother and husband gone, the illustrious princess could now shine in her own right. Planned together with her husband's Tahtakale mosque (*c.* 1561–63), the complex at Edirnekapı was executed at the height of Sinan's artistic powers.

The chief architect was primarily involved at that time with the rebuilding of aqueducts outside the walls of Istanbul, ruined by the flood of 1563, and the construction of the Büyükçekmece bridge (1565–67/68) en route to Edirne. The Mağlova aqueduct, built between 1563 and 1565, is a masterpiece of monumental stone sculpture, integrating structural boldness

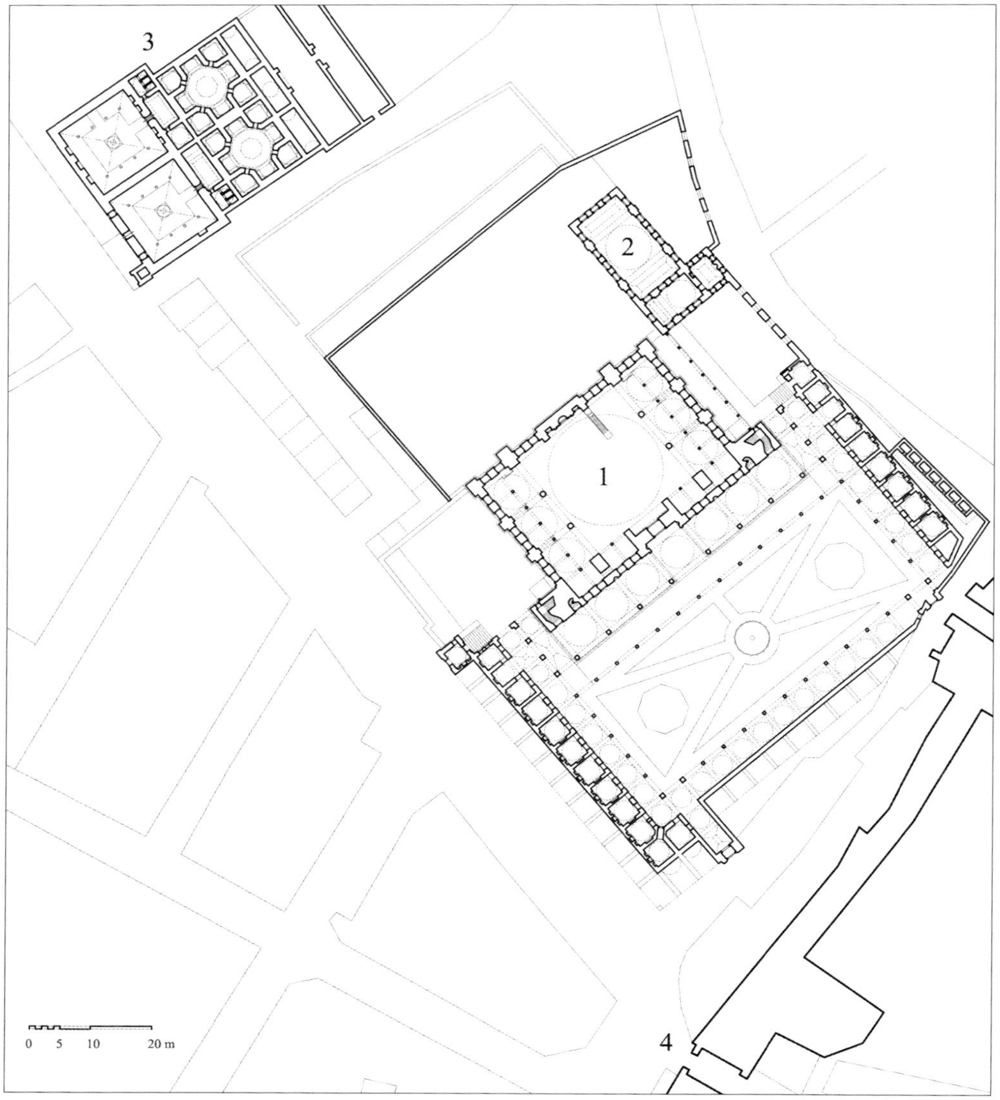

286 Plan of the Mihrümah Sultan complex, Edirnekapı:

1. Mosque and madrasa
2. Güzelce Ahmed Pasha mausoleum with school
3. Double bath with street fountain
4. Edirne gate

with formal elegance in its 'skeletal aesthetics' (illus. 110).[104] While he supervised these engineering projects, he directed his creative energies in the field of mosque design to the memorials commissioned by Mihrümah for her late husband and herself. With its four colossal tympanum arches and walls perforated by rows of arched windows, the Edirnekapı mosque, celebrated as a *tour de force* of structural lucidity and stylistic refinement, is attuned to Sinan's artistic explorations in aqueduct design. Innovations introduced in this mosque and that of Rüstem Pasha, with its unprecedented octagonal baldachin, would be elaborated on a gigantic scale at the Selimiye in Edirne (1568–74).

The Edirnekapı mosque is thought to have initially been planned with two minarets, but the second one was never built.[105] Goodwin speculates that it was Selim II who deprived his sister of the use of twin minarets.[106] In addition to his personal disdain for Mihrümah, the official decline of her status to the sister of the reigning sultan may have required a renegotiation of decorum. The mosques later built by Sinan in the capital for Selim II's daughters, İsmihan and Shahsultan, likewise lacked twin minarets, a choice that seems to reflect the diminished prominence of princesses as their numbers increased. The one-time permission granted for double minarets at Mihrümah's mosque in Üsküdar thus signifies her special distinction as the reigning monarch's only daughter, who formed a formidable coalition with his cherished wife and his omnipotent grand vizier. The multiplication of princesses married to viziers under Selim II and Murad III would give rise to competing palace factions characteristic of the late-sixteenth-century regime.[107]

Goodwin's compelling hypothesis rests on his dating of the mosque and madrasa complex in Edirnekapı, which bears no foundation inscription, to around 1565–70, whereas some scholars believe it was built in 1562–65 during Süleyman's reign, and others have proposed an even earlier date in the 1550s.[108] Based on the madrasa professor's appointment in

287 Axonometric projection of the Mihrümah Sultan complex, Edirnekapı.

1568–69 and the registration of Mihrümah's endowment deed in 1570, Kuran places the completion of the complex after Süleyman's death.[109] Archival documents provide additional evidence to settle the controversy in favour of a completion date during Selim II's reign. A permit issued by Süleyman in August 1563 shows that Mihrümah had previously obtained her father's sanction to build a mosque complex at Edirnekapı, most likely in 1562, when the construction permit of her husband's mosque at Tahtakale was procured.[110] The princess had even obtained decrees for the provision of timber required in the construction of her mosque, the building site of which had been selected and prepared. However, since the endowment administrator of the late grand vizier Kara Ahmed Pasha (d. 1555), Hüsrev Kethüda, had also bought places near the site and was about to build a mosque for his deceased patron, she requested her father to renew her previous permit and to forbid the construction of the rival mosque. The reissued imperial permit is addressed to the kadi of Istanbul:

My daughter, may her honour be perpetual, was previously given an august permit from my lofty court to build a noble Friday mosque and a caravansaray free of charge at the protected metropolis of Istanbul inside the Edirne gate. Even plots of land had been selected and prepared for it, in addition to noble orders bestowed for acquiring its timber. But since Hüsrev [Kethüda], the endowment administrator of the late vizier Ahmed Pasha who was in charge of some of [the latter's] affairs, obtained lands close to those plots and had started to build a mosque, she requested him to be prohibited and my previous imperial permit to be reconfirmed. Therefore, I command that in accordance with my earlier imperial permit a noble Friday mosque and a caravansaray free of charge be built by her in that place, and that the aforementioned endowment administrator be prohibited from constructing a mosque on that site.[111]

288 Mihrümah Sultan complex, Edirnekapı, from the north with the Byzantine city walls.

Kara Ahmed Pasha's endowment deed, drawn up in 1555, just before he was executed as a result of the machinations of Mihrümah and Hürrem to reinstate Rüstem Pasha, does not specify the site of his planned mosque complex.[112] He had acquired plots of land and commercial properties near Edirnekapı shortly before his death, but construction was delayed during the vindictive Rüstem Pasha's second grand vizierate between 1555 and 1561.[113] The project seems to have regained momentum thereafter, when Mihrümah decided to erect her own mosque on nearly the same site. The resulting controversy was resolved in her favour by Süleyman's imperial permit, reissued in 1563. Sinan's mosque complex for Kara Ahmed Pasha was eventually built inside the neighbouring Topkapı gate (1565–71/72).[114]

Hüsrev Kethüda unsuccessfully attempted to preempt Mihrümah's building project with two fatwas he obtained from the mufti Ebussuud. The first outlines the legal dispute that arose between him and the princess's representative, Mehmed Beg, the late Rüstem Pasha's former steward who now served as the administrator of his endowed funds:

> A place at the interior of the gate of a large city, busy in traffic and featuring numerous quarters, is afflicted by the absence of a noble Friday mosque and a fountain, besides the lack of lodging for visitors who suffer difficulties when they come to the bazaar held outside that gate. Therefore, a large group made up of neighbourhood dwellers and others apply to the vizier Zayd [Kara Ahmed Pasha] with a supplication, begging him to develop that place, and the latter agrees to build there a noble Friday mosque, spacious caravansarays free of charge (*sebīl ḫānlar*) sufficient for the needs of travellers, and lodgings (*meskenler*), and he also agrees to bring water to that place, which he promises to develop and rehabilitate. He buys some houses and shops there for this purpose, but passes away when he has just started to prepare the building materials. A noble sultanic permit is obtained for that project together with imperial orders addressed to various locations for the preparation of building materials. But as these preliminary arrangements are being made, other important matters take precedence before the construction starts. In the meantime, Bakr [Mehmed Beg], who is the endowment administrator of the endowed funds (*vaḳf aḳçesi*) of another deceased vizier called ʿAmr [Rüstem Pasha], obtains a noble sultanic permit to build a noble Friday mosque and a madrasa on the aforementioned site without making known the previous sultanic permit given to Zayd's party. He then collects building materials, buys some lots, and intends to start construction work. If Zayd's representative [Hüsrev Kethüda] tells ʿAmr's endowment administrator, 'Your noble permit has been obtained without reporting the existence of the earlier noble permit bestowed to us; it cannot annul our noble permit and consequently we

289 Mihrümah Sultan complex, Edirnekapı, from the northeast.

shall proceed with construction work in accordance with it', can the noble permit given to ʿAmr's party completely cancel and nullify the one previosly donated to Zayd's party, or not?

Ebussuud's subtle response reads: 'When the second permit is obtained without taking into consideration the first, it cannot annul the latter; but what is preferable is to petition the imperial court on this matter and act in accordance with the sultan's subsequent firman.'[115] The mufti's tactful answer implies that it was ultimately Süleyman's decision that would determine the outcome of the dispute.

The second, shorter fatwa favours Kara Ahmed Pasha's project over that of Mihrümah because the charitable services it promised to provide were more suitable for a site located next to a city gate. The legal reasoning is as follows:

If the buildings proposed by ʿAmr's party [Rüstem Pasha] are only a Friday mosque and a madrasa, whereas those planned by Zayd's party constitute an extensive ensemble completely addressing the needs of the residents and visitors of that district, amply providing all the charitable buildings needed and requested by them, which noble permit gains precedence for the benefit of God – may He be exalted – and the people?

The way in which the legal problem was posed loaded the dice in favour of Hüsrev Kethüda; the mufti was left little choice but to answer: 'If the charities provided from Zayd's side are more extensive in themselves, in addition to being more profitable to the people in every respect in terms of meeting all their needs, let them act according to the first permit.'[116]

The permit reissued by Süleyman in 1563 favoured his daughter's party, despite the existence of a previous permit given to Kara Ahmed Pasha's representative. The sultan's licence allowing Mihrümah to construct a Friday mosque and a free of charge caravansaray seems to have responded to the judgment of the second fatwa that a complex serving the needs of travellers was more appropriate for a city gate. The fact that the princess went ahead with her original building programme combining a mosque and a madrasa (mentioned in the first fatwa) testifies to her bargaining power in the negotiation of decorum, perhaps with the help of additional imperial decrees and fatwas that have not come down to us.

Mihrümah's mosque complex was not completed by the time

290 Mihrümah Sultan mosque, Edirnekapı, from the south.

her brother ascended the throne. On 8 August 1565 Süleyman granted his daughter an imperial permit for the construction of a bath-house 'near the mosque newly being built at the inner side of the Edirne gate'.[117] Another decree addressing the kadi of Istanbul in March 1566 indicates that she had just obtained permission to legally exchange with other properties several endowed rental rooms and shops near her mosque 'which is being built near the Edirne gate'. Those endowed properties included four shops belonging to Kara Ahmed Pasha's widow, Fatma Hatun, a daughter of Selim I.[118] Two other decrees, issued by Süleyman in April 1566, inform the city prefect that the sultan had created a public fountain at the market-place of the custom-house in Edirnekapı, the costs of which were to be covered from his privy royal purse. A new source of water, inspected by a committee of experts including the chief architect Sinan and the superintendent of royal waterworks, was incorporated into Bayezid II's pre-existing channel to feed the fountain.[119]

Mihrümah herself created a channel that conducted water from the suburb of Küçükköy to the ablution fountain of her mosque and to her income-producing double bath with a public fountain on its Divanyolu façade.[120] In 1571 she obtained a decree from her brother Selim II commanding the kadis of Aydıncık and Marmara to help her agent in having sufficient marble cut for her 'bath-house that is being built near the Edirne gate'.[121] Clearly, then, it took some time to implement the building permits obtained during Süleyman's reign. The mosque and madrasa must have been finished by 1568–69, before the appointment of the first professor and Sinan's departure for Edirne to build the Selimiye. The incomplete bath-house is omitted from Mihrümah's waqfiyya, registered in September 1570, which outlines the components of her complex as follows (illus. 288):

> Adjacent to the inner courtyard of the admirable mosque, a madrasa with lofty foundations and pillars consisting of seventeen praiseworthy chambers, unequalled in cheerfulness and costliness and unique in decoration and ornament, was built. And around the venerable courtyard, sixty-two strongly contructed shops and a house across from it containing three shops underneath with an adjacent grocery store were erected.[122]

The *Tuḥfe* mentions the mosque, madrasa, and bath-house. An addendum in red ink reads: 'The mausoleum of [Güzelce] Ahmed Pasha (d. 1580) the grand vizier is there.'[123] Attached to a school for Koran recitation, the mausoleum of Mihrümah's son-in-law and his descendants is incorporated into the grounds of her complex, but it was supported by a separate endowment.[124]

Pervitich's cadastral map of 1930 depicts rows of vaulted shops (now lost) enveloping the outer walls of the madrasa and the garden of the mosque.[125] Plots of land extending behind the qibla wall of the mosque may have been acquired in 1566, when the princess obtained permission to exchange endowed properties. The legal dispute probably discouraged meddling with other waqf properties during the initial stages of construction. This would explain the shape of the forecourt shared by the mosque and the madrasa, the irregularity of which could have been avoided if it had been possible to shift the ensemble further south, away from the Byzantine city wall.[126]

A terrace raised on vaulted substructures elevates the main components of the complex from its bustling site, increasing its exposure on the crown of the hill (illus. 364). Edirnekapı was a major city gate that connected the ceremonial artery of Divanyolu to Edirne. Its custom-house and the market held there on Fridays made it a lucrative commercial site, comparable to the landing station in Üsküdar.[127] Endowed shops organically blended with the urban fabric of Edirnekapı that once surrounded Mihrümah's mosque and madrasa. The ashlar masonry of the mosque contrasts with the alternating courses of stone and brick used in the outer walls of the madrasa, the elementary school-cum-mausoleum, and the lower belt of shops. This contrast visually heightens the primacy of the mosque, with which the inner courtyard walls of the madrasa are unified through the use of cut stone.

The garden court enclosed by the mosque and madrasa offers a serene urban oasis with four unconventional entry points. The stairs of the main portal facing the ceremonial avenue lead under a domed gatehouse to the east entrance of the mosque. Another domed gate provides access to the west entrance. Two asymmetrical gates communicate with the narrow north lane that runs parallel to the city wall. The chief architect introduced the combination of a mosque and a U-shaped madrasa around a fountain

291 Mihrümah Sultan mosque, Edirnekapı, interior view of the domical superstructure.

court in the grand admiral Sinan Pasha's complex at Beşiktaş (1554–55/56), posthumously built under the supervision of his brother, Rüstem Pasha. In the Edirnekapı complex, the seventeen madrasa rooms for fourteen students and staff occupy only the courtyard's lateral wings. Because space for additional dormitory rooms is lacking, the north wing has a domical arcade. The absence of a classroom, also missing in the Beşiktaş complex, implies that the mosque served this function.

The seven-domed portico of the mosque was once fronted by a second portico. Its slanting wooden roof concealed the awkward juncture between the low madrasa colonnades with lozenge capitals and the higher columns of the mosque bearing muqarnas capitals.[128] It also narrowed the width of the courtyard, where the kiosk-like domed ablution fountain with two concentric arcades originally occupied a central position, flanked by two sixteen-sided raised garden platforms. The north façade of the mosque recalls that of Mihrümah's smaller mosque in Üsküdar, fronted by a double portico with five domes. The central domes of both buildings rest on four-point support systems, most commonly used in sultanic mosques (illus. 4). Each of the domes has a prominent square base with a window-pierced tympanum arch rising above the double portico.

The three half-domes of the Üsküdar mosque are eliminated in the cubical base of its counterpart in Edirnekapı, which features four immense fenestrated tympanum arches crowned by a single dome. Four polygonal weight turrets capped with onion domes rise above the internal piers and bear the thrust of the tympanum arches, whose stepped extrados resemble those of the Süleymaniye (illus. 174). Unlike the earlier domes of the İskele, Şehzade Mehmed, and Süleymaniye mosques, which are supported by flying buttresses, that of the Edirnekapı mosque constitutes a continuous shell seamlessly raised on a drum without external props. It emanates organically from the body of the mosque, entirely dominating the lower domes of the portico and the lateral aisles.

The dominating solitary dome represents a move away from the pyramidally massed sillhouettes of Sinan's previous royal mosques. The polyphony of cascading half-domes, smaller domes, and exedras gives way here to the monophony of a dome unique in both senses of the word: single and singular. The elimination of subordinate domical elements frees up the mosque's façades, allowing them to be taller and to be transformed into transparent screens perforated with multiple tiers of windows. Sinan's treatment of the structural skeleton as a lattice for fenestration has been compared to the luminous screen-wall effect

292 Mihrümah Sultan mosque, Edirnekapı, interior toward the east.

293 Mihrümah Sultan mosque, Edirnekapı, interior toward the qibla wall.

of late Gothic architecture, in so far as the massive structure of Ottoman masonry permits.[129] The qibla wall, rendered translucent with six tiers of windows, forms a veritable façade turned towards the city (illus. 290). The stepped buttresses above it, abutting each weight turret as if to affirm the stability of the dome, are less structural than aesthetic in function. Visually continuous with the stepped extrados of the tympanum arch above, they frame the qibla façade, giving it a triangular profile culminating with the dome.

The Edirnekapı mosque exhibits striking parallels with the concurrently designed mosques of Rüstem Pasha (*c.* 1561–63) and Kara Ahmed Pasha (1555, 1565–71/72). The rectangular plan of each mosque features a central baldachin and internal lateral galleries supported on columnar arcades. To preserve the unity of central space, the loggias that flank the north portal (surmounted by a prominent upper balcony) incorporate twin tribunes for muezzins. Each of the three mosques has two side entrances and an arched main portal without the customary muqarnas hood or foundation inscription.

Mihrümah's mosque also makes conspicuous references to the Süleymaniye, where internal upper galleries raised on columns had been introduced for the first time. In both mosques there is a similar proportional relationship between the lofty central domes, which rest on four pendentives, and the lower lateral galleries. Particularly notable is the analogy between the pair of colossal red granite columns that support the lateral tympana on top of three grand arches, behind which extend the side galleries (illus. 180, 291, 292). The four red granite columns of Mihrümah's mosque, thought to have been removed from the church of Saint John the Baptist in the Hebdomon, contribute to a grandeur of scale unmatched by any of Sinan's other non-sultanic mosques.[130] The logistic problems faced in transporting the Süleymaniye's four red granite columns would certainly have been remembered by contemporaries, who must have noticed the counterparts of these precious columns in Mihrümah's mosque.

The square baldachin of the princess's mosque can be read as a truncated version of the one in her father's mosque, abbreviated by the decorous omission of its two half-domes and hence of allusion to the imperial iconography of Hagia Sophia (illus. 181, 291). A similar subtractive strategy had been followed in the design logic of Mihrümah's mosque in Üsküdar by eliminating one half-dome of the Şehzade mosque's quatrefoil plan. Her first mosque, covered by a small dome, had cross-referenced her brother's princely mosque with its sultanic ambitions. Her second mosque is surmounted by a considerably larger dome (20.25 metres wide, 37 metres high), which slightly surpasses in size that of the Şehzade and daringly quotes the central core of the Süleymaniye: the paramount imperial monument of the capital. The Edirnekapı mosque surpasses in monumentality Rüstem Pasha's and Kara Ahmed Pasha's grand vizierial mosques, covered by 15.2-metre and 12-metre domes respectively. Even though the princess was ultimately denied the use of twin minarets, her widowhood mosque flaunts the largest and highest dome Sinan ever built for a royal woman (Appendix 1).

Although crowned by an abbreviated version of the domed baldachin of the Süleymaniye, the glowing interior of Mihrümah's mosque does not retain the sombre atmosphere of her father's (illus. 293). In the Süleymaniye light is screened off by the complex superstructure that reduces the height of walls, and by external lateral porticoes covered with overhanging eaves. Mihrümah's mosque is designed to maximize the light it draws in from its soaring square baldachin and its taller wall surfaces, which are punctured by a record number of 204 windows; bathed with light, the interior seems crystalline. The four colossal free-standing piers of the Süleymaniye emphasize structural strength and material solidity; by contrast, the externally protruding piers of the Edirnekapı mosque are almost imperceptible from the interior and their invisibility creates the illusion of a weightlessly suspended ethereal dome, carried on the four points of the pendentives where the tympanum arches converge.[131]

The illusion of weightlessness is countered by an emphasis on structural clarity and architectonic purity. The near absence of muqarnased elements, which are confined to the four colossal column capitals and to the mihrab hood, is striking. The windows, casting patches of light on wall surfaces, constitute the main ornaments of the mosque. The theme of luminosity hesitantly introduced in the İskele mosque finds a more forceful and eloquent expression in Mihrümah's second mosque with its sheer qibla wall (illus. 293). Above the white marble mihrab that quotes the standard mihrab verse (3:37) some of the original stained glass windows, fitted with intricate plasterwork lattices, are preserved. The three arched windows directly over the mihrab bear inscriptions. The central one repeats the pious invocation carved on the mihrab of the İskele mosque: 'Allah, May His Glory be exalted!' The flanking windows serially quote the profession of faith.

The painted decorations, executed in 1956, are not based on original remains. Photographs taken after the devastating 1894 earthquake show completely barren walls and plaster fallen on the floor of the derelict sanctuary, which was built in an area particularly prone to earthquake damage.[132] The inscription programme may have verbalized the theme of divine light resonating with Mihrümah's name. It is unclear whether the calligraphic roundel in monumental *thuluth* at the centre of the dome, written in 1940, was based on the remains of an original inscription. It quotes the Light verse (24:35) which refers to God as the light of the heavens and the earth, who, 'light upon light', guides those whom He chooses towards His light.[133]

Unlike the mosque of her husband, lavishly clad in floral İznik tiles, Mihrümah's own mosque featured simpler painted decorations, a contrast that challenges our modern assumptions about the ornate character of the 'female aesthetic'. It was through structural grace and the metaphor of light that Sinan articulated the gendered identity of his royal patron. The endowment deed, which praises the princess as the founder of numerous pious foundations that 'filled the pages of the book of the universe', describes God's creation of the cosmos in the form of an elegant Friday mosque, crowned with the 'roof of the sky' and ornamented by brilliant stars, the sun, and the moon: a sublime mosque filled with angels and replete with artistry.[134] It eulogizes Mihrümah's microcosmic mosque as a unique masterpiece of unmatched beauty, covered by a brilliantly lit heavenly dome transparent like a bubble and engulfed by divine light like another Mount Sinai:

> It is built in an unrepeatable strange manner and an unimaginable wonderful style, featuring unassailable foundations, lofty columns, and artistic grace. It embodies the most beautiful of all beautiful characteristics, the like of its beauty being hitherto unseen and perhaps unheard of. The exterior of its heavenly dome is a spherical bubble and an overwhelming illuminated summit, like a Mount Sinai that is a place of descent for flashes of light.[135]

Evliya Çelebi, who once again misattributes the princess's mosque to her father, perceptively comments on its pavilion-like palatial quality resembling the legendary Iram (an ancient Near Eastern garden palace built with precious marble columns as an earthly imitation of paradise):

> The royal mosque (*cāmiʿ-i selāṭīn*) of Mihrümah Sultan, the daughter of Süleyman Khan – may God's mercy and pardon be upon him – is a lofty mosque built on an elevated site at the inner face of Edirnekapı. It is the columnar Iram pavilion of all royal mosques. It was built during the year [empty] by Sultan Süleyman in the name of his chaste daughter, all of its expenses having been covered from the imperial treasury. Its length and width are [empty] feet. Its mihrab, minbar, and muezzin's tribune are extremely artistic, but it does not have an imperial tribune. Its courtyard is completely shaded by tall plane trees and its sides are madrasa chambers. It has a bath-house and a suq, but lacks a hospice and a hospital. Its minaret is a single-galleried tall minaret with twelve facets.[136]

Ayvansarayi draws attention to a martyr's tomb attached to the walls of the forecourt: 'One of the ghazis of the conquest [of Constantinople] is buried against the land wall within the courtyard of the congregational mosque. [His grave] became a place of pilgrimage.'[137] Today the graves of two martyred ghazis, Gülzar Dede and Zambak Dede, still constitute a popular visitation site.[138] Converted Byzantine churches with adjoining tombs along the land walls became the focus of a popular cult of martyrs that flourished after the conquest of Constantinople.[139] According to an unconfirmed tradition, Mihrümah's mosque replaced the church of Saint George (Hagia Georgios), which she is said to have bought and to have substituted with a surrogate church built across from her own mosque, at the other side of Edirnekapı.[140]

Whether the princess's mosque replaced that church or not, it did contribute to the Islamization of its district. Mihrümah's insistence on providing her mosque with a madrasa, rather than a charitable caravansaray, shows her preference for a building programme that expressed the primacy of religion. The graves of venerated ghazis within its courtyard must have augmented the association of its site with the memories of holy warfare. Edirnekapı was the gate through which Ottoman armies ceremonially marched off to and returned from military campaigns in Christian territory.[141] The symbolic association of this route with war against the 'infidel' was once again underlined by Selim II's selection of Edirne as the site of his sultanic mosque, built and endowed with the spoils of Cyprus. The mosques of sister and brother, punctuating as landmarks both ends of the imperial highway extending between Istanbul and Edirne, not only commemorated their royal patrons, but also displayed Sinan's full-blown artistic vision.

The Edirnekapı mosque was a revolutionary monument for its time, hailed as one of the chief architect's most imaginative works, pushing the technological limits of his age. He strove to design a unique memorial, aesthetically befitting his illustrious female patron.[142] Mihrümah's pioneering mosque introduced the idea of a single-domed baldachin flooded with light. That idea would be brought to its conclusion in the mosque of Selim II, who trumped his sister with the imperial allusion to Hagia Sophia of the Selimiye's larger dome. Nevertheless, it was the legacy of Mihrümah's elegant mosque that would inspire the luminous single-domed royal mosques of the eighteenth and nineteenth centuries.[143] In modern Turkey, it is still one of the most copied works of Sinan.

2. RÜSTEM PASHA

The two principal monuments built by Sinan for Rüstem Pasha are a mosque complex overlooking the seaport of Rodoscuk (modern Tekirdağ) and a world famous mosque in Tahtakale, along the commercial harbour of the capital (illus. 294, 295). Together with four smaller, generic mosque complexes in Thrace and northwest Anatolia, which have either vanished or changed beyond recognition, the Rodoscuk complex was created during the grand vizier's lifetime. The construction of these provincial monuments overlapped with the building of the Süleymaniye, giving Rüstem Pasha the advantage of riding the tidal wave of a grand imperial project coordinated through decrees issued by his cabinet. The prestige mosque at Tahtakale was built by his wife after his death as a distinctive memorial. Having considered the grand vizier's rise to power and his relationship with princess Mihrümah, I shall primarily focus here on those aspects of his career and personality that shed light on his patronage of architecture.

The career of the Bosnian Croat Rüstem Pasha, a swineherd originating from a village near Sarajevo, is an Ottoman success story.[144] Rapidly rising through the ranks of chief stable master, governor-general of Diyarbakır, and governor-general of Anatolia (Kütahya), he became third vizier in 1539, second vizier in 1541, and rose to the grand vizierate in 1544. As the longest-serving grand vizier of Süleyman's reign, he headed the imperial council for fourteen-and-a-half years (g.v. 1544–53, 1555–61). His tenure was briefly interrupted by his deposition after being implicated in prince Mustafa's execution, which aroused the unforgiving hatred of the janissaries. The grand vizier Kara Ahmed Pasha would pay with his life for replacing him between 1553 and 1555, thanks to the machinations of Mihrümah and Hürrem who were eager to have their collaborator restored to office.[145]

Rüstem Pasha commanded the sultan's full confidence, due partly to his own talents and partly to his alliance with the two sultanas,[146] but he was a highly controversial figure whose achievements were overshadowed by accusations of political intrigue and bribery. Anonymous petitions sent to the sultan complained that the avaricious grand vizier and his steward hoarded an immense fortune through extortion.[147] Even Mustafa Āli, who praises Rüstem Pasha's impeccable administrative skills and financial acumen that filled the state treasuries, admits that he introduced bribery into the Ottoman government. Nevertheless, offices were then sold for reasonable fees, with 'justice' and 'moderation', and only to worthy individuals, who enjoyed long terms in office as the pasha's protégés, with their names carefully recorded in a register. Noting how in his own time, namely three to four decades later, one had to frequent the palaces of forty to fifty grandees and eunuchs to attain even a short-lived government post, Āli enthusiastically exclaims: 'One would give one's life for that [grand] vizier and the laws of his period!'[148]

The *bailo* Bernardo Navagero characterizes Rüstem Pasha just before his demotion in 1553 as the 'absolute master of the whole empire':[149]

> This pasha is fairly small rather than large, with a red face, and such a flushed countenance that it resembles a keelblock

(*lazarino*). His external appearance seems rather strong and vigorous, but it is said that he has some indisposition at the moment. He displays above all great cleverness in his eyes, showing that he was born as a man of business. He is extremely diligent and sober, never having drunk wine. He has an outstanding endurance for hard work. Besides dealing with the affairs of the *Gran-Signore*, he gives audiences all week except Fridays from the afternoon hours until sunset. He has an extraordinary memory of things, in particular of the *Gran-Signore*'s forces and what needs to be watched out for. He is famous among many for being arrogant and quick-tempered, but I have found him to be humane and likeable ... He is ambitious beyond measure, and nothing pleases him more than being told that none of the Ottoman rulers has had a wiser and more prudent adviser than he. He is most avaricious and money can induce him to do whatever a person wants. He is by nature an enemy of Christians, more so than any of his predecessors, and he says the infidels (*giaur*) are not to be trusted, yet he seems to have a higher opinion of those Christians who give him more [money].[150]

Navagero remarks that the pasha used the sultan's and his own money to acquire the favour of the populace, especially the janissaries, and that he sought to augment Süleyman's grandeur by cutting superfluous spending to increase in every possible way the imperial treasury revenues.[151] He owned 1,500 slaves, 200 to 300 of whom were pages, and had an annual income of 24,000 ducats, with additional presents whose value exceeded 60,000 ducats per year.[152] Because the miserly Rüstem spent very little, he amassed an 'infinite quantity of money.' Though he appreciated all kinds of presents, he did not care much for jewels and did everything to promote 'those silk and gold Bursa textiles of his, sometimes wearing vests made of these'.[153]

Rüstem Pasha is said to have owned silk looms in Bursa, and during his grand vizierate substantial silk-weaving manufactories staffed with court artisans were established in Istanbul. The covered market that he built in 1551 near his birthplace at Sarajevo, known as Bursa Bedesteni, specialized in the sale of textiles produced for him in Bursa. The pasha endowed four other *bedestens* in Afyon, Van, Erzurum, and Erzincan.[154] As part of his fiscal policy of accumulating wealth, he fostered the consumption of domestic fabrics by restricting the importation of Italian textiles.[155] Reports addressed to the Venetian Senate contain bitter complaints that the sale of imported cloth and luxury goods had drastically been reduced during his regime, when the Jews of Istanbul replaced Italian merchants as the intermediaries of the Levantine trade.[156] The Hapsburg ambassador Busbecq wrote in 1555 that of all the pashas Rüstem 'enjoyed most influence and authority' with the sultan because of his foresight and fiscal measures:

A man of keen and far-seeing mind, he had been instrumental in promoting Soleiman's fame. If you wish to know his origin, he was a swineherd; yet he was not unworthy of his high office but for the taint of mean avarice. This was the only quality in him which aroused

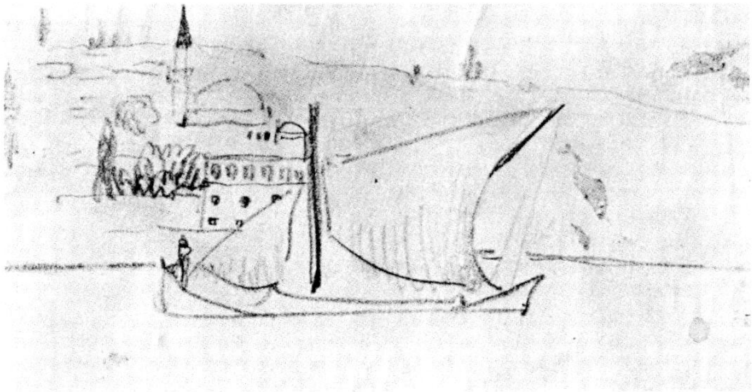

294 Le Corbusier, Sketch of Rodoscuk (Rodosto), 1911.

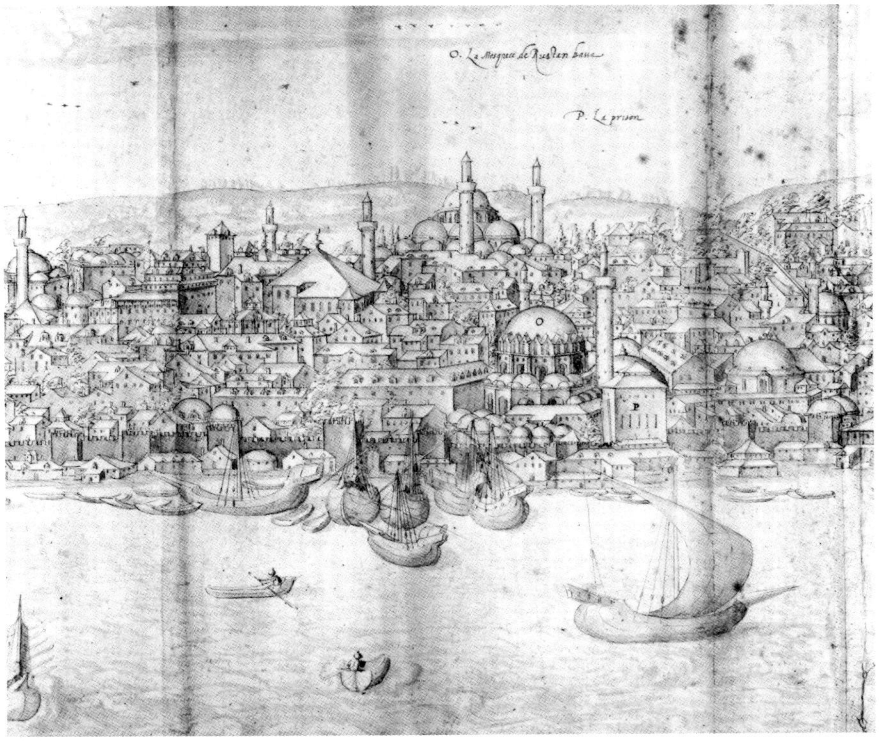

295 Rüstem Pasha mosque Tahtakale, behind a prison tower of the Byzantine sea walls (Baba Cafer Zindanı) with the mosque of Bayezid II on the hilltop; detail from a prospect of Istanbul, *c.* 1566–82, sepia ink drawing on paper.

> the Sultan's suspicion; otherwise he enjoyed his affection and approval. Yet even this vice of his was employed in his master's interest, since he was entrusted with the privy purse and the management of his finances, which were a cause of considerable difficulty to Soleiman. In his administration he neglected no source of revenue, however small, even scraping together money by selling the vegetables and roses and violets which grew in the Sultan's gardens; he also put up separately for sale the helmet, breastplate, and horse of every prisoner; and he managed everything else on the same principle. The result was that he amassed large sums of money and filled Soleiman's treasury.[157]

In 1562 Busbecq portrayed the grand vizier, who had recently passed away, as 'avaricious and mean', constantly thinking of his 'own interests and enrichment'.[158] He 'never deviated from his customary rudeness' and was 'always gloomy and brutal, and wished his words to be looked upon as orders'.[159]

Antonio Erizzo (1557) reports that the grand vizier was universally disliked. Having aroused 'a quasi-immortal envy and hatred' in all, his only remaining friend was the grand mufti Ebussuud.[160] The coalition between Rüstem and Ebussuud coloured the ethos of institutionalized Sunni orthodoxy during the second half of Süleyman's reign. The grand vizier was also affiliated with the austere Nakshbandi order that repudiated music and dance in sufi rituals. The tenets of the Nakshbandi path, upholding rigid adherence to the shariʿa, shaped the puritanical outlook of Rüstem, who disliked not only 'heterodox' dervishes but also poets.[161] Having become a fervent disciple of the Nakshbandi shaykh nicknamed Hekim Çelebi, whose devotees included the sultan himself, the pasha is said to have 'never deviated from that shaykh's advice for twenty years.'[162] While he was chief stablemaster at the imperial palace, he had embraced the shaykh's favourite student, Mahmud Çelebi, as his mentor and 'second father', nicknaming him Baba (Father) Çelebi. With his proper madrasa education, Mahmud Çelebi continually guided his pupil 'towards the path of God and charitable deeds'.[163]

According to the historian Celalzade, the devout grand vizier never missed the congregational prayers, relished listening to Koran recitations, zealously obeyed the prescriptions of the shariʿa, and went out of his way to establish pious foundations to make the thankful populace pray for the continued prosperity of the sultan's reign:

> In order to make students value the study of theology he built lofty madrasas in numerous locations for the love of God, along with Friday mosques, countless masjids, convents, caravansarays in required places for the comfort of travellers, elementary schools for teaching religious knowledge to Muslim children, pavements on roads and straits that presented difficulties of travel, and fountains for the thirsty in arid places, taking pains to build bathhouses that provided income for his endowment.[164]

None of the former grand viziers matched the legion of pious endowments left by Rüstem, who sought to rectify his unpopular public image and gain merit in God's eyes by creating an empire-wide infrastructure of charitable works contributing to urban renewal (Map 4). His view of architectural patronage as a 'public relations' strategy parallels that of his ally Hürrem Sultan. Like the queen, he sponsored a multitude of monuments, formally modest yet functionally magnanimous. The only exception, celebrated as a masterpiece of Sinan, is his posthumously built mosque at Tahtakale. Āli comments on the pasha's abundant pious foundations and gives an inventory of the astonishing assets he left at the time of his death:

> He was strongly inclined to establish pious foundations. Besides his many good works in the two Harams [Mecca and Medina], he built inside Istanbul a Friday mosque and in Rodoscuk another Friday mosque with a hospice and a madrasa. In Hama and in many other towns and villages his caravansarays, which offer plenty of food, and his Friday mosques, masjids, madrasas, and libraries are numerous. After having established so many pious foundations and having made expenditures on behalf of the chaste sultana [Mihrümah], at the time of his death, they found 1,700 slave servants, 2,900 horses destined for holy warfare, 1,150 bridled camels forming more than 183 trains, 80,000 turbans, 780,000 gold coins [46,800,000 aspers], 5,000 caftans and robes of honour, 1,100 gold caps, 209 arms, 2,000 armours and cuirasses, 600 silver saddles, 500 jewel-inlaid gold saddles, 1,500 silver-gilt helmets, 130 pairs of gold stirrups, 760 gilded swords, 1,000 silver-gilt rapiers, and 32 priceless jewels. Assessors appraised their value as 11,200,000 aspers. They additionally calculated 100,000,000-aspers-worth of silver in the form of coins, ingots, and bars. Moreover, in 815 places of Rumelia and Anatolia were found cultivated farms of his. Furthermore, 476 water wheels were counted. The value of carpets, rarities, and miscellaneous items was not calculated. As the late pasha was fond of Koran recitation and of beautifully calligraphed volumes of the Koran, 8,000 Koran manuscripts belonging to him were found, 130 of them richly bound and illuminated in gold. More than 5,000 volumes of varied books were also uncovered.[165]

Rüstem Pasha expired on 9 July 1561 from 'dropsy', probably a cancerous tumour.[166] The *bailo* Gerolamo Ferro says that he left a testament to free all his slave servants with the exception of eunuchs and young pages, whom he bequeathed to the sultan. He also granted 40,000 ducats [2,400,000 aspers] for the liberation of Muslim prisoners.[167] His waqfiyyas (registered in 1544,

1557, 1560, 1561, and 1570) enumerate the pious foundations created during and after his lifetime, naming his father variously as Abdurrahman (1557, 1560), Abdurrahim (1560), and Mustafa (1561). The last name, repeated in the posthumous waqfiyya (1557) of his brother, the grand admiral Sinan Pasha, implies that their Catholic father may have converted to Islam, as did their sister, Nefise.[168]

Rüstem Pasha focused on creating countless income-producing structures before founding the pious foundations that would be supported by their revenues – an economically rational method through which he established his immense waqf empire (Map 4). An endowment deed recorded in 1560, a year before his death, acknowledges that he had established numerous revenue-generating structures, but not as many charities. He therefore decided to endow a portion of his armoury (*cebeḫāne*), whose sale would raise extra cash for additional pious foundations.[169] Another waqfiyya written in January 1561, shortly before his demise, catalogues all the pious foundations he had created up to that point. The list ends with a charitable khan free-of-charge, built at Tahtakale, and 'a noble Friday mosque that is going to be constructed with the surplus revenues of the waqf.' Selling the contents of his previously endowed armoury would generate funds earmarked to buy real estate properties for the waqf of that mosque. The site of the projected mosque is not specified, but since it is mentioned right after the khan in Tahtakale, the pasha may have had the same quarter in mind. This is all the more likely because he had endowed many other commercial structures at this site, along the port of the Golden Horn dotted with shipping wharfs.[170]

Preoccupied with his declining health, the grand vizier was resolved to build his own mosque if God should permit him to live long enough. Otherwise, his illustrious wife (the executor of his will) would oversee its construction.[171] He appointed his steward Mehmed Kethüda as the administrator of his endowed armoury funds, and his daughter Ayşe Sultan as the administrator and overseer of his endowment following his death. The surplus of his waqf would be given to her, and subsequently to her descendants. Should her family line cease, the waqf would be overseen by grand viziers who would select appropriate endowment administrators. Thereafter the waqf's surplus funds would finance the construction of public fountains and paved roads.[172]

A posthumous waqfiyya, dated September 1570, records the landed properties bought for the endowment of the Tahtakale mosque by Mihrümah's steward, Behram Kethüda, acting as her proxy. The pasha had designated for that purpose 100,000 gold coins (6,000,000 aspers), plus one-eighth the value of items sold from his armoury (25,000 gold coins, equalling 1,500,000 aspers). The total sum obtained from the armoury sale (12,000,000 aspers) closely approximates the amount cited above in Āli's inventory (11,200,000 aspers). The waqfiyya does not specify the construction costs of the Tahtakale mosque, built with surplus income yielded by the pasha's waqf and endowed with funds (7,500,000 aspers) that were converted into real estate.[173]

Rüstem Pasha's endowments may well have been distributed according to the logic of a larger commercial-industrial strategy that he had in mind. In any case, his enormous waqf with sixteen revenue collectors was spread throughout the empire (Map 4).[174] His record-breaking number of income-producing properties included villages, arable fields, farms, workshops, tanneries, bakeries, 157 mills, 11 water wheels, more than 563 shops, 273 rental rooms and 54 warehouses, 15 commercial caravansarays, 5 covered bazaars (*bedesten*), and 32 commercial bath-houses.[175] These properties were endowed to support five masjids (Istanbul [2], Galata, Edirne, Esztergom), seven elementary schools (Istanbul [2], Üsküdar, Rodoscuk, Hayrabolu, Kütahya, Esztergom), five madrasas (Istanbul, Medina, Rodoscuk, Hayrabolu, Kütahya), one hospice (Rodoscuk), two convents serving as guest-houses (Hums, Sapanca), thirteen free-of-charge caravansarays (Rodoscuk, Büyükkarışdıran, Zelinje in Bosnia, Skopje, Üsküdar, Sapanca, Dibek, Akbıyık, Lefke, İnönü, Bolvadin, Kalkanlı, Tahtakale), twenty public fountains, six paved roads, and free-of-charge bridges in Bosnia. Additional funds were allotted for two mosques restored by the pasha in Gümüş (Yörgüç Pasha mosque) and Kastamonu (Atabey mosque).[176] He also endowed seven Friday mosques, with or without complexes, in Tahtakale, Rodoscuk, Sapanca, Dibek (Bolu), Samanlı (Yalova), Büyükkarışdıran, and Mount Benefşe in Daday. With the exception of the last two, all of them are included in Sinan's autobiographies which mention another Friday mosque at Bolvadin. The *Tuḥfe* lists the pasha's mosques as follows:

> The noble Friday mosque of the late Rüstem Pasha in Tahtakale, madrasa: 1 [in the Mahmutpaşa quarter]; the noble Friday mosque and hospice in Sapanca; the noble Friday mosque and madrasa in Rodoscuk; the noble Friday mosque in Samanlı; the noble Friday mosque in Bolvadin; two caravansarays in the place called Dibek near Bolu and the noble mosque in Bolu.[177]

The Bolvadin mosque is omitted from the pasha's endowment deeds, but his waqfiyya of 1557 lists a charitable caravansaray, a commercial bath-house, and fifty shops in that town near Afyon at the intersection of several Anatolian land routes.[178] It must have been created posthumously, because the *Tezkiretü'l-bünyān* refers to it as the 'Friday mosque built in the town of Bolvadin for the soul of Rüstem Pasha'.[179] Known today as the Marketplace (Çarşı) mosque, it is a simple cubical structure crowned by a relatively large dome (13.87 metres). Constructed with alternating courses of rubble masonry and brick, its rebuilt wooden-pillared portico and brick minaret no longer display their original form.[180]

Among the two mosques omitted from Sinan's autobiographies, the one in Daday was endowed in 1561. This extant mosque at Mount Menekşe (Benefşe Dağı) is dramatically sited on a hilltop in a village fifteen kilometres away from Kastamonu. A Koran endowed by the pasha refers to it as the 'Friday mosque of Mahmud Efendi on Mount Benefşe.' It was built in honour of that Nakshbandi shaykh, next to his dervish convent (now lost). The mosque is a modest single-minaret rectangular building with a hipped roof and alternating courses of rubble stone and brick.[181] Also omitted from Sinan's works is the mosque in Büyükkarışdıran (Kırklareli in Thrace). Only the foundation walls and minaret base of this largely rebuilt rectangular structure with a hipped roof are original. Mentioned as a future project in Rüstem Pasha's earliest waqfiyya dated 1544, it was accompanied by a charge-free double caravansaray, a guest-house (*tābḫāne*), an elementary school, a public fountain, a paved road, a commercial bath-house, and shops.[182] The double caravansaray, the only structure designed by Sinan, dominated this roadside complex sited on a Rumelian land route. It was completed by 1550 when the Venetian diplomat Catharin Zen visited it:

> We rode until we reached a fountain near the hamlet of Calistrano ... in which there are two very beautiful caravansarays built for the grand vizier Rüstem Pasha together with an attractive residence (*casa*) where he stays when he goes there, as do all other visitors. A beautiful mosque has been built there for the said pasha, as well as bridges and roads paved with stones because the countryside is muddy.[183]

The three small mosque complexes designed by Sinan for the pasha in Sapanca, Dibek, and Samanlı were all located on land routes clustered around the bay of İzmit at the east side of the Sea of Marmara. Endowed in 1557, the mosque near Lake Sapanca is located on an avenue connecting the small town of Sapanca to the capital, an avenue largely used for transporting firewood and timber.[184] An imperial decree sent to the kadis of İzmit and Adapazarı in 1552 informs them that Rüstem Pasha had resolved to construct a caravansaray in Sapanca. The sultan appointed Mehmed Çavuş to build it and ordered the kadis to help him buy required materials (Appendix 4:4).[185] The charitable caravansaray was built together with a Friday mosque, an elementary school, a 'convent' (*zāviye*) functioning as a guest-house, a paved road, and commercial structures including a bath-house. Sinan's autobiographies mention the mosque, hospice, caravansaray, and bath-house.[186] Except for the single-domed bath-house, all of the dependencies have disappeared.[187] The dilapidated small mosque, entirely rebuilt in 1932, is once again a generic rectangular structure covered by a hipped roof, with an independent minaret preserving only its original base.[188] Endowed in 1560, the Samanlı mosque near the port of Yalova (Yalakabad) was situated on the caravan route connecting Istanbul to Bursa. It has disappeared, together with its charitable caravansaray, paved road, and commercial dependencies.[189] The vanished mosque in Dibek near Bolu was likewise sited along an imperial avenue.[190] Also endowed in 1560, it was once accompanied by a charitable double caravansaray, a guest-house (*misāfirḫāne*), a paved road, and a public fountain.[191]

Like the three smaller mosque complexes near the Bay of İzmit, the two major monuments that Sinan built for the grand vizier are sited in commercial ports: Rodoscuk, on the north shore of the Sea of Marmara (in the sanjak of Gallipoli under the jurisdiction of his brother, the grand admiral), and Tahtakale, along the Golden Horn. Their lucrative sites convey the grand vizier's commercial vision, centred on the Sea of Marmara. He owned a large ship, which he used in trading with Egypt,[192] and which he loaned with its galley slaves for the construction of the Süleymaniye complex.[193] All the grand vizier's mosques were situated on major trade routes and ports, with the exception of the remote mosque in Daday, dedicated to a Nakshbandi shaykh he was attached to. They are a lasting tribute to his talent in optimizing the state's and his own financial resources while improving his prospects for the other world.

THE COMPLEX IN RODOSCUK (TEKİRDAĞ)

A 1911 sketch of Rodosto (Rodoscuk) by Le Corbusier shows Rüstem Pasha's domed mosque complex crowning a hilltop from which it visually commands the harbour (illus. 294).[194] Sinan's autobiographies list the mosque, madrasa, hospice, and caravansaray of this complex (illus. 296, 297).[195] The pasha's waqfiyya of 1557 mentions additional structures: an elementary school, a commercial double bath, four public fountains, six paved streets (one of them fronting the mosque), forty-five warehouses, eight tanneries, two shops abutting a charitable caravansaray, and ten shops nearby.[196]

The port of Rodoscuk was an extension of Via Egnatia, the Roman imperial highway that constituted the 'left branch' of the Ottoman road system in Rumelia, linking the capital to the Adriatic Sea. The port specialized in the commerce of legal merchandise (agricultural products, salt, wine, wood, leather, and textiles) and the illegal traffic of grain to Europe. During the 1550s the kadis of Istanbul and Gallipoli were repeatedly ordered to stop the clandestine sale of grain to foreign ships anchored in Rodoscuk.[197] Catharin Zen described the town in 1550 together with the grand vizier's mosque complex that was under construction then:

> Rodesto is a town situated along the coast; it has a fine harbour, mosques, and caravansarays, but no covered bazaar (*bagistano*). It is mostly inhabited by Christians and abounds in vineyards and fruit trees. It has lots of water but not of good quality. It also has some fish and its own kadi, and its dues are submitted to Constantinople. This is the landing station (*scala*) for the commerce of cargo arriving from

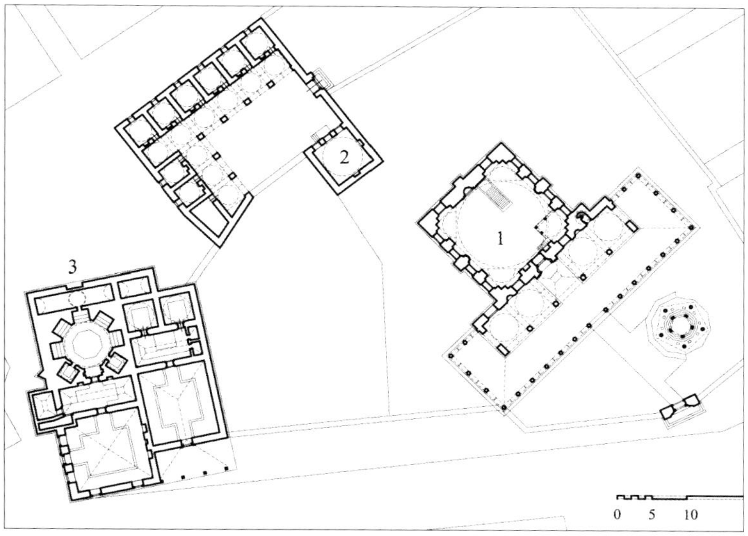

296 Plan of the Rüstem Pasha complex, Rodoscuk: 1. Mosque. 2. Madrasa. 3. Bath-house.

Anatolia and Edirne; nowadays they ship loads of grain more than is customary. Rüstem Pasha is having a mosque with its own hospice (*imarath*) constructed there, following a plan that is sufficiently prominent according to their standard. This territory is on the left route that extends from Constantinople to Greece.[198]

Two decrees issued in 1552 concern the construction of the grand vizier's complex in Rodoscuk. One of them orders the kadi of Thessaloniki to send lead,[199] and the other commands the custodian of timber in İzmit to dispatch without delay 10,000 planks of wood.[200] The Turkish foundation inscription carved on a rectangular panel on the muqarnas-hooded portal of the mosque shows that it was completed just before the grand vizier's deposition from office. Contained in paired cartouches in four lines of *thuluth*, it states that 'Rüstem, the grand vizier, intending to win God's approval, / Made this station (*maḳām*, abode) resemble the flower garden of paradise.' It asks that the patron be rewarded in the other world and ends with a chronogram: 'When this soul-reviving place with a pleasant breeze was completed, / The planet of Mercury wrote a beautiful date on the surface of the moon: "May God make the reward of this Friday mosque the favour of Eden! 960 (1552–53)".'[201]

Although the mosque itself is well preserved (restored in 1841 and 1955–71), its dependencies are in a ruined state (illus. 298).[202] The precinct wall has disappeared, except for an arched stone portal aligned with the north gate of the mosque, which is fronted by an off-centre ablution fountain. The portal is built at an angle conforming to the direction of the avenue paved by the pasha. The dilapidated madrasa occupies a lower terrace on the southeast side of the mosque.[203] The largely ruined double bath to the east of the madrasa is situated on a lower platform. The caravansaray and hospice, no longer extant, were located at the west side of the mosque, in what is now a park. The dependencies

297 Axonometric projection of the Rüstem Pasha mosque.

298 Rüstem Pasha mosque from the north.

299 Rüstem Pasha mosque, Rodoscuk, from the southwest.

300 Rüstem Pasha mosque interior.

of the complex flanked both sides of the hilltop mosque on a terraced terrain, while commercial structures occupied the lowest level along the waterfront.

The ashlar masonry mosque, built of yellowish grey limestone, stands out from its dependencies, which were constructed with alternating courses of stone and brick. It is a domed cube, fronted by a monumental five-bay double portico. The unusual round arches of the outer portico and the primitive capitals of its columns, in the shape of truncated cones, display a marked provincial character. The sturdy minaret at the northwest corner has a single gallery encircled by a muqarnas frieze. The double portico conceals the relatively small size of the mosque, which is covered by a 13.28-metre dome raised on squinches (illus. 299). The height of the portico reaches the lead-covered drum of the dome, pierced with windows and reinforced by pairs of flying buttresses at each corner. The visually continuous lead-covered superstructures of the portico and the single-dome conceal the octagonal stone base of the drum and the stone walls, giving the mosque a somewhat heavy and sombre appearance.

The east, west, and south façades are each propped by a central buttress. The lateral walls feature two tiers of windows, awkwardly crushed against the buttresses. Judging by their clumsy composition, Goodwin doubts that the mosque was fully supervised by Sinan.[204] Despite the closeness of Rodoscuk to the capital, the chief architect presumably assigned this project to one of his assistants after drawing its plan, since he was fully preoccupied at that time with the construction of the Süleymaniye. Inside the prayer hall, angular muqarnas corbels under the squinches are among the awkward provincial characteristics of the mosque (illus. 300). The unusual composite buttresses with semicircular pilasters at the centre of each lateral wall recall those of Mihrümah's mosque in Üsküdar. The muqarnas-hooded rectangular north portal and the marble mihrab are well proportioned yet plain, as is the minbar. The now unadorned interior, redecorated in a Europeanizing manner in 1841, no longer preserves its original paintings and inscriptions.[205]

Mehmed Aşık in the 1590s briefly describes the complex: 'Rüstem Pasha built in Rodoscuk a long and wide caravansaray (*ribāṭ*, stable), a banqueting house for guests, and a hospice, appointing for each fireplace inside the caravansaray a table where free meals are served to travellers.'[206] Evliya Çelebi records the foundation inscription of the mosque, located at the city's crowded market-place, and notes its large congregation and its tall, artistic minaret.[207] The complex did not elicit detailed commentary from travellers who apparently perceived it as a generic monument.

At the time it was built, however, the mosque must have been a novelty with its double portico, the earliest provincial examples of which appear in the mosques of Sultan Süleyman (Damascus, 1554–58/59) and Hürrem Sultan (Svilengrad, 1559–60). The complex in Rodoscuk was a grand vizierial foundation decorous for a bucolic port on a major land route, and noteworthy for the extensive services it provided to travellers, merchants, and townsmen. As Rüstem Pasha's premier provincial foundation, it stood out in monumentality from his smaller mosque complexes. It even had an advantage over the grand vizier's principal prestige mosque in Tahtakale, in that the latter lacks a complex of its own. Yet, naturally, it was built and decorated in an idiom befitting the capital: lavishly decorated with

İznik tiles, it boasts a more majestic double portico and a lofty octagonal baldachin.

THE MOSQUE IN TAHTAKALE

The Tahtakale mosque was created to perpetuate the late grand vizier's memory (illus. 301, 302). In the fall of 1562, a written permit from Sultan Süleyman and several fatwas of Ebussuud legitimized the construction of the posthumous mosque. These documents record the official procedures followed in procuring its site that took a year to clear up, both physically and legally. Because the mosque replaced a pre-existing masjid, Sinan built a substitute (*bedel*) in Yenibahçe, using the materials of the old one.[208] The demolished building in Tahtakale was a converted Byzantine church called Kenise Mescidi (Church Masjid), also known by the name of its fifteenth-century founder, Hacı Halil. In a fatwa appended to Rüstem Pasha's waqfiyya of 1570, the following hypothetical question was posed to Ebussuud by the late grand vizier's waqf administrator, his former steward Mehmed Kethüda:

> The donor of a pious foundation, Zayd [Rüstem Pasha], creates numerous charitable endowments, building masjids and madrasas and other edifices. Before he is able to build others, just as he is about to pass away, he makes a last will (*vaṣiyyet*) for the construction of a Friday mosque he had previously intended to create and requests his endowment administrator to build the Friday mosque, to arrange all of its necessities and requisites, and designate its upkeep expenses and personnel salaries in whatever manner is deemed decorous with the permission of the executor of his will (*vaṣī*) [Mihrümah Sultan]. Then the endowment administrator, with the oversight of the will's executor, searches for a decorous site (*maḥall-i münāsib*), and the people of a district say they urgently need a Friday mosque. In that place no landed property is found because its land belongs to the waqf of the noble Ayasofya mosque, as do some of the buildings on that site, while the remaining buildings belong to the endowments of other persons. With a sultanic permit, the latter structures are exchanged (*istibdāl*) with better buildings, and the shops of Ayasofy a are bought for their full fee. The land rent (*muḳāṭaʿa*) is assessed on the basis of revenues yielded by all the buildings and shops at their time of prosperity. That rent is paid fastidiously month by month. Is it lawful according to the shariʿa to build a Friday mosque on that site?[209]

Ebussuud's affirmative answer reads: 'It is, God knows best!' Several other fatwas obtained from him concern the legal details of exchanging waqf properties and establishing a posthumous endowment.[210]

Sultan Süleyman's permit, appended to the same waqfiyya, was given to the endowment administrator Mehmed Beg on 20 February 1562, after he had obtained Ebussuud's undated fatwa. Addressed to the kadi of Istanbul, it justifies the demolition of the masjid in Tahtakale because it was not spacious enough for its congregation, and approves the exchange of neighbouring waqf properties in accordance with the shariʿa. After recapitulating what was explained in Ebussuud's fatwa, it decrees:[211]

> On the said site let him [Mehmed Beg] build a noble Friday mosque for the soul of the above-mentioned deceased pasha, in accordance with the permission of the noble shariʿa; let the Friday prayers be performed and the khutba be read there along with prayers recited for the soul of the afore-mentioned and for the continuation of my imperial reign.

A title-deed obtained by Mehmed Beg on 25 October 1562 provides additional details about the site, which the chief architect Sinan personally surveyed with a committee of experts:

> In the metropolis of Istanbul, near Tahtakale, a Friday mosque and exalted sanctuary was eminently needed. In that place, the masjid known as Hacı Halil Mescidi, whose plot measured 248 mason's cubits, was ordered to be enlarged as a Friday mosque for the expansive soul of His Highness the late Rüstem Pasha in accordance with the noble fatwa and the sultan's decree. The pride of his peers and equals, Sinan Agha, who is presently the chief architect, went to that place together with a large group of experts (*ehl-i vuḳūf*). For the needs of the afore-mentioned Friday mosque, a plot belonging to the waqf of Ayasofya, measuring 3,788 mason's cubits and comprising twenty-three cauldron makers' shops and one butcher's shop, was acquired.[212]

The title-deed goes on to itemize adjoining real estate properties belonging to various endowments, whose plots were rented from the waqf of Hagia Sophia and whose buildings were exchanged with others. One of the plots of land measured 216 mason's cubits; it was complemented by four smaller parcels of unspecified size. The site of the masjid was thus expanded to more than seventeen times its original size. The pasha's savvy endowment administrator designated some of that land for the mosque, reserving the rest for the construction of income-producing structures. The three commercial khans surrounding the south and east sides of the mosque have been identified as its dependencies (illus. 301). The charitable khan mentioned in the waqfiyya might have been the one next to the neighbouring prison tower of the Byzantine sea wall, known today as Kurşunlu or Zindan Han and associated with Rüstem Pasha (illus. 295).[213]

A permit given by Sultan Süleyman on 28 November 1562 concerns the water supply of the mosque. It states that the late Rüstem Pasha's representatives had just added 1.5 measures (*lüle*) of water to the imperial Kağıthane water channel for the

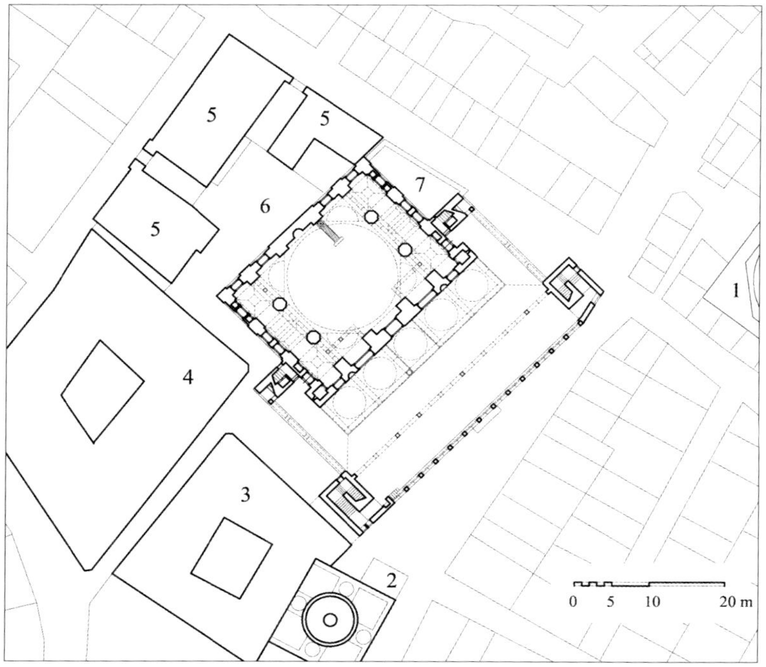

301 Plan of the Rüstem Pasha mosque, Tahtakale: 1. Pre-existing bath-house. 2. Ablution fountain at the head of Uzunçarsı. 3. Küçük Çukur Han. 4. Büyük Çukur Han. 5. Burmalı Han (law court). 6. Courtyard of the law court. 7. Cemetery garden.

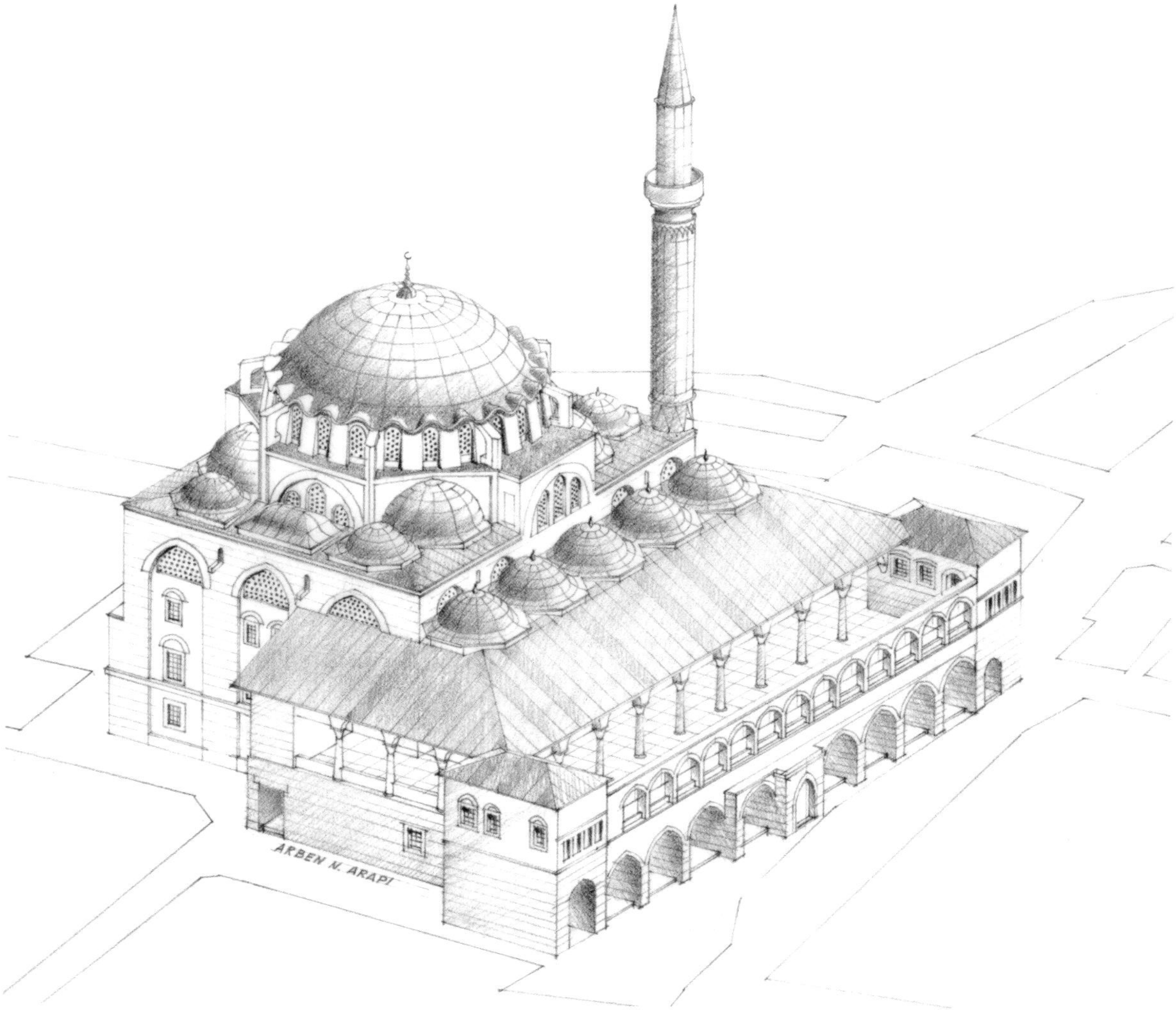

302 Axonometric projection of the Rüstem Pasha mosque.

303 Rüstem Pasha mosque, Tahtakale, from the east with surrounding khans and ablution fountain.

mosque, which was still under construction. The sultan orders the same amount of water conducted to the mosque and bestows on it full water rights in perpetuity.[214] The text accompanying a miniature painting of the Kırkçeşme water distribution system identifies the 'aqueduct of Tahtakale' built for Rüstem Pasha as the water source for his 'graceful' mosque (illus. 119).

Dispatches sent to the Venetian Senate during the spring and summer of 1562 show that Mihrümah Sultan had requested materials for her husband's mosque. On May 18 the *vicebailo* reports, 'I have let the Sultana know that your illustrious Highness has written to me about the glass panes (*vedri*) and lanterns (*ferrali*) desired by her.'[215] Another dispatch, of 19 May, reports that the pasha's steward (Mehmed Beg) was 'presently supervising a certain building that the sultana is having built'. He had been particularly busy that morning 'ordering many things for the building'.[216] The *bailo*'s dispatch, dated 3 August, asks that the materials requested by the sultana be promptly sent because she kept asking for them every morning.[217]

It is unclear when Rüstem Pasha's mosque was completed, since like most posthumously built monuments it lacks a foundation inscription. Some architectural historians have assumed that it must have been finished by 1561, before the pasha's demise, and others have proposed a completion date of 1562.[218] As the site was not cleared until the fall of 1562, its construction probably extended into 1563. The pasha must have communicated his wishes concerning the location, layout, and decoration of his projected mosque to his wife and waqf administrator, but the details of its programme could not have been finalized until Sinan drew its plan in consultation with the building supervisor Mehmed Beg, who received instructions from the widow princess. It was the combined deliberations of this trio that in the end shaped what a decorous memorial for the grand vizier should look like.

What could be more appropriate for the financial wizard than a glorious mosque in the very centre of commercial activity at the bustling port of the capital? Perched on the pedestal of a vaulted substructure containing income-producing warehouses and shops, the ashlar masonry mosque dominates the tightly knit urban fabric of mixed masonry around it.[219] Its monumental dome (15.2 metres wide) looms over the smaller domes of its side wings and porticoes, the whole encircled by the lower domical superstructures of khans bubbling around it. Before a broad modern artery was cut in front of it, the mosque was not fully exposed to the Golden Horn, from which it was separated by the no-longer-extant Byzantine sea wall near a prison tower (illus. 295).

Elevating the mosque above a massive basement not only exploited the commercial potential of the site, but also increased its visibility: its octagonal dome and minaret rise high above the functional buildings of the harbour (illus. 303, 304). In turn, Rüstem Pasha's mosque is situated directly below the Süleymaniye and appears as if it has been placed in the sultan's shadow. This visual juxtaposition articulates the relative status of the monarch and his son-in-law, and establishes an implicit dialogue between the skyline and waterfront. The grand vizier's mosque is situated at the intersection of two commercial arteries: its main north façade borders Uzunçarşı, a major thoroughfare extending between the sea wall and Divanyolu, on which the pasha had endowed ten shops and sixteen rental rooms for bachelors.[220] Thanks to the diagonal orientation of the mosque

304 Rüstem Pasha mosque with the Süleymaniye on the hilltop, Tahtakale.

towards Mecca, that section of Uzunçarşı is widened to form a small triangular piazza that provides an ideal perspective of the building. Sinan took advantage of this prospect to expose the stately stone arcade of the north façade, extending between two gate pavilions above an elevated stone terrace. Under that palatial arcade, which commands vistas of the Golden Horn, is an arched central fountain flanked by four vaulted shops on each side (illus. 305, 306).

Lack of space on the upper terrace prompted Sinan to move the ablution fountain down to the street level, in the form of a protruding square kiosk that frames the triangular 'viewing' plaza (illus. 301 [2]). Although very poorly restored, the ablution kiosk enhances the palatial character of the mosque, to which it is connected by an arch that crosses a narrow alley. Its octagonal water tank and surrounding seats were under a domed canopy carried on twelve columns (now covered by an ungainly pyramidal roof of concrete), with four projecting domical porches at cardinal points.[221] The innovative ablution kiosk and the double porticoed mosque terrace recall their counterparts in Mihrümah's Üsküdar mosque, with its north façade along the waterfront mimicking a shore pavilion (illus. 280).

Behind the qibla wall is another 'viewing' plaza, surrounded by commercial structures and known as the courtyard of the law court (*mahkeme*). The unassuming west façade is fronted by a small cemetery garden lined with shops. Even though an expansive space had been cleared up, there was no attempt to redefine the urban tissue with a garden enclosure isolating the mosque from surrounding structures. The new income-producing buildings erected nearby made maximum use of premium property by conforming to pre-existing street patterns. The mosque lacks the customary precinct wall that indicates where profane space stops and sacred space begins. Instead, its commercial basement, continuous with the plane of mercantile activity, has a superimposed stone terrace, on top of which the serene sanctuary is isolated from the frenetic activity of the market below.[222] What differentiates it from 'upper-storey' (*fevḳānī*) mosques typical of commercial districts is its monumental scale

305 Rüstem Pasha mosque from the northeast showing basement with shops and public fountain surmounted by the upper terrace arcade.

306 Rüstem Pasha mosque double portico with gate pavilion and outer arcade overlooking the street.

and magnificence. Four enclosed staircases act as transitional spaces that transport the privileged users of the mosque into a visually stunning space inspiring tranquility and peace. The two principal staircases, punctuating both ends of the north façade, are surmounted by gate pavilions for the custodians and muezzins, which give access to the stone-paved terrace. The two subsidiary staircases at the south corners of the terrace mount to the lateral gates of the mosque, continuing up another storey to its internal upper galleries.

The double porticoed north façade has an arched central portal flanked by two enormous rectangular iron-grilled windows which are similar those on the façade of Kara Ahmed Pasha's mosque in Topkapı (1565–71/72) (illus. 307, 375). As we have seen, the mosque of the rival grand vizier was planned shortly before his execution in 1555, but not allowed to be built on its originally intended site at Edirnekapı, where Mihrümah erected her own mosque. The five-domed first portico of the Tahtakale mosque has tall columns with muqarnas capitals. The second portico covered by a slanting wooden roof rests on smaller columns with lozenge capitals; the spandrels of its ogee arches are decorated with eight white-on-blue İznik tile roundels inscribed with the revered names. A sense of 'restorative oasis' pervades the courtyard, which has two raised prayer platforms. The absence of a real garden enclosure is compensated for by the exquisite floral İznik tiles that profusely decorate the north façade of the mosque and its whole interior with variegated flowers and blossoming 'paradise trees', which evoke an unearthly hanging garden raised on vaulted substructures (illus. 307–12).

The sheer number of tiles must have been even more overwhelming at the time the mosque was inaugurated, for it was the first grand vizierial foundation to boast 'classical' İznik tiles recently introduced at the Süleymaniye (*c.* 1556–59). Rüstem Pasha's smaller mosque provided an opportunity to display to their fullest advantage the innovative products of the İznik ateliers. Its celebrated tiles go a step further than the Süleymaniye's experimental revetments by magnifying patterns to assure their legibility from a distance. The hand of many artists and different ateliers is borne out in the variety of tile sizes that would become standardized during the last quarter of the century.[223] The tiles are celebrated for their wealth of floral designs, which are combined with more traditional patterns. Pioneered by court artists in the 1550s, the new floral idiom exhibits a creative outburst in the pasha's mosque with its abundance of semi-naturalistic flowers (including forty-one variants of tulip compositions) and its blue-ground blossoming tree panels (illus. 307, 311).[224] The prayer hall also inaugurates ogival and wavy-vine repeat-panels (illus. 312), inspired directly by textile patterns that became fashionable during the grand vizierate of Rüstem Pasha. His strategic economic measures had a profound impact on the silk-weaving industry and during his regime the tile workshops in İznik were reorganized to cater to the growing needs

307 Rüstem Pasha mosque north façade with large iron-grilled window and İznik tile panel depicting a blossoming tree at the left side of the portal, Tahtakale.

308 Rüstem Pasha mosque interior toward the qibla wall.

309 Rüstem Pasha mosque, Tahtakale, interior toward the anti-qibla wall.

311 Rüstem Pasha mosque, detail of mihrab tiles.

310 Rüstem Pasha mosque, interior view of the domical superstructure.

312 Rüstem Pasha mosque, floral İznik tiles with undulating vine motif framed by white stone mouldings.

of the construction industry.[225] It is therefore not unlikely that textile designers employed in the pasha's own silk looms contributed to the decorative programme of his posthumous mosque.[226]

The abundance of tiling in the Tahtakale mosque is generally attributed to the idiosyncratic personal taste of Rüstem Pasha with his collector's penchant for hoarding, which presumably dictated a decorative programme at odds with Sinan's selective use of tiles to accentuate architectural elements.[227] Noting the unusually large variety of repeat-pattern modular tiles, Walter Denny suggests that many different designers worked in a competitive atmosphere fomented by the grand vizier who undertook a 'personal act of patronage that would demonstrate the capabilities of the Ottoman ceramic artisans' and provide a 'powerful advertisement' for their products.[228] It is unlikely, however, that the tiles were 'collected' before the site and dimensions of the mosque had been determined. Tiles with modular repeat patterns were probably commissioned together with custom-made unified-field panels conforming to specific dimensions, which could only be produced on the basis of full-size paper cartoons after the mosque's design became finalized in 1562.[229]

Rüstem Pasha may well have left behind instructions that influenced the flamboyant use of İznik tiles, but such wasteful extravagance seems out of character with his penny-pinching, austere disposition. It is more plausible that the unique decorative programme, never again repeated by Sinan, was envisioned in consultation with Mehmed Beg and Mihrümah Sultan as an attribute appropriate for a posthumous memorial. The wealthy princess with a taste for conspicuous consumption apparently did not spare any expense in creating a monument worthy of her departed husband as the executor of his last will. Extensive tile revetments are a typical characteristic of Ottoman palaces and mausolea, conceived as eternal garden pavilions for the dead. The lavish use of tile revetments in the pasha's mosque not only amplifies its palatial aura, but also imbues it with funerary associations that are manifested in its eschatological inscription programme.

The unprecedented octagonal domed baldachin of the mosque, too, may have been inspired by the affiliation of the octagon with funerary architecture. It was, in fact, designed simultaneously with Rüstem Pasha's octagonal domed mausoleum, commissioned by his widow at the funerary garden of Şehzade Mehmed's complex to underscore his familial connection with the dynasty (illus. 154, 313). Dated by an inscription to 968 (1560–61) and endowed by Mihrümah in 1562, the mausoleum also enshrines the body of her only son who died from the plague shortly before his father. It has innovative İznik tile revetments with unique imitation-marble joggled voussoirs around its upper windows (illus. 314, 315).[230] The panels at ground level, which depict floral medallions sprouting from vases, find a parallel in the mihrab of the Tahtakale mosque (illus. 311).

313 Rüstem Pasha mausoleum, Istanbul, at the Şehzade Mehmed complex.

The mosque was Sinan's earliest experiment with the octagonal-baldachined plan type, which paved the way for the Selimiye in Edirne, and thereafter became a standard scheme in his late mosques at the capital (illus. 5). An often cited model for the octagonal baldachin is the church of SS Sergius and Bacchus in Istanbul, transformed during the late fifteenth century into a convent mosque known as Küçük Ayasofya. Its ground plan, with eight free-standing supports, a projecting apse, and a U-shaped ambulatory with an upper gallery, was more closely paraphrased in the Selimiye than in the Tahtakale mosque. The tentative octagonal baldachin of the pasha's experimental rectangular mosque is not as visually pronounced as that of the Selimiye, where Sinan would create a more fully centralized, square inner space. The tripartite spatial configuration of the Tahtakale mosque remains conceptually closer to the Süleymaniye, with its central domed space flanked by side wings. The eight asymmetrical piers, aligned with the rectangular walls, do not fully harmonize with the octagonal zone of transition under the dome. Four of them are incorporated into the north and south walls as pilasters, while the remaining four are paired alongside the lateral gallery colonnades, supported on white and green marble columns with lozenge capitals. One wonders whether a puzzling feature of Rüstem Pasha's memorial mosque, the prominent yet unreachable private balcony projecting over its main gate on marble

314 Rüstem Pasha mausoleum interior, Istanbul.

315 Rüstem Pasha mausoleum, arched İznik tile panel.

consoles extending between the north piers, was meant to represent the absence of its departed patron (illus. 309).[231]

Sinan must have designed the pasha's mosque and that of his widow in Edirnekapı, the royal permit of which was reissued in 1563, around the same time.[232] Their shared elements include high domes flanked on the sides by triple arches resting on two supports with muqarnas capitals (four octagonal piers in one case and colossal red granite columns in the other), two side entrances, and tall façades with novel window compositions. The four-piered square baldachin of Mihrümah's mosque, with its monumental fenestrated tympanum arches and red granite columns, paraphrased the central core of her father's Süleymaniye mosque. The princess's royal aspirations were further announced by the grandiose dome of her mosque. Her husband's mosque, crowned by a smaller octagonal domed baldachin (15.2 metres wide and 22.8 metres high), had no such royal ambitions. Nevertheless it flaunts the largest dome that Sinan ever built for a grand vizier in the capital (Appendix 1).

The horizontally stratified exterior of Rüstem Pasha's mosque is austere and minimally articulated. The internal configuration of its side wings, covered by flat-roofed cloister vaults, is masked on the exterior by cradle vaults flanked by two small domes (illus. 302–3). Surrounded by four tympana and four exedral half-domes, the main dome is raised on a tall octagonal base. Unlike post-Selimiye mosques with octagonal baldachins, most of which have domes surrounded by eight weight turrets and square plans with projecting mihrabs, Rüstem Pasha's rectangular mosque features eight traditional flying buttresses around its dome (illus. 5). The undulating serpentine lips of its Byzantinizing dome – perhaps an allusion to the church that once stood on its site – recall the wavy cresting along the octagonal dome base of the pasha's mausoleum (illus. 295, 313).[233]

The mosques of husband and wife in Tahtakale and Edirnekapı supplant the pyramidal massing of the princess's earlier mosque in Üsküdar with their dominant single domes. The pasha's mosque is not as luminous as the tileless interior of his wife's, whose iconography revolves around the metaphor of light. The distinctive mood of the tile-covered sanctuary relies on the carefully controlled manner in which light is permitted to colour its interior space. The zone above the first stringcourse, which defines the upper limit of tile revetments, is lined with triple windows and transparent tympanum arches of bottle-glass. The reduced number of windows on the lower zones increases the area of walls faced with tile revetments and eliminates glaring reflections on their glassy surfaces. The dramatic upward surge of light creates an otherworldly, transcendental ambience.[234]

İznik tiles cloak virtually every surface up to the first stringcourse. A second stringcourse, encircling the springing points of the eight arches that support the dome, outlines a transitional belt of light between the walls and the superstructure. The dome cornice above the tile-covered pendentives is surrounded by another belt of windows. Contrary to general opinion, the tile programme, bilaterally symmetrical along the mihrab axis, was carefully worked out as Denny has shown. Its unity was later on undermined by haphazard repairs that resulted in surfaces patched with an incongruous collage.[235] Unlike the matching tiles of Rüstem's small mausoleum, those of his mosque represent an aesthetic of unity in variety. The diversity of designs was an outcome of the immense quantity of tiling required, which no single workshop in İznik had the capacity to meet within a short time. Modular-repeat patterns are mostly used on large wall surfaces and on the octagonal piers whose upper facets are linked with custom-made pointed arch motifs. Arched unified-field panels with blossoming 'paradise trees' appear on the north façade, the mihrab, and the minbar canopy. The spandrels of the gallery arcades and the dome pendentives are decorated with discs that mimic porphry roundels. In an attempt to unify the wide variety of designs, a single type of border tile and a 45 degree vertical 'bevel' moulding were used throughout the building.[236]

The gilded paintings preserved on the minbar hood and the wooden ceilings of the muezzin's tribunes that flank the north portal hint at the extravagance of the original painted decorations, now lost. The domical superstructure was repainted during the nineteenth century in a Europeanizing manner that brutally clashed with the tiles; the paintings have recently been removed and replaced with whitewashed plain surfaces. The stone-carved and tilework inscriptions in monumental *thuluth* are largely intact. The calligraphic tiles alternate blue-on-white and white-on-blue inscriptions, a unique combination repeated in the painted calligraphy of upper galleries in the Selimiye.

Overshadowed by ornamental patterns, the inscriptions have largely been ignored by scholars. Their cumulative message emphasizes the divine creator's control over the fate of humankind, both in this world and the next. By begging the merciful God to reward obedient worshippers who follow the path of orthodoxy, the inscriptions underscore the memorial character of the mosque built for the salvation of the pious Rüstem's soul. Quotations from the Koran are accompanied by hadith and unusual Arabic supplicatory prayers specifically composed for the mosque. It is tempting to speculate that the epigraphic programme was conceived by the pasha's venerable mentor and 'second father', the Nakshbandi shaykh Baba Çelebi, who signed as a witness the waqfiyyas of Rüstem and Mihrümah. This madrasa-educated 'cream of philosophers', 'one of the best imams of the age', was renowned for his knowledge in every science. As an accomplished calligrapher, he had copied Ebussuud's famous commentary on the Koran for Sultan Süleyman. One even wonders whether he designed the inscriptions of his disciple's mosque himself.[237]

The Koranic quotations on the porticoed north façade set the tone for those inside the prayer hall by stressing the importance of worshipping the divine creator. The heavily damaged façade preserves two rectangular white ground tilework window lunettes at both ends, but their placement has been reversed during incompetent repairs. The left lunette (which should have been on the right) cites the beginning of a verse, the rest of which is inscribed on the other lunette. It encourages the congregation to obey the basic requirements of orthodox worship in order to be among the 'rightly guided' (9:18). Above the central portal is a rectangular marble panel carved with a verse glorifying God as the artistic creator of the universe: 'He is Allah, the Creator, the Shaper out of naught, the Fashioner. His are the most beautiful names. All that is in the heavens and the earth glorifieth Him, and He is the Mighty, the Wise (59:24).'

The theme of the divine creator's glory is echoed on the painted central roundel of the dome (illus. 310). It is inscribed with a popular verse from the Fatir sura that announces the forgiving nature of God, whose power firmly holds the heavens and the earth in place (35:41). The white-on-blue tilework roundels marking the eight pendentives list the revered names. The rectangular blue-on-white calligraphic tile panels on the qibla wall resonate with those of the parallel north façade that stress orthodox worship. Placed over the muqarnas hood of the white marble mihrab and above the pair of windows that flank it, they are legible from the main entrance (illus. 308). The mihrab panel cites the common fragmentary verse containing the word 'mihrab' (3:37). The window lunettes quote two verses (72:18–19) announcing the indivisible oneness of God and the Prophet's subordinate role as His messenger. They urge the mosque's congregation to worship only Allah.

The remaining inscriptions are rectangular white-on-blue lunette tiles surmounting the windows and doors of the upper galleries. They proceed counter-clockwise, starting at the west side of the anti-qibla wall and ending at its east side. In the west gallery, the first lunette quotes a hadith reported by the caliph ʿUmar, which declares that places of worship are only for Allah. The second and third lunettes are inscribed with an invocation: 'We submit to Allah as our Lord and to Islam as our religion and to Muhammad (May God commend and salute him!) as His Prophet and Messenger.' The fourth and fifth lunettes feature another invocation: 'O God! Remove us from the Fire and make us enter Paradise together with the righteous ones by showing your mercy. O, the most merciful of all!' The sixth lunette pleads for divine support in both worlds: 'O God! Give us forgiveness and health in the world and the Hereafter.' The seventh lunette quotes a related fragmentary verse: 'Thou art my Protecting Friend in the world and the Hereafter. Make me to die submissive (unto Thee), and join me to the righteous (12:101).'

The east gallery is similarly inscribed with supplications imploring divine blessing in both worlds. The first lunette on the qibla wall and the second one on the east wall are inscribed with an invocation that is interrupted because the third and fourth lunettes following them are missing: 'O God! I turn my face unto you, and I submit myself to you, and I entrust you with my affairs, and I rely upon you willingly; there is no salvation and no refuge....' The fifth lunette quotes another fragmentary prayer: '... and Paradise, and I seek protection in you and [protection] from the anger of your Fire.' The sixth lunette cites the end of a verse from the Baqara sura, which once again asks God's favour in both worlds: 'Our Lord! Give unto us in the world that which is good and in the Hereafter that which is good, and guard us from the doom of Fire (2:201).' The seventh lunette is inscribed with verses exalting God's majesty and greeting His messenger: 'Glorified be thy Lord, the Lord of Majesty, from that which they attribute (unto Him). And peace be unto those sent (to warn) (37:180–81).'

As a group, these supplications are made on behalf of both the congregation and the patron's soul. The enchanting garden-like ambience of the microcosmic mosque implies that the devout pasha is destined to reside in paradise. Contemporary descriptions liken it to the gardens of paradise and its radiant superstructure to the dome of heaven. Attributing its construction to Mihrümah, the historian Ramazanzade Mehmed (*c.* 1562–65) praises it as follows:

> Her Highness the Sultana's pious deed on behalf of the late Rüstem Pasha's soul (couplet): 'She built such a luminous Friday mosque, / That those who saw it would think it was [made of] light.' In Istanbul, near Tahtakale, Her Highness the afore-mentioned Sultana built a Friday mosque and noble sanctuary resembling paradise. Ever since the azure dome of the sky has been sparkling with the rays of the moon and the sun [an allusion to Mihrümah's name], no such ornamented and pleasant-looking building has ever been erected, designed, or founded on the surface of the earth and under the heavens. The arch of its unrivalled mihrab is a vault of the universe and the arcades of its agreeable galleries are a rarity of the age (couplet): 'Its gate is the qibla of the sun, / Its mihrab is a canonically lawful prostration place.' Its interior and exterior are completely clad in tiles (*kāşī*), and its spherical dome, composed of lofty strata and elevated tiers like the fourth heaven, has been designed in the same form as the soaring roof of the sky.[238]

Hasanbeyzade also identifies the princess as the patroness of the mosque: 'For her husband Rüstem Pasha's soul she built in Tahtakale an artistic and elegant Friday mosque.'[239]

The pasha's waqfiyya of 1570 confirms Mihrümah's active contribution to the mosque recalling the pavilions of paradise:

> Her Highness, the aforementioned Sultana, in accordance with her magnanimous fame, brought forth various types of kindness and favour, and with his [Rüstem's] own pure money and property ordered in the metropolis of Constantinople, near Tahtakale, the construction of an ornate and elegant upper-storey (*fevḳānī*) Friday mosque, with a purified floor and a heart-attracting, lofty painted vault which in elegance is a Chinese picture gallery and in beauty the envy of the sublime garden of paradise, as if it were a sign of the pavilions of paradise, in all respects unequalled and hitherto unseen, a rarity of the age, and encompassing all kinds of artistry. And near it ... she ordered the construction of a well-built ablution fountain (*şādırvān*), whose spouts flow with the water of life and whose vault is like the rainbow, as well as shops whose revenues yield a surplus after covering the expenses of that Friday mosque. She endowed all of these for the expansive soul of her illustrious husband, the aforementioned Rüstem Pasha, may God bless his soul.[240]

Evliya Çelebi identifies Rüstem Pasha's mosque, frequented by a crowded congregation, as a work of Sinan and recognizes the similarity of its smaller octagonal baldachin to that of the Selimiye. He says this 'brilliantly illuminated upper-storey mosque, covered from head to foot with China ceramics (*kāşī-yi çīn*), defies description in words and has a basement filled with warehouses and shops.'[241] He often compares unusually ornate mosques he encounters during his travels to that of Rüstem Pasha, which he singles out as a paragon of decorative flamboyance.

The consecutively built mosques of Rüstem Pasha in Tahtakale and of Mihrümah Sultan in Edirnekapı share a familial aura stamped by the vision of the widow princess. Unlike later princess-vizier couples who chose to create jointly endowed mosque complexes in the capital, Süleyman's only daughter and son-in-law kept their identities separate. The two unique mosques Mihrümah commissioned from Sinan individualized the public images of husband and wife, permanently inscribing their memory on the cityscape of the capital. Rüstem Pasha's smaller mosque along the Golden Horn decorously expressed his subordinate status with respect to his wife, whose royal mosque crowns the last hill of the city. The aspiration of these complementary mosques to aesthetic uniqueness and novelty is demonstrated by their waqfiyyas, registered during the same year.

With its ambitious royal references, Mihrümah's widowhood mosque in Edirnekapı expressed her confident self-image as an incomparably wealthy and influential princess. The memorial she commissioned for her late husband defined the upper limit of decorum for a grand vizier. Through the combined efforts of the building supervisor Mehmed Beg and Sinan, the illustrious princess succeeded in creating the ultimate grand vizierial mosque on behalf of her late husband: unmatched with its octagonal domed baldachin, its extravagantly tiled interior, and its singular inscription programme.

III. İSMİHAN SULTAN AND THE GRAND VIZIER SOKOLLU MEHMED PASHA

1. THE COUPLE İSMİHAN AND SOKOLLU

Sited next to their palace overlooking the port of Kadırgalimanı (Kadırga) near the Hippodrome, İsmihan Sultan and Sokollu Mehmed Pasha jointly commissioned one of Sinan's most distinguished mosque complexes. It was planned concurrently with a smaller funerary madrasa complex in the holy necropolis of Eyüp, built to enshrine the couple's infants, who perished in rapid succession (illus. 318–21). These mutually endowed projects were complemented by three monuments (in Lüleburgaz, Payas, and Azapkapı) designed by Sinan for Sokollu as personal memorials, which are discussed separately under his individual patronage (illus. 16, 316, 317).

İsmihan was the first of three daughters born to prince Selim's Venetian chief consort Nurbanu in 1544. In 1562 the prince's rank as heir apparent was bolstered by their triple wedding.[242] İsmihan, then about eighteen, was given to the second vizier Sokollu Mehmed Pasha, a Bosnian Serb who was about forty years older than she, as a reward for his contribution to the prince's victory at the battle of Konya. Sokollu had been brought up in Sultan Süleyman's palace after being levied from the village of Sokolovići in Višegrad (see Chapter 1). The Venetian diplomat Marino Cavalli (1567) reports that he owed his swift promotion to having rescued Haseki Hürrem Sultan from drowning one day when her boat capsized, thanks to his strong physique. The grateful queen thence caused his rapid rise through the ranks of chief gatekeeper (1541), grand admiral (1546), and governor-general of Rumelia (1549), to third vizier in 1554.[243]

As a vizier, Sokollu was closely involved with the ageing sultan's measures to control the rivalry between the two remaining contenders to the throne.[244] Sent to Konya with an army to support Süleyman's candidate in 1559, he was the architect of prince Selim's success. Spending that winter in Aleppo, he returned to Istanbul in the spring of 1560 and with Rüstem Pasha's death in 1561 became second vizier. Soon after his marriage, he succeeded the late Semiz Ali Pasha as grand vizier in 1565 and accompanied Süleyman to the campaign of Szigetvár, where the sultan passed away. His skill in concealing the monarch's death to ensure the smooth accession of his father-in-law Selim became proverbial; he also revealed political acumen in gaining the submission of unruly *kul*s during the the new ruler's enthronement. Sokollu would serve as grand vizier for fourteen years under three successive rulers until he was stabbed to death in 1579 by a vindictive Bosnian dervish of the persecuted Hamzawi order. He was officially declared a martyr and ceremonially buried next to his offspring at the domed mausoleum built by Sinan in Eyüp (illus. 318–19).[245] His royal widow died during childbirth in 1585, a year after her second marriage to the handsome governor-general of Buda, whose repudiated wife (forcefully divorced by imperial decree) is said to have moved the stones and mountains of the city to tears with her wailing. İsmihan lies buried at the imperial mausoleum of her father at Hagia Sophia, in the august company of her mother and siblings.[246]

Dynastic histories written by Sokollu's protégés contributed to the glorification of Süleyman's 'golden age' and idealized the pasha's grand vizierate under three sultans as the continuation of classical ideals.[247] He reached the apogee of his authority as the true master of the empire and the maintainer of its grandeur during his father-in-law's sultanate, between 1566 and 1574. It was in those years that he and his royal wife commissioned from Sinan their major architectural memorials. The accession of Murad III marked the decline of Sokollu's authority. The new sultan's envious inner circle viciously opposed the grand vizier's policies, and their hostility culminated with the purge of his protégés just before his assassination. Sokollu attracted much criticism for bolstering a nepotistic regime through a network of protégés dominated by his Bosnian relatives and dependents. Mustafa Āli observes that the pasha, nicknamed 'the Tall' (*ṭavīl*), was the most privileged and autonomous of all Ottoman grand viziers. He became the 'virtual emperor' during Selim II's reign, when 'he gave and took as he wished and was independent in his office after his heart's desire.'[248] Relatives whom he convinced to convert to Islam were appointed to provincial governorships, while those who remained Orthodox Christian held influential ecclesiastical posts.[249]

316, 317 Portraits of Sokollu Mehmed Pasha, 1570s, oil on paper.

İsmihan Sultan's involvement in the much-maligned harem politics of the period helped secure Sokollu's position during the reigns of her father and brother.[250] European sources abound in eye-witness accounts of the grand vizier and his relationship with his much younger wife. According to dynastic tradition, he had to leave the mother of his two sons upon marrying the princess.[251] Nevertheless, his cherished sons, Kurd Kasım Beg (d. 1571) and Hasan Beg (d. 1604–5), were allowed to stay with him and rose to high offices as provincial governors.[252] Marino Cavalli (1567) reports that the 'intelligent and prudent' grand vizier, who matched his royal wife in religious 'bigotry', enjoyed unparalleled authority as the true 'emperor' of the Ottoman dominions.[253] Andrea Badoaro (1573) notes that the pasha possessed 'great majesty' and lived in 'grand pomp', but was generally disliked by the populace because he held his own interests above those of the people.[254]

Marcantonio Barbaro (1573), who gave his signed self-portrait to Sokollu as a token of friendship (illus. 91), describes the grand vizier in his mid-sixties as having a well-built body, healthy complexion, grave presence, and optimal memory. He was patient, indefatigable, gracious, pious, sober, peace-loving, non-vindictive, unrapacious, and extremely rich thanks to the infinite gifts he received. Despite his supreme authority, however, he was by nature 'extremely cautious and timid': to avoid the calumny of envious rivals, he notified the sultan of all his proceedings in writing.[255] Barbaro characterizes Sokollu's wife as 'young and pretty enough'. Every year she gave birth to a son, but each of them passed away shortly thereafter.[256] Antonio Tiepolo (1576) says the couple only had three surviving infants, two daughters and a son, their many other sons having died from 'falling sickness'. He surmised that the robust pasha would have had a longer life ahead of him, were it not for the 'appetite' of his wife 'with whom he cannot afford to fall short of the proper duties of marriage, not only because she is a sultana, but also a young woman thirty years old!'[257] A Ragusan ambassador in Rome informed the pope that the only person Sokollu seemed to be afraid of was his royal wife, who exercised complete control over him and occasionally insulted him as 'Vlach' (Valachian) which, in this instance, meant 'bumpkin.'[258]

Gerlach (1573–77) concludes that this was the disadvantage of marrying a princess: 'Men who are willing to take sultanas as brides essentially become slaves of their wives, who reserve the right to remind them, "You were once my father's slave", and they must obey whatever their wives demand.'[259] According to his informant (Sokollu's German clockmaker, Oswald), the pasha's royal wife 'was small and ugly in countenance, but cheerful and entertaining in disposition.'[260] The grand vizier humbly obeyed her wishes, only visiting her palace quarters when she chose to summon him by a eunuch.[261] She carried a dagger like a cavalry soldier, and had a hundred select concubines from her household of 300 women dressed up like male pages in silk costumes and bejewelled gold belts fitted with daggers.[262] The pasha's household was staffed with 200 male pages and a hundred household servants.[263] Gerlach reports that the sultana possessed her own great treasure, overflowing with jewels presented as gifts to her husband, who was 'richer than any German prince'.[264] Sokollu used his enormous income from gifts to build mosques and caravansarays for the salvation of his soul.[265] His 900 slaves, kept in a castle-like edifice of his palace in Kadırga, were employed in these construction projects, along with Greek stonemasons who received a daily wage of seven to fifteen aspers.[266] Peçevi confirms that Sokollu owned about a thousand galley slaves used in construction work.[267]

For her pious foundations İsmihan Sultan received donations of crown lands from her father that complemented her daily salary. But her wealth was moderate compared to that of her aunt, princess Mihrümah, Süleyman's only daughter, who had inherited a fortune from her husband.[268] The greater number of princesses during Selim II's reign seems to have contributed to their diminished privileges. Peçevi reports that İsmihan's royal father had granted her 100,000 gold coins (6,000,000 aspers) when she expressed her desire to build a 'new palace' at the Hippodrome, but Sokollu gallantly made that grant a gift to his wife by building the palace with his own money.[269] According to Gerlach's account of 1576, the sultan had donated 70,000 thaler for the construction of the palace, to which the couple moved because they believed their castle-like old palace (*alten Burg*) at Kadırgalimanı to be haunted by evil spirits, causing the deaths of their children one by one.[270] The old palace, not far removed from the new one, seems to have been abandoned just around the time the couple's mosque complex was completed in 1574. Sokollu's waqfiyya, registered that year, refers to both palaces: 'the old house of felicity at Kadırgalimanı' and 'the new house of felicity'.[271]

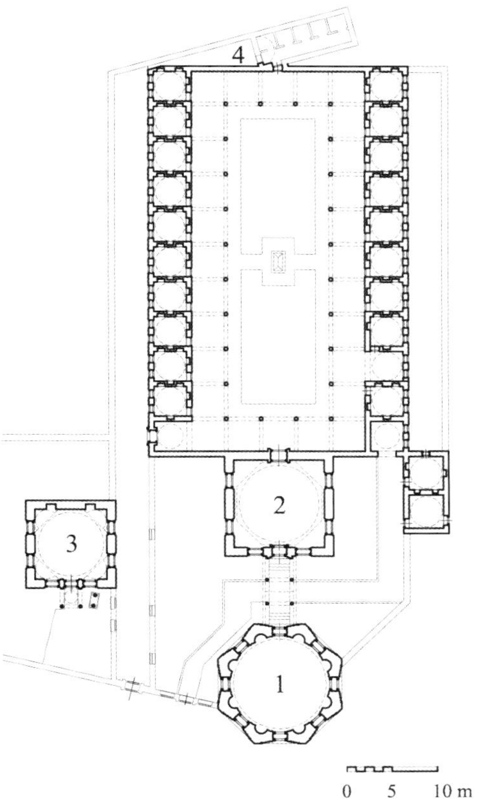

318 Plan of the funerary madrasa complex of İsmihan Sultan and Sokollu Mehmed Pasha, Eyüp: 1. Mausoleum with street fountain. 2. Madrasa. 3. School for Koran recitation. 4. Latrines.

319 İsmihan-Sokollu complex, Eyüp, with the mausoleum of Siyavuş Pasha across the street and the smaller mausoleum of Mirmiran Mehmed Pasha.

Sinan's autobiographies list four palaces built for the grand vizier: one at Kadırgalimanı, one near Hagia Sofia at Ahırkapı (Hippodrome), and two summer palaces, in Üsküdar (İstavroz) and Halkalı.[272] The *Tuḥfe* specifies that 'the palace of Mehmed Pasha at Kadırgalimanı' was a pre-existing structure extensively remodelled by the chief architect.[273] The Frenchman Du Fresne Canaye (1573) was thoroughly unimpressed by the humble edifices of the pasha's quarters, where the grand vizier daily held public and private audiences, although he was told that the princess's private quarters were truly magnificent (illus. 13[1–4]). The pasha's cautious sense of decorum and fear of arousing envy had caused him to construct his own quarters in such a modest fashion.[274]

The new palace did prove luckier for the couple, as their son İbrahim (d. 1622) outlived his parents and inherited their properties along with the administration of their lucrative waqfs. It was he who sold the Kadırga palace to Ahmed I in 1609 to make space for the sultan's mosque complex.[275] İbrahim had been honoured with the royal title of 'khan', matching his mother's name ('İsmihan' means 'with the name of Khan'). During the eighteenth century his descendants, who owed their wealth and prestige to the endowments they administered, were considered to be among the few candidates eligible to succeed the Ottoman sultanate should the reigning sultan's lineage cease.[276] The pious endowments set up by Sokollu came to be named İbrahim Khanzade (Sons of İbrahim Khan) after the aristocratic family of his son.[277]

The waqfiyyas of İsmihan Sultan (January 1573) and Sokollu Mehmed Pasha (April 1574) enumerate their endowed monuments.[278] That of the princess lists her two Friday mosques, in Kadırgalimanı and the Rumanian village of Mangalya, along with her madrasa in Eyüp (illus. 318–21).[279] Her monuments in the capital were all works of Sinan, unlike the modest provincial mosque in one of the fiefs donated by her father in 1568.[280] Her endowment deed praises the 'golden lineage' of the Ottoman dynasty, which for 299 years since its emergence had developed the world with endowed religious monuments. Following the example of her forebears, 'Her Highness İsmihan Sultan' built and endowed for her last journey to the other world 'pious monuments decorously suited to her title of khan (*ism-i ḫāna lāyıḳ*) and befitting her exalted prestige (*sümüvv-i şāna münāsib*).' Aware of this world's transcience, she had fully devoted herself to 'piety, divine worship, pious foundations, and good deeds'. Her endurance and resignation on the path of God was such that she even accepted His divine decree after six of her 'darling children fell like pearls of pure tears from her moist eyes, one after the other, to the earthen grave, becoming concealed from her sight like the soul and sliding away from her eyes like drops filled with blood.'[281]

According to the stipulations of her waqfiyya, the princess

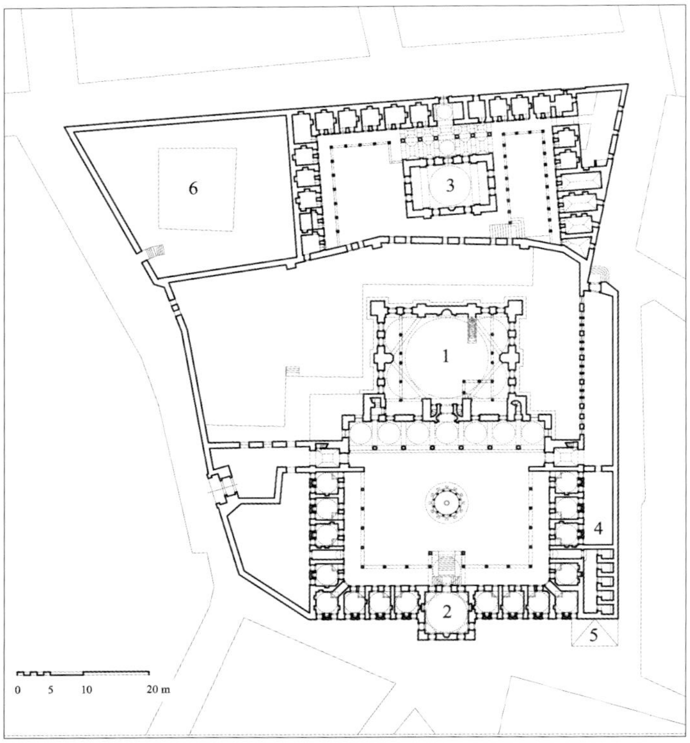

320 Plan of the İsmihan Sultan and Sokollu complex, Kadırgalimanı: 1. Mosque. 2. Madrasa. 3. Convent. 4. Latrines. 5. Reservoir with street fountains. 6. Pre-existing masjid of Helvacıbaşı İskender.

321 Axonometric projection of the complex at Kadırgalimanı.

was to administer her own waqf jointly with her household steward, Hüsrev Kethüda b. Abdurrahman. After her death, the endowment would be administered by her children and grandchildren over the generations, replaced by the freed slaves of her husband should their bloodline cease.[282] The princess's endowed properties included villages and agricultural lands in Rumelia donated by her father in 1568, and real estate including a residence with three ground-storey shops near the Kadırga mosque for its two imams. The surplus income of her waqf was to be used in repairing dilapidated mosques, masjids, and madrasas; in buying clothes for poor children; and in renovating paved roads and bridges. Every year twenty women (selected from orphan girls, poor widows, and the needy daughters of her freed female slaves) would each be given a marriage dowry of 4,000 aspers.[283]

The tragic demise of her children provided an impetus for the twenty-nine-year-old princess's architectural patronage. Her

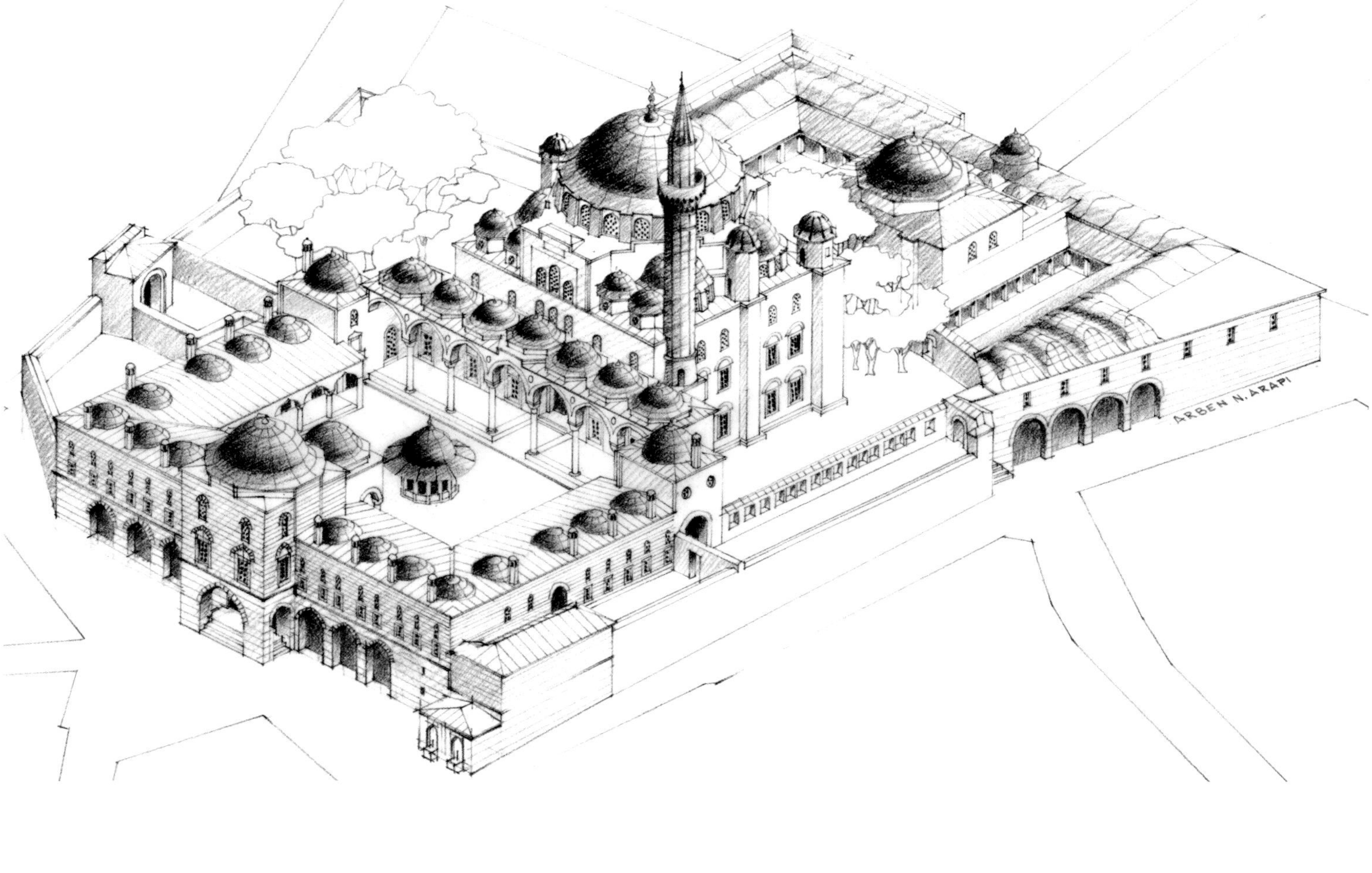

madrasa, adjacent to the mausoleum of her offspring in Eyüp, and her mosque at Kadırga were conceived as complementary structures built simultaneously with the new palace (illus. 318–21). The domed mausoleum where Sokollu eventually intended to be buried with his progeny is endowed separately in his waqfiyya (Map 3). Its Turkish foundation inscription gives 976 (1568–69) as the date of completion.[284] Carrying the same date, the Arabic inscription of the madrasa refers to its foundress as 'Her Highness the Sultan[a], daughter of Selim Khan'.[285] Sinan's small complex also includes a domed school for Koran recitation endowed by Sokollu and dated by its inscription to 987 (1579).[286] The public fountains created by the grand vizier in the vicinity of the complex range in date from 1567–68 to 1570–71.[287]

Sokollu's waqfiyya explains that he built the madrasa in Eyüp and the mosque in Kadırgalimanı – completed in 979 (1571–72) according to its foundation inscription – as gifts for his wife, even though İsmihan's waqfiyya claims these two monuments as her own (illus. 322).[288] The princess's authorial voice and agency, then, were materialized through the mediation of her husband. This was also the case with the new palace, created around that time at her initiative but as yet another gift from Sokollu. The grand vizier's waqfiyya indicates that he added his own madrasa and dervish convent next to the mosque at Kadırgalimanı (illus. 320, 321):

> He constructed a lofty madrasa and house of knowledge at the courtyard of the joy-giving Friday mosque and soul-expanding place of worship which he built with a thousand artful wonders and heart-alluring decorations at Kadırgalimanı near the Hippodrome as a gift (*ihdā'*) for his illustrious wife, Her Highness the Sultana, who is the sun of the summit of the sultanate… And for the group of dervishes, who divest themselves from the contamination of the gilded wheel of fortune by retiring like a spider to the corner of contentment and who substitute litanies in praise of God for worldly quarrels, he built behind that light-filled Friday mosque a convent with thirty defectless rooms embodying beautiful characteristics.[289]

The text goes on to narrate how Sokollu brought water from a source discovered in the suburbs to the mosque complex and its neighbourhood. Some of that water was conducted 'to the heart-stealing ablution fountain (built between the above-mentioned elevated royal (*sulṭānī*) mosque and the madrasa of lofty construction.' The ablution fountain in turn was connected to 'the famous fountainhouse (*çeşmesār*) built next to the courtyard gate': the extant reservoir with public fountains at the northwest corner of the courtyard façade facing the street below (illus. 323). The rest of the water flowed into his 'house of felicity' and its surplus was donated to the residences of his confidants and leading household officers.[290]

Additional fountains were created inside two caravansarays endowed by Sokollu across from the 'old house of felicity'. One of them, known as the 'Dormitory of Tasters', seems to have been a former service courtyard of the Kadırga palace.[291] The grand vizier also endowed a 'prison for slaves' surrounded on all sides by streets, probably the palace prison mentioned above by Gerlach. Other endowed structures in that neighbourhood included a bakery, a large house, six shops under the madrasa, four shops under the convent, a block with fifteen newly built rental rooms near the mosque, fourteen shops near the gate of the new palace, and empty plots near the palace and the Kumkapı Gate of the Byzantine sea walls, where rental rooms would be built in the future with the waqf surplus. Sokollu moreover bought and endowed a 'grand residence' for the shaykh of the dervish convent.[292] The convent behind the qibla wall of the mosque had not been finished when its designated Halveti shaykh, Mustafa Muslihüddin Nureddinzade Efendi, passed away in 1574 (February–March) (illus. 324–25).[293]

Sinan probably designed the complex some time before 1568, before he left for Edirne to build the Selimiye. Since the foundations of the sultan's mosque were not laid until 1569, the chief architect must have been relatively free while its building materials were being collected. Hence, he could have supervised the early stages of construction at the Kadırga mosque, continuing to check its progress during short visits to the capital. Marcantonio Barbaro assumed that the complex was being built for the grand vizier himself. On 20 August 1569, during an audience at Sokollu's palace, he had witnessed the grand admiral of the navy (Müezzinzade Ali Pasha) oversee the grand vizier's neighbouring 'building with a baton in his hand as if he were a foreman or supervisor of the builders'. The grand admiral, a seasoned building supervisor who had overseen construction work at the Kırkçeşme aqueducts in the early 1560s as the agha of janissaries, must have contributed galley slaves under his command to the workforce of the Kadırga complex.[294]

On 2 September 1569 the *bailo* informed the Senate that 'the building of the magnificent pasha is close to being covered'. Sokollu promised him that the Christian prisoners used in constructing it would be liberated 'once that building gets covered and he no longer needs so many workers.'[295] Two weeks later, Barbaro liberated ten of the slaves. In the meantime, thirteen others had converted to Islam to improve their lot. As they were still being kept in the grand admiral's service, they repented of their decision with bitter tears. But the *bailo* could no longer ask that they be set free, for they had 'become Turks'.[296]

On 11 June 1569 he placed an order for 900 Murano oil lamps for 'one of the mosques' Sokollu was building, accompanied by drawings indicating their size and shape, along with a large lantern for the palace.[297] The superstructure of the Kadırga mosque must have been covered around that time. Between 1569 and 1572 Sokollu and his wife sent orders to

Dubrovnik for large quantities of window glass and lamps.[298] A decree addressed to the kadis of Alacahisar and Skopje on 20 December 1570 asks them to transport 5,000 qintars of lead with rented carts to Sofia for the needs of the grand vizier's 'prosperous buildings in the protected city of Istanbul'.[299] Ongoing construction work is recorded in a decree sent on 5 February 1571 to the kadi of Molova on the island of Mitilini: he is ordered to send in all haste as many builders and carpenters as possible, with their tools, to work for a wage at the grand vizier's 'construction in Istanbul', and record their names in a register.[300]

Like the decrees cited above, the Turkish foundation inscription carved over the north portal of the courtyard facing the street identifies the grand vizier as the patron of the mosque which replaced a demolished church (illus. 322):

> The namesake of the Glory of the World [the Prophet Muhammad]; namely, the grand vizier,
> Whose fortune is everlasting and prosperity is eternal,
>
> He demolished the church of the base infidels,
> And built a place of worship that is the foremost in the city.
>
> That house of blasphemy and darkness became an abode of worship.
> In truth this is one of the greatest miracles of the Muslims.
>
> While considering this conquest (*feth̤*), the unseen voice composed the following chronogram:
> 'This Friday mosque of the Faith is a conquest pertaining to Muhammad (*feth̤-i Muḥammedī*),' in nine hundred seventy nine, 979 (1571–72).[301]

322 İsmihan-Sokollu complex, Kadırgalimanı, foundation inscription on the north courtyard portal.

323 İsmihan-Sokollu complex, elevation of the north façade.

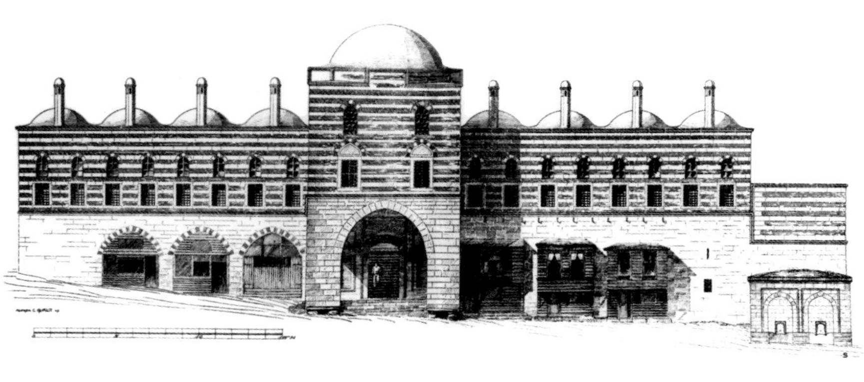

Such punning on the names of the Prophet and Mehmed Pasha (written identically) is also encountered in the foundation inscriptions of other monuments sponsored by the grand vizier.[302] The *double-entendre* of this chronogram implies that the 'conquest [literally, opening] pertaining to Muhammad', namely the Islamization of the mosque site, was Mehmed's personal feat.

The dismantled church has not yet been identified, although scholars once thought it might have been Hagia Anastasia. Spolia embedded in the mosque walls were discovered during repairs in 1930; they included a reversed window slab with a carved image of the Virgin and Christ child, and the fragmentary statuette of an apostle.[303] The demolition of the Christian sanctuary coincided with the sale of waqf estates belonging to churches and monasteries in the Balkans in order to increase the state's taxable lands. Enforced by imperial decrees throughout Rumelia between 1567 and 1571, this policy may have had repercussions in the capital.[304] Sokollu himself had three churches and a synagogue razed in 1567 to make way for his covered market and caravansaray in Belgrade.[305] The theme of conquest emphasized in the foundation inscription of the Kadırga mosque also found expression in the name given to Sokollu's adjoining madrasa and convent: Fethiye (pertaining to conquest).[306] The church of the Orthodox patriarchate in Istanbul, which Murad III later converted to a Friday mosque (1586–88) to commemorate his conquests in Georgia, would bear the same name. The theme of conquest manifested in the Kadırga complex is in keeping with the prevailing ethos of its years of construction, dominated by naval battles against the 'infidel' in the Mediterranean: the Cyprus campaign between 1568 and 1570–71, and the battle of Lepanto in 1571.

The power of Islam is celebrated inside the Kadırga mosque with four pieces of the Kaʿba's black stone, framed by gilt-brass and set into various focal points: above the muqarnas hood of the mihrab, above the door and canopy arch of the minbar, and above the north portal

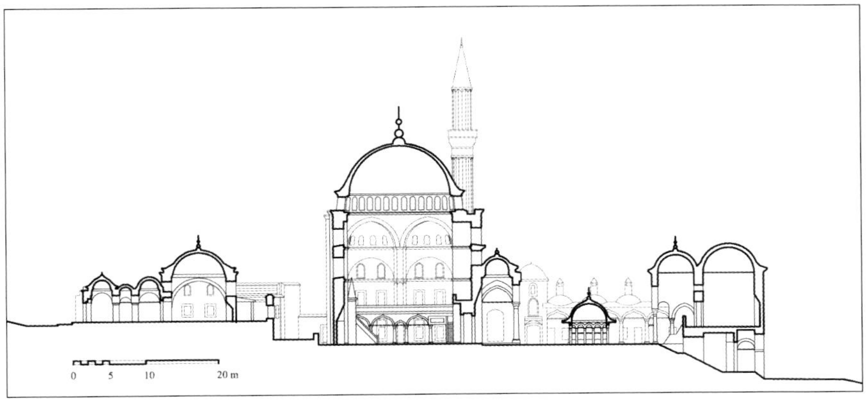

324 İsmihan-Sokollu complex, Kadırgalimanı, cross-section.

325 İsmihan-Sokollu from the south, with axially aligned domes of the convent and mosque.

aligned with the mihrab axis. Ayvansarayi mentions one of these stones as 'an object of pilgrimage'. The venerable relics must have been mementos of the renovation of the Kaʿba under Selim II (1567–74), who claimed to have undertaken the victorious Cyprus campaign to improve the safety of the overseas hajj route. Perhaps the sultan presented the stones as gifts to his daughter and son-in-law, or they were acquired by the agents of Sokollu, who established pious foundations of his own in Mecca.[307]

The foundation inscription of the Kadırga mosque blatantly advertises the grand vizier's patronage while excluding İsmihan's. Not even mentioning his presentation of the mosque to her as a gift, it silences the voice of his wife, who must have contributed to the design and decoration of the mosque. Like Barbaro, Gerlach thought that the mosque was built for the pasha.[308] It still carries his name today. Ayvansarayi explains why it popularly came to be named after Sokollu:

> The above-mentioned is an upper-storey (*fevḳānī*) mosque. It was converted from a church. The wife of the aforesaid [Sokollu Mehmed] Pasha, İsmihan Sultan, the daughter of His Majesty Sultan Selim Khan the Second, built it and brought it to life during the time of his grand vizierate. Because the aforesaid [Mehmed Pasha] added and appended a madrasa in front of it [and built] a *şadırvan* in its courtyard and a dervish lodge, it is generally known as the Friday Mosque of Mehmed Pasha.[309]

The suppression of the young princess's identity as the builder of the mosque, affirmed by her waqfiyya, implies that she was a relatively unassertive patroness of architecture, preferring to keep a lower public profile than her mother, Nurbanu, and such royal women as Hürrem, Mihrümah, and Shahsultan (Süleyman's sister). Sinan's autobiographies list the monuments commissioned by these four women under their own names or titles, but they identify the Kadırga complex as Sokollu's foundation. The mosque complex of Shahsultan and Zal Mahmud Pasha in Eyüp is similarly listed in the chief architect's autobiographies under the pasha's name rather than that of his wife (İsmihan's younger sister). Clearly, then, husbands overshadowed wives as the patrons of jointly endowed complexes.

Kadırgalimanı (Port of Galleys) facing the Sea of Marmara was the ancient Port of Julian, converted in the middle Byzantine period into an arsenal called Kontoskalion. The Ottomans renovated it as their first arsenal prior to the construction in 1513–14 of the new one at Kasımpaşa along the Golden Horn.[310] Pierre Gilles (1547–51) describes the silted port:

> It is now filled up. If it was the port that stands west of the Church of [Sergius and] Bacchus, it is now almost demolished and enclosed by a wall. There is only a small part of it remaining. This is a pool of water where the women wash their linen. The people tell you that they have seen some three-decked galleys that have been sunk there. It is now called Caterga Limena or the Port of the Three-Decked Galleys by the present inhabitants.[311]

According to Reinhold Lubenau (1587–88) Sokollu had filled the remaining basin of 'Caderga Limani' because of the stench that affected his nearby palace.[312] The reclaimed land formed a public square known as Kadırga Meydanı, to which the main

326 İsmihan-Sokollu complex, Kadırgalimanı, from the northeast with the Marmara Sea and Küçük Ayasofya (SS Sergius and Bacchus) in the background.

327 İsmihan-Sokollu complex, the view of the courtyard fountain and mosque when emerging from the north portal staircase.

entrance of the Sokollu palace opened. It is no longer possible to determine the exact relationship between the north façade of the mosque complex and the palace located further north.[313]

The palatial north façade of the complex has an arched central gate bearing the foundation inscription, above the vestibule of which is raised the domed classroom of the madrasa, built with alternating courses of stone and brick (illus. 323). The madrasa rooms are elevated on massive vaulted substructures in stone that incorporate six shops and the reservoir with public fountains mentioned in Sokollu's waqfiyya. The lofty arched portal of this monumental façade is connected to the fountained courtyard above by a steep staircase. The success of the complex lies in its organic integration with the hilly terrain and neighbouring streets. The inward-looking convent, concealed behind blind walls, is built on a higher level than the marble-paved fountain courtyard shared by the mosque and U-shaped madrasa, while the north façade of the complex overlooks a small irregular plaza at the lowest level (illus. 324).

The monumental domes of the madrasa classroom (6.4 metres), the mosque (13 metres), and the ritual hall of the convent (6 metres) are aligned along the central north–south axis (illus. 325). The inclusion of a monumental dervish convent in the complex was a novelty. The few other mosque complexes with substantial madrasa-like convents mentioned in Sinan's autobiographies are those of Sokollu in Payas (*c.* 1567–74) and the queen mother Nurbanu in Üsküdar (1571–86). Unlike these two complexes, the one in Kadırga lacks a hospice-cum-caravansaray for travellers. Conceived as an urban foundation, its madrasa and convent address the communal needs of a residential quarter.

The contrast between the striped masonry outer walls of the madrasa and the ashlar masonry mosque visually accentuates their hierarchy. The most effective picturesque vistas are oblique perspectives glimpsed from two diagonal streets approaching the small plaza in front. One of them winds up from the public square of Kadırga Meydanı to the northwest corner of the madrasa, and the other one descends from a hilltop behind the palace to the bevelled northeast corner of the precinct wall (illus. 326). Two other streets approaching the middle of the plaza converge in front of the north portal. The irregular precinct encircled by streets is surrounded by rubble masonry walls along its south, east, and west sides. Two unassuming gateways on the east and west walls provide access to the lateral portals of the fountain courtyard. The southeast corner of the precinct contains the walled-in masjid of Helvacıbaşı İskender, built in 1546. A window-pierced curtain wall with a small gate separates the higher convent from the rest of the complex. The cemetery garden that extends between it and the mosque is a potent site of memory, packed with the tombstones of shaykhs and waqf administrators descending from İbrahim Khan.[314]

The south portal of the convent, facing a sloping street, is capped by a small onion dome. A windowless rubble masonry outer wall, stepped along the slope, shields from the outer world the ascetic dervishes of the Halveti order. Only the hemispherical dome of the otherwise hidden ritual space of the convent is visible from the street above (illus. 325). The sloping terrain of its courtyard, higher to the east than the west, is divided into two platforms connected by a staircase. The edge of the higher platform is occupied by the free-standing domed ritual hall constructed with alternating courses of ashlar stone and brick. The south façade of the masjid-like domed hall is fronted by a five-bay double portico. The U-shaped convent is built with cheaper rubble and brick. It comprises single and double-storey rooms covered by flat wooden roofs and fronted by porticoes with overhanging eaves. Its thirty residential rooms for dervishes are complemented by windowless cells for periodic retreat, a kitchen, a bath, and ablution spouts.[315]

Mentioned only in the *Tuhfe*, the convent approaches residential vernacular architecture in its informal wooden details and relatively cheaper materials. Its domed hall, the focal point of Halveti rituals, is the earliest surviving example of its type in Sinan's oeuvre. The 'pseudo mihrab' at the centre of the north wall is a niche axially aligned with the mihrab of the mosque, behind that wall. It marks the position of the shaykh, who constituted the symbolic qibla of disciples forming a circle around their master. Some of the whitewashed painted decorations and monumental *thuluth* inscriptions of the hall are visible on old photographs. The four pendentives of its dome were painted with roundels bearing the names of the four caliphs. The shaykh's niche was flanked by roundels inscribed 'Hasan' and 'Husayn', while the 'Allah' and 'Muhammad' roundels were placed above the gate facing the qibla direction: a curious semiotic reversal of the traditional position of mihrab and portal, signifying the primacy of the 'true mihrab' inside the mosque.[316]

The Kadırga mosque and its madrasa are usually compared with the complex of the grand vizier Kara Ahmed Pasha at Topkapı, thought to have been completed in the early 1560s (illus. 370–71).[317] The construction of that complex, however, was delayed when Mihrümah Sultan appropriated its site at Edirnekapı for her own mosque and madrasa. Completed around 1570, these two rival monuments constitute relevant comparanda for the Kadırga complex, with which their final stages of construction overlapped. The striking parallels that exist between the complexes in Topkapı and Kadırga may not have been fortuitous, for it was Sokollu's household steward, Hüsrev Kethüda, who supervised the delayed construction of Kara Ahmed Pasha's complex.[318] Spread on a flat terrain, this complex with its U-shaped madrasa featuring a central classroom and its hexagonal-baldachined mosque grouped around a fountain courtyard prefigures the basic layout of its counterpart at Kadırga.

In adapting the scheme of the Topkapı complex to the steep slope of Kadırga, Sinan sculpted a more compact, three-dimensional configuration and increased the proportional harmony and spatial unity of the hexagonal baldachined mosque. The ascent from the staircase under the madrasa classroom gradually reveals the mosque in dramatic perspective (illus. 327). At the entrance to the small courtyard, the mihrab axis passing through the mosque portal is momentarily impeded by the central ablution fountain. The onion dome of the fountain canopy rests on tiny polychrome pointed arches supported by twelve slender columns with muqarnas capitals. The variegated arcades of the madrasa and the north façade of the mosque create dynamic rhythms (illus. 328).

With its marble pavements, the intimate courtyard comes closer to sultanic prototypes than do the planted garden courts of Kara Ahmed Pasha's and Mihrümah's comparable complexes. In all three monuments the outer walls of the madrasas are of alternating cut stone and brick, whereas their inner walls are revetted in ashlar masonry to match the accompanying mosques. The north portico of the Kadırga mosque is raised on six tall white marble columns with muqarnas capitals. Decorated with porphyry roundels, it supports seven domes and is linked to the lower foliate ogee arcade of the madrasa by lateral gatehouses surmounted by domed chambers for the mosque's caretakers. This solution resolves the problematic juncture of arches with different profiles and proportions (illus. 326).

With its moderate size and single-galleried minaret, the Kadırga mosque resembles grand vizierial foundations, albeit with regal touches reflecting İsmihan's status as a princess. Unlike the five-domed porticoes of the Rüstem Pasha and Kara

328 İsmihan Sultan mosque, Kadırgalimanı, north façade and ablution fountain.

Ahmed Pasha mosques, İsmihan's mosque boasts a seven-domed portico like that of her aunt Mihrümah in Edirnekapı. Yet the young princess's mosque is crowned by a smaller dome (13 metres wide and 22.8 metres high) in comparison to its counterpart in Edirnekapı. The economy observed in its scale may have been a corollary of its equivocal status as a royal mosque inserted in a jointly endowed grand vizierial complex, which was popularly associated with the overly circumspect and cautious Sokollu.[319] The complexes that this grand vizier commissioned in his own name have mosques with even smaller domes (Lüleburgaz 12.5 metres, Azapkapı 11.8 metres, Payas 8 metres) that fall short of the upper limit of decorum observed in the 15.2-metre dome of Rüstem Pasha's Tahtakale mosque.

The restraint that informed the scale of the Kadırga mosque was amply compensated for by its impeccable design and the sheer opulence of its decorative programme. Just as İsmihan's waqfiyya praises its decorousness, befitting her 'title of khan', that of Sokollu identifies her mosque as a 'royal' (*sulṭānī*) edifice. As the centrepiece of a complex mutually endowed by the couple, the Kadırga mosque conflates royal and grand vizierial status. Its moderate size is effectively concealed by the grandeur of its porticoed north façade, fronted by an unprecedented marble-paved forecourt. The mosques built in the capital during the 1560s for Rüstem Pasha, Kara Ahmed Pasha, and Mihrümah Sultan all have simpler arched portals without the muqarnas hood that distinguishes the mosque at Kadırga, whose façade recalls that of the Süleymaniye (illus. 178, 326).

In the classical manner, the interior configuration of the mosque is reflected by its clearly articulated exterior. Like Mihrümah's mosque in Edirnekapı, it is crowned by a dome that eliminates flying buttresses. The two lateral piers that internally support the hexagonal base of the dome are externally expressed as weight turrets, capped by mini-domes like those of Kara Ahmed Pasha's mosque. Two additional domed buttresses mark the corners of the qibla wall. They are counterbalanced by pairs of miniature twin cupolas with hexagonal drums along the north façade, which cover the deep internal galleries flanking the buttresses of the central portal.

The prayer hall replaces the six free-standing marble columns that support the hexagonal baldachin of Kara Ahmed Pasha's mosque with differently shaped piers, skilfully integrated into the walls or pulled close to them. The substitution of unusually high piers for columns permits the creation of a loftier dome, enveloping a superbly unified central space (illus. 329–31). The bases of the polygonal piers attached to the lateral walls are hidden behind elegant arcades that support the upper galleries. The muqarnas-corbelled squinches under the four exedral half-domes define a dematerialized and scintillating transitional zone around the central dome, a zone framed by two string courses that encircle the prayer hall. The unifying force of the central hexagon is accentuated by strong arches extending from pier to pier and delineating six pendentives with İznik tiles around the main dome. The conflict between the circular dome and the rectangular ground plan, left unresolved in Sinan's previous mosques with hexagonal baldachins, is finally solved (illus. 4).

Compared to the 204 windows that brighten the interior of Mihrümah's mosque in Edirnekapı, the 100 windows of the Kadırga mosque allow controlled illumination to permeate the prayer hall from all sides.[320] Unlike the Edirnekapı mosque, which lacks İznik tiles and muqarnas detailing, the Kadırga mosque balances structure with decoration. The seductive power of its internal space is achieved by its lavish yet disciplined use of İznik tiles, which enhance the perception of architectural forms by accentuating window lunettes, pendentives, and the central qibla arch. İsmihan's mosque thus presents a subtle critique of Rüstem Pasha's mosque, whose tile revetments overwhelm and compete with their architectural support.

The balanced sense of proportion that permeates the structure is also manifested in its ornamental skin, a masterpiece of harmoniously coordinated designs and calligraphy in multiple media. In terms of decorative richness and harmony, the mosque is generally recognized as Sinan's most successful work. The central arch of the qibla wall is praised by Goodwin as 'the finest single wall of tile ever created by İznik'. It is reminiscent of the qibla wall in the Süleymaniye, with its similar pair of calligraphic roundels (illus. 179, 183, 330). But now the decorative vocabulary and technical perfection of tiling has reached an apogee, with a broader colour spectrum that includes green. The qibla wall of the Kadırga mosque more effectively coordinates writing and decorative patterns on tilework by adjusting their scale to the subjectivity of vision: the naturalistic flowers and giant tulips that decorate its upper zones are boldly magnified to assure their visibility from the ground level (illus. 332). The İznik tiles spread beyond the qibla wall and the external north façade to which they are confined in the Süleymaniye. They contribute to the centralized spatial effect of the prayer hall by articulating additional architectonic units: two tiers of rectangular window lunettes and roundels along the galleried side walls, and the dome pendentives. The restored stained glass windows surround the interior space in similar fashion.[321]

The mosque was once painted as lavishly as it was tiled. Its painted decorations have been renovated more sensitively than usual, but the remains of original painting reveal what has been lost. Some are preserved above the vestibule of the north gate, on the brackets of the projecting private balcony above that gate (reserved for Sokollu and his retinue), and under the ceilings of the muezzin's tribune and the lateral galleries (illus. 333–34). Dominated by red, these gilded paintings with black contours combine blue and white, like the tiles. They would have harmonized with the twenty-nine carpets of varying sizes İsmihan Sultan endowed for her mosque, some with mihrab designs.[322]

The mosque has a meticulously coordinated inscription programme. Upon climbing the staircase of the north portal celebrating the theme of conquest, one first encounters the profession of faith carved in a rectangular frame at the centre of the mosque façade, on the stone base of the main dome. The central arch of the portico beneath it has another rectangular frame, inscribed with a Koranic ultimatum about the necessity of congregational worship at fixed hours (4:103). The same theme is echoed across the courtyard by a hadith carved above the domed porch of the madrasa classroom, dedicated to the study of the Prophet's traditions and theology: 'Worship is the pillar of religion; whoever abandons it has left the Faith'. Another hadith, inscribed on the classroom portal, declares the importance of knowledge: 'Striving for knowledge is a sacred duty of all Muslim men and women.' The reference to women is particularly meaningful in a complex whose centrepiece was endowed by a princess. It endorses the access of women to the pursuit of religious knowledge despite their exclusion from the institutional setting of the madrasa.

The inscriptions concentrated on the mosque façade are Koranic. A gilded epigraph carved under the muqarnas hood of the portal greets the congregation (36:58): 'God the Most High has said in His Holy Book: The word from a Merciful Lord (for them) is: Peace!' The lunette tiles quote the Fatiha sura, which beseeches the merciful God, the 'Owner of the Day of Judgment', to guide believers in the 'right path' of the favoured ones, not in the path of those who go astray (1:1–7). This plea is fulfilled by the spiritual journey inside the mosque, replete with inscriptions that turn its fabric into a visual medium for contemplation and a visionary experience of the divine.

Upon entering the sanctuary, one stands directly under its domed baldachin before approaching the mihrab, glittering with tiles, as the final destination of the longitudinal axis that starts at the street portal.[323] The viewer's gaze is first arrested by the superstructure, charged with cosmic allusions by the central inscription roundel of the dome (illus. 329–30). It quotes a popular verse from the Fatir sura that refers to the undeviating heavens and earth, held firmly in place by the omnipotence of the forgiving God (35:41). The preamble of İsmihan's waqfiyya, which describes the creation of the universe in the form of an exquisitely decorated domed mosque, implicitly turns her mosque into a microcosm of the universe, presented to humankind as a 'sign' of the divine creator's greatness.[324]

The four exedral half-domes diagonally surrounding the central dome cite two verses from the Jumʿa sura, starting at the right side of the qibla and proceeding counter-clockwise (62:9-10). They recommend the canonical congregational prayers along with the 'remembrance of Allah' (*dhikr*). These verses resonate with the six pendentive roundels which invoke remembrances of God by a selection of divine epithets. The ninety-nine beautiful names of God are inscribed on sixteen rectangular İznik tile panels over the upper gallery windows and on an inscription band above the central arch of the anti-qibla wall.

The presence of a Halveti convent behind the qibla wall charges these inscriptions with special significance as a visual

329 İsmihan Sultan mosque, Kadırgalimanı, interior view of the domical superstructure.

330 İsmihan Sultan mosque, Kadırgalimanı, interior toward the qibla wall.

331 İsmihan Sultan mosque, Kadırgalimanı, interior toward the east, with wooden preacher's lectern fronting the central arch.

333 Paintings on the vestibule ceiling and consoles above the north gate, with black stone embedded on the lintel.

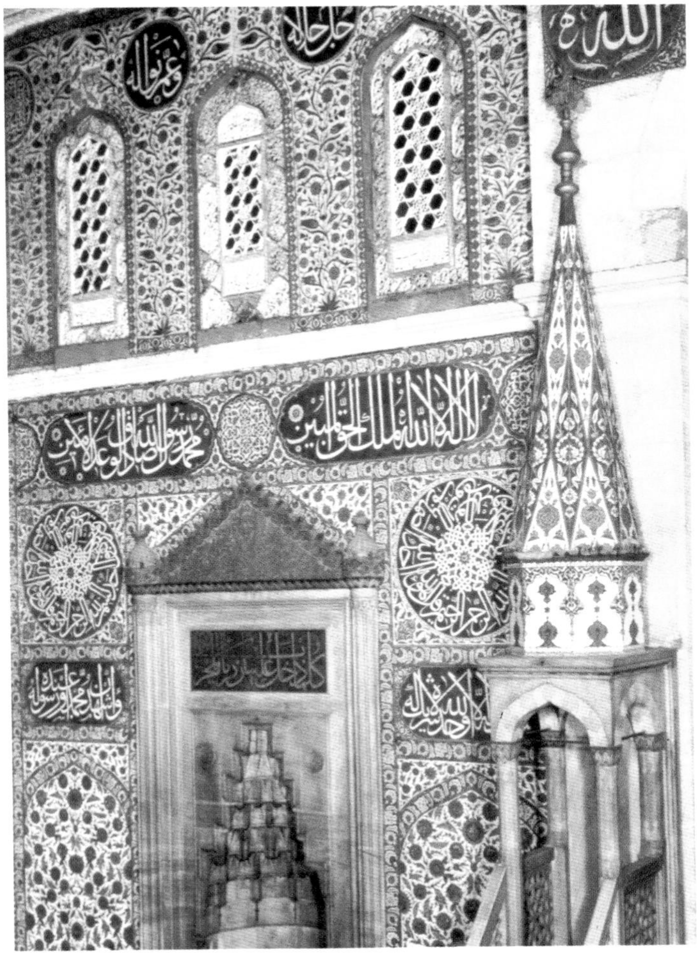

332 İznik tiles on the minbar cap and the qibla wall with black stones inset above the mihrab's muqarnas hood and the minbar canopy.

334 Painted decoration under lateral gallery ceiling.

counterpart to the oral recitations of the sufis. The rituals daily practised inside the domed convent hall involved the loud recitation by a chanter (*dhākir*) of litanies and prayers (*vird*), preceded by the *dhikr* of God's beautiful names, and accompanied by praises of the Prophet and his Companions.[325] The ultimate goal of oral recitation for the Halvetis was to achieve unity with God: a visionary experience of the divine essence through the consubstantiation of its light in the devotee's heart. The implicit dialogue between the mosque and convent is underscored by a hadith inscribed above the portal of the ritual hall. It declares those who perform the *dhikr* as having the highest station in God's eyes: 'The messenger of God, peace be upon him, said: The highest rank among the people according to God are the reciters of litanies' (*dhākirūn*).[326] Sokollu's waqfiyya requires the convent shaykh to deliver sermons to the congregation of the mosque after the Friday prayers from the inlaid woodwork lectern endowed by him (now placed in front of the east gallery arcade).[327] Upon performing the daily prayers inside the mosque, the thirty dervishes of the convent were required to offer invocations there on behalf of the souls of the Prophet, Sokollu, and the reigning sultan.[328]

The two engaged rectangular piers of the qibla wall are surmounted by square İznik tile panels inscribed 'Allah' and 'Muhammad, the Prophet of Allah'. The anti-qibla piers and the side walls are decorated with square and round tile panels invoking the names of the four caliphs, Hasan, and Husayn.[329] The central arches of the lateral gallery arcades feature two unusual rectangular calligraphic panels in Turkish. Read sequentially from right to left, they praise the four caliphs: 'They are Ebu Bekir, ʿÖmer, ʿOs̱mān, ʿAli', 'They who are the most virtuous of all the Companions'.[330] Recalling sufi litanies, the paired panels assert the preeminence of the four Sunni caliphs over Hasan and Husayn. These panels affirm the adamant adherence of the Halveti order to Sunni orthodoxy and the struggle of its devotees against 'heretics' and 'heterodoxy'. The names of Hasan and Husayn, relegated to a subordinate position inside the mosque, occupy a prominent place above the 'pseudo-mihrab' of the convent described above.[331]

The visually enticing qibla wall of the mosque displays a densely packed collection of inscriptions on marble, tiles, and stained glass. It presents a spectacular vision of the oneness of God and the prophethood of Muhammad. Above the muqarnas hood of the marble mihrab, the standard verse using the word 'mihrab' is carved inside a rectangular frame (3:37). A flanking pair of tilework cartouches spell out the monotheistic formula. The two roundels above them cite the Ikhlas sura, the most explicit disavowal of the Christian tenet of the Holy Trinity, declaring the oneness of the merciful God, who neither begets nor was begotten (112:1–4). Another pair of cartouches above these roundels reads: 'There is no god but God, the Just Sovereign, the Manifest,' and 'Muhammad is the Prophet of God, the Faithful Keeper of Promises, the Trustworthy.'

The upper zone of the central mihrab arch, featuring two tiers of triple windows, exalts God alone. The pair of tilework roundels above the first tier of windows has pious exclamations: 'May His Glory be exalted!' 'And may His Gift be eternal!' The inscriptions in stained glass on the first tier of windows urge the congregation to pray and repent before it is too late: 'Hasten to prayer before passing away', 'Wherever you turn, the face of God is there', 'Hasten to repentance before death.' The central window of the uppermost tier exclaims: 'O, God! Glory be to God, the Lord of this world and the next!' A verse from the Baqara sura, which begs God to reward believers in both worlds, is quoted on two rectangular lunette tiles that flank the central qibla arch (2:201): 'Our Lord! Give unto us in the world that which is good, and in the Hereafter that which is good, and guard us from the doom of Fire.'

The qibla wall discloses the gist of the 'right path' that will ensure the well-being of pious worshippers in this world and the next. The opposite wall, encountered before leaving the prayer hall reiterates the theme of conquest, introduced by the foundation inscription outside, which applauds the destruction of 'blasphemy and darkness.' Two rectangular inscription panels on the piers, at both sides of the private balcony, quote a verse that celebrates the victory of truth over falsehood: 'And say: Truth hath come and falsehood hath vanished away. Lo! falsehood is ever bound to vanish! (17:81).' Before leaving the prayer hall with this comforting assurance, one encounters above its gate the piece of the Kaʿba stone that complements the other three affixed to the mihrab and minbar (illus. 332–33).

It is tempting to speculate that the inscription programme of the mosque was conceptualized by the Halveti shaykh Nureddinzade for whom the convent was originally built. Had he not passed away in 1574, he would have delivered Friday sermons at the mosque. Sokollu, who at one point 'took a vow of repentance and penitence', became an ardent disciple of Nureddinzade, who was appointed with Ebussuud's recommendation as the shaykh of the neighbouring convent of the Küçük Ayasofya mosque (SS Sergius and Bacchus) at Kadırga. The humbly clad ascetic shaykh's moving sermons at that convent mosque blended the internal spiritual essence of sufism with the external doctrines of the shariʿa. His 'magnetic force' attracted a 'limitless sea' of devotees, including Sultan Süleyman, princess Mihrümah, Sokollu, and most likely his pious wife, İsmihan.[332]

The personal imprint of Nureddinzade, an avid champion of Sunni orthodoxy known for his sharp criticism of those who deviated from the 'right path', can perhaps be detected in the inscriptions which denounce 'infidels', 'falsehood', and 'heterodoxy'.[333] Before passing away, he requested Sokollu to appoint in his place the Halveti shaykh Mehmed b. Ömer, known as Kurd Efendi, who had been trained by the same spiritual master (Bali of Sofia). Kurd Efendi (d. 1587–88) was invited from Sofia as the first shaykh of Sokollu's Fethiye convent. His popular Friday sermons inside the mosque, which attracted both commoners and the elite, interpreted the Prophet's traditions and expounded commentaries on the Koran, followed by special 'assemblies for recitation and meditation'.[334]

The complex at Kadırga exemplified the symbiosis of sufism with orthopraxy during the second half of the sixteenth century. The sublime mosque which Hasanbeyzade characterizes as an 'assembly place of angels', is portrayed in İsmihan's waqfiyya as 'paradise-like' and 'joy-increasing'.[335] Its captivating mihrab arch was a 'corner of delight', and its bright dome 'a mirror of the moon and the Pleiades at the summit of elegance, reflecting the countenance of pleasure.'[336] Sokollu's waqfiyya similarly highlights the sense of delight elicited by the 'joy-giving' and 'soul-expanding' mosque, embodying 'a thousand artful wonders and heart-alluring decorations'.[337]

Modern architectural historians have ranked the mosque,

hailed in its foundation inscription as the 'foremost sanctuary in the city', among Sinan's finest masterpieces. Goodwin evaluates it as one of the chief architect's 'two greatest achievements', a 'final statement' on the ideal grand vizierial mosque, as the Selimiye is on the ideal sultanic mosque.[338] The Kadırga mosque can be interpreted as a commentary on the classical synthesis of the Süleymaniye, an ambition befitting İsmihan's royal image and Sokollu's reverence for the Süleymanic 'golden age'. It represents the glorious culmination of classical ideals rather than a prelude to change. Its backward-looking reverential aesthetic orientation is exemplified by its reformulation of the traditional plan of Kara Ahmed Pasha's mosque, unlike the Selimiye that further explores innovations introduced in Mihrümah's pioneering Edirnekapı mosque. Withholding the urge for bold experimentation, the stunning mosque, personifying İsmihan and her husband as a couple, embodies the measured restraint of classical magnificence.'

2. SOKOLLU MEHMED PASHA

Sokollu Mehmed Pasha was one of Sinan's foremost patrons. His scores of pious foundations extended from the Balkans to the Hijaz, many of them concentrated along the main pilgrimage and trade route of the empire (Map 5). The grand vizier's architectural patronage was broader in geographical scope than that of Rüstem Pasha, whose charitable socio-religious monuments were largely focused around the Sea of Marmara (Map 4). Sokollu's global vision echoed that of his first master, Sultan Süleyman, who had emphasized the creation of complexes along the main diagonal route of the empire, culminating in Mecca and Medina. The major mosque complexes that Sinan designed for Sokollu on the same route are located in Lüleburgaz, on the Istanbul–Edirne highway, and in Payas, near Aleppo. Another complex commissioned by the grand vizier in Havsa, near Edirne, is discussed under the monuments of provincial governors because it was a memorial financed with the 'canonically lawful income' of the estate he inherited from his late son, Kurd Kasım Pasha (d. 1572).[339] Sokollu's two provincial mosque complexes were complemented in the capital by his prestige mosque in Azapkapı, outside the walls of Galata.

Antonio Tiepolo (1576) perceptively surmises that the grand vizier's greatest ambition was to amass a fortune surpassing that of Rüstem Pasha, a manifestation of the latter's 'aspiration for grandeur, although everyone calls it avarice.'[340] Sokollu's architectural patronage was driven by the same ambition: to outstrip the pious foundations of the most prominent grand vizier of the Süleymanic era. His waqfiyya of 1574 asserts that more than any of his predecessors he gave 'splendour and adornment' to the office of the grand vizierate by endowing refined monuments that added 'beauty and elegance' to the 'palace of the world'. Replenishing the 'flower garden of the religion and the state', he contributed to the well-being of the empire and its subjects through pious foundations that 'enlivened the rituals of religion and rejuvenated the meeting places of the manifest shariʿa'.[341]

The anonymous Venetian author of a 'Relazione' of 1579 applauds the 'magnificent' monuments that the 'prudent and most illustrious' grand vizier erected throughout the empire and in the capital – mosques, colleges, caravansarays, bath-houses, shops, bridges, and aqueducts – as 'works worthy not only of his virtue but also of his grandeur'.[342] Gerlach (1573–77) concludes that Sokollu surpassed former grand viziers by commissioning an unprecedented number of impressive monuments supported by extensive endowments. Employing his slaves in their construction, he reserved his annual income from gifts (worth a million ducats) to build pious foundations for the salvation of his soul.[343]

The historians Āli and Peçevi concur that no other grand vizier attained such 'great majesty' and created as many pious foundations as Sokollu.[344] Āli only lists his major monuments, omitting the complexes he jointly sponsored with his wife and the one he built for his late son:

> In Istanbul near Galata [Azapkapı] he built a noble Friday mosque; and in the town called Burgos [Lüleburgaz] a Friday mosque, a madrasa, and an elegant hospice; he caused the castle of Payas to be rebuilt and established near it a visit-worthy hospice and a Friday mosque and a library, in addition to pious works in many other places including the two Holy Cities, the enumeration of which would be so verbose that an abridged account has been deemed preferable.[345]

Peçevi, a relative of Sokollu, finds him guilty of nepotism but maintains that unlike Rüstem Pasha he rejected bribes. The historian poses the following question to the grand vizier's two confidants (his steward, Kaytas Kethüda, and his treasurer, Hadım Hasan Agha), inquiring how so many pious foundations were financed without resorting to bribery:

> You say that the late grand vizier did not take bribes and that his fiefs did not yield more than 15,000,000 to 16,000,000 aspers; then what was the source for the expenditures of his two palaces [Kadırgalimanı and Hippodrome], worth 100,000,000 aspers; the Burgaz complex, worth 30,000,000 aspers; the Havsa complex, worth 15,000,000 aspers; and his various other endowed monuments at Kasımpaşa [Azapkapı] in Istanbul, Aleppo, Damascus, Mecca, and Medina? They answered: 'The gifts given to our late pasha were two to three times more than the bribes that grand viziers receive nowadays. His buildings and most of his expenses were financed by those presents. Moreover, he had 1,000 galley slaves who worked in his constructions. For the erection of the new palace [at the Hippodrome] near the new mosque of Sultan Ahmed Khan, the late Sultan Selim had donated 100,000 gold coins

[6,000,000 aspers] since it was created with his chaste daughter's initiative, but the late pasha did not take it and presented it to the sultana. In other words, there was no end to such gifts. Apart from all this, he was a grand vizier for nearly sixteen years; simply calculate his fief revenues of 16,000,000 aspers (that equal 400,000 gurush) for a period of sixteen years, and add to that amount his annual income of 100,000 gurush as a vizier for nine years, and then ask how so much money was spent on these buildings.' Indeed we calculated a sum of 70 to 80 times 100,000 gurush. And then they joked: the additional assets he accumulated before he rose to the vizierate 'are money for your pocket!'[346]

When Sokollu passed away, his royal widow and their son İbrahim Khan applied to the imperial council for the authorization of an inspection to consolidate all his waqfs.[347] The two Turkish versions of the grand vizier's abridged waqfiyya (compiled in 1574 on the basis of four extensive waqfiyyas) enumerate his foundations differently. One of them uses a geographical classification, moving from Medina to Becskerek in Transylvania (Map 5), while the other one groups them according to building types.[348] The former waqfiyya expresses the wish that Sokollu may continue to build additional monuments in the remaining part of his life, thereby turning the face of the earth into the envy of the garden of Eden.[349] It is explained that the pious foundations were recorded as the 'lawful last will' of the grand vizier, who pronounced the profession of faith after announcing his testament.[350] This explains why the waqfiyyas list some incomplete monuments as if they had already been built.

The version grouped according to building types starts by listing seven Friday mosques, sited in Azapkapı (Istanbul), Burgos (Lüleburgaz), Becskerek (near Temesvár), Szigetvár, Kayapınarı (Sidhirókastron), Bor (Karaman), and Payas.[351] Of the seven masjids commissioned by Sokollu, four were in Aleppo: the renovated ʿUmari masjid founded by the caliph ʿUmar near the old tannery; a masjid above the courtyard fountain of his newly built large khan (Khan al-Gumruk); and two masjids outside Bab Antakiyya (above the fountain of his newly built khan, and at his new tannery along the Quwayq river). Three other masjids were located near the Büyükçekmece bridge; at the centre of Sokollu's covered bazaar in the Bulgarian town of Balçık, subordinate to Varna; and in his birthplace, the village of Sokolovići, subordinate to Višegrad.[352] The waqfiyya also mentions two madrasas (Kadırgalimanı, Lüleburgaz), a school for Koran recitation (Eyüp), eight elementary schools (Azapkapı, Lüleburgaz, Kayapınarı, Sokolovići, Becskerek, Bor, Payas, Medina), three dervish convents (Kadırgalimanı, Szigetvár, Payas), three hospices (Lüleburgaz, Višegrad, Payas), a hospital (Mecca), many fountains (Eyüp, Kadırgalimanı, Azapkapı, Lüleburgaz, Belgrade, Višegrad, Sokolovići, Payas, Aleppo, Medina), a paved road (Lüleburgaz), and bridges (on the Tunca river near Edirne, and the Drina river at Višegrad).[353]

The income-producing structures endowed to support these pious foundations, entrusted to four waqf administrators subordinate to a chief administrator, are far too numerous to count.[354] Sokollu's many khans and covered markets (*bedesten*) invigorated commercial traffic in such cities as Belgrade, Varna, Balçık, Sidhirókastron, Edirne, Istanbul, Gallipoli, Bor, Niğde, Antioch, Aleppo, Damascus, and Saida (Sidon). They were complemented by shops, houses, warehouses, bakeries, bath-houses, workshops, mills, dairy farms, market-places, arable fields, and numerous villages (donated by the sultans or purchased from owners). The grand vizier acted as the chief administrator and overseer of his waqf; upon his demise, his male descendants would serve as chief administrators and future grand viziers would act as overseers. Secondary administrators were to be selected from Sokollu's male progeny, and if their lineage ceased, from his freed household slaves and their descendants. Depending on their qualifications, his sons and slave servants would be given preference over 'outsiders' in all staff appointments.

Sinan's autobiographies mention Sokollu's complexes in Kadırgalimanı, Eyüp, Azapkapı, Lüleburgaz, Payas, and Havsa ('built for the soul of his son, Kasım Beg'). They also list the grand vizier's hospice and caravansaray in Bosnia (Višegrad), his masjid at Büyükçekmece, his caravansaray in Aleppo (Khan al-Gumruk), his commercial baths (Edirne, Mecca, Medina), and his bridges (Višegrad, Marmaracık near Çorlu, Sinanlı in Hayrabolu).[355] Monuments omitted from the chief architect's oeuvre must have been created by regional architects and builders, such as the Ragusan stonemasons imported from Dubrovnik for several buildings that Sokollu and his relatives commissioned in Bosnia and Herzegovina.[356]

I shall briefly survey the grand vizier's smaller mosque complexes before turning to his principal foundations in Lüleburgaz, Payas, and Azapkapı. The now-lost Friday mosque and elementary school in Becskerek, accompanied by a commercial bath-house and shops, commemorated Sokollu's conquest of that stronghold in 1551.[357] It was supported by revenues from mills, villages, and fields donated to him by the sultans in Becskerek and Temesvár.[358] The masjid, elementary school, and fountain in Sokolovići were endowed for the soul of Sokollu's father, who converted to Islam and adopted the name Cemalüddin Sinan Beg. Only the rebuilt masjid with a hipped roof and wooden portico remains from this small complex that celebrated the Islamization of Sokollu's birthplace and expressed his lifelong preoccupation with kinship ties.[359]

The demolished Friday mosque and dervish convent in Szigetvár memorialized the victorious Hungarian campaign of 1566, during which Sokollu had successfully concealed Süleyman's death, a cornerstone of his career. The sultan's internal organs were buried in a golden vessel in a domed mausoleum erected outside the castle of Szigetvár.[360] The monuments that Sokollu added next to that mausoleum, which was protected by a small fort (*palanka*) surrounded by a moat, expressed his personal devotion to the martyred sultan of the ghazis.[361] A decree addressed by Selim II to the governor-general of Szigetvár in 1577 enumerates the components of this complex, whose wardens are reduced from fifty to twenty-five to improve their low wage: 'a sanctified mausoleum, dervish lodge, Friday mosque, and fort.'[362] Another imperial decree sent that year to the governor of Bosnia instructs him to transfer Mevlana Shaykh Ali of the Halveti order (a disciple of Nureddinzade) from Sarajevo to Szigetvár, where he would be the shaykh, imam, and Friday preacher of the mosque and convent adjoining Süleyman's mausoleum.[363]

The campaign of Szigetvár had been conducted under the spiritual leadership of the Halveti Shaykh Nureddinzade, for whom Sokollu later built a convent in Kadırgalimanı. Given the grand vizier's devotion to the Halveti order, it is not surprising that the guardianship of Süleyman's mausoleum was entrusted to a shaykh from that order. The hallowed funerary complex in Szigetvár, a memorial to the victorious expedition masterminded by Sokollu on behalf of the martyred sultan, combined imperial structures (the mausoleum and fort) with the grand vizier's personal foundations. The masjid at the head of the Büyükçekmece bridge similarly linked the grand vizier's identity with Süleyman's memory. The sultan had commissioned the bridge, as well as a caravansaray and public fountain, along the Istanbul–Edirne highway in 1565, before leaving for the Szigetvár campaign. The masjid and commercial structures that Sokollu added next to these imperial buildings, completed in 1567–68, stamped his own identity on the small complex in Büyükçekmece, which was a prelude to his monumental complex in Lüleburgaz.[364]

The grand vizier's Friday mosque and elementary school in the 'new market-place' (*bāzār-i cedīd*) of Kayapınarı at Sidhirókastron have vanished. The complex is described in the itinerary of the *bailo* Lorenzo Bernardo in 1591: 'In Genibazar (Yeni Bazar, new market-place) is a place resembling a serraglio, approximately a mile-and-a-half in circumference, built by the grand vizier Mehmed Pasha ... for his own soul, where there is a stable for horses, a mosque, a bath, and many shops for the articles sought by those who go to the bazaar held there every Friday.'[365] Supported by revenues from that region and Thessaloniki, this complex was accompanied by a commercial bath, caravansaray, shops, warehouses, and rental rooms. The no-longer-extant masjid at the centre of Sokollu's income-producing covered bazaar at Balçık was complemented by another covered market and khan he built in Varna. The extant Friday mosque above his covered market at Bor is a modest upper-storey structure with a single minaret, surmounted by a lead-covered hipped roof. Once accompanied by an elementary school, its endowment was supplemented by another covered market nearby in Niğde.[366]

Among the four masjids endowed in Aleppo, only the renovated ʿUmari masjid and the octagonal masjid raised on piers above the courtyard fountain of the Khan al-Gumruk survive. Following the war of the princes in Konya, Sokollu had wintered at that city in 1559–60. Perhaps it was then that he bought and built some of his commercial properties there that turned him into the 'biggest landlord' of Aleppo.[367] A number of these structures may have been created under the supervision of his son, Kurd Kasım Pasha, and his cousin, Derviş Pasha, both of whom served as governor-generals in Aleppo.[368] Sokollu's properties in Aleppo, complemented by others in the Arab provinces, supported his masjids in that city, his Payas complex, and his pious foundations in Mecca and Medina.

The grand vizier's charities in the two Holy Cities have disappeared. His two bath-houses in Mecca and Medina are only mentioned in the *Tuḥfe*.[369] A royal letter addressed to the Sharif of Mecca in 1576 explains that Sokollu wanted to buy a courtyard house near the Meccan Haram to lodge the sick and to build a commercial bath-house nearby to cover its services. The Sharif is asked to help the grand vizier's man in buying timber and appropriate properties near the Haram.[370] The bath-house and hospital in Mecca were completed around the time of Sokollu's death.[371] His endowments to the Prophet's mosque in Medina expressed his special devotion to his namesake Muhammad, with whom he is compared in the inscriptions of his pious foundations in Istanbul, Lüleburgaz, and Payas. Several imperial decrees dated 1568 document the construction of his commercial bath-house and waterworks in Medina, where he also built a madrasa and elementary school.[372] The kadi and shaykh al-Haram of Medina were ordered to appoint talented hydraulic experts to assist the water channel builder (*ṣu yolcusı*) Cemalüddin in the construction of Sokollu's water conduit and water dispensers.[373] The governors of Alexandria and Suez were ordered to send building materials for the bath-house that was still under construction in 1578, a year before his death.[374]

Sokollu's pious foundations marked the territories of the empire with an enduring record of memories associated with his life and career. They promoted Islamic socio-religious institutions, urban and agrarian development, commerce, and travel. Like the bridges he constructed in Thrace and Bosnia, his monuments marking focal points of passage reflected his visionary preoccupation with communications and connections throughout the empire. That vision also manifested itself in his unrealized state projects such as the creation of a canal in the Suez, and another one connecting the Don with the Volga. The grand vizier's immense waqf was truly imperial in conception, befitting his image as the 'virtual emperor' of the Ottoman dominions.[375] Differing in functional programme and style, the three principal monuments Sinan designed for him in Lüleburgaz, Payas, and Azapkapı made explicit the dichotomy between the centre and periphery of the empire. The primacy of the capital was expressed by the prestige monuments Sokollu and his wife chose to build there.

THE COMPLEX IN LÜLEBURGAZ

According to Gerlach, it was Sultan Süleyman who donated to Sokollu the ancient castle of 'Bergasch', where the foundations of his complex there were laid in 1565 (illus. 335–36).[376] It is sited along the historical Istanbul–Edirne highway over a flat terrain with ample grounds, unlike the sloping and cramped urban setting of the complex in Kadırgalimanı. A domed porch (popularly known as *dua kubbesi*, prayer dome) straddles the east–west axis of the shop-lined avenue (*arasta*), powerfully articulating the two halves of the complex: the religious-educational core (Friday mosque, madrasa, elementary school) at the south, and the service block for travellers (hospice, guest-house, and double caravansaray) at the north. Raised on an octagonal drum, the domed porch functions like a 'monumental keystone' at the intersection of the sacred qibla axis and the profane east–west axis (illus. 337). According to oral tradition, under this 'prayer dome' shop owners solemnly pronounced prayers at daybreak before the gates of the complex were ceremonially opened.[377] It was also there that the caravansaray keeper graciously bid his guests goodbye each morning to the sound of beating drums (illus. 338).[378]

The cross-axial composition of the complex, with its nodal 'prayer dome', is shared by Sokollu's other major roadside foundations in Payas and Havsa, whose visual unity may have been recognized by passengers who traversed the empire's main highway. The construction chronology of the complexes in Lüleburgaz (1565–69/70) and Payas (1567–74) overlapped with those in Eyüp and Kadırgalimanı in the capital. In 1567 Marcantonio Pigafetta encountered in 'Berghaz' more than 200 chained Christian slaves who expected to be freed after the completion of construction work. They were building 'a large and beautiful caravansaray with a very capacious hospice' across from whose gate 'a mosque of marble and stone' was being erected. Moreover, they were going to create along the caravansaray façade 'a very long row of shops between which will pass the usual street from Istanbul to Edirne'.[379] Lambert Wyts, who saw the grand vizier's recently finished complex in 1572, says it was built between 1566 and 1570.[380]

These dates are confirmed by imperial decrees. The earliest, addressed on 16 September 1565 to the kadi of Pınarhisar, orders him to help Sokollu's men in buying timber for his charitable caravansaray in Lüleburgaz (Burgos, Bergos).[381] Another orders the kadi of Skopje on 1 December 1567 to send seventy carpenters (*neccār*) with their tools to the grand vizier's 'noble Friday mosque' that was being built in Lüleburgaz. Copies of this decree were dispatched to other kadis to enlist additional carpenters from Serres (40), Thessaloniki (60), Edirne (100), Mitilini (40), and Gallipoli (30).[382] Yet another decree given to the pasha's steward (Kethüda Beg) on 13 July 1568 orders the kadis of Çorlu, Silivri, and Rodoscuk (Tekirdağ) to send enough masons (*bennā*) with their tools to the hospice (*ʿimāret*) that was being built for the grand vizier in Lüleburgaz.[383] Two decrees from August 1568 concern the purchase of lead from Bulgarian towns for 'some buildings' erected by the grand vizier.[384] The kadis of Sofia, Dubnica, Radomir, Samokov, and Kustendil in Bulgaria were ordered to supply carts so that the grand vizier's lead, kept in storage at Sofia, could be carried to Lüleburgaz.[385]

Dispatches sent to the Venetian Senate in March and June 1568 indicate that Sokollu had requested window panes and oil lamps 'for his mosque.'[386] On 8 January 1568 Marcantonio Barbaro reported that the grand vizier went to join Selim II, who was hunting in Edirne, and inspect the royal mosque there along with his own complex in 'Bergas'. The *bailo* refers to the latter complex as a collection of 'most superb edifices; that is, a mosque, a bath, and a caravansaray with rooms for the use of travellers, built with the most beautiful marbles, very large columns, and valuable stone' (illus. 339).[387] We learn from Barbaro's dispatch of 3 January 1569 that on his way back to Istanbul, the sultan 'lodged in Bergas, a place two days away from Edirne, where the Magnificent Pasha built a mosque and a palace (*serraglio*) comprising buildings of great value and cost'. There the grand vizier 'received His Majesty very honourably and regally, presenting to him as a gift the palace he had built together with all its furnishings'. The palace Sokollu presented to his royal father-in-law included furnishings of gold cloth, beautiful horses, young slaves, and gardens planted with fruit trees and flowers.[388]

Decrees issued between 1568 and 1570 concern Sokollu's endowment and the populating of Lüleburgaz with tax-exempt settlers. In March 1568 the kadi of Lüleburgaz was ordered not to allow the sale of animals, leather, fruits, and cotton in places other than the market-place of the town because those who sold their goods elsewhere to avoid paying taxes harmed the grand vizier's waqf.[389] A decree addressed in December 1568 to the kadi of Pınarhisar acknowledges that the inhabitants of Lüleburgaz suffered greatly from those who continually traversed their town; therefore, new settlers willing to live there would from now on be exempt from taxes.[390] Another decree sent to the kadis of Lüleburgaz and Babaeski in February 1570 orders them to accompany Yahşi Çavuş, who is arriving from the capital, in marking with 'signs' the borders of seven pieces of land donated to Sokollu in Babaeski as his freehold property and in preparing a register of those borders.[391]

The complex was completed in 1569–70, according to Turkish inscriptions in *thuluth* script, carved in cartouches on two gates under the 'prayer dome'. The inscription on the gate of the hospice-cum-caravansaray emphasizes the affinity between the grand vizier and his namesake, the Prophet Muhammad Mustafa:

In name Muhammad and in nature Mustafa,
Namely, the grand vizier of Sultan Selim Khan,

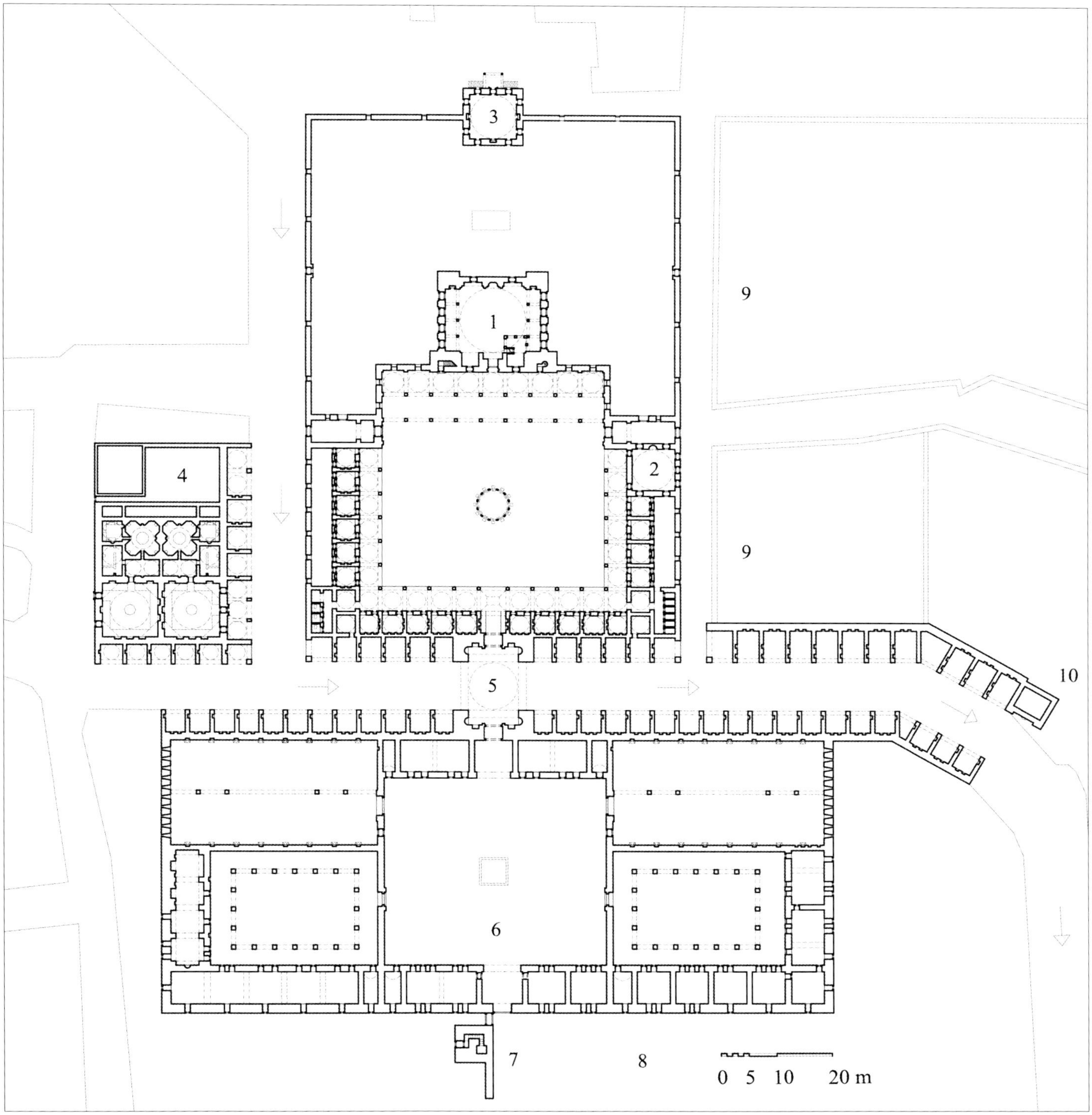

335 Plan of the Sokollu Mehmed Pasha complex, Lüleburgaz, with arrows pointing the direction from Istanbul to Edirne: 1. Mosque. 2. Madrasa. 3. Elementary school. 4. Double bath. 5. Prayer dome. 6. Double caravansaray, with guest-rooms, and hospice [hypothetical reconstruction]. 7. Watchtower of waqf administrator's residence. 8. Site of royal palace. 9. Residences for the professor, preacher, imam, and four muezzins. 10. Public fountain and route toward the bridge.

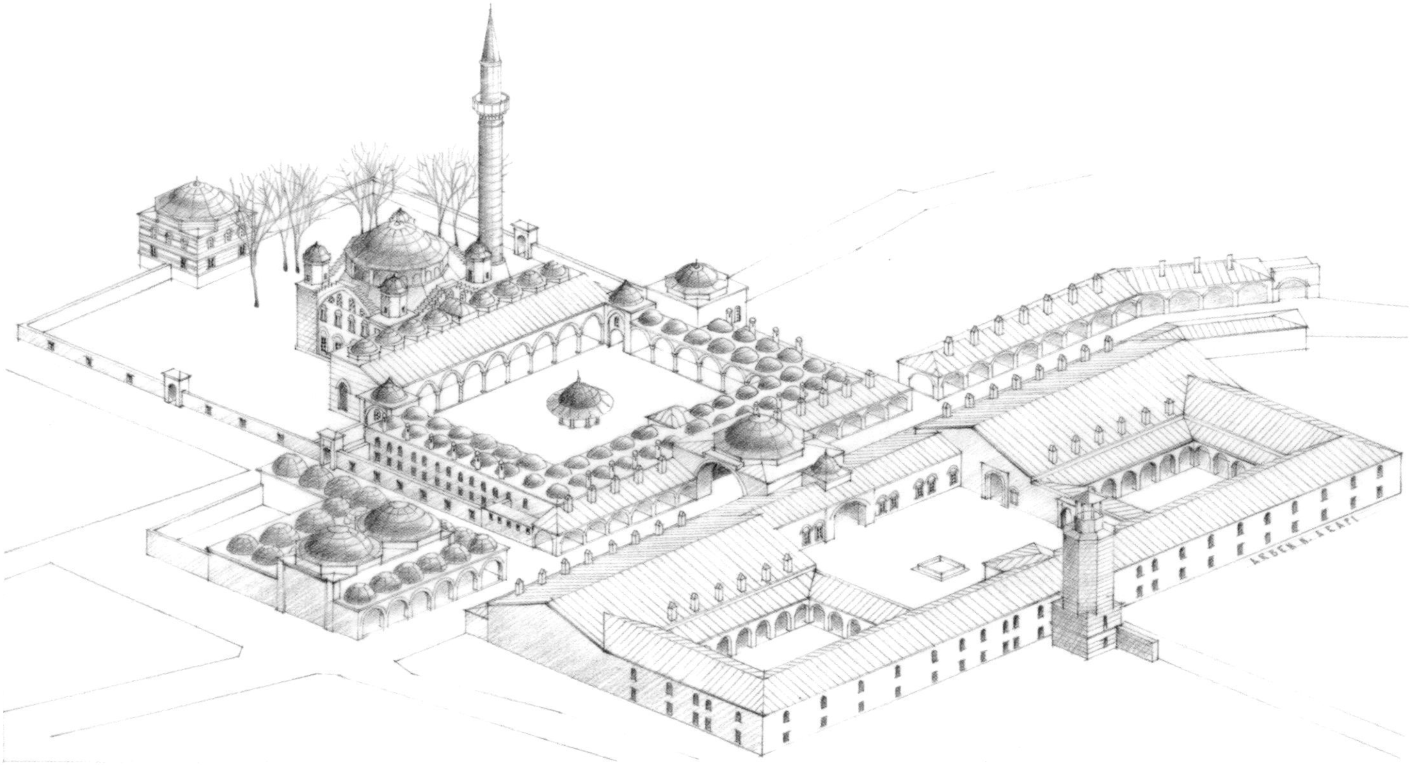

336 Axonometric projection of the Sokollu complex, Lüleburgaz.

337 Luigi Mayer, *Borgas with Shop-lined Artery and Prayer Dome*, c. 1801, print.

338 Luigi Mayer, *Caravansera at Borgas*, c. 1801, print.

339 Sokollu complex, Lüleburgaz.

Built this caravansaray in the year 977; we wish
That God make paradise his lot.
Its date was pronounced by the divine voice:
'Those who came to this caravansaray all moved along'
[977 (1569–70)].[392]

The chronogram alludes to the caravansaray-like world through which the passangers of life pass on to the eternal afterworld. The pendant inscription over the gate of the courtyard shared by the mosque and the madrasa once again likens the virtuous grand vizier to the Prophet:

The just Asaph (vizier of Solomon) and vizier with a good name,
That Muhammad of glorious virtue,

Showed kindness and made Burgos prosperous
With a collection of charitable constructions, that man of Faith,

[... plastered over ...] may you perpetually keep him,
O God, at the head of the state.

The divine voice pronounced its date:
'The Aqsa Mosque and the House of the Pious
[977 (1569–70)].'[393]

Sokollu's waqfiyya describes the components of the complex in detail, starting with its paradise-like pastoral site, bordered by a river where 'an extremely delightful city composed like the Pleiades and called Burgos came into being'. The grand vizier paid utmost attention to the 'renewal and expansion' of that city, which was 'like the moon along a highway resembling the Milky Way'.[394] He built there 'a decorated Friday mosque' covered with a skylike dome, which resembled the columnar garden palace of Iram. It was endowed with seven large, six medium-sized, and twelve small carpets (*ḳaliçe*), along with two prayer carpets (*seccāde*). Among its personnel, thirty readers of sections of the Koran would recite the holy book for the Prophet's soul after the morning prayers, for the soul of 'Sultan Süleyman Khan Ghazi' after the noon prayers, and for the continuation of the reigning sultan's rule following the afternoon prayers.[395]

In the delectable courtyard of the mosque, Sokollu built an artistic madrasa endowed with magnificent manuscripts covering all the sciences. Behind the mihrab, 'beyond the heart-stealing pool of the flower garden', he constructed a 'lofty elementary school (*mekteb*) resembling the pavilions of the rose garden of paradise'. Across from the Friday mosque, for the grandees and common people alike he created a monumental hospice (*ʿimāret*) and banqueting house (*ziyāfetḫāne*) which comprised a kitchen, bakery, commissariat, 'seven internal and six external lofty guest-rooms (*tābḫāne*) in addition to two large caravansarays (*ḫān*), each with thirty-two fireplaces, which were a sign of the caravansaray of the world in spaciousness and solidity'. Free food was served to distinguished travellers at every guest-room on two round tables. Ordinary guests were given food individually at each fireplace of the double caravansaray.[396] The grand vizier also stipulated that his old and invalid manumitted household slaves should be given free food from his hospice twice a day, along with a stipend of one asper.[397]

The waqfiyya goes on to explain that water originating from two sources, Büyükkaynarca and Küçükkaynarca, was collected in a place 6,260 cubits away from the city. A channel and an aqueduct conducted those springs to a water distribution tower near the elementary school and to two reservoirs by the bridge on the river.[398] The waqfiyya also mentions the 'lovely palace' built to lodge the sultan whenever he travelled between Istanbul and Edirne. That royal palace, adjacent to the residence of the endowment administrator (namely Sokollu and his descendants) seems to have been located behind the northwest corner of the hospice. The administrator's residence 'near the hospice', was composed of several courtyards and included a 'great tower'.[399] A surveillance tower, constructed with alternating courses of stone and brick, is all that remains from this residence behind the northeast side of the hospice.[400]

Across the street running along the west side of the mosque and madrasa Sokollu also built individual residences with courtyards for the leading personnel of his complex (the madrasa professor, imam, and four muezzins), each according to his status.[401] He constructed on the 'two sides of the felicitous town a beautiful paved road', since the region suffered from flooding and mud. This endowed road can perhaps be identified as the one running along the east and north sides of the mosque and madrasa block. The waqfiyya applauds the regular plan of the 'heavenly' city that came into being with Sokollu's efforts: 'In short, in that orderly town, composed like the Pleiades, he made manifest so many lofty buildings and magnificent works that when they are not judged by the eye, describing their details with agreeable words is impossible and inconceivable.'[402]

The vast complex was a veritable orthogonally planned city. Its income-producing endowed structures included the grounds of a yearly market fair (*pāzār yiri*) held near the pre-existing bridge (sited beyond the northwest corner of the complex), and fifty-three masonry shops covered with lead roofs (only thirty-two of which are extant). Twelve of these shops abutted the right and left sides of the madrasa façade, eighteen were adjacent to the caravansaray, twelve adjoined the houses of the imam and muezzins, and eleven were grouped around the commercial double bath. Near that bath were constructed a sesame oil press, a linseed oil press, a public eating house specializing in sheep heads, and a straw storage with an adjacent empty plot. Close to the bridge a candle manufactory, a soap manufactory, and three tanneries (provided with two reservoirs) were built under a single roof.[403] The fair held along the road extending from the bridge up to Sokollu's shop-lined *arasta* is mentioned in 1550 by Catharin Zen, who referred to 'Bargas' as a large hamlet (*casale*) with the vestiges of an ancient castle. It had a caravansaray and a mosque with a hospice before Sokollu transformed it into a prosperous town: 'In this hamlet they hold a fair during Easter that lasts three days, in which one sees a large amount of merchandise because people

340 Sokollu mosque, Lüleburgaz, from the southwest.

341 Sokollu mosque ablution fountain.

342 Sokollu mosque, Lüleburgaz, from the north.

343 Sokollu mosque interior.

gather from all surrounding areas, along with the 'Uruzi' [*yürük*, nomads], who are people inhabiting the countryside with their animals.'[404]

Sinan's autobiographies list the mosque, madrasa, hospice, and caravansaray in Lüleburgaz.[405] The axially composed regular plan is the most impressive aspect of the complex, which only preserves some of its components today. The caravansaray and hospice block, demolished in 1935, is known from hypothetical reconstructions based on photographs and prints. It constituted an integrated grand block with several courtyards, differing from Sinan's earlier treatment of its constituent units as independent structures. Its novel layout, repeated in Payas (1567–74) and Havsa (1573–77), formed the model for its counterpart in Nurbanu Sultan's Üsküdar complex, dated 1579–80 (illus. 261–62).[406] The flat roofs of the caravansaray and hospice compound contrasted with the domical superstructures of the bilaterally symmetrical southern block, comprising religious and educational functions (illus. 338).[407]

The alignment of domed units along the qibla axis – the 'prayer dome,' ablution fountain, prayer hall, and elementary school – resonates with the composition of the mosque complex in Kadırga, which lacks the hospice-cum-caravansaray block. Unlike the ashlar masonry mosque and U-shaped madrasa, the school is built with alternating courses of stone and brick. The partially destroyed double bath, surrounded by shops, is situated across a street to mark its independent commercial status. The historical Istanbul–Edirne avenue passing through the *arasta* bends towards the direction of the bridge. Ideal perspective views of the complex, dominated by the mosque dome (12.5 metres) with smaller domes bubbling around it, would have been glimpsed by travellers on the avenue. The precinct wall of the garden with a pool exposes the domed cube of the mosque, simpler than the baldachined mosques of Sokollu and his wife in the capital. It is given a semblance of structural complexity by the stepped extrados of its tympanum arches and its four weight turrets with domical lead caps punctuating the corner buttresses (illus. 340). Its distant but noticeable resemblance to Mihrümah Sultan's Edirnekapı mosque (*c.* 1563–70), seen by all travellers upon leaving Istanbul for Edirne, visually affiliates this provincial monument with prestige mosques in the capital (illus. 288–89).

Three gates provide access into the serene garden court of the mosque, surrounded by madrasa rooms. The undulating wooden baroque canopy of the central ablution fountain bears the monogram of Mahmud II, who extensively renovated the mosque in 1839 (illus. 341). The inner core of the marble fountain, an elegant dodecagonal domed baldachin, is original. Its pointed arches with alternating voussoirs are supported by columns on muqarnas capitals; the marble panels featuring spouts are carved in low relief with foliate niches flanked by naturalistic flowers. The two domed gatehouses at the east and west sides of the garden court bridge the taller columns of the double portico fronting the mosque and the lower madrasa arcades. The classroom is unconventionally shifted to the end of the west wing because the centre of the north wing is occupied by the gate communicating with the 'prayer dome'.

The relatively small mosque, which constitutes a variant of the domed cube, is aggrandized by its unusually wide, nine-bay double portico opened up at both ends with iron-grill windows that provide vistas of the qibla garden. The minaret at the northwest corner was rebuilt in 1934, after being demolished during the Bulgarian invasion of 1910–12.[408] The low dome over the double porticoed façade is carried on a sixteen-sided blind drum, delineated in red with pseudo-arched windows framed by rectangles (illus. 340, 342). The dome is overpowered by the pair of heavy weight turrets capped with onion domes. Comparison of the awkward proportions of this façade with its sophisticated counterpart in Kadırga (illus. 326) displays its provincial character, also reflected in the simpler decorative programme of the mosque, without İznik tile revetments.

The well-lit prayer hall features three tiers of windows (illus. 343). Window frames that come too close to the dome arches show the supervising architect's inability to coordinate the interior and exterior elevations. The refined arcades of the internal side galleries, supported on white marble columns with muqarnas capitals, are decorated with alternating marble voussoirs. These galleries are fitted into the thick lateral arches carrying the central dome on four pendentives that descend close to the ground level. The private balcony above the deeply inset doorway is raised on three pointed-arched recesses, with a Bursa-arched muezzin's tribune at the west side. The muqarnas-hooded marble mihrab, topped by a triangular pediment with two finials, and the latticework minbar are finely proportioned. The painted decorations of the prayer hall, entirely renewed in 1983, are in red, black, and white. They replaced Europeanizing paintings and original inscriptions rendered in white on a blue background.[409] The designs, consisting of palmettes, medallions, geometric interlaces, and vegetal scrolls, lack the semi-naturalistic floral motifs that became the hallmark of the classical decorative idiom. The intricate plasterwork window grills of the qibla wall have lost their original stained glass inlays.

The epigraphy in monumental *thuluth* underscores the paradisical allusions of the mosque emphasized in the waqfiyya, together with Sokollu's special attachment to the Prophet. The carved stone inscription above the muqarnas-hooded portal welcomes the congregation into the gardens of paradise (39:73). The rectangular frame of this verse is flanked by two inscriptions invoking the beautiful names of God: 'O, the All-Bounteous!', 'O, the Most Compassionate!' The arched window lunettes on both sides of the portal quote the Fatiha sura, which begs the merciful God to reveal the 'straight path' (1:1–7). Inside the prayer hall, the central roundel of the dome quotes the cosmic verse alluding to the heavens and earth held in place by the divine creator's power (35:41), which is repeated on the domes of the Kadırga and Azapkapı mosques. The standard mihrab verse (3:37) is carved on the mihrab, and the two arched window lunettes that flank it cite the Ikhlas sura affirming the unity of God (112:1–4). A rectangular painted panel over the mihrab spells out the profession of faith and is accompanied by two roundels inscribed 'Allah' and 'Muhammad'. The four dome pendentives bear roundels painted with the names of the four caliphs. The names of Hasan, Husayn, and the Companions to whom the Prophet is said to have promised paradise are inscribed on the lunettes of the upper gallery windows: Zubayr, ʿAbd al-Rahman b.ʿAwf, Saʿd b. Malik, Saʿid b. Zayd, Abu ʿUbayda (ʿAmir b. al-Jarrah). These names, unique in the epigraphic programmes of Sinan's mosques, underline the Prophet's role as an intercessor capable of providing access to paradise.

European travellers who stayed in Sokollu's complex were particularly impressed by its magnificence. The Frenchman Du Fresne-Canaye (1573) comments on the grand vizier's rehabilitation of the derelict old town and describes the complex together with its small yet lavish royal garden palace:

> In Bergas Mehmed Pasha has certainly displayed the extent of his riches, for he has built all of this large town at his own expense in a place that was practically uninhabited, unhealthy, and without trees. He erected there a sumptuous caravansaray with stables for horses and separate rooms for travellers, and he brought there springs of very sweet water. In front of the caravansaray he erected a beautiful and superb mosque, ornamented with pretty marble columns and a fountain in the middle of its court. There are also baths for men and women. On the other side one sees the palace (*sérail*), small but delicious, at the centre of a garden in which, after mounting three to four steps, one enters a corridor or portico that surrounds and envelops the whole palace. Under its roof are very lively colourful paintings and it has clear fountains even in its most private spaces. There are not more than eight rooms, narrow and small, one next to the other, and most Turkish houses are built in this manner. Besides the hospice, the mosque, the palace, and the baths, there are many shops also covered with lead, showing that the money spent on this place was enormous and worthy of Mehmed Pasha's dignity. When the *Grand Seigneur* and the Sultanas pass through this route, they lodge in the palace.[410]

The Venetian ambassador Jacopo Soranzo, who enjoyed his stay at the 'commodious hospice' in 1574, praises the 'very grand monument created by Mehmed Pasha', with its richly endowed 'caravansaray and hospice containing many rooms', its 'most beautiful and graceful mosque, though not very large', and its many shops fulfilling all the needs of travellers. He describes the royal palace in much the same way as Du Fresne-Canaye does: 'We saw near this place a very beautiful *serraglio* built by Mehmed Pasha for the person of the *Signore*, in which there are four handsome rooms at the centre of a portico (*zardacco*, Turkish *çardak*) that encircles it all around, and near that portico is a pond with beautiful fish; then there is a surrounding garden with many fountains that present an agreeable sight.'[411]

The *bailo* Paolo Contarini (1580) describes the complex in detail, mentioning the special accommodations for women travellers and the royal palace:

> Finally we arrived in Borgassi, where there is a mosque built by Mehmed Pasha with a large courtyard in front of it – enclosed like a Carthusian cloister with vaulted cells and lead covered domes, and planted with very tall trees (not found in our parts) to create shade – and a large garden behind the mosque. Mehmed Pasha also built a very beautiful bath, and a caravansaray divided into two sections with twenty-four rooms in each, featuring a quadrangular courtyard in the middle surrounded by vaulted porticoes covered with lead. There are four large portals, two of which serve as entrances, one for the women, and the other for the kitchen and bakery, all of them similarly built with vaults in an excellent manner and covered with lead ... We also saw a *serraglio* built by the same Mehmed Pasha, with a superb edifice in the middle of a garden that is enclosed by walls; it is encircled by a portico in their fashion and has a fishpond at one side.[412]

Ottoman travellers provide briefer descriptions of the complex, simply enumerating its components.[413] Evliya Çelebi mentions the annual market fair, the 'fortress-like' caravansaray, and the royal palace, pointing out that the whole complex was constructed of masonry except for the wooden awnings of shops. Completely covered with 'indigo-blue lead', its buildings 'rose and fell like the waves of the azure sea', an analogy triggered not only by the blue colour reflected on the lead surfaces but also by the conventional use of silver to depict water in Ottoman painting.[414] Evliya eulogizes with great enthusiasm the mosque 'Koca Mimar Sinan' built for Sokollu, praising its paintings and its unparalleled artistic inscriptions (now transformed), which reminded him of those in the Prophet's mosque in Medina:

> This ornate Friday mosque is the pious work of that wise vizier, but language falls short of its description. Nevertheless, as much as we are able to, we shall attempt to describe it like a drop in the ocean and a particle in the sun. Firstly, being sited inside the town, no rest can be found in it from large congregations. It is a locus of worship, an excursion spot, and a pleasurable outing place. It has an outer courtyard with jets of water and a pool, zand an esteemed [inner] courtyard, shaded by many hundred plane trees, cypresses, chestnuts, and other beautiful trees, where all travellers and the community of Muslims obey and praise God. In summer and winter the rays of the fiery-temperamented sun cannot penetrate into its courtyard. The four sides of this great courtyard are surrounded by cells and porticoes composed of candle-like columns that are covered by domes resembling indigo-coloured bowls, each of them a sign of the dome of heaven. And the interior of the mosque is so decorated and artistic that in the Ottoman lands there is no vizierial mosque comparable to this one, except for the mosque of Zal Mahmud Pasha in Eyüp and the mosque of Süleyman Khan's eunuch [Hadım] İbrahim Pasha inside the Silivri gate in Istanbul. But compared to them this Burgos mosque is a more artistic, lovely, and light-filled mosque ... Around its big dome it is adorned with strata of suspended oil lamps and its interior is decked out with a muezzin's tribune and upper galleries. The eulogists of the world remain helpless in praising the windows around its minbar and mihrab. And when the exemplary chameleon-like designs of their rare Murano glass illuminates the mosque, the sura 'God is the light of the heavens' becomes revealed, light upon light.[415]

Despite Evliya's enthusiasm, the mosque in Lüleburgaz does not come close in magnificence to the baldachined prestige mosques the chief architect built in the capital for Sokollu (Azapkapı) and his wife (Kadırga). An enormous nine-bay double portico, which dwarfs its five-bay counterpart at Rüstem Pasha's provincial mosque in Rodoscuk (*c.* 1550–52/53) gave it the illusion of monumentality. As a variant of the domed cube, the plan of the Lüleburgaz mosque decorously conformed to the traditional programmes of provincial roadside complexes dominated by service buildings catering to travellers. Providing pleasant retreats for the enjoyment of weary passengers, its two garden courts were ideal 'excursion spots'.

The axial plan of the complex can be read as a metaphor for the ephemeral 'caravansaray of the world' from which the pious passengers of life pass on to the promised eternal realm of paradise. This inbuilt narrative dimension, implied by the inscriptions and the waqfiyya, is articulated by the aligned gates of the caravansaray and mosque under the hinge of the 'prayer dome'. The two gates prescribed an itinerary that chanelled Muslim travellers from the profane space of the caravansaray into the sacred space of the mosque, with its Edenic gardens. Non-Muslim guests of the hospice and caravansaray were spectators to this timeless narrative, ritually enacted on the architectural stage of the complex. The two educational institutions appended to the mosque block synthesized the primary function of Sokollu's compound as a deluxe roadside complex with its secondary role as an urban foundation. With its enormous scale projecting the settlement and future growth of Lüleburgaz, the luxurious complex contributed to the emergence of a flourishing town.

THE COMPLEX IN PAYAS

Sokollu's mosque complex in the strategic port of Payas (modern Yakacık, ancient Baiae) fostered urban development in a forsaken caravan station along the hajj route (illus. 344, 345). The town is located between two formidable mountain passes at the juncture of Anatolia and Syria: the Gülek pass north of Adana and the Belen (Bakras) pass near İskenderun, where in the 1550s Sinan designed a small roadside complex for Sultan Süleyman (illus. 44, 45). The *Tuḥfe* lists Sokollu's caravansarays in Payas and Aleppo [Khan al-Gumruk] after the sultan's complex: 'And on the Aleppo road the caravansaray and convent (*tekye*) built in the mountain pass of Bakras [by Sultan Süleyman]; and at Payas on the Aleppo road the caravansaray built by the grand vizier Mehmed Pasha; and the caravansaray built by the above-mentioned [pasha] in Aleppo.'[416] The same source mentions Sokollu's Friday mosque and hospice in Payas.[417] The exclusion of the complex from the *Teẕkiretü'l-ebniye* implies its relatively loose connection with Sinan, who designed its plan, but probably entrusted its execution to the local masters employed in the grand vizier's constructions in Aleppo.

The mosque complex in Payas was part of Sokollu's effort to create a secure caravan station for pilgrims and merchants, along with a port that combined military and commercial functions. Sited about 700 metres from the coastline, the complex is adjacent to a former Crusaders' castle that was ordered rebuilt with state funds in 1567, on the eve of the Cyprus campaign. Provided with a new imperial arsenal for ship construction, the rejuvenated port of Payas would play a strategic role during that campaign and after the conquest of Cyprus in 1570–71 its military functions were supplemented by its emerging role as a trading port of Aleppo, where Sokollu endowed numerous commercial structures. With the customs dues of its landing station endowed to the grand vizier's waqf, Payas remained a vital commercial harbour even after it was eclipsed by the neighbouring port of İskenderun, created in the 1590s.[418]

The mosque complex in Payas, with its cross-axial layout spread on a flat terrain, recalls its counterpart in Lüleburgaz. The historical hajj route that passed through its covered market (*arasta*) along the north–south qibla axis intersects with the east–west axis under a 'prayer dome' raised on four pendentives. The complex is appended to both sides of the spine-like cross-vaulted market, the north and south gates of which have wall fountains. On the east side lies a gigantic service block that comprises a caravansaray with stables, a guest-house, and a hospice. The west side, bisected by the east–west axis passing through the gates of the castle and caravansaray, is taken up by a mosque with an adjoining convent, and a bath-house adjacent to an elementary school. As in Lüleburgaz, the flat roofs of the hospice and caravansaray constrast with the domical superstructures of socio-religious and educational edifices. Once covered with lead, the complex was dominated by the large domes of its mosque, bath-house, and 'prayer dome'. Three monumental arched gates connect the shop-lined artery to the caravansaray, the bath-house, and the courtyard shared by the mosque and U-shaped convent.

Under the 'prayer dome', a Turkish inscription in *taʿlīḳ* script is carved over the monumental gate of the caravansaray, facing the open public space in front of the castle (illus. 346). Its placement and content underline the functional primacy of the caravansaray block, equal in size to the castle:

> The Asaph of Sultan Selim, son of the Solomon of the Age, that azimuth of the Glory of the World [the Prophet] and the possessor of good character,
>
> Comprehending the perishability of this transitory world, saw the impermanence of the banner of the misery-filled abode of death.
>
> He built and endowed this khan for God's approval, thereby building up beforehand his halting station in the next world.
>
> May God accept this unmatched good work, which in fact does not ordinarily fall to everyone's lot.
>
> The endower and patron of this work said its chronogram: 'I endowed this khan for travellers for the sake of God', 982 (1574–75).[419]

Curiously enunciating Sokollu's own voice, the unusual chronogram refers only to the khan, the *raison d'être* of the complex. It can be taken as the completion date for the whole ensemble.

Sokollu's waqfiyya lists the main components of the complex as a khan, a convent, and a mosque (confusingly referred to as both a masjid and a Friday mosque):

> In the sanjak of Uzeyr (ʿAzir), the castle with lofty foundations known among the people as Payas was located on a great highway and an immense thoroughfare, but it remained a feared place and a rarely frequented caravan station. When visitors and pilgrims arrived there in untimely fashion they were left stranded outside the castle. As there was no refuge and shelter to offer protection from the tricks of the warden and the adversities of rain, they suffered numerous afflictions and strange infections. His Highness, the above-mentioned influential and well-informed vizier, built in that frightful place a lofty khan (*ḫān*), which in spaciousness and solidity is a sign of the guest-house of the world, and a convent (*zāviye*), with a wonderful edifice where splendid food is amply served to each guest like the blessings of paradise, and an elevated masjid (*mescid*) functioning as a heart-stealing sanctuary for worshipping guests and residents.[420]

The waqfiyya explains that the dervishlike grand vizier endowed the convent (*ḫānḳāh*) he built around the courtyard of his Friday mosque (*cāmiʿ*) to dervishes, without specifying their order. The convent's shaykh was allocated a private house nearby. Like the

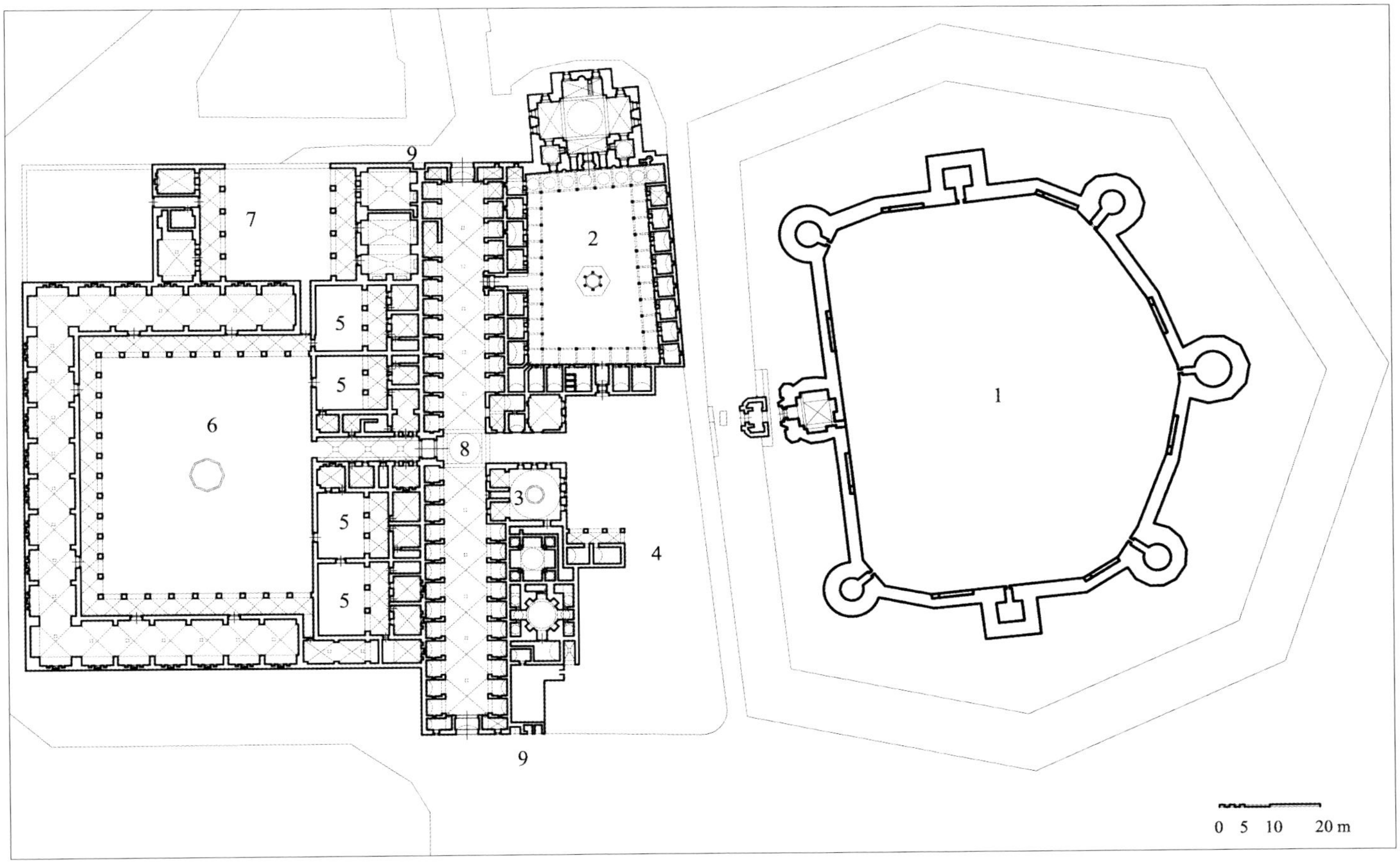

344 Plan of the Sokollu Mehmed Pasha complex, Payas: 1. Fortress. 2. Mosque and convent courtyard. 3. Bathhouse. 4. Elementary school (hypothetical reconstruction). 5. Guest-rooms with private courts. 6. Caravansaray with stables. 7. Hospice. 8. Prayer dome. 9. Public fountains.

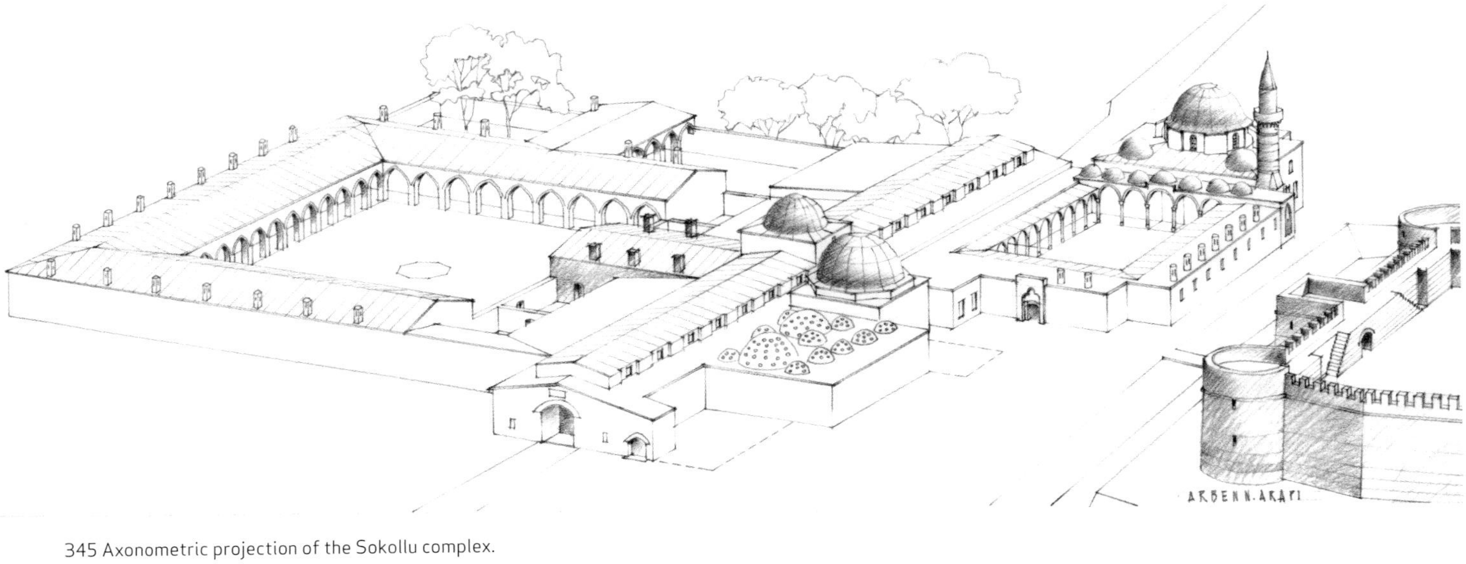

345 Axonometric projection of the Sokollu complex.

346 Sokollu complex from the fortress, Payas.

Halveti shaykhs of Sokollu's two other convents in Szigetvár and Kadırgalimanı, the shaykh in Payas had to deliver sermons in the Friday mosque twice a week. His disciples, residing in cells around the mosque courtyard, received two aspers each, in return for which they had to pray for the souls of the Prophet, the reigning sultan, and the founder of the complex. The waqfiyya stipulates that the convent should never be converted to a madrasa, a telling clause testifying to the common fate of many dervish convents. Among the dependencies of the complex, the waqfiyya also mentions its elementary school and its hospice comprising guest-houses (*tābḫāneler*), a kitchen, and a bakery. The privileged visitors to those guest-houses were each served two plates of food and two loaves of bread on round tables. The same amount of food was given to less distinguished guests lodged with animals in front of the khan's fireplaces.[421] Sokollu also created a water channel:

> Near the protected metropolis of Aleppo, he restored a pleasant and heart-alluring place at the edge of the sea called Payas, building there a flourishing hospice, a noble Friday mosque, and a charming convent. From the mountainous region at the east side he brought pleasing waters by an independent channel, making them flow into many places in those innovatively organized buildings.[422]

The income-producing endowments of the complex comprised forty-eight shops, a bath-house, and a bakery.[423] The donor also endowed the revenues of the 'landing station (*mülk iskele*) he constructed at the edge of the sea as his own property', along with many houses in Payas and landed properties nearby.[424]

Decrees document the construction chronology on the eve of the Cyprus campaign of the imperial castle and its dependent structures.[425] On 22 October 1567 the governor of Adana, Derviş Mehmed Beg, was ordered to oversee the renovation of the dilapidated castle in Payas, which was subordinate to the sanjak of Uzeyr, 'a frightful and dangerous' place by the sea where passengers were attacked by 'infidel' pirates. Using 10,000 gold coins from the Aleppo treasury for the repairs, the governor had to appoint wardens to guard the castle and have its environs populated with tax-exempt settlers.[426]

Another decree addressed to the governor on 2 March 1568 responds to his report notifying the court that the foundations of 'the castle and other planned buildings' had been laid, and that the governor of Uzeyr and other officials were sent orders to supply timber. The other buildings may be a reference to Sokollu's complex. The decree announces that Derviş Kethüda was on his way from Istanbul to Aleppo with money from the imperial treasury that would cover the wages of stonemasons and lime-burners. As soon as he arrived with 'the plan of the building and the description of the circumstances of the building', the governor of Adana was to start its construction. He is instructed to remedy the shortage of labourers he had previously reported by recruiting them from the sanjaks of Adana, Uzeyr and other neighbouring places. For the required food provisions of the builders (*bennā*) and labourers (*ırġad*), he is asked to enlist butchers, bakers, and cooks from the same places. He is reminded to make sure that the thickness of the castle walls be not less than four cubits, so that enemies could not score a victory from the sea.[427]

On 16 May 1568 the building supervisor was informed that İskender Beg, the governor-general of Aleppo, had sent a letter to the court reporting the impossibility of having the razed castle rebuilt on its old foundations. In his letter, he specified the length and width of the new foundations, already at ground level. The recipient of the decree is instructed to take extra money from the treasury of Aleppo if the 10,000 gold coins given earlier should prove insufficient.[428] The present castle with eight towers, then, replaced the razed fortress, whose weak foundations were entirely rebuilt. When its walls and towers reached twelve cubits above the ground, an order from the court specified that they should be heightened to sixteen cubits. In 1568 many shops and warehouses were built at the port of Payas, where an imperial arsenal was created for the construction of ships.[429] That year the governor-general and the finance minister of Aleppo were ordered to build ten ships at the new arsenal of Payas with timber cut from nearby forests.[430] Given the presence of enemy ships, the governor of Adana was instructed in 1570 to dig trenches and guard with additional wardens and weapons the ships that were being built in the arsenal dockyards.[431]

A decree addressed to the governor and the kadi of Uzeyr on 26 April 1573 indicates that the caravansaray had by then reached completion. The sultan accepts their suggestion to move the weekly bazaar held in Uzeyr on Thursdays to 'the khan that has been built near the town of Payas', and orders them to encourage the settlement of up to 300 households exempt from taxes.[432] On 16 November 1574 the kadi of Uzeyr and the governor-general and the finance minister of Aleppo were instructed to settle 500 tax-exempt Muslim and non-Muslim households in the

347 Sokollu complex, Payas, vaulted shopping artery with portal connected to the mosque courtyard on the left.

348 Sokollu mosque from the south.

349 Sokollu mosque, detail of muqarnas-hooded north portal.

350 Sokollu mosque, Payas, interior.

new town (a number raised to 800 later on):

> Subordinate to Aleppo, the site called Payas is a passage place and a halting station for the people and joyful pilgrims, but it remains uninhabited and desolate in addition to being an area where the ships of the base infidels renew their water supplies. Since they pillage and plunder the goods and chattels of travellers, a castle has been built on that site through my auspicious favour. To make it flourishing and prosperous, let five hundred households exempt from taxes be settled there.[433]

On 29 September 1574 the construction of a bridge was ordered in Payas, again using state funds from Aleppo.[434] The extant bridge, about fifty metres away from the south end of the *arasta*, is sited on the road to Belen, where the leaking caravansaray of Sultan Süleyman's complex was renovated in 1570. The salaries of the mosque staff were increased in 1574, the same year the neighbouring halting station in Payas was completed.[435] On 1 October 1574, the governor of Uzeyr was instructed to prepare a ship in Payas for carrying stones and another one for raking the silted harbour.[436] Another decree, dated 25 April 1574, informs the governor of Adana and the finance minister of Aleppo that the twenty wardens appointed to guard the castle at Payas had to be supplemented by twenty others whose wages would be paid from Aleppo.[437]

Decrees issued between 1575 and 1580 concern the construction of a moat around the castle, a project supervised by the governor of Adana and financed by the treasury of Aleppo.[438] The decree sent on 5 August 1577 to the governor-general and the finance minister of Aleppo complains that the digging of the moat had been delayed. They are ordered to appoint Abdülnebi, 'one of the architects of Aleppo (*Ḥaleb miʿmārlarından*)', who had visited the capital to promise he would complete the moat quickly and cheaply if ten persons were assigned for the job from the castle of Aleppo together with 'master masons' (*üstādlar*) of his own choice.[439] The moat was finished in 1580, when an architect was sent from the capital to prepare a correct estimate of its costs.[440] Another structure erected in 1577 is the fortified square tower near the seashore, about a kilometre away from the main castle. The governor and the kadi of Uzeyr and Mustafa Çavuş were ordered to build this 'strong tower in the manner of (*üslūb*) the Maiden's Tower across from the imperial palace in Istanbul' on a site they deemed 'decorous and appropriate' (*vecih ve münāsib*), and to have it guarded by four artillerymen and a sufficient number of wardens. Evliya Çelebi says the watch tower protected the customs house of the landing station.[441]

Like the imperial castle, Sokollu's mosque complex seems to have been constructed by local masters imported from Syria and south Anatolia, where Ottoman and Mamluk architectural practices creatively mingled. The grand vizier's constructions in Aleppo make it all the more likely that some of the masons were brought in from that city. The treatment of the complex as a single organically integrated block, in which individual buildings are not free-standing structures, recalls the spatial organization of Mamluk complexes. Its regional architectural features include the trefoil arch, monumental portals articulated with striped polychrome masonry, and the construction technique of the shopping arcade and caravansaray block dominated by cross vaulting (illus. 347).

The Ottoman style is reduced to its basic common denominator, the cube and the hemispherical dome, in the 'minimalist' architecture of the complex. The provincial character of the mosque is reflected in its simple proportions, the heavy flying buttresses of its small dome with pendentives raised on a window-pierced octagonal drum, the squat proportions of its single-galleried cylindrical minaret with a pointed cap, its cubical walls with few windows, its asymmetrical eight-bay portico, its striped polychrome muqarnas-hooded portal and mihrab, and its lack of tile revetments commonly used in such cities as Aleppo and Damascus (illus. 348–50). The only remaining inscriptions inside the whitewashed prayer hall are painted roundels with the revered names on its arched window lunettes. The right side of the polychrome marble mihrab has been cut off to accommodate a wooden minbar, suggesting that the sanctuary may initially have been designed as a masjid and subsequently converted into a Friday mosque.

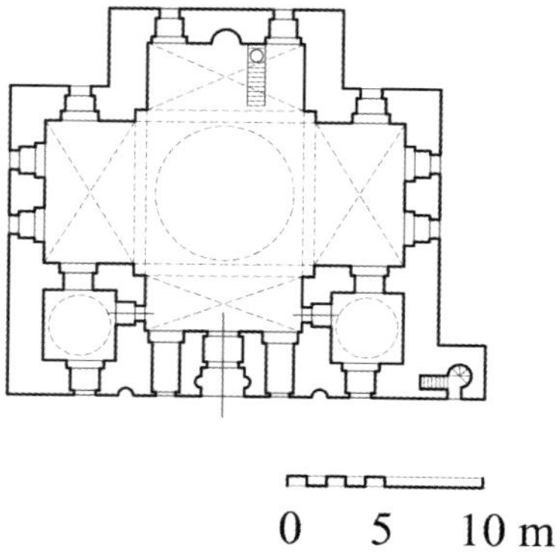

351 Plan of the Sokollu mosque.

The ambiguous status of the Friday mosque in Payas is hinted at by its classification in the *Tuḥfe* at the end of the list of masjids (an ambiguity also reflected in Sokollu's waqfiyya). The absence of a monumental assembly hall for sufi rituals in the fountained garden court of the convent implies that the mosque itself fulfilled that function. Its atypical cruciform plan, composed of a central dome (8 metres) and four cross-vaulted iwans, recalls that of the Belen mosque, which the *Tuḥfe* identifies as a convent (*tekye*) (illus. 45, 351). With its two small double-storey rooms flanking both sides of its gate, the unusual plan of the Payas mosque harks back to multifunctional early Ottoman convent-masjids featuring attached guest-rooms. The corner rooms, marked by external domes, exemplify the longer life the T-type plan enjoyed in the recently colonized provinces of Diyarbakır and Aleppo.[442]

Ottoman writers generally attribute the creation of the whole town of Payas, including its imperial fortifications and bridge, to Sokollu. Hasanbeyzade, for instance, writes: 'On the road to Aleppo and Damascus, [he built] the Payas castle with solid foundations, a noble mosque, khans, a bath-house, shops, and other charitable buildings that are beyond description and narration.'[443] Evliya Çelebi, who stayed there for two days in 1648 during his pilgrimage to Mecca, gratefully acknowledges the food he ate in Sokollu's many hospices administered by the sons of İbrahim Khan and adds: 'But from all his pious foundations, the most necessary and indispensable one is this city of Payas, a passage place of hajj pilgrims, which was once a dangerous pass he rendered prosperous. It is now a charming city, safe and well-kept, flourishing and adorned, filled with gardens, vineyards, and rose-gardens.'[444]

Evliya says the populous city of 850 mudbrick houses had armed soldiers, pass guards, and tax-exempt inhabitants, who protected pilgrims and merchants from 'infidel pirates' and 'mountain robbers,' enabling them to travel safely by land and sea.[445] The castle was kept by wardens who guarded the port with cannons, and 'since it is the port of Aleppo, it is a major frontier'. He nevertheless notes the deteriorated state of the silted harbour:

> In old days it is said to have been a very fine port.
> With the passage of time it is no longer as prosperous …
> Some ships still enter it, but big caravels, *burtuns*, and galleons do not come to moor there. All ships anchor at some distance in the open sea. It is a safe and anchor-holding harbour, protected from the eight winds.
> And at the left side of the castle moat is an exhilarating law court of the Prophet's manifest shariʿa.[446]

Evliya comments on the 'Aristotle-like' grand vizier's incredible wealth in 'that age of abundance', so much so that Sokollu did not even glance at the account book recording the great sum spent on this complex. His lavishly decorated mosque was the only one in Payas where the khutba was pronounced on Fridays, all the rest being convents (*zāviye*). Evliya identifies Sokollu as the patron of the bridge, castle, bath-house, bazaar, khan, hospice, mosque, and madrasa (apparently the convent was converted into a madrasa despite the waqfiyya stipulation):[447]

> And in front of the castle gate is a mulberry tree. And in this place is a fortress-like huge khan with iron gates. The date over its gate is 1007 [1598, *sic*]. The gate of this khan faces the castle gate. The khan is very elaborate, embellished, prosperous, and flourishing with many private rooms, stables for horses and camels, a hospice, a banqueting house, and a wide courtyard. It is a retreat and a house of kindness for all travellers. And near this khan is an artistic and wonderful mosque similar to the mosque of [Hadım] İbrahim Pasha inside the Silivri gate of Istanbul. Its mihrab and minbar are very artistic. Its length and width are eighty feet, and it is a very charming and adorned, lovable mosque. Its courtyard is an excursion spot and an outing place, like a sign of the gardens of paradise. It has a large congregation, being located inside the town, and is a light-filled structure that resembles a royal mosque (*selāṭīn miṣāl*). In the middle of its mirth-increasing, spacious courtyard is a latticed pool surrounded by ablution spouts that flow night and day for the renewal of ablutions. And the environs of that pool are decked with many citrus trees. Under their shade, breathing the air infused with the pleasing odour of lemon and orange blossoms, the brains of the populous congregation become perfumed and scented as they worship God. This mosque has two gates; one of them is the gate of the prayer hall opening towards the qibla, which has another chronogram [empty], and the other gate faces the mulberry tree. And the interior of the mosque is an illuminated dome of light. Its iron-grilled windows with mother-of-pearl-inlaid shutters have intricately inlaid Murano glass and crystal panes through which brilliant sunlight enters the interior of the mosque. The likes of its ornate muezzin's tribune are not to be found in any other mosque. Neither are its candlesticks and many hanging pendants and embroidered silk carpets found in other mosques. In short, the castle, mosque, khan, hospice, masjid [mekteb?], madrasa, bazaar, and bath-house – all of them masonry buildings entirely covered with indigo-blue lead – constitute a flourishing city. All of these charitable and pious constructions were the works of the martyred ghazi Sokollu Mehmed Pasha.[448]

Compared to Sokollu's complex in Lüleburgaz, the one in Payas is described by fewer European travellers, as it lay beyond the itinerary of diplomatic delegations. The Austrian Baron Johann Christoph Tayfel (1588), who travelled there by ship from Cairo, attributes the 'enlargement of the port of Payas (Beas), where Syria begins', to the late grand vizier Mehmed Pasha, who built its castle and adjoining complex:

> The said Pasha also ordered there the construction of a very strong castle, with an important caravansaray, near which is a beautiful mosque, a bath, a school, and a bazaar. The caravansaray contains many beautiful rooms and fountains, as well as provisions given to all travellers, both Christians and Turks: wood, candles, and food for three days without any payment.[449]

Tayfel and his companions moved on with a caravan via Bakras to Aleppo, 'the third major city after Hormuz and Babylonia (Baghdad), where merchandise arriving from India was unloaded 'thanks to the neighbouring port'. He notes the continuing importance of Tripoli, where many European merchants resided, as the port of Aleppo.[450] Smaller than Tripoli yet closer to Aleppo, Payas functioned as a secondary port particularly linked with Egypt and Cyprus.

A decade later, Fynes Moryson (1596) refers to 'Bias' as a 'pleasant village' six miles away from İskenderun, the new port of Aleppo that suffered from 'pestilent aire'. He observes that Payas abounded with fruits, 'silkeworms', and 'all things necessarie to sustaine life'.[451] Despite the competition since the 1590s of İskenderun as the preferred port of foreign merchants, the Jewish pilgrim Samuel D. Yemshel (1641–42) identifies Payas as an active port of Aleppo where he spent a day on his way back from Jerusalem:

> From Belen (Bakras) we arrived at a city along the seashore called İskenderun. Continuing to move on our way, we arrived at noon in the city of Payas. There are many fresh waters here, but they are not drinkable. The town is on the coast. Because this is the port of Aleppo, the ships of Europeans and Egyptians come here. They sell their merchandise to the Aleppines and leave with the goods they take from Aleppo. It has a strong small castle, a mosque, a bath-house, and approximately 130 shops where goods imported from Egypt are sold. We rested here on Saturday. Beyond a tower on the castle walls extend many gardens. The road from Aleppo to Payas is five days. The road to Tripoli, which is the port of Damascus, is three days away [from Payas].[452]

The resilience of Payas as a port and caravan station until the eighteenth century bears testimony to its founder's astute vision.[453] Imperial decrees show that Sokollu's pious foundation could not have been created without the support of the state apparatus through which his building activities were steered and the town was populated. As in Büyükçekmece and Szigetvár, his monuments in Payas were seamlessly appended to imperial edifices in a manner that blurred the boundary between private and state patronage. This contributed to the assumption that the whole town was the personal creation of the grand vizier, whose identity became conflated with the centralized imperial government he personified.

THE MOSQUE IN AZAPKAPI

Sokollu's early career as a grand admiral of the Ottoman navy may have played a role in the creation of the imperial arsenal in Payas, next to which he built his own pious foundation. The prestige mosque he subsequently commissioned Sinan to design in Azapkapı is sited near the Kasımpaşa arsenal outside Galata, which he had refurbished during his tenure as grand admiral between 1546 and 1549 with the construction of 117 covered storage spaces behind each ship vault (illus. 352, 353).[454] When Selim II ordered Sokollu to rebuild the fleet decimated in Lepanto, eight new vaults for ship construction were added to the Kasımpaşa arsenal on grounds borrowed from an imperial garden that bordered the Golden Horn. There, the grand vizier supervised the construction of eight mahones, supplemented by 150 galleys completed in record time during the winter of 1572. The reassurance he gave to the grand admiral, Kılıç Ali Pasha, who questioned the feasibility of refitting the whole fleet in a short time, became legendary: 'This exalted state is so powerful and mighty that it is possible to overhaul the whole armada with anchors of silver, ropes of silk thread, and sails of atlas, should a firman order it!'[455]

During the peace negotiations of 1573, which affirmed Ottoman supremacy in the Mediterranean, Sokollu is said to have boasted to Marcantonio Barbaro: 'We cut your arm by conquering Cyprus and you cut our beard by destroying our fleet; a severed arm does not grow back, but a shaved beard grows even thicker than before!'[456] In the winter of 1574 Sokollu was once again ordered by Selim II to refit the fleet at the arsenal for the reconquest of Tunis from Spanish invaders. This time he prepared 268 galleys, 15 mahones and 15 galleons with which the fort of Goletta was conquered that summer under the command of the grand admiral Kılıç Ali Pasha and the vizier Koca Sinan Pasha.[457]

The Azapkapı mosque alongside the imperial arsenal, then, marked yet another site associated with memories of Sokollu's career extending all the way back to his youthful days as a grand admiral. It was commissioned towards the end of his life as a personal memorial, prominently inserted into the seascape of the capital. It complemented the less visible mosque complex that he and his wife had endowed next to the old arsenal in Kadırgalimanı. The commemorative dimension of Sokollu's Azapkapı mosque is proclaimed by its foundation inscription, which emphasizes the proximity of its location to the shipbuilding ateliers of the arsenal where he had revamped the fleet in 1572 and 1574. The Turkish inscription, in two lines of *thuluth*, is carved on a rectangular marble panel with eight compartments, placed inside the northwest staircase of the upper-storey mosque:

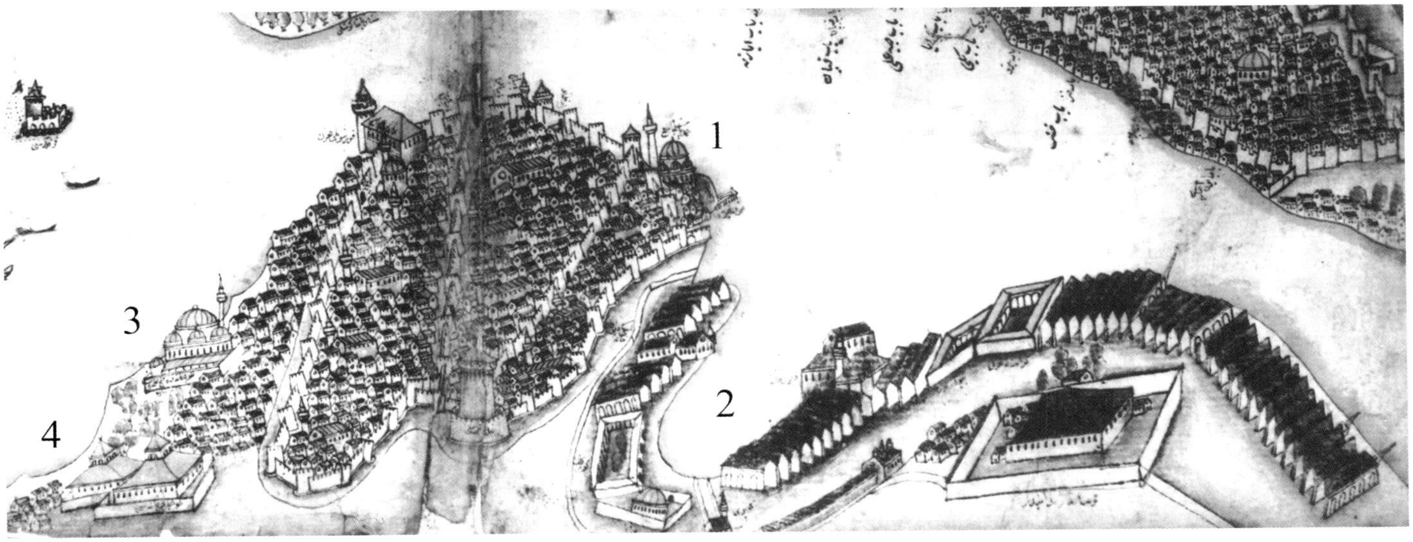

352 Detail from the Piri Reis map (illus. 104): 1. Azapkapı mosque. 2. Kasımpaşa arsenal. 3. Kılıç Ali Pasha mosque. 4. Tophane (cannon foundry).

The grand Asaph, the praiseworthy Muhammed, the Pasha
  of the epoch,
The donor of this admirable pious foundation and the
  source of favour and munificence,

Having built this adorned Friday mosque along the seashore,
Duplicated its edifice in masonry at the present time.

The people of the Faith gathered on the site of the arsenal,
And prayed five times a day to request God's mercy for
  its founder.

With hands lifted in worship, the mysterious voice said its
  date:
'The mosque of the Asaph, the sanctuary of God, the
  place of worship,' 985 (1577–78).'[458]

This inscription implies that Sokollu had erected a simpler mosque near the arsenal (*dārü's-ṣanā'a*) which he subsequently monumentalized by rebuilding it in masonry.[459] Its foundations were probably laid sometime after 1572, before the compilation of the grand vizier's waqfiyya in 1574, to celebrate his efforts in resuscitating the armada together with Kılıç Ali Pasha. Gerlach mentions Sokollu's mosque 'in Galata by the seashore' in 1576, pointing out that he owned galley slaves kept at the imperial arsenal together with those of the grand admiral and the sultan. The grand vizier likely used those slaves as labourers in building the Azapkapı mosque, just as Kılıç Ali Pasha did later on in the construction of his waterfront mosque at Tophane (1578–83) outside the other end of the Galata walls (illus. 352).[460] On 27 June 1578 a memorandum sent by the Venetian Senate to the *bailo* in Istanbul mentions the preparation of bottle-glass requested by the grand vizier.[461] Another letter dated 22 October 1579 informs the *bailo* that the eight large mosque lanterns Sokollu

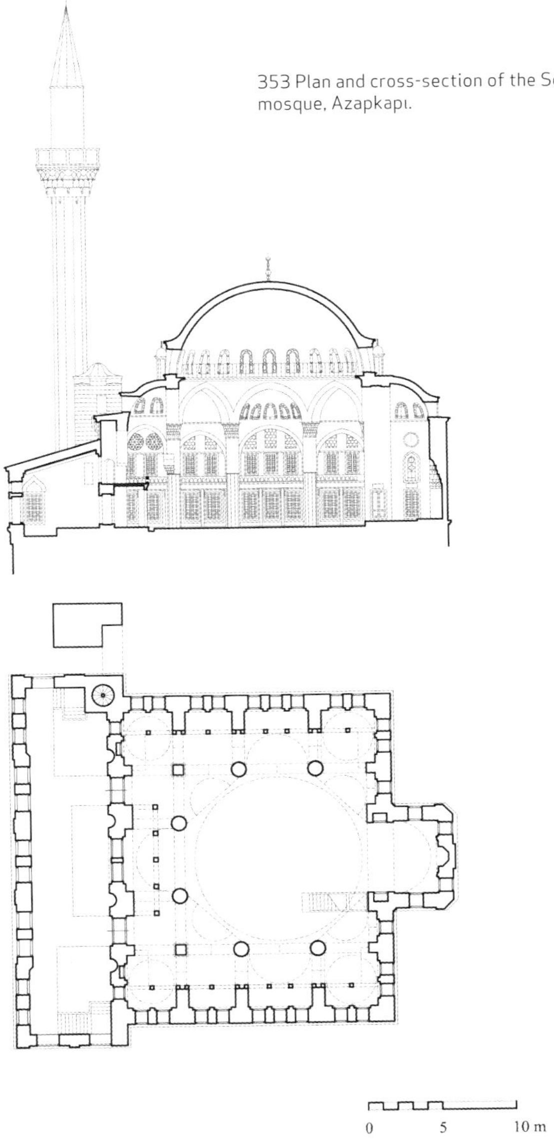

353 Plan and cross-section of the Sokollu mosque, Azapkapı.

354 Thomas Allom's view of the Golden Horn with the Azapkapı mosque (left) and the Süleymaniye (right), from Robert Walsh's *Constantinople* . . . (London, 1838).

had solicited would be sent there soon.[462] These orders from Murano must have been intended for the Azapkapı mosque.

Sokollu's waqfiyya describes the mosque that would be completed within a few years as if it already existed in 1574, likening it to a bubble by the waterfront (illus. 354):

> And near the capital, Kostantiniyya, which is the beauty mole of the face of Rum and the pupil of the eye of all cultivated lands, outside the Azapkapı (*ʿAzebler ḳapusı*) gate of Galata's city wall, he built along the seashore a heart-attracting upper-storey (*fevḳānī*) Friday mosque and a pleasure-giving sanctuary like the vault of the heavens, peerless on the face of the earth. The arch of its captivating mihrab is a corner of pleasure and the stairs of its minbar are the unreachable ladder of the sky of salvation. Verse: 'The new moon turned its stature into an arc, / To become a gold doorknocker on its gate.' The sumptuous and soaring dome became a pleasant bubble on the lip of the sea.[463]

The waqfiyya also mentions the 'charming' elementary school built 'behind the imperial arsenal' at the north side of the mosque, two fountains near the mosque (one of them inside the Azapkapı gate and the other outside it), and the well next to the mosque staircase (removed during modern renovations).[464] Moreover, two reservoirs were endowed, near the elementary school and at the Kasımpaşa landing station further north.[465]

The school was accompanied by two houses, one endowed for its teacher, who served as the imam of the mosque, and the other for the four muezzins. On behalf of his late mother's soul, the residents of these houses had to read the Koran manuscripts donated by the grand vizier to his school. She was buried nearby, next to her two sons, who had passed away in their youth while they were being educated as royal pages (they had been recruited from Sokolovići with Sokollu's effort).[466] The grand vizier also endowed Koran manuscripts for his mosque, where thirty sections of the holy book were read daily as a pious offering to the Prophet. The waqfiyya stipulates that five sections of the Koran be recited at the mosque for its founder, five sections for the soul of his mother, ten sections for the souls of his brothers (Mustafa and İbrahim) interred in Kasımpaşa, and ten others for his late sons buried in Eyüp. Sokollu also endowed nineteen large, sixteen medium-sized, and six small carpets (*ḳaliçe*) for his mosque, together with four prayer carpets (*seccāde*).[467]

The pious foundation in Azapkapı was supported by income-producing structures constructed in its neighbourhood, named after the dormitory of marines (*ʿazeb*). The inhabitants of that quarter included captains engaged in commercial traffic, merchants, and artisans such as carpenters and caulkers.[468] We learn from Sokollu's waqfiyya that the vaulted substructure of his *extra-muros* upper-storey mosque contained eleven warehouses and three shops (illus. 355). In its vicinity, forty-six two-storey masonry shops were built in three rows, along with twenty-four places for two-oared boats (*pereme yirleri*) on the waterfront. Five more shops were constructed outside the Galata wall, separated by a street from the mosque, along with a commercial double bath inside the Azapkapı gate.[469] Other endowed commercial properties were spread along the seaside gates of Galata and at the Kasımpaşa landing of the arsenal, where twenty places for two-oared boats were created.[470]

Sinan's autobiographies mention the Azapkapı mosque and its bath-house, but they omit the elementary school, no longer

355 Sokollu mosque, Azapkapı, from the west.

extant.[471] The seventeenth-century author Eremya Çelebi describes the environs of the Azapkapı gate: 'Here there is a large mosque and a landing stage continually overflowing with all kinds of provisions. On both sides one can observe many large shops for ironworkers who forge large iron cannonballs needed in ships and other objects. Ships are caulked here before navigating, and they are supplied with sails, ropes, and other implements.'[472] Some of the endowed commercial structures near the mosque must have been rebuilt after they were destroyed in a fire recorded by Selaniki:

> On the night of 30 May 1596, a fire erupted by God's decree near the late Mehmed Pasha's mosque outside Galata, burning the shops in front of it and the upper-storey cells used as warehouses of tools and implements for ships. Until the magnificent viziers and janissaries arrived to extinguish it, that whole wing was consumed by flames.[473]

Today the cleared area around the mosque is occupied by a modern park created between 1938 and 1941 that raised the ground level around it. It was then that the basement arches and gates of the extensively renovated mosque were walled over.[474] The north façade of the mosque is dwarfed by the Atatürk bridge that looms over it, separating it from the arsenal dockyards further to the north. A print by Thomas Allom captures the former eminence of the mosque along the waterfront and its inescapable visual connection with the looming Süleymaniye across the Golden Horn (illus. 354). The site also encourages a dialogue with Rüstem Pasha's octagonal-baldachined Tahtakale mosque on the opposite shore. Sokollu's memorial monument, the second mosque with an octagonal support system designed by Sinan in the capital, competes with its predecessor by cultivating the post-classical idiom inaugurated in the Selimiye (illus. 5). Both grand vizierial upper-storey mosques lack accompanying complexes, and both are raised on vaulted basements with commercial substuctures. Lacking precinct walls, they seamlessly merge with their bustling neighbourhoods. The dome of the Azapkapı mosque, surrounded by eight weight turrets, and its projecting mihrab unequivocally allude to the Selimiye (illus. 355–56). It is a scaled-down grand vizierial version of the sultanic mosque built for Sokollu's father-in-law, during whose reign he enjoyed unlimited authority as the true master of the empire.

The nearly square plan of the more centralized Azapkapı mosque differs from the laterally set, rectangular layout of Rüstem Pasha's mosque in Tahtakale. Its amply fenestrated, screen-like façades are typical of the post-classical idiom. Its moderately scaled 11.8-metre dome, smaller than the domes of Rüstem Pasha's mosque (15.2 metres) and that of İsmihan Sultan in Kadırga (13 metres), is in keeping with Sokollu's cautious restraint. Unlike the Tahtakale mosque, which remained partially hidden behind the Byzantine sea walls, the fully-exposed Azapkapı mosque is perched at the very edge of the Golden Horn. Its innovative features include a free-standing minaret with a fountain attached to its base, placed at the northeast rather than the usual northwest corner. It is connected to the body of the mosque across a lane by means of a lofty arch supporting a domed room for muezzins. Its position on firmer ground away from the narrow waterfront has the additional advantage of increasing the audibility of the call to prayer. Having suffered damage, the minaret was rebuilt during the nineteenth century in a Europeanizing style, this was in turn replaced in the 1950s with the present one in the classical manner.[475]

A unique characteristic of the mosque is its covered upper-storey vestibule, a substitute for the traditional domed portico, which lends it a palatial aura (illus. 357). Featuring a slanting shed roof, the vestibule is lined with a row of rectangular windows surmounted by arched openwork lunettes typical of Sinan's late style. The north façade is raised on a basement with two arched gates at both ends and vaulted shops (now walled in). The stringcourse moulding that separates the basement from the

356 (top) Sokollu mosque, Azapkapı, from the southeast.

357 Sokollu mosque, Azapkapı, from the northwest.

358 (top) Sokollu mosque, Azapkapı, interior toward the qibla wall.

359 Sokollu mosque interior toward the anti-qibla wall.

360 Sokollu mosque interior, detail of west gallery with bookshelves.

upper-storey mosque envelops the whole building, as in several mosques designed by Sinan in the late 1570s and 1580s (Kılıç Ali Pasha, Muradiye, Mesih Mehmed Pasha).

Another deviation from the norm is the north façade of the prayer hall, reached by two stairways at both ends of the basement. The conventional mosque gate flanked by two prayer platforms, each with a mihrab, is replaced here by a pair of gates inserted between three prayer platforms with four mihrabs. The small platforms at both ends have single mihrabs; the wider central platform with two mihrabs has superimposed pairs of windows in the middle, which provide late-coming worshippers with a view of the prayer hall.[476] The rectangular windows omit the standard lunettes with inscriptions, and the façade is entirely composed of contiguous window frames, doors, and mihrabs. The two arched gates, which lack muqarnas hoods, facilitated the circulation of the congregation in the absence of gates on the lateral walls (the idiosyncratic mosque of the grand admiral Piyale Pasha (*c.* 1565–73) near the Kasımpaşa arsenal also has a façade with two gates).[477]

The tall lateral façades of the Azapkapı mosque, structurally freed from the autonomous octagonal baldachin, no longer reflect the configuration of inner space (illus. 355–56). Perforated by inventively grouped windows with contiguous or closely spaced frames in three tiers, these façades are subdivided into rectangular fields by vertical strips of masonry. Their asymmetrical composition echoes the off-centre disposition of the domical superstructure, which is shifted to the south of the central axis of the prayer hall. This visual imbalance is compounded by the covered vestibule, which, unlike the double portico of Rüstem Pasha's mosque, is not treated as an element independent from the lateral façades. The 'lopsidedness' of the superstructure is caused by the repetition of the half-dome over the projecting mihrab at the north side of the mosque. Hence, the four small domes that mark the corners of the prayer hall are unevenly spaced in relation to the central dome. The window-pierced drum is encircled by eight tall weight turrets with domical caps that articulate the internal piers. They alternate with four shallow exedras framed by stepped extrados and four half-domes, whose undulating lips resemble those of the dome crowning Rüstem Pasha's mosque. With the exception of the stone weight turrets, all surfaces of the superstructure are covered by lead.

As Jale Erzen notes, the innovative unclassical aspects of Sinan's post-Selimiye mosques in the capital have generally been disparaged as symptoms of decline.[478] Kuran criticizes the lack of coordination between the off-centre domical superstructure and the substructure of walls, which he says 'lessens the mosque's aesthetic impact'.[479] Goodwin detects signs of Sinan's 'declining power' in the interior configuration (illus. 358, 359).[480] He draws attention to the 'inevitable weakness' of a plan that requires secondary columns to support the northwest and northeast exedras, resulting in cluttered north corners: 'The overall effect is a busy one except in the central area of the hall, while from the outside the quantity of windows gives the impression that they were inserted everywhere possible, just as at Zal Mahmud Pasha.'[481] The U-shaped inner gallery, mimicking that of the Selimiye, adds to the crowded feeling inside the prayer hall. The upper galleries are raised on dainty Bursa arches, which alternate with the inner buttresses featuring built-in bookshelves (illus. 360). The arches that span the buttresses above the galleries partially mask the topmost tier of windows on the lateral walls.

Conceived as a delightful shore pavilion, the radiant prayer hall is portrayed in its waqfiyya as a heavenly dome of pleasure. With its view-commanding, multi-tiered windows it prefigures the palatial façades of Shahsultan and Zal Mahmud Pasha's jointly endowed mosque (1577–90) along the Eyüp waterfront, to which I shall turn next. The windows of its west galleries offer spectacular seascape vistas. Their ground-level 'booths', separated by buttresses, constitute intimate private spaces recalling palatial alcoves designed to afford delectable views (illus. 360). The sumptuous stained glass windows of the qibla wall were renewed in 1941 together with the damaged İznik tile revetments of the eight dome spandrels, which were replaced with modern replicas manufactured in Kütahya; these bear roundels with revered names. The remaining İznik tiles are said to have been stolen, but the internal walls, almost entirely covered with windows, hardly have any surface available for tile revetments.[482]

Unlike the lavishly tiled mosque of İsmihan Sultan in Kadırga, the main ornaments of Sokollu's mosque are profuse windows, which bathe its cheerful interior with light. The stained glass windows, painted decorations, and inscriptions have been completely renewed. The only inscription on the superstructure is a painted calligraphic roundel that quotes the same cosmic verse repeated on the domes of the Kadırga and Lüleburgaz mosques (35:41).[483] The standard mihrab verse (3:37) carved above the muqarnas hood of the mihrab is accompanied by the profession of faith painted under its framing arch. The carved stone inscriptions on the rectangular window lunettes of the mihrab recess quote the Throne verse (2:255), which affirms God's absolute sovereignty over the heavens and the earth.

Evliya Çelebi provides a brief description of Sokollu's charming mosque, which he attributes to Sinan:

> It is an illuminated mosque in the manner of royal mosques. All its windows overlook the sea. And all its domes and its well-proportioned minaret with a single gallery are strongly built. Because this mosque is sited on a narrow plot on the lip of the sea, its minaret has been placed on the left side across a lane. It is a lofty, well-proportioned stone minaret. And being located by a landing station, this crowded mosque has a very large congregation.[484]

İsmihan Sultan's mosque at Kadırga, often associated with Sokollu, reinterpreted the classical synthesis of the Süleymaniye. The grand vizier's own mosque in Azapkapı is a miniature version of the Selimiye, with which it begs comparison. Built during Murad III's reign, at a time when Sokollu's authority was beginning to dwindle, it is a personal memorial touting his service to the imperial naval forces during Selim II's sultanate, dominated by military expeditions in the Mediterranean. The anti-Safavid war initiated in 1578, just when the mosque was reaching completion, signalled the emergence of new political orientations. The end of the classical era, anticipated by the manneristic features of the Azapkapı mosque, would be signalled by the grand vizier's assassination the following year.

IV. SHAHSULTAN AND THE VIZIER ZAL MAHMUD PASHA

With its domed mausoleum where they lie buried side by side, the posthumously built mosque complex of Shahsultan and Zal Mahmud Pasha is a poignant memorial to their legendary love (illus. 361–62). The waqfiyya of their jointly endowed complex, registered in 1593, explains that they passed away within two weeks in 1577 and were entombed together in Eyüp according to their last will.[485] Unlike her siblings, who were interred at the imperial mausoleum of their parents, Selim II and Nurbanu Sultan, at Hagia Sophia, Shahsultan preferred to be buried with her beloved husband.[486]

Born in Manisa in 1545, Shahsultan was one of three 'famous sultanas' who married favoured statesmen in a triple wedding in 1562, the year their father became heir apparent to the throne. The ranks of the fortunate bridegrooms corresponded to the relative seniority of each princess: the 'old sultana', İsmihan, was given to the second vizier Sokollu Mehmed Pasha; the 'second sultana', Gevherhan, to the grand admiral Piyale Pasha; and the 'third sultana', Shahsultan, to the janissary agha Çakırcıbaşı Hasan.[487] Shahsultan's first husband had accomplished the sensitive mission of strangling the rebel prince Bayezid and his sons at the Safavid court. Upon marrying the seventeen-year-old princess, he was promoted sanjak governor of Bosnia (1563–64), and then to governor-general of Rumelia (1570–71), but he died shortly thereafter in 1574, having attained the honourary rank of vizier.[488]

That year the twenty-nine-year-old princess married the Bosnian-born vizier Zal Mahmud Pasha. Her second husband's main claim to fame was his strength as a wrestler, which had won him the title 'Zal' (the mythical Persian hero) after he had strangled prince Mustafa in 1553. Both of Shahsultan's husbands, then, contributed to her father's enthronement by eliminating rival princes. Peçevi gives the pasha's short biography and recounts the romantic myth that he and his wife expired in each other's arms:

> Exiting from the honourable imperial palace as chief gatekeeper, he subsequently attained fame as the governor-general of Aleppo [1564–65] and Anatolia [1566]. Then he rose to the rank of vizier [1567] and married among the sultan's daughters the widow of the governor-general of Rumelia, Hasan Pasha. During the execution of prince Mustafa, when the afflicted victim managed to escape from the clutches of executioners and started to flee towards the sultan [Süleyman],

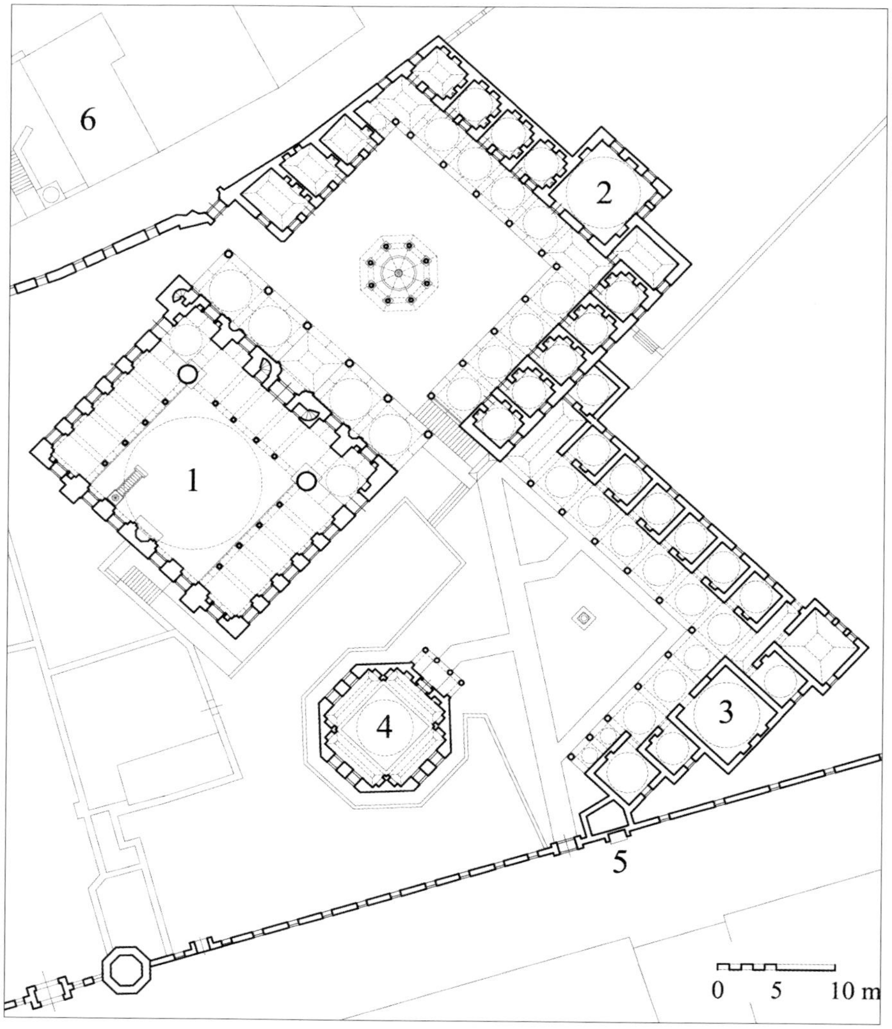

361 Plan of the Shahsultan and Zal Mahmud Pasha complex, Eyüp: 1. Mosque, 2. Madrasa of Shahsultan, 3. Madrasa of Zal Pasha, 4. Mausoleum, 5. Dated public fountain, 6. Pre-existing masjid of Silahi Mehmed Beg.

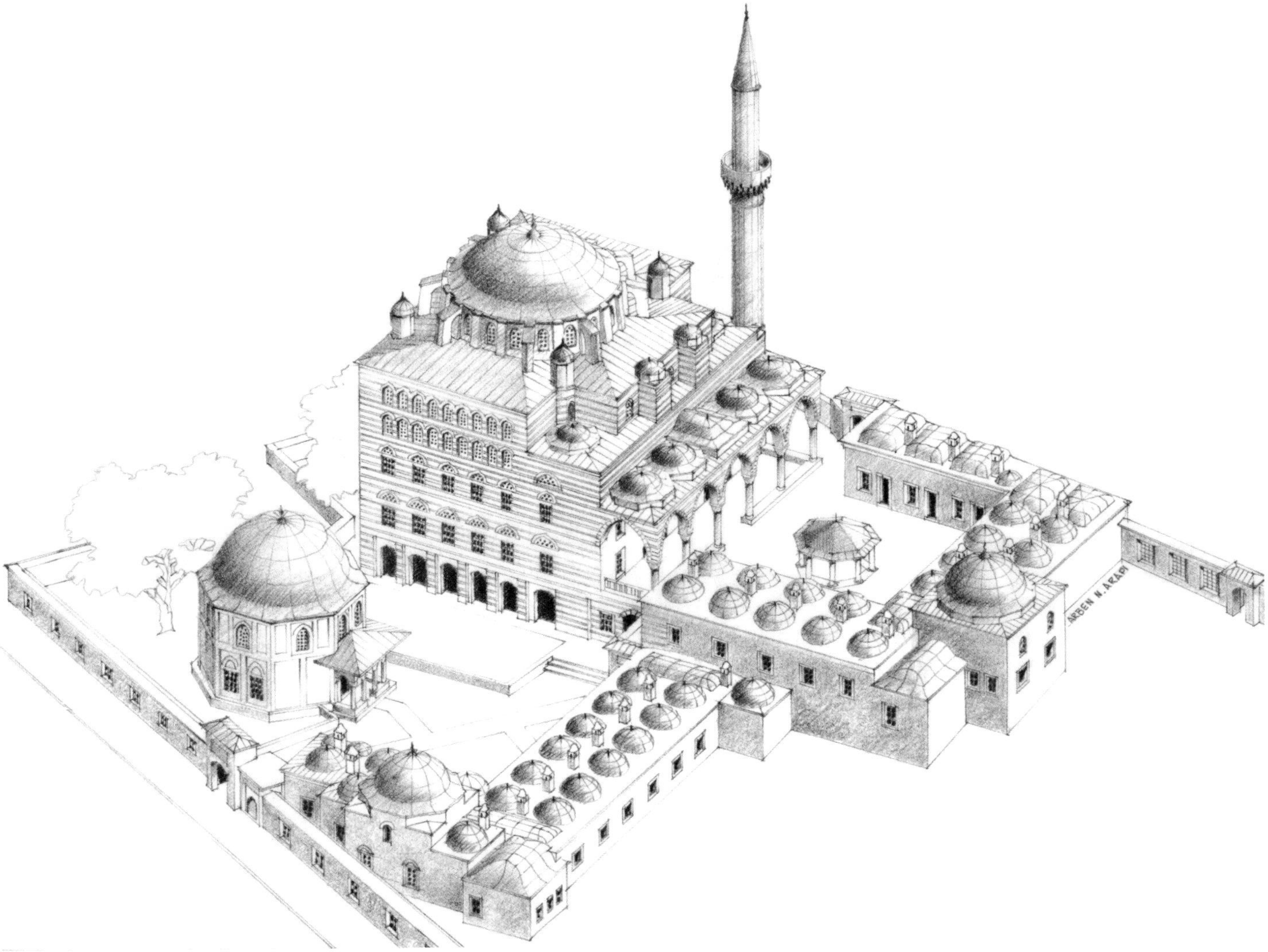

362 Axonometric projection of the Shahsultan and Zal Pasha complex, Eyüp.

> the above-mentioned [Mahmud], being an unequalled wrestler, had caught him and thrown him down. For that reason, he was seen worthy of his title [Zal]. In terms of justice and generosity he was a man of moderation, esteemed and respected among his peers. It is related that he became ill on the same day with his wife, the sultana, and that they both gave up their souls together after exchanging vows of mutual forgiveness and embracing each other. This was attributed to the perfection of their love, to such a degree that has not befallen any husband and wife.[489]

The Venetian diplomat Jacopo Ragazzoni (1571) refers to the pasha as the fifth vizier, who is 'a native of Bosnia, forty-eight years old, brave, strong in body, but not too intelligent'.[490] Nor did Marcantonio Tiepolo (1576) find Murad III's brother-in-law particularly praiseworthy: 'Although he is a very good person, he has negligible understanding of things and consequently is not much esteemed.'[491] His happy marriage with Shahsultan lasted only about three years (1574–77). The enamoured couple did not, however, pass away on the same day. We learn from their joint waqfiyya that the vizier died first on 22 October 1577, with his devoted wife following him to the other world after thirteen days. Gerlach's diary gives an eyewitness account of their successive funeral processions to Eyüp:

> On 22 October [1577] the deceased vizier Mahmud Pasha was buried. At the head of his coffin, decked with a coloured fabric in the manner of their cenotaphs, stood a turban. In front of it walked many people and the priests chanted various hymns for God to have mercy on him. Before the coffin paraded his chief gatekeeper, his steward, and other high-ranking Turks. His weeping servants walked by the side of the coffin and behind it. Then rode his son,

363 Shahsultan and Zal Pasha complex, Eyüp, from the north end of the upper street.

364 Eyüp with the mosque of Shahsultan and Zal Pasha, the shrine complex of Ayyub al-Ansari, and the hilltop mosque of Mihrümah Sultan in Edirnekapı at the upper-right corner.

who wore a black robe and a turban like the pashas who followed him, [Sokollu] Mehmed, [Güzelce] Ahmed, and [Koca] Sinan. The governor-generals of Rumelia and Anatolia and the agha of janissaries wore smaller turbans and black attire. Otherwise, no particular order was observed as the crowd moved to and fro until [they reached] Eyüp, where he was buried. His widow is Sultan Selim's daughter. Her father had given him a beautiful residence at the Hippodrome (Atmeydan).[492]

The pasha's residence was the palace of İbrahim Pasha (d. 1536) in the Hippodrome, loaned to Zal the year he rose to the vizierate.[493] Apparently born to an earlier wife, the late vizier's son Mehmed Beg, who was old enough to ride on a horse during the funeral, would grow up to hold various provincial governorships.[494] Gerlach reports that on 26 October 1577 fifty young pages and thirty older servants of the deceased pasha's household were transferred to the imperial palace; among the remaining slave servants those without letters of manumission were sold by his widow.[495] On 4 November, the princess herself was buried in Eyüp 'without special pomp':

> At the head of her coffin was a bejewelled small woman's hat of gold and in its middle a belt of gold with jewels, the width of a palm, worth many thousand ducats. Many people walked in front of it and at the back. Behind them rode [Sokollu] Mehmed Pasha and the chief army judge of Rumelia, followed by [Lala] Mustafa Pasha, [Güzelce] Ahmed Pasha, [Koca] Sinan Pasha, the chief army judge of Anatolia, the governor-general of Rumelia, and the janissary agha, all attired in black. The janissaries wore turbans instead of their usual headgear.[496]

The couple's hitherto unknown waqfiyya explains in detail how their posthumous monument was financed and built (Appendix 2). The pasha and princess had each left behind a written will, donating one-third of their inheritance for the construction of a joint mosque and madrasa complex.[497] Shahsultan's will requested her reigning brother, Murad III, and her royal sisters to give up their legal shares of the remaining two-thirds of her inheritance, which they generously did.[498] Shahsultan selected her mother Nurbanu Sultan (d. 1583) as the executor of her will. She begged the influential queen mother, a notable 'patroness of charitable foundations', to diligently oversee the commencement and completion of the mosque complex in accordance with the reigning monarch's 'sublime judgment'.

365 Mosque of Shahsultan and Zal Pasha, Eyüp, from the west.

The princess chose Hüseyin Agha b. Abdülmuin, the chief finance minister who had been her husband's council scribe, as endowment administrator. Whoever occupied the grand vizierate – at that time her brother-in-law Sokollu (d. 1579) – would oversee the endowment.[499]

Shahsultan's project could not have been in better hands. The mosque complex was built under the joint supervision of the queen mother and the endowment administrator, facilitated by orders from the sultan and the overseeing grand vizier. Hüseyin Agha was handed a sum of 5,875,663 aspers, a third of the pasha's inheritance (2,857,655 aspers), plus that of the princess, which included the shares given up by her siblings (3,018,008 aspers). Shahsultan's richer estate comprised her own assets, her marriage dowry, and the inheritance from her late husband.[500] The properties that she endowed included fourteen villages in Plovdiv donated by her royal father in 1568.[501] Her husband's more modest endowments consisted of shops in Ankara and Plovdiv, and a public fountain and a bath-house with its own water channel in the Macedonian town of Prilep.[502]

The money was loaned out at interest and within a year and a half available funds rose to 6,007,155 aspers.[503] The mausoleum in Eyüp, the first structure to be built, cost 600,000 aspers.[504] Hüseyin Agha then spent 1,251,563 aspers to create an income-producing caravansaray and mills in Plovdiv.[505] Subsequently, the foundations of the mosque and its two madrasas were laid, probably around 1578–79. Because Hüseyin Agha was sent to the Safavid campaign (1578–90), he was absent for an extended period; to avoid further delays, a new endowment administrator was appointed in his stead, the couple's former household steward Mustafa Kethüda b. Abdurrahman.[506] It was he who completed the mosque and its twin madrasas, together with a water channel, and in parallel rows along an avenue bordering the Golden Horn twenty-four rental rooms, six shops, and a candle factory. Six of the rental rooms were endowed for the two imams and four muezzins; the largest room at the head of the seaside row was reserved for the waqf administrator. These structures cost 5,976,819 aspers.[507] Total construction expenses, then, amounted to 7,828,382 aspers.

Because revenues from the pasha's waqf were weaker than those of the princess, Mustafa Kethüda merged them into a single endowment in 1585–86 with the sultan's and grand vizier's permission. This merger had been recommended by the late queen mother, Nurbanu, before her death in 1583. Thereafter, the couple's accounts were no longer kept separately but were mixed together.[508] A decree sent by Murad III to the kadi of Eyüp and to the endowment administrator on 5 June 1583 indicates that there was not enough space for Shahsultan's madrasa (the upper madrasa attached to the mosque courtyard). The sultan authorizes them to buy a plot of land measuring 30 by 70 cubits from neighbouring waqfs.[509]

One of the imperial orders appended to the waqfiyya of 1593 approves the preparation of an endowment deed in April 1590, when the construction of the mosque, two madrasas, mausoleum, and commercial structures had just been completed (illus. 363). The sultan accepts Mustafa Kethüda's request to link the twin madrasas institutionally.[510] Professors of the lower-ranking 'outer' (*ḫāric*) madrasa along the Golden Horn, named after Zal Mahmud Pasha, would be promoted to Shahsultan's higher-ranking 'inner' (*dāḫil*) madrasa adjacent to the mosque courtyard.[511] The waqfiyya stipulates that endowment administrators and staff should be selected from the best of the pasha's and princess's freed household slaves, implying that they had no offspring.[512]

The complex took more than a decade to build, with delays caused by the change of waqf administrators and the queen mother's death. The inflation of 1584–85 seems to have had an additional adverse impact, possibly resulting in the use of cheaper materials in the madrasas and a sparse decorative programme. The date of construction has been a source of scholarly controversy, given the absence of a foundation inscription on the mosque portal. The chronogram of the public fountain adjacent to the gate of the precinct wall communicating with the avenue along the Golden Horn has added to the confusion. Ayvansarayi's description of the 'Friday mosque of Zal Mahmud Pasha' miscalculates the date yielded by that chronogram as 1551–52:

> Its builder was Mahmud Pasha and his illustrious wife, Shahsultan ... The two of them are buried in a tomb. There is a gallery (*mahfil*) in the blessed mosque but it is not elevated. There is a madrasa in the space before it and a *şādırvān* in the courtyard. [Because it is built on sloping ground], the mosque has a single storey on one side and two storeys on the side of the tomb. There is another madrasa of his opposite the tomb, and a fountain at the gate of the tomb courtyard. This is the chronogram of the fountain: 'Parched tongues composed this date: Fountain of soul-reviving water of life', 958 (1551–52)'.[513]

In actuality, the chronogram yields the date of 998 (1589–90); Ayvansarayi himself provides a correct reading of 'the chronogram of Zal Pasha's fountain' elsewhere:

> The patroness of the pious foundation Shahsultan
> Together with His Highness Zal Mahmud Pasha,
>
> In the service of God made this water free.
> May God make the fountain of paradise her recompense.
>
> Thirsty ones composed its date:
> 'Fountain of the soul-reviving water of life,'
> 998 (1589–90).[514]

On the basis of the misread chronogram, some scholars have dated the building to the early 1550s. Finding this date too early on stylistic grounds, others have ascribed it to the 1560s. Yet another group has dated the complex to the late 1570s, assuming that its construction was completed before the demise of the pasha, who is thought to have died in 1580.[515] Kuban, for instance, proposes a completion date before 1579, when the first madrasa professor was appointed, and he dismisses the fountain as an unrelated, pre-existing structure created in 1551. Kuran speculates that the complex was built between 1575 and 1580; he disregards the same fountain as a later addition of 1589–90, extraneous to Sinan's work.[516]

The chronogram of the fountain precisely coincides with the completion date of 1590 provided by the waqfiyya. The inscription clearly highlights the princess's priority as the primary patron, but Ayvansarayi names both the fountain and the mosque after her husband, even though he recognizes Shahsultan's contribution to them – another demonstration of husbands overshadowing their wives in the authorship of collaborative monuments. Sinan's autobiographies likewise identify the mosque complex as the pasha's work. The *Tuḥfe* refers to it as the 'noble Friday mosque of Zal Pasha in Eyüb Ensari, madrasa 2; his mausoleum is there [and he is buried] with his Sultan[a].'[517] The *Teẕkiretü'l-ebniye* omits the twin madrasas. The silencing of the princess's voice is particularly troubling both because she contributed more funds and more valuable endowed properties to this mutual project than did her husband, and because her dynastic connections were far more powerful than his. Selective amnesia erased her contribution from the collective memory, just as in the case of her older sister İsmihan Sultan, whose mosque in the jointly endowed complex in Kadırgalimanı was similarly named after her husband Sokollu.

Today the complex in Eyüp carries the name of Zal Mahmud Pasha. The highly unusual design of the mosque and the peculiarly asymmetrical layout of its madrasas have raised doubts about Sinan's having designed it. Most scholars attribute the complex to him, but Kuban thinks it may have been created by an assistant, because 'one is hard put to categorize this mosque as a work of Sinan consistent with his artistic development.'[518] It is not so easy to dismiss the chief architect's involvement in this major project, however, when one considers the high rank of its patrons and the clout of its building supervisors. The complex must have been designed by Sinan and intermittently supervised by him, even though it was completed after his demise in 1588.

Near the venerated shrine of Abu Ayyub al-Ansari, the site of the complex is referred to in its waqfiyya as 'a joy-giving and delight-increasing place along the waterfront' (illus. 106, 364, Map 3).[519] It was originally much closer to the shoreline, which has now been extended by a modern avenue:

> The noble Friday mosque has two venerable courtyards and an illuminated tall minaret. Its upper courtyard is surrounded by the rooms of the inner (*dāḫil*) madrasa, with an elegant ablution fountain (*şādırvān*) of flowing water in its centre for the believers. That unmatched cheerful courtyard is paved with marble. There are two grand avenues on both sides and two solid portals open to these

avenues. Across from the unequalled gate of the mosque is an elegant domed classroom surrounded by ten rooms for talented students and a room for the assistant professor, with several latrines in a far corner. The lower courtyard is reached from the delightful fountain courtyard with a flight of stairs constructed of hewn stone. It is a cheerful, clean, and spacious courtyard, containing the mausoleum and the outer (*ḫāric*) madrasa, which comprises an elegant classroom, ten student rooms, several latrines on one side, and a water well. Its portal opens to a public avenue and adjacent to its wall is a decorated fountain with flowing water. At the middle of that courtyard is the mausoleum of the two deceased founders, contained inside a garden. The boundary of this complex (*mecmuʿ*) is bordered on both sides by public avenues, with one side [south] adjacent to Mustafa Kethüda's property and some Muslim graves, and the other side [north] bounded by an endowed vegetable garden.[520]

The *extramuros* site of the complex permitted the incorporation of a mausoleum. Its funerary character is not shared by the non-sultanic mosque complexes that Sinan built inside the walled city, where with special permission from the sultan only a few mausoleums were allowed.[521]

The complex in Eyüp is a celebrated example of the chief architect's skill in taking advantage of irregular sites for picturesque effects. Its organic, asymmetrical composition on a sharply sloping terrain is characteristic of his later works, such as the non-funerary mosque complexes of Shahsultan's sister and brother-in-law in Kadırgalimanı and of her mother in Üsküdar.[522] Composed of two separate levels, linked by two staircases at the north and south sides of the mosque, the complex is sandwiched between parallel avenues, to which its two arched portals open. Whichever portal one enters presents an 'image staged in sequence'.[523] From the upper portal, one encounters the mosque on the right and the paved fountain court with Shahsultan's madrasa on the left. Straight ahead, an axially aligned staircase descending to the garden court below provides a fragmentary glimpse of the pasha's lower madrasa and the Golden Horn. From the seaside gate, one traverses an oblique stone path that extends between the octagonal mausoleum with a cemetery garden at the right and the pasha's L-shaped madrasa fronted by a well at the left. Ascending the staircase abutting the mosque portico transports the visitor from the charming setting of the funerary garden into the more formal stone courtyard above.

The complex obeys an experiential visual logic, a 'logic of *parcours*' that was a function of the lateral circulation path connecting its two entrances.[524] The monumental mausoleum with a double shell dome stands out as the only ashlar masonry building of the compound. The remaining structures are built with courses of stone alternating with brick or cheaper materials, thus highlighting the mausoleum as the focal point and *raison d'être* of the funerary complex.[525] The madrasas are visually subservient to the emphatic monumentality of the single-minaret mosque, which dominates the waterfront and the processional upper avenue connecting Divanyolu and Eyüp (illus. 363, 365). They are built of modest materials: stone and brick arcades, plastered rubble masonry walls, and columns of stone. Their unorthodox layout, with off-centre classrooms, unevenly spaced arcades, and non-matching columns topped by varying lozenge capitals, has puzzled scholars.[526]

The position of classrooms in each madrasa seems to have been intentionally shifted to assure an optimal view of the Golden Horn seascape praised in the waqfiyya. The staggered composition of different-sized cells along the east wing of the lower madrasa also responds to the prized vista of the waterfront. The classroom along that wing is axially aligned with the staircase linking the two madrasas to ensure its visibility from the courtyard above (illus. 366). Only the east wings of each madrasa feature striped stone and brick masonry to match the mosque, with which they are seen together upon entering the gate from the upper street and proceeding to the staircase. The remaining wings feature arcades in plain brick, a measure likely enforced by economic cutbacks. Once again, the design logic is visual and experiential: it accentuates the ideal perspective of the lateral enfilade that starts above and slopes down towards the funerary garden.

The palatial aspect of the monumental mosque is reinforced by its horizontal courses of stone and brick, characteristic of residential architecture.[527] Its tallest east façade, lined with four parallel rows of windows overlooking the funerary garden, dramatically rises to a great height above the doors and windows of its basement, composed of five vaulted storerooms (*maḫzen*) for the mosque's furnishings (illus. 362).[528] Each of the remaining façades displays a different elevation.[529] The north façade, facing the paved fountain courtyard, is fronted by a striped masonry five-bay portico supported on marble columns with muqarnas capitals. The central portal is topped by a simplified flattened muqarnas hood, which is flanked by arched window lunettes frugally ornamented by geometric interlaces in low-relief plasterwork, painted red and white.

The bold prismatic form of the cubic mosque with its flat façades departs from the pyramidal massing of Sinan's 'classical' mosques, in which the structure of inner space is mirrored externally. The masking of the interior configuration behind structurally independent, screen-like tall façades is characteristic of the chief architect's late works, as is the multitude of windows with openwork lunettes flooding the sanctuary with light. The elimination of lateral domes, half-domes, and exedras in favour of a dominating single dome resonates with the hilltop mosque of princess Mihrümah at Edirnekapı (*c.* 1563–70), visible from the Eyüp waterfront (illus. 364). Whereas in the Edirnekapı mosque the lateral galleries are surmounted by small domes, here they

366 Superstructure of the Shahsultan and Zal Pasha mosque, Eyüp, with partial views of the twin madrasas.

extend up to the drum level of the main dome and are covered by shed roofs (illus. 365–66). Dominated by the enveloping façades, the dome is almost lost from view. It no longer grows directly from the mosque's outer walls as in Edirnekapı, but sits above the inner square baldachin, whose support system is externally expressed by four octagonal weight turrets capped with onion domes. The much larger dome of Mihrümah's ashlar masonry mosque dispenses with flying buttresses, but the medium-sized dome here is conservatively braced with pairs of flying buttresses at each corner.

Sinan's classical conception of spatial unity is no longer palpable inside the mosque in Eyüp, whose interior features a U-shaped upper gallery typical of his post-Selimiye works (illus. 367). Upon entering the prayer hall from the north portal, one is confronted with a surprise: the low ceiling under the narthex-like north gallery delays one's encounter with the central dome, which is cut off by a screen of five arches carried on four marble columns between two massive round piers. The lateral upper galleries, freed from the structural constraints of the domed baldachin, have curtain walls with continuous linear strips of windows covered by flat vaults that lend the interior and exterior of the mosque a unique appearance (illus. 368, 369). The dome, seemingly suspended in mid-air with the concealment of its south piers inside the qibla wall, appears unexpectedly lofty. Its mighty arches are fully exposed, unlike their counterparts in Mihrümah's Edirnekapı mosque. The pull of gravity is strongly felt in Shahsultan's lower and smaller domed baldachin, the four pendentives of which descend to the gallery level.

The well-lit space is simple yet majestic. With the exception of the north wall, fenestration proliferates on all sides. The omission of muqarnas detailing everywhere but on the mihrab hood recalls the Edirnekapı mosque, where the architectonic clarity of the structural skeleton reigns supreme. The centre of the qibla wall, framed by the robust arch of the dome, has three linear rows of windows topped by a bullseye window. Their hexagonal honeycomb grills are fitted with clear bottle-glass, from which blazing light enters the interior. Stained glass borders with discreet cartouches are sparingly used to outline the frames of the upper windows. A stringcourse moulding that runs above the second tier of windows defines an upper semicircle, illusionistically delineating a window-pierced tympanum. Interrupted by the massive lateral arches of the dome, the stringcourse encircles the galleries in an attempt to tie together the mosque walls visually.

The luminous interior is enveloped in whiteness: limpid windows of clear glass, plain white stone walls, and milky arcades without polychrome voissoirs contribute to the aura of pristine purity. The chaste ambience is accentuated by the sparseness of painted decorations (dominated by red, blue, white, and black). Restored in 1955–63, they are mainly concentrated in the dome, the pendentives, and the gallery ceilings. The dearth of ornament, perhaps due to economic shortfalls, turns the pattern-forming patches of light entering through the windows into the primary adornments of the ethereal space. The plain white marble mihrab is accompanied by an intricately carved filigree-work minbar, whose conical cap preserves original gilt medallions. The mihrab is surrounded by a simple white-ground İznik-tile border, awkwardly cut at the top by a window frame added during modern renovations.[530]

The rectangular inscription of the mihrab quotes a less common verse including the word 'mihrab' (3:39); this alternative verse appears in some other late mosques attributed to Sinan. Three of the ground-level windows on the qibla wall are decorated with narrow İznik tile inscription bands beneath their arched openwork lunettes. They quote a sura (113:1–5), which contrasts the merciful creator's divine light with the darkness of evil, followed by another sura (114:1–6) asking God to safeguard worshippers from the darkness of evil forces. The popular verse

367 Mosque of Shahsultan and Zal Pasha, Eyüp, upper gallery.

from the Fatir sura inscribed on the central roundel of the dome affirms the forgiving nature of God, whose absolute power keeps the heavens and the earth from deviating beyond their fixed orbits (35:41). Eight painted roundels with the revered names decorate the four pendentives and the qibla and anti-qibla walls.

The only other inscription is outside, carved on a rectangular white marble panel above the north portal. It highlights the importance of congregational prayers as a means of gaining entry into paradise: 'God the exalted and sublime said: And [those] who pay heed to their prayers (23:9); these will dwell in Gardens, honoured (70:35).' By implication the mosque, whose windows command delightful vistas of gardens along the Golden Horn, becomes a heavenly mansion promised to believers in paradise. This is precisely the theme emphasized in the waqfiyya, which praises the belvederes of the mosque as recalling those in paradise, its interior bathed in divine light, and its entrancing architectural beauty. Capable of transporting the congregation into states of spiritual rapture, the prayer hall constitutes a physical medium for visionary experience, guiding the contemplative gaze in its quest for the divine. According to the waqfiyya, it sharpens ocular vision and bestows eyesight to the blind:

368 Mosque of Shahsultan and Zal Pasha, Eyüp, interior toward the qibla wall.

369 Mosque of Shahsultan and Zal Pasha, interior view of the domical superstructure with subsidiary flat vaults.

> Truly, the noble mosque is a charming and immaculate sanctuary whose large, well-proportioned dome and hitherto unseen four arches embody manifest skill. Its exterior has a matchless and peerless, delicate minaret. Its interior comprises large and small prayer spaces (*muṣalla*) on both sides, two large [lateral] upper galleries (*fevḳāniyye*) providing additional prayer places, and two pleasant and unequalled small tribunes (*mahfil*) for the chanters and muezzins [at the north gallery]. The ornate and fanciful minbar is attractive and agreeable, and the charming marble mihrab is unrivalled. The windows are like doors opening from the belvederes of paradise (*ġurfe-i cinān*) for the eyes of praying worshippers, and those open doors provide vistas for eyes desirous of encountering God ... by revealing the miracle-filled illumination of the true path. Men entering there for the joy of God are granted spiritual states (*ḥālet*). It is a meeting place for people caught in rapture and ecstasy (*vecd ve ḥāl*). This beautiful and alluring mosque is joy-giving and illuminated to such a degree that the eyes of men, normally limited to perceiving the visible world, are almost freed from the concealment of the sublime hosts of angels and fairies. And it embodies such a degree of charm and delight that it is possible for even the blind eye to behold brightness from its world-viewing windows. All of its sides are agreeable and well-proportioned, and its many beautiful heavenly arches are limitless. Its high dome has not hitherto been seen by the eyes of the stars under the green dome [of heaven], and nor has the engineer of the firmaments fashioned its Iram-like plan (*ṭarḥ*) on the surface of the earth.[531]

This extraordinary eulogy ends with an accolade: 'Whoever saw that artistic mosque said "Well done!" to its Sinimmar-like architect [Sinimmar was the builder of the legendary Khawarnaq palace] and a thousand times "Bravo!" to its intelligent endowment administrator, who supervised its construction.'[532] The endowment administrator in question, Mustafa Kethüda, eventually rose to the rank of vizier (Sarı Mustafa Pasha) and was buried in the mosque cemetery next to his former masters.[533] Working for patrons no longer living seems to have given Sinan greater freedom to explore unusual aesthetic effects in this distinctive mosque, which has been appraised as a 'highly original experiment that owes nothing to previous schemes'.[534] With its 12.4 metre dome rising to a height of 21.8 metres, the mosque of Shahsultan and Zal Mahmud Pasha is an inventive variant of the single-domed vizierial mosque, upgraded with royal features in accord with the princess's rank. Its striped masonry walls differ from the ashlar masonry of most of Sinan's vizierial and royal mosques in the capital. An early example of a single-domed vizierial mosque with striped masonry is that of Hadım İbrahim Pasha at Silivrikapı (1551). Alternating courses of stone and brick were also used in two modest domeless mosques designed by Sinan for another Shahsultan (the sister of Süleyman) – one along the waterfront of Eyüp (1537, 1555–56) and the other outside the Yenikapı gate (*c.* 1552).

With its striped masonry fabric, the mosque of Shahsultan and Zal Mahmud befitted the relatively marginal status of its patrons: a princess who was the reigning monarch's sister rather than his daughter, and a 'lightweight' fifth vizier. The use of mixed masonry had the advantage of accentuating the mosque's quasi-palatial aura, particularly decorous for a rural suburban setting dotted by shore palaces. The couple's unique mosque recalls a blocklike Italianate palazzo, perhaps inspired by queen Nurbanu's distant Venetian recollections. The omission of twin minarets must have been dictated by the joint patronage of the mosque, which conflates the ranks of its two patrons.

The mosque of princess Mihrümah in Edirnekapı provided the principal model for the square baldachin, typical of royal foundations (illus. 3). The most obvious parallel between the single-domed mosques in Edirnekapı and Eyüp is their four-point support systems articulated externally by four dome-capped weight turrets. What distiguishes one from the other is Sinan's post-classical idiom, also manifested in the concurrently built Muradiye mosque of Shahsultan's reigning brother in Manisa (1583–86/87). I have argued earlier that the vague affinity of the Muradiye with the mosque in Eyüp may reflect the queen mother Nurbanu's unifying vision (illus. 241–44). We have seen that Evliya Çelebi noticed the stylistic affinity between these two light-filled mosques, even though he found that of the sultan 'more ornate'.[535] Before describing the mosque of 'Zal Pasha', he mentions the elevated shore palaces in its neighbourhood: 'It is a well-cultivated district along the shore, with a thousand residences, vineyards, and gardens, and containing many palaces and meadows; its residences boast multiple storeys and pleasant vistas.'[536] It is the novel design of the mosque that elicits Evliya's enthusiasm:

> The Friday mosque of Zal Pasha is sited inside an Iram garden with two public avenues on both sides. It is such a bright mosque that within the Ottoman domains no other illuminated vizierial mosque like it exists. It is a world-famous mosque adorned with 366 (*sic*) crystal windows. One climbs up from the north side to its courtyard by a stone staircase; beneath it are many student cells. From the south side one ascends to the courtyard by another staircase of [empty] steps because one side of the mosque is built on a steep slope. If one were to fully describe the style and manner and mode of construction of this mosque, it would fill a volume. The science of architecture (*ʿilm-i miʿmārī*) displayed in this mosque does not exist in any other mosque. And the imagination-pleasing skills manifested [on façades] outside its central dome are beyond limit. Architects of our time are incapable of creating such charming artistry (*şīrīnkārlıḳ*). The skilful filigree-work of its minbar, mihrab, and muezzin's tribune is only seen in the minbar of the Sinop castle. And the three sides of its courtyard are decorated with madrasa cells. The music of birds in the rose meadows and flower gardens that surrounds its four sides is life-prolonging. And its date is this: [empty]. Its minaret is very artistic and high. The great old architect Sinan has clearly manifested his artistic power (*yed-i ṭūlā*) in the edifice of this mosque.[537]

Evliya's description once again shows the erasure from collective memory of Shahsultan's role as patron. The separate waqfiyyas of her sister İsmihan and brother-in-law Sokollu identified the individual buildings endowed by each of them in their joint mosque complex at Kadırga. The union of Shahsultan's and her husband's endowments into a single administrative unit with one waqfiyya may have inspired Sinan to invent a novel mosque type for them. The one-of-a-kind mosque defies the chronological and typological categories used in tracing the chief architect's supposedly linear stylistic evolution. Its uncustomary design fuses the identity of its two patrons as a couple: it is more modest than other vizierial mosques on account of the somewhat inconsequential pasha's rank as fifth vizier, yet it is enhanced by regal touches warranted by the dynastic pedigree of the minor princess. Ever mindful of decorum, Sinan conceived a singular monument that eloquently materialized the wills of his deceased patrons. The palatial feel of the lofty mosque, rising at the water's edge inside an ambrosial funerary garden, accentuated its Edenic associations, attuned to the couple's wish to be permanently reunited in paradise.

Chapter 9

GRAND VIZIERS

I. KARA AHMED PASHA
ISTANBUL, TOPKAPI (1555, 1565–71/72)
II. SEMİZ ALİ PASHA
MARMARA EREĞLİSİ (*c.* 1561–65)
BABAESKİ (*c.* 1569–75, 1585–86)

I. KARA AHMED PASHA

Kara Ahmed Pasha was married to Fatma Sultan, an undistinguished daughter of Selim I who is not among Sinan's patrons. I have therefore included his mosque complex, sited within the Topkapı gate along the Byzantine land walls, under the patronage of grand viziers (illus. 370, 371). Neither of the two patrons considered in this chapter was married to a prominent princess, and the short terms during which they each held the grand vizierate did not prove conducive to substantial architectural patronage. Unlike the more celebrated grand viziers Rüstem and Sokollu, who sponsored several monuments supported by richer endowments, they each left behind a single posthumously created mosque complex. Kara Ahmed Pasha's mosque is distinguished by the antique flavour of its hexagonal domed baldachin, carried on six spoliated red granite columns with muqarnas capitals. Dates ranging from the mid-1550s to the mid-1560s have been proposed for his complex, which is presented as a future project in his waqfiyya, recorded shortly before his execution in 1555.[1]

I have already discussed under Mihrümah Sultan's patronage the legal dispute that arose when her representative, Mehmed Kethüda, and Hüsrev Kethüda, the endowment administrator of the late Kara Ahmed Pasha, both set out to build mosque complexes for their patrons within the Edirne gate (Edirnekapı). The ensuing feud was settled in August 1563 with Sultan Süleyman's decree that favoured his daughter's party and prohibited the pasha's posthumous construction near the same site. Kara Ahmed Pasha's complex within the neighbouring Topkapı gate was not completed until 1571–72, significantly later than its generally assumed date of inauguration. This embeds it in an entirely different context than hitherto imagined. Unravelling its enigmatic construction history requires an understanding of its patron's position *vis-à-vis* political factions in the Ottoman court.

Educated in the imperial palace, the swarthy, Albanian-born grand vizier nicknamed Ahmed Pasha 'the Black' (Kara) distinguished himself primarily by military exploits. Rising through the ranks, he became the agha of janissaries and as the governor-general of Rumelia participated in the Hungarian campaign of 1543. He was appointed second vizier while he served as the commander-in-chief of Süleyman's second Safavid expedition in 1548–49. Commanding another campaign to Hungary in 1552, he and the governor-general of Rumelia, Sokollu Mehmed Pasha, together conquered Temesvár. In 1553–55 Kara Ahmed Pasha replaced the deposed grand vizier Rüstem Pasha, held responsible for the execution of prince Mustafa, who was particularly favoured by the janissaries. Busbecq reports that the appointment of the new grand vizier, 'a man of greater courage than judgment', had 'soothed the grief and calmed the feelings of the soldiers, who, with the usual credulity of the vulgar, were easily led to believe that Soleiman had discovered the crimes of Roostem and the sorceries of his wife and had learnt wisdom, though it was too late.'[2]

Accompanied by Sokollu's Rumelian troops, the grand vizier marched to Nakhchivan in 1555, directing successful operations against Georgian fortresses. That year Sokollu was appointed third vizier in Amasya, where a peace treaty was signed with the Safavids. On 29 September 1555, shortly after the court had returned to Istanbul, Kara Ahmed Pasha was strangled in front of the sultan's private audience chamber. His brief grand vizierate lasted less than two years, between 1553 and 1555. The historian Celalzade attempts to legitimize the pasha's execution by citing his lack of sagacity and his incompetence as a grand vizier, who displayed innate shortcomings of character and signs of corruption and who sought the company of 'ignoramuses and mischief makers', being by nature an unrefined person who 'caressed the low and nurtured the vulgar'.[3]

The reason for his execution has been variously explained as

370 Plan of the Kara Ahmed Pasha complex, Topkapı:

1. Mosque
2. Madrasa
3. Mausoleum
4. Elementary school

371 Axonometric projection of the Kara Ahmed Pasha mosque and madrasa.

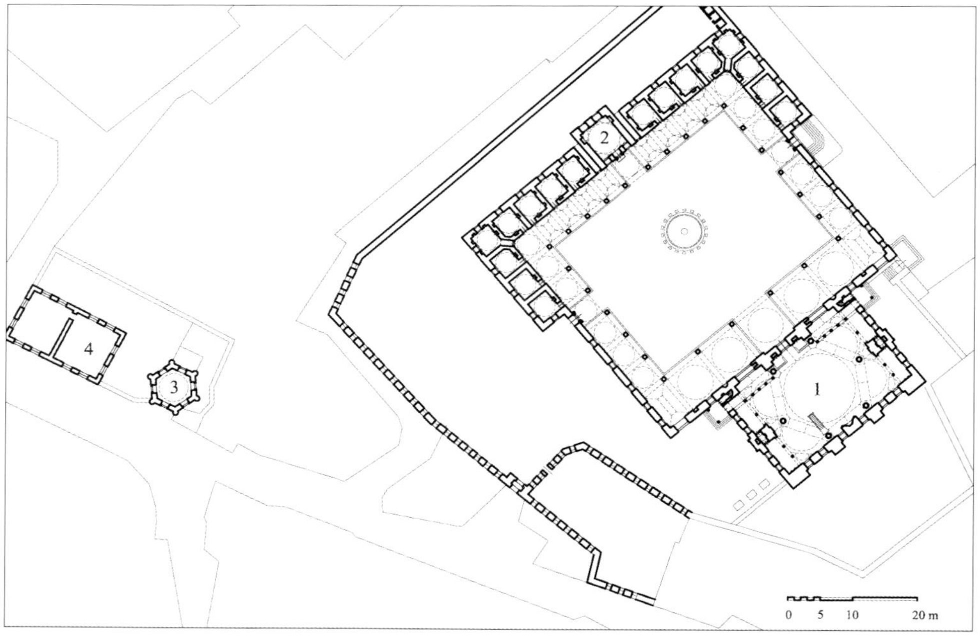

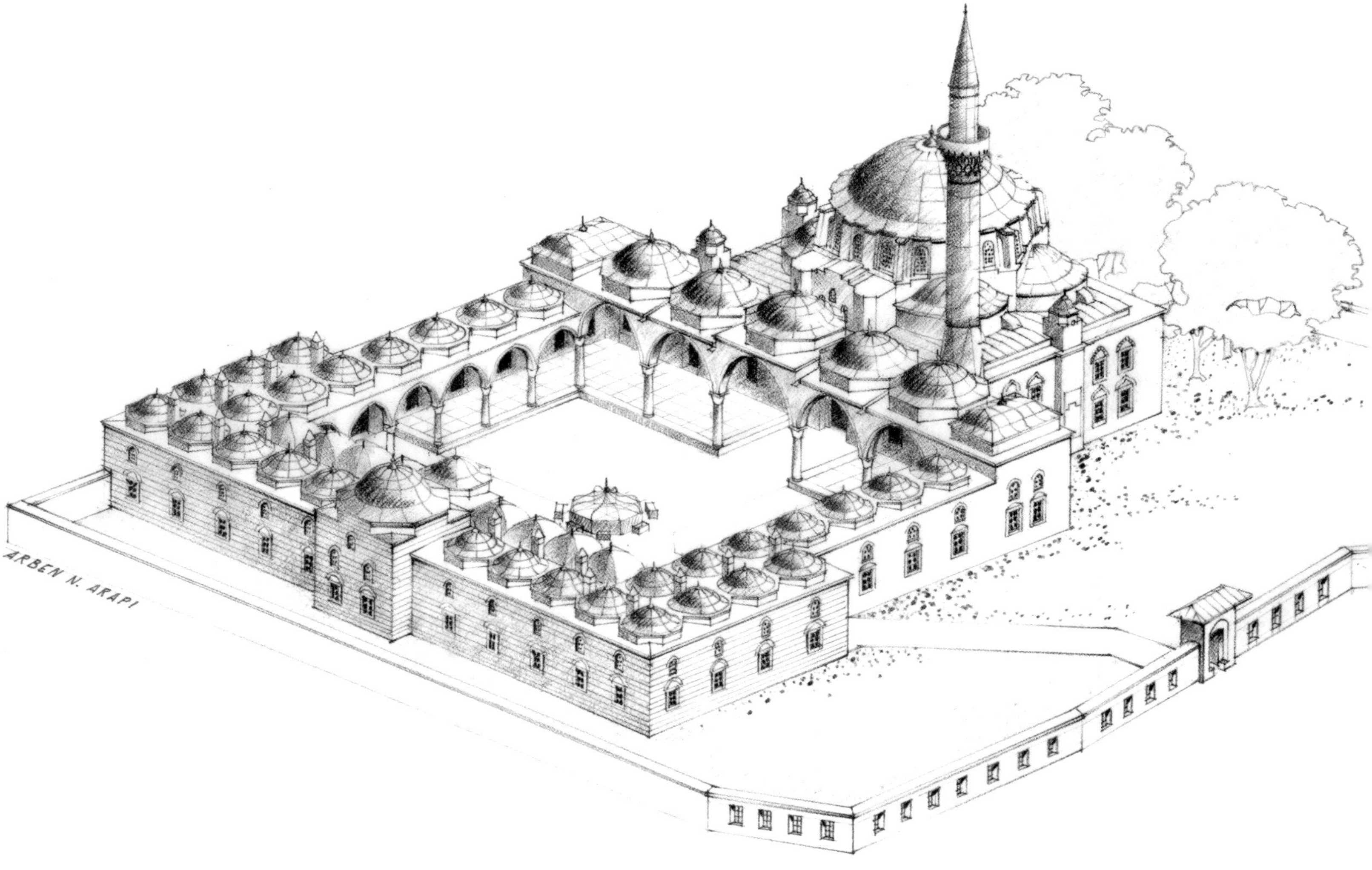

his devotion to prince Mustafa, the conspiracy of Hürrem and Mihrümah to reinstate Rüstem Pasha, and the fraudulent financial administration of Egypt during his tenure. Daniele Barbarigo (1564) explains that the grand vizier had plotted with the new governor-general of Egypt (Dukakinzade Mehmed Pasha, also of Albanian descent) against the former holder of that post, Semiz Ali Pasha, who rose to the vizierate in 1553. To discredit Semiz Ali in the sultan's eyes, Kara Ahmed accused him of appropriating a vast personal treasure in Cairo through extortion. The accused vizier, in turn, obtained an incriminatory letter that his accuser had written to the new governor-general of Egypt, promising him protection and urging him to amass a treasure there without fear. Barbarigo reports the comment of Semiz Ali Pasha (g.v. 1561–65), who handed the letter over to the sultan: 'The people believed he had been killed to restore Rüstem Pasha to office, but it was because of this letter.'[4]

Mustafa Āli defends the 'brave and intelligent' grand vizier, who had fallen victim to the 'deceit of women'. Among 'the Albanian stock' he was 'a rare possessor of good character and a follower of the path of valour and toughness', acclaimed for his religiosity and justice.[5] According to Āli, there was not even a legitimate reason to depose him, let alone execute him, and the permission granted for the construction of the pasha's mausoleum next to his posthumously built mosque was a token of his innocence: 'In Istanbul, the noble Friday mosque near the gate of Topkapı was built after his death; the placement of his body by its side signified that he was not one bit immersed in the sea of sin.'[6] The disgraced pasha's coffin had originally been buried without ceremony in a cemetery inside the Topkapı gate.[7] His domed mausoleum, constructed over his grave many years after his death, proclaimed his exoneration.

A now-lost inscription panel placed over Kara Ahmed Pasha's sarcophagus provided his brief biography, followed by additional information about the construction of his mausoleum and mosque complex:

> The deceased namesake of [Güzelce] Ahmed Pasha entered
> The sultan's palace and served it,
> He exited it and became the agha of janissaries.
> At the time of his dismissal, he was given the vizierate.
> He remained four years in the post of agha,
> Serving another three years as vizier.
> He was appointed commander-in-chief in Iran and Hungary,
> Becoming famous as the conqueror of Temesvár.
> He fought the holy war like the mythical hero Rustam.
> Becoming a royal bridegroom, he took the grand vizier's seal.
> He was the brother [-in-law] of Rüstem Pasha;
> Replacing him as grand vizier, he reached eminence.
> He conducted the holy war in the land of Georgians,
> Where all the unruly ones obeyed him.
> His predecessor and brother [-in-law] succeeded him again;
> His destiny allowed him less than two years [as grand vizier].
> Sultan Süleyman executed him;
> In 962 (1555) he attained martyrdom.
> The foundations of the noble Friday mosque had been laid,
> This service was abandoned for many years.
> Then Sultan Selim II ascended the throne,
> He permitted [its construction] since [the pasha] was innocent.
> His pious foundation thus became fully realized,
> His soul found joy and glory at that time.
> The deceased [pasha] had been buried there,
> His mausoleum was built after seven years.
> He became celebrated for his virtuousness;
> A turban ornamented the head of his sarcophagus.
> His face was permanently whitewashed,
> With the intercession of the Prophet.
> Through his servants' souls he became happy,
> May those who served [his construction] be blessed.
> With martyrdom he set out for the [eternal] abode,
> They pronounced the date 'Merciful Pasha,' year 962 (1555).[8]

The inscription proclaims the innocence of Ahmed Pasha 'the Black', the namesake of the vizier Güzelce Ahmed Pasha (d. 1580, Mihrümah's son-in-law). His 'blackened face' became 'whitewashed' by the permission granted to resume construction of his mosque, whose foundations were abandoned for many years until Selim II's reign (r. 1566–74), when the pasha was fully exonerated.

The inscription implies that the mausoleum was built seven years after the pasha's death in 1555. This coincides with the date given on an inscription over the west portal of the mosque forecourt, which provides the foundation date of the mosque 969 (1561–62) and records repairs made in 1108 (1696–97). The date carved on the gate of the mausoleum 966 (1558–59), however, complicates its chronology and suggests that the mausoleum was created during the grand vizierate of Rüstem Pasha (d. 1561) before the construction of the mosque.[9] Fatma Sultan, the wife of Kara Ahmed Pasha, lies buried in the cemetery outside her husband's posthumous mausoleum.[10] Ayvansarayi mentions the modest masjid with a hipped roof she built at Topkapı and her elementary school in Karagümrük near Edirnekapı, pointing out that the couple's waqfs were interlinked.[11]

Registered on 21 July 1555, approximately two months before his death, Kara Ahmed Pasha's endowment deed does not specify the site of his projected mosque complex.[12] It was to be built 'in a decorous (*münāsib*) quarter of Istanbul' and would comprise an artistic Friday mosque, a madrasa with sixteen dormitories and a classroom, a dervish convent whose shaykh would deliver sermons at the mosque, a hospice, and an elementary school.[13] After the grand vizier's demise, his household steward Firuz Kethüda was to serve as the administrator and overseer of his waqf. Upon the cessation of the latter's bloodline, the pasha's other manumitted slaves would administer his endowment. If none of them were to survive, the sultan would appoint an appropriate administrator, who had to read the waqfiyya once every month.[14]

The pasha endowed 3,000,000 aspers, whose accumulated interest would finance the construction of his mosque complex, and real estate properties including his palatial residence near Yenibahçe, in the Topkapı quarter, composed of two courtyards and a vast garden with a pool that measured more than 40 *jarīb* (10,000 square feet).[15] His mosque complex must have been built on the grounds of this garden estate after the prohibition in 1563 of its construction near Edirnekapı. Its originally intended site was in all likelihood in Karagümrük near Edirnekapı, where his wife endowed the elementary school mentioned above by Ayvansarayi. The foundation of both a Friday mosque and a masjid in Topkapı by husband and wife can be explained as the unforeseen outcome of the enforced change of site from Edirnekapı to Topkapı, where Fatma Sultan must have built her masjid beforehand. The siting of the pasha's mausoleum as an independent structure outside the walled precinct of his mosque and madrasa complex once again implies that the location of the complex was an afterthought.[16] Neither the hospice nor the dervish convent mentioned in the waqfiyya was built in the programatically scaled down complex, appended next to the cemetery where the pasha had been buried.

Composed by the pasha's slave servant Haydar, an inscription panel that once hung inside the mosque gave its foundation and completion dates:

> The foundation date of the late grand vizier Ahmed Pasha's noble Friday mosque: The construction of this Friday mosque began on a Sunday during the year 972 and was completed seven years after that auspicious year [979]. The foundations of the noble Friday mosque were laid in timely fashion on the 22nd day of the month of Şaban, which was the Persian New Year's Day [22 Şaban 972 / 25 March 1565]. Praise be to God, who facilitated the completion of the perfect grand vizier Ahmed's pious foundation. May all the angels, human beings, and jinns perform prayers in it, standing and bowing, sitting and prostrating in worship. Haydar, the humble servant of Ahmed, pronounced its date: It was completed in the year 979 (1571–72).[17]

The foundations of the mosque, then, were laid ten years after the pasha's death, and its construction was completed within seven years between 1565 and 1571–72. Konyalı, who recorded the inscription in 1950, dismissed it as unreliable, claiming that its unidentified author was not well enough educated to compose a literate chronogram.[18] He proposed that the mosque complex must have been finished in 1558–59, the date carved over the gate of the pasha's mausoleum.

The author of the chronogram cited above was none other than Haydar b. Abdullah, the overseer of Ahmed Pasha's endowment, who together with Hüsrev Beg b. Abdullah, the administrator of the same endowment, signed the chief architect Sinan's undated waqfiyya (*c.* 1583–85).[19] These two individuals must have acted as witnesses because of the proximity of the pasha's complex to that of the chief architect in Yenibahçe, where he endowed a masjid and an elementary school next to his garden mansion. Ayvansarayi records the inscription on the now-lost tombstone of Hüsrev Beg in the cemetery of Kara Ahmed Pasha's mausoleum, which praises his completion of the mosque complex:

> Hüsrev Beg passed away from this evil world to eternity.
> O God, let paradise be his abode!
>
> He caused the auspicious mosque, the charitable work of
> the vizier Ahmed Pasha,
> To be completed and made [the pasha's] soul joyful.
>
> O Asarī! He journeyed to the garden of paradise.
> They composed [a chronogram] for Hüsrev Beg; the date is:
> 'Place of the Gardens of Paradise.'[20]

The construction supervisor can be identified as Hüsrev Kethüda, the grand vizier Sokollu's household steward, who was himself a prolific patron of architecture. Sinan designed for him two madrasas in Ankara and Istanbul, a school for Koran recitation in Istanbul (at Vefa), a caravansaray in İpsala, along with three bath-houses in Istanbul (Ortaköy), İzmit, and Çatalca.[21]

The construction of Kara Ahmed Pasha's mosque and madrasa in Topkapı between 1565 and 1571–72 overlapped with the supportive grand vizierate of Sokollu (g.v. 1565–79), who had fought side-by-side with its patron and was promoted to the vizierate under his regime. The projected mosque complex was delayed during the second grand vizierate of the vindictive Rüstem Pasha (g.v. 1555–61), who is known to have persecuted his rival's allies.[22] The erection of a grandiose memorial in the name of an executed grand vizier was apparently deemed undecorous during Süleyman's reign. The project seems to have regained some momentum after Rüstem's demise in 1561, giving rise to the legal dispute with his wife Mihrümah in 1563, but the construction of the mosque complex at Edirnekapı was prohibited during the equally vengeful grand vizierate of Semiz Ali Pasha (g.v. 1561–65), the former governor-general of Egypt against whom Kara Ahmed Pasha had conspired.

The mosque complex at Topkapı, built concurrently with that of Mihrümah in Edirnekapı (1563–70), approached completion around 976 (1568–69), the date carved on a now-lost public

372 Kara Ahmed Pasha mosque, Topkapı, from the west.

fountain located near the mausoleum of Kara Ahmed Pasha. The mosque and its water channel were finished around 1568–69, but the complex as a whole was inaugurated in 1571–72.[23] We learn from dispatches sent by the *bailo* Marcantonio Barbaro to the Venetian Senate in 1569 that the former slave servants of the late pasha had resolved to present gifts to his 'nearly complete' mosque (illus. 372). For that purpose, the court translator Dragoman İbrahim Beg requested a mosque lamp from the Murano factories.[24]

A list of objects endowed for the mosque in Topkapı confirms that some of them were presented as gifts by former servants and allies: Sokollu Mehmed Pasha gave three Korans and three carpets; Hasan Kethüda (a steward of Sokollu) gave one carpet and one prayer carpet; the vizier Lala Mustafa Pasha (formerly a boon companion attached to the patron's household) donated three carpets; the vizier's steward Mustafa Kethüda gave one Koran and one carpet; and one prayer carpet apiece was donated by other individuals (Kenan Agha, Mustafa Agha, Yazıcı Hüsrev Agha, Süleyman Beg, Fazlı Çavuş). The inventory of objects lists a rosary with a thousand beads, fifteen Koran manuscripts, eighteen carpets (*ḫaliçe*), and five prayer rugs (*seccāde*), one of which was a white 'Baghdadi' featuring nine mihrabs.[25]

The mosque complex, sited between Yenibahçe and Edirnekapı, is built at a distance from the Topkapı gate where a weekly market was held on Tuesdays.[26] The mausoleum and elementary school are located across a lane, outside the window-pierced, ashlar masonry precinct wall of the mosque and madrasa. The much-altered elementary school, built with alternating courses of stone and brick, faces the cemetery of the mausoleum, which is enclosed by its own precinct wall. The 'inelegantly tall' ashlar masonry mausoleum has a hexagonal exterior and a dodecagonal interior, with an atypically bulbous double-shell dome raised on an eighteen-sided drum.[27]

Located in a rural setting with ample grounds, the mosque and U-shaped madrasa share an unusually spacious garden court. An off-centre nonagonal ablution fountain, recently covered by an unbecoming domed canopy, marks the intersection of the lateral courtyard entrances and the mihrab axis of the mosque.[28] Domical arcades extend between the mosque portico and the side wings of the madrasa, whose domed classroom is aligned with the mihrab axis. The madrasa is fronted by a portico with eight-faceted vaults; its outer walls of alternating courses of stone and brick do not match the ashlar masonry lateral walls of the mosque courtyard to which it is appended.

Kara Ahmed Pasha's mosque and madrasa complex is generally compared with that of the grand admiral Sinan Pasha in Beşiktaş, posthumously built under the supervision of his then-deposed brother, Rüstem Pasha between 1554 and 1555–56 (illus. 4). The comparable U-shaped madrasa in Beşiktaş lacks a domed classroom (as does Mihrümah's Edirnekapı complex).

With its hexagonal baldachin flanked by double domes on each side, the late grand admiral's modest mosque in Beşiktaş, built with alternating courses of stone and brick befitting his lower status, paraphrases the plan of the Üç Şerefeli mosque in Edirne. The higher-ranked ashlar masonry grand vizierial mosque in Topkapı further develops the hexagonal plan type by substituting four exedral half-domes for the pair of lateral domes, thereby eliminating awkward triangular areas. Its side wings are more fully integrated with the central baldachin, but its insufficiently unified interior space, featuring cumbersome lateral piers, is in keeping with its planning date of around 1555.

An undated fatwa obtained by Hüsrev Kethüda from Ebussuud to preempt Mihrümah's rival project in Edirnekapı indicates that Kara Ahmed Pasha, who bought properties near that city gate, had ordered some building materials before he passed away:

> He buys some houses and shops there for this purpose, but passes away when he has just started to prepare the building materials. A noble sultanic permit is obtained for that project, together with imperial decrees addressed to various locations for the preparation of building materials. But as these preliminary arrangements are being made, other important matters take precedence before the construction starts.[29]

The six rectangular *cuerda seca* window lunettes decorating the qibla wall of the mosque and the ogee-arched lunettes of two niches with bookshelves on the porticoed north façade are datable to around 1555 in technique, design, and colour scheme (yellow, green, blue, turquoise, white) (illus. 373, 374). This is the last work of Sinan in which *cuerda seca* tiles appear. The preparation of custom-made tiles for the Topkapı mosque well in advance of its construction indicates that Sinan had drawn its plan around 1555. His autobiographies list the mosque, madrasa, and mausoleum, whose execution he must have delegated to one of his assistants.[30] A likely candidate is Davud, who may have supervised the construction of another hexagonal-baldachined mosque just around the time the complex in Topkapı was completed: that of Nurbanu Sultan in Üsküdar, whose foundations were laid in 1571 (illus. 4).[31]

373 Kara Ahmed Pasha mosque, Topkapı, *cuerda seca* tile lunette on the qibla wall.

374 Kara Ahmed Pasha mosque, Topkapı, *cuerda seca* tile lunette of niche on the north façade.

Kara Ahmed Pasha's mosque is fronted by a five-domed portico carried on columns with muqarnas capitals and flanked by cradle vaults at each end. The conical hood of the muqarnas-galleried minaret, whose shaft is decorated with an upper and lower band of six-pointed stars in tilework, was replaced by a stone cap in 1896–97, when it was renovated together with the damaged central dome.[32] The large iron-grilled windows at each end of the portico command vistas of the surrounding garden, which provides access to the porticoed lateral gates of the prayer hall (illus. 372). The north gate of the mosque is flanked by two enormous iron-grilled windows, comparable to the pair on the double porticoed façade of Rüstem Pasha's Tahtakale mosque (*c.* 1561–63) (illus. 307, 375). The huge windows suggest that the Tophane mosque may initially have been planned with a double portico, which would have limited the amount of light entering from its north façade. A change of programme might explain the disproportionately large size of its five portico domes.[33]

The mosques in Tophane, Tahtakale, and Edirnekapı share simple arched portals without the customary muqarnas hoods and foundation inscriptions. Other analogous characteristics of these three interrelated mosques with linked destinies are their rectangular plans with side aisles featuring lateral gates, and their arcaded upper galleries carried on small columns. Flanking their north portals, they each have twin muezzin's tribunes surmounted by a lofty private balcony. The rectangular north portal of the Topkapı mosque is framed by a monumental arch dressed in white marble and carved with distinctive low-relief cartouche motifs (illus. 375). The plain brick window lunettes on the north façade lack tile revetments, unlike the two unusual niches with bookshelves.

The structural frailty of the north façade, pierced with two oversize windows, is counterbalanced by the thickening of the

375 Kara Ahmed Pasha mosque, Topkapı, north façade with large iron-grilled windows flanking the portal.

other walls, which are reinforced by heavy buttresses that limit the volume of light filtering into the dimly lit prayer hall (illus. 376, 377). The projecting buttresses of the qibla wall are complemented by the massive central buttresses of the side walls, which contain internal staircases and are externally punctuated with weight turrets capped by mini domes (illus. 372). The lateral façades have two tiers of rectangular windows featuring blind lunettes, while the central part of the qibla wall features three-tiered windows. The slightly ogee-arched profiles of the window lunettes find a parallel in the mosque of the vizier Hadım İbrahim Pasha within the neighbouring gate of Silivrikapı (1551). The simple façades of the Topkapı mosque differ from their taller counterparts in the Tahtakale and Edirnekapı mosques, which are distinguished by innovative window compositions. The internal system of supports is externally expressed by six flying buttresses that surround the window-pierced base of the low dome, which is reinforced by pilaster-shaped engaged buttresses.

The six colossal red granite columns of the hexagonal baldachin are thought to have originated from the neighbouring church of Hagia Romanos.[34] Their muqarnas capitals are heightened by impost blocks to carry the six dome arches. The columns are grouped in pairs close to the qibla and anti-qibla walls, with the two lateral ones connected to the heavy piers by means of scallop shell squinches. The piers mark the midpoints of the gallery arcades on each side, whose ogee arches with joggled voussoirs are carried on small columns with lozenge capitals. The piers that bisect these galleries are connected to the north and south walls by two large pointed arches that partially mask the side wings; these wings are covered by flat vaults and provided with their own mihrabs.

The use of columns limits the height of the dome and results in a relatively cramped central space appended with unintegrated side wings.[35] An unresolved problem is the awkward concealment of the red granite column behind the finely sculpted minbar. The muqarnas-hooded marble mihrab is inscribed with the standard verse (3:37). The two tiers of stained glass windows above it have intricate plasterwork grills composed of six-pointed stars and hexagons, bordered by cartouches. The painted decorations of the prayer hall have changed over time.[36] What has been lost during successive renovations can be gleaned from the exquisite gilded paintings of a wooden ceiling beneath one of the muezzin's tribunes (illus. 378, 379). Featuring a central medallion and corner-pieces forming foliate arches at both ends, its composition recalls bookbindings and Uşak carpets. The low relief plasterwork designs combine vegetal scrolls, rosettes,

376 Kara Ahmed Pasha mosque, interior toward the qibla wall.

377 Kara Ahmed Pasha mosque, interior toward the east.

378, 379 Kara Ahmed Pasha mosque, Topkapı, painted wooden ceiling of the muezzin's tribune.

palmettes, *saz* leaves, and Chinese cloud bands. Outlined in black on a light blue background, they are painted in red, white, yellow, and gold. The original gilded blue conical cap of the minbar suggests that the domical superstructure also had a colour scheme dominated by blue and gold. This is insinuated by a Persian poem inscribed in one of the cupboards: 'I have heard that this domed roof (the sky) is overlaid with gold.'[37]

The few remaining Koranic inscriptions, in monumental *thuluth*, signal an otherwise generic programme. The central roundel of the dome quotes the Ikhlas sura affirming the unity of the merciful God (112:1–4). The painted roundels on the six dome arches, accompanied by a pair above the northern private balcony, bear the revered names. The *cuerda seca* window lunettes on the qibla wall cite the Fatiha sura that begs the merciful God, the owner of the Day of Judgment, to guide the congregation toward the 'straight path' (1:1–7).

The mosque is briefly described by Evliya Çelebi, who emphasizes its monumentality: 'Sited inside the Topkapı gate on a hill, it is a large Friday mosque in the manner of royal mosques.'[38] He indirectly critiques it in a comparison with the grand vizier Semiz Ali Pasha's hexagonal-baldachined mosque in Babaeski (*c.* 1569–75), to which I shall turn next. He finds the latter mosque more spacious, luminous, and ornate.[39] Evliya thus recognizes Sinan's improvement of the hexagonal-baldachin plan type at a later point of his career (illus. 4). With its 12-metre-wide dome, the mosque of Kara Ahmed Pasha was the first grand vizierial mosque designed by Sinan in the capital, but its construction was preceded by that of Rüstem Pasha in Tahtakale. Crowned by a larger dome, the latter mosque, built under the supervision of Mihrümah Sultan outshines its rival with more fashionable underglaze-painted İznik tiles that completely cover its wall surfaces.

The troubled building history of the disgraced pasha's memorial monument confirms the importance of winning the sultan's and grand vizier's support in negotiating the politics of monumental mosque construction. Realized a decade after its initial conceptualization, Kara Ahmed Pasha's mosque comes chronologically much closer than previously assumed to İsmihan Sultan's mosque at Kadırgalimanı, completed, according to its inscription, in 1571–72. Hailed as the finest version of the hexagonal-baldachin plan type, the latter mosque was built, not a decade after the inauguration of its less sophisticated counterpart in Topkapı, but around the same time.[40] What would have been a highly innovative grand vizierial mosque when it was first designed in 1555 could not help but turn into a relatively outdated, *retardataire* structure when it finally came into being during the apogee of Sinan's career.

II. SEMİZ ALİ PASHA

Sinan designed a modest Friday mosque in the Thracian port of Marmara Ereğlisi and a monumental mosque complex in

Babaeski, en route to Edirne, for Ali Pasha 'the Fat' (Semiz). The pasha, born in Brazza at Hercegovina to a family of converts to Islam, was admitted into the imperial palace as a relative of Çeşte Bali (the steward of the grand vizier İbrahim Pasha). Becoming the agha of janissaries in 1546, he was promoted to the governor-generalship of Rumelia and then of Egypt (1549–53).[41] Summoned to the capital as third vizier in 1553, he became second vizier in 1555, and succeeded Rüstem Pasha as grand vizier in 1561, holding that post for four years until his death on 25 June 1565.[42]

Celebrated for his corpulence, sense of humour, and gentle character, the jolly pasha endeared himself both to European and to Ottoman contemporaries. Mustafa Āli reports that he was so tall and huge 'that a horse capable of carrying him could rarely be found'. This 'jovial and witty vizier of great glory' was 'prudent and wise, and inclined towards justice and fairness'. His witticisms became so famous that they were recorded in books of jokes.[43] In 1562 Busbecq, who developed a close friendship with the grand vizier during peace negotiations, characterized him in his late sixties as a likeable and exceptionally clever administrator:

> By origin a Dalmatian, he is the only really civilized man whom I ever met among those Turkish barbarians. He is of a mild and calm disposition, polite, highly intelligent; he has a mind which can deal with the most difficult problems, and a wide experience of military and civil affairs. He is now well advanced in years and has continually held high office. He is tall of stature, and his face has a serious expression which is full of charm. He is devoted to his master, and nothing would please him better than to obtain for him the peace and quiet which would enable him to support in greater comfort his age and infirmities. He is anxious to obtain by courtesy and fairness – in fact, by treating me as a friend – the objects which Roostem [Rüstem Pasha] sought to gain by bullying and intimidation and threats.[44]

Busbecq then contrasts the 'different character' of these two grand viziers:

> Ali, throughout his life, had been freed from any suspicion of meanness, and was therefore never afraid that his courtesy or easiness of approach would incur the Sultan's blame. Roostem, on the other hand, was always avaricious and mean, and his first thoughts were always of his own interests and enrichment. My interviews with Roostem were always brief; whereas Ali purposely extended them over several hours, and his kindliness made the time pass pleasantly... I almost always went [to him] without having taken a meal, in order that I might have as clear a brain as possible for conversation with a man of such keen intellect... He used sometimes to say that wealth and honour and dignity had been abundantly showered upon him, but that now his sole desire was to serve his fellow men and so make his name live in the grateful memory of future ages.[45]

Daniele Barbarigo comments on how much the aged Sultan Süleyman was attached to the grand vizier, who had fallen ill in 1564, about a year before his death from diphtheria.[46] When he recovered a little but was unable to walk, he was permitted to ride up to the public audience hall of the imperial palace on a horse, a privilege never before granted to any grand vizier.[47] Unlike most of Süleyman's grand viziers and viziers, Semiz Ali Pasha was not married to a princess; in fact he refused the widow Mihrümah's marriage proposal in 1561–62.[48] His waqfiyya, registered in late December 1565, about six months after his death, shows that he had a consort named Hesna bint-i Abdullah, known as 'the spouse of Ustad Hasan' from a previous marriage, to whom he assigned a modest daily stipend of two aspers. He appointed his trusty steward, Ferruh Kethüda, the executor of his will, which stipulated that one-third of his inheritance be added to his pre-existing waqfs for additional charities. The steward was also entrusted with collecting the revenues to be inherited by the pasha's young son, Mehmed Beg.[49]

Gerlach reports that Semiz Ali Pasha, while less wealthy than his successor, Sokollu, had nevertheless left behind a fortune worth eight million gold coins (480,000,000 aspers).[50] Renowned for his lack of avariciousness and his refusal to accept bribes, he established a smaller endowment than did Rüstem Pasha or Sokollu. The income of his endowed properties was gathered by revenue collectors based in Istanbul and its suburbs (Haslar), Çatalca, Edirne, Plovdiv, Skopje, Komotini, Trikkala, İznik, Bursa, Alaşehir, and Cairo.[51] The properties he endowed included several structures built by Sinan: his palace at the İshak Pasha quarter near the Hippodrome, his suburban garden palace in Eyüp, a caravansaray at the flea market (Bitpazarı) of Istanbul, a covered market named after him in Edirne, and a caravansaray in Bursa.[52]

Concentrated in Istanbul, Edirne, and Thrace, the pasha's pious foundations comprised two works of Sinan: a madrasa in Edirnekapı (Karagümrük) and a Friday mosque in Marmara Ereğlisi.[53] These were complemented by structures omitted from the chief architect's autobiographies: a Friday mosque at the village of Akviran in Silivri (a suburban port of the capital where the pasha endowed a commercial bath-house), a masjid in Eyüp, two masjids in Edirne, a bridge in Sofia, and four public fountains (two in Eyüp and two in Marmara Ereğlisi).[54] Semiz Ali Pasha also left a testament for a Friday mosque and hospice to be built in his memory in the town of Babaeski, funded by the surplus of his endowments.[55] The waqfiyya stipulates that his waqf should be staffed by his freed slaves selected by the endowment

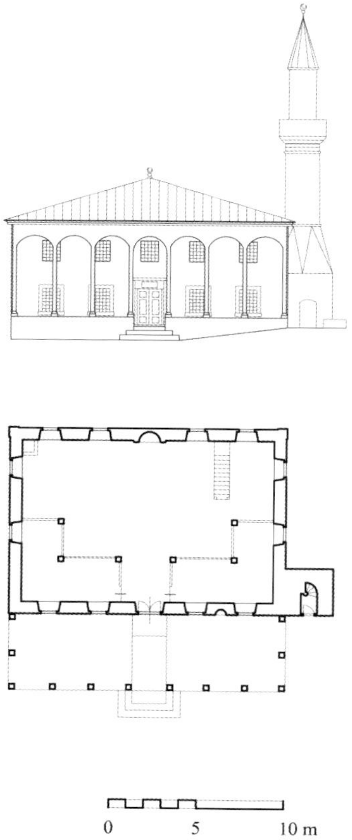

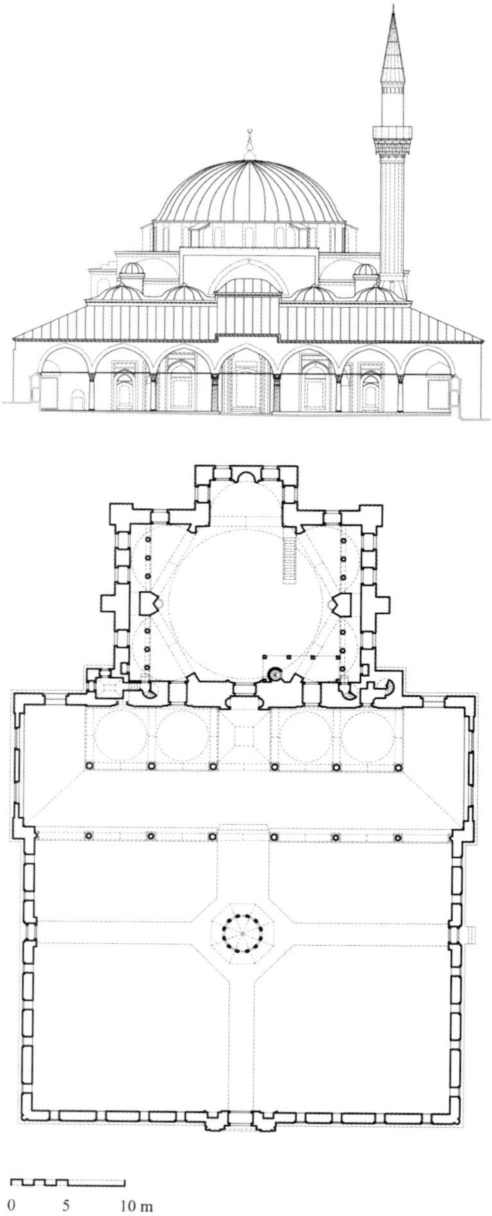

380 (above) Plan and elevation of the Semiz Ali Pasha mosque, Ereğli.

381 (right) Plan and elevation of the Semiz Ali Pasha mosque, Babaeski.

administrator, Mustafa Beg b. Abdülmennan.[56] It explains that the executor of the pasha's will, Ferruh Kethüda, first prepared his master's tomb near the shrine of Eyüp and then completed the mosque at Akviran.[57] A decree addressed to the kadi of Silivri on 3 July 1565 orders him to assist Mustafa Çavuş, the building supervisor of the late pasha's mosque at Akviran, in buying bricks and lime needed for its construction.[58]

This unknown mosque, finished soon after the pasha's demise, must have been a simple structure. So is the mosque that Sinan designed for him in the port of Marmara Ereğlisi (*c.* 1561–65). Extensively remodelled in 1865–86, it is a rectangular building constructed of alternating courses of stone and brick, fronted by a rebuilt wooden portico and covered by a hipped roof (illus. 380).[59] The hitherto unknown waqfiyya's specification concerning the posthumous construction of a mosque with a hospice in Babaeski reveals that the complex there could not have been built in the 1560s, as is usually assumed.[60] Moreover, the projecting mihrab of the hexagonal-baldachined mosque is a telltale sign pointing to its post-Selimiye date (illus. 4). Ferruh Kethüda probably commissioned it in the late 1560s from Sinan, who had built his own Friday mosque in the Balat quarter of Istanbul (1562–63).[61] The construction of the complex in Babaeski overlapped with that of the Selimiye in Edirne (1568–74), whose dependencies continued to be built throughout the 1580s (illus. 381). The Babaeski mosque seems to owe the harmony of its proportions to the sporadic personal oversight of Sinan, but awkward details visible upon closer inspection signal the work of a subordinate to whom he delegated its construction.

The chief architect's autobiographies mention the mosque and its no-longer-existing madrasa, but not the hospice included in the waqfiyya.[62] Evliya Çelebi counts among the dependencies of the mosque its madrasa, caravansaray, hospice, bath-house, and shops.[63] Today the only extant dependency is a single-domed commercial bath-house, located at a distance from the mosque in the town centre. Four fragmentary account books recording the expenditures of the complex between 1573 and 1577 testify to its ongoing construction in those years. They do not identify its architect but do provide the names of some master masons, lead casters, artisans, and decorators, imported from Edirne, Kırkkilise (Kırklareli), and Istanbul. The master masons included Hüseyin and Mustafa, who built the mosque portal, Usta Hızır, and Usta Hüsam.[64] Specialized masters (*üstādān*) were assisted by predominantly non-Muslim labourers (*ırġadān*), who ranged in number from nine to twenty-three and were paid five to six aspers a day.[65]

A fragment of the first account book from 1574 records the expenses of 'the new bath-house, and the new caravansaray, and shops' in Babaeski.[66] The second includes payments made between April 1574 and April 1575 for the gates of the mosque and bath-house, and for building materials. Under construction at that time were the mosque and its minaret (each covered by wooden scaffolding), the bath-house and its water channel, the caravansaray, and the shops.[67] A third account book, detailing expenses between September 1573 and September 1575, lists the costs of iron grills for the mosque's windows, lead for its roofs, chains for oil lamps, and materials used by painters.[68] Fees were paid to 'cart drivers for materials carried from Edirne to Babaeski', and for renting carts to 'transport painters from Edirne to Babaeski'.[69] The painters Nakkaş Osman and Nakkaş Mahmud were paid wages, along with the master mason Süleyman Halife, who carved an inscription.[70] A fourth account book, assembled between September 1576 and August 1577, lists the cost of materials (including indigo blue and gold leaf) for painting the prayer hall, which seems to have been completed around 1575.[71]

We learn from an imperial decree of 23 April 1584 addressed to the endowment administrator of Semiz Ali Pasha's waqf, that the mosque courtyard had not yet been built due a shortage of funds. On the administrator's behalf the kadi of Istanbul had requested an imperial permit for the construction of the missing courtyard, since surplus funds from the waqf had accumulated in the meantime. The sultan orders him 'to build a courtyard at the noble Friday mosque in a decorous (*münāsib*) manner', if the endowment is sufficient.[72] A follow-up decree sent on 12 September 1585 to the waqf administrator reads:

> The kadi of the protected metropolis of Edirne, Muslihüddin, has sent a letter, reporting that the above-mentioned deceased [grand vizier's] noble Friday mosque in Babaeski has remained incomplete because its front [portico] and its courtyard have not yet been built. He requested my imperial decree for its completion, since it would become completely ruined were it to stay in that condition. As long as the endowment permits, I order it to be completed: I command you to finish the front and the courtyard of the afore-mentioned noble Friday mosque if its endowment is sufficient.[73]

382 Semiz Ali Pasha mosque, Babaeski, from the southwest.

The shortage of funds not only explains the slow progress of construction, but also suggests possible cutbacks in the materials for dependencies, judging by their wholesale disappearance. Lambert Wyts, who passed through Babaeski in 1572, reported the ongoing construction of Semiz Ali Pasha's mosque (*mesquita*), bath (*bagno*), caravansaray (*caravassaray*), and hospice (*hospital*).[74] The Venetian ambassador Jacopo Soranzo (1575) says the complex had recently been built with the efforts of the pasha's descendants: 'This place, with a mosque and certain other edifices there, has been built a short time ago by the relatives of Ali Pasha, for his soul.' Soranzo stayed at the 'caravansaray neither large nor commodious', which had 'some small rooms where we lodged, though tightly'.[75] Late-sixteenth-century European travellers generally comment on the monumental mosque, only briefly mentioning its 'good enough' caravansaray and other dependencies.[76]

The Babaeski mosque, no longer surrounded by dependencies, is sited on a caravan station along the Istanbul–Edirne highway between Lüleburgaz and Havsa (illus. 382).[77] In the latter stations Semiz Ali Pasha's successor, Sokollu, commissioned two mosque complexes from Sinan, the first for himself and the second in memory of his late son Kasım Pasha. The larger complex in Lüleburgaz (*c.* 1565–69/70) features a cubical domed mosque fronted by a nine-bay double portico, while the smaller complex in Hafsa (1573–77) has a simpler mosque with a single

383 Semiz Ali Pasha mosque, Babaeski, interior view of the domical superstructure.

384 Semiz Ali Pasha mosque interior toward the qibla wall.

385 Semiz Ali Pasha mosque interior toward the west, with a marble preacher's lectern attached to the central pier.

three-bay portico. European travellers were more impressed with the services offered to passengers at these two complexes, which featured grand double caravansarays appended to hospices and guest-houses. By contrast, the relatively modest complex in Babaeski stood out from its neighbours by the unusually elaborate plan of its hexagonal-baldachined mosque, fronted by a double portico and a fountained garden court. It is the only example of a baldachin type mosque that Sinan ever built outside the capital.

One approaches Babaeski from the direction of Istanbul by crossing a bridge aligned with the modern highway that borders the west façade of Semiz Ali Pasha's mosque. The most impressive perspective of the pyramidally layered silhouette of the mosque is from that bridge, towards which its qibla façade is turned.[78] Like other posthumous monuments, the Babaeski mosque lacks a foundation inscription. A repair inscription on the north portal of its walled garden courtyard, which features a dodecagonal ablution fountain, records renovations made in 1832–33, when the mosque was redecorated with Europeanizing paintings. The muqarnas-galleried minaret raised on a tall base at the northwest corner of the prayer hall was rebuilt in 1934, having collapsed during the Bulgarian invasion of 1911–12.[79]

Three other complexes featuring mosques with hexagonal support systems were built in the capital around the same time as the complex in Babaeski (illus. 4): that of the grand vizier Kara Ahmed Pasha in Topkapı (1555, 1565–71/72), of İsmihan Sultan and Sokollu in Kadırga (*c.* 1567/68–1571/72), and of the queen Nurbanu Sultan in Üsküdar (1571–86). The 14-metre dome of Semiz Ali Pasha's provincial mosque is larger than those of its peers in Istanbul (Appendix 1). With its projecting mihrab, the nearly square plan of the Babaeski mosque comes closest to that of Nurbanu Sultan, prior to its expansion with double-domed side aisles between 1584 and 1586. Fronted by double porticoes, both mosques have free-standing lateral supports (piers in Babaeski and porphyry columns in Üsküdar), with their remaining four piers integrated in pairs into the qibla and anti-qibla walls.

The more elaborately piled-up pyramidal superstructure of Semiz Ali Pasha's mosque comprises a central dome surrounded by five exedral half-domes raised on fenestrated tall stone drums. The six flying buttresses that surround the drum of the central dome are supplemented by lateral stepped buttresses and four dome-capped weight turrets at each corner. The openwork geometric window lunettes that flood the interior with light are typical of Sinan's late works. The imposing five-bay double portico, completed around 1586, has iron-grilled windows at both ends that command vistas of the rural riverside setting.

The well-proportioned muqarnas-hooded portal is carved with a verse that welcomes the congregation into the gardens of paradise (39:73). A thematically matching fragmentary verse decorates the inner face of the portal on the anti-qibla wall: '[These are] Gardens of Eden which they enter (13:23).' The painted decorations of the cheerful interior were renewed in 1987. The original gilded paintings and inscriptions, executed by artists imported from Edirne, must have been unusually sophisticated for a provincial mosque. The effect of spatial unity inside the prayer hall is powerful. It is crowned by a lofty dome raised on six arches with unusual muqarnas-corbelled spandrels, which are seamlessly integrated with the V-shaped piers (illus. 383).

The awkward distribution of some windows reveals the apparent difficulty Sinan's assistant faced in coordinating the interior and exterior elevations. The internal windows of the mihrab recess are set too close together, and the muqarnased arch above the mihrab encroaches on the upper windows (illus. 384). The two free-standing lateral piers are pulled close to the side walls, whose narrow arcaded upper galleries are carried on delicate marble columns with lozenge capitals. A distinctive detail clearly points to the workmanship of stonemasons from Edirne: two marble preacher's pulpits in the form of truncated cones attached to the lateral piers, which resemble those adjacent to the piers of the mihrab recess in the Selimiye mosque (illus. 224, 229, 385).[80] The muqarnas-hooded marble mihrab with a triangular pediment, inscribed with the standard mihrab verse (3:37), also resembles that of the Selimiye. It is accompanied by an elegant latticework minbar, and a Bursa-arched muezzin's tribune at the west side of the entrance portal.

Evliya Çelebi is among the few Ottoman travellers to describe in some detail the mosque complex in Babaeski:

> The monumental Friday mosque of Ali Pasha along the river was founded by one of Süleyman's viziers, a prudent vizier known as Semiz Ali Pasha. In this town he has built a Friday mosque, which is as if it were a royal mosque. It resembles the mosque of [Kara] Ahmed Pasha inside the Topkapı gate in Istanbul. But compared to it, this one is more spacious, luminous, and ornate, and an exemplary perfect building. A madrasa, hospice, bath-house, caravansaray, and shops belong to the great charity of this Ali Pasha, all of them monumental works. The dome of the mosque, which reaches the sky, is visible from the distance of a day's journey, like the rising and falling waves of a sea of indigo-coloured lead. This exemplary work is the creation of Koca Mimar Sinan, who in this mosque has displayed elegant skills and graceful artistry, building a minaret so tall that it is as if it were the minaret of Rüstem Pasha.[81]

As the only provincial version of the hexagonal-baldachin scheme that Sinan was so fond of experimenting with in the capital, Semiz Ali Pasha's mosque differs from typical roadside complexes grouped around mosques with basic domed cubes. It owed its complex design in part to the chief architect's presence in nearby Edirne, from which skilled artisans were borrowed. Another reason for its distinctiveness was its conceptualization as the principal monument of the deceased grand vizier, who had not lived long enough to create a major mosque complex befitting his stature. To suit its patron's eminent status, the mosque in Babaeski transgressed codes of decorum observed in other provincial foundations. Accompanied by relatively modest dependencies, it forcefully called attention to itself by mimicking the prestige mosques of the capital. As the main focus of Semiz Ali Pasha's memorial complex, the mosque aspired to remind travellers of its departed patron's fame and to fulfil his sole desire recorded by Busbecq, 'to make his name live in the grateful memory of future ages'.

VIZIERS

I. SOFU (BOSNALI, HACI) MEHMED PASHA

Sofu Mehmed Pasha's mosque in Sofia is among the very few monuments in the Balkans attributed to Sinan, whose autobiographies omit the hospice and madrasa that once accompanied it (illus. 386, 387).[1] The mosque was remodelled in 1903 as a Byzantinizing cathedral church with a bell tower.[2] Its minaret and five-bay portico were eliminated and only its structural skeleton remains: a cube crowned by a dome with muqarnas-corbelled squinches carried on eight pointed arches.[3] Its Bosnian-born patron, educated in the imperial palace, was nicknamed Sofu (devout) or Hacı (hajj pilgrim) on account of his steadfast piety. We learn from the *Tezkiretü'l-bünyān* that the chief architect knew him from the Moldavian campaign of 1538, when 'Sofu Mehmed Pasha, who was the governor-general of Rumelia' and a man of 'considerable foresight' convinced the grand vizier to dismantle a bridge built by Sinan over the Pruth river.[4]

Becoming fourth vizier in 1539, the pasha, together with the new governor-general of Rumelia, led an army to Hungary in 1541.[5] Before Sultan Süleyman arrived in Buda (conquered twice in 1526 and 1529), Sofu Mehmed Pasha's vanguard forces had defeated the fleeing Hapsburg army. After its third conquest that year, Buda – the kernel of Budapest – became the capital of a new province comprising the Hungarian territories of the empire. The pasha eventually rose to the post of second vizier, from which he was demoted to become the governor of Baghdad and Bosnia. He passed away in 1557, soon after his promotion as the governor-general of Buda.[6] Mustafa Āli says he was poisoned by a Jewish physician, who confessed he had caused the death of 'forty other Mehmeds'.[7]

The Arabic waqfiyya of Sofu Mehmed Pasha, registered in January 1548, refers to him as the 'second vizier'. It mentions his Friday mosque, madrasa, and hospice in Sofia; and his now-lost monuments in the capital (a Friday mosque outside the city walls and a hadith college near his palace).[8] A later waqfiyya, recorded in 1554–55, covers his endowments in Banjaluka (Friday mosque, caravansaray, and bath-house) where he was based as the sanjak governor of Bosnia.[9] Besides Sofu (Bosnalı) Mehmed Pasha's Friday mosque in Sofia, Sinan's autobiographies list his mosque in Diyarbakır (an unknown monument); his hadith college and nearby palace in the Hocapaşa quarter of Istanbul; his school for Koran recitation (unidentified but probably in the capital); and his palace in Bosnia.[10] In the summer of 1544, the Frenchman Jérome Maurand described the 'very beautiful' public audience hall of the vizier's palace in the capital, whose figural tiles depicted trees with 'naturalistic' peacocks and parrots. At that time Sofu Mehmed Pasha was serving as the lieutenant governor of Istanbul while the sultan's court was away in Bursa.[11]

A poem composed by the poet Zaifi gives a completion date of 954 (1547–48) for the pasha's mosque, madrasa, and hospice in Sofia.[12] The same date is carved on the Turkish foundation inscription of the mosque, preserved in the Bulgarian Archaeological Museum. Like the waqfiyya of 1548, the inscription refers to the patron of the 'noble Friday mosque', built during Sultan Süleyman's reign as 'the vizier of the age, Mehmed Pasha b. Abdülmuin'. It asks God to accept his pious foundation and ends with a chronogram: 'The House of God, the Assembler, the Everlasting, the Eternal' [954 (1547–48)].[13] This confirms that the patron was a vizier during the inauguration of his mosque in Sofia, where he had once been based as the governor-general of Rumelia.[14]

The waqfiyya indicates that the mosque complex was located outside the centre of Sofia, on a plain called Pınarcık. Its south

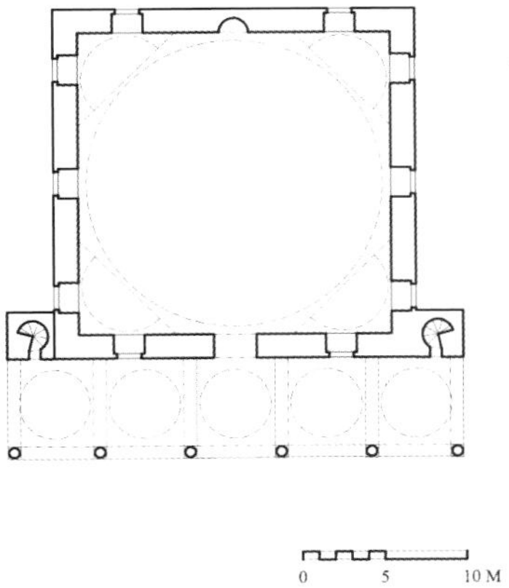

386 Reconstruction plan of the Sofu Mehmed Pasha mosque, Sofia.

387 Sofu Mehmed Pasha mosque, Sofia, now the church of Sveti Sedmocislenitse.

and north sides had empty plots; on the east it was bordered by a highway known as 'the road of the ghazis' (*ġāziler yolı*), and along its west side passed another road that led to the convent (*zāviye*) of Shaykh Bali Dede.[15] The latter can be identified as the Halveti shaykh Sofyalı Bali, celebrated as a champion of holy war against the 'infidel'.[16] The site of the mosque, then, was closely associated with the memories of holy warfare. Legends related by Bulgarian historians identify it as the place where Sultan Süleyman had camped en route to Hungary in 1526, claiming that the mosque was built to commemorate the locus of the imperial tent and the conquest of Buda.[17]

It is therefore no coincidence that the pasha, whose vanguard forces reconquered Hungary in 1541, chose that site for his mosque complex. The waqfiyya explains that behind the qibla wall of the mosque was the hospice (*ʿimārat*) which comprised a guest-house and caravansaray (*tābkhāna wa iṣṭabl*), a kitchen, a commissariat, and latrines. The madrasa, composed of sixteen cells and endowed with a manuscript library, was located at the north side of the mosque courtyard, which was planted with trees and featured a pool with an ablution fountain.[18] The pasha's income-producing endowments in Sofia included a bath-house, a khan, shops, neighbouring villages, and arable lands.[19]

The mosque, converted into a church, is situated in what is now a park. Located far from the centre of the old city, its site marked the entrance into the Rumelian capital from a road connected with the mining town of Samokov. Also known as the Hospice (İmaret) mosque or the Black (Kara) mosque because of its black granite walls, it was the largest single domed structure that Sinan designed beyond Edirne with its 18.3-metre dome.[20] Evliya Çelebi likens the vizierial mosque of 'Koca Derviş Mehmed Pasha' to a royal foundation and mentions its madrasa, its hospice (whose caravansaray housed a hundred horses), and its bath-house:

> They call this the Hospice Mosque; it is an illuminated place of worship. It has a lofty dome like a royal mosque. Its interior and exterior are very artistic. It has an extremely spacious courtyard and the domes on top of all the columns are covered with indigo blue lead. And its tall minaret is high and well-proportioned. This light-filled mosque is the work of Sultan Süleyman Khan's architect, Koca Sinan. Among vizierial mosques, it is in this place of worship that the famous architect's artistic power is most clearly manifest.[21]

The mosque must have impressed Evliya with the sheer size of its dome and the simple majesty of its proportions. Popular legends preserved the memory of its association with holy warfare and perhaps prompted its conversion into a cathedral church, thereby preserving its structural core for posterity.

II. HADIM İBRAHİM PASHA

With its domed cube fronted by a five-bay portico, Hadım (Eunuch) İbrahim Pasha's mosque within the Silivri gate conformed to codes of decorum observed in early-sixteenth-century vizierial mosques (illus. 388, 389).[22] In the capital Sinan articulated the rank of grand viziers with innovative baldachin-type mosques graced by internal galleries raised on precious columns. The subordinate status of viziers was expressed in simpler mosques with octagonal zones of transition – either domed cubes like the Silivrikapı mosque or variants of the baldachin type lacking internal columnar arcades.

Hadım İbrahim Pasha, a chief white eunuch of Süleyman's palace, held the post of governor-general of Anatolia before becoming fourth vizier in 1544. As a vizier he was appointed lieutenant governor of Istanbul during the Safavid campaign of 1548–49.[23] Bernardo Navagero refers to him in 1553 as third

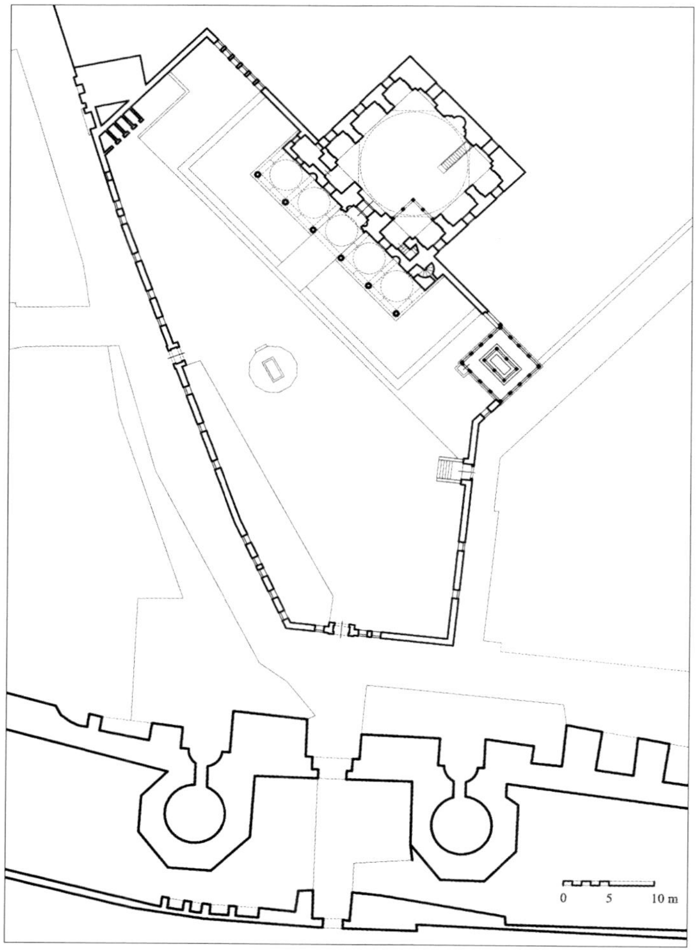

388 Plan of the Hadım İbrahim Pasha mosque and mausoleum, Silivrikapı.

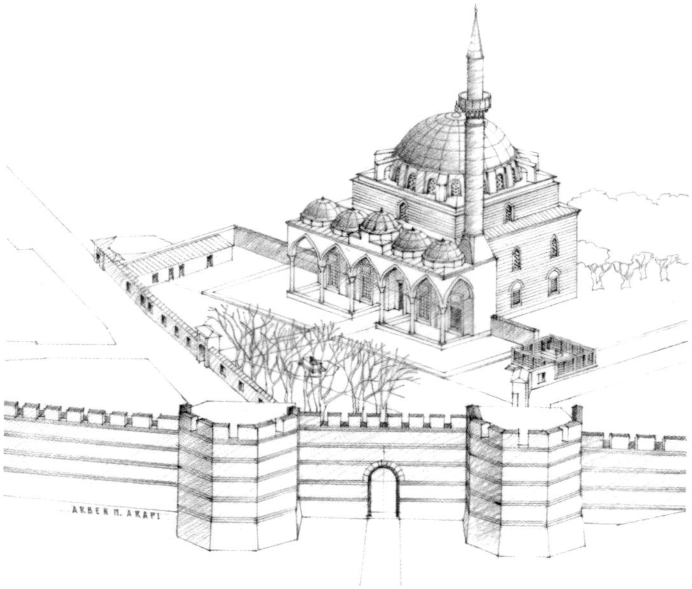

389 Axonometric projection of the Hadım İbrahim Pasha mosque and mausoleum.

vizier and describes him as an eighty-year-old eunuch of Bosnian origin.[24] After prince Mustafa's execution that year, the pasha rose to the rank of second vizier and was sent from the sultan's camp in Aleppo to Bursa to strangle the late prince's son. Returning to the capital, he replaced the deposed grand vizier Rüstem Pasha's brother, Sinan Pasha, as the lieutenant governor of Istanbul (1553–55).[25] When the sultan's court came back to the capital in 1555, he was asked to retire from office on account of his old age, and he passed away in 1562.[26] Mustafa Āli characterizes the retired pasha as one of the few eunuchs who was 'restrained by modesty' and whose 'propriety and dignity was not questioned by anybody'.[27]

According to its foundation inscriptions cited below, the funerary mosque at Silivrikapı was completed in 1551 while its patron was third vizier. A waqfiyya registered on 21 January 1562 lists the pious foundations the pasha created in Istanbul: a Friday mosque and an upper-storey (*fevḳānī*) elementary school inside the Silivrikapı gate; a monastic church converted into a masjid near the İsakapı gate, which was accompanied by a madrasa and an elementary school; another elementary school near the Arcadius column; and a water well for travellers outside the Yenikapı gate.[28] The pasha apparently chose to build his monuments in the sparsely populated outskirts of the city, along the Byzantine land walls settled by predominantly Christian communities, in order to foster Islamization.[29] The income-producing properties that he endowed comprised villages donated by the sultan; arable fields, mills, and shops in Rumelia; and real estate properties in Edirne and Istanbul (including two palaces in the İshakpaşa and Sinanağa quarters).[30]

Properties endowed near the Silivrikapı mosque consisted of three baths, as well as shops and houses (some of them earmarked for the use of the four muezzins, imam, preacher, and schoolteacher). Until flowing water was brought to the mosque, water would be pulled from the well in its garden cultivated by a salaried gardener. The staff of the mosque and elementary school would preferably be selected from the pasha's manumitted slaves and their descendants. During his lifetime the founder would administer his own waqf, to be replaced upon his death by Müslihüddin Hoca and thereafter by the governors of Kütahya (a city where the pasha had resided as the governor-general of Anatolia). The endowment would be overseen by the chief white eunuchs of the imperial palace, once again an office the patron had held in the past.[31] The castrated, childless donor thus expressed his sense of corporate identity in the selection of administrators and overseers for his relatively modest waqf.

Sinan's autobiographies mention the Hadım İbrahim Pasha's mosque, bath-house, and mausoleum at Silivrikapı, along with his masjid and madrasa at İsakapı.[32] The only remaining structure in Silivrikapı is the landmark mosque and its mausoleum at one of the busiest entry points into the capital (illus. 390). It is theatrically staged by the archway of the Byzantine city gate,

390 Hadım İbrahim Pasha mosque, Silivrikapı, from the northwest.

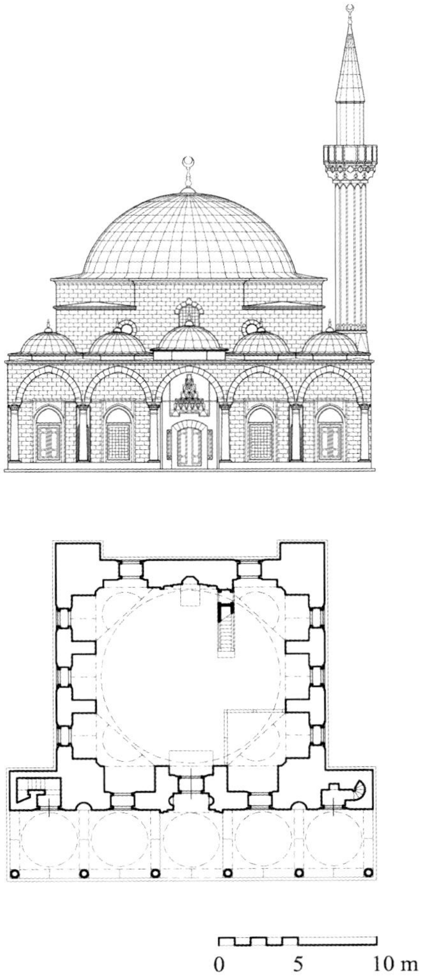

391 Plan and elevation of the Bali Pasha [Hüma Hatun] mosque, Yenibahçe.

with which the main door of its ashlar stone precinct wall is aligned. The precinct with three gates and an arched public fountain in one corner contains a garden court with a well, a reservoir, latrines, an off-centre ablution fountain, and the pasha's humble mausoleum at the west side of the mosque portico. The transparent white marble open-air mausoleum, surrounded by rectangular iron-grilled windows, overlooks a narrow street to encourage the prayers of passers-by.

The closest comparison to the Silivrikapı mosque, built with alternating courses of stone and brick, is the ashlar masonry mosque of Bali Pasha in the Yenibahçe quarter, dated to 910 (1504–5) by the chronogram of its foundation inscription, which identifies its builder as 'Hüma Hatun, the daughter of the vizier İskender' (illus. 391).[33] Like several other monuments jointly endowed by husbands and wives, the mosque was named after Hüma Hatun's husband. Puzzled by the inclusion of this early mosque and its no-longer-extant mausoleum in the chief architect's autobiographies, scholars generally agree that it was renovated by Sinan at an unknown date.[34] I shall take a brief detour to discuss his contribution to this mosque before comparing it with the one in Silivrikapı. The autobiographies refer to it as the mosque of Bali Pasha in Yenibahçe, but Sinan's waqfiyya calls it the 'Friday mosque built by Hüma Hatun' to which he endowed a water channel that conducted water from his own neighbouring masjid and elementary school.[35]

Ayvansarayi claims that Hüma Hatun was a daughter of Bayezid II and that she completed the mosque of her husband, the vizier Bali Pasha (d. 1494), upon his death (both were buried together in its no-longer-extant mausoleum). However, as the inscription indicates, she was actually the daughter of the vizier İskender Pasha, who had been executed by his royal father-in-law, Selim I, in 1515. We shall see in Chapter 12 that her brother, Osmanshah Beg, commissioned from Sinan two mosques – one for his late royal mother, a daughter of Selim I, in the capital (now lost), and the other for himself in Trikkala.[36] A waqf register of Istanbul, compiled in 1546, lists the 'Friday mosque of Bali Pasha' as a monument whose waqfiyya had not yet been registered because its endower was still alive.[37] A later

392 Hadım İbrahim Pasha mosque, Yenibahçe, interior toward the qibla wall.

393 Hadım İbrahim Pasha mosque, Silivrikapı, interior toward the west.

register (*c.* 1578–80), which identifies the mosque with both Bali Pasha and his wife Hüma Hatun, summarizes her waqfiyyas of 1563 and 1572, by which she donated houses to the endowment of the mosque.[38] Another waqfiyya of 'Bali Pasha b. Abdurrahman', registered in 1566, records his endowments for 'the noble Friday mosque built by Hüma Hatun', appointing as the administrator of his waqf 'Hüma Hatun, the daughter of the late İskender Pasha'.[39]

Sometime before 1546, Sinan either completed the mosque (whose foundations may have been laid by Hüma Hatun's executed father in 1504–5) or extensively rebuilt it.[40] Whatever the circumstances of its construction, its plan furnished a model for the vizierial mosque of Hadım İbrahim Pasha. There is little difference between the spatial organization of these single-domed mosques with three deep recesses on each side and two others flanking their gates. They share almost identical ground plans, although their elevations differ considerably. The blind dome of Bali Pasha's mosque (11.8 metres wide), set on an archaic octagonal base without a window-pierced drum, was rebuilt in 1937, having collapsed in the earthquake of 1894.[41] The ground-level recesses surrounding the prayer hall on three sides support narrow upper galleries and are independent from the transition system of the dome, raised on pendentives.

Now I am returning from my detour to Hadım İbrahim Pasha's mosque, whose eight internal buttresses articulating deep recesses rise all the way to the top of the walls and are treated as an integral part of the superstructure (illus. 392, 393).[42] Its bright interior is illuminated by three tiers of windows and the arches of its recessed alcoves delineate an inner arcade parallel to the eight upper arches carrying the dome. The conch-shell squinches of the 12-metre dome are not expressed externally as an octagonal base; instead, the dome rests on a cubical base that contributes to the layered composition of the external façades. Its lead-covered Sinanesque drum, whose engaged pilaster buttresses alternate with windows, is reinforced at each corner by paired flying buttresses. The ashlar masonry north façade is distinguished from the other walls, constructed with stone and brick courses. The five-domed portico rests on arches with a slightly ogee profile that are supported by marble columns with alternating muqarnas and lozenge capitals. The portico extends beyond the mosque walls to mask the base of the stone minaret (rebuilt in 1763–64), which is balanced on the opposite corner by a room.[43]

With its mixed masonry, its deeply recessed archaic muqarnas-hooded portal, and its conch-shell squinches, the mosque recalls early examples of the domed-cube scheme: the mosques of the vizier Çoban Mustafa Pasha in Gebze (1520s) and Hürrem Sultan in Avratpazarı (1538–39). Its ornate and exceptionally refined pre-classical decorative programme includes underglaze-painted tiles, used by Sinan for the first time in place of the *cuerda seca* tiles that decorate the complexes of Hürrem Sultan, Şehzade Mehmed (1543–48), and Kara Ahmed Pasha (*c.* 1555). The unusual tiles dominated by abstract foliate designs have a rare colour scheme of blue, turqoise, light purple, white, and black. A few naturalistic tulips and carnations, which timidly appear

394 Hadım İbrahim Pasha mosque, Silivrikapı, underglaze İznik tile lunette and roundel on the north façade.

among the monumental *thuluth* inscriptions of the ogee-arched lunette tiles in the portico, foreshadow the floral idiom that would emerge during the second half of the 1550s in the Süleymaniye complex (illus. 394). The comparable ogee-arched portico lunettes of the grand vizier Kara Ahmed Pasha's mosque within the neighbouring gate of Topkapı feature the last known examples of *cuerda seca* tiles (illus. 374).

The epigraphic programme of the Hadım İbrahim Pasha mosque emphasizes the duty of congregational prayers and invites worshippers into paradise. Two of the gates in the precinct wall have carved Turkish chronograms in *thuluth* script, composed by the poet Kandi. The one on the principal gate facing Silivrikapı reads:

> Thank God! This Friday mosque came into being on its site,
> For the house of the world becomes prosperous with the beauty of charitable works.
>
> The vizier who is the possessor of justice made with good fortune
> This exalted Friday mosque, aided by the Eternal God.
>
> With glory and honour; Kandi said its date:
> 'İbrahim Pasha made this Friday mosque adorned and strong', the year 958 [1551].[44]

The inscription on the gate facing the avenue of Silivrikapı reads:

> 'İbrahim Pasha made this exalted Friday mosque
> With prosperity [. . . broken . . .] in a joy-bringing year',
>
> So that the gathered community may perform the five prayers
> With litanies praising God day and night.
>
> The well-wisher Kandi said its completion date:
> 'This sanctuary was created with honour at a consecrated time', the year 958 [1551].[45]

A third poem by Kandi, carved on a rectangular panel under the muqarnas hood of the mosque gate, provides the same completion date; it is flanked by two square panels that spell out the profession of faith. The inscription emphasizes the site of the mosque along a road:

> The Asaph (Solomon's vizier) with pure faith, İbrahim,
> It is he who made this charitable building.
>
> Thank God, it reached completion,
> This roadside attained honour with his Friday mosque.
>
> Kandi said the date for this Friday mosque:
> 'House of the Guide to the Right Path [God] and place of worship of the Righteous,' the year 958 [1551].[46]

The arched lunettes on the north façade feature white-on-blue calligraphic tiles framed by black-and-turquoise borders with vegetal scrolls. The verse inscribed on the lunette over the minaret door welcomes the congregation into the gardens of paradise (39:73). The tile roundel above it rotates invocations of divine epithets: 'O, the Most Compassionate! O, the All-Bounteous!' The corresponding door lunette at the northeast corner quotes a similar verse inviting the congregation into the heavenly abode (13:24). The roundel on top of it rotates other divine epithets: 'O, the All-Sufficing! O, the Intercessor! O, the Enricher!' The removed tile panel of the window lunette at the righ side of the central portal (now kept at the Vakıf Türk İnşaat ve Sanat Eserleri Müzesi) complemented its counterpart on the left, which quotes a fragmentary hadith: 'The hypocrite inside a masjid is like a bird in a cage.' The missing part of that hadith on the second panel concerns the true believer: 'The believer in a masjid is like a fish in water.'

Inside the prayer hall, the dome quotes the Fatiha sura, which asks the 'Lord of the Worlds' and the 'Owner of the Day of Judgment' to reveal 'the straight path' of favoured ones (1:1–7). The spandrels of the eight arches carrying the dome are painted with roundels bearing the revered names. The divine epithets cited on the north façade are echoed inside by the ninety-nine beautiful names of God, painted in monumental *thuluth* on the arched lunettes of ground-level windows bordered with vegetal scrolls. Each of the recessed alcoves on the side walls has its own low-relief plasterwork mihrab, with a foliate ogee arch framed inside a rectangle (illus. 393). Decorative niches with foliate arches flank the window lunettes.

Framed by a monumental pointed arch, the muqarnas-hooded white marble mihrab is unique in its composition (illus. 392). Its arched lunette tile, with a blue-on-turquoise inscription cartouche surrounded by blue-and-white vegetal scrolls, quotes the standard mihrab verse (3:37). Composed of two cartouches, the inscription band above the mihrab arch affirms the necessity of worship at fixed hours (3:103). The exquisitely carved white marble minbar, with its dainty fluted cap matching the conch-shell squinches, is decorated with gilded *saz* leaves, palmettes, rosettes, and Chinese cloud bands, accompanied by openwork geometric interlaces. The muezzin's tribune at the northwest corner of the prayer hall is raised on Bursa arches.

The religious inscriptions resonate with Kandi's chronograms, which emphasize the piety of the patron, who built the mosque for the performance of litanies praising God and of the five daily prayers by 'righteous' congregations seeking the 'right path.' They articulate the aged patron's concern for religious uprightness and for a final reward in paradise. His preoccupation with ritual propriety is recorded by Ayvansarayi:

> [Hadım İbrahim Paşa] endowed a special building in order to take the greatest care [in determining] the time of the blessed call to prayer. Erecting two tall columns inside it, he set a wooden beam across their tops, and placed several hourglasses [on it] that could be turned with pulleys. Whoever dwells in that house watches those timepieces and, when the time for the call to prayer arrives, he strikes that plank. The muezzin, anticipating the sound, notes it, ascends the minaret and recites the call.[47]

Particularly impressed with this mosque, Evliya Çelebi uses it as a comparison for provincial non-royal mosques that he considers artistic (*muṣannaʿ*), such as those of Sokollu in Lüleburgaz and Payas.[48] He finds the paradisaical sanctuary spiritually moving and aesthetically pleasing:

> The late pasha, who retired while he was Süleyman Khan's grand vizier [*sic*], built at the inner side of Silivrikapı a spiritual single-storey mosque which is, as it were, a lofty pavilion of the sublime paradise. The interior of its courtyard is decorated with tall trees and its manner of construction is extremely artistic and joy-giving because its builder was Mimar Sinan.[49]

Built at a time when the chief achitect was busy laying the foundations of the Süleymaniye, the mosque in Silivrikapı decorously expressed its patron's vizierial rank through the elaboration of the dome-on-a-cube theme. It is distinguished by its sophisticated decorative programme and its creative interpretation of the recessed plan type introduced in the Bali Pasha mosque. Modernizing the superstructure of its model with a dome supported on eight engaged piers forming an internal arcade, it embodies both traditional and innovative features. Its plan provided a model for the mosques of some provincial governor-generals, such as those of Dukakinzade Mehmed Pasha in Aleppo, Behram Pasha in Diyarbakır, and Hacı Ahmed Pasha in Kayseri.[50] Anticipating the more elaborate octagonal schemes of later vizierial mosques of ashlar masonry in the capital, the Silivrikapı mosque effectively bridged past and future.

III. PERTEV MEHMED PASHA

Pertev (Light-Ray) Mehmed Pasha's mosque complex, visually dominating the harbour of İzmit at the confluence of major land and sea routes, was posthumously built in accordance with his will (illus. 395, 396). The harmonious proportions of the single-domed ashlar masonry mosque, the most impressive component of the loosely ordered complex, were due in part to the proximity of İzmit to the capital. The largely ruined dependencies were constructed with cheaper materials, as in the grand vizier Semiz Ali Pasha's comparable posthumous complex, whose mosque owed its refinement to the closeness of Babaeski to Edirne.

The Albanian-born Pertev Pasha had been brought up in the imperial palace, from which he exited as chief gatekeeper. He was promoted to janissary agha in 1544, a post he occupied for about a decade. He became the governor-general of Rumelia in 1553, fourth vizier in 1555, and third vizier in 1561.[51] Marcantonio Donini (1562) was not particularly impressed by him: 'He is over 55 years old, and an Albanian relative of [the second vizier] Ferhad Pasha, being married to the mother of the latter's wife; he uses few words, lacks deeds, and is somewhat simple and uninformed about the affairs of the world.'[52] His non-royal wife, Fütuha Hatun, the widow of Şehzade Mehmed, was the mother of princess Humashah (Huma), who had married Ferhad Pasha.[53] In 1565 Pertev Pasha became second vizier and a year later he was appointed the commander-in-chief of a campaign in Transylvania, where he distinguished himself by conquering several strongholds. Disgraced as a commander during the naval battle of Lepanto, however, he was dismissed from his post in 1571 (illus. 397). Mustafa Āli praises the deposed vizier's 'moral qualities' and 'honest character'.[54] He passed away in his mid-sixties on 9 October 1572 and was buried at the family mausoleum built by Sinan in Eyüp for 'the ray (*pertev*) of the light of God'.[55]

Having served as the building overseer of the Şehzade Mehmed mosque, Pertev Pasha must have cultivated a close relationship with the chief architect, who built for him a palace at the public square of Vefa, where the office of royal architects was located (illus. 157).[56] Sinan seems to have paid personal attention to the late pasha's impressive mosque in İzmit, delegating its construction to one of his talented associates. The *Teẕkiretü'l-bünyān* confirms that it was posthumously built: 'For the soul of the late Pertev Pasha, a mosque in İznikmid (modern İzmit).'[57]

An undated Turkish waqfiyya written before the pasha's death states that he endowed 20,000 florins (1,200,000 aspers) for the construction of a Friday mosque on an unspecified site.[58] If the interest yielded by that sum proved insufficient for a 'solidly built' and 'beautifully designed' mosque decorated with utmost care, it would be supplemented by other income from the pasha's waqf.[59] Endowed with twenty-one religious manuscripts, the mosque was to be furnished with six oversize Korans displayed on wooden reading stands next to the mihrab and a 'sufficient number' of large carpets. It would be accompanied by

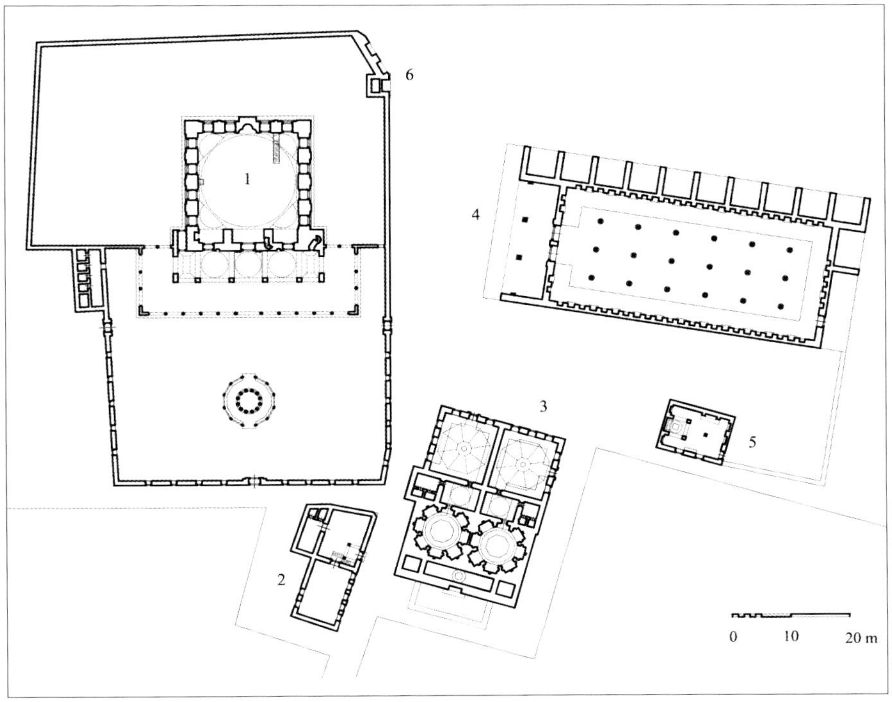

395 Plan of the Pertev Mehmed Pasha mosque, İzmit, with hypothetical reconstruction of the complex:

1. Mosque
2. Elementary school
3. Double bath
4. Caravansaray with shops
5. Hospice
6. Reservoir with public fountains

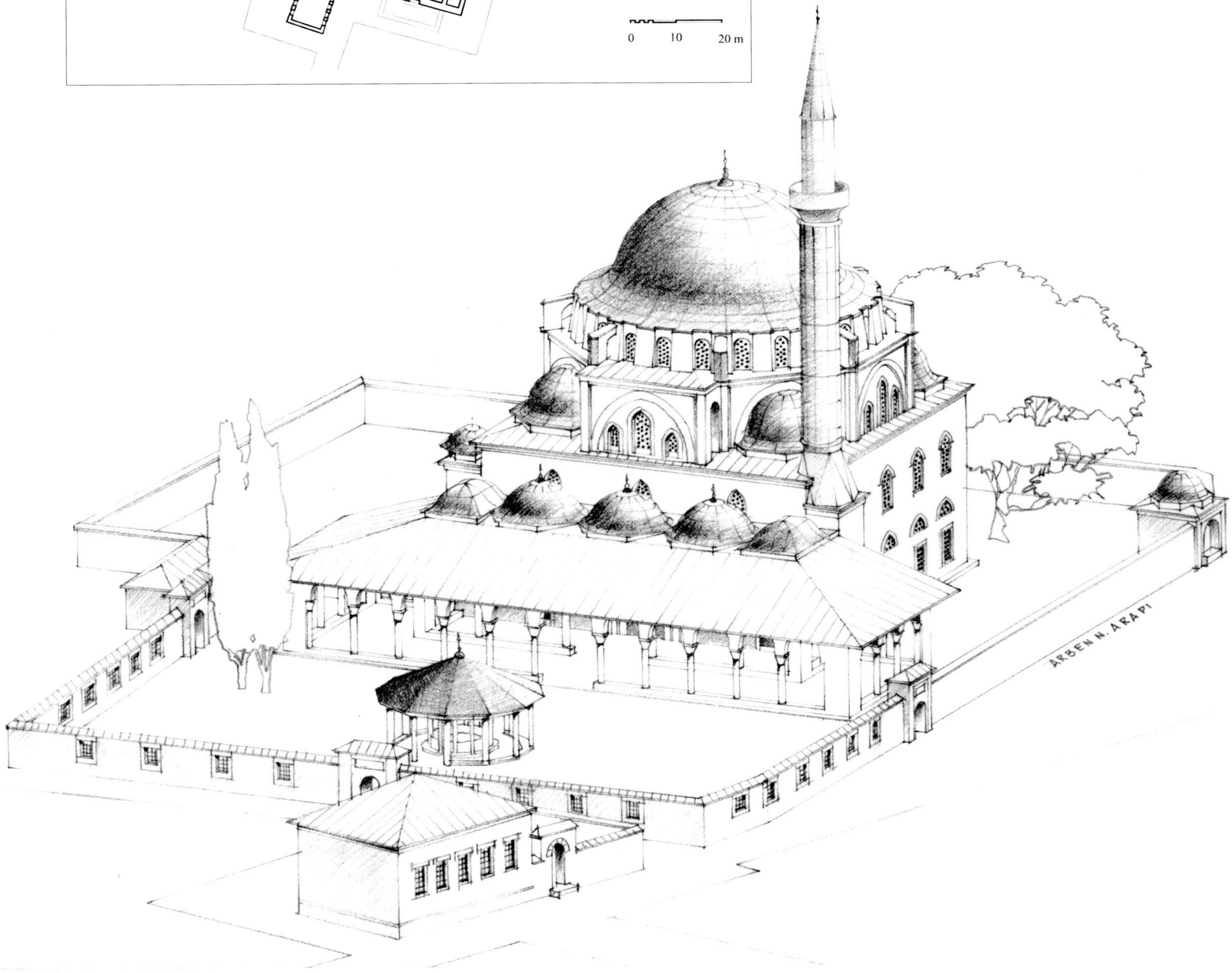

396 Axonometric projection of the Pertev Mehmed Pasha mosque.

397 The second vizier Pertev Mehmed Pasha presiding over a council meeting at his palace, c. 1581, watercolour on paper, from Lokman, *Shāhnāma-i Salīm Khān*.

an elementary school and a charge-free caravansaray with twelve fireplaces. The caravansaray, built with rubble masonry and bricks (*seng ü kīl*), was to be covered by a roof of terracotta tiles (*kiremid*), unless the waqf funds should prove sufficient to construct it in stone (*kārgīr*) and cover it with a lead roof. After the collection of additional surplus funds, the caravansaray guests would each be served free food once a day.[60] To support naval warfare, the waqf surplus would also cover the lodging costs of oarsmen at houses in the neighbourhood of the mosque.[61] This suggests that the site of the complex near the imperial arsenal of İzmit, where warships were built, was chosen before the demise of the pasha who endowed lands, mills, and shops near İzmit, along with commercial properties on the waterfront of the city (a warehouse for flour merchants and six others for marines).[62] He also endowed properties in such places as Gallipoli, Silistra, Malkara, and Istanbul, as well as his palace in Vefa.[63]

The waqfiyya, which mentions properties endowed as late as March 1571, seems to have been written just before the pasha, referred to as Selim II's vizier, left for Lepanto in the spring of that year. It asks God to increase his pomp, suggesting that the site of his projected mosque complex near İzmit's imperial arsenal may have been selected to commemorate the naval battle he was hoping to win.[64] Pertev Pasha stipulated that upon his death, his steward Sinan Kethüda b. Abdülmennan should serve as the administrator of his waqf, which would be overseen by grand viziers.[65] The steward would be succeeded by the manumitted slaves of the pasha, who asked his children not to meddle in the affairs of his pious foundation.[66] He assigned a daily stipend to each of these living children (three sons and two daughters) and thereafter to their descendants. Upon his demise, thirty sections of the Koran would daily be read for his soul at the mausoleum Sinan built for him in Eyüp. Eight other persons would recite the monotheistic formula, litanies praising God, and special prayers for his departed spirit. When the mother of his children, Fütuha Hatun, passed away, one section of the Koran would be read for her soul in the mausoleum; a section of the Koran was already being recited there for the pasha's late son, Ahmed, and his parents, who must have converted to Islam.[67]

The posthumous construction of the Pertev Pasha mosque was supervised by his steward, Sinan Kethüda, who probably received detailed instructions from his departed master. An imperial decree addressed on 13 August 1573 to the kadis of İzmit and other cities in northwest Anatolia (Kandıra and Taşköprü) concerns the provision of building materials for which the late pasha's steward, Sinan, had requested a firman. The kadis are informed that 'stones and timbers and lime are needed for the deceased Pertev Pasha's mosque, which is going to be built in İznikmid' (İzmit). The existence of imperial stone quarries in İzmit and the abundance of timber from neighbouring forests must have facilitated the collecting of building materials. The presence of skilled stone cutters in the state quarries of İzmit contributed to the high quality of carved detailing in the mosque. A copy of the same decree sent to the kadi of Samokov and to Mehmed Çavuş orders them to allow the pasha's men to buy the iron tools required for constructing the mosque and to transport them in rented carts. Another copy dispatched to the kadi of Kratovo orders him not to let anyone hinder the buying of lead or the renting of carts.[68]

Like most posthumously built mosques, Pertev Pasha's lacks a foundation inscription; dated inscriptions in *taʿlīḳ* script are instead carved on the precinct wall of the mosque. One of them is located on a public fountain at the southwest corner of the precinct wall: 'The gracious fountain of Pertev Mehmed Pasha, the year 987 (1579–80)' (illus. 398).[69] The other, above the west gate of the forecourt, gives the same completion date: 'The noble mosque of Pertev Mehmed Pasha, the year 987 (1579–80).'[70] This date is repeated in a third inscription inside the prayer hall, painted in monumental *thuluth* on the west pier abutting the gate and signed by an otherwise unknown calligrapher: 'Written by the humble Mehmed, the scribe of the majuscule script (*el-kātib el-müṣennā*), the year 987 (1579–80).'[71]

The waterfront complex is located outside the ancient walls of the upper city. The seventeenth-century French traveller Jean-Baptiste Tavernier describes the shipbuilding yards along the quay, lined by warehouses stacked with timber used in the construction of ships and houses.[72] In 1646 Evliya Çelebi saw warehouses, shops, khans, and coffeehouses along the quay of the bustling commercial port.[73] Pertev Pasha's *extramuros* complex formed the nucleus of a new settlement called the 'quarter of the new Friday mosque' (Yeni Cuma Mahallesi). It combined the characteristics of a roadside complex with the urban functions of an elementary school. Turning its qibla wall towards the quay, the mosque is situated in the midst of two walled gardens planted with trees. The forecourt is surrounded by a rubble masonry precinct wall (rebuilt in 1962) featuring iron-grilled windows and three gates. The refined marble ablution fountain in the forecourt is composed of a domed central core with twelve white marble columns, whose muqarnas capitals carry pointed arches with red and white marble joggled voussoirs. Its rebuilt outer canopy, with a conical lead roof, is supported on twelve modern columns that replaced the original wooden pillars seen in old photographs.[74] The original urban fabric around the complex has completely vanished with the creation of roads and a park that now contains the ruined dependencies.[75] Built of rubble masonry and covered with wooden roofs, the dependencies diagonally oriented at the west side of the mosque were an elementary school, a caravansaray with a small hospice kitchen, and a double bath.[76] These unassuming structures accentuated the primacy of the ashlar masonry mosque, fronted by a handsome double portico.

The dated inscriptions of the west gate and the precinct fountain indicate that the main seaside approach to the complex was from the southwest. The triple-arched fountain on the bevelled southwest corner of the precinct wall faces an open public space that provides an ideal perspective of the mosque (illus. 398). Its layered walls rise in three clearly defined zones: the cubical block of walls; the high octagonal zone of transition, featuring four exedral half-domes and triple-windowed tympanum arches; and the lead-covered drum of the dome pierced by windows and reinforced with engaged pilasters and eight flying buttresses. The austere exterior, which reflects the interior structure, displays a classical harmony of proportions no longer evinced in other mosques that Sinan designed in the capital in those years, such as the mosque of Sokollu at Azapkapı (*c.* 1573–77/78).

The prayer hall, crowned by a lofty single dome raised on four squinches with muqarnas corbels, is spatially extended at the north side by three vaulted recesses arranged in two storeys. The upper gallery has a private balcony flanked by two muezzin's tribunes. Over-sized windows in three tiers bathe the interior with light, as if to evoke the patron's name (illus. 399). The ground-level windows have openwork arched lunettes of bottle-glass and the qibla wall boasts lavish stained-glass windows with inscriptions and intricate plasterwork grills. The muqarnas-hooded and pediment-crowned marble mihrab is fitted inside a tall arch, featuring a bullseye window on top and two tiers of windows at each side. The standard mihrab verse (3:37) is carved on a rectangular panel beneath the bullseye window, whose inscriptions in stained glass quote the profession of faith.

The painted decorations, restored in 1952–61, are dominated by red, blue, black, and white. The Koranic epigraphy glorifies the divine creator and His revelation transmitted by the Prophet Muhammad (the founder's namesake) to guide worshippers towards the correct path. The central roundel of the dome affirms God's absolute power in keeping the heavens and the earth in their fixed orbits (35:41). The spandrels of the eight dome arches have painted roundels bearing the revered

398 Pertev Mehmed Pasha mosque with fountain at the southwest corner of the precinct wall, İzmit.

399 Pertev Mehmed Pasha mosque interior.

names. The four squinches under them continuously quote two verses from the Anʿam sura. Starting at the right of the qibla wall and moving counter-clockwise, they declare the unity of the divine creator, whose revelation guided Muhammad to turn away from the idolaters (6:79–80).

The white-on-blue inscription band that encircles the prayer hall between the first two tiers of windows recalls its tilework counterpart in the grand admiral Piyale Mehmed Pasha's mosque (*c.* 1565–73) near the Kasımpaşa arsenal (illus. 430).[77] Both bands cite the Jumʿa sura (62:1–11), which recommends believers to perform the congregational prayers and 'haste unto remembrance of Allah', encouraging them to be guided by God's 'scripture and wisdom' and His revelation taught by the messenger Muhammad. The declaration that the dead will inevitably return to the omniscient creator, who is the ultimate judge of their actions, is particularly appropriate for a posthumous memorial mosque (62:8). The theme of the inevitability of death is repeated in the mother-of-pearl-inlaid wooden doors (28:88) of the sanctuary.

Evliya Çelebi provides the sole early description of Pertev Pasha's mosque and its dependencies, among which he praises as the best in İzmit the stone caravansaray with lead-covered vaults:[78]

> Resembling a royal mosque, Pertev Pasha's mosque
> sited at the lip of the sea is an illuminated mosque
> with a lead-covered dome and a single minaret . . .
> It is a gracious mosque that is extremely luminous and
> decorated, being the work of Koca Mimar Sinan.[79]

Crowned by an unusually large dome (16.39 metres), the mosque comes close to its vizierial counterparts in the capital. Decorously designed as a variant of the domed cube, it is a worthy tribute to the memory of its deceased patron: a provincial prestige mosque that commemorates its donor's status as if he had never been deposed from the vizierate.

IV. FERHAD PASHA

Sinan designed two provincial mosques for Ferhad Pasha, one of them erected in Kastamonu during his lifetime and the other posthumously built in Çatalca. The Hungarian-born pasha was brought up in the imperial palace and later became its chief gatekeeper.[80] Appointed the agha of janissaries after prince Mustafa's execution in 1553, he was downgraded as the sanjak governor of Kastamonu in 1557.[81] The cause of Ferhad's demotion was his strict disciplinary measures, about which the janissaries complained bitterly to the reinstated Rüstem Pasha (g.v. 1555–61), accusing him of protecting their tyrannical agha as his prospective son-in-law and threatening to sack the grand vizier's palace. The same janissaries also sent an audaciously defiant petition to Sultan Süleyman:

> It is preferable to be an infidel than a janissary under his governance. You, the illustrious sultan, think he is a man, but he is the devil himself, may he be damned! What a pity you trust him, God forbid, and that he was brought up under your breeding . . . What was our crime to deserve such a Hungarian infidel who has only recently departed from among the infidels and whose mouth still retains the odour of pork meat! You assign him to us and he unfairly tramples on our honour and good name with all kinds of insults; if we are guilty kill us with your own hands so that we may be relieved from him. You are the son of a just sultan who did not trust anyone and took care of the affairs of his *kul*s himself. You, however, trust a regiment of tyrants. . . . We are sick and tired of you, your sons, and your pashas, and are ready to rebel ... We wish we had died in the place of prince Mustafa! . . . We would long ago have contemptuously killed this Hungarian infidel, but instead we protected your honour and petitioned you directly. If you dismiss him, fine, otherwise know that the responsibility of the ensuing sedition and mischief is yours. It is not possible to remain passive; by God we shall rebel, be aware and informed of this! You currently forbid wine, so inspect and see how many taverns this agha whom you trust as devout (*ṣofi*) has created along the waterfront [of Istanbul].[82]

Appreciative of Ferhad's unflinching loyalty despite janissary opposition, the sultan rewarded Ferhad in 1558 with marriage to his cherished granddaughter, Huma Sultan (Humashah, the daughter of Şehzade Mehmed). He returned from Kastamonu to the capital as the fifth vizier and become fourth vizier upon Rüstem Pasha's death in 1561.[83] The secretary of the Venetian embassy reported in 1562 that the forty-year-old Ferhad Pasha owed his position primarily to having married the princess, 'very much loved' by the sultan. He was 'a man with considerably less experience' than the other viziers in administering the state, 'neither having much practice in the affairs of the world, nor possessing great understanding'.[84] He became third vizier in 1565 but was forced to retire around 1568, early in Selim II's reign.[85]

According to Selaniki, when the retired vizier passed away on 6 February 1575, his men accused a sufi physician of poisoning their master 'at the instigation of the felicitious grandees'. Mustafa Āli points out that some believed it was the grand vizier Sokollu who 'signalled the murderer to make him drink poison'.[86] Ferhad Pasha left five sons and three daughters born from the princess. He was ceremonially buried in a humble oper air tomb next to the holy mosque in Eyüp by the grandees and the ulama. Selaniki acknowledges that 'among the great viziers no such calligrapher, famed as a penman, had held the office of the vizierate.'[87] Āli praises the calligraphic skills and religiosity of Ferhad Pasha, who was deposed after serving as a vizier for ten years:

> He was a person talented in calligraphy, perfect in the *naskh* script, and famed as a devout man (*ṣofi*); nevertheless, during his tenure as agha [of janissaries] he had proven to be a copious reprimander and an advocate of capital punishment.[88]

The sanctimonious pasha (a student of the renowned calligrapher Ahmed Karahisari) had accumulated several thousand gold coins by selling for a hundred pieces of gold each of the Koran manuscripts he had meticulously copied. His will stipulated that this canonically lawful income should be used in washing and wrapping his corpse.[89] Huma Sultan endowed one of the Koran manuscripts, which her beloved husband had written and given her as their wedding present, to her burial in Şehzade Mehmed's mausoleum. She inscribed it with the following poignant plea:

> This Koran was given to me by His Highness Ferhad Pasha on the night I came to him. After I die let nobody hinder this Koran from being read by my grave. I have endowed it. Let it remain by my side with no interference from any of my children. Let it be read for my soul for the approval of God and the pure soul of the Prophet. And let the readers sincerely offer their reading for the benefit of my soul. Let it remain night and day beside my head. Whoever does not fulfil this last will should know that on the Day of Judgment I shall hold him responsible in the presence of God with my two hands seizing his collar![90]

Despite her keen devotion to Ferhad Pasha, the sultana remarried soon after his death. In 1576 Antonio Tiepolo reported that the pasha's widow, 'a woman of great spirit who was much beloved and esteemed by the sultan', had recently been wedded to the vizier Kara Mustafa Pasha.[91] She inherited the palace Sinan had built for Ferhad Pasha at the time of their marriage on a plot removed from the Old Palace.[92] The chief architect must have delegated the construction of the pasha's two provincial mosques to his associates.

A waqf register indicates that 'Ferhad Pasha b. Abdullah' had endowed for his pious foundations income-producing properties in Istanbul, Kastamonu, Çatalca, and Yenice-i Karasu, but his waqfiyya has not come to light.[93] The foundation inscription of his generic mosque in Kastamonu indicates that he commissioned it early in his vizierate in response to a plea made by Seyfi Dede (illus. 400). The pious pasha had likely become a devotee of that sufi shaykh during his stay in Kastamonu:

> In name Seyfi Dede, in mystical stature the pole of wise men,
> When he requested for himself an adorned Friday mosque,
>
> The Khusraw of the age, the vizier Ferhad Pasha,
> Built this charming and sublime and adorned Friday mosque.
>
> A wise man wrote two adorned chronograms:
> One is, 'quite a pleasant building'; the other one is 'quite an alluring building', 967 (1559–60).

The extensively rebuilt rubble masonry mosque covered by a hipped roof has a single-galleried ashlar stone minaret datable to the eighteenth century and a modern wooden pillared portico.[94]

According to the *Tezkires*, Ferhad Pasha's Friday mosque in Çatalca was posthumously built for 'his soul' (illus. 401).[95] A stone-carved Turkish inscription panel with a wooden frame is nailed on top of its arched gate which lacks a muqarnas hood. It is a crude copy of an inscription carved on the public fountain

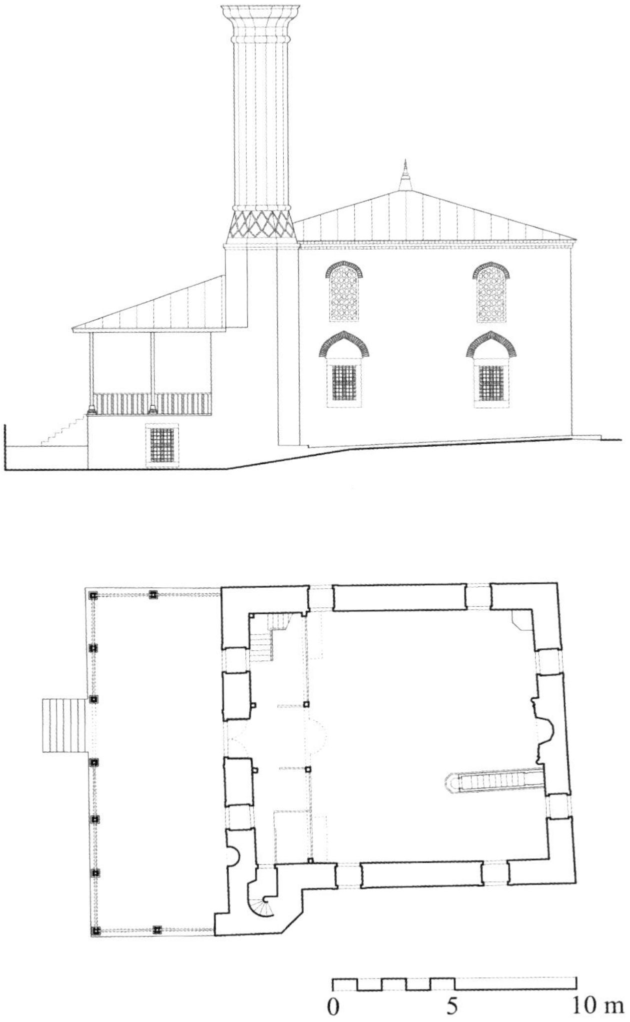

400 Plan and elevation of the Ferhad Pasha mosque, Kastamonu.

at the southeast corner of the precinct wall. The identical inscriptions read: 'Fatiha for the soul of the patron of the pious foundation, the late vizier Ferhad Pasha, the year 1006 (1597–98).'[96] Mentioned in Sinan's autobiographies, the mosque can tentatively be dated to 1575–88, even though some of its details may have been completed in 1597–98.[97]

Built under the supervision of Ferhad Pasha's relatives and freed slaves, the single-domed mosque stands in the middle of a raised garden courtyard on a steep hill (illus. 402). It forms a simple yet charming complex with an elementary school (named after an unidentified Ramazan Agha who may have been one of the pasha's household servants) and a public fountain, which respectively occupy the precinct's northeast and southeast corners. Preceded by a handsome double portico, the ashlar masonry mosque is a domed cube with a muqarnas-galleried minaret. It is crowned by a modest 9.2-metre dome supported on four pendentives above a blind octagonal base. Its triple-domed first portico, raised on columns with muqarnas capitals,

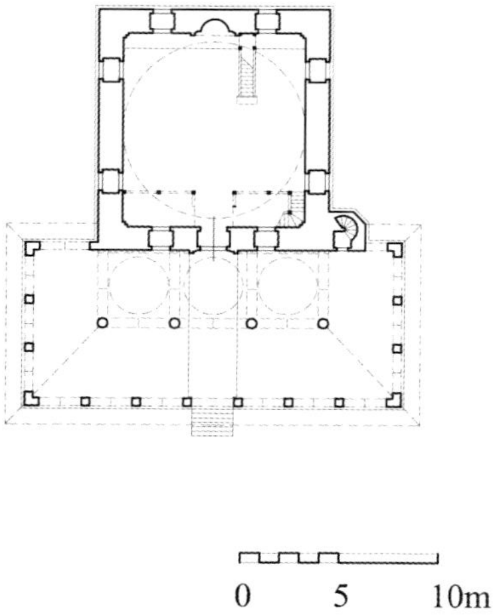

401 Plan of the Ferhad Pasha mosque, Çatalca.

is encircled by an outer portico whose slanting wooden roof is carried on smaller columns and pilasters with lozenge capitals. The simple prayer hall, which has lost its original painted decorations, is lit by two tiers of windows that flank its muqarnas-hooded mihrab, its gate, and the niches at the centre of each lateral wall (illus. 403). The wooden minbar and pillared upper gallery along the anti-qibla wall date from modern repairs.

Despite its small size, Evliya Çelebi found the mosque utterly delectable. He eulogizes it as the most impressive landmark of Çatalca, a town replete with palatial residences in extensive gardens:

> The most elaborate and adorned and prosperous Friday mosque is that of Ferhad Pasha, a vizier of Süleyman Khan who reached the reigns of Selim II and Murad III. That he was a gallant vizier is apparent from his mosque. Sited in the middle of the city on an elevated terrain inside a tree-planted garden along an avenue, it is an illuminated mosque with a single tall minaret. True,

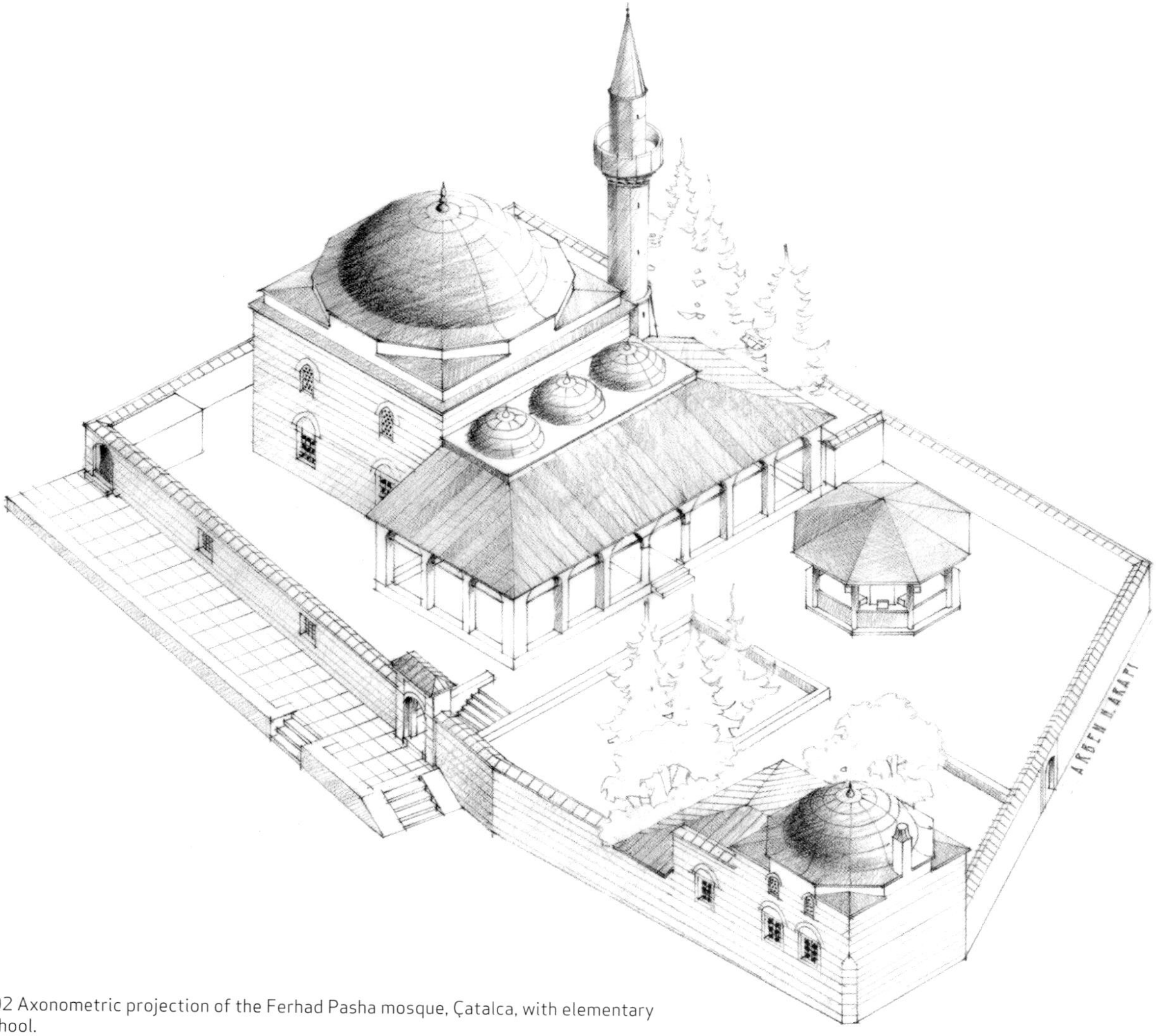

402 Axonometric projection of the Ferhad Pasha mosque, Çatalca, with elementary school.

403 Ferhad Pasha mosque, Çatalca, interior.

> it is small, yet it is an extremely artistic and adorned and flawless and exemplary mosque that is exhilarating. It is a mosque of light with an entirely lead-covered superstructure. In truth, Koca Mimar Sinan, who is the builder of Süleyman Khan's mosque, has invented all kinds of moldings (*zıhlar*) and displayed a variety of artistic exertions (*taṣarruflar*) in this mosque. Night and day it is not free from congregations.[98]

Compared to the monumental mosque complex posthumously built in İzmit for the deposed second vizier Pertev Mehmed Pasha (the husband of Ferhad Pasha's mother-in-law), the mosque in Çatalca is surprisingly unpretentious. Its low-profile patron was celebrated more for his steadfast piety and his excellence in penmanship than for statesmanship. The memorial mosque that Sinan designed for him in Çatalca reflects not only his lowered status as a discharged third vizier, but also his personal humility.

V. MESIḤ MEHMED PASHA

Mesih Mehmed Pasha's funerary mosque at Yenibahçe, commissioned while he was third vizier, was completed before his dismissal from the grand vizierate, a post that he occupied for only four-and-a-half months (illus. 404, 405). The *Tuḥfe* lists it as 'the noble Friday mosque of the grand vizier Mesih Pasha [and] his mausoleum', but it is excluded from the *Teẕkiretü'l-ebniye*.[99] The Bosnian-born Mesih (Messiah) began his career as a white eunuch, who served as chief of the inner pantry and treasury of the imperial palace.[100] To restock the palace kitchens and pantry that burned in 1574, he was sent to Cairo as the governor-general of Egypt, a post he held for five years and ten months.[101] Upon returning to the capital in 1581, he became the third vizier.[102] The Venetian ambassador Jacopo Soranzo (1581), clearly unimpressed with the pasha, reports that he owed this post to his success in financial matters (illus. 406):

> He is by birth Bosnian, and he was made a eunuch upon being placed in the palace, and after some time he became the sultan's treasurer. Exiting the said palace, he went as a pasha to Cairo where he governed with infinite cruelty and extortions, being inhuman and extremely avaricious. Returning from that governorship with a great treasure, he had the means to make his way to the rank of vizier, not having merited such an exalted office, for which he is completely unfit. Therefore, there is nothing worth reporting about him except that he is ugly and monstrous in appearance, being small and hunchbacked, with an emaciated face.[103]

The *bailo* Paolo Contarini (1583) notes Murad III's affection for the third vizier, whose financial acumen helped remedy the deficit of the imperial treasury:

> The eunuch Mesih Pasha is by nature a just man, diligent, and loved by His Majesty for the great work he accomplishes with much personal toil in collecting what debtors in Rumelia owe to the treasury. He is cruel but fearful, and with little courage; therefore he desires peace and procures it.[104]

Mustafa Āli laments the pasha's cruelty in collecting arrears from debtors; he notes that unlike the Messiah Jesus, who used his power to resuscitate the dead, this Messiah tyranically extinguished lives. When Āli refused on one occasion to pay back a loan and demanded a just trial in the shariʿa court, the pasha 'shamelessly' replied: 'Did they first ask the Divine Law before they removed my testicles, so that I too should handle such matters according to the Divine Law?'[105]

Mesih Pasha became second vizier in July 1584 and lieutenant grand vizier in November 1585, substituting for Özdemiroğlu Osman Pasha, who left the capital for a Safavid campaign.[106] The *bailo* Gianfrancesco Morosini (1585) observes the devoutness and asceticism of the lieutenant grand vizier, then over seventy, whose primary objective was to make debtors pay their debts to the treasury:

> This man is very dexterous and understands better than his predecessors the affairs of the government, but is esteemed little for not having any experience in military matters, and because he is believed to have little courage. He is renowned for being quite cruel and avaricious, as most of these eunuchs are, and he is also extremely obstinate in his opinions. His council will be useful to us, for he will never make the *Grand Signore* go into war, having his view set on the conservation of money ... He makes a grand profession of piety, and owing to his devoutness he dresses

very humbly and eats with extreme sobriety. He moreover keeps a rather humble residence, and the room where he holds audience is poorly adorned in comparison to those of other viziers, even though it is commonly believed he has much money.[107]

Mesih Pasha rose to the grand vizierate on 1 December 1585 when the news of Osman Pasha's death arrived. According to Selaniki, he was deposed with a fatwa of Çivizade Efendi on 15 April 1585.[108] But Peçevi claims that he resigned because of a disagreement with the sultan about an appointment, asserting that he did not 'want to be one of those viziers whose word carries no weight.' He was keen on governing autonomously by laconic pronouncements:

> He was so independent in his government and judgment that while he governed he never contradicted the word he once uttered; he either said yes or no to those who sought his assistance. If they insisted on their request he would send them away curtly, without prolonging the conversation.[109]

The retired pasha passed away several years after his retirement in 1589 and was buried at his funerary mosque.[110]

The earliest decree authorizing the construction of Mesih Pasha's mosque is dated 13 March 1584, while he was still third

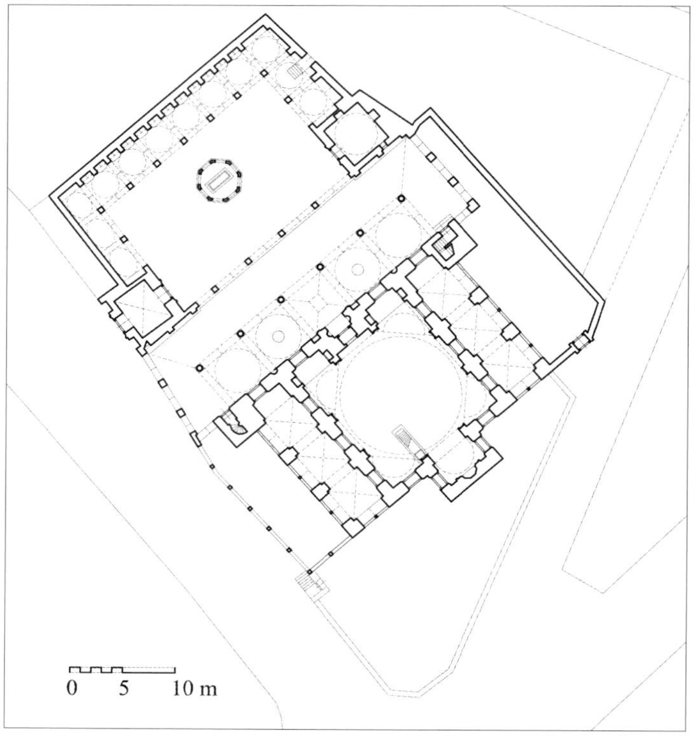

404 Plan of the Mesih Mehmed Pasha complex, Yenibahçe.

405 Axonometric projection of the Mesih Mehmed Pasha complex.

406 *Mesih Pasha*, c. 1586, watercolour on paper.

vizier. Addressed to the kadi of Istanbul, it approves the kadi's petition concerning the legality of the Friday mosque the vizier wanted to build on the site of 'the dilapidated masjid of Hasan Pasha,' because its waqf lacked funds for repairs, and neighbourhood residents had requested a Friday mosque as none existed nearby.[111] Ayvansarayi explains that the demolished masjid was replaced by another that Mesih Pasha built nearby, on a 'suitable site in Karagümrük'.[112] A decree sent to the 'lieutenant of the chief architect' on 2 April 1584 orders him to assist the construction of the vizier's Friday mosque: 'When this [decree] arrives and the preparation and provision of needed building materials and timber for his noble Friday mosque is requested, prepare with his own money the required materials, timber, carpenters, labourers, and whatever else is necessary, and have him be given the assistance he needs.'[113] This document confirms the involvement of the chief architect's office in Mesih Pasha's mosque, the plan of which was designed either by Sinan before he left for Mecca or by the royal architect Mehmed Subaşı, who on 28 February 1584 was appointed Sinan's lieutenant 'until he goes to and returns from the noble hajj'.[114]

On 18 April 1584 the kadi of Sidhirókastron was ordered to allow the purchase of 1500 qintars of lead for the vizier's mosque.[115] The kadi of Istanbul and the superintendent of water channels (İsmail Çavuş) were instructed on 10 June to inspect the water source for the mosque:

> Since the Friday mosque that is being built by my vizier Mesih Pasha in Istanbul needs water, he has discovered three measures (*maṣura*) of water in the city's vineyards outside Edirnekapı. As he requests my imperial permission for the addition of that water to the pipe (*künk*) of Mahmud Pasha's mosque, with one measure flowing to his own mosque, and one measure given to that water channel, I have ordered that, when this [decree] arrives, you go to the said water source and see whether the mentioned amount of water has been discovered there, and whether it is possible to add it to the pipe of Mahmud Pasha's mosque.'[116]

Two decrees sent to the kadi of Istanbul on 2 and 9 April 1585 (just before the pasha's retirement on 15 April) approve the construction of a public fountain next to his mosque in the Hasan Pasha quarter, whose residents urgently needed water.[117]

The inscription of the triple fountain at the southwest corner of the precinct wall (refurbished in 1817–18) explains that it was created by 'His Highness the pasha named Mesih, who resolved to bring life to religion' with the fountain's 'water of life' in the year 994 (1585–86).[118] The same date is given in the foundation inscription of the mosque, which identifies its patron as a grand vizier. The middle panel carved under the muqarnas hood of the gate cites two Koranic verses: 'Everyone that is thereon will pass away; there remaineth but the Countenance of thy Lord of Might and Glory' (55:26–27). The right and left panels, carved in Turkish above the two flanking niches of the gate, articulate the same theme by referring to the patron's awaited union with God and explaining that, in hope of preparing his place in paradise, the 'divinely inspired' pasha resolved to build his mosque. The inscription echoes that of the fountain in its allusion to Mesih's power to give life like his namesake, the Messiah Jesus. It highlights the grand vizier's justice and pious asceticism by calling him a 'monotheist of pure faith' (*muvaḥḥid-i pāk dīn*) and emphasizes the rapid completion of the mosque, without 'idle chatter', a reference to the patron's celebrated laconicism, mentioned above by Peçevi:

> Thanks be to God, that the just Asaph, the monotheist of
> pure faith,
> Erected this Friday mosque without idle chatter.
>
> He brought it to life with divine revelation, as his Jesus-like
> nature
> Became a proof of union with God and the road to paradise.
>
> That grand vizier's name is the soul-reviving Messiah
> (Mesih),
> In both worlds make the water of his desire flow for the
> love of God.

The divine voice said the chronogram for its completion:
'This place (*maḳām*, abode) became a glorious and esteemed house of worship', 994 (1585–86).[119]

It was later in 1587, shortly before his death, that the retired pasha obtained the sultan's permission to be buried next to his mosque:[120]

> Since Mesih Pasha, may his eminence be enduring, has sent a petition to my threshold of felicity, requesting my imperial permission to have his grave (*ḳabr*) dug and be prepared at the noble Friday mosque he has built in the capital Istanbul, I order that when my imperial decree arrives, let him have his grave dug and prepared at the place he deems decorous and fitting (*vecih ve münāsib*) in the noble mosque he has built at the capital, Istanbul.[121]

The last document, dated 1588, asks the new water channel superintendent Davud Agha's permission to conduct additional water to the retired pasha's mosque from the water channel of Mahmud Pasha.[122]

Sited at the junction of two streets, the mosque sits on the edge of a hill sloping from east to west; its vaulted substructure is lined with eight shops and a triple-arched public fountain at the southwest corner (illus. 407). The sloping site is used to full advantage in exposing the ashlar masonry mosque to the open public space in front of the fountain. The post-classical façades have two levels of windows separated by a stringcourse moulding corresponding to the gallery level inside. Comparable mouldings divide into two zones the façades of several other late mosques attributed to Sinan – Sokollu in Azapkapı (*c.* 1573–77/78), Kılıç Ali Pasha in Tophane (1578–80/81), and the Muradiye in Manisa (1583–86/87). The windows of Mesih Pasha's mosque are grouped within large framing arches (like those of the Tophane and Manisa mosques) fitted with varied openwork geometric lattices (illus. 408). Light pours through these windows into the bright side wings and upper galleries, leaving the central core of the mosque relatively dim. Eight stone weight turrets rising above the internal piers encircle the tall window-pierced and lead-covered drum of the dome. The four shallow exedral half-domes at the corners, the half-dome over the projecting mihrab, and the drumless triple domes above the lateral galleries are hardly visible from below.

Ayvansarayi mentions an elementary school (no longer extant) above the public fountain, built by the founder of the original masjid, Hasan Pasha, who was 'buried before the mihrab'.[123] Perhaps that is why Mesih Pasha's tomb was unconventionally placed in the middle of the mosque forecourt, where one would normally expect to find an ablution fountain. The modest grave, surrounded by a transparent octagonal white marble enclosure with eight iron-grilled windows, recalls that of the vizier Hadım İbrahim Pasha at Silivrikapı. By occupying the traditional locus for an ablution fountain, the tomb metaphorically turns the deceased patron's castrated body into the resuscitating 'water of life', mentioned in the inscription quoted above. It thus alludes to the impotent eunuch's 'life-giving' power and underscores the funerary character of his memorial mosque as a veritable *maḳām*.

The tomb is not the only departure from 'classical' norms in Mesih Mehmed Pasha's idiosyncratic mosque. As Kuran observes, the arcaded forecourt without madrasa rooms is 'the first of its kind in a vizier's mosque of the classical period'.[124] As in the earlier mosque of Kılıç Ali Pasha at Tophane, a row of ablution spigots is installed under the north arcade of the rectangular forecourt. The inscription band carved in monumental *thuluth* above that arcade is a hadith of the Prophet concerning the necessity of minor ablutions (*wuḍū*) for performing worship (*ṣalāt*). The forecourt, designed as a funerary garden, is entered from a domed gatehouse at each end. The five-bay double portico of the mosque has an inner row of tall columns with unfinished muqarnas capitals, surrounded by an outer row of lower columns with lozenge capitals.

Another departure from the norm is the spatial duality of the octagonal-baldachined mosque with a projecting mihrab, which reintroduces appended side wings that fragment the unity of inner space (illus. 404, 409). Covered by cross vaults, the independent side wings feature external entrances from gates at the east and west façades of the mosque (illus. 408, 410). At ground level, the square prayer hall is defined as a cube, spatially separate from the lateral cross-vaulted wings, with which it communicates by two gates and iron-grilled windows featuring rectangular İznik tile lunettes. The windows are treated as if they opened onto the outside world, like the doors, which are 'not internal communicating doors, but designed as external doors and much stronger than would otherwise be necessary' (illus. 411, 412).[125] The independent lateral wings support triple-domed upper galleries that are spatially continuous with the prayer hall, an arrangement reminiscent of the Selimiye mosque, where ground-level outer porches become inner galleries at the upper level.[126] The eight engaged piers, incorporated into the walls at the ground floor, emerge at the gallery level as free-standing supports that expose the octagonal baldachin. The anti-qibla wall has an attractive private balcony above its gate, with a triple arcade carried on two columns; the flanking upper galleries functioned as twin tribunes for muezzins and Koran readers.[127]

While the upper galleries expand the prayer hall, crowned by a 12.8 metre dome, the side wings that spatially fragment its ground level distantly recall the attached *tabhane*s of early Ottoman multi-functional convent mosques.[128] The pasha's lost waqfiyya may have specified the intended purpose of these 'oratories', most likely used for meditative sufi rituals and the recitation of monotheistic litanies. Mesih Pasha's sufi bent was mani-

407 Mesih Pasha mosque, Yenibahçe, from the southwest.

408 Mesih Mehmed Pasha mosque, Yenibahçe, detail of east façade.

fested by a pious foundation he created in Cairo (1575–80) for the Egyptian Shaykh Nur al-Din al-Qarafi and his family.[129] Comparable lateral halls also appear in the nearby vizierial mosque of Nişancı Mehmed Pasha in Karagümrük (1584/85–1588/89), built around the same time (illus. 5). Its waqfiyya shows that its dependencies once included a Halveti convent whose shaykh and dervishes invoked monotheistic litanies in the mosque.[130]

The sparsely decorated, austere prayer hall is in keeping with Mesih Pasha's ascetic proclivity. The few İznik tile revetments are confined to the narrow mihrab recess and to window lunettes. The muqarnas-hooded white marble mihrab is accompanied by a refined lacelike minbar. The mihrab quotes a less common variant (3:39) of the standard verse using the word mihrab, which appears in several late mosques attributed to Sinan: 'And the angels called to him [Zachariah] as he stood praying in the sanctuary [mihrab].' The painted inscription of the central dome cites the Fatiha sura (1:1–7) which affirms the unity of the merciful God, 'the Owner of the Day of Judgment', and begs Him to show the 'straight path'. The calligraphic İznik tile lunettes over the windows are read in a counter-clockwise direction, starting at the northwest corner of the prayer hall and terminating at the northeast. Their white-on-blue monumental *thuluth* inscriptions quote two verses from the Jumʿa sura, which declares the necessity of congregational prayers and recommends the 'remembrance of Allah' (62:9–10).

The funerary mosque of Mesih Mehmed Pasha and that of the vizier Nişancı Mehmed Pasha in nearby Karagümrük, to which I shall turn next, were created concurrently. They are generally attributed to the architect Davud, whose name is mentioned in the foundation inscription of a third funerary mosque built in Çarşamba (1584–85) for the chief black eunuch Mehmed Agha.[131] The mosques of all three Mehmeds are variants of the post-Selimiye octagonal baldachin type with projecting mihrabs, but that of Mesih Mehmed Paşa has more dynamically composed façades and stands out from the others with its innovative fenestration (illus. 5). It is perhaps more reasonable to connect the architect Mehmed Subaşı with Mesih Pasha's mosque, which he was ordered to oversee in the decree quoted above before being sent to complete the Muradiye of Manisa in 1586. But the unusual plan of the mosque must have been approved by Sinan, who returned from Mecca to the capital in 1585, still in charge of the bureau of royal architects.[132]

The post-classical innovations manifested in Mesih Pasha's mosque must partly have been informed by the ascetic piety of its patron, who likely dictated a special programme including segregated spaces for sufi rituals. The central core of the mosque retains its cubic form as a reminder of the patron's vizierial status, while its octagonal-baldachined upper section, extended

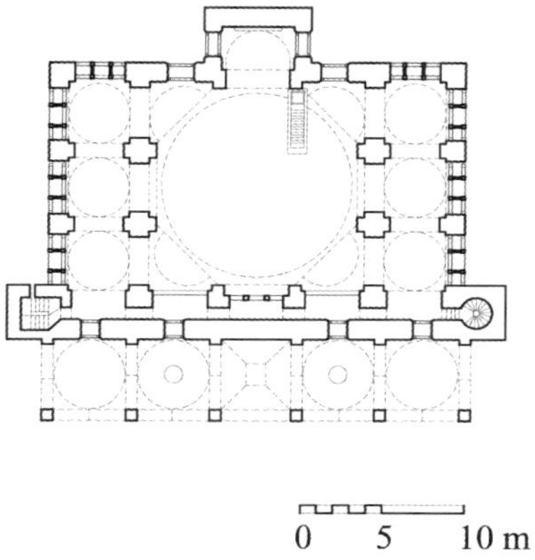

409 Plan of the Mesih Pasha mosque, Yenibahçe, at upper gallery level.

411 Mesih Pasha mosque, interior toward the qibla wall.

410 Mesih Pasha mosque, interior of the cross-vaulted west-side wing.

412 Mesih Pasha mosque, interior toward the west.

by spacious galleries, invites comparison with grand vizierial prototypes. Its complex plan differs from previous mosques that Sinan had designed for viziers, using simpler variations of the domed cube with octagonal zones of transition. It emulates grand vizierial models, yet omits their lavish inner arcades and keeps within the bounds of vizierial decorum at the level of its ground plan. It is as if the unique layout of the mosque, which subtly blurs the distinction between two patronage levels in its aspiration for higher status, predicts Mesih Pasha's rise to the grand vizierate.

VI. NİŞANCI MEHMED PASHA

Nişancı (Chancellor) Mehmed Pasha was one of the few freeborn Muslims to rise to the vizierate from the ranks of the imperial chancery during the age of Sinan. The mercurial vacillation of his status between vizier and chancellor during the construction of his funerary complex exemplifies the instability of government posts under Murad III (illus. 413, 414). The mosque itself, once accompanied by a double madrasa and a dervish convent, which have entirely disappeared, is an innovative variant of the octagonal scheme shared by other vizierial foundations. Like several late works attributed to Sinan, it is omitted from the *Tezkiretü'l-ebniye* and only mentioned in the *Tuhfe* as 'the noble Friday mosque of the vizier Nişancı Mehmed Pasha and his mausoleum'.[133] Its distinctive plan articulates the lofty aspirations of its patron, who was celebrated for his commitment to maintain the fading glory of the classical age in a period of transition.

Mehmed was the son of a chief judge of Aleppo and his wife, the sister of Nişancı Celalzade Mustafa Çelebi, the most renowned chancellor of Süleyman's reign. After studying religious law, Mehmed left the scholarly career path to join the ranks of secretaries at the chancery of the imperial council through the mediation of his mentor and maternal uncle, Celalzade. Becoming chief secretary (*reisülküttab*), he eventually rose to the post of chancellor (*nişancı*, *nişancıbaşı*) when his uncle died in 1567.[134] It was his duty to inscribe the sultan's monogram (*tughra*) on official documents and to supervise the writing of dynastic law codes; hence the title of chancellor became an inalienable component of his identity. His nickname 'Boyalı Nişancı' (Painted Chancellor) may have alluded to the inks and paints he used in designing illuminated *tughras*. The biographer Atai praises the talented pasha, who wrote poetry under the pen-name 'Nāmī,' as 'the blossom of China and Cathay in every skill' and the 'creator of graceful artificial flowers [of speech] and resounding witticisms'.[135]

After briefly serving as the governor-general of Aleppo (*c.* 1574–76), where his father had been a chief judge, the pasha returned to the capital, where he was appointed chancellor a second time in 1577, rising to the rank of fourth vizier in October 1580.[136] Dismissed in March 1582, he was reappointed chancellor a third time in 1583. Gianfrancesco Morosini (1585–86) observes that the chancellor retained the title of pasha 'for having been a vizier of the Porte, deposed at the request of [Koca] Sinan Pasha.' He continued to exercise considerable influence in authenticating decrees:

> He is a man more than seventy years old, esteemed as the most intelligent and experienced in this Porte, very observant in their law, and one who makes a profession of being just and incorruptible ... All the decrees pass from his hand, and quite often he tears up the commands of the grand vizier and even of the *Grand Signore*.[137]

The pasha rose to the vizierate again in 1586, reverted to the rank of chancellor in 1587, and was appointed sixth vizier in 1588–89.[138] The sultan ordered him to simultaneously serve as chancellor in 1591,[139] the same year the *bailo* Lorenzo Bernardo referred to him as the third vizier:

> Mehmed Pasha, the third vizier, is a native Turk from Ankara, against the ordinary custom of this Porte, which did not use to admit native Turks to the rank of vizier ... He is about sixty-five years old, with a long face and beard, and an aquiline nose. He appears to have a placid nature, talks courteously, professes to be just, and is famous for his prudence.[140]

According to Selaniki, the elderly pasha, then the sixth vizier, died from 'dropsy' on 10 June 1594, but the gate inscriptions of his funerary garden cited below give the date of his death as 1001 (1592–93).[141] Selaniki, who served for four years as keeper of the inkstand under Nişancı Mehmed, remarks how his colleagues had 'sighed with a sense of loss' upon his advancement to the vizierate, as he was an irreplaceable chancellor learned in the religious and secular laws.[142] The historian portrays the pasha as a resolute upholder of ancient dynastic laws, who complained about changes in the circumstances of the age, 'ruminating on the conduct of the people and the state of affairs introduced by the innovators':[143]

> He was pious, a man of God, and very zealous. He did not deviate from the ancient path of the forefathers. As he refused to conform to the disposition of the people of the age and opposed their aspirations, he was not sought after by upstart dignitaries (*nev-devlet*). He had a natural aptitude for excellent verse and truth-filled prose. He left behind two sons and five daughters. During his lifetime he married his daughters to the sons of chief judges ... hoping they would benefit his pious foundations and the affairs of his waqfs. But in that respect, all his sons-in-law collaborated in opposing his sons and the last wishes of the deceased [vizier]. He was buried inside Istanbul in the mausoleum near his Friday mosque. All the pillars of the state, the great viziers, the honourable ulema, and the venerable shaykhs accompanied his funeral up to his mausoleum, an event that served as an examplar to the whole world and produced a feeling of loss.[144]

Atai mentions among the pasha's pious works 'his noble Friday mosque, and madrasa, and sufi convent in Istanbul alongside the imperial avenue [Divanyolu]', pointing out that he had married 'each of his five chaste daughters to five members of the ulema, to whom he assigned fifty aspers a day as madrasa professors'.[145] Ayvansarayi cites the chronogram of the foundation inscription of the mosque and observes that some of its dependencies were completed posthumously:

> The date of the noble mosque is written in prose on the arch of its exalted gateway: 'It was begun with the help of God, the Sovereign, the All-Bounteous, in the year nine hundred ninety-two, 992 (1584–85). And it was completed with the help of the Lord, whose aid is implored, in the year nine hundred ninety-seven, 997 (1588–89).' There are two madrasas of brick and stone in the mosque courtyard,

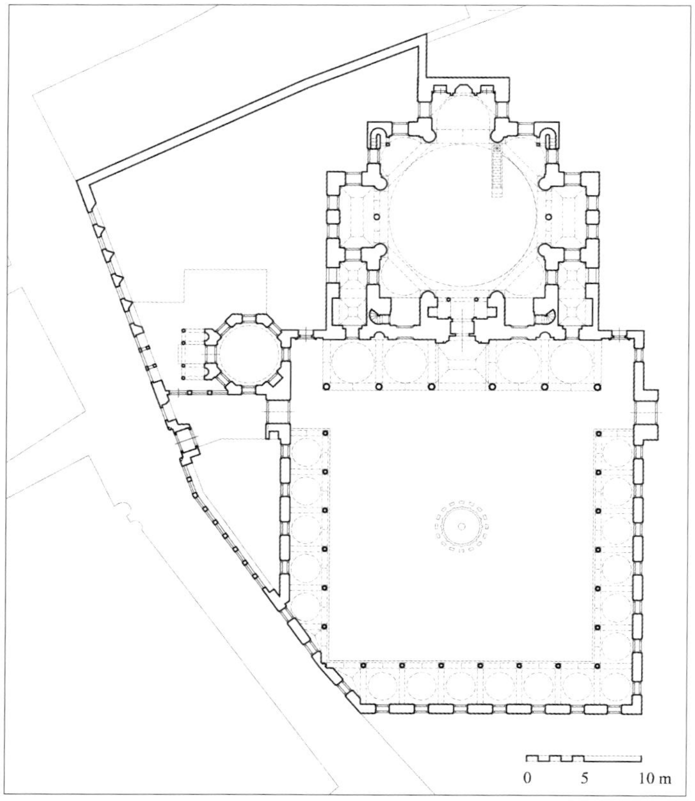

413 Plan of the Nişancı Mehmed Pasha complex, Karagümrük.

> one of them upper-storey, and the other lower-storey.
> Subsequently, when the waqf increased in size,
> the adjoining dervish lodge was built in accordance
> with [Mehmed Pasha's] will.[146]

The chronogram shows that the foundations of the mosque were laid in 1584–85, during the deposed vizier's third term as chancellor; he was reappointed to the vizierate twice before its completion in 1588–89. The extant Arabic foundation inscription, carved in four lines of *thuluth* under the muqarnas hood of the mosque portal, explains that 'the vizier Mehmed b. Pir Ahmed' built the Friday mosque to seek God's approval in accordance with the Prophet's saying: 'Whoever builds mosques for God and for the Day of Judgment [God will build an abode for him in Paradise].' Above the inscription is a distinctive emblem of the patron's identity: a *tughra* of Murad III that must have been designed by the pasha himself (illus. 415). Another striking identity marker is a Turkish poem composed by Nişancı Mehmed himself, which is inscribed above one of the gates of his funerary garden:

414 Axonometric projection of the Nişancı Mehmed Pasha complex.

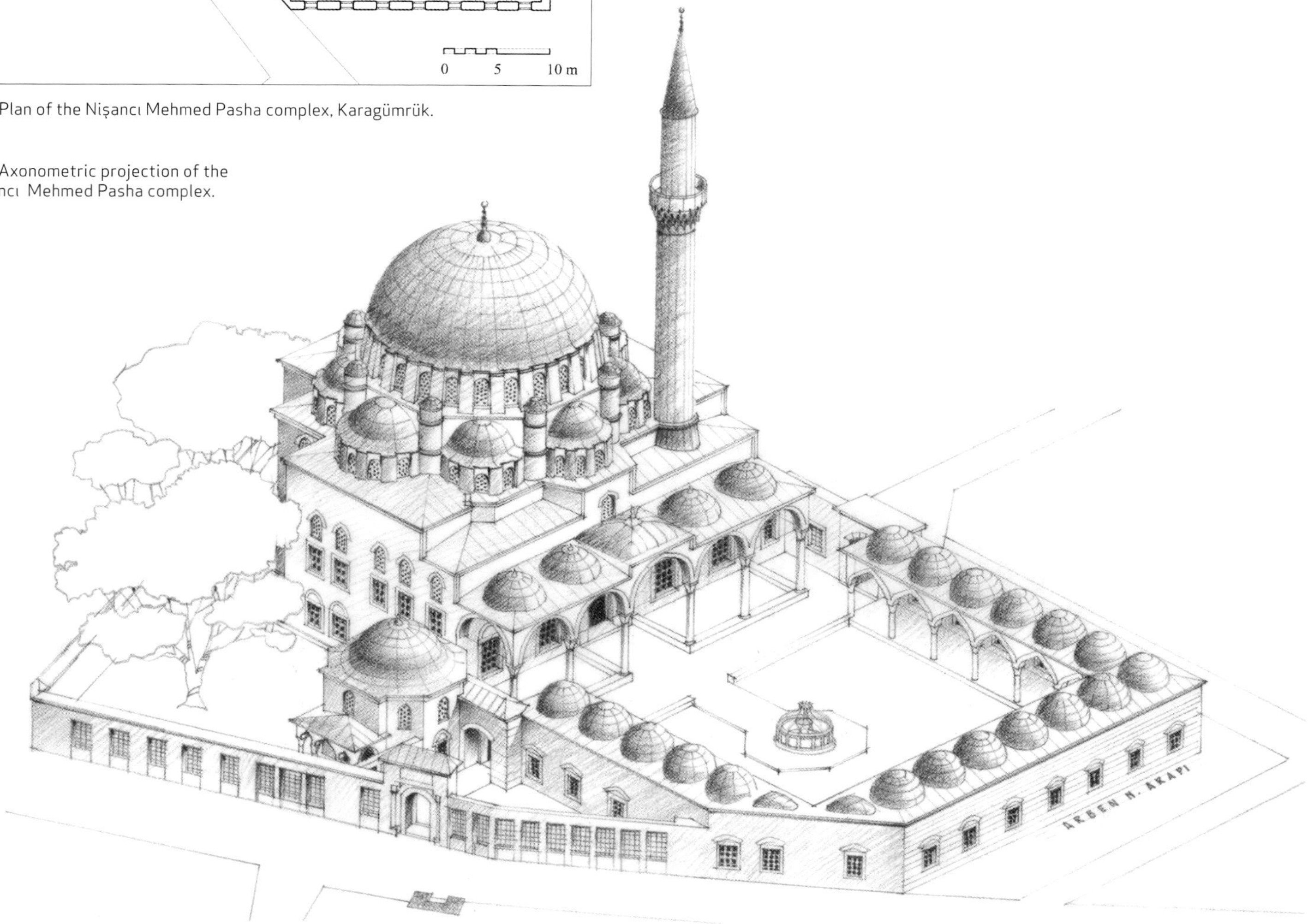

This is a noble verse by the late and pardoned patron of the pious foundation:
Whenever brethren come to his grave,

Seeing him all one with the earth,
Let them show compassion and opening their hand in prayer,

Say: May the All-Compassionate have mercy on him!
If those who query the state of Nāmī ask: How does he fare?

Lying at the halting station of his grave, he asks for prayer.
May the end of those who recite the Fatiha for his soul be fortunate, in the year 1001 (1592–93).

A Turkish poem composed by Sinan's biographer, Sai, is inscribed above another gate of the funerary garden; it ends with a chronogram for the pasha's death: 'They said Nişancı Pasha became united with God' (1001/1592–93).[147]

The pasha's posthumous waqfiyya, dated 13 July 1600, was authorized with the testimony of his son and two daughters, who attested that their father had passed away before registering his endowments.[148] The endowment deed mentions two madrasas and a Halveti convent (*ḫānḳāh*) among the dependencies of the 'joy-giving noble Friday mosque and exalted paradise-like sanctuary'. One of the madrasas, 'built near the mosque with thirty-two cells', functioned as a hadith college. It was staffed with a resident shaykh well versed in Muslim tradition, who daily received fifteen aspers; with a gatekeeper; and with thirty students assigned two aspers a day. After the dawn prayers, each student had to recite a section of the Koran at the patron's mausoleum on behalf of the souls of the Prophet Muhammad, other prophets, the pasha, his parents, his mentors, and his defunct relatives. The second madrasa must have been built posthumously: 'Under each of the separate domes existing in front of the mentioned mosque let there be built a cell with a fireplace, and when those cells are built, let ten of them be inhabited by students receiving four aspers a day.' The remaining cells of the madrasa were to be occupied by two assistant professors and a gatekeeper; its professor, receiving a salary of fifty aspers, had to offer classes on the religious sciences and other desirable disciplines 'in the mentioned mosque, in whichever place he chooses'.[149] The eleven-cell convent was headed by a Halveti shaykh paid ten aspers a day; it housed ten disciples, who received three aspers each. After performing the afternoon prayers in the mosque, they had to recite there 'monotheistic litanies' (*tevḥīd-i şerīf*) conforming to the shariʿa. Their shaykh would deliver sermons in the mosque on Fridays and on holy nights.[150]

The waqfiyya also lists endowed monuments outside the capital, apparently modest structures that have disappeared: a Friday mosque and a water dispenser in Aleppo, a masjid and an elementary school in Galata, a Friday mosque at the Aydınlı village of Üsküdar, a Friday mosque in the Anatolian village of Kuş, a masjid and a hospice in Tosya near Ankara (the birthplace of the pasha's mother and uncle Celalzade), and three Friday mosques in villages near his own place of birth in the province of Hüdavendigar near Bursa, in the region called 'Mihallü Emlāki'.[151] These pious foundations, which memorialized sites associated with the patron's life and career, were endowed with income from villages in the Hüdavendigar province and real estate in Bursa, Edirne, Aleppo, Galata, and Istanbul (including the pasha's palace in the Nişancı quarter near Fatih, not far from his mosque complex).[152] It is noteworthy that unlike most of his convert colleagues from the Balkans, the Muslim-born Anatolian vizier did not establish any endowments in Rumelia.

415 Nişancı Mehmed Pasha mosque, Karagümrük, foundation inscription and *tughra* on the north portal with flattened muqarnas hood.

The construction chronology of Nişancı Mehmed Pasha's prestige mosque in Istanbul can be traced from documents. The 'Nisangibassi' had requested Murano oil lamps and glass panes from the Venetian Senate on 12 October 1584; these were shipped out at the end of that year.[153] Murad III's earliest surviving decree, issued on 12 September 1585 and given to the *nişancıbaşı* himself, orders the kadis of Thessaloniki and Sidhirókastron to allow the sale of 2,000 qintars of lead for the dome of the Friday mosque being built in Istanbul by 'Mehmed Pasha, my former vizier who is now in the service of my imperial *tughra*'.[154] A month later the kadi of Samokov and the overseer of its mines were commanded to authorize the sale of 500 qintars of iron for the pasha's mosque.[155] On 10 February 1586 the kadi of Kosovo was asked to help the pasha's man, Zaim Mehmed, buy and transport 3,000 qintars of lead.[156]

Several decrees concerning the preparation of stone, marble, and columns were issued when the pasha was reinstated to the vizierate. The kadi of Mihaliç was instructed on 7 May 1586 to have stone cut for the arches of the 'vizier Nişancı Mehmed Pasha's' mosque when his man arrived there.[157] The kadis of

Aydıncık, Marmara, and Rodoscuk were sent a decree on 14 July 1586 concerning the food provisions for marble cutters under their jurisdiction, to be bought with the money of 'my vizier Mehmed Pasha for the needs of the noble Friday mosque that is being built for him.'[158] Another decree addressed to the kadi of Samanlı (near Yalova) orders him to buy the marble columns said to exist at the garden of a non-Muslim subject for the 'vizier Mehmed Pasha's noble Friday mosque' when the vizier's men arrive there.[159] The kadi of İzmit was instructed on 2 September 1586 to assist the purchase of two marble columns for the 'noble Friday mosque the vizier Mehmed Pasha is building in Istanbul' and to have them loaded on a ship.[160] A decree dispatched to the kadi of Devrekani (near Kastamonu) on 24 April 1587 shows that the pasha had in the meantime been demoted to the rank of chancellor. The kadi is asked to send the marble needed for the mosque of 'Mehmed Pasha, who is in the service of the noble *tughra*'.[161]

On the same day, the chief architect Sinan received a decree that responded to his letter concerning the masons, stone cutters, and carpenters who refused to work in Nişancı Mehmed Pasha's mosque even though their wages had been raised after the drastic devaluation of 1584–85. He is ordered to urge those builders to continue working at the pasha's mosque and to punish those who refused to do so.[162] The fact that, a year before his death, Sinan sent a petition to the sultan about the reluctant workforce of the mosque demonstrates his involvement in its construction, which he probably supervised periodically. It is likely that he personally designed the innovative structure, with whose patron he must have developed a close rapport thanks to numerous construction-related decrees authenticated by his seal. It is tempting to speculate that the combined artistic visions of the chief architect and his discerning patron, a visually sensitive *tughra* designer, engendered this exemplary monument.

Some scholars attribute the exceptional sculptural unity of the mosque's central space to the chief architect himself, accepting the fact that it must have been executed by one of his talented assistants.[163] Ranking it as one of Sinan's 'most original' monuments, Kuran regards its similarity to the mosque of Cerrah Pasha (a hexagonal-baldachined vizierial mosque that Davud built as chief architect in 1593–94) as a clue pointing to Davud's hand in both buildings (illus. 4).[164] Like Mesih Mehmed Pasha's concurrently built mosque, that of Nişancı Mehmed Pasha has elements that go counter to 'classical' code: its forecourt without madrasa cells, its disregard for the principle of spatial unity in reintroducing lateral halls recalling early Ottoman convent-mosques, and its cross-shaped central space that departs from canonical quadrangular plans (illus. 416, 417).[165]

The ceremonial avenue of Divanyolu cuts through the bevelled northeast corner of the forecourt of the ashlar masonry mosque. The north and west walls of the forecourt are built with alternating courses of stone and brick, while its more visible east wall facing Divanyolu is of ashlar masonry. Surrounded by iron-grilled windows, the forecourt garden has a central twelve-sided ablution fountain, depicted in early photographs with an open ogival metal canopy (it now features a pyramidal roof supported by eight modern columns).[166] Two projecting portals at both sides of the five-bay mosque portico, which rests on tall white columns with muqarnas capitals, provide access to the forecourt, a space surrounded by lower domical porticoes composed of dainty ogee arches supported on columns with lozenge capitals. The lost dependencies seem to have been grouped at the west side of the complex.[167] The enfilade of lateral gates, and the position of the mausoleum at the side of the mosque, recalls the composition of the complex of Shahsultan and Zal Mahmud Pasha in Eyüp (illus. 361–62, 413–14).

Appended to the southeast corner of the forecourt, the octagonal domed mausoleum of ashlar masonry differs from the modest open-air tombs of Hadım İbrahim Pasha's and Mesih Pasha's vizierial mosques (illus. 419). The enclosed funerary garden is reached from two arched gates. One of them is along the curtain wall that extends between the aligned portals of the forecourt and the precinct wall along Divanyolu; the other is located between the mosque and the mausoleum. Exceptionally large iron-grilled rectangular windows on the curtain wall and the precinct wall facing the avenue invite the users of the mosque and passers-by to offer prayers for its patron's soul.

The skilfully layered exterior of the mosque is crowned by an unusually lofty dome whose octagonal base is surrounded by eight tall weight turrets alternating with four half-domes and four exedras. The base of the multi-faceted and muqarnas-galleried minaret is integrated into the north wall of the mosque, behind its portico. The façades of the mosque have three classically restrained rows of windows. The north corners of the cruciform prayer hall are filled with rooms, while its south corners are empty, as in the grand vizier Piri Mehmed Pasha's T-type convent mosque in Silivri, built by Sinan's predecessor in 1530–31 (illus. 85).[168]

Nişancı Mehmed Pasha's mosque reinterprets its antiquated prototypes with an octagonal baldachin supported on column-like engaged semicircular piers topped by muqarnas capitals (illus. 418). The central dome resting on eight arches is surrounded by four half-domes that alternate with exedras as in Sokolu Mehmed Pasha's Azapkapı mosque, completed a decade earlier (illus. 353). The 14.2-metre dome of the vizier's mosque is larger than that of the illustrious grand vizier (11.8 metres), and among the non-royal mosques of the capital, it is second only to the 15.2-metre dome of Rüstem Pasha's mosque in Tahtakale (Appendix 1). Nevertheless, it conforms to vizierial prototypes in its omission of internal arcades supporting upper galleries. The four precious columns that articulate the boundaries of the central domed cube, however, create the illusion of a continuous arcade, recalling those of grand vizierial mosques. As in the vizier Mesih Mehmed Pasha's mosque, the ground level of Nişancı

Mehmed's mosque differs from its upper level, which is surrounded by a continuous U-shaped gallery (illus. 418, 420). The projecting mihrab constitutes a single tall unit, while the three other half-domed units are divided into two levels by means of upper galleries linked up to the corner spaces above the lateral rooms. The semi-domed lateral recesses are screened off from the central domed cube with ogee arches supported on red porpyhry columns featuring muqarnas capitals: one at each side and two in front of the anti-qibla vestibule, which is surmounted by a private balcony.

The balcony above the gate is flanked by two vaulted spaces that probably functioned as tribunes for the muezzins. A late-Ottoman muezzin's tribune raised on wooden pillars is clumsily inserted into the northeast corner of the prayer hall, where it blocks an inscribed window lunette. The two dainty marble preacher's pulpits at the southeast and southwest corners of the prayer hall, each supported on a porphyry colonnette, are reached from staircases incorporated into the walls of adjacent windows. They recall the pulpits with precious columns attached to the piers of the Süleymaniye mosque, and the star-studded minbar hood also finds a parallel in Sultan Süleyman's mosque, which represented the glory of the classical age so cherished by Nişancı Mehmed Pasha.

The long vaulted rooms at the north corners have separate doors from the north portico and communicate with the prayer hall through arched gateways and iron-grilled windows. Goodwin speculates that these *tabhane* rooms could have been inspired by 'deliberate revivalism'.[169] Mosques with lateral *tabhane* rooms enjoyed a longer life in southeast Anatolia and Syria, where examples attributed to Sinan include those of Hüsrev Pasha in Aleppo (*c.* 1546–47) and Çerkes İskender Pasha in Diyarbakır (*c.* 1551–65). The closest parallel, however, is Sokollu's cruciform convent mosque in Payas (*c.* 1567–74), inaugurated just around the time Nişancı Mehmed Pasha ruled that town as the governor-general of Aleppo. The presence of a Halveti convent in the chancellor's complex suggests that the segregated lateral rooms of his mosque functioned as retreats for the devotional rituals of dervishes. His waqfiyya stipulates the recitation of monotheistic litanies by dervishes in the mosque, where the madrasa professor would hold classes, perhaps in the iwan-like semi-domed lateral recesses. The fragmented spatial layout of the mosque, then, responded to a functional programme accommodating the needs of the dervishes and madrasa students, whose dormitories lacked assembly halls.

Inscriptions on the north façade of the mosque foreshadow themes elaborated inside the prayer hall: the enumeration of divine attributes echoing the litanies recited by dervishes, and the importance of both inner and outer forms of worship. The muqarnas-hooded twin mihrabs of the façade have rectangular panels that quote hadith: 'Whoever builds a masjid for God, God the Most High will build an abode for him in paradise', 'Prayer is the

416 Nişancı Mehmed Pasha complex, Karagümrük, from the north.

417 Nişancı Mehmed Pasha mosque from the south.

418 Nişancı Mehmed Pasha mosque, Karagümrük, interior.

pillar of religion, and whoever abandons it demolishes religion.' The four arched window lunettes of the façade, carved with gilded inscriptions against a green background in monumental *thuluth* script, cite the ninety-nine beautiful names of God, as do the lunettes of the prayer hall and those of the *tabhane* rooms. Only the lunettes flanking the mihrab recess feature Koranic inscriptions; they quote an unusual verse from the Baqara sura which indirectly compares the mosque to the Kaʿba: 'God the Most High said: And when Abraham and Ishmael were raising the foundations of the House (Abraham prayed): Our Lord! Accept from us (this duty). Lo! Thou, only Thou, art the Hearer, the Knower (2:127).' The muqarnas-hooded mihrab with a triangular crested pediment quotes a variant of the standard mihrab verse (3:39) that appears in some late mosques of Sinan.

The renovated painted inscriptions of the domical superstructure consist of Koranic verses that emphasize the importance of congregational prayers, the recitation of the Koran, and the remembrance (*dhikr*) of God.[170] The central roundel of the dome is inscribed with an atypical verse recommending worship from sunset until the dark of night, and the recital of the Koran at dawn (17:78). Its eight arch spandrels bear roundels with the revered names. The half-dome over the mihrab recess cites verses that promise paradise to obedient worshippers (23:9–11). The verse quoted on the east half-dome emphasizes turning towards God at every place of worship (7:29). The west half-dome is inscribed with a verse from the Jumʿ a sura that recommends the remembrance of God after the performance of the congregational prayers (62:10). The exedras sequentially quote a verse declaring the remembrance (*dhikr*) of God as more important than the mere performance of obligatory worship (*ṣalāwat*):

> Recite that which hath been inspired in thee of the Scripture, and establish worship. Lo! Worship preserveth from lewdness and iniquity, but verily remembrance of Allah is more important. And Allah knoweth what ye do (29:45).

The thematically unified epigraphy reflects the harmonious coexistence of diverse modes of orthodox worship in the

419 Nişancı Mehmed Pasha complex, prayer windows of the mausoleum and the forecourt gate.

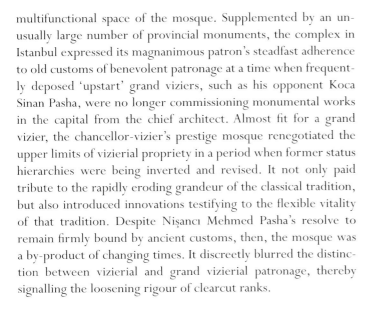

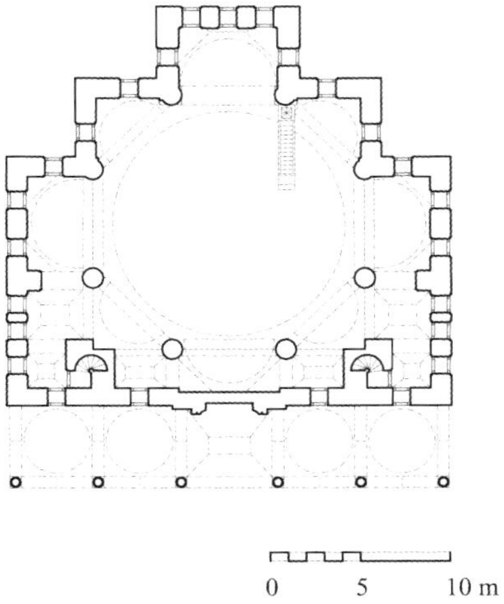

420 Plan of the Nişancı Mehmed Pasha mosque, Karagümrük, at upper gallery level.

multifunctional space of the mosque. Supplemented by an unusually large number of provincial monuments, the complex in Istanbul expressed its magnanimous patron's steadfast adherence to old customs of benevolent patronage at a time when frequently deposed 'upstart' grand viziers, such as his opponent Koca Sinan Pasha, were no longer commissioning monumental works in the capital from the chief architect. Almost fit for a grand vizier, the chancellor-vizier's prestige mosque renegotiated the upper limits of vizierial propriety in a period when former status hierarchies were being inverted and revised. It not only paid tribute to the rapidly eroding grandeur of the classical tradition, but also introduced innovations testifying to the flexible vitality of that tradition. Despite Nişancı Mehmed Pasha's resolve to remain firmly bound by ancient customs, then, the mosque was a by-product of changing times. It discreetly blurred the distinction between vizierial and grand vizierial patronage, thereby signalling the loosening rigour of clearcut ranks.

Chapter 11

GRAND ADMIRALS

I. SİNAN PASHA
ISTANBUL, BEŞİKTAŞ (1554–55/56)

II. PİYALE MEHMED PASHA
ISTANBUL, KASIMPAŞA (TERSANE, *c.* 1565–73)

III. KILIÇ ALİ PASHA
ISTANBUL, TOPHANE (1578–80/81)

I. SİNAN PASHA

There was no precedent for the monumental mosque complexes that Sinan designed in the suburbs of Galata for grand admirals, a new group of patrons, whose status had recently risen.[1] The unusually spacious, idiosyncratic mosques of these complexes reinterpret archaic plan types associated with the ghazi ethos, since they commemorate the conquests of seafaring ghazis. Built to accommodate large congregations in neighbourhoods predominantly inhabited by mariners, they were erected by workforces dominated by galley slaves and financed with the spoils of naval victories.

Barbaros Hayreddin Pasha (Barbarossa) was the first navy commander honoured in 1534 with the title grand admiral (*kapudan paşa*) and governor-general of islands (*cezair beylerbeyi*). With its capital in Gallipoli, the newly created province that came under his jurisdiction included Ottoman-controlled islands supplemented by sanjaks in Rumelia, Anatolia, and recently subjugated territories in North Africa.[2] Barbarossa built a modest complex outside the walls of Galata, next to his endowed shore palace near the landing station of Beşiktaş.[3] Overlooking a public square called Deve Meydanı (Camel Square), this complex comprised a masjid, madrasa, hospice, and mausoleum.[4]

Sinan's autobiographies list only the mausoleum, built in 1541–42, during the lifetime of Barbarossa (d. 1546), along with the two commercial bath-houses he endowed in the quarters of Zeyrek (Çinili Hamam) and Karagümrük.[5] The octagonal ashlar masonry mausouleum is the only remaining part of the grand admiral's humble complex. It is no coincidence that the monumental mosque complex of Sinan Pasha is located across from the mausoleum of the venerated 'sea wolf' (illus. 421, 422). Barbarossa's legendary exploits, recorded in his *vita* of the early 1540s (*Ġāzavātāme*, Book of Ghazas), had turned him into a saintly figure whose hallowed burial place became the site of ceremonial visitations.[6] A seventeenth-century expanded version of his *vita* explains that the investiture ceremonies of grand admirals took place there:

> His sacred mausoleum is in Beşiktaş. He is the patron saint (*pīr*) of grand admirals because in the Ottoman state he was the first to become a *ḳapudān paşa*. It is he who regulated in the Ottoman state the affairs of the sea and the imperial arsenal. Presently, when grand admirals receive a robe of honour, they wear it in the place where the late Hayreddin Pasha is entombed and offer prayers there. Food is distributed, and the poor and needy eat it. May his soul rejoice! He was a saintly person (*velī*), a ghazi, and a warrior of Islam (*mücāhid*) whose revelations and miracles became manifest countless times. May God bless his soul![7]

The revered mausoleum was also visited before the annual departure of the fleet from the port of Beşiktaş. A dispatch sent to Genoa on 28 March 1566, for instance, describes how the grand admiral Piyale Pasha had launched the armada that day at the Kasımpaşa arsenal, and 'according to custom went with grand pomp to the sepulchre of Barbarossa' before leaving the capital the next day.[8] Marcantonio Pigafetta (1567) reports that Piyale Pasha visited the sacred mausoleum each time he departed with the fleet, staying there a day and a night to offer sacrifices and beg God for victory against the 'infidels' for the love of Barbarossa.[9] These annual visitations are crucial for understanding the symbolic significance of the site chosen for Sinan Pasha's posthumously built mosque complex. It was in his mosque that Lala Mustafa Pasha and Piyale Pasha, the commanders of the

421 Plan of the Sinan Pasha complex, Beşiktaş, with the mausoleum of Barbarossa.

422 Axonometric projection of the Sinan Pasha complex and the Barbarossa mausoleum.

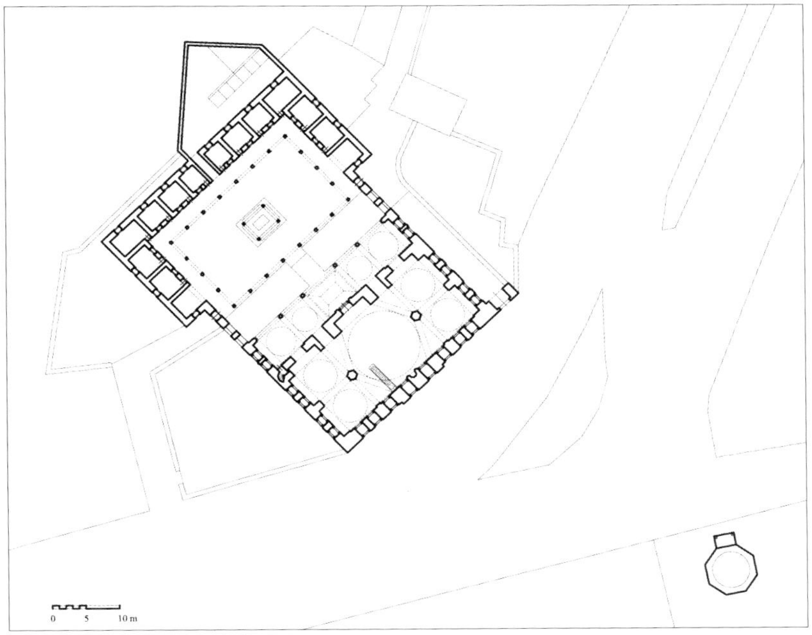

423 Sinan Pasha mosque, Beşiktaş, from the southeast, with the mausoleum of Barbarossa.

victorious Cyprus campaign, performed the prayers of the sacrificial feast with the army before sailing away with the armada in May 1570. Firing cannon balls in front of the Topkapı Palace, they left for Mediterranean waters as the sultan and a crowd of spectators prayed for the victory of the 'soldiers of Islam' over the 'enemies of the Faith'.[10] A year later, the vizier Pertev Mehmed Pasha and the grand admiral Müezzinzade Ali Pasha accompanied the 'soldiers of Islam' during the Friday prayers at the 'Beşiktaş mosque', where they begged for victory before departing for the Lepanto campaign, unaware of the disaster that awaited them.[11]

Sinan Pasha's Friday mosque, which turns its qibla wall towards the mausoleum of Barbarossa, added a veneer of religious orthodoxy to the rituals of veneration enacted there (illus. 423). Its patron was the younger brother of the Croatian-born grand vizier Rüstem Pasha (g.v. 1544–53, 1555–61). The two brothers, recuited as swineherds from a Bosnian village near Sarajevo, rose to power during Süleyman's reign after being educated in the imperial palace.[12] The younger of the two, Sinan Pasha, served as the sanjak governor of Herzegovina before he replaced Sokollu Mehmed Pasha as grand admiral in 1548, two years after Barbarossa's demise. Mustafa Āli portrays 'Kapudan Sinan Pasha', who passed away holding the rank of grand admiral and governor-general of islands in 1554, as irritable, arrogant, and explosive in his outbursts of anger: 'He was not blessed with a long life because he was viciously contentious, impetuous with words, dreadful, and tyrannical!'[13]

Among the few achievements of the grand admiral, who apparently eclipsed his brother in bad temper, was the seizure of Tripoli in Libya from Spanish forces in 1551 with a fleet guided by the seasoned corsair, Turgud Reis.[14] According to Bernardo Navagero (1553), the forty-year-old, hot-tempered Sinan Pasha enjoyed immense authority thanks to the clout of his grand vizier brother, ten years older than he:[15]

> The *Grand Signore*'s present Captain of the Sea has little experience with maritime affairs, since he has not had any duty or practice related to the army: he is obeyed and esteemed more than any other captain on account of his brother. There is nothing he commands that is not carried out and he wants to be recognized by all as a leader. He has little courtesy and speaks with no reservation. He is irascible, or better said furious ... His brother, the Pasha, loves him extremely and favours him excessively, and cannot support any talk against him. He therefore does all that enters his head without any fear whatsoever, and everyone stays quiet even if greatly abused ... Believed to be a man about forty years old, he is huge and stocky, with a dark-coloured countenance, and a great vivacity in his eyes.[16]

Navagero adds that Rüstem Pasha had appointed his brother as grand admiral to ensure prince Selim's accession to the throne: 'There is no securer way to prevent Mustafa's succession than to prohibit with the armada his passage [to the capital].'[17] Domenico Trevisano (1554) concurs that the grand vizier and the grand admiral had made plans to assure prince Selim's entry into the capital following the sultan's death, where he would seize the imperial treasury and buy the favour of the janissaries who supported his rival.[18] Sinan Pasha was designated lieutenant governor of Istanbul in 1553, the year his brother and Sultan Süleyman left for a campaign at the Safavid front. After prince Mustafa's execution during that campaign and Rüstem Pasha's dismissal from the grand vizierate, Sinan Pasha was replaced by a new lieutenant governor (Hadım İbrahim Pasha) but was allowed to keep the post of grand admiral.[19] Dernschwam records his death shortly thereafter, on 21 December 1554, pointing out that he had accumulated a fortune from the sale of Christian slaves captured from Naples and Sicily and owned 700 galley slaves, kept in the towers of Galata.[20]

The Spanish galley slave Pedro, attached to the pasha's service for twelve years, reports that his master had died from 'hydropsy' following surgery on a dark tumescent cyst (his brother, too, would die from a cancerous tumour).[21] Sinan Pasha was ceremonially buried at the cemetery of the mosque complex built in Üsküdar for his sister-in-law, Mihrümah Sultan, near her garden palace, where the deposed Rüstem Pasha was spending his two years of exile (1553–55):[22]

> They placed his body in a coffin of cypress wood, and an escort of four pashas carried it to a mosque that had been built by his brother [*sic*] in Scutari, distant by a league from Constantinople. A solemn cortège like that of the pope accompanied it, for he was not a grandee of minor importance. They sacrificed sheep all over the place and cooked large quantities of rice and meat for distribution as a charity.[23]

Pedro was among the galley slaves who had built the grand admiral a palace with three courtyards at the Hippodrome just before his death.[24] He says that the pasha kept sixty-three women there, four of whom had given birth to his children, but that the most important among them was his oldest son's mother, who commanded the rest like an abbess.[25] Pedro adds that only one of the pasha's daughters survived and describes how his possessions were entrusted to princess Mihrümah, whom he appointed as the executor of his will:

> The Sultana was designated the executor of his testament and all his possessions were carried to her, cartloads of gold and silver. Certainly there was more than a million ducats of money, and another million worth of jewels and movable properties. He left behind two daughters and a son, and as far as I know two of them subsequently died and only a daughter remained.[26]

Pedro mentions the sale of the pasha's slaves, with the exception of a hundred 'destined for the construction of a mosque at the site of the sepulchre [of Barbarossa]'. They, too, would be sold after the completion of that building.[27]

According to its foundation inscriptions, cited below, Sinan Pasha's posthumously built mosque complex in Beşiktaş was completed in 1555–56. Its construction process and costs are outlined in the posthumous Arabic waqfiyya of 'the late Sinan Pasha, son of the late Mustafa Beg b. Abdülmecid', registered on 26 August 1557. The waqfiyya, mentioning the grand admiral's only remaining daughter, Meryem Hatun, was approved in a court hearing on the basis of testimony provided by his household steward, Keyvan Kethüda.[28] The latter testified that Sinan Pasha had endowed his properties in a waqfiyya drawn up on 16 June 1554, prior to his death in late December, when he appointed his steward as the administrator of his waqf and his brother (Rüstem Pasha b. Mustafa Beg b. Abdülmuin) as its overseer.[29]

The ailing Sinan Pasha stipulated the construction of a Friday mosque, madrasa, and elementary school under the supervision of his steward, with his brother acting as building overseer. He also requested that real estate properties be bought to maximize the revenues of his waqf, for which he additionally endowed a third of his inheritance. His income-generating endowments included his palace at the Hippodrome, real estate properties in Herzegovina and the capital (Fener, Kasımpaşa, Tophane), mills in İzmit and Herzegovina, and 1,900,000 aspers. The waqfiyya explains how Keyvan Kethüda increased the total amount of endowed cash to 3,273,800 aspers, with which he set out to build the mosque complex soon after the pasha's demise (Appendix 2).[30]

He built the Friday mosque, madrasa, and elementary school in Beşiktaş, along with neighbouring commercial properties (fifty shops, forty-one rental rooms, a bakery, and a butcher's store) for 1,841,398 aspers. The grand admiral's complex replaced a pre-existing masjid and convent endowed by Mehmed b. Durmuş (an early sixteenth-century poet nicknamed Deli Birader) with the permission of its waqf administrator. The former complex had once been accompanied by a bath-house, but it was demolished by the grand vizier İbrahim Pasha (d. 1536) because it had turned into a scandalous hub of licentiousness frequented by the city's prettiest boys and their aficionados. Keyvan Kethüda built a new bath-house with three adjacent shops in Beşiktaş for 263,667 aspers, together with seven other shops and eight rooms that cost 15,862 aspers. He then constructed a dervish convent (*zāwiya*) near the Friday mosque for 28,430 aspers and a masjid in the new quarter (*yeñi maḥalle*) that emerged near Sinan Pasha's complex for 24,246 aspers. For the demolished masjid of Deli Birader, a surrogate masjid was built in Yenibahçe for 75,509 aspers.[31]

The grand admiral's six pious monuments (mosque, madrasa, elementary school, convent, and two masjids) were supported by a large number of newly built shops, rooms, and mills in Istanbul and its suburbs (Galata, Tophane, Kasımpaşa, Hasköy) which cost 510,663 aspers. The money that remained (514,025 aspers) was loaned out at a legally approved interest rate to cover staff wages and repair expenses. Salaried personnel were assigned not only to the six pious monuments posthumously built for Sinan Pasha, but also to others created during his lifetime: a masjid near Gül Camii in the Fener quarter of Istanbul (the now-ruined Sinan Pasha Mescidi, converted from a Byzantine chapel); a Friday mosque at Hısn-ı Nova (Novum Castrum) in Herzegovina; another Friday mosque with an elementary school near Foça in Herzegovina; and an elementary school in Sarajevo.[32] The chief architect's autobiographies list the grand admiral's palace at the Hippodrome; his Friday mosque, madrasa, and bath-house in Beşiktaş; his masjid in Yenibahçe; and his tomb in Üsküdar.[33]

A supplementary waqfiyya registered in September 1562, shortly after Rüstem Pasha's demise, records the increased salaries of personnel and additional expenditures covered by one-third of the grand admiral's inheritance (2,427,155 aspers). At the law court where this waqfiyya was authorized, Keyvan Kethüda provided a detailed account of how he spent this sum to witnesses that included the representatives of Mihrümah Sultan and Meryem Hatun.[34] New constructions in Beşiktaş included two bridges (720,025 aspers) and the repair of a conduit that carried water to Sinan Pasha's Friday mosque and its bath-house (21,948 aspers). Additional funds were devoted to the pasha's neighbouring dervish convent (*zāwiya*) with ten rooms (120,000 aspers), and its hospice (*ʿimārat*) serving free food to the dervishes (350,674 aspers).[35]

The convent and hospice was staffed with new personnel, unmentioned in the earlier waqfiyya, which cites only the convent keeper. It was to be headed by an erudite shaykh, chosen from the followers of the Nakshbandi shaykh Ahmed Bukhari, buried in Bursa. This shows that, like his brother, Sinan Pasha must have been affiliated with the Nakshbandi order. The shaykh was to preach to the congregation of the mosque on Fridays and holy days. After he and his ten disciples performed the five congregational prayers in the mosque, they would assemble at the convent to recite designated suras from the Koran, praises of God, and pious aphorisms: Praise be to God! Thanks be to God! There is no God but God! God is Great, the succour of those who seek aid! I ask for God's forgiveness! There is no God but God, and Muhammad is His messenger! Then they would pronounce the following invocation:

> O God, for whom this place was built, the King, the Benefactor, send the rewards of our prayers and recitations, which were for your generous self, to the soul of your slave, Sinan Pasha, and place him among those for whom one has no fear and who are not sad on the Day of Judgment; the one who answers our prayers, Amen!

After eating at the convent kitchen, the dervishes would repeat the same invocation. On Friday nights and holy nights the shaykh and his disciples had to stay awake to mention (*dhikr*) God's names, standing and kneeling in worship inside the mosque and at the convent.[36]

The only surviving components of Sinan Pasha's complex are its mosque and U-shaped madrasa. The historical avenue running parallel to the shore, which separated the complex from Barbarossa's mausoleum, has been replaced with a widened modern artery that obliterated the urban fabric seen on the Pervitich map of 1922. The map identifies the convent (tekké Sinan-Pacha) near an alley connected to the east gate of the mosque's forecourt. It shows two cemetery gardens at both sides of the qibla wall, flanked by rows of shops facing the avenue. The bath-house, demolished in 1957, was located at a distance across the same avenue, at the edge of the Dolmabahçe Palace.[37]

Beşiktaş was the neighbourhood where grand admirals generally resided.[38] The North African traveller al-Tamgruti (1589–91), who stayed in the grand admiral Uluç Hasan Pasha's palace, described the carefree district (illus. 101):

> We rested three days at the house of the captain which is in a place called Beşiktaş, situated at the east side of Galata. It is in fact in the neighbourhood of Galata that the [grand] admirals, who command the ships and all the marines, reside. They live there so as to keep the ships continually under the watch of their eyes and ears. This quarter is not one of high-ranking people nor of merchants; it is largely inhabited by foreigners and poor people, who reside in it because life there is easygoing.[39]

According to the seventeenth-century travelogue of Eremya Çelebi, the shoreline was dotted with garden palaces and the mixed population of the suburban town included Armenians and Greeks with their own churches, some Jews, and Muslims, who had 'a large mosque, a bath-house, and a market'.[40] Evliya Çelebi says the mosque of Sinan Pasha, sited on a flat pasture a hundred paces away from the landing station, had an outer precinct planted with plane trees, on one corner of which was a law court. The hospice no longer functioned, and a vast plain extended between the qibla wall of the mosque and the landing station.[41] Ayvansarayi mentions among the dependencies of the complex its madrasa and 'upper-storey' elementary school, specifying that the court of justice was located at the left side (east) of the mosque.[42]

The mosque and madrasa block, constructed with alternating courses of stone and brick, turns its qibla façade to the modern avenue that separates it from Barbarossa's ashlar masonry mausoleum, now situated in a park (illus. 423). Unlike other posthumously built complexes attributed to Sinan, which generally lack foundation inscriptions, the mosque has two chronograms, one inscribed above its gate and the other around the ablution fountain of its paved courtyard framed by the U-shaped madrasa without a classroom. The Turkish inscription carved around the rectangular white marble fountain basin was composed by the poet Sıhri Mehmed Efendi, nicknamed Kız Memi (Girl Mehmed):[43]

> For the love of God, he was a generous patron.
> His wealth, flowing like water, built the *sebīl.*
>
> Today he was the source of many works of charity.
> May God have mercy on him tomorrow.
>
> If it be said that he is one destined for Paradise, it is true.
> For his works are proof of it.
>
> He was grand admiral and governor-general.
> He humbled many non-believers.
>
> As to being a second Joseph, there is no dispute,
> Since good character and great comeliness are his.
>
> For the sake of the people of Merve and Safa [outside Mecca],
> The Friend [Abraham] built the spring of Zemzem in the Kaʿba.
>
> O Sıhrī, the voice expressed its date.
> 'Selsebil, fountain of the water of life', the year 963 (1555–56).

The gilded Arabic inscription, carved in cartouches above the arched gate of the mosque, which lacks a muqarnas hood, echoes the praises of God and the monotheistic litanies that the Nakshbandi dervishes of the convent were required to invoke:

> In the name of Allah, the Beneficient, the Merciful.
> Praise be to God! And thanks be to God! And there is no god

But God! And God is Great! And there is no power
Nor strength but in God, the most powerful!

This noble Friday mosque was built by the late Sinan Pasha,
In the month of Muharram in the year six-hundred-and-sixty-six [November/December, 1555].[44]

The main components of the mosque complex, then, were completed in 1555–56. Sinan, who was building the Süleymaniye at that time, may have periodically checked its construction. Although architectural historians have generally assumed that the mosque was begun in the early 1550s during the patron's lifetime, his two hitherto unnoted waqfiyyas leave no doubt that its foundations were laid after his death.[45] Therefore, the claim that the miserly Rüstem Pasha completed his brother's mosque in a less spectacular manner than originally planned remains unsubstantiated.[46] The use of striped masonry and simple shed roofs over the domeless madrasa cells and their porticoes appropriately expressed the deceased grand admiral's status as lower than that of viziers. The modest forecourt is surrounded by irregular madrasa rooms of varied size, fronted by short columns with simple capitals. This is Sinan's first experiment in the capital with a U-shaped madrasa confronting a mosque, a scheme he had used earlier in Sofu Mehmed Pasha's complex at Sofia (*c.* 1547–48). As in Mihrümah Sultan's Edirnekapı mosque (1563–70), the madrasa lacks a classroom.

Sinan's historicist reinterpretation of the ancient hexagonal-baldachined plan of the Üç Şerefeli mosque has been regarded as an archaism reflecting his 'loss of interest in the building after the death of its founder'(illus. 52, 53).[47] Attributing such independence to the chief architect underestimates the input of Rüstem Pasha and Keyvan Kethüda, who supervised its construction. The trio must have deemed the old sultanic mosque in Edirne, associated with the 'good old days' of the ghazis, a particularly decorous model for the grand admiral's unprecedented memorial. The chief architect adapted the layout of the antiquated imperial mosque for his defunct non-royal patron by subtractive transmutation, reducing its scale, omitting its multiple minarets, and translating its domical forecourt into a functional madrasa.

Sinan Pasha's mosque is crowned by a 12.6-metre dome, approximating in size the domes of mosques built for viziers and governor-generals (Appendix 1). Its exceptionally large space was designed to accommodate crowded congregations that performed collective prayers in it prior to the annual departure of the fleet from Beşiktaş. The mosque was originally fronted by a double portico, a familial feature it shares with the mosques of Rüstem Pasha (Tekirdağ, Tahtakale) and Mihrümah Sultan (Üsküdar, Edirnekapı). The five-domed first portico mentioned by Evliya Çelebi was incorporated into the prayer hall in 1749 to accommodate even larger congregations. The embedding of its columns (uncovered during repairs in 2002) within walls added to the sombreness of the prayer hall, which is lit with evenly spaced windows in three tiers.[48] The second portico covered by a shed roof preserves its original form.

The mosque improves upon its forerunner in Edirne in its more refined support system, featuring two hexagonal piers; in its proportionally loftier main dome; and in its better integration of the double-domed side aisles with the central space. Nevertheless, the disturbing triangular areas between the main dome and the lateral domes, externally expressed as turrets with whorl caps, remain unresolved. The chief architect would create a more satisfactory layout in his next trial with the hexagonal scheme in the grand vizier Kara Ahmed Pasha's mosque, which was designed in 1555, but postponed following the pasha's execution that year to reinstate Rüstem Pasha (illus. 4). Sinan Pasha's mosque in Beşiktaş was inaugurated the same year, when his brother reclaimed the grand vizierate. Comparing the two hexagonal-baldachined mosque and madrasa complexes designed by Sinan in those years reveals the codes of decorum through which the differing ranks of their patrons were represented architecturally.[49]

Unlike the grand vizier's more innovative ashlar masonry mosque, ornamented with *cuerda seca* tiles datable to around 1555, that of the grand admiral was built with cheaper striped masonry and features simpler painted decorations. Its prayer hall, repainted in the nineteenth century and more recently, has lost its original decorative programme.[50] The plain white marble minbar and muqarnas-hooded mihrab are relatively humble, as is the Bursa-arched muezzin's tribune at the right side of the gate. An inventory appended to the waqfiyya of 1557 lists the objects and furnishings endowed for the mosque: Koran manuscripts, pulpits, candlesticks, incense burners, damascened mirror globes (*ṭop-ı āyine*), ostrich eggs, oil lamps from Damascus, crystal rosaries, and two Kaʿba covers. These were complemented by a kilim for the minbar, four prayer carpets (*ḳaliçe-i seccāde*), three large carpets (*ḳaliçe*) donated by Rüstem Pasha, four red carpets with mihrabs (11 cubits each), two smaller red carpets with mihrabs (6 cubits each), a 5.5-cubit carpet, and an 8-cubit carpet given by the chief armourer.[51]

Sinan Pasha's posthumous mosque complex is still the primary landmark of Beşiktaş. It propelled the Islamization of that neighbourhood, which previously lacked a Friday mosque. Its extensive socio-religious, educational, and commercial structures contributed to the urban development of this suburban township at a time when the capital was experiencing a major population boom. The pasha's monumental mosque without a mausoleum of its own permanently linked his identity to the revered Barbarossa, the patron saint of grand admirals. It represented a veritable 'invention of tradition' with its rituals connected to Barbarossa's mausoleum and its reformulation of an ancient plan type that set a model for the mosques Sinan would design for future grand admirals.

II. PİYALE MEHMED PASHA

Like Sinan Pasha's mosque in Beşiktaş, that of his successor, Piyale Mehmed Pasha, reinterprets an archaic plan type: it is composed of six domed modules in the manner of multi-unit early Ottoman Great Mosques (illus. 424, 425). Because it is cited only in the *Tuḥfe* and deviates from Sinan's mainstream works, its eccentricity is often attributed to another court architect and to the patron's taste.[52] Located behind the dockyards of the Kasımpaşa arsenal, the mosque complex stimulated the creation of a new settlement. Its now-lost dependencies, omitted from the chief architect's autobiographies, comprised a madrasa, dervish convent, elementary school, bath-house, and market.[53] Also known as the Tersane (Arsenal) mosque, its site was intimately associated with the post of its patron, who as grand admiral held daily audiences at the neighbouring arsenal (illus. 103–4, 352[2]). A Venetian secretary observed in 1562 that Piyale Pasha 'never fails to punctually hold his usual council meetings, both in his own residence [in Aksaray] and in the arsenal, where he goes almost every day to discuss with the captains issues concerning the armada.'[54]

The pasha was a Croat from Hungary: according to the Austrian ambassador Jacob von Betzek (1564–65), he had invited to the capital his Hungarian mother, who was then living with him, though still a Christian.[55] After being brought up in Süleyman's imperial palace, from which he exited as chief gatekeeper in 1547, Piyale was appointed grand admiral and sanjak governor of Gallipoli in 1554. Together with the seasoned corsair Turgud Reis, he conquered the castle of Reggio in southern Italy and the port of Oran in Algeria in 1555, vanquishing Bizerta in Tunisia the following year. He was promoted to governor-general of islands in 1558, after conquering Ciudadela in Majorca and pillaging Sorrento, near Naples. One of the grand admiral's greatest exploits was the conquest of the island of Jerba in 1560, where he captured forty ships, 4,000 slaves, and a huge booty from Spanish forces.[56] Busbecq says the pasha and his men had made their 'last will and testatement' before setting out on that dangerous campaign, thinking they might never come back from it. But they returned with great pomp. The grand admiral first 'sent a galley to Constantinople to announce his victory' and then made his own triumphal entry into the capital with the fleet:[57]

> In September the victorious fleet returned to Constantinople with the prisoners, spoils, and captured vessels, a sight as joyful to the Turks as it was mournful and deplorable to us Christians. The first night it anchored at the rocks off Constantinople, so that it might enter the harbour by day with greater pomp and before a greater crowd of spectators. Soleiman had gone down to the colonnade adjoining the entrance of the harbour and forming the continuation of his garden [the Marble Kiosk at the Topkapı Palace], so that he might have a nearer view of the arrival of the fleet and of the Christian officers exhibited upon it. On the poop of the flagship were displayed [the grand admiral] Don Alvaro de Sandé and the admirals of the Neapolitan and Sicilian fleets, Don Berenguer de Requesens and Don Sancho de Leyva. The captured galleys were towed along, stripped of their oars and bulwarks and reduced to mere hulks, so that in this condition they might seem small, shapeless, and contemptible in comparison with the Turkish vessels.[58]

In 1562 Sultan Süleyman rewarded his grand admiral (whom he is said to have esteemed more than his grand vizier, Rüstem Pasha) with marriage to the eighteen-year-old princess Gevherhan Sultan, one of prince Selim's daughters.[59] That year Marcantonio Donini described the opium-eating Piyale Pasha as follows:

> He neither has the experience nor the intelligence required of a grand admiral, being very timid. Yet he has excellent advisers, who alleviate the weight of most things expected from his post. He occasionally eats opium to liberate himself from all worries and troubles, and especially from the sea. He is of the Hungarian nation and approximately thirty-seven years old, with a pleasant and human nature and a mediocre intellect.[60]

In 1566, the year after an unsuccessful expedition to Malta, the grand admiral accomplished his second-greatest feat: the conquest of the island of Chios (Sakız) from the Genoese, followed by a lucrative raid on the Apulian coast in southern Italy.[61] He congratulated his father-in-law Selim II's accession to the throne with 'unmatched gifts' and 'angel-faced slaves' from his recently acquired booty and was promoted to the rank of fifth vizier. He continued to hold the post of grand admiral for about two more years, guarding the capital as lieutenant governor in 1567–68 while the new sultan wintered in Edirne with his court.[62]

Marcantonio Pigafetta (1567) reports that the admiral-cum-vizier 'rarely followed the court with the other pashas, remaining instead in Constantinople to take care of the armada and manage the affairs of all the mariners.'[63] According to Marino Cavalli (1567), although the pasha did not get along with his brother-in-law, the grand vizier Sokollu, he was still reputed to be the best counsellor in maritime matters, 'having made a name as very skilful and experienced, and a man of war because of which he is esteemed and greatly loved by the mariners'.[64] In 1568 he was deprived of the office of grand admiral because the envious Sokollu convinced the sultan that nobody should possess such great power on the sea and hold the vizierate at the same time. Thereafter Piyale came to hate his brother-in-law and sided with the court's pro-war faction, which opposed the grand vizier's peace policy.[65]

Raised to the rank of third vizier in 1568, he nevertheless remained known as 'Kapudan Piyale Pasha' because his fourteen-year vocation as naval commander had become inseparable from his identity.[66] He continued to command the fleet on several occasions during his decade-long vizierate: as third vizier he was the commander-in-chief of naval forces at the victorious Cyprus campaign of 1570, and as second vizier he commanded an expedition in 1573, during which the coasts of Apulia and Messina were pillaged. The Frenchman Du Fresne Canaye describes how the vizier and the grand admiral Kılıç Ali Pasha sailed away with an impressive armada launched at the Kasımpaşa arsenal in 1573, after kissing the sultan's hand and visiting Barbarossa's mausoleum in Beşiktaş with all the grandees. Piyale's amorous wife and her older sister İsmihan watched the departure of the flotilla from Sokollu's palace in Üsküdar, to which the grandees moved on their 'caiques' from Beşiktaş. The sultana, 'seeing that her beloved husband was about to part, and that she had no means of holding him back, made the grandest lamentations in the world, and no consolation could appease her sighs.'[67]

When the fleet returned without having won a victory against the Spaniards in Sicily, Sokollu is said to have used this as an occasion to discredit his rival.[68] The Venetian diplomats who signed the post-Lepanto peace treaty of 1573 commented that the war-oriented fifty-year-old second vizier had many children from the sultan's daughter and lived prosperously with a large retinue of slaves. His addiction to opium relieved him from cares and made him live merrily, even if dimwittedly.[69] Antonio Tiepolo (1576) described Piyale Pasha, who preserved his rank as second vizier under Murad III, as 'very sick, though not too old'. He had lost the sultan's favour because of his feebleness, increased by 'an herb he uses for his pleasure because it uplifts his spirit'.[70]

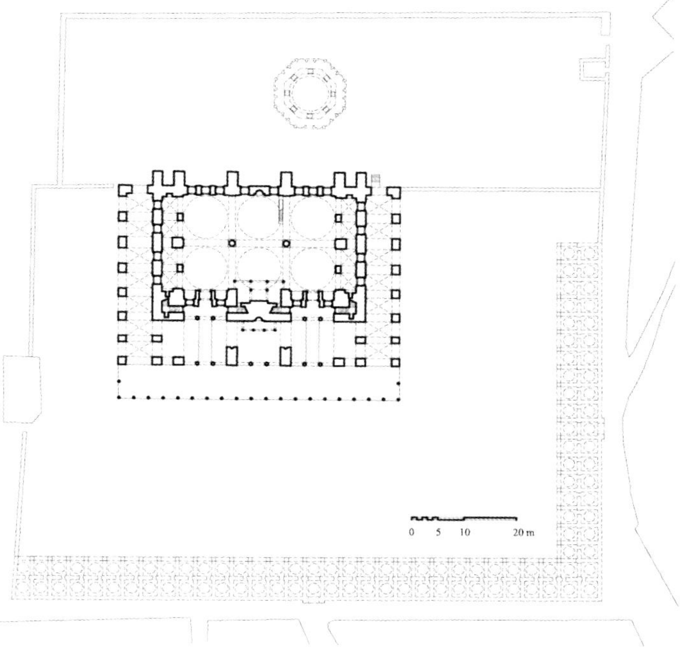

424 Plan of the Piyale Pasha mosque and mausoleum, Kasımpaşa, with hypothetical reconstruction of madrasa and convent cells.

425 Axonometric projection of the Piyale Pasha complex.

In 1577 Gerlach recorded in his diary that the pasha, suffering from strangury (painful urination), had piously given up listening to musical instruments. He passed away on 20 January 1578 and was buried at the mausoleum of his mosque complex in Kasımpaşa.[71]

Ayvansarayi lists the pious foundations of Piyale Pasha, who had conquered 'sixty-seven islands in fourteen years'.[72] His mosque in Kasımpaşa was called 'Büyük (Big) Piyale Pasha' to differentiate it from his now-lost masjid in the same quarter, 'Küçük (Small) Piyale Pasha':[73]

> The island of Chios was initially conquered by the hand of [Piyale Pasha]. He built a noble Friday mosque and a single bath there. There is also a Friday mosque of his in Kilid-i Bahr [Gallipoli]. The embellished garden called Tunus Bağı [Tunisian Vineyard] in Üsküdar was also built by him. It is stipulated that the tax levy from the quarter of the noble Friday mosque [in Kasımpaşa] be paid from his waqf so as not to be a burden to the people of that quarter ... The Küçük Piyale Pasha mosque in Kasımpaşa and the water dispenser (*sebīl*) surmounted by an upper-storey elementary school near Mercan Çarşı at the entrance to the Uzunçarşı in Istanbul are also charitable works of the aforesaid pasha.[74]

The building chronology of the Tersane mosque can be deduced from the two previously unknown Turkish waqfiyyas of 'Piyale Pasha b. Abdurrahman', dated 2 April 1565 and 25 November 1573. The first, registered a few days before the grand admiral left for the ineffective Malta expedition, shows that he had already built his masjid 'outside Galata in the place called Kozludere'.[75] He endowed funds for building 'the noble Friday mosque whose construction he initiated', along with a garden in Kozludere and real estate properties at the capital and Gallipoli. For this purpose he set aside 50,000 gold coins (3,000,000 aspers), sixty-eight pieces of headgear encompassing 186 *miskāls* of gold, as well as silver belts and candlesticks. After the building costs of the mosque were covered, the remaining funds would be used for the wages of its personnel as specified in the waqfiyya. The staff would be appointed by the mufti, who was the overseer of the endowment, which was administered by Piyale Pasha himself.[76]

The foundations of the mosque, then, were laid in 1565, perhaps as a pious offering in anticipation of victory in Malta, which did not prove forthcoming. Booty from the conquest of Chios in 1566, the year the pasha rose to the vizierate, may have been dedicated to the ongoing construction completed by 1573. The second waqfiyya registered that year mentions only the completion of the 'noble Friday mosque near Okmeydanı (Archery Field)' and a nearby elementary school, implying that other dependencies were added later.[77] It raises the formerly designated salaries of the mosque staff and stipulates the construction of rent-free houses nearby for the imams and muezzins. Income-producing properties added to the waqf included real estate in Galata and its suburbs; the empty plots of shops that had abutted the pasha's palace (in Aksaray) but were burnt in the fire of 1569; his house and garden in Chios; olive groves in Athens; properties at Kite and Gallipoli; and a village in the sanjak of Nikopolis, donated by the sultan in May 1573.

Based on the completion date of 1573 given by Ayvansarayi, it has been assumed that the Tersane mosque must have been created by another architect while Sinan was busy with the Selimiye in Edirne (1568–74). The first waqfiyya, however, reveals that it was commissioned earlier, in 1565, while its founder was still a grand admiral.[78] Given the high rank of the patron, married to princess Gevherhan, it is difficult to imagine that the chief architect was not consulted at least during the planning stages. In all likelihood Sinan designed the mosque in consultation with naval architects attached to the Kasımpaşa arsenal, who were mostly renegades like Michele Benedetto (called Mandolo da Rodi), a Greek master from Rhodes who was the chief architect of the arsenal in 1554. This Rhodian master had under his command three to four galley architects (receiving fifteen aspers a day), as well as carpenters and blacksmiths (paid eight to twelve aspers), who were imported from Rhodes, Chios, Mytilene, and Gallipoli.[79]

Piyale Pasha may personally have overseen the construction of his mosque, initiated shortly after he served as a building overseer during the renovation of Istanbul's flood-damaged aqueducts in 1563–64. Selaniki records Sultan Süleyman's decree ordering him to oversee the rebuilding of those aqueducts: 'The corps of ships' captains (*rü'esā*) and marines (*ʿazebān*) and galley slaves (*forṣa*) under the command of His Highness Kapudan Piyale Pasha, together with the janissary master builders (*üstād*) and novices commanded by the janissary agha [Müezzinzade] Ali Agha, should diligently work, taking turns to complete the repairs with great effort, and thereafter be promoted in rank according to custom.' A contemporary chronicler wrote that the janissary corps proved much more effective in this project, demonstrating how seamen were 'worthless on land'.[80] The workforce of Piyale Pasha's mosque must have been dominated by the building crew of the arsenal and galley slaves, less experienced in monumental constructions than novices and janissaries. Its building supervisor was probably the pasha's steward, Kurd Kethüda, who testified at the law court that approved the second waqfiyya.[81]

The only structures that accompany the Tersane mosque today are the patron's domed octagonal mausoleum and the ruins of the double bath located at a distance. Evliya Çelebi narrates how by God's will the grand admiral discovered a treasure when he started to build his mosque, finding at its north side six urns filled with gold, which were still displayed at his water dispenser in Uzunçarşı. With this canonically lawful income he built next to his mosque 'a convent, a tomb for himself, a bath-house, and a market-place'.[82] Our traveller also mentions the pasha's nearby garden palace and explains how he developed its unpopulated neighbourhood with the order of Sultan Süleyman:[83]

> As the deceased Koca Piyale Pasha owned 12,000 slaves, he had them build at the far end of Kasımpaşa a Friday mosque, and madrasa, and dervish convent. In order to create a large following for the mosque, which lacked a congregation, he dug a canal from the old arsenal and brought water all the way to the Piyale Pasha mosque which is one hour away. Both sides of the canal were lined with multi-story houses in vineyards and gardens, and the environs of the mosque became cultivated (*ʿimār*) and a crowded congregation came into being. After Piyale Pasha's death, the canal was not cleaned, and it became filled with soil and debris carried by flooding rainwaters. When caiques and two-oared boats could no longer navigate it, everyone built houses further down, and nowadays the canal remains abandoned.[84]

Evliya describes the glistening mosque 'entirely covered with pure lead' at the mouth of the stream, with its qibla side raised on an elevated platform (illus. 426). Its spacious tree-planted outer courtyard featured four gates; the one on the west lined by madrasa rooms at its right and left sides. The artisans of the arsenal would hang out at the convent, whose kitchen distributed food each night to the poor.[85] Ayvansarayi's description provides additional details about now-lost structures:

> The rooms of the madrasa are on one side of [the forecourt], and the cells of the dervish lodge are on the other. There is a water dispenser (*sebīl*) outside the [west] gate. And inside the courtyard is a well, and a stone spigot (*taş muşluk*), and privies. In the cemetery of the [founder's] tomb there is an upper-storey elementary school overlooking the market, and there is an exalted double bath in its market.[86]

Baha Tanman has hypothetically reconstructed the domed dormitory cells of the dervish convent and madrasa that once lined the two wings of the mosque forecourt: the twenty-eight cells of the convent along the north wing, and the seventeen madrasa cells along the west. The functions of their omitted assembly halls were presumably fulfilled by the mosque itself.[87] Its spacious inner galleries and outer porticoes must have served as gathering spaces for students and dervishes, in addition to providing space for crowded congregations on special occasions. The witnesses who signed the second waqfiyya include the preacher and the imam of the mosque who were shaykhs. Later on Shaykh İbrahim was appointed the imam and preacher, as well as the spiritual guide of the convent. He subsequently served as the preacher of the Cerrah Mehmed Pasha mosque, built by the second husband of the grand admiral's widow, Gevherhan.[88]

426 Piyale Pasha mosque, Kasımpaşa, from the northwest.

A Venetian print dated 1571 depicts the miraculous apparition of a cross over Piyale Pasha's mosque, which then moved to several churches converted to mosques, forecasting the hoped-for recovery of Constantinople by Christian forces at the time of Lepanto (illus. 32).[89] Evliya Çelebi identifies some of the mementoes of victory displayed at the mosque complex of 'ghazi Piyale Pasha'. One of them, suspended from the dome of his 'light-filled' mausoleum, was an intricately carved model of Chios contained inside a glass ball.[90] The bronze window grilles of the mosque were said to have been made of the church bells its patron collected from places he conquered from the 'infidels'.[91] Other spolia seen today include the two monumental granite columns at the middle of the mosque (apparently removed from the Podium Temple at Alexandria Troas), and smaller granite columns used in the inner and outer colonnades.[92]

Like Piyale Pasha's exotic 'Tunisian' garden in Üsküdar, his mosque has unusual details that seem to have been inspired by curiosities that he encountered in distant lands.[93] The minaret, uncustomarily placed at the centre of the north façade in the manner of 'Arab' mosques, may carry the memory of monuments the pasha saw in North African territories that fell under his jurisdiction. The cushion voussoirs of the external lateral porticoes and of some arches inside the prayer hall are a shared feature of late medieval Mediterranean architecture (especially monuments built by the Crusaders and the Mamluks), only rarely seen in the Ottoman context.[94] Another rarity is a sizeable group of slender white marble columns whose 'Corinthianizing' foliate capitals were intact in the 1930s, when Martiny surveyed the mosque: they were used in the portico that once surrounded the mausoleum, in the mosque's lateral upper porticoes (recently restored with crude modern replicas of the original capitals), and in the canopy of the no-longer-extant ablution fountain of the forecourt (illus. 427–29).[95] The fountain basin was an antique white marble sarcophagus with classicizing reliefs and Latin inscriptions.[96] The columns and their capitals may have been spolia, perhaps originating from one of the Mediterranean islands. It is more likely, however, that they were created for the mosque complex by one of the renegade artisans employed at the Kasımpaşa arsenal, possibly a Greek or Italian master originating from Chios, where the pasha had a mosque built in his name. The columns could also have been carried from a distance on ships of the armada, given that in 1566 Piyale Pasha had ordered 100 columns from Dubrovnik for a garden he was creating in Euboia (Negroponte).[97]

The six-dome plan of the Tersane mosque (each dome 8.9 metres wide) comes close to that of the grand vizier Atik Ali Paşa (d. 1511) in Karagümrük.[98] It is generally considered incompatible with the chief architect's style, but, as Tanman remarks: 'Why is it not possible that Sinan, who throughout his career experimented with new solutions for monuments with centralized plans, tried out in this case designing a mosque based on a scheme abandoned for a hundred years, producing in it similar effects of spatial unity and airiness?'[99] The mosque modernizes early Ottoman prototypes with its novel elevations and superstructure. For their heavy, free-standing piers it substitutes two slender granite columns and concealed buttresses that no longer interfere with the unity of inner space. Its up-to-date internal galleries, surrounding the prayer hall on three sides, effectively hide the inner buttresses. External porticoes envelop the mosque, except on the qibla side, which is reinforced by tapering buttresses with domical weight turrets. The two-tiered lateral porticoes are complemented by a spacious double portico incorporating flying buttresses to the north. Other modern features include the increased amount of light pouring in from a large number of windows, the decorative programme comprising high quality İznik tiles, and the monumental *thuluth* inscriptions attributed to the famous calligrapher Hasan Karahisari who designed the calligraphy of the Süleymaniye and Selimiye mosques (illus. 430).[100]

The six domes on pendentives, raised above blind drums without stone bases, are entirely sheathed with lead. Some scholars find it inconceivable that Sinan was responsible for these ungainly 'closed-up' domes.[101] Tahsin Öz speculates that the mosque, with its peculiar superstructure floating above the pointed arches of its fenestrated tympana, must have been a naval warehouse that Piyale Pasha extensively remodelled.[102] This hypothesis is certainly far-fetched, but the patron may have wished to establish a visual dialogue between the pronounced tympana arches of his mosque and the row of arched vaults at the neighbouring arsenal, where galleys were kept. The uninterrupted, undulating lead cover of the windowless roofscape of the mosque evokes the wavy seas. A similar analogy is used by Sinan's biographer Sai for the multiple domes of the Şehzade and Süleymaniye complexes, which he likens to bubbles on the surface of the sea.[103] According to a popular tradition recorded in Edwin Grosvenor's guidebook (1865), Piyale Pasha drew the plan of his mosque to resemble a warship and would climb its minaret and 'imagine himself afloat'.[104] While this too may seem far-fetched, the sixteenth-century poet Taşlıcalı Yahya did compare the lead-covered domes and minarets of the Istanbul skyline to ships cruising the harbour at full sail.[105] Perhaps the vaguely mimetic maritime allusions of Piyale Pasha's mosque were not lost on its users, dominated by seafarers and artisans affiliated with the Kasımpaşa arsenal.

Unlike Sinan Pasha's striped masonry mosque in Beşiktaş, the Tersane mosque is built of cut stone. Nevertheless, economy was observed in those areas of the façades that would have been concealed under painted plaster: its side walls, for instance, are built with cheaper masonry (rubble stone, brick, and mortar) up to the tympana level (illus. 427). The central position of the single-galleried minaret (rebuilt in the nineteenth century) relegates the two mosque gates without muqarnas hoods to either side of the north façade.[106] The middle of the untypical façade has a muqarnas-hooded mihrab, fronted by a triple-arched mini baldachin resting on four white marble columns with muqarnas capitals. According to Evliya Çelebi, the wall around the mihrab was inscribed 'from head to foot' with poetic couplets and bold calligraphic designs.[107]

Fronted by triple arcades, the recessed gates are inscribed with Koranic passages welcoming the congregation into the gardens of paradise (16:32, 39:73). The upper galleries inside the prayer hall are reached from staircases incorporated into tower-like, dome-capped buttresses at the east and west corners of the north façade. The arcades of the lateral inner galleries are supported on piers. From the muezzin's tribune, raised on six columns at the centre of the anti-qibla wall, stairs lead up to the minaret. The balcony above the tribune is flanked by galleries that surmount the twin gates. Gerlach (1575) says the wall behind it was inscribed 'from top to bottom, like a tablet (*Taffel*), with Arabic scriptures' from the Koran.[108] His description, not unlike Evliya's remarks about the exterior of the same wall, brings to mind the densely inscribed walls of multi-domed early Ottoman mosques.

The whitewashed interior of Piyale Pasha's mosque no longer preserves its painted inscriptions and decorations (illus. 430). The renewed stained glass windows along the qibla wall have also lost their original character. The plain white marble minbar is accompanied by a muqarnas-hooded mihrab whose lower İznik tiles were recently stolen; it is inscribed with a variant of the typical mihrab verse (3:39).[109] The only other remaining inscription is the white-on-blue İznik tile epigraphic band that encircles the prayer hall on three sides, interrupted along the anti-qibla wall. Starting and ending at the west corner of the qibla wall, it quotes the Jumʿa sura (62:1–11), which emphasizes the

427 Piyale Pasha mosque, Kasımpaşa, from the west, prior to restoration.

428 Piyale Pasha mosque, from the southeast with restored lateral portico.

importance of the scriptures God revealed to Muhammad, together with the necessity of congregational prayers and the continual 'remembrance of Allah'. Those who do not follow the guidance of the divine scriptures are likened to 'the ass carrying books'. The remaining part of the epigraphic band quotes the Ikhlas sura, which contests the Christian doctrine of the Holy Trinity by declaring the absolute unity of God who 'begetteth not, nor was begotten' (112:1–4).

Piyale Pasha's ashlar masonry mausoleum behind the qibla wall occupies a lower platform on the sloping terrain.[110] A poem recorded by Ayvansarayi, which seems once to have been inscribed on a panel inside the mausoleum, declares: 'This is the mausoleum of the ghazi named Piyale Pasha / The joy of the feast of spiritual enlightenment becomes manifest by visiting it.' The poem then summarizes his career, concluding that the pasha was 'no doubt a saintly person (*velī*)' because his name had the same numerical value with the word 'saint' (*evliyā*). It ends with the wish that God may accept his mosque and give joy to his soul together with the souls of the ghazis by granting him a place in the garden of paradise.[111] This inscription, encouraging the veneration of the pasha's mausoleum, is evidence of the attempt to create a second hallowed landmark outside the walls of Galata for the visitation of seafarers, complementing the saintly mausoleum of Barbarossa in Beşiktaş. Piyale Pasha lies buried with his many sons and daughters in his mausoleum, which contains thirteen sarcophagi. His royal widow, said to have been a 'lady of great spirit', established a modest waqf of her own after the death of her second

429 Piyale Pasha mosque, restored lateral portico column with classicizing capital.

430 Piyale Pasha mosque, interior.

husband, Cerrah Mehmed Pasha (d. 1604), and was subsequently entombed at Selim II's imperial mausoleum next to Hagia Sophia.[112]

The Tersane mosque, whose deliberate archaism evokes memories of the ancient era of frontier warriors, immortalized the image of its patron as a victorious seafaring ghazi. Despite the small size of its domes, commensurate with Piyale Pasha's status as a grand admiral at the time of its conception, the mosque is gargantuan in scale. It must have housed large crowds during such ceremonial occasions as the annual launching of the fleet from the arsenal. Designed towards the end of Süleyman's reign, during which Piyale Pasha accomplished his greatest military exploits, the one-of-a-kind mosque exemplifies the elasticity of Sinan's codes of decorum, which could comfortably accommodate diverse identities and memories. The personal taste of the opium-eating pasha, portrayed by Mustafa Āli as a humane and venerable vizier who 'followed his own fancy', marked the eccentric designs of his mosque and his 'Tunisian Vineyard'.[113] The latter is identified by Katib Çelebi as 'one of the wonders of the world'.[114] Not failing to recognize the comparable uniqueness of Piyale Pasha's mosque, the geographer Mehmed Aşık refers to it in the 1590s as 'a rarity of countries in the seven climes'.[115]

III. KILİÇ ALİ PASHA

The unconventional plan of Kılıç Ali Pasha's mosque on the waterfront of Tophane – a small scale replica of Hagia Sophia – has long puzzled architectural historians (illus. 431, 432). Even though it is included in all three autobiographies of Sinan, some scholars find it incomprehensible that he should have 'reverted' to a longitudinal plan after having achieved his life-long ambition to create a perfectly centralized space at the Selimiye in Edirne.[116] The building is thus often attributed to another royal architect and explained by the patron's 'special fascination' with Hagia Sophia.[117] However, Goodwin proposes that it was Sinan who 'deliberately produced a modified copy of the interior of the church across the water', being intrigued by its design, which he had an opportunity to study during its renovation in the 1570s.[118] Denny regards the historicist mosque as 'Sinan's last homage and his last challenge to the great *paragone* of Ottoman architecture, which, as the Master himself revealed in his autobiography, was one of his great obsessions.'[119]

I find it more likely that the chief architect and his patron jointly selected Hagia Sophia as an appropriate model, in keeping with the reinterpretation of ancient prototypes in the former mosques of grand admirals outside the walls of Galata. Sinan adapted the plan of the archaic Byzantine church, recently renovated as Selim II's funerary mosque (1573–76/77), to his patron's non-royal status by omitting its porticoed forecourt, reducing its four minarets to one, and shrinking its dimensions. Decorum was observed by keeping the 12.7-metre dome of the grand admiral's mosque smaller than that of his adjoining bath-house (14.1 metres). Sinan translated the structural scheme and elevations of Hagia Sophia into the modern Ottoman idiom of clearly articulated forms, substituting cut stone for its brick masonry. He responded to the exuberance of Hagia Sophia's opulent mosaic-sheathed interior with a lavish decorative programme combining an abundance of stained glass windows with İznik tile revetments, surrounding the prayer hall on all sides. The mosque of Kılıç Ali Pasha evokes its inimitable, world-famous model through selective quotations of recognizable features (illus. 54–57): its superstructure that combines a central dome with two half-domes flanked by exedras; its starkly cubical dome base, reinforced by prominent buttresses; its fenestrated tympana arches; its processional axis culminating in an apse-like mihrab covered by a half-dome; its lateral galleries with screens of two-tiered columns cut off from the central space; and its U-shaped upper gallery, whose arcades alternate single and paired columns. The porphyry columns that grace the interior are spolia; they were in all likelihood carried on the imperial fleet's ships with which Kılıç Ali Pasha was ordered to transport marble and columns for royal constructions.[120]

Before turning to the question of why Hagia Sophia was selected as a fitting prototype for the Tophane mosque, let us consider the identity of its patron and the context in which it was built (illus. 433).[121] Unlike his predecessors Sinan Pasha and Piyale Pasha, who were educated in the imperial palace, Kılıç Ali rose to the post of grand admiral through the ranks of ghazi-corsairs, as had Barbarossa. Christened Giovanni Dionigi Galeni, he was born to a fisherman's family in the village of Le Castella on the coast of Calabria, at the tip of southern Italy. On his way to become a priest in Naples, the boy was captured by Ottoman corsairs and began his humble career as a rower on galleys. Upon converting to Islam, his name was changed to Uluç (Renegade) Ali, and he joined the ranks of Ottoman naval officers in 1551 as a ship captain (*reis*). Attached to the coterie of the famous corsair Turgud Reis, he participated in all the naval campaigns commanded by the grand admiral Piyale Pasha. After Turgud Reis's death in 1565, he became the governor-general of islands. Joining the Cyprus campaign with his contingent of Algerian ships, he subsequently commanded the left wing of the fleet in Lepanto, where he managed to save his ships by brilliant manoeuvres. As a reward for his partial victory in that otherwise disastrous campaign, Selim II in 1571 conferred on him the honorific title 'Kılıç' (Sword), together with the post of grand admiral.[122]

During the winter of 1572 the new grand admiral cooperated with the grand vizier Sokollu in rebuilding at the Kasımpaşa arsenal the fleet destroyed at Lepanto. His hesitant forays into Mediterranean waters during the summers of 1572 and 1573 were followed in 1574 by an order to prepare with Sokollu another large fleet, this time in response to the recent conquest of Tunis by Spanish forces.[123] That effort culminated with the grand admiral's second major victory in 1574, just before Murad III ascended the throne: the reconquest of Tunis after a raid on the coasts of Calabria and Messina.[124] The impressive booty of that campaign included thousands of slaves and five thousand artistically decorated cannons, captured at the Spanish fort of Goletta and displayed as mementoes of victory in front of the sea walls of the Topkapı Palace and along the shores of the imperial Cannon Foundry (Tophane), where the triumphant grand admiral would build his mosque complex a few years later (illus. 100[2], 101[4], 166, 352[3]).[125]

Kılıç Ali Pasha retained his post under Murad III until his demise in 1587. In the absence of naval campaigns during this sultan's reign, which was dominated by a protracted war at the Safavid front (1578–90), the grand admiral concentrated his efforts on reorganizing the Kasımpaşa arsenal and overseeing building projects at the Topkapı Palace with his numerous team of galley slaves.[126] The *bailo* Paolo Contarini (1583) reports that the admiral not only upgraded the unused galleys of the arsenal, but also offered his galley slaves for the building projects of the sultan and grandees to win their favour:

> He is a man extremely diligent in his duty, as much as one can imagine, and is universally loved by all his men for his generosity, just as he is feared for his severity, since he never enters where they work without giving large donations to the slaves, nor does he fail to castigate with utmost discipline those who do not fulfil their duties.

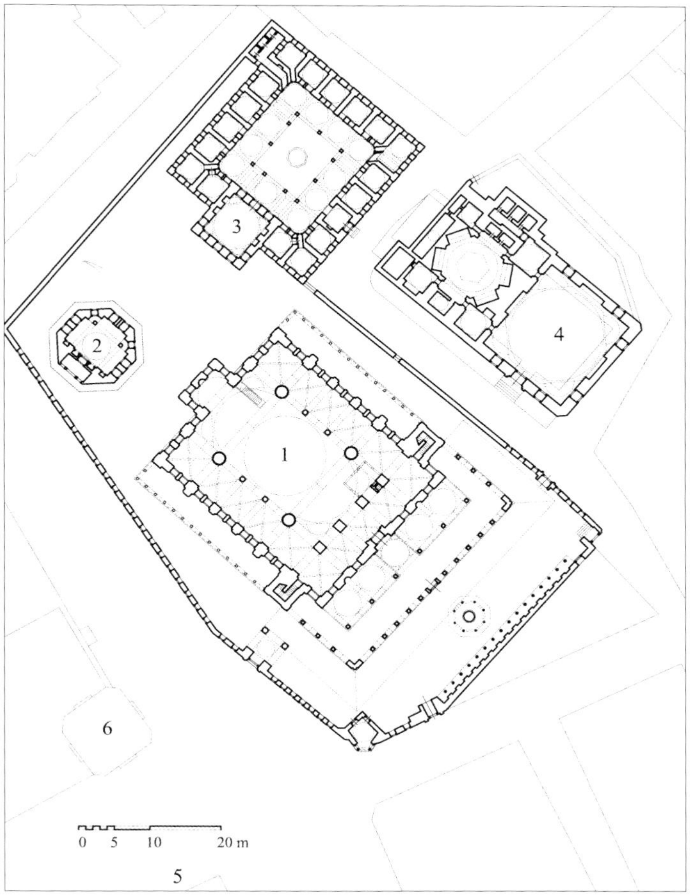

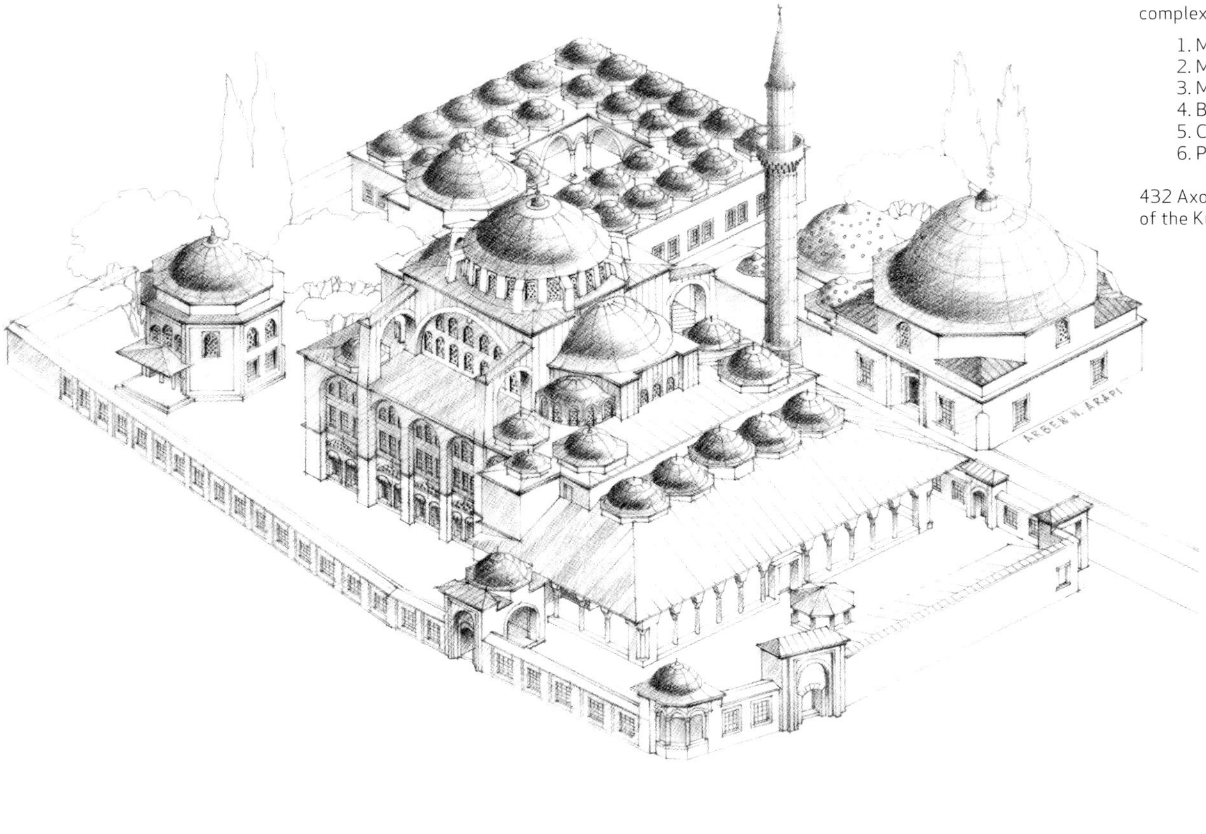

431 Plan of the Kılıç Ali Pasha complex, Tophane:

1. Mosque
2. Mausoleum
3. Madrasa
4. Bath-house
5. Cannon foundry
6. Public fountain (1732)

432 Axonometric projection of the Kılıç Ali Pasha complex.

> He has 5,000 slaves, of whom 800 are carpenters and as many are caulkers, all most excellent, who receive twelve aspers per day when they work at the arsenal, while the rest are paid eight aspers. Others who possess another skill are paid at least four aspers, but those who lack experience are employed by him in the constructions of the sultan, the pashas, and other grandees. In this way the grand admiral procures their gratification and favour.[127]

433 Kılıç Ali Pasha, c. 1586, watercolour on paper.

Gianfrancesco Morosini (1585) makes a similar observation about the pasha, noting that he was greatly esteemed for his generosity and that he served the sultan not only as his grand admiral but also as his full-time construction overseer: 'He never parts from the buildings that they erect for His Majesty, to which he goes in person with his slaves.' With his 3,000 slaves, he fulfilled the same service for the sultanas and the viziers, thereby securing his post.[128] Morosini says, however, that the grand admiral, illiterate and quite advanced in age, was mainly preoccupied with strengthening the armada and trying to convince the sultan to wage new naval battles:

> They say this man is close to eighty years old, but he is still so healthy and vigorous that it amazes everyone. He is of the Calabrian nation, born most humbly in a place called Li Castelli. He does not know how to read and write, and as he was taken quite young as a slave, everything he knows he has learned while rowing oars, a fact he is never ashamed of confessing.[129]

One of the military constructions that Kılıç Ali Pasha had been ordered to oversee was a fortress at the strategic port of Navarino (Pylos) on the southwest corner of the Morean peninsula.[130] Selim II's decrees instructed the pasha and the governor of Morea in September 1573 to build the fortress with state funds according to a plan (*resm*) dispatched by a court messenger. The royal architect, Mimar Şaban, would be assisted by an unnamed foreign architect attached to the grand admiral's service; it was he who had designed the plan of the castle in the 'European manner' (*Frenk üslūbu*).[131] The extant Navarino fortress with its hexagonal bastion does have an Italianate plan; its completion was marked in 1576–77 with the construction of a Friday mosque (now demolished) named after Murad III.[132] The grand admiral's architect, most likely an Italian renegade like him, may subsequently have been employed in the construction of the Tophane mosque.

We learn from Contarini (1583) that Kılıç Ali Pasha, who had a large number of Italian renegades under his service, built a 'very large hamlet' (*casale*) near the Kasımpaşa arsenal, which was called 'New Calabria'. In it skilled artisans taught their crafts of galley building and maritime arts: 'I dare say with truth that the Turks did not know at all the true art of navigation with galleys before Ucchiali's [Uluç Ali] governance.'[133] Gerlach (1576) confirms the pasha's eagerness to establish contact with Calabria, his place of birth, where he attempted to construct a fortress soon after the one in Navarino was finished. But the grand admiral was forced to flee from Calabria, leaving behind five hundred of his men, when the Spanish general Andrea Doria suddenly showed up with sixty galleys.[134]

In 1578–79, the year the pasha started to build his mosque complex, he was put in charge of overseeing the construction of Murad III's domed bedchamber at the imperial harem of the Topkapı Palace, one of Sinan's few extant pavilions, profusely decorated with İznik tiles.[135] On 7 March 1579 the *bailo* Nicolò Barbarigo saw Kılıç Ali Pasha personally oversee the construction of his own mosque, not far from the Venetian embassy on the hills of Tophane.[136] For this project the grand admiral likely employed the Kasımpaşa arsenal's idle staff of blacksmiths, painters, carpenters, and ship-designing architect-engineers, headed by their own chief architect.[137] Sinan may have designed the Tophane mosque in consultation with these architects, many of whom were renegades, such as the Ragusan galley artisan Marcus, who adopted the name İbrahim after converting to Islam in 1576.[138]

When Kılıç Ali Pasha passed away in 1587, he was buried at the domed mausoleum of his mosque complex. Selaniki decribes how the nearly ninety-year-old, virile grand admiral, who simply could not resist the charms of pretty maidens, expired:

> On 27 June 1587 Kapudan Kılıç Ali Pasha performed the Friday prayers at the Tophane mosque. Being extremely eager to accomplish pious deeds and distribute donations,

> he disbursed all the money he had with him to the poor and the wretched; and when that amount did not suffice, he borrowed more from those who accompanied him and gave it out as alms. Then in the evening he stayed at his residence. More than twenty days ago he had been afflicted with a troublesome illness. The expert doctor diagnosed his infirmity and took thoughtful precautions by prescribing useful medications so that he rapidly recovered his health. His age had approached ninety, but passion and worldly desire were his close companions. Unable to resist sexual intercourse with very beautiful concubines, he often resorted to intimacy and familiarity with them. The doctor had strongly forbidden this with the warning, 'by all means it is necessary to abstain from friendly intercourse with women, for the life of the frail is a precious entity', but he did not obey that prohibition. And the news reached the imperial council that his soul left his body to the other world that night while he was fooling around with a virgin concubine.[139]

The generous grand admiral's habit of distributing alms to the poor each Friday, while seated under the portico of his mosque, was still remembered at the time Evliya Çelebi wrote his travelogue. During the inauguration ceremony of his mosque, attended by the viziers and grandees, the ignorant Kılıç Ali, with his 'Frankish' accent, had allegedly risen in the middle of the recitation of a poem eulogizing the Prophet and asked: 'What is this gu-gu-gu? Are we in a tavern, a *boza* (fermented millet) shop, or what?' The accompanying viziers are said to have politely informed him what the chanting was all about.[140] The fictitiousness of this anecdote is implied by the grand admiral's waqfiyya of 1581, which stipulates his special wish to have poetry praising the Prophet chanted after the Friday prayers in his mosque, and selected suras from the Koran recited there daily for the salvation of his soul.[141]

Selaniki explains that the grand admiral's inheritance was confiscated by the sultan because he had no legal inheritors.[142] An early waqfiyya of 'Kapudan Ali Pasha b. Abdülmennan', registered in April 1576, mentions his children, who apparently passed away before his death. It refers to him as a warrior of the faith and a ghazi who possessed good morals, sagacity, and a 'bravery never before seen by Muslim eyes'. The waqfiyya records the pasha's endowment of his shore palace with three courtyards in Beşiktaş, which featured two prisons – one old and one new – for non-Muslim captives. The palace was endowed for his own use and, following his death, that of his children and grandchildren. Upon the extinction of their progeny it would be inhabited by his manumitted slaves, but only the Muslim men and women among them. Thereafter, its rent was to be sent to the Prophet's mosque in Medina.[143] This might be the palace depicted on a map of the Bosphorus sketched in 1588 (illus. 101[6]). The map identifies the palace as that of Uluç Hasan Pasha, a manumitted Venetian-born slave of Kılıç Ali Pasha, who rose to the post of grand admiral (1588–91) and was subsequently buried at his former master's mausoleum in Tophane.[144]

The second waqfiyya, registered in May 1581, endows for Muslim men and women the Friday mosque 'at Tophane outside Galata'. The grand admiral who 'protected Islam on the seas' was 'generous like the ocean'. He endowed numerous commercial properties in the neighbourhood of his mosque: a bath-house (built by Sinan), 8 shops adjacent to the north side of the mosque forecourt, 18 shops abutting the southeast and south sides of the precinct wall, 44 additional shops nearby, 56 upper-storey rooms, 7 warehouses, a smelting-house (*ḳālkhāna*), two slaughterhouses, 17 shops across from the dormitories of cannoniers, a public eating house specializing in sheep heads, 27 ground-storey and 17 upper-storey rooms, an empty plot for keeping 50 two-oared boats, and a house accompanied by nine rental rooms at the Defterdar Ebulfazl quarter of Tophane. These were complemented by properties in Beşiktaş, Galata, and Istanbul (including a now-lost bath-house built by Sinan near the Fener gate).[145] Outside the capital, the grand admiral endowed villages, vineyards, five Aegean islands, and the island of Samos, donated in July 1580 upon his request by Murad III for the waqf of his mosque.[146]

The founder designated himself as the administrator of his endowment, a task to be fulfilled after his demise by his freed slaves and their descendants, who would be given precedence over 'outsiders' in staff appointments. The waqf would be overseen by the mufti, like those of the grand admirals Sinan Pasha and Piyale Pasha.[147] The date of the second waqfiyya coincides with the completion date given in the foundation inscriptions 988 (1580–81) of the mosque. It mentions only the neighbouring bath-house, indicating that the madrasa was added later on. An addendum made in late July 1587, about a month after 'the late Kapudan Ali Pasha b. Abdullah's' death, concerns the appointment of a keeper for his domed mausoleum, which must have been built together with the mosque.[148] Sinan's autobiographies list the mosque, the mausoleum, and the two commercial bath-houses in Tophane and Fener.[149] They omit the madrasa, whose first professor was appointed in 996 (1587–88) with a high daily salary of fifty aspers.[150]

Imperial decrees provide additional details about the building chronology of the mosque, initiated simultaneously with the war on the Safavid front that took precedence over naval campaigns. In a decree handed over to the arsenal superintendent on 25 June 1578, the sultan orders the kadi and the overseer of iron mines in Samokov to allow the man sent there by 'my grand admiral Ali, who has started the construction of a noble Friday mosque in the metropolis of Galata' to buy iron and timber.[151] Another decree, addressed on 3 May 1579 to the inspector and the overseer of lead mines in Skopje, authorizes them to permit the sale of lead needed for the 'Friday mosque that is newly being built by my grand admiral, Ali, the governor-general of islands', when his man arrives there.[152] The kadis of Galata and Haslar (Eyüp) were ordered that year to allow the construction of shops on an empty plot outside the Tophane gate.[153]

We learn from a dispatch sent to the Venetian Senate on 9 February 1579 that Cafer Agha of the arsenal requested 12,000 discs of bottle-glass (*rui*) for the grand admiral's mosque, whose decoration would begin in three to seven months, when its superstructure was expected to be covered.[154] A month later the *bailo* Barbarigo reported that the grand admiral had requested for his mosque two glass lanterns of gilded wood, custom-made on the basis of a drawing indicating measurements: 'He said to me that he would pay for one lantern and wanted the second one given to him as a gift signifying friendship, and that these two lanterns should be the same as those that were previously sent to the Magnificent Pasha (Sokollu).' Since the lanterns would cost no more than a hundred ducats, Barbarigo took the liberty of announcing to the grand admiral that the Signoria would gladly send both lanterns free as a sign of affection for his person.[155] These two galley lanterns were once displayed on each side of the mihrab of the Tophane mosque.[156] A final dispatch from Venice, dated 15 April 1581, announces the shipment of glass panes (*lastre*) requested by the grand admiral.[157] Various decrees issued in 1584, such as a permit for the water channel of the bath-house in Fener, suggest that the details of the pasha's endowment took more time to finalize.[158]

The many income-producing structures constructed in the vicinity of the complex, extending from the walls of Galata all the way to the pasha's endowed shore palace in Beşiktaş, considerably expanded the commercial potential of this suburban area. The Tophane quarter was largely inhabited by seafarers and the international staff of the imperial Cannon Foundry, where the Frenchman Jerome Maurand had seen forty to fifty German artisans employed in 1544.[159] The grand admiral's mosque complex contributed to the Islamization of that quarter, from which the English embassy was transferred to Galata in 1594 because its inhabitants disturbed the Muslims by their lewd behaviour and by playing music during the congregational prayers (illus. 101[5]).[160] The seventeenth-century Armenian author Eremya describes the neighbourhood with its rowdy mariners who would congregate in a tree-planted public square extending between the hill of the Cannon Foundry and the jetty, along the eastern flank of Kılıç Ali Pasha's mosque:

> This place [Tophane] is filled with state-owned cannons. Look, [and you will see] large and small cannons of every type are lined up outside. Those brought from Hungary do not resemble any others; they are so wide that a person can sit inside them. They are inscribed with names and images of the cross. Many cannon balls rest on the ground, ready for shipment. Mariners sit under the shade of big plane-trees nearby. This is a broad jetty, completely stacked with goods. None of the jetties we have seen so far or will see next are as large as this one. The quarter where one encounters rogues, scoundrels, and licentious mariners has the Friday mosque of Kılıç Ali Pasha, a light-filled bath-house … and the dormitories of cannoniers where the chief cannonier resides.[161]

The cannoniers of Tophane were closely affiliated with the imperial armada.[162] Hence, the site of the mosque in front of the Cannon Foundry, at the edge of the sea, was particularly fitting for the grand admiral's memorial (illus. 434). According to the geographer Mehmed Aşık, the complex was built on a piece of land reclaimed from the sea:

> Outside the workshop [Cannon Foundry] along the seashore are many huge cannons. And near this workshop, the late Kapudan Kılıç Ali Pasha built a decorated and joy-giving Friday mosque and a life-bestowing bath-house and a lofty madrasa for the study of the sciences. And the mausoleum of the afore-mentioned Ali Pasha is near his Friday mosque. The Friday mosque, bath-house, madrasa, and mausoleum are sited on the lip of the sea. For their construction, a certain amount of ground was reclaimed by filling up the sea.[163]

Edwin Grosvenor (1895) recounts a popular story, according to which the architect of the mosque had fitted into sockets on each side of its main gate revolving colonettes to assure the people of its strong foundations (illus. 436). Because they were afraid to enter the mosque, thinking it might sink back into the sea, the architect promised them: 'As long as these cylinders turn in their places, it will be evident that the mosque has not settled a hair's breadth, and you can go in.'[164]

The site by the waterfront, against the backdrop of the Cannon Foundry perched on a hilltop behind the northeast corner of the mosque, was filled with reminders of naval victories against Christian powers, including the cannons Kılıç Ali Pasha captured at Goletta in 1574. The traveller Samuel Kiechel (1588) says the late grand admiral, 'who was a great enemy of the Christians', had built his 'stately and beautiful' mosque there as his personal 'memorial'.[165] Little remains of the urban fabric that once surrounded the complex, except for the public square, where a free-standing royal fountain was built in 1732. The north wall of the mosque forecourt had to be pulled back when the avenue stretching between Tophane and Beşiktaş was widened in the 1950s. This contributed to the cramped appearance of the double-porticoed north façade, hidden from the avenue behind a modern blind wall. The Pervitich map of 1927 depicts the eight shops mentioned in the waqfiyya that formerly abutted the north

434 Tophane waterfront with cannons and the mosque of Kılıç Ali Pasha: the multi-domed eighteenth-century Cannon Foundry in the background replaced an earlier structure with pyramidal roofs.

435 Kılıç Ali Pasha mosque, Tophane, from the northeast.

436 Kılıç Ali Pasha mosque, cental portal of the north façade.

wall. It also shows the original form of the modified window-pierced precinct wall surrounding the funerary garden, which once had a gate providing access to the pasha's mausoleum, whose façade is turned toward the public square.[166]

The present precinct wall around the mosque and its mausoleum garden has five gates. The narrow forecourt preserves its original free-standing domed ablution fountain encircled by eight columns, and has rebuilt spigots along the arcaded north wall. A domed water dispenser punctuates the northeast corner of the precinct wall, emphasizing the orientation of the mosque towards the public square (illus. 435). The inner gate of the *sebil*, opening to the forecourt, is inscribed with a fragmentary Koranic verse that alludes to the life-giving properties of water: '[We made] every living thing from water (21:30).'[167] Sinan had created similar corner *sebils* abutting the precincts of Selim II's mausoleum (1576–77) at Hagia Sophia and Piyale Pasha's mosque at Kasımpaşa (*c.* 1573).

The intimate fountain courtyard extends in front of the spacious double portico with its broad cantilevered overhanging roof supported on wooden struts. Resting on tall marble columns with muqarnas capitals, the five-domed inner portico is fronted by a second portico of smaller columns featuring lozenge capitals. The exquisite central portal features a triangular 'flattened muqarnas' hood, carved with mirrored calligraphy (illus. 436). A screen of iron grills separates the double portico from the forecourt, a separation of zones further accentuated by a white marble gate fitted into the central arch of the outer colonnade. Flanked by a pair of columns with muqarnas capitals, this arched gate, framed by a triple arcade, has a rectangular *thuluth* inscription spelling out the profession of faith. Its alignment with the mosque gate and the ablution fountain accentuates the axial approach to the prayer hall. Unusual wooden benches extend in front of the iron-grilled outer portico. Old photographs show healers and apothecaries seated on the

437 Kılıç Ali Pasha mosque, an old photograph showing wooden benches in front of the iron-grilled double portico with overhanging eaves.

benches with their goods displayed on wooden chests – an infiltration of the commercial public space surrounding the mosque into its courtyard (illus. 436).[168]

The most monumental gate of the fenestrated precinct wall, preceded by a domed porch, faces the public square. The recessed portal of the octagonal mausoleum, crowned by a prominent double-shell dome, is inscribed with a Turkish epigraph in *ṭaʿlīḳ* script, apparently added after the grand admiral's demise: 'This is the noble mausoleum of the patron of the pious foundation, the late ghazi Kılıç Ali Pasha, 995 (1587).'[169] Grosvenor records a now-lost inscription: 'His cord of life was relaxed by age, and he himself was bent like his bow. So he embarked in the wooden skiff of his coffin, and rests already beneath the soil, which during his lifetime he almost never trod.'[170]

The arched lunette of the main precinct gate features a carved and gilded foundation inscription in Turkish, composed of paired cartouches in four lines of *thuluth*. It attributes the prosperity enjoyed by the flourishing site to the just reign of Murad III, when such humble imperial servants as Kılıç Ali Pasha attained glory:

> In the state of Murad Khan, with justice –
> Thanks be to God – the world found order.
>
> Each of his servants relishes glory and high rank,
> How can not every abode (*maḳām*) prosper, then?
>
> He exerted himself and built this beautiful Friday mosque:
> That lion of the [battle] field named Ali Pasha.
>
> Men of God composed its chronogram:
> 'Your Friday mosque became a most excellent Kaʿba
> [*beytü'l-ḥarām*)', the year 988 (1580–81).[171]

Another gilded Turkish inscription is carved on the arched lunette of the north gate near the water dispenser. Composed of two lines of *thuluth* with paired cartouches, it wishes that the founder of the mosque be rewarded in paradise:

> Because the lord of the sea, that is to say Ali Pasha, grand admiral of the age,
> Built this Friday mosque, let Paradise be his place!
>
> Ulvī saw it, and the Divine Voice composed its chronogram:
> 'May this abode (*maḳām*) be a place of worship for the Faithful,' the year 988 (1580–81).[172]

The absence of inscriptions on the other precinct gates shows that the bevelled northeast corner, punctuated by the domed water dispenser, staged the primary approach. The main components of the complex – the mosque and mausoleum – are built of ashlar masonry, whereas the single bath and the madrasa are constructed of alternating courses of stone and brick. A striking feature of the mosque is its immense superstructure entirely covered with lead, as are several other late works of Sinan.[173] The drumless exedras with 'tunnel vault' windows cut into their curved surfaces find a parallel in Selim II's mausoleum at Hagia Sophia (1576–77) and in the mosques of Nurbanu Sultan (1571–86), and Molla Çelebi (1570–84). The sculpturally articulated, dynamic façades of Kılıç Ali Pasha's mosque are subdivided into two horizontal tiers by a stringcourse moulding – as in the mosques of Sokollu in Azapkapı (*c.* 1573–77/78), Mesih Mehmed Pasha (1584–85/86), and the Muradiye in Manisa (1583–86/87). Tapering pilaster-like strips of masonry frame the arches fitted with superimposed windows and openwork lunettes (illus. 438, 439). The innovative façades with multi-tiered window compositions recall those of Mesih Mehmed Pasha's mosque, initially overseen by the architect Mehmed Subaşı, before he was sent to complete the Muradiye in 1586. Perhaps the same architect, Sinan's favourite who acted as his lieutenant in 1584, supervised the construction of the Tophane mosque (Appendix 4:4).[174]

Light pours into the mosque from its qibla wall with a projecting mihrab and its lateral galleries with unique two-tiered colonnades, but the dimly lit central space promotes an aura of mystery akin to that of Hagia Sophia (illus. 440–42). The modernity of the Tophane mosque is expressed by substituting slender round piers for the four massive angular piers of its archaic Byzantine model, whose bulky external buttresses are eliminated to free the façades. The intricate stained glass windows of the qibla wall are complemented by unusually large arch-shaped lunettes spanning the ground storey of the cross-vaulted side galleries (illus. 442). Denny interprets these stained-glass lunettes, juxtaposed with unusual quadripartite rib vaults (composed of two torus mouldings that intersect at the centre of each lateral bay), as a deliberate use of Gothic elements by Sinan.[175] The stained glass windows, renewed and signed in 1912 by Tevfik of Bursa, were refurbished again in 1959–60.[176] The originals may indeed have been inspired by churches the Calabrian grand admiral encountered during his Mediterranean expeditions, such as the Gothic cathedrals of Cyprus which had recently been converted into mosques.

438 Kılıç Ali Pasha mosque, Tophane, from the south.

The striking rib vaults of the Tophane mosque recall the cross-vaulted lateral wings of Mesih Mehmed Pasha's mosque (illus. 410). Comparable cross vaults also appear in the basement of Murad III's domed bedchamber in the harem of the Topkapı Palace, whose construction was supervised by Kılıç Ali Pasha in 1578–79. Hollow roundels fitted with geometric openwork grills, another distinctive motif seen on the arch spandrels of that basement, is repeated in the upper gallery spandrels of the pasha's mosque.[177] Contarini mentions a highly unusual visit that Murad III paid to the mosque at Tophane, visible from his newly built bedchamber:

> The Captain of the Sea ... is much loved by His Majesty who recognizes that he has no other person in his empire more intelligent in maritime affairs. Therefore, in the past and now, he has bestowed on him the greatest favours. When I was in Constantinople [1580–83] His Majesty went one day with only four youngsters of his seraglio in a caique to view the mosque that the captain had ordered built in Tophane, across from the seraglio. And not wanting it to be known by others that he and his attendants went to see the place of the Tophane and the artillery, he rapidly returned back to his seraglio.[178]

The İznik tiles covering the mihrab recess of Kılıç Ali Pasha's mosque, and the rectangular lunettes of all ground-level windows, were probably ordered together with those of the sultan's bedroom pavilion. The original painted decorations of the mosque are preserved only on the woodwork ceiling of the Bursa-arched muezzin's tribune attached to the pier at the northwest corner.[179] An artistic mother-of-pearl-inlaid wooden preacher's lectern fronts the southeast pier. The white-on-blue calligraphic tilework lunettes are complemented by painted and stone-carved inscriptions in monumental *thuluth* script, executed by Demircikulu Yusuf Efendi (d. 1611). This calligrapher, a slave-servant of the superintendent of iron mines in Bulgaria, had taken writing lessons from Derviş Mehmed, a student of Ahmed Karahisari.[180]

The exclusively Koranic inscriptions glorify God and stress the necessity of communal worship for those expecting a reward in paradise. Those on the north façade introduce themes elaborated inside the prayer hall. The four tilework window lunettes on the façade quote a verse from the Hashr sura, hailing the one and only God's divine epithets (59:23). The mirrored calligraphy of the central portal also acclaims the divine epithets (39:62). The rectangular inscription under it cites a thematically related verse from the Hashr sura that resonates with the window lunettes on the same wall (illus. 436):

> He is Allah, the Creator, the Shaper out of naught,
> the Fashioner. His are the most beautiful names.
> All that is in the heavens and the earth glorifieth Him,
> and He is the Mighty, the Wise (59:24).

Inscriptions above the pair of arched gates at both ends of the façade emphasize the rewards awaiting those who perform the congregational prayers. The one over the left gate reads: 'God the Exalted and Blessed said: And those who are attentive in their worship, these will dwell in Gardens, honoured (70:34–5).' The other gate quotes a related verse: 'God the Exalted and Blessed said: Be guardians of your prayers, and of the midmost prayer, and stand up with devotion to Allah (2:238).'

Upon entering the prayer hall, one encounters the majestic domical superstructure with its entirely renewed painted

439 Kılıç Ali Pasha mosque, detail of the east façade.

440 Kılıç Ali Pasha mosque, Tophane, interior toward the qibla wall.

441 Kılıç Ali Pasha mosque upper gallery with alternating double and single columns featuring muqarnas and lozenge capitals.

442 Kılıç Ali Pasha mosque cross-vaulted lateral aisle with stained glass windows and İznik tile lunettes.

443 Kılıç Ali Pasha mosque, Tophane, interior view of the domical superstructure.

inscriptions, which closely echo in content those of the Selimiye (illus. 443).[181] The roundel of the main dome is inscribed with the Ikhlas sura, which encompasses the essence of the Koranic message concerning the indivisible unity of God, who 'begetteth not nor was begotten' (112:1–4). This sura presents an aniconic vision of divine oneness, in contrast to Hagia Sophia's figural representation of Christ, alluding to the doctrine of the Holy Trinity. The contrast would have been recognized by the users of the Tophane mosque, as the Pantokrator mosaic on the dome of Hagia Sophia was still on view at that time (a Koranic inscription roundel replaced it in the early seventeenth century).[182]

The four pendentives, the two half-domes, and the exedras emphasize the duties of worshippers and the requirement of congregational prayers. The pendentive roundels quote verses from the Jumʿa sura sequentially, in a counter-clockwise direction starting at the southeast and ending at the southwest (62:9–11). They urge believers to cease trading with the call for prayer on the 'day of congregation and haste unto remembrance of Allah.' The two half-domes continuously cite a verse that lists the basic obligations of rightly guided believers who observe 'proper worship and payeth the poor due' (9:18). The two exedras at the west side quote a verse alluding to the worship and remembrance of the all-knowing God (29:45). The southeast exedra refers to the all-knowing God's omnipresent countenance wherever one turns (2:115). The northeast exedra invites believers to revere God by turning their faces toward Him at every place of worship (7:29).

The small semi-dome over the mihrab recess urges the congregation to bow down in worship (22:77). The muqarnas-hooded white marble mihrab under it has a carved rectangular inscription quoting the standard mihrab verse (3:37). The İznik tile calligraphic roundel above it invokes divine epithets: 'O, the Most Compassionate! O, the All-Bounteous!' The flanking rectangular tilework lunettes are inscribed with the Fatiha sura (1:1–7) presenting the gist of the Koran. The remaining İznik tile window lunettes on three sides of the prayer hall start at the left of the qibla wall and follow a counter-clockwise direction. They quote verses from the Baqara sura (2:255–59) which encompasses all essential points of the revelation; hence its precedence as the second sura of the Koran. The long sequence begins with the Throne verse, asserting the absolute sovereignty of God over the heavens and the earth. The next verse refers to those who reject false deities in favor of Allah (2:256). It is followed by a verse (2:257) that identifies God as the 'Protecting Friend' of believers who 'bringeth them out of darkness into light.' By contrast, disbelievers doomed to hellfire are plunged 'into darkness' by false deities. The next verse declares that 'Allah guideth not wrongdoing folk (2:258)' and the sequence ends with a miraculous story proving how 'Allah is able to do all things' (2:259).

The prominence given to the Fatiha sura and the Throne verse, widely quoted in mausoleums, befits the funerary character of the grand admiral's mosque. Like the Selimiye, its epigraphy is pervaded by a preoccupation with the triumph of Islam. It is therefore no coincidence that both mosques engaged in a pointed dialogue with Hagia Sophia, the ultimate symbol of the victory of Islam under Ottoman imperial rule. Sinan had created the Selimiye as a competitive response (*naẓīre*) to the unsurpassed monumentality of the dome of Hagia Sophia to meet the challenge of 'infidel' architects who claimed that its size could never be matched under Muslim rule. Kılıç Ali Pasha's decorously scaled-down mosque, in turn, mimicks the overall layout of the recently renovated Hagia Sophia. The native Byzantine architectural tradition of Calabria (also featuring Norman and Gothic churches) may have played a role in the selection of the former cathedral church of Constantinople as a model for the Italian grand admiral's memorial. The emulation of the ancient sultanic mosque, associated with the conquest of the city by the victorious ghazis, underscored his image as one of them: 'the lion of the battle field' who spent most of his life on the seas fighting holy wars.

As one of the foundation inscriptions announced, the patron's ability to erect such an ambitious mosque demonstrated the prosperity of the empire under Murad III's thriving reign. If a slave-servant could create a mini-Hagia Sophia in Ottoman guise, the sultan he served was surely capable of much greater architectural feats. This conceit left its imprint on the popular perception of the Tophane mosque, as suggested by a story recounted by the vassal Moldavian prince Cantemir in the early eighteenth century:

> The Turks claim that he had the foundations of this mosque laid in just one night, during which its walls reached window level. The following morning, when the people who passed by it saw such a large construction, for which they had not previously noticed any preparations, they spoke of this as a miracle. The sultan thus summoned the patron of that construction and asked him how he had accomplished such a miraculous feat. In response, the pasha answered: 'This is not mine but my sultan's monument, because it has been constructed by the slaves of the sultan's galleys. My aspiration, on the other hand, was merely to show my dexterity and to prove the grandeur of the Ottoman empire. If a private patron like me is capable of creating such a monument with only the help of galley slaves, then what can the united power of the Ottomans not accomplish against the forces of enemies?[183]

Grosvenor's guidebook of Constantinople (1895) narrates a similar story about the mythified mosque:

> The Ottomans have a tradition that the bay was filled, the foundations were laid, and the wall raised to the base of the lower windows in a single night. Mourad III, looking across from the Seraglio in the morning, was astonished, and cried, 'It is the work of djins', the genii of the Arabian Nights. 'Nay', replied the Kapoudan Pasha, 'all this has been done by your Majesty's prisoners of war. So many have been your victories, and so countless are your captured slaves, that far greater things than this can be accomplished in less an amount of time.'[184]

Kılıç Ali Pasha's small replica of Hagia Sophia was thus understood as an expression of Ottoman imperial might. Its proud message addressed not only its Muslim users, who included the grand admiral's own circle of Italian renegades, but also the European admirers of Hagia Sophia residing in Tophane and Galata. The mosque proclaimed the glory of Islam at a time when victorious Ottoman naval campaigns in Europe were becoming rare. Its reference to Hagia Sophia was not lost on Evliya Çelebi, who regards this work as a manifestation of Sinan's artistic power:

> It is as if it were a royal mosque (*cāmiʿ-i selāṭīn*). Sited on a spacious flat terrain, it is a charming (*şīrīn*) ground-storey mosque, the like of which does not exist in Istanbul. It has been built exactly in the manner (*ṭarz*) of Ayasofya the Great.[185]

The matching colossal calligraphic roundels with revered names that were added to both the Tophane mosque and Hagia Sophia in the nineteenth century further accentuated their likeness. As if to assert the power of Islam even more forcefully, these roundels replaced smaller ones.[186]

Kılıç Ali Pasha's mosque was certainly more assertive than those commissioned by his predecessors Sinan Pasha and Piyale Pasha. Its four-point support system had long been a prerogative of royal mosques, like its mighty, window-pierced tympanum arches and its dome flanked by two half-domes (illus. 3). With its stately mass evoking solidity rather than grace, the mosque projected its patron's unprecedented prestige despite his never having risen to the vizierate as had Piyale Pasha. His enhanced rank, acknowledged by the favours Murad III is said to have showered upon him, exemplified the mutation of the traditional hierarchies of status.

In part, the grand admiral owed these favours to his intimate interaction with the otherwise secluded monarch during his supervision of building projects at the Topkapı Palace, projects that also brought him into close contact with Sinan. The striking parallels between the sultan's bedroom pavilion and the Tophane mosque point to the chief architect's involvement in both projects. Since the shariʿa did not permit Murad III to commission a mosque of his own in the capital, the vacuum of sultanic patronage was filled by ambitious monuments built for royal women and for specially favoured grandees now competing in rank with the viziers. The victory mosque of Kılıç Ali Pasha was one of these extraordinary monuments, conforming to codes of decorum, yet at the same time subverting them with its unmistakable allusions to imperial grandeur.

PROVINCIAL GOVERNORS AND ADMINISTRATORS

RUMELIA

I. SOFU (HACI, KARAGÖZ) MEHMED BEG
HERCEGOVINA, MOSTAR (1557–58)

II. OSMANSHAH BEG
GREECE, TRIKKALA (*c.* 1566/67–1570)

III. SOKOLLU KASIM BEG (PASHA)
HAVSA (1573–77)

WESTERN AND CENTRAL ANATOLIA

IV. FİRDEVS BEG (PASHA)
ISPARTA (*c.* 1565–69/70)

V. CENABİ AHMED PASHA
ANKARA (KURŞUNLU, 1565–66)

VI. LALA (TÜTÜNSÜZ) HÜSEYİN PASHA
KÜTAHYA (*c.* 1566–70)

VII. HACI (DOĞANCI) AHMED PASHA
KAYSERİ (KURŞUNLU, *c.* 1576–85/86)

EASTERN ANATOLIA

VIII. LALA MUSTAFA PASHA
ERZURUM (1562–63)

IX. KÖSE HÜSREV PASHA
VAN (KURŞUNLU, 1567–68)

X. HADIM ALİ PASHA
DİYARBAKIR (*c.* 1541–44)

XI. ÇERKES İSKENDER PASHA
DİYARBAKIR (*c.* 1551–65)

XII. BEHRAM PASHA
DİYARBAKIR (*c.* 1564/65–1572/73)

XIII. MELEK (MELİK) AHMED PASHA
DİYARBAKIR (*c.* 1587–91)

SYRIA AND THE ARAB LANDS

XIV. DİVANE (DELİ) HÜSREV PASHA
ALEPPO (KHUSRAWİYYA, *c.* 1546–47)

XV. DUKAKİNZADE MEHMED PASHA
ALEPPO (ʿADİLİYYA, 1556–65/66)

RUMELIA

Mehmed II's law code specifies that 'the governor-generals (*beglerbegi*) are one tier (*ṭabaḳa*) below the viziers.'[1] At that time there were only two governor-generals, one of Rumelia and one of Anatolia. As Ottoman territories expanded, new provinces were created, so that by the end of the sixteenth century the number of governor-generals reached thirty-two, with the *beglerbegi* of Rumelia enjoying precedence over the rest. The governor-generals of such important provinces as Rumelia, Buda, Egypt, Damascus, and Baghdad were often granted the honorary rank of vizier. As 'viceroys of the sultanate' (*salṭanat vekīli*), governor-generals supervised provincial administration through subordinate sanjak governors (*sanjak begi*). The sanjak governors, in turn, were ranked above the two army judges (*kazasker*) of the imperial council, since in the sanjaks they represented the sultan with symbols of sovereignty, the kettledrum and standard.[2]

The mosque complexes of governor-generals were built mostly in capital cities that came under their jurisdiction, where each of them presided over a miniature court with a *divan* of its own. The standardized plans of mosques commissioned by governor-generals and sanjak governors are domed cubes fronted by single or double porticoes with three to five bays. They can hardly be distinguished from provincial mosques representing higher levels of patronage. Sinan's autobiographies claim authorship of only a few Friday mosques in Rumelia, among which that of Sofu Mehmed Pasha in Sofia has already been discussed under the patronage of viziers. The chief architect's mosques in this region exhibit a pragmatic spirit in their stern architecture, dominated by simple yet well-proportioned forms, and in their restrained decorative programmes, lacking İznik tiles and naturalistic floral paintings.[3]

The only work attributed to Sinan in Hungary is the no-longer-extant mosque and mausoleum complex of Sokollu Mustafa Pasha (d. 1578) in Buda, the administrative capital of a new province established in 1541 (illus. 444). The patron was the grand vizier Sokollu Mehmed Pasha's favoured paternal cousin, who served as the governor-general of Buda for twelve years (1566–78), receiving the honorary rank of vizier in 1574.[4] His architectural patronage sheds light on the shared concerns of pre-eminent provincial administrators whose building projects were aimed to foster urban development, improve travel conditions, and promote Sunni Islam. The pasha's profile as a

444 Sketch of Buda (Ofen) and Pest, c. 1570s, ink on paper.

prolific patron of architecture emerges from his rare biography and his fragmentary waqfiyya, registered sometime after 1574, which refers to him as 'the governor-general of the province of Buda with the title of vizier, the father of charity, Mustafa Pasha b. Abdülmennan'.[5] The monuments he commissioned were spread throughout Bosnia and Hungary where the Bosnian-born pasha sought to 'strengthen the Prophet's shariʿa' as a token of gratitude for having been 'blessed with conversion to Islam', thereby leaving a permanent record of his memory on the 'pages of Time'. He improved communications in underdeveloped places by building bridges, paved roads, and caravansarays, transforming his birthplace, Rudo, into a prosperous town settled with 500 tax-exempt households. He provided it with a Friday mosque, an elementary school, a weekly bazaar, and a caravansaray at the head of a bridge spanning the Lim river.[6]

The prestige mosque and mausoleum that Sinan designed for him in Buda were complemented by other public works by local architects that contributed to the urban development of the city and its environs.[7] Endowed with five thermal baths and four caravansarays, these monuments were dedicated to the souls of the Prophet, his daughter Fatima, and the four Sunni caliphs: a masjid for the first caliph, Abu Bakr, accompanied by an elementary school near the convent of Hindi Baba; a masjid for the second caliph, ʿUmar, in the quarter of the 'central thermal bath' (*orta ılıca*); a masjid created by a 'heretic' that was rebuilt for the third caliph, ʿUthman, near the convent of Gülbaba; the renovated Friday mosque of the late İbrahim Çavuş in the quarter of tanners, to which new waqfs dedicated to the Prophet were assigned; another Friday mosque for the Prophet, with an elementary school and a madrasa, in Pest, which the pasha linked to Buda with a new bridge resting on boats; a masjid for the fourth caliph, ʿAli, at the nearby castle of Fülek; and a masjid for Fatima in the *varoş* (Hungarian: suburb) of the fort of Földvár subordinate to Buda.[8]

The domed Friday mosque in Buda, also dedicated to 'the soul of the Prophet', had a madrasa whose professor was 'a shariʿa-abiding mufti' sorely needed in that city.[9] The mosque was built next to the pasha's endowed riverfront palace, described by Marcantonio Pigafetta in 1567 as 'sufficiently beautiful according to their fashion and located along the Danube at the foot of the hill, above which extends the walled city'.[10] The waterfront mosque and palace were sited in the *varoş* of Buda, whose outer walls had been created by the pasha as an extension of the ancient hilltop city comprising a castle and citadel.[11] We shall see in this chapter that the expansion of towns with the addition of outer walls was a distinctive characteristic of Ottoman urbanism in the age of Sinan, whose provincial Friday mosques were often located in the newly created suburban extensions of pre-existing cities or in new settlements founded along major imperial routes. Sokollu Mustafa Pasha must have owed his access to Sinan's services to his intimate connection with the grand vizier. His mosque and mausoleum in Buda, the only monuments he commissioned from the chief architect, simultaneously commemorated his personal fame and his public office. Other privileged patrons of Sinan's 'signature' mosques in Rumelia were similarly distinguished by their special kinship ties with the viziers, the grand vizier, or the sultan himself.

I. SOFU (HACI, KARAGÖZ) MEHMED BEG

As the most impressive domed mosque of Mostar, the capital of the sanjak of Hercegovina, Hacı Mehmed Beg's Friday mosque has long been attributed by local tradition to Sinan (illus. 445). The chief architect's autobiographies list the Friday mosque of 'Sofu Mehmed Pasha in Hercegovina', whereas the founder of the Mostar mosque (nicknamed Karagöz Beg) was not a pasha but a large-scale fiefholder (*zaʿīm*) identified in his Arabic waqfiyya (1570) as 'al-Hajj Mehmed Beg al-Zaʿim'.[12] The

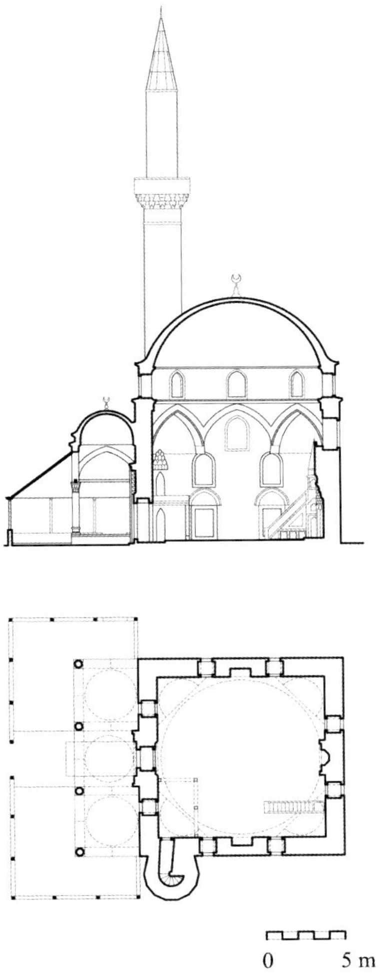

445 Plan and cross-section of the Karagöz Mehmed Beg mosque, Mostar.

Arabic foundation inscription of the mosque explains that it was built during Süleyman's reign by the 'brother of the most illustrious vizier, the owner of pious foundations, al-Hajj Mehmed Beg b. Abu al-Sa'adat' in the year 965 (1557–58).[13] Without citing a source, local scholars generally identify the patron, thought to have been born in Potoc near Mostar, as the brother of Rüstem Pasha. However, the grand vizier's only known brother is the grand admiral Sinan Pasha, and the 'most illustrious vizier' referred to in the inscription has yet to be identified.[14]

The Bosnian-born vizier Sofu Mehmed Pasha (d. 1557), mentioned in the chief architect's autobiographies as the patron of a mosque in Hercegovina, was also known as Hacı Mehmed Pasha.[15] It is likely that the autobiographies confused the title of the patron of the mosque in Mostar, referring to him as a pasha rather than a beg. Therefore, Karagöz Mehmed Beg's mosque can tentatively be attributed to Sinan. The same patron was in charge of overseeing the construction of the famous Mostar bridge. An archival document dated 1557 shows that the bridge was being 'built with the oversight (*neẓāret*) of Karagöz Beg by the order of Hadım Haydar Pasha, the governor of Hercegovina'.[16] The latter was a white eunuch, who upon being deposed from the vizierate in 1553 was appointed the sanjak governor of Hercegovina, where he originated, until his death in the early 1560s.[17]

A decree addressed to the rulers of Dubrovnik in 1556 requests salaried Ragusan masons to be sent 'for the construction of a bridge in the township of Mostar in the sanjak of Hercegovina', a state project ordered with an imperial decree sent to 'the kadi of Mostar and the overseer (*nāẓır*) Mehmed'. Dispatched with their tools, the masons would 'get their wages from the expense account kept by the overseer'.[18] Karagöz Mehmed Beg built his own mosque at Mostar just around that time in 1557–58. Since the royal architect of the bridge has been identified as Mimar Hayrüddin, it is likely that the mosque too was built by him, perhaps on the basis of a plan drawn by Sinan (Appendix 4:4). The Mostar bridge was erected between 1557 and 1566–67, during which period its construction overseer completed his complex, endowed in 1570.[19] According to his waqfiyya, the mosque was accompanied by a madrasa, an elementary school for teaching the Koran to Muslim children, and a hospice (*'imāret*) for guests. The founder also endowed income-producing structures in Mostar that included a nearby khan and forty-two shops. These were complemented by other properties in Potoc (a mosque and elementary school) and in Konjic (an elementary school).[20]

The only remaining structures from the charming little complex, sited a hundred metres away from the bridge on the main avenue of Mostar, near its suq, are the mosque, an L-shaped madrasa, and an ablution fountain (*ṣādırvān*), surrounded by a rubble masonry precinct wall containing a cemetery garden (illus. 446).[21] Covered by cradle vaults, the madrasa is composed of four small rooms, one large room, and a classroom that had an endowed library. The ashlar masonry mosque is a simple domed cube fronted by a double portico and provided with a slender muqarnas-galleried minaret. The triple-domed first portico, carried on four marble columns with muqarnas capitals, is extended with a second portico, featuring a sharply slanting shed roof that rests on small octagonal pillars. The colourfully painted portal has a triangular 'flattened muqarnas' hood. In accordance with local building tradition, the lead-covered domes of the mosque (built by a workforce of imported Ragusan masons) are of cut limestone instead of brick.

The patron's humble status is reflected by the modestly scaled main dome (10.65 metres wide) with a window-pierced octagonal stone drum, carried by eight pointed arches on muqarnas-corbelled squinches in each corner. The simple muqarnas-hooded mihrab and plain minbar, painted like the portal in lively colours with abstract foliate and geometric designs, signals the provincial character of the well-proportioned mosque. The ground-level windows of the brightly lit prayer hall feature openwork arched lunettes of bottle-glass and the lateral walls have

446 Karagöz Mehmed Beg mosque, Mostar, from the north.

central cupboards, as in the comparable provincial mosques of Sokollu Kasım Beg (a sanjak governor) in Havsa and Ferhad Pasha (a deposed vizier) in Çatalca, both of them fronted by triple-domed porticoes. Future research may yield more information about the architect and the little-known patron of the mosque in Mostar, to which Sinan's contribution could not have been more than a plan dispatched from the capital.

II. OSMANSHAH BEG

The imposing mosque that Sinan designed for the sanjak governor Osmanshah Beg in Trikkala announces its patron's privileged stature as Sultan Süleyman's beloved nephew (illus. 447, 448).[22] Said to have been even more acclaimed than the viziers, its founder was born to a daughter of Selim I and the executed vizier İskender Pasha (d. 1515).[23] Despite his distinguished lineage as a prince, the mosque that Osmanshah commissioned in the sanjak he governed has one single-galleried minaret, conforming to codes of decorum formulated for non-royal provincial governors. The omission of the second minaret underscores his identity as a minor prince descending from the reigning sultan's sister.

The absence of twin minarets is offset by the unusually grand scale of the mosque, which bears a striking resemblance to that of the vizier Sofu Mehmed Pasha in Sofia (1547–48), thereby emphasizing the patron's special status, approximating that of a vizier. Both monuments are composed of a single-domed prayer hall fronted by a five-bay portico. Osmanshah's mosque has a more imposing double portico, deviating from the three-domed norm typical for Rumelian sanjak governors. Moreover, it boasts the second-largest dome among mosques beyond Edirne attributed to Sinan. With its 17.98-metre-wide dome, it approaches in scale its vizierial counterpart in Sofia (18.3 metres), although it differs from the Sofia mosque in its cheaper masonry with alternating courses of stone and brick.[24]

Osmanshah, who passed away in his early seventies in 1570, is buried behind the qibla wall of his mosque in an octagonal mausoleum built of rough cut stone.[25]

Mustafa Āli portrays Osmanshah Beg as a spirited governor who surpassed even the viziers in pomp and circumstance. Cherished by his reigning uncle Süleyman, who granted all his wishes, he was a carefree prince, 'moderate in terms of justice and injustice'. As he preferred hunting and entertainment to governing, he had his steward (*kethüda*) preside over public audiences in his place.[26] Peçevi describes the prince, nicknamed Kara (Black) Osmanshah Beg because of his dark complexion, in similar terms:

> Although he was officially called a governor, he actually was more magnificent and imposing than governor-generals and even viziers. He would now be the joint governor of the sanjaks of Morea and Lepanto, and then of the sanjak of Bosnia. Whichever one he desired was granted to him by His Majesty, the Sultan [Süleyman] … He has bath-houses and monuments in some summer pastures of Morea. Being a man of pleasure, he would spend his time in diversion and friendly conversation with boon companions in summer pastures and places of temperate climate. Not participating in military campaigns, he was a fortunate one following his own fancies. Whenever the triumphant Sultan used to be troubled by one of his sons, he would declare: 'I will fetch Kara Osman and designate him [crown prince] in your place!' At the province of Morea, some of his modes of behaviour and demeanour are still famous and talked about today as part of the people's folklore.[27]

In 1569, a year before his demise, 'the sanjak governor of Trikkala and Lepanto, Osmanshah Beg', endowed new properties for his late father İskender Pasha's elementary school and mausoleum in Istanbul's Güngörmez quarter near the Hippodrome. The witnesses who signed the waqfiyya included Osmanshah's only heir (Mustafa Beg b. Süleyman Beg, the son of his deceased brother), his steward Mehmed (Memi) Kethüda, and the staff of his Friday mosque in Trikkala.[28] Osmanshah Beg had previously commissioned the chief architect Sinan to design a Friday mosque and madrasa in memory of his late royal mother (d. 1538) in the Kovacı Dede quarter of Istanbul, near Aksaray. The waqfiyya of this lost complex, mentioned in Sinan's autobiographies, was registered by the prince in accordance with his mother's will in 1538.[29]

Given Osmanshah's close connections with the imperial court in Istanbul, where he managed his parents' waqfs, he could easily have obtained a plan from Sinan for the Trikkala mosque. The structure is mentioned only in the *Tuḥfe*, with no reference to its dependencies.[30] We do not know when its foundations were laid, but an annual account book of Osmanshah's waqfs from the year 974 (1566–67) shows that together with its charitable

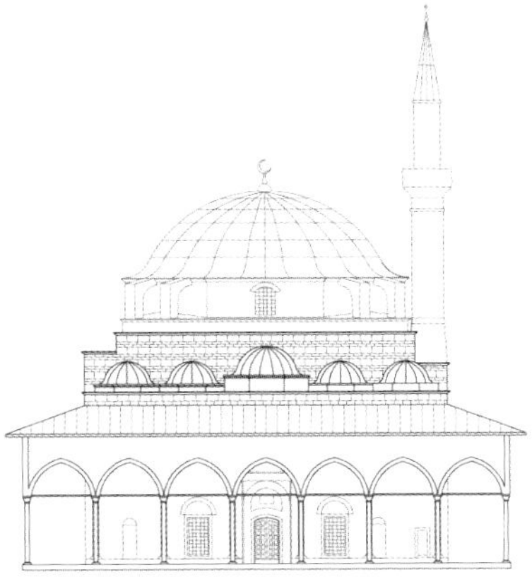

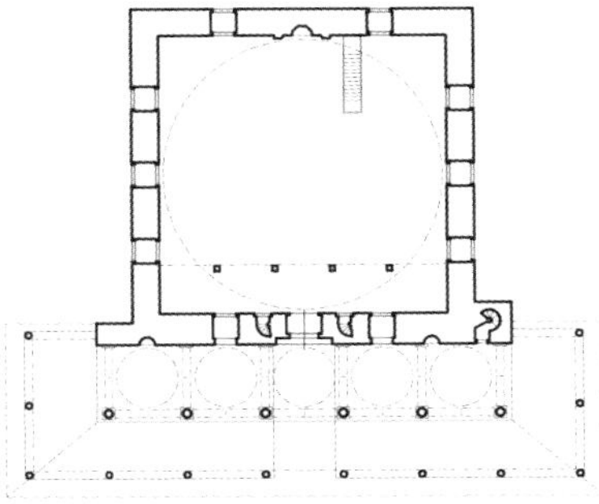

0 5 10 m

447 Plan and elevation of the Osmanshah Beg mosque, Trikkala, showing the missing double portico hypothetically reconstructed.

448 Osmanshah Beg mosque and mausoleum from the south.

kitchen (*maṭbaḫ*) it was already functioning at that time.[31] The mosque complex in Trikkala was likely built sometime after the prince returned from Bosnia to Greece in the 1560s. Prior to that, he endowed a no-longer-extant Friday mosque in Banjaluka, where he had been transferred in 1556 as the sanjak governor of Bosnia. Because Osmanshah expired before having had a chance to register the waqfiyya of his pious foundation in Trikkala, an endowment deed was posthumously prepared by his nephew Mustafa Beg according to his will. The surviving portion of this undated, fragmentary waqfiyya explains that the late Osmanshah Beg b. İskender Pasha had founded his mosque in Trikkala 'during his lifetime while he was in good health.' His endowments include 154,000 aspers loaned at interest and various landed properties, farms, mills, and bath-houses in Greece. Unfortunately, the sections of the fragmentary waqfiyya concerning the mosque dependencies are lost.[32]

Today the only remaining structures of the complex are its recently restored mosque, whose preachers belonged to the Halveti order, and its mausoleum.[33] The mosque has lost its original portico and all of its painted decorations and inscriptions. Its well-proportioned cubic body, with three tiers of windows, is dominated by a large dome raised on pendentives above an octagonal drum, with paired buttresses in each corner. Its provincial character is reflected in its unlayered massing and its unadorned simplicity. Its arched portal lacks a muqarnas hood and its thick minaret of ashlar stone, recently renovated, has a plain gallery. According to Evliya Çelebi, however, the mosque had an elaborately decorated interior and was accompanied by a U-shaped madrasa, an elementary school, a hospice, a khan, and a bath-house.[34] The functional programme of the complex, then, came close to that of Sofu Mehmed Pasha in the outskirts of Sofia, where once again Sinan designed only the mosque.[35] Osmanshah's complex was located outside the city, along a river in a joyful, tree-planted meadow frequented in the evenings by merchants, artisans, and 'loyal lovers' who gathered there for pleasurable discourse. Evliya reports: 'It is a prosperous monument whose edifices are covered with indigo-blue lead from head to foot, but being located at the city's periphery, it is deprived from a large congregation.'[36] He raves about the suburban mosque, far more impressive than its eight counterparts inside the city:

> Its like is not found in any land, except in Tire and Manisa and Bursa and Istanbul. Although it is small, its architecture is extremely splendid. It is a decorated, prosperous, and illuminated edifice, a joy-giving, graceful, and exemplary Friday mosque. The gilded pendants hanging in it, the artifice of its mihrab and minbar, its charming artistry (*şīrīkārlıḳ*), and the various skills (*taṣarruflar*) exerted all over it make eulogizers fall short of praise. In short, it is a light-filled mosque whose beauty and grace is beyond description and verbalization with jewel-scattering words. In truth, this mosque is a house of God built by Koca Mimar Sinan b. Abdülmennan Agha, the builder of Sultan Süleyman Khan's mosque. He has exerted in it his best effort, displaying a mastery (*kārgerlik*) that no previous architect or engineer had ever achieved in the ninth heavenly sphere; may it last until the end of Time. The azure dome of this light-filled

> mosque rests on top of four-cornered walls, as if it were the mosque of Selim I in Istanbul; its interior is completely devoid of lofty columns. The circumference of its indigo-coloured dome is surrounded by iron railings to hang oil lamps. Its qibla gate [across the mihrab] is extremely artistic, and the date on its lofty threshold is [empty]. And its external portico has on top of six exemplary columns five lofty domes, each of which resembles the dome of heaven. And its courtyard paved with white marbles is of decorated marble work. It is a joy-giving courtyard surrounded by domes raised on tall columns and decked with the cells of madrasa scholars.'[37]

Evliya's glowing description seems to have been prompted by the rarity of a mosque built in the manner of Sinan in this part of the empire. With its mausoleum enshrining the body of its legendary royal patron, the complex perpetuated Osmanshah's remembrance in folklore. Evliya hence embellishes his architectural description with fanciful tales about the prince, whose 'generous disposition' was obvious from his charitable mosque complex in Trikkala.[38]

III. SOKOLLU KASIM BEG (PASHA)

Kurd [Wolf] Kasım Beg's mosque complex in Havsa (originally Hafsa) was a posthumous memorial built by the grand vizier Sokollu Mehmed Pasha for his beloved son, who passed away as the sanjak governor of Hercegovina in 1572 (illus. 449, 450). Sited at the final road-station of the highway connecting Istanbul to Edirne, it was accompanied by more monumental grand vizierial complexes that Sinan designed along the same route for Sokollu himself (Lüleburgaz, *c.* 1565–69/70) and Semiz Ali Pasha (Babaeski, *c.* 1569–75). The late Kasım Beg's status as a sanjak governor is expressed by the modest scale of his single-minaret mosque, a domed cube fronted by a triple-domed portico (now missing). Its grand vizierial counterparts in Lüleburgaz and Babaeski feature seven- and five-domed double porticoes respectively.

Born from a concubine of Sokollu, Kurd Kasım Beg held various provincial posts thanks to his father's influence. The dates of his tenure as the governor-general of Aleppo have yet to be determined. He spent the last months of his life as the sanjak governor of Hercegovina (October 1571 to April 1572), a demotion that reduced his status from pasha to beg.[39] Nevertheless, an imperial decree issued on 13 May 1573 for the posthumous construction of the Havsa complex invokes the more prestigious title, 'the former governor-general of Aleppo, Kasım Beg, who recently passed away'.[40] Shortly before his demise, the Venetian diplomat Jacopo Ragazzoni (1571) described the youthful governor of Hercegovina, who was based in the sanjak capital Mostar, three days' journey from Ragusa:

> This sanjak governor is young, twenty-two years old. He is greatly cherished by his father, who has no son other than him [actually Sokollu had another son from a slave concubine, Hasan Pasha.] He is a minor son, born from a slave, and because none of the sons of the Sultana, the *Grand Signor*'s daughter, are alive, this one is all the more loved by him, especially after having fathered a son a few months ago whom he named Mehmed after his father. This sanjak governor is by nature avaricious, as all Turks universally are. Respected and feared by many, thanks to being the son of the person who governs the whole Ottoman empire, he is able to extract more than 80,000 scudi annually from his sanjak, whose former governors in the past did not derive a third of that amount.[41]

For the memory of his late son, Sokollu commissioned along the Dubrovnik caravan route a bridge and a caravansaray at Trebinje, constructed by Ragusan stonemasons between 1572 and 1574. The Frenchman Pierre L'Escalopier describes this pious foundation dedicated by the grand vizier to his son's soul:

> On 11 March 1574 we traveled almost all day long on foot over cracked roads and arrived quite late in Trebinje, named after a river carrying the same name that passes from there, over which is a long bridge of stone and a nearby caravansaray covered with lead, built by [Sokollu] Mehmed Pasha ... The pasha's son died as the governor of this province [Hercegovina], and his father had that hospice built so that passengers would offer prayers to God on behalf of his son.[42]

The mosque complex in Havsa was likewise created by Sokollu for the soul of his son. An undated fragment of 'the late Kasım Pasha's' Arabic waqfiyya mentions both of these monuments. It refers to a 'long bridge' in Hercegovina, accompanied by 'a sumptuous carvansaray' with a masjid and a source of running water, and a nearby pavement.[43] The complex in Havsa comprised 'two large khans facing each other', next to which were built a hospice with 'kitchen, commissariat, bakery, wood storage, and latrines'. Near these was constructed a 'noble masjid' and a water channel.[44] Sokollu's own waqfiyya, registered in 1574, provides another description of the late 'Kurd Kasım Pasha's' complex in Havsa, financed with the legal share of the 'canonically lawful property' that the grand vizier inherited from his son:

> Near the protected metropolis of Edirne, in an auspicious town called Hafsa which was a passage place of the people and a thoroughfare of the high and low, a guest-house (*mihmānḫāne*) was most urgently needed. In that place he [Sokollu] built for the soul of the aforementioned deceased [Kasım Pasha] two lofty khans facing one another on both sides of a delightful porch (*ṣoffa*), and a lofty noble masjid in front of it, conducting tasteful waters there.[45]

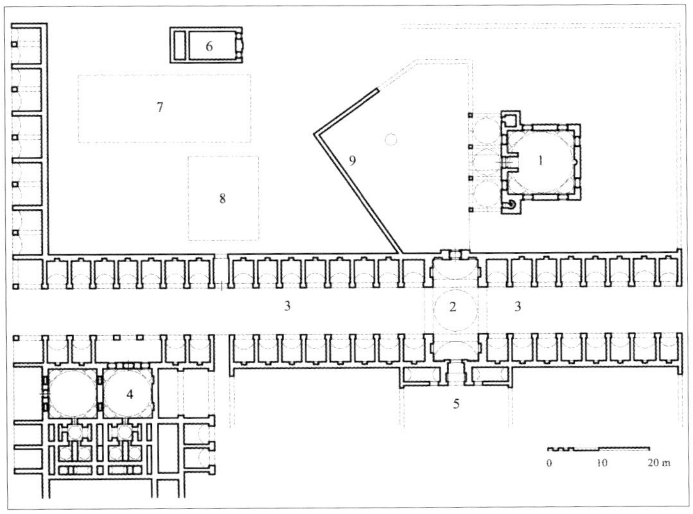

449 Plan of the Sokollu Kasım Beg complex, Havsa: 1. Mosque with missing portico, hypothetically reconstructed. 2. Prayer dome. 3. Reconstruction of *arasta*. 4. Double bath with corner fountain. 5. Site of double caravansaray with guest-rooms and hospice. 6. Pre-existing masjid. 7. Modern elementary school. 8. Modern structure. 9. Excavated wall.

450 Sokollu Kasım Pasha mosque and prayer dome, Havsa, from the west.

The complex is mentioned in all of Sinan's autobiographies, and identified in the *Tezkiretü'l-ebniye* as a posthumous construction: 'In the town of Hafsa, a noble Friday mosque for the soul of [Sokollu] Mehmed Pasha's son, Kasım Beg.' By referring to the patron as 'Kasım Pasha, the son of Mehmed Pasha', the *Tuhfe* captures the ambiguous status of the grand vizier's son who was simultaneously called 'beg' and 'pasha': an ambiguity that informed the ambitiousness of his complex, which was entirely designed by Sinan. The chief architect's autobiographies list not only the mosque, but also its hospice, caravansaray, and bath-house.[46]

The decree of 13 May 1573 mentioned above orders the kadis of Bulgaria to provide rental carts for the transportation to Sofia of lead bought in Yanova, 'for the caravansaray newly built in Hafsa for the late Kasım Beg's soul'.[47] This shows that the caravansaray-cum-hospice block was the first structure to be built, as in the grand vizier's own complex at Lüleburgaz. In 1575, the kadis of Bulgaria were once again asked to provide rental carts to transport the grand vizier's lead, stored in Sofia, to 'the building in the town of Hafsa near Edirne'.[48] The kadi of Haskovo, near Edirne, was sent a decree in August 1576, ordering him to assist the steward Mustafa Kethüda, who had been appointed building supervisor (*emīn*) of the grand vizier's new charitable construction in Havsa. The supervisor was probably the former steward of Kasım Beg, described by Ragazzoni in 1571 as an old man who administered the sanjak of Hercegovina 'with acute prudence'. The kadi had to help the building supervisor buy bricks, timber, wooden planks, stone, lime, and other required materials.[49]

The new construction was almost certainly the mosque, built after the completion of the caravansaray-cum-hospice block and the income-producing structures that included a double bath and shops. In May 1575, Gerlach reported that the construction of the mosque had just begun: 'In the beginning of this month, [Sokollu] Mehmed Pasha built a beautiful church three miles away from Edirne on the road to Istanbul; a hundred and twenty slaves were sent there with their guards to cut stone.'[50] The Venetian ambassador Jacopo Soranzo, who passed from Havsa on 21 June 1575 en route to Istanbul, stayed in the guest-house of the double caravansaray while the neighbouring mosque was undergoing construction together with an elementary school:

> Capsa is a small place, but each day it grows larger because [Sokollu] Mehmed Pasha recently had a most beautiful caravansaray built there which is divided into two parts, having in between them a beautiful superstructure that joins them together. And the edifice of that caravansaray is continuous, its two parts unified into one; together they are 135 paces long and 25 wide. It has, in addition, a commodious place to lodge leading persons, with its own fountains; and on the other side of the caravansaray are baths, kitchens, and every other convenience. He also had a long stretch of shops built, which he managed to have inhabited with all sorts of donations and other favours. Now he is having a beautiful mosque built together with a school to discipline boys, besides buildings for the commodity of travellers ... This edifice is extremely beautiful, with a lot of graceful artifice (*molto vago artificio*) according to the manner of these lands, all covered with lead and of immense cost. We lodged in the above-mentioned place, which was built with many vaulted rooms, adjacent to one another, featuring a portico in front and a courtyard that was divided by a big wall from the large courtyard of the caravansaray.[51]

The *bailo* Paolo Contarini (1580) described the completed complex as follows:

> We arrived at a place called Cafsa, built by [Sokollu] Mehmed Pasha, where he had a beautiful mosque erected. And upon exiting from the mosque one finds a very high vault covered with lead, which is like a city gate, and one enters into a courtyard surrounded by porticoed rooms for lodging, where we stayed, and it has a fountain in the middle. It moreover has two large stables for lodging twenty-four men and horses, and in the middle a large square house (*casa*) for keeping goods. He has created many shops of cut stone to sell merchandise for the needs of travellers. There is also a place set apart for women. We found there fruits and eggs; there is also a sufficiently beautiful bath for men in the middle and for women beyond it. They give food to those who lodge in the eighty-eight rooms of the two caravansarays. At the entrance is a square place with four arches of cut stone, and a dome in the middle, covered with lead. It has a kitchen and magazines to keep rice, butter, and other provisions. Twice a day they give to lodging guests bread, and rice with meat. To this mosque are endowed, besides other revenues, the income of a caravansaray in Edirne.'[52]

Recorded by Evliya Çelebi, the foundation inscription above the arched roadside gate under the 'prayer dome', leading into the mosque's courtyard, provides the completion date of the complex: 'When Azmi saw it, he prayed and said its date: May God make this solid building last; the year 984 (1576–77).' Today the inscription, in *thuluth* on a rectangular marble panel, is faded and only partially legible.[53] Another foundation inscription above the muqarnas-hooded portal of the mosque explains that it was built by the grand vizier for his son, with the hope of securing for him an abode in paradise, but its chronogram is no longer legible:

> His Highness, the pious pasha and the venerable vizier,
> May his power and life be enduring, [and] his generosity
> perpetual,
>
> Built this Friday mosque as a charity on behalf of his son,
> Creating an unequalled and unmatched lofty abode
> (*maḳām*).
>
> The well-wisher Azmi saw it and said its date:
> 'For its owner may his Friday mosque [yield ?]
> paradise.'[54]

Unlike the pious foundations of governors, generally located in the provinces where they ruled, that of Kasım Beg is a highly visible roadside complex along the main thoroughfare of the empire, supplementing Sokollu's own complexes on the same route. It was composed of two main blocks, a mosque and a hospice-cum-caravansaray, bisected by a shopping artery (*arasta*) lined with shops on both sides of the Istanbul-Edirne highway. The components of the roadside complex were visually tied together by a domed baldachin (*dua kubbesi*, prayer dome) as in Sokollu's foundations in Lüleburgaz and Payas.[55] The only remaining structures of the complex are its extensively renovated Friday mosque (whose triple-domed portico is missing), the lofty baldachin (whose dome resting on four pendentives collapsed and was rebuilt), and the dilapidated income-producing double bath built at a distance in the northwest corner of the *arasta*. The integrated block of the double caravansaray and hospice, with special rooms for privileged guests and women, must have resembled its counterparts at Sokollu's own complexes in Lüleburgaz and Payas. It was destroyed during an earthquake in 1752, together with the rows of shops that formed an *arasta* along the north-south axis.[56] The historical highway passing under the 'prayer dome' was connected to a pre-existing stone bridge, mentioned by Dernschwam in 1553, whose ruins can still be seen under the modern bridge at the southwest side of the complex.[57]

The ashlar masonry mosque is crowned by a medium-sized renovated dome (about 13 metres wide) carried on squinches. With its unlayered massing and simple elegance, the mosque befits the status of a privileged sanjak governor who once held the title of pasha. It was the clout of Kasım Beg's father that secured Sinan's services in designing this mosque complex. The chief architect, who was then building the Selimiye in Edirne (1568–74), could have overseen the laying of foundations at Havsa in 1573, but he must have delegated construction to one of his subordinates. The prayer hall, lit by three tiers of windows, has completely lost its original painted decorations and inscriptions (illus. 451).[58] Its lateral walls have central cupboards as in the comparable mosques of Karagöz Mehmed Beg in Mostar (1557-58) and Ferhad Pasha in Çatalca (*c.* 1575–88), which also feature three-bay porticoes.

Evliya Çelebi was impressed by the ornateness of the mosque: 'With its great dome, lofty minaret, and spacious courtyard, it is an extremely artistic Friday mosque, as if it were a royal mosque (*cāmiʿ-i selāṭīn*). The interior of the mosque is so decorated and illuminated that it is as if it were the Rüstem Pasha mosque [in Tahtakale].'[59] He explains that with the money he inherited from his deceased son Sokollu Mehmed Pasha had developed the small settlement around the complex 'into a flourishing large town resembling an emporium' (*şehr-i bender*).[60]

With its modestly scaled memorial mosque featuring a triple-domed portico, the complex conformed to codes of decorum established for sanjak governors. This 'signature' monument designed by Sinan was distinguished from other generic examples of its type by its unusually monumental service block for travellers. The grand vizier's intimate involvement in its construction process, expedited by means of royal decrees issued through his mediation, ensured the provision of high quality materials and a skilled workforce. Jacopo Soranzo even preferred it to Sokollu's own complex in Lüleburgaz: 'Although the

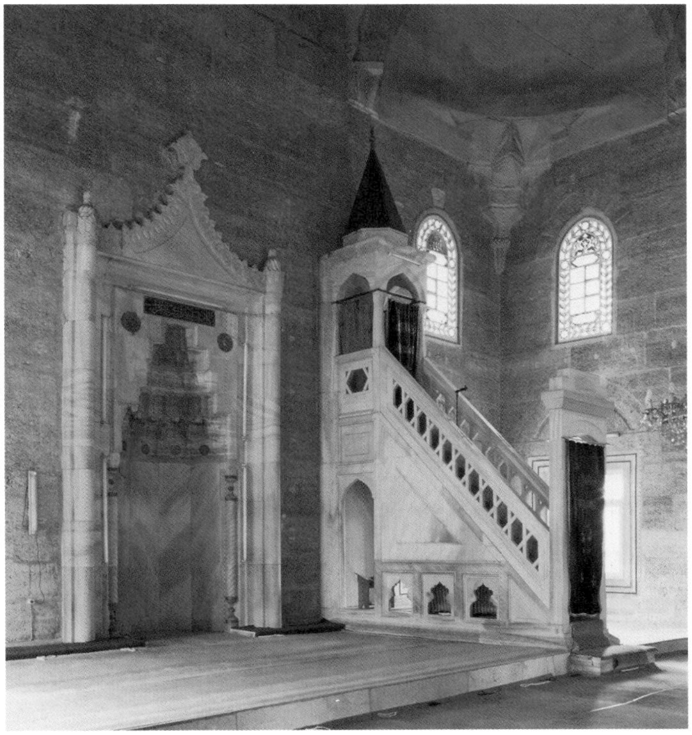

451 Sokollu Kasım Pasha mosque, Havsa, interior.

building in Capsa is not as large, it can nevertheless be judged as having greater artifice (*artificio*) and architecture (*architettura*).'[61]

WESTERN AND CENTRAL ANATOLIA

The four mosques that governor-generals commissioned from Sinan in the provincial capitals of western and central Anatolia (Isparta, Ankara, Kütahya, Kayseri) complemented those he designed for higher ranking patrons in the same region (Map 1): the vizier Pertev Pasha (İzmit), the grand vizier Rüstem Pasha (Samanlı, Sapanca, Dibek-Bolu, Bolvadin), the crown prince Selim (Karapınar near Konya), and Murad III (Manisa). Stylistically, these four mosques are barely distinguishable from others excluded from the chief architect's autobiographies, such as the vizier Lala Mustafa Pasha's mosque complex at Ilgın, near Konya (1576–77), a domed cube with a three-bay portico, which is a smaller version of the one built for his pupil, prince Selim, at Karapınar during the 1560s. With the exception of the Muradiye in the princely capital, Manisa, none of these mosques has İznik tiles or refined painted decorations executed by court painters sent from Istanbul.[62]

Sinan's mosques in Western and Central Anatolia are outnumbered by their pre-Ottoman and early-Ottoman counterparts, which visually dominate the urban landscape of this region, where the dissemination of the 'classical' idiom does not seem to have been a high state priority. Unlike roadside complexes lining the principal highway cutting diagonally across Anatolia, which were spatially dominated by dependencies serving the needs of travellers, mosques designed by Sinan in regional capitals had a primarily urban character. Omitted from his autobiographies, their few dependencies must have been simple structures that have generally disappeared.

IV. FİRDEVS BEG (PASHA)

The little-known patron of this mosque, a domed cube fronted by a five-bay portico, was the governor of the sanjaks of Teke and Hamid, whose capitals were Antalya and Isparta respectively (illus. 452, 453). Sinan's autobiographies identify the founder as 'Firdevs Beg'.[63] A Turkish waqfiyya recorded in October-November 1565 refers to him as 'one of the viziers of His Highness, the late Sultan Süleyman Khan, the governor of the sanjaks of Teke and Hamid in the province of Anatolia ... Firdevs Pasha b. İskender Pasha b. İshak Pasha'. Although he was merely a sanjak governor, the Muslim-born Firdevs Beg is identified here as a pasha who furthermore enjoyed the honorary title of vizier, perhaps because he descended from a distinguished family of pashas. If he is the same person as Firdevs Agha, the chief court messenger of prince Selim's household during the Konya war of 1559, he may subsequently have been rewarded with the governorship of these two sanjaks. Later on, he became the sanjak governor of Lepanto and was martyred there during the disastrous Ottoman campaign in 1571.[64]

The waqfiyya explains that the founder had newly built 'in the quarter of the Old Mosque (*cāmiʿ-i ʿatīḳ*) of Isparta, on a plot of land he owned, a noble Friday mosque with a masonry dome' for the salvation of his soul and the forgiveness of his sins. For this pious foundation, he endowed a number of shops nearby and a covered bazaar built of masonry (*kārgīr bezzāzistān*).[65] The court records and endowment registers of Isparta show that the dependencies of the 'Firdevs Beg' mosque included a dervish convent (*tekke, zāviye*) entrusted to a shaykh. The patron had endowed 300,000 aspers for the construction of his covered bazaar and convent. The interest of the remaining sum would be used for distributing food from the convent kitchen for the personnel of the mosque and convent as well as the city's poor residents.[66]

Sinan's autobiographies do not mention the now-lost convent and the still extant Bedesten.[67] The Friday mosque is located at the commercial centre of Isparta, in the quarter of the Seljuk-period Great Mosque renovated by and named after Kutlu Beg (*c.* 1429), the first Ottoman governor of the city formerly ruled by the Hamidoğlu principality. The foundation of the new mosque paralleled the urban growth of Isparta, whose seventeen quarters, listed in a register dated 1522, rose to twenty-four around 1567, with the quarter of the Great Mosque showing a considerable increase in population. Late-sixteenth-century registers reveal that Firdevs Beg's Friday mosque was the only one in the city other than the Great Mosque.[68] It must have reinforced the policy of Sunni orthodoxy promoted by the centralized state in this region, settled with rebellious pro-Safavid Turkmen

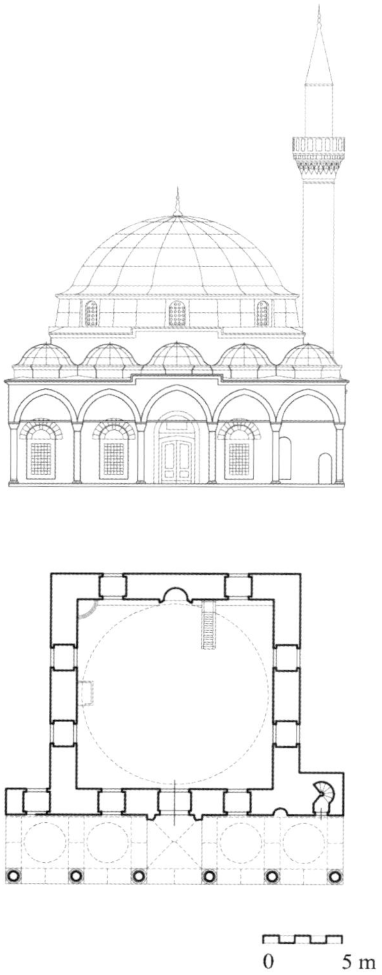

452 Plan and elevation of the Firdevs Beg mosque, Isparta.

453 Firdevs Beg mosque, from the west.

tribes. The waqfiyya refers to the mosque as if it was completed by 1565, but an intriguing chronogram composed by a disgruntled dervish dates its inauguration to the year 977 (1569–70): 'Always oppression!'[69]

The extensively renovated ashlar masonry mosque of beige limestone lacks a foundation inscription.[70] With its polygonal muqarnas-galleried minaret, its layered yet simple massing, and its few windows organized in two tiers, the mosque exemplifies an unsophisticated regional interpretation of Sinan's 'classical' idiom. Its lead-covered, medium-sized dome (12.38 metres) is raised on four pendentives and sits on a tapering window-pierced drum also covered with lead, which omits the typical paired flying buttresses in each corner. The five-domed portico with spoliated marble columns has a simple arched gate flanked by two windows on each side, without the customary paired mihrabs. Inside the prayer hall, which has lost its original painted decorations, the muqarnas-hooded mihrab and minbar are plain structures of greyish white marble. With its artless monumentality and ambitious five-bay portico (more appropriate for governor-generals and viziers), Firdevs Beg's mosque was a worthy memorial for a nobly descended sanjak governor boasting the honorary titles of pasha and vizier.

V. CENABİ AHMED PASHA

The funerary mosque that Cenabi Ahmed Pasha commissioned in Ankara, where he was based for many years as the governor-general of the province of Anatolia, is a basic domed cube with a single-galleried minaret and an unassuming triple-domed portico (illus. 454, 455). The capital of the province he governed was temporarily transferred from Kütahya to Ankara between 1542 and 1566, the years during which the princes Bayezid and Selim were successively appointed the sanjak governors of Kütahya. The capital moved back to Kütahya with Selim II's accession in 1566.[71] The site of Cenabi Ahmed Pasha's mosque, then, was intimately tied to his official seat in Ankara. His domed octagonal mausoleum of ashlar masonry, raised on a garden platform at the east side of the walled precinct, is omitted from Sinan's autobiographies.[72]

This Muslim-born pasha was the son of the governor-general Ulama Pasha (d. 1557), whose father had been a fiefholder in the sanjak of Teke near Antalya, settled with pro-Safavid Turkmen tribes. Ulama joined the Safavid order as a fervent disciple of Shah Isma'il, becoming a leading dignitary under Shah Tahmasp, but defected to Sultan Süleyman's court in 1531–32 and was rewarded with the governorship of various provinces. Educated in the sultan's palace, his son Ahmed eventually became the governor-general of Anatolia, a post he is said to have held with justice for nearly twenty years (*c.* 1544–65).[73] During the war of princes at Konya in 1559, Cenabi Ahmed Pasha was ordered by the sultan to leave Ankara with his troops to support prince Selim, who emerged at that time as the victorious heir-apparent.[74] A miniature painting that depicts a wine-drinking party at the crown prince's court in Kütahya, where he was based as sanjak governor between 1561-62 and 1566, identifies his loyal supporter as 'Cenab Pasha, your servant' (illus. 30). The governor-general is seated on a separate carpet marking his higher status from the begs comprising the prince's entourage: Kurd Beg, Gülabi Beg, and Turak Beg (executed in 1561–62).[75] Yet Cenabi Pasha's humble pose and attire express his submissive role as the 'servant' of his lavishly dressed royal master, destined to become the next sultan.

Like prince Selim, the pasha was a heavy drinker and an aspiring poet whose entertaining poems became popular among jugglers and acrobats. Mustafa Āli notes his grave addiction to wine and his doctors' consensus that he would die if he ever quit drinking. Known by the pen-name 'Cenābī' (Majestic), Ahmed Pasha had been brought up as an ideal courtier: 'He was extremely dignified, courteous, and agreeable in virtues; throughout his life he was not once seen laughing too loud, and when he did laugh his sparkling teeth of pearl were never visible; even in private he was not seen sitting cross-legged or leaning against a pillow, unlike other men of fortune.'[76] A biographical compendium of poets describes him as an eloquent poet of agreeable character, good breeding, and perfect manners, and reports that while he 'bloomed' in Sultan Süleyman's palace, 'cultivated with the waters of the imperial garden', he was nicknamed 'Ahmed the Rose' (Gül Ahmed) because of his youthful beauty. Had he not died in 969 (1561–62), the compendium asserts, he would certainly have risen to the vizierate.[77]

If Cenabi Ahmed Pasha did pass away that year, his mosque must have been finished four years after his death: its Turkish foundation inscription gives the completion date of 973 (1565–66) (illus. 456, 457).[78] According to the historian Uzunçarşılı, however, the pasha remained the governor-general of Ankara until 1565.[79] Unlike most posthumously inaugurated monuments, his mosque has a foundation inscription which refers to him as if he were still alive. Carved under the muqarnas hooded portal of the mosque in two lines of *thuluth*, the inscription alludes to his honorary title of vizier (*āṣaf*, Solomon's vizier) and his penname Cenabi (*cem cenāb*):

> Sultan Süleyman's Asaf, Ahmed Pasha of Jam-like majesty
> Built and made in this world a most beneficial abode
> (*maḳām*).
>
> Oh God, may this building remain solid like a pole of
> firmness,
> Perpetually for the people of the world, with the aid of the
> Most Noble One's protection.
>
> For the completion of this fortunate Friday mosque, Mahfī
> said

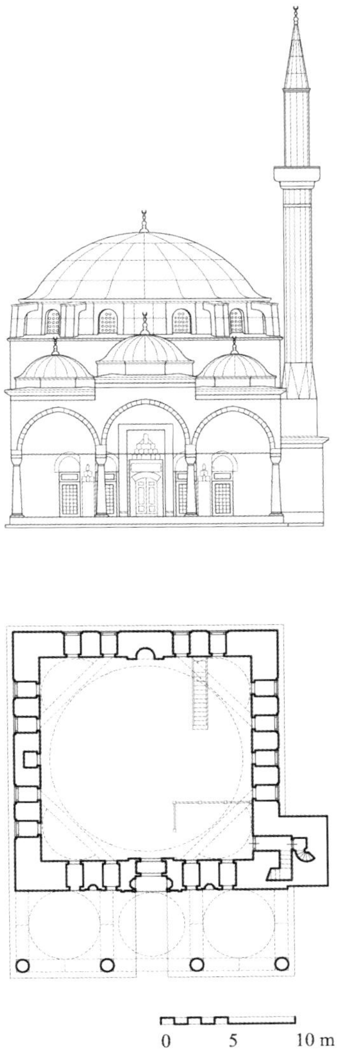

454 Plan and elevation of the Cenabi Ahmed Pasha mosque, Ankara.

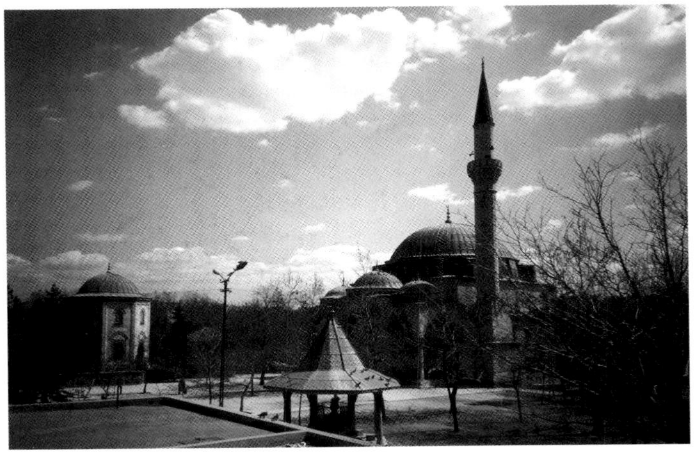

455 Cenabi Ahmed Pasha mosque, Ankara, with mausoleum and ablution fountain.

456 Cenabi Ahmed Pasha mosque, Ankara, from the north.

457 Cenabi Ahmed Pasha mosque from the west.

The date: 'May the high and low make this building a place of worship', the year 973 (1565–66).'[80]

Some clumsy architectural details of the mosque – the off-centre placement of its gate, the lack of correspondence between its three-domed portico and the composition of its north façade, and the differing window arrangements of its east and west façades – hint that Sinan's plan was executed by an inexperienced royal architect sent from the capital, or by a local one not so familiar with the 'classical' idiom.[81] No such incongruities are to be found in the comparable mosque with a five-domed portico, which the Aleppine architect Cemalüddin built for prince Selim in Karapınar (1560–63/64) to commemorate his victory in nearby Konya (illus. 203–8).[82] The smaller three-domed portico of Cenabi Ahmed Pasha's mosque is in keeping with his deferential disposition as a courtier. Even though as the governor-general of Anatolia he was entitled to five domes, the pasha seems to have chosen a modest plan so as to express his obedient respect for prince Selim: the sanjak governor of Kütahya, subordinate to his jurisdiction.

The local masons who executed the pasha's beige ashlar masonry mosque continued to use some archaic features inherited from the Rum Seljuk architectural tradition, such as the muqarnas-hooded portal and the mihrab framed by rectangular border friezes with carved geometric interlaces (illus. 458, 460). Characteristics associated with the chief architect's style include the layered façades articulated by horizontal mouldings, and the lead-covered hemispherical dome raised on a window-pierced drum with engaged pilasters and paired flying buttresses in the corners. The slender stone minaret with its plain gallery is well proportioned. The relatively large dome (14.4 metres) is supported on eight pointed arches with conch-shell squinches. The white marble minbar and the muezzin's tribune at the northwest corner are plain structures. The painted decorations and inscriptions of the prayer hall no longer preserve their original character.

The mosque was the only one built in Sinan's manner in Ankara during the classical period (illus. 459). Evliya Çelebi says the city had very few mosques with lead-covered domes and attributes that of Cenabi Ahmed Pasha to Sinan, mentioning its bath-house and convent for Mevlevi dervishes, surrounded on all three sides with rose gardens. Also known as Kurşunlu (Leaded) or Yeni (New) Cami, the mosque was located at the edge of the outer castle, which according to Evliya had been created by the same pasha beneath the inner hilltop castle containing a citadel.[83] The pasha's unprecedented 'New Mosque' occupied a highly visible site inside the Kayseri gate of the outer castle, also known as the Cenabi gate. It was located along an urban avenue leading to the commercial district under the citadel hill, crowded by khans and a covered market where Ankara's distinctive textiles of mohair yarn (angora) were marketed.[84]

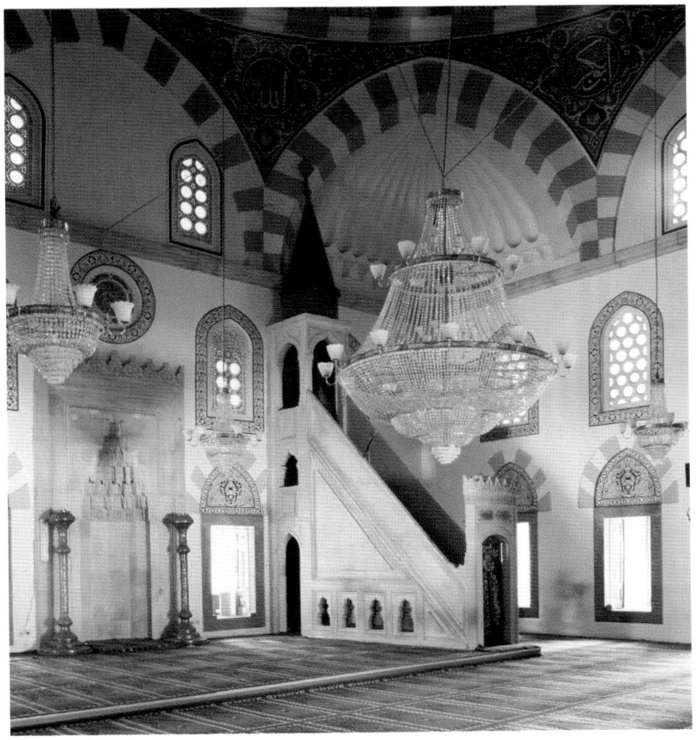

458 Cenabi Ahmed Pasha mosque interior.

459 Anonymous, *View of Ankara*, eighteenth century, oil on canvas.

460 Cenabi Ahmed Pasha mosque, north façade.

The funerary mosque memorialized the modest persona of its patron, a subservient courtier ironically nicknamed 'Majestic'. Its now-lost Mevlevi convent also expressed his sufi piety. Perhaps the convent commemorated Mevlana Celalüddin Rumi's spiritual support, which was believed to have sealed prince Selim's victory in the Konya war, a war in which Cenabi Ahmed Pasha participated.[85] Erected while the victorious crown prince held court in the subordinate sanjak of Kütahya, the pasha's humbly restrained mosque in Ankara paid respect to the future sultan of the empire.

VI. LALA (TÜTÜNSÜZ) HÜSEYİN PASHA

The Albanian-born Lala Hüseyin Pasha commissioned his mosque while he was based in Kütahya as the governor-general of Anatolia (illus. 461, 462). Educated in Sultan Süleyman's palace as a relative of the vizier Pertev Pasha, he was appointed prince Selim's tutor in 1560 (hence his nickname Lala, or tutor). Upon his pupil's accession, the lucky tutor was promoted to governor-general of Anatolia in 1566, the year the capital of that province moved back from Ankara to Kütahya.[86] In 1568–69, he became the governor-general of Konya and Cyprus, subsequently rising to the governor-generalship of Rumelia. He passed away in 1572 as a vizier of the imperial council in Istanbul.[87] According to Mustafa Āli's rather unflattering biographical entry on this undistinguished vizier (also nicknamed Tütünsüz, or avaricious), Hüseyin Pasha was by nature inclined towards injustice and avarice and owed his rank largely to his close relationship with Pertev Pasha and Selim II.[88]

A Turkish waqfiyya dated February 1570, which refers to 'Hüseyin Paşa b. Abdurrahman' as the governor-general of Rumelia, records the endowments he made to his Friday mosque and elementary school in Kütahya. The pasha also constructed an income-producing bath-house, shops, and houses next to his mosque, in whose vicinity he bought vacant plots and gardens that were rented out to create a 'new quarter'.[89] The witnesses of the waqfiyya include Mimar Ahmed, who may have been the architect responsible for executing the mosque on the basis of a plan by Sinan.[90]

The ashlar masonry mosque of beige sandstone is a domed cube, fronted by a five-bay portico facing a tree-planted courtyard with an octagonal marble fountain covered by a modern wooden canopy.[91] Resting on four white marble columns with lozenge capitals and curtain walls at each end that have ogee-arched grilled windows, the portico is crowned by two lateral vaults and three domes in the middle. The unusual muqarnas-galleried cylindrical brick minaret, decorated with bands of locally produced green-glazed tiles arranged in geometric patterns, pays tribute to the regional architectural tradition of Kütahya. The north façade of the mosque has a simple arched gate and lacks the customary pair of flanking mihrabs.

Compared to the roughly contemporary mosque with

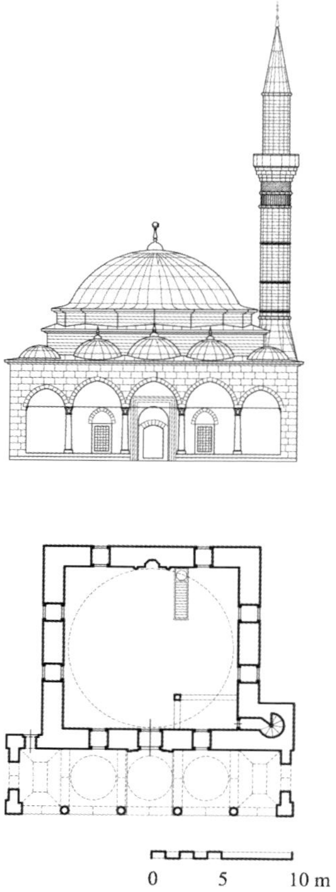

461 Plan and elevation of the Lala Hüseyin Pasha mosque, Kütahya.

462 Lala Hüseyin Pasha mosque, from the northwest.

a triple-domed portico built in Ankara for the previous governor-general of Anatolia, Cenabi Ahmed Pasha (1565–66), the Kütahya mosque boasts a wider façade, but it is crowned by a smaller dome (12.46 metres), raised on pendentives over a sixteen-sided windowless drum without the usual engaged pilasters and flying buttresses in each corner. Unlike its counterpart in Ankara, the mosque in Kütahya has plain, unlayered façades without alternating voussoirs around the arches of its porticoes and its two tiers of windows. Such awkward details as the asymmetrical composition of windows on the lateral walls and the lack of alignment between the gate and mihrab imply that an inexperienced architect executed Sinan's plan. The white marble mihrab without a muqarnas hood and the plain minbar are accompanied by an unassuming wooden muezzin's tribune at the northwest corner of the prayer hall. The extensively renovated mosque has lost its original painted decorations and inscriptions.

In 1671–72 Evliya Çelebi mentions the 'quarter of Hüseyin Pasha' among the neighbourhoods of the 'lower walled suburb' (*aşağı varoş*), which the Ottomans added to the inner and outer castles of Kütahya, perched on a hilltop.[92] The palace of the governor-general of Anatolia was located in the suburban extension of the city, replete with gardens and villas. Evliya praises 'the mosque of Hüseyin Pasha in the new quarter (*yeni maḥalle*)' as an 'extremely charming and illuminated excursion spot' whose courtyard was planted with tall plane-trees. Constructed 'very solidly', this was 'a gracious Friday mosque with a lead-covered superstructure'.[93]

The mosque commemorated Lala Hüseyin Pasha's presence in Kütahya as the governor-general of Anatolia (1566–68/69), prior to which he had resided there as prince Selim's tutor (1561/62–66). Endowed in 1570, when the pasha had graduated to the more prestigious post of governor-general of Rumelia, it celebrated the reestablishment of Kütahya as a provincial capital. Much like the mosque of his pupil in Karapınar and that of his predecessor Cenabi Ahmed Pasha in Ankara (both of them built during the 1560s), Lala Hüseyin Pasha's mosque expressed its patron's rise to fortune after the war of Konya which secured prince Selim's destiny as future sultan. With its new quarter named after the pasha, the mosque memorialized his intimate connection with the prince-turned-sultan and with Kütahya, where he accumulated substantial real estate properties before his eventual rise to the vizierate.

VII. HACI (DOĞANCI) AHMED PASHA

Hacı Ahmed Pasha's mosque complex commemorated his stay in Kayseri as the governor-general of the Karaman (Konya) province (illus. 463, 464).[94] This Muslim-born descendant of the Kızıl Ahmedli branch of the İsfendiyarid dynasty of Kastamonu, extinguished by the Ottomans, was educated in Sultan Süleyman's palace, from which he exited as chief falconer (hence his nickname Doğancı, or falconer). He became the chief of the imperial stables in 1556 and was appointed the governor-general of Karaman in 1558, just before the war of princes. He then served as the governor-general of Rum (Sivas) and of Damascus (*c.* 1563–69). He eventually retired to Istanbul, where as a royal companion he accompanied Selim II and Murad III during hunting parties. Passing away in 1588 as a grizzled man of over a hundred, he was buried in a domed octagonal mausoleum that Sinan built for him in 1576–77

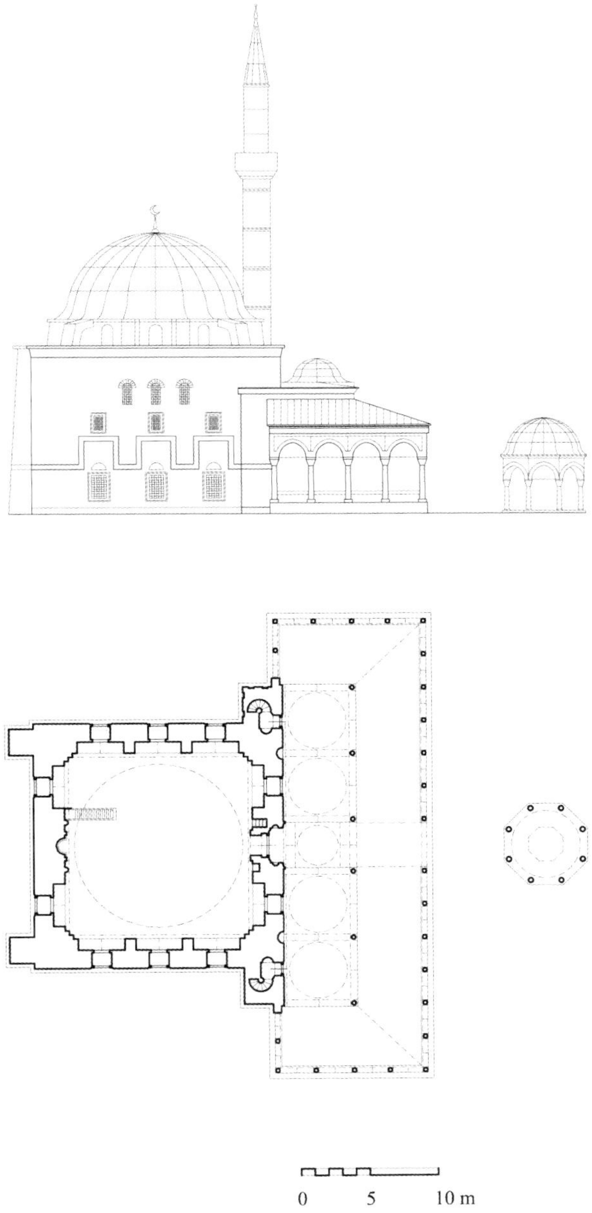

463 Plan and elevation of the Hacı Ahmed Pasha mosque, Kayseri.

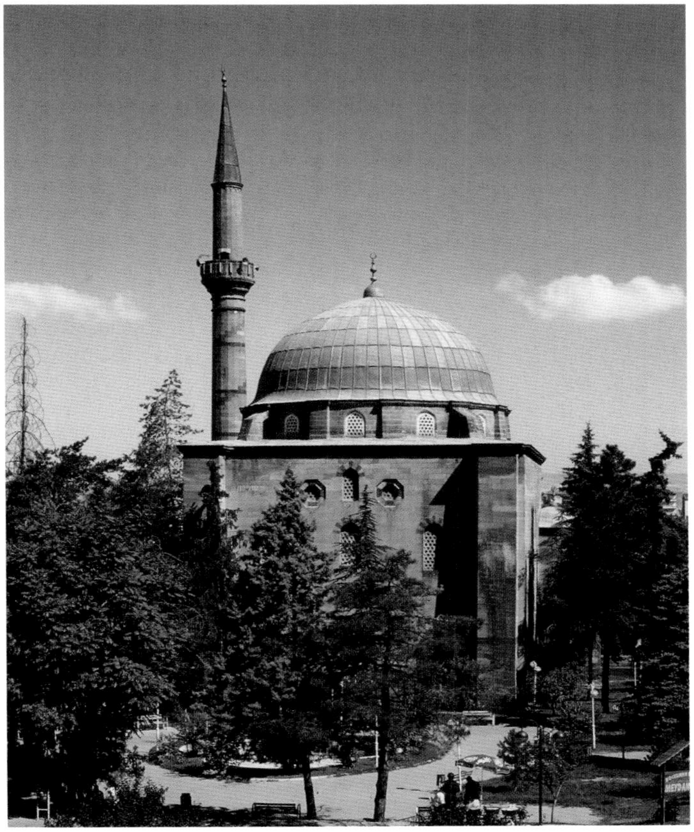

464 Hacı Ahmed Pasha mosque, from the south.

465 Hacı Ahmed Pasha mosque, double portico.

466 Hacı Ahmed Pasha mosque, Kayseri, interior.

next to his palace in Üsküdar.[95] The chief architect's autobiographies also list 'Hacı Pasha's' nearby masjid in Üsküdar.[96]

Mustafa Āli mentions him among the governor-generals of Süleyman's reign, after his more famous relative Şemsi Ahmed Pasha, who commissioned Sinan to build an exquisite little mosque complex next to his palace on the waterfront of Üsküdar. Both Ahmeds were retired governor-generals who spent the last years of their lives in the capital as privileged companions of the sultans:

> Hacı Ahmed Pasha, too, descended from the Kızıl Ahmedlis. For many years he served as the chief stable master. Thereafter, his honour increased as he became the governor-general of Karaman [Konya], and Rum [Sivas], and Damascus. But in falconry he was vastly superior among his peers and admired for his nimble talent. Even when he was over a hundred years old, he continued to accompany each royal hunt. Nevertheless, his avariciousness was self-evident, and during his lifetime his companionship with men of quality was a rarity.[97]

Recorded in 1581–82, the pasha's Turkish waqfiyya refers to him as 'His Highness Ahmed Pasha, the son of the late Mahmud Beg, who became famously known as *el-ḥācc* [Hacı] Ahmed Pasha.' It highlights the retired (*müteḳaʿid*) pasha's distinguished descent from the İsfendiyarid dynasty, whose ancestry allegedly went back to the Prophet's martyred general, Khalid b. al-Walid.[98] It then lists the pious endowments of the pasha, who likely performed the hajj (hence his nickname Hacı) while he governed Damascus: a Friday mosque and a hospice comprising two guest-rooms [*tābḫāne*], a storehouse, a kitchen, and wood storage in Kayseri, accompanied by a khan with thirteen fireplaces where guests were served a bowl of soup and two loaves of bread twice a day; a palace-like elementary school in Kayseri for teaching the Koran to Muslim children; a Friday mosque and elementary school in the town of Akyazı; an elementary school in Bendereğli; another elementary school in the village of Üskübü; a convent (*ḫānḳāh*) near the pasha's palace in Üsküdar, composed of five dormitory rooms for dervishes and their shaykh, with a sixth room functioning as a kitchen; a mausoleum built for the pasha next to that convent; and a conduit that carried water from the village of Bulgurlu to his reservoir (*siḳāye*) in front of the same convent and to a neighbouring public fountain near the masjid of the Emir Ahur (İmrahor) quarter in Üsküdar, where the pasha had endowed his palace, which included two courtyards and a garden with tile-revetted kiosks.[99]

The sites of Hacı Ahmed Pasha's pious endowments in Anatolia and Üsküdar were intimately associated with his noble lineage and career. His convent in Üsküdar is attributed in the *Tuḥfe* to his relative Şemsi Ahmed Pasha, whose waqfiyya does not include a dervish lodge.[100] A biography of Halveti shaykhs also identifies that convent as the '*zāviye* of Şemsi Ahmed Pasha'.[101] Another source referring to it as the 'convent of the İsfendiyar masjid in Üsküdar' implies that it may have been a collective familial foundation of the aristocratic İsfendiyarid clan.[102]

Sinan's autobiographies mention the Friday mosque of 'Hacı Pasha, who retired from the governor-generalship of Damascus' in Kayseri, but omit its now-lost dependencies.[103] An imperial decree handed over to the pasha's man and addressed to the kadi of Kayseri in 1576 permits 'Hacı Ahmed, who retired as governor-general of Damascus', to use his own money to reopen a sealed old gate on the city wall 'near the mosque he is building there'.[104] This suggests that the mosque must have been commissioned soon after the pasha's retirement in the early 1570s. His waqfiyya, dated 1581–82, enumerates the components of his complex, including a garden and a bathhouse he endowed near it, as if they existed at the time.[105] But the chronogram of the foundation inscription of the mosque yields the completion date of 994 (1585–86). Carved in two lines of *thuluth* on a rectangular panel above the arch of the muqarnas-hooded portal, it reads:

> You laid its foundations in the month of Zilhicce,
> I wish that its founder may receive prayers until Doomsday.
>
> I said its date: 'The province has become prosperous,
> Since Ahmed Pasha built his Friday mosque in Kayseri.'[106]

We learn from a petition made to the imperial court in 1646–47 by the administrator of Hacı Ahmed Pasha's waqf in

Kayseri that the patron of the mosque had died before he could make proper provisions for the water supply of his pious foundation, which used the surplus water of the city's public fountains.[107] The administrator found a water conduit abandoned for fifty years and offered to repair it for the needs of the mosque and double bath, promising to conduct the surplus water to public fountains. Identified as 'Hacı Paşa Camii' by Evliya Çelebi, the mosque is the most monumental one commissioned from Sinan by provincial administrators in western and central Anatolia.[108] Either supervised by a royal architect or a local master on the basis of a plan dispatched from the capital, it must have been executed by the skilful masons of the Kayseri region, where the chief architect himself originated.[109]

The mosque's unlayered domed cube of light grey ashlar masonry is preceded by an impressive five-domed double portico carried on two rows of white marble columns with lozenge capitals and decorated with alternating voussoirs and roundels (illus. 465).[110] The prayer hall is extended with recessed alcoves on all four sides that function as hidden buttresses, as in the mosques of Hadım İbrahim Pasha at Silivrikapı (1551), Dukakinzade Mehmed Pasha in Aleppo (1556–65/66), and Behram Pasha in Diyarbakır (*c.* 1564/65–1572/73). Perhaps its plan was inspired by its predecessor in Aleppo, which Hacı Ahmed Pasha may have seen during his governorship of Damascus in the 1560s. The prayer hall is heavily buttressed at each corner, and the qibla wall is cautiously reinforced with an extra pair of external buttresses. The rebuilt multi-faceted, plain-galleried minaret has lost its original character. The three tiers of windows on the tall façades are accentuated with dark grey frames and alternating voussoirs. A continuous course of dark grey stone passes above the ground-level windows, echoing the rhythm of their rectangular frames. The tree-planted forecourt has a central ablution fountain under an elegant lead-covered domed canopy whose arches rest on eight columns with lozenge capitals.

A medium-sized dome (12.3 metres) resting on pendentives crowns the rigidly cubical mass of the mosque. It is raised on a window-pierced stone drum reinforced with engaged pilasters and a flying buttress in each corner. Because the lead-covered dome with an unusually bulbous hemispherical profile was a novelty in Kayseri – a city dominated by pyramidal, conical, or saucer-like domical vaults in stone masonry – the mosque came to be known as Kurşunlu Cami (Leaded Mosque). The original painted decorations and inscriptions of the sober prayer hall, encircled by a U-shaped upper gallery with a projecting balcony above the gate, are no longer extant. The well-proportioned muqarnas-hooded marble mihrab, featuring a panel carved with the standard mihrab verse (3:37), is accompanied by a plain marble minbar (illus. 466). A muezzin's tribune occupies the northwest corner of the prayer hall.

Hacı Ahmed Pasha's mosque is one of two Friday mosques in Kayseri for which Sinan claims authorship in his autobiographies. The other one, commissioned by Çerkes Osman Pasha (d. 1553–54), has disappeared.[111] In the course of the sixteenth century, Kayseri (a sanjak centre subordinate to the province of Karaman) grew into a vigorous commercial hub of interregional trade. By the 1580s it became the second largest Anatolian city after Bursa and a gathering place for merchants seeking to buy cotton cloth, raw cotton, and leather.[112] Built during the peak of prosperity in Kayseri, Hacı Ahmed Pasha's mosque complex is located next to a public park that may have been the garden he endowed in his waqfiyya. It was sited within a gate of the outer castle of the city, along an artery linked to the bustling commercial district at the foot of the inner castle.[113] Unlike the three mosques designed by Sinan in Isparta, Ankara, and Kütahya, the one in Kayseri was once accompanied by a hospice-cum-caravansaray serving the needs of travellers. The complex perpetuated the memory of its patron, a retired governor-general of the province of Karaman: its foundation inscription proudly proclaims that the 'province has become prosperous since Ahmed Pasha built his Friday mosque in Kayseri'.

EASTERN ANATOLIA

The mosque complexes governor-generals commissioned from Sinan in eastern Anatolia represent a collective attempt to Ottomanize with Sunni institutions this contested border region along the Safavid frontier (Map 1). The Ottomanization of the former Akkoyunlu capital, Diyarbakır (Amid), ruled by the Safavids between 1507 and 1515, started soon after the commander Bıyıklı Mehmed Pasha conquered it during Selim I's reign and became its first governor-general (1515–21) holding the honorary title of vizier. Owing its strategic importance to being 'the key to the lands of Iran and the capital of the Akkoyunlu rulers', Diyarbakır became the administrative centre of a pivotal province.[114]

Following Selim I's 'sultanic order', Bıyıklı Mehmed Pasha built there a symbolically charged, prominent Friday mosque to announce the inauguration of Ottoman rule.[115] With its centralized quatrefoil plan featuring four half-domes and its lateral guest-houses (*tabhane*), this single-minaret mosque fronted by a seven-domed portico emulated Istanbul's sultanic mosques on smaller scale (illus. 86). It initiated a hybrid architectural idiom blending Ottoman plan types and forms with local modes of construction and decoration: Mamluk striped masonry and polychrome marble revetments juxtaposed with Persianate tiles.[116] The idiom would have a broader impact beyond Diyarbakır: its variants appeared throughout eastern Anatolia and Syria-Palestine during the age of Sinan. Unlike Bıyıklı Mehmed Pasha's inaugural mosque memorializing the city's conquest, the group of Friday mosques in Diyarbakır attributed to the chief architect are variants of the domed cube scheme. Their omission from the *Tezkiretü'l-ebniye* hints at Sinan's marginal contribution to them, probably in the form of plans sent from or approved in Istanbul.[117]

The Amasya Peace Treaty of 1555 had temporarily fixed shifting Safavid-Ottoman borders, until it was broken under Murad III by a protracted war (1578–90) that resulted in the conquest of Tabriz, Shirvan, and Georgia. The mosques Sinan designed during the 1560s for Lala Mustafa Pasha in Erzurum and Köse Hüsrev Pasha in Van were sited in the capitals of newly established provinces constituting major military bases.[118] Differing from their counterparts in Rumelia and other parts of Anatolia, the chief architect's mosques in the east feature such regional forms as trefoil arches, striped masonry, and locally produced tile revetments that began to imitate those of İznik in the 1560s.[119] These monuments contributed to the visual integration of major cities recently conquered from the Safavids and Mamluks (Erzurum, Van, Diyarbakır, Aleppo, Damascus, Jerusalem) into the Ottoman territorial boundaries.

467 Lala Mustafa Pasha, c. 1570s, watercolour on paper.

The governor-generals of this strategic frontier zone extending from eastern Anatolia into Syria-Palestine were often transferred from one provincial capital to the next, a mobility that encouraged interregional networks and artistic correlations. It was their shared vision, centrally coordinated through Sinan's office, that contributed to the creation of a visually unified belt architecturally marking the newly established eastern boundaries of the empire. More distant provincial capitals characterized by greater administrative autonomy in Azerbayjan, Iraq, Egypt, Yemen, and North Africa remained beyond that visually Ottomanized belt.

VIII. LALA (KARA) MUSTAFA PASHA

Erzurum was an important commercial and military centre on the main thoroughfare for caravans and armies crossing the Ottoman-Safavid border. Dominated by monuments with pyramidal or conical vaults from the Seljuk and Ilkhanid periods, the city was under Akkoyunlu rule for thirty years before Shah Isma'il conquered it in 1502. Added to the Ottoman domains in 1518–19, it became the centre of a province in 1534, provided with a new law code in 1540. Governor-generals resided there from 1548 onwards, and its population considerably increased after the Amasya Peace Treaty of 1555, which revived the caravan trade between Iran and Bursa.[120] Archival documents show that the governor-generals of Erzurum initially imported architects from Diyarbakır until a chief architect was appointed to their own province in 1555.[121]

Lala Mustafa Pasha's Friday mosque in Erzurum was built during his brief tenure as governor-general in 1562-63. Brought up in Süleyman's imperial palace, this Bosnian-born pasha (the younger brother of the deposed vizier Divane Hüsrev Pasha, d. 1545) was appointed the tutor (*lala*) of prince Selim in 1556.[122] He notoriously became the chief originator of intrigues by which the prince came into conflict with his brother Bayezid, culminating with the Konya war of 1559, which turned Lala Mustafa's royal pupil into heir apparent and resulted in Bayezid's execution at the Safavid court in 1562. In 1560 prince Bayezid's supporter Rüstem Pasha discharged the scheming tutor (replaced by Lala Hüseyin) and tried to exile him to the distant Hungarian sanjak of Pozega, but with prince Selim's intervention Lala Mustafa Pasha was appointed the governor-general of Van to monitor prince Bayezid's activities in Iran. During his tenure there, about 300 individuals migrated from Van to join the refugee prince's forces, followed by streams of smaller migrant groups disgruntled with the Ottoman regime. The pasha was ordered to catch and execute such defectors.[123]

Dismissed from his post in 1561, he became the governor-general of Erzurum in 1562 and remained posted there for thirteen months until he was appointed governor-general of Aleppo and then of Damascus. The pasha, who in 1569 was summoned back to the capital as a vizier by his grateful pupil Selim II, attained fame as the conqueror of Cyprus (1570–71). Thereafter he conquered Tbilisi, Shirvan, and Kars for Murad III (1578–79, illus. 40). Returning to the capital from the Safavid front, he passed away in 1580 at over seventy years of age, without realizing his lifelong ambition to become grand vizier (illus. 467). He was buried in an open baldachin-type tomb next to the shrine in Eyüp.[124] Having inherited a vast fortune from his wife, Fatma Hatun, the granddaughter of the Mamluk sultan Qansu al-Ghawri, Lala Mustafa Pasha was married in 1575 to the Ottoman princess Huma Sultan (the daughter of Şehzade Mehmed and the widow of the late vizier Ferhad Pasha). Notwithstanding his reputed stinginess, the wealthy pasha established numerous waqfs: a mosque and elementary school in Erzurum (1563); a mosque, hospice, khan, and school in Qunaytira near Damascus on the road to Jerusalem (1567); another mosque, hospice, and convent at Jenin in Lajjun, between Damascus and Jerusalem (1567); mosques at Nicosia and Famagusta in Cyprus (1579); a mosque, convent, hospice, double caravansaray, and school at Ilgın, near Konya, along the road to

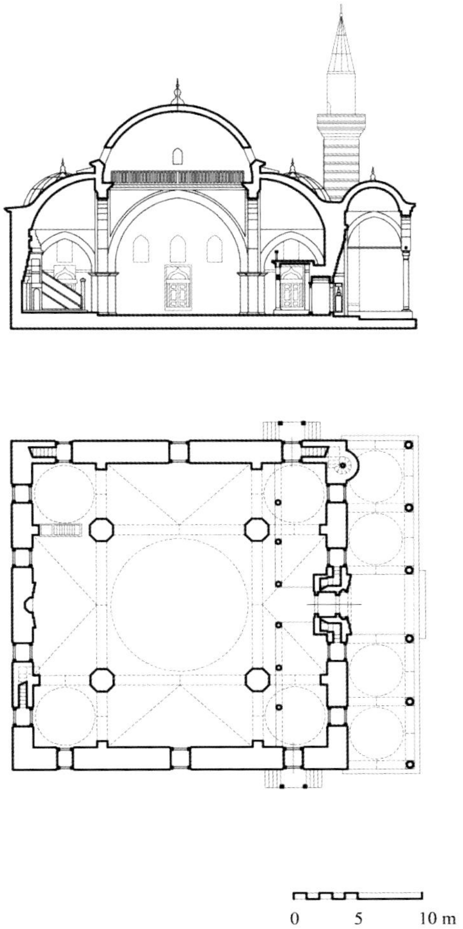

468 Plan and cross-section of the Lala Mustafa Pasha mosque, Erzurum.

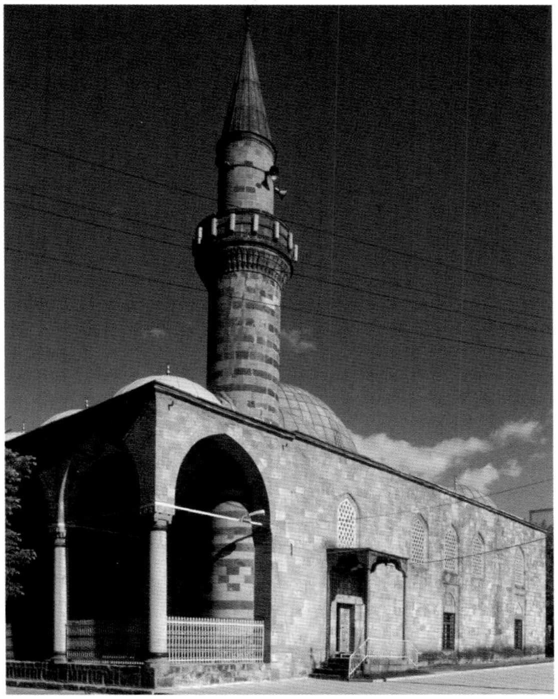

469 Lala Mustafa Pasha mosque, from the northwest.

Cyprus (1577); two mosques in Tbilisi and Kars (1579, illus. 49, 50), and a water dispenser in Medina.[125]

Sinan's autobiographies mention only the Friday mosque in Erzurum, which was completed in 970 (1562–63) according to its Arabic foundation inscription (illus. 468, 469).[126] The inscription is carved in three lines of *thuluth* in a highly unusual location, above the muqarnas-hooded mihrab:

> This Friday mosque was built to request the mercy of the Merciful God, in the days of the shadow of the All-Knowing God, Sultan Süleyman Khan b. Sultan Selim Khan,
>
> By Mustafa Pasha b. Abdülmukim, the tutor of the sultan's son Selim, God perpetuate his [Selim's] shadow with the help of eternal favour.
>
> May God accept the charity of its builder with His universal generosity; and its date was divinely inspired: 'A masjid founded upon piety (9:108)', the year 970 (1562–63).[127]

An Arabic waqfiyya registered in October 1563 refers to the pasha as the governor-general of Erzurum and explains that he built a single-minaret Friday mosque with an ablution fountain in its courtyard next to the residence that Sultan Süleyman had constructed for governor-generals. The mosque was accompanied by an elementary school that replaced a ruined pre-Ottoman structure known as the Kaʿba masjid.[128] Omitted from Sinan's autobiographies, the elementary school, built with elaborately carved reused stones and located at the west side of the mosque, was demolished in 1983. Its Turkish foundation inscription explained that Lala Mustafa Pasha had rebuilt the ornate Kaʿba masjid as a beautifully decorated school for children in 969 (1562).[129]

The pasha endowed his Friday mosque, located in the outer castle of Erzurum, with properties legally bought from fiefholders and Georgian amirs in accordance with a permit he obtained from the sultan in May 1563. His income-producing endowments in Erzurum included twenty-six shops built in two parallel rows next to the mosque courtyard, nearby houses, as well as ten shops and ten storehouses near the governor-general's residence. He also endowed a neighbouring princely dwelling, known as 'the palace' (*sārāy*), which Sultan Süleyman had built for the heir-apparent (*velīʿahd*) prince Selim. For his mosque, the pasha endowed six large Korans with their own lecterns, two big copper candle-holders, light fixtures, fourteen large carpets, two prayer carpets to be hung at the mihrab during religious holidays (one of them depicting the Kaʿba), and seven kilims with mihrab designs. An appendix dated 1578 adds new endowments, mostly villages in Georgia that the pasha conquered as the commander of Murad III's Safavid campaign that year,

470 Lala Mustafa Pasha mosque, Erzurum, interior.

471 Lala Mustafa Pasha mosque, window lunette with underglaze tiles.

when the army camped in Erzurum. The waqf would be administered by the sons of the founder after his demise and overseen by the governor-generals of Erzurum.[130]

Prince Selim must have stayed at the Erzurum palace in 1559, when he and the vizier Sokollu pursued his fleeing brother Bayezid over the Safavid border. In the fall of that year, Selim passed from Erzurum to Diyarbakır and Aleppo before returning to his sanjak at Konya in December.[131] It is unclear how his palace was acquired by his former tutor. By building his own mosque next to it, Lala Mustafa Pasha may have intended to celebrate Selim's confirmed status as heir-apparent following Bayezid's execution in July 1562. Moreover, the location of the mosque next to the governor-general's residence broadcast the ambitious pasha's official image as a servant of the state and religion.

The ashlar masonry mosque of grey basalt is crowned by a small dome (10.56 metres) resting on an octagonal drum with paired flying buttresses in each corner. Raised on pendentives, the central dome is carried on four octagonal piers; it is surrounded by four cradle vaults, with four tiny domes tucked in the corners. The quatrefoil-plan prayer hall is fronted by a five-domed portico of the same height, carried on columns with muqarnas capitals. The configuration of inner space is hardly reflected on the unlayered outer façades of the mosque, whose low domical superstructure is not externally articulated. Its plan, conspicuously deviating from the standard layout of Sinan's generic provincial domed cubes, is a simpler variant of Bıyıklı Mehmed Pasha's mosque in Diyarbakır, whose *tābḫānes* it leaves out (illus. 86). Its simple façades with few windows arranged in two tiers, and its unelevated domical superstructure, lacking window-pierced drums, signal the work of a local architect who apparently executed a design prepared by Sinan. The muqarnas-galleried, disproportionately short and thick cylindrical minaret decorated with bands of red and dark grey stone is uncustomarily inserted into the northwest corner of the portico. Old photographs show that the portico was once extended on three sides by overhanging eaves carried on wooden struts (removed in 1962).[132]

The muqarnas-hooded portal at the centre of the north façade is complemented by two gates with staircases at the northeast and northwest corners of the lateral façades. Inside the prayer hall, the plain muqarnas-hooded stone mihrab is accompanied by a modern wooden minbar and muezzin's tribune (illus. 470). An upper gallery, resting on arches with six marble columns, extends along the anti-qibla wall. The tribune for pashas (*paşa mahfili*) at the southwest corner was once reached from a private gate (blocked during recent repairs) by a staircase built into the wall, an unusual feature recalling the imperial tribunes of sultanic mosques.[133]

The arched lunettes of the lateral gates and all windows were decorated both internally and externally with twenty-eight matching underglaze-painted tile panels. Those outside the mosque have largely disappeared, but most of the ones inside the prayer hall are preserved.[134] The centre of each lunette has a horizontal cartouche scalloped at both ends and filled with white inscriptions in monumental *thuluth* script against a dark blue background decorated with designs in blue, turquoise, red, and white. The panels are densely covered with small floral rosettes, palmettes, *saz* leaves, and vegetal scrolls (illus. 471). Together with other tiles from the second half of the sixteenth century in eastern Anatolia, they form a distinct group, characterized by 'a brackish red, strident new blue, crackled glaze and overcrowded designs'.[135] The tiles of Lala Mustafa Pasha's mosque may have been produced in Diyarbakır, which inspired the quatrefoil plan of the mosque, but as Julian Raby suggests, the potters could also have been sent from İznik to carry out this commission in Erzurum. He speculates that the 'itinerant İznik potters may then have made their way to the provincial capital of Diyarbakır and there either have been assimilated into the already existing local industry or set up their own workshop'.[136] Whatever their provenance, the tiles in Erzurum are closely related to the square and rectangular tiles produced in Diyarbakır after the 1560s in the manner of İznik.

The inscriptions of the tilework lunettes combine Koranic verses with hadith. The pair on the north façade spells out the Basmala and the profession of faith.[137] Inside the prayer hall, the window lunettes of the anti-qibla wall and the lunettes of the lateral gates are inscribed with hadith: 'The messenger of God, on him be peace, said: Trade (handicraft) protects man from impoverishment; the messenger has spoken the truth.' 'The messenger of God, God bless him and grant him salvation, said: Whoever builds a masjid for God, God will build an abode for him in paradise.' 'The messenger of God, on him be peace, said: Prayer is the pillar of religion and whoever performs it erects (the pillar of) religion and whoever destroys it pulls down; the messenger has spoken the truth.'[138]

Following a counter-clockwise direction, the remaining window lunettes quote Koranic verses that recommend congregational prayers and other duties of rightly guided orthodox believers: a theme particularly appropriate for a city ruled until recently by the Shiʿi Safavids. Starting with the Basmala, the panels on the west wall cite a verse from the Baqara sura: 'Unto Allah belong the East and the West, and whithersoever ye turn, there is Allah's countenance. Lo! Allah is All-Embracing, All-Knowing (2:115).'[139] The lunettes of the qibla wall also begin with the Basmala and quote fragmentary verses from the same sura (2:144, 238) that urge the congregation to turn toward the qibla and to perform the congregational prayers. Lunettes on the east wall start with the Basmala and cite a verse, which outlines the basic duties of orthodox believers (9:18). Painted roundels bearing the names of Allah, Muhammad, Abu Bakr, and ʿUmar decorate the dome pendentives; curiously the names of Hasan and Husayn are omitted. The dome itself is inscribed with a verse rotated four times, which promises God's reward to those with righteous conduct (17:84).[140]

Evliya Çelebi attributes the mosque to Sinan and describes its location along an avenue near the governor's palace (*paşa sarayı*), in front of which extended a public square for polo games:

> It was built by Süleyman Khan's vizier Lala Mustafa Pasha with a lofty dome in the manner (*ṭarz*) of Istanbul and its whole edifice is covered by pure lead. Its length and width are eighty-eight feet. Its mihrab, minbar, and muezzin's tribune are of plain beauty (*sāde güzeli*). Its interior lacks noteworthy pendants. It has external prayer platforms (*ṭaşra ṣoffa*), but its courtyard is narrow.[141]

The mosque, which introduced a provincial variant of Sinan's 'classical' idiom to Erzurum, proclaimed its patron's identity as a privileged governor-general who had once been the crown prince Selim's tutor. Its elaborate plan resonates not only with the victory mosque of Bıyıklı Mehmed Pasha in Diyarbakır, but also with the sultanic mosque of the heir-apparent Şehzade Mehmed in the capital. It differs significantly from the pasha's later mosques along such road-stations as Ilgın and Qunaytira, designed as generic domed cubes and accompanied by extensive complexes addressing the needs of travellers. The more ambitious urban mosque adjacent to the governor's palace in Erzurum, the only prestige monument the pasha commissioned from Sinan, expressed his intimate affiliation with the sultan-to-be. With its foundation inscription expressing the hope that God eternally perpetuate the prince's fortune, this assertive monument hints at Lala Mustafa Pasha's aspiration to attain the grand vizierate during the reign of his royal pupil. As his critical personal secretary Mustafa Āli professed, however, the covetous pasha became the apt subject of the saying: 'The inordinately greedy are deprived!'[142]

IX. KÖSE HÜSREV PASHA

Delegates from the fortified city of Van had surrendered its keys during the siege of Tabriz in 1534, but as soon as Süleyman's army withdrew the Safavids reoccupied it. The city became the capital of a strategic Ottoman province when it surrendered a second time, in 1548. Köse Hüsrev Pasha, who commissioned Sinan to design a mosque and madrasa in Van, had been brought up in the imperial palace. After serving as the sanjak governor of Anteb (Ayntab) and Pasin (Erzurum), he became the governor-general of Van in 1561. He was one of those sent on a sensitive mission to Qazvin in 1562 to oversee the execution of prince Bayezid and his sons. After their elimination, he returned to Van, where he intermittently served as governor-general for about a decade. In the interim periods he was transferred to such provinces as Damascus, Diyarbakır, Erzurum, and Aleppo. While serving as governor-general of Diyarbakır in the Safavid campaign of 1587, he was martyred and buried in a posthumously built mausoleum adjacent to his mosque in Van (illus. 472, 473).[143]

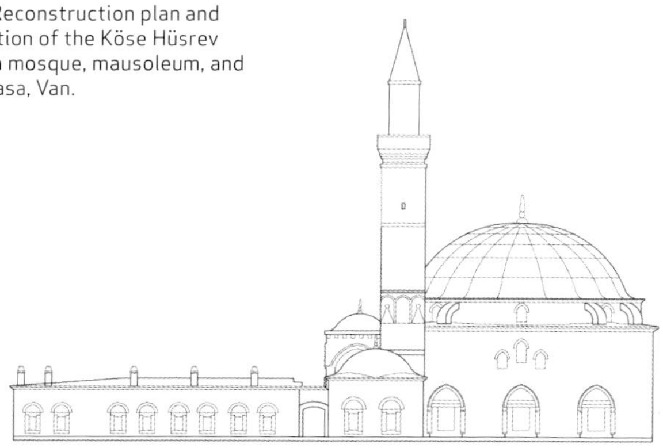

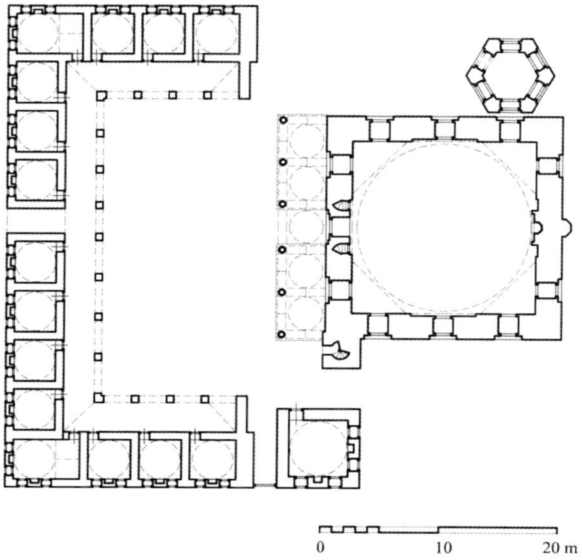

472 Reconstruction plan and elevation of the Köse Hüsrev Pasha mosque, mausoleum, and madrasa, Van.

According to Mustafa Āli, Köse Hüsrev Pasha did not deserve the rank of *beglerbegi* because he was addicted to wine and opium. However, Selaniki eulogizes the pasha as 'unequalled in sagacity and shrewdness', for he was 'an expert who knew the inner truth of *ḳızılbaş* affairs in the victorious frontier.' Having succeeded in assuring the alliance with Shah Tahmasp's court during the 'prince Bayezid affair', he was 'wise, a prudent counsellor, and a noble person capable of being in charge of matters of state and religion'.[144] Köse Hüsrev Pasha's mosque complex must have been a potent signifier of the Sunni Ottoman regime in Van, whose governor-generals received orders during the 1560s to keep under surveillance the *ḳızılbaş* populations settled in their province.[145]

The Friday mosque and madrasa, mentioned only in the *Tuhfe*,[146] belonged to a larger complex built while the pasha reinforced the outer walls of the city. On 24 November 1568 he was ordered to strengthen the walls of Van's mudbrick outer castle (*varoş ḥiṣari*) with stone revetments, using the help of soldiers and

473 Köse Hüsrev Pasha mosque and mausoleum.

notables. The costs of this project, completed in 1572, were covered by the treasury of Diyarbakır.[147] An earlier imperial decree addressed to the governor-general and sanjak governor of Van on 10 October 1566 commanded them to prepare timber and building materials for the Friday mosque and bath-house whose construction had been 'ordered by imperial decree'.[148]

The Persian foundation inscription of the mosque, addressing the predominantly Persian-speaking population of Van, gives the completion date of 1567–68. Signed by the calligrapher Yusuf, it features two lines of *thuluth* carved on a rectangular marble panel under the pointed arch of the mosque gate:

> When His Majesty, the pasha with the power of Khusraw [Hüsrev]
> Built such a lofty paradise like this,
>
> A[n unseen] voice said its date:
> 'He built a house for you pious ones' [968 (1567–68)].[149]

The martyred pasha's mausoleum, attached to the southeast corner of his mosque, was built posthumously; it communicates with the prayer hall by means of a window converted into a gate. The Turkish inscription on its north gate gives the date 996 (1587–88), names an architect from Mardin (a sanjak of Diyarbakır) called Şaban b. Abdullah, and ends with the phrase: 'Glory to God, his abode became paradise.' The hexagonal mausoleum of white stone, crowned by a twelve-sided pyramidal vault, follows the model of medieval east Anatolian tomb towers (*kümbet*). Its rectangular windows and gates, framed by trilobed arches resting on twin colonettes, are elegantly carved with geometric designs and muqarnas friezes.[150]

A seventeenth-century topographic miniature of Van depicts the inner hilltop castle for the janissary garrison and the outer castle below it (illus. 474). The inner castle has a domed mosque with one minaret, adjacent to the janissary agha's residence.

474 Map of Van, seventeenth century: 1. Citadel mosque of Sultan Süleyman. 2. Residence of the janissary agha. 3. Hüsrev Pasha mosque. 4. Governor-general's palace. 5. Pasha gate. 6. Middle gate.

Known today as the Castle Mosque, or Kale Camii, it was built for Sultan Süleyman in 1534. It is crossed out in the *Tuhfe*, where it was initially listed as a work of Sinan. This pre-Ottoman mosque may have been remodelled by him while he accompanied the sultan's army that year. The same miniature depicts Köse Hüsrev Pasha's mosque next to the governor-general's palace (Paşa Sarayı) between the Pasha Gate (Paşa Kapısı) and the Middle Gate (Orta Kapı). It is identified as the 'Leaded Noble Friday Mosque' (*ḳurşunlu cāmiʿ-i şerīfdür*).[151]

The mosque, whose dome is no longer covered with lead, is known today as Kurşunlu Cami (Leaded Mosque), or Hüsreviye. An undated waqfiyya mentions the mosque; its courtyard surrounded by a madrasa with twelve chambers and a classroom; a hospice (*ʿimāret*) comprising a kitchen, pantry, stable, wood storage, and guest-rooms (*tābḫāneler*); and an elementary school adjacent to the guest-rooms. The courtyards of the mosque and hospice were provided with fountains to which water was brought by a channel. At the school poor children would be taught the Koran and the madrasa professor had to subscribe to the Hanefi rite. The complex was endowed with 100,000 aspers, plots of land, and many commercial properties built in its neighborhood: shops, a double caravansaray, and a double bath. The waqf administrator would be Hüsrev Pasha himself, and thereafter his children.[152] A waqf register dated 1571 also lists a convent (*zāviye*) entrusted to a shaykh and ten dervishes, probably none other than the hospice-cum-guest-house.[153] Today only the mosque, mausoleum, and dilapidated double bath built at a distance are extant. Damaged by a fire in 1915, the complex was partially restored between 1967 and 1983; it has been in the process of excavation and renovation since 1996. The demolished U-shaped madrasa around the mosque forecourt has been reconstructed on the basis of old photographs and recent excavations that uncovered the hospice at its north side. The ruins of the caravansaray at the east side are waiting to be excavated.[154]

Kuran speculates that the mosque and madrasa designed by Sinan must have been built either by a royal architect sent from the capital or by a local master. Others have suggested that these buildings may have been executed by the non-Muslim city architect of Van, Selman, who is mentioned in a decree dated 1556.[155] The mosque introduced a regional variant of the chief architect's style to Van with the unlayered massing of its domed cube fronted by a no-longer-extant, five-domed portico. The conical hood of its muqarnas-galleried, thick cylindrical minaret was rebuilt in 1997. The striped masonry fabric of the mosque finds a parallel in such neighbouring provincial capitals as Diyarbakır, Aleppo, and Damascus. The polychrome façades have only a single tier of windows with blind-arched lunettes, surmounted in the middle by a group of three small upper windows. The walls are composed of alternating courses of red and white stone up to the first tier of windows, with the rest in black and white. All three colours are mixed in the minaret. The relatively low building is crowned by a large hemispherical dome (14.84 metres) resting on squinches above a polygonal stone drum pierced with windows and reinforced by sixteen flying buttresses, an unusually large number. Inside the prayer hall the eight pointed arches that carry the dome descend close to the ground level.

The north façade has an arched central gate with no muqarnas hood. It is flanked by two windows and lacks the customary paired mihrabs. On the qibla wall, the muqarnas-hooded mihrab (blown up with dynamite by treasure hunters in 1992) is externally expressed as a projection with a conical cap. The damaged mihrab is framed by a trefoil arch resting on twin colonettes, within a rectangular outer frame bordered by a muqarnas frieze. The minbar and the painted decorations of the prayer hall have vanished. The tile revetments of the dadoes, recalling those of Diyarbakır mosques, are thought to have been removed during the Russian occupation. Some of the hexagonal underglaze tile fragments, preserved in the Van museum, are identical in design to those of the Bıyıklı Mehmed Pasha and Çerkes İskender Pasha mosques in Diyarbakır (discussed below), but they use a different colour scheme: instead of light-purple and blue, the potters have introduced a combination of indigo blue, emerald green, and greenish yellow. Other fragments with cloud bands, stems, and floral motifs in white against a dark blue ground (with some touches of light blue) resemble the rectangular border tiles of Behram Pasha's mosque in Diyarbakır. The tiles were likely produced in Diyarbakır, the province from which Şaban of Mardin, the architect of Köse Hüsrev Pasha's mausoleum, originated.[156]

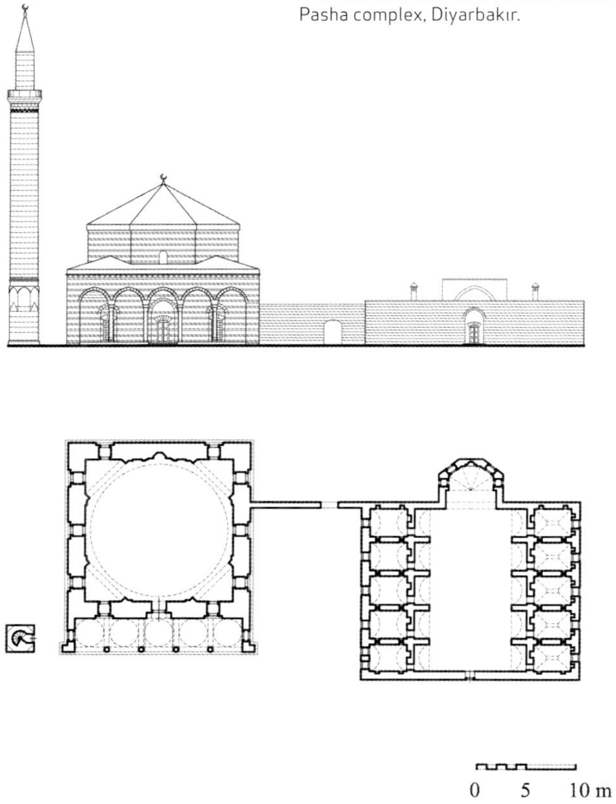

475 Plan and elevation of the Hadım Ali Pasha complex, Diyarbakır.

476 Hadım Ali Pasha mosque, from the north.

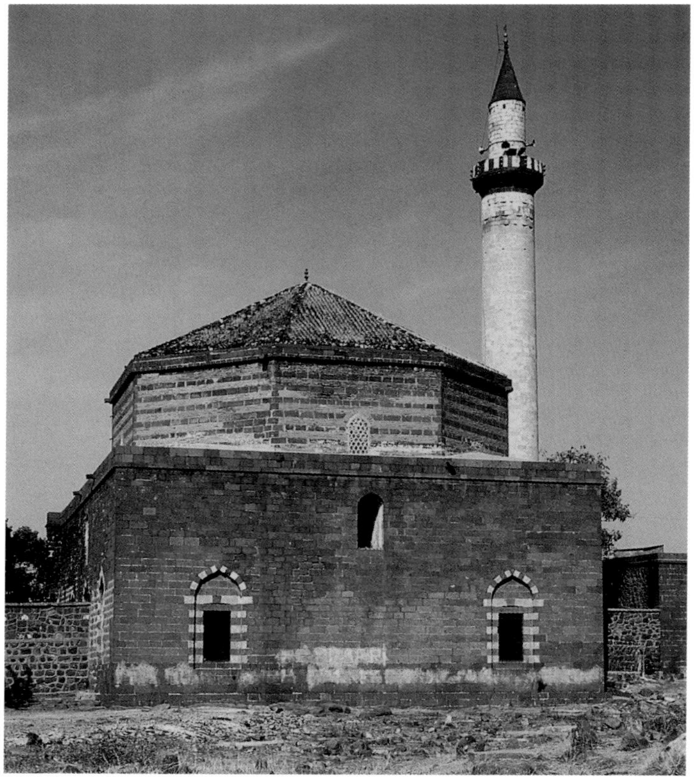

477 Hadım Ali Pasha mosque, from the south.

Evliya Çelebi mentions other waqfs of the pasha in eastern Anatolia and locates his mosque in Van next to the governor-general's palace:[157]

> It was built by one of Sultan Süleyman Khan's viziers, Koca Hüsrev Pasha, who has a covered bazaar and a market-place of masonry in Bitlis and a colossal khan in the plain of Rahva. He built this charming Friday mosque while he was governing Van. It is a light-filled mosque, the domes of which are completely covered with indigo-colored lead. Its central dome is extremely artistic. The finials gilt with pure gold dazzle one's eyes when the world-illuminating sun shines on them. Inside the mosque are precious and artistic pendants. The windows on its four sides are extremely ornate, fitted with crystal and Murano glass. Its mihrab, minbar, and muezzin's tribune are very skilfully executed. It has a tall minaret in the manner (*ṭarz*) of Istanbul. All around its courtyard are madrasa cells. Because this illuminated mosque is inside the city's Middle Gate, near the palace of pashas (*paşa sarayı*), the pashas frequent it every Friday. In the city of Van there is no other lead-covered building than this one.'[158]

Like Lala Mustafa Pasha's mosque in Erzurum, then, that of Köse Hüsrev Pasha represented its patron's official identity by its siting. The mosque-centred complex, the first of its kind in Ottoman-ruled Van, represented an attempt to promote Sunni orthodoxy and urban development in a provincial capital still subject to the Shiʿi propaganda of Safavid agents.

X. HADIM ALİ PASHA

The Friday mosque and madrasa complex of Hadım (Eunuch) Ali Pasha, the first in a series of four extant complexes attributed to Sinan in Diyarbakır, is sited at the periphery of the city at the southwest corner of the outer castle, between the Mardin and

478 Hadım Ali Pasha mosque, Diyarbakır, interior.

Urfa gates.[159] Its eunuch founder, originally from Janina in Albania, served as governor-general in various provinces, although the exact dates of his tenure have yet to be established and are approximate here: Maraş (1540), Diyarbakır (1541–44), Erzurum (1544–48), Buda (1551–52), Diyarbakır (1553), Karaman (Konya, 1554), Buda (1556–57), Timisvár (1557–59), and Egypt (1559–60/61). He passed away at Cairo in 1560–61 and was buried there at the Qarafa cemetery.[160] Mustafa Āli portrays the thrifty pasha, known for his military exploits, as follows:

> He was just, generous, kind, merciful, moderate in behaviour, perfect in avoiding injustice and oppression, fully in command of his office, and a saint of high respect. When he passed away while he possessed the province of Egypt, only 2,000 gold coins were found in his treasury, which signalled his integrity and resignation (to the Divine will).'[161]

The dependencies of Hadım Ali Pasha's mosque in Diyarbakır included a commercial bath-house (now-lost) and a domeless madrasa with a projecting iwan whose plan conforms to local traditions.[162] The mosque and madrasa are cited in the *Tuhfe* (illus. 475).[163] Unlike the typically Ottoman mosque with a quatrefoil plan built near the inner castle of Diyarbakır by its first governor-general, Bıyıklı Mehmed Pasha, that of Hadım Ali Pasha is a modest structure perpetuating regional traditions of construction. It lacks a foundation inscription and is generally dated to 1534–37 because its founder is believed to have been based in Diyarbakır at that time.[164] However, primary sources reveal his presence there in the early 1540s, a date more compatible with Sinan's tenure as chief architect.[165]

The unassuming mosque is a domed cube fronted by a five-bay portico (illus. 476, 477). Its hemispherical dome, raised on an unusually tall octagonal drum of striped masonry with alternating courses of brick and black stone (basalt) is hidden under a pyramidal outer shell, as are the five domes of its portico. Its pyramidal superstructure resembles that of the Shaykh Safa mosque, a late-fifteenth-century Akkoyunlu monument renovated under Ottoman rule in 1531 by a local architect from Diyarbakır, Ustad Ahmed al-Amidi. The starkly cubical walls of Hadım Ali Pasha's ashlar masonry mosque feature only a few windows arranged in two tiers. Its portico, built of alternating courses of black and white stone, is carried on white stone columns with plain capitals. The north façade with an arched central gate lacks the customary paired mihrabs. The octagonal ablution fountain in the forecourt has been renovated with a pyramidal-roofed canopy. The once free-standing cylindrical minaret of white stone has a plain gallery.

The large dome (14.4 metres) covering the prayer hall is raised on squinches above eight pointed arches that descend close to the ground level, as in the Shaykh Safa mosque (illus. 478). The mihrab with its muqarnas hood framed by a trefoil arch (as in Bıyıklı Mehmed Pasha's mosque) is carved with painted geometric patterns composed of octagons interlocking with eight-pointed stars. The ornate wooden minbar, also with geometric designs, has a conical cap in the Ottoman manner. The prayer hall preserves the locally produced tile revetments of its dadoes, which run around the four walls, a characteristic of mosques in Diyarbakır.

The main field of hexagonal tiles has geometric patterns composed of hexagons interlocking with six-pointed stars, rendered in black contour lines filled with ultramarine blue, turquoise, and white. These underglaze-painted tiles closely mimic their *cuerda seca* predecessors in the Shaykh Safa mosque, which also includes a few experimental underglaze examples. The rectangular border tiles are identical to those in the Shaykh Safa and Bıyıklı Mehmed Pasha mosques: their rosettes, cloud bands, and scrolling stems are painted in black against a pale blue background (a few are blue on white).[166] The architectural modesty of Hadım Ali Pasha's mosque complex, reflecting the persistence of local traditions of construction and decoration, can perhaps be attributed to the proverbial frugality of its patron. If Sinan did design its plan, the architect who executed it must have been more familiar with the regional Akkoyunlu building tradition than with the metropolitan style of Istanbul.

XI. ÇERKES İSKENDER PASHA

Çerkes (Circassian) İskender Pasha's Friday mosque goes one step further in Ottomanizing the local building tradition of Diyarbakır (illus. 479, 480). This Circassian-born governor-general was descended from a noble family of amirs belonging to the Kabartay tribe, settled north of the Caspian Sea and subordinate to the Kazan Khanate. When his father was killed during a Muscovite raid, he sought refuge in the Ottoman domains, together with his uncle Amir Süleyman Beg, his mother, and his siblings.[167]

İskender joined the household of Divane Hüsrev Pasha, with whom he moved from Karaman to Diyarbakır in 1521 while the latter served there as governor-general. After holding various posts, he became the joint finance minister of Diyarbakır,

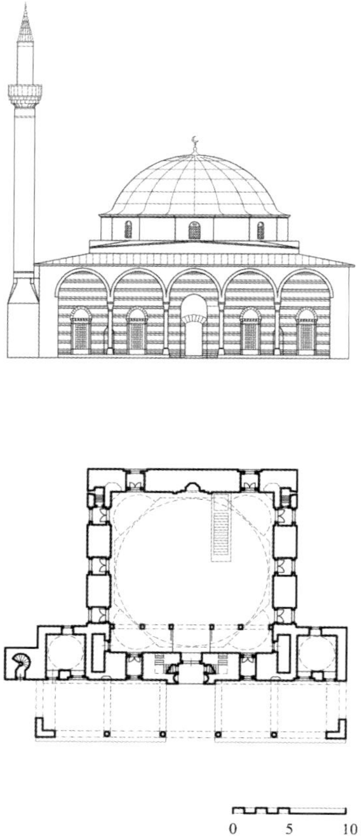

479 Plan and elevation of the Çerkes İskender Pasha mosque, Diyarbakır.

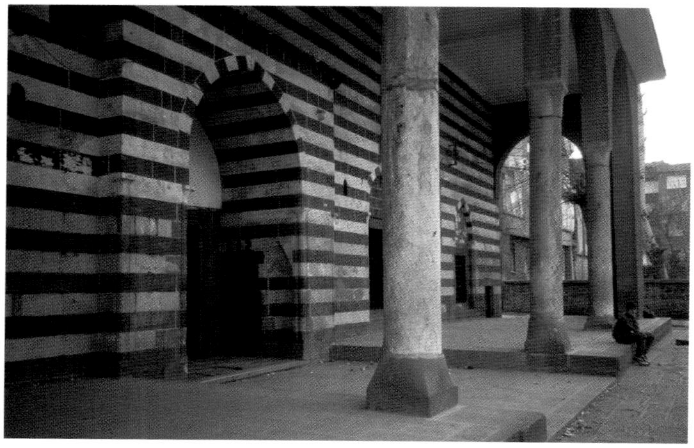

480 Çerkes İskender Pasha mosque, north façade.

Damascus, and Aleppo in 1546, and was called to the capital as the finance minister of Anatolia the following year. In 1548 he was bold enough to accept the post of governor-general in Van, a border city reconquered from the Safavids, which was 'so dreadful' that nobody else wanted to remain confined there.[168] He conquered the castle of Khoy in Iran the same year and raided Erivan the next. In 1551 he became governor-general of Erzurum, where he fought valorously against Georgians allied with the Safavid forces and conquered the castle of Ardanuç. To seek revenge, Shah Tahmasp sent an army to Erzurum under the command of his son, İsma'il Mirza. Outnumbered by Safavid forces, the pasha lost the battle, and many of his men and relatives died, including his uncle Amir Süleyman.[169]

As a reward for bravely defending the castle of Erzurum, Çerkes İskender Pasha was promoted governor-general of Diyarbakır, a post he held for fourteen years (*c.* 1551–65). He subsequently became the governor-general of Baghdad (1566) and of Egypt (1569). Deposed within two years from this last post, he returned to Istanbul, where he died in 1571.[170] According to Mustafa Āli, the Circassian pasha was intelligent, venerable, mature, fear-inspiring, and courageous. Fluent in Arabic and Persian, he sought the company of scholars and poets, being particularly fond of discussions related to sufism and jusrisprudence. Always inclined toward justice, mercy, and kindness, this 'Alexander of the age' and 'Aristotle of the epoch' fully deserved the rank of pasha, being a man of the sword and a man of the pen.[171]

Çerkes İskender Pasha's mosque in Diyarbakır lacks a foundation inscription. Its endowments are recorded in an Arabic waqfiyya registered in 1565, at the end of his tenure there, but the mosque is generally dated by scholars to 1551, on the basis of local tradition.[172] The pasha's endowment deed lists his pious foundations in Van, Erzurum, and Diyarbakır, the three provincial capitals where he governed between 1548 and 1565.[173] The no-longer-extant madrasa-cum-masjid he commissioned from Sinan in Van may have been inspired by the one that his master Divane Hüsrev Pasha had built in Diyarbakır during the 1520s.[174] The waqfiyya also refers to the extant Friday mosque with a hipped roof renovated by İskender Pasha at the castle of Ardanuç, an Akkoyunlu monument whose pre-existing endowments he amplified with new ones. He endowed one asper a day for a Koran reader at that mosque for the soul of his late uncle, Amir Sulayman, who had been martyred by the Safavids and was buried in an adjoining mausoleum.[175] Another Friday mosque, accompanied by a bath-house, was built by the pasha in the castle of Ahlat, near Lake Van, conquered in 1548. Omitted from Sinan's autobiographies, this ashlar masonry mosque is a domed cube with a three-bay portico. The Persian foundation inscription on its gate is dated 972 (1564–65); the two inscriptions on its minaret give the date 978 (1570) and identify its builder as the chief architect of Ahlat.[176]

481 Çerkes İskender Pasha mosque, Diyarbakır, interior.

The waqfiyya is imbued with a zeal to implant Sunni orthodoxy in the eastern provinces of the empire. It specifies that the preachers and imams of the pasha's Friday mosque in Diyarbakır should subscribe to the Hanefi rite, like the imam and professor of his madrasa-cum-masjid in Van. Lamenting the Safavid destruction of many madrasas and mosques in the region, the endowment deed prays that God help the conquest of lands in Iran. Çerkes İskender Pasha endowed the prestige mosque he commissioned from Sinan in Diyarbakır with two bath-houses featuring their own water channels, with shops and rental rooms, and mills outside the city. Properties endowed near the mosque at the quarter of Bab al-Jabal (Mountain Gate) included a bath-house with four adjacent shops, the founder's own residence, a garden surrounding the mosque on three sides (east, south, and west), and three large residences with an empty plot at the qibla and west sides of the mosque.[177]

The bath-house near the mosque was demolished after a fire in 1912, but the pasha's neighbouring residence is partially extant.[178] Evliya Çelebi claims that the bath-house had been designed by the patron himself, as he was skilled in the 'science of architecture'.[179] He may also have contributed to the distinctive layout of his mosque, which reflects his sufi bent and his fondness for scholars. The waqfiyya explains that the quadrangular structure featured a lofty single dome, a minaret 'devoid of defect', a lead-covered domical portico with seven arches and windows, two rooms at the northeast and northwest corners 'for the destitute among men of knowledge and learning', an octagonal pool at the north surrounded by iron lattices and ablution spouts, and latrines at the west, featuring a central iwan for ablutions.[180]

The mosque is an unlayered domed cube with two lateral cells functioning as *tābḫānes* for needy scholars and dervishes. It is fronted by a five-bay portico resting on white marble columns with plain capitals; the portico domes mentioned in the waqfiyya have been replaced by a flat concrete roof. The lateral guest-rooms recall those of the founder's former master, Divane Hüsrev Pasha, in Aleppo (*c.* 1546–47), also attributed to Sinan.[181] There is in addition a local precedent for such guest-rooms in Diyarbakır itself in the mosque of Bıyıklı Mehmed Pasha (illus. 86). Unlike the detached guest-rooms with external gates, the unusual narrow rectangular cells at the northeast and northwest corners of İskender Pasha's mosque communicate with the prayer hall; they can perhaps be identified as the 'secluded' spaces for Koran chanters mentioned in the waqfiyya. The large staff included fourteen chanters of sufi litanies glorifying God, three chanters of the 'Fathiyya prayer' (*vird*), fifteen Koran reciters, and two readers of a tenth portion of the Koran (*ʿashr*). One of these readers chanted his portion of the Koran after the noon prayers in 'the secluded place' at the west side of the mosque, while the other used the corresponding space in the east following the afternoon prayers.[182] Two small raised alcoves built into the corners of the qibla wall, about two metres above ground level and reached from passages through the windows, may have fulfilled a similar function.

With its lead-covered hemispherical dome, Çerkes İskender Pasha's mosque comes closer to Sinan's 'classical' idiom than that of Hadım Ali Pasha with its pyramidal outer shell. The large dome (about 15 metres wide) is raised on squinches above eight pointed arches on a sixteen-sided drum pierced with eight windows. The drum, the muqarnas-galleried cylindrical minaret, and the projecting low guest-rooms are built of unstriped white ashlar masonry. The remaining walls of the mosque are constructed with alternating courses of white and black stone. The north façade with a central arched gate features two small muqarnas-hooded mihrabs (missing in Hadım Ali Pasha's earlier mosque) and lateral doors with steps that descend into the guest-rooms. Aligned with the central portal is the ablution fountain, protected by an ungainly modern canopy of concrete added during repairs in 1953.[183]

The arched central portal lacks a muqarnas hood; its vestibule is surmounted by an internal upper balcony for the patron and his retinue, flanked by muezzin's tribunes. The rectangular mihrab of white and pink marble is bordered by a muqarnas frieze and has a conical muqarnas hood, framed by a trefoil arch (illus. 481). The badly repaired wooden minbar features a canopy with a mini dome. The continuous tile revetments of the dadoes, mentioned by Albert Gabriel in 1940, seem to have been removed around 1948, when some samples were stored at the local museum.[184] These consist of hexagonal modules with arabesques forming six ogival compartments as in Bıyıklı Mehmed Pasha's mosque. Painted under the glaze in a 'dull purple' and a 'new blue' wash, they were accompanied by rectangular border tiles with scrolling stems, rosettes, and cloud bands.[185] The original painted decorations and inscriptions of the prayer hall are lost.[186]

The striped masonry mausoleum at the east side of the mosque is not mentioned in the waqfiyya. Perhaps intended for

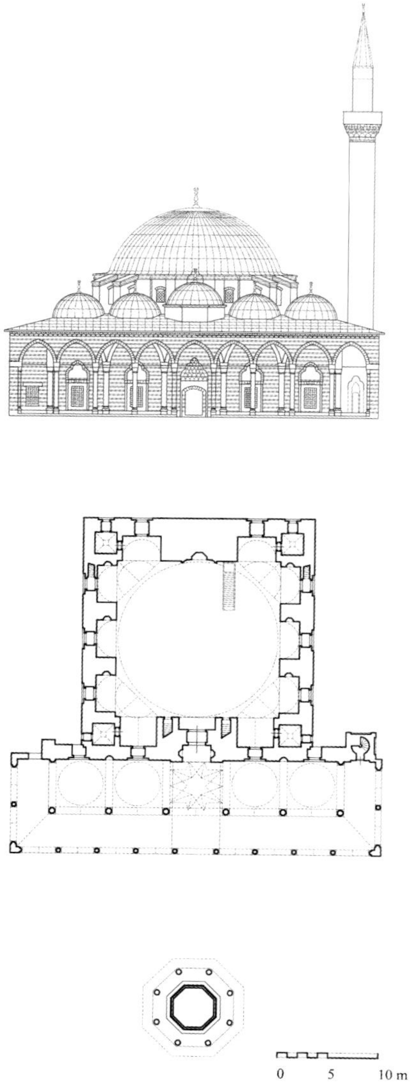

482 Plan and elevation of the Behram Pasha mosque, Diyarbakır.

483 Behram Pasha mosque, north façade.

484 Behram Pasha mosque, double portico with muqarnas-hooded portal.

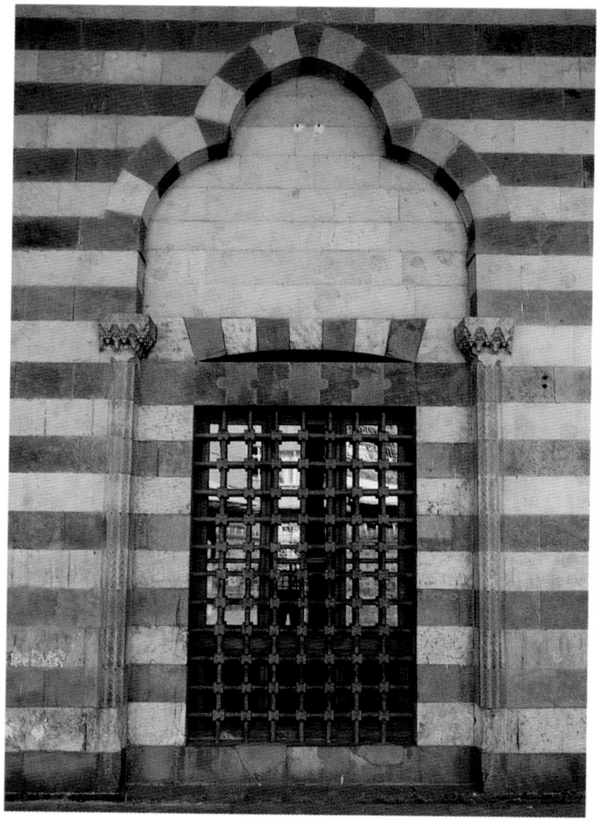

485 Behram Pasha mosque, window with trefoil-arched lunette on the north façade.

the founder, it contains the bodies of some of his descendants.[187] İskender Pasha himself passed away in Istanbul after his retirement and was buried with his oldest son Ahmed Pasha (the governor-general of Rakka, Lahsa, and Abyssinia) in a mausoleum at Kanlıca, along the Bosphorus. Attributed to Sinan, the open-air mausoleum is located at the waterfront mosque of the pasha's namesake, Bostancı İskender Pasha, who died in Cyprus and was buried there.[188] The mosque in Diyarbakır, endowed with a large waqf for the benefit of Çerkes İskender Pasha's progeny, contributed to the development of a prosperous commercial quarter. Accompanied by a palatial residence, it is a worthy reminder of its founder, who equitably governed the provincial capital for many years. His esteemed descendants, known as the 'sons of İskender' (İskenderoğlu), continued to live in Diyarbakır well into the twentieth century and still administer his waqf.[189]

XII. BEHRAM PASHA

Compared to its forerunners in Diyarbakır, Halhallı (Bangled) Behram Pasha's mosque, located near the Mardin Gate at the southwestern quadrant of the quadriparite city, comes closest to Sinan's 'classical' idiom (illus. 482, 483).[190] Its Muslim-born patron was the son of Kara Şahin Mustafa Pasha, a Bosnian recruit educated in Sultan Süleyman's palace. His father initially governed the sanjak of Ghazza and then became the governor-general of Yemen (1556–60) and of Egypt (1560–64), with the honorary rank of vizier. Later on Behram Pasha and his brother Rıdvan Pasha also governed Yemen.[191] Mustafa Āli states that the sons of viziers should not be given appointments as *beglerbegi*s while their fathers are viziers because 'carried away by their rank and majesty and following their personal whims, [they] never cease to demonstrate their power and might through their governorship'. As an example he refers to Behram Pasha, who coming from Yemen became the governor-general of Diyarbakır.[192]

The date of Behram Pasha's tenure in Diyarbakır is uncertain (probably between 1564–65 and 1567–68). He subsequently became the governor-general of Yemen, and participated in the Cyprus campaign of 1570–71 as the governor-general of Rum (Sivas). He took part in the Safavid campaign of 1578–79 while he was the governor-general of Erzurum. After being transferred to Aleppo around 1580, he was reappointed to Diyarbakır, at which time he participated in the Safavid campaign of 1581–82.[193] He passed away in 1585 and was buried according to his will in Aleppo, in a mausoleum at the south side of the Friday mosque he had endowed there with a waqfiyya dated 1583. His older brother Rıdvan Pasha (who governed such provinces as Ghazza, Yemen, Erzurum, and Anatolia) was buried next to him in 1586. The funerary mosque in Aleppo, known as the Bahramiyya, is not cited among Sinan's works.[194]

The mosque built for Behram Pasha in Diyarbakır was completed in 980 (1572–73), during Selim II's reign, according

486 Behram Pasha mosque, interior.

487 Behram Pasha mosque, detail of underglaze tile revetments on the lateral recesses with mihrabs.

to the Arabic foundation inscription in two lines of *thuluth* carved above the arch of its muqarnas-hooded portal (illus. 484):

> This noble Friday mosque was built by the meek slave Behram Pasha, may God fulfill his wishes;
>
> Who was among the slaves of the late Sultan Süleyman Khan, in the days of the reign of the great Sultan Selim Khan; the year 980 (1572–73).[195]

The mosque is thought to have been built in eight years between, 1564–65 and 1572–73.[196] A Turkish waqfiyya recorded in February 1569 (at the end of his tenure in Diyarbakır) lists the properties that Behram Pasha endowed for 'the noble Friday mosque he built in the city of Amid (Diyarbakır)', and for his elementary school and masjid in Ruha (Urfa) subordinate to Diyarbakır.[197] The income-producing properties endowed in Diyarbakır included a new bath-house (known today as Paşa Hamamı) near the Shaykh Matar mosque, and a new khan with warehouses and shops comprising workshops for silk thread production near the 'İskenderiyye mosque' (Çerkes İskender Pasha). He also endowed forty shops and a commercial caravansaray in Urfa that contained his masjid, and a bath-house and landed properties in Malatya. After the pasha's death, his waqf was to be administered by his male descendants and overseen by the governor-generals of Diyarbakır.[198]

The white stone ashlar-masonry mosque is an unlayered domed cube with two tiers of windows, preceded by a lofty five-domed double portico of striped masonry. Its hemispherical dome sits on a sixteen-sided, window-pierced drum with Sinanesque engaged pilasters and pairs of flying buttresses in each corner (missing in the two previous mosques of Diyarbakır). The rebuilt muqarnas-galleried cylindrical minaret is attached to the northwest corner of the projecting portico. The portico is carried on white marble columns with plain capitals; the two central supports of the outer portico are bundled composite pilasters, each with a 'braided' middle section set between black and white drums. Similar knotted composite pilasters support the extensively rebuilt, pyramidal-roofed octagonal ablution fountain, which is axially aligned with the central portal of the north façade. Flanked by a pair of small mihrabs, the lavish rectangular portal features a conical muqarnas hood framed by a trefoil arch. The two windows on each side have twin colonettes and lunettes with matching trefoil arches (illus. 485).

A large dome on squinches (15.9 metres wide), resting on eight muqarnas-corbelled pointed arches, covers the prayer hall surrounded by dadoes decorated with tiles (illus. 486, 487). The central space is extended by deep alcoves on all sides, as in the mosques of Hadım İbrahim Pasha at Silivrikapı (1551), Dukakinzade Mehmed Pasha in Aleppo (1556–55/56), and Hacı Ahmed Pasha in Kayseri (*c.* 1576–85/86). The lateral alcoves have their own muqarnas-hooded mihrabs framed by trefoil arches, and the upper galleries on three sides are reached from four staircases built into the walls. The four small cells inserted into the corners of the prayer hall recall the pair in the northeast and northwest corners of Çerkes İskender Pasha's mosque and the raised alcoves at both ends of its qibla wall. The corner cells in Behram Pasha's mosque (which omits the archaic *tabhane*s of İskender Pasha's mosque) probably functioned as secluded retreats for the chanting of sufi litanies and prayers. Among the mosque staff, the waqfiyya mentions a shaykh who daily recited the names of God (*ẕikrullāh*), ten chanters of litanies praising God, two chanters of the 'Fathiyya prayer' (*vird*), ten readers of a tenth part of the Koran, thirty readers of a thirtieth part of the Koran for the founder's soul, and a eulogizer of the Prophet Muhammad.[199]

The dadoes that surround the prayer hall on all sides feature two types of unusually large, square underglaze tiles, decorated with palmettes flanked by *saz* leaves and rosettes linked by floral stems. These innovative tiles, which depart from the traditional hexagonal format and colour scheme of tiles used in the earlier mosques of Diyarbakır, are rendered in blue, turquoise, and red on a white ground. The two types of rectangular border tiles have a design of counterset cresting, painted alternately in dark blue and turquoise (with cloud bands in white and red against the turquoise). Produced locally in Diyarbakır, the tiles mimic those made in İznik in both design and colour scheme, but the resemblance is not total, and the relief-red falls short of İznik's brilliant scarlet.[200] Framed by a muqarnas border freeze, the rectangular mihrab, with its muqarnas hood within a trefoil arch, has colourfully painted arched panels featuring geometric patterns. The ornately carved polychrome minbar of white, black, and pink marble is crowned by a conical cap. Dated 1321 (1903–4), the renovated painted decorations on the domical superstructure feature Koranic inscriptions.[201]

Evliya Çelebi recounts that Behram Pasha, a native of Ghazza, imported skilled builders and marble cutters to Diyarbakır from his birthplace and from Jerusalem for the replication of an artistic bath-house he had seen in the Arab lands. This 'exemplary' bath-house in Diyarbakır (Paşa Hamamı) was built with loads of imported marble 'carried by hundreds of camels'.[202] The plan of the equally exemplary mosque resembles that of Dukakinzade Mehmed Pasha in Aleppo (ʿAdiliyya), whose window lunettes are decorated with underglaze tile revetments in the manner of İznik. One wonders whether Behram Pasha had seen the mosque in Aleppo, where he later built his own mosque. If so, he may have asked Sinan to design one like it in Diyarbakır.

Whether its construction was overseen by an architect sent from the capital or by a local master, Behram Pasha's mosque must have been the creation of a team of talented masons from Diyarbakır who left their distinctive mark on its fabric. Goodwin praises the mosque as the most impressive example of its kind in the city: 'It is, indeed, the prince of provincial mosques,

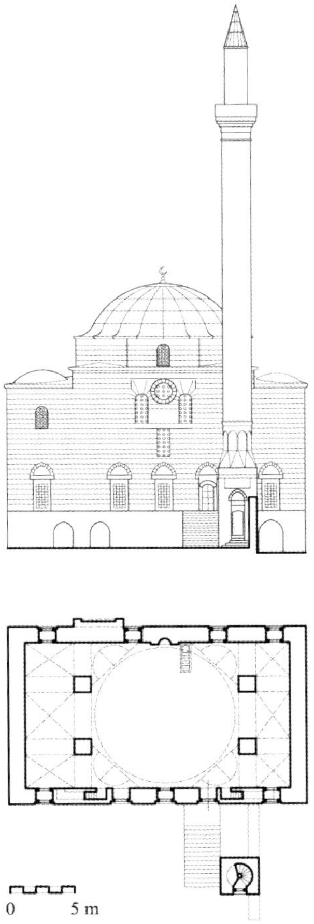

488 Plan and elevation of the Melek Ahmed Pasha mosque, Diyarbakır.

as splendid in its decoration as it is in proportions within the limits of the severe local style.'[203] The mosque of Behram Pasha represents a truly outstanding synthesis of local traditions of polychrome stone masonry and İznik-inspired tilework, anchored by an unmistakably Ottoman structural skeleton.

XIII. MELEK (MELİK) AHMED PASHA

The upper-storey mosque of Melek Ahmed Pasha, sited on a major shop-lined artery connected to the Urfa Gate (Rum Gate) at the west side of Diyarbakır, is the latest monument attributed to Sinan in that city (illus. 488). Among the commercial structures endowed to support this 'light-filled Friday mosque near the Rum Gate' Evliya Çelebi mentions a monumental caravansaray and a bath-house inside the same gate. The caravansaray is lost; the extant bath-house dated by several chronograms to 975 (1567–68) was completed before the mosque. According to local tradition, the mosque and bath were both planned in 972 (1564–65). Construction of the mosque is thought to have been delayed by the building of Behram Pasha's mosque in the same city and then by Melek Ahmed's duties in the Safavid campaign of 1578.[204]

Neither the date of the mosque nor the details of its patron's career have been firmly established. It is believed that the Muslim-born Melek (Melik) Ahmed Pasha was born in Diyarbakır to a local notable who lost his fortune towards the end of his life. He inherited from his father a farm in Payas near Aleppo, whose ownership he shared with his relative Alaüddin Beg. The two partners managed to accumulate considerable wealth from agriculture and trade in silk cloth produced on looms they owned in Diyarbakır.[205] They were then employed for many years as tax farmers of public revenues (*mültezim*) in Diyarbakır. Melek Ahmed Pasha was appointed the governor-general of Mosul in 1585 and dismissed in 1587.[206] He returned to his hometown and resumed his position as tax farmer. His main claim to fame was his ruthlessness in collecting taxes with *mültezim* Alaüddin Beg. When these two notorious tax farmers were executed in 1591, the historian Selaniki hailed the release of Diyarbakır from their vicious clutch and its purification from their 'bodies contaminated with malignance'.[207]

Melek Ahmed Pasha's mosque is thought to have been built between 1587 and 1591.[208] He passed away before completing its courtyard, at the left side of which he owned a large residence (converted in the seventeenth century into a khan by Dilaver Pasha).[209] Because the mosque lacks a foundation inscription and its waqfiyya has disappeared, its date of construction remains hypothetical. Noting the striking departures of its asymmetrical plan from classical norms (it lacks a portico and its unusually monumental minaret is free-standing), Kuran is reluctant to accept it as a work of Sinan.[210] Whether it was designed by the chief architect or not, this idiosyncratic mosque was certainly executed by a local master.

The basement of the mosque is taken up by warehouses and shops. An off-centre monumental gateway on the asymmetrical street façade, composed of a muqarnas hood framed by a trefoil arch, is connected to a vaulted passage that passes under the mosque to a garden court in the back. A flight of stairs leads to the off-centre main gate with a simple arch on the equally asymmetrical north façade. Both façades are built of striped masonry and the blind lateral walls of cheaper black stone. The plan of the upper-storey mosque reinterprets that of the Shaykh Safa mosque in Diyarbakır, composed of a central octagonal domed baldachin carried on two lateral supports and flanked by side aisles. The pasha's mosque has upper galleries that are missing in its model. Its relatively small dome (11.49 metres) raised on squinches rests on eight pointed arches. Both the octagonal striped masonry drum of its hemispherical dome and the base of its minaret quote selected details from the Shaykh Safa mosque, seamlessly blending them with Ottoman forms.

The hexagonal tile revetments that cover the dadoes of the Shaykh Safa mosque are replaced in the pasha's mosque with locally produced versions of square and rectangular İznik tiles, almost identical to those of the Behram Pasha mosque. The muqarnas-hooded mihrab is also faced with tiles, unlike any other mihrab in Diyarbakır. The staircase that leads to the upper gallery at the east side is lined with hexagonal underglaze-painted tiles (in indigo, cobalt blue, and white) echoing old designs encountered in the *cuerda seca* tiles of the Shaykh Safa mosque. Relegated to a staircase, these archaistic tiles are marginalized by the modern ones of the prayer hall which closely mimic the İznik canon.[211] The mosque of Melek Ahmed Pasha, then, enters into a pointed dialogue with the pre-Ottoman building tradition of Diyarbakır. Its recognizable references to the Shaykh Safa mosque were perhaps intended to expresses its patron's indigenous identity. This hybrid monument befits the status of a demoted provincial governor of minor importance, whose life and career were firmly grounded in Diyarbakır.

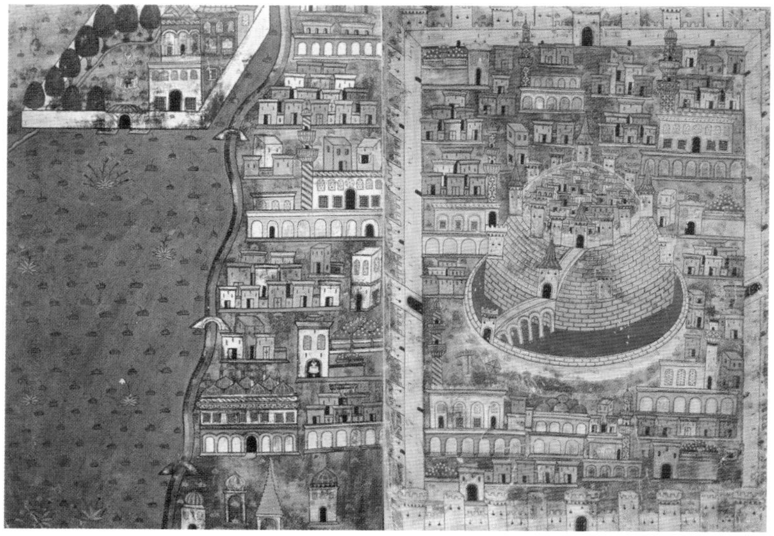

489 Matrakçı Nasuh, Map of Aleppo, c. 1537, watercolour on paper, from *Beyān-ı Menāzil-i Sefer-i ʿIrāḳeyn*.

SYRIA AND THE ARAB LANDS

The territories of the Mamluk sultanate and its satellites, conquered under Selim I, were initially grouped as three provinces: Diyarbakır, ʿAla' al-Dawla (Maraş), and ʿArab (Syria, Palestine, Egypt, and Hijaz). Early in Süleyman's reign the latter province became subdivided into three provinces: Aleppo (Haleb), Damascus (Şam), and Egypt (Mısır). By the end of the sixteenth century, the empire had more than thirty provinces, among which nine were subject not to the regular fief system (*timār*), but to tax revenues (*sālyāne*) directly collected for the imperial treasury.[212] The architecture of these relatively autonomous Arab provinces (Egypt, Baghdad, Basra, Yemen, Abyssinia, Lahsa, Tripolitania, Algeria, and Tunisia) was only minimally Ottomanized during the age of Sinan, a telling sign of their incomplete integration into the centralized provincial system of the empire.

Friday mosques commissioned from Sinan by the governor-generals of Arab lands, like those in Diyarbakır, are listed only in the *Tuhfe*. They comprise the mosques of Maktul (Executed) Ayas Pasha in Basra, Murad Pasha in Baghdad, and Divane Hüsrev Pasha and Dukakinzade Mehmed Pasha in Aleppo (Map 1). The grafting of the Syrian stone masonry tradition onto the Ottoman architectural style created a vibrant and flexible regional idiom. By contrast, the more distant province of Iraq retained its 'foreign' character with its brick-and-tile construction in the Safavid manner. The mosque-cum-convent complexes of Abu Hanifa and Shaykh ʿAbd al-Kadir al-Gilani, commissioned by Sultan Süleyman after the conquest of Baghdad in 1534, adapted the local architectural tradition to Ottoman plan types using brick and Persianate tiles (illus. 35). The unknown mosque of Ayas Pasha (the executed brother of Koca Sinan Pasha) may have commemorated his victorious Basra campaign of 1545–46. The campaign, which he commanded as the governor-general of Baghdad, had restored the sultan's authority against powerful local leaders. Murad Pasha's extant mosque in Baghdad, known as the Muradiya, was completed in 1570–71 according to its Turkish foundation inscription, which identifies its patron as the governor-general of that province during Selim II's reign. Extensively renovated, this brick mosque with a white-washed interior has a typically Ottoman ground plan, but its elevations entirely conform to the regional building tradition.[213]

The rectangular plan of Murad Pasha's mosque has a central octagonal domed baldachin resting on two lateral columns on each side and flanked by aisles with three bays. Its five-domed, narthex-like portico lacks columns; rising above its northwest corner is a muqarnas-galleried cylindrical minaret with geometric brick-and-tile patterns and a domical fluted cap in the local manner. The drumless plain brick dome with a slightly pointed profile differs from its more bulbous Safavid counterparts, which are raised on higher drums and lavishly decorated with polychromatic tiles. The unlayered mosque with plain brick façades has two tiers of windows, framed by arches in rectangular compartments. In the absence of a stone masonry building tradition, the architect who presumably executed a plan designed by Sinan had no choice but to translate it into regional forms, using Baghdadi arch profiles and squinch nets.

The only other mosques commissioned from the chief architect by the governor-generals of Arab provinces are located in Aleppo, whose hinterland extended into southeast Anatolia. This explains their visual affiliation with the Ottoman-style mosque architecture of Diyarbakır, even though their income-producing commercial dependencies (excluded from Sinan's autobiographies) generally elaborated local Mamluk prototypes which were monumentalized and transformed with new inputs. Like their counterparts in Diyarbakır, the mosques of Aleppo feature domes raised on squinches, trefoil arches, striped ablaq masonry, polychrome marble mihrabs and minbars, and underglaze tile revetments. These monuments were complemented by Sinan's previously discussed hajj-route complexes for higher-level patrons – in Payas (Sokollu), Damascus (Sultan Süleyman), and Jerusalem (Hürrem Sultan) – and others created by local architects.[214]

During the age of Sinan Aleppo emerged as the principal international emporium of the Levant, where consulates were established by the Venetians in 1548, the French in 1557, and the English in 1583. It was then that major mosque-centred waqfs lined the east-west commercial artery extending from the citadel to Bab Antakiyya (Antioch Gate): Hüsrev Pasha (*c.* 1546–67), Dukakinzade Mehmed Pasha (1556–65/66), Sokollu Mehmed Pasha (*c.* 1574), and Behram Pasha (*c.* 1583).[215] Beyond this commercial artery was an *extramuros* royal garden palace near the public square of Gök Meydan, where Sultan Süleyman had stayed in 1535 during the campaign of the Two Iraqs. Matrakçı Nasuh's pictorial representation of Aleppo dating from that year depicts the royal palace across the Quwayk river and the prominent citadel at the centre of the city, with a public square extending in front of it (illus. 489).[216] The east–west commercial artery that subsequently became lined with mosque complexes visually linked these two foci: the sultan's palace (renovated by royal decree in 1559) and the citadel, at the foot of which was located the official residence of Ottoman governor-generals. Known as the Dar al-ʿAdl (Palace of Justice), the residence of governors was a remodelled Mamluk-period palace which marked the new status of Aleppo as a provincial capital.[217]

Unlike Damascus, the prestigious seat of former Islamic dynasties where sultanic mosque-cum-hospice complexes were built for Selim I and Süleyman I, Aleppo was Ottomanized primarily by the commercially lucrative complexes of non-royal patrons, who concentrated their building campaigns on the central market area. Attributed to the chief architect, the first two of these complexes, known as the Khusrawiyya and ʿAdiliyya, were sited near the official palace of governor-generals at the southwest corner of the citadel. Although the principal commercial artery of Aleppo developed westward by the successive accretion of mosque-centred pious foundations, 'the cumulative effect amounted to a kind of urban policy.'[218]

That 'policy' seems partly to have been coordinated from the capital by Sinan, who also claims authorship for the centrepiece of Sokollu's enormous waqf in Aleppo, the Khan al-Ghumruk, whose courtyard features a domed masjid raised above a fountain in the Ottoman manner. The grand vizier's khan is listed in the *Tuhfe* along with his mosque complex in Payas, the new port of Aleppo reached from Bab Antakiyya, beyond which Sokollu created a new tannery near the Quwayk river, accompanied by another khan featuring a masjid atop a fountain.[219] Like Sokollu, who wintered in Aleppo in 1559–60, Sinan was

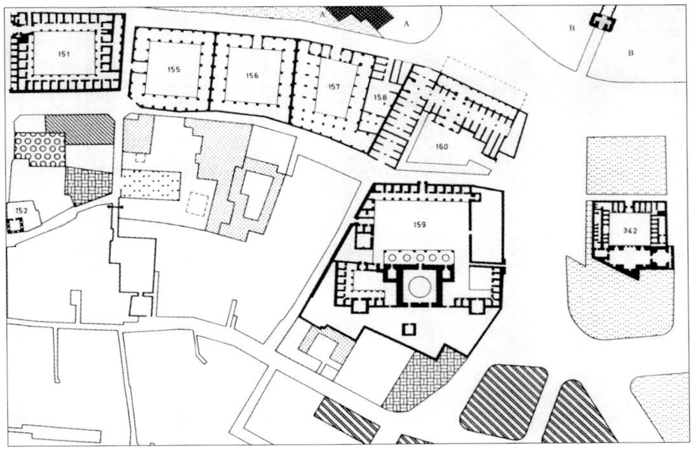

490 Hüsrev Pasha complex on a plan of Aleppo.

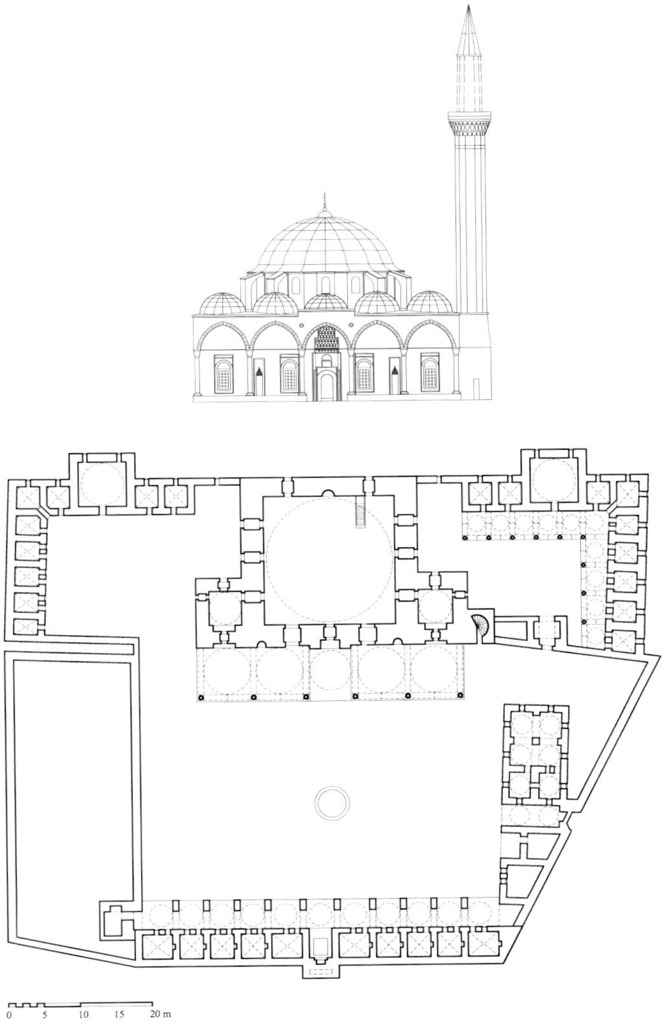

491 Reconstruction plan of the Hüsrev Pasha complex, Aleppo, with mosque elevation.

familiar with the city, where he had briefly camped in 1535 with Süleyman's army during the campaign of the Two Iraqs. Moreover, he was in contact with such capable Aleppine architects as Cemalüddin (who built prince Selim's Karapınar complex in 1560) and Abdülnebi (who completed the moat of the Payas castle after visiting Istanbul in 1577).[220] Local architects no doubt played a decisive role in the urban restructuring and reorientation of Aleppo that was not the outcome of a 'master plan', but of a dynamic process guided by the remarkably consistent collective vision of Sinan and his palace-educated patrons who served as its governor-generals.

XIV. DİVANE (DELİ) HÜSREV PASHA

The mosque complex of Divane (Crazy) Hüsrev Pasha at the foot of the citadel was completed soon after his death in 1545, according to the Arabic foundation inscription carved on its gate (illus. 490, 491): 'And places of worship are only for Allah, so pray not unto anyone along with Allah (72:18); it was founded during the reign of the greatest sultan, Süleyman – may his victory be glorified – and built by the vizier Hüsrev Pasha.' The inscription ends with a couplet whose chronogram yields the date 953 (1546–47): 'Born pious from his mother, / He is now well-protected in a refuge. // A sanctuary in Aleppo whose date is: / 'A noble masjid he founded'.[221]

The Bosnian-born patron of this prominent mosque complex (the older brother of Lala Mustafa Pasha) was educated in the imperial palace and served as the governor-general of various provinces such as Karaman and Diyarbakır before he was transferred to Syria. He is thought to have been the governor-general of Aleppo in 1532–34 and of Damascus in 1534–35. During Sultan Süleyman's campaign of the Two Iraqs he was promoted to governor-general of Egypt with the honorary rank of vizier (1535–36). He then became the governor-general of Anatolia and Rumelia before being appointed vizier of the imperial council in 1541.[222] He was dismissed from that post in 1544, together with the grand vizier Hadım Süleyman Pasha, when the two engaged in a scandalous fight in the imperial council; the joint dismissal cleared up the way for the grand vizierate of Rüstem Pasha.[223]

Utterly lost in despair, the 'Crazy' Hüsrev Pasha starved himself to death, fearing he might be poisoned.[224] He was buried in an exuberantly decorated domed octagonal mausoleum that Sinan built for him in 952 (1545–46), next to the elementary school the vizier had founded in 947 (1540–41) at the Yenibahçe quarter.[225] Mustafa Āli says Hüsrev Pasha owed his nickname to being unrestrained, audacious, dauntless, and wild.[226] His pious foundations include a madrasa-cum-masjid complex in Diyarbakır (*c.* 1521–28), a Mamluk-style water dispenser with an upper-storey elementary school in Cairo (1535–37), and the Khusrawiyya complex in Aleppo.[227] Their differing styles exemplify the regional diversity among these provinces, a visual counterpart to the flexibility of Ottoman colonization policies that favoured the cultivation of local customs.

Ibn al-Hanbali's (d. 1563–64) biographical dictionary of Aleppine grandees explains that Hüsrev Pasha's mosque complex in Aleppo was commissioned after he attained the rank of vizier and that it was completed in 1544–45. We learn from the same source that his manumitted slave Ferruh b. Abdülmennan el-Rumi supervised the construction, which was the work of a 'Christian architect from Rum' (the Ottoman lands in Anatolia and Rumelia).[228] Assuming that the complex was built soon after the pasha left Syria for Egypt, some scholars have dated it to 1535–37, arguing that Sinan could have designed it while he passed through Aleppo with Süleyman's army.[229] Kuran, however, speculates that it was probably created after the pasha became a vizier at the imperial council (1541–46), by an architect sent from Istanbul with Sinan's plan.[230] If so, the complex should have been grouped in this book under the patronage of viziers, but I have chosen to treat it together with the foundations of governor-generals because the pasha's waqfs in Syria were most probably consolidated soon after he left for Egypt. The mosque may have been designed by Sinan later on, around 1541, after the preliminary construction of some of the income-producing commercial properties.

The modern Aleppine historian Kamil al-Ghazzi summarizes three Arabic waqfiyyas of Hüsrev Pasha (dated April 1558, December 1559, and November 1566), which he acquired from a descendant of the pasha living in Damascus. The first two were set up by the founder's brother 'Mustafa b. Sinan', that is, Lala Mustafa Pasha, who was then the tutor of prince Selim in Konya.[231] These two short waqfiyyas are appendices to a now-lost earlier endowment deed. They list new properties that generated additional income for the waqf's already existing employees. The third waqfiyya was recorded in 1566, while Lala Mustafa Pasha was based in Syria, as the governor-general first of Aleppo (*c.* 1563–65) and then of Damascus (*c.* 1565–68/9).[232]

This is an updated version of an earlier waqfiyya dated 1561, which in turn must have been based on a lost endowment deed that was recorded during Hüsrev Pasha's lifetime, judging by its reference to the founder as if he were still alive. It stipulates that the pasha would administer his own waqf and be succeeded after his death by his sons and the descendants of his sons; upon the extinction of their lineage their successors would be the founder's freed slaves and the children of his freed slaves. The waqfiyya of 1561 describes the complex, which comprised a Friday mosque in the al-Biza quarter of Aleppo, near 'the palace of felicity' (*dār al-saʿāda*), surrounded by a garden at the south, a street at the east, the forecourt of the mosque at the north, and a madrasa at the west. The location of the hospice (*takiyya, al-ʿimārat*) entrusted to a shaykh – comprising thirteen guest-rooms, kitchen, bakery, commissariat, wood storage, and stable – is not specified. Its components probably surrounded the mosque forecourt, which features a central ablution fountain without a domed canopy.[233] The nearby 'palace of felicity' was the official residence of governor-generals where Hüsrev Pasha must have resided in the early 1530s.[234]

The site of the mosque encompassed the burial place of Hüsrev Pasha's wife: the waqfiyya of 1561 stipulates the recitation of the Koran in the mosque for the soul of 'Shah-i Khuban bint Shadi Pasha', the mother of the pasha's son, Kurd Beg.[235] The updated waqfiyya of 1566 mentions the still extant mausoleum in the garden cemetery behind the qibla wall of the mosque, where Kurd Beg (a governor of sanjaks in Syria-Palestine) was buried next to his mother (illus. 490).[236] The site of Hüsrev Pasha's complex finds a parallel in several provincial mosques built next to the palaces of governor-generals (such as those of Sokollu Mustafa Pasha in Buda, Lala Mustafa Pasha in Erzurum, and Köse Hüsrev Pasha in Van already considered in this chapter). Highly visible, the Khusrawiyya reshaped the contours of the large open public space in front of the citadel gate, which had housed the horse market in the Mamluk era and was still used for a weekly market.[237] The principal entrances of the pasha's complex at the north and east accentuated its dialogue with the monuments of previous dynasties: the looming citadel and the Madrasa Sultaniya (1223) founded by the Ayyubid ruler al-Zahir Ghazi (illus. 490[342]). Several endowed structures had been demolished to make way for it.[238]

Sinan's autobiographies list only the Friday mosque and madrasa, without mentioning the hospice.[239] Income-producing endowed structures extending along the north and west sides of the mosque's precinct included stables, rental rooms and shops, a qaysariyya or covered market – the Khan al-Shuna located across a narrow street at the north side of the forecourt (illus. 490[160]) – and a khan whose north façade faced the gate of the 'palace of felicity'. These were complemented by more distant commercial structures, such as the Khan of Kurd Beg in the Farafra quarter (a renovated Mamluk building named after the pasha's son) and a pre-Ottoman bath-house known as Hammam al-Sitt (adjacent to the ʿAdiliyya complex).[240] The endowments also comprised landed properties and mills in the provinces of Aleppo and Damascus. A significant portion of the waqf revenues was allocated to provide food for the staff of the complex, its students, and hajj pilgrims travelling on their way to Mecca and Medina. The thirteen guest-rooms were supplemented by the lateral *tābḫānes* of the mosque, where the poor and needy dervishes must have found shelter. The madrasa is an L-shaped structure at the west side of the mosque.[241] The other charitable dependencies have been substantially modified.[242]

492 An early photograph of the Hüsrev Pasha complex, Aleppo, with the mosque of Dukakinzade Mehmed Pasha in the background.

493 Hüsrev Pasha complex, with the citadel in the background.

The only building to have survived without major alterations is the ashlar masonry mosque, fronted by a five-domed portico carried on columns with muqarnas capitals. Its unlayered domed cube is flanked by lower *tabhanes*, which enjoyed a longer life in the provinces of Aleppo and Diyarbakır, where Hüsrev Pasha succeeded in 1521 the governor-general Bıyıklı Mehmed Pasha (whose mosque in Diyarbakır features two *tabhane* cells, illus. 86). Attached to the western *tabhane*, the faceted minaret crowned by a typically Ottoman conical cap has a band of blue-and-white tiles under the muqarnas frieze of its gallery. Once covered by lead, the large hemispherical dome (about 18 metres wide) of the mosque sits on a Sinanesque drum, pierced with sixteen windows, and reinforced by engaged pilasters and paired

494 Hüsrev Pasha mosque, Aleppo, underglaze tile lunettes from the north façade (top) and the prayer hall (bottom).

flying buttresses in each corner.[243]

Rising high above its dependencies with lower roofs, the mosque, which is crowned by the largest dome in the city asserts its primacy as the centrepiece of the complex, the first of its kind in Aleppo (illus. 492, 493). It stands out from the small hypostyle mosques founded by Mamluk patrons, surpassed in monumentality only by the ancient Great Mosque. Unlike the Khusrawiyya, Mamluk complexes were generally centred on madrasas, convents, or hospitals, with small bulbous domes accentuating the mausoleums of their founders. The spatial composition of the pasha's complex as a free-standing structure surrounded by a low precinct wall was a novelty in the urban fabric of Aleppo, until then dominated by the façades of complexes organically composed as single structural units responding to pre-existing street networks.[244] The Khusrawiyya also inaugurated institutions affiliated with the Ottoman regime: a mosque with a Hanefi imam, a madrasa with a Hanefi professor, and a charitable hospice entrusted to a shaykh.

The mosque built by local masons placed under the supervision of the non-Muslim architect from 'Rum', mentioned by Ibn al-Hanbali, combines imported and indigenous elements. Its unresolved details include portico arches that collide with the windows and with the twin mihrabs on the north façade. Regional modes of decoration (the joggled voussoirs of arches and the geometric-patterned polychrome marble inlays of the portal and mihrab), are juxtaposed with underglaze blue-and-white tiles in the Ottoman manner (illus. 494). The four arched window lunettes on the north façade are decorated with somewhat crude tiles. The two that flank the muqarnas-hooded portal have central rectangular cartouches with identical inscriptions (black-on-white) which combine the Basmala with the profession of faith. The window lunettes in the prayer hall feature higher-quality square tiles, decorated with scrolls, palmettes, and rosettes conforming to a diagonal diaper grid. Similar blue-and-white tiles made for the Dome of the Rock in the 1540s suggest that those of the Khusrawiyya were either manufactured in Jerusalem or by potters imported from that city.[245]

The spacious prayer hall is dominated by the large dome with muqarnas-corbelled squinches, raised on eight pointed arches with joggled voussoirs. A private balcony above the gate overlooks it. The rectangular mihrab, with a crested pediment featuring painted vegetal scrolls, is intricately decorated with polychrome geometric interlaces. Above its semicircular niche, which lacks the customary muqarnas hood, is a cartouche carved with the profession of faith. The inscription band encircling the niche atypically quotes part of a verse that urges the congregation to face the qibla (2:143). The ornate wooden minbar, with an Ottoman style conical cap, is complemented at the northwest corner of the prayer hall by a muezzin's tribune that rests on marble columns. The dome has painted cartouches inscribed with verses that praise the beautiful names of God (59:23–24).

Evliya Çelebi, who quotes the foundation inscription of the mosque, attributes it to Sinan:

> The old Friday mosque of Hüsrev Pasha is an extremely artistic and decorated, elegant mosque. And its lofty single dome reaching the heavens is an indigo-coloured dome. And its mihrab and minbar feature variegated designs [like the works] of Mani. And its courtyard is completely paved with white marbles as if it were a seamless polished field. In its middle is an ablution fountain resembling a Shafiʿi pool. All around it are water spouts where worshippers renew their ablutions before approaching the presence of God. At the four sides of this courtyard are domes raised on well-proportioned marble and porphyry columns in various colours. And all of these structures are covered with lead. And it has a tall minaret in the Ottoman manner (*rum ṭarzı*) which is like the bride of Aleppo.[246]

Hüsrev Pasha's mosque complex, enshrining the bodies of some of his family members, including the son of his brother Lala Mustafa Pasha, marked the political centre of Aleppo with a combination of personal and communal memories.[247] Representing

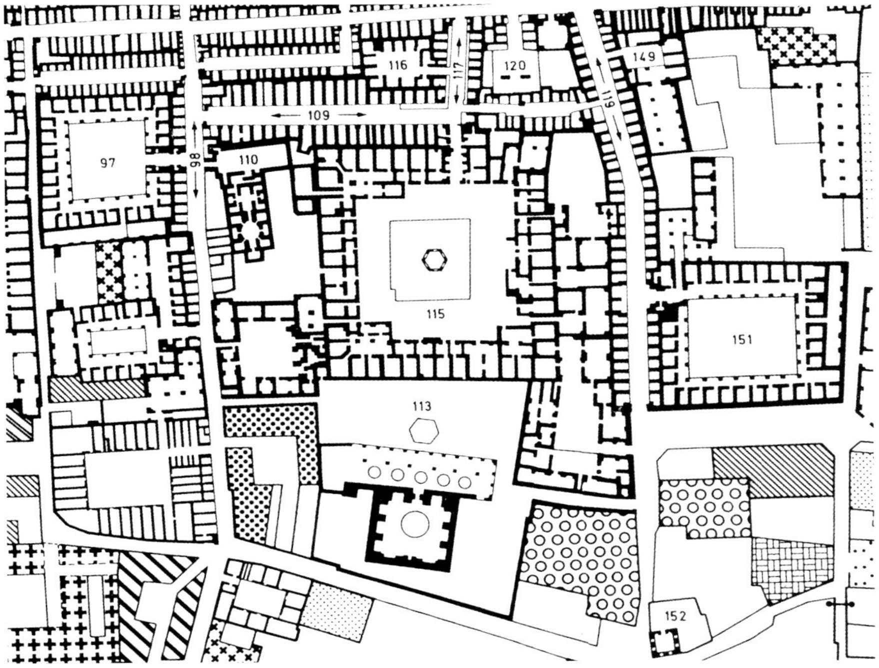

495 Dukakinzade Mehmed Pasha complex on a map of Aleppo.

the patron's official identity as an embodiment of the state, it set the stage for future mosque complexes that contributed to the Ottomanization of this flourishing provincial capital.

XV. DUKAKİNZADE MEHMED PASHA

Dukakinzade Mehmed Pasha's mosque complex, endowed in 1556 and posthumously completed in 1565–66, further extended the east-to-west axis of Aleppo initiated by the Khusrawiyya (illus. 495, 496). It came to be known as the ʿAdiliyya because of its proximity to the governor-general's palace, the Dar al-ʿAdl, also known as Dar al-Saʿada.[248] The Muslim-born patron of this complex was the grandson of the Albanian ruler Duca-Jean. His father, Dukakinzade (Duke's Son) Ahmed Pasha, had been brought up in the imperial palace following the Ottoman conquest of Albania under Mehmed II. Ahmed Pasha rose to the grand vizierate in 1514, but was executed by Selim I in 1515 after being implicated in a janissary revolt. His son Mehmed, born to a granddaughter of Bayezid II, was educated in the imperial palace.[249] He too married an Ottoman princess descending from Bayezid II's family, Gevher-i Müluk Sultan. Dukakinzade Mehmed Pasha, his wife, and their children are buried in a family cemetery at Eyüp.[250] The pasha's royal mother, who passed away in Aleppo after returning from a pilgrimage to Mecca in 1552, lies buried in a Mamluk-style domed mausoleum on the site of her house, next to which the pasha later built the ʿAdiliyya complex (illus. 495 [152]). The Arabic inscription of the mausoleum refers to her as the mother of 'the amir of grand amirs, His Highness Mehmed Pasha' and identifies her as 'Gevher Melikshah Sultan, the daughter of Ayşe Sultan, daughter of Sultan Bayezid Khan'.[251]

The aristocratic patron of the ʿAdiliyya complex held various provincial posts before he became the governor-general of Aleppo (1551–53). He was appointed the governor-general of Egypt in December 1553, during the favourable grand vizierate of the Albanian-born Kara Ahmed Pasha, with whom he shared ethnic and family ties (the grand vizier's wife, Fatma Sultan, was a granddaughter of Bayezid II). Kara Ahmed Pasha was executed in 1555 partly due to an incriminatory letter he had sent to his protégé, urging him to freely amass a big treasure in Egypt.[252] Reinstated as grand vizier, the vindictive Rüstem Pasha dismissed Dukakinzade from the governorship of Egypt in March 1556; he returned to the capital, where he passed away in January 1557.[253] Mustafa Āli says the pasha, renowned for his illustrious descent from the Albanian duke (*duca*, synonymous with *beg*), was 'a gentlemanly and dignified governor-general'.[254] The monuments he commissioned from Sinan are mentioned only in the *Tuhfe*: his tomb in Eyüp; a no-longer-extant Friday mosque in Konya Ereğlisi; and the ʿAdiliyya mosque in Aleppo.[255]

Dukakinzade Mehmed Pasha had already started to build the commercial dependencies of his future mosque complex near his

496 Plan and elevation of the Dukakinzade Mehmed Pasha mosque, Aleppo.

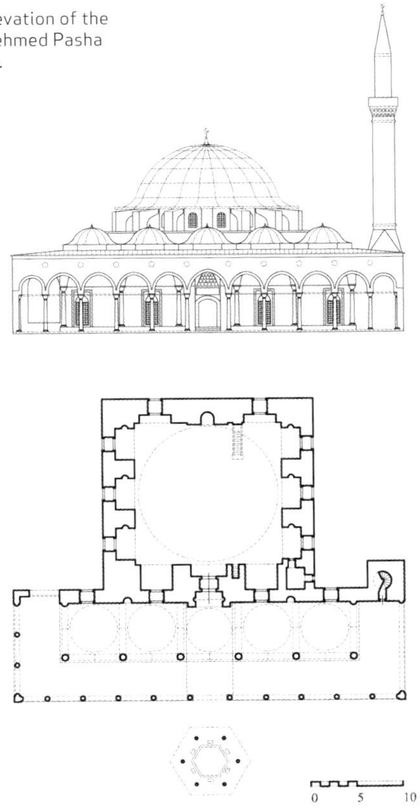

mother's mausoleum when he moved to Egypt in 1553. His Arabic waqfiyya, registered in November 1556, refers to the deposed pasha as 'His Highness Mehmed Pasha the son of the late Ahmed Pasha b. Dukakin.' It records the commercial buildings he had created in the vicinity of the 'palace of felicity' (*dār al-sa'āda*) in Aleppo (illus. 495): two khans (Khan al-Farra'in [151], Khan al-Nahhasin [97]), four suqs comprising two rows of shops [98, 109, 117, 119], and three qaysariyyas [116, 120, 149]. The waqfiyya stipulates the construction of a new khan at the north side of the hill known as Tallat 'A'isha, paid for by the founder's own funds and not those accruing from his waqf. Its boundaries would be the Hammam al-Sitt (belonging to the Khusrawiyya waqf [110]) and the pasha's adjacent suq at the west [98]; his other suq at the east [119]; and the northern suqs to which the lofty gate of the new khan would open [109, 117]. This must have been the Khan al-'Ulabiyya, the largest in the complex [115]. The pasha endowed 30,000 gold dinars (1,800,000 aspers) that would first be loaned out at interest. With its yield, the endowment administrator was to build near the public square adjacent to Tallat 'A'isha 'a noble Friday mosque'.[256]

Clearly, then, neither the Khan al-'Ulabiyya nor the mosque aligned with it along the central north-south axis of the complex had yet been built (illus. 495 [113, 115]). The plan of the mosque may have been designed by Sinan after its patron returned to Istanbul, and executed either by a royal architect sent from the capital or by one residing in Aleppo. The waqfiyya stipulates that the pasha's endowment would be administered by himself; after his demise it was to be managed by his sons and their descendants. When their lineage ceased, they would be succeeded by the sons of the pasha's manumitted slaves. The pasha determined the wages of the staff of his waqf, including the personnel of the projected mosque, which some scholars misdate to 1555–56, the year the waqfiyya was recorded.[257]

The Turkish foundation inscription carved on the mosque portal confirms that it was completed a decade after the waqfiyya was registered. The inscription refers to the founder as 'the governor-general Mehmed Pasha b. Dukakin' for whose soul the Friday mosque had been built and completed with great care. The chronogram provides the posthumous completion date of 973 (1565–66): 'May the station and home of the deceased [pasha] be paradise.'[258] A less prominent inscription in Arabic is engraved on the strap hinges nailed to the upper part of the two wooden door panels. Each half asks God's forgiveness and names a Syrian craftsman: (the inlayer) Muhammad al-Shami, and al-Hajj Khalil b. al-Hajj Yusuf al-Halabi.[259]

Two imperial decrees show that construction work on the projected khan was still going on in 1559, three years after its mention in the waqfiyya. They respond to a complaint that the surplus water of the 'imperial palace' (*sarāy-ı 'āmire*) in Aleppo, which used to flow to the 'Hospital of Argun Kamil' (Maristan Argun, 1354), had dried up because it was diverted to the khan

497 Dukakinzade Mehmed Pasha mosque, Aleppo, north façade.

498 Dukakinzade Mehmed Pasha mosque, portal.

presently being built for Dukakinzade Mehmed Beg. The kadi and finance minister of Aleppo are ordered to find out whether the hospital's water was taken against the shariʿa, and if so to redirect it to its original destination.[260]

Unlike the Khusrawiyya, the ʿAdiliyya complex did not have a madrasa, but it was provided with a hospice (*ʿimārethāne*) adjacent to the west side of the mosque and a guest-house (*misāfirhāne*) adjoining the north side of the hospice. These otherwise unknown charitable structures, omitted from the waqfiyya, seem to have been added later on. They are mentioned in a document that records their extensive renovation in 1141 (1728–29).[261] The *Tuhfe* attributes only the mosque to Sinan, excluding the solidly vaulted suqs and the double-storey khans with graceful proportions that monumentalized Mamluk models with innovative features. This is often the case in other provincial mosques commissioned from the chief architect, whose income-generating dependencies were created by local builders.[262]

According to Ibn al-Hanbali (d. 1563–64), the complex took over the sites of dismantled endowed structures along with the maydan at the edge of the hill known as Tallat ʿA'isha, where the Mamluks had held polo games. The Khan al-ʿUlabiyya replaced the maydan, while the adjacent mosque occupied the peak of the small hill, slightly elevated above its surroundings. Heghnar Watenpaugh notes the symbolic significance of appropriating the maydan: used for martial exercises crucial for the training and military culture of the Mamluk troops, it was 'a site rich in associations with the previous ruling group'.[263] The demolition of old buildings and the dissolution of several waqfs entailed the erasure of past memories to make way for new ones.

In contrast to the Khusrawiyya complex, whose income-producing endowments are distributed in various quarters, the ʿAdiliyya is a more compact compound, fully integrated with the commercial structures concentrated in adjacent plots. Compared to the highly visible mosque complex of Hüsrev Pasha, encircled on all sides by avenues, that of Dukakinzade is inserted into a dense urban fabric. None of its commercial structures open to the unporticoed paved forecourt of the mosque, behind which extends a cemetery-garden surrounded by walls. The commercial structures hinder an axial approach to the mosque, which is reached by two lateral entrances from the east and west, through long corridors with simple gates. Gevher Melikshah's mausoleum, supported by a separate waqf, is located near the more prominent eastern gate (illus. 495 [152]).

Designed at the height of Sinan's career, the ʿAdiliyya mosque comes closer to his 'classical' idiom than does the Khusrawiyya (illus. 497). No longer featuring lateral *tabhane* rooms, it is an ashlar masonry domed cube preceded by a trademark lofty double portico. The five-domed first portico is extended by a second one of the same height, and both rows of columns are luxuriously surmounted by muqarnas capitals. The second portico is covered by a flat rather than slanting roof, which creates

499 Dukakinzade Mehmed Pasha mosque, Aleppo, underglaze tile window lunette on the north façade.

a rigidly cubical appearance. Circular *oeil-de-boeuf* apertures embellish the spandrels of the outer portico. The exquisite muqarnas-hooded portal of striped ablaq masonry is flanked by two windows and a mihrab on each side (illus. 498).

The pointed-arched window lunettes on the north façade and inside the prayer hall are decked with matching underglaze tiles datable to the 1560s (consisting of square modules and rectangular borders) in blue, turquoise, and tomato red against a white ground (illus. 499). Their central rectangular frames, with white inscriptions against a dark blue background, are surrounded by palmettes, rosettes, *saz* leaves, and vegetal scrolls. Comparable underglaze tiles comprising tomato red in their colour scheme make their appearance in Diyarbakır in the mosque of Behram Pasha (*c.* 1564/65–1572/73), who later on built another mosque in Aleppo (*c.* 1583). It is unclear where the higher-quality tile revetments of the ʿAdiliyya were created; a likely place of production is İznik itself.

I have speculated earlier that Behram Pasha's mosque in Diyarbakır may have been inspired by the ʿAdiliyya, with which it shares a similar plan, used earlier by Sinan in Hadım İbrahim Pasha's Silivrikapı mosque (1551). Both provincial mosques boast lavish double porticoes, and their prayer halls crowned by domes raised on squinches are extended on all four sides by recessed alcoves with their own mihrabs (the more developed plan of Behram Pasha's mosque features an upper gallery missing in the ʿAdiliyya). They each have a monumental canopied ablution fountain axially aligned with the central arch of their double portico.[264] The fountain in the marble-paved forecourt of the ʿAdiliyya was once covered by a conical hood (now replaced with a domed canopy) resting on six columns. Unlike the simple water-tank of the Khusrawiyya, which Evliya Çelebi likens to a Shafiʿi pool, this is a typically Ottoman *şadırvan*, unprecedented in Aleppo. The use of a comparable plan fronted by a domed ablution fountain at the Hacı Ahmed Pasha mosque in Kayseri (*c.* 1576–85/86) is in keeping with the interregional links of central Anatolia with Diyarbakır and Aleppo, links reinforced by the similar plan types Sinan used in these three mosques.

500 Dukakinzade Mehmed Pasha mosque, Aleppo, interior.

The muqarnas-galleried slender minaret of the ʿAdiliyya has a conical cap in the Ottoman manner. The hemispherical dome of the mosque, originally covered with lead, sits on a drum pierced by sixteen windows, which is bolstered by Sinanesque engaged pilasters and paired flying buttresses in each corner.[265] Compared to the dome of the Khusrawiyya, that of the ʿAdiliyya is smaller (it covers an area about 255 square metres instead of 290).[266] The dome resting on eight pointed arches is raised on muqarnas-corbelled squinches with a provincial flavour (illus. 500). The handsome rectangular mihrab, richly inlaid with polychrome marbles (white, pink, and black) in the Mamluk manner, is accompanied by a matching Ottoman-type minbar with a conical cap. The inscription band under the muqarnas hood of the mihrab quotes one of the two Koranic passages (3:39) generally inscribed on the mihrabs of Sinan's mosques. The muezzin's tribune at the northwest corner of the prayer hall is supported on three slender pink marble columns with muqarnas capitals.

The tilework lunettes of the mosque cite a mixture of Koranic passages and hadith, as in those of Lala Mustafa Pasha's contemporary mosque in Erzurum (1562–63). Each pair on the north façade is inscribed with a hadith concerning the next world, a theme appropriate for a mosque commemorating a deceased patron. The first hadith declares that this world is understood by earthly possessions while the next is achieved by good deeds. The second hadith asserts that whoever builds a masjid for God, God will build an abode for him in paradise. Starting at the right side of the mihrab and moving counterclockwise, the lunette tiles in the prayer hall quote the Fatiha sura, which begs the merciful God, the 'owner of the Day of Judgment', to show the 'straight path' to favoured ones (1:1–7). The last two window lunettes on the west wall are inscribed with two hadith that resonate with their counterparts on the north façade: 'The world is carrion and dogs seek it'; 'Life in this world is short; spend it in obedience (to God).' The lunette panel above the gate, surmounted by a private balcony, is inscribed with the beautiful names of God and echoes the painted inscriptions in a band of cartouches around the base of the dome above. The names of Allah, Muhammad, the four caliphs, Hasan and Husayn are calligraphed without roundels in monumental *thuluth* over the plain arch spandrels that carry the dome.

The ʿAdiliyya mosque attractively blends a provincial version of Sinan's architectural idiom with a distinctive decorative skin combining tiles in the manner of İznik with Aleppine polychrome masonry. The waqf that Dukakinzade Mehmed Pasha established as a retired officer safeguarded the real estate properties he had accumulated in Aleppo as a source of income for his projected mosque, his progeny, and his household slaves. Some members of his family are known to have settled in Aleppo, in a mansion (*dār*) at the quarter of al-Biza, near the ʿAdiliyya complex. His descendants, who continued to live there well into the twentieth century, came to be known as the ʿAdili family after the waqf they administered. They also maintained the mausoleum of Gevher Melikshah and were buried in the cemetery of their ancestor's mosque, which perpetuated his memory over the generations while contributing to the commercial prosperity of Aleppo.[267]

Chapter 13

OFFICERS OF THE IMPERIAL COUNCIL AND OTHER DIGNITARIES

THE GRAND MUFTI AND ARMY JUDGES
I. MOLLA ÇELEBİ
ISTANBUL, FINDIKLI (*c.* 1570–84)

FINANCE MINISTERS AND CHANCELLORS
II. DEFTERDAR MUSTAFA ÇELEBİ
EDİRNE (*c.* 1569–74)

MINOR OFFICERS OF THE IMPERIAL COUNCIL AND THE GRAND VIZIER'S HOUSEHOLD
III. ÇAVUŞBAŞI MAHMUD AGHA
ISTANBUL, SÜTLÜCE (*c.* 1538–39)
IV. DRAGOMAN (TERCÜMAN) YUNUS BEG
ISTANBUL, DRAMAN (BALAT, 1541–42)
V. HÜRREM ÇAVUŞ
ISTANBUL, YENİBAHÇE (KARAGÜMRÜK, *c.* 1560/61–1562/63)
VI. FERRUH KETHÜDA
ISTANBUL, BALAT (1562–63)

THE GRAND MUFTI AND ARMY JUDGES

Only the highest-ranking jurists of the ulema commissioned Friday mosques from Sinan. These generally domeless sub-vizierial mosques are all sited in Istanbul, where their patrons held office (Map 2). The grand muftis (*şeyhülislam*) who headed the ulema as the absolute representatives of the sultan's religious authority were not members of the grand vizier's imperial council, despite the great influence they came to exercise in state affairs. The only *şeyhülislam* for whom the chief architect designed a Friday mosque is Fenarizade Muhyiddin Mehmed Çelebi (d. 1547–48); his mosque with a hipped roof and wooden portico recalls a masjid. Sited above the valley of Tophane, and popularly known as the Çukurcuma or Muhyiddin Çelebi mosque, it was rebuilt after a fire in 1823. Only its minaret base and the foundations of its rectangular walls, constructed with alternating courses of stone and brick, are now preserved.[1]

Next in rank within the ulema hierarchy were the army judges (*kazasker*) of Rumelia and Anatolia, who unlike the grand muftis did belong to the imperial council. Mehmed II's law code specified that the army judge of Rumelia was the more important of the two, and that they were both superseded in status by the governor-generals and sanjak governors.[2] Three army judges commissioned Sinan to design Friday mosques in the capital: Amasyalı Kızıl Abdurrahman Çelebi, Mevlana Ensari Ahmed Çelebi, and Molla Çelebi. The first of these mosques, completed in 962 (1554–55) and sited in the Yenibahçe quarter, was demolished during the creation of a modern avenue. Known as the mosque of Kazasker Abdurrahman Çelebi, this rectangular building was crowned by a wooden dome protected under a lead-covered hipped roof. Fronted by a wooden portico, its walls of alternating courses of stone and brick had two tiers of windows.[3]

The Friday mosque that Sinan designed in Üsküdar for Kazasker Ahmed Çelebi, the army judge of Anatolia, was entirely rebuilt in the nineteenth century. Its rectangular masonry structure is crowned by a wooden hipped roof and features an onion-domed wooden minaret raised from its roof. The patron is buried next to the modest, masjid-like mosque which Ayvansarayi dates to 975 (1567–68). Recorded in 1588, its Arabic waqfiyya explains that the Friday mosque of 'al-Mawla Ahmad Efendi al-Ansari' was located in the 'new quarter' of Üsküdar, named after him as Kazasker Mahallesi, near the mosque of the late queen mother Nurbanu.[4]

I. MOLLA ÇELEBİ

Compared to the two previous mosques, that of the retired army judge Mehmed Vusuli Efendi (Molla Çelebi) in Fındıklı is unusually monumental and unlike them features a hexagonal domed baldachin (illus. 501).[5] Its deviation from the norm can be attributed to its patron's privileged status, thanks to his influential mother-in-law, the poetess Hubbi Hatun (d. 1589–90), who was a lady-in-waiting (*musahibe*) of Selim II and Murad III. Because he owed his position to her mediation, he was nicknamed 'Hubbi Mollası' (Hubbi's Mullah).[6]

The autobiographical notes interpolated by Mehmed Vusuli Efendi into his history of Selim II's reign, which he dedicated to Murad III, indicate that his father, Abdullah Agha, had been the chief gatekeeper of prince Selim's court at Manisa in the 1540s.[7]

501 Plan and elevation of the Molla Çelebi mosque, Fındıklı.

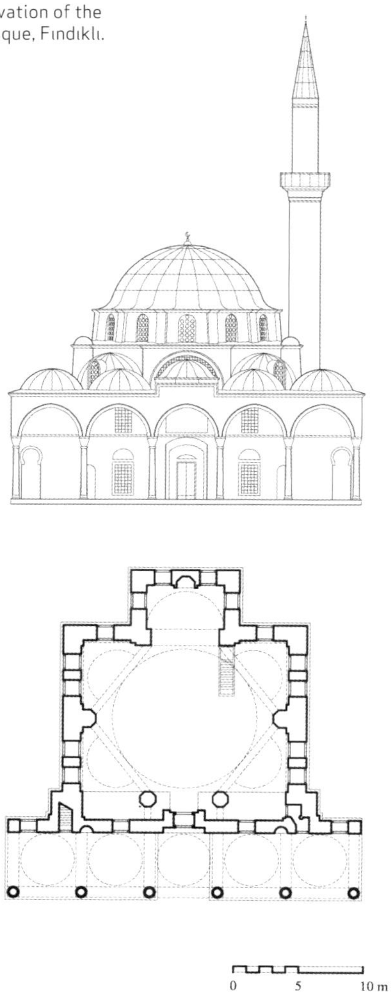

502 Plan of the Kazasker İvaz Efendi mosque, Eğrikapı, with hypothetical reconstruction of wooden porticoes.

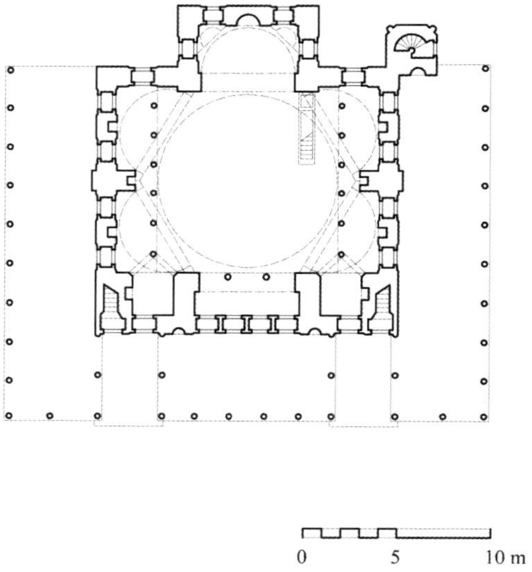

During a hunting party that the prince organized while guarding Edirne in 1548, the author was appointed to his first teaching position in Bursa.[8] When Selim moved to Bursa before the war of princes in 1558, Molla Çelebi came to meet him as 'an opportunity for advancement' and was designated the kadi of Konya.[9] Soon after Selim's accession to the throne, he became the kadi of Bursa and was promoted to the kadi of Istanbul in 1567. He then rose to the post of army judge of Anatolia (1568–70), thereafter serving as the kadi of Istanbul three times in the 1570s and 1580s.[10] He died in 1589–90 and was buried in a mausoleum next to that of his mother-in-law in Eyüp, where he had endowed a convent in 1584 (Map 3).

Molla Çelebi's Friday mosque and now-lost bath-house in Fındıklı are listed in all of Sinan's autobiographies. The *Tuhfe* refers to 'the noble Friday mosque of Kazasker Molla Çelebi near the shore on the road to Beşiktaş' and to his bathhouse along the seashore.[11] The chronology of these buildings is a matter of controversy. The mosque lacks a foundation inscription and is assumed to have been completed the same year as the bathhouse, whose Turkish chronogram, recorded by Evliya Çelebi and

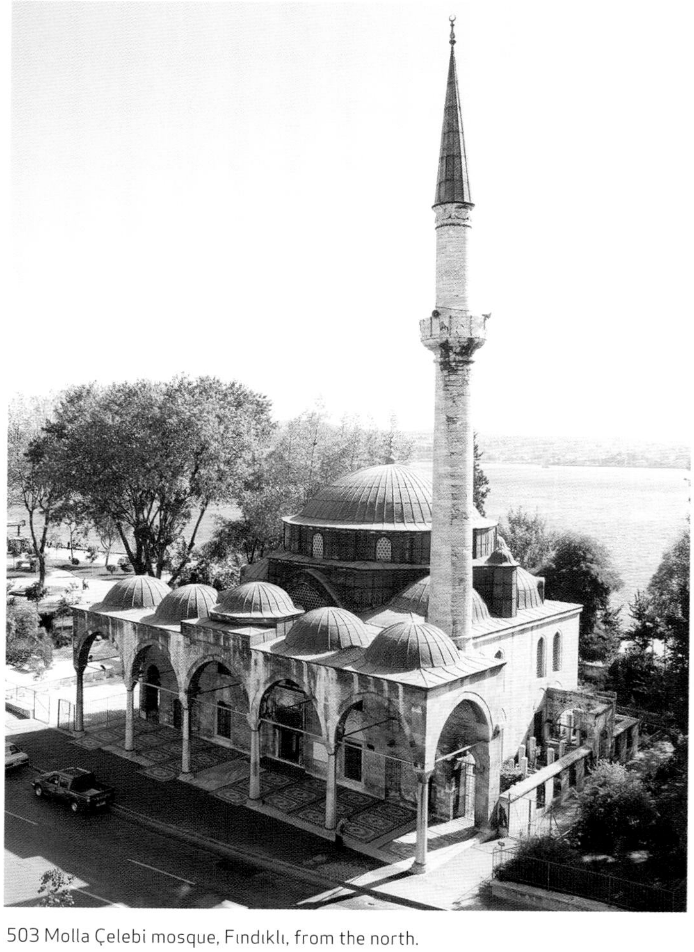

503 Molla Çelebi mosque, Fındıklı, from the north.

Ayvansarayi, has been calculated variously to yield the dates of 959 (1551–52), 969 (1561–62), and 979 (1571).[12] The chronogram reads: 'Visit the Molla's bathhouse along the lip of the sea.'[13]

The more likely date of the bath chronogram is 1571, judging by a hitherto unnoted Arabic waqfiyya of 'Mevlana Mehmed the son of the late amir Abdullah, the army judge of Anatolia', registered in February 1570. It shows that 'the bathhouse built in the place known as Canfeda near Tophane' was completed around that time.[14] The waqfiyya also endows properties in Bursa for the madrasa Molla Çelebi built in that city for the soul of his late father. The interest yielded by an endowed sum of 25,000 gold coins and by rents from the bathhouse and abutting shops in Fındıklı would be used to finance the construction of a 'noble madrasa' for teaching the hadith and a 'noble masjid' on the empty plot next to the bathhouse.[15] On the same site near a landing station (now Kabataş İskelesi), rooms were to be built for hajj pilgrims. A sum of twenty aspers a day was assigned to cover the costs of cooking their food. If the founder should die before his wife (Hubbi Hatun's daughter), she would receive a daily stipend of fifty aspers to pray for his soul. Upon her death, thirty aspers of that sum would be used to pay fifteen Koran reciters at the projected masjid on behalf of her soul. The surplus of the endowment was to be split among the founder's children and their progeny over the generations.[16]

Clearly, then, the mosque did not exist in 1570. A second Arabic waqfiyya, registered in July 1584, shows that a 'Friday mosque' (*cāmiʿ*) had been built instead of a masjid, and a madrasa functioning as a hadith college (*dār al-ḥadīth*) would be created in the future (it never seems to have materialized).[17] The mosque, generally dated to 1561–62, should therefore be redated to sometime between 1570 and 1584. It was probably completed around 1584, well after Molla Çelebi lost his rank of army judge of Anatolia in 1570, and during his intermittent tenure as kadi of Istanbul. The second waqfiyya, which identifies Molla Çelebi as the 'retired' army judge of Anatolia, emphasizes the highest post he occupied during his career. The historian Selaniki likewise refers to him in 1582 as 'Molla Çelebi, who retired from the post of army judge of Anatolia'.[18] This is precisely how Ayvansarayi identifies the patron of the mosque: 'Molla Çelebi who had been dismissed from the office of *kazasker* of Anatolia.'[19]

The waqfiyya of 1584 endows the patron's summer and winter residences in order to bring income to his pious foundation. Upon his death, the waqf would be administered and overseen by his sons and their descendants, who would live in those palaces. The summer residence comprised a garden with pools and edifices in 'the place known as Fındıklı, near the garden of Canfeda', which abutted its west side.[20] Canfeda can be identified as the powerful stewardess of the imperial harem, Kethüda Canfeda Hatun.[21] The newly developing suburb of Fındıklı was dominated by garden residences owned by the female attendants

504 Molla Çelebi mosque, Fındıklı, interior.

of the imperial harem and by leading members of the ulema such as the grand mufti Ebussuud Efendi.[22]

This was an ideal site for the Friday mosque of Molla Çelebi, since he was both a prominent member of the ulema and associated through his mother-in-law with the imperial harem. Old photographs show that the ashlar masonry double bath at the west side of the mosque (demolished when the avenue along the north was widened in 1957) had two undressing halls covered by hipped wooden roofs. The ashlar masonry mosque, with a hexagonal domed baldachin and a five-domed portico, belongs to a type Sinan had experimented with before. Its projecting mihrab is a distinctive feature of post-Selimiye mosques; examples with hexagonal baldachins include those of the queen mother Nurbanu in Üsküdar and the grand vizier Semiz Ali Pasha in Babaeski (illus. 4).[23] The less monumental mosque of Molla Çelebi is comparable in scale with that of another army judge, Kazasker İvaz Efendi, in Eğrikapı, which was completed in 1586 but has been excluded from Sinan's autobiographies (illus. 4, 502).[24] Once surrounded by a U-shaped portico, the Eğrikapı mosque has an unusual north façade with two lateral gates and multi-tiered windows. By comparison, the façade of the Fındıklı mosque is relatively traditional. Nevertheless, both mosques share post-classical characteristics and are crowned by small domes appropriate to the ranks of their patrons (Molla Çelebi 11.8 metres, İvaz Efendi 9.8 metres).[25]

The mosque in Fındıklı has changed relatively little despite extensive repairs after two fires in 1723 and 1724, when its damaged portico was replaced with a wooden one. The present five-domed portico raised on white marble columns with lozenge capitals was built in 1958 (illus. 503). Its simple arched portal lacks a muqarnas hood. The nearly cubical walls of the mosque are surmounted by a layered domical superstructure entirely covered with lead, as in several late-Sinan mosques. The main dome with squinches rests on a twelve-sided drum reinforced by four weight turrets that alternate with four exedral half-domes and a half-dome over the mihrab. The insetting of windows into the curved surfaces of these drumless half-domes by opening 'stunted tunnel vaults' (as in the İvaz Efendi mosque) is another characteristic of Sinan's later works. The four weight turrets with domical caps rise above the internal engaged piers abutting the lateral walls of the prayer hall and those incorporated into the corners of the mihrab recess (illus. 504). The two free-standing octagonal piers at the north are not expressed externally. Featuring a plain gallery, the rebuilt neoclassical cylindrical minaret is decorated with garlands. The spatially unified, light-filled prayer hall no longer preserves its original painted decorations and inscriptions. Its plain muqarnas-hooded mihrab is accompanied by a late-Ottoman wooden minbar.

Construction-related decrees jointly addressed to Sinan and the kadis of Istanbul suggest that he must have collaborated closely with Molla Çelebi, who held that post while his mosque was being built. Mimicking vizierial foundations in smaller scale, the aspiring mosque commemorates its patron's former rank as an army judge. It negotiates the upper limit of decorum thanks to Molla Çelebi's special connection with the imperial palace through his late father and mother-in-law.

FINANCE MINISTERS AND CHANCELLORS

The viziers, army judges, finance ministers, and chancellor constituted the 'four pillars of the state', who sat at the imperial council hall (illus. 12).[26] Headed by the chief finance minister (*başdefterdar*), the finance ministers (*defterdar*) were ranked after the army judges in Mehmed II's law code.[27] The chancellor (*nişancı*), who signed the sultan's monogram on imperial decrees, came next in rank, superseding the finance ministers if he held the honorary title of vizier or governor-general.[28]

Among the Friday mosques commissioned from Sinan by chancellors, we have already considered that of the vizier Nişancı Mehmed Pasha boasting an octagonal domed baldachin.[29] His relative and mentor, Nişancı Celalzade Mustafa Çelebi (d. 1567), was the most famous chancellor of Süleyman's reign, but never rose to the vizierate. He commissioned from Sinan a Friday mosque along the shore of Eyüp next to his residence, which was considerably more modest than the vizierial mosque of Nişancı Mehmed Pasha. The rectangular structure, completely rebuilt on old foundations after a fire in 1780, preserves nothing of the original fabric except for the base of the brick minaret. Built of rubble masonry with two rows of windows, it is covered by a wooden hipped roof with terracotta tiles. It may originally have featured a small dome, judging by Evliya Çelebi's description of it as 'elaborate and perfect like a royal mosque'.[30] The mosque that gave the quarter its name (Nişanca) was once accompanied by a bathhouse and a convent for Halveti dervishes. Its patron is buried in the cemetery behind the qibla wall of the mosque together with his brother Salih Efendi, who also held the post of chancellor (d. 1565).[31]

Sinan's autobiographies mention several Friday mosques commissioned by finance ministers: Abdüsselam Çelebi in İzmit, Ebulfazl Mehmed Efendi at Tophane, Süleyman Çelebi near the Üsküblü fountain in Istanbul, and Mustafa Çelebi in Edirne. The first, endowed in 1525 by the Jewish-born chief finance minister Abdüsselam (d. 1526–27), is too early to have been created during Sinan's tenure as chief architect, though he may have contributed to its construction or renovation. It was entirely rebuilt after an earthquake in the nineteenth century.[32] The second, built for the finance minister of Anatolia, Defterdar Süleyman Çelebi, is a remodelled fifteenth-century masjid founded by the chief falconer, Çakır Ağa. Completely rebuilt after a fire in 1874, it is described by Evliya Çelebi as having a wooden dome surmounted by a four-hipped roof covered with lead.[33]

The Friday mosque of Ebulfazl Mehmed Efendi on a hilltop of Tophane has disappeared without a trace, but it can be reconstructed on the basis of photographs recording its ruins after a fire in 1916 (illus. 505).[34] Its Arabic foundation inscription, carved on the arched lunette of its gate, which lacked a muqarnas hood, named the reigning monarch, Sultan Süleyman, and the patron, ending in a chronogram that yielded the date 961 (1553–54).[35] The Muslim-born patron was the son of the celebrated historian İdris-i Bidlisi. After being demoted from his position of finance minister in 1541, he twice occupied the post of chief finance minister (1566–67 and 1569–70). According to Atai, Ebulfazl passed his retirement 'in Tophane, on a hill overlooking the sea', where he built a pleasant residence and a paradise-like garden, spending his time with the pursuit of knowledge, worship, and spiritual conversations with friends. Next to his garden, he added a Friday mosque, an elementary school, and a tomb for himself in 1553–54, but he was buried in Damascus, where he died while performing the hajj in 1574–75.[36] Known as Defterdar Camii, the view-commanding mosque was a monumental rectangular structure built of alternating courses of stone and brick and covered by a wooden hipped roof. Fronted by a spacious wooden portico on a terrace reached by stairs, it featured two rows of windows and a projecting cylindrical minaret with a plain gallery at its northwest corner.

II. DEFTERDAR MUSTAFA ÇELEBİ

The only extant Friday mosque of Sinan named after a finance minister is that of Defterdar Mustafa Çelebi in Edirne (illus. 506, 507). It is a domed cube, constructed of alternating courses of stone and brick and preceded by a three-bay portico of ashlar masonry resting on marble columns with muqarnas capitals. Prominently located along the Istanbul-Edirne highway, the mosque has a muqarnas-galleried, multi-faceted stone minaret.

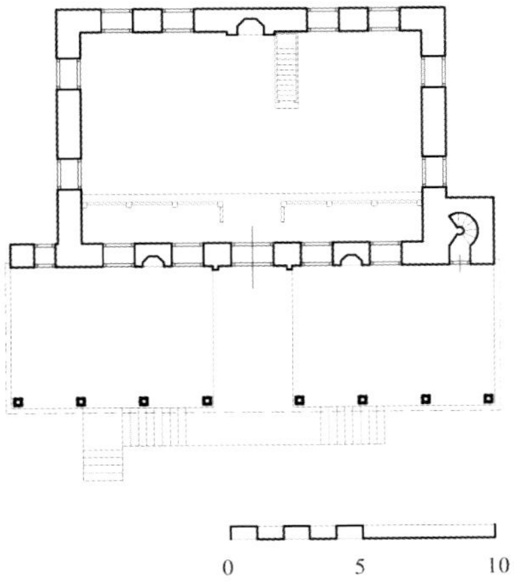

505 Reconstruction plan of the Defterdar Ebulfazl Efendi mosque, Tophane.

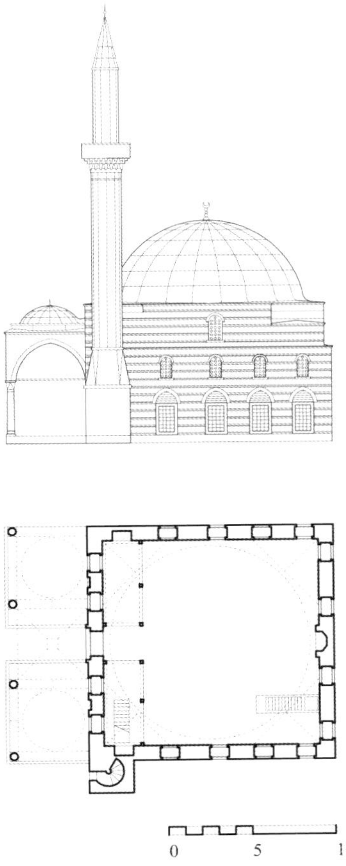

506 Plan and elevation of the Defterdar Mustafa Pasha mosque, Edirne.

The lead-covered dome, raised on squinches above an archaic octagonal drum, collapsed during an earthquake in 1752 and was rebuilt after many years between 1953 and 1962. Consequently, the painted decorations of the prayer hall, featuring a muqarnas-hooded mihrab and a modern wooden minbar, have vanished. Defterdar Mustafa Çelebi's mosque comes close in plan type to those of sanjak governors. The circumstances of its construction remain obscure in the absence of a waqfiyya and a foundation inscription on its plain portal without a muqarnas hood. Nor do we have much information about the patron of this mosque, which is thought to have been created during the construction of the Selimiye in Edirne.[37]

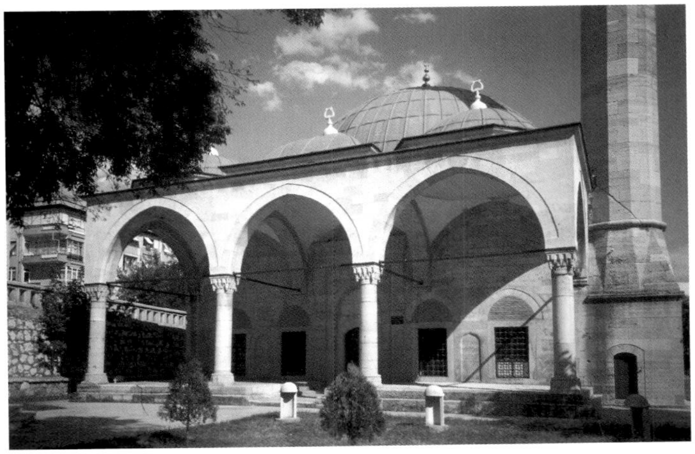

507 Defterdar Mustafa Pasha mosque, from the north.

MINOR OFFICERS OF THE IMPERIAL COUNCIL AND THE GRAND VIZIER'S HOUSEHOLD

Lower-ranking officers of the imperial council, such as the chief court messenger and chief court interpreter, were proud enough to commission Friday mosques from Sinan, as were the household stewards of some grand viziers. The simple mosques with hipped roofs designed for them by the chief architect are located on the outskirts of the walled city (Yenibahçe, Balat) and in its outlying suburbs (Sütlüce). These mosques could therefore accommodate garden cemeteries where their patrons were buried.

III. ÇAVUŞBAŞI MAHMUD AGHA

Among the Friday mosques Sinan designed for minor officers of the imperial council is that of Sultan Süleyman's chief court messenger, Çavuşbaşı Mahmud Agha, in Sütlüce, outside the walls of Galata (illus. 508). Mehmed II's law code counts the *çavuşbaşı*, a master of ceremonies in the service of the grand vizier, among the servants of the imperial council who were not allowed to sit there.[38] Sited on a slope overlooking the Golden Horn, the Sütlüce mosque is thought to have been completed in 945 (1538–39), on the basis of its dated fountain and a repair

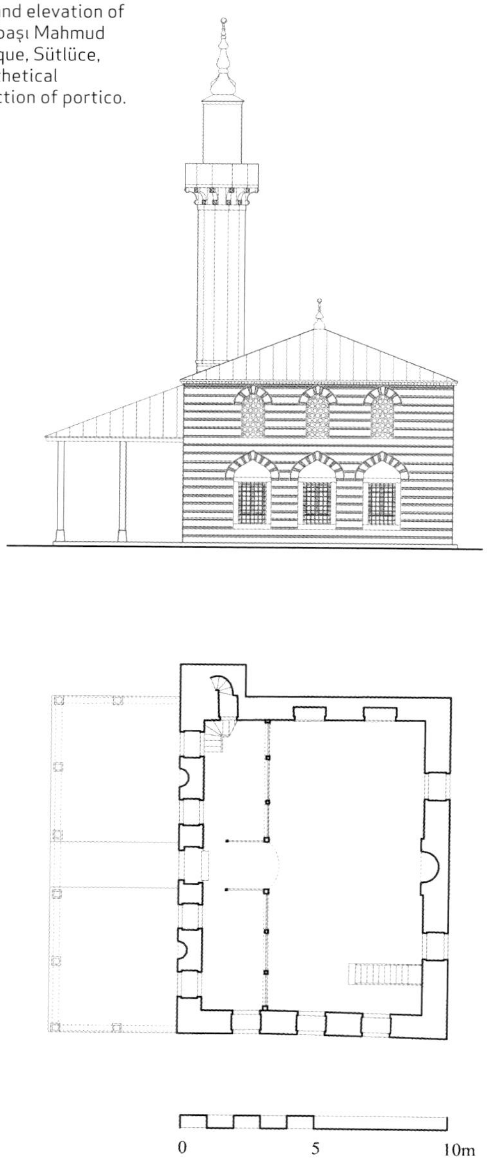

508 Plan and elevation of the Çavuşbaşı Mahmud Agha mosque, Sütlüce, with hypothetical reconstruction of portico.

inscription added to its gate in 1307 (1889).[39] Its patron is buried in the cemetery of the mosque; the Arabic inscription on his tombstone, which is dated Şaban 957 (August–September 1550), refers to him as the late 'Mahmud b. Abdullah'. The cemetery was once almost a museum of tombstones including those of the Halveti Shaykh İshak Karamani (d. 1526–27), his calligrapher disciple Ahmed Karahisari (d. 1555–56), and the latter's pupil Hasan Karahisari (d. 1593–94). The rectangular mosque, built with alternating courses of stone and brick, has a wooden roof with terracotta tiles. According to Evliya Çelebi, its four-hipped roof was originally covered by lead.[40] Despite various renovations, the mosque preserves the fabric of its walls with two tiers of windows, but its rebuilt superstructure, its wooden portico (now walled-in), and the upper part of its brick minaret no longer maintain their original form.

IV. DRAGOMAN (TERCÜMAN) YUNUS BEG

The post of chief interpreter emerged in the early sixteenth century as part of the staff of the chief secretary (*reisülküttab*) of the imperial council. The funerary mosque of the influential Greek-born chief interpreter, Dragoman Yunus Beg, in Draman (Balat) is dated to 948 (1541–42) by the chronograms of two foundation inscriptions (illus. 509, 510).[41] One of these is in Turkish, carved in three lines of monumental *thuluth* over the arched mosque gate without a muqarnas hood:

> Yunus Beg, who with dignity and glory became
> The translator (*tercümān*) of the world-adorning Shah,
>
> Built this noble masjid (*mescīd*)
> When God assisted and favoured him.
>
> The divine spirit said its date at that time:
> 'House of piety and abode of the righteous.'[42]

The second inscription, in *taʿlīḳ* script, consists of two Persian couplets attributed to the famous jursist Ebussuud Efendi. It is carved outside the east gate of the precinct wall, reached by a steep staircase from the avenue below:

> O Lord, how fit it is that for this place
> There is sun instead of shade.
>
> When Ridwan [gatekeeper of Eden] saw that building,
> He said its date: 'A gate of Paradise', 948 (1541–42).[43]

Ayvansarayi points out that the patron first built an elementary school and then a Friday mosque, but passed away before the completion of his complex. He was buried behind the mihrab of the mosque, and his brother Mustafa Agha finished the complex, building a hadith college at one corner. Ayvansarayi adds that Abdülmümin Efendi of Bosnia, a disciple of the Halveti shaykh Nureddinzade, who was a Friday preacher in the mosque, built a convent (*zaviye*) there. Being the owner of a house adjoining the mosque courtyard, he endowed it to the shaykh of the mosque, and was buried beside Yunus Beg when he died in 1004 (1595–96).[44]

The Friday mosque and madrasa are listed in all the autobiographies of Sinan as the works of 'Dragoman Yunus Beg', and their site is identified as 'near Balat' (once a primarily Jewish neighbourhood, named today after the founder as Draman).[45] No trace remains of the neighbouring elementary school or the Halveti convent, which was staffed with eighteen dervishes.[46] A waqf register of Istanbul, dated 1546, records the waqfiyya of 'Yunus Beg b. Abdurrahman', the sultan's translator, which was registered in May 1541. His endowments included 453,540 aspers, real estate properties in the capital, and a bathhouse in Plovdiv. One of the houses near the Friday mosque was earmarked as the residence of its shaykh. When surplus funds reached

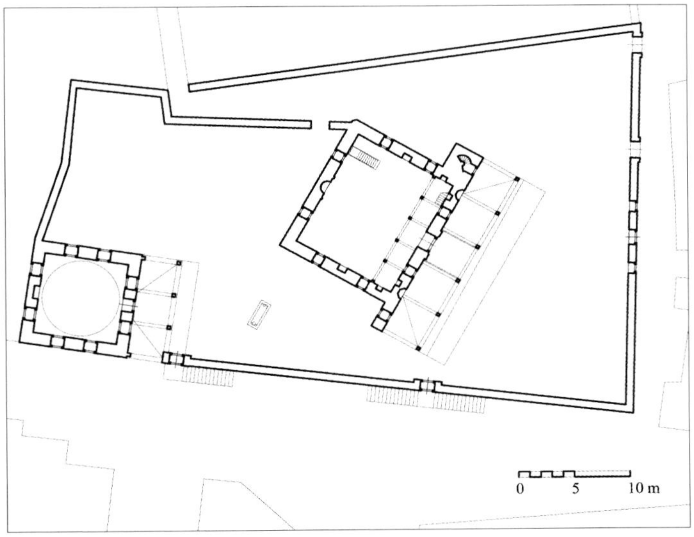

509 Reconstruction plan of the Dragoman Yunus Beg complex, Draman.

5,000 aspers, a new house would be bought for the shaykh. Two other neighbouring houses were reserved for the imam and muezzin, while individual rooms were set aside for the janitor and the shaykh's disciples. Administered by Yunus Beg himself, the endowment would revert to his freed slaves upon his death. Among the staff of the Friday mosque (*cāmiʿ*), referred to as a masjid in its foundation inscription, the waqfiyya covers the salary of the shaykh, who delivered Friday sermons. It also records the wages of a teacher and an assistant for the elementary school.[47]

The programme of the mosque complex, then, housed sufi functions from the very beginning. Its founder became chief court interpreter in 1525, under the grand vizier İbrahim Pasha (d. 1536). He is identified as 'Yunus Beg son of Abdurrahman' in Venetian archival documents that record his six embassies to Venice, the first two as a young cavalry soldier of the court, and the latter ones as a rich and powerful '*dragomanno*' (1519, 1522, 1529, 1532–33, 1537, 1542). Yunus is said to have been a native of Modone, the son of a Giorgio Taroniti; he had Christian relatives in Zante including his sister Marietta and her

510 Hypothetical axonometric projection of the Dragoman Yunus Beg complex.

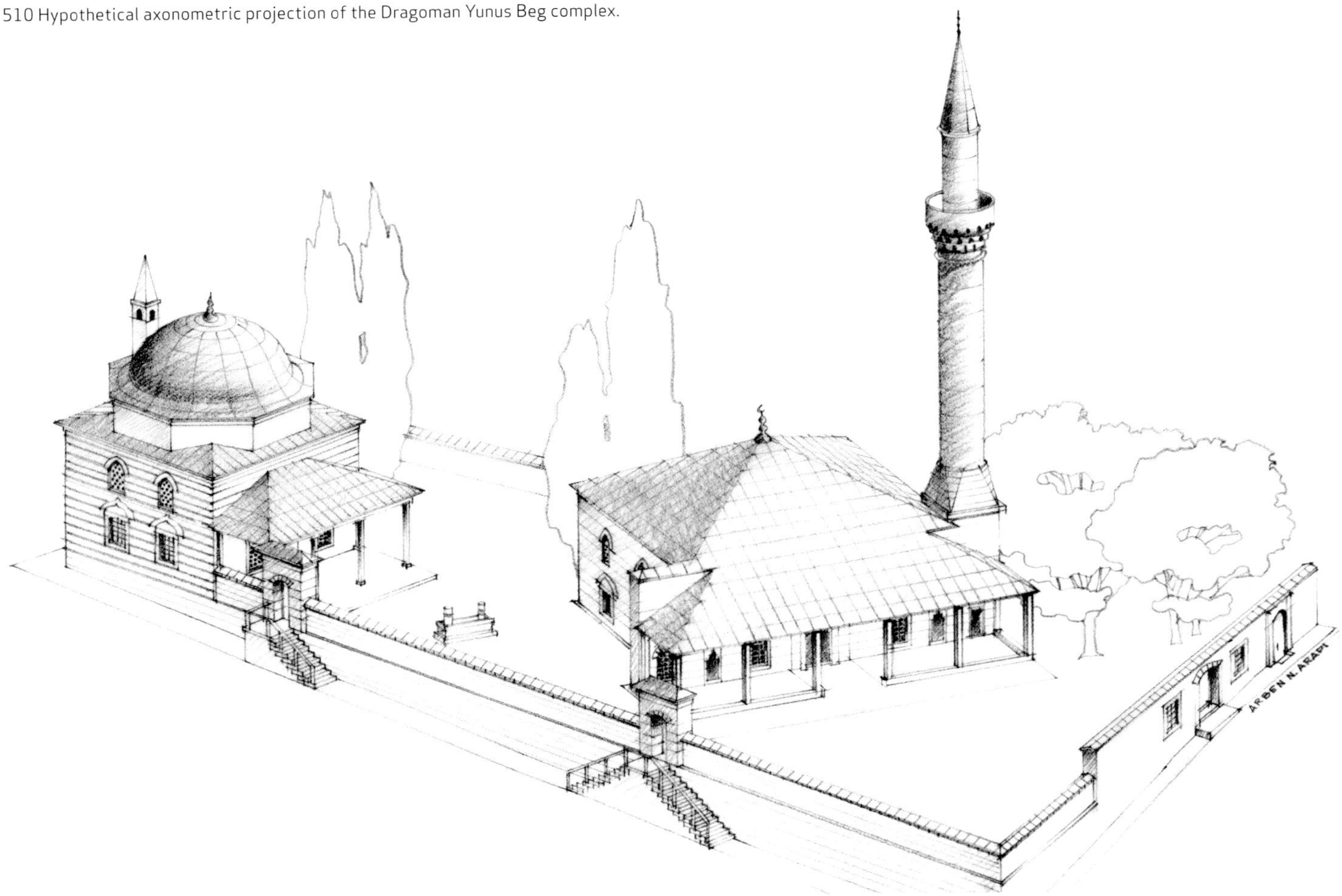

son Nicolò Stefani. His brother Mustafa Agha (d. 1565) was the chief gatekeeper and then the chief messenger of the sultan's court.[48] The renegade Yunus Beg spoke Greek, Latin, and Italian. He is portrayed as a notoriously avid person who often complained about the diplomatic gifts he received. Primarily concerned with making money, he was engaged in trade (particularly of textiles). Though he was judged negatively by the members of the Venetian Senate, they tried to please him in every possible way because they could not afford to offend him.[49]

Johann Maria Malvezzi's dispatches from Istanbul to the Austrian Hapsburg ruler Ferdinand testify to the continuing influence of Yunus Beg during the last decade of his life. On 26 December 1549, Malvezzi wrote that the 'old Jonus' was ready to help them in diplomatic negotiations with Rüstem Pasha and Sultan Süleyman, who 'deferred to him a great deal in all negotiations'. In return for his services, he was promised funds to support the mosque he had built:

> Because the said Jonus does not have children,
> I promised him that Your Majesty will set up and give
> provisions after his death for his mosque (*meschitta*),
> which is particularly dear to him for having been built
> by him; and he very much desires to leave it rich with
> a good income for his honour and [the salvation of]
> his soul.[50]

On 9 May 1550, Malvezzi reports the appointment of a pro-French 'new *dragoman*' because 'Jonusbey has been very ill.'[51] He passed away from 'hydropsy' on 22 June 1551.[52]

Overlooking the Golden Horn, Yunus Beg's Friday mosque is raised on a high terrace whose east side rests on a steep retaining wall along an avenue. Its only surviving dependency is the madrasa, which functioned as a hadith college – a domed cube occupying the southeast corner of the walled precinct. The east façade of the madrasa, facing the avenue below, is built of ashlar masonry, unlike its less visible walls of cheaper rubble stone.[53] The rectangular ashlar masonry mosque, originally surmounted by a lead-covered hipped roof, has a muqarnas-galleried, multifaceted stone minaret. Inscriptions show that the mosque, damaged in the Balat fire of 1729, was renovated in 1730–31, followed by later repairs in 1746, 1873, and 1914. Its windows were altered with round-arched profiles and its wooden portico was replaced by a covered hall with a flat roof.

More recently, the hipped roof has incongruously been replaced by a lead-covered dome, fronted by a new portico with five small domes resting on six marble columns. The modern Kütahya tiles that embellish the prayer hall have nothing to do with the original decorative programme. These aggressive interventions by the congregation were intended to 'improve' and 'Sinanize' the mosque in a manner that anachronistically imitates the grand master's domed masterpieces, with no regard for codes of decorum. No such audacity could have been contemplated by the rich and powerful patron of the mosque. At a time when higher-ranking sub-vizierial officers of the imperial council were commissioning humble hipped-roof mosques with alternating courses of stone and brick, Yunus Beg's ashlar masonry mosque was already a bold proclamation of honour and prestige.

V. HÜRREM ÇAVUŞ

This mosque was built in Yenibahçe during Sultan Süleyman's reign for one of the messengers of the imperial council, Hürrem Çavuş (illus. 511). The post of *çavuş* is ranked in Mehmed II's law code as being comparable to that of scribes.[54] These minor officers served the imperial council, acclaimed the sultan in ceremonial parades, went abroad as ambassadors, acted as couriers in royal construction projects, and were often trained as architects – like Mehmed Çavuş, or Sinan's successors, Davud Çavuş and Dalgıç Ahmed Çavuş (Appendix 4:4, 4:5).[55] Next to nothing is known about the patron of the mosque. A late-

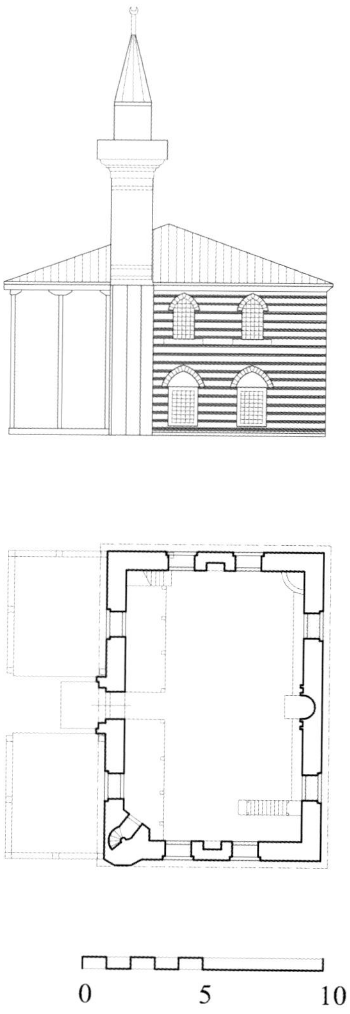

511 Plan and elevation of the Hürrem Çavuş mosque, Yenibahçe, with hypothetical reconstruction of portico.

sixteenth-century register of Istanbul waqfs records the waqfiyya of 'Hürrem Beg b. Abdülhalim', dated November 1568, with which the patron endowed income-producing properties for his 'noble Friday mosque and elementary school in the quarter of Karabaş', near Yenikapı. These properties included seven shops and forty-four rental rooms adjacent to the mosque courtyard, thirty rental rooms and a bakery with a well nearby, and other real estate in the capital. The waqfiyya lists the salaries of the Friday mosque and elementary school staff (the latter had not yet been built, according to a marginal note).[56]

Hürrem Çavuş must have been well acquainted with Sinan, since he also endowed a house for the imam of the chief architect's neighbouring masjid at Yenibahçe.[57] He is buried in the cemetery behind the mihrab of his own mosque; the date inscribed on his tombstone is 968 (1560–61). According to a chronogram cited by Ayvansarayi, the construction of the mosque was completed in 970 (1562–63), shortly after the patron's demise:

> Hürrem Çavuş, with perfect zeal,
> Made firm this place of prayer.
>
> May he be enveloped in God's mercy!
> May the highest Paradise be his abode!
>
> Hatibī, hearing the year of [its] completion,
> Composed a chronogram: 'House of prayers',
> 970 (1562–63).[58]

A now-lost inscription was painted in black on the pointed-arched stone lunette of the mosque portal which lacks a muqarnas hood. Under the popular hadith, promising a place in paradise to whoever builds a mosque for God, was written the dates of foundation and various repairs: 968 (1560–61), 1260 (1844) and 1319 (1901–2). The first date implies that the foundations of the mosque were laid just before the death of Hürrem Çavuş and completed posthumously. It was accompanied by an elementary school that no longer exists and a public fountain facing the street.[59]

Situated in a walled enclosure, the rectangular mosque preserves its original fabric of alternating courses of stone and brick, with two tiers of windows. Featuring a hipped roof with terracotta tiles, it has a rebuilt wooden portico protected by walls. The short, thick cylindrical stone minaret with a plain gallery is integrated into the northwest corner of the mosque. The side walls of the prayer hall each have a pair of superimposed windows and a rectangular cupboard in the middle. The muqarnas-hooded mihrab is accompanied by a modern wooden minbar. This is one of the few hipped-roof mosques attributed to Sinan that has not been altered beyond recognition.

VI. FERRUH KETHÜDA

Just as grand viziers saw their power augmented during the reign

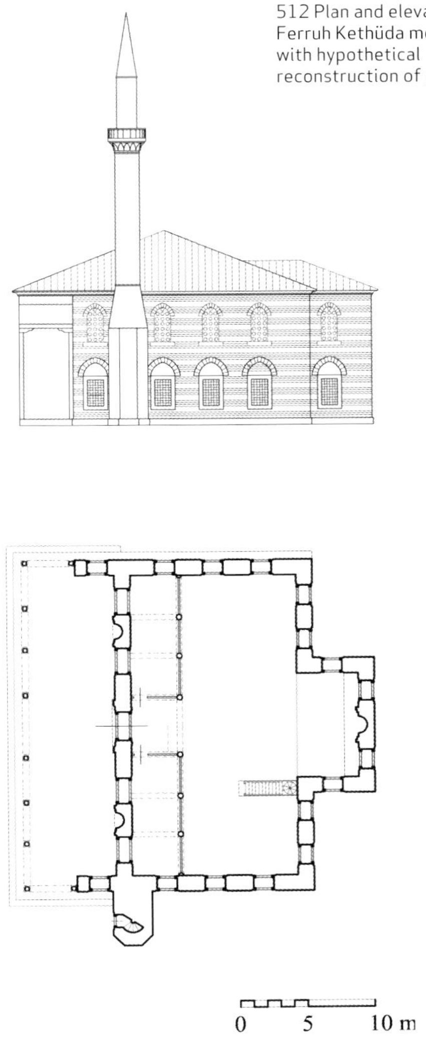

512 Plan and elevation of the Ferruh Kethüda mosque, Balat, with hypothetical reconstruction of portico.

of Süleyman, their household stewards emerged from obscurity into the public domain. The Friday mosque that Sinan designed for Ferruh Kethüda, the steward of Semiz Ali Pasha, is situated inside the Balat gate along the Golden Horn, next to a preexisting bathhouse (illus. 512). Another of Sinan's Friday mosques, built in İzmit for Mehmed Kethüda, the steward of Rüstem Pasha, has not survived in its original form. The remains of its basement suggest that it was a rectangular structure with a hipped roof.[60] Both Mehmed Kethüda and Ferruh Kethüda became the waqf administrators of their deceased patrons, whose Friday mosques were posthumously created under their supervision: Rüstem Pasha in Tahtakale and Semiz Ali Pasha in Babaeski.[61] It is not surprising, then, that these two stewards had access to Sinan for their own Friday mosques.

The Balat mosque, completed in 1562–63, was endowed soon after Semiz Ali Pasha's death with a Turkish waqfiyya dated March 1566. It explains that 'Ferruh Kethüda b. Abdülhalim' endowed a Friday mosque and convent inside the Balat gate, as well as a paved road connecting the Balat gate to the Eyüp gate and an elementary school in Kocamustafapaşa (the headquarters of the Sünbüli-Halveti order).[62] In the mosque courtyard the patron created an ablution fountain, along with a public fountain outside. Next to the mosque he built 'an elegant convent (*zāviye*) comprising ten cells (*ḥücre*); and an upper ritual hall (*cemiyyetḫāne*) and a porch (*ṣoffa*); and under the ritual hall a pantry (*kiler*), and next to the pantry a kitchen (*maṭbaḫ*), and a cell known as the library (*kitābḫānelik*)'.[63]

The waqfiyya stipulates that the shaykh of the convent was to deliver sermons at the mosque on Fridays and holy nights, and that the post was earmarked for Mevlana Shaykh Sinan Efendi, the son of shaykh Mevlana Yakub Efendi of Ioannina, so long as he lived. After his demise, he would be replaced with one of his disciples belonging to the Halveti order, and the endowed house he lived in would pass to his successor.[64] The mosque and convent were surrounded by a host of endowed houses, rooms, shops, storehouses, and plots of land. Outside the Balat gate, the patron endowed additional shops, rooms, and shore residences with garden kiosks (*köşk*) overlooking the Golden Horn where he, his wife (Münteha Hatun), and their descendants would reside before these reverted to the waqf upon the extinction of their lineage. Administered by the patron himself, the waqf would be managed after his death by his children and their progeny.[65]

Shaykh Sinan Efendi (Sinaneddin Yusuf), a famous scholar celebrated for his interpretations of the Koran, had given up his post as a madrasa professor to join the Halveti order. He was renowned for his melodic recitations of the Koran and his spiritually moving sermons filled with 'deep and subtle secrets'. He left Ferruh Kethüda's complex to spend the last years of his life as the *shaykh al-haram* of Medina (d. 1579–80), where he was buried.[66] The convent, known as Balat Tekkesi, remained connected with the Sünbüli branch of the Halveti order, to which Shaykh Sinaneddin Yusuf belonged, until it was closed down in 1925.[67] Sinan's autobiographies mention only the Friday mosque, omitting its convent, which came close to vernacular architecture and housed sixteen dervishes.[68] This was also the case with the mosque of Dragoman Yunus Beg, discussed above, whose Halveti convent (formerly the residence of its shaykh) is not listed among the chief architect's works. Ferruh Kethüda's mosque complex comprised a low-ranking madrasa not mentioned in the waqfiyya of 1565; by 1566–67 it had a professor who received a humble salary of thirty aspers.[69] Today the only structures remaining from this complex are its mosque, popularly known as Balat Camii, and a public fountain with a pointed arch at the northwest corner of its irregular walled precinct. The patron is buried in the cemetery behind the mosque.

The rectangular mosque with its projecting mihrab and two tiers of windows preserves its original wall fabric of alternating courses of stone and brick. The present concrete hipped roof with terracotta tiles replaced the wooden one that collapsed in 1938. The rebuilt portico has eight tall pillars that rest on square stone bases. The large rectangular portal without a muqarnas hood is topped by a crested frieze. The Arabic foundation inscription carved above its arch states that the mosque was built to achieve closeness to God and the intercession of the Prophet Muhammad, by the grand vizier Ali Pasha's servant Ferruh Kethüda, during the reign of Sultan Süleyman in the year 970 (1562–63).[70]

The upper part of the cylindrical stone minaret with a plain gallery was rebuilt after an earthquake in 1766. The muqarnas-hooded marble mihrab is accompanied by a modern white marble minbar that replaced a wooden one. The woodwork details of the mosque have been entirely renewed and its painted decorations are lost. Evliya Çelebi attributes the mosque to Sinan and describes the topographic city views along the hajj route that were once painted on its outer portico walls:

> The qibla wall of its outer prayer platform (*ṭaşra ṣoffası*)
> has been painted by a masterful painter from head
> to foot with halting stations (*menziller*) from the Noble
> Jerusalem to Egypt and from Egypt all the way to
> Medina and Mecca, depicting their shape and image
> along with their rivers and mountains and dangerous
> passes, in such a way that if Erjenk and Mani came
> [to see these], they could not find any fault with them.[71]

Evliya's description was not a figment of his imagination, given that the mosque's first shaykh, Sinaneddin Yusuf Efendi, wrote a pilgrimage manual entitled *Menāsik-i Ḥacc* (Rites of the Hajj).[72] The relatively generic hipped-roof mosque of Ferruh Kethüda, then, was individualized by its unusual paintings of pilgrimage stations described in its shaykh's hajj manual.[73] The stipulations of the waqfiyya firmly linked the funerary mosque complex with the memory of its founder, who endowed it in perpetuity for the descendants of his family and the disciples of its celebrated shaykh.

Chapter 14

AGHAS AND ATTENDANTS OF THE INNER IMPERIAL PALACE

I. KAPIAĞASI MAHMUD AGHA
ISTANBUL, AHIRKAPI (1553–54, 1574–75)
II. BOSTANCIBAŞI İSKENDER PASHA
ISTANBUL, KANLICA (1559–60)
III. ODABAŞI BEHRUZ AGHA
ISTANBUL, YENİKAPI (1562–63)
IV. ŞEMSİ AHMED PASHA
ISTANBUL, ÜSKÜDAR (1580–81)
V. MEHMED AGHA
ISTANBUL, ÇARŞAMBA (1584–85)

The aghas of the inner imperial palace (*enderun*) and the sultan's confidants had been relatively insignificant patrons of architecture until they rose to prominence in Murad III's reign. The monumental ambitions of the mosque complexes commissioned in the 1580s by the chief black eunuch of the harem, Mehmed Agha, and the royal companion Şemsi Ahmed Pasha (the retired governor-general of Rumelia) articulated the upwardly revised status of their patrons in the post-classical social order. These monuments challenged norms of decorum observed in the humbler mosque complexes that Sinan had built during Süleyman's reign for comparable patrons: Mahmud Agha (the chief white eunuch), Behruz Agha (the chief of the privy chamber), and Bostancıbaşı İskender Pasha (the former chief gardener and retired governor-general of Egypt). The mosques of patrons belonging to this group are invariably situated in the capital and its suburbs.

I. KAPIAĞASI MAHMUD AGHA

As the chief white eunuch of Süleyman's imperial palace (*kapı ağası* or *babüssaade ağası*), Mahmud Agha commissioned a neighbourhood masjid at Ahırkapı (formerly the Nahlbend quarter), later converting it into a Friday mosque and amplifying it with a complex. Rebuilt after a fire in 1895, only what was originally the cut-stone basement of the upper-storey mosque remains intact (illus. 513, 514). The extensively remodelled mosque, covered by a hipped roof with terracotta tiles, features a single tier of round-arched modern windows and a cylindrical brick minaret with a plain gallery. The square prayer hall is appended to another one that has replaced its portico. Unaware that the Friday mosque was initially built as a masjid, Kuran speculates that the thick walls may once have supported a dome.[1] The masjid was more likely covered by a hipped roof and it is datable to 1553–54 on the basis of a Persian chronogram inscribed on its gate:

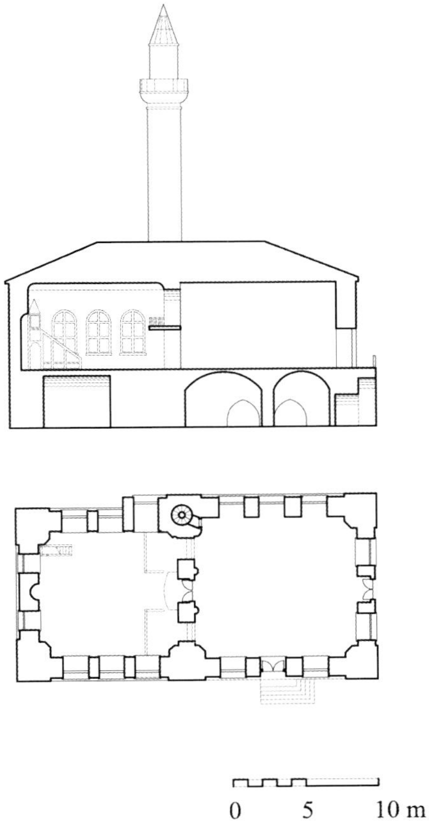

513 Plan and cross-section of the Kapıağası Mahmud Agha mosque, Ahırkapı.

Mahmud Agha, that sun of felicity,
Mine of prosperity and spring of generosity,

[Built] his masjid as a pious deed.
He composed the date: 'Charitable building of Mahmud',
961 (1553–54).[2]

Previously unnoted archival documents reveal that the masjid was subsequently converted into a Friday mosque. In a decree

514 Kapıağası Mahmud Agha mosque, Ahırkapı.

dated 1570, Selim II grants permission for the exchange of a house 'adjacent to the masjid of Kapıağası Mahmud in the Nahlbend quarter' with another one in Kadırgalimanı, so that the courtyard of the masjid could be enlarged.[3] Another order addressed to the kadi of Istanbul in 1574 permits the transformation of Mahmud Agha's masjid because it 'has the capacity of being converted into a noble Friday mosque', which, according to a petition sent by the inhabitants of that quarter, was greatly needed.[4] In 1579, the acceptance of Mahmud Agha's request to be buried next to his 'noble Friday mosque built for the love of God' was communicated with a royal permit sent to the kadi of Istanbul by Murad III.[5]

The masjid was probably converted into a Friday mosque simply by the addition of a minbar. According to Ayvansarayi, it was accompanied by a madrasa, an elementary school, a public fountain, and a cemetery containing the founder's grave. Sinan's autobiographies list the Friday mosque, madrasa, and tomb. Only the remodelled mosque and the arched public fountain across the street are extant.[6] Mahmud Agha's waqfiyya of 1575 endows his Friday mosque and elementary school, without mentioning the madrasa, which must have been added later on. The two buildings were bounded by public streets on three sides and by the waqfs of the founder and another person on the fourth side. The endowments of this small complex included the founder's residence, comprising two courtyards and a garden adjoining the mosque, where he would live during his lifetime; after his death it would be rented out. Another house with two courtyards next to the elementary school was endowed for the waqf administrator, along with smaller houses for the two muezzins and the imam. Since the chief white eunuch had no progeny, his freed slaves and their descendants would administer the waqf.[7] The complex, situated near the Topkapı Palace where Mahmud Agha held office, sought to perpetuate his memory in the neighbourhood in which he resided: a touching testament to the childless patron's longing to establish roots.

II. BOSTANCIBAŞI İSKENDER PASHA

The mosque complex of Bostancıbaşı (chief gardener) İskender Pasha is sited at the head of the Kanlıca jetty on the Asian shore of the Bosphorus (illus. 515). A waqfiyya recorded in 1544 shows that the Christian-born patron 'İskender Agha b. Abdülhay' had endowed an elementary school on that site along with another school in the nearby village of Sırapınarı while he served as Sultan Süleyman's chief gardener. For this pious foundation, administered and overseen by himself, he assigned income-producing real estate properties in the capital. After his death, his freed slaves and their sons would administer the waqf, and chief gardeners would oversee it.[8]

A Friday mosque attributed to Sinan was added next to the elementary school at Kanlıca in 1559–60, the year İskender Pasha came back to Istanbul, having been dismissed as the governor-general of Egypt.[9] Prior to that, he had created a complex in Cairo (no longer extant), endowed with a waqfiyya registered in March 1558 and consisting of a Friday mosque, a dervish convent, and a *sabil-kuttab* (water dispenser surmounted by an elementary school).[10] The Friday mosque in Kanlıca, dated by its foundation inscription to 967 (1559–60), was endowed by 'İskender Pasha b. Abdülhannan' with another waqfiyya, registered in December 1559. It lists his former pious foundations in two villages subordinate to Yoros, on the Asian shore of the Bosphorus, amplified by the new mosque: in the village of Kanlıca (Kanlıcak) a Friday mosque and an elementary school, and in the village of Sırapınar another elementary school next to the mosque of the late chief gardener Mustafa Agha.[11]

An imperial decree handed over to a servant of the deposed pasha on 25 August 1560 shows that the mosque was still under construction at that time. Addressed to the kadi of Yoros, it reads:

> The former governor-general of Egypt, İskender …
> has sent a letter to my threshold of felicity,
> [explaining that] he has endowed a two-oared market
> boat (*bazar peremesi*) for the Friday mosque he is
> presently building in the village of Kanlıca (Kanlıcak)
> under your jurisdiction, and he requests my noble
> order so that nobody else operates a *pereme* [there].
> In accordance with his petition, when the above-
> mentioned assigns a *pereme* for the endowment of his
> Friday mosque, do not allow anyone to interfere or
> to operate a market boat there.[12]

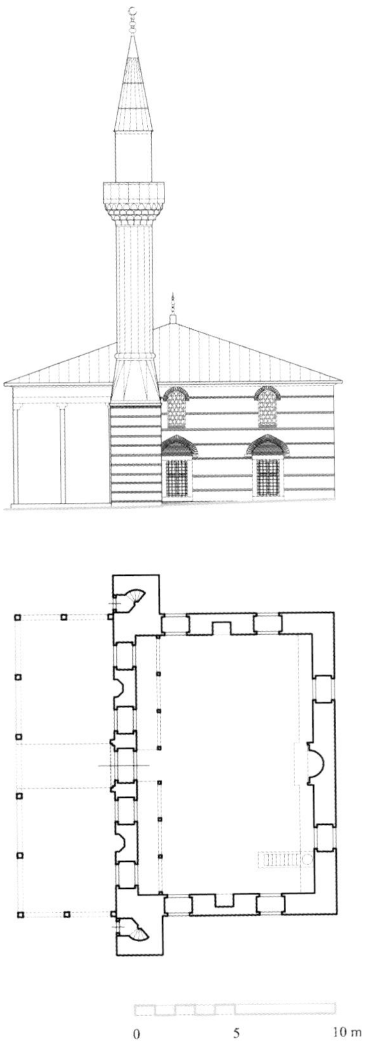

515 Plan and elevation of the Bostancıbası İskender Pasha mosque, Kanlıca, with hypothetical reconstruction of portico.

Another waqfiyya, registered in 1561, endows additional income-producing properties, including houses and shops in Kanlıca and the market boat mentioned above.[13] Two short waqfiyyas recorded in 1567 mention the elementary schools built by the pasha in the suburbs of Istanbul to fulfil the wills of his three dead sons, along with new properties assigned to his own waqf.[14] Bostancıbaşı İskender Pasha must have created these last endowments in 1565–66, when he was appointed the lieutenant governor of Istanbul as the retired 'former governor-general of Anatolia.' Reappointed governor-general of Anatolia, he passed away in 1571 two days after the conquest of Famagusta in Cyprus, where he was buried.[15] Mustafa Āli describes the pasha as a greedy governor-general who gave out fiefs only in return for bribes, a singular person 'neither just nor unjust', 'neither pious nor impious', and 'neither immature nor mature'.[16]

Sinan's autobiographies list İskender Pasha's Friday mosque, madrasa, bathhouse, and tomb in Kanlıca.[17] Surrounded by a precinct wall with three gates, the additively created complex was altered during the construction of a road in 1925, when its wooden domed bathhouse was demolished. The costs of that bathhouse, executed by the architect Üstad Manol and his two Greek assistants (Yorgi and Yani) under Sinan's supervision, are recorded in an account book stamped with the chief architect's seal in 1565 (the year İskender Pasha was based in Istanbul as lieutenant governor).[18] The madrasa, omitted from the pasha's waqfiyyas, is also lost and the elementary school is transformed beyond recognition. The ashlar masonry open-air mausoleum, atypically located close to the shore, at the north side of the mosque (rather than behind its qibla wall), is a rectangular structure with sixteen iron-grilled windows (now protected by a lead-covered wooden roof). Inside it are two undated marble cenotaphs with late-Ottoman inscriptions identifying 'the late Ghazi İskender Pasha' and his 'late son Ahmed Pasha'. Çerkes İskender Pasha (d. 1571), the patron of a mosque designed by Sinan in Diyarbakır, was apparently buried there with his son when his namesake was interred in Cyprus.[19]

The mosque portal is inscribed with an Arabic foundation inscription whose chronogram yields the completion date of 967 (1559–60). The patron is identified as 'the noble leader (*ṣadr ʿālī*), the generous İskender Pasha', who erected the building (*binā*) for the love of God.[20] The extensively renovated mosque of roughly cut stones alternating with widely spaced brick courses has two tiers of windows. Its new flat wooden ceiling is protected by a terracotta-covered hipped roof and its wooden-pillared portico has been transformed into a covered hall. The muqarnas-galleried, multi-faceted ashlar stone minaret was renovated after an earthquake in 1895. Stripped of its original decorations, the prayer hall has a muqarnas-hooded mihrab, accompanied by a modern wooden minbar. Evliya Çelebi describes the mosque complex 'at the head of the jetty':

> It is a Friday mosque with quadrangular walls, a four-hipped, lead-covered roof with a dome [underneath], and a single minaret. Its courtyard has tall trees. It is the work of the famous architect Sinan Agha. In addition there are two elementary schools, and it lacks such things as a madrasa or a hadith school. It has a very small bathhouse. On one of the basins of this bathhouse, a talented marble carver has depicted the image of an elephant that astonishes the beholder.[21]

The low-relief carving of the elephant, a Byzantine spolia, is now kept at the Türk ve İslam Eserleri Müzesi.[22] One of the two elementary schools that Evliya mentions may have been the madrasa, probably a simple classroom without dormitory cells.[23] This is the only mosque complex attributed to Sinan in the outer reaches of the Bosphorus, whose bucolic shores came under the jurisdiction of chief gardeners. Judiciously downscaled in accordance with the status of its patron as a retired governor-general, it inscribed İskender Pasha's memory on the suburban landscape of Istanbul by commemorating his nickname: Bostancıbaşı.

III. ODABAŞI BEHRUZ AGHA

The Friday mosque of Odabaşı Behruz Agha, the chief of Sultan Süleyman's privy chamber, is sited at the outskirts of the capital in Yenikapı (illus. 516). We have seen in Chapter 4 that it was thanks to this agha's favourable recommendation that the sultan had handed over the key of the Süleymaniye to Sinan during its inauguration ceremony. The chief architect's autobiographies mention the mosque of Odabaşı Behruz Agha and its bathhouse (now lost) at Yenikapı (Şehremini).[24] Ayvansarayi cites the chronogram: 'On the main portal, it is written that the noble Friday mosque was completed in the year 'Obligation of obedience to God', 970 (1562–63).' He mentions the elementary school and a public fountain, noting that the location of the patron's grave was not known.[25] The elementary school at the north side of the mosque has entirely been rebuilt, but the nearby public fountain is extant and the cemetery at the south is surrounded by a precinct wall with rectangular grilled windows. The mosque, built with alternating courses of stone and brick, is a masjid-like structure covered by a hipped roof. Its multifaceted ashlar stone minaret, featuring a plain gallery, was rebuilt after it collapsed during an earthquake in 1766. Severely damaged by a fire in 1782, the mosque itself was extensively refurbished in 1836 and more recently in 1969. It preserves its original wall fabric with two tiers of windows, but its wooden-pillared portico has been replaced by an enclosed hall.

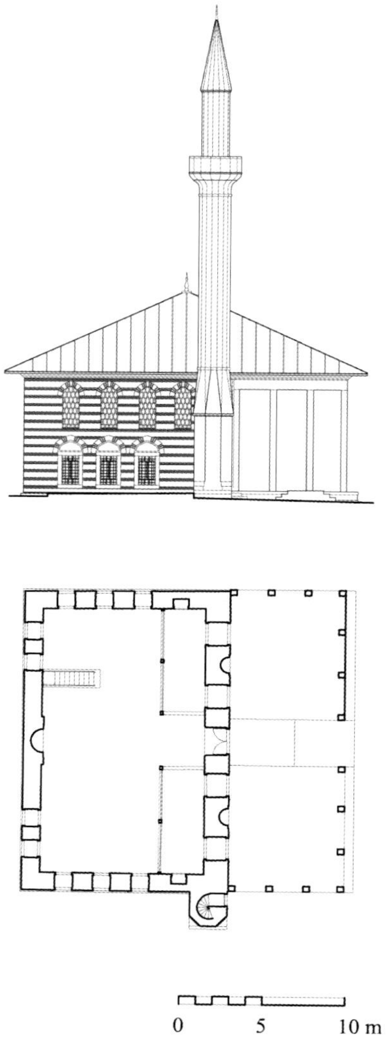

516 Plan and elevation of the Odabaşı Behruz Agha mosque, Yenikapı, with a hypothetical reconstruction of the portico.

IV. ŞEMSİ AHMED PASHA

As one of Murad III's favourite royal companions, Şemsi Ahmed Pasha commissioned a delightful funerary mosque complex next to his shore palace in Üsküdar (illus. 517, 518). Sinan's Muslim-born patron boasted noble descent from both sides of his family: his mother was an Ottoman princess and his father was Mirza Mehmed Beg of the Kızıl Ahmedli (İsfendiyaroğlu) dynasty of Kastamonu, which had been extinguished by Mehmed II. He moreover claimed a fabricated paternal genealogy that went back to Khalid b. al-Walid (d. 641–42), a celebrated Arab commander whose armies conquered Syria at the time of the Prophet.[26]

In a history he dedicated to Murad III, Şemsi Ahmed Pasha explains that his forebears, skilled in falconry and fighting like Khalid b. al-Walid, had accompanied Ottoman sultans to hunts and wars ever since they became the *kul*s of Mehmed II. As the sanjak governor of Bolu, his father was martyred while fighting against the Georgians during Selim I's reign. After being raised in Sultan Süleyman's imperial palace, Ahmed held such posts as chief falconer, chief hunter, and agha of the cavalry troops. Whenever he accompanied the sultan's hunts, he would recount entertaining stories and recite poems composed under the penname 'Şemsī' (Pertaining to the Sun). During the 1550s and 1560s he served as the governor-general of Damascus, Rum (Sivas), Anatolia, and Rumelia.[27]

As the governor-general of Rumelia, he left the capital for Sofia in 1565 with such pomp that the people of Istanbul who watched the spectacle of his lavishly clad retinue had never seen a *beglerbegi* display such 'majesty and grandeur'. A witty conversationalist and poet, the aspiring Şemsi Ahmed Pasha was ordered to retire at the beginning of Selim II's reign (1567–68), when his disgraced older brother Mustafa Pasha was dismissed from the vizierate.[28] The retired governor-general of Rumelia, holding the honorary title of vizier, was appointed the sultan's boon companion by Sokollu and Ebussuud. He retained his fiefs yielding 250,000 aspers, but 'after retiring with the rank of vizier he did not advance beyond royal companionship (*muṣāhib*).'[29]

517 Plan of the Şemsi Ahmed Pasha complex, Üsküdar.

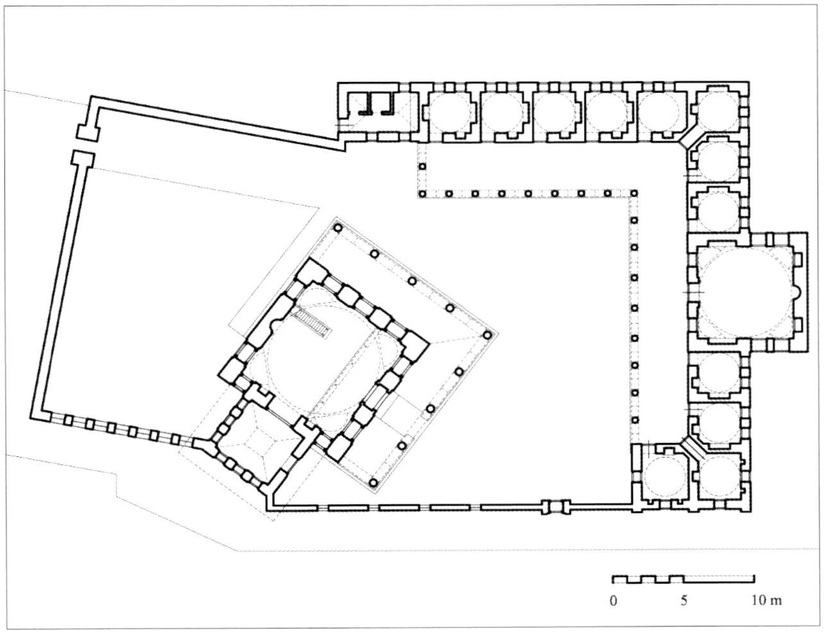

518 Axonometric projection of the Şemsi Ahmed Pasha complex.

519 Şemsi Ahmed Pasha complex, Üsküdar, with Istanbul in the background.

The Venetian ambassador Costantino Garzoni (1573) reports that Selim II frequently visited Ahmed Pasha's residence in Üsküdar. Staying there for two or three days, the sultan enjoyed drinking wine at the same table with his boon companion and playing chess with his royal mother, to whom the sultan himself was related.[30] Schweigger (1577–81) remarks that Selim II had relished drinking wine with the 'famous Turkish poet named Şemsi Pasha', who entertained him with stories, jokes, and rhymes, and that now Murad III sought his company.[31] The pasha came to wield considerable power during the reign of the new sultan, who increasingly relied on the advice of favourites belonging to his inner palace circle.[32] Gerlach (1577) observes that Murad III's hunting escort, as the son of a sultana, could visit the imperial palace whenever he wanted to. He was honoured and feared by all the grandees: whenever he paid a visit to the grand vizier Sokollu, he was treated as if he were the sultan himself.[33]

Mustafa Āli portrays Şemsi Ahmed Pasha as Süleyman's 'hunting companion', Selim II's 'drinking and carousing comrade', and Murad III's 'confidant in matters of the state and religion'.[34] But he had also heard the resentful pasha boast to his steward Koçi Kethüda that he had revenged the Kızıl Ahmedli dynasty by persuading Murad III to accept a hefty bribe of 40,000 ducats: 'Just as they extinguished our hearth, I, too, precipitated the extinguishing of theirs, because from now on he [Murad] cannot resist taking bribes, and their dynasty will not survive with bribery.' By congratulating the pasha on following in the footsteps of his ancestor Khalid b. al-Walid, who first introduced bribery in the Islamic domains, Āli certainly did not win his favour.[35] He complains about the ungenerous pasha's lack of patronage, lamenting that his 'sunlike' (Şemsī) glory was 'like the dying flame of a candle'.[36] Despite the exorbitant boat fares that Āli paid to frequent his court in Üsküdar, the envious pasha failed to recommend his poetic talents to the sultan. During one of these visits, those gathered there asked Şemsi Pasha why he modestly lived in Üsküdar, at the periphery of the capital. He wittily replied: 'Üsküdar is a way-station of mankind, a place where countless people come with business from the lands of Anatolia, Damascus, Aleppo, and especially Egypt and Iraq.' Because they met with him before visiting the palaces of the viziers in Istanbul, they gave him 'the cream of the gifts'. Had he lived in the 'lofty capital', the best presents would go to the viziers![37]

No doubt, circumspection and discretion also governed Şemsi Pasha's choice to reside in Üsküdar, the traditional place

520 Aerial view of the Şemsi Ahmed Pasha complex, Üsküdar.

of retirement for deposed grandees, who were not supposed to meddle in affairs of state as he did.[38] Moreover, his waterfront residence was conveniently situated across from the Topkapı Palace, where he frequented the sultan's private living quarters (illus. 278 [2], 519). Şemsi Pasha's mosque complex may have been planned in 1579, when 'the amir of amirs who previously retired as the governor-general of Rumelia' obtained the sultan's permit to conduct water to his garden in Üsküdar.[39] The foundation inscription of the mosque gives the completion date of 988 (1580–81), the year the pasha passed away. According to Ayvansarayi, it was finished posthumously:

> The aforesaid [pasha] was initially a boon companion of Sultan Süleyman Khan and was later a gentleman-in-waiting to Sultan Selim Khan and Sultan Murad Khan ibn Selim Khan ... [He] built the famous palace that bears his name for His Majesty the abovementioned sultan. In connection with it, he was also assisted by God in building the nearby noble Friday mosque and exalted madrasa ... He passed away to the abode of immortality during the time the abovementioned Friday mosque was being built.[40]

It is unclear from this passage which sultan the pasha built his palace for, but the sources we have considered above indicate that it was already frequented by Selim II. Probably created on a royal estate loaned for the use of his family, the palace named after Şemsi Ahmed Pasha was sited along the seashore next to his madrasa, with its gardens extending behind his mosque complex up to that of Rum Mehmed Pasha on a hilltop (illus. 84, 278 [2]).[41]

A waqfiyya recorded in 988 (1580–81) lists the pasha's pious foundations in Üsküdar, Bolu, and Gerede. It refers to him as 'Ahmed Pasha, son of the late Mirza Pasha al-Khalidi from the side of His Highness [Khalid b.] al-Walid, and renowned like the sun as Şemsi Pasha.' His mother is identified as Şahnisa Sultan, the daughter of Bayezid II's son prince Abdullah.[42] The waqfiyya explains that the pasha developed the city of Bolu because it was the noble place of his birth, valued by the people as a road station located along a grand highway. He built there a Friday mosque whose courtyard was surrounded by a hospice and a convent (*ḫānḳāh*) featuring five cells for dervishes. In Gerede, sited on a major highway near his birthplace, he built a charitable khan that was free to travellers.[43]

According to the waqfiyya, he also embellished Üsküdar, his 'seat of honour and place of residence', with monuments resembling the Pleiades (illus. 84, 519–20). He built 'near his palace along the seashore' an agreeable Friday mosque 'whose heart-ravishing silver dome is a bubble on the lip of the sea, and each of whose polished polychrome marble panels is a world-illuminating mirror of the eight paradises'. In the pleasant forecourt of this 'luminous' Friday mosque, the pasha, of 'sunlike countenance', constructed an exquisite madrasa functioning as a hadith college (*dārü'l-ḥadīs*) and comprising twelve cells and a beautiful classroom.[44] He also built a 'royal mausoleum', in which 'the noble substance of his body' would be 'buried and cherished like a hidden treasure'.[45] He created these pious foundations as lasting memorials on the 'face of Time' so that the people's tongues would perpetually utter his praise.[46]

Şemsi Pasha's pious foundations memorialized aspects of his life and career. Those in Damascus, where he had served as governor-general, were created first and recorded in a waqfiyya dated 1554: a mosque and convent in a garden with a pool near the citadel.[47] Next came the ones in Bolu and Gerede, towns located in northwest Anatolia, where the Kızıl Ahmedli dynasty had once ruled. Evliya Çelebi, who saw Şemsi Pasha's palace in Bolu, says the town had been donated to his family as a permanent estate.[48] An imperial decree dated 1564 grants Ahmed Pasha, then the governor-general of Anatolia, ownership of the villages he had requested for endowing the 'guesthouse of the Friday mosque he built in Bolu.'[49] Known today as the İmaret Camii (Hospice Mosque), this unpretentious hipped-roof mosque of mixed masonry was once accompanied by a hospice listed in the *Tuḥfe* as a work of Sinan.[50]

All of the chief architect's autobiographies claim authorship for the Friday mosque, madrasa and mausoleum of Şemsi Ahmed Pasha's prestige monument in Üsküdar.[51] The neighbouring convent (*tekye*), mentioned only in the *Tuḥfe*, is omitted from the pasha's waqfiyya. We have seen that this Halveti convent was endowed by his relative and namesake, Hacı Ahmed Pasha, for whom Sinan built a mosque in Kayseri.[52] The Turkish foundation inscription of the Friday mosque in Üsküdar, placed over its gate which lacks a muqarnas hood, confirms that it was completed posthumously. Carved in four lines of *thuluth* above an arch with joggled voussoirs in white and red marble, the inscription wishes the deceased patron a place in paradise:

> Because Şemsi Pasha built this noble Friday mosque,
> We hope that the Abode of Peace will be the place of the deceased [founder].
>
> O Ulvi, when the Unseen One saw it, he pronounced its date:
> 'May this abode (*maḳām*) be a place of worship for the community of the Prophet!' 988 (1580–81).[53]

The mosque complex occupied a highly visible site near a jetty that was 'not as large as that of Tophane, but teeming with those passing to and from Anatolia'(illus. 104, 278[2]).[54] A now-lost inscription carved above the gate of the mausoleum explained that the pasha's sepulchre faced the waterfront so that boat passengers would offer prayers for his soul:

> His mausoleum on the seashore
> Şemsi built for the following reason:
>
> When they pass along this seashore,
> May acquaintances remember him with prayers.
>
> O God, by the truth of the light of the Prophet,
> Free that slave of yours from hell-fire.[55]

The mausoleum is appended to the mosque like the projecting alcove of a shore pavilion. Another vanished inscription was a Turkish couplet begging for divine forgiveness at the last breath of 'Şemsi, the helpless', an expression used in the pasha's own poems.[56] Shaped like a sun-disk, the gilded finial that once glistened on the mosque dome (but is now replaced with a crescent) also alluded to the founder's pen-name.[57] Adjoining the north-west side of the mosque complex, the shore palace named after the pasha was yet another identity marker.

Evliya Çelebi describes the 'small mosque on the lip of the sea' as such a 'charming' edifice that onlookers would think it a 'decorated pavilion'.[58] Much like Mihrümah Sultan's more monumental royal complex nearby, it was designed to resemble a shore palace (illus. 278 [1,2]). Kuran ranks the tiny complex as one of Sinan's 'most remarkable works', a veritable 'architectural gem'.[59] It is a celebrated example of the chief architect's skill in organically blending architecture with the natural landscape. Eliminating one wing of the typical U-shaped madrasa scheme, he creates an asymmetrical, L-shaped design open to spectacular vistas. The irregular courtyard extending between the mosque and madrasa is poetically framed by a wall pierced with iron-grilled windows, giving 'the impression that one is in a picture gallery looking at framed Bosphorus seascapes'.[60]

The complex has two gates, one facing the land and the other the sea; the land gate opens to a cemetery garden containing the tombstones of Şemsi Pasha's relatives. The courtyard is visually unified by two L-shaped porticoes whose domeless shed roofs are supported by dainty ogee arches resting on columns with lozenge capitals. The portico of the mosque collapsed and was rebuilt in 1940, along with its muqarnas-galleried minaret, whose concealed base is incorporated into the northwest corner of the prayer hall. The portico of the madrasa boasts two pairs of green and pink porphyry columns aligned with its classroom gate. The madrasa is built of alternating courses of stone and brick, but its ashlar masonry seaside rooms are visually harmonized with the mosque-cum-mausoleum to stress the primacy of the waterfront view. The dome of the classroom (6.9 metres) is subordinated to the higher and larger dome (8.2 metres) of the mosque, which is raised on squinches above an octagonal stone drum whose windows alternate with four lead-covered exedras.

The kiosk-like mausoleum is covered by a cradle vault with a pointed profile. Brilliantly lit by two tiers of windows, it is spatially continuous with the prayer hall, from which it is separated by a bronze-grilled arch flanked by two rectangular niches for books. The communication between the mausoleum and prayer hall, a feature common in the shrines of saints, connotes the holiness of Şemsi Pasha's body, which is compared to a hidden treasure in his waqfiyya.[61] The pasha used every opportunity to advertise in his writings not just his royal lineage but also his spurious descent from the Prophet's general, Khalid b. al-Walid, which conferred a saintly aura upon him.

The painted decorations and inscriptions of the mosque were considerably changed during restorations in 1940. Konyalı says the centre of the dome was originally inscribed with the Light verse (24:35), appropriately resonating with the patron's refulgent penname, while its rim was encircled by the Throne verse (2:255) common in the epigraphy of funerary monuments.[62] The unadorned, muqarnas-hooded marble mihrab, inscribed with the standard mihrab verse (3:37), is accompanied by a modern wooden minbar, and the muezzin's tribune is raised above the mosque entrance. The Koranic inscription carved over the gate of the classroom greets those who enter the gardens of paradise (13:24), a theme elaborated in the waqfiyya.

Surrounded by delectable gardens, the palatial mosque complex represented a heavenly abode, an eternal resting place replete with light imagery alluding to its patron's pen-name. Viewed from the sea in relation to neighbouring garden pavilions and Rum Mehmed Pasha's antiquated vizierial mosque perched on a hilltop behind it, the modern complex designed by Sinan decorously projected the refined courtly tastes of its poet patron. With his diminutive yet stunning memorial monument, the sultan's treasured confidant of 'sunlike countenance'

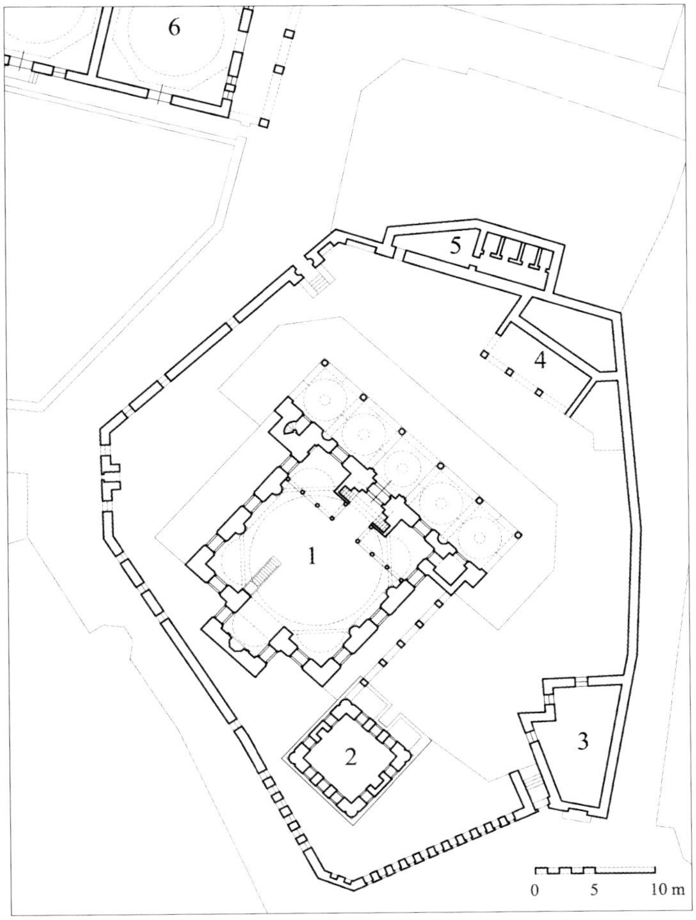

521 Plan of the Mehmed Agha complex, Çarşamba:

1. Mosque
2. Mausoleum
3. Site of the convent shaykh's house with street fountain next to precinct gate with foundation inscription
4. Ablution fountains
5. Latrines
6. Double bath

522 Elevation of the Mehmed Agha mosque, Çarşamba.

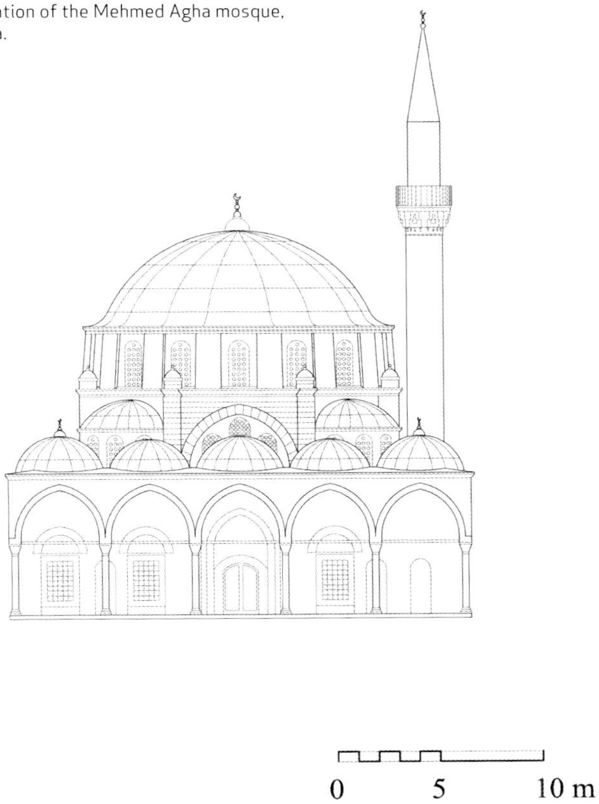

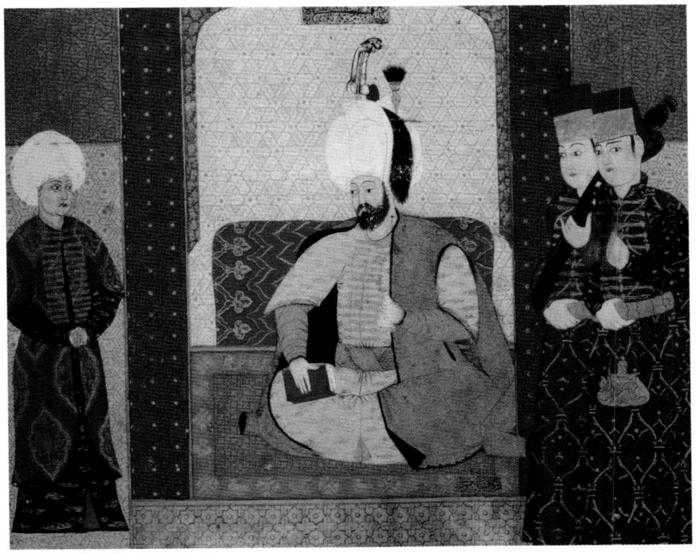

523 The chief black eunuch Mehmed Agha presenting Seyyid Lokman's manuscript to Murad III, 1583, watercolour on paper, from Lokman, *Zübdetü't-tevārīḫ*.

inscribed his fame at the political centre of the capital, albeit in a discreet suburban location.

V. MEHMED AGHA

The funerary mosque complex of Habeşi (Abyssinian) Mehmed Agha, who served as the chief black eunuch of the imperial harem for many years (1574–91), announced the unparalleled escalation of his status by emulating vizierial prototypes (illus. 521, 522).[63] Heading the queen mother Nurbanu Sultan's harem faction, he eclipsed the chief white eunuchs in authority, thanks to his intimacy with Murad III, who spent most of his time in the women's quarters (illus. 523). Mehmed Agha's rise to power culminated in 1586–87 with his appointment as the overseer of imperial waqfs and of pious endowments made to the two Holy Cities, a position formerly held by chief white eunuchs.[64] This is commemorated by an inscription over the gate of the domed vestibule of the imperial harem, facing the second court of the Topkapı Palace, where the agha held public audiences each Wednesday. Dated 996 (1587–88), it praises the just ruler Murad III, who augmented the importance of that previously less illustrious audience gate (*bāb-ı dıvān*), following the advice of his chief black eunuch, Mehmed Agha.[65]

An eighteenth-century biographical compendium of black eunuchs traces their rise to power to the late sixteenth century:

> Let it be known that during the age of the paradise-abiding late sultans, Süleyman I and Selim II, even though histories record the existence of chief black eunuchs (*dārü's-saʿāde aġası*), in that period the service of the imperial harem was generally the responsibility of the chief white eunuchs (*ḳapu aġaları*) and chief treasurers (*ḫazīnedār başılar*). Hence, for those well-read in history, it is apparent that the chief black eunuchs were not famous and prominent at that time. In the year 1574–75, at the beginning of Sultan Murad III's reign, Mehmed Agha was favoured as the agha of the abode of felicity and attained success over time in illustrious works, being honoured with overseeing the waqfs of the Two Harams.[66]

The compendium begins with the biography of Mehmed Agha because he was the first chief black eunuch to achieve fame. He came to wield such power that 'most of his clients and trainees were blessed with the rank of the vizierate'. Among the agha's pious foundations, the biography lists the castle he created in İsmail Geçidi, a previously uninhabited pass in Rumania along the Danube, and his mosque complex in the 'Çarşamba Pazarı' quarter of Istanbul, where he was eventually buried.[67] Selaniki records Mehmed Agha's death on 26 January 1591; the meeting of the imperial council was cancelled for his stately funeral service at the mosque of Mehmed II, after which the agha was 'buried near his own Friday mosque'. He reports that the people criticized his misdeeds and composed the following unfavourable chronogram: 'Departed from this world, that black calamity!' All his belongings were sold and the proceeds ordered to be added to his waqf.[68]

Mehmed Agha's pious foundations are registered in two waqfiyyas. The first, dated 1582, endows a water dispenser (*sebīl*) with a 'charming novel design' (*ṭarḥ-ı cedīd-i dilfirīb*) in the Hace Rüstem quarter, along the processional avenue of Divanyolu near Hagia Sophia. Among the witnesses who signed the waqfiyya was the architect Davud, who seems to have been entrusted with this project, and is referred to as 'Davud Beg b. Abdullah, the former superintendent of water channels.'[69] Occupying a highly visible site, the no-longer-extant water dispenser with an upper-storey elementary school was constructed in 1579–80: an unfamiliar combination seemingly inspired by Mamluk *sabil-kuttabs*, like the one in Medina that Mehmed Agha obtained permission to restore in 1578.[70]

Several imperial permits issued by Murad III between 1579 and 1581 allowed the chief black eunuch to conduct water from the sources he had discovered outside the city walls to the elementary school-cum-water dispenser he built 'for the love of God' at the Hace Rüstem quarter and to another water dispenser at Irgadpazarı (near Constantine's column). These documents show that 'Davud Çavuş b. Abdullah' was the superintendent of water channels at that time.[71] It was he who inspected the water sources in question with a committee of water channel experts (Ali, Hızır, Hüseyin, Hamza, Nasuh, and Muhyiddin).[72] Recorded by Ayvansarayi, the foundation inscription of the water dispenser with an elementary school gives the date 988 (1580–81). It identifies the patron as Mehmed Agha, the favoured servant (*bende-i maḳbūl*) of Murad Khan, during whose reign the world flourished thanks to his subjects devoted to charitable works; this statement is repeated in the foundation inscription of Kılıç Ali Pasha's mosque complex at Tophane, also dated 988 (1580–81).[73] The chief black eunuch added a madrasa built of stone and brick near his water dispenser-cum-elementary school in 1582–83, a work attributed to Sinan in the *Teẕkiretü'l-ebniye*.[74]

The second waqfiyya, recorded on 5 February 1591, shortly after Mehmed Agha's demise, enumerates all his pious foundations.[75] The list constitutes an impressive collection: a Friday mosque in the Begcügez (Beyceğiz, now Çarşamba) quarter of the capital, accompanied by a madrasa for the study of hadith (*dārü'l-ḥadīs̱*) composed of ten cells, a convent (*zāviye*), and a public fountain; another Friday mosque at İsmail Geçidi; a masjid in Üsküdar; a madrasa with ten cells and a classroom in the Hace Rüstem quarter, accompanied by a water dispenser with an upper-storey elementary school and a public fountain; another water dispenser and fountain at the crossing of four roads in the Irgadpazarı quarter; a fountain near the Hagia Sophia mosque next to the rooms of the chief white eunuch Cafer Agha (d. 1557); ablution fountains in the courtyard of the Friday mosque of Mercan Agha near the Old Palace (a masjid endowed in 1474 by an agha of the imperial harem); a fountain in front of Mehmed Agha's own residence near the Old Palace; another fountain and open prayer space (*muṣalla*) near the Edirnekapı gate; and five fountains in Üsküdar.[76]

These charities were supported by real estate properties that Mehmed Agha endowed in the capital and its suburbs, along with 8,400 aspers whose interest would maintain his numerous fountains, created under the supervision of his protégé Davud. Income-producing properties built in the neighbourhood of his mosque complex included a double bath, shops, and rental rooms for married couples. Two houses were earmarked for the imam of the mosque and the shaykh of the convent.[77] The agha also endowed his own two-courtyard residence near the Old Palace, donated to him by Murad III. His garden at the queen mother Nurbanu Sultan's 'new quarter' in Üsküdar was likewise made a waqf, along with neighbouring commercial properties. His charitable fountains nearby were created in the mid-1580s when he supervised the posthumous enlargement of the late queen's mosque as her waqf overseer, a project he likely entrusted to the architect Davud.[78]

The only property Mehmed Agha endowed outside the capital was İsmail Geçidi, which Murad III had donated to him in 1589–90 in response to his request to build a castle with a new settlement so that bandits would not harass passengers there.[79] Outside that castle the agha created a town along the Danube named after himself: Bağdad-ı Mehmedabad. Inside the castle he constructed a Friday mosque, and outside it he founded a water dispenser. The revenues of İsmail Geçidi would be used for the upkeep of Mehmed Agha's pious foundations, with a percentage distributed to the poor in Mecca, Medina, and Jerusalem. The waqfiyya of 1591 specifies that a bathhouse and shops should be built there without delay, using the late agha's endowment funds.[80] Documents confirm the posthumous construction between 1591 and 1593 of a bathhouse, elementary school, shops, and a khan in İsmail Geçidi, a town endowed to the Two Harams.[81] Since the chief black eunuch had no progeny, he bequeathed the professorship of his madrasa in Istanbul and other salaried positions of his waqfs to his worthy manumitted slaves and their children, who would be given precedence over outsiders. His endowment was to be overseen by chief black eunuchs who succeeded him.[82]

Let us now turn to Mehmed Agha's mosque complex in Istanbul, for which he bought a large number of houses from non-Muslims in the 'Begcügez' and 'Patrikān' quarters.[83] This suggests an attempt to Islamize the neighbourhood near the Orthodox Patriarchate, whose church would soon be converted into a Friday mosque called Fethiye by Murad III (1587–88). The deeds of houses bought in 1584 include among their witnesses the architect Davud Çavuş, who is identified in the foundation inscription of the mosque as its architect.[84]

524 Mehmed Agha complex, Çarşamba, from the southeast.

525 Mehmed Agha mosque, from the south.

Carved within a rectangular frame in four lines of *thuluth*, arranged in sixteen compartments, this unusually long inscription appears above the east gate of the precinct wall facing the street (illus. 521[3]). It lists the names of the patron and the architect, together with the completion date of 1585:

> The humble servant of the world [ruler] Murad Khan,
> That virtuous Mehmed Agha,
>
> Namely, the *darüssaade ağası*:
> Expended such zeal on pious works!
>
> He built this noble Friday mosque.
> It became the sum of the mosques of mercy.
>
> For its founder, may God make this pious work
> A reason for Paradise on the morrow!
>
> God is his pardoner, the Prophet is his intercessor.
> May the Sunna and obligatory worship be carried out here!
>
> Come what may, let prayers be accepted in it!
> May it be that which fulfils the needs of the Muslims!
>
> Its perfect architect was Davud.
> He built [it] by inscribing art with his soul.
>
> Asari, the Voice, expressed its date:
> 'House of God and mosque of the Community',
> 993 (1585).[85]

Given that none of Sinan's mosque complexes mention his name in their foundation inscriptions, the reference here to the architect Davud is extraordinary. Mehmed Agha's mosque and mausoleum, mentioned only in the *Tuhfe*, was probably omitted from the *Tezkiretü'l-ebniye* as a recognition of Davud's authorship, even though the chief architect must have approved their plan (illus. 524, 525). The complex was built in 1584–85, when Sinan had left the capital for Mecca, and its commercial bathhouse was added in 1585–86. Having created countless waterworks, the founder had developed special ties with the water channel superintendent Davud, who signed the waqfiyya of his small complex along Divanyolu in 1582. Doubtless the chief black eunuch himself selected Davud as the architect of a new bathhouse in the imperial harem of the Topkapı Palace, constructed in 1585 during Sinan's absence from the capital.[86] He also must have been instrumental in Davud's promotion to chief architect in 1588.

The precinct gate bearing the foundation inscription of Mehmed Agha's mosque complex is flanked on its right side by an arched public fountain. Above the fountain is a renewed wooden house thought to have been endowed for the shaykh of the convent.[87] Two other gates provide access to the courtyard, which surrounds both the mosque and the mausoleum, the only structures of the complex listed in the *Tuhfe*.[88] With the exception of the double bath, the other dependencies mentioned in the waqfiyya have disappeared. We learn from Ayvansarayi that the convent and hadith college were located outside the precinct wall, like the bathhouse:

> He [Mehmed Agha] is buried in an exalted tomb near the noble mosque. The chronogram for his death by Sai Nakkaş Mustafa Agha reads: 'May God illuminate that Mehmed's grave!' 999 (1590–91). He built a fountain near his tomb, which adjoins the courtyard gate of the noble mosque. A Halveti convent and an adjoining exalted double bath were built opposite the mosque. Nihadi composed the chronogram: 'Illuminated mansion and pure bath', 994 (1585–86). This is the chronogram on the arch of the courtyard gate of the mosque … [Mehmed Agha's] *darülhadis* is opposite it.[89]

Mehmed Agha's waqfiyya stipulates that the shaykh of the convent should have twelve dervishes as his disciples.[90] Its first Halveti shaykh, Yayabaşızade Hızır Efendi, had turned to the sufi path after beginning his career as a madrasa professor. He moved to Mehmed Agha's convent from that of Hacı Ahmed Pasha in Üsküdar (listed in the *Tuhfe* as Şemsi Ahmed Pasha's convent).[91] The learned shaykh, who 'captured hearts' with his conversation, taught Koranic interpretation at the hadith college of the complex built by Mehmed Agha, who had become his devotee.[92] As the 'army shaykh' of Mehmed III's Eger campaign, he was martyred in 1596–97, soon after predicting victory to the demoralized sultan, who was on the verge of fleeing the battlefield.[93] The next shaykh of the convent, Shaykh Abdülmecid Sivasi (d. 1639), would became the prime target of the anti-sufi Kadızadeli movement (discussed in the Epilogue) when he was appointed the Friday preacher of Sultan Ahmed I's new mosque at the Hippodrome.

Attached to the southeast corner of the prayer hall, the chief black eunuch's mausoleum is an ashlar masonry domed cube, privileged over the more cheaply constructed stone-and-brick mosque. Its façade was once fronted by a wooden portico, but this and another portico extending along the east side of the mosque have both disappeared. The placement of the foundation inscription on the precinct gate, next to the mausoleum rather than on the portal of the mosque, also accentuates the primacy of the founder's burial place. The section of the precinct wall corresponding to the mausoleum is given additional transparency with a contiguous set of grilled rectangular windows, encouraging the prayers of passers-by (illus. 524).

The square mosque with a projecting mihrab and a polygonal muqarnas-galleried stone minaret is a variant of the octagonal-baldachin scheme Sinan experimented with in several post-Selimiye vizierial foundations in the capital (illus. 5).[94] Dimly lit with two tiers of widely spaced windows, the mosque is fronted by a five-domed portico of ashlar stone carried on marble columns with muqarnas capitals. The 11.8-metre dome, raised on squinches, rests on pointed arches springing from eight piers with muqarnas capitals. The two columnar piers abutting the side walls of the prayer hall are semicircular, unlike those incorporated into the north and south walls. The north side of the prayer hall has an upper balcony reached from two staircases near the entrance and flanked by twin muezzin's tribunes. The internal piers are expressed externally by eight cylindrical weight turrets that encircle the window-pierced drum of the dome, which is reinforced with engaged pilaster-shaped tapering buttresses. The turrets alternate with four exedral half-domes, a half-dome over the mihrab, and fenestrated tympana at the east and west sides.

The ablution fountains are placed along the precinct wall at the north, across from the mosque portico as in the mosques of Kılıç Ali Pasha (1578–80/81) and Mesih Mehmed Pasha (1584–85/86). Compared to these two mosques, that of Mehmed Agha has less innovative façades with fewer windows. The muqarnas-hooded white marble gate of the prayer hall is inscribed with an incomplete verse (23:9) that promises paradise to those who 'pay heed to their prayers'. Above it is a glorification of God in mirrored calligraphy: 'He is the everlasting!' The only remaining rectangular tilework window lunette on the north façade quotes a verse from the Fatiha sura.

The epigraphic programme of the mosque in a newly Islamized neighbourhood stresses the necessity of worship to avoid punishment in hell, the dire fate of unbelievers and idolaters. The muqarnas-hooded marble mihrab, carved with a verse (3:39) used in the mihrabs of some post-classical mosques, has eight painted cartouches invoking God's beautiful names. The mihrab recess is faced with İznik tiles that clash with the Europeanizing paintings of the domical superstructure. The rectangular window lunettes that flank the mihrab quote the following verses (98:5–7):

> And they are ordained naught else than to serve Allah, keeping religion pure for Him, as men by nature upright and to establish worship and to pay the poor-due. That is true religion (5). Lo! those who disbelieve, among the People of the Scripture and the idolaters, will abide in fire of hell. They are the worst of created beings (6). (And) lo! those who believe and do good works are the best of created beings (7).

Proceeding in a counterclockwise direction starting at the right side of the entrance, the calligraphic İznik tile lunettes that surround the prayer hall quote the Throne verse (2:255). The eight arch spandrels carrying the dome bear roundels inscribed with the revered names. The painted roundel at the centre of the dome cites the popular cosmic verse that affirms God's power to hold the heavens and earth in their orbits (35:41). The two squinches at the east side repeat a fragmentary verse (10:25): 'And Allah summoneth to the abode of Peace, and leadeth whom He will [to a straight path].' The two squinches at the west side are inscribed with a verse from the Baqara sura (2:115): 'Unto Allah belong the East and the West, and withersoever ye turn, there is Allah's countenance.' The half-dome above the mihrab quotes the beginning of a verse from the Anʿam sura (6:79): 'Lo! I have turned my face toward Him Who created the heavens and the earth, as one by nature upright, and I am not one of the idolaters.'

Mehmed Agha's mosque bears a striking resemblance to those of his namesakes, the viziers Mesih Mehmed Pasha (a white eunuch) and Nişancı Mehmed Pasha, both of them built in the mid-1580s (illus. 5). Sometimes attributed to the architect Davud, these two vizierial mosques with mausoleums are more expensively constructed of ashlar masonry, and crowned by larger domes (Appendix 1).[95] The slightly smaller size and mixed masonry fabric of the chief black eunuch's mosque underscore his relatively lower status. Yet by appropriating a plan type suitable for viziers, it projects its patron's exalted self-image. With its domed mausoleum, the mosque complex enshrines the memory of the childless Mehmed Agha, the 'patron saint' of the chief black eunuchs who served as the overseers of his waqf over the generations.

Chapter 15

MERCHANTS AND TRADESMEN

I. KASAP USTASI HACI EVHAD
ISTANBUL, YEDİKULE (1585)

II. BEZİRGANBAŞI HACI HÜSREV
ISTANBUL, KOCAMUSTAFAPAŞA (RAMAZAN EFENDİ, 1585–86)

Sinan designed only two Friday mosques for patrons not of the tax-exempt ruling elite in Istanbul during the mid 1580s, one for the master butcher (*kasap ustası*) Hacı Evhad and the other for the chief merchant (*bezirganbaşı*) Hacı Hüsrev. Relegated to the outskirts of the capital, these masjid-like mosques once featured wooden domes under their hipped roofs and each was accompanied by a convent for the Halveti order of dervishes. Sheathed in İznik tiles like the comparable mosque of the felt cap maker Takkeci İbrahim Efendi (1591–92) outside the Topkapı gate, which preserves its wooden inner dome and pillared portico, these charming mosques resembled garden pavilions.[1] Their vanished residential facilities for dervishes had an affinity with vernacular architecture, much like the convents of other mosques designed by Sinan, which are omitted from his autobiographies.[2] The two mosques included in this chapter are deluxe versions of the many generic masjids that the chief architect's office created in the capital for the heads of artisanal guilds.

I. KASAP USTASI HACI EVHAD

The Friday mosque of Kasap Ustası Hacı Evhad [Evhadüddin] in Yedikule was part of a small complex with a convent, a bathhouse, two public fountains, and a cemetery garden (illus. 526).[3] Of these dependencies, only the single bath, not listed among Sinan's works, has survived, although the original wooden roof of its undressing hall has been rebuilt in concrete. Photographs show the rubble masonry convent with a row of dervish cells, fronted by a wooden pillared portico facing the mosque courtyard.[4] The mosque is surrounded by a rebuilt precinct wall with two gates, each featuring an adjacent public fountain. Pierced by rectangular iron-grilled windows, the wall provides glimpses of the cemetery. One window has an inscription giving the name of the patron, buried behind the qibla wall of his mosque: 'The patron of charitable works, el-Hac Evhadüddin, may God have mercy on him, 993 (1585).'[5]

The gate of the mosque lacks a muqarnas hood; above its arch decorated with alternating voussoirs of red and white marble is a Turkish foundation inscription, carved in two lines of *thuluth*:

> Hacı Evhad, who built this decorated Friday mosque,
> Expended money for the sake of God.
>
> It is befitting to that patron of charitable works, if
> I call him the most generous butcher of the world.
>
> The humble Azizi composed its date:
> 'Hacı Evhad, your Friday mosque is the like of the
> Haram [Kaʿba]', the year 993 (1585).[6]

The mosque, which preserves its walls with two tiers of windows, was extensively rebuilt in 1945, when its missing wooden pillared portico became substituted with a new one.[7] Built of alternating courses of stone and brick, the prayer hall has a flat wooden ceiling surmounted by a hipped roof with terracotta tiles. Originally lead-covered, the roof had an internal wooden dome. The muqarnas-galleried tall, sixteen-sided stone minaret is decorated with vertical mouldings joined to form arches.

The façade featuring paired mihrabs had İznik tiles on its arched window lunettes; these tiles and the ones that once decorated the qibla wall have all disappeared. Old photographs show a round-arched, simple mihrab in the prayer hall; it has now been replaced by a muqarnas-hooded one in plaster. It is accompanied by a modern wooden minbar and a wooden upper gallery along the anti-qibla wall; at the middle of each lateral wall is a cupboard. The mosque seems to have functioned as the ritual hall of the neighbouring convent, which comprised residential cells and kitchen facilities for dervishes of the Halveti-Sünbüli order.[8] According to Ayvansarayi, the waqf was overseen by master butchers, who shared the founder's profession.[9] Sited near the slaughterhouses and tanneries of Yedikule, the mosque complex commemorated the corporate identity of its charitable patron and his affiliation with the Halveti order of dervishes.

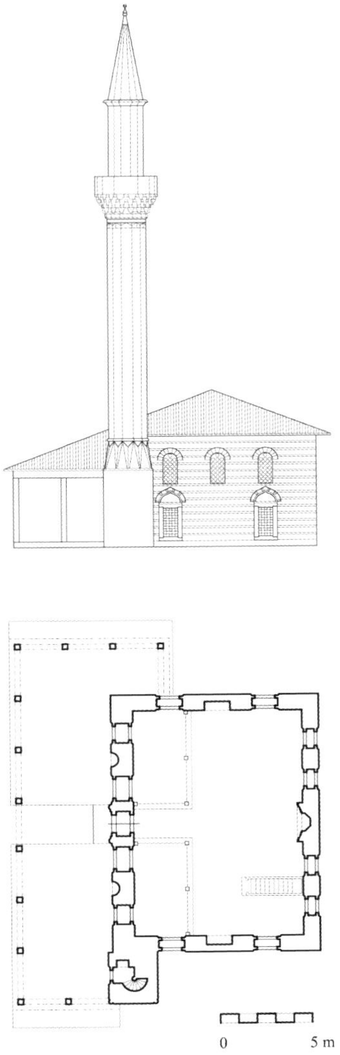

526 Plan and elevation of the Hacı Evhad mosque, Yedikule, with hypothetical reconstruction of the portico.

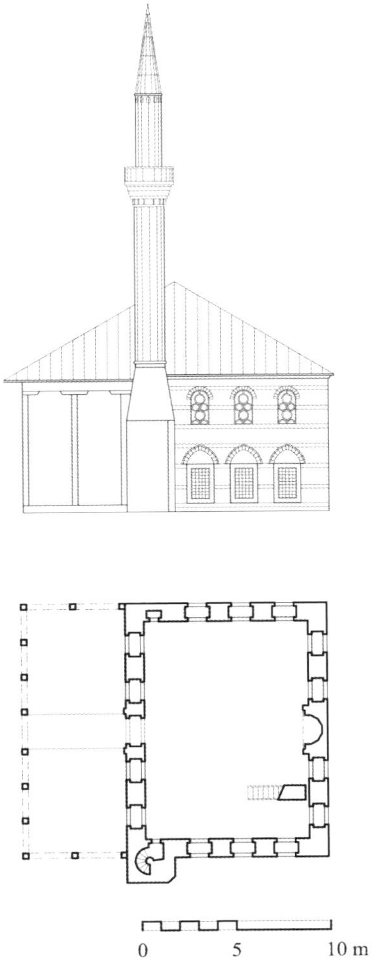

527 Plan and elevation of the Bezirganbaşı Hacı Hüsrev (Ramazan Efendi) mosque, Kocamustafapaşa, with hypothetical reconstruction of the portico.

II. BEZİRGANBAŞI HACI HÜSREV (RAMAZAN EFENDİ)

Hacı Hüsrev's mosque near the headquarters of the Halveti-Sünbüli dervish order in Kocamustafapaşa is also known after the name of its first shaykh, Ramazan Efendi (illus. 527, 528). This shaykh, who founded the Ramazani branch of the Halveti order, came to Istanbul from Afyon Karahisar around 1585, just before the construction of the mosque-cum-convent complex, which is dated by an inscription to 994 (1585–86). He served as its shaykh for more than three decades, until he passed away in 1616 and was succeeded by his offspring and their disciples over the generations.[10]

Ayvansarayi refers to the building as the 'Bezirgan (merchant) mosque in Kocamustafapaşa' and lists the shaykhs of its convent. Its builder, Hacı Hüsrev, was buried there and the foundation inscription of the mosque was composed by Sinan's biographer Sai:

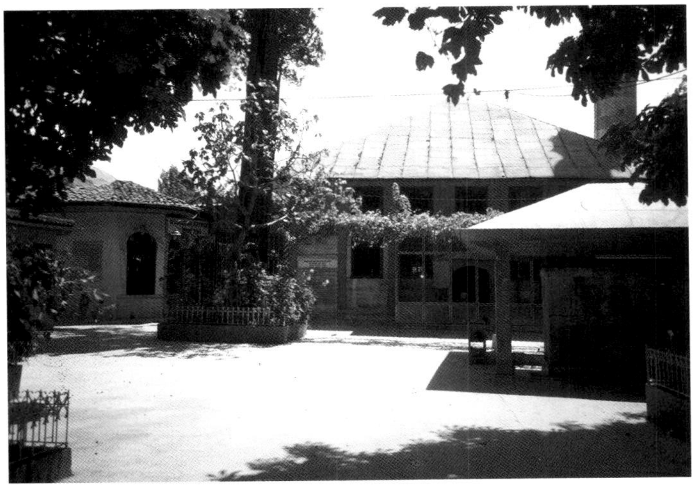

528 Bezirganbaşı Hacı Hüsrev mosque and mausoleum from the north with ablution fountain.

Thanks be to God! Murad, the Khan of the age
Became by his justice known to all horizons.

In particular when, like the stars, there burn
Many torches (*çırāḳ*, disciples) in the edifice of this mosque.

Hacı Hüsrev, the servant (*ġulām*) of Hace İmad,
Found merit in a charitable foundation such as this.

He built this mosque, and the pure in heart
Were all filled with longing for worship.

A convent (*tekyegāh*) for the dervishes
He built, with many arches and vaults.

When it was finished, the prayerful Sai
Composed the date: 'Kaʿba of the Lovers [of God]',
994 (1585–86).'[11]

The chronogram, *'Kaʿbetü'l-ʿuşşāḳ'*, is shared by the foundation inscription of the Muradiye mosque in Manisa, which similarly had a dervish convent among its dependencies.[12]

A biographical compendium of Halveti shaykhs describes Ramazan Efendi as the spiritual guide of the 'illiterate' (*ümmī*) and those in search of enlightenment in the path of God. His disciple Hace Hüsrev had donated to him a garden near Kocamustafapaşa where the shaykh supervised the construction of a Friday mosque and convent.[13] A waqfiyya dated 1593 identifies the founder as 'el-Hac Hüsrev b. Abdullah', who was 'the steward of the old covered bazaar' (*bezzāzistān-ı ʿatīḳ ketḫüdāsı*) and 'the pride of merchants'. It explains that, with the sultan's permission, he built in the garden of his own residence a Friday mosque, and at the north side of the mosque courtyard a joy-giving convent (*ḫānḳāh*) comprising ten cells for the sufis. The site, known as the 'garden of Yazıcızade', was located near the Kocamustafapaşa mosque. The convent was to be assigned to a pious shayh capable of delivering Friday sermons to congregations gathered in the mosque.[14] At the time its shaykh was Mevlana Ramazan b. Halil; upon his death, he was to be succeeded by a disciple talented in interpreting the hadith, delivering Friday sermons, and spiritually guiding the resident sufis. The sufis were to assemble at the convent on Monday and Thursday nights, praising God with repeated invocations and monotheistic litanies.[15]

It is unclear whether the lost convent comprised an assembly hall like that of Ferruh Kethüda's mosque in Balat.[16] Outside the mosque courtyard were built eighty-four endowed rooms, one of them earmarked for the imam, two for the muezzins, and one for the janitor. The remaining eighty rooms would be rented out to married couples to finance the salaries of employees, among whom the shaykh was the most highly paid (ten aspers a day). The founder would administer his waqf during his lifetime; after his death, he would be succeeded by his freed slaves and their descendants over the generations.[17]

The extensively rebuilt complex includes a Friday mosque, with a mausoleum at its east side where Ramazan Efendi is buried with six of his successors, and a paved forecourt featuring a rectangular ablution fountain. A cemetery garden extends behind the mosque and mausoleum. The precinct wall surrounding the complex is entered from an arched stone portal facing an avenue at the west side. The ten dervish cells at the north side of the mosque courtyard have disappeared, along with the dependencies of the convent.[18] During renovations in 1973, a number of authentic elements were obliterated when the precinct wall was rebuilt and the lush green courtyard, featuring informal cobblestone paths, was paved with marble. Goodwin describes the old courtyard: 'The garden, rather than a court for it is full of flowers and trees, is a retreat from the mud of the streets of the quarter beyond the precinct wall.'[19] The rectangular white marble ablution fountain is carved with arch motifs that frame low relief rosettes, naturalistic flowers, and cypresses. It has a modern lead-covered canopy, supported on marble columns.[20]

Built with alternating courses of stone and brick, the mosque has a muqarnas-galleried stone minaret. It was once fronted by a portico with wooden pillars; its present walled-in façade with two tiers of quadrangular windows was built in 1818–19, after a fire destroyed the original in 1782. The prayer hall, now covered with a flat wooden ceiling, had a wooden dome beneath its four-hipped leaded roof. The north wall of the mosque, hidden behind the present façade, has a central arched gate with joggled alternating voussoirs of pink and white marble. The unusual keystone of the arch has a spherical boss, decorated with a circle surrounded by six circles from which twelve rays emanate. It has been suggested that this may have been a symbol of the Halveti devotion to the Twelve Imams.[21] The foundation inscription is carved above it in a rectangular frame, in three lines of *thuluth*, composed of twelve cartouches. The gate is flanked on each side by two tiers of quadrangular iron-grilled windows, with a pointed-arched mihrab in between.

Exquisite İznik tiles – decorated with palmettes, rosettes, *saz* leaves, naturalistic flowers, and spring blossoms – cover the north façade and the interior of the prayer hall to the height of the upper windows (illus. 529). Modular tiles used on the walls are complemented by custom-made lunette tiles delineating pointed arches within rectangular frames. The muqarnas-hooded marble mihrab is accompanied by an elegant minbar sparsely carved with geometric lattices. The only inscriptions in the mosque appear in modern wooden roundels between the upper windows, calligraphed with the revered names, and on a rectangular panel inscribed with the typical verse (3:37) that hangs above the mihrab. The floral tiles that transform the prayer hall into an eternally blooming garden, echoing the bucolic setting outside, entirely lack inscriptions. Perhaps this was a deliberate strategy: to encourage inner forms of worship among

529 Bezirganbaşı Hacı Hüsrev mosque, Kocamustafapaşa, interior.

Ramazan Efendi's following dominated by the 'illiterate' in search of spiritual guidance.[22]

In Katib Çelebi's view, the Halveti leadership increasingly revelled in the illiteracy of initiates, playing on the social and entertainment value of sufi association in order to attract a larger following. This was the reason why the 'brutish common people' flocked to them, and votive offerings and pious gifts poured into their lodges. The adherents of the seventeenth-century anti-sufi Kadızadeli movement, to be discussed in the Epilogue, criticized the Halvetis for glorifying illiteracy and thus encouraging the masses to ignore the sacred law.[23] Primarily drawing on an unlettered popular base, Ramazan Efendi, 'renowned as *ümmī*', inspired his dervish disciples to burn like 'torches' with longing for God and spiritually enlightened 'the pure in heart' among the congregation of the 'Kaʿba of Lovers'.[24] With its mausoleum enshrining the venerated bodies of the shaykh and his successors, the intimate mosque-cum-convent complex, named Bezirgan Tekkesi after its merchant founder, became one of the foremost sufi shrines of the capital.

SİNAN'S LEGACY

The canonical style perfected by Sinan lived on well into the eighteenth century, with a tenacity not unlike Palladio's. The codes of decorum embodied in his mosque-centred complexes, however, remained limited to a particular context. They had already begun to disintegrate towards the end of his half-century-long career, with the transformation of the classical Ottoman order. Nevertheless, Sinan's canon proved flexible enough to accommodate the rise of new types of patrons, whose mosque complexes boldly negotiated the upper limits of decorum during the reign of Murad III. Distinguished by their close relationship with the sultan, these privileged patrons included the queen mother Nurbanu Sultan, the chief black eunuch Mehmed Agha, the royal companion Şemsi Ahmed Pasha, and the grand admiral Kılıç Ali Pasha.

After Sokollu Mehmed Pasha's demise in 1579, traditionally regarded as the end of the classical centralized regime, short-lived coalitions formed by competing palace factions began to interfere with the autonomy of the grand vizier's cabinet. The result was a system of government in which the sultan himself, his personal circle of advisers, and especially the royal women and eunuchs were increasingly involved in the administration of the state. This trend culminated in the seventeenth century with the so-called 'reign of women', characterized by the growing political dominance of the imperial harem (illus. 530, 531). Süleyman I and Selim II had delegated the administration of the state to such powerful grand viziers as Rüstem Pasha and Sokollu, trendsetters whose vision shaped the cultural politics of the empire for many years. These omnipotent grand viziers and their royal wives were among Sinan's foremost patrons. During the reign of Murad III, the grand vizierate became an unstable, short-term post that did not favour sustained architectural patronage on a large scale. During this period neither the sultan nor his grand viziers commissioned major works from Sinan; their role as patrons fell to the sultanas, viziers, and ascendant dignitaries, who strove for higher status through architectural visibility in the capital.

The Albanian-born Koca Sinan Pasha, celebrated as the conqueror of Yemen and Tunisia, personified a new breed of grand vizier, who bought his way into power; so fabulous was his wealth that the people imagined he practised alchemy.[1] The five short terms during which he occupied the grand vizierate (1580–82, 1589–91, 1593–95, 1595, 1595–96) testify to the mercurial instability of his position. In an age plagued by economic difficulties, he survived disgrace thanks to the wealth with which he could finance the state in cases of emergency.[2] Hasanbeyzade remarks that in his prodigious patronage of pious foundations Koca Sinan Pasha was rivalled only by Sokollu.[3] The chief architect's autobiographies, however, list just one work commissioned by this pasha: a palace near the Hippodrome.[4] They do not take credit for any of the provincial mosque complexes he sponsored local architects to build in such places as Bulaq (Cairo), Saʿsaʿa, Qtaifa (Kadife), Damascus, Yenişehir (Bursa), and Kaçanik (Skopje). They also omit the pasha's suburban mosques in the capital (Okmeydanı, outside Galata; and Salacak, in Üsküdar), seemingly undistinguished works that have disappeared without a trace.[5]

Nor did the Croatian-born Siyavuş Pasha, who held the grand vizierate three times (in 1582–84, 1586–89, and 1592–93) and is acknowledged in the preface of the *Teẕkiretül-bünyān*, commission any significant public works from the chief architect.[6] Sinan's autobiographies do not mention the pasha's premier mosque complex at Harmanlı in Bulgarian Thrace (*c.* 1584–87).[7] They list only his family tomb in Eyüp (illus. 319), together with his two palaces in Üsküdar and a third near the Süleymaniye complex.[8] It was Siyavuş Pasha who appointed Davud, the superintendent of water channels, as Sinan's successor in 1588. The chief architect, who had recommended his favourite, Mehmed Subaşı, to replace him as lieutenant in 1584, does not seem to have been particularly close to Davud whose signature is notably missing among the ten royal architects who signed his waqfiyya (*c.* 1583–85) (Appendix 4:4).[9] The new chief architect largely owed his position to the ties he had cultivated with

530 Sultan Osman II enthroned at the Topkapı Palace in the presence of white and black eunuchs, 1620, watercolour on paper, from Mehdi, *Shāhnāma*.

the chief black eunuch Mehmed Agha and the harem faction to which Siyavuş Pasha belonged. From Davud the pasha commissioned only a madrasa in memory of his royal wife and Murad III's youngest sister, Fatma Sultan, who expired during childbirth in 1590.[10] Adjoining their palace near the Süleymaniye (illus. 167[19]), this madrasa was just one among many monuments she requested him to construct as the proxy of her will (Friday mosque, dervish convent, elementary school, hospice, caravansaray, public fountain, stone bridge, and pavements).[11]

Besides the female relatives and favourites of Murad III, viziers rather than grand viziers stood out as the leading patrons of Sinan's late mosques in the capital. Those of Mesih Mehmed Pasha and Nişancı Mehmed Pasha renegotiated codes of decorum in the 1580s with their octagonal-baldachin plans that approximated grand vizierial prototypes (illus. 5). An even more ambitious mosque complex was built by the new chief architect Davud for the vizier Cerrah [Surgeon] Mehmed Pasha, who married the sultan's sister Gevherhan (the widow of Piyale Pasha) in 1578 and owed his nickname to having circumcised the crown prince Mehmed in 1582.[12] This vizierial mosque near Avratpazarı, dated by an inscription to 1002 (1593–94), is a particularly monumental variant of the hexagonal-baldachin scheme developed by Sinan (illus. 5, 532, 533). It is part of a complex comprising a domed mausoleum facing the street, an arched public fountain (dated 1594–95) at the bevelled corner of the precinct wall, and an income-producing double bath.[13] An independently endowed madrasa created earlier in 1586–87 for the pasha's royal wife is situated across the street.[14] The complex exemplifies the increasing visibility of public fountains and mausoleums in mosque complexes built during the 1580s inside the walled city, such as those of Mehmed Agha, Mesih Mehmed Pasha, and Nişancı Mehmed Pasha.

These mosque-centred complexes would soon be ousted by smaller madrasa-centred ones with prominent water dispensers and mausoleums, which became the norm for non-royal patronage in Istanbul from the 1590s onwards. The noticeable dearth of mosque construction at that time explains why Selaniki dedicates a chapter to the inauguration of Cerrah Mehmed Pasha's complex on 15 May 1594. The Friday prayers that day were attended by a crowded congregation, including 'all the pillars of the state, the great ulema, and the honourable shaykhs'. On the evening before (the holy night of Berat), the people had gathered there in a huge assembly to 'enliven the night with active religious exercises and supplications' under the moving spiritual guidance of the Halveti Shaykh Hasan Efendi, the 'fountainhead of mysteries and the recourse of the righteous'. Selaniki concludes his narration by praising the architectural style of the mosque:

> Near Dikilitaş [Avratpazarı], which is a distinguished and select site in the city of Istanbul, the newly built noble Friday mosque and elegant sanctuary of the unequalled vizier, His Highness Mehmed Pasha, which was constructed with the help and divine assistance of God, reached completion with perfect elegance and solidity. Being excellent in its beautiful manner and attractive style, it was admired by the inhabitants of the world.[15]

Compared to the mosques of his namesakes Mesih Mehmed Pasha and Nişancı Mehmed Pasha, that of Cerrah Mehmed Pasha is less innovative (illus. 5).[16] The smaller mosque that Davud built for the chief black eunuch Mehmed Agha similarly avoids experimentation, preferring instead to mimic prestigious vizierial prototypes designed by the grand master. The 'manneristic' inventions of Sinan's post-Selimiye mosques in the capital were

531 Feast given by the queen mother at the imperial palace in the presence of the wife of the French ambassador Girardin, second half of the seventeenth century, watercolour on paper.

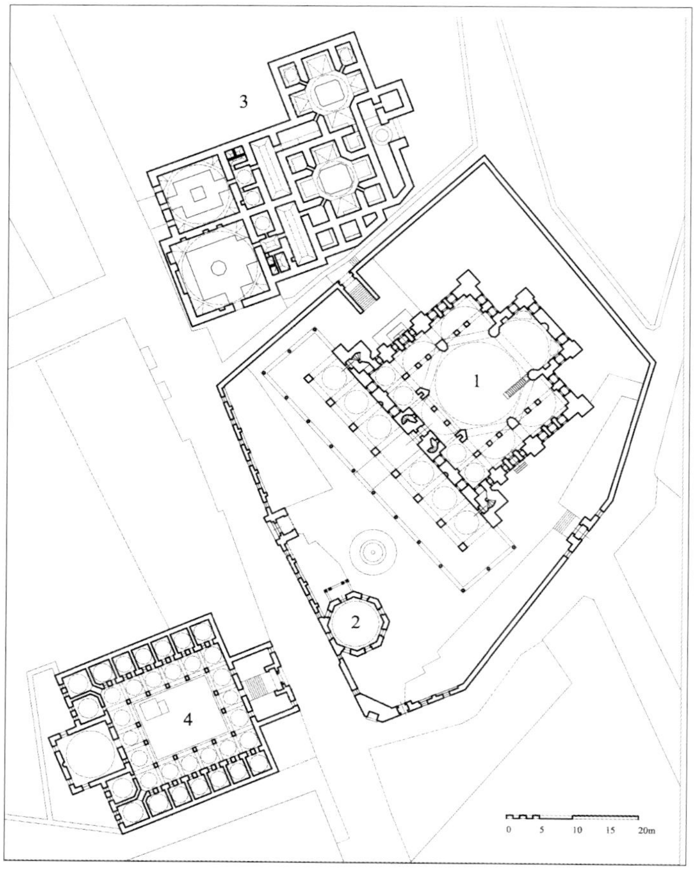

532 Plan of the Cerrah Mehmed Pasha complex, Avratpazarı: 1. Mosque. 2. Mausoleum. 3. Double bath. 4. Madrasa of Gevherhan Sultan.

discontinued during the tenure of his immediate successors. The crushing weight of his legacy also generated somewhat conservative plan types in royal mosques commissioned at the turn of the seventeenth century: those of the queen mother Safiye Sultan and her grandson Ahmed I, to which I shall turn after considering new patterns of non-royal patronage.

Cerrah Pasha's mosque-centred complex was the last example of its kind to be built in Istanbul until the revivalist mosque of Hekimoğlu Ali Pasha reinterpreted its design in 1734.[17] The kernel of a post-classical architectural paradigm emerged in the capital during Davud's tenure as chief architect (1588–98), a paradigm further elaborated under his successors, Dalgıç Ahmed (1598–1606) and Mehmed (1606–22).[18] From the seventeenth century onwards, madrasa-based funerary complexes became the rule for vizierial and grand vizierial patronage in the capital, where mosques were erected primarily for some of the sultans and their mothers.

The madrasa complexes of grandees, generally sited along or near the Divanyolu, enhanced the architectural unity of that ceremonial axis.[19] The earliest surviving examples of such small *intramuros* complexes were commissioned from Davud in the 1590s by the grand vizier Koca Sinan Pasha and the influential

533 Louis-François Cassas, Sketch of the Cerrah Pasha mosque, c. 1786, pencil on paper.

Venetian-born chief white eunuch, Gazanfer Agha. An earlier madrasa complex, accompanied by a water dispenser with an upper-storey elementary school, which Davud had created on Divanyolu for the chief black eunuch Mehmed Agha (1579–82), is only partially extant.[20] Prominently sited on crossroads, the madrasa complexes built for Sinan Pasha and Gazanfer Agha each includes a projecting water dispenser and a monumental domed mausoleum. Surrounded by nearly transparent window-pierced precinct walls, these monuments engage in a more intimate dialogue with public urban space than do Sinan's grand mosque complexes, which are relatively self-sufficient microcosms.

The madrasa complex of Koca Sinan Pasha (d. 1594) is visually dominated by his sixteen-sided domed mausoleum of ashlar masonry facing Divanyolu (illus. 534, 535).[21] Other components of the complex are a U-shaped madrasa, built of alternating courses of stone and brick, and a pyramidal-roofed octagonal 'water dispenser' (*sebīlḫāne*) that punctuates the corner where Divanyolu intersects with a street. The foundation inscription on the gate of the water dispenser gives the completion date of 1002 (1593–94) along with the names of the chief architect, Davud, and his patron. This new emphasis on artistic authorship is anticipated by earlier inscriptions that mention Davud's name: on the precinct gate of Mehmed Agha's mosque (1584–86) at Çarşamba, and on a fountain of the Pearl Kiosk at the Topkapı Palace, financed by Koca Sinan Pasha (1588–89) as a gift for Murad III.[22] Within sixteen cartouches, the *thuluth* inscription of the water dispenser quotes a hadith on the relative merits of providing water to an animal, a tree, and a believer (equalling twenty, forty, and seventy years of fasting respectively). The inscription is as much a reminder of the chief architect Davud's expertise in hydraulic engineering as it is a celebration of his patron Koca Sinan Pasha's engagement in this increasingly popular form of charity.[23]

The other madrasa complex Davud designed for Gazanfer Agha (d. 1599) was authorized by an imperial decree addressed to the kadi of Istanbul in 1593 (illus. 536, 537). The sultan explains that his esteemed chief white eunuch has been 'wanting to build a madrasa for two years' and because a church in an Islamic neighbourhood had recently been razed, the agha had

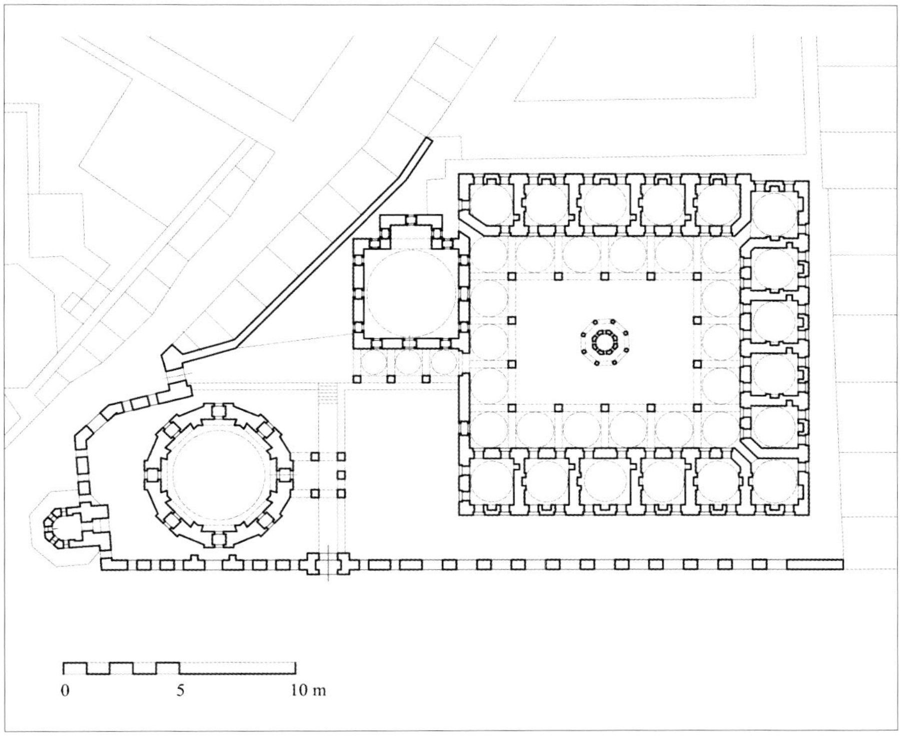

534 Plan of the Koca Sinan Pasha complex, Divanyolu.

535 Koca Sinan Pasha complex.

requested permission to use its empty plot for the construction of his madrasa and mausoleum.[24] Murad III permits Gazanfer Agha's project which was completed around 1596, judging by the date of his waqfiyya. The endowment deed refers to the site close to Divanyolu as 'a crossroad in Kırkçeşme' and praises the 'novel design' of the madrasa complex comprising a paradise-like lofty mausoleum and an elegant water dispenser *(sebīl)*.[25]

The intimate ashlar masonry complex abutting the Valens aqueduct is composed of an asymmetrical, U-shaped madrasa, appended to a twelve-sided domed mausoleum in its forecourt. The fenestrated precinct wall allows the monumental mausoleum, which dominates the complex, to be seen from the street. The domed octagonal water dispenser, serving passers-by to attract their prayers on behalf of the founder's soul, protrudes from the bevelled corner where two streets meet.[26] A painting in the *Dīvān* of the poet Nadiri, who served as the professor of the madrasa from its foundation until 1601, depicts him with a row of students in the domed classroom, with the Valens aqueduct seen in the background. The mounted figure paying a visit to the complex is Gazanfer Agha (illus. 538). The painting captures the personalized nature of patronage relationships engendered by such intimate complexes, which embody an ethos more worldly than that of their mosque-centred counterparts, an ethos of early modernity emerging at the turn of the seventeenth century.[27]

The shrunken scale of these tiny complexes is foreshadowed by the *extramuros* funerary madrasa created by Sinan for Sokollu and his royal wife in Eyüp (1568–69), whose scheme now is transplanted inside the city walls (illus. 318, 319). It has been suggested that the dramatic surge in the number of madrasa complexes during the seventeenth century may well have been rooted in the perceived needs of the time and the renewed emphasis on interpreting the law, triggered by the challenge of the Kadızadeli movement.[28] The Kadızadelis were named after their founder, the Friday mosque preacher Kadızadeli Mehmed (d. 1635), who studied with the disciples of the conservative theologian Birgili Mehmed (d. 1573), a virulent critic of Ebussuud's more lenient interpretation of Islam. Relying on Birgili's treatise, 'The Way of the Prophet Muhammad', the proponents of this movement (*c.* 1633–56, 1665–83), who opposed innovations introduced after the lifetime of the Prophet, primarily targeted the sufi path and the performance in mosques of such sufi rituals as the remembrance of God *(dhikr)*. The growing tension between innovation and fundamentalism was aggravated by the fact that orthodox-minded Friday mosque preachers had to compete with sufi shaykhs for preacher posts *(vaiz)*, which were particularly dominated by Halveti shaykhs.[29]

The new preference for madrasa-centred complexes may also have responded to a critique voiced by Mustafa Āli in 1586–87: he regarded the redundant construction of so many Friday mosques at the political centre of the empire, rather than in needy provincial towns, a blatant show of prestige having little to do with piety.[30] It must have become increasingly difficult to find a legal justification for the construction of more Friday mosques in Istanbul, which had reached a saturation point by the late sixteenth century. The paradigm shift in the capital from mosque-centred monumental complexes to more modest ones grouped around madrasas (sometimes featuring sufi convents

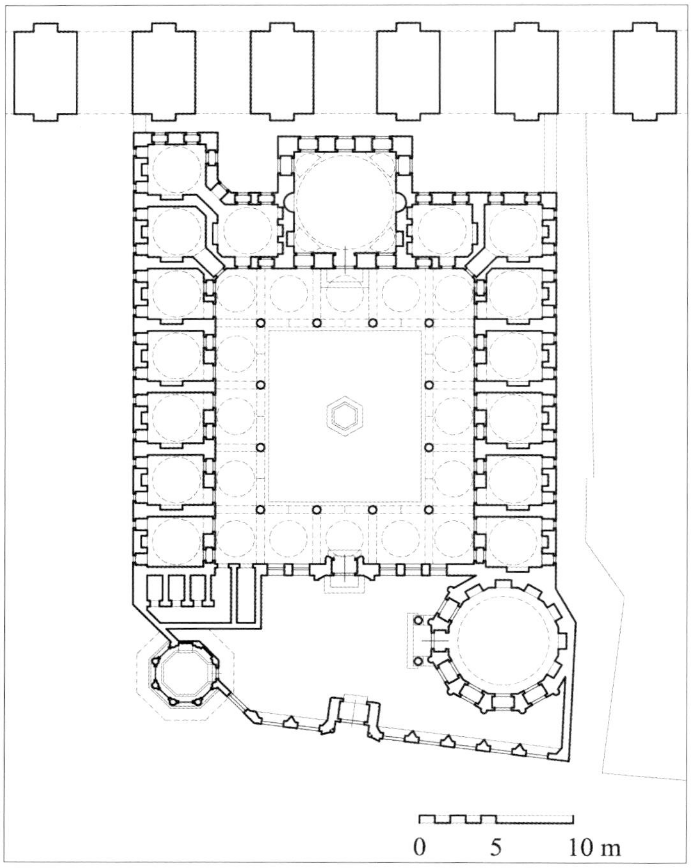

536 Plan of the Gazanfer Agha complex, Unkapanı, in front of the Valens aqueduct.

537 Gazanfer Agha complex.

and masjids) also responded to practical constraints, namely the reduced availability of building sites and the diminished wealth of non-royal patrons.

Economic realities had drastically changed under the impact of such factors as inflation, budget deficits caused by the expanded army, lack of military expansion abroad, and unrest in the provinces, expressed by recurrent Celali rebellions.[31] After quoting the expenses of Sultan Süleyman's monumental architectural projects, the court historian Lokman remarked with some exaggeration during the late 1580s that the same buildings would now cost twice as much because of rampant inflation.[32] The Süleymaniye complex had been built for 53,782,980 aspers, equivalent to 896,383 Ottoman gold pieces. The mosque complex of Sultan Ahmed I at the Hippodrome (1609–17) would cost about 180,341,803 aspers, but as the asper had dramatically been devalued, this corresponded to 1,381,245 gold coins.[33] The Yeni Valide (New Queen Mother) mosque in Eminönü, completed by Turhan Sultan in the mid-1660s, cost 154,000,000 aspers. This sum did not include the expenses of its foundations, which had been laid in the 1590s by another queen mother, Safiye Sultan.[34] Clearly, then, the favourable economic circumstances that had encouraged the boom in Friday mosque construction in the age of Sinan were over.

During the 1590s, the adverse effects of inflation on various branches of the construction industry began to be vividly registered in imperial decrees issued on behalf of the chief architect, Davud. These documents show how far officially fixed prices lagged behind market forces, and how the state's authority in enforcing repeatedly issued orders had diminished.[35] Weakened central authority and provincial disorder induced by the Celali revolts meant that long-distance building operations (and state-protected industries such as the manufacture of İznik tiles) could no longer be effectively coordinated from the capital. The seventeenth century also saw the emergence of local chief architects in many more provincial cities than in Sinan's time, a development that precipitated the decentralization of architectural practice.

The shrinking number and scale of monuments commissioned in Istanbul found a parallel in major provincial centres. In Aleppo and Damascus, for instance, smaller waqfs, dominated by sufi convents and no longer grouped around monumental Friday mosques, became the norm during the seventeenth century.[36] In less developed towns, on the other hand, the ongoing construction of monumental domed mosques by sub-royal patrons diminished the architectural primacy of Istanbul.[37] The emergence of a decentralized state was paralleled by the ascendance of autonomous provincial elites and the rise of flourishing cities, such as İzmir, that began to approximate the capital.[38] This trend would culminate in the eighteenth and nineteenth centuries with the appearance of even more powerful local notables, whose provincial mosques asserted their autonomy *vis-à-vis* the capital.

538 The chief white eunuch Gazanfer Agha visiting his madrasa complex, c. 1605, watercolour on paper, from Nadiri, *Dīvān-Nādirī*.

It was only on the level of limited royal patronage that monumental mosque complexes continued to be built in Istanbul during the seventeenth century. The wives of sultans, princesses, and princes largely disappeared as mosque patrons, leaving only the sultans and queen mothers. The last crown prince sent to govern Manisa, Murad III's eldest son Mehmed, was robbed from the opportunity to build a mosque of his own in that city, where his tutor had been ordered to oversee the completion of his father's Muradiye complex. When the prince was enthroned as Mehmed III (r. 1595–1603), he refrained from constructing a sultanic mosque in Istanbul, delegating that function to Safiye Sultan, his forceful mother. Although Murad III never married the Albanian-born Safiye, as the heir apparent's mother she stood out among his more than forty *haseki*s.[39] When she attained the all-powerful position of queen mother during her son's reign, she undertook the construction of an imposing mosque complex at the capital. The obstacles Safiye and, later on, her grandson Ahmed I faced in legitimizing their mosque complexes in Istanbul reveal the unfavourable circumstances for grand architectural initiatives. The intertwined stories of these two royal mosques, both of which perpetuated Sinan's legacy by paraphrasing the quatrefoil plan of the Şehzade Mehmed mosque, disclose the tensions even the foremost royal patrons now had to resolve in the negotiation of decorum.

The queen mother commissioned her mosque complex from the chief architect Davud soon after 1596, when her son Mehmed III victoriously returned to the capital from the Eger campaign in Hungary (illus. 539). The mosque was located on a highly visible site along the waterfront of Eminönü, near the imperial garden of the Topkapı Palace, where Safiye Sultan resided. Selaniki explains that in 1597, a site next to the landing station of 'Emin İskelesi' (Eminönü) was prepared for her Friday mosque, madrasa, hospice, and caravansaray by demolishing the houses she had bought from Jewish residents. The gatekeeper Kara [Black] Mehmed Agha (the steward of the chief black eunuch Osman Agha) was appointed the construction supervisor, with the grand vizier Hadım [Eunuch] Hasan Pasha acting as building overseer.[40]

On 8 April 1598, while the foundations of the mosque were being dug in accordance with the selected plan (*resm*), the sultan sent a memorandum dismissing the grand vizier because he gossiped about how he had bribed the queen mother for his position and conspired against the chief white eunuch Gazanfer Agha.[41] For the second foundation ceremony, held on 20 August 1598 at an auspicious time determined by casting a horoscope, the meeting of the imperial council was cancelled. Attended by all the pillars of the state and religion, the ceremony affirmed that the queen mother's construction was not just her personal affair. Should God allow the completion of this 'royal monument', Selaniki writes, it was destined to become 'an exemplar of the ages'. But, alas, the chief architect Davud died from the plague in the beginning of September 1598 and was succeeded by the superintendent of water channels, Dalgıç Ahmed Çavuş.[42]

After losing its original architect, the mosque continued to experience setbacks. In 1600 its building supervisor was dismissed because he had not properly compensated owners of demolished buildings and waqfs on the construction site in accordance with the shariʿa. The accusations directed against him exhibit the increasing difficulty of obtaining a legal building site in the packed capital. Among the structures dismantled for the queen mother's mosque were a Christian church and a Jewish synagogue whose congregations had secured written permissions from the sultan and the kadi's court for the replacement of their sanctuaries with new ones. However, since the law court's permits had been signed not by the kadi himself but by his assistant, they were deemed invalid. The assistant judge was swiftly dismissed, and the kadi of Istanbul tore down the surrogate church that had been constructed elsewhere by the builders of the mosque. The kadi then visited the grand mufti, who had been threatened by the queen's building supervisor with losing his post should he refuse to sign the permit for the synagogue, which was to be built next. The grand mufti wrote a letter of protest to the sultan and his mother, declaring that their mosque complex (apparently perceived as a joint endeavour) was illegal:

539 Victory procession of Sultan Mehmed III in Istanbul after the Eger campaign, *c.* 1596, watercolour on paper, from Talikizade, *Shāhnāme*.

> Your pious foundation meant to redeem you in the next world is legally contaminated, and illegitimate affairs do not endure; it is decorous and appropriate that your affairs pertaining to the shariʿa should be strengthened by a pious supervisor observant of the shariʿa.

The culpable building supervisor was replaced by Nasuh Agha, the steward of gatekeepers.[43]

The queen mother's construction, dubbed 'oppression' (*ẓulmiye*), remained incomplete after her grandson Ahmed I (r. 1603–17) exiled her in 1603 to the Old Palace, where she died in 1619.[44] We learn from the Venetian *bailo* Agostino Nani (1600–3) that the sixty-year-old queen mother had already been temporarily chased to the Old Palace and banned from building her mosque during her son's reign because the army 'attributed to her many disorders, and in particular spending money for an extremely superb mosque that she was having built.' She had to 'withdraw from the construction of that building' upon returning to the Topkapı Palace.[45] This must have happened in 1600, when the imperial cavalry troops, who demanded the unpopular Safiye's exile, tore to pieces her wealthy Jewish agent Esther Kira, the tax farmer of the customs house in Eminönü, whom they held responsible for the debased coins they were paid with. Another revolt in 1603 resulted in the assassination of the chief white and black eunuchs, Gazanfer and Osman Agha.[46]

The mosque of Safiye Sultan caused considerable resentment because it was deemed an unnecessary expense, undertaken during an economic recession and military campaign on the western frontier of the empire, for which she and others had donated money in 1599.[47] Besides legal controversies, the perennial competition between the proponents of war and peace turned Safiye Sultan's construction project into a backdrop for public dissent. What also hindered the completion of her mosque must have been its sultanic typology, which blatantly subverted codes of decorum established during the age of Sinan. The negotiation of consensus was hopelessly blocked by the contestation of her begrudged status. The completion of the mosque had to wait until the mid-seventeenth century, when the 'reign of women' empowered another queen mother to negotiate and bypass classical codes of decorum more effectively. Turhan Sultan (the mother of Mehmed III's namesake Mehmed IV) dared to complete the beleaguered mosque in Eminönü after a fire in 1660–61 exposed its walls, which had been concealed under filth and debris by the Jewish residents of the neighbourhood.[48] Since the walls had risen one cubit above the ground, up to the window level, its ground plan did not change substantially (illus. 540, 541). It was finished in three years according to its original plan, after removing a single row of stone.[49]

The İznik tile-revetted royal pavilion attached to the imperial tribune, from which the second patroness surveyed construction work, is dated by an inscription to 1074 (1663–64). By glorifying Turhan Sultan as the mother of Sultan Mehmed IV, who had conquered lands in Christendom, this inscription underscores the legitimization of the mosque through her son's military victories.[50] Popularly known as Yeni Valide, the mosque complex preserves Turhan Sultan's memory as the exalted matriarch of the dynastic family. She lies buried in its monumental domed mausoleum with her son Mehmed IV, several eighteenth-century sultans, and other male and female members of the royal family.[51]

Safiye Sultan's double-minaret mosque, modelled on that of Şehzade Mehmed with its quatrefoil plan and marble-paved imperial forecourt, was meant to surpass the mosque complex of her rival and arch-enemy, Nurbanu Sultan, in Üsküdar. The hexagonal-baldachined mosque with two minarets that Sinan had designed for Nurbanu grew in hesitant stages with the addition of side aisles and a porticoed forecourt cautiously planted with trees (illus. 261–62).[52] These posthumous modifications in the mid-1580s paved the way for the more audacious plan of Safiye Sultan's mosque, prominently sited at the foot of the imperial palace. From the viewpoint of its architect, Davud, the queen mother's mosque must have been a competitive artistic response to Sinan's legacy. From the perspective of its patroness, its sultanic pretensions could be justified by its conception as a joint memorial for herself and her son, the conqueror of Eger. Forbidden from completing it, Safiye Sultan resorted to having a simpler, single-minaret mosque built in Cairo (illus. 542).

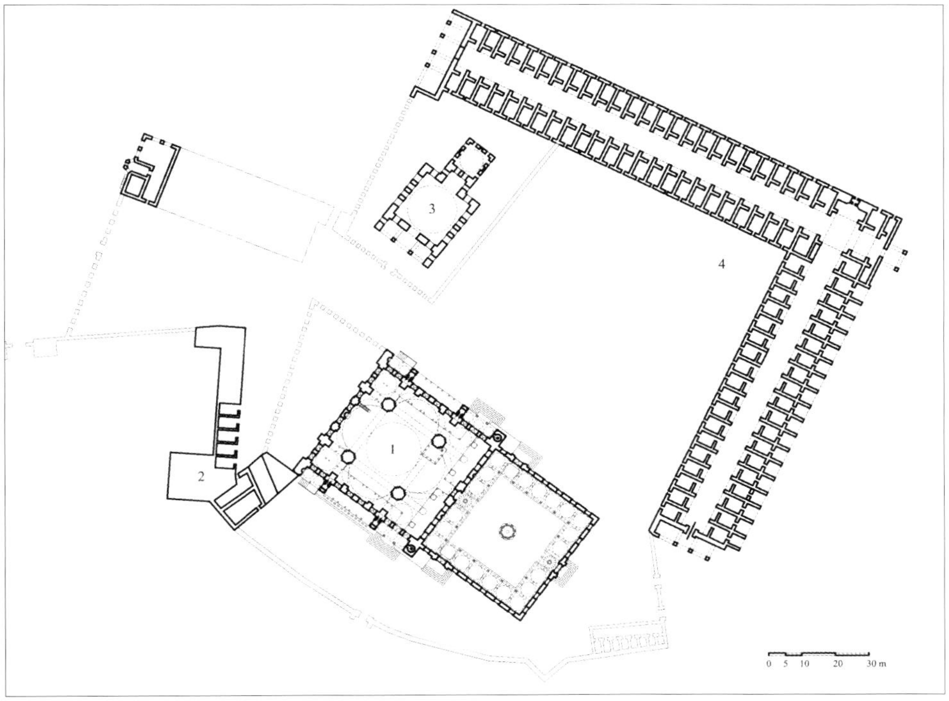

540 Yeni Valide complex, Eminönü:

1. Mosque
2. Ramp to the royal pavilion
3. Mausoleum
4. Covered bazaar

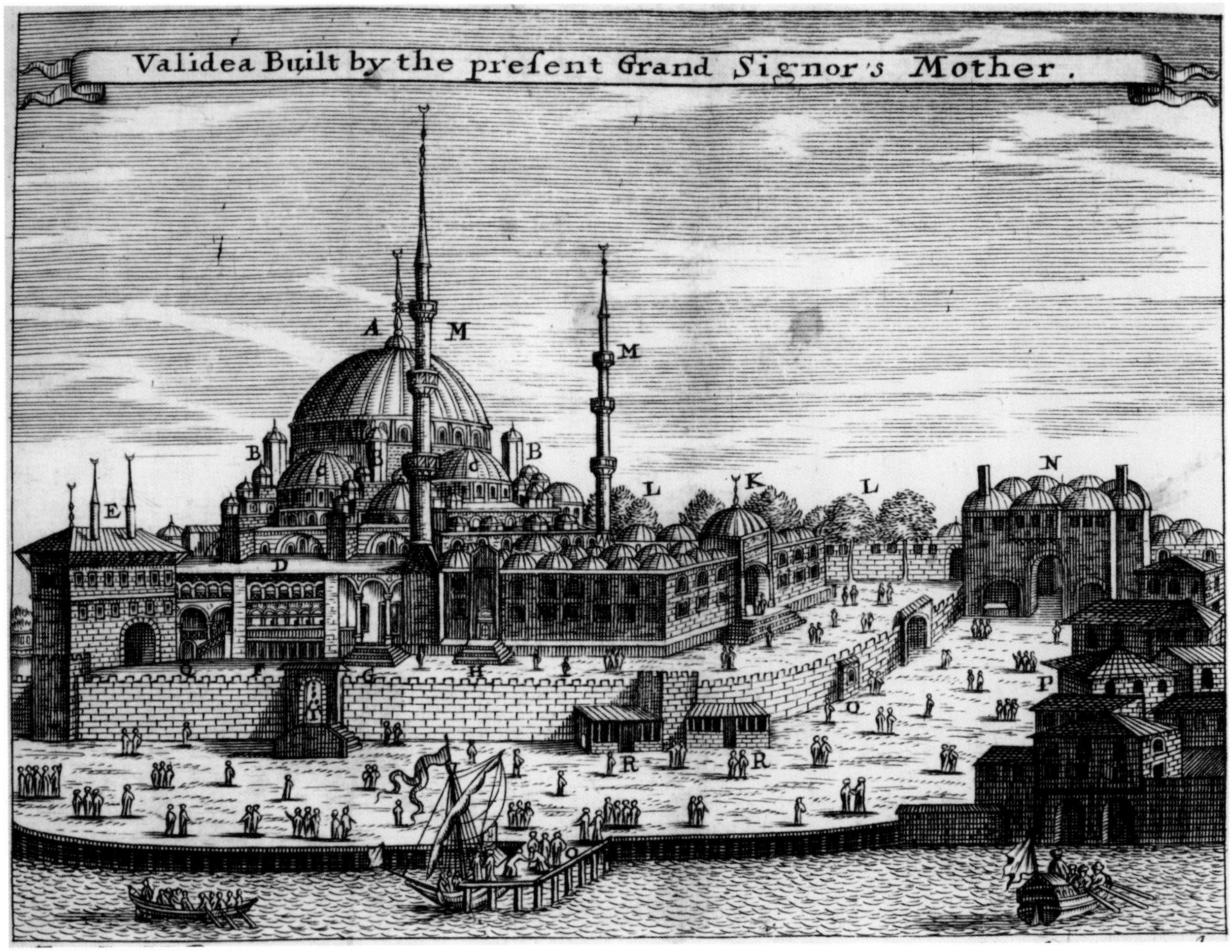

541 G.-J. Grelot, Yeni Valide complex, *c.* 1683, engraving.

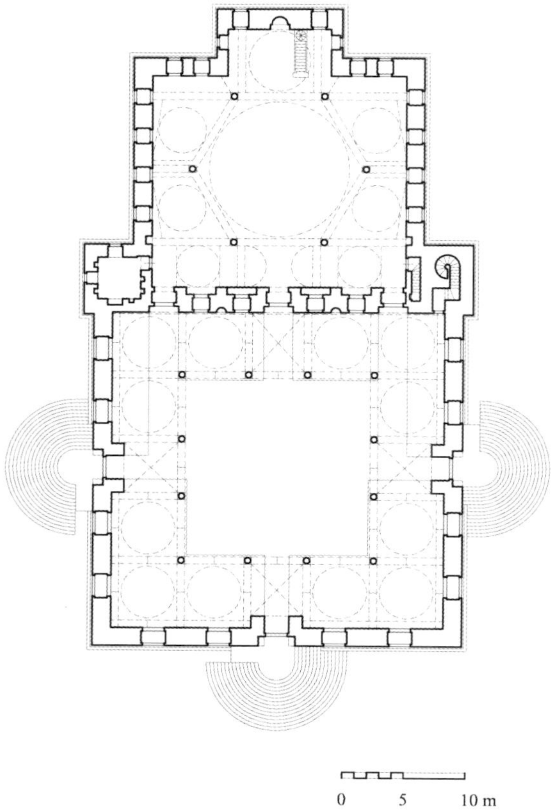

542 Plan of the Safiye Sultan (Malika Safiyya) mosque, Cairo.

Known today as the Malika Safiyya mosque, its hexagonal-baldachin plan (recalling that of Nurbanu's mosque) boasts an unprecedented marble-paved imperial forecourt, and its foundation inscription, dated 1019 (1610–11), refers to her as the 'mother of our late lord, Sultan Mehmed Khan'.[53]

The fourteen-year-old new ruler Ahmed I must have perceived his grandmother's assertive mosque in Eminönü as an encroachment on his authority. The Venetian *bailo* Simone Contarini wrote in 1613 that the sultan founded his own mosque at the Hippodrome to display his disdain towards the old queen mother, whose request to complete her waterfront mosque he firmly refused (illus. 543, 544). Contarini adds that the sultan's mosque, located on the site of two palaces in return for which he had legally exchanged other properties, would be similar to the Süleymaniye. It would exceed its model in length by ten *braccia* and would have two extra minarets. Great sums were going to be spent on this '*superbissima*' mosque (1,830,000 scudi per year), which was expected to reach completion within five years. It was abhorred by many, Contarini reports, because it absorbed funds that could instead be spent on a war against the Christians. Aware of the necessity to legitimize its construction, the sultan wanted to count as a military victory the recent suppression of the Celali rebellions in Anatolia (1608) by Kuyucu Murad Pasha. Contarini also mentions the youthful monarch's plan to invade Candia in Crete so as to justify the continuation of his disputed project.[54]

The Sultan Ahmed mosque has recently been interpreted as part of its patron's aspiration to model himself after the glorious image of Sultan Süleyman.[55] Cristoforo Valier (1616), who notes Ahmed's desire to surpass the legendary memory of Süleyman, recognizes his need to justify the construction of the new mosque with a grand conquest that was not forthcoming.[56] The internal victory against the Celalis in 1608 had provided only a temporary boost from recent humiliations against external enemies. At the western border of the empire, a peace treaty signed with the Hapsburgs in 1606 had forced the sultan to address as his equal Rudolf II, who would no longer pay the annual tribute required since the days of Süleyman. In 1603, at the eastern front, the Safavid ruler Shah ʿAbbas had won back such strongholds as Tabriz and Erivan, conquered under Murad III. Soon after laying the foundations of his mosque in 1609, Sultan Ahmed declared war against the Safavids, a war that was still going on when the mosque was inaugurated in 1617. The twenty-eight-year-old monarch passed away that year and was buried in a posthumously built mausoleum within his complex. He did not live long enough to see the completion in 1619 of the loosely arranged dependencies of his mosque (a hospice, a madrasa, a school for Koran recitation, an elementary school, a hospital, four water dispensers, a bath-house, shopping arcade, and rental houses), only some of which survive today.[57]

Sultan Ahmed took utmost care to obtain a legal site for his construction. He was initially presented with the option of completing Safiye Sultan's mosque but decided in favour of building a 'New Mosque'. To avoid the controversies raised by the queen's illicit construction, he rejected the first site proposed: the palace of the late grand vizier Rüstem Pasha in the Mahmudpaşa quarter. Although that palace decorously overlooked the Golden Horn from an elevated and airy hilltop next to the Topkapı Palace, it was located in a heavily inhabited area that would have necessitated the expropriation of too many properties. Moreover, the narrowness of streets would have disturbed neighbourhood residents during the transportation of building materials, requiring the demolition of additional structures. The present site on the Hippodrome, overlooking the Sea of Marmara rather than the Golden Horn, was preferred because it required only the demolition of two large palaces designed by Sinan for the couples Mihrümah-Rüstem and İsmihan-Sokollu, which the sultan purchased from their heirs.[58]

The biographer of the chief architect Mehmed Agha, who designed the mosque complex, praises the monarch's sensitivity concerning the selection of an appropriate site:

> The benevolent Shah did not consent to the tearing
> down of districts
> He did not wish that abodes and dwellings be
> removed.

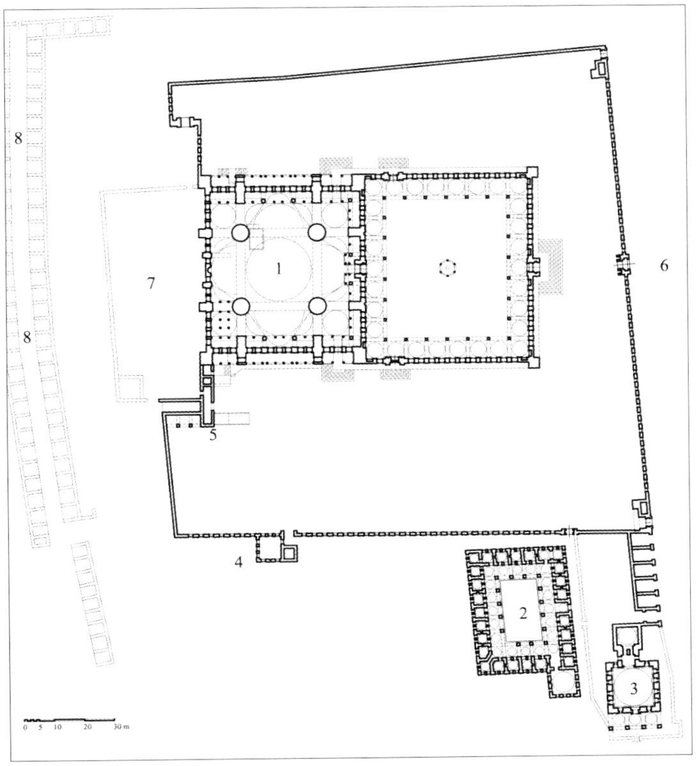

543 Plan of remaining parts of the Sultan Ahmed complex, Atmeydanı: 1. Mosque. 2. Madrasa. 3. Mausoleum. 4. Elementary school. 5. Royal pavilion. 6. Hippodrome. 7. Garden platform. 8. *Arasta*.

544 Sultan Ahmed complex, Istanbul, from the east, with the bath-house of Hürrem Sultan at the lower-left corner.

> In the city of Istanbul, there were many aged palaces,
> There were none, either man or jinn, dwelling
> in those houses.
>
> The buildings occupied one of the finest locations of
> the city.
> They had become filled with the nests of owls.[59]

When the sultan consulted the grand mufti to confirm the propriety of building a mosque on the Hippodrome, he was told that the public square surrounded by grand palaces lacked a large enough congregation. A chronicle written by the royal imam explains that this legal hindrance was to be countered by replacing some of the old structures there with houses.[60] The author praises the proximity of the Hippodrome to the Topkapı Palace, which drew people 'like a magnet' from all over the world, sufficient to fill 'many mosques like Ayasofya'.[61]

The closeness of Hagia Sophia must surely have made the 'New Mosque' appear superfluous to its critics. Those opposed to its construction only needed to remember Mustafa Āli's advice to Murad III in 1581: that the shariʿa did not permit the sultans to waste the public treasury on 'unnecessary' building projects, nor to construct charitable foundations, without having enriched themselves with the spoils of Holy War.[62] Like Safiye Sultan's mosque, that of Ahmed I faced opposition from pro-war parties, who considered its costs unjustified. While reservations about the necessity of a mosque in the sparsely inhabited Hippodrome were apparently neutralized, the sultan was unable to offset the second legal hurdle underlined by Āli. The grand mufti and other jurists regarded the mosque as illegitimate because Ahmed had won no victory against the Christians.[63] As the Frenchman Guillaume-Joseph Grelot (1683) observes, however, the steadfast ruler chose not to pay too much attention to the ulema's criticisms:

> However Sultan Achmet, though he had not by any conquest extended the bounds of the Empire, resolved to Build a Mosquee, to the end he might eternize his name, since his achievements did not suffice to recommend him to posterity. And though the Mufti, the Mullas, the Cheiks, and other Doctors of the Law, laid before him the sin of undertaking to erect such a costly fabrick, since he had never been in any other Combats, than those which are daily to be seen for the exercise of the Pages, and the divertisement of the Prince, nevertheless he gave little heed to their admonitions, but carried on the work with a vigor answerable to his resolution; and when he had finished the Pile, because he had slighted his Chaplains exhortations, called it *Imansis Gianisi* [Imansız Camisi], or the Temple of the Incredulous. It is also called the New Mosquee, as being one of the last that was Built.[64]

The sultan's insistence on founding a legally suspect grand mosque asserted the primacy of his imperial prerogatives over codes of decorum reached by collective consensus. Historians recount how Sultan Ahmed descended from his high pavilion at the construction site during the initial foundation ceremony on 9 November 1609 in order to dig the ground with his own hands, using a gold mattock with a velvet-covered handle. During the second foundation ceremony, held on 4 January 1610, the construction of the qibla wall was initiated at a lucky hour determined by astrologers.[65] Headed by the grand mufti, the ulema and shaykhs consecrated the building with prayers, but Evliya Çelebi reports that they urged the sultan to undertake the conquest of Crete so as to provide legal revenues for his mosque in the manner of Sultan Süleyman.[66]

The French diplomat Jean de Gontaut-Biron (1609–10) says the ruler frequently came to the construction site, watching it from his elevated pavilion, in which he sometimes stayed overnight to encourage the rapid completion of the mosque.[67] Account books mention the now-lost İznik tiles of this royal pavilion (*ḳaṣr-ı hümāyūn*), which was subsequently attached to the imperial tribune at the southeast corner of the mosque and served as a space where the sultan could rest and hold audiences.[68] The unprecedented inclusion of a palatial structure in the programme of the mosque parallels the new blend of temporal and religious functions in the public ceremonies that were held at the construction site by the increasingly visible monarch. These ceremonies included annual recitations of the Prophet's nativity poem (*mevlud*). The first such ceremony, recorded in 1614, is described as having been attended by all the statesmen, ulema, and shaykhs who gathered for 'sociable conversation' (*ṣoḥbet*) at the mosque, 'whose scaffoldings were decorated with oil lamps'. It was on that occasion that the finance minister Kalender Efendi, who had served as the building supervisor, was promoted to the vizierate.[69] The completion of the dome in 1617 was once again celebrated with the recitation of the Prophet's nativity poem to an assembly so large that the Muslims spilled beyond the precinct wall, filling the public space of the Hippodrome.[70] Account books list expenses for incense and rosewater, sweetmeats, food for 'the high and low', fruits, candies, drinks, and coffee consumed on that festive occasion.[71]

The stipulation of Sultan Ahmed's waqfiyya (dated 1613) about the annual chanting of the nativity poem on the Prophet's birthday explains why for centuries his successors continued to observe this ritual at his mosque, where the order and rank of dignitaries was regulated by a particular etiquette (illus. 545).[72] It was Murad III who had first introduced the *mevlud* ritual into a sultanic mosque, the Hagia Sophia. In 1599 the grand mufti banned its practice at royal mosques as an 'ugly innovation' during which endowment administrators served candies and sherbets only to the grandees, while the poor were bypassed.[73] The Sultan Ahmed mosque's revived *mevlud* festivities corrected this objectionable inequity by serving food and drinks to both 'high and low'. The consumption of coffee, a beverage rejected in some conservative circles as a suspect innovation, within the sacred space of the sultanic mosque, underscores its function as a locus for sociable interaction: an instance of the expansion of the public sphere during the seventeenth century, an epoch of urban 'mass' culture.[74]

545 Annual celebration of the birth of the Prophet Muhammad at the Sultan Ahmed mosque, *c.* 1788, print.

The famous sufi shaykhs appointed to lecture at the Sultan Ahmed mosque included Abdülmecid Sivasi (the Friday preacher), Aziz Mahmud Hüdai (the Friday preacher of Mihrümah Sultan's mosque in Üsküdar, appointed to lecture at the sultanic mosque on the first Monday of each month), and Cerrah Şeyhi İbrahim Efendi (the Friday preacher of Cerrah Mehmed Pasha's mosque, who delivered Sunday sermons at the sultan's mosque).[75] The Halveti shaykh Abdülmecid Sivasi (d. 1639) in particular became a target of the Kadızadeli movement, whose proponents denounced such innovations as shaykhs preaching in Friday mosques, sufi rituals for the remembrance of God, supererogatory prayers on holy nights, commemorations of the Prophet's birthday, and coffee.[76] These openly debated religious controversies were another harbinger of the expanded public sphere in a period of crisis, characterized by recurrent rural and urban revolts. The Kadızadelis ultimately failed because of the narrowness of their vision, as no city was further removed from the simplicity of Medina in the days of the Prophet than the Ottoman capital. Their call for rigid austerity ran counter to the mainstream religious culture that had matured during the age of Sinan. The humanizing urge of popular Islam and sufism, which balanced the aridity of orthodox-minded religion, was vindicated with the dissipation of the Kadızadeli movement: after the abortive siege of Vienna in 1683, its last influential proponent was banished from the capital.[77]

The Sultan Ahmed mosque heralded the dawning ethos of early modernity not only in the increasingly civic and sociable touch of its religious rituals, but also in the 'baroque' overtones of its new architectural sensibility. Its designer, the chief architect Mehmed Agha, who in 1617 signed one of the four water dispensers in the complex, was a former water channel superintendent who had studied with Sinan.[78] Like his predecessors, Davud and Dalgıç Ahmed, he too emulated the grand master's legacy in the 'New Mosque', whose stated programme was to outshine the Süleymaniye. Its quatrefoil plan with four half-domes, however, paraphrases the layout of Şehzade Mehmed's mosque (also commissioned by Süleyman). This design choice not only accentuated the implicit competition of Sultan Ahmed's mosque with that of his grandmother, but also eliminated the costly search for colossal internal columns used in the Süleymaniye.

Rather than replicating the Süleymaniye, the 'New Mosque' indirectly alludes to it through recognizable references: its four comparable minarets of unequal height around the courtyard, which are supplemented with two others along the qibla wall, and its analogous lateral façades with ablution spigots and external porticoes, now extending beyond the mosque walls to its forecourt. Raised on four colossal fluted piers, the central dome (23.5 metres wide, 43 metres high) falls between those of the Şehzade and Süleymaniye mosques in size. The proportionally higher domical superstructure exaggerates the pyramidal massing of Süleyman's two royal mosques, abandoned in the Selimiye.[79] Anti-classical innovations introduced in the latter mosque, dominated by a single dome, are overlooked in favour of reviving Sinan's 'classical' idiom. The decision to reinterpret the scheme of the Şehzade mosque, rather than of the Süleymaniye or Selimiye, tacitly admits the forbidding perfection of the chief architect's two supreme masterpieces.

Despite its conservative revivalism, the pyramidal superstructure of the Sultan Ahmed mosque embodies a new taste for flamboyance and exuberant ostentation. The domical composition of the courtyard façade, more dramatic and elaborate than that of the Süleymaniye, has two additional weight turrets and an extra central exedra rippling under the half-dome (illus. 178, 546). The cylindrical drums no longer feature engaged buttresses, and their graceful curvilinear forms subdue the tensions between the curve and rectangle of the Süleymaniye. Sinan's preoccupation with dome size gives way here to a new emphasis on dramatic buildup and verticality. The elaboration of the Süleymaniye's two-tiered domical superstructure with a third tier finds a counterpart in the multiplication of its minarets from four to six. The triple minarets along each lateral façade create perspectival effects representing a theatrical 'baroque' aesthetic of exaggeration. Compared to the sober austerity of the Süleymaniye's decorative programme, the dazzling spectacle of İznik tiles covering the whole interior of the Sultan Ahmed mosque reflects a preference for unrestrained ornamental splendour (also observed later on in the Yeni Valide mosque). The extensive use of tile revetments and the unprecedented royal pavilion heighten the palatial character of the mosque, which is axially aligned with the first gate of the Topkapı Palace.

546 Sultan Ahmed mosque, Atmeydanı, north façade from the forecourt.

The visual juxtaposition of the Sultan Ahmed mosque with Hagia Sophia revives an age-old competition, another theme it shares with the Süleymaniye.[80] The decision to confront the ancient monument with a stunning mosque in the 'modern' Ottoman style involved a grand urban gesture, the remodelling of the Hippodrome. Fully exposed to the public gaze, the sultan's royal mausoleum is situated at the entrance to the piazza, instead of the garden behind the qibla wall of the mosque. It enters into a dialogue with Hagia Sophia's imperial mausoleums across from it – where Sultan Ahmed had built the mausoleum of his father – and signals the major change he introduced in the 'father-to-son' system of dynastic succession: the move to 'seniority', that is, the succession of the oldest male member of the dynasty, whether he was the brother, cousin, nephew, or son of the sultan.[81] This meant that princes were no longer executed by their reigning brothers, but kept under close house arrest in the 'cage' of the imperial harem as potential alternatives to the sultanate.

The bodies of strangled princes buried in the mausoleums of Selim II and Murad III thus became the chilling mementos of an old imperial order, abandoned by Sultan Ahmed I, who is glorified by the inscription of his mausoleum as the 'Shah powerful as Solomon (Süleyman)'.[82]

The contiguity of the city's oldest and newest sultanic mosques inevitably invited an aesthetic comparison. Comparing these intentionally paired monuments, Prince Cantemir (1673–1723) interprets the Sultan Ahmed mosque as an attempt to surpass the Hagia Sophia in terms not of monumentality but of magnificence.[83] Like the Masjid-i Shah, built around the same time by Shah ʿAbbas along the new maydan of Isfahan (1611–38), the Sultan Ahmed mosque (1609–19) adjoining Istanbul's reconfigured main public square has been disparaged by modern critics for its uninhibited extravagance. Goodwin finds its few innovations 'ungainly or monotonous, since the dominant ideals were size and splendour'. To some extent the mosque does achieve the grandeur to which it aspires, but it 'lacks Sinan's economy of purpose, born of creative thinking'.[84] Although the showiness of the Sultan Ahmed mosque is generally criticized by architectural historians, who tend to regard everything after Sinan's restrained classicism as a decline, it never failed to impress contemporary audiences and still remains the favourite of the general public.

Grelot, who discussed his architectural drawings of the Sultan Ahmed mosque with Louis XIV's minister Colbert, judged it as 'the most beautiful [mosque] in Constantinople, if not in all the East'.[85] Likewise, Evliya Çelebi considers it 'the most beautiful of all sultanic mosques in Istanbul', and regards the 'charming artistry of its architectural style unequalled by the mosques of any land'.[86] The biographer of the chief architect Mehmed Agha, who in 1613 wishes Sultan Ahmed a victory against the 'heretic' Safavid Shah, eulogizes the incomplete 'New Mosque' as the leader of all sultanic mosques, drawing particular attention to the imperial symbolism of its six minarets:[87]

> Indeed, each of these minaret shafts became a tree,
> Which made manifest the lineage of the shah of the
> world.
>
> The balconies of the minarets are equal in number to the
> generations of the Ottoman dynasty,
> Which all resemble the litanies of the righteous.
>
> The fourteen sultans became the shahs of the world.
> And this is the reason for the balconies being ten and
> four.
>
> The entire edifice is naught but a symbol.
> In it are many of these unique sorts of creations.
>
> That holy place proclaims all of the sultans.
> Is it any wonder that it is the commander of the army of
> mosques?[88]

This poem shows that the minarets were originally meant to have fourteen rather than sixteen galleries, numerically corresponding to Ahmed's position as the fourteenth ruler of the dynasty: another parallel with the Süleymaniye whose ten minaret galleries represented its patron's lineage according to Sinan's biographer.[89]

The Sultan Ahmed mosque is generally regarded as 'the last great mosque of the classical age'.[90] After the completion of the queen mother Turhan Sultan's mosque in Eminönü, the humiliating second siege of Vienna (1683) marked the end of Ottoman expansion in Europe and opened the floodgates to territorial loss. Thereafter the tension between innovation and fundamentalism, manifested by the Kadızadeli movement, would be played out against a new religio-political climate, the coordinates of which emerged over time as, roughly, pro- and anti-West. During the second half of the seventeenth century, the sultans preferred to reside in Edirne and refrained from building new mosques in Istanbul, to which they were eventually forced to return by a revolt in 1703.

It was not until the middle of the eighteenth century, after a long pause of more than a century, that the sultans resumed construction of mosques in the capital. No longer commemorating grand victories, these scaled down sanctuaries with few dependencies introduced fashionable styles diverging from Sinan's 'classical' idiom. The earliest examples inside the city walls include the Nuruosmaniye (1756) and Laleli (1763–64), followed by others in Üsküdar and along the shores of the Bosphorus, sites unprecedented for sultanic foundations previously confined to the hilltops of the walled peninsula. Some of these mosques accompanied Europeanizing shore palaces built to project the modernizing self-image of the dynasty, while others commemorated internal reforms constituting the new triumphs of the day: the mosque of Selim III in Haydarpaşa (1804) beside the barracks of his modern army called the 'New Order', and Mahmud II's Nusretiye (Victory) mosque near the parade grounds of the new artillery barracks in Tophane that celebrated the extermination of the janissary corps (1826).

The late-Ottoman mosques of Istanbul, erected mostly for the sultans and their mothers, were generally domed cubes. No longer reflecting a preoccupation with monumental scale and structural experimentation, their novelty was largely confined to the exuberant plastic treatment of their surfaces. Their variegated arch profiles, Europeanizing sculptural reliefs, and painted ornaments broadcast the dynasty's rapidly changing identity. Dubbed 'baroque' or 'rococo' by architectural historians because of their flamboyant decoration with curvilinear forms, these mosques did not introduce new plan types. Their most notable typological invention was to relieve the monotony of the domed cube with royal pavilions attached to their increasingly palatial façades: an innovation launched at the Beylerbeyi mosque Abdülhamid I built for his mother in 1777–78. Suites of royal apartments, exemplifying the new accessibility of sultans accompanied by large official retinues, replaced former royal tribunes tucked at the corner of qibla walls to maintain imperial seclusion. Flanked by stone-capped twin minarets, without the customary lead-covered conical hood, these royal suites (recalling the appended *tabhanes* and royal balconies of multi-functional early Ottoman mosques) supplanted the paved imperial forecourts of previous sultanic mosques in the capital.[91]

Among the masterpieces of Sinan, it was Mihrümah Sultan's mosque at Edirnekapı that exercised the strongest influence on the capital's light-filled late-Ottoman mosques. The more complex quatrefoil plan of the Şehzade Mehmed mosque, on the other hand, provided the favoured model for ambitious provincial mosques. Before its adoption in the mosques of Safiye Sultan and Ahmed I, two smaller variants of this plan type had appeared in Murad III's mosque at the newly fortified town of Navarino (*c.* 1576–77) and in Abdurrahman Pasha's mosque in Tosya (1584). The same plan was thereafter reinterpreted in several non-royal provincial monuments as a potent signifier of regional authority: the Mosque of the Strangers (Jamaa Gureba) built for the Ottoman garrison in the Tunisian island of Djerba (1640), the so-called Mosquée de la Pêcherie (1659–60) in Algiers founded by the town's janissary corps, the Sidi Mahrez mosque (1692–97) in Tunis dedicated to the patron saint of the city under the regency of Muhammad Beg, the now-lost mosque of Eğribozlu Ahmed Pasha in Thebes (1666–67), and the Fethiye mosque in Athens (1670s).[92]

The quatrefoil plan type was once again revived in the sultanic mosque of Mehmed II in Istanbul, rebuilt after an earthquake in 1766. Acquiring symbolic status as an icon of power, the same plan engendered unusually monumental descendants in the increasingly autonomous provinces of the empire: the mosque of Muhammad ʿAli (1824–48) inside the citadel of Cairo, and the mosque of Khalid b. al-Walid (1908–13) in Homs built for sultan Abdülhamid II by the Ottoman governor of Syria to commemorate the burial site of the Prophet's celebrated general. The legacy of Sinan's mosques, still a global source of inspiration for contemporary mosque architecture, continues to live more strongly than ever with the recent outburst of mosque construction in Turkey. Generally modelled on the chief architect's works, these mosques, crudely built in concrete, often boast former royal prerogatives such as twin minarets and monumental domes accompanied by half-domes. More ostentatious prestige monuments with four minarets, such as the Kocatepe mosque in Ankara and the Sabancı mosque in Adana, are neo-Ottoman pastiches that proudly quote recognizable elements from the chief architect's grand sultanic masterpieces.[93]

Exhausting all the possible combinations, Sinan brought to an end the evolution of mosque types in Ottoman architecture. The richly varied typology of his mosques, encoding the stratification of social and territorial status, was intimately bound with the centralized order of the state, which he visually articulated as a veritable architect of empire. An impermanent mix of imperial bounty, territorial expansion, economic prosperity, religious fervour, and longing for eternal glory were among the factors that converged with his artistic genius in sparking an explosion of architectural creativity in mosque construction. The changing identities of the dynasty and the ruling elite within the post-classical imperial order contributed to modified patterns of patronage at the overdeveloped capital, where Sinan's graduated mosque typology gave way to a less calibrated, two-tiered paradigm of religious architecture at the turn of the seventeenth century: non-royal madrasa complexes and royal mosques. This was paralleled by an erosion of former hierarchies between the empire's centre and periphery, and a growing emphasis on non-religious construction projects signalling the emergence of a new 'worldliness'. The codes of decorum that once guided Sinan's architectural canon were now a distant memory. What remained were his intensely alluring monuments, some of the most enduring architectural masterpieces ever created.

REFERENCES

INTRODUCTION

1 Kostof, 1985. Nationalist scholarship, on the other hand, has denied the influence of Hagia Sophia and insisted on the Turkic origins of Ottoman architecture. For Sinan's treatment in histories of world architecture, see Matthews, 2000.

2 Farago, ed., 1995; Howard, 2000; Jardine and Brotton, 2000; and Mack, 2001.

3 Matthews, 2000 and 2002; McQuillan, 2001. Studies on Sinan which compare his works with those of Italian architects include Kuban, 1997 and 1999; Erzen, 1996; Vogt-Göknil, 1986.

4 Babinger, 1914; idem., 'Sinan', EI(1) 4:428–32; Otto-Dorn, 1937. A recent example is the biographical novel *Sinan: The Turkish Michelangelo*, De Osa, 1982.

5 Translated in Kuban, 1997, p. 50, from Gurlitt, 1912, p. 57.

6 Babinger, 1914.

7 The five versions of Sinan's autobiographies are discussed in Chapter 4. Babinger uses the versions published in Edhem Paşa and M. de Launay, 1873; Sai, 1897.

8 Egli provides a summary of the chief architect's biography and an analysis of selected monuments tracing the development of his style and his responses to particular patron's wishes; see E. Egli, 1954. His monograph remains the only one to take into consideration Sinan's patrons.

9 Taut, 1938; analyzed in Bozdoğan, 1997.

10 The emphasis on structural rationalism is encountered earlier in a treatise on Ottoman architecture commissioned by Sultan Abdülaziz for the Vienna International Exhibition; see Edhem Paşa and de Launay, 1873. The rationalist interpretation of this treatise finds a parallel in a monograph on early Ottoman architecture by Leon Parvilée, who belonged to the circle of Viollet-le-Duc; see Parvilée, 1874. The engineer Auguste Choisy, the grand succesor of Viollet who exclusively interpreted architecture in terms of the history of construction, presented Ottoman architecture as a derivative tradition imitating Byzantine construction. See, Choisy, 1883, which refers to the sultanic mosques of Istanbul as 'les derniers monuments de l'art byzantin', pp. 122; and regards the Selimiye in Edirne as 'la dernière forme que revêtit l'idée de Sainte-Sophie', pp. 139–41.

11 This view is further elaborated in Kuban, 1987 and 1997.

12 Eldem, 1939. Eldem's style and the movement he belonged to are analyzed in Bozdoğan, 2001.

13 Eldem, 1939, p. 220. For an elaboration of this view, see Kuban, 1987.

14 I thank Sibel Bozdoğan for this reference, Behçet Bedreddin, 'Türk İnkilap Mirası' *Mimar*, 1933. Newly emerging as a professional body, Turkish architects claimed that the children of Sinan should be more entitled to build modern Turkey than the foreign experts employed by the state.

15 Sai, 1989, pp. 139–40.

16 An early-seventeenth-century architectural treatise refers to him as 'Sinan Agha, known as the Great Architect [*koca miʿmār*]', Cafer Efendi, 1987, p. 53.

17 See Chapter 4(II).

18 Araz, 1954.

19 I disagree with Uğur Tanyeli who argues that the 'myth of the creative genius' was entirely the construction of modern scholarship on Sinan; see his introduction in Erzen, 1996, II–III.

20 Examples include Goodwin, 1971; Kuran, 1986 and 1987.

21 Kuban, 1997, pp. 235–38. The longitudinal plans of the Süleymaniye and Kılıç Ali Pasha mosques, for example, are considered oddities reflecting idiosyncratic patron's wishes, ibid., p. 16: 'The sole rationale behind the schemes of Süleymaniye or Kılıç Ali Paşa Mosque could have been the demands of the patrons.'

22 Wittkower, 1949. For a critique of Wittkower's paradigm; see Payne, 1994.

23 Kuban, 1997, p. 233. For an early comparison between Sinan's works and twentieth-century architecture; see Kocainan, 1939.

24 Exceptions include Bates 1978b; Mülayim, 1989; Yerasimos, 1987, 2000 and 2002; Cezar, 1988; Erzen, 1991b, 1996; Akın, 1995; Tanman, 2001. Kuban argues that the rationalism of Sinan's architecture was not understood by his contemporaries, who lived in a society characterized by medieval irrationalism in thought, science, and literature; see Kuban, 1997, pp. 9–15. He criticizes 'semantic interpretations' which are 'very much in vogue in contemporary art historical theory' where 'new meanings are sought in the artistic object quite beyond the formal-functional level.' He prefers 'empirical' analyses without recourse to 'Western criteria', but ironically his own model of formal evolution is the very basis of traditional Western art historiography, ibid., pp. 201–12.

25 Goodwin, 1971 and 1993; Stierlin, 1985; Petruccioli, ed., 1987; Burelli, 1988; Bartoli et al., 1992.

26 Haider, 1986; Hillenbrand, 1994.

27 Gurlitt, 1907, p. 94; Gabriel, 1926; Kuban, 1958, 1963, 1997; Batur, 1968; Kuran, 1968.

28 For a critique of the typological method which overlooks 'secondary forms', see Erzen, 1996, especially p. 53.

29 An exception is Kuran's comprehensive survey of Sinan's works accompanied by a catalogue; see Kuran 1986. Unfortunately this useful catalogue is excluded from the English translation (Kuran, 1987).

30 For an unintegrated collection of essays by scholars from different disciplines on the historical, political, social, and cultural settings of Sinan's age; see Bayram, ed., 1988. Several Ottomanist historians have analyzed architectural patronage without a formal reading of buildings; see Barkan, 1972–79; Kreiser, 1985; Peirce, 1993, 2000; Faroqhi, 2000; Singer, 2002.

31 Only a few scholars have acknowledged the importance of patronage for understanding Sinan's oeuvre; see E. Egli, 1954; Bates, 1978a, 1978b, 1993; and Yerasimos, 1987. The latter writes: 'To this date the evolution of Sinan's work has been ... considered as an intrinsic evolution supposedly based solely on earlier models and on his own search for perfection. The addition of a new parameter, the status, function, or even personality of the patron, would help clarify some questions', p. 124.

32 In addition to interpretative contextual studies, more systematic morphological and structural inquiries need to be pursued for a richer understanding of Sinan's corpus.

33 Kuban, 1997, p. 3.

34 Sinan experimented more boldly with mosques; in other building types he was 'satisfied with minor spatial plays or formal variations, rather than developing totally new suggestions', Kuban, 1997, p. 63. Sinan's foremost aspiration to build monumental sanctuaries for God is articulated in his autobiographies; see Chapter 4(I–II).

35 For the argument that 'the theoretical vacuum abandoned the artist to his own devices in the process of creation', see Kuban, 1997, p. 237. Kuban regards variations in Sinan's mosque plans 'purely as the expression of an artistic will', ibid., p. 58.

36 Tietze, 1982.

37 These texts are discussed in Chapter 3(IV).

38 Bourdieu, 1984.

39 Necipoğlu, 1992a, 1993.

40 The only non-sultanic mosque that paraphrases Hagia Sophia is that of Kılıç Ali Pasha; for an interpretation of this unusual choice; see Chapter 11.

41 Hillenbrand, 1994, p. 123. Among the typical characteristics of mosque design, Hillenbrand lists the 'indifference to exterior façades' and the 'emphasis on the interior', ibid., pp. 126–28. Also see, Erzen, 1996, pp. 55–70.

42 Halbswachs, 1980; and Nora, 1984–.

43 For the roles of spectacle and theatricality in the Roman building tradition, see Taylor, 2003.

44 The few studies that consider the programmes of tile decoration in Sinan's mosques include Yenişehirlioğlu, 1982, 1985; and Denny, 1977, 1998. Kuban dismisses Koranic inscriptions as 'completely meaningless' for the congregation which he assumes to have been illiterate; see Kuban, 1997, p. 206.

45 Written sources on Islamic architecture are often dismissed as prosaic and uninformative; see Hillenbrand, 1994, pp. 26–30; and Kuban, 1997, pp. 9–15, 27–31, 235–38. Kuban argues that the rationalism of Sinan's architecture was not understood by his contemporaries, a dichotomy that made architectural discourse 'quite independent from the architecture itself', ibid., p. 205.

46 Studies on the architectural patronage of Ottoman women include Bates, 1978a and 1993; Peirce, 2000; Singer, 2002; Thys-Şenocak, 1994, 1998, 2000.

CHAPTER 1

1 İnalcık and Quataert, eds, 1994, p. 11. For the ghazi identity of the early Ottoman state, see Kafadar, 1995.

2 Kafadar, 1995.

3 Bayezid's title was secured 'from the *fainéant* ʿAbbasid Caliph in Cairo, al-Mutawakkil I', Bosworth, 1967, p. 138.

4 İnalcık and Quataert, eds, 1994, p. 20.

5 Sümer, 1991, pp. 353–54. The meeting in Cairo is recorded in the *Rūznāme* of Haydar Çelebi, cited in ibid., p. 349.

6 For the conquest of the 'capital of the righly guided caliphs' and the pronunciation of the 'khutba of the caliphate' (*ḫutbe-i ḫilāfet*), see Rüstem Paşa, ÖNB, Codex Vindobonensis Palatinus, Mxt. 339, fols 208r–210v. Süleyman's claim to the universal caliphate is discussed in İnalcık, 1993, pp. 78–81; İnalcık and Quataert, eds, 1994, p. 20; and Imber, 1992, 1997. For his short-lived experiment with messianic rulership, see Fleischer, 1992.

7 See Chapter 2(II) and 4(I).

8 İpşirli, 1994, p. 21. For Selim I's possession of the seven climes and four corners, 'yidi iḳlīm ile dört köşeye mālik', see Lokman, 1987, fol. 47r. The queen mother Safiye Sultan's letter to Queen Elizabeth in 1593 refers to her reigning son, Mehmed III, as 'the Khan of the seven climes at this auspicious time and the fortunate lord of the four corners'; see Skilliter, 1965, p. 131.

9 Necipoğlu, 1989. The Ottoman claim for the heritage of the eastern and western Roman empire is discussed in İnalcık, 1993, pp. 78–79.

10 İnalcık, 1993, pp. 78–81; Imber, 1997, pp. 99–111.

11 Imber, 1997, pp. 99–111. Bearing a marginal note by Ebussuud, the 1552 waqfiyya of a hospice built in Jerusalem by the sultan's wife refers to Süleyman as 'the holder of the Great Imamate (*ʿimāmet-i ʿuẓmā*) and the sultan who inherited from father to son the Grand Caliphate (*ḫilāfet-i kübrā*)'; see Stephan, 1944, pp. 179–80.

12 Gibb, 1962.

13 Rüstem Pasha, IÜ, Ms. 2438, fols 181v–82r.

14 Hasanbeyzade, 1980, p. 59.

15 The 'decline' paradigm has been challenged by several scholars; for a synthetic overview of the debate; see Kafadar, 1991a, 1991b, 1993. Late-sixteenth-century transformations are discussed in İnalcık and Quataert, eds, 1994, pp. 22–43.

16 Talikizade, 1983, fols 5r–10v.

17 Hillenbrand, 1994, p. 31.

18 Chapters 5 and 6. For the organization of the hajj under the Ottomans, see Faroqhi, 1994.

19 Necipoğlu, 1996.

20 Talikizade, 1983, fols 6v–7r.

21 Talikizade, TSK, A.3592, fols 116v–117v.

22 Matrakçı Nasuh, 1976.

23 Goffman, 2002, p. 172.

24 Talikizade, 1983, fols 10r–v.

25 Busbecq, 1927, pp. 22–23.

26 Cantemir, 1734, pp. 33–34.

27 Al-Tamgrouti, 1929, p. 63.

28 Sadeddin, 1992, 4:297.

29 Necipoğlu, 1991, pp. 26–30.

30 He also recommends 'silence' and 'piety'; see Lutfi Paşa, 1991, p. 72; note 325, p. 75.

31 Rüstem Paşa, ÖNB, Codex Vindobonensis Palatinus, Mxt. 339, fols 220r–v. Riding on horseback and carrying arms was a privilege of the *askeri* class denied to ordinary citizens; see Lutfi Pasha, 1991, p. 98.

32 See the anonymous treatise entitled *Ḳāwānīn-i Yeñiçeriyān* (Customs of the Janissaries), in Petrosiyan, ed., 1987, fols 102v–105r, 112r.

33 Du Fresne Canaye, 1897, p. 126.

34 Āli, Nuruosmaniye Library, Ms. 3409, fol. 3r.

35 Edhem Paşa and de Launay, 1873, p. 14.

36 Talikizade, 1983, fols 9v–10r. The discovery of a treasure to finance the construction of Hagia Sophia, when Justinian runs out of money, is mentioned in the *Diegesis* translated into Turkish and Persian; see Mango, 1992, p. 47.

37 For the economic dimension of decorum, see Chapter 3(IV).

38 Talikizade, 1983, fol. 9v.

39 Hadidi, 1991, p. 17.

40 I thank Cornell Fleischer for this reference: Mevlana İsa, *Cāmiʿ ü'l meknūnāt*, dated 950 (1543), IÜ, T.3263, fol. 63v: 'Ḫuṣūṣā bu zamanda oldı meşhūr / Mesācidden bilād ü şehir maʿmūr. // Bilürsün mescidin mildir fināʾsı / Bu dem bir milde on mescid bināsı.'

41 Eberhard, 1970.

42 Talikizade, TSK, R.1299, fol. 21v: 'ṣadā-yi ozān yirine nidā-yi ezān oḳunub.'

43 Newman, 2001.

44 Cited in Babayan, 1996, pp. 128–29.

45 Newman, 2001.

46 Imber, 1997, pp. 65–67.

47 Ibn Khaldun, 1967, 1:449–50.

48 Āli, 1979, 1:81.

49 İnalcık, 1993, p. 81.

50 Gibb, 1962, p. 288.

51 Ibid., p. 294.

52 İnalcık and Quataert, eds, 1994, pp. 16–17.

53 Āli, Nuruosmaniye Library, Ms. 3409, fol. 3r; also see Āli, 1979–82, 1:25.

54 Suzuki, 1990, p. 887.

55 Peirce, 1993, p. 66–67.

56 Koçi Beg, 1998, p. 83.

57 Ibid., p. 86.

58 Ibid., pp. 86–87.

59 Albèri, 1840–55, 1:88–89; 2:17, 26.

60 Lutfi Paşa, 1991, pp. 62, 73.

61 Repp, 1986, pp. 272–96; Imber, 1992 and 1997.

62 Al-Tamgrouti, 1929, pp. 61–63.

63 Fleischer, 1992, p. 167.

64 Cornell Fleischer's forthcoming book on the Süleymanic age analyses these developments.

65 Fleischer, 1992, pp. 172–73.

66 Ibid., 1992, p. 173.

67 The first version completed in 1534 was finalized around 1561 during Celalzade's retirement; see Celalzade, 1981, pp. 13–14.

68 For the seat of the chief architect under the portico of the imperial council, see Chapter 5(I). Celalzade's mosque is discussed in Chapter 13.

69 Translated from Āli's *Künhü'l-aḫbār* in Fleischer, 1986, p. 254; also see Kafadar, 1995, p. 28.

70 For the fluidity of early Ottoman identities, see Kafadar, 1995.

71 Dernschwam, 1992, pp. 96, 99–100, 118.

72 Cantemir, 1979–80, 1:xxxix–xl.

73 Hobsbawm, 1990.

74 For the Topkapı Palace, see Necipoğlu, 1991; the lost palace of Sokollu Mehmed Pasha is discussed in Artan, 1993, 1994; and Stichel, 1996.

75 Dernschwam, 1923, pp. 87–89. Some villagers willingly gave away one to two sons in order to be exempted from service in war, but others gave away their eight-to-nine-year-old sons to women to avoid the levy; see Gerlach, 1674, p. 314. Āli, 1979–82, 2:29–30.

76 For their mosques, see Chapters 8 and 12.

77 Anonymous, *Cevāhirü'l-menāḳib*, IÜ, T.2578, fols 15v–16v.

78 See Chapter 8.

79 Kafadar, 1994, p. 604.

80 See Chapter 7.

81 Petrosiyan, ed., 1987, fols 10r–10v.

82 Ibid., fol. 16r.

83 Ibid., fols, 12v–13r. Āli, 1997, pp. 231–32.

84 Petrosiyan, ed., 1987, fols 9r–10r.

85 Dernschwam, 1992, pp. 64–65, 88–89, 128.

86 Beckingham, 1987, pp. 260, 269.

87 Āli, 1997, p. 320.

88 Albèri, 1840–55, 1:400–1, 406.

89 Gerlach, 1674, pp. 266, 349, 384, 398.

90 Ibid., pp. 349, 383; Samardzić, 1995, p. 298.

91 Āli, Nuruosmaniye Library, Ms. 3409, fols 121r–v; Lutfi Paşa, 1991, p. 61.

92 Gerlach, 1674, pp. 180, 318, 334.

93 For the parades of sultans, see ibid., pp. 43, 205, 311, 361, 400.

94 For non-royal processions, see ibid., pp. 40, 97–98, 186–87, 265–66, 268, 270, 392–93, 402, 445, 449.

95 Albèri, 1840–55, 2:369.

96 Āli, 1979–82, 1:19, 35.

97 Āli, 1997, pp. 177–78.

98 Albèri, 1840–55, 3:267, 270–71.

99 Mango, 1993, 'The Development of Constantinople as an Urban Center', p. 128. For the construction and endowment of churches, family chapels, and palaces in Renaissance Italy, see Goldthwaite, 1993.

100 Selaniki, 1989, 1:131, 250, 318; 2:707.

101 Ibid., 1:250.

102 Goffman, 1990.

CHAPTER 2

1 See lists of mosques in Sai, forthcoming 2005; Kuran, 1986, p. 22. The TM lists 104 Friday mosques, the TB 80, and the number ranges between 71 and 81 in TE manuscripts.

2 Sai, 1989, fol. 5r; the epitaph is quoted in Chapter 4(III).

3 Kuran, 1986, p. 22.

4 For the patrons of masjids, see Cezar, 1988, p. 72, chart 4; and Kuran, 1986, pp. 305–19.

5 Johansen, 1981–82, pp. 150–51.

6 Ergenç, 1981.

7 Barkan and Ayverdi, eds, 1970; Kayako, 1992.

8 Kafescioğlu, 1996, pp. 284–316.

9 BA, Tapu Defteri no. 670, dated 986–88 (1578–80); and Ankara Tapu ve Kadastro Umum Müdürlüğü nos. Eski 542 and 543, dated 1003–12 (1595–1603).

10 Ebussuud, TSK, A.786, fol. 18v; Düzdağ, 1972, p. 60.

11 İnalcık, 1993, pp. 80–81. For Ebussuud's fatwas condemning the Safavid 'redheads', see Düzdağ, 1972, pp. 109–12.

12 Eberhard, 1970, pp. 48–53.

13 Ebussuud, TSK, A.786, fols 16v–17r.

14 BA, AE. Kanuni, no. 6, dated the end of B. 953.

15 Düzdağ, 1972, pp. 59–62, 73–76.

16 Ebussuud, TSK, A.786, fols 17r, 8r, 468v.

17 Ebussuud, TSK, A.786, fol. 17r.

18 Barkan, 1942; Eyice, 1963; Emir, 1994.

19 Cited in Barkan, 1942, p. 354.

20 VGM, D.2225, dated C. 761. For the inscription, see Tüfekçioğlu, 2001, pp. 130–33.

21 Ayverdi, 1969.

22 The term *tābḫāne* (sometimes spelled *tāvḫāne*) implies a heated winter-room with a fireplace. Other terms used for guest-houses include: *ḫalvetḫāne* (also hot room in a bath-house), and *mihmānḫāne* or *misāfirḫāne* (guest-house).

23 Ayverdi, 1969.

24 For a list of Sinan's *ʿimaret*s, see Kuran, 1986, pp. 362–67.

25 BA, MD. 23, #135, p. 164, dated 25 Ca. 981. Gerlach and Schepper attribute the mosque to Hain Ali Pasha (executed in 1524) who rebelled as the governor-general of Cairo; see Gerlach, 1674, p. 510; Schepper, 1857, p. 188. Its madrasa and hospice, probably added after 1538, are mentioned among Sinan's works; see Kuran, 1986, p. 366, no. 366; p. 351, no. 264.

26 For a list of his *imaret*s and caravansarays, see Kuran, 1986, pp. 362–76.

27 For Safavid rituals, see Chapter 2 (I).

28 Ibn Battuta, 1983, pp. 194-95, 213-18.

29 İsmail b. İsmail b. İsfendiyari, *Ḫulviyāt-i Şāhi*. IÜ, T.5849, fol. 275v. For Sinan's endowment, see Chapter 4(III).

30 Düzdağ, 1972, pp. 83–88.

31 Ebusuud, TSK, A.786, fols 464r–v.

32 Ibid., fols 465r–v.

33 Ibid., fols 360r–v, 464v.

34 Ibid., fols 463r–64r, 466r–68v.

35 Aydemir, 1968, p. 239; Düzdağ, 1972, p. 196.

36 Ocak, 1991; Düzdağ, 1972, pp. 193–95.

37 Clayer, 1994, 119-20; for Shahsultan, see Chapter 8.

38 Materials given from the Süleymaniye for the convent's construction in the 1550s are cited in TSK, H. 1425, fol. 70r: 'Fil ṭamı yirinde emr-i şerīfle binā olınan zāviye bināsıyçün cāmiʿ -i şerīf esbābından bervech-i ḳarż virilen esbāblar'; also see fol. 96r. The 'Fildamı zāviyesi' is listed in the waqfiyya of Süleyman; Kürkçüoğlu, 1962, pp. 193–98, 199. This no-longer-extant convent-masjid in Koska is described in Ayvansarayi, 2000, p. 101.

39 For Nureddinzade, see the complex of Sokollu and his wife at Kadırgalimanı in Chapter 8.

40 See Selim II's biography in Chapter 6.

41 For these complexes, see Chapters 7 and 8.

42 Āli, Nuruosmaniye Library, Ms. 3409, fols 140r–41r.

43 The alliance between Sokollu, Ebusuud and Nureddinzade is mentioned in Āli, 1979–82, 1:43–44.

44 Selaniki, 1989, 1:61–2. For the prohibition of wine and the punishment of those not performing the five daily prayers in mosques, see Marciana Library, IT. VII, 193 (7490), Dispacci, dated 16 February 1560.

45 Selaniki, 1989, 1:62.

46 Al-Halabi, 1990, 1:254–55, 260–61.

47 Ergenç, 1981, pp. 1265–74; Johansen, 1981, pp. 143–44.

48 Imber, 1997, pp. 65–67.

49 TSK, K.888, fol. 341r, dated 11 Ş. 959.

50 BA, MD. 14, #609, p. 430, dated 22 Ca. 978.

51 TSA, D.548 1, fol. 2v 'cāmiʿ-i şerīf olmasına der-i devletde emr-i şerīf ḫarcı', 'cāmiʿ olmasına ʿarż olunduḳda ʿarż içün ücret.'

52 Johansen, 1981, 144–45.

53 Ibid., pp. 145–50.

54 Āli's criticism is quoted in Chapter 1(II).

55 TSA, E.463/1, dated Z. 962.

56 TSA, E.5209/5, dated the beginning of Ca. 982.

57 Ebussuud, TSK, A.786, fol. 13r.

58 BA, MD. 52, #920, p. 344, dated 7 R. 992.

59 See Chapters 8, 10, and 11 for the mosques of these pashas.

60 Ebussuud, TSK, A.786, 128r–v; Düzdağ, 1972, p. 104.

61 Some sources attribute the attempt to convert churches in Istanbul into mosques to Selim I and others to Süleyman I, placing this event at various times between 1517 and 1539; for the differing reports; see Patrinelis, 1969. A survey of churches conducted under Selim I, when many of them were converted into mosques, is mentioned in a decree dated 24 Ra. 972 (1564), published in Ahmed Refik, 1988, pp. 45–46, no. 4. Manuel Malaxos's *Patriarchal History of Constantinople* written in 1578 confirms the date of 1538–39 provided in Ebussuud's fatwa. It states that in 1537 a fatwa was issued, followed by a firman of Sultan Süleyman which ordered that all churches in Istanbul be demolished or converted into mosques. This order was opposed by the grand vizier Lutfi Pasha (g.v. 1538–41) and the Greek patriarch Hieremias; who found two aged janissaries to provide the testimony about the city's partial surrender, after which the privileges of churches were renewed; cited in Patrinelis, 1969, pp. 567–68.

62 Düzdağ, 1972, pp. 104–7.

63 An example involving the construction of a surrogate church and synagogue is the queen mother's mosque (Yeni Valide) in Eminönü, discussed in the Epilogue. Ebussuud (TSK, A.786, fol. 129v) allows new churches in *dhimmi* villages without a masjid or elementary school. For the remodelling of Serbian churches, see Ćurčić, 1988.

64 See Chapter 8. Another mosque that replaced a church in Istanbul was that of Kazasker İvaz Efendi (1586); it is compared with the mosque of Molla Çelebi in Chapter 13.

65 Ebussuud, TSK, A.786, fols 137r–v.

66 BA, MD. 62, #403, p. 181, dated 11 Ra. 996. The kadi of Kratova is ordered to send lead for the converted church (Patrik Kilisesi), copies were sent to Novaberde, Sidrekapsi, Çirmen.

67 See Kreiser, 1985.

68 Gerlach, 1674, p. 212.

69 Fotić, 1994.

70 Ibid., pp. 39–41, 50.

71 See Sokollu's patronage in Chapter 8.

72 For his waqfiyya dated early Ca. 1004 (January 1596), which mentions the conversion of the church, see Bayram, 1999.

73 Mehmed Aşık, TSK, E.H.1446, fol. 356r.

74 Arguing that service to the 'House of God' is a form of prayer, the shaykh enlisted a large group of volunteers, including local artisans and shipyard workers, to transform the church into a Friday mosque; ibid., fols 356r–69r.

75 BA, MD. 62, #209, p. 95, and #145, p. 65, dated L. 995.

76 Ćurčić, 1988.

77 Dodds, 1992, p. 19.

78 Āli, 1979-82, 1:54.

79 Lubenau, 1914, 2:164–65.

80 Steinach von, 1881, p. 217.

81 Albèri, 1840–55, 1:151.

82 Kreiser, 1985, p. 79. Bayezid's son and successor Mehmed I conquered Byzantine settlements (Hereke, Gebze, Darıca, Pendik, Kartal) near Constantinople for the endowment of his T-type mosque complex in Bursa; see Solakzade, 1297, p. 133.

83 For the mosque's initial construction with 'booties from two ghazas', see Beşir Çelebi, 1946. The foundation inscription only mentions Mehmed I; see Tüfekçioğlu, 2001, pp. 111–15.

84 For the laying of foundations before the campaign, see Yusuf bin Abdullah, 1997, pp. 125; Solakzade, 1297, pp. 167; Gökbilgin, 1952, pp. 213–14. Murad II's pious monuments endowed with lands conquered by his own sword are listed in Āli, IÜ, T.5959, fol. 61r; and Solakzade, 1297, pp. 187–88.

85 Gökbilgin, 1952, pp. 357-58; Kreiser, 1985, p. 79; Sadeddin, 1992, 3:237–38, 261–62.

86 Celalzade, 1981, fol. 26r; Lokman, TSK, H. 1524, fols 280v–82r.

87 Sadeddin, 1992, 4:284; Celalzade, 1997, pp. 641–43.

88 Sadeddin, 1992, 4:295–6; al-Rihawi, 1975.

89 For Gülşeni's convent in Cairo, see Hulvi, 1993, pp. 529, 531–33; Sadeddin, 1992, 4:341; illustrated in Behrens-Abouseif, 1994, plate 4.

90 Repp, 1986, pp. 250, 252.

91 Ibid., p. 252; TSK, A.786, fols 455r–56v, 461v–62r.

92 Meriç, 1965, p. 24.

93 Āli, Nuruosmaniye Library, Ms. 3409, fol. 118v; Lokman, TSK, H. 1524, fol. 282v.

94 Āli, Nuruosmaniye Library, Ms. 3409, fols 118v–19r.

95 Āli, TSK, R. 1290, fols 9r, 11v.

96 The garden associated with Mehmed II's son Prince Cem was called 'Cem bāġı'; see Vusuli, Fatih Millet Kütüphanesi, Ali Emiri, T.321, fols 44r, 52r–v, 54r.

97 The garden is referred to as 'Sulṭān Cem bāġçesi' in Rüstem Pasha, ÖNB, Codex Vindobonensis Palatinus, Mxt. 339, fols 286v–88r.

98 See Chapter 6.

99 A nineteenth-century document refers to the Konya mosque as the 'mosque of Sultan Selim known as the Süleymaniye'. For sources on the mosque, thought to have been completed during Selim II's reign, see Konyalı, 1997, pp. 528–35. Ebussuud's fatwa is mentioned in Repp, 1986, p.284.

100 Konyalı, 1997, p. 535.

101 Konyalı, 1994, pp. 629–96. The renovation (*tecdid*) of the hospice (*imaret*) of Mevlana's shrine complex is mentioned among Sinan's works only in the TM; see Meriç, 1965, p. 38; Kuran, 1986, p. 363, no. 307.

102 See Chapter 6.

103 Kreiser, 1985, p. 79; see Chapter 6.

104 Wratislaw, 1862, p. 41; Lubenau, 1912, 1:119.

105 Evliya, TSK, B.304, 3:154r–55v.

106 Palerne, 1991, pp. 254-55. The same observation is made in Lubenau, 1912, 1:164.

107 Necipoğlu, 1996; Vatin, 1995.

108 Dernschwam, 1992, p. 122.

109 BA, MD. 5, #1555, p. 564, dated 17 L. 973.

110 BA, MD. 35, #334, p. 131, dated 5 C. 986.

111 Vatin, 1995, p. 97.

112 Murad III's order in 1588 to illuminate minarets on holy nights is cited in Selaniki, 1989, 1: 198. For coloured illuminations see Dernschwam, 1992, p. 132. Inscriptions spelling out victories are mentioned in Grelot, 1683, p. 226.

113 Herosolimitano, 2001, p. 7.

114 Schweigger, 1964, pp. 192–93.

115 Rüstem Pasha, ÖNB, Codex Vindobonensis Palatinus, Mxt. 339, fol. 248v.

116 Ibid, fol. 286v.

117 Feridun Ahmed Beg, 1264–65, 1:524–27.

118 Ibid., 1:527–29.

119 Ibid., 1:528–29.

120 Selaniki, 1989, 1:69.

121 Feridun Ahmed Beg, TSK, H. 1339, fols 250v, 263r, 264r.

122 Gerlach, 1674, p. 199.

123 Dzaja and Weiss, eds, 1995, p. 441.

124 Ibid., pp. 484, 492.

125 Albèri, 1840–55, 3:326.

126 See Chapter 11.

127 Müstakimzade, 1928, pp. 510–11. For this masjid, see Kuran, 1986, p. 308, no. 117.

128 See Chapter 14.

129 See Chapter 10.

130 Albèri, 1840–55, 1:152–53.

131 Kayoko, 1992.

132 Cezar, 1988, pp. 1398–1400.

133 Koçi Beg, 1998, pp. 85–86.

134 Ibid., pp. 72–73.

135 Cezar, 1988, pp. 60–61.

136 See Chapter 8.

137 Al-Halabi, 1990, 1:117, 170.

138 Ebussuud, TSK, A.786, fol. 18v.

139 Dernschwam, 1992, p. 103.

140 Laguna, 1983, p. 277.

141 L'Escalopier, 1921, p. 40.

142 Du Fresne-Canaye, 1897, pp. 105–6.

143 Gerlach, 1674, p. 231.

144 Özcan, ed., 1994, p. 49.

145 Petrosiyan, ed., 1987, fol. 33v.

146 See Chapter 8.

147 Al-Halabi, 1990, 1:758, 2:502–3.

148 Aydemir, 1968, pp. 21-36; Repp, 1986, pp. 254–55.

149 TSK, E.H. 1515, margins of fols 182r; 149v. Also see al-Halabi, 1990, 1:757–58, who says unjust endowment administrators could be dismissed by the judge.

CHAPTER 3

1 Barkan, 1942, p. 354; Gökbilgin, 1952, pp. 216–17; Lokman, TSK, H.1523, fol. 146r. Āli (IÜ, T.5959, fol. 61r) describes how the sultan served food with an apron: 'ḫatta itmām-ı binā ḥīninde bizẕat bir peştemal ḳuşanub, evvelki gün ṭaʿām-ı fuḳarāyı kendüler ḳotārmışlardur.'

2 Barkan, 1972–79, 2:1–14, 'imāret-i ʿāmire/şerīfe/cedīde'; 2:15–20, 'ʿimāret ve cāmiʿ-i şerīf.'

3 For documents on the Selimiye, see Chapter 6. For the term 'ʿimāret', see Ergin, 1939.

4 For Sinan's roadside complexes, see Küçükkaya, 1990; Müderrisoğlu, 1993.

5 Dernschwam, 1992, pp. 31–32, 38, 43, 49, 51. Clock towers were introduced in Bosnia and Hercegovina during the late sixteenth century, unlike other parts of the empire where they were generally absent until the nineteenth century.

6 Barkan, 1942; Orhonlu, 1984 and 1990.

7 Lescalopier, 1921, pp. 27–28.

8 TM in Meriç, 1965, p. 50. For caravansarays along the hajj route, see Sauvaget, 1937.

9 Lokman, TSK, H.1524, fols 288r–v.

10 This entry in TM (Sai, TSA, D.1461/4) is undeciphered in Meriç, 1965, p. 49: 'Ve ḥalep yolunda baḳraşma derbendinde binā olınan kārvānsaray ve tekye.'

11 Lead was given from the Süleymaniye complex in 1551 for the caravansaray, 'Ḥalebe tābiʿ olan Baḳraşda binā olınān ḫān-ı cedīd', TSK, H.1425, dated 16 B. 958, fol. 45v. For the Arabic inscriptions of the caravansaray (*al-khān*), the mosque (*al-jāmiʿ*), and bath-house, see Müderrisoğlu, 1993, pp. 432, 434, 440. The double caravansaray was repaired in 1570 by Selim II (BA, MD. 14, #605, p. 425, dated 22 Ca. 978) who increased the salaries of the mosque's personnel in 1574 after renovating it (BA, MD. 25, #2550, p. 274, dated 10 C. 982).

12 Orhonlu, 1990.

13 Müderrisoğlu, 1993, p. 427.

14 Cafer Efendi, 1987, p. 91. Also see the related words: 'built up, flourishing' (*ʿumrān* in Arabic, *şenlik* in Turkish, and *ābādānī* in Persian).

15 Lokman, TSK, H.1524, fol. 291v.

16 See Chapters 7 and 8.

17 See Chapter 12.

18 See Chapter 12.

19 TM in Meriç, 1965, p. 29.

20 Lokman, TKS, H.1321, fol. 88v.

21 Lokman, TSK, H.1321, fol. 88r.

22 Selaniki, 1989, 1:123.

23 The letter composed by the sultan's teacher Hoca Sadeddin in cited in Āli, IÜ, T.5959. The decrees are in BA, MD. 38, #374, p. 194, dated 7 C. 987; and MD. 39, #115, p. 47, dated 10 S. 987. The kadis of Karaman are ordered to send builders to Kars in BA, MD. 39, #329, p. 169, dated 26 R. 987.

24 Āli, TSK, H.1365, fols 195r–97v. The towers were built by the janissary agha (İbrahim Kethüda), and the governor-generals of Damascus (Sokollu Hasan Pasha), Erzurum (Mehmed Pasha), Karaman (Mehmed Pasha), Diyarbakır (Behram Pasha and his brother Rizvan Pasha), Rum (Mahmud Pasha), and Anatolia (Cafer Pasha).

25 Ibid., fols 198r–v.

26 Ibid., fols 195r–97v.

27 Ibn Khaldun is quoted in Chapter 1(I). For new trends under the Seljuks; see Ettinghausen, Grabar, and Jenkins-Madina, 2001.

28 Blair and Bloom, 1994.

29 Necipoğlu, 1993; O'Kane, 1996.

30 Translated in O'Kane, 1996, p. 507.

31 Blair and Bloom, 1994, pp. 6–8.

32 Golombek and Wilber, 1988, 1:254–63.

33 Ayverdi, 1972, pp. 46–118; Aslanapa, 1986, pp. 38–42; Necipoğlu, 1990.

34 Golombek and Wilber, 1988, 1:302–7, 314–15.

35 Humphreys, 1972; Blair and Bloom, 1994, pp. 70–96.

36 Translated in O'Kane, 1996, p. 510.

37 Ousterhout, 1995.

38 For Mamluk features in early Ottoman architecture, see Tanman, 1999.

39 The same architect signed Sultan Mehmed I's madrasa in Merzifon in 817 (1414); see Sönmez, 1989, pp. 347–51, 403–9.

40 Ibid., pp. 415–22.

41 The foundation inscription identifies the building as an 'ʿ*imāret*'; see Ayverdi, 1972, pp. 406–15.

42 Necipoğlu, 1996.

43 Goodwin, 1971, pp. 94–97.

44 The mosque's architect was Usta Müslihüddin; see Necipoğlu, 1991, pp. 15, 212–17.

45 Aslanapa, 1986, pp. 48–54, 66–73.

46 Evliya, TSK, B.304, 3:152r–v.

47 Necipoğlu, 1996.

48 For Safavid architecture, see Blair and Bloom, 1994, pp. 188–90.

49 For Mughal architecture, see Blair and Bloom, 1994, pp. 267–86.

50 Necipoğlu, 1989.

51 Necipoğlu, 1992b.

52 Kritovoulos, 1954, pp. 147, 149.

53 Kuran, 1994.

54 Necipoğlu, 1992a.

55 Kritovoulos, 1954, p. 140.

56 After a man was found murdered in the courtyard of the church, the patriarch departed from it because 'the area around that church had no houses and there were no neighbours in the vicinity'; see Phillipides, 1990, p. 57.

57 The Friday mosque is identified in its Arabic foundation inscription as a '*masjid jāmiʿ*'; see Ayverdi, 1973, p. 386.

58 Royal loggias existed above the vestibules of some T-type convent-masjids, but previous Great Mosques did not feature tribunes separating the ruler from the rest of the congregation. For Mehmed's ceremonial emphasis on seclusion, see Necipoğlu, 1991.

59 Tursun Beg, 1978, fols 56r, 59r–v.

60 Vasari, 1963, 2:183.

61 For the paradisiac associations, see Tursun Beg, 1978, fols 58v–60v. The four cypresses in the forecourts of the mosques of Mehmed II, Selim I, and Şehzade Mehmed are described in Mehmed Aşık, TSK, E.H.1446, fols 388v, 390v. For the eight cypresses around the domed atrium fountain of Hagia Sophia, see Cyril Mango and John Parker, 'A Twelfth-Century Description of St. Sophia', in Mango, 1993, p. 242. Two of the eight cypresses remained at the time of Mehmed II; see Şemsüddin Karamani, IÜ, T.259, p. 39: 'ol ṣādırvān eṭrāfında sekiz dāne servilerden ḥaremde henüz iki servi mevcuddur.'

62 For a more detailed description of the plan, see Necipoğlu, 1986.

63 Quoted in Chapter 4(II).

64 Ayverdi, 1973, pp. 385–86.

65 Mesarites, 1957, pp. 865–67, 894–97; Kafescioğlu, 1999.

66 Restle, 1981.

67 Bruschi, 1994, pp. 139–42. The early Christian church of S. Lorenzo was rebuilt according to its original plan when it collapsed in 1573.

68 Russian sources mentioning Fioravanti's invitation to Istanbul are cited in Raby, 1980, pp. 29–33. Also see A. Ghisetti Giavarina, 'Aristotele Fioravanti', DBI, 48: 95–100. He may have been summoned by the sultan in the mid-1470s, but turned down the invitation.

69 Alberti, 1989, pp. 195, 199.

70 Kostof, 1985, p. 459.

71 The invitation to a builder from Venice is cited in Babinger, 1978, p. 386; and Raby, 1982, p. 4.

72 Babinger and Heydenreich, 1952.

73 Condivi, 1999, p. 132, note 50. In 1519 Michelangelo received a letter from Tommaso di Tolfo who recalled that in Florence about fifteen years ago the artist had spoken of his wish 'to come and see this country'. The letter urges him to join the court of Selim I, who had recently paid a large sum for the antique statue of a naked female and was not opposed to figural representation, unlike his father; see Sarre, 1909.

74 Condivi, 1999, p. 37. Also see p. 94 for Bayezid's invitation.

75 Reproduced in Millon and Lampugnani, 1994, pp. 603–4, no. 287.

76 Ibid., 1994, pp. 600–2, nos. 282, 284.

77 Ackerman, 1986, p. 197; Foschi, 1998.

78 Translated in Smith, 1992, p. 212.

79 Ibid., pp. 199–215.

80 For the Greek manuscript copied in 1474, see Raby 1980, p. 386. The *Diegesis* is analysed in Dagron, 1984; and Mango, 1992.

81 Translations made for Mehmed II and later on for Bayezid II are discussed in Yerasimos, 1990. Also see Tauer, 1953.

82 Smith, 1987.

83 Cited in Foschi, 1998, p. 92; and idem., 2002, p. 8.

84 The *Diegesis* records Justinian's boast to have surpassed the Temple of Solomon during the inauguration of Hagia Sophia. For the image of Hagia Sophia as the 'New Jerusalem' and its association with the Holy Land and the Temple of Solomon (believed to be the source of the spiral columns of St Peter's tomb), see Foschi, 1998, pp. 34–36, 92–98.

85 Manners, 1997. Manners dates this map to Mehmed II's reign, but the inclusion of his posthumously built mausoleum suggests a date in the beginning of Bayezid II's reign, before the construction of the latter's mosque complex.

86 Noting that Bayezid II's mosque and St Peter's were both designed around the same time, Chastel writes: 'Faisant la part des informations qui ont pu être échangées, il convient peut-être de placer dans une méme perspective le développement monumental de Stamboul et celui de Rome en leur commun "revival" du plan central'; see Chastel, 1965, pp. 18–24.

87 The Buondelmonti maps may have been among the sources of the twin towers and lanterned dome of St Peter's, see Foschi, 1998 and 2002.
88 Some scholars believe that Bramante's fragmentary plan was not for a central-plan Greek-cross church; for the complicated chronology of proposed plans see Bruschi, 1994; Bredekamp, 2000.
89 Millon and Smyth, 1988, p. 102.
90 Drums proposed for St Peter's by different architects are discussed in Millon and Lampugnani, 1994, p. 612, no. 303; p. 645, no. 370; pp. 658–64; also see Millon and Smyth, 1988, pp. 94–155.
91 Cited in Millon and Smyth, 1988, p. 96.
92 Cited in Connors, 1996.
93 Ibid., p. 45.
94 Ibid., pp. 44–45.
95 Ibid., p. 48.
96 Jardine, 2002, p. 415.
97 One of these merchants was Sir Dudley North, 'who was a builder himself; and no foreigner ever looked more closely into the manner of the Turkish buildings than he had done', ibid., pp. 336, 414–20.
98 For the critiques of Mehmed's complex, see Kafescioğlu, 1999.
99 The waqfiyya identifies it as a '*cāmi*ʿ*-i şerīf*'; see Barkan and Ayverdi, eds, 1970, p. 42.
100 Beysanoğlu, 1987, 2:520–31.
101 For the mosques in Diyarbakır and Elbistan, see Aslanapa, 1986, pp. 152–55.
102 Murray, 1971, pp. 145, 159–61; and Bruschi, 1994, p. 162.
103 Behrens-Abouseif, 1994, pp. 163–64, 179, 184–90, 244–50. The dome of Sidi Sariya, containing the tombs of Ottoman dignitaries, dates from the Fatimid period (1141).
104 Exceptions with cross-axial plans are the mosques of Süleyman in Belen (Bakras), Lala Mustafa Pasha in Erzurum, and Sokollu Mehmed Pasha in Payas.
105 *Tabhane*-like spaces only appear in the 1580s in the unusual vizirial mosques of Mesih Mehmed Pasha and Nişancı Mehmed Pasha in Istanbul; see Chapter 10.
106 Necipoğlu, 1986, pp. 225–27.
107 For architectural descriptions by Venetian diplomats, see Concina, 1994, pp. 35–56.
108 For Barbaro's comments on these mosques, see Chapters 6 and 8.
109 Howard, 2003.
110 I owe the staircase reference to Howard Burns; see Palladio, 1965, p. 35.
111 For the often made comparison with Palladio, see Kuran, 1987, p. 246. Palladio's approach to design is discussed in Kostof, 1985, pp. 453–83; Burns, 1991; and Payne, 1999, pp. 170–213.
112 The two cities are compared in Kostof, 1985, pp. 453–83.
113 See Chapter 13.
114 For Ottoman ambassadors to Venice, see Pedani, 1994. Architects who held the rank of *çavuş* are listed in Appendix 4.4 and 4.5.
115 Francesco Dei Marchi, *Architettura militare*, quoted in De Maio, 1978, p. 322, note 64.
116 Oral communication with Howard Burns. The five engravings of Sangallo's wooden model by Antonio Salamanca are reproduced in Millon and Lampugnani, 1994, pp. 644–46, no. 370. For the piers of the Şehzade and Süleymaniye mosques, see Chapter 6.
117 Plans kept at the chief architect's office are mentioned in Cafer Efendi, 1987, pp. 53–54, 56. For medieval sources on engineering and mathematics that informed Islamic architectural practice, see Necipoğlu, 1995.
118 Flachat, 1766, p. 225.
119 See Hajnoczi, 1991, for this manuscript given as a gift to Hungary by Abdülhamid II in 1877 (Codex MS. Lat. 32, University Library of Budapest).
120 The designs for St Peter's are reproduced in Millon and Lampugnani, 1994, p. 612, no. 303; p. 614, no. 308; p. 621, no. 322.
121 For the Portuguese captain see Appendix 4.2; the grand admiral's architect is discussed in Chapters 5(II) and 11.
122 Bruschi, 1994, p. 162.
123 Lateral colonnades also appear in several project plans for St Peter's in Rome; see Bruschi, 1994, pp. 167–69; Murray, 1971, p. 145.
124 See Chapter 6.
125 Erzen, 1988.
126 Cited in Bruschi, 1994, p. 123.
127 Palladio, 1965, Book IV, pp. 79–80.
128 Ruhi Edrenevi, *Tārīḫ-i āl-i ʿoṣmān*, Berlin, Staatsbibliothek, Or. Quart. 821, fol. 190r. Sinan 'strengthened with a new arch' the dome of Bayezid II's mosque in 981 (1573–74); see TM in Meriç, 1965, p. 24.
129 For another classification, see Erzen, 1996: pre-classical 1538–57, classical 1557–70, post-classical 1570–85.
130 Erzen, 1981 and 1988.
131 Kuran, 1987, p. 251.
132 See his eulogies of decoration and epigraphy in the Süleymaniye and Selimiye mosques, discussed in Chapter 6. Sinan's role in devising ornamental schemes is recognized in Yenişehirlioğlu, 1982, 1985.
133 See Chapter 5(I).
134 See Chapter 6.
135 BA, MD. 19, #59, p. 21, dated 8 M. 980; and MD. 19, #63, p. 23; published in Ahmed Refik, 1977, pp. 112–13, nos. 16 and 18.
136 BA, MD. 26, #751, p. 261, dated 23 C. 982.
137 Necipoğlu, 1990, p. 155.
138 Önkal, 1992, pp. 85–89.
139 BA, MD. 28, #438, p. 188, dated beginning of Ca. 984.
140 For the combination of Persian poetry, hadith, and Koranic verses in the T-type mosque and mausoleum of Mehmed I in Bursa, see Ayverdi, 1972, pp. 46–118.
141 Evliya, 1896–1938, 1:152.
142 I owe this reference to Cemal Kafadar: Hilmi, 1995, pp. 197–205.
143 Prepared in 985 by the mufti of Istanbul, Zekeriya Efendi, the census is recorded in Süleymaniye Kütüphanesi, Hacı Mahmud Efendi, no. 6321, fol. 17r. See Chapter 2(I) for the population of Istanbul that reached 500,000 around this time.
144 Laguna, 1983, pp. 280–81.
145 For the concept of contextual literacy, see Bierman, 1998.
146 For a comparison of the Selimiye dome to a 'mirror globe', see Sai, 1989, 15r–v.
147 The mirror globes are referred to as 'runde Spiegel wie Kugeln von Damaskin Eisen', Lubenau, 1912, 1:119.
148 Gerlach, 1674, p. 513.
149 Wratislaw, 1862, pp. 40–41.
150 The cost of gilding the 'ball of the dome' for the Süleymaniye is given in Barkan, 1972–79, 1:18, no. 38. Evliya, 1896–1938, 1:151, 163.
151 BA, MD. 7, #1006, p. 348, dated 7 N. 975.
152 Barkan, 1972–79, 2:16, no. 24; and 2:194, no. 496.
153 Ibid., 2:194, no. 497; 2:195, no. 498.
154 Yenibahçe was a meadow for the grazing of janissary hounds. For the city's urban development, see Halil İnalcık, 'Istanbul', EI(2), 4:224–48.
155 Grelot, 1683, pp. 58–59.
156 Laguna, 1983, p. 318.
157 İnalcık, 1998, p. 260.
158 Erzen, 1991a.
159 Vatin and Yerasimos, 1994, 2001.
160 Al-Tamgrouti, 1929, p. 57; Gerlach, 1674, p. 187.
161 Necipoğlu, 1992a.
162 Sinan was ordered on 26 December 1573 to send the pulleys bought from Samokov for the Selimiye's construction for the needs of Hagia Sophia, if they are no longer required; BA, MD. 23, #44, p. 259, dated 2 N. 981.
163 BA, MD. 16, #375, p. 194, dated Z. 979.
164 BA, MD. 10, #291, p. 194, dated 979 (1572).
165 BA, MD. 21, #615, p. 258, dated 16 Z. 980; and #654, p. 276, dated 23 Z. 980.
166 Selaniki, 1989, 1:95–96.
167 BA, MD. 22, #171, p. 82, 20 S. 981.
168 İnalcık, 1998, p. 267.
169 See the Selimiye in Chapter 6.
170 BA, MD. 21, #462, pp. 191–92, 21 Za. 980.
171 BA, MD. 26, #696, p. 243, dated 13 C. 982.
172 Selaniki, 1989, 1:3–4.
173 Çeçen, 1988.
174 BA, MD. 3, #82, dated 25 N. 996; and #68, dated 20 N. 966.
175 BA, MD. zeyl 2, #694, p. 265, dated M. 982.
176 BA, MD. 14, #80, p. 64, dated 28 S. 975; MD. 23, #359, p. 169, dated 28 B. 981; MD. zeyl 2, #728, p. 276, dated M. 982; MD. 40, #495, p. 221, dated 29 Ş. 987.
177 BA, MD. 21, #304, p. 126, dated 20 Ş. 980; MD. 21, #318, p. 131, dated 20 Ş. 980. See Ahmet Refik, 1977, p. 145, no. 9, for the appointment of the former water channel superintendent Davud as 'ḳaldırıcılar nāẓırı.'
178 TSK, K.888, dated 16 N. 959, fol. 425v.
179 BA, MD. 3, #72, p. 29, dated 23 N. 966; published in Aykut et al. eds, 1993, pp. 38–39.
180 BA, MD. 3, #788, p. 272, dated 17 Ca. 967; published in Aykut et al., eds, 1993, p. 358.
181 BA, MD. 7, #1417, p. 491, dated 15 Za. 975.
182 Selaniki, 1989, 1:76–77.
183 Marciana Library, Venice, IT. Cl.VII (8872), Marcantonio Barbaro, dispatch sent from Pera on 1 October 1569, fols 193r–94r: '... si potrebbe veder sopra un minuto ritratto di tutto Costantinopoli cavato dal naturale, che ho mandato.'
184 Ibid., dispatch dated 15 October 1569, fol. 204v.
185 Ibid., dispatch dated 15 October 1569, fols 203v–204r.
186 BA, MD. 9, #201, p. 75, dated 20 Ş. 977 (given to Mehmed Çavuş).
187 BA, MD. 19, #280, p. 132, dated 17 S. 980.
188 Āli, Nuruosmaniye Library, Ms. 3409, fol. 4r: 'Ve ol cāmiʿ-i şerīf şehzādelere maḫṣūṣ olan resmle bünyād olunmamışdur. Selāṭīn-i ʿoṣmāniyye bünyād itdükleri üzre iki mināre ve çifte şerefelü, ḫuṣūṣā ecdād-ı ʿiẓāmları cāmiʿleri gibi vüsʿatle ābād ḳılınmışdur.'
189 Peçevi, 1864–67, 1:19, 263–64.
190 Tietze, 1982, p. 579.
191 Ibid., pp. 578–79.
192 Ibid., pp. 581, 583–85.
193 Ibid., pp. 580–81.
194 Ibid., pp. 581–82.
195 Āli, 1979–82, 1:66.
196 Tietze, 1982, p. 583.
197 Ibid., pp. 584–85.
198 Ibid., pp. 588–89.
199 The manuscript, now in Budapest, is described in Hajnoczi, 1991.
200 Payne, 1994, pp. 34–51.
201 Alberti, 1989, pp. 36–37, 94, 315.
202 Payne, 1999, 113–43.
203 Palladio, 1965, p. 38.
204 Āli, IÜ, T. 5959, fol. 577v.
205 I thank Cemal Kafadar for this reference, TSA, E.6650, also E.6926: '... şişḫāne tuğlalar ki şimdiki

ḥalde sulṭānımuñ dīvānḫānesinde vāḳiʿ olmuş ola, ol ṭuġlalardandur, ve daḫı evlerinüñ mecmūʿ-i ḳapuları ve manẓaraları bi'l-cümle ḳoz aġacı taḫtalarındandur ve dürlü dürlü ṭoġrama tavanlardur ol emṣālde şöyle ki sancāḳ beglerine lāyıḳ olandur.' The value of this house was estimated as 25,000 aspers by the royal architects 'Murad Halife and Camcı Mimar'.

206 Dernschwam, 1992, p. 157.
207 D'Ohsson, 1788–1824, 4:234–35.
208 Celalzade, 1990, p. 453.
209 Celalzade, 1981, fol. 26r.
210 Alberti, 1989, p. 13; also see p. 199.
211 BA, MD. 5, #313, p. 134, dated 7 R. 973.
212 BA, MD. 3, #799, p. 274, dated end of Ca. 967; published in Aykut et al., eds, 1993, p. 362.
213 BA, MD. 40, #739, p. 319, dated 27 N. 987.
214 See Chapter 2(i).
215 Translated and analysed in İnalcık, 1999, pp. 275–376.
216 Ćurčić, 1988, pp. 60–65.
217 Ibid., p. 68.
218 Ibid., p. 69.
219 Dernschwam, 1992, pp. 57, 101.
220 Dodds, 1992, p. 18.
221 Cited in Ćurčić, 1988, p. 68, note 43.
222 See Chapter 11.
223 In his description of Bursa, for example, Evliya Çelebi first lists royal mosques and then non-royal ones (*cāmiʿ hā-yi selāṭīn ve ġayr-i selaṭīn*); see Evliya, TSK, B.304, 2:223v.
224 Celalzade, 1981, fols 12r–13v.
225 Evliya, TSK, B.304, 2:223v.
226 Meriç, 1965, pp. 23–29.
227 Sai, TSA, D.1461/4, fol. 14v: 'Tetimme-i ebniye-i cevāmiʿ-i ezān vüzerā ve ḥükkām.'
228 Ibid., fol. 15r: 'tetimme-i cevāmiʿ-i ḥükkām', fol. 16r: 'tetimme-i cevāmiʿ-i ḥükkām.'
229 Ayvansarayi, 2000.
230 An exception was Kılıç Ali Pasha's mosque; see Chapter 11.
231 Examples include the mosques of Bayezid II's son-in-law by Güzelce Hasan Beg (1499) in Hayrabolu, and that of the governor-general Süleyman Pasha inside the Cairene citadel (illus. 87). For the mosque in Hayrabolu, see Yüksel, 1983, pp. 146–48.
232 Bursa textiles are grouped in three grades in BA, D.BRZ, no. 2, 20611, dated 932–35 (1525–28). Timbers follow the same classification in a decree handed over to Sinan in 1568, BA, MD. 7, #1425, p. 494, dated 16 Za. 975 (1568).
233 Cantemir, 1979–80, 2:249.
234 Turan, 1963, pp. 174–75.
235 BA, MD. 12, #939, p. 490, dated 7 Ra. 976; and #2220, p. 809, dated 12 Ra. 976: 'binā olınacaḳ ḳubbe ziyāde büyük ve küçük olmayub, iʿtidāl üzre ola.' For Mustafa's tomb built by Sinan's assistant Mehmed Çavuş and completed in 1573, see Önkal, 1992, pp. 159–63.
236 BA, MD. 3, #635, p. 290, dated 27 Ra. 967: 'iḫtiṣār üzre mescid.'
237 TSK, H.1425, fols 99r–v.
238 Chapter 4(II).
239 Yerasimos, 1987, pp. 125–26.
240 Evliya, TSK, R.1457, 6:226v.
241 BA, MD. 29, #425, p. 177, dated end of Za. 984.
242 The names of these churches are identified in BA, MAD. 5675, dated 1032 (1622–23), fol. 22r: 'cāmiʿ-i şerīf-i Ayaṣofya-i kebīr ve ṣaġīr der ḳalʿa-i Lefkoşe (Nicosia) ve Maġosa (Famagusta) der cezīre-i Ḳıbrıs.'
243 BA, MD. 12, #1211, p. 638, dated 17 Z. 979.
244 See Chapter 7.
245 Cihangir's mosque is discussed together with the Şehzade Mehmed mosque in Chapter 6.
246 Both complexes had shops and a bath-house among their income-generating dependencies. A covered market and caravansaray were added after Selim II's death to the Selimiye.
247 Barkan, 1972–79, 1:1–45. The total cost is specified in: TSK, H.1425, fol. 100r: '303 kere yüzbiñ daḫı altmış biñ 960 aḳçe ṣarf olunub, cāmiʿlerine 546 biñ kerre 100 biñ daḫı 97 biñ 560 akçe ṣarf olunmuşdur.' 'Sikke ḥasene 9,016,000 / Beher ḥasene fī 60, beḥesāb-i naḳdiye: 540,960,000 / Beḥesab-i ḥaml 5409 / Kusur 6000.'
248 Barkan, 1972–79, 1:15–16, 30–40.
249 30,000,000 aspers came from the yearly revenues of Egypt, and the rest from the daily stipend of the sultan from the treasury and the sale of produce from the imperial gardens; see Barkan, 1957–58, p. 289.
250 TSA, D.2336, lists a total of 21,930,000 aspers, paid between 15 L. 975 and 17 B. 982.
251 See the Selimiye in Chapter 6.
252 TSA, D.3902, and D.5481. The construction initiated in 1559 (beginning of B. 966) was completed in 1561 (end of Z. 968) when its accounts were prepared by the kadi of Sarajevo.
253 Kunt, 1983, p. 50.
254 Gerlach, 1674, p. 449.
255 Ibid., pp. 33, 266–67
256 For Sokollu, see Chapter 8.
257 Gerlach, 1674, p. 414.
258 For portraiture, see Istanbul, 2000.
259 Rossi, 1982, p. 55.
260 Faroqhi, 1994, pp. 7–8, 28, 125, 148.
261 BA, MD. 33, #1, p. 1, dated 3 N. 985.
262 Cafer Efendi, 1987, pp. 53–54.
263 TSA, E.1175.
264 Chapter 4(I–II).

CHAPTER 4

1 For these texts and their manuscript copies, see Şeşen, 1986; Sai, 1989, pp. 19–34; Sai, 2002, pp. 13–16. The three unicum drafts and the TE are published in Meriç, 1965. Howard Crane and Ezra Akın's critical edition and English translation of all known manuscripts, which I have edited, will be published soon; see Sai, forthcoming 2005.
2 Şeşen (1986). Some scholars have attributed the *Tuḥfe* to the poet Asari and think it was composed in the 1590s after the deaths of Sinan (d. 1588) and Sai (d. 1595); see Kuran (1986, 1987) and Meriç (1965). That Sai was the author of all five autobiographical texts is suggested by the similarity of their prefaces and their nearly identical biographical sections.
3 For the bath-house, see Chapter 14. TSA, D.1461/1 is the account book of the Kanlıca bath-house; D.1461/2 entitled 'Defter-i ḫarc-ı vaḳf-ı sinān aġa' is dated 10 L. 946; D.1461/3 is the Untitled Treatise ('Adsız Risāle' in Meriç, 1965, pp. 5–7); D.1461/4 contains the *Risāletü'l-miʿmāriyye* and TM (Meriç, 1965, pp. 8-52).
4 TSA, D.1461/1, fol. 1v: 'Defter-i müfredāt ve iḫrācāt-ı binā-kerden-i ḥammām be-ḳażā-i Anaṭolı der ḳaṣaba-i ḳanlıca be fermān-ı ḥażret-i pādişāh ... bemaʿrifet-i ḳıdvetü'l-emācid ve'l-ekārim sinān aġa ser-miʿmārān-ı ḫāṣṣa.' It lists building materials and the names of master masons (*üstādān*), masons (*bennāyān*), carpenters (*neccārān*), foremen (*muʿtemedān*), labourers (*ırġādān*), porters (*ḥammālān*), iron smiths (*ḥaddādān*), water channel experts (*üstādān-ı rāh-ı āb*), diggers of water channels (*laġımciyān*) and novices (*ʿacemiyān-ı miʿmārān*) employed in the bath's construction in the year 973. The construction was headed by Üstad Manol and his two assistants Yorgi and Yani, fol. 5r.
5 "El-faḳīr sinān ser-miʿmārān-ı ḫāṣṣa.'
6 "El-faḳīrü'l ḥakīr sinān', 'bende-i miskīn kemīne derdmend/ser-miʿmārān-ı ḫāṣṣa müstemend.'
7 Sai, 1989, fols 2r–2v.
8 TE in Meriç, 1965, pp. 62–63.
9 Kuran dates the TB to 1582–83, but it lists mosques completed around 1585–86: Hacı Ahmed Pasha in Kayseri, Hacı Hüsrev (Ramazan Efendi) in Istanbul, and the Muradiye in Manisa. According to Saatçi, the earliest known manuscript of the TB (Süleymaniye Kütüphanesi, Hacı Mahmud Efendi, no. 4911) might have been Sai's autograph copy because of its marginal notes; see Sai, 1989, pp. 25–27. This is unlikely because it was written after the death of Hasan Karahisari (d. 1593–94), who is referred to in it as the 'late' calligrapher (ibid., fol. 10r); whereas Sai's preface indicates he presented the TB to Sinan during his lifetime.
10 Mosques completed around 1585–86 are listed in TM and TE. The inclusion of Melek Ahmed Pasha's mosque in Diyarbakır (*c.* 1587–91) in the *Tuḥfe* does not justify the hypothesis that it was written after Sinan's death. Not all of the mosques listed in the autobiographies reached completion when the chief architect died in 1588. For example, the mosque complex of Shahsultan and Zal Mahmud Pasha in Eyüp (included in TM and TE) was initiated in 1577, but not completed until 1590.
11 Goldthwaite, 1980, p. 411.
12 TE in Meriç, 1965, p. 58.
13 Meriç, 1965, p. 5. Repeated almost verbatim in TE (pp. 69-71) and with some variations in *Risāletü'l miʿmāriyye* (p. 11) and TM (pp. 16-17).
14 Meriç, 1965, *Risāletü'l-miʿmāriyye*, p. 12; TM, p. 16.
15 Sai, 1989, fol. 2v.
16 Petrosiyan, ed., 1987, fol. 13v.
17 Uzunçarşılı, 1984–88, 1:20–21. According to Koçi Beg the *devşirme* levy used to be applied only to Albanians, Bosnians, Greeks, Bulgarians and Armenians in the classical age.
18 Koçi Beg, 1998, p. 31. Uzunçarşılı rejects the claim that Armenians were excluded from the levy; see Uzunçarşılı, 1984–88, p. 17. The anonymous author of the 'Customs' dates the corruption of the *devşirme* system to 1582, when Murad III approved the conscription of urbanized Christians from the three capital cities and of Turks whose parents paid bribes to have their names recorded as Christians; Petrosiyan, ed., 1987, fols 15v–16r, 23v–24r.
19 For the Süleymaniye's second building supervisor Sinan, see Barkan, 1972-79, 1:14-16. The waqfiyya refers to him as the 'building supervisor (*binā emīni*) Sinan Çelebi', and as 'Sinan Agha the sultan's building supervisor' (*el-emīn el-ebniye el-sulṭāniye*). The misattribution of Konyalı, 1948, is repeated in Ateş, 1990. The waqfiyya is correctly identified with the building supervisor of the Süleymaniye in Bilge, 1972–73, pp. 164–75.
20 Konyalı, 1948, pp. 29–44.
21 Ibid, pp. 44–45. This is logically impossible because Sinan was conscripted under Selim I before İbrahim Pasha's grand vizierate under Süleyman.
22 Ibid., pp. 15–16.
23 BA, MD. 12, #338, p. 157, dated 24 Za. 978.
24 'Miʿmārbāşı oğlunuñ ḳapu ketḫüdāsına virildi.'
25 Āli, IÜ, T.5959, pp. 504-6.
26 Konyalı, 1948, p. 57.
27 BA, MD. 23, #513, p. 240, dated 11 N. 981. Published in Konyalı, 1948, p. 41; Ahmed Refik, 1977, p. 116, no. 23; Göyünç, 1985.
28 Güyünç, 1985, argues for a Turkish origin; Sıvaslıyan, 1985, claims the names are typically Armenian. For those who believe Sinan was Greek, see note 36 below.
29 Göyünç, 1985, p. 40.
30 Konyalı, 1948, pp. 106-8.

31 Published in Barkan, 1972-79, 2:227, no. 551; in Atatürk Kitaplığı, Muallim Cevdet, Ms. 0.91: 'Ya'ḳūb-şāh ermeni, mi'mār', dated 895 (1489-90).
32 See Chapter 5(I). Documents on this architect are published in Meriç, 1958. For the argument that the name of Yakubshah and his son Hüdaverdi were common among Armenians, and the hypothesis that he had not established a waqf because he was non-Muslim, see Yerasimos, 2002, pp. 41-42.
33 BA, TSA, D.9105, dated 976; see fol. 17v for the name 'Ḳudanşāh' along with other Armenian stone cutters with Turkish names. For Armenian sewer diggers (*lağımān-i ermeniyān*) originating from Karaman, Kayseri, and Akşehir, see fol. 2v.
34 Barkan, 1972–79, 1:235–36, 250–314, 320–23; 2:71–72, 118–21, 140, 142.
35 Yerasimos, 2002, pp. 75–76, 78.
36 Following Cevdet's preface to the TB (see Sai, 1897), Babinger (1914), Otto-Dorn (1937), and Konyalı (1948) identify Sinan as a Greek whose father was named Hristo.
37 Other errors include Sinan's date of death in 1578 (12 Ca. 986), which we know was a decade later in 1588; and the claim that he was married twice but had no children (Sinan's waqfiyya indicates that he did have children). An Azerbayjani Turkish student of the Viennese art historian Heinrich Glück, Mehmed Ağaoğlu, expresses doubts about the reliability of the *Ḳuyudāt* the whereabouts of which Ahmed Cevdet could not remember twenty-five years after he wrote his preface; see Ağaoğlu, 1926. The *Kuyudāt* is flatly dismissed as a forgery in Konyalı, 1951, p. 292.
38 Cited in Rifat Osman, 1927; reproduced in Konyalı, 1951, p. 290.
39 Konyalı argues that Rifat Osman forged this marginal note on which water was sprinkled to make it appear ancient; see Konyalı, 1951, p. 293. Similarly Meriç doubts the authenticity of the note which he dismisses as 'hearsay'; see Meriç, 1938, p. 199. Works in which this note is cited as conclusive evidence include Ağaoğlu, 1926, pp. 861–62; and İnan, 1937, 1956.
40 Reported in Konyalı, 1948, pp. 105–6.
41 Ankara Vilayet Salnamesi, cited in 'Kayseri', *Yurt Ansiklopedisi*, Istanbul, vol. 7, 1982–83, p. 4699.
42 The epitaph, quoted later in this chapter, is recorded in Ayvansarayi, 1985, pp. 386–87. The lunar (Hijri) calendar is shorter than the solar calendar (100 solar years equal 103 lunar years).
43 Sai, 1989, fol. 3r.
44 Uzunçarşılı, 1984–88, 1:14, 16.
45 Meriç, 1965, p. 16.
46 Ibid., p. 70.
47 Sai, 1989, fol. 3r.
48 Uzunçarşılı, 1984–88, pp. 40–42.
49 Ibid., 1:37, 53–55; Petrosiyan, ed., 1987, fol. 21r. The novices educated in these dormitories were placed under the jurisdiction of the Agha of Istanbul, ibid., fol. 112r. Novices employed at the imperial gardens were placed under the chief gardener's jurisdiction, ibid., fol. 139v.
50 Uzunçarşılı, 1984–88, 1:400. For workshops and craftsmen at the janissary agha's palace that included a chief carpenter; see Petrosiyan, ed., 1987, fol. 77r.
51 Sai, 1989, fol. 2v. Repeated in TE, Meriç, 1965, pp. 56–57.
52 Konyalı, 1948, pp. 145–47.
53 Unlike novices lodged near the Old Chambers of the janissaries, who were subordinate to the Agha of Istanbul, those in the palace gardens were placed under the supervision of the chief gardener (Bostancıbaşı).
54 Cafer Efendi, 1987, p. 31.
55 Ibid., p. 28.
56 Ibid., p. 32.
57 Ibid., p. 32.
58 For the role of practical geometry in Islamic architectural practice, see Necipoğlu, 1995.
59 TE, in Meriç, 1965, p. 56.
60 Babinger, 1978, p. 201.
61 Sai, 1989, fols 3r–3v.
62 Cafer Efendi, 1987, p. 9.
63 Sai, 1989, fol. 3v.
64 Ibid., fol. 4r. Sinan's appointment as chief architect is generally dated 1538, but Lutfi Pasha who offered him the post became grand vizier in 1539.
65 Ibid., fols 4r–v.
66 Ibid., fol. 4v.
67 Ibid., fol. 2v.
68 For the classification of mathematical sciences and engineering in Islamic sources, see Necipoğlu, 1995.
69 For architects' signatures, see Sönmez, 1989.
70 Meriç, 1965, p. 17.
71 Sai, 1989, fol. 5r.
72 Kuran, 1986, p. 22; Sai, forthcoming 2005.
73 Kuran, 1986, p. 20.
74 Meriç, 1965, pp. 6–7.
75 Ibid., pp. 45–47, 124–29.
76 A telling example is the so-called mosque of Mustafa Pasha in Bolu, which owes its mention in the TE to scribal error: a conflation of the *Tuḥfe*'s entry on Rüstem Pasha's mosque in Bolu (Dibek) with the next, crossed out, entry on Mustafa Pasha's mosque in Gebze. The Bolu (Dibek) mosque thus disappears from the derivative lists of the TE. Kuran's identification of this imaginary mosque with that of Kara Mustafa Pasha at Ilgın near Konya is not convincing; see Meriç, 1965, pp. 25, 80. Another scribal error in the TE invents a mosque for Rüstem Pasha's steward, Kethüda Mehmed Beg, in Trikkala by conflating the crossed out line in the TM, 'Mehmed Beg the Kethüda of Rüstem Pasha', with the next entry on Osmanshah's mosque in Trikkala; ibid., pp. 26, 85.
77 Ibid., p. 17.
78 One example is the chief black eunuch Mehmed Agha's mosque, completed in 1585, whose foundation inscription identifies Davud as its architect. Some mosques, on the other hand, are only mentioned in the TE, which cites monuments overlooked in earlier drafts: the mosques of Haseki Hürrem Sultan at the bridge of Mustafa Pasha near Edirne (now Svilengrad) and of Hacı Evhad in Yedikule.
79 Dervish convents that belonged to the dependencies of Sinan's Friday mosques in Istanbul include those of Şehzade Cihangir, Ferruh Kethüda, Dragoman Yunus Beg, Shahsultan (Shaykh Merkez Efendi), Piyale Pasha, Mehmed Agha, and Nişancı Mehmed Pasha.
80 Condivi, 1999, pp. 9, 30, 33, 94, 97.
81 Ibid., XIII, p. 4; Sai, 1989, fol. 2v.
82 Ibid., pp. 4, 109.
83 A rare example of an early-sixteenth-century autobiography is that of the grand admiral Barbarossa, a seafaring ghazi; see Galotta, ed., 1983.
84 Cafer Efendi, 1987, p. 23.
85 For the *Diegesis* and its translations, see Chapter 3(II); Dagron, 1984; and Mango, 1986, 1992.
86 Yerasimos 1990, pp. 26-33. Dagron sees in the *Diegesis* an implicit critique of Justinian who squandered untold riches to surpass Solomon's temple, but raised an imperfect monument that had to be renovated by his successor; see Dagron, 1984.
87 Yerasimos, 1990, p. 34.
88 Barkan, 1972–79, 1:107; Yerasimos, 1990, p. 34.
89 Yerasimos, 1990, p. 33.
90 Meriç, 1965, p. 16.
91 Ibid., pp. 18–19.
92 For the model, see Chapter 5(II).
93 Meriç, 1965, p. 21.
94 Another reason given for the collapse of the dome is that it was too high, but in fact the second dome that replaced it was 20 or 30 feet higher than the first one, not lower; see Mango, 1992, p. 48.
95 Alberti, 1989, p. 39.
96 Smith, 1998, p. 304, note 52.
97 Smith, 1992, pp. 199–215.
98 Ibid., pp. 212–13.
99 Smith, 1998, pp. 294–95, 299–300, 317.
100 Ibid., pp. 295, 303. Other humanist commentators also praised Brunelleschi's *ingenio*, a leitmotif in Manetti's biography; ibid., pp. 301–3.
101 Alberti, 1989, p. 24.
102 The mythical histories of Hagia Sophia say it was built with supernatural intervention in about sixteen years (seven and a half years were taken up by the preparation of materials), even though the whole project was completed in five to six years; see Mango, 1992, pp. 49–50.
103 Cafer Efendi, 1987, p. 107.
104 Ibid., p. 68.
105 Meriç, 1965, pp. 51–52.
106 Ibid., pp. 51–52.
107 Sai, 1989, fol. 13v.
108 Ibid., fol. 13v.
109 The same technique was used in the Mostar bridge, built by the royal architect Mimar Hayreddin. The exposed stone blocks of the recently destroyed bridge are connected by iron clamps sealed with lead, a technique used by the Romans.
110 Eyyubi, 1991, especially pp. 196–98, 226–36.
111 Sai, 1989, fol. 9r.
112 Ibid., fols 5v–6r.
113 Ibid., fols 6r–v.
114 Selaniki, 1989, 1:3-4.
115 Selaniki says the survey made during Süleyman's reign by 'Koca Mimar Sinan Agha and the non-Muslim known as Kiriz Nikola' was taken up again in 1591 by the grand vizier Koca Sinan Pasha; ibid., 1:232–33.
116 Sai, 1989, fols 6v–7r.
117 Ibid., fols 6v–7r.
118 Ibid., fol. 8r. A topographic painting identifies both the renovated 'old aqueducts' (*kemer-i 'atīk*) and the new ones (illus. 119).
119 Ibid., fol. 7r–v.
120 Ibid., fol 7v, this analogy is repeated in the epitaph of Sinan's tomb.
121 Ibid., fol. 13r.
122 Ibid., fol. 12v.
123 Ibid., fol. 13r.
124 Ibid., fol. 13r.
125 Ibid., fols 12v–13r.
126 The account books of the Süleymaniye list the cost of 255 pieces of 'jugs (*sebū*) for the noble mosque's dome'; Barkan, 1972–79, 2:171, no. 418.
127 Sai, 1989, fol. 9r.
128 Ibid., fols 9v–10r. The elaborate search for marbles and columns for the Süleymaniye is discussed in Chapter 5.
129 Ibid., fol. 9v.
130 For the obelisk at the Hippodrome, see Müller-Wiener, 1994, pp. 64–71. For Fontana's operation and his book (*Della Trasportatione dell'Obelisco Vaticano*, published in Rome in 1590), see Dibner, 1950. The kadi of Istanbul was ordered to assist Sinan during the transportation of Kıztaşı in 1551; TSK, H.1425, fol. 43v.
131 Alberti, 1989, pp. 25, 163.
132 Sai, 1989, fol. 9v. For these columns, see Yerasimos, 2002, pp. 100–2; I discuss them further in Chapters 5 and 6.
133 Sai, 1989, fol. 10v.
134 For theories concerning the type of centering used at the Pantheon, see Taylor, 2003, pp. 174–211. Scaffolding and centering timbers from the

Süleymaniye were reused at the Büyükçekmece bridge (Appendix 2). Eaton describes the following method of dome construction: 'In some parts of Asia, I have seen cupolas of a considerable size, built without any kind of timber support. They fix firmly in the middle a post about the height of the perpendicular wall, more or less, as the cupola is to be a larger or smaller portion of a sphere; to the top of this is fastened a strong pole, so as to move in all directions, and the end of it describes the inner part of the cupola; lower down is fixed to the post another pole, which reaches to the top of the outer part of the perpendicular wall, and describes the outside of the cupola, giving the difference of thickness of the masonry at top and bottom, and every intermediary part, with the greatest possible exactness. Where they build their cupolas with bricks, and instead of lime use gypsum, finishing one layer all round before they begin another, only scaffolding for the workmen is required to close the cupola at top'; Eaton, 1799, p. 236.

135 Sai, 1989, fol. 10v.
136 Ibid., fols 11r–v.
137 Ibid., fols 11r–v.
138 Yerasimos, 2002, pp. 131–32.
139 Sai, 1989, fols 11v–12r.
140 Ibid., fol. 12r.
141 Āli, IÜ, T. 5959, pp. 503–8.
142 Sai, 1989, fol. 11r.
143 Ibid., fols 15r–v.
144 The minaret of the Üç Şerefeli is 67.65 metres, those of the Selimiye are 70.9 metres: Kuran, 1968, p. 181.
145 Sai, 1989, fol. 15v.
146 Kuban, 1997, p. 137; Yerasimos, 2002, p. 139.
147 In the published edition of TB, the term circumference (*devr*) is replaced by the word depth (*derinlik*); see Sai, 1897, pp. 71–72.
148 Evliya, TSK, B. 304, 3:154v.
149 Evliya, 1896–1938, 1:149–50.
150 Sai, 1989, fol. 15v.
151 Ibid., fols 15r–v.
152 Meriç, 1965, p. 61.
153 Sai, 1989, fol. 15v.
154 Dagron, 1984, p. 200; Yerasimos, 2002, p. 114. One of the Turkish translations that mentions Hızır is by Şemsüddin Karamani, IÜ, T. 259, pp. 19, 26. It is also with the help of Hızır that a treasury is discovered when the emperor runs out of money, Āli, IÜ, T. 5959, p. 499.
155 Evliya, 1896–1930, 3:443–44.
156 Sai, 1989, fol. 9r; TE in Meriç, 1965, p. 59.
157 Sai, 1989, fol. 11v.
158 Yerasimos, 1990, pp. 32–35.
159 Sai, 1989, fol. 2v.
160 Evliya, TSK, B. 304, 3:155v.
161 For Dayezade, see Sönmez, 1988, pp. 101–2.
162 The TE manuscript bearing Hafiz İbrahim's seal once belonged to Ekrem Hakkı Ayverdi. It is now kept in Kubbealtı Akademisi Kültür ve Sanat Vakfı (no. VI / 1). I thank Aydın Yüksel for providing a copy of it. For the Cairo manuscripts, see Sai, forthcoming 2005.
163 Ehl-i hüner, maʿrifet ehli, erbāb-ı naẓar, erbāb-ı ḥikmet, erbāb-ı teʾlīf; see Sai, 1989, fols 2v, 9r, 14v: Meriç, 1965, pp. 12, 21, 59, 63, 71.
164 Ateş, 1990, p. 63.
165 Sai, 1989, Hızır in fols 6r, 7r, 7v, 13r; Lokman in fols 2v, 11v–12r.
166 Necipoğlu, 1995, pp. 197–215.
167 For examples, see Mango, 1986; Mesarites, 1957.
168 Eyyubi, 1991, p. 190.
169 Āli, IÜ, T. 5959, pp. 504–6.
170 Celalzade, 1981, fol. 519v.
171 Kuban, 1997, pp. 235–38; Matthews, 2002, p. 70.
172 Kuban, 1997, pp. 58, 237.
173 Published in Konyalı, 1948, pp. 120–21; Saatçi, 1988, pp. 134–37, no. 51.
174 Konyalı, 1948, pp. 52, 72. The term 'muʿallim', meaning master architect, is misinterpreted by Konyalı as an 'instructor' of architecture.
175 The waqfiyya is dated to 1586 in Bilge, 1972–73; and to between 1566 and 1583 in Ateş, 1990, p. 62 (because it refers to 'the late' Sultan Süleyman). I think *c.* 1583–85 is a likely date; the architect Mahmud who signed the waqfiyya died in 1586 (Appendix 4.4).
176 Ateş, 1990, pp. 84–85.
177 Ibid., p. 70.
178 Ibid., p. 85.
179 Also see Chapter 14 for Davud's close relationship with the chief black eunuch of the harem, Mehmed Agha.
180 For the landed property in Ağırnas, see Chapter 4(1). BA, MD. 28, #961, p. 370, dated 5 N. 984.
181 Konyalı, 1948, p. 109, identifies it as the village of Soğanlıbahçe near Bakırköy.
182 Ateş, 1990, pp. 63, 80.
183 Ibid., p. 69.
184 Ibid., p. 72.
185 Ibid., p. 70.
186 Ibid., p. 103.
187 Konyalı, 1948, p. 139.
188 The Bali Pasha mosque is discussed together with that of Hadım İbrahim at Silivrikapı in Chapter 10.
189 Hızır b. Abdullah's endowment is recorded in an inscription at the portico of the Bali Pasha mosque; it is published in Kreiser, 1982.
190 Ateş, 1990, p. 59.
191 The renovation expenses of that residence are mentioned in BA, KK. 7098, dated M. 960 to Z. 963 (1552–56), fols 42v–43r: 'becihet-i ücret-i neccārān berāy-i sāḫten-i bölmehā-i odahā-i kātibān-i şehnāme-i şāh der ḫāne-i Fetḫullāh Çelebi şehnāmegūy.'
192 Cited in Konyalı, 1948, pp. 141–42.
193 Ateş, 1990, pp. 77–78.
194 Ibid., p. 69.
195 Ibid., pp. 68, 80–81.
196 Quoted in İzgi, 1997, 1:126–27.
197 For the use of the quadrant by Italian architects, see Trachtenberg, 1997, pp. 223–32.
198 A document identifies him as 'müneccim ve rasıt Molla Fütuh'; see Akmandor, 1968, p. 3.
199 Ateş, 1990, pp. 67–68. This book was compiled by the ruler of the İsfendiyaroğlu dynasty of Kastamonu, İsmail Beg (d. 1479).
200 The masjid is hypothetically dated to 981 (1573–74) in Kuran, 1986, p. 314, no. 141.
201 Konyalı, 1948, pp. 72–73.
202 Ateş, 1990, p. 70–71.
203 BA. MD. 31, #551, p. 250, dated the beginning of B. 985.
204 The janissary agha's palace, depicted in the panorama of Melchior Lorichs, is mentioned in the Süleymaniye account books; 'sedd der-cānib-i aġa-i yeniçeriyān'; see Barkan, 1972–79, 2:136.
205 Cited in Bilge, 1972–73, pp. 144–45.
206 For the compass comparison, see Aslanapa, 1986, p. 205.
207 Ateş, 1990, p. 68.
208 Ibid., p. 69.
209 Ibid., pp. 82–83. Under the Third and Fourth madrasas facing the Golden Horn are twenty chambers for the *mülāzims*, and two upper-storey rooms; see Kuran, 1986, pp. 75–76.
210 Konyalı, 1948, p. 78.
211 Ateş, 1990, p. 69.
212 Barkan, 1971, pp. 155–59.
213 Selaniki, 1989, 2:629.
214 Barkan and Ayverdi, eds, 1970, p. 290, no. 1703.
215 For the waqfiyyas and the tombstone inscribed 'miʿmār-ı sulṭānī ʿātīḳ ḫoca Sinānü'd-dīn Yusuf ibn-i ʿAbdullāh', see Konyalı, 1953.
216 Barkan and Ayverdi, eds, 1970, p. 290, no. 1703; Konyalı, 1953, pp. 15–21, 29–40.
217 Ayvansarayi, 1864–65, 1:206–7.
218 Kunter, 1960; Barkan and Ayverdi, eds, 1970, pp. 382–84, no. 2252.
219 Sinan's student Mehmed Agha was a devotee of Shaykh Vişne Mehmed Efendi of the Halveti order (the first shaykh and Friday preacher of Nurbanu Sultan's complex in Üsküdar); see Cafer Efendi, 1987, pp. 42–43.
220 TE in Meriç, 1965, p. 57. Repeated in the TB; see Sai, 1989, fol. 3r. Nevertheless, Sinan's devotion to the martyred Imams, Hasan and Husayn, is revealed in the preface of the TB, where their names are invoked after the four Sunni caliphs. Their death anniversary on the tenth of Muharram was commemorated by the annual feast at his residence.
221 Kuban argues that the rationalism of Sinan's architecture was not understood by his contemporaries who lived in a society characterized by medieval irrationalism in thought, science and literature; see Kuban, 1997, pp. 8–14.

CHAPTER 5

1 Turan, 1963 and 1965; E. Afyoncu, 1999.
2 White, 1846, pp. 171–72.
3 Angiolello, 1909, pp. 133–34.
4 TSA, D. 9587, fol. 4r: 'cemāʿat-i miʿmārān ve neccār ve ḫarrāṭ maʿa şākirdāneş, yigirmibir neferdür.'
5 Extracts are published in Meriç, 1958.
6 Ibid., p. 71, #179, #186.
7 Ibid., p. 71.
8 Necipoğlu, 1991, pp. 47–48.
9 Lokman, TSK, H. 1523, fol. 16r.
10 Turan, 1963; E. Afyoncu, 1999, pp. 207–8.
11 Cafer Efendi, 1987, pp. 33–34.
12 Ibid., p. 37. Under Dalgıç Ahmed Agha 'however many public buildings he created, all of them were built by the above-mentioned Mehmed Agha.'
13 BA, D.BŞM. 40816, dated 934–37, pp. 55, 61.
14 TSA, D. 7844.
15 BA, D.BŞM 40816, dated 934–37, p. 38, lists among the 'cemāʿat-i müteferriḳa': 'Rüstem meremmetī-yi sarāy-i cedīd', 'Naṣuḥ meremmetī-yi bāġçe-i ʿāmire', and 'Ḫayrüddin mermerī'. The water channel servants and other experts are listed on pp. 28, 67.
16 Necipoğlu, 1991, pp. 47, 207–8.
17 Cited in Turan, 1963.
18 Ruhi, Berlin, Staatsbibliothek, Or. Quart. 821, fols 152v, 177v.
19 'Murād ḫalīfe nām usta', ibid., fols 149v, 152v, 177v.
20 Barkan and Ayverdi, eds, 1970, p. 286, no. 1686. The waqfs of Mimar Sinan b. Abdullah (Atik Sinan) and Mimar Murad are recorded in the Hagia Sophia endowment register of 1519, Ayasofya Tahrir Defteri, Atatürk Kitaplığı, Ms. Muallim Cevdet 0.64, p. 270.
21 Ruhi, Berlin, Staatsbibliothek, Or. Quart. 821, fol. 193v.
22 Meriç, 1958, pp. 27–28.
23 Ayvansarayi, 1864–65, 1:213; Edhem Paşa and de Launay, 1873.
24 Meriç, 1958.
25 Ibid., pp. 48 (#8, #10), 62 (#123, #124), 65 (#140): 'yaʿḳub-şāh miʿmār naḳd 3,000, cāme ʿan murabbaʿ bā-postin-i samur sevb.' For the unsubstantiated view that no chief architect existed before Sinan's predecessor Acem Alisi, see Yerasimos, 2002, p. 42.
26 BA, KK. 1867, p. 50, dated 22 C. 976: 'ādet-i zemistāni-yi ser miʿmārān-ı ḫāṣṣa, naḳdiyye 3000,

cāme ʿan murabbaʿ bā-postin-i samur: (1) ṣof-i elvān 1, (2) postin-i samur ḳıymet dāden fermūde, (3) berā-yi sancaḳ ʿan kemḫā çift 3; BA, KK.1768, dated 977–78, fol. 73v: ʿādet-i zemistānī fī sinān aġa ser-miʿmārān-i ḫāṣṣa: naḳd 3000, cāme an murabbaʿ bā postin-i samur: (1) ṣaru 1 kıṭʿa, (2) samur ... (3) kemḫā-i ḳırmızı berāy-i sancaḳ 3 çift'; BA, KK.1767, fol. 65r: ʿādet-i zemistānī-yi sinān aġa ser-miʿmārān-i ḫāṣṣa vācib, sene 977: (1) naḳdiyye 3000 ḥasene (2) cāme an murabbaʿ sepīd samur sevb: (1) ṣof kıṭʿa 1, (2) postin-i samur 2 nim, (3) kemḫā-i frengī berā-yi sancaḳ 3 çift.'

27 Atatürk Kitaplığı, Muallim Cevdet, Ms. 0.91, p. 588: 'Yaʿḳub-şāh ermeni, miʿmār', published in Barkan, 1972–79, 2:227.

28 Meriç, 1958, p. 57 (#86), dated 29 B. 912. Meriç says it is unclear whether Yakubshah was from Amasya as well, p. 28.

29 He must have remained a Christian according to Yerasimos, 2002, p. 41.

30 Meriç, 1958, p. 27.

31 For bibliography and the unsubstantiated claim that he was a slave of Azeri Turkish origin, see Özkan Ertuğrul, 'Acem Ali', VIA 1:322–23.

32 Meriç, 1958.

33 'Alaüddin ḫalīfe-i miʿmār' received 2000 aspers and a robe on 19 C. 911; see Meriç, 1958, p. 54, no. #59. Meriç hypothesizes that Yakubshah was suceeded sometime after 1509 by his chief assistant Mimar Ali bin Abdullah, but does not identify the latter as Acem Alisi; ibid., p. 31.

34 Ibid., pp. 30–31.

35 Kunter, 1960, pp. 438, 441.

36 The two sons of Acem Alisi, Hamza Çelebi and Hasan Çelebi, are mentioned in ibid., p. 442. Hamza's name no longer appears among the corps of architects in wage registers dating from the 1520's, when his father occupied the post of chief architect. For the architect Ali b. Abdullah and his son Hamza, see Meriç, 1958, p. 31, p. 70 (# 182).

37 For Alaüddin's constructions at the Topkapı Palace, see Necipoğlu, 1991, pp. 23, 80–82, 98, 146, 194, 197, 253, p. 276 (note 41).

38 Murad Halife's adopted son, İbrahim, is variously identified as his 'slave' and 'son.'

39 Sai, 1989, fol. 4r.

40 BA, KK.62, dated 21 M. 951, p. 60.

41 Cited in E. Afyoncu, 1999, p. 208: BA, D.BRZ, no. 20617, Bab-ı Defteri, Büyük Ruznamçe, dated M. 961, pp. 4–5, 'sinān ser miʿmārān, 65.'

42 For Sinan's annual allotment, see note 26 above.

43 Hezarfen, 1998, p. 75.

44 Petition examples from the year 994 (1586) are quoted in E. Afyoncu, 1999, pp. 213–16.

45 BA, MD. 2, #1037, p. 101, dated 20 Ş. 963, quoted in Turan, 1963, p. 184.

46 BA, MD. 4, #2109, p. 202, dated 16 B. 968.

47 E. Afyoncu, 1999, p. 215.

48 Ibid., p. 214. See Ahmet Refik, 1977, p. 127, no. 37 for a decree sent in 1582 to Sinan to appoint sixteen to seventeen architects for Ferhad Pasha's eastern campaign.

49 Documents related to the search for marbles are published in Barkan, 1972–79, 2:11–100.

50 Ibid., 2:27, no. 53.

51 Ibid., 2:33–34, 56–57, nos. 70–73, 114–15.

52 Ibid., 2:11–77.

53 BA, MD. 2, #852, p. 82, dated 10 B. 963.

54 Martal, 1989, p. 1621–22.

55 BA, MD. 30, #293, p. 121, dated 18 B. 985.

56 Ayn Ali Efendi, 1979, p. 94.

57 Özcan, ed., 1994, p. 36. The same number is repeated in Hezarfen, 1998, p. 94.

58 E. Afyoncu, 1999, p. 29.

59 Ibid., p. 23.

60 Ibid., pp. 28–29.

61 Ibid., p. 23.

62 Evliya, 1986–1938, 1:620–21.

63 Tanpınar, 1996, p. 147.

64 Cantemir, 1979–80, 3:378–80.

65 For this assumption, see Orhonlu 1981.

66 Barkan, 1943, pp. 396–37.

67 BA, MD. 7, #1139, p. 397, dated 25 N. 975. It is unclear whether this is the same person as the architect Hayrüddin who built the bridge of Mostar; see Chapter 5(II).

68 BA, KK.67, dated 5 M. 980, p. 5.

69 Cited in Dündar, forthcoming, from BA, MD. 2, # 1714, p. 187.

70 BA, MD. 2, #13, pp. 1–2, dated beginning of Ra. 963, quoted in Turan, 1963, p. 198; and O. Kılıç, 1997, pp. 194–98.

71 Orhonlu, 1984, pp. 11–26.

72 BA, MD. 39, #33, p. 12, dated 11 L. 987: 'Mezbūr miʿmārbaşı davud bege virilmişdür, dīvānda.' The decree addressed to the finance officer of Damascus orders him to give Zaim Davud, 'the chief architect of Damascus the Noble (*şām-ı şerīfde miʿmārbaşı*)', two hundred gold coins from the treasury, and to send to the court the report prepared by the kadi of that province about construction costs.

73 BA, MD. 39, #103, p. 44, dated 26 L. 987.

74 VGM, Defter 522, p. 5: 'Miʿmārbaşı sinān aġa mektub gönderüb şām-ı şerīfde zeʿāmet ile miʿmār ve ehl-i ḫibre ve cāmiʿ-i beni umeyyede ḳurşuncı ve ṣuyolcı olan davud fevt olub hizmeti muʿaṭṭal ḳalmaġın şām sākinlerinden naḳḳāşoġlı isḥaḳ maḥaldur deyü ...' 'ʿan miʿmārān, ibtidā-yi vaẓīfe-i isḥaḳ ki ehl-i ḫibre ve miʿmār şüd der şām-ı şerīf be-cāy-i davud ʿan züʿemā ki müteveffā şüd bā-teẕkere-i reʾīsü'l-küttāb fī 17 Ca. sene 996.' Also listed are 'meḥmed b. manṣūr, miʿmār 15' (beginning of M. 998); 'ibtidā-i vazīfe-i yusuf veled-i ḳadir ki miʿmār-ı mesācid ve medāris ve cevāmiʿ ve binā-i sāʾire şüde der şām-ı şerīf' (28 Ra. 996).

75 Atallah, 2000.

76 BA, MD. 61, #256, p. 104, dated 16 L. 994.

77 BA, MD. 3, #1106, p. 445, dated 18 Ş. 967, see Chapter 6.

78 BA, MD. 5, #1492, p. 544, dated 7 L. 973: '... muḳaddemā ḥaleb şeyḫlerine baş olan miʿmār ʿabdülḳādirīñ babası naṣreddīn ẕikr olunan taşcılara baş taʿyīn idüb bile gönderesin.'

79 The governor-general and finance officer of Aleppo are ordered to appoint for this project 'ḥaleb miʿmārlarından ʿabdülnebī', BA, MD. 31, #300, p. 126, dated 20 Ca. 985.

80 His task was administrative according to Behrens-Abouseif, 1994, p. 24; also see Bates, 1985.

81 Meriç, 1965, p. 23, read this faded TM entry partially. I propose the following reading, also incomplete: 'Ve sene 958'de mıṣır vālīsi ʿali paşaya hükm-i şerīf vardur, mıṣırda miʿmārbaşı olan ḳara muṣṭafā kāʿbe-i muʿaẓẓamaya varub pirinc-i muṭallādan mīzāb-ı raḥmetīñ ḳuṣūrun tecdīd itmiş, sāc āġacı ile mezbūr ... ve mevlāna meḥmed çelebi kadı-yi mekke-i mükerreme ...' Lokman confirms that the architect of Egypt, Mimar Mustafa, went to Mecca to repair the roof of the Kaʿba; Lokman, TSK, A.3595, pp. 85–92. An order sent in 1552 for this project to the governor-general of Egypt [Semiz] Ali Pasha is preserved in TSK, H.888, fol. 322r, dated 28 B. 959. It acknowledges receiving the pasha's letter concerning the petition of the kadi and overseer of Mecca about repairing the ceiling, pavements, and rain spout of the Kaʿba.

82 BA, MD. 7, #980, p. 341, dated 4 N. 975: 'Evlād-ı ʿarabdan mıṣır müteferriḳalarından yaḥyā nām miʿmārın binā ʿilminde mahāreti olmaġın...'

83 BA, MD. 7, #990, p. 343: 'binā olınan şu yolı meşāliḫine ʿilm-i hendese ile terāzūya almasınuñ ṭarīḳin bilür kimesne lāzım olub ḫuṣūṣ-ı mezbūrda senüñ mahāretin olduġı iʿlām olunmaġın...'.

84 BA, MD. 25, #2390, p. 258, dated 21 Ca. 982.

85 Lokman, TSK, A.3595, pp. 87–88/94–95.

86 Selaniki, 1989, 1:94–95.

87 See Chapter 5(II).

88 BA, MD. 23, # 564, p. 267, dated 11 L. 981.

89 BA, MD. 23, #227, p. 112, dated 15 B. 981; ibid., #448, p. 212, dated 28 B. 981.

90 BA, MD. 36, #909, p. 346, dated 9 R. 987.

91 BA, MD. 58, #779, p. 306, given to Sinan's man Kabil Çavuş on 17 N. 993.

92 Kütükoğlu, 1983, p. 294.

93 Eviya, TSK, B.304, 1:202r–204v.

94 Ibid., fol. 204v. The workshop of carpenters (*doġramacıyān*) in Vefa had been built by Sultan Süleyman, ibid., fol. 202r.

95 Ibid., fol. 204v.

96 Ibid., 204v.

97 Ibid., fols 204v–205v.

98 Ibid., fol. 305v.

99 Mentioned in the unillustrated Vienna manuscript of the *Sūrnāme-i Hümāyūn* (PAL.VIND.Cod.HO 70), Prochàzka-Eisl, 1992, p. 267. The procession took place on 17 C.

100 'Āverden-i yekī ez ustādān resm ü timṣāl-i cāmiʿ-i şerīf-i süleymāniye', ibid., p. 266, on the day 16 C.

101 Intizami, TSK, H.1344, fol. 189v; Atasoy, 1997, pp. 62–63.

102 Prochàzka-Eisl, 1992, p. 267; Intizami, TSK, H.1344, fol. 127b 'taşcıyān'. The next day was the chief architect's procession.

103 For the parade of masons (bennālar) on the first day of the month C. (23.6.1582), see Prochàzka-Eisl, 1992, pp. 227–28; TSK, H.1344, fols 171v–72r.

104 Prochàzka-Eisl, 1992, pp. 253–69.

105 Yücel and Pulaha, eds, 1995, pp. 66, 200.

106 Captured in 1552 and freed around 1557, Pedro stayed at Sinan Pasha's prison in the imperial arsenal, inside a tower of the Galata walls where seven hundred galley slaves shared his fate. Pedro also mentions another tower-prison at Galata in which the sultan's two hundred galley slaves were kept; see Laguna, 1983, pp. 76–78, 87. The palace at the Hippodrome is listed in Kuran, 1986, p. 382, no. 378.

107 Laguna, 1983, pp. 99–112.

108 Ibid, pp. 100–1, 105.

109 Ibid., pp. 102–5.

110 Ibid., p. 107. For bonuses Mehmed II distributed to speed up the construction of the Topkapı Palace, see Necipoğlu, 1991, p. 14.

111 BA, MD. 58, #237, p. 83, dated 17 Ca. 993.

112 The decree was given to the Nişancı Pasha's man; BA, MD. 62, #127, p. 55, dated 16 Ca. 995.

113 BA, MD. 62, #145, p. 65, dated 16 Ca. 995.

114 BA, MD. 31, #383, p. 171, dated 2 C. 985, and handed over to the 'miʿ mār kātibi' on 17 C. 985.

115 BA, MD. 52, #734, p. 276, dated 25 S. 992. The stones are referred to as 'kārhenklerden çıḳan aʿlā pehlu ve sāʾir arşun ṭaşlar.'

116 Barkan, 1972–79, 2:74, no. 137.

117 Ibid., 2:379.

118 Ibid., 2:156–57, nos. 375–76, dated 957.

119 Ibid., 2:157, no. 378, dated 24 Z. 959.

120 BA, MD. 7, #1425, p. 494, dated 16 Za. 975.

121 BA, MD. 22, #346, p. 180, dated 28 Ra. 981.

122 Cited in Ahmet Refik, 1977, pp. 128–30, no. 40.

123 VGM, 635/1 Mükerrer, p. 6.

124 Cafer Efendi, 1987, p. 83.

125 TSK, H.1425, fol. 107v, dated Ca. 959.

126 Selaniki says the survey made during Süleyman's reign

was taken up again in 1591 by the grand vizier Koca Sinan Pasha; Selaniki, 1989, 1:232–33. However, a document referring to a survey made for Koca Sinan Pasha for the Sapanca project is dated 1582 and it does not mention Kiriz Nikola. I have not been able to locate this document (BA, Cevdet, Bayındırlık kısmı no. 3) cited in Akmandor, 1968, p. 3. Akmandor identifies the committee members, 'Ser Mimaranı Hassa Koca Sinan, Ser Mimar Mehmet, Ser Mimar Davut Ağa, müneccim ve rasıt Molla Futuh, Mimar Çavuş, Su Yolcu Yusuf, Su Yolcu Ali.'

127 Cantemir, 1979–80, 2:251–52. The archive was probably located at the royal storehouse in the first court of the Topkapı Palace, where both the city prefect and the chief architect had their official seats; see Chapter 5(I).

128 BA, MD. 3, #23, p. 8, dated 16 N. 966; published in Aykut et al., 1993, pp. 11–12.

129 BA, MD. 58, #660, p. 260, dated 13 N. 993.

130 BA, MD. 39, #545, p. 284, dated 7 S. 988; ibid., #622, p. 321, dated 29 S. 988.

131 BA, KK.62, p. 79, dated 25 M. 951.

132 BA, KK.62, p. 345, dated 18 R. 951.

133 Ibid., p. 841, dated the end of Za. 951.

134 BA, MD. 14, #837, p. 585, dated 26 Ca. 978.

135 BA, MD. 23, #742, p. 334, dated 15 Za. 981.

136 BA, MD. 35, #181, p. 75, dated 10 Ca. 986; ibid., #594, p. 237, dated 16 B. 986.

137 BA, MD. 22, #641–42, p. 323, dated 15 Ca. 981: '… senüñ adamlaruñdan binā olınacaḳ ḳalʿayı frenk üslūbunda māʿen resm eyleyen miʿmāruñ ḳalʿa-i mezbūre bināsında bile olmasında lāzım olmaġın.' Cited in G. Tanyeli, 1996, p. 86.

138 For the castle, see G. Tanyeli, 1996.

139 See Chapter 11.

140 BA, MD. 23, #58, p.30, dated 25 Ca. 981.

141 BA, MD. 21, #570, p. 237, dated 3 Z. 980.

142 Cited in Barkan, 1972–79, 2:247.

143 BA, KK.67, p. 1018, dated 20 L. 980: '… üslūb-ı sābıḳ üzre saḳf yazılu ve gül ve lāciverd ile olub arşun dıvār olursa ikiyüz biñ aḳçe ve saḳfı sāde olub arşun dıvār olursa seksenbiñ aḳçe ve eger saḳf sāde olub dolma dıvār olursa yitmişbiñ aḳçe ile olur deyü taḫmīn …'.

144 BA, MD. 12, #849, p. 438, dated 19 Ra. 979.

145 BA, MD. 10, # 391, #253, dated 19 B. 979.

146 For the appointment of Ahmed Beg, see BA, MD. 12, # 1093, p. 574–75, dated 7 Za. 979.

147 BA, MD. 23, #6, pp. 3–5, dated 21 Ca. 981.

148 BA, MD. 22, #624, p. 313, dated 13 Ca. 981.

149 BA, MD. 23, #88, p. 43, dated 25 Ca. 981.

150 The architect from Egypt is discussed in Chapter 5(I).

151 TM in Meriç, pp. 25, 50; TE in ibid., p. 82.

152 BA, MD. 7, #398, p. 154, dated 20 Ca. 975.

153 Evliya, TSK, B.304, 1:58r; BA, KK.1767, dated S. 977: 'Teslim be sinān aġa ser miʿmārān-ı ḫāṣṣa ki iḫrācāt-ı mermerhā berāy-i ḥarem-i şerīf-i mekke-i mükerreme rusūm-i berevāt bā-teẕkere dāde.'

154 TSA. E.2491.

155 Esin, 1985, pp. 227–30.

156 'Bu bir ḳ ubbedür ve ḳırāyaṭı [sic. ḳırāṭı] elli biñ aḳçe olur', 'ṭulı ve arżı on arşūn', 'bu ḳubbeden yuḳarusu müseddes olur.'

157 'Tulı ve arżı on arşun', written twice on each hall; 'tābḫāne bu iki ḳubbe olur, taḫmīnen yitmiş biñ aḳçe olur.'

158 'Bu görinen kārnāme ki ḳırayāṭ ola [ḳırāṭ] taḫmīni yüz yigirmi biñ aḳçe olur', 'feemmā tekyenüñ važʿı budur ve hem bunı ṭaleb iderler.'

159 The waqfiyya of the 'zawiya' dated 822 is in DGM, Defter 590 (p. 69, no. 58), translated in D.1967 (p. 90, no. 28). The endowment administrator was İlyas b. Shaykh Mahmud Burhan Abdal Ata.

160 For the effects of the earthquake in Çorum, see Meriç, 1958, p. 37.

161 For this method used in Ottoman and Italian architectural practice, see Necipoğlu, 1986, pp. 231–34.

162 Celalzade, 1981, fol. 377v: 'eṭvār-i ġarībede resmler ve ṭarḥlar bünyād idüb getürdiler ʿizz-i ḥużūr-ı salṭanata ʿarż olunub, maṭbūʿ ve mevzūn olan üslūb iḫtiyār olundı.'

163 Sai, 1989, fol. 9r.

164 Celalzade, 1981, fols 519v–20v.

165 TSA, E.3946/4: 'cāmiʿ-i şerīf … ve eṭrāfında olan ebniye-i cedīde ve ʿatīkanuñ resmleri ve binā olunması fermān olunan ʿimaretüñ resmi taḥrīr ve taṣvīr olunub irsāl olına deyü sorulmaġın, miʿmār ḥüseyin çavuş ḳulları ile ẕikr olınan … cāmiʿ-i şerīfüñ ve sāʾirüñ resmi emrleri üzre bi't-tamām olub, irsāl olundı.'

166 An inventory of the inner treasury compiled in 1505 lists a chest full of plans kept together with a one cubit long architect's measuring stick of brass: '1 ṣanduḳ kārnāme ve 1 ḳıṭʿ a pirinc binā ẕirāʿ 1', cited in Necipoğlu, 1986, pp. 241–42.

167 TSK, Yeni 1815: 'Ber mūcib-i ḥisāb-ı kārnāme-i miʿmār sinān aġa mesāḥa mucibince cemʿān.' The annotations of this plan are published in Bilge, 1969.

168 Bilge dates the plan after 1563, but since only two of the aqueducts required rebuilding it is unclear why all of them are surveyed; see ibid., pp. 18–34.

169 The accusations are recorded in a decree of 1577, published in Ahmed Refik, 1977, pp. 140–41, no. 2.

170 See Chapter 7.

171 See Chapter 6.

172 Cafer Efendi, 1987, pp. 53–54, 56–57. Sinan's drawings were probably kept at the chief architect's office in Vefa.

173 Necipoğlu, 1986, 1995. Filarete's treatise refers to plans provided with a grid divided into *braccia*, and some plans of Bramante and Antonio da Sangallo the Younger feature a grid on the drawing paper; for an example, see Millon and Lampugnani, 1994, p. 408, fig. 8.

174 Meriç, 1958, p. 34, nos. 176–77; Necipoğlu, 1986, pp. 234–35.

175 An old photograph of the partially extant buttress is reproduced in Necipoğlu, 1991, p. 128, fig. 73. The annotations on the working drawing read: 'bu cānib-i maṭbaḫdur', 'bu maḥal maṭbaḫ kenarınuñ ger-mesidür', 'bu dıvāruñ ardı ḥammāmdur', 'bu maḥal ḥammām cāmekānınuñ pencereleridür', 'bu ḥammā-muñ cāmekānıdur', 'bu maḥal ḫazīne pencereleridür', 'bu maḥal ḫazīne-i ʿāmire pencereleridür.'

176 'Divār bu çizdür, içerdeki çiz ḫazīne dıvārına yasdan-ması resmidür'.

177 Cafer Efendi, 1987, pp. 65, 67–68, fols 52r, 54v.

178 Barkan, 1972–79, 1:18, no. 39. Istanbul paper was manufactured locally at a workshop renovated in the 1520s (BA, D.BŞM, dated 934–37, p. 56): 'becihet-i ḫarc-ı meremmet ve vasīʿ-kerden-i odahā-i kaġıḫāne-i ḫāṣṣa.'

179 Barkan, 1972–79, 1:51–52, 2:184 (nos. 461–63, 465, 467–68).

180 Ibid., 1972–79, 2:13, no.15.

181 Sai, 1989, fol. 9v. For the origin of the four columns, see Yerasimos, 2002, pp. 100–2, and chapter 6.

182 Barkan, 1972–79, 1:27, no. 45(d) lists the costs of special brass window grills unlike others made of iron: four of them flanked the sultan's private mihrab and the main mihrab of the mosque, while seven were for Hürrem's mausoleum.

183 TSA, S.P. E.153B.

184 See Sokollu's complex at Payas in Chapter 8.

185 Necipoğlu, 1986.

186 For Italian models, see Millon and Lampugnani, 1994.

187 BA, D.BŞM.BNE 15963, dated 1180–83: 'aḥşabdan inşā olınan cāmiʿ -i şerīfüñ resmi meṣārifi, 7021.'

188 I thank Machiel Kiel for this reference, Plyviou, 1994.

189 TSA. S.P.78, fol. 2r, dated B. 1003: '… ṭop-ı sırça-i resm-i cāmiʿ-i sulṭān süleymān ḫān, ʿaded 1, ḳıymet 1,200.'

190 Cited in Necipoğlu, 1986, pp. 237–38.

191 Prochàzka-Eisl, 1992, p. 267.

192 Intizami, TSK, H.1344, pp. 189–90.

193 Hezarfen, 1998, p. 241; Nutku, 1987, p. 58.

194 'Hediyye-i neccārān be-maʿrifet-i Aḥmed Aġa, ser-miʿ mārān-ı ḫāṣṣa, köşk döşemesi ile māʿan ve üç şah-nişīnle önü aşma çardağı ve fıskiyeli bir muşannaʿ nesne idi', Hezarfen, 1998, p. 229; Nutku, 1987, p. 72.

195 Meriç, 1958, p. 14.

196 Sai, 1989, fol. 10v.

197 Barkan, 1972–79, 1:15–16.

198 Ibid., 1:32–33.

199 Gerlach, 1674, p. 267.

200 Eyyubi, 1991, pp. 176–222.

201 Ibid., pp. 238, 242.

202 Marciana Library, Venice, IT. Cl. VII(8872), Pera 20 August 1569, fol. 154v.

203 Selaniki 1:173; Bostan, 1992.

204 Gerlach, 1674, p. 361.

205 Selaniki, 1989, 1:134.

206 See Chapter 11; and Atasoy, 1997, p. 110.

207 For Sokollu's use of galley slaves, see Chapter 8.

208 See Düzdağ, ed., *Gazavāt-i Hayreddin Paşa*, 2 vols., [no date], 2:127.

209 Laguna, 1983, pp. 96–97.

210 BA, MD. 26, #823, p. 284, dated 7 B. 982.

211 Cohen, 1989, pp. 470–75.

212 BA, MD. 58, #703, p. 276, dated 17 N. 993.

213 BA, MD. 60, #58–59, p. 25, dated 28 L. 993; BA, MD. 64, #14, p. 4, dated 28 Ş. 996.

214 BA, MD. 30, #365, p. 154, dated S. 985; ibid., #667, p. 289, dated 5 B. 985.

215 For the decrees, see Chapter 6.

216 Celalzade, 1981, fol. 520v; Barkan, 1972–79, 1:44.

217 Barkan, 1972–79, 2:4.

218 Documents published by Barkan are analysed in Rogers, 1982; and Yerasimos, 2002.

219 The account books of the Sultan Ahmed mosque are used in Nayır, 1975.

220 TSK, H.1424, copied in 1615–16.

221 BA, MD. 36, #821, p. 310, dated 9 R. 987.

222 Cited in Jardine, 1996, p. 376.

223 Barkan, 1972–79, 2:1.

224 TSK, H.1425, fol. 5v.

225 Barkan, 1972–79, 2:1–2.

226 Ibid., 2:2–3.

227 Ibid., 2:3.

228 BA, MD. 7, #2170, p. 794, dated 6 Ra. 976.

229 Barkan, 1972–79, 2:31, no. 69.

230 Sai, 1989, fols 11r–v.

231 Barkan, 1972–79, 2:44, no. 88.

232 Ibid., 2:78, no. 145.

233 Ibid., 2:37.

234 Ibid., 2:78, no. 143.

235 Sai, 1989, fols 10v–11v.

236 Barkan, 1972–79, 1:70.

237 See Chapter 4(II).

238 BA, MD. 60, #415, p. 178, dated 18 M. 994.

239 Manetti, 1970, p. 94.

240 Condivi, 1999, p. 9.

241 Burns, 1991.

242 Goldthwaite, 1980, p. 394.

243 See Chapter 4(II).

244 Cafer Efendi, 1987, p. 69.

245 Ibid., pp. 68–69.

246 Barkan, 1972–79, 1:95–105.

247 Ibid., 1:137.

248 Ibid., 1:131.

249 Cited in ibid., 1:107.

250 TSA, E.2941.
251 Barkan, 1972–79, 1:160–61; also see Yerasimos, 2002, pp. 61–62.
252 Goldthwaite, 1980, pp. 123–24.
253 TSA, D.3902 and D.5481; also see Appendix 2.
254 Barkan, 1972–79, 1:97; for the workforce also see Yerasimos, 2002, pp. 51–71.
255 Barkan, 1972–79, 1:22–24.
256 Ibid., 1:108–30.
257 Uzunçarşılı, 1984–88, 1:114.
258 An account book of expenses for non-Muslim galley slaves used in the construction of the Selimiye's outer enclosure shows that the 55 unskilled slaves (*irgadān-i kefere*) were paid one asper each, while the forty slaves skilled in the crafts (*ehl-i ṣanāyiʿ-i kefere*) received two aspers (TSA, D.3719/1, dated 995/1586–87, fol. 1v).
259 Uzunçarşılı, 1984–88, 1:115.
260 BA, MD. 10, #241–242, p. 159, dated 4 L. 979.
261 Barkan, 1972–79, 1:112.
262 Betzek, 1979, pp. 26–27.
263 In 1568 the kadis on the road from Istanbul to Edirne were ordered to sell food to the galley slaves coming to work at the Selimiye; see BA, MD. 7, #2376, p. 866, dated 6 Ca. 976.
264 Necipoğlu, 1991, p. 71.
265 Barkan, 1972–79, 1:147. For a detailed analysis of the religious affiliation of skilled masters, see Yerasimos, 2002, pp. 71–79.
266 Barkan, 1972–79, 1:143–44.
267 Ibid., 1:143, 145, 147.
268 Ibid., 1:71.
269 Ibid., 1:72.
270 Ibid., 1:73–76.
271 Ibid., 1:145–46.
272 Ibid., 1:146, 150–51.
273 Ibid., 1:149–51. According to Yerasimos, non-Muslims from the Kayseri region were mostly Armenian; see Yerasimos, 2002, p. 78.
274 Barkan, 1972–79, 1:146.

CHAPTER 6

1 Fleischer, 1992.
2 Bernardo Navagero (1553), in Albèri, 1840–55, 1:72–73; Marino Cavalli (1560), 1:275; Daniele Barbarigo (1564), 2:17, 26.
3 ASV, Archivio Proprio Costantinopoli, Busta 5, Bernardo Navagero, June 1551, fol. 130v.
4 Angelo Rachanis, dated end of November 1551, in Dzaja and Weiss, 1995, p. 629.
5 Sai, 1989, fols 14v–15r.
6 Selaniki, 1989, 1:53.
7 Bates, 1978b.
8 Lokman, TSK, H.1524, fol. 287v.
9 Ibid., fols 280r–87v. Churches were converted into mosques in such places as Belgrade, Buda, Esztergom, Pécs, Székesfehérvár, Szigetvár, Temesvár, and Eszék.
10 Süleyman also sponsored a convent mosque for Shaykh Ahmed Bukhari (d. 1531–32) at Otakçılar near Eyüp, a convent-masjid in Koska for Hekim Çelebi (d. 1566), and a convent-masjid in Eyüp for Shaykh Haydar Baba (d. 1567–68).
11 Lokman, TSK, H.1524, fols 289r–91v.
12 Āli mentions the following monuments: Süleymaniye, water supply systems in Istanbul and Edirne, the Büyükçekmece bridge, the two complexes in Baghdad, the mosque in Konya, the mosque complex at Gök Meydan in Damascus, a church converted to a mosque at Caffa in Crimea (where the sultan had served as governor during his princehood), the Great Mosque of İznik (a converted church) renovated after a fire, the Dome of the Rock in Jerusalem decorated with ceramic tiles, and the posthumous mosque complexes of Selim I, Şehzade Mehmed, and Şehzade Cihangir in Istanbul; see Āli, Nuruosmaniye Library, Ms. 3409, fols 117v–19r. Āli also mentions some monuments built by the sultan's wife and daughter under his patronage. Süleyman's patronage is also covered in Ramazanzade Mehmed, 1862, pp. 286–302; Peçevi, 1864–67, 1:423–28; and Hasanbeyzade, 1980, p. 60.
13 Eyyubi, 1991, pp. 138–42.
14 See Hürrem's patronage in Chapter 7.
15 Dijkema, 1997, p. 55–56, no. 34.
16 For a decree in 1573 concerning the tax-exempt status of Süleyman's irrigation canal in Karbala, see BA, MD. 24, #652, p. 245, dated 26 M. 981.
17 Dated 1 C. 973, published in Ateş, 1987.
18 Ibid., pp. 13–14.
19 Ibid., p. 11.
20 Fleischer, 1992, p. 164–67.
21 For Süleyman's building activities and inscriptions in Jerusalem, see Meinecke, 1988; Hillenbrand, 2002.
22 Āli, Nuruosmaniye Library, Ms. 3409, fol. 4r; Peçevi, 1864–67, 1:19.
23 'Şehzādelerin güzīdesi sulṭān meḥemmedim.'; see Ayvansarayi, 2000, p. 18.
24 Talikizade, TSK, A.3592, fol. 73r; Celalzade, 1981, fols 376v–77r.
25 Ali, Nuruosmaniye Library, Ms. 3409, fol. 66r.
26 Celalzade, 1981, p. 376v.
27 Talikizade, TSK, A.3592 fol. 73v.
28 Ibid., fols 10v–11r.
29 TSK, E.H.3003, fol. 99v.
30 Sai, 1989, fols 4v–5r.
31 For the mausoleum, see Önkal, 1992, pp. 139–40.
32 Ramazanzade Mehmed, 1862, p. 299.
33 Ayas Pasha, *Tārīḫ*, BN, Ms. Schefer no. 1021, fols 184r–85r.
34 Celalzade, 1981, fol. 378r.
35 Ibid., fol. 379r.
36 Lutfi Pasha, 2001, p. 300.
37 In 1544–45 Süleyman once again met with his sons Selim and Bayezid, accompanied by the new grand vizier Rüstem Pasha, in a hunting expedition at Gümülcine (Komotini); see Ayas Pasha, *Tārīḫ*, BN, Ms. Schefer 1021, fol. 190r. In 1546, Hürrem visited Selim in Manisa with her youngest son Cihangir; see Emecen, 1989, p. 33.
38 Dzaja and Weiss, eds, 1995, p. 398.
39 The Venetian diplomats Navagero (1553) and Trevisano (1554) report that Hürrem and Rüstem Pasha were resolved to ensure prince Selim's succession even though the queen was more favourably inclined to her younger son Bayezid; see Albèri, 1840–55, 1:76–78, 116, 174–75. In 1558 Antonio Barbarigo wrote that Hürrem and Rüstem supported prince Bayezid; ibid., 3:149.
40 TSK, E.H.3003, fols 8r–16r.
41 Celalzade, 1981, fols 378r–v.
42 Āli, Nuruosmaniye Library, Ms. 3409, fol. 66r.
43 Navagero writes: 'Il Gran Signore e sua madre l'han voluto onorare con una belissima moschea e sontuosissima', in Albèri, 1840–55, 1:76; also see Trevisano in, ibid., 1:116: 'e fu sepolto in Costantinopoli, essendo onorata la sua sepoltura dal padre e dalle madre con una bellissima moschea fabbricata a suo nome, cosa non più fatta.'
44 Petrosiyan, ed., 1987, fol. 33v.
45 Marcantonio Donini (1562) says Pertev Pasha was a relative of the vizier Ferhad Pasha (the husband of prince Mehmed's daughter Humashah, also known as Huma), being married to the mother of Ferhad's wife; see Albèri, 1840–55, 3:187–88. Pertev's wife Fütuha Hatun (d. 1571) is buried in his family tomb at Eyüp; see Haskan, 1993, 1:242–45.
46 TSA, E.12321, #63, fols 27v–28r, dated 5 L. 951; published in Sahillioğlu, ed., 2002, p. 50.
47 The site is referred to in 1546 as 'karye-i Azadlu der mevzi-i Davud Paşa çayırı', in Barkan and Ayverdi, eds, 1970, p. 340. A firman sent in 1553 to the kadi of Haslar (Eyüp) shows that the Azadlu village was a quarry for dressed blocks of 'cubit stone' (*arşun ṭaşı*). The kadi is ordered to 'find a sufficient number of carts in the appropriate season according to the old tradition (*ʿādet-i ḳadīme*), and after loading them with cubit stones arriving from the Azadlu village, to send them to the imperial complex of Süleymaniye; see Barkan, 1972–79, 2:169, no. 411 (dated 5 R. 960).
48 The mausoleum has one gate, the 'gates' may refer to its pair of wooden doors or the doors of its walled precinct. TSA, E.12321, #112, fols 52v–53r, dated 23 L. 951; Sahillioğlu, ed., 2002, pp. 91–92.
49 Ibid., #50, fols 21v–22r; #112, fols 52v–53r; #261, fols 111v–112r; #426, fol. 173v; see Sahillioğlu, ed., 2002, pp. 40, 91–92, 203, 309.
50 Ibid., #38, fol. 17v, dated 5 L. 951; Sahillioğlu, ed., 2002, p. 32.
51 Ibid., #522, fols 217v–18v; #541, fol. 225v; #545, fol. 226v; Sahillioğlu, ed., 2002, pp. 377, 389, 391.
52 Filori Defteri, TSA, D.1992, fol. 33r: on 29 Ca. 952, 'yapı usta aḥmede yigirmi filori inʿām'; fol. 42v: on 13 B. 953, 'miʿmāra onbeş filori inʿām olundı'; fol. 54v: on 3 Ca. 954, 'sulṭān meḥemmed cāmiʿinüñ kemer buluşduġına müjdegān içün yigirmi filori inʿām.'
53 Saatçi, 1988, pp. 43–45, no. 15. The construction was started in Ra. 951 and completed in B. 955; the chronogram gives the completion date: 'Maʿbad-i ummat-i rasūl-i mubīn, sene 955.' The dates provided in Sai's TB for the mosque (Ra. 950 [sic. 951] and B. 955 / June–July 1543 and August–September 1548) must be a scribal error; Sai, 1989, fol. 5r.
54 Öziş and Arısoy, 1986, p. 137.
55 The Persian chronogram of the madrasa gives the completion date of 954 (1547–48); see Ayvansarayi, 1985, pp. 199–200; Saatçi, 1988, p. 36, no. 12.
56 Mausoleums include those of Rüstem Pasha and his son from Mihrümah Sultan (d. 1561), Bosnalı İbrahim Pasha married to Murad III's daughter Ayşe Sultan (d. 1603), Murad III's daughter Hatice Sultan, Mehmed III's son Şehzade Mahmud, the open baldachin tomb of Şehzade Mehmed's daughter Fatma Sultan, the Mufti Bostanzade Mehmed (d. 1598), the vizier Destari Mustafa Pasha married to Ayşe Sultan (d. 1616); see Aslanapa, 1986, pp. 188–89; Önkal, 1992, pp. 138–43.
57 Sinan had passed through Diyarbakır during the campaign of the Two Iraqs (1534–36).
58 Mehmed Aşık, TSK, E.H.1446, fol. 389v.
59 Ibid., fol. 390v.
60 Evliya, 1986–1938, 1:164–65.
61 These walls are lined with hollow acoustic resonators hidden behind groups of three stone roundels, each with a hexagonal openwork grill at its centre.
62 TSK, Y.Y. 999.
63 For the mausoleum tiles, see Yenişehirlioğlu, 1980.
64 Kuban, 1997, p. 73.
65 Goodwin, 1971, p. 211.
66 Önkal, 1992, pp. 139–40.
67 Saatçi, 1988, pp. 29–31, no. 10.
68 The mosque's inscriptions are analysed in Haider, 1986.
69 The roundel above the sultan's private mihrab cites the al-Ikhlas sura (112:1–4) acknowledging God's oneness; it is accompanied by another roundel on the east wall that rotates divine epithets: 'O! The All Bounteous! O! The Most Passionate!'
70 Celalzade, 1981, p. 378v.
71 TSK, E.H.3003, fols 16r–17r.
72 Sai, 1989, fols 4v–5r.
73 Ibid., fol. 5r.

74 Ibid., fol 5r.
75 Lokman, TSK, H.1524, fols 283v–84r.
76 Āli, Nuruosmaniye Library, Ms. 3409, fol. 4r.
77 Ibid., fol. 66r.
78 Peçevi, 1864–67, 1:263–64.
79 Based on the erroneous foundation date given in Sai's TB (see reference 53 above), which gives the false impression that the mosque was founded before the prince's death, some scholars are inclined to accept Peçevi's rumour; see Kuban, 1997, p. 64; Yerasimos, 2000, pp. 254–55.
80 See comparative chart in Chapter 3(IV).
81 Among earlier princes Süleyman Pasha (son of Orhan I) had endowed a madrasa in İznik and Yakup Beg (son of Murad I) built a mosque in İznik. For restrictions imposed on later princes, see Peirce, 1993, p. 20.
82 Albèri, 1840–55, Trevisano, 1:116.
83 Önkal, 1992, pp. 127–29; the tomb of the princes Murad, Mahmud, and Abdullah also contains two princesses.
84 For Cihangir see Navagero and Trevisano, in Albèri, 1840–55, 1: 77, 116–17. The latter writes: 'non avendo sua maesta voluto mai darlo al governo di alcun sangiaccato, ma tenerlo appresso di se, perche era di natura piacevole ed insieme anco di debole complessione, ed anche perche era gobbo, e d'aspetto non degno d'aver carica del governo di alcuna provincia.'
85 Evliya, TSK, B.304, 1:132v.
86 Ayvansarayi, 1985, pp. 416–17.
87 TSA, D.43/16, fol. 2r.
88 TSA, D.9435, fol. 1v: 'ṭopḫāne bağçesinde vāḳi' olan cāmi'-i şerīfüñ binası'; fol. 2r 'mu'allimḫāne ve imām odaları.'
89 Ayvansarayi, 2000, pp. 395–96. The convent had thirteen dervishes; see M. Kılıç, 1997, p. 271, no. 122.
90 Kuran, 1986, p. 302, cat. no. 98.
91 Lokman, TSK, H.1524, fol. 284v. For the convent at Fildamı built in the 1550s with materials given from the Süleymaniye, see Chapter 2(I). Also see M. Kılıç, 1997, p. 269, no. 15: 'Koska'da Hakīm Çelebi Zāviyesi, 14 postnişīn.'
92 TSK, H.3003, fol. 99v.
93 See Chapter 6.
94 See the Muradiye in Chapter 6.
95 Quoted in Chapter 4(II).
96 Chesneau, 1887, p. 28–29. See Hugone Favolio (1545) who similarly attributes the mosque to Süleyman, cited in Yerasimos, 2000, p. 255.
97 Necipoğlu, 1996.
98 Evliya, 1896–1938, 1:162, 164.
99 See Chapter 4(II).
100 Rüstem Paşa, IÜ, Ms. 2438, fols 252v–53r.
101 Ibid., fol. 286v.
102 Translated in Imber, 1997, pp. 75–76; for the Arabic version see Çulpan, 1966; and Saatçi, 1988, pp. 49–52, no. 17. Çulpan also provides Ebusuud's longer original text, shortened to fit the available space for the inscription.
103 According to the inscription, the mosque was inaugurated at the end of Ca. 957 (June 1550) and completed at the end of Z. 964 (October 1557). The dates given in different sources are discussed in Barkan, 1972–79, 1:47–48.
104 The undated Turkish waqfiyya is thought to have been registered in 1557 (Kürkçüoğlu, 1962, p. 3), but it must have been written later, around 1559, because it mentions the mausoleum of the 'late' Hürrem Sultan (d. 1558). The completion of the twin madrasas in 1559 is revealed in an account book of their expenses (312,953 aspers); see TSA. D.6774: 'Binā-i medrese ki 'an ibtidā'-i binā-i mezbūr ilā 15 şevvāl el-mükerrem sene 966.' Kuran dates the twin madrasas facing the Golden Horn (named Third and Fourth madrasas) to 966 (1558–59), Kuran, p. 350, cat. nos. 260–61. For the completion of the water channels in 1559, see BA, MD. 3, #23–24, p. 8, dated 16 N. 966, published in Aykut et al., 1993, pp. 11–12.
105 A document in the Genoa state archives (A.S. 2170, #209, 29 November 1566) describes the tent erected on the site of the sultan's mausoleum.
106 BA, MD. 7, #670, p. 240, dated 7 B. 975.
107 Lokman, TSK, H.1524, fol. 286r.
108 Kürçüoğlu, 1962, p. 23.
109 Mehmed Aşık, TSK, E.H.1446, fol. 392v: 'erkān-ı ḫamse-i dīn-i islām.'
110 Kürkçüoğlu, 1962, pp. 32–33; Lokman, TSK, H.1524, fol. 286r.
111 ASV, Archivio Proprio Costantinopoli, Busta 5, Bailo Bernardo Navagero, November 1550, fols 23r–v. The *bailo* was asked to order from Venice glass panes and oil lamps for the mosque that would surpass others in 'bellezza et grandezza': '... scrivesse a Venetia, che li fussero mandati delli vedri quanto numero ne bisognano, e di che coloro e, di che grandezza tutto e scritto qui in questa scatola, si desideravà anco aver certe cesendelli per essa Moschea e se li sara de una mostra', ibid., fols 130r–v, dated June 1551.
112 Zen, 1878, p. 30.
113 Dernschwam, 1992, pp. 124, 137, 188.
114 Gilles, 1988, pp. 83–84, 155–56.
115 Lokman, *Tārīkh-i Sulṭān Sulaymān*, Chester Beatty Library, Dublin, Ms. 413, fol. 119r.
116 Lokman, TSK, H.1524, fol. 285r: 'Ve bünyān-i lāzımeden başka eṭrāfında birkaç maḥalle ve ekābir ve vüzerāya sarāylar yapılmaġa sarāy-ı 'atīk-ı 'āmireden bervech-i tanṣīf belki ziyāde yir ayırub, himmet-i şāhāne maṣrūf olunmuşdur ki şerḥ ḳılınur. Evvelā bir 'aẓīm ḥavli ve bāġçe yapılub, ṭaşraları ṭaraf ṭaraf ve köşe köşe meydānlar olub, ve cevāniblerinde ḥammām ve dükkānlar, ve cāmeşū odaları yapılub ...'.
117 Barkan, 1972–79, 2:202–3, nos. 535–38; 2:531.
118 Ibid., 2:201, no. 532.
119 Evliya, 1896–1938, 1:156.
120 See Chapter 4(III).
121 The fountain dated 1207 (1792) must have replaced an earlier structure. Another explanation for its name is that calculated amounts of water were distributed from it to the complex.
122 Also known as the hall of mausoleum keepers (*türbedār odası*), this seems to be the school for Koran recitation (*dārü'l-ḳurrā*) mentioned in Sinan's autobiographies and in the chronicle of Celalzade, 1981, fols 524v–25r.
123 Lokman, TSK, H.1524, fol. 286r; Evliya, 1896–1938, 1:153.
124 See Chapter 4(II).
125 Du Fresne-Canaye, 1897, p. 103; Meriç, 1965, p. 51.
126 Evliya, 1896–1938, 1:151.
127 Lokman, TSK, H.1524, fol. 285v.
128 Eyyubi, 1991, p. 150.
129 Kostof, 1985, p. 462.
130 Kuban, 1987, p. 84.
131 Barkan, 1972–79, 2:177–82, nos. 437, 443–44, 445, 447–50; 2:184–84, nos. 461, 464, 466, 469; 2:186, nos. 476–77; 2:187, nos. 479, 481–82.
132 Inscriptions on the mihrab and the main dome are sometimes attributed to Ahmed Karahisari (d. 1556), but the TB and Süleymaniye account books only mention his student and adopted son Hasan Karahisari who signed the mosque's foundation inscription in 1557. For the attribution to Ahmed Karahisari, see Derman, 1989.
133 The Europeanizing paintings executed by Fossati during the reign of Abdülmecid were replaced in the 1960s with those seen today. Ramazanzade Mehmed, 1862, pp. 286–91.
134 Sai, 1989, fols 10r–v.
135 Kürkçüoğlu, 1962, p. 22.
136 Mango, 1986; Dagron, 1984.
137 Necipoğlu, 1985, pp. 107–11.
138 The other faces of the piers bear roundels with the Fatiha sura.
139 Kürkçüoğlu, 1962, p. 46.
140 Önkal, 1992, pp. 144–48.
141 Translated by T.S. Halman, in Kemal Sılay, ed., *An Anthology of Turkish Literature*, Bloomington, Indiana, 1996, p. 177.
142 Du Fresne-Canaye, 1897, pp. 103–4.
143 Cited in Rogers, 1999, pp. 307–8. The garden is referred to as a 'jardinet tout fleuri', in Du Fresne-Canaye, 1897, pp. 103–4.
144 Pigafetta, 1890, p. 147; Müller-Wiener, 1977, pp. 466–67.
145 Necipoğlu, 1986, p. 238, fig. 23.
146 Du Fresne-Canaye, 1897, p. 104. For the cenotaphs added later on to the mausoleum, see Önkal, 1992, pp. 149–58.
147 Wratislaw, 1862, p. 64.
148 The eight tile-faced pendentives of the dome bear roundels inscribed with the names of Allah, Muhammad, the four caliphs, Hasan and Husayn; the muqarnas capitals beneath them are carved with God's beautiful names; see Önkal, 1992, p. 154.
149 Meriç, 1965, p. 51.
150 Lokman, TSK, H.1524, fols 285r–86r. Also see Hasanbeyzade, 1980, p. 60.
151 Celalzade, 1981, fol. 522r.
152 Sai, 1989, fol. 10r; Celalzade, 1981, fol. 522r.
153 Sai, 1989, fols 9r–v.
154 Reinhold Lubenau (1587–88) imagines that the four columns belonged to king Solomon's palace in Jerusalem; see Lubenau, 1914, pp. 164–66. Two of the columns arrived from Alexandria and two were found in Istanbul according to Celalzade, 1981, fol. 522r. One of the TB manuscripts (Süleymaniye Kütüphanesi, Ali Emiri, T. 921, fol. 36r) gives the weight of the two columns that arrived via Alexandria (83,000 qintars and 79,000 qintars); their value was calculated as one asper per 80 dirhams. The two columns arrived from Alexandria in 1552, and another column came from Baalbek in 1554; see Barkan, 1972–79, 2: nos. 30. 31, 36–39: 1:342.
155 Kürkçüoğlu, 1962, pp. 17, 23.
156 Barkan's documentation is summarized in Yerasimos, who accepts Sai's report concerning the origin of the four columns; see Yerasimos, 2002, pp. 97–102. Al-Tamgrouti, 1929, p. 54.
157 Kuran, 1986, p. 89; Kuban, 1997, p. 83.
158 Āli, Nuruosmaniye Library, Ms. 3409, fol. 117v.
159 Sanderson, 1931, pp. 70–71; Moryson, 1907, p. 95.
160 Albèri, 1840–55, 1:391.
161 Evliya, TSK, B.304, 3:155v.
162 Evliya, 1896–1938, 1:157.
163 Carlier de Pinon, 1909–11, pp. 190–92. Similarly, Jean Palerne (1581–83) writes with reference to the Süleymaniye: '... laquelle surpasse, à la verité, Saincte Sophie en beaux marbres: mais non en architecture; la hauteur de laquelle ils ont jamais sceu attaindre'; Palerne, 1991, p. 254. Also see, Pigafetta (1567), 1890, pp. 145–46; and Du Fresne-Canaye (1573), 1897, p. 103.
164 Evliya, 1896–1938, 1:158–59.
165 Evliya's comparison comes close to that of the Moroccan traveler al-Tamgrouti (1589–91) who concludes unlike him that the Ottoman's tried 'in vain' to imitate Hagia Sophia: 'The architecture of Hagia Sophia offers more solidity, it is more grandiose in character, and more massive in appearance; that of Süleymaniye is more elegant, more agreeable, and more spacious'; see al-Tamgrouti, 1929, pp. 53–54.
166 Celalzade, 1981, fol. 6r.

167 Yahya Beg's chronogram is cited in Ayvansarayi, 2000, p. 20; also see Ayvansarayi, 1864–65, 1:17.

168 Celalzade, 1990, pp. 438–39; Sadeddin, 1992, 4:295–96; Lokman, H.1524, fol. 136v. The camping site at 'Gök Meydan' is identified as 'Sulṭān Maṣṭabası' in Ayas Pasha, *Tārīḫ*, BN, Ms. Schefer 1021, fol. 124v; and Rüstem Paşa, ÖNB, Codex Vindobonensis Palatinus Mxt. 339, fols 178v–79r.

169 Discussed in Chapter 2(II); see Sauvaire, 1896; al-Rihawi, 1975, pp. 222–24.

170 VGM, D.2142, #5, no. 89, pp. 343–53, dated 924 and copied in 947. Another copy of the Arabic waqfiyya is in TSK, E.H.3031.

171 Meinecke, 1978, pp. 578–80; al-Rihaawi, 1975, pp. 224–25.

172 The Arabic inscription of the hospice, dated 962 (1554–55), refers to the 'just ruler' Süleyman's renovation of the *ʿimārat al-Salīmiyya*; see al-Rihawi, 1975, pl. III, p. 223.

173 Mamluk institutions had kitchens for sufis and students but not *ʿimaret*s for the public; see Behrens-Abouseif, 1994, p. 164.

174 Mehmed Aşık, E.H.1446, fol. 227r: '… cevāmiʿ-i diyār-ı ʿArab resm ve ṭarzı üzre… diyār-ı ʿArab mināreleri resmindedür… miʿmārān-ı diyār-ı ʿArab ṭarḥ ve resmidür.'

175 Later governors ceremonially performed their first Friday prayers in this mosque; see Kafescioğlu, 1999, p. 74, note 23.

176 Published in Sauvaire, 1896, p. 253.

177 Celalzade, 1981, fols 439v–44r.

178 His governorship is dated between 29 December 1551 and 17 December 1552 up to November 1554 in Laoust, 1952, p. 185. The dates 1551–52 to 1555 are given in Mehmed Süreyya, 1996, 5:1583. According to the pasha's own chronicle, however, he was appointed to Damascus when the sultan returned from the Persian campaign to Amasya (1554–55), Şemsi Ahmed Pasha, ÖNB, HO.22/1, fols 61v–64r.

179 The date of 962 (1554–55) which Mustafa Āli gives for Süleyman's 'Friday mosque and madrasa in Gök Meydan at Damascus' refers to the laying of its foundations; see Āli, Nuruosmaniye Library, Ms. 3904, fol. 118v. The Turkish inscription of the mosque, composed by Şemsi Pasha, gives the completion date of 966 (1558–59), and al-Ghazzi provides the dates 962 (1554–55) to 967 (1559–60); see Rihawi, 1975, p. 219, pl. 3.

180 VGM, Mücedded Anadolu Salis (3/2), Defter 588, pp. 153–61, dated 15 B. 964. The Arabic waqfiyya is summarized in Jafar Hasani, 'Takīyya as-Sulaimanīyya fī Dimashq', *Magallat al-Magmaʿ al-ʿilm al-ʿarabī* 31 (1956):222–450.

181 BA, MD. 7, # 899, p. 314, dated 975 (1567–68) gives the salaries of the four professors in Mecca, cited in Faroqhi, 1994, pp. 95–96.

182 For al-ʿAlmawi, see Sauvaire, 1896, pp. 253–54.

183 BA, MD. 7, #398, p. 150, dated 19 Ra. 975.

184 BA, MD. 7, #1642, p. 584, dated 3 M. 975.

185 BA, MD. 21, #414, p. 172, dated 14 Za. 980.

186 BA, MD. 28, #459, p. 195, dated the beginning of Ca. 984.

187 TSA, D.3697/2, dated 15 Ra. 1005.

188 Barkan, 1972–79, 1:36, no. 9.

189 Ibid., 1:37–38, no. 4, dated from 2 Z. 960 to the beginning of M. 961.

190 Ibid, 2:9, no. 15.

191 Cited in Müderrisoğlu, 1993, 1:123. See, BA, MD. 4, #89823, p. 87, dated N. 967: 'Şām beglerbegi mektub gönderüb anda binā olınan ʿimāret-i ʿāmirenüñ miʿ mārı olan Todoros nām zimmīnüñ ʿimāreti itmāma irişdirüb … mīrī akçe ile miʿ mār olma buyuruldı.'

192 For these complexes, see Kafescioğlu, 1999.

193 TM in Meriç, 1965, pp. 23–24.

194 TE in Meriç, 1965, pp. 83, 106; Sai, 1897, pp. 31, 38.

195 Kuran, 1986, pp. 68–72.

196 Āli, Nuruosmaniye Library, Ms. 3904, fol. 118v, gives 959 (1551–52) as the completion date of tile revetments at the Dome of the Rock. For signed tilework at the Dome of the Rock see Meinecke, 1988; and Hillenbrand, 2002. The drum tiles are dated earlier, to 1545–46. The nearby Dome of the Chain has later tiles dated 1561–62.

197 Al-Halabi, 1990, 1:49, 53.

198 Sauvaire, 1896, p. 254.

199 Ibid., pp. 253–54.

200 Mehmed Aşık, TSK, E.H.1446, fol. 225v.

201 Ibid., fol. 226r.

202 Goodwin judges the small mosque 'no more important a domed square than many a vezir's mosque in spite of the twin minarets which announce that it was a royal foundation'; see Goodwin, 1971, p. 256.

203 Mehmed Aşık, TSK, E.H.1446, fol. 18r.

204 Ibid., fol. 18r.

205 Ibid., fol. 18r.

206 Evliya, 1896–1938, 9:540–41.

207 Ibid., 9:544, 552.

208 BA, MD. 3, # 317, p. 122, dated 966 (1558–59); Faroqhi, 1994, pp. 32–42, 69.

209 Kafescioğlu, 1999, pp. 71, 74.

210 Ibid., pp. 70, 78–79, 91.

211 See Chapter 5(I).

212 For the war of princes, see Turan, 1961.

213 The couple's youngest daughter Fatma Sultan (born *c.* 1559) was married in 1580 to Siyavuş Pasha.

214 For Nurbanu, see Chapter 7.

215 Albèri, 1844–50, 3:179–83.

216 Cavalli, 1914, pp. 9–10.

217 Lokman, 1987, fols 56r–v. For the sultan's habit of colouring his grey beard, tinging his eyelids, his 'costumes of gold and silk of every colour' and his 'extremely large turban', see Costantino Garzoni (1553), in Albèri, 1:401–3.

218 Peçevi, 1864–67, 1:438–39.

219 Selaniki, 1989, 1:78. Marcantonio Donini mentions Selim's desire to conquer Cyprus in 1562; see Albèri, 1984–50, 3:182.

220 Düzdağ, 1972, pp. 108–9, no. 478; Repp, 1986, pp. 284, 289.

221 Piri, TSK, R.1294, fols 4r–5v, written in Cyprus in 979 (1571–72).

222 For Gothic churches converted in the name of the sultan, see Chapters 2(II) and 5(II). The church converted into a mosque by Lala Mustafa Pasha in Famagusta is identified in his waqfiyya of 1579 as the place where Muawiya had prayed, VGM, Defter 746, dated 17 Ra. 987. The discovery of a mihrab from time of the Prophet's companions in a church converted by Selim II is mentioned in Lokman, TSK, A.3595, fol. 100r.

223 Selaniki, 1989, 1:88–90.

224 Ibid., 1:87–88.

225 Lokman, 1987, fols 56r–v.

226 Selaniki, 1989, 1:98; Atai, 1989, 2:340.

227 Selaniki, 1989, 1:98.

228 Lokman, TSK, A.3595, fols 55ff; Selaniki, 1989, 1:94–96; Āli, IÜ, T.5959, fols 459r–60r; Atai, 1989, 2:224; Hasanbeyzade, 1980, pp. 85–86. For the castle of Navarino, built in the name of the sultan by its conqueror Kılıç Ali Pasha, see Selaniki, 1989, 1:96.

229 VGM, Defter 608, dated end of Ş. 965 (1558); Defter 741, dated 12 Z. 977 (1570); D.2134, #1, dated end of Ş. 965 (1558), #2, dated C. 977 (1569).

230 At the funerary garden of Hagia Sophia, provided with a gardener who planted its trees and flowers, Murad III also built a smaller mausoleum for princes (his own children) and a water dispenser (*sikāye*); VGM, Defter 2148, #16, dated N. 987; Defter 1550, pp. 79–157, dated beginning of Ra. 987; Defter 2136, pp. 127–30, dated beginning of Ra. 987.

231 The planned madrasas are mentioned in Āli, IÜ, T.5959, fol. 152v.

232 Genoa, Archivio di Stato, no. 2170, dated 19 February 1575, describes Murad III's visitation of Eyüp and funerary imperial mosques (Mehmed II, Bayezid II, Selim I, Süleyman I, and finally Hagia Sophia): 'poi ando à Santa Sofia ora la fan nominato Selimia dal nome de Soltan Selim.'

233 The images are repoduced in Necipoğlu, 1996.

234 Önkal, 1992, pp. 164–70; for the undated smaller mausoleum of princes added next to the mausoleum for the children of Murad III; see pp. 175–77.

235 BA, MD. 4, #545, p. 51, dated 24 B. 967; MD. 3, #993, p. 339, dated 18 Ş. 967 (published in Aykut et al., eds, 1993, p. 445). Cited in Müderrisoğlu, 1993, p. 472.

236 Cited in Müderrisoğlu, 1993, p. 472; Küçükdağ, 1997, pp. 10–11, 38–40.

237 BA, MD. 3, #1107, p. 374, dated 18 Ş. 967; published in Aykut et al. eds, 1993, p. 490.

238 BA. MD. 3, #1108, p. 374, dated 18 Ş. 967; published in ibid., p. 490.

239 BA, MD. 3, #1106, p. 374, dated 18 Ş. 967; published in ibid., p. 490: ' … cemālü'd-dīn nām miʿmār getürilmesi iʿlām olınmağın . . .'.

240 Cited in Küçükdağ, 1997, p. 51; dated Ra. 971: 'Sulṭāniye nām maḥalde binā olunan ʿimāret-i ʿāmirem kilārına …'. Curiously the hospice is referred to by the sultan as 'my hospice'. Another letter addressed on 10 Za. 973 (29 May 1566) to the prince's tutor calls it 'my son's hospice': 'oğlumun ḳarapınar'da binā itdüği ʿimāret.'

241 Barkan, 1942, pp. 355–56; Müderrisoğlu, 1993, pp. 474–75; Eyice, 1965; and Küçükdağ, 1997.

242 Lokman, TSK, H.1321, fols 87r–v.

243 Küçükdağ thinks that the complex was called Sultaniye because its real patron was the sultan; see Küçükdağ, 1997, p. 25.

244 Ibid., pp. 93–96.

245 BA, MD. 7, #1404, p. 486, dated 13 Za. 975; MD. 7, #1848, p. 665, dated 9 S. 976; cited in Müderrisoğlu, 1993, pp. 472–73.

246 Lokman, TSK, H.1321, fol. 87v.

247 Müderrisoğlu, 1993, pp. 469–70. Three of the other fountains are still extant.

248 Müderrisoğlu, 1993, p. 469.

249 Ibid., p. 473.

250 Ibid., p. 473; Küçükdağ, 1997, pp. 12–15.

251 The ongoing archaeological survey of the site, initiated in 1989–90, is summarized in Müderrisoğlu, 1993; and Küçükdağ, 1997.

252 Only thirty-six of the endowed shops were discovered during archaeological investigations; some of them may have faced the street of the fountain.

253 The school mentioned by Evliya Çelebi was restored in 1784; see Küçükdağ, pp. 66–69.

254 The complex planned in Istanbul was realized by a talented royal architect according to Kuran, 1986, pp. 157–61; and Eyice, 1965, pp. 136–37. The role of the Allepine architect Cemalüddin, who worked under Sinan's orders, is recognized in Müderrisoğlu, 1993, pp. 107–8, 480; and Küçükdağ, 1997, pp. 32–33.

255 Sokollu returned to Istanbul in the spring of 1560, when the sultan's decree appointed the architect Cemalüddin for his son's building project; see G. Veinstein, 'Soḳollu Meḥmed Pasha', EI(2), 9:707.

256 Cited in Dündar, 2001, pp. 168–69: ' … Şehzade hazretlerinin Sultāniye nam mahalde bina olunan cāmi-i şeriflerine hāssa mimārlarından altı bin timara

mutasarrıf Mimar Mehmed cāmi-i mezbūrun ibtidāsından inhāsına değin hizmet eylemeğin ...'.

257 He is identified as Mimar Mehmed [Subaşı], who supervised in 1573 the repair of pavements at the capital, in Dündar, 2001, 169.

258 For the no-longer-extant second portico, see Kuran, 1986, p. 158; and Müderrisoğlu, 1993, p. 493.

259 A portal with a similar conch shell appears in the mausoleum of Mehmed III (1012/1603), attributed to the chief architect Mimar Dalgıç Ahmed; see Önkal, 1992, p. 191, illus. 90. A niche fountain with comparable conch shell hoods on three sides was added by Murad III in 998 (1590) to a room in the Çinili Köşk at the Topkapı Palace; see Ayverdi, 1973–74, p. 751; Eldem, 1969–74, 1:74.

260 Kuran, 1987, p. 115.

261 Kuran, 1973; Gooodwin, 1971, p. 302.

262 Müderrisoğlu, 1993, pp. 465–68; Eyice, 1965, p. 133. Additional inscriptions record repairs in 1263 (1847).

263 Küçükdağ thinks the prince's name was omitted because the real patron was Süleyman; see Küçükdağ 1997, p. 25.

264 I have slightly modified the translation of Pickthall.

265 After appearing at the dome of the Süleymaniye, this verse was commonly used on the domes of several Sinan mosques.

266 Evliya, TSK, B.304, 1:16r.

267 Müderrisoğlu assumes without supporting evidence that the second minaret must have been added after Selim became sultan; see Müderrisoğlu, 1993.

268 For the mosque in Konya, see Kuran, 1986, p. 157 (who finds it difficult to relate it to Sinan's style in the 1560s); and Goodwin, 1971, pp. 117–22.

269 Lokman, 1987, fol. 54r.

270 See the Muradiye complex in Chapter 6.

271 Le Corbusier, 1989, p. 72. Bruno Taut described the Selimiye as a city crown (*die Stadt Krone*), cited in Kuban, 1997, p. 127.

272 Sai, 1989, fol. 14b.

273 Ibid., fols 15r–v.

274 Dayezade reports that when one of the Russian ambassadors came to Edirne, the first thing he did was to visit the Selimiye because of its fame among 'Christian nations.' He had the mosque's picture drawn by an artist in his retinue to show it to his king; see Sönmez, 1988a, p. 105.

275 Selim's tenure as lieutenant governor is discussed under the Şehzade Mosque in Chapter 6. Reluctant to return to Manisa in 1550, Selim begged his father to be permanently posted in Edirne so that he could remain closer to the capital than his more popular half-brother Mustafa, but his wish was denied as it went against dynastic customs; see Dzaja and Weiss, 1995, pp. 398, 423, 426.

276 Selaniki, 1989, 1:66.

277 BA, MD. 7, #1006, p. 348, dated 7 N. 975.

278 The register is discussed in Chapter 3(IV).

279 The first building supervisor was Edirne Hassa Harcı Emini Müteferrika Halil Beg; for the second supervisor, see Chapter 5(III): BA, MD. 7, #1367, p. 475, dated 8 Z. 975; MD. 7, #1529, p. 539, dated 8 Z. 975; MD. 7, #1578, p. 559, dated 23 Z. 975; MD. 7, #1589, p. 564, dated 24 Z. 975. Money given for the kiosk is documented in BA, KK. 1768 Büyük Ruznamçe, dated 977–78 (1570–71), fol. 32r: (M. 978) 'teslim be-ḫalīl çelebi emīn-i binā-i cāmiʿ-i şerīf der Edirne kim mühimmāt-ı köşk-i cedīd ve ġayri der sarāy-i ʿāmire.'

280 BA, MD. 7, #1981, p. 722, dated the beginning of Ra. 976: 'Edirnede binā olınacaḳ cāmiʿ-i şerīf ve ʿimāret-i ʿāmire mühimmātı içün.'

281 Genoa, Archivio di Stato, no. 2170, # 300, dated 15 October 1569: 'se a Cargato alchuna grossa Colone per Rodosto sopra alchune galeaze per eser poi condote per tera in andrinopoli per la Nova moscheta del Gran. Sr.'

282 Venice, Marciana Library, IT. Cl. VII (8872), fol. 45v, dispatch sent from Pera.

283 Ibid. fol. 110v, dated 27 May 1569.

284 BA, KK.1867, p. 83, 25 L. 976: 'inʿ ām be sinān aġa ser miʿmārān-ı ḫāṣṣa der vaḳt-i nihāden-i temel-i binā-i cāmiʿ-i şerīf-i ḥażret-i pādişāh-ı ʿālempenāh ḫullide mülkuhu der Edirne, cāme-i mīrahūrī ʿan serāser, 1 sevb.' Lala Mustafa Pasha became sixth vizier at the time the sultan went to Edirne to lay the foundations of his mosque; see Mehmed Zaim, Süleymaniye Library, Hafid Efendi. Ms. 237, fol. 300v.

285 Lokman, TSK, A.3595, pp. 55–57, 152–54.

286 Lubenau, 1912, 1:119; Wratislaw, 1862, p. 41.

287 Selaniki, 1989, 1:84–90.

288 Evliya, TSK, B.304, 3:154r–55v: 'benim ḥimāyemde olan sedd-i islām edirnem'de bir cāmiʿ inşā idüb . . . '.

289 Kafadar, 1995, pp. 148–49.

290 Beşir Çelebi, 1946.

291 Evliya, TSK, B.304, 3:154v.

292 Dayezade identifies the site as the former dormitory of Halberdiers (Teberdarlar) at the Old Palace; published in Sönmez, 1988a, pp. 103–4, 121.

293 See Chapters 3(II) and 4(II).

294 Evliya, TSK, B.304, 3:154v, 169r; for the myth concerning the dome of Hagia Sophia, see Necipoğlu, 1992a.

295 See Chapter 2(II).

296 Sanderson, 1931, p. 71.

297 The Old Palace was founded by Murad I (r. 1360–89). A decree orders Sinan to prepare an estimate for the bath he proposed to build for novices, BA, MD 9, #136, p. 50, dated 3 L. 977. Also see BA, KK. 1768 Büyük Ruznamçe 977–78 (1570–71), fol. 32r, for a payment made for that bath: 'mühimmāt-ı binā-i ḥammām-ı cedīd der sarāy-ı ʿatīḳ-i Edirne.' The bakery's site, originally belonging to the dormitory of Halberdiers (Baltacılar), was located near the janissary barracks; see BA, MD. 12, # 907, p. 473, dated 5 Ca. 979; MD. 12, # 949, p. 495, dated 7 Ra. 979; MD. 14, #1008, p. 699, dated 13 B. 978; MD. 14, #1456, p. 979, dated end of S. 979.

298 In 1568 kadis on the road from Istanbul to Edirne were ordered to provide food in return for money to galley slaves sent to work at the mosque (BA. MD. 7, #2376, p. 866, dated 6 Ca. 976); in 1570 the janissary agha was ordered to recruit a hundred novices for the mosque (BA, MD. 9, #122, p. 46, dated 3 L. 977); the kadi of Aydıncık was instructed in 1570 to send stone cutters from Aydıncık and Kapıdağ with their tools to Edirne according to a register with Sinan's seal listing their names (BA, MD. 9, #11, p. 4, dated 25 N. 977); in 1571 the sultan responded to Sinan's progress report about the mosque and those employed in its construction (BA, MD. 12, #985, p. 514, dated 15 Ra. 979).

299 BA, MD. 9, #216, p. 82, dated 20 L. 977.

300 The kadi of Ferecik was ordered in 1568 to send columns found at İnoz (Enez) and to cut stones according to a specified dimension from the local quarry of coloured stone (*rengāmiz ṭaş maʿdeni*), BA, MD. 7, #2145, p. 785, dated 3 Ra. 976.

301 Red stone was quarried in 1570 at Kırkkilise (Kırklareli) in Thrace; BA, MD. 9, #36, p. 14, dated 20 N. 977.

302 BA, MD. 7, #2657, p. 963, dated 25 Ca. 976.

303 BA, MD. 17, #15, p. 9, dated 25 M. 979.

304 The kadi of Aydıncık was ordered in 1568 not to allow anybody to quarry marble there without an imperial permit because this created a shortage (BA, MD. 7, #2170, p. 794, dated 6 Ra 976); in 1570 he was instructed to urgently send skilled stone cutters with their tools to the quarries (*kārhenkler*) of the Marmara Island (BA, MD. 14, #506, p. 350, dated 12 R. 978); he was asked in 1570 to send a report about how much marble was quarried in Aydıncık for the mosque under the supervision of Hüsrev Reis and Mehmed Reis (BA, MD. 14, #175, p. 125, dated 15 S. 978); the kadi of Ereğli in Thrace was ordered in 1570 to unload the marble that arrived by ship from Aydıncık (BA, MD. 14, #588, p. 415, dated 22 Ca. 978); in 1572 Sinan was informed that marble had arrived from Aydıncık at the port of Ereğli (BA, MD. 16, #341, p. 179, Z. 979).

305 BA, KK. 1768, fol. 101v, dated N. 978, money given in 1571 to a ship captain in Galata for the cutting of marble in the Marmara Island: 'berā-yi bürīden-i seng-i mermer der cezīre-i marmara ki cāmiʿ -i şerīf der maḥmiyye-i Edirne.' An order sent to the grand admiral in 1571 reports that the architect Kara Hasan (*miʿmār ḫalīfelerinden Ḳara Ḥasan*) had previously supervised twenty-five galley slaves to cut marble column bases and capitals at the Marmara Island; now he needed to borrow from the arsenal the same slaves with their tools to cut 850 marble frames (*söve*); the admiral is asked to provide a state ship to carry Hasan and his crew to that island (BA, MD. 10, #180, p. 113, dated 29 Ş. 979).

306 In 1572 the kadis of Thessaloniki and Sidhirókastrón were asked to send 4000 qintars of lead; copies of the same order were sent to the kadis of Sofia, Kratova, and Skopje for 3000 qintars of lead (BA, KK. 67 Ahkam Defteri, p. 23, dated 6 M. 980); in 1573 the kadi of Skopje was ordered to provide 8,000 more qintars of lead in addition to the previously sent quantity of 12,000 qintars (BA, KK. 67, pp. 841, 1030, dated 26 L. 980).

307 The chief gardener of Edirne was asked in 1572 to prepare an estimate with experts for the water channel (BA, MD. 10, # 246, p. 161, dated 4 L. 979); in 1574 he was ordered to send a register of costs for the completed channel that yielded 1 *lüle* and 1 *maṣura* of water (BA, MD. 26, #795, p. 277, dated 7 B. 982); money was sent to chief gardener of Edirne for the channel in 1574: 'berā-yi averden-i āb-ı cāmiʿ-i şerīf-i cedīd ki ḥāliyā binā şüde-est der maḥrūsa-i mezbūre, ki der ḳarye-i ḳaya ẓāhir şüde-est' (BA, KK. 1770, fol. 28v, dated R. 982). Documents about the calligrapher and the completion of dome arches are cited below.

308 Cited in Chapter 3(III).

309 BA, KK. 67, Ahkam Defteri, p. 776, dated 22 Ş. 980.

310 BA, KK. 67, p. 1007, dated 25 L. 980, sent to the kadi of Chios: 'Presently among the painters (*naḳḳāşlardan*) of Sakız, since it is important and necessary that the non-Muslims named Nikola Todoros, and the other [Nikola] his son, and Papa Kargopuli, and Yani the son of Papalya, and Kosta Papas must be sent for the needs of the noble mosque that is being built in Edirne, I order that when my noble decree arrives immediately send the aforementioned painters with their tools to my sublime porte, and write down their [family] relations [as guarantors] so that they are sent to Edirne, arrive there, and perform the required service in return for wages.'

311 BA, MD. 21, #461, p. 191, dated 21 Za. 980.

312 BA, MD. 22, #522, p. 267, given to Lutfi Çavuş on 27 R. 981.

313 BA, KK. 1770, fol. 13v, M. 982 (1574): 'teslim be sinān aġa ser miʿmārān-ı hāṣṣa ki ṭilā-i ʿalemhā ve pencerehā-i cāmiʿ-i şerīf der Edirne.'

314 BA, MD. 26, #770–73, p. 267, dated 28 C. 982.

315 BA, MD. 26, #848, p. 292, dated 15 B. 982.

316 The endowments included villages close to Edirne and real estate near the Selimiye complex including a

bath-house, rental rooms with an empty plot on the qibla side, other vacant parcels adjacent to the mosque, and houses bought from their owners. The waqfiyya mentions the mosque, madrasa, and *darülkurra* in Edirne, and the mausoleum at Hagia Sophia (VGM, Defter 2113, dated Ramazan 987; Defter 1550, dated the beginning of Ra. 987; Defter 2136, dated the beginning of Ra. 987).

317 BA, MD. 27, #967, p. 403, dated 15 Z. 983: '... cāmiʿlerinüñ ḥaremi taḫta ḥavli ile dutılub cevānibde ḳapu olmamaġile cemāʿat-i müslimīn cāmiʿ-i şerīfe vārduḳda müzāyaḳa çekdükleri iʿlām olunmaġın.'

318 BA, MD. 34, #467, p. 221, dated 11 Ra. 986.

319 BA, MD. 35, #416, p. 164, dated 5 C. 986.

320 BA, MD. 52, #586, p. 224, dated 10 M. 992, given to the water superintendent İsmail Çavuş.

321 The grand admiral was ordered to send the slaves with a guardian to Hüseyin Çavuş, BA, MD. 52, #707, p. 267, dated 16 S. 992.

322 See documents published in Meriç 1963; and Tuncay, 1969.

323 BA, MD. 73, #682, p. 302, dated 29 Za. 999. The fruit market seen in old photographs was a large two-storey caravansaray; see Kuran, 1986, p. 174.

324 Abdüllatif who was the shaykh of Selim II's *darülkurra* in Tire was appointed to the newly built hadith college in Edirne, where he was ordered to start his service on 23 October 1574; BA, MD. 26, #827, p. 285, dated 7 B. 982.

325 For the convincing argument that the eastern row of shops in the *arasta* was built by Sinan, see Kuruyazıcı, 1986.

326 Kuban, 1997, p. 133.

327 The minarets are 70.89 metres tall.

328 Kuban, 1997, pp. 127–28.

329 Sai, 1989, fol. 15v. For the association of the Dome of the Rock with the Last Judgment and the throne of God, see Raby and Johns, eds, 1992; Grabar, 1996.

330 The forecourt fountains of other sultanic mosques in Edirne, such as the Üç Şerefeli and the mosque of Bayezid II also lack canopies. Assuming that Sinan had left the forecourt incomplete, Kuban attributes its construction to an associate of his and thinks the pot-shaped roofless ablution fountain was never finished. He criticizes the awkward joining of the north arcade with the shorter arcades on both sides; see Kuban, 1997, pp. 145, 148.

331 For the church, see Müller-Wiener, 1977, pp. 177–83.

332 Projecting mihrabs also exist in some early Ottoman T-type mosques, such as those of Atik Ali Pasha in Istanbul and Piri Mehmed Pasha in Silivri, see illus. 85, 88.

333 Kuban, 1997, p. 143.

334 The paintings were uncovered during a restoration in the 1980s.

335 The symbolism of the muezzin's tribune is interpreted in Akın, 1995. He sees in it the distant memory of pools used in early Ottoman convents and convent-mosques representing the *axis mundi* and emphasizing mystical unification with the divine.

336 Burelli, 1988, p. 75.

337 Kuban, 1997, pp. 137–39.

338 Procopius's ekphrasis is translated in Mango, 1986, pp. 74–75; Sai, 1989, fol. 15r–v.

339 Sai, 1989, fols 14r–15v.

340 Evliya, TSK, B.304, 3:155r.

341 Ibid., 3:155r.

342 Adapted from the translation in Dijkema, 1997, pp. 58–59, no. 37.

343 A white-on-blue and blue-on-white scheme is only used in the inscriptions of the Rüstem Pasha mosque in Tahtakale.

344 Concerning the duty of congregational prayers, the white-on-red epigraphic bands above both wings of the qibla wall (4:103, 33:56) are dated 1223 and seem to be later additions. The lower white on blue bands (113:1–5, 114:1), also dated 1223, are prayers for refuge and protection from fears of the unknown, hellfire, and from evil in man's heart. The latter may be based on original inscriptions, as they are visually continuous with the epigraphic band of the mihrab recess.

345 The first lunette on the right wing of the qibla wall reads: 'Our Lord! Give unto us in the world that which is good and in the Hereafter that which is good, and guard us from the doom of Fire (2:201).' The second lunette is a variation on the same theme: 'Those who say: Our Lord! Lo! we believe. So forgive our sins and guard us from the punishment of Fire! (3:16).' The third lunette reads: 'Thou art my Protecting Friend in the world and the Hereafter. Make me to die submissive (unto Thee), and join me to the righteous (12:101).' The two tilework window lunettes on the left wing of the qibla wall continuously quote two verses from the al-ʿImran sura; the third lunette under the sultan's royal loge bears no inscription. One of the inscribed lunettes begs for God's guidance and mercy: 'O Lord! Cause not our hearts to stray after Thou hast guided us, and bestow upon us mercy from Thy Presence. Lo! Thou, only Thou art the Bestower (3:8).' The other lunette alludes to God's role as arbiter during the Last Judgment: 'Our Lord! it is Thou Who gatherest mankind together to a Day of which there is no doubt. Lo! Allah faileth not to keep the tryst (3:9).'

346 The full poem is quoted in Rifat Osman, 1999, p. 37: 'Yazdı Tīgī levḥ-i bāb-ı cennete tāriḫini / Cāmiʿ-i şāh selīmü'l-ḳalb imām-ı cemʿ-i dīn.'

347 See the Epilogue.

348 He calls it a 'retirement cell' (*ıtıkāf hücresi*); see Tanman, 2001, pp. 151–161, 239–45. It once had an ablution chamber, removed in 1837, according to Rifat Osman, 1999, p. 33.

349 Some of the tiles on that wall, removed by the occupying Russian forces in 1877, are copied in painting; see Rifat Osman, 1999, p. 32.

350 When the missing parts of the verses are added they correspond to the order of beautiful names recited in the *Vird-i Settār* of the Halveti order according to Tanman, 2001, pp. 153–54. Between the lunettes are squared kufic panels, repeating the names of Muhammad and ʿAli. Tanman interprets the unusual prominence of ʿAli as a reference to the genealogy of the Halveti order.

351 Sai, 1989, fol. 15v.

352 Ibid., fol. 14v.

353 Ibid., fol. 15v.

354 VGM, Defter 2136, p. 127.

355 Selaniki, 1989, 1:95.

356 Mehmed Aşık, TSK, E.H. 1446, fol. 397v–98v.

357 Evliya, TSK, B.304, 3:154v; Sönmez, 1988a, pp. 104, 118; Cantemir, 1979–80, 2:270–71.

358 Hibri Abdurrahman, ÖNB, Codex Vindobonensis Palatinus, Mxt. 21, fols 12r–v.

359 Ibid., fols 12v–13r.

360 Ibid., 1:89v.

361 Ibid., 3:155b.

362 Ibid., 3:155r–56v.

363 Araz, 1954.

364 Sönmez, 1988a, pp. 105–6.

365 Goodwin, 1971, p. 266.

366 See Chapter 2(II).

367 Selaniki, 1989, 1:432.

368 Ibid., 1:427–32; Kafadar, 1986a, 1991a, 1993.

369 For the sultan's illness (*mal caduco*), see an anonymous 'Relazione' dated 1579, in Albèri, 1840–55, 1:463–64; Giovanni Moro (1590) in ibid., 3:332.

370 Gianfrancesco Morosini (1585), in Albèri 3:283–84; Giovanni Moro (1590), in ibid., 3:328; Āli, IÜ. T.5959, fols 497v–98r.

371 Āli, IÜ. T.5959, fols 497v–98r; and Salomone Cormano's report published in Rosedale, 1904, pp. 19–33.

372 Lorenzo Bernardo (1592), in Albèri, 1840–55, 2:351; Giovanni Moro (1590), in ibid., 3:332.

373 For the lavish festivities, see Atasoy, 1997.

374 Cited from Morosini's report of 1585, in Peirce, 1993, p. 238.

375 For the queen's death on 22 Za. 991 (7 December 1583), see Selaniki, 1989, 1:140–41. The prince's departure for Manisa is discussed in Emecen, 1989, p. 37.

376 Hasanbeyzade, 1980, pp. 151; also see pp. 97, 161.

377 Lokman gives the completion date of 1576 (M. 984), IÜ, F.1404, fol. 49r; and TSK, H.1321, fol. 103v. In 1577 the kadi of Mecca was ordered to have the floors under the finished domes paved (BA, MD. 33, #1, p. 1, dated 3 N. 985). That year the text of a foundation inscription was sent to Mecca (BA, MD. 31, #858, p. 386, dated 1 Ş. 985).

378 The madrasa is mentioned in VGM, Defter 2136, dated middle of Ş. 1006 (1598).

379 See Chapter 5.

380 Lokman gives the date M. 984 (1576) for the initiation of renovations in Medina, Lokman, IÜ, F.1404, fol. 49r. That year, the governor of Jidda, Ahmed Beg, who had been in charge of repairs in Mecca was appointed to supervise the construction of a madrasa and hospice for the sultan in Medina (BA, MD. 28, #180, p. 76, dated 25 B. 984; and MD. 28, #381, p. 165, beginning of Ca. 984). Murad III's waqfiyya dated 1598 is in VGM, Defter 2136, mid Ş. 1006.

381 The appointment of Mimar İlyas in 1589 was announced to the kadi of Mecca in BA, MD. 64, #121, p. 45, dated 11 R. 997. The Sharif of Mecca was asked to help in this project; BA, MD. 64, #128, p. 46, dated 14 R. 997.

382 See the waqfiyya cited above. In 1578 the minbar of the Prophet's mosque was ordered to be replaced with a new one for which the architect Zeynizade was sent from Egypt (BA, MD. 36, #909, p. 346, dated 9 R. 987); in 1579 money was sent for the minbar and other repairs at the Prophet's mosque and mausoleum (MD. 40, #201, p. 88, dated 12 Ş. 987); an elementary school on top of a water dispenser was ordered in 1580 (MD. 43, #533, p. 282, dated 29 Ş. 988). Decrees dated 1585 and 1588 identify the chief court painter Lutfullah as the building supervisor of a water dispenser, convent, and hospice in Medina (MD. 60, #58–59, p. 25, dated 28 L. 993; MD. 64, #14, p. 4, dated 28 Ş. 996); the sultan endowed villages in Egypt for his new hospice whose waqfiyya was sent to Medina in 1589 (MD. 72, # 236, p. 121, 26 Ca. 1002).

383 A decree issued in 1595 explains that the convent was endowed for sufis; BA, MD. 73, #500, p. 214, dated 25 N. 1003.

384 Discussed in Chapter 3(I). The sultan's waqfs in Kars are recorded in VGM, Defter 458, dated 999, pp. 348–51.

385 A decree addressed to the building supervisor of the convent in Konya shows that its rooms and assembly hall were close to completion and that lead was being sent from Istanbul (BA, MD. 53, #671, #673, p. 233, dated 21 Z. 992): '...ḳonyada ḫānḳāh-ı şerīfde binā olınan ḥücrāt ve cemīʿetḫāne mühimmi içün ... '. For the Turkish inscription dated 992 (1584–85), which mentions Murad III's construction of a 'ḫānḳāh' with rooms 'buyūt' housing Mevlevi dervishes, see Konyalı, 1997, pp. 649–50.

386 The convent of the shaykh Yahya Efendi in Beşiktaş is

attributed to Murad III in Hasanbeyzade, 1980, pp. 151–52. The mausoleum and madrasa of this convent are included in Sinan's autobiographies; see Kuran, 1986, p. 334, no. 203; p. 354, no. 275. For a domed mosque with four half-domes built in the name of Murad III at the castle of Navarino in 1576–77, see G. Tanyeli, 1996; BA, MD. zeyl 13, #295, p. 112, dated 984.

387 The decrees and foundation inscription, which gives the dates 991 M. and 994 Z., are published in Su, 1940.

388 Emecen, 1983–87, p. 188, no. 1.

389 Ibid., pp. 178–79, 188–89 (nos. 2, 3). The Arabic waqfiyya dated 982 (1584) is mentioned in Su, 1940, p. 8.

390 TSA, D.6947, fols 1r–28v, dated the beginning of Ra. 984.

391 BA, MD. 30, #521, p. 224, dated 13 Ra. 985; published in Su, 1940, p. 21, where 'ṭurre' is misread as 'ṭaşra.'

392 BA, MD. 34, #57, p. 29, dated 14 M. 986.

393 BA, MD. 30, #521, p. 224, dated 13 Ra. 985; published in Su, 1940, p. 22.

394 TSA, D.7006/1, dated beginning of Ş. 988, fols 30v–37v; another copy of the same waqfiyya is in TSA, D.7006/2, fols 39r–49r.

395 Emecen, 1983–87, p. 180; pp. 190–91, nos. 4 and 7.

396 Su, 1940, p. 23.

397 Ibid., p. 24.

398 Ibid., p. 24; Emecen, 1983–87, p. 181.

399 Su, 1940, p. 24; Emecen, 1983–87, p. 181.

400 BA, MD. 49, #444, p. 132, dated 19 C. 991: '... içine ḳaraçav çatılub yan ḳubbeleri yıḳılub dörd cānibe cedīd temel ḳazılub ve öñine ṣoffa temeli ḳazılmaġile ...'; published in Su, 1940, p. 25.

401 BA, MD. 49, # 447, p. 133, dated 19 C. 991; published in Su, 1940, pp. 25–26.

402 Dated 26 C. 991, published in Su, 1940, p. 26.

403 Emecen, 1983–87, p. 182.

404 BA, MD. 58, #885, p. 346, dated 8 L. 993; cited in Emecen, 1989, p. 103. Given to the 'naḳḳāşbaşı' on 10 L. 993, the decree mentions 'ḫāṣṣa naḳḳāşlarımdan üstād meḥmed ḫalīfe ile oniki nefer naḳḳāş.'

405 ASV, Senato, Deliberationi Costantinopoli, Segreta, Registro 6, fol. 175r (12 October 1584); and fol. 181r (29 December 1584); Evliya, 1999, pp. 96–97.

406 Su, 1940, p. 29.

407 Mehmed Aşık, TSK, E.H. 1446, fols 323v–24r.

408 Emecen, 1983–87, p. 183.

409 The construction of the outer precinct wall had to wait until 1602; see Emecen, 1983–87, pp. 183–84.

410 Ibid., p. 185.

411 TSA. D.7006/1–2 drawn up in Ra. 984 and D.6974, fols 1r–28v. The kitchen (*maṭbaḫ*) and pantry (*kilār*) entrusted to a shaykh is mentioned in D.7006/1, fol. 22r. The pre-existing hospice was expanded in 1589 according to Emecen, 1989, p. 103.

412 Emecen, 1983–87, pp. 180, 185.

413 TSA, D.7006/1, fols 38r, 40v; D.7006/2, fols 54r, 58r.

414 Goodwin, 1971, p. 318.

415 The octagonal library between the madrasa and mosque, added in 1812 by Karaosmanzade Hüseyin Ağa, may have replaced the elementary school. Kuran finds it difficult to attribute either the madrasa or the hospice to Sinan; Kuran, 1986, pp. 217–19.

416 See the map of Manisa and its monuments in Evliya, 1999, pp. 322–23.

417 For Hafsa Sultan's complex, see Emecen, 1989, p. 95; Yörükoğlu, 1984.

418 This resemblance is noted in Kuran, 1986, p. 219.

419 Ibid., p. 222.

420 See Chapter 8.

421 For renovations between 1952 and 1964, see Kuran, 1986, p. 221.

422 Su, 1940, pp. 5–6.

423 Ibid., p. 5. Cited in Evliya, 1999, pp. 96–99.

424 Evliya, 1999, p. 96.

425 Goodwin, 1971, p. 321.

426 Hasanbeyzade, 1980, p. 151.

427 Evliya, 1999, pp. 94–95.

428 See Chapters 7 and 8.

429 B. Spuler, 'Ḳirim', EI(2), 5:136–43; Ürekli, 1989.

430 In 1538 Sahib Giray had built the fortress of Gözleve and its landing station with imperial permission; see Gökbilgin, ed., 1973, pp. 45–46; Ürekli, 1989, pp. 35, 40, 85.

431 Gökbilgin, ed., 1973, pp. 134, 136; Ürekli, 1989, pp. 42–44.

432 The mosque is mentioned in all autobiographies, but the non-extant mausoleum is only cited in TM; see Kuran, 1986, p. 303, no. 102; p. 332, no. 201. For the hypothesis that Sinan may briefly have visited Crimea to lay the foundations of the mosque, leaving its completion to an assistant, see Aslanapa, 1986, pp. 207–8.

433 The inscription in two lines reads: 'Giray ḫānuñ Gözleve cāmiʿ-i şerīfidür, / Sene 1552 tāriḫinde', followed by the Basmala and the date 1324 (1906–7).

434 The plan and photograph published in Aslanapa, 1989, pp. 206–7, show a walled-in portico (now opened up) and collapsed minarets (now intact).

435 Ibid., pp. 207–8.

436 Spuler, 'Ḳirim', EI(2) 5:137.

437 Özcan, ed., 1994, p. 53.

438 Evliya Çelebi, 1986–1938, 7:564–66.

439 Ürekli, 1989, pp. 47–57.

CHAPTER 7

1 Peirce, 1993, p. 58.

2 Busbecq similarly reports that the queen was accused of sorcery, ibid., p. 63.

3 S. A. Skilliter, 'Khurrem', EI(2), 5:66–67. Hans Dernschwam (1553–55) says the sultan's 'Russian' wife was brought up in his sister's household and then given to his mother before joining the imperial harem; Dernschwam, 1923, p. 136. Mekki (1557–58) says the queen was of Russian origin and a former concubine of Süleyman's mother who presented her to him while he was a prince; see Kamil, 1937, p. 78. She is referred to as 'Ḫürremşāh' in Ālī, Nuruosmaniye Library, Ms. 3409, fol. 123v.

4 Zen (1524), in Albèri, 1844–50, 3:93–97; Bragadin (1526) in ibid., 3:102.

5 Peirce, 1993, p. 59.

6 The marriage is mentioned in Daniello de' Ludovisi (1534), Albèri, 1844–50, 1:28. For an undated description of the wedding, see Peirce, 1993, pp. 61–62.

7 Hürrem's letters to Süleyman are published in Uluçay, 1956; cited in Peirce, 1993, pp. 63–65.

8 The letters of Hürrem and her daughter Mihrümah to Sigismund I and Sigismund II are published in Uçtum, 1980.

9 Dernschwam, 1923, pp. 136–37; Busbecq is cited in Peirce, 1993, p. 90.

10 For Rüstem Pasha's promotion of the brothers of his wife, born from the queen 'ḫürremşāh', see Ālī, Nuruosmaniye Library, Ms. 3409, fol. 123v.

11 Kamil, 1937, p. 78.

12 Examples include Bülbül Hatun's mosque in Ladik (1517), a domed cube with a three-domed porch; and Hüsnishah Hatun's mosque in Manisa (1490–91) which has a five-domed portico and paraphrases the layout of the Üç Şerefeli mosque in Edirne; see Yüksel, 1995, pp. 335–40, 419. For the single-domed mosque with a three-domed portico built in Edirne for Mehmed II's wife Sitti Sultan (1484), see Bayrakal, 2001, pp. 77–82.

13 Rüstem Pasha, ÖNB, Codex Vindobonensis Palatinus, Mxt. 339, fols 282r–v.

14 Talikizade, TSK, A.3592, fols 29v–30r.

15 The waqfiyya is published in Kürkçüğlu, 1962, p. 46; for the title deed, see Stephan, 1944, p. 171.

16 See the patronage of Mihrümah in Chapter 8.

17 Süleyman's initial repair of the Meccan water channel built 'during the caliphate of Harun al-Rashid by Zubayda Khatun', is mentioned after his conquest of Belgrade (1521) in the chronicle of Kemalpaşazade, 1996, p. 123. The author reports that famous histories record the 'previous Islamic sultans' who repaired that channel.

18 Like Talikizade, the geographer Mehmed Aşık recognizes Hürrem's patronage of the Meccan water channel; he says the people of the city and pilgrims prayed for her soul whenever they used its water; see Mehmed Aşık, TSK, E.H. 1446, fol. 165v.

19 Ramazanzade, 1862, p. 301. This information is repeated later on by Ālī, Nuruosmaniye Library, Ms. 3409, fols 118v–19r; Hasanbeyzade, 1980, p. 62.

20 Cited from Jacopo Ragazzoni (1571) in Skilliter, 1982, pp. 517.

21 Peirce, 1993, pp. 128–29.

22 The Turkish and Arabic versions are summarized in Taşkıran, 1972. Copies of the waqfiyya dated 947 (1540) are in TIEM, no. 2191; and VGM, Defter 608/2. Copies of the waqfiyya dated M. 958 (1551) include TIEM, no. 2194; Süleymaniye Library, Esad Efendi, Ms. 3752; Süleymaniye Library, Şehid Ali Paşa, Ms. 943; and VGM, Defter 2142.

23 It is shown on von Vincke's Ankara map of 1838; see Cezar, 1983, p. 52, fig. 30.

24 Daye Ayşe Hatun's masjid in Kağıthane was upgraded into a Friday mosque, its foundation inscription gives the date 951 (1544–45); see Ayvansarayi, 2000, p. 319.

25 Belonging to Bayezid II's waqf, this converted church incorporated the tombs of two martyred Arab warrior saints. Toklu Dede, the keeper of the tombs after the conquest of Constantinople, was subsequently buried next to them. Hürrem donated funds for oil used in the convent-masjid's lamps. For this building, see Müller-Wiener, 1994, pp. 206–8; Ayvansarayi, 2000, pp. 159–62; Vatin and Yerasimos, 2001, p. 110.

26 A decree of 1549 donates a hundred aspers from the poll tax of Jews for the salaries and food expenses of the shaykh and dervishes of the queen's convent in 'Balat'; TSA. E.7788 (dated middle of Z. 955). For the conversion of this convent into a madrasa, see Atai, 1989, pp. 168–69. It is referred to as 'medrese-i ḳahriyye, nām-ı dīger ḫānḳāh, der bāb-ı ṭop, 50 [aspers]', in a list of madrasas published in Özergin, 1973–74, p. 278.

27 This 'new madrasa sited near the Edirne Gate', complemented the higher-ranked madrasa attached to Hürrem's mosque complex at Avratpazarı; see the account book of her waqf dated 965 (1558) in Taşkıran, 1972, pp. 185–89. The now lost madrasa is mentioned in Sinan's autobiographies; see Kuran, 1986, p. 342, no. 232.

28 Dernschwam, 1923, pp. 136–37; another version of same story is found in the travelogue of Sandys, 1621, pp. 158–59.

29 Meriç, 1965, p. 24.

30 The quarter, known later on as Avratpazarı, is referred to as 'Hacı Revvas' (Başçı Hacı Mahmud) in TIEM, no. 2191, fols 29v–31r.

31 Ayvansarayi, 2000, p. 114.

32 Cited in Taşkıran, 1972, pp. 85–86; Saatçi, 1988, pp. 145–47, no. 55. The expansion was approved by Ahmed I to whom it was petitioned by the chief white eunuch administering the late queen's waqf.

33 Taşkıran, 1972, pp. 102–3.

34 Ibid., pp. 114–15; Saatçi, 1988, pp. 17–19, no. 5. The first line of the inscription mentioning the patron is effaced; the building reached completion in the month of R. 947 (August–September 1540).
35 A much later completion date, 957 (1550), is given in Kuran, 1986, p. 40.
36 TSA, D.3904, fol. 1r.
37 Ibid., fol. 3r.
38 Taşkıran, 1972, p. 43.
39 TSA, D.3904, fol. 1v.
40 Ibid., fol. 1v, the 'site of the kitchen' (*cā-yi maṭbaḫ*) cost 44,000 aspers. Other expenses include the boiler of the bath-house (in the Jewish quarter), houses, and shops.
41 Ibid., fol. 1v.
42 Ibid., fol. 3v: 'bāha-i kāşī berā-yi ḳalḳān-ı bāb-ı ḥarem-i maṭbaḫ ve pencerehā; bāb 1: 1300; pencere 6: 1620.
43 TSA, E.9517 (dated end of M. 946); E.9099 (dated R. 946); E.7766 (dated beginning of R. 947).
44 Barkan and Ayverdi, eds, 1970, pp. 434–35, no. 2496.
45 Taşkıran, 1972, pp. 47, 133–34.
46 Kürkçüoğlu, 1962, pp. 40–42.
47 TIEM, no. 2191, fol. 42r.
48 Özcan, 1994, p. 49; also discussed under the Şehzade Mehmed complex in Chapter 6.
49 For the 'Forum Arcadii', see Müller-Wiener, 1977, pp. 250–53. The column was removed after being damaged during an earthquake in 1719.
50 Taşkıran, 1972, pp. 100, 187.
51 TIEM, no. 2191, fol. 42r.
52 Dernschwam, 1923, pp. 97–98. For the khan of Bayram Pasha, see Necdet Sakaoğlu, 'Avrat Pazarları', ISTA, 1:430–31. Reinhold Lubenau (1587) reports that the weekly market at Avratpazarı specialized in the sale of 'tulip bulbs, diverse Turkish plants and flowers, as well as a medley of edibles'; Lubenau, 1914, 2:155.
53 Taşkıran, 1972, p. 80.
54 Laguna, 1983, p. 320.
55 Sanderson, 1931, p. 77.
56 Barkan and Ayverdi, eds, 1970, p. 341, no. 2023.
57 Examples attributed to Sinan include the masjid of Muhsine Hatun (wife of the grand vizier İbrahim Pasha) at Kumkapı, the masjid of the daughter of the mufti Çivizade at Davudpaşa, and the Friday mosque of Hamami Hatun in Samatya; see Kuran, 1986, p. 279, no. 29; p. 307, no. 115; p. 314, no. 142. In the district of Davudpaşa Süleyman's sister Shahsultan built a convent, later converted into a madrasa; see Chapter 8.
58 Originally the masjid was called Etmekçibaşı; see Ayvansarayi, 2000, p. 231; Barkan and Ayverdi, eds, 1970, p. 342, no. 2026. Another neighbouring masjid built by a woman is that of Keyçi (Kiçi) Hatun, endowed in 1485.
59 Kuran, 1987, pp. 46, 48.
60 The al-Ikhlas sura (112:1–4) inscribed at the centre of the dome affirms the oneness of God.
61 A comparable building with an octagonal courtyard is the madrasa Sinan built for Rüstem Pasha near his palace at Cağaloğlu; see Kuran, 1986, p. 345, no. 243. For the hospital, see ibid., p. 361, no. 299.
62 Evliya, 1896–1983, 1:165.
63 Stephan, 1944, p. 180.
64 The Turkish waqfiyya dated 1552 is published in Stephan, 1944. The Arabic waqfiyya dated 1557 is preserved in Istanbul, Türk ve İslam Sanatı Müzesi (TIEM, no. 2192).
65 The accounts of expenses for Hürrem's other waqfs, dated 1558 and 1560, also refer to her as prince Mehmed's mother; published in Taşkıran, 1972, pp. 118, 185.
66 The title deeds of villages and lands Süleyman donated for Hürrem's pious foundation in Jerusalem between May 1550 and July 1560 identify her as the 'mother of prince Selim'; see Singer, 2002, pp. 44–46, 68. One wonders whether these documents were copied after Selim's victory in Konya.
67 Meriç, 1965, p. 25. For the madrasa of Haseki Sultan in Jerusalem, see Baltacı, 1976, p. 567. Kuran misidentifies the mosque as a reference to Süleyman's renovation of the Haram; see Kuran, 1986, p. 273, no. 11.
68 The hospice in Mecca is listed in all autobiographies, while the one in Medina is just mentioned in the TE; see Kuran, 1986, p. 362, nos. 304–5.
69 TSA, E.5221/2 (dated the middle of R. 956) and E.5404/13 (dated the middle of Ca. 956).
70 See Chapter 5(I).
71 TSK, K.888, fol. 405v, dated 10 N. 959 (10 August 1552).
72 Singer, 2002, p. 107.
73 Ibid., pp. 105–6.
74 TSK, K.888, fol. 283r (dated 2 B. 959). Nakkaş Mehmed's building activities in Jerusalem are discussed in Chapter 5.
75 Ibid., fols 283r–87v (dated 23 B. 959). For the emissary Abdülkerim and the successive waqf administrators of the queen's complex in Jerusalem, see Singer, 2002, pp. 99–118.
76 Süleyman's earliest inscriptions on the windows of the Dome of the Rock are dated 935 (1528–29); his latest inscriptions date from 972 (1564–65). The date 959 (1551–52) is given for the completion of tile revetments at the Dome of the Rock in Āli, Nuruosmaniye Library, Ms. 3409, fol. 118v. The tiles on the drum are dated 952 (1545–46), while the lower walls were signed in 959 (1551–52) by 'Abdallah al-Tabrizi; see Hillenbrand, 2002, p. 45. The Dome of the Chain has tiles dating from 960 (1561–62); ibid., p. 56.
77 TIEM, Ms. 2192, fol. 12r.
78 Peirce, 1993, pp. 204–5; Singer, 2002, pp. 71–80. Hürrem's hospice was known among the Christians as the 'Hospital of St. Helena'.
79 Burgoyn, 1987, p. 487; Myres, 2000.
80 Stephan, 1944, pp. 182–83.
81 For the chief architects of Jerusalem, see Atallah, 2000.
82 Singer, 2002, pp. 150–56.
83 See Chapter 6.
84 Dernschwam, 1923, pp. 22–23. For the bridge, see Eyice 1964; Kuran, 1986, p. 402, no. 462.
85 TE in Meriç, 1965, pp. 83, 105; Sai, 1897, p. 32.
86 Albèri, 3:148.
87 For one of her fountain inscriptions, see Dijkema, 1997, p. 55, no. 34.
88 Taşkıran, 1972, pp. 185–93. Süleyman donated villages in 1557 for Hürrem's waqf in Vize (Thrace), TSA, E.765, dated 12 Ca. 964. For the bath-house near Hagia Sophia, see Kuran, 1986, p. 390, no. 414.
89 BA, MD. 3, #117, p. 48, dated 11 L. 966; published in Aykut et al., eds, 1993, p. 57, no. 117.
90 Turan, 1961.
91 See Chapter 6.
92 Marcantonio Donini (1562), in Albèri, 1844–50, 3:184–85.
93 BA, MD. 3, #871, p. 298, dated 26 Ca. 967; published in Aykut et al., eds, 1993, pp. 393–94, no. 871.
94 Ibid., #1102, p. 373, dated 17 Ş. 967; published in Aykut et al., eds, 1993, p. 488, no. 1102.
95 Ibid., #1193, p. 398, dated 3 N. 967; published in Aykut et al., eds, 1993, p. 524, no. 1193.
96 Ibid., #1272, p. 426, dated 29 N. 967; published in Aykut et al., eds, 1993, p. 558, no. 1272.
97 Ibid., #1496, p. 503, dated 18 Z. 967; published in Aykut et al., eds, 1993, p. 647.
98 For the photograph (Abdülhamid Album, no. 90412), see Eyice, 1964, p. 741; and Ayverdi, 1981–82, 4:147.
99 Betzek, 1979, pp. 19–20.
100 Du Fresne-Canaye, 1897, pp. 44–45.
101 Soranzo, 1856, p. 52.
102 Pigafetta, 1890, p. 211; Lescalopier, 1921, p. 33; Gerlach, 1674, p. 514.
103 Evliya, TSK, B.304, 3:147v.
104 For her dowry, see Jacopo Ragazzoni (1571), in Albèri, 1844–50, 3:97; cited by Skilliter, 1982, p. 517.
105 For the 'Venetian Sultana', see Skilliter, 1983. Arbel thinks the queen had a Corfiote Greek origin because Giacomo Soranzo (1566) reported that a poor man from Corfu claimed to have found Nurbanu's impoverished Corfiote mother, Regina Quartani (Quartano, Kartanou). Like Paros, Corfu was Venetian territory and several members of the noble Greek family of Quartani had belonged to local councils. The *bailo* appended the woman's letter behind which Nurbanu scribbled: 'Let my mother be brought here without delay!'; see Arbel, 1992, pp. 248–51, 257. The letter, however, seems rather suspect and using it as evidence for Nurbanu's descent from the Quartani family is problematic.
106 Cavalli, 1914, pp. 10–11; cited in Arbel, 1992, p. 248.
107 Morosini (1585), in Albèri, 1844–50, 3:280. According to Costantino Garzoni (1573) she was 'una sua schiava di Corfu di casa Baffo', ibid., 1:403. This is repeated by Andrea Badoaro (1573) who says she was 'Corfiutta di Casa Baffo', ibid., 1:362.
108 Paolo Contarini (1583) says she loved the Venetians because she remembered being born as a 'gentile-donna veneziana' and her house on the canal, ibid., 3:235. Arbel believes that Nurbanu and the Republic kept alive rumours about her identity as the scion of a Venetian patrician family to encourage diplomacy, see Arbel, 1992.
109 Cited in Peirce, 1993, pp. 222–23.
110 Some of Nurbanu's letters were written on her behalf by the Jewess Esther Kira; see Skilliter, 1982.
111 Ibid., p. 525.
112 For the birth of the three sultanas and Fatma Sultan's birth in 968 (1560–61) after the war of the princes in Konya, see Vusuli, Fatih Millet Kütüphanesi, Ali Emiri T.321, fols 15v, 17v–18r, 54r.
113 Cited in Peirce, 1993, p. 93.
114 Ibid., pp. 129, 213–14.
115 Albèri, 1844–50, 2:237.
116 Ibid., 3:234–35.
117 Ibid., 3:235; cited in Peirce, 1993, p. 91.
118 Cited in Peirce, 1993, p. VII.
119 During the extensive renovations of the harem quarters in the Topkapı Palace, Murad III resided in his mother's Yenikapı palace between the Edirnekapı and Topkapı gates near the land walls; see Necipoğlu, 1991, pp. 165, 172.
120 Selaniki, 1989, 1:140–41.
121 BA, MD. 52, #466, p. 183 (dated 14 Z. 991).
122 Her Arabic waqfiyya is in VGM, Defter 1550 [Kasa 121], pp. 25/50 to 40/89, dated the beginning of R. 990 (translated into Turkish in VGM, Defter 1766, no. 27, pp. 136–70). For the posthumous approval of Nurbanu's endowment by Murad III, who appointed Pir Ali b. Mustafa as the administrator of her waqf, see VGM, Defter 1766, pp. 168–70. A Turkish summary of her waqfiyya is in TSK, E.H.3064, fols 1v–9r.
123 For the convent in Üsküdar and its first shaykh, see Tanman, 1988a, pp. 12–14; Tanman, 1988b, p. 320. The convent in Lapseki had a shaykh and ten sufis; the one in Üsküdar was staffed with a shaykh, thirty sufis, and a gatekeeper; see TSK, E.H.3064, fols 3v, 4v.

124 VGM, Defter 1766, pp. 137, 155.

125 The building supervisor Mustafa belonged to the royal cavalry troops (*sipahioğlan*); see BA, MD. 14, #1326, p. 900, dated 21 N. 978; repeated in MD, 12, #102, p. 49, dated 23 N. 978.

126 BA. MD. 12, #105, p. 50, dated 23 N. 978. Repeated in MD. 14, #1685, p. 1142, dated 25 N. 978.

127 BA, MD. 14, #1415, p. 953, dated 26 Z. 978; MD. 10, #535, p. 328, dated 4 M. 979; MD. 14, #1511, p. 1021, dated 10 M. 979; MD. 17, #10, p. 6, dated 25 M. 979.

128 BA, MD. 12, #1080, p. 566, dated 4 Za. 979.

129 BA. MD. 21, #775, p. 328, dated 11 M. 981.

130 BA, MD. 26, #264, p. 111, dated 4 R. 982.

131 BA, MD. 28, #607, p. 251, dated the beginning of Ca. 984.

132 BA, MD. 30, #141, p. 59, dated 3 S. 985.

133 BA, MD. 34, #60–63, dated 14 M. 986.

134 Mehmed Aşık, TSK, E.H. 1446, fols 394r–v. The same date is given in Evliya, 1896–1938, 1:476; and İnciciyan, 1976, p. 134.

135 Gerlach refers to it in 1578 as the church of the king's mother in Üsküdar (Kaysers Mutter kirche ausser Scutari); see Gerlach, 1674, pp. 499–500; Schweigger, 1964, pp. 135–36.

136 BA, MD. 25, #634, p. 251, dated 19 B. 986. The Horse Market is mentioned in Nurbanu's waqfiyya; TSK, E.H. 3064, fol. 2v; VGM. Defter 1766, p. 143.

137 BA, MD. 35, #720, p.284, dated 27 B. 986. Copies of the same order are in MD. 39, #182–185, pp. 75–76, dated 27 L. 987. Another decree explains that these lands were previously the 'paşmaḳlıḳ' of the sultan's aunt Mihrümah Sultan, MD. 39, #238, p. 96, dated 20 Za. 987. The revenue collectors of Nurbanu's waqf were based in Üsküdar, Yanbolu, Rodoscuk, and Yeni–il; for her endowed properties, see BA, Vakfiye 18/5, dated 990 (1582).

138 BA, MD. 37, #660, p. 59, dated 29 Z. 986: Hasan Mehter was given a timar worth 3000 aspers for his service in the noble mosque of 'vālide sulṭān ḥażretleri.' MD. 37, #701, p. 63, dated 2 M. 987: 'Mehmed came for his services in the noble mosque.'

139 BA. MD. 39, #578, p. 301, dated 13 S. 988.

140 Kuran, 1986, p. 187; Tanman, 1988.

141 BA, MD. 42, #289, p. 65, dated 23 Ca. 989. The bath in Ayakapı is mentioned in Nurbanu's waqfiyya; VGM, Defter 1766, p. 136; TSK, E.H. 3064, fol. 2r. This single bath dated 989 (1581–82) is cited among Sinan's works in his autobiographies; see Kuran, 1986, p. 400, no. 457.

142 The decree dated 25 R. 997 is published in Ayvansarayi, 1985, pp. 362–63. For the endowed baths of Nurbanu's complex – near the mosque, near the shore of Üsküdar (Yeşil Direkli Hamam), at Dikilitaş (Çemberlitaş), Ayakapı, and Yenikapı); see Konyalı, 1950, p. 84; Ayvansarayi, 2000, p. 489. The baths are listed in the wafiyya; see VGM, Defter 1766, pp. 137–40. They are also mentioned in Sinan's autobiographies; see Kuran, 1986, pp. 400–1, nos. 457, 459, 460. For fountains around Nurbanu's complex, see Çeçen, 1991b, pp. 44–54.

143 The new building supervisor appointed in 1584 for this project was Çaşnigir Ahmed Agha (BA, MD, 53, #310, p. 111, dated 26 B. 992). He became promoted chief armourer in 1585; see Selaniki, 1:157.

144 BA, MD. 52, #241, p. 100, dated 14 L. 991. A copy was sent to the kadi of Marmara and the steward of the marble quarry (*kārhenkçiler ketḫüdāsı*), MD. 52, #242, p. 100 (here 2000 cubits of slabs for steps are mentioned instead of 200 cubits).

145 BA, MD. 60, #261, p. 106, dated 9 Z. 993. For the inscription of 992 (1584–85), see Saatçi, 1988, pp. 118–20, no. 44. The bath at Çemberlitaş is listed among Sinan's works in TM, Meriç, 1965, p. 45.

146 BA, MD. 61, #100, p. 37, dated 3 B. 994: the kadi of Üsküdar is ordered to provide the builders and carpenters requested by a letter of the chief architect Sinan for the bath-house of the sultan's mother. The order was handed over to the water channel superintendent İsmail Çavuş, with a copy sent to the kadi of Galata. The bath-house in Üsküdar is listed in all autobiographies of Sinan; see Kuran, 1986, p. 401, no. 460.

147 VGM, Defter 1766, pp. 137–44. For the bath-house near the complex, see Kuran, 1986, p. 401, no. 459.

148 TSK, E.H. 3064, fol. 1v.

149 The dome size of Nurbanu's mosque is also surpassed by those of Rüstem Pasha (15.2 m) and Nişancı Mehmed Pasha (14.2).

150 See the Muradiye in Chapter 6.

151 Two other mosques designed by Sinan in the 1580s have unusual forecourts without madrasa cells: Mesih Mehmed Pasha and Nişancı Mehmed Pasha (see Chapter 10). The original domed ablution fountain of the forecourt in Nurbanu's mosque, destroyed by a collapsed tree and replaced with a new one, is illustrated in Konyalı, 1950, pp. 77, 82.

152 Kuban, 1997, p. 110; Günay, 1998, p. 73; Tanman, 1988a, p. 4; Kuran, 1986, p. 189.

153 Konyalı, 1950, p. 80; Ayvansarayi, 1985, p. 125; Ayvansarayi, 2000, p. 489; Saatçi, 1988, pp. 116–17, no. 43.

154 Ayvansarayi cites another chronogram composed by Murad III for his mother's mosque: 'As a pure charity this new light-filled mosque was built in the present year, / By the Valide Sultan as a fountainhead of pious merit.// Muradi wrote the following chronogram for the charity of his mother: / 'May her mosque count as a good deed for the Valide Sultan!' 990 (1582–83)'; Ayvansarayi, 1985, p. 117.

155 For Mehmed Agha's patronage ties with Davud, see Chapter 14.

156 The brothers Hacı Ferhad and Hacı Mehmed of Konya had obtained the queen's permission in 1582–83 to use leftover materials in the Tabaklar mosque; see Ayvansarayi, 2000, p. 512. Mimar Kurban Nasuh is said to have been executed in 995 (1586) for building his masjid in the Debbağlar quarter with materials stolen from Nurbanu's complex; cited in Konyalı, 1976–77, 1:193–205.

157 Palerne, 1991, pp. 273.

158 VGM, Defter 1766, p. 164.

159 Schweigger, 1964, pp. 135–36.

160 VGM, Defter 1766, p. 139, mentions Mehmed Agha's waqfs in Üsküdar at the Debbağlar quarter near the complex. The costs of his garden wall are recorded in a document dated 1585–86, TSA, D.6161, fol. 1v: 'Becihet-i iḫrācāt-ı dıvār-ı bostān-ı ḥażret-i aġa-yi dārüssaʿāde der üsküdar be-maʿrifet-i Pir ʿAli aġa el-mütevellī ve Muṣṭafā Beg bevvāb el-vāḳiʿ fī şehr-i ramażān el-mübārek sene 993 ila ġāye-i ṣafer sene 994.' For the water Mehmed Agha conducted in 1585 to his fountains in Üsküdar, see BA, MD. 60, #262, p. 106, dated 9 Z. 993. Another order concerns the addition of the water Mehmed Agha brought from Bulgurlu for his fountains to the queen mother's water channel; see BA, MD. 60, #266, p. 107, dated 9 Z. 993.

161 Like Hürrem's waqfiyya, that of Nurbanu requires the hospital physicians to treat patients kindly, as if they were close relatives.

162 For the appointment of the professor, see Kuran, 1986, p. 187.

163 For the convent, see Tanman, 1988a and 1988b.

164 Similar windows appear in the Kazasker İvaz Efendi mosque, completed in 1586, but omitted from Sinan's autobiography.

165 See Chapter 2.

166 Stylistically the mosque tiles are dated to *c.* 1585 in Denny, 1998, pp. 100–6. The façade inscriptions are recorded in Konyalı, 1976–77, 1:145. From right to left: lunette 1 (48:3), 2 (48:3), 3 (smaller lunette of the minaret door, half of the monotheistic formula), 4 (39:53), 5 (39:53); 6 (39:53), 7 (39:53), 8 (other half of the monotheistic formula on the second minaret door), 9 (48:4), 10 (48:4).

167 This calligrapher was a follower of Şeyh Hamdullah (d. 1520) rather than of Ahmed and Hasan Karahisari; see Derman, 1989, p. 289.

168 For the convent in Kadırgalimanı, see Chapter 8.

169 Mehmed Aşık, TSK, E.H. 1446, fols 394r–v.

170 Evliya, 1896–1938, 1:473–76.

171 Examples include the posthumous complexes of Bayezid II's mother in Tokat (1485) and Selim I's mother in Trabzon (1505–14); see Yüksel, 1983, pp. 49–54, 380–88. The complex of Süleyman's mother in Manisa (1522–23) was posthumously amplified in 1538.

CHAPTER 8

1 She is also known as Devletshahi or Shahi Sultan. For her biography, see Uluçay, 1980, pp. 32–33; Suraiya Faroqhi, 'Shah Sultan', EI(2) 9:199–200.

2 Baha Tanman, 'Merkez Efendi', ISTA 5:396–97; Hulvi, 1993, pp. 460–68. Merkez Efendi was the shaykh of the Koğacı Dede convent in Aksaray before he moved to Hafsa Sultan's convent in Manisa (*c.* 1512–29); see Hulvi, 1993, pp. 463–64.

3 Ayvansarayi, 2000, p. 255.

4 Hürrem's donations are discussed in Chapter 7. For Shaykh Merkezzade Ahmed Efendi, who is buried in Uşak (d. 970/1562–63), see Hulvi, 1993, pp. 469–70.

5 Ibid., p. 464.

6 Ibid., p. 467; Ayvansarayi, 2000, p. 280.

7 Āli, Nuruosmaniye Library, Ms. 3409, fols 121r–v; Lutfi Paşa, 1991, p. 61.

8 Cited in Faroqhi, EI(2) 9:199.

9 Copies of her Turkish waqfiyya are in TSK, E.H. 3032; VGM, Defter 1993, dated the middle of Ş. 977 (Istanbul Esas 7, 945/2640). A shorter, undated version is in TSK, E.H. 3064, fols 18v–20v.

10 Mihrümah's representative Behram Kethüda come to the shariʿa court to testify about Shahsultan's will to leave a third of her property to her waqf; see TSK, E.H. 3032, fols 39r–44v.

11 Mehmed Çelebi b. Ali is identified as the waqf administrator in TSK, E.H. 3064, fols 19v, 20r.

12 Shaykh Yakub died in 979 (1571–72). For the complex at Davudpaşa, see Ayvansarayi, 2000, p. 148; Hulvi, 1993, p. 479. The madrasa was endowed by Shahsultan with one third of the inheritance of her late granddaughter Vasfihan Sultan (daughter of İsmihan and Hüseyin Pasha) and Fatma Hatun (daughter of Hüseyin Pasha by another woman); see TSK, E.H. 3064, fols 18v–20v. The conversion date of 981 (1573–74) is given in Baltacı, 1976, pp. 436–37.

13 TSA, E. 5404/15, dated middle of R. 970.

14 Esra Güzel Erdoğan, 'Şah Sultan Camii', ISTA 7:124–25.

15 TM in Meriç, 1965, p. 24. The mosque is cited in all autobiographies of Sinan; see Kuran, 1986, p. 302, no. 97.

16 Hulvi, 1993, p. 467; Ayvansarayi, 2000, pp. 279–82; Baha Tanman, 'Şah Sultan Camii', ISTA 7:125–27; Haskan, 1993, 1:85–89, 263–65.

17 TSA, E.463/1, dated Z. 962; cited in Chapter 2.

18 Ayvansarayi, 2000, p. 280; Saatçi, 1988, p. 67, no. 23.

19 Evliya, TSK, B.304, 1:119r; Tanman, ISTA, 7:125–27. A domed mausoleum for Shaykh Merkezzade Ahmed Efendi (d. 1813) was built at the southeast corner of the mosque.

20 TSK, E.H.3032, fol. 11v: '… köşki baʿde vefātihā muʿallimḫāne olmaḳ içün vaḳf eylediler.'

21 Ayvansarayi, 2000, p. 280. TSK, E.H.3064, fols 18v–19v: 'ḳaṣaba-i Eyüb ḳurbinde bir cāmiʿ-i şerīf ve zāviye ve mekteb-i laṭīf.' TSK, E.H.3032, fol. 11r, mentions one room and one hall at the shaykh's male quarters and one room and one hall at the refectory of dervishes: 'bir oda ve bir ṣoffa şeyḫ-i mezbūra selāmlıḳ ve bir oda ve bir ṣoffa dervişlere taʿāmḫāne ola.' The number of dervishes was nineteen according to a later source; see M. Kılıç, 1997, p. 269, no. 16.

22 TSK, E.H.3032, fols 21v–23r; TSK, E.H.3064, fols 20r–v. The palace is identified as Hançerli Sultan Sarayı in Ayvansarayi, 2000, p. 280.

23 TSK, E.H.3032, fols 7v–8r: 'cāmiʿ-i şerīf ḥareminde olan türbeleri.' The mausoleum is interchangeably identified as 'her mausoleum' and 'her mother's mausoleum' in TKS, E.H.3064, fols 9v–10r, 19v: 'cāmiʿ-i mezbūr ḳurbinde vāḳiʿ türbelerinde', 'vālideleri türbelerinde.' Shahsultan also endowed an elementary school for her late mother near Silivrikapı; TSK, E.H.3032, fol. 18r. Shahsultan's '*mekteb* in the Arabacı Bayezid quarter outside the Silivri Kapı' is mentioned in Ayvansarayi, 2000, p. 148.

24 For the tombstones of Shahsultan, her unnamed mother, her granddaughter Neslihan (born from İsmihan and Hüseyin Pasha), Neslihan's sister Vasfihan, and Fatima Hatun (Hüseyin Pasha's daughter from another woman); see Haskan, 1993, 1:263–65.

25 She was buried in her mausoleum at Eyüp according to Ayvansarayi, 2000, p. 148. For the unsubstantiated assertion that Shahsultan and her daughter İsmihan were buried at Selim I's complex, inside the now-lost mausoleum of Hafsa Sultan, see Uluçay, 1980, p. 33; Mehmed Süreyya, 1996, 1:42.

26 TSK, E.H.3032, fol. 11v; also see TSK, E.H.3064, fol. 18v.

27 TM and TE in Meriç, 1965, pp. 28, 77; Sai, 1897, p. 29.

28 Ayvansarayi, 2000, pp. 255–56. Konyalı, 1950, pp. 156–59.

29 Baha Tanman, 'Merkez Efendi', ISTA 5:396–97, 400.

30 Merkez Efendi endowed on 28 September 1552 the double bath with adjacent shops near the Yenikapı gate to subsidize prayers for his own soul, the souls of his sons Derviş Çelebi and Ali Çelebi, and the soul of 'my son Ahmed Beg's mother Shahsultan, the daughter of Sultan Selim Khan.' He designates himself waqf administrator, a post that would pass upon his demise to his son 'Ahmed Çelebi.' This document (VGM, Küçük Evkaf Evvel, Defter 623, dated 9 L. 959, no. 333, p. 329) has led Emel Esin to conclude that Shahsultan was married to Merkez Efendi in Manisa where their son Ahmed was born (*c.* 1512–20), before she married Lutfi Pasha in 1523; see Esin, 1977–79. However, neither the princess's own endowment deed, nor other historical sources refer to this unlikely marriage, which could not have taken place after Shahsultan's divorce in 1541, when Merkez Efendi had reached his eighties. Her waqfiyya assigns a stipend to the daughter of the shaykh's son without identifying him as her own son ('oğlı … merḥūm şeyḫ aḥmed çelebinüñ ḳızı selīme ḫatūn'); TSK, E.H.3032, fol. 14v. Nor do Hulvi's biographies of Merkez Efendi and his son Ahmed mention the marriage; Hulvi, 1993, pp. 461–70. More research is needed to clarify this puzzling issue.

31 The mosque is dated to *c.* 1552–72 in Kuran, 1986, p. 287, no. 52. The double bath near Yenikapı and its adjacent shops (endowed earlier by Merkez Efendi) is mentioned among Shahsultan's waqfs in TKS, E.H.3064, fol. 18r: 'yeñi bāġçe ḳurbinde ḥammām.'

32 TSK, E.H.3032, fols 12r–13r.

33 TSK, E.H.3064, fol. 19v.

34 TKS, E.H.3032, fol. 14r. For the mausoleum with twelve cenotaphs, see Konyalı, 1950, p. 157; Ayvansarayi, 2000, pp. 255–56.

35 TSK, E.H.3032, fol. 12r; E.H.3064, fols 16v–17r, 18v.

36 Demolished in 1958, the mosque is referred to in Sinan's autobiographies as the 'mosque of Osmanshah's mother'; see Konyalı, 1950, p. 183; Kuran, 1986, p. 291, no. 65. Osmanshah's own mosque in Trikkala is discussed in Chapter 12. His mother is referred to as Hanım Sultan in her posthumous waqfiyya dated N. 976 (1569); TSK, E.H.3038, published in Uzunçarşılı, 1976.

37 Kuran, 1986, p. 298, no. 86. Konyalı thinks this could be Bayezid II's daughter Hatice Sultan or his granddaughter Neslişah Sultan both of whom built modest mosque complexes near Edirnekapı; Konyalı, 1950, pp. 50–51.

38 TSK, E.H.3032, fol. 2v; VGM, Defter 1993, p. 11. Hürrem and Mihrümah are also compared to Rabiʿa; see Chapters 7 and 8.

39 Her name is generally spelled 'Mihrimah' in modern publications, but I have preferred the spelling used in her waqfiyya and in contemporary sources.

40 Bernardo Navagero (1553) in Albèri, 1840–55, 1:98–99.

41 Āli, Nuruosmaniye Library, Ms. 3409, fol. 122r.

42 Bernardo Navagero (1553) in Albèri, 1944–50, 1:98–99. According to Daniello de Ludovisi (1534) the jealous grand vizier İbrahim Pasha had caused the chief stablemaster Rüstem's appointment to the province of Diyarbakır to banish him away from the sultan, who admired his intelligence and frequently listened to his advice; ibid., 1:12.

43 '*Kehle-i iḳbāl*', Āli, Nuruosmaniye Library, Ms. 3409, fols 122r–v.

44 Domenico Trevisano (1554) in Albèri, 1840–55, 1:117, 175.

45 For these letters, see Uluçay, 1956, pp. 88–93.

46 Uçtum, 1980.

47 In Albèri, 1840–55, 1:90, 92–93.

48 In Kamil, 1937, pp. 72–73, 81.

49 For how he cured Mihrümah, see Laguna, 1983, pp. 112–15, 118.

50 For the date of her death in 985 (1578), see Lokman, TSK, H.1321, fol. 105r; Gerlach, 1640, p. 449.

51 Marcantonio Donini (1562) says Mihrümah gave money to support Bayezid according to her late mother's wish; in Albèri, 1840–55, 3:184.

52 ASV, Dispacci al Senato, Costantinopoli Filza 3C, dispatch #79 of Daniele Barbarigo, dated 12 October 1562, fol. 235r: '… ha mostrato di haver sentito per questa morte assai dolore, che non senti per quella di Rustem bassa suo marito.' Prince Bayezid had named his oldest daughter Mihrümah; see Kamil, 1937, p. 41.

53 Marcantonio Donini (1562) in Albèri, 1840–55, 3:184–85.

54 Ahmed Refik, 1924, p. 30.

55 ASV, Dispacci al Senato, Costantinopoli Filza 3C, dispatch #73 of Daniele Barbarigo, dated 1 September 1562, fols 220r–v.

56 Ibid., dispatch #79 by Daniele Barbarigo, dated 12 October 1562, fol. 235r.

57 For her wish to reside in the sultan's palace and take the place of her mother, see ibid., fol. 236v; Ahmed Refik, 1924, p. 29.

58 Peirce, 1993, pp. 65, 68.

59 Selaniki, 1989, 1:43.

60 ASV, Senato, Dispacci Costantinopoli Filza 3C, dispatch #43 of Gerolamo Ferro, dated 16 November 1561, fol. 136r. For Ahmed's Croatian origin; see Betzek, 1979, p. 35; and Wyts (1572), ÖNB, Codex Vindobonensis Palatinus, 3325*, fol. 112v. He was Albanian according to Peçevi, 1864–67, 1:440.

61 ASV, Senato, Dispacci Costantinopoli, Fiza 3C, dispatch #32 by Gerolamo Ferro, dated 10 July 1561, fol. 107r.

62 Selaniki, 1989, 1:186; Peçevi, 1864–67, 1:440–41.

63 Peirce, 1993, pp. 127–29.

64 In Albèri, 1840–55, 1:312.

65 Ibid., 1:400–1.

66 Gerlach, 1674, p. 449.

67 An account book of Mihrümah's waqfs for her complexes in Üsküdar and Edirnekapı, Süleyman's tomb, and the tomb of Rüstem Pasha is in TSA, D.3850, dated the beginning of M. 1047 (1637). Her waqfiyya of 1562 for her husband's tomb and water dispenser is in VGM, Defter 635/2, no. 8, dated the beginning of Ra. 970.

68 In 1561 Ayşe Sultan became both the *mütevelli* and *nazır* of her late father's waqf; see Yüksel, 1995, pp. 272–73. Mihrümah's waqfiyya of 1570 also appoints her daughter as waqf administrator and overseer; VGM, Defter 632/2, no. 10, dated R. 978, pp. 83–90.

69 Koçi Beg, 1998, pp. 85–86. For Mihrümah's numerous landed properties, see VGM, K.28, dated 965 (1557–58).

70 Hasanbeyzade, 1980, p. 62.

71 For the madrasa, see Kuran, 1986, p. 344, no. 243. The repair in 1557 of Rüstem Pasha's palace at the 'Serv' quarter of Mahmudpaşa is documented in TSA, D.6856, dated 964–65. It was inherited by his daughter Ayşe Sultan, who in 1612 endowed it for herself; after her death it would be inherited by her daughter Safiye Hanım and her descendants, thereafter it would be sold to yield alms for the poor in Mecca and Medina; see VGM, Defter 653/2, no. 17, dated 2 Ra. 1021. The neighbourhood of that palace came to be known as Cağaloğlu after it passed on to the descendants of Cigalazade Sinan Pasha, who married in succession two daughters of Ayşe Sultan and Ahmed Pasha. For the wedding of a grand-daughter of Cigalazade Sinan Pasha in 1596, the 'late Rüstem Pasha's palace where he resided' was prepared; see Selaniki, 1989, 2:561, 571. Rüstem Pasha's palace in Edirne where Cigalazade moved with his family upon his deposition in 1596 is mentioned in ibid., 2:650.

72 Sinan's autobiographies list Rüstem Pasha's palaces near the Hippodrome (Kadırgalimanı), at Üsküdar, and outside the city walls; see Kuran, 1986, p. 380, nos. 370–72. The one outside the city walls (near Yeşilköy and Bakırköy) is referred to elsewhere as Mihrümah Sultan's garden palace, known as İskender Çelebi Bahçesi; see Sai, 1989, fol. 12r. For Mihrümah's garden palace in Üsküdar, see Necipoğlu, 1997, pp. 40–41. In 1560 the newly built palace of Mihrümah at the Hippodrome was granted a source of water with her father's permission; see TSA, E.9512, dated the beginning of Z. 967. A decree approves the donation of water to 'the palace built at the Hippodrome for Her Highness Mihrümah Sultan'; BA, MD. 4, #1143, p. 112, dated 13 Za. 967. The palace Ayşe Sultan inherited at Atmeydanı was endowed by her in 1595; see VGM, Defter 635/2, no. 2, dated 27 B. 1003. Ayşe Sultan's Hippodrome palace (also known after her husband's name as 'Ahmed Paşa Sarayı') was sold to Sultan Ahmed I in 1609 for 30,000 filorins, to create space for his sultanic mosque; the sale document is in TSA, D.10748, dated 1026 (1617).

73 For Rüstem Pasha's waqfiyya and Mehmed Beg's role as his building supervisor and waqf administrator, see the next section on his patronage. Also see Mihrümah's waqfiyya of 1570, VGM, Defter 632/2, no. 10, dated R. 978, pp. 88–89.

74 In 1572 (N. 978) the endowment administrator

Mehmed Beg (Kethüda) made a payment for the expenses of the completed water channel: ''an taḥvīl, Meḥmed Beg mütevellī-yi evḳāf-ı ḥażret-i mihrümāh sulṭān ... ki pīş ezīn bā fermān-ı 'ālīşān ki iḫrācāt-ı rāh-ı āb-ı cebel 'arafat', BA, KK.1768, Büyük Ruznamçe, fol. 108r. Rüstem Pasha's waqfiyya of 1570 shows that she had borrowed 125,000 gold coins (7,500,000 aspers) for her Meccan water channel from his endowed money obtained from the sale of his armory (*cebeḫāne*); a sum she reimbursed later; VGM, Defter 648, p. 177: ' ... cümle yüzyigirmibeş biñ filori sulṭān ḥażretleri alub, ... 'arafatdan mekke-i mükerreme ve kā'be-i mu'aẓẓama ... şu getürmege ḫarc buyurmuşlardur.'

75 Selaniki, 1989, 1:95; Atai, 1989, pp. 169, 269. According to Atai the water channel construction for which she spent money 'like water' lasted nine years between 970 (1562–63) and 979 (1571–72); it was inaugurated on 20 Za. 979 (1572).

76 Venice, Marciana Library, IT. Cl. VII (8872), dispatch dated 11 June 1569, fol. 116v.

77 Her requests were made through Sokollu, her husband's former steward Mehmed Kethüda, and her own letters; see Venice, Marciana Library, IT. Cl. VII (8872) dispatch dated 11 June 1569, fol. 116v; 11 November 1569, fols 117r, 227r–v; 4 January 1569, fol. 263v; ASV, Senato, Costantinopoli (Segreta), Registro 5, fol. 23r. For her aqueduct spanning a forty-day journey across the desert crossed by pilgrims arriving from Cairo, also see Barbaro's report (1573) in Albèri, 1840–55, 1:312.

78 These mosques are discussed under Shahsultan in Chapter 8.

79 Bates, 1993, pp. 52–53; Bayrakal, 2001, pp. 61–66.

80 Dernschwam, 1923, pp. 31, 56–58.

81 Laguna, 1983, pp. 160–61.

82 Ibid., pp. 160–61: 'Fu designata a esecutrice testamentaria la sultana e a lei furono portati tutti i beni, carrettate di oro e da argento.' The mosque in Beşiktaş is discussed in Chapter 11. For Sinan Pasha's marble cenotaph at the cemetery of Mihrümah's Üsküdar mosque, dated 961 (1553–54) and attributed to the chief architect in the *Tuḥfe*, see Kuran, 1986, p. 328, no. 188.

83 Kamil, 1937, p. 49.

84 Tombstones at the cemetery of the mosque are identified in Konyalı, 1976–77, 1:221–30. The second domed mausoleum of the grand vizier Ethem Pasha was added in 1892. Also see Ayvansarayi, 2000, pp. 492–93.

85 For Mahmud Hüdayi's appointment as preacher at Mihrümah's mosque and Ayşe Sultan's construction of his mosque-cum-convent (*cāmi' ü ḫānḳāh*) complex, see Hasanbeyzade, 1980, 2:160-61. Her waqfiyya dated 1595 endows her mausoleum in a garden that contained the convent with eleven rooms she donated to the shaykh along with a fountain, and funds for the repair of the nearby İmrahor masjid converted into a mosque; VGM, Defter 635/2, no. 2, dated 27 B. 1003. Ayşe Sultan's donations in 1612 to the shaykh's mosque together with water from her garden is recorded in ibid., no. 17, dated 2 Ra. 1012. For Cigalazade Sinan Pasha's endowments to the shaykh's shrine complex in 1606, see VGM, Defter 611, no. 16, dated the beginning of Z. 1012. The shaykh's complex created with contributions from his disciples is described in Baha Tanman; it was entirely rebuilt after a fire in 1855, 'Aziz Mahmud Hüdai', ISTA 1:505–7.

86 VGM, Defter 635/2, no. 1, dated mid. Ra. 957, p. 3; Süleymaniye Library, Esad Efendi, Ms. 3752, dated 956, fols 17r–v.

87 For the waqfiyya of Shahsultan who chose Mihrümah as the executor of her last will, see Chapter 8. Hürrem is compared to Rabi'a in a title deed attached to her waqfiyya; see Chapter 7. Mihrümah's devotion to Shaykh Nureddinzade is discussed in Samardzić, 1995, p. 106.

88 Süleymaniye Library, Esad Efendi, Ms. 3752, dated 956, fols 21r–v.

89 VGM, Defter 635/2, no. 1, dated mid Ra. 957, pp. 1–32; ibid., no. 7, dated the beginning of Z. 965 (1558), pp. 62–78; Süleymaniye Library, Esad Efendi, Ms. 3752, dated 956, fols 15v–27r. Catharin Zen (1550) mentions paved avenues with bridges endowed by Mihrümah on the Istanbul-Edirne highway, Zen, 1878, p. 19.

90 For slightly different readings, see Konyalı, 1976–77, pp. 1:216–17; Peirce, 1993, p. 201; Ayvansarayi, 2000, p. 492; Saatçi, 1988, pp. 37–39, no. 13.

91 Kuran, 1986, p. 288, no. 56; p. 344, no. 239; p. 363, no. 308.

92 The fountain carries a repair inscription of 1092 (1689) which likens Mihrümah to the Queen of Sheba; see Egemen, 1993, p. 597; Saatçi, 1988, pp. 40–42, no. 14.

93 Eremya, 1988, pp. 47–48; İnciciyan, 1976, p. 134.

94 Kuran, 1987, p. 67.

95 Ibid., p. 55.

96 For a photograph showing the Europeanizing paintings that were replaced with new ones during repairs in 1955–63, see Kuban, 1997, p. 63.

97 VGM, Defter 635/2, no. 1, dated mid Ra. 957, p. 4: 'ṭarz-ı ṣoffa ve ġuref-i bedi' el-taṣvīri ḫayret-fezā-yi hünermendān-ı ṣāhib-i naẓar'; Süleymaniye Library, Esad Efendi, Ms. 3752, dated 956, fols 17v–18r. The waqfiyya description is paraphrased in Konyalı, 1950, p. 179.

98 Ramazanzade Mehmed, 1862, p. 302.

99 Mehmed Aşık, TSK, E.H.1446, fol. 393v.

100 Evliya, 1896–1938, 1:473–75. Mihrümah's waqfiyya only mentions one caravansaray (*ḫān*). This was either a double caravansaray, or one of the caravansarays was the one Rüstem Pasha endowed 'at the west side of the Üsküdar jetty.' For his charge-free caravansaray along the shore and his elementary school near the garden palace (at the İmrahor quarter in Doğancılar), see Yüksel, 1995, pp. 244–45, 248; Konyalı, 1976–77, 1:332, 2:54.

101 The demolished hospice was located at the left side of the madrasa according to Konyalı, 1976–77, 1:290, 445.

102 Peçevi, 1864–67, 1:427–28.

103 Evliya, TSK, B.304, 1:141v–43r.

104 Kuran, 1987, p. 250.

105 Kuban, 1997, pp. 101–2.

106 Goodwin, 1993, p. 49.

107 Selim II's four daughters formed influential couples: İsmihan and Sokollu, Gevherhan and Piyale Pasha, Shahsultan and Zal Mahmud Pasha, Fatma Sultan and Siyavuş Pasha.

108 The date 1550 is given in H. Egli, 1997, p. 62. For the date 1556–60; see Müller-Wiener, 1977, p. 441. The date 1562–65 is proposed in Konyalı, 1950, p. 160; Sözen, 1975, p. 184; Burelli, 1988, p. 42; Günay, 1998, pp. 37–38.

109 He rightly rejects the assumption that she died before her father in 1557; see Kuran, 1986, p. 123.

110 The permit of her husband's mosque is in VGM, Defter 635/1 Mükerrer, dated mid C. 969, p. 5.

111 Cited in Konyalı, 1950, p. 161; VGM, Defter 635/1 Mükerrer, no. 6, dated mid Z. 970, p. 6.

112 Published in Yaltkaya, 1942, p. 96.

113 Rüstem Pasha is known to have taken revenge from the supporters of his executed rival by dismissing them from their positions.

114 See Chapter 9.

115 VGM, Defter 635/1 Mükerrer, no. 10.

116 Ibid., no. 11.

117 BA, MD. 5, #63, p. 24, dated 11 M. 973: 'edirne ḳapusınuñ iç yüzinde müceddeden binā olınān cāmi'i ḳurbinde ḥammām binā itmek istid'ā itdügi ecilden izn-i şerīfim muḳarrer olub.' Based on this document, Konyalı thinks the mosque must have been completed before 1565; see Konyalı, 1950, p. 162. The wording is ambiguous; it can also be read as 'near the mosque that has newly been built'. But this is unlikely judging by the same wording used in Selim II's decree of 1571 cited below, which refers to Mihrümah's incomplete bath-house.

118 Cited in Konyalı, 1950, p. 162; VGM, Defter 635/1 Mükerrer, no. 7, dated the beginning of N. 973.

119 BA, MD. 5, #1413, p. 517, dated 17 N. 973; ibid., #1443, p. 527, dated 25 N. 973.

120 Kazım Çeçen, 'Sinan'ın Yaptığı Su Tesisleri', in Bayram, ed., 1988, 1:449. The inscription of the bath fountain shows that Cigalazade İbrahim Beg rebuilt it after a fire in 1142 (1729–30).

121 BA, MD. 14, #80, p. 64, dated the beginning of M. 979; repeated in BA, MD. 17, #28, p. 18, dated the beginning of S. 979: 'hemşīrem mihrümāh dāmet 'ismetuhā ṭarafından maḥrūse-i istanbulda edirneḳapusı ḳurbinde binā olınān ḥammāmı mühimmi içün mermer lāzım olmagıñ ...'.

122 VGM, Defter 635/2, no. 10, dated R. 978, pp. 83–90.

123 TM in Meriç, 1965, p. 24.

124 Kuran, 1986, p. 322, no. 170. Kuran dates the mausoleum to 1580–81, but it existed in 1576 when Gerlach described the burial ceremony of Ahmed Pasha's son near Edirnekapı, where Rüstem Pasha [sic] had built a pretty mosque and tomb for the children of the family; see Gerlach, 1674, p. 187. In 1595 Ayşe Sultan made an endowment for the thirty Koran reciters at her husband's mausoleum in Edirnekapı; see VGM, Defter 635/2, no. 2, dated 27 B. 1003. She married Feridun Ahmed Beg in 1582, and was buried in her own tomb at the mosque-cum-convent complex of Aziz Mahmud Hüdayi in Üsküdar.

125 Pervitich, 1999, plate 31.

126 The irregular design of the madrasa leads Kuran to speculate that it was planned after the mosque had already been built; see Kuran, 1987, p. 132.

127 The Friday market is mentioned in İnciciyan, 1976, p. 48.

128 For a photograph showing the sockets and the traces of the slanting portico roof on the madrasa walls, see Goodwin, 1971, p. 254, fig. 243.

129 Ibid., p. 254.

130 Grosvenor, 1895, 2:661; Müller-Wiener, 1977, p. 441.

131 Günay, 1998, p. 37; Burelli, 1988, p. 47.

132 For damages and repairs, see Konyalı, 1950, p. 164; Kuran, 1987, pp. 129–30; Kuban, 1997, p. 101.

133 For the new inscriptions, see Derman, 1989, p. 291.

134 VGM, Defter 635/2, no. 10, p. 83. The cosmos is similarly compared to a domed Friday mosque in İsmihan Sultan's waqfiyya for her mosque in Kadırgalimanı; see Chapter 8.

135 Ibid., p. 85.

136 Evliya, TSK, B.304, 1:47r: 'sā'ir cāmi'-i selāṭīnlerüñ ḳaṣr-ı irem ẕātül-'imādıdur.'

137 Ayvansarayi, 2000, p. 26.

138 Vatin and Yerasimos, 2001, p. 143; Goodwin, 1971, p. 255.

139 Mihrümah's mother Hürrem Sultan assigned an endowment to the convent-mosque of Toklu Dede in Ayvansaray, featuring the venerated tombs of two Arab martyrs and the ghazi warrior Toklu Dede. Her convent later transformed into a madrasa called Kariye was also located near the land walls; see Chapter 7.

140 Grosvenor, 1895, 2:662; Konyalı, 1950, pp. 161, 163, 166; Müller-Wiener, 1994, pp. 441–42. For the church at the east side of Edirnekapı (Eglise Grecque St. George), see the map in Pervitich, 1999, plate 31, no. 519. The 'Hagios Georgios' church is depicted with a hipped lantern roof in Paspates, 1877, pp. 386–87.

141 Mihrümah's mosque is said to have been associated more than any other sanctuary 'with the European wars of the Empire' because 'the sultans always performed their devotions here before setting out to military expeditions in the West'; see Grosvenor, 1895, 2:662.

142 The novelist Arthur Straton construes the mosque as the sublimation of Sinan's unrequited erotic passion for Mihrümah in his novel on the chief architect; see Straton, 1972, pp. 180, 183.

143 Examples in Istanbul include the Nuruosmaniye (1755), Ayazma (1760), Nusretiye (1826), Mecidiye (1848), Ortaköy (1850), and Dolmabahçe (1855) mosques; see Kuban, 1997, p. 100; Günay, 1998, p. 38.

144 For his origin from 'Serraglio di Bosnia', see Bernardo Navagero (1553), in Albèri, 1840–55, 1:88, 98–99. The two brothers Rüstem and Sinan Pasha are identified as swineherds from Bosnia in Dernschwam, 1923, p. 58. Also see Āli, Nuruosmaniye Library, Ms. 3409, fols 122r–23v.

145 See Chapter 9.

146 Rüstem's political inclination towards the brothers of his wife born from the queen called 'Ḫurremşāh' is noted in Āli, Nuruosmaniye Library, Ms. 3409, fol. 123v.

147 For the petitions, see Gökbilgin, 1955. A very positive view of Rüstem Pasha is provided in Celalzade, 1981, fols 502r–503v. .

148 Āli, Nuruosmaniye Library, Ms. 3409, fols 122v–23r.

149 '... padrone assoluto di quell'imperio', in Albèri, 1840–55, 1:74, 88.

150 Ibid., 1:90–91.

151 Ibid., 1:89, 92–93.

152 Ibid., 1:61–62, 88.

153 Ibid., 1:89, 92–93. The Meccan Sharif's envoy, Mekki, says that the pasha accepted textiles, but refused jewels, gold, and silver as diplomatic gifts; see Kamil, 1937, p. 68.

154 Yüksel, 1995, p. 229, note 25.

155 Gökbilgin, 1955, pp. 32–33.

156 Navagero notes the decline in Venetian trade and the rise of Jewish intermediaries, in Albèri, 1840–55, 1:101; also see, Domenico Trevisano (1554), ibid., 1:183; Marino Cavalli (1560), ibid., 1:274–75.

157 Busbecq, 1927, pp. 29–30.

158 Ibid., pp. 191–93.

159 Ibid., pp. 190–93.

160 Erizzo says that the pasha was 'by nature austere, a great enemy of Christians, and very avaricious'; see Albèri, 1840–55, 3:136–37. Marino Cavalli (1560) concurs that Rüstem Pasha 'loved nothing but money', pointing out that he was the 'worst man' in the empire, 'without reason, without any conscience, nearly a tyrant, and uncourteous'; ibid., 1:295.

161 For his dislike of poets, see Āli, Nuruosmaniye Library, Ms. 3409, fol. 124r. One of the complaints against the pasha was that he cancelled the income of shaykhs established since the days of Bayezid II; see Gökbilgin, 1955, p. 18.

162 Peçevi, 1864–67, 1:465; Kamil, 1937, p. 75. For the convent Süleyman endowed for Hekim Çelebi, see Chapter 6.

163 Atai, 1989, 2:357–58. According to the Meccan envoy Mekki, Baba Çelebi was the teacher of Rüstem Pasha's daughter; see Kamil, 1937, p. 77.

164 Celalzade, 1981, fols 502v–503r.

165 Āli, Nuruosmaniye Library, Ms. 3409, fols 123r–v.

166 Busbecq, 1927, p. 183.

167 ASV, Dispacci al Senato, Costantinopoli, Filza 3c, dispatch #32 of Gerolamo Ferro, dated 10 July 1561, fol. 107r.

168 The waqfiyya of 'Abdülmecid b. Mustafa Beg b. Sinan Pasha' is discussed in Chapter 11. A register from the kadi court at Sarajevo, dated 1557, records the sale of a house by the endowment administrator of Rüstem Pasha's covered bazaar in that city on behalf of Nefise Hanım, the grand vizier's sister and the daughter of Mustafa; see Christine Woodhead, 'Rüstem Pasha', EI(2) 8:640–41.

169 VGM, Defter 635/2, no. 4, dated the beginning of S. 968, pp. 151–53; for an inventory of the endowed portion of his armoury, see Yüksel, 1995, pp. 268–69.

170 VGM, Defter 635/2, no. 5, dated the beginning of Ca. 968, pp. 153–66. The mosque is referred to on p. 156: 'maḥmiyye-i mezkūrede evḳāf-ı mezbūre zevāidiyle binā olınacaḳ cāmiʿ-i şerīf.' The wages of the mosque's personnel are listed on pp. 156–57. Across the khan at Tahtakale he endowed rental rooms for Jews and storehouses. For the pasha's shops and properties near Tahtakale see ibid., pp. 140–41; Yüksel, 1995, pp. 243, 246–47.

171 VGM, Defter 635/2, no. 5, dated 1561, p. 159: '... eger ecel ... fırṣat virür ise ẕikr olan cāmiʿ-i şerifi bizzāt nefs-i nefīs-i pür taḳdīsleri binā idüb muḳaddemā vaḳf itdükleri cebeḫāne bahāsıyla ʿaḳārāt iştirāʿ ideler ... taḳdīr-i rabbānī heminān olmaz ise ol zamānda kendülerinüñ celīle-i ḥaliletül-ẕātı ve bānū-yı samiyetül-semātı olan sulṭān-ı ʿaliyyetül-şān ... himmet buyuralar.'

172 Ibid., pp. 153–54.

173 VGM, Defter 648, dated the end of Ra. 978, p. 175: 'merḥūm Rüstem Paşa ... yüz biñ filorisin vaḳf ve tescīl-i ṣaḥīḥ-i şerʿ -ī idüb ve cebeḫānesinde olanı her ne ise añı daḫī vaḳf idüb, kendüler civār-ı raḥmete riḥlet bıyurduḳdan ṣoñra beyʿ olunub, sümni vaḳf olmaḳ şart ve ẕikr olan nuḳūd mevżiʿ-i revāc ve iʿ tibār ve mevżiʿ-i raġbet ve iştihārda ʿaḳārāta tebdīl olunması n daḫī şart idüb ve vaḳfından rūḥıyçün bir cāmiʿ-i şerīf binā olunmasın şart idüb, ve ḥalīle-i celīle-i .... Mihrümāh Sulṭān ... ḥażretlerinden vaḳflarınuñ uṣūl ve furūʿunda saʿ ī-i cemīl eylemelerin tevḳiʿ idüb.'

174 Yüksel, 1995, pp. 274–75.

175 Ibid., p. 267.

176 For a detailed index of monuments, see ibid., pp. 219–81.

177 TM in Meriç, 1965, p. 25. Meriç has misread Bolvadin as 'Silivri' and was unable to read Dibek.

178 Yüksel, 1995, pp. 228–29.

179 Sai, 1897, p. 31. Also see TM in Meriç, 1965, p. 25; TE ibid., p. 82.

180 Kuran, 1986, p. 292, no. 68.

181 Known as Menekşe Camii, it is now in Talipler Köyü; see Çifci, 1995, pp. 127–28; Yüksel, 1995, pp. 231, 276.

182 Kuran, 1986, p. 370, no. 335; Yüksel, 1995, pp. 230–31, 276; Küçükkaya, 1990, pp. 195–96, 229. The village had been donated to the grand vizier by Sultan Süleyman as his freehold property in 1549; see VGM, Defter 635/1, pp. 9–10, dated 2 Ra. 956. A summary of the waqfiyya from 1544 is included in Barkan and Ayverdi, eds, 1970, p. 432, no. 2493.

183 Zen, 1878, p. 19.

184 The construction of bridges, water channels, fountains, and pavements with state funds at Sapanca between 1551 and 1555 is recorded in BA, MAD. 55, fols 244v–45r, 288v–89r, 391v.

185 TSK, H.1425, dated 14 B. 959, fol. 301r.

186 Yüksel, 1995, pp. 256–58, 278; Kuran, 1986, p. 257, nos. 451–54.

187 For the bath, see Kuran, 1986, p. 396, no. 439. The ruined *imaret* and caravansaray are discussed in ibid., p. 363, no. 309; p. 371, no. 337.

188 Ibid., p. 293, no. 72.

189 Yüksel, 1995, pp. 232, 276, 279. Kuran lists the mosque and caravansaray among Sinans works; see Kuran, 1986, p. 293, no. 71; p. 370, no. 334. These buildings are included in the autobiographies; TM in Meriç, 1965, p. 25; TE in ibid., p. 80; Sai, 1897, p. 30.

190 TM in Meriç, 1965, p. 25: 'Iki han [Dibek] nam mahalde, Bolu kurbünde', 'Camii şerif Boluda.' Meriç was not able to decipher 'Dibek.' The mosque in Dibek near Bolu is misidentified in TE (due to a scribal error) as the mosque of Mustafa Pasha in Bolu; I explain the error in Chapter 4. Noting that there was no such mosque in Bolu, Kuran hypothesizes that this might have been Lala Mustafa Pasha's mosque and caravansaray at Ilgın; see Kuran, 1986, p. 284, no. 45; p. 368, no. 328.

191 VGM, Defter 635/2, no. 2, pp. 145–48; no. 3, pp. 149–51.

192 Dernschwam, 1992, p. 84.

193 The ship's galley slaves ranged between 119 and 127 in number; see Barkan, 1972–77, 1:134–35.

194 Le Corbusier, 1989, pp. 77–78.

195 Kuran, 1986, p. 295, no. 73; p. 345, no. 244; p. 364, no. 310; p. 371, no. 338.

196 Yüksel, 1995, pp. 261–64, 279–280.

197 Ortaylı, 1996, pp. 195–96, 199.

198 Zen, 1878, pp. 33–34.

199 TSK, H.1425, dated 26 Ra. 959, fol. 129r: 'rodoscuḳda binā itdügi binası.'

200 Ibid., fol. 157r, dated 14 R. 959: 'rodoscuḳda olan binası içün taḫta.'

201 The chronogram reads: 'ṣafḥa-i māha ʿutārid yazdı bir tārīḫ -i hūb, 960 / ḫayrını ʿadn eylesün bu cāmiʿüñ luṭf-i ḳadīm.' A photograph of the inscription is published in Tuncel, 1974, p. 110, fig. 52. Another inscription records repairs in 1841, ibid., p. 111, fig. 53.

202 Tuncel, 1974, pp. 31–35.

203 Baltacı, 1976, p. 347.

204 Goodwin, 1971, p. 214.

205 The few inscriptions invoke the divine epithets as in Mihrümah's İskele mosque. They are accompanied by painted roundels with standard names.

206 Mehmed Aşık, TSK, E.H.1446, fol. 361v.

207 Evliya, TSK, B.308, 8:381r.

208 TM in Meriç, 1965, p. 30: 'Yenibağçede āhar mescide bedel bina olunan Rüstem Paşa mescid-i şerifi.' For the masjid at Yenibahçe, which was demolished in 1957, see Yüksel, 1995, pp. 239–40, note 50; Ayvansarayi, 2001, pp. 129–30.

209 VGM, Defter 635/1 Mükerrer, p. 7. The fatwa implies that the site was chosen after the pasha's death: 'mütevellī rāy-i vaṣī ile bir maḥall-i münāsib tetebbuʿ itdükde...'

210 Ibid., pp. 7–9.

211 Ibid., dated the end of C. 969, p. 5. Cited in Konyalı, 1950, pp. 203–4. A copy of this decree is in TIEM, no. 2404.

212 VGM, Defter 635/1 Mükerrer, dated 26 S. 970, pp. 6–7; cited in Konyalı, 1950, pp. 205–6.

213 For Küçük Çukur Han, Büyük Çukur Han, and Burmalı Han (thought to have housed a law court), see Yüksel, 1995, p. 243, note 55; pp. 246–47.

214 VGM, Defter 635/1, the beginning of R. 970, p. 4; cited in Konyalı, 1950, p. 207.

215 ASV, Dispacci al Senato, Costantinopoli, Filza 3C, dispatch #55 of Andrea Dandolo Vicebailo, dated 18 May 1562, fol. 170r. For eight lanterns (*otto Ferali grandi ordinarii da Moschea*) ordered later on for Sokollu's Azapkapı mosque, see Chapter 8.

216 Ibid., dispatch #56 of Andrea Dandolo, dated 19 May

1562, fol. 172v: 'il checagia [kahya], che allhora si ritrovava sopra certa fabrica che fà fare la sultana ... in questa mattina devendo ordinar molte cose per essa fabrica ...'.

217 Ibid, dispatch #71 of Daniele Barbarigo, dated 3 August 1562, fol. 217r.

218 The completion date of 1562 is accepted in Konyalı, 1950, pp. 205–6; Kuran, 1986, p. 135; Burelli, 1988, p. 52; Goodwin, 1993, p. 50; Denny, 1998, p. 39; Kuban, 1997, p. 102; Günay, 1998, p. 79. The date *c.* 1555–61 is given in Müller-Wiener, 1977, p. 454. The completion date of 1561 is proposed in Aslanapa, 1986, p. 217; and H. Egli, 1997, p. 84.

219 For the plan of the basement, see Kuran, 1986, p. 135.

220 Yüksel, 1995, p. 248.

221 Pervitich, 1999, p. 152, plate 76, no. 270.

222 Burelli, 1988, pp. 52, 54.

223 Denny, 1998, p. 45.

224 Aslanapa, 1986, p. 217; Denny, 1998, pp. 37–52.

225 Necipoğlu, 1990, 1992b.

226 For a textile designer who prepared cartoons in 1593 for tiles made in İznik for the Shore Kiosk at the Topkapı Palace, see Necipoğlu, 1990, p. 155.

227 Kuban, 1997, pp. 105–106; Burelli, 1988, p. 61; H. Egli, 1997, pp. 86–87. The popular tradition that Rüstem Pasha established a private tile workshop in Kütahya is not based on written evidence.

228 Denny, 1977; and 1998, p. 38.

229 For the use of cartoons, see Chapter 3(III); Denny, 1998, p. 38.

230 For the mausoleum, see Mihrümah's patronage discussed earlier in this chapter.

231 Goodwin notes that 'the only access is by ladder' and adds, 'its importance is that it gives access to the roof'; Goodwin, 1971, p. 251. A small stairway affixed to the exterior of the balcony provides access to the dome; see Burelli, 1988, p. 55.

232 Kuban, 1997, pp. 102–3: 'It can be argued that Sinan built this mosque after designing the Edirnekapı Mihrimah Sultan.' For the similarities between the two mosques, see Kuran, 1987, pp. 141–48.

233 The Byzantinizing style of the dome is noted in Goodwin, 1971, pp. 250, 252; and Aslanapa, 1986, pp. 216–17. The undulating rim of the dome and its flying buttresses were added after the earthquake of 1766 according to Doğan Kuban, 'Rüstem Paşa Camii', ISTA 6: 370–72.

234 The 'mystical atmosphere' inside the mosque is noted in Aslanapa, 1986, p. 217; and Kuban, 1997, p. 106.

235 Damages caused by a fire in 1660 were followed by other repairs; see Denny, 1998, pp. 38, 52.

236 Ibid., p. 52.

237 Kamil, 1937, p. 77. He signed the following waqfiyyas: VGM, 635/2, p. 32 (1550), p. 166 (1561), p. 82 (1562), p. 90 (1570).

238 Ramazanzade, 1862, pp. 302–3. The chronicle ends with prince Bayezid's death in 1562 and omits Mihrümah's Edirnekapı complex which had not yet been built.

239 Hasanbeyzade, 1980, 2:62. The mosque is likewise attributed to the princess in İnciciyan, 1976, p. 52.

240 VGM, Defter 648, p. 176.

241 Evliya, TSK, B.304, 1:89v.

242 For the wedding, see Lokman, TSK, H.1321, fol. 87v.

243 Cavalli, 1914, pp. 12–13. For his biography, see Gilles Veinstein, 'Soḳollu Meḥmed Pasha', EI(2) 9:706–11; Ahmed Refik, 1924; and Samardzić, 1994 and 1995.

244 Mekki (1557) portrays the third vizier Mehmed Pasha as young, polite, shy, tall, and well-built; see Kamil, 1937, p. 70.

245 For the funeral, see Selaniki, 1989, 1:125; Hasanbeyzade, 1980, 2:105.

246 For her second husband Kalaylıkoz Ali Pasha, see Peçevi, 1864–67, 2:28. İsmihan's burial is recorded in Selaniki, 1989, 1:155. Her infant Mahmud, who died in fifty days, was buried with his siblings at Sokollu's tomb; ibid., p. 156.

247 For Sokollu's patronage of historical manuscripts, see Necipoğlu, 2000, pp. 22–61.

248 Āli, Nuruosmaniye Library, Ms. 3409, fols 125v–26r; Āli, 1979–82, 1:36, 2:72.

249 Veinstein, EI(2) 9:708.

250 For the two slave concubines she presented to Murad III, see Chapter 6.

251 The pasha had two sons 'from his first wife' according to Cavalli, 1914, p. 12. It is unclear whether these sons were born from the same mother according to Samardzić, 1994, p. 85. For the claim that Sokollu divorced two of his wives before marrying İsmihan, see Veinstein EI(2), 9:708.

252 For a petition prince Selim wrote to the grand vizier Semiz Ali Pasha, asking him to send away Sokollu's sons and their concubine mother to a distant place; see ASV, Dispacci Costantinopoli, Senato, Filza 3C, dispatch #74 of Daniele Barbarigo, dated 21 September 1562, fol. 223r: 'haveva in casa alcuni figliuoli, havuti con una sua schiava ... sua altezza scrisse al magnifico Ali Bassa, che dovesse far che essi figliuoli insieme con la madre fusseso mandati in qualche loco lontano di quà, accioche sua figliuola non se li vedesse tutto il giorno inanzi.' They were sent away to Mehmed Pasha's 'great displeasure', but the princess then consented to have his sons return back home to his 'supreme content'.

253 Cavalli, 1914, p. 12.

254 Albèri, 1840–55, 1:364–65. Also see Costantino Garzoni (1573) in ibid., 1:402, 404.

255 Ibid., 1:312, 319–21, 330.

256 Ibid., 1:320, 405.

257 Ibid., 2:156–57.

258 Samardzić, 1994, p. 298.

259 Gerlach, 1674, p. 349.

260 Ibid., p. 349.

261 Ibid., pp. 383–84.

262 Ibid., p. 349.

263 Ibid., p. 130.

264 Ibid., pp. 58, 398.

265 Ibid., p. 187.

266 Ibid., pp. 38, 130, 266, 379.

267 Cited in Chapter 1(II). The galley slaves of the late Sokollu paraded during the 1582 royal circumcision; see Atasoy, 1997, pp. 46–47, 81.

268 In 1575 İsmihan received a stipend of 300 aspers, her younger sister Gevherhan was paid 250 aspers, and Mihrümah 600 aspers. Murad III's chief consort Safiye had a higher stipend of 700 aspers; see Peirce, 1993, pp. 127–29.

269 The 'new palace' (*yeñi sarāy*) was near the 'new mosque of Sultan Ahmed Khan'; see Peçevi, 1864–67, 1:11.

270 Gerlach, 1674, p. 267. In 1578 the *bailo* promised to lend a young painter residing in the Venetian embassy for a building Sokollu was having constructed in his palace; see ASV, Senato Dispacci, Costantinopoli, Filza 12, dispatch of Niccolò Barbarigo, dated 3 August 1578, fol. 167r.

271 VGM, Defter 572, pp. 31–32: 'ḳadırġa limanında ... dārüs-saʿāde-i ʿatīḳa;' p. 33: 'dārüs-saʿāde-i cedīde.'

272 Kuran, 1986, pp. 383–84, nos. 384–87. The old and new palaces are discussed in Artan, 1993 and 1994; Stichel 1996. For the palace in Üsküdar, see Necipoğlu, 1997.

273 TM in Meriç, 1965, p. 40.

274 Du Fresne-Canaye, 1897, pp. 55–56.

275 For the governor-general of Bosnia, İbrahim Pasha's sale of his property in the Kabasakal Sinan Agha quarter known as the 'palace of Mehmed Pasha' to Sultan Ahmed, see TSA, D.10748, dated Ca. 1018. The sale document is published in Ahmed Refik, 1924, p. 305; and Eldem, 1984–87, 2:22–27.

276 For İbrahim Khan who is buried in Eyüp next to his father, see Ayvansarayi, 2000, p. 364; and Cantemir, 1979–80, 1:149, 175–77. It is generally assumed that he was born in 1565, but Gerlach reports in 1578 that the couple's only son was four to five years old; see Gerlach, 1674, p. 318. Also see Tiepolo, cited above, who says in 1576 that the couple had an infant son and two daughters.

277 The waqfs of İbrahim Khanzade are recorded in VGM, Küçük Evkaf 43, Defter 2, dated 21 Ca. 1233, which lists all waqfs of Sokollu and İsmihan: 'vaḳf-ı merḥūm ve maġfūrunleh vezīr-i aʿẓam-ı asbaḳ şehīd meḥmed paşa eşşehīr be-ibrāhīm ḫānzāde ve merḥūm ismiḫān sulṭān.'

278 Both were written in Turkish by Abdülgani b. Emirshah, a professor employed in İsmihan's madrasa at Eyüp. Sokollu's waqfiyyas are compiled in abridged form in VGM, Defter 572/20, dated the end of Z. 981, pp. 27–62 (translated into modern Turkish in Defter 2104/323, pp. 442–78); Fatih Millet Kütüphanesi, T.933; and Süleymaniye Kütüphanesi, Lala Ismail 737. Copies of İsmihan's waqfiyya, dated beginning of N. 980, are in Lala İsmail 737; and VGM, Defter 572.

279 VGM, Defter 572, p. 149; Lala İsmail 737, fol. 34v, the quarter known today as Kadırgalimanı is referred to as 'the Çatladıkapı quarter near the Hippodrome.'

280 For fiefs granted to her in 1568, see VGM, Defter 572, pp. 141, 149–51. Now a museum, the mosque in Mangalya is an ashlar masonry structure covered by a hipped roof and fronted by a wooden pillared portico attached with a single-galleried minaret; see Ayverdi, 1977, 1:42–43, 49, figs. 67–78.

281 Süleymaniye Kütüphanesi, Lala İsmail 737, fols 32r–33v. Her name is spelled 'Esmahan' in some modern publications, but I have used the waqfiyya's spelling: 'İsmihan'.

282 Ibid., fols 37v–38r; VGM, Defter 572, pp. 141, 145.

283 The house endowed for imams was in the Helvacıbaşı İskender quarter; see VGM, Defter 572, pp. 143–44, 147–49. She also endowed the rents of a market in 'Poğonya nahiyesi' at the sanjak in Avlonya; ibid., p. 159.

284 For tombstones and inscription, see Bacqué-Grammont, Laqueur, and Vatin, 1990, pp. 31, 33, 37, 208–9. The inscription is also recorded in Ayvansarayi, 1985, p. 390.

285 Ibid., p. 31.

286 Ibid., p. 40. The Turkish foundation inscription explains that the grand vizier had commissioned it to honor the Koran. For Sokollu's *dārül-ḳurrā* with a shaykh assigned to teach students the chanting of sections from the Koran at the mausoleum, see Fatih Millet Kütüphanesi, T.933, fols 20r–v; VGM, Defter 572, pp. 29, 51.

287 Most of Sokollu's inscriptions were composed by the poet Nihadi. For the fountain inscriptions, see Egemen, 1993, pp. 571, 573.

288 Fatih Millet Kütüphanesi, T. 933, fol. 19v: 'ḥālīleleri olan sulṭān ḥażretlerine ihdā' itdükleri cāmiʿ-i dilgüşā', fol. 20v 'ḥālīle-i celīlelerine ihdā' itdükleri medrese-i şerīfe.'

289 Ibid., fol. 20r; also see VGM, Defter 572, p. 29.

290 Fatih Millet Kütüphanesi, T. 933, fol. 20v; VGM, Defter 572, p. 31.

291 The khans are not mentioned in the undated waqfiyya; see VGM, Defter 572, p. 32: 'dārü's-saʿāde-i ʿatīkalarına ḳarīb ... vaḳf ḫānları ... ḫān-ı mezbūr muḳābelesindeki ḫān-i cedīd.' The former khan was called 'çaşnigirler oṭaları'.

292 Fatih Millet Kütüphanesi, T.933, fol. 20r.

293 Atai, 1989, p. 213.
294 For the grand admiral, see Chapter 5. Venice, Marciana Library, IT. Cl. VII(8872), dispatch of Marcantonio Barbaro, dated 20 August 1569, fol. 154v.
295 Ibid., fol. 159r.
296 Ibid., dispatch dated 17 September 1569, fols 187r, 189r.
297 Ibid., fol. 116v. The drawings are published in Carboni, 1989.
298 Han, 1973.
299 BA, MD. 14, #948, p. 645, dated 22 B. 978. On the same date the kadi of Sofia was ordered to send the lead that arrived there to the port of Ahyolu; ibid., #949, p. 654.
300 BA, MD. 14, #1296, p. 885, dated 10 N. 978.
301 Ayvansarayi, 1985, p. 111; idem., 2000, p. 214.
302 See the next section on his individual patronage.
303 For Paspates's identification of the church as Hagia Anastasia, see Müller-Wiener, 1977, pp. 461–62. The spolia are described in Konyalı, 1950, p. 151.
304 Fotić, 1994.
305 Andrejević, 1983.
306 For Sokollu's convent known as Fethiye (fetḥiye nāmı ile meşhūr zāviyeleri civarında vāki‘ cāmi‘-i Meḥmed Paşa), see Atai, 1989, 2:363. The pasha's waqfiyya endows two carpets for the 'medrese-i fetḥiye', VGM, Defter 2104/323, pp. 463–78.
307 Ayvansarayi, 2000, p. 214. Another piece of the black stone is seen in Sultan Süleyman's mausoleum, built by Selim II between 1566 and 1567–68.
308 Gerlach, 1674, p. 253.
309 Ayvansarayi, 2000, p. 214.
310 Müller-Wiener, 1994, pp. 6–27, 35–39.
311 Gilles, 1988, p. 92.
312 Lubenau, 1914, 2:181–82.
313 For the location of the palace, see Artan, 1993, pp. 202–3, figs. 1–2.
314 For the tombstones, see Bacqué-Grammont, Laqueur, Vatin, 1990.
315 Tanman, 1988b, pp. 311–19.
316 Ibid., pp. 311–19.
317 Kuran, 1986, pp. 111–12, 120; Goodwin, 1971, p. 272.
318 See Chapter 9.
319 For Sokollu's cautiousness and 'timid' character, see the descriptions of Marcantonio Barbaro (1573), in Albèri, 1840–55, 1:320, 330–31; Jacopo Ragazzoni (1571), ibid., 2:98; Antonio Tiepolo (1576), ibid., 2:158.
320 The number of windows is given in Kuran, 1986, pp. 111, 126.
321 The stained glass windows of the qibla and anti-qibla walls were renewed in 1881; see Müller-Wiener, 1977, p. 461; Goodwin, 1971, p. 272.
322 VGM, Defter 572, pp. 149–50: 'miḥrāblu ġāyet büyük ḳaliçe 2 ḳıṭ‘a; vasat el-ḥāl ḳaliçe 6 ḳıṭ‘a, bunuñ daḫi ikisi mihrābludur; ve vaşat el-ḥālden dört ḳaliçe onyidi ḳıṭ‘a; ġāyetde kuçek ḳaliçe 4 ḳıṭ‘a.'
323 Inscriptions on the domical superstructure were renewed on the basis of originals by Halim Özyazıcı according to Derman, 1989, p. 291. A photograph taken prior to their restoration shows nineteenth-century decorations; see Konyalı, 1950, p. 154.
324 Süleymaniye Library, Lala İsmail 737, fols 32r–33v. The same analogy is made earlier in Mihrümah's waqfiyya of 1570 for the Edirnekapı mosque.
325 The loud *dhikr* and rotation (*devrān*) of the Halvetis was criticized in some orthodox circles; the Nakshbandis preferred silent *dhikr* and stillness; see Clayer, 1994, pp. 41–42.
326 Tanman, 1988b, p. 315.
327 VGM, Defter 572, p. 50: 'vā‘iẓ içün vaẓ‘ itdügi kürside her cum‘a gün ba‘de ṣalavat el-cum‘a müslümanlara va‘ẓ ve naṣiḥat eyleye.'
328 Ibid., p. 50. The shaykh was paid twenty-five aspers (half the pay of the madrasa professor); his thirty disciples received three aspers each (the madrasa students were paid four aspers).
329 They are accompanied by the following phrases: 'May the prayers and peace of God be upon them!' 'May God be pleased with him!' 'May God be pleased with all of them!'
330 'Ebu Bekir, ‘Ömer, ‘Oṣmān, ‘Alidür', 'Olar kim cümle aṣḥāb afżālidür.'
331 Clayer, 1994, pp. 85–91, 114–41. Nurbanu's mosque in Üsküdar, also accompanied by a Halveti convent, features unusual roundels inscribed 'Hasan' and 'Husayn' above its mihrab; see Chapter 7.
332 For Nureddinzade, see Atai, 1989, pp. 212–14; Clayer, 1994, pp. 81–90, 114–41. The coalition between Sokollu, Ebusuud, and Nureddinzade is mentioned in Āli, 1979–82, 1:43–44.
333 Nureddinzade may have collaborated with the professors of Sokollu's and İsmihan's madrasas in the selection of inscriptions. Albdülgani b. Emirshah, the professor of İsmihan's madrasa at Eyüp, wrote the couple's waqfiyyas. For the names of professors, see Baltacı, 1976, pp. 197–200, 421–23.
334 Atai, 1989, p. 363; Clayer, 1994, pp. 93–94.
335 Hasanbeyzade, 1980, p. 86: '*cāmi‘-i melā'ik mecāmi‘*.'
336 VGM, Defter 572, p. 149; Süleymaniye Kütüphanesi, Lala İsmail 737, fol. 34v.
337 Fatih Millet Kütüphanesi, T.933, fol. 20r.
338 Goodwin, 1971, p. 276.
339 Fatih Millet Kütüphanesi, T. 933, fol. 46r: 'irs-i şer‘ile intiḳāl iden māl-ı ḥelāl.'
340 Albèri, 1840–55, 2:157–59. Garzoni says Sokollu's annual income from fiefs was four thousand ducats and gifts that surpassed a million ducats (60,000,000 aspers) each year; ibid., 1:402, 404–7.
341 VGM, Defter 572, p. 28.
342 Albèri, 1840–55, 2:443–44.
343 Gerlach, 1674, pp. 38, 266–67, 378, 414, 449, 451.
344 Āli, Nuruosmaniye Library, Ms. 3409, fol. 125v–126r; Peçevi, 1864–67, 1:11–12.
345 Ibid., fol. 126r. Hasanbeyzade mentions Sokollu's mosque complexes at Kadırgalimanı, Kasımpaşa iskelesi (Azapkapı), Havsa, Burgos (Lüleburgaz), and Payas and his many other monuments only rivalled in number by those of Koca Sinan Pasha; see Hasanbeyzade, 1980, p. 86.
346 Peçevi, 1864–67, 1:11–12.
347 Ahmed Refik, 1924, pp. 315–16. Decrees sent by Murad III in 1581 upon the request of his sister to the kadis and governors of Karaman, Payas, Aleppo, Damascus, Tripoli, Hama, and Homs ordered them to inspect the accounts of Sokollu's waqf administrators (BA, MD. 42, #280–85, pp. 62–64, dated 23 Ca. 989).
348 The waqfiyya dated the end of Z. 981 mentions four individual waqfiyyas (müstaḳil vaḳfiyeler) with four groups of (*sınıf*) waqfs and four *mütevelli*s on p. 32; see VGM, Defter 572/20, pp. 27–62 (translated into modern Turkish in Defter 2104/323, pp. 442–78). The undated waqfiyya (Fatih Millet Kütüphanesi, T.933; and Süleymaniye Kütüphanesi, Lala İsmail 737) lists monuments in the following geographical order: Medina, Aleppo, Payas, Bor, Istanbul, Büyükçekmece, Burgos, Balçık, Sidhirókastron, Sokolovići, and Becskerek.
349 Fatih Millet Kütüphanesi, T.933, fols 46r–v.
350 Süleymaniye Kütüphanesi, Lala İsmail 737, fols 47r–48v: 'bu kitāb-ı ‘anberīn niḳāb içre mufaṣṣalan meẕkūr ve maṣṭūr olan umūr-ı ḥasene ve ḫayrāt-ı mustaḥseneyi vaṣiyyet-i şer‘iyye ... ile vaṣiyyet eyledi ve ḳabl el vaṣiyyet kelīme-i şehādet getürüb.'
351 VGM, Defter 572, p. 28.
352 Ibid., p. 28. For the masjids and other waqfs in Aleppo, see Watenpaugh, 1999, pp. 122–51.
353 VGM, Defter 572, pp. 28–32.
354 The chief administrator is referred to as '*‘umūmī mütevellī*' or '*mütevellī-i kebīr*', ibid., pp. 478–95. For the waqfs in Rumelia, see Gökbilgin, 1952, pp. 508–15. The pasha's endowments in Edirne supported the complex in Lüleburgaz.
355 The last two bridges are omitted from Sokollu's waqfiyyas; see Kuran, 1986, pp. 402–3, nos. 465–67.
356 For Dubrovnik masons, see Samardzić, 1995, pp. 117–18, 263–69.
357 Fatih Millet Kütüphanesi, T.933, fols 2r–3r; Gökbilgin, 1952, pp. 513–14.
358 Ibid., fols 1r–5v, 45v. For Sokollus conquest of Becskerek, see Celalzade, 1981, fols 414r–15r, 421r.
359 Fatih Millet Kütüphanesi, T.933, fol. 45r; Ayverdi, 1981–82, 2:422–3.
360 Ayverdi, 1977, 1:252–6; 252–53.
361 They are described in his waqfiyya as 'the Friday mosque outside the castle of Szigetvár, constructed on the site where the late Sultan Süleyman's body was temporarily enterred', and the 'dervish lodge (ḫānḳāh) built adjacent to that mosque', VGM, Defter 572, pp. 28–29.
362 BA, MD. 29, #270, p. 111, dated 7 Za. 984: 'merḥūm sulṭān süleymān vefāt itdükde emāneten ḳonulduġı maḥalde türbe-i şerīfe ve hānḳāh ve cāmi‘ ve palanḳa.'
363 BA, MD. 30, #459, p. 194, dated 5 Ra. 985. He was the shaykh of Hüsrev Beg's dervish convent at Sarajevo; for his biography see Atai, 1989, pp. 465–66.
364 Küçükkaya, 1990, pp. 90–93; Müderrisoğlu, 1993, pp. 503–23; Kuran, 1986, p. 316, no. 150; p. 374, no. 350; p. 403, no. 468.
365 Bernardo, 1886, p. 34.
366 For the *bedesten* in Bor, see Cezar, 1983, p. 219.
367 Watenpaugh, 1999, pp. 122–48.
368 The dates of their governorship is not clear; for Kasım Pasha's career see Chapter 12.
369 Kuran, 1986, p. 398, nos. 446–47.
370 BA, MD. 28, #2, p. 1, dated 19 Ca. 984; ibid., #30, p. 14.
371 Another order sent to the kadi of Mecca in 1583 indicates that the bath-house and real estate properties (shops, storehouses, houses) supporting the Meccan hospital had been built under the supervision of the scribe Katib Ali, who died shortly after the grand vizier. The scribe's father-in-law claimed that Ali had built these commercial structures for himself. An official was sent from the capital to inspect this matter upon the request of Murad III's sister İsmihan Sultan; see BA, MD. 51, #167, p. 53, dated 16 B. 991.
372 A decree addressed to the kadi of Medina explains that Sokollu obtained a fatwa authorizing the exchange of properties for his water dispenser there; BA, MD. 7, #716, p. 256, dated 15 B. 975.
373 BA. MD. 7, #971, p. 273, dated 28 B. 975; ibid., #774, p. 274. For the wages of Koran readers and water distributers Sokollu endowed villages in Tripoli, see BA, MD. 7, #1807–8, p. 649, dated 2 S. 976.
374 BA, MD. 35, #434, p. 170, dated 20 C. 986; ibid., #435, p. 170.
375 He is referred to as 'pādişāh-ı ma‘nevī', in Āli, Nuruosmaniye Library, Ms. 3409, fol. 125r.
376 Gerlach, 1674, p. 510.
377 Aslanapa, 1986, p. 270.
378 Evliya, TSK, B.304, 3:108r.
379 Pigafetta, 1890, p. 199.
380 Wyts, ÖNB, Codex Vindobonensis Palatinus 3325*, fol. 107r.
381 BA, MD. 5, #527, p. 210, dated 21 Ra. 973, given to the 'pasha's man Keyvan.'

382 BA, MD. 7, #625, p. 226, dated 29 Ca. 975.
383 BA, MD. 7 #1751, p. 627, dated 18 M. 976.
384 BA, MD. 7, #1928, p. 701, dated 21 S. 976, addressed to the kadis of Skopje, Kratova, İştib, Köprüli, and Varna.
385 BA, MD. 7, #1940, p. 706, dated 24 S. 976.
386 ASV, Dispacci Costantinopoli, Senato, Filza 3, dispatch #4 of the *bailo* Giacomo Soranzo, dated 23 March 1568, fol. 32r; ibid., #16, dated 5 June 1568, fol. 98r; ibid., #18, dated 14 June 1568, fols 122r–v; ibid., #31, dated 3 Sept 1568, fol. 237v.
387 Marciana Library, IT. Cl. VII (8872), fol. 54r: '... per veder la fabrica della Moschea, che fà far sua Maestà, anco à Bergas, dove sua Magnificènza fà diversi superbissime fabriche; cioè una Moschea, un Bagno, un Carvansserà, che i stantia ad uso commune di viadanti, con bellissimi marmori, grandissime colone, et ricche pietre.'
388 Ibid., fol. 262r.
389 BA, MD. 7, #993, p. 344, dated 4 N. 975.
390 Cited in Müderrisoğlu, 1993, p. 538 (BA, MD. 7, p. 853, B. 976).
391 BA, MD. 9, #144, p. 54, dated 7 N. 977: 'yir yir ʿalāmetler vażʿ idüb.... sınurnāme-i hümāyūn virile.'
392 Cited in Müderrisoğlu, 1993, pp. 528–29.: 'Bu kārvānsarāya gelen oldı hep revān.'
393 Ibid., p. 330: 'Mescidü'l-akṣā ve beytü's-ṣāliḥīn'; Ayvansarayi, 1985, p. 295.
394 Fatih Millet Kütüphanesi, T.933, fol. 21r.
395 VGM, Defter 2104, pp. 463–78.
396 Fatih Millet Kütüphanesi, T.933, fols 21r–v; Süleymaniye Library, Lala İsmail 737, fols 43v–44r. The elementary school is generally identified by architectural historians as a *darülkurra*.
397 Fatih Millet Kütüphanesi, T. 933, fol. 22r.
398 Ibid., fols 21v–22r; VGM, Defter 572, p. 31.
399 Fatih Millet Kütüphanesi, T. 933, fol. 22r; Süleymaniye Kütüphanesi, Lala İsmail 737, fol. 45r: 'pādişāh-ı ʿālempenāh ḥażretleri saʿādetle istanbuldan edirneye gelüb gitdükçe ḳonmaġiçün bir sarāy-ı dilārā binā idüb ...' Also see Gökbilgin, 1952, p. 511.
400 Müderrisoğlu thinks the tower was part of the old Byzantine fort and locates the royal palace at the west side of the caravansaray; see Müderrisoğlu, 1993, pp. 543, 575. The tower is identified as the tomb tower of Zindan Baba in Aslanapa, 1986, p. 254.
401 These residences are hypothetically reconstructed in Müderrisoğlu 1993, p. 547; Küçükkaya, 1990. p. 574.
402 Fatih Millet Kütüphanesi, T. 933, fols 21v–22r; Süleymaniye Kütüphanesi, Lala İsmail 737, fols 44v–45v: 'ol şehr-i saʿādet menzīlüñ iki cānibine ... bir zībā ḳaldırım binā itdüler.'
403 VGM, Defter 572, pp. 34–35.
404 Zen, 1878, p. 18.
405 Kuran, 1986, p. 297, no. 82; p. 348, no. 253; p. 364, no. 313; p. 373, no. 344.
406 Jean Palerne (1582) thought that the Lüleburgaz caravansaray copied that of Nurbanu; see Palerne, 1991, pp. 302–3.
407 The hypothetical reconstruction proposed by Ali Saim Ülgen has domes, but old photographs and prints show flat roofs; see Müderissoğlu, 1993, pp. 541, 558.
408 Ibid., p. 547. For repairs in 1839, 1934, and 1952–68, see Küçükkaya, 1990, p. 96.
409 Aslanapa, 1986, pp. 250–53.
410 Du Fresne-Canaye, 1897, pp. 48–49.
411 Soranzo, 1856, pp. 56–57.
412 Contarini, 1856, pp. 36–37. Also see Reinhold Lubenau who describes the endowment administrator's residence with a tower where Sokollu used to stay, and the adjacent palace; Lubenau, 1912, 1:122–23.
413 Mehmed Aşık, TSK, E.H.1446, fol. 397r; Hasanbeyzade, 1980, p. 86. In 1632 the local historian of Edirne, Abdurrahman Hibri, refers to the 'royal palace (*hünkār sarayı*)'; cited in Müderrisoğlu, 1993, p. 539.
414 Evliya, TSK, B.304, 3:107v–108r. He says the town was overseen by the sons of İbrahim Khan.
415 Ibid., 3:107v–108r.
416 TM in Meriç, 1965, p. 49.
417 Ibid., pp. 32, 38.
418 For Sokollu's landing station, see Müderrisoğlu, 1993, pp. 610–14. The complex is described in idem., 1995.
419 Müderrisoğlu, 1993, pp. 580–81.
420 Fatih Millet Kütüphanesi, T.933, fol. 19v.
421 Süleymaniye Kütüphanesi, Lala İsmail 737, fol. 47v; VGM, Defter 572, pp. 28–29.
422 VGM, Defter 572, p. 32.
423 Müderrisoğlu, 1993, p. 631, identifies the halls adjacent to the convent's north gate, across from the bath-house, as the bakery.
424 It was a 'royal donation (*temlik-i sulṭānī*)', VGM, Defter 572, p. 40: 'leb-i deryāda binā itdükleri mülk iskele.'
425 Müderrisoğlu, 1993, pp. 610–14.
426 BA, MD. 7, #372, p. 146, dated 18 R. 975; also see the decrees sent to the finance minister of Aleppo, ibid., #373, p. 146; to the sanjak governor of Uzeyr, ibid., #374, p. 146. The governor of Adana was ordered to repair the castle and send timber for ships built in Egypt on 22 December 1667 (ibid., #612, p. 221, dated 29 C. 975).
427 BA, MD. 7, #964, p. 335, dated 3 N. 975: '... bināsı fermān olınan Payas ḳalʿasınuñ üzrine varılub ḳalʿa ve sāʾir binā olınacaḳ yirler tabʿ ve taḥṣīs olunub, ve aṣlı ile resm olunub ... binā kārnāmesi ve binā aḥvāli taṣvīr olunub ...'.
428 BA, MD. 7, #1429, p. 469, dated 19 Z. 975. The finance minister of Aleppo was ordered to provide extra money for the castle (ibid., #1530, p. 539, dated 8 Z. 975).
429 Müderrisoğlu, 1993, p. 612, note 101.
430 Cited in Müderrisoğlu, 1993, pp. 612–13 (BA, MD. 7, # 1964, p. 716, dated 27 S. 976).
431 BA, MD. 9, #81, p. 30, dated 977; MD. 9, #35, p. 14, dated 20 N. 977.
432 BA, MD. 21, #654, p. 276, dated 23 Z. 980: 'payas ḳaṣabası ḳurbinde binā olınan ḫān.'
433 BA, MD. 26, #909, p. 316, dated 1 Ş. 982; see Müderrisoğlu, 1993, p. 619.
434 BA, MD. 26, #689, p. 240, dated 12 C. 982; see Müderrisoğlu, 1993, pp. 632–33.
435 The finance minister of Aleppo is informed about the leaking roof of the khan in Bakras and ordered to go there with experts to record the damaged places and to report the measurements in detail (BA, MD. 14, #605, p. 425, dated 22 Ca. 978). For the salary increase of the imam and preacher of Sultan Süleyman's mosque in Bakras, see BA, MD. 25, #2550, p. 274, dated 10 C. 982.
436 BA, MD. 26, #709, p. 247, dated 14 C. 982: 'taş gemisi ... liman ayrıtlanmaḳ içün daḫi bir ṭaraḳlu gemi...'.
437 BA, MD. 24, #418, p. 155, dated 3 M. 982.
438 BA, MD. zeyl 2, #544–45, p. 206, dated M. 983; MD. 27, #472, p. 204; MD. 29, #222, p. 92, dated 24 L. 984.
439 BA, MD. 31, #300, p. 126, dated 20 Ca. 985, given to Abdülnebi.
440 BA. MD. 39, #545, p. 284, dated 7 S. 988; ibid. #622, p. 321, dated 29 S. 988.
441 Cited in Müderrisoğlu, 1993, pp. 607–10.
442 Other examples of mosques with *tabhane*s are those of Çerkes İskender Pasha in Diyarbakır and Hüsrev Pasha in Aleppo; see Chapter 12.
443 Hasanbeyzade, 1980, p. 86.
444 Evliya, TSK, B.304, 3:20r.
445 Ibid. 3:20r–v.
446 Ibid., 3:19v–20r.
447 Ibid., 3:20v.
448 Ibid., 3:19v–20r.
449 Tayfel, 1598, pp. 47–48.
450 Ibid., pp. 48–51.
451 Moryson, 1907, 2:68–69, 60–61.
452 Yemşel, 1956, p. 101.
453 Photographs testify to the severe damages Payas suffered during the eighteenth century, when it was ruled by local notables; see Müderrisoğlu, 1993, pp. 592–94.
454 According to Domenico Trevisano (1554) Sokollu used a royal garden once belonging to the grand vizier İbrahim Pasha for those constructions; see Albèri, 1840–55, 1:144–45. He mentions the arsenal superintendent (*proto*) Mandolo da Rodi who received a daily wage of fifteen aspers and one sixth of the value of each new galley that was built there.
455 Katip Çelebi, 1973, pp. 140–41.
456 Ahmed Refik, 1924, p. 414.
457 Katip Çelebi, 1973, pp. 144–46.
458 Ayvansarayi, 1985, p. 112. The broken inscription panel was copied by the modern calligrapher Halim Özyazıcı in a new version placed over the northwest gate of the mosque's basement; see Derman, 1989, p. 291, fig. 19. For the identical old and new inscriptions, see Saatçi, 1988, pp. 96–101, nos. 35–36; he misreads 'maḥallinde' as 'maḥfelinde.'
459 'Sāḥil-i deryāda yapmış iken bu zībā cāmiʿi, / Kārgīr itdi mükerrer ol bināyı.'
460 Gerlach, 1674, pp. 266, 493–94.
461 ASV, Senato Deliberatione Costantinopoli (Secreta), Registro 5 (1575–79), dated 27 June 1578, fol. 89v: 'Habbiamo fatto ordinare anco li due mille Rui cristallini, richiesti dal predetto Magnifico Bassà.'
462 Ibid, Registro 4, dated 22 October 1579, fol. 27v: 'Habbiamo intesa la richiesta fattavi per il detto Bassà delli otto Ferali grandi ordinarii da Moschea.' Ibid., 4 Feb 1579, fol. 31v: 'Li Diese Ferali da Moschea ultimamente richiesti per quel Magnifico Bassà sono fornito del tutto, et preparati per mandarsi de li con la prima occassione di passaggio.'
463 Fatih Millet Kütüphanesi, T.933, fol. 20r; Süleymaniye Kütüphanesi, Lala İsmail 737, fol. 42r; cited in Konyalı, 1950, p. 32.
464 Fatih Millet Kütüphanesi, T.933, fol. 20v; Süleymaniye Kütüphanesi, Lala İsmail 737, fol. 43r; VGM, Defter 572, pp. 29, 31, 33.
465 VGM, Defter 572, p. 31.
466 For their recruitment, see Chapter 1. Fatih Millet Kütüphanesi, T.933, fol. 43r.
467 VGM, Defter 2104/323, pp. 463–78.
468 Katip Çelebi, 1973, p. 217; Evliya, 1896–1938, 1:433–4.
469 VGM, Defter 572, p. 33. The still extant double bath at the 'Yolcuoğlu' (Yolcuzade) quarter had two endowed shops adjacent to its façade and a residence across the street. It is known as Yeşildirek Hamamı after the columns supporting its two domes.
470 Ibid., pp. 33–34.
471 Kuran, 1986, p. 296, no. 80; p. 398, no. 445.
472 Eremya, 1988, p. 35.
473 Selaniki, 1989, 2:601.
474 For repairs, see Kuran, 1987, pp. 144–46. A photograph of shops demolished in 1885 is reproduced in Müller-Wiener, 1977, p. 380.
475 The minaret was rebuilt after it cracked during a fire in 1807 according to Ayvansarayi, 2000, p. 364.
476 For the elevation of the façade, see Erzen, 1981, p. 104.
477 See Chapter 11. Another mosque with a façade featuring two gates is that of Kazasker İvaz Efendi in

Ayvansaray (*c.* 1586, illus. 4.7), but it is omitted from Sinan's autobiographies.
478 Erzen, 1996, pp. 144–53.
479 Kuran, 1987, p. 149.
480 Goodwin, 1971, p. 285.
481 Ibid., p. 286.
482 Konyalı, 1950, p. 36.
483 For the renewal of inscriptions, see Derman, 1989, p. 291.
484 Evliya, TSK, B.304, 1:129r.
485 BA, Evkaf 20/25, dated end of M. 1002 (October 1593), fol. 9r. The pasha died on 10 Ş. 985 (fols 6v–7r) and Shahsultan passed away thirteen days later. Some studies wrongly date their deaths to 1580; see Uluçay, 1980, p. 41; Mehmed Süreyya, 1996, 1:43.
486 For her siblings in Selim II's tomb, see Önkal, 1992, pp. 164–70.
487 The three princesses are referred to as 'büyük sulṭān ḥażretleri', 'ikinci sulṭān ḥażretleri', and 'üçüncü sulṭān ḥażretleri' in Lokman, TSK, H.1321, fol. 87v.
488 Āli, Nuruosmaniye Library, Ms. 3409, fols 133r–v.
489 Peçevi, 1864–67, 1:441–42.
490 Albèri, 1840–55, 2:99.
491 Ibid., 2:156.
492 Gerlach, 1674, p. 393.
493 Selaniki, 1989, 1:58–59. Pigafetta (1567) says the very beautiful palace of İbrahim Pasha was possessed by the fifth vizier Mahmud Pasha; see Pigafetta, 1890, p. 149. The palaces of Güzelce Ahmed Pasha and Zal Mahmud Pasha at the Hippodrome are mentioned in 1577 in Gerlach, 1674, p. 312.
494 He became the governor of Shirvan in 1587–88 and of Tomanis in 1591; see Selaniki, 1989, 1:260; Ayvansarayi, 1985, p. 318.
495 Gerlach, 1674, p. 397.
496 Ibid., p. 402.
497 BA, Evkaf 20/25, fols 6v–7r.
498 Among her inheritors only her brother and her two sisters Gevherhan and Fatma Sultan are mentioned, to the exclusion of İsmihan and the queen mother Nurbanu; ibid., fol. 8r.
499 Ibid., fol. 7r.
500 Ibid., fol. 8v.
501 Ibid., fols 12r–13r; Gökbilgin, 1952, p. 502.
502 BA, Evkaf 20/25, fol. 12r.
503 Ibid., fol. 8v.
504 Ibid., fol. 9r.
505 Ibid., fols 9r, 10v, 11v.
506 Ibid., fol. 9r.
507 Their boundary was a landing station, the waterfront, the endowment of Defterdar Mustafa Pasha's mosque, and the avenue along the Golden Horn; ibid., fol. 12v.
508 Ibid., fol. 13r.
509 BA, MD. 49, # 297, p. 85, dated 15 Ca. 991; cited in Dündar, 2000, p. 171.
510 BA, EV.HMH. 30, fol. 3a, no. 2, dated B. 1002, fols 4r–v.
511 Ibid., fols 9v–11v.
512 BA, EV.HMH. 30, dated end of Ş. 994 (August 1586), no. 1, fols 2v–3r.
513 Ayvansarayi, 2000, p. 277. Egemen, 1993, p. 777, also gives the date 958 (1551–52).
514 Ayvansarayi, 1985, p. 114: 'çeşme-i mā'i ḥayāt-ı cānfezā.' For the correct reading, also see Saatçi, 1988, pp. 138–40, no. 52.
515 Goodwin, 1971, p. 257, accepts Eyice's dating for the mosque between 1560 and 1566. For the date 1566–68 and the view that the fountain of 1589–90 was added later; see Aslanapa, 1986, p. 242. The date 1577 with a question mark is proposed in Günay, 1998, p. 41.
516 Kuban, 'Zal Mahmud Paşa Külliyesi', ISTA 7:542–43; Kuran, 1986, pp. 196–99.
517 Meriç, 1965, p. 26.
518 Kuban, 1997, p. 114. Elsewhere, he attributes the mosque to Davud due to its similarity with the Yeni Valide mosque in Eminönü featuring comparable collosal piers and a gallery over the entrance; idem., 'Zal Mahmud Paşa Külliyesi', ISTA 7:543. The whole complex is attributed to Sinan in Kuran, 1986, p. 199. Goodwin writes, 'it is likely that Sinan conceived the plan of the mosque and left the building of the lesser areas to subordinates'; Goodwin, 1971, p. 257.
519 BA, Evkaf 20/25, fols 23r–v. An annual rent (*muḳāṭaʿa*) was paid by the endowment administrator for the land leased for 320 aspers from the waqf of Abu Ayyub al-Ansari.
520 Ibid., fols 9v, 10v–11r.
521 Vatin and Yerasimos, 1994.
522 Pinon, 1987, p. 109; Günay, 1998, p. 41.
523 H. Egli, 1997, p. 89.
524 Alain Borie, 'Sinan's Külliyes: Architectural Composition', in Petruccioli, ed., 1987, p. 120.
525 The unconventional mausoleum plan with a cross inscribed in an octagon has been compared to that of the grand admiral Kılıç Ali Pasha built in the early 1580s; see Kuran, 1987, p. 213. The third person buried in it is unidentified.
526 Their irregularity is attributed to the interruption of construction work with the Selimiye in Edirne that thrust the project into 'less than competent hands'; see Goodwin, 1971, pp. 257–58.
527 Ibid., p. 258; Günay, 1998, p. 43.
528 BA, Evkaf 20/25, fol. 17v.
529 The minaret was rebuilt in the classical style after an earthquake in 1894; see Kuran, 1987, p. 205.
530 Photographs showing the tilework border intact confirm that the ungainly window frame is a later addition; see H. Egli, 1997, p. 91, photo 148.
531 BA, Evkaf 20/25, fols 11r–v.
532 Ibid., fol. 11v.
533 The first madrasa professor was Kethüda Mustafa Efendi (987/1579–80); see Baltacı, 1976, pp. 465–67. For the career of Sarı Mustafa Pasha, see Mehmed Süreyya, 1996, 4:1205.
534 Günay, 1998, p. 43.
535 Evliya, 1999, pp. 94–98.
536 Evliya, 1896–1938, 1:394.
537 Evliya, TSK, B.304, 1:118r.

CHAPTER 9

1 The date 1553–55 is given in Goodwin, 1971, p. 244; he proposes a later date (1561–62) in idem., 1993, pp. 46–47. The complex is dated to 1554–58 in Aslanapa, 1986, p. 222; to the late 1550s in Kuban, 1997, pp. 96–97; to 1558–1560 in Kuran, 1987, p. 111; and 1558–65 in Günay, 1998, pp. 68–69.
2 Busbecq, 1927, p. 33.
3 Celalzade, 1981, fols 500r–502r.
4 Albèri, 1840–55, 2:31–32.
5 Āli, Nuruosmaniye Library, Ms. 3409, fol. 124r.
6 Ibid., fol. 124r.
7 His coffin was left outside the first gate of the Topkapı Palace by the chief executioner and gatekeepers; it was picked up by his brother and servants; see Lokman, TSK, H.1524, fol. 177r.
8 Konyalı, 1950, p. 23; Ayvansarayi, 1985, pp. 148–49.
9 For these inscriptions, see Konyalı, 1950, pp. 18, 23; and Yaltkaya, 1942.
10 Konyalı who saw her tombstone says it did not have a date; he thinks she passed away before her husband in 1553; Konyalı, 1950, p. 26. For the unsubstantiated claim that she married after her husband's death the eunuch vizier Hadım İbrahim Pasha (d. 1562–63) as her 'adopted friend', see Erdoğan, 1938, p. 33. For this little known princess, also see Uluçay, 1980, p. 31.
11 Ayvansarayi, 2000, pp. 159, 175, 222. For her extant masjid at Topkapı, see Semavi Eyice, 'Fatma Sultan Mescidi', VIA 12:264.
12 Dated 2 N. 962, the waqfiyya is published in Yaltkaya, 1942.
13 Ibid., p. 96.
14 Ibid., pp. 92, 95.
15 Ibid., pp. 88–89.
16 The plot of land for the mosque complex must have been bought later on near the pre-existing mausoleum according to Kuran, 1987, p. 111.
17 Konyalı, 1950, pp. 17–18.
18 Ibid., pp. 16–18, 23.
19 Konyalı, 1948, p. 82.
20 Ayvansarayi, 2000, p. 159; Konyalı, 1950, pp. 18–19.
21 Kuran, 1986, p. 355, no. 279; p. 368, no. 326; pp. 392–93, nos. 423–25. The endowments of 'Hüsrev Kethüda b. Abdülmennan' are recorded in Ankara, Tapu ve Kadastro, Yeni no. 33, Eski no. 2262/2204, dated Ş. 990 (1582).
22 Upon regaining his post, Rüstem Pasha took revenge from the supporters of his executed rival by dismissing them from their positions; see Turan, 1958.
23 For the fountain inscription, see Egemen, 1993, p. 107, no. 129. It was destroyed during road construction and only its tank remained according to Konyalı, 1950, p. 21.
24 Marciana Library, IT. Cl. VII(8872), dated 12 January 1569, fol. 272v: 'volendo metter nella Moschea dal g. Achmat Bassà suo patrone, alla qual hora che è quasi finita tutti li suoi schiavi li offeriscono alcuna cosa.' Also see ASV, Dispacci Costantinopoli, Senato, Filza 4, dispatch #7 of Marcantonio Barbaro, dated 16 April 1569, fol. 42r: 'Il qual S[igno]r Ibraino mi hà pregato anco, che dovendo lui presentar qualche cosa, come è ordinario, alla Moschea del g. Achmat Bassà suo patrone, che fu primo visir, desidera che V[ostro] Ser[eni]tà li facia mandar un di quelli cesendelli, che si pongono nelle Moschee: dicendo egli, che di là si sà la sorte, che ordinariamente si sogliono mandar per tal effetto.' ASV, Senato Deliberazione Costantinopoli, Secreta, Registro 4, dated 11 June 1569, fol. 18v, indicates that the oil lamp requested by İbrahim Beg would soon be sent as a gift to certify the Senate's affection for him.
25 The inventory is published in Yaltkaya, 1942, p. 83. For Lala Mustafa Pasha's early career as a boon companion of Kara Ahmed Pasha, see Āli, Nuruosmaniye Library, Ms. 3409, fol. 124v.
26 The market is mentioned in İnciciyan, 1976, p. 36.
27 Goodwin, 1993, pp. 46–47; idem., 1971, p. 248; Kuran, 1986, p. 325, no. 177.
28 For the original wrought-iron canopy covering the ablution fountain, see Müller-Wiener, 1977, p. 486, illus. 589.
29 VGM, Defter 635/1 Mükerrer, no 10, fully cited under Mihrümah's patronage in Chapter 8.
30 Kuran, 1986, p. 282, no. 39; p. 325, no. 177; p. 341, no. 231.
31 See Chapter 7.
32 Konyalı, 1950, p. 15.
33 Their large size led Ernst Egli to hypothesize that the plan was altered after the hiatus in construction work; he believes the mosque was originally designed with side aisles covered by two small domes. This 'may be true' according to Kuban, 1997, p. 96. But Kuran rejects this hypothesis; see Kuran, 1987, p. 112.
34 Müller-Wiener, 1977, p. 487.
35 I agree with the view that the 'effect is obfuscated and convoluted' inside the prayer hall; see H. Egli, 1997, p. 73. Following the lead of Gurlitt and Gabriel, Kuban praises the classicizing scheme with free-standing columns: 'The central space created by the

hexagonal dome sitting on ostentatious columns is as effective as that under the octagonal baldachin of Selimiye'; see Kuban, 1997, pp. 97–98.

36 For inscriptions recording repairs, see Konyalı, 1950, p. 14; Yaltkaya, 1942, p. 97.

37 Cited in Konyalı, 1950, p. 16: 'Shenīdem ke berīn tārim zer-endūd-est.'

38 Evliya, 1896–1938, 1:310.

39 Evliya, TSK, B.304, 3:170r.

40 Kuran writes that it took 'another ten years' before Sinan produced this 'ultimate version' of the hexagonal scheme; see Kuran, 1987, p. 114.

41 See Chapter 5.

42 The pasha's waqfiya of 1565 refers to him as Ali Paşa b. Hüseyin; VGM, Defter 1961, no. 441, pp. 444–62 (translated from the Arabic original in Defter 585, dated the beginning of C. 973). For his biography, see R. Mantran, ''Ali Pasha Semiz', EI(2) 1:398; Āli, Nuruosmaniye Library, Ms. 3409, fols 124v–25v; Peçevi, 1864–67, 1:24; Daniele Barbarigo (1564) in Albèri, 1840–55, 2:30–32.

43 Āli, Nuruosmaniye Library, Ms. 3409, fols 124v–25v.

44 Busbecq, 1927, p. 190.

45 Ibid., pp. 193–95. His gentle character is also noted by Mekki (1557) in Kamil, 1937, p. 68; Andrea Dandolo (1562) in Albèri, 1840–55, 3:171; and Marcantonio Donini (1562) in ibid., 3:185.

46 In 1562, Marcantonio Donini estimated that the pasha was about sixty-seven years old; see Albèri, 1840–55, 3:185. For Daniele Barbarigo (1564), see ibid., 2:26–31. The pasha's death from '*maraż-ı ḫunnaḳ*' is recorded in Selaniki, 1989, 1:8.

47 Ibid., 2:27–31.

48 For Mihrümah's proposal, see Chapter 8.

49 VGM, Defter 585, p. 19; Defter 1961, pp. 457–62.

50 Gerlach, 1674, p. 449.

51 VGM, Defter 1961, pp. 446–57; Gökbilgin, 1952, pp. 502–3.

52 Kuran, 1986, p. 371, nos. 339–41; p. 381, nos. 375–77. He also owned an estate with three courtyards in Plovdiv, and a second palatial residence in the capital at Kızıltaş (Koska) featuring three courtyards and a garden kiosk; VGM, Defter 1961, pp. 446–48.

53 Kuran, 1986, p. 346, no. 346; p. 294, no. 75.

54 VGM, Defter 1961, pp. 445–46.

55 Ibid., pp. 459–460; VGM, Defter 585, p. 19.

56 VGM, Defter 1961, pp. 457, 461.

57 Ibid., pp. 462–63. For the tomb in Eyüp, a simple marble sarcophagus only mentioned in the TM and dated 973 (1565–66), see Kuran, 1986, p. 328, no. 187.

58 BA, MD. 6, #1335, p. 605, dated 4 Z. 972.

59 Kuran, 1986, p. 294, no. 75.

60 The following dates have been proposed: 1561–65 in Tuncel, 1974, p. 14; *c.* 1565 in Günay, 1998, p. 72; 1560s in Goodwin, 1971, p. 303; 1561–64 in Aslanapa, 1986, p. 228; and late 1560s in Kuran, 1986, p. 294, no. 74.

61 For the mosque in Balat, see Chapter 13.

62 Kuran, 1986, p. 294, no. 74; p. 345, no. 246. For the madrasa, see Baltacı, 1976, p. 559; Küçükkaya, 1990, p. 220; Müderrisoğlu, 1993, pp. 652–53.

63 Cited in Müderrisoğlu, 1993, p. 640.

64 BA, EV.HMH. 18, dated from the beginning of M. 982 to 25 Z. 982, fol. 2v: 'ḥüseyin ve muṣṭafā sāḫten-i bāb-ı cāmiʿ' 'ʿan yed-i usta ḫıżır', fol. 6r: 'baha-i ḳurşun-ı ḫām ʿan yed-i usta ḥüsām', fol. 5v: 'ücret-i ırġadān berā-yı sāḫten-i mināre be-maʿ rifet-i usta ḫıżır.'

65 BA, EV.HMH. 18, dated from the beginning of Za. 981 to 29 L. 982.

66 Gökbilgin, 1952, pp. 503–4, note 827.

67 BA, EV.HMH 18, dated the beginning of M. 982 to 25 Z. 982.

68 BA, EV.HMH 15, dated from the beginning of Ş. 981 to the end of B. 983.

69 Ibid., fol. 2r: 'ücret-i ʿarabacıyān berā-yı esbāblar ʿan edirne ilā babaeskisi', 'becihet-i kirāye-i ʿaraba berā-yı naḳḳāşlar ʿan edirne ilā babaeskisi.'

70 Ibid., fols 2v–3v.

71 BA, Ali Emiri, Murad III, no. 350.

72 BA, MD. 52, #934, p. 349, dated 12 R. 992: 'cāmiʿ-i şerīfe münāsib olduġı üzre ḥarem binā idüb …'.

73 BA, MD. 58, #818, p. 329, dated 17 N. 993. 'cāmiʿ-i şerīfüñ öñi ve ḥaremi henüz binā olunmayub cāmiʿ-i mezbūre nātamām ḳalmışdur … cāmiʿ-i şerīf-i mezbūruñ vaḳfında müsāʿde olduḳça öñini ve ḥaremini itmām eyleyesin.'

74 Wyts, ÖNB, Codex Vindobonensis Palatinus, 3325*, fol. 107v.

75 Soranzo, 1856, pp. 55–56.

76 Paolo Contarini (1580) mentions 'a mosque built by Ali Pasha, and a good enough caravansaray'; Contarini, 1856, p. 36. Also see Gerlach, 1674, p. 511; Lubenau, 1912, 1:121.

77 The geographer Mehmed Aşık, who visited Babaeski in 1578–79 and 1589–90, only mentions the mosque, bath, and little suq; see Mehmed Aşık, TSK, E.H.1446, fol. 397r.

78 The historical bridge built in 1043 (1633–34) replaced an earlier one mentioned by the Austrian diplomat Jacob von Betzek in 1564–65; see Betzek, 1979, p. 20.

79 For repairs, see Tuncel, 1974, pp. 14–19; Küçükkaya, 1990, pp. 201–3; Müderrisoğlu, 1993, p. 636.

80 See photographs of the pulpits in Aslanapa, 1986, p. 231; and Goodwin, 1971, pp. 260, 265, 303.

81 Evliya, TSK, B.304, 3:170r.

CHAPTER 10

1 Kuran, 1986, p. 273, no. 9.

2 Abdülhamid II requested that the converted structure should not resemble a mosque and covered its remodelling expenses as a church; see Eren, 1968.

3 I am grateful to Machiel Kiel, who gave me a copy of his forthcoming study on this mosque.

4 Sai, 1989, fols 3v–4r.

5 Lutfi Paşa, 2001, pp. 132–33; Rüstem Pasha, ÖNB, Codex Vindobonensis Palatinus, Mxt. 339, fols 221v–22r.

6 For the biography of Hacı (Sofu) Mehmed Pasha, see Mehmed Süreyya, 1996, 4:1073. Some of the dates given in this source are contradicted by primary sources. For instance the pasha is said to have died at Buda in 1551, but a list of the governor-generals of Buda indicates he died there in 1557; see Gévay, 1841, p. 59.

7 Āli, Nuruosmaniye Library, Ms. 3409, fol. 127r.

8 VGM, Mücedded Rumeli Vakfiyesi Defteri 2, no. 988, dated mid Z. 954, pp. 51–64. He is identified as 'al-wazīr al-thānī … Meḥmed Pāşā b. ʿAbd al-Muʿīn', on p. 51.

9 These buildings are no longer extant; see Mujezinović, 1998, 2:196–97.

10 Kuran, 1986, pp. 262–63; p. 273, no. 9; p. 346, no. 346; p. 356, no. 282; p. 383, no. 382. The TM mentions the 'palace of Sofu Mehmed Pasha' inside the city and the 'palace of the Bosnian Mehmed Pasha outside the city walls'; see Meriç, 1965, p. 41. The 'palace of Mehmed Pasha in Bosnia' is identified by Kuran with Sokollu, but it must have belonged to Sofu Mehmed Pasha who governed in Bosnia; see Kuran, ibid., p. 384, no. 384. Meriç has misread an entry in TM as 'Āmidde Sofu Mehmed Paşa Camii – Medrese der Van.' The madrasa in Van belongs to the previous entry on the mosque of İbrahim Pasha in Amid (Diyarbakır); see Meriç, 1965, p. 27.

11 Maurand, 1901, pp. 189–97.

12 Zaifi, *Külliyāt*, TSK, R.822, fol. 126r.

13 The inscription is published in Eren, 1968, p. 70.

14 This contradicts the dates given in Mehmed Süreyya, who says he became second vizier in 1537–38, the governor-general of Baghdad in 1545, of Bosnia in 1547, and of Buda in 1551; see Mehmed Süreyya, 1996, 4:1073.

15 VGM, Mücedded Rumeli Vakfiyesi Defteri 2, no. 988, p. 52. For the tomb of Shaykh Bali Efendi near Sofia, see Eren, 1968, p. 69.

16 For that shaykh, see Clayer, 1994, pp. 69–81.

17 Eren, 1968, p. 69.

18 VGM, Mücedded Rumeli Vakfiyesi Defteri 2, no. 988, p. 52.

19 The madrasa containing a library was demolished in 1928, the hospice served free food until 1878; see Eren, 1968, p. 69.

20 Machiel Kiel's forthcoming study compares it to the mosque of the governor Osmanshah in Trikkala, covered by a dome 17.98 metres wide.

21 Evliya, 1986–1938, 3:398–99.

22 Examples of early-sixteenth-century single-domed vizirial mosques with three- to five-bay porticoes include those of Çoban Mustafa Pasha in Eskişehir and Gebze, Güzelce Kasım Pasha in Bozüyük, and Cezeri Kasım Pasha in Eyüp.

23 Rüstem Pasha, ÖNB, Codex Vindobonensis Palatinus Mxt. 339, fols 238r, 250v.

24 Albèri, 1840–55, 1:89.

25 Dernschwam, 1923, pp. 56–59, 118, 137; Domenico Trevisano (1554) in Albèri, 1840–55, 1:121, 177–78, 191; 'Relazione Anonima, 1553', in ibid., 1:247, 256; Busbecq, 1927, p. 28.

26 Rüstem Pasha, ÖNB, Codex Vindobonensis Palatinus Mxt. 339, fol. 280r. For the unsubstantiated claim that the eunuch pasha had married princess Fatma Sultan, the widow of Kara Ahmed Pasha (d. 1555), see Erdoğan, 1938, p. 33.

27 Āli, Nuruosmaniye Library, Ms. 3409, fol. 127r.

28 He is referred to as 'İbrāhīm Pāşā ibn ʿAbd al-Muʿīn', TIEM 2187, dated 15 Ca. 969; cited in Erdoğan, 1938, pp. 30–33; Konyalı, 1950, pp. 106–7; Gökbilgin, 1952, pp. 504–6. Another copy of the waqfiyya is in VGM Defter 1961, dated 15 Ca. 969, pp. 41–76 (translation of the Arabic waqfiyya in VGM, Istanbul Hamis, Defter 574, no. 41, pp. 87–97).

29 An earlier waqfiyya dated 2 January 1542 shows that the madrasa in İsakapı and the mosque and school in Silivrikapı were built later; see VGM, Defter 1961, no. 3, dated the middle of N. 948, pp. 240–51 (translation of the Arabic waqfiyya in 618/1 Mücedded Anadolu, no. 68, p. 117).

30 Erdoğan, 1938, pp. 30–32; Konyalı, 1950, p. 107; Gökbilgin, 1952, pp. 504–6.

31 Erdoğan, 1938; Konyalı, 1950, pp. 99–101.

32 Kuran, 1986, p. 259; p. 279, no. 28; p. 311, no. 128; p. 323, no. 172; p. 338, no. 220; p. 390, no. 414.

33 Konyalı, 1950, p. 41. Eyice unconvincingly argues that the chronogram could also yield the date 950 (1543–44) which coincides with Sinan's tenure; see Eyice, 1991, pp. 510–11. For a comparison of the Silivrikapı mosque with that of Bali Pasha, see Goodwin, 1971, p. 244; Kuran, 1987, pp. 103–4.

34 Goodwin, 1971, p. 174; Kuran, 1986, p. 272, no. 6; Müller-Wiener, 1977, pp. 382–83; Yüksel, 1983, pp. 180, 256–57. For the argument that the mosque was entirely built by Sinan around 1546–48, see Eyice, 1991.

35 Ateş, 1990, p. 67.

36 Ayvansarayi, 2000, pp. 70–72. For the identity of Hüma Hatun, see Uzunçarşılı, 1976, p. 473, note 12. It is unclear whether her mother was a daughter of Selim I (Hanım Sultan) or another woman. For İskender Pasha's mausoleum (with a tombstone dated

1515) and his elementary school near the Sultan Ahmed mosque at the Hippodrome; see Yüksel, 1983, pp. 297, 439.
37 Barkan and Ayverdi, eds, 1970, p. 216, no. 1254.
38 BA, Istanbul Tapu Defteri no. 670, pp. 559–61: 'vaḳf-ı hümā ḫātūn', dated the beginning of Z. 970; ibid., p. 561, dated the beginning of Ş. 980. The mosque is referred to both as 'Bali Paşa cāmiʿi' and as the mosque of the foundress 'vāḳıfe-i mezbūreniñ cāmiʿi.'
39 VGM, Anadolu Başlar, Defter 1211, the beginning of N. 973, pp. 237–39 (translation of the Arabic waqfiyya in Defter 579); the mosque is identified as 'hümā ḫatun binā itdügi cāmiʿ-i şerīf.' The identity of Bali Pasha is unclear. Perhaps he was Enderunlu Bali Pasha who served as the governor-general of Anatolia, Diyarbakır, and Buda; see Mehmed Süreyya, 1996, 2:357.
40 It is thought that the mosque was either left incomplete or was damaged in the earthquake of 1509; see Eyice, 1991, p. 509.
41 The fallen domes of the five-bay portico were rebuilt in 1975; see Kuran; 1987, p. 103.
42 Ibid., pp. 103–4.
43 For repairs, see ibid., p. 103; Müller-Wiener, 1977, p. 417.
44 Konyalı, 1950, p. 94; Erdoğan, 1938, p. 30.
45 Konyalı, 1950, p. 93.
46 Ibid., pp. 95–96; Erdoğan, 1938, p. 30; Ayvansarayi, 1985, p. 128; Saatçi, 1988, pp. 57–59, no. 20.
47 Ayvansarayi, 2000, pp. 32–33.
48 See Chapter 8.
49 Evliya, TSK, B.304, 1:89r.
50 See Chapter 12.
51 Franz Babinger, 'Pertew Pasha', EI(2) 8:295–96; Erdoğan, 1942.
52 Albèri, 1840–55, 3:187–88.
53 'Pertau' had married 'the widow of Mahomet', according to Busbecq, 1927, p. 81. Mekki (1557) says the fourth vizier Pertev Pasha had two children from Şehzade Mehmed's daughter Hanım Sultan; see Kamil, 1937, p. 70.
54 Āli, Nuruosmaniye Library, Ms. 3409, fols 127v–28r.
55 He was about sixty-five years old in 1571 according to Jacopo Ragazzoni; see Albèri, 1840–55, 2:98. For the inscription of his tombstone and the family mausoleum, see Kuran, 1986, p. 327, no. 185; Haskan, 1993, 1:242; Ayvansarayi, 1985, pp. 120–21.
56 For the two palaces Sinan built for Pertev Pasha in Vefa and outside the city walls, see Kuran, 1986, p. 379, nos. 368–69.
57 Sai, 1897, p. 30; Aktuğ, 1990, pp. 24–25.
58 TIEM, 3406, undated waqfiyya, cited in Erdoğan, 1942. Another copy is in Bayezid Umumi Kütüphanesi, no. 5157; and in VGM, Defter 740 (no. 1, undated waqwiyya; no. 2, *temliks* donated in M. 977 (1570) and renewed in M. 980 (1572); no. 3, posthumous additions to the waqf dated Ca. 980).
59 VGM, Defter 740, p. 29.
60 Ibid., pp. 30–33; Erdoğan, 1942, pp. 236–37.
61 VGM, Defter 740, p. 34.
62 İzmit was the fief of Pertev Pasha for seven years according to Evliya, TSK, B.304, 2:242r. For his endowments in İzmit, see VGM, Defter 740, pp. 18–21; Erdoğan, 1942, pp. 238–39.
63 For the palace, see VGM, Defter 740, pp. 34–45; Erdoğan, 1942, p. 239.
64 VGM, Defter 740, p. 17 refers to him as Sultan Selim II's 'vüzerā ḳullarından ... pertev paşa tecāvez allāhu ʿanhu nümāyişehā.' Erdoğan says the waqfiyya was written in 977 (1569) without an explanation; see Erdoğan, 1942, pp. 238–40.
65 VGM, Defter 740, pp. 24–25.
66 Erdoğan, 1942, p. 239–40.
67 VGM, Defter 740, p. 28; Erdoğan, 1942, p. 238. His wife is referred to as 'Fütūha bint-i Rabbü'l-aʿ lā' and her tombstone is dated 979 (1571); see Haskan, 1993, 1:242.
68 BA, MD. 22, #474, p. 243, dated 14 R. 981.
69 Erdoğan, 1942, p. 235; Müderrisoğlu, 1993, p. 684.
70 Erdoğan, 1942, p. 235; Müderrisoğlu, 1993, p. 683, fig. 198a.
71 Erdoğan, 1942, p. 235. Sai's TB similarly refers to monumental *thuluth* inscriptions as '*müṣennā*'; see Chapter 3(III).
72 Cited in Müderrisoğlu, 1993, pp. 689–90.
73 Evliya, TSK, B.304, 2:242r.
74 Aktuğ, 1990, pp. 12–14.
75 The complex was ruined in the earthquake of 1719. For repairs in 1131 (1718–19), 1178 (1764–65), 1274 (1857–58), 1937, 1946, and 1959–60, see Müderrisoğlu, 1993, p. 694.
76 The waqfiyya mentions the staff of the modest hospice kitchen among the caravansaray's employees. For the dependencies, see ibid., pp. 701–5.
77 See Chapter 11.
78 Evliya, TSK, B.304, 2:242r.
79 Ibid., 2:242r.
80 Āli, Nuruosmaniye Library, Ms. 3409, fol. 128r.
81 Rüstem Pasha, ÖNB, Codex Vindobonensis Palatinus, Mxt. 339, fols 278v–79r.
82 Gökbilgin, 1955, pp. 29–32, 46–50. Ferhad was replaced by the janissary agha (Güzelce) Ahmed in 965 (1557–58), who married in 1561 the daughter of the late Rüstem Pasha and Mihrümah.
83 Rüstem Pasha, ÖNB, Codex Vindobonensis Palatinus, Mxt. 339, fols 282v, 293v.
84 Marcantonio Donini (1562), in Albèri, 1840–55, 3:187–88.
85 Selaniki 1:15, 36. In 1567 he is still mentioned as the third vizier by Pigafetta, 1890, p. 136.
86 Selaniki, 1989, 1:111. After a trial, Shaykh Şuca was sent to prison on 8 February 1575; Āli, Nuruosmaniye Library, Ms. 3409, fol. 128r.
87 Selaniki, 1989, 1:110–11. For the open-air mausoleum of 'Ferhad Pasha b. Mustafa', whose tombstone near the courtyard gate of the Eyüp mosque is dated L. 982; see Haskan, 1993, 1:190–91.
88 Āli, Nuruosmaniye Library, Ms. 3409, fol. 128r.
89 Ibid., fol. 128r.
90 Ahmed Refik, 1924, pp. 261–63.
91 Albèri, 1840–55, 2:154. For her second husband, see Chapter 12.
92 For the palace near the forecourt of Bayezid II's mosque, see Kuran, 1986, p. 376, no. 356. Süleyman had scolded Sinan in 1557 for delaying the Süleymaniye with the construction of Ferhad Pasha's neighbouring palace; see Sai, 1989, fol. 10v; and Chapter 4(II).
93 VGM, Dolab Defteri 1747, dated M. 1181.
94 Çifci, 1995, pp. 118–20; Kuran, 1986, p. 275, no. 16. The mosque was renovated in 1166 (1752–53), 1195 (1781), and 1815. Damaged in an earthquake in 1943, it was rebuilt in 1958 and 1968–70. Kuran thinks the mosque may originally have had a dome.
95 Sai, 1879, p. 31; TE in Meriç, 1965, p. 84.
96 Kuran, 1975, pp. 76–77, figs. 11–12.
97 It is dated *c.* 1575–80 and its construction is attributed to the pasha's wife Hüma Hatun in Kuran, 1986, p. 276, no. 15.
98 Evliya, TSK, B.304, 3:171r.
99 TM in Meriç, 1965, p. 26; Kuran, 1986, p. 287, no. 53. Mesih Pasha's mosque is only listed in one copy of the TE; see Meriç, ibid., p. 85.
100 He became chief treasurer of the inner palace during Selim II's accession in 1566 according to Selaniki, 1989, 1:65.
101 He was chief of the inner pantry before Selim II's accession according to Peçevi, 1864–67, 2:18.
102 A.H. de Groot, 'Mesih Mehmed Pasha', EI(2) 6:1024.
103 Albèri, 1840–55, 2:243.
104 Ibid., 3:241.
105 Āli, 1979–82, 2:31.
106 Selaniki, 1989, 1:150–51.
107 Albèri, 1840–55, 3:287–89.
108 Selaniki, 1989, 1:164–65, 167–68.
109 Peçevi, 1864–67, 2:18.
110 Ibid., 2:18–19. Morosini says he was in his late seventies in 1585. He died at ninety in 1589 according to A.H. de Groot, EI(2) 6:1024. He passed away in 1591–92 according to Ayvansarayi, 2000, p. 214.
111 TSA, E.317/264, dated the beginning of Ra. 992.
112 Ayvansarayi, 2000, pp. 193–94, 213. On 27 April 1588 a permit allowed Mesih Pasha 'who retired from the grand vizierate' to build with his own money a new masjid requested by the inhabitants of the Hadice Sultan quarter near Karagümrük (TSA, E.317/268, dated the end of Ca. 996).
113 BA, MD. 52, #854, p. 322, dated 21 Ra. 992 (mi'mārbaşı ḳā'immaḳāmına ḥükm).
114 BA, MD. 52, #714, p. 269, dated 16 S. 992.
115 BA, MD. 52, #920, p. 344, dated 7 R. 992.
116 BA, MD. 53, #134, p. 49, dated 1 C. 992.
117 TSA, E.317/266, dated the beginning of R. 993; BA, MD. 58, #36, p. 12, dated 8 R. 993.
118 Ayvansarayi, 1985, p. 386; Egemen, 1993, p. 596. The two-faceted fountain with one arch facing Mevkufatçı Sokak and two others facing Eski Ali Paşa Sokak was repaired by Beyhan Sultan in 1233 (1817–18).
119 The second couplet is misinterpreted in Crane's translation; I have followed Saatçi's reading: 'Itdi iḥyā vaḥiy-yi ḥaḳḳile çün ol ʿīsā-yi nefs / Vuṣlāt-ı ḥaḳḳa tarīḳ cennete oldı delīl;' Crane, 2000, pp. 213–14; Saatçi, 1988, pp. 128–30, no. 45; Kuran, 1986, p. 233, note 43.
120 Ayvansarayi, 2000, p. 213.
121 TSA, E.317/267, dated the end of N. 995.
122 The memorandum of the mosque's waqf administrator to Davud Agha is in TSA, E.3778/2, dated 8 Ra. 996 (6 February 1588).
123 Ayvansarayi, 2000, pp. 213–14.
124 Kuran, 1987, p. 234.
125 Goodwin, 1971, p. 271.
126 Ibid., p. 270.
127 Ayvansarayi, 2000, p. 213: 'The *müezzins* and Qur'an readers (*devrhan*) who take part in Friday prayer perform their duties in the small gallery at the right side [of the mosque], and at other times they remain in the small gallery on the left side [of the mosque].'
128 Calling the side wings 'oratories', Goodwin speculates that their present use as spaces for private prayer might reflect their original function; see Goodwin, 1971, pp. 270–71.
129 Behrens-Abouseif, 1994, pp. 159, 180.
130 See Chapter 10.
131 Kuran speculates that 'the novel features that appear in the Mesih Pasha mosque may have directly or indirectly been inspired by Sinan', even though Davud contributed to its design and execution; see Kuran, 1987, p. 234. The mosque is attributed to Davud in Müller-Wiener, 1977, p. 439; and in Aslanapa, 1986, p. 307.
132 The mosque generally attributed to Davud 'could just as easily be by Mehmed or some other subordinate of the master', according to Goodwin, 1971, p. 270.
133 TM in Meriç, 1965, p. 26.
134 His father was Pir Ahmed Çelebi; for his biography, see Ayvansarayi, 2000, p. 233; Atai, 1989, 2:337; Fleischer, 1986, p. 219, note 13.
135 Atai, 1989, 2:337.
136 Selaniki, 1989, 1:128. Of all the chancellors appoint-

ed between 1573 and 1597 only Mehmed Pasha achieved a position as the governor-general of a province; see Fleisher, 1986, pp. 220–21.
137 Albèri, 1840–55, 3:295.
138 The dates given in the sources vary; see Atai, 1989, 2:337–38; Ayvansarayi, 2000, p. 233; Mehmed Süreyya, 1996, 4:1043–44; Selaniki, 1989, 1:212, 395.
139 Selaniki, 1989, 1:238.
140 Bernardo, 1886, p. 42.
141 The sixth 'vizier Nişancı Mehmed Pasha' died from 'maraż-ı istisķā' on 21 Ramadan 1002 according to Selaniki, 1989, 1:318. Atai says he died as the seventh vizier and Sai's chronogram, which gives the date 1001 (1592–93) for the pasha's death, is quoted in Atai, 1989, 2:337–38.
142 Selaniki, 1989, 1:129. According to Āli, despite his genealogy, Nişancı Mehmed was not a learned man and hence a poor chancellor; Nuruosmaniye Library, Ms. 3409, fol. 257r.
143 Selaniki, 1989, 1:129–30.
144 Ibid., 1:318.
145 Atai, 1989, 2:337–38.
146 Ayvansarayi, 2000, p. 233. He mentions repairs in 1251 (1835–36).
147 The chronogram reads: 'Didiler vāṣıl-ı ḥaķķ oldı nişānī pāşā.'
148 He is referred to as the late vizier 'Meḥmed Pāşā el-Tevķīʿi el-Vezīr', VGM, Defter 2111, dated the beginning of M. 1009, pp. 258–68 (translation of the Arabic original, Defter 572, pp. 233–44). The site of the mosque complex is described as 'between [the quarter] of Küçük Karaman and Edirnekapı, at the place called Zincirlikuyu.'
149 VGM, Defter 2111, pp. 264–65; Defter 572, pp. 237–40: 'cāmiʿ ķurbinde binā olınan otuziki bāb oṭalar dārü'l-ḥadīş olub … cāmiʿ-i şerīf-i mezkūruñ öninde vāķiʿ olan ḫurde ķubbeler altında ocaķluca birer ḥücre binā olunub, ve ẕikr olınan ḥücerāt binā olunduķda …'.
150 For Shaykh Yunus Halife, who was the shaykh and preacher in the mosque of 'Nişancı Mehmed Pasha zaviyesi', see Hulvi, 1993, p. 609. The convent with eleven members is listed in Zakir Şükri Efendi, 1980, p. 62.
151 VGM, Defter 2111, pp. 264–68; VGM, Defter 572, pp. 237–43. The no-longer extant mosque and school in Galata is mentioned in Ayvansarayi, 2000, p. 364; see note 2725, p. 364. For the pasha's waqf in Aleppo, the Khan al-Hibal was built in 1003 (1594), but his mosque there is no longer extant; see Watenpaugh, 1999, pp. 151–52.
152 For the endowed palace, see VGM, Defter 2111, pp. 262–63.
153 ASV, Senato, Deliberationi Costantinopoli (Secreta), Registro 6, dated 12 October 1584, fol. 175r: 'Habbiamo fatto ordinar li dui mille Rui, la mità tondi et la mità quadri, et li cinquanta cesendeli per il Nisangibassi ricercati colle ultime nostre.' Ibid., 29 December 1584, fol. 181r: 'Li Cesendeli et Rui per quel Serenissimo Signor et per il Nissangibassi sono fatti, et si manderanó con primo passaggio di mare.' Ibid., 7 February 1584 (i.e., 1585), fol. 203r: 'Havemo fatti ordinar li altri cesendeli, et lastre di cristallo per il Magnifico Nisangibassi lequali con li altri vedri che egli se fece ricercare che sono gia fatti vi si manderanno colla prima nave.'
154 BA, MD. 58, #747, p. 293, 17 N. 993. Repeated on 24 October 1585 for 3,000 qintars of lead (BA, MD. 60, #13, p. 15, end of L. 993).
155 BA, MD. 60, #33, p. 15, dated end of L 993 (24 October 1585).
156 BA, MD. 60, #337, p. 143, dated 20 S. 994.
157 BA, MD. 60, #547, p. 230, dated 18 Ca. 994.
158 BA, MD. 61, #121, p. 44, dated 27 B. 994, given in the imperial council to Mehmed Pasha himself.
159 BA, MD. 61, #166, p. 63, dated 3 N. 994.
160 BA, MD. 61, #89, p. 33, dated 18 N. 994.
161 BA, MD. 62, #105, p. 47, dated 16 Ca. 995.
162 BA, MD. 62, #127, p. 55, 16 Ca. 995.
163 Aslanapa, 1986, p. 307; Günay, 1998, p. 45; Kuban, 'Nişancı Mehmed Paşa Camii', ISTA 6:85–87.
164 Kuran, 1987, pp. 226, 234, 239. For the attribution of Nişancı Mehmed Pasha's mosque together with the Mesih Pasha and Cerrah Pasha mosques to Davud, see Goodwin, 1971, pp. 336–37.
165 Kuran, 1987, pp. 236–37.
166 See the old photograph in Aslanapa, 1986, p. 308.
167 The street running parallel to the west side of the mosque was called 'Tekye Sokak' (Convent Street); see Ayverdi, 1958, plate 5; Pervitich, 2000, plate 34, p. 178. The site of 'Çukur Medrese' (Sunken Madrasa) is shown at the west side of the forecourt in Müller-Wiener, 1977, p. 447.
168 The plan also recalls such late fifteenth-century T-type mosques with projecting mihrabs as that of Davud Pasha; see Aslanapa, 1986, p. 115.
169 Goodwin, 1971, p. 337.
170 For renovations see Kuran, 1987, p. 236; Müller-Wiener, 1977, p. 449.

CHAPTER 11

1 The mosques of grand admirals are recognized as a distinctive subgroup in Yerasimos, 1987, pp. 125–27.
2 Aldo Gallotta, 'Khayr al-Dīn Pasha', EI(2), 4:1155–58; idem., 1983.
3 Lutfi Pasha, 1991; Gallotta, ed., 1983.
4 Barbarossa also endowed a convent and hospice complex in his birthplace, the island of Mytelene; see his waqfiyyas dated 1534 and 1548, VGM, Defter 571, dated 2 Ra. 941; and BA, Vakfiye 6/47, dated the beginning of Z. 954. His masjid and hospice in Beşiktaş were being built at the time of his death according to a dispatch of the *bailo* Alessandro Contarini, dated July 1546; see ASV, Archivio Proprio Costantinopoli, Busta 4, fol. 81r. For the now-lost 'Hayreddin İskelesi Mosque', see Ayvansarayi, 2000, pp. 410–11.
5 Kuran, 1986, p. 320, no. 163; pp. 388–89, nos. 406–7.
6 Gallotta, ed., 1983; Katip Çelebi, 1973, p. 34.
7 Gallotta, ed., 1983, p. 28.
8 Genoa, Archivio di Stato, 2170, dispatch #168, dated 28 March, 1566.
9 Pigafetta, 1890, p. 194.
10 Selaniki, 1989, 1:77–78.
11 Ibid., 1:81.
12 See Rüstem Pasha's biography in Chapter 8.
13 Āli, Nuruosmaniye Library, Ms. 3409, fol. 134r.
14 Katip Çelebi, 1973, pp. 88–89.
15 Albèri, 1840–55, 1:71, 88.
16 Ibid., 1:70.
17 Ibid., 1:78–79. In 1544, when Hürrem Sultan invited prince Selim to Bursa to a meeting with the grand vizier Süleyman Pasha and the second vizier Rüstem Pasha, she sent 'Kapudan Sinan Pasha' (then the chief court taster or *çaşnigirbaşı*) to accompany him from Uşak to Bursa; see Vusuli, Fatih Millet Kütüphanesi, Ali Emiri, T. 321, fol. 14v.
18 Albèri, 1840–55, 1:173–74.
19 Domenico Trevisano (1554) in ibid., 1:175, 177–79; and Dernschwam, 1923, pp. 32, 41–42, 57–58.
20 Dernschwam, 1923, p. 141.
21 Laguna, 1983, pp. 125–60.
22 For the pasha's exile in Üsküdar, see Dernschwam, 1923, p. 57.
23 Laguna, 1983, pp. 160–61.
24 Ibid., pp. 99–105. During the royal circumcision in 1582, goods from the imperial commissariat were stored in the late Sinan Pasha's residence at the Hippodrome ('kapudan iken vefat iden Sinan Paşa evlerinde'), Selaniki, 1989, 1:132–33.
25 Laguna, 1983, pp. 300–1.
26 Ibid., pp. 118, 160–61.
27 Ibid., pp. 161–63.
28 VGM, Defter 2113 (Kasa Defteri 110), sıra no. 49, dated the beginning of Za. 964, pp. 7–106 (translated from Arabic into Turkish in Defter 2148, sıra no. 8, pp. 123–272).
29 The waqfiyya was written in the middle of B. 961, and the pasha died in M. 962; see VGM, Defter 2148, pp. 125–31.
30 The cash was increased with the sale of slaves and of properties in Hercegovina; VGM, Defter 2148, pp. 129, 131–32.
31 VGM, Defter 2148, p. 132. For Deli Birader and the complex he built next to the garden of his residence, see Aşık Çelebi, 1971, fols 294r–96r.
32 VGM, Defter 2148,, pp. 139–42. For the Byzantine chapel converted into of a masjid (Kızıl Mescit), see Semavi Eyice, 'Sinan Paşa Mescidi', ISTA 7:5; Ayvansarayi, 2000, p. 261.
33 Kuran, 1986, p. 295, no. 76; p. 316, no. 149; p. 328, no. 188; p. 346, no. 248; p. 382, no. 378; p. 397, no. 442. The bath-house in Beşiktaş was demolished in 1957 and the masjid in Yenibahçe was destroyed during a fire in 1918. For the masjid, see Ayvansarayi, 2000, pp. 142–43.
34 The Arabic waqfiyya is in VGM, Kasa Defteri 94, dated the beginning of M. 970, pp. 1–68. The testimony of Mihrümah Sultan was represented by her steward Behram Kethüda and Meryem's agent was Mehmed Beg b. Abdülmennan (the former steward of Rüstem Pasha, now acting as his endowment administrator).
35 Also listed are the burial and feast expenses of Sinan Pasha's funeral (110,000 aspers), farms bought in Hercegovina (140,000 aspers), and building expenses of the Beşiktaş mosque (796,300 aspers). Upon subtracting these expenditures that equalled 1,046,300 aspers from the total sum, the remaining 1,380,855 aspers were added to the waqf.
36 VGM, Kasa Defteri 94, pp. 20–26.
37 Pervitich, 1999, pp. 31, 35. For the vanished masjid of Sinan Pasha in the Yıldız quarter of Beşiktaş, see Ayvansarayi, 2000, p. 419.
38 It is unclear whether Sinan Pasha had a palace in Beşiktaş besides the one he commissioned from Sinan at the Hippodrome. A palace was owned in Beşiktaş by Cağaloğlu (Cigalazade Yusuf Sinan Pasha who successively married two grand-daughters of Rüstem Pasha and Mihrümah Sultan); he held the post of grand admiral twice in the 1590s. For 'the state-owned (*mīrī*) shore palace in Beşiktaş named after Cağaloğlu', which was demolished and converted into a royal palace in 1680, see Silahdar, 1928, 1:732–33.
39 Al-Tamgruti, 1929, pp. 68–69.
40 Eremya, 1988, p. 39–40. See also İnciciyan, 1976, p. 114.
41 Evliya, TSK, B. 304, 1:134v–35r.
42 Ayvansarayi, 2000, pp. 408–10.
43 Cited in Ayvansarayi, 2000, p. 409.
44 Saatçi, 1988, pp. 63–65, no. 22.
45 Kuran, 1987, p. 105; Goodwin, 1993, p. 105; Kuban, 1997, pp. 94–95.
46 Aslanapa, 1986, p. 220; Kuban, 1997, p. 95; H. Egli, 1997, p. 71.
47 Kuban, 1997, pp. 94–95.
48 The date given by Hammer von Purgstall is cited in Kuban, 1997, p. 94. Evliya mentions the external prayer platforms (*ṭaşra yan ṣoffalar*) covered with five domes raised on columns; TSK, B. 304, fols 134b–35a.

49 For Kara Ahmed Pasha's mosque, see Chapter 9.
50 For the dates of repairs, see Kuran, 1986, p. 295, no. 96; Müller-Wiener, 1977, pp. 459. The light verse (24:35) on the dome was written by the calligrapher Kazasker Mustafa İzzet Efendi (1801–76) and the window lunettes with the beautiful names of God were calligraphed by Alaeddin Bey (1844–87); see Derman, 1989, p. 291.
51 VGM, Kasa Defteri 121, undated, attached to Kasa Defteri 110.
52 The mosque is attributed to Sinan in Aslanapa, 1986, pp. 278–81; and Tanman, 1989. Others exclude it from Sinan's corpus: Goodwin, 1971, pp. 276–77; Kuban, 1997, p. 118; Kuran, 1987, p. 126. A European architect may have contributed to its design, according to Martiny, 1936.
53 Only the mosque is listed in TM, Meriç, 1965, p. 26.
54 Marcantonio Donini (1562), in Albèri, 1840–55, 2:189–90. For Piyale Pasha's palace near Atpazarı in Aksaray, see Selaniki, 1989, 2:777–78. A decree addressed to the water channel superintendent Hasan in 1567 permits the water sources discovered outside the city walls by Piyale Pasha to be conducted to his palace with the water channel of Bayezid II; see BA, MD. 7, #113, p. 39, dated 20 S. 975.
55 Betzek, 1979, p. 36. His Hungarian origin is mentioned by Jacopo Ragazzoni (1571) in Albèri, 1840–55, 1:98; Badoaro (1573), ibid., 1:365; Garzoni (1573), ibid., 1:407. Gerlach says Piyale was the son of a Hungarian shoemaker; he had been taken in his childhood from Tolna in Hungary where he still kept in touch with some friends; see Gerlach, 1674, pp. 37–38, 229. Piyale was the son of a cobbler and found as an infant in Hungary while Sultan Süleyman was hunting there, according to Pigafetta, 1890, pp. 156–57. His origin is described as 'di nazione croato, vicino ai confini d'Ungheria', in Albèri, 1840–55, 2:243. He is identified as a Croat in Katip Çelebi, 1973, p. 207; and Āli, IÜ, T. 5959, fol. 461v.
56 Şerafettin Turan, 'Piyāle Paşa', IA, 9:566–69; F. Babinger, 'Piyale Pasha', EI(2) 8:316–17; Ayvansarayi, 1985, pp. 265–66.
57 Busbecq, 1927, pp. 169–77.
58 Ibid., pp. 174–75.
59 Piyale divorced his previous wife to marry the sultana according to Gerlach, 1674, p. 268. For Gevherhan, see Uluçay, 1980, pp. 41–42. Marino Cavalli (1560) reports that Süleyman valued the loyal and prudent grand admiral's advice more than that of Rüstem Pasha; see Albèri, 1840–55, 1:295.
60 Ibid., 3:188–89.
61 Katip Çelebi, 1973, pp. 115–20.
62 Selaniki, 1989, 1:57–58, 66; Katip Çelebi, 1973, pp. 114–15.
63 Pigafetta, 1890, pp. 156–57.
64 Cavalli, 1914, p. 13.
65 Antonio Tiepolo (1576), in Albèri, 1840–55, 2:159, 162.
66 He is referred to as 'Vezir Kapudan Piyale Paşa' in Peçevi, 1864–67, 1:441.
67 Du Fresne-Canaye, 1897, pp. 139–40.
68 Antonio Tiepolo (1576), in Albèri, 1840–55, 2:159. The planned attack on Sicily and Nàvplion in Greece (Anabolu) did not materialize because of wretched weather conditions; see Katip Çelebi, 1973, pp. 143–44. For the raid of Messina, see Peçevi, 1864–67, 1:354–55.
69 Badoaro (1573), in Albèri, 1840–55, 1:365; Garzoni (1573), ibid., 1:407.
70 Ibid., 2:156.
71 His fief of 100,000 ducats reverted to the sultan, and his other properties were inherited by his widow and children. His horses, furs and jewels were sold in the covered bazaar on 27 January; see Gerlach, 1674, pp. 448–49.
72 Ayvansarayi, 2000, p. 352.
73 Ibid., p. 347.
74 Ibid., p. 352.
75 VGM, Defter 573, no. 1, dated the beginning of N. 972, p. 112.
76 Ibid, p. 113: 'bināsına şurūʿ eyledügi cāmiʿ-i şerīfüñ bināsına kifāyet itdügi ḳadar ṣarf oluna.'
77 VGM, Defter 573, no. 2, pp. 116–18: 'oḳ meydanı ḳurbinde binā bıyurduḳları cāmiʿ-i şerīf', 'muḳaddemā cāmiʿ-i şerīf-i mezbūr ḳurbinde bir mektebḫāne-i dilpezīr ve muʿallimḫāne-i lā-naẓīr binā olunub …'. Also see the waqfiyyas in BA, Evkaf 4/34, nos. 1–2, dated B. 981 (1573).
78 Ayvansarayi, 2000, p. 351.
79 Bernardo Navagero (1553), in Albèri, 1840–55, 1:67. Also see Domenico Trevisano (1554), ibid., 1:145.
80 Selaniki, 1989, 2:2–3; Eyyubi, 1991, pp. 174, 184–86.
81 VGM, Defter 573, no. 2, pp. 116–17.
82 Evliya, 1896–1938, 1:419.
83 Ibid., 1:420, 496.
84 Ibid., 1:416–17.
85 Ibid., 1:421.
86 Ayvansarayi, 1864–65, 2:25–26; idem., 2000, p. 351. For the domed water dispenser similar to that of the grand admiral Kılıç Ali Pasha's mosque in Tophane, see Egemen, 1993, pp. 133, 695.
87 Tanman, 1989. A late Ottoman source mentions only seven dervishes at the convent of Piyale Pasha; see M. Kılıç, 1997, p. 272, no. 155.
88 The convent was associated later on with the Kadiriye order, but it is unclear whether its first shaykhs were from that order. The waqfiyya's witnesses include the preacher (*hatib*) Shaykh Mahmud and the imam Mevlana Derviş Halife b. Abdullah. For Shaykh İbrahim, see Atai, 1989, 2:765. Known as 'Cerrah Şeyhi İbrahim Efendi', he was assigned to preach on Sundays in the Sultan Ahmed mosque; see Topçular Katibi, Süleymaniye Kütüphanesi, Esad Efendi, Ms. 2151, fol. 186v.
89 The print is discussed in Chapter 2.
90 Evliya, TSK, B. 304, 1:126v.
91 Ibid., 1:125r–v.
92 I am indebted to Kutalmış Görkay for the hypothetical source of the two monumental granite columns. These columns may have inspired the plan of the mosque according to Goodwin, 1971, p. 277. Kuban similarly writes: 'Perhaps the choice of plan was the result of two columns he discovered in a campaign'; see Kuban 1997, p. 118.
93 For the garden, see Konyalı, 1976–77, 1:173.
94 For rare examples of cushion voussoirs in Ottoman architecture, see Tanman, 1999; Goodwin, 1971, p. 279, note 102. A contemporary example is the grand vizier Semiz Ali Pasha's fountain in Karagümrük, dated by an inscription to 973 (1565–66); see Egemen, 1993, pp. 124, 126.
95 Martiny, 1936. The two columns of the canopy over the sarcophagus used as an ablution font were still standing in 1930. For the unsubstantiated hypothesis that the capitals were created in eighteenth- or nineteenth-century repairs, see Baha Tanman and Yıldız Demiriz, 'Piyale Paşa Külliyesi', ISTA 6:256–57.
96 It is seen in a photograph published by Martiny and described by Gerlach (1575) as 'einen alten Grabstein daraus man einen Wasser-Stein gemacht gefunden von weissem Marmel mit figuren und diesen grossen Buchstaben: V. CNEI POMPEI PHILIMI PHILUMENAE FILIAE ET SIBI'; Gerlach, 1674, p. 90.
97 For Piyale Pasha's mosque, bath, and khan in Chios, see Evliya, 1896–1938, 9:119–21. The columns he ordered from Dubrovnik are mentioned in Samardzic, 1995, p. 125. Similar classicizing capitals flank the portal of Mehmed III's tomb at Hagia Sophia, featuring a conch-shell hood. Dated 1017 (1608–9), it was built by the chief architect Dalgıç Ahmed; see Önkal, 1992, p. 191, illus. 191.
98 Built with alternating courses of stone and brick, Atik Ali Pasha's mosque featuring six domes raised on two central piers is fronted by a three-bay domical portico; see Müller-Wiener, 1977, pp. 374–75.
99 Tanman, 1989, p. 88.
100 The calligrapher is identified in Ayvansarayi, 2000, p. 351.
101 Kuban, 1997, p. 119.
102 Öz, 1962–65, 2:54.
103 Sai, 1989, fols 4v, 10r.
104 Grosvenor, 1895, 2:672–73; cited in Martiny, 1936, p. 168.
105 For Yahya's poem, see Necipoğlu, 1996, p. 34.
106 Twin gates also appear in the later mosques of Sokollu at Azapkapı and Kazasker İvaz Efendi at Eğrikapı.
107 Evliya, TSK, B. 304, 1:125v.
108 Gerlach, 1674, p. 90.
109 The paintings of arched lunettes on the qibla wall are original according to Aslanapa, 1986, p. 281. Four İznik tile window lunettes said to have been removed from the mosque are kept in European museums; see Önder, 1986. It is unclear whether these lunettes decorated the qibla wall, whose painted lunettes imitate tile patterns.
110 For a photograph and plan showing its no longer extant portico, see Martiny, 1936, illus. 11 and 33.
111 Ayvansarayi, 1985, pp. 265–66.
112 She is described as 'donna di grandissimo spirito' by Morosini in 1585; see Albèri, 1840–55, 3:289. Her waqfiyya of N. 1018 (1609), once belonging to the Edwin Binney 3rd collection, is now at the Los Angeles County Museum. She endowed a madrasa located across from the Cerrah Pasha mosque in Istanbul (illus. 532[4]) and two provincial mosques.
113 Āli, IÜ, T. 5959, fol. 461v.
114 Katib Çelebi, 1973, p. 208.
115 Mehmed Aşık, TSK, E.H. 1446, fol. 393v.
116 Kuran, 1987, p. 220.
117 Kuban, 1997, p. 111.
118 Goodwin, 1971, p. 287.
119 Denny, 1983, p. 126. Also see Aydın H. Polatkan, 'Kılıç Ali Paşa Camisi ve Ayasofya: Bir Historisist Deneme', in Nur Akın et al., *Osmanlı Mimarlığının 7 Yüzyılı "Uluslarüstü Bir Miras"* 1999, pp. 69–75.
120 In 1574 he was ordered to bring to Istanbul fifteen columns from Bozcaada (Tenedos) for royal use when the armada passed by that island (BA, MD. 26, #823, p. 284, dated 7 B. 982).
121 For biographical details, see Svat Soucek, 'ʿUlūdj ʿAlī', EI(2) 10:810–11; Haluk Şehsuvaroğlu, 'Kılıç Ali Paşa' IA, 6:679–81.
122 Selaniki, 1989, 1:84.
123 See Sokollu's biography in Chapter 8.
124 Selaniki, 1989, 1:96, 97–99.
125 Katip Çelebi, 1973, p. 145.
126 He oversaw the construction of Murad III's bedroom at the imperial harem in 1578–79, the renovation of the shore pavilion of Bayezid II in 1583, and the construction of a royal bath at the harem in 1583–85; see Necipoğlu, 1991, pp. 167–70, 172, 231–32, 240.
127 He often liberated his skilled slaves for 200 to 300 sequins and allowed their masters to work without chains on their feet for an agreed period; the promise of liberation made them labour with great enthusiasm; see Albèri, 1840–55, 3:221–22.
128 Ibid., 3:296.
129 Ibid., 3:296.
130 Selaniki, 1989, 1:86–87, 96. Orders were sent in 1573 to the kadis of Lepanto, Trikkala, and

Negroponte for the importation of labourers (*cerahor*) for that castle and their food provisions (BA, MD. 23, #97–98, p. 48, dated 25 Ca. 981).

131 See Chapter 5(II).

132 G. Tanyeli, 1996.

133 Albèri, 1840–55, 3:222–23.

134 Gerlach, 1674, pp. 238, 244, 373.

135 Necipoğlu, 1991, pp. 167–70.

136 ASV, Senato, Dispacci Costantinopoli, Filza 13, dispatch # 1, dated 7 March 1579: 'si trovava nel luogo, dove fà fabricare la sua Moschea.'

137 For robes of honour given in 1585–86 to Kılıç Ali Pasha, the arsenal's chief architect (*Tersāne mi' mārı*), and the arsenal's supervisor and steward for a galley built by architects and engineers (*mi' mārān u mühendisān*), see Selaniki, 1989, 1:173. The tombstone inscription of the ship architect Mimar Mustafa (d. 1007/1598–99) in Kasımpaşa is recorded in Ayvansarayi, 1985, p. 148.

138 Gerlach, 1674, p. 176.

139 Selaniki, 1989, 1:186. The grand admiral's fame as a womanizer 'overly immoderate in venereal matters', is noted by Contarini (1583); see Albèri, 1840–55, 3:224.

140 Evliya, TSK, B. 304, 1:132v.

141 VGM, Defter 574, no. 21, dated the middle of R. 989, pp. 48–52 (translated from Arabic into Turkish in Defter 1766, no. 3, pp. 277–87). The following suras are specified in Defter 1766, pp. 283–84: Muhammad (47), al-Mulk (67), Ya-Sin (36), and al-Baqara (2).

142 Selaniki, 1989, 1:186. The grand admiral's wife Selime Hatun, who died on a ship while accompanying him, was buried in an island; she built an upper-storey masjid at Fındıklı (between Tophane and Beşiktaş), which burnt in a fire in 1912; see Ayvansarayi, 2000, p. 400, note 2911.

143 VGM, Defter 572, no. 48, pp. 124–26, dated the beginning of M. 984. The palace was bordered by the seashore at the south, public streets at the west and north, and the property of Mehmed Çelebi b. Turmuş (known as Deli Birader) at the east.

144 For a demolished masjid of Kılıç Ali Pasha near his palace in Beşiktaş, see Ayvansarayi, 2000, p. 420.

145 VGM, Defter 574, pp. 48–52; Defter 1766, pp. 277–87.

146 The donation was not officially recorded until 1584; see TIEM, no. 2235, dated the middle of Ş. 992.

147 VGM, Defter 1766, pp. 283–84.

148 VGM, Defter 574, no. 22, dated the end of Şaban 995, pp. 51–52 (translated from Arabic into Turkish in Defter 2225, no. 97, p. 220).

149 Kuran, 1986, p. 283, no. 41; p. 325, no. 178; p. 393 no 427; p. 394 no. 429.

150 Baltacı, 1976, pp. 279–81. The mausoleum and other dependencies were not designed by Sinan according to Kuban, 1997, p. 113. Kuran thinks that neither the bath-house (which he dates to 1583) nor the madrasa (which he says was added in the early seventeenth century) are Sinan's works; see Kuran, 1987, p. 220. The otherwise unknown elementary school of the complex is only mentioned in Ayvansarayi, 2000, p. 382.

151 BA, MD. 35, #65, p. 29, dated 19 R. 986, given to Tersane Emini Hasan Çelebi.

152 BA, MD. 36, #604, p. 228, dated 6 Ra. 987. A copy was sent to the kadi of Sofia asking for his help in this matter (ibid., #605, p. 228).

153 BA, MD. 36, #642, p. 243, dated 11 Ra. 987.

154 ASV, Senato, Dispacci Costantinopoli, Filza 13, dispatch #74 of the secretary Gabriel Cavazza, dated 9 February 1579, fols 504r–v.

155 Ibid., dispatch #1, dated 7 March 1579, fols 3v–4r: 'dui ferali di legno dorati con li suoi vetri.' The lanterns previously given to the grand vizier Sokollu were intended for his mosque at Azapkapı, completed in 1577–78.

156 They are described in Goodwin, 1971, p. 288. For the design of a gilded lantern drawn on paper and executed in 1599 for the boat of Mehmed III, see Rogers, 1999, p. 309, fig. 2.

157 ASV, Senato, Dispacci Costantinopoli, Filza 13, Registro 6, dispatch of the *bailo* Paolo Contarini, dated 29 June 1580, fol. 33r: 'Habbiamo fatto ordinare li 400 ver da Fanale secondo la mostra mandato richiesti già dal Magnifico capo del mare.' Ibid., 15 April 1581, fol. 52v: 'Quante alle lastre di verro, che ne ricercate in nome del Magnifico Bassà et Capitanio del Mare, ne sono state fatte.'

158 An order to the kadi of Eyüp permits one *lüle* of water to be added to the Kağıthane channel for Kapudan Ali Pasha's fountain inside the Fener gate and his bath-house (BA, MD. 52, #797, p. 298, dated 8 Ra. 992). Another decree sent in 1584 to the kadi of Galata allows the taxes of those living in the bath-house, shops, rooms, and houses the grand admiral built around his mosque to be collected by his men instead of the Tophane police (BA, MD. 52, #985, p. 364, dated 19 Ra. 992).

159 Maurand, 1901, pp. 202–5.

160 The embassy was based in the house of Arap Ahmed Pasha; see Ahmed Refik, 1988b, pp. 15–16, no. 30.

161 Eremya, 1998, p. 39. Also see İnciciyan, 1976, p. 112.

162 Bostan, 1992, pp. 176–77, 239–41.

163 Mehmed Aşık, TSK, E.H. 1446, fol. 393v.

164 Grosvenor, 1895, 2:674.

165 Kiechel, 1987, p. 454.

166 Pervitich, 2000, p. 108, plate 34. The precinct wall was moved closer to the funerary garden in the 1950s; for renovations, see Müller-Wiener, 1977, pp. 430–31; Eyice, 'Kılıç Ali Paşa Külliyesi', ISTA 4:558.

167 The *sebil* is attributed to Kılıç Ali Pasha in Egemen, 1993, p. 133, no. 172; Ayvansarayi, 2000, p. 382. For the unsubstantiated view that the *sebil* was transferred there from across the avenue, when it was widened under Abdülaziz; see Semavi Eyice, 'Kılıç Ali Paşa Külliyesi', ISTA 4:558.

168 Grosvenor, 1895, 2:676.

169 Saatçi, 1988, pp. 112–13, no. 41.

170 Grosvenor, 1895, 2:676.

171 For a slightly different translation, see Ayvansarayi, 2000, p. 382; Saatçi, 1988, pp. 107–9, no. 39.

172 For a slightly different translation, see Ayvansarayi, 2000, p. 382; Saatçi, 1988, pp. 110–11, no. 40.

173 Examples include the mosques of Molla Çelebi, Shahsultan and Zal Mahmud Pasha, and Kazasker İvaz Efendi. According to Kuban, the flying buttresses were 'probably an intervention for reinforcement purposes after an unidentified earthquake.' He adds that the lead 'which goes down to the walls is another sign that the entire covering system of the building has undergone major reparations'; Kuban, 1997, p. 113. As Kuran writes, there is 'no evidence it underwent a major reconstruction', with the exception of the minaret renewed in the Crimean War; see Kuran, 1987, p. 218. In my opinion the lead sheathing is original; it reveals that cheaper materials were used instead of cut stone on the drums of the domical superstructure.

174 For Mesih Pasha's mosque, see Chapter 10.

175 Denny, 1983, p. 120.

176 Kuran, 1986, p. 214.

177 For Murad III's bedchamber, see Necipoğlu, 1991, pp. 165–72; Goodwin, 1971, p. 327.

178 Albèri, 1840–55, 3:224.

179 An artistic mother-of-pearl inlaid wooden preacher's pulpit is placed in front of the southeast pier.

180 Derman, 1898, pp. 289, 291.

181 The paintings were renewed in 1959–60 according to Kuran, 1987, p. 218. For a photograph showing nineteenth-century Europeanizing paintings, see Konyalı, 1950, p. 137.

182 Necipoğlu, 1992a, pp. 210–13.

183 Cantemir, 1979–80, 2:313–14.

184 Grosvenor, 1895, 2:673–76.

185 Evliya, TSK, B. 304, 1:132r–v.

186 The roundels of the Tophane mosque were calligraphed by Sultan Abdülmecid (1823–61), for whom Hagia Sophia was renovated by the Fossati brothers; see Derman, 1989, p. 291.

CHAPTER 12

1 Akgündüz, 1990, 1:320.

2 Tevki'i Abdurrahman Paşa, 1912–13, pp. 527–28.

3 Kiel, 1990.

4 He was executed in 1578 by the chief stable master Ferhad Agha belonging to the anti-Sokollu faction; see Gévay, 1841, p. 61. For his biography, see Peçevi, 2:26–28.

5 The anonymous biography entitled *Cevāhirü'l-menāḳıb* is in Fatih, Millet Kütüphanesi, Ali Emiri, no. 1031. The waqfiyya is in TSA, D. 7000; it is summarized in Káldy-Nagy, 1972.

6 *Cevāhirü'l-menāḳıb*, fols 32r–v, 74v–89r; Mujezinovic, 1998, 2:124–25. A copy of the waqfiyya of the complex in Rudo, dated 963 (1555), is in Sarajevo, Gazi Hüsrev Beg Library, Ms. 421.

7 For a list of monuments, see Káldy-Nagy, 1972.

8 TSA, D. 7000, fols 5r–8r; *Cevāhirü'l-menāḳıb*, fols 172r–74v.

9 *Cevāhirü'l-menāḳıb*, fols 170v–71v.

10 The palace was bounded by the river and by streets on three sides; see TSA, D. 7000, fol. 7r; *Cevāhirü'l-menāḳıb*, fol. 171r. The palace is described in Pigafetta, 1890, pp. 126–27; and Gerlach (1573), 1674, pp. 10–16.

11 For the mosque site, see a map of Buda published in Ayverdi, 1977–82, 1:89. The walls of the *varoş* of Buda were built by Mustafa Pasha according to Peçevi, 1864–67, 2:26–8. The mosque with a lead-covered dome is described in Evliya, 1896–1938, 6:242.

12 TM in Meriç, 1965, p. 26; TE in ibid., p. 84. A copy of the waqfiyya is preserved in Sarajevo, Gazi Hüsrev Pasha Library, Ms. 178, dated the beginning of N. 977. It is summarized in Mujezinovic, 1998, 3:175–79.

13 Mujezinovic, 1998, 3:177–78.

14 Ibid, 3:178; Pašic, 1994, p. 67; Amir Ljubovic, 'Karagöz Bey Külliyesi', VIA, 24:403–4. Rüstem Pasha's brother Sinan Pasha served as the governor of Hercegovina before becoming grand admiral in 1548; see Chapter 11.

15 For his mosques in Sofia and Banjaluka (the capital of Bosnia), see Chapter 10.

16 The document dated M. 965 is cited in Adrejevic, 1990, pp. 41–42; and Çulpan, 1975, p. 161: 'bi-neẓāret-i ḳaragöz beg bi-emr-i ḫadım ḥaydar pāşā mīrlivā-i hersek'.

17 Āli, Nuruosmaniye Library, Ms. 3409, fol. 127r. For the governors of Hercegovina, see Popovic, 1966–67. Haydar Pasha sent a lieutenant to govern Hercegovina between 1552 and 1557; Popovic gives no names of governors for the years 1557–61. Haydar Pasha seems to have occupied the post between 1553 and *c.* 1561–63. The next governor was a relative of Sokollu Mehmed Pasha, Sinan Beg Boljanic (1563–67).

18 The decree dated 15 Ş. 963 is cited in Andrejevic, 1990, p. 42. He misreads the date as 15 Ş. 973 (8.III.1566).

19 For the dates of the bridge and written sources, see Çulpan, 1975, pp. 158–63. The foundation inscription

of the bridge is cited in Mujezinovic, 1998, 3:148–51.

20 Mujezinovic, 1998, 3:179.

21 Pašic, 1994, pp. 67–69; Kuran, 1986, p. 283, no. 41. Kuran says the mosque was designed in Istanbul and executed by a royal architect.

22 The patron's name, Osmanshah, is misread as Osman Pasha in Meriç, 1965, pp. 26, 85. The TE misidentifies the patron, who was a sanjak governor, as the 'vizier Osmanshah'; ibid., p. 85.

23 For the founder's identity, see Uzunçarşılı, 1976, pp. 474–78. For Osmanshah's sister Hüma Hatun and her mosque in Yenibahçe, generally named after her husband Bali Pasha; see my discussion of the Hadım İbrahim Pasha mosque at Silivrikapı in Chapter 10.

24 I thank Machiel Kiel for providing the dome dimensions of the mosque in Trikkala (17.98 metres inside, 21.2 metres outside) and the mosque in Sophia (18.3 metres inside).

25 I have followed the well-documented biographical details given in Uzunçarşılı, 1976. For a conflicting and unreliable biography, see Mehmed Süreyya, 1996, 4:1306.

26 Cited in Uzunçarşılı, 1976, pp. 475–76.

27 Peçevi, 1864–67, 1:45. He misidentifies the prince as the son of Kara Mustafa Pasha.

28 TSA, D.7062, dated B. 977; see facsimile and summary in Uzunçarşılı, 1976, p. 477. Mehmed Süreyya claims Osmanshah died in 1567–68; so does Atai, 1989, 2:104. For his father's complex near the Hippodrome, see Yüksel, 1983, p. 297.

29 The waqfiyya calls her 'Hanım Sultan', (TSK, E.H.3038, dated Ş. 945); see facsimile and summary in Uzunçarşılı, 1976, pp. 472–74. For the mosque and madrasa, whose patron is identified in Sinan's autobiographies as the 'mother of Osmanshah', see Kuran, 1986, p. 291, no. 65; p. 344, no. 241.

30 Kuran, 1986, p. 291, no. 64.

31 TSA, D.1659, fols 1r–4v: 'Defter-i meṣārif-i cāmiʿ-i şerīf ve maṭbaḫ ... [torn] ḥażret-i ʿosmānşāh ... fī sene 974.' The complex is dated around 1550–60 in Alexandra Yerolimpos, 'Tırḫāla' EI(2) 10:539–40. The madrasa mentioned by Evliya is not included among Trikkala's madrasas in Özergin, 1973–74, p. 281.

32 TSA, D.3681, dated *c.* 1571–72; for facsimile and summary, see Uzunçarşılı, 1976, pp. 477–78. Uzunçarşılı says the complex comprised a mosque, madrasa, hospice and mausoleum; ibid., p. 477.

33 The Halveti Shaykh Mehmed of Malkara (d. 1604–5), a disciple of the militant Shaykh Nureddinzade, served as the first preacher of the mosque in Trikkala according to Atai, 1989, 2:595–96.

34 Evliya, 1896–1938, 8:203. For photographs of the mosque and mausoleum before its restoration, see Babinger, 1924; Orlandos, 1929. Also see, Kuran, 1986, p. 291, no. 64.

35 See Chapter 10.

36 Evliya, 1986–1938, 8:204.

37 Ibid., 8:203–4.

38 Ibid., 8:204–5.

39 Popovic, 1966–67, p. 98.

40 BA, MD. 21, #772, p. 327, dated 11 M. 981: 'muḳaddemā ḥaleb beglerbegisi iken fevt olan ḳāsım beg.'

41 Albèri, 1840–55, 2:80–81.

42 Lescalopier, 1921, p. 27. Paolo Contarini (1580) says the bridge had collapsed. Sokollu built 'the bridge and a most beautiful caravansaray covered by lead to lodge travellers for the love of one of his sons, who died as the governor of Hercegovina'; see Contarini, 1856, p. 13.

43 Süleymaniye Kütüphanesi, Lala İsmail 737, fols 47r–48v.

44 Ibid., fols 75r–v.

45 Fatih Millet Kütüphanesi, T.933, fol. 23r.

46 TM, in Meriç, 1965, p. 26; TE, in ibid., p. 84.

47 See reference 40 above.

48 BA, MD. zeyl 2, #621, p. 237, dated M. 982.

49 BA, MD. 28, #214, p. 90, dated beginning of C. 984, it was given to 'ḳoca ḳapucı' who brought a memorandum from 'ketḫüda beg.' Ragazzoni refers to the steward of Kasım Beg as 'chiaiagà' (kahya); see Albèri, 1840–55, 2:80–81.

50 Gerlach, 1674, p. 89. The 'church' and 'caravansaray' was completed by 1578; ibid., p. 511.

51 Soranzo, 1856, pp. 54–55. The now-lost elementary school is also mentioned in Ahmed Badi Efendi's guidebook of Edirne; cited in Küçükkaya, 1990, p. 204.

52 Contarini, 1856, pp. 35–36.

53 Cited in Reyhanlı and Altun, 1974–75, p. 75; and Müderrisoğlu, 1993, p. 660.

54 The chronogram reads: 'Şaḥibine cumʿasını yaz ey ?? darüs'selām.' Cited in Reyhanlı and Altun, 1974–75, pp. 75–76; and Müderrisoğlu, 1993, p. 659.

55 Reyhanlı and Altun, 1974–75; Reyhanlı, 1977–79.

56 The mosque whose dome, portico and minaret with a muqarnased single gallery were severely damaged during the Balkan war of 1912, has been restored without its portico. For the wrong assumption that the mosque originally had two minarets, see Reyhanlı and Altun, 1974–75, p. 71; and Aslanapa, 1986, p. 273. Ahmed Badi Efendi mentions the Friday mosque, double khan, bath-house, hospice, elementary school and masonry shops damaged in the 1165 earthquake when part of the mosque's dome, the khans and shops were destroyed; cited in Küçükkaya, 1990, p. 206.

57 Derschwam's description is cited in Müderrisoğlu, 1993, p. 662.

58 The inscriptions seen today include the standard mihrab verse (3:37), the revered names calligraphed on the eight arch spandrels carrying the dome, and the cosmic verse on the dome (35:41).

59 Evliya, TSK, B.304., fol. 169v.

60 Ibid., 3:169r–v.

61 Soranzo, 1856, p. 56.

62 The mosque complex in Ilgın is misattributed to Sinan in Kuran, 1986, p. 284, no. 45; p. 368, no. 328. He thinks this must be the Mustafa Pasha mosque in Bolu, mentioned in TE and TB, a scribal error deriving from TM's entry on Rüstem Pasha's mosque at Bolu (Dibek); see Chapter 4(I) and Appendix 1.

63 TM in Meriç, 1965, p. 28; TE, ibid., p. 85. The mosque is hypothetically dated 1561 in Kuran, 1986, p. 277, no. 22.

64 It is unclear why the sultan, who died in 1566, is referred to as 'late'. VGM, Defter 589 (Mücedded Anadolu 3/3), no. 107, dated 2 R. 973, pp. 64–65. I have not been able to identify the pasha's family. A register of the sanjak of Hamid, dated 1568, shows that its governor Firdevs Beg had a fief yielding an income of 239,066 aspers; see Arıkan, 1988, p. 131. For prince Selim's chief messenger (*ser-çavuşān*) Firdevs Agha, see Āli, TSK, R.1290, fol. 12v. Firdevs Beg's death in Lepanto is mentioned in Katip Çelebi, 1973, p. 140.

65 VGM, Defter 589, p. 64.

66 Arıkan, 1988, p. 141.

67 For the *bedesten*, see Cezar, 1983, pp. 203–4, illus. 150–51.

68 For Kutlu Beg's waqfiyya dated 1429 and the names of quarters, see Feridun Emecen, 'Isparta', VIA 19:196–99.

69 The chronogram, 'hep ẓulm', is cited in Böcüzade, 1983, p. 78.

70 For repairs after an earthquake in 1914, when the openwork window lunettes were filled in with masonry, see Kuran, 1986, p. 277, no. 22. The lead cover of the ashlar masonry *bedesten* was removed to repair the dome of the mosque in 1610 according to Böcüzade, 1983, p. 78.

71 Uzunçarşılı, 1932, pp. 158–61.

72 A second mausoleum was added in 1171 for İsmail Paşazade Hacı Esad; see Dağlıoğlu, 1942, p. 215. For the mosque; see Kuran, 1986, p. 274, no. 12; Başkan, 1993.

73 For the biographies of father and son, see Āli, Nuruosmaniye Library, Ms. 3409, fols 132v–33r; Peçevi, 1864–67, 1:36–37. Cenabi Ahmed Pasha's tenure in Ankara ended in 1565 according to Uzunçarşılı, 1932, pp. 159–60.

74 Āli, TSK, R.1290, fols 5r–6r.

75 For this painting, dated *c.* 1561–62, see Istanbul, 2000, pp. 226–27.

76 Āli, Nuruosmaniye Library, Ms. 3409, fols 132v–33r; Kınalızade, 1989, 1:265; Peçevi, 1864–67, 1:37.

77 Aşık Çelebi, 1971, fol. 68r. The same date is given for his death in Āli and Peçevi; see reference 73 above.

78 For the unsubstantiated rumour that the chief architect Sinan's son Mehmed Beg, who served as sanjak governor of Ankara, may have supervised the mosque's construction, see Dağlıoğlu, 1942, p. 214.

79 Uzunçarşılı, 1932, pp. 159–60.

80 Dağlıoğlu, 1942, p. 213.

81 Repair inscriptions dated 1802–3 (1217) and 1887–88 (1305) are cited in ibid., p. 214. For more recent repairs in 1940 and 1959–70, see ibid., p. 213, note 3; Kuran, 1986, p. 274, no. 12. For a detailed description of the mosque, see Başkan, 1993.

82 See Chapter 6.

83 Evliya, TSK, B.304, 2:357r.

84 Faroqhi, 1987, pp. 25, 33–36. For a sketchy plan of Ankara by Baron von Vincke, dated 1838, where Cenabi Ahmed's mosque is shown inside the Kayseri gate, see Cezar, 1983, p. 52, illus. 30. Also see the modern city plan on pp. 47–48, illus. 26.

85 The Mevlevi convent functioned until the abolishment of dervish lodges in the Republican period, and the mosque's cemetery contains the tombstones of Mevlevi dervishes; see Dağlıoğlu, 1942, pp. 214. Rumi's spiritual support that assured the prince's victory is discussed in Chapter 2(II).

86 Uzunçarşılı, 1932, pp. 158–61.

87 He was buried near a dervish lodge in Otakcılar at Eyüp according to Ayvansarayi, 2000, p. 309. For his masjid at Tavşantaşı in the Nişanca quarter of Kumpkapı, see ibid., p. 106. For his biography, see Mehmed Süreyya, 1996, 3:724; Selaniki, 1989, 1:58–59.

88 Āli, IÜ, T.5959, fol. 461v; Peçevi, 1864–67, 1:442–43.

89 VGM, Defter 2138 (Kasa 98), dated the beginning of N. 977, p. 105: 'cāmiʿ-i mezbūr ḳurbinde alınan arāżi ve bagçeler ki icāreye virilüb maḥalle-i cedīde olmuşdur.'

90 The waqfiyya also mentions the pasha's wife, Kamer Hatun, ibid., pp. 105–6.

91 For repairs in 1835 (1250), 1892–93 (1310), 1962–66, and 1970–71, see Kuran, 1986, p. 284, no. 43. The painted calligraphy is dated by an inscription to 1310 (1892–93). For a detailed description of the mosque hypothetically dated to 1566–68, see Altun, 1981–82, pp. 256–260, 549–54.

92 Evliya, 1896–1938, 9:18–19.

93 Ibid., 9:19–25.

94 Even though Kayseri was only a sanjak centre, it boasted an official residence for governor-generals (Paşa Sarayı); see Faroqhi, 1987, pp. 56, 58.

95 For biographical details and the unconfirmed statement that the pasha was appointed a second time as the governor-general of Konya in 1571–72, see Mehmed Süreyya, 1996, 1:208. For the mausoleum, see Kuran, 1986, p. 323, no. 171.

96 Kuran, 1986, p. 310, no. 127.
97 Āli, Nuruosmaniye Library, Ms. 3409, fol. 133r.
98 VGM, Defter 503, dated 989, pp. 326–36 (adapted to modern Turkish in Defter 1988, no. 113). After the pasha's death, the waqf would be administered by his sons and his freed slaves. The waqf's overseer was the pasha's 'beloved son, His Highness Mehmed Beg, the pride of amirs and notables'.
99 VGM, Defter 503, pp. 327–33. For a list of income-producing endowed properties, see Çayırdağ, 1981, p. 556.
100 See Chapter 14; TM in Meriç, 1965, p. 27.
101 The convent's first Halveti shaykh was Yayabaşızade Hızır Efendi (d. 1596–97), in whose honour the chief black eunuch Mehmed Agha would later build a mosque complex in Istanbul (Çarşamba); see Hulvi, 1993, pp. 606–7.
102 'Üsküdār'da İsfendiyār Mescidi Zāviyesi, 4 postnişīn'; see M. Kılıç, 1997, p. 270, no. 72.
103 TM in Meriç, 1965, p. 26: 'Cami-i şerif-i Ahmed Paşa, Kızıl Ahmedlüdür, der Kayseriyye'; and TE in ibid., p. 81, note 194: 'Kayseriyyede merhum [Şam Beglerbegiliginden müteka'id] Hacı Paşa Camii.'
104 The ambiguous wording can also be read as 'the mosque he built there', BA, MD. 28, #1014, p. 389, dated 12 N. 984: 'şām beglerbegisi olub tekā'üd iden ḥacı aḥmed binā itdügi cāmi'-i şerīfinüñ ḳurbinde ḥiṣār dıvarı olub ḳal'a içine giden ḳadīmī ḳapusı olub...'.
105 VGM, Defter 503, pp. 328–35.
106 Çayırdağ, 1981, p. 555.
107 Cited in Faroqhi, 1987, p. 62.
108 Evliya, 1896–1938, 3:178–89.
109 For the hypothesis that it may have been built by the architect of Ali Pasha's mosque in Tokat (1573) or by another imperial architect trained in the capital; see Goodwin, 1971, pp. 314–17.
110 Kuran, 1986, p. 278, no. 26.
111 Ibid., p. 256.
112 Faroqhi, 1987, pp. 42–43.
113 Ronald Jennings, 'Ḳaysariyya', EI(2) 4:844; Faroqhi, 1987, pp. 42–62 (see Kayseri map on p. 57).
114 Hoca Sadeddin, 1992, 4:226.
115 A petition by the pasha to Selim I requests a village to be donated for the waqf of 'the mosque he built in Diyarbakır by sultanic order' (*emr-i pādişāhī ile Amid-i maḥrūsede binā itdügi cāmi'*); see Beysanoğlu, 1987, 2:525–26.
116 The mosque is discussed in Sözen, 1971, pp. 65–69; and Yüksel, 1983, p. 424. For its tiles, see Raby, 1977–78, pp. 431–32.
117 Four of the five mosques mentioned in the *Tuḥfe* are extant. That of Sofu Mehmed Pasha in Diyarbakır seems to be a figment of imagination according to Kuran, 1986, p. 295, no. 77.
118 Another mosque Sinan's autobiographies mention in this region is that of Memi Kethüda (a steward of the Old Palace) in Ulaş near Sivas; for this unknown mosque; see Kuran, 1986, p. 286, no. 51.
119 For tiles produced in Diyarbakır, see Raby, 1977–78.
120 Cevdet Küçük, 'Erzurum', VIA 11:321–29.
121 (BA, MD. 2, #1714, p. 187) cited in Dündar, forthcoming.
122 For his biography, see Turan, 1958; Bekir Kütükoğlu, 'Mustafa Paşa', IA 8:732–36.
123 O. Kılıç, 1997, pp. 41–49.
124 For his mausoleum, an open baldachin raised on four columns, and his tombstone dated 988 (1580), see Haskan, 1993, 1:216–17.
125 His endowments are recorded in separate waqfiyyas. For his waqfs in Cyprus, see VGM, Defter 746, dated 14 Ra. 987 (1579); his waqfs at Erzurum are recorded in VGM, Defter 608, dated Ra. 971 (1563); those in Jenin, Qunaytira, Erzurum, Ilgın, and Nablus are recorded in VGM, Defter 2134 (Haremeyn 734), no. 3, dated 4 C. 982 (1574); no. 4, dated Ra. 971 (1563); no. 5, dated 25 Z. 974 (1567); no. 6, dated Za. 981 (1574).
126 For the mosque mentioned in Sinan's autobiographies, see Kuran, 1986, p. 284, no. 44.
127 Gündoğdu, 1992, pp. 12–13, 18.
128 VGM, Defter 608, no. 213, dated the beginning of Ra. 971, pp. 184–98 (translated into Turkish in Defter 2134, pp. 96–129). For a summary, see Konyalı, 1960, pp. 242–45.
129 Gündoğdu, 1992, pp. 51–56.
130 The endowed properties and the appendix dated 987 are summarized in Konyalı, 1960, pp. 244–45.
131 Āli, TSK, R.1290, fols 13r. Turan, 1961, pp. 117–57.
132 Gündoğdu, 1992, illus. 11 on p. 26; Konyalı, 1960, pp. 232, 235.
133 Gündoğdu, 1992.
134 They are reproduced in colour in Gündoğdu, 1992.
135 Raby, 1977–78, p. 455.
136 Ibid., pp. 434–35, 455. The tiles are attributed to İznik in Gündoğdu, 1992.
137 Gündoğdu, 1992, pp. 69–70.
138 Ibid., pp. 71–73.
139 Ibid., pp. 75–77.
140 Other inscriptions carved on stone record various repairs in 1670, 1721, 1836–39, 1851, 1870, and 1889. The building underwent more recent restorations in 1962 and 1971; see Gündoğdu, 1992, pp. 14–15, 64–68.
141 Evliya, TSK, B.304, 2:287r.
142 Āli, IÜ, T.5959, fol. 462r.
143 Turan, 1958, pp. 126, 128, 134, 151, 153–54, 156. Hüsrev Pasha was based in Van for more than ten years (*c.* 1561–62/63, 1568–71, 1580s) according to O. Kılıç, 1997, pp. 204–5, 232. For his career, see Mehmed Süreyya, 1996, 2:684. He was transferred in 1586 from Van to Diyarbakır and died in 1587 according to Selaniki, 1989, 1:116, 177, 196.
144 Āli is cited in Turan, 1958, p. 126, note 1; Selaniki, 1989, 1:116; 196.
145 O. Kılıç, 1997, pp. 41–49.
146 Kuran, 1986, p. 283, no. 42; p. 342, no. 234.
147 Cited in O. Kılıç, 1997, pp. 205–6.
148 Ibid., p. 233.
149 Uluçam, 2000, 1:41, illus. 34. I thank Wheeler Thackston for the translation. 'Ḥaẓrat-i pāshā-yi khusraw iqtidār / Chun binā kard īn chunīn khuld-i barīn // Guft hātif baḥr-i tārīkhash ravān / Qad banā baytan lakūmu'l-ṣāliḥīn.'
150 O. Kılıç, 1997, p. 232; Uluçam, 2000, pp. 45–46.
151 Published with a key in O. Kılıç, 1997, pp. 248–49. For Kale Camii, see Kuran, 1986, p. 301, no. 94.
152 VGM, Defter 585/1, no. 2/2, pp. 2–7; summarized in O. Kılıç, 1997, pp. 217–40; and Uluçam, 2000, pp. 38–50.
153 O. Kılıç, 1997, p. 230. The madrasa had eleven students, ibid., p. 226.
154 Uluçam, 2000, pp. 38–50.
155 Kuran, 1986, p. 283, no. 42; p. 342, no. 234. The complex is attributed to an assistant of Sinan in Semavi Eyice, 'Hüsrev Paşa Külliyesi', VIA 19:49–51. For the attribution to Mimar Selman, see O. Kılıç, 1997, p. 218, note 108; and Dündar, forthcoming.
156 The tiles are attributed to Diyarbakır in Raby, 1977–78, pp. 435, 444.
157 The palace is described in Evliya, 1896–1938, 4:182.
158 Ibid., 4:181. For the waqfiyya of the double caravansaray in Rahva, each with twelve fireplaces, see VGM, Defter 585/1, no. 10/3, pp. 7–9.
159 See map in Sözen, 1971, pp. 21–22.
160 Tayyib Gökbilgin, 'Ali Paşa', IA, 1:332–33; Mehmed Süreyya, 1996, 1:287; Āli, Nuruosmaniye Library, Ms. 3409, fol. 132r; and Peçevi, 1864–67, 1:36. According to Gökbilgin, the pasha governed Diyarbakır beween 1537–40/41; Mehmed Süreyya gives the same dates. An unpublished prosopography by Bacqué-Grammont, however, dates the pasha's presence in Diyarbakır between 1541–44, pp. 19–20. Bali Pasha, the governor-general of Diyarbakır, was replaced by Hadım Ali Pasha in 948 (1541) according to the chronicle of Rüstem Pasha, ÖNB, Codex Vindobonensis Palatinus, Mxt. 339, fol. 224r.
161 Āli, Nuruosmaniye Library, Ms. 3409, fol. 132r.
162 For the bath-house, see Sözen, 1971, p. 211. He identifies a rectangular vaulted structure at the northeast side of the mosque as a space for the performance of *dhikr*. The free-standing minaret became attached in the eighteenth century to a prayer hall reserved for Shafi'i congregations at the east side of the mosque.
163 See Kuran, 1986, p. 278, no. 27; p. 338, no. 219.
164 Sözen, 1971, pp. 76–79; Kuran, 1986, p. 278, no. 27; Tuncer, 1996, pp. 127–37. Kuran finds it unlikely that Sinan designed the mosque because he had not been appointed chief architect between 1534–37.
165 See reference 160 above.
166 The same potters were responsible for the tiles of the Shaykh Safa and Ali Pasha mosques according to Raby, 1977–78, pp. 444–45.
167 İskenderoğlu, 1989, pp. 1–4. For his career see Ayvansarayi, 2000, pp. 469–70; Mehmed Süreyya, 1996, 3:809; Abdülkadir Özcan, 'İskender Paşa', VIA, 22:565–66.
168 Āli, Nuruosmaniye Library, Ms. 3409, fol. 133v.
169 Özcan, 'İskender Paşa', pp. 565–66.
170 For his biography, see Beysanoğlu, 1987, 2:568. Bacqué-Grammont places his tenure there between 1554–65; see his unpublished prosopography, pp. 57–58. I have followed the dates proposed by Özcan, 'İskender Paşa', p. 565.
171 Āli, Nuruosmaniye Library, Ms. 3409, fol. 133v; Peçevi, 1864–67, 1:38; Özcan, 'İskender Paşa', p. 566.
172 The date 1551 is given in Sözen, 1971, pp. 81–85; Goodwin, 1971, p. 310; and Kuran, 1986, p. 282, no. 37. It was built between 1554 and 1557 according to Beysanoğlu, 1987, 2:569.
173 VGM, Defter 591, dated 27 Ra. 973, no. 13, p. 40. Another version of the Arabic waqfiyya is in Defter 581, no. 185, pp. 170–72 (translated into Turkish in Defter 1766, no. 11, p. 53).
174 The madrasa in Van was destroyed during the Russian occupation; see Özcan, 'İskender Paşa', p. 566. The entry in TM reads: 'In Amid (Diyarbakır) the Friday mosque of İskender Pasha, madrasa in Van' (*Amidde İskender Paşa Cāmi' i, Medrese der Van*). This is misread in Meriç, 1965, p. 27, as 'Amidde Sofu Mehmed Paşa Camii – Medrese der Van.' The madrasa in Van belongs to the entry above, referring to İskender Pasha's mosque in Amid. For Hüsrev Pasha's madrasa-cum-masjid in Diyarbakır, see Sözen, 1971, pp. 70–72.
175 For İskender Pasha's extant domeless mosque in Ardanuç and the tomb of Süleyman Pasha attached to its west side, see Osman Aytekin, 'İskender Paşa Külliyesi, Artvin'in Ardanuç Kalesinde XVI. Yüzyılda Yapılmış olan Külliye', VIA, 22:570–71.
176 Özcan, 'İskender Paşa', p. 566; Ali Boran, 'İskender Paşa Camii, Ahlat'ta Osmanlı Döneminde Yapılmış İlk Cami', VIA, 22:568–69.
177 VGM, Defter 1766, pp. 2–5.
178 For the mosque's site, see the city map published in Sözen, 1971, pp. 21–22. For the residence, see İskenderoğlu, 1989, p. 28, plates 5–6.
179 Evliya, 1896–1938, 4:40.
180 VGM, Defter 591, p. 41; Defter 581, p. 172.
181 See Chapter 12.
182 VGM, Defter 1766, pp. 14–15.
183 For the repairs, see İskenderoğlu, 1989, p. 59.

184 The tiles had disappeared when Kurt Erdmann visited Diyarbakır around 1958; see Sözen, 1971, pp. 83–85.
185 Raby, 1977–78, pp. 434, 444.
186 The inscriptions are dated 1379 (1960); see Sözen, 1971, pp. 83–85.
187 The poet Yusuf Efendi, a descendant of İskender Pasha's family, is one of the persons buried there; see İskenderoğlu, 1989, p. 33. The mausoleum is believed to have been built by the pasha or his sons; see Sözen, 1971, p. 177.
188 For the mosque and tomb in Kanlıca, see Chapter 14 and Ayvansarayi, 2000, pp. 469–70. The marble cenotaphs of İskender Pasha and his son Ahmed bear late-Ottoman inscriptions without dates. Another tradition claims that the pasha was buried at the mausoleum next to his mosque in Diyarbakır; see Özcan, 'İskender Paşa', p. 566.
189 For a family tree, see İskenderoğlu, 1989, pp. 65–99.
190 Described in Goodwin, 1971, p. 310; Sözen, 1971, pp. 86–91; Kuran, 1986, p. 272, no. 7; Tuncer, 1996, pp. 154–55.
191 J.R. Blackburn, 'Muṣṭafā Pasha, Ḳara Shāhīn', EI(2) 7:720.
192 Āli, 1979–82, 1:79–80.
193 For 'Behram Paşa (Halhallı)', see Mehmed Süreyya, 1996, 2:366 where his tenure in Diyarbakır is dated from 1564–65 to 1567–68. He governed Diyarbakır for three years (1564–67) according to Beysanoğlu, 1987, 2:573. Bacqué-Grammont calls him 'Mustafa Paşazade Halhallı Behram Pasha' in his unpublished prosopography, p. 27. According to Selaniki, Behram Pasha was the governor-general of Sivas during the Cyprus campaign, the governor-general of Erzurum in 1578–79, and of Diyarbakır in 1581–82; see Selaniki, 1989, 1:78, 118, 130.
194 For Behram Pasha's wish to be buried in Aleppo where he may have been based as governor-general around 1580, and his Arabic waqfiyya dated 1583 which records his endowments for the Bahramiyya mosque in Aleppo; see Watenpaugh, 1999, pp. 104–22.
195 Gabriel, 1940, p. 200; Beysanoğlu, 1987, 2:578.
196 No source is cited for this assumption; see Sözen, 1971, p. 86; Aslanapa, 1986, pp. 238–39; Beysanoğlu, 1987, 2:573.
197 VGM, Defter 616, no. 65, dated end of Ş. 976, pp. 128–32.
198 VGM, Defter 616, pp. 129–30.
199 VGM, Defter 616, p. 130.
200 Raby, 1977–78, pp. 435–36, 447–56.
201 The squinches are inscribed with verses from the al-Jumʿa sura (62:9–10); the central dome quotes verses from the al-Mulk sura glorifying the absolute power of the forgiving God (67:1–3).
202 Evliya, 1988, pp. 167–68. For the bath, see Beysanoğlu, 1987, 2:580.
203 Goodwin, 1971, p. 310.
204 Evliya, 1896–1938, 4:32–33, 38, 40–41. For the bath-house with a pyramidal roof, see Sözen, 1971, p. 211. Chronograms composed by local poets for the bath-house, begun in 972 (1564–65) and completed in 975 (1567–68), are cited in Beysanoğlu, 1987, 2:618. The same information and the delay of the mosque is mentioned in Ali Emiri, 'Sahib-i Cami Melek Ahmed Paşa', *Amid-i Sevda* 6 (1325): 81–88.
205 Beysanoğlu, 1987, 2:618; Ali Emiri, 1325, pp. 81–84.
206 Ali Emiri, 1325, pp. 86–87.
207 Mehmed Süreyya, 1996, 4:1081. For 'Melik Ahmed's' role as an avaricious '*mültezim*' and his associate Alaüddin Beg, see Selaniki, 1989, 1:247, 258, 260–61, 274, 289. For his career and the mosque, also see Beysanoğlu, 1987, 2:618–25.
208 The dates 1587–91 are given in Ali Emiri, 1325, p. 86; Sözen, 1971, pp. 95–99; Beysanoğlu, 1987, 2:620. The date 1591 is given in Goodwin, 1971, p. 309; Kuran, p. 286, no. 50; Aslanapa, 1986, p. 313.
209 Ali Emiri, 1325, p. 86; Beysanoğlu, 1987, 2:624.
210 Kuran, 1986, p. 286, no. 50. It is attributed to an assistant of Sinan in Tuncer, 1996, pp. 162.
211 The tiles are described in Raby, 1977–78, pp. 437, 454.
212 Halil İnalcık, 'Eyālet', EI(2) 2:721–24.
213 For the Turkish foundation inscription and a more detailed description, see Uluçam, 1989, pp. 66–89, plates 131–40. The inscription dated 978 (1570–71) is cited in Ayvansarayi, 2000, p. 469. For the mosque, also see Kuran, 1986, p. 289, no. 59.
214 Examples of fortified hajj-route complexes commissioned by governor-generals include that of Lala Mustafa Pasha in Qunaytira and those of Koca Sinan Pasha in Qutayfa (Kadife) and Saʿsaʿa. Ottoman mosques in Damascus and Aleppo are discussed in Kafescioğlu, 1999. For those in Cairo, see Behrens-Abouseif, 1994.
215 For these monuments and further bibliography, see Watenpaugh, 1999.
216 A decree dated 1559 orders the renovation of the royal palace at Aleppo in Gök Meydan with state funds; see BA, MD. 3, #613, p. 279, dated 4 Ra. 967. For the 'imperial garden' (*hünkār bāğçesi*) at the west side of Aleppo, see Evliya, 1896–1938, 9:377.
217 The Ayyubid Dar al-ʿAdl (1190), the tribunal of justice where rulers used to hold public audiences, seems to have been located at the southeast corner of the citadel. The palace of Ottoman governor-generals at the southwest corner must have been a different structure. It is identified as a Mamluk palace in Watenpaugh, 1999, p. 96.
218 Ibid., pp. 61–62. Watenpaugh attributes the 'coherence of building habits' in the absence of a master plan or municipal body to 'the awareness of a local tradition', without considering the contribution of Sinan.
219 For Sokollu's four masjids in Aleppo and his complex in Payas, see Chapter 8.
220 See Chapter 5.
221 Herzfeld, 1956, 1:279, no 278; Gaulmier, 1942–43, pp. 14–15.
222 Unreliable dates are given in the biographical entry of Mehmed Süreyya, 1996, 2:684. I have followed Jean-Louis Bacqué-Grammont, 'Khosrew Pasha, Dīvāne or Deli', EI(2), 5:35; and Abdülkadir Özcan, 'Hüsrev Paşa, Deli', VIA, 19:40–41.
223 The fight was provoked by Rüstem Pasha according to Āli, Nuruosmaniye Library, Ms. 3409, fol. 127r.
224 Lutfi Paşa, 2001, p. 300.
225 For the mausoleum built next to the pasha's endowed market, fountain and elementary school, see Ayvansarayi, 2000, p. 72. The chronograms of the mausoleum and school are cited in Ayvansarayi, 1985, pp. 115–17.
226 Āli, Nuruosmaniye Library, Ms. 3409, fol. 127r.
227 For the complex in Diyarbakır, see Sözen, 1971, pp. 70–72, no. 20. The water dispenser in Cairo is discussed in Bates, 1991; and Behrens-Abouseif, 1994, p. 179.
228 Cited in Watenpaugh, 1999, pp. 66–68. The supervisor was 'Furukh b. ʿAbd al-Mannān al-Rūmī', and the non-Muslim architect is referred to as 'miʿmār rūmī naṣrānī.'
229 E. Egli, 1954, pp. 57–58; Goodwin, 1971, p. 202; Aslanapa, 1986, pp. 180–81.
230 Kuran, 1986, p. 281, no. 35.
231 The waqfiyyas are summarized in Gaulmier, 1942–43, pp. 13–27.
232 For Lala Mustafa Pasha, see Chapter 12.
233 VGM, Defter 583, no. 132, dated the beginning of the year 969, pp. 148–50 (translated from Arabic into Turkish in Defter 2114, pp. 510–21).
234 For the palace of pashas (*paşa sarayı*) under the citadel, see Evliya, 1896–1938, 9:378.
235 VGM, Defter 583, pp. 148–50; VGM, Defter 2114, p. 521.
236 Gaulmier, 1942–43, p. 15; Watenpaugh, 1999, p. 78. For 'Kurd Beg b. Hüsrev Paşa', a companion of prince Selim who governed such sanjaks as Ma'arra, Jerusalem and Safed, see the unpublished prosopography of Jean-Louis Bacqué-Grammont, p. 64.
237 Watenpaugh, 1999, p. 92.
238 Ibid., pp. 91–92.
239 Kuran, 1986, p. 281, no. 35; p. 340, no. 227. Kuran identifies the domed hall at the east side of the mosque as the classroom of a second madrasa.
240 Gaube and Wirth, 1984, pp. 131–32; Watenpaugh, 1999, pp. 70, 79–80.
241 The domed hall and rooms at the mosque's east side are identified as a twin madrasa complementing the one at the west side in Kuran, 1986, p. 140, no. 227.
242 Following an earthquake in 1821, the complex underwent extensive repairs in 1884, 1911, and 1919; see Watenpaugh, 1999, p. 71, note 15.
243 For the size of the dome, see ibid., p. 73.
244 Ibid., pp. 82–83.
245 For identical tiles removed from the Dome of the Rock, see Hillenbrand, 2002, plate VII after p. 32.
246 Evliya, 1896–1938, 9:374–75.
247 For the burial of Lala Mustafa Pasha's son, the governor-general Mehmed Pasha (d. 1578), in the same cemetery, see Watenpaugh, 1999, p. 79.
248 Ibid., 1999, p. 96.
249 He is believed to have first married a daughter of Bayezid II (Ayşe Hanım Sultan) and then one of his granddaughters (Fatma Sultan, the daughter of Selim I); see Abdülkadir Özcan, 'Dukakinzāde Ahmed Paşa', VIA 9:550–51. However, the mausoleum inscription of the mother of Dukakinzade Mehmed Pasha in Aleppo identifies her as Ayşe Sultan's daughter Gevher Melikshah Sultan; see reference 251 below.
250 For Gevher-i Müluk, a daughter or granddaughter of Bayezid II, who was buried near the elementary school she built next to the mosque complex of İsmihan Sultan and Zal Mahmud Pasha in Eyüp; see Mehmed Süreyya, 1996, 4:1049; Uluçay, 1980, pp. 26–27. The extant tombs in that cemetery are identified in Haskan, 1993, 1:176–78.
251 For the inscription, see Herzfeld, 1956, 1:419–20. The mausoleum is discussed in Watenpaugh, 1999, pp. 49–51.
252 See Kara Ahmed Pasha's biography in Chapter 9.
253 Rüstem Paşa, IÜ, Ms. 2438, fols 284r, 287v.
254 Āli, Nuruosmaniye Library, Ms. 3409, fols 128v–29v.
255 Kuran, 1986, p. 271, no. 4; p. 275, no. 18. Kuran was unable to locate the site of Dukakinzade's tomb in Eyüp; ibid., p. 321, no. 166. For the tomb and its cemetery, see Haskan, 1993, 1:176–78. Kuran misidentifies the caravansaray of Sokollu Mehmed Pasha in Aleppo as that of Dukakinzade Mehmed Pasha; ibid., p. 367, no. 325.
256 VGM, Defter 607 (Mücedded Anadolu 21), dated the end of Z. 963, pp. 1–3.
257 The mosque is dated 963 (1555–56) in Watenpaugh, 1999, pp. 95–96.
258 The chronogram is: 'Menzīl ve me'vāsı ola merḥūmuñ dārü's-selām.' The correct date, 973 (1565–66), is given in Kuran, 1986, p. 271, no. 4.
259 Gaube, 1978, p. 27, no. 36; Watenpaugh, 1999, p. 1.
260 BA, MD. 3, #643 and #646, pp. 228–29, dated 25 Ra. 967; published in Aykut et al., eds, 1993, pp. 293–94.
261 VGM, Defter 512, pp. 18–20: 'duḳākīn meḥmed

pāşānıñ medīne-i ḥalebde binā eyledigi ʿadliyye cāmiʿ-i şerīfi ... ġarb ṭarafına muttaṣıl ... ʿimāretḫāne ... yine ʿimāretḫāne-i meẕkūruñ şimāl ṭarafına muttaṣıl olan misāfirḫāne.'

262 TM in Meriç, 1965, p. 28.

263 Watenpaugh, 1999, pp. 96–97.

264 The same plan was reinterpreted at the mosque of Hacı Ahmed Pasha in Kayseri (*c.* 1576–85/86), whose patron had served as the governor-general of Damascus during the 1560s; see Chapter 12.

265 The lead-covered domes of the mosque are mentioned in Evliya, 1986–1938, 9:375.

266 Watenpaugh, 1999, p. 98.

267 Ibid., pp. 99–100.

CHAPTER 13

1 Kuran, 1986, p. 289, no. 58; Konyalı, 1950, pp. 61–62.

2 Akgündüz, ed., 1990, 1:318–20.

3 Kuran, 1986, p. 271, no. 2; Konyalı, 1950, p. 131. The mosque at Çapa, damaged in a fire in 1908, was demolished in 1950.

4 Ayvansarayi, 2000, p. 511; Kuran, 1986, p. 271, no. 2; Konyalı, 1976–77, 1:86; M. Baha Tanman, 'Ahmed Çelebi Mesidi', ISTA, 1:121. The waqfiyya is in VGM, Defter 609/24, no. 137, dated 1 Ra. 996, pp. 112–14 (translated from Arabic into Turkish in Defter 1767, no. 72, pp. 299–306).

5 For the biography of Molla Çelebi who wrote poems with the pen-name Vusuli, see Aşık Çelebi, 1971, fols 79a–80a; Kınalızade, 1989, 2:1044–46.

6 Mustafa Uzun, 'Hubbī', VIA, 18:265–66.

7 Vusuli, Fatih Millet Kütüphabesi, Ali Emiri, T. 321, fol. 22v.

8 Ibid., fol. 25v.

9 Ibid., fols 40v–41v.

10 Ibid., fols 58v, 60v, 61r; Selaniki, 1989, 1:52, 182–83. For a summary of his career, see Ayvansarayi, 2000, pp. 401–2.

11 TM in Meriç, 1965, p. 27; Kuran, 1986, p. 288, no. 57; p. 395, no. 434.

12 M. Baha Tanman, 'Molla Çelebi Camii', ISTA 5:483–84; Aslanapa, 1986, p. 224; Konyalı, 1950, pp. 182–83; and Kuran, 1986, p. 288, no. 57.

13 Ayvansarayi, 1985, p. 374 'Leb-i deryāda seyrān eyle ḥammāmın monlānuñ 979/1571;' Evliya, 1896–1938, 1:445.

14 VGM, Defter 624, no. 1, dated the beginning of N. 977, pp. 1–4 (translated from Arabic into Turkish in Defter 1967, no. 33, pp. 134–47).

15 Defter 1967, pp. 141–43. The madrasa professor would receive twenty aspers, the masjid's imam five aspers, its muezzin three aspers, its janitor two aspers, and its fifteen reciters of sections from the Koran two aspers each.

16 Ibid., pp. 142–47.

17 VGM, Defter 624, no. 2, dated the end of B. 992, pp. 4–5 (translated from Arabic into Turkish in Defter 1967, pp. 148–54).

18 Selaniki, 1989, 1:136.

19 Ayvansarayi, 2000. p. 401.

20 The winter residence with two courtyards was located in the Kızıltaş quarter; see Defter 1967, pp. 149–51.

21 The list of baths in the 'Untitled Treatise' mentions 'the bath-house of Molla Çelebi near Tophane.' The word 'Tophane' is crossed out and replaced with 'Canfeda', a reference to the neighbouring garden of the stewardess mentioned in the waqfiyya. 'Canfeda' is misread as 'Can feneri', in Meriç, 1965, p. 7, note 30.

22 The shore mansion of Perizad Hatun, one of the imperial harem's female attendants, and her husband Arap Ahmed Pasha (d. 1586), became the English embassy from 1583 to 1594. Sinan built a domed mausoleum there for the married couple. For a posthumous masjid-cum-convent, endowed in 1599–1600, next to that mausoleum in accordance with the late Perizad Hatun's will; see M. Baha Tanman, 'Keşfī Cafer Efendi Tekkesi', ISTA 4:549–51. Ebussud's garden is mentioned in Eremya, 1988, pp. 39, 252.

23 See Chapters 7 and 9.

24 For the career of İvaz Efendi, see Ayvansarayi, 1985, p. 233. For his death as the Kazasker of Rumelia in 1586, see Selaniki, 1989, 1:178. He was buried at Eğrikapı in front of the mihrab of the mosque he had built there. Murad III visited the late İvaz Efendi's tomb to offer prayers and distribute alms; it was located 'in the quarter of Eğrikapı in the place where a church became a Friday mosque'.

25 For İvaz Efendi's mosque, see Müller-Wiener, 1977, pp. 428–29; Goodwin, 1971, p. 259. Its wooden U-shaped external portico was demolished in 1935.

26 Āli, İÜ. T. 5959, fols 90r–93v.

27 Akgündüz, ed., 1990, 1:320–22.

28 Ibid., p. 320.

29 See Chapter 10.

30 Kuran, 1986, p. 290, no. 61. Evliya, TSK, B. 304, 1:89v.

31 Atai, 1989, 2:114; Ayvansarayi, 2000, pp. 313–14; Haskan, 1993, 1:75–77.

32 Kuran, 1986, p. 271, no. 3.

33 Ibid., p. 301, no. 301; Konyalı, 1950, pp. 67–69; Evliya, 1896–1938, 1:312.

34 Kuran, 1986, p. 276, no. 19; Konyalı, 1950, pp. 63–66; Müller-Wiener, 1977, pp. 398–99; Ayvansarayi, 2000, p. 386.

35 Konyalı, 1950, pp. 64–65.

36 Atai, 1989, 2:188–89.

37 The mosque is hypothetically dated 1576 with a question-mark in Kuran, 1986, p. 275, no. 275.

38 Akgündüz, ed., 1990, 1:318, 321.

39 Konyalı, 1950, p. 58.

40 For the tombs, see Ayvansarayi, 2000, pp. 321–23. The mosque is discussed in Kuran, 1986, p. 274, no. 13; Konyalı, 1950, pp. 57–60.

41 Ayvansarayi, 2000, p. 127; Konyalı, 1950, pp. 70–71.

42 Konyalı, 1950, p. 71.

43 Ayvansarayi, 2000, p. 127; Konyalı, 1950, p. 70.

44 Ayvansarayi, 2000, pp. 127–28.

45 Kuran, 1986, p. 305, no. 106, p. 354, no. 354; see also Müller-Wiener, 1977, p. 400; Konyalı, 1950, pp. 70–73; and M. Baha Tanman, 'Dırağman Külliyesi', ISTA 3:49–51.

46 Atai, 1989, 2:759; Hulvi, 1993, p. 604; M. Kılıç, 1997b, p. 269, no. 17.

47 Barkan and Ayverdi, eds, 1970, pp. 417–18, no. 2438, dated M. 948.

48 Pedani, 1994, pp. 144–53, 242.

49 Ibid., p. 147.

50 Dzaja and Weiss, 1995, p. 386.

51 Ibid., pp. 440–41.

52 Ibid., p. 608.

53 Kuran, 1986, p. 354, no. 276.

54 Akgündüz, ed., 1990, p. 323.

55 For Sinan's successors, see Akalın, 1958; Erdoğan, 1955; Mülayim, 1996.

56 BA, Istanbul Tapu Defteri 670, pp. 1090–92, 'vaḳf-ı mescid-i ḫürrem beg ibn ʿabdülḥalīm', dated the end of Ca. 976: 'vaḳf-ı cāmiʿ-i şerīf ve mekteb der maḥalle-i ḳarabaş ... ḥālā mekteb yoḳdur.' See the folded map in Müller-Wiener, 1977, for the Hürrem Çavuş mosque near the Karabaş masjid in Karagümrük near Yenibahçe.

57 BA, Istanbul Tapu Defteri 670, p. 1093. Under 'maḥalle-i miʿmār sinān aġa ... der ḳurb-i yeñibāġçe' is listed the waqf of Hürrem Çavuş. A 'hüccet' dated Z. 970 (1563) endowed a house for the imam of Sinan's masjid: 'mescid-i mezbūrda imām olanlar sākin olalar.'

58 Ayvansarayi, 2000, pp. 113–14.

59 The inscriptions are cited in Konyalı, 1950, pp. 117–18; Kuran, 1986, p. 280, no. 33. For the wrong assumption that the patron died after building his mosque, school and fountain in 961 (1554), see Mehmed Süreyya, 1996, 2:271.

60 For the mosque in İzmit, see Kuran, 1986, p. 285, no. 48.

61 See Chapters 8 and 9.

62 VGM, Defter 570, no. 32, dated the end of Ş. 973, p. 57 (adapted from Ottoman-Turkish to modern Turkish in Defter 2111, pp. 140–47).

63 Defter 2111, p. 141. A librarian receiving five aspers was responsible for the library.

64 Ibid., p. 145. The first shaykh Sinaneddin Yusuf Efendi is mentioned in Ayvansarayi, 2000, p. 62; for his father Shaykh Yakub; see Shahsultan's patronage in Chapter 8.

65 Ibid., 141–47.

66 Hulvi, 1993, pp. 483–85.

67 Ayvansarayi, 2000, pp. 62–63.

68 Kuran, 1986, p. 276, no. 21; Müller-Wiener, 1977, p. 381; Konyalı, 1950, pp. 86–88; M. Baha Tanman, 'Ferruh Kethüda Camii ve Tekkesi', ISTA 3:294–95. For the number of dervishes in the convent; see M. Kılıç, 1997, p. 269, no. 2.

69 Baltacı, 1976, pp. 98–99; Atai, 1989, 2:280.

70 Konyalı, 1950, p. 87.

71 Evliya, TSK, B. 304, 1:89r.

72 Konyalı, 1950, p. 88. For a copy of the manuscript, dated Receb 968 (1561), see TSK, H. 146.

73 The Friday mosque in Çorlu, attributed to Sultan Süleyman by its extant Turkish inscription dated 928 (1521–22), also had architectural paintings on its façade, described as representations of 'Latin, Greek [Orthodox], and Turkish [Muslim] churches' in Du Fresne-Canaye, 1897, p. 49. The mosque, its hospice-cum-caravansaray, and its fountain were 'very artistically and perspectivally painted with churches' according to Gerlach, 1674, p. 510.

CHAPTER 14

1 Kuran, 1986, p. 282, no. 38; Konyalı, 1950, pp. 127–28.

2 Ayvansarayi, 2000, p. 58; Konyalı, 1950, p. 127.

3 TSA, E. 5209/6, dated the end of S. 978.

4 TSA, E. 5209/5, dated the beginning of Ca. 982.

5 TSA, E. 5217/7, dated the beginning of M. 987.

6 The tombstones of the cemetery were removed after 1940; see Kuran, 1986, p. 324, no. 324; the ruins of the elementary school are described by Konyalı, 1950, pp. 129–30.

7 VGM, Defter 582, no. 362, dated the end of C. 983, p. 485 (adapted from Ottoman-Turkish to modern Turkish in Defter 1967, pp. 294–307). He also endowed a well at Rumelihisar and a public fountain outside the Yenikapı gate of Istanbul.

8 Barkan and Ayverdi, eds, 1970, p. 31, no. 197, dated M. 951.

9 For the pasha's appointment to Egypt in 1556 and his return to the capital in 1559, see Winkelhane and Schwarz, 1985, pp. 25–26; Ayvansarayi, 2000, p. 468; Rüstem Pasha, ÖNB, Codex Vindobonensis Palatinus, Mxt. 339, fols 281r, 284v–85r.

10 The convent was built for Shaykh ʿAbd al-Wahhab al-Shaʿrani; see Winkelhane and Schwarz, 1985, pp. 67–73; Behrens-Abouseif, 1994, p. 180.

11 VGM, Defter 2113, no. 29, dated Ra. 967, p. 168 (translated from Arabic into Turkish in Defter 2142, no. 73, pp. 297–310). Cited in Konyalı, 1950, p. 121; Winkelhane and Schwarz, 1985, p. 39.

12 BA, MD. 3, # 1480, p. 498, dated 3 Z. 967, published in Aykut et al., eds, 1993, p. 641, where the village of 'Kanlıcak' is misread as 'Çamlık'.

13 VGM, Defter 2113, no. 30, dated 26 Ş. 968, p. 175 (translated from Arabic into Turkish in Defter 2142, pp. 305–7). The endowed 'market caique' is also mentioned in Ayvansarayi, 2000, p. 470; for other endowments, see Konyalı, 1950, pp. 121–22.

14 VGM, Defter 2113, dated mid R. 975, p. 175 (translated from Arabic into Turkish in Defter 2142, p. 307). His three late sons endowed one third of their inheritance for the following structures built by the pasha: an elementary school in Eyüp for Mehmed and Mustafa Beg, and another elementary school for Mahmud Beg in the village of Koçlu subordinate to Üsküdar; see VGM, Defter 2113, dated mid R. 975, no. 31, p. 177 (translated in Defter 2142, pp. 308–10).

15 He participated in the Szigetvár campaign as the 'former governor-general of Anatolia' and attended the Cyprus campaign as the 'governor-general of Anatolia'; see Selaniki, 1989, 1:15, 41, 54, 78. For his death in Cyprus, see Ayvansarayi, 2000, pp. 468–69.

16 Āli, Nuruosmaniye Library, Ms. 3409, fol. 133v.

17 Kuran, 1986, p. 277, no. 23; p. 337, no. 214; p. 322, no. 169; p. 390, no. 412.

18 The account book is discussed in Chapter 4(1); for the bath-house and other dependencies; see Konyalı, 1950, pp. 119–28; M. Baha Tanman, 'İskender Paşa Külliyesi', ISTA, 4:207–8.

19 For the mausoleum and the confusing identity of the bodies buried there, see Ayvansarayi, 2000, p. 470; Winkelhane and Schwarz, 1985, p. 14; Kuran, 1986, p. 322, no. 169; Konyalı, 1950, p. 123. For Çerkes İskender Pasha, see Chapter 12.

20 Konyalı, 1950, p. 119.

21 Evliya, 1896–1938, 1:466.

22 Inventory no. 1225; see Haluk Kargı, 'İskender Paşa Külliyesi', VIA, 22:571–72.

23 Kuran, 1986, p. 337, no. 214.

24 The entry in TM on the 'Friday mosque of Odabaşı at Yenikapu' is misread as the mosque of '[Ferruh?] Paşa' in Meriç, 1965, p. 27. For the mosque and bath-house, see Kuran, 1986, p. 290, no. 62; 396, no. 437.

25 I have slightly changed the translation in Ayvansarayi, 2000, p. 33.

26 J. H. Mordtmann, 'Isfendiyār Oghlu', EI(2) 4:108–9. The Meccan Sharif's envoy to Istanbul in 1557 wrote that this alleged ancestry could not be true because the Arab commander had left behind no descendants according to hadith experts; see Kamil, 1937, p. 71. For Şemsi Pasha's biography, see Akkaya, 1995; Ayvansarayi, 2000, pp. 496–97; Bayraktar, 1980–81.

27 Şemsi Ahmed Pasha, BN, Supplement Turc 1144, fols 38v–40v; Aşık Çelebi, 1971, fols 250r–51r; Āli, Nuruosmaniye Library, Ms. 3409, fol. 133r.

28 For Şemsi's retirement, see BN, Supplement Turc 1144, fols 81r–v. His parade is described in Selaniki, 1989, 1:6, 21. Mustafa Pasha was dismissed from the vizierate because of his incompetence in the Malta campaign (1565–66) and died during a pilgrimage to Mecca in 1568–69; see Āli, Nuruosmaniye Library, Ms. 3409, fols 128r–v. He sold his residence once belonging to the late (Kara?) Ahmed Pasha for 110,000 florins, settled his pious foundations in Bolu and other places, and left for Damascus. Buried in Muʿalla, he left behind three sons and a daughter; see Selaniki, 1989, 1:64.

29 Hasanbeyzade, 1980, 2:83–84, 97; also see Āli, 1979–80; 1:43–46.

30 Ahmed Pasha's father was the son of a daughter of Bayezid II according to Garzoni; see Albèri, 1844–50, 1:402, 404.

31 Schweigger, 1964, p. 135.

32 After his accession to the throne, Murad III summoned the retired Şemsi Ahmed Pasha from Bolu as his royal companion according to Āli, IÜ, T. 5059, fol. 504r.

33 Gerlach, 1674, p. 311.

34 Āli, Nuruosmaniye Library, Ms. 3409, fol. 133r.

35 Āli, IÜ, T. 5959, fol. 504v.

36 Āli, 1979–82, 1:42.

37 Ibid., 2:97–98, 227.

38 For Rüstem Pasha's retirement in Üsküdar, see Chapter 8. Likewise the grand vizier Koca Sinan Pasha spent his retirement in 1582 at his garden in Üsküdar, before he was exiled to Malkara in Thrace; see Selaniki, 1989, 1:136–37, 211. The retired grand vizier Siyavuş Paha was allowed to come to his city palace in 1596, after having spent many years in his Üsküdar garden; ibid., 2:618–19.

39 The new source of water discovered in a nearby mountain would be conducted via the water channel of the royal garden of Haydarpaşa; see BA, MD. 40, #122, p. 55, dated 12 Şaban 987; addressed to the water channel superintendent Davud Çavuş.

40 I have slightly modified the translation in Ayvansarayi, 2000, pp. 496–97.

41 Şemsi Pasha's shore palace is cited among royal gardens in various registers; it was replaced in the eighteenth century by the royal Şerefabad Palace. For its site, see Konyalı, 1976–77, 1:81–82; 2:251–62; Eldem, 1969–74, 2:374–88.

42 An undated Turkish copy is in Süleymaniye Kütüphanesi, Lala İsmail 737, fols 15v–24v; see fols 17r–v. An abbreviated copy, dated 988 (1580–81) is in VGM, Defter 456; see pp. 103–5, 175. Şemsi Pasha's mother is misidentified by modern historians as a daughter of Bayezid II; see Mordtmann, EI(2), 4:198–99.

43 Süleymaniye Kütüphanesi, Lala İsmail 737, fol. 21v.

44 Ibid., fols 23v–24r. The madrasa professor received a modest wage of twenty aspers and the students two aspers each; ibid., fol. 26v.

45 Ibid., fol. 26v: 'cism-i şerīf ve ʿunṣūr-ı laṭīfleri ol türbe-i hümāyūn içre genc-i nihān gibi medfūn ve maḥzūn ḳılına.'

46 Ibid., fols 24v–27r.

47 He was governor-general of Damascus between 959 (29 December 1551 to 17 December 1552) and 961 (7 December 1553 to 25 November 1554) according to Laoust, 1952, p. 185. For his madrasa, convent and khan in Damascus, see Kafescioğlu, 1999, p. 74.

48 Evliya, TSK, B. 304, 2:277v.

49 BA, KK. 81, dated 6 Za. 971, p. 528: 'Bolıda binā itdügi cāmiʿüñ misāfirḫānesi evḳāfı olmayub...'.

50 Yüksel, 1993, pp. 73–88. TM in Meriç, 1965, p. 38.

51 Kuran, 1986, p. 303, no. 100; p. 352, no. 269; p. 333, no. 200.

52 See Chapter 12.

53 I have slightly modified the translation in Ayvansarayi, 2000, p. 497. Also recorded in Ayvansarayi, 1985, p. 111; Konyalı, 1950, p. 105; Konyalı, 1976–77, 1:284; and Saatçi, 1988, pp. 114–15, no. 42.

54 Eremya Çelebi, 1988, pp. 48–49.

55 I have slightly modified the translation in Ayvansarayi, 2000, p. 497. Also recorded in Konyalı, 1950, p. 106; and Konyalı, 1976–77, 1:284–85.

56 Cited in Konyalı, 1950, p. 107; see the inscription photographs in Konyalı, 1976–77, 1:285, 386–88. For a ghazal of the pasha using the same wording, 'şemsī-i bī-çāre', see Akkaya, 1995, p. 99.

57 For the lost finial, see Konyalı, 1950, p. 106. It is described in Eremya Çelebi, 1988, p. 48.

58 Evliya, 1896–1938, 1:474, 'ḳaṣr-ı müzeyyen'.

59 Kuran, 1987, p. 199.

60 Ibid., p. 199.

61 The damaged artistic bronze grill was replaced with a new one during repairs in 1940; for a photograph of the dilapidated mausoleum see Konyalı, 1976–77, 1:386–88.

62 Ibid., 1:286–88; Konyali, 1950, p. 106. The central roundel of the dome (calligraphed by İsmail Hakkı Altınbezer) now quotes the cosmic verse alluding to God's power in keeping the heavens and earth in their orbits (35:41); the Throne verse on its rim is preserved; see Derman, 1989, fig. 21.

63 Āli, IÜ, T. 5959, fol. 94r.

64 Ülkü Altındağ, 'Dārüssaāde', VIA, 9:1–3. A decree dated 28 May 1588 informs the governor-general of Anatolia about Mehmed Agha's appointment as the overseer of the 'ḥaremeyn-i şerīfeyn' waqfs; BA, MD. 62, #563, p. 249, dated 2 B. 996.

65 Necipoğlu, 1991, p. 174.

66 Ahmed Resmi Efendi, 2000, pp. 85–87.

67 Ibid., pp. 85–87.

68 Selaniki, 1989, 1:229–30.

69 TSK, E.H. 3001, dated 990, fol. 37v: 'davud beg b. ʿabdullāh nāẓır-ı rāh-ı āb-ı sābıḳ.'

70 Two decrees sent to the kadi of Medina in 1578 concern the permit of the dilapidated Mamluk period elementary school Mehmed Agha wanted to rebuild there along with a water dispenser (*sebīl*) and a convent with rooms for the poor; BA, MD. 35, # 196 and #241, pp. 81 and 97, dated *c.* 986.

71 TSA, E.7830/1, dated the beginning of Ca. 987; E.7830/5, dated mid Ş. 988; E.7830/4, dated the beginning of Ş. 988. Also see, BA, MD. 36, #942, p. 364, dated 9 R. 987; and MD. 39, #569, p. 297, dated 11 S. 988.

72 A title-deed prepared by the kadi of Istanbul in 1580 shows that Davud Çavuş (*ṣuyolı nāẓırı*), the administrator of Bayezid II's waqf, and Ali Çelebi b. Mustafa (*ṣuyolı ketḫüdāsı*) inspected the water sources with a committee of water channel experts (*ṣuyolcı*) who signed the document as witnesses: Ali Çelebi, Üstad Hızır b. Abdullah, and Hamza (TSA, E.7830/3, dated the beginning of Ra. 988). Another title deed dated 1579 concerns four hundred aspers for the damage of a garden from which the water channel passed, paid by the legal representative of Mehmed Agha, the water channel superintendent Davud Çavuş; witnesses include Üstad Hızır b. Abdullah and Üstad Muhyiddin b. Abdullah (TSA, E.7830/2, dated 22 Şevval 987). Yet another title-deed dated 1581 concerns the inspection of additional water sources added to Bayezid II's channel with a committee of experts including the water channel superintendent Davud Beg b. Abdülmennan, Üstad Hüseyin b. Abdullah, Üstad Ali b. Abdullah, and Üstad Nasuh b. Abdullah (TSA, E.7830/6[1], dated mid Z. 988). One last title-deed dated 1581 was signed by the witnesses Hüseyin Çavuş b. Abdullah, Davud Çavuş b. Abdullah, Üstad Nasuh b. Abdullah, and Hızır Çavuş (TSA, E.7830/6[2], dated mid Z. 988).

73 Ayvansarayi, 1985, p. 385. For the inscription in Tophane, see Chapter 11.

74 Kuran, 1986, p. 343, no. 236; Zeynep Ahunbay, 'Mehmed Ağa Medresesi', ISTA, 5:356–57.

75 TSK, E.H. 3028, dated 10 R. 999.

76 Ibid., fols 15v–29r. For Mercan Agha mescidi, later converted into a Friday mosque, see Barkan and Ayverdi, eds, 1970, p. 84, no. 452; and Ayvansarayi, 2000, p. 221.

77 TSK, E.H. 3028, fols 29r–50r.

78 Ibid., fols 35v, 53v–55v. Mehmed Agha's involvement in the expansion of the queen mother's complex is discussed in Chapter 7. For his fountains in Üsküdar, see Egemen, 1993, p. 541.

79 TSK, E.H. 3028, fols, 50r–51v. The donation of İsmail Geçidi on 18 December 1589 to Mehmed Agha is recorded in TSA, E. 10807 (30062), dated 9

Safer 998. Also see the *temliks* (1589–90) in VGM, Defter 744, no. 1, dated the beginning of Ca. 998; no. 2, dated mid M. 998; no. 3, dated 23 Ca. 998.

80 TSK, E.H.3028, fols 50r–51r.

81 In 1593 the kadi of İsmail Geçidi requested masons and carpenters for these buildings, TSA, E.7377/1, dated the end of Ra. 1001. Between 1591 and 1593 materials and workers were requested from neighbouring kadis for the bath-house; see BA, MD.68, #58, p. 29, dated 14 Z. 999; MD. 69, #124, dated 10 Za. 1001.

82 TSK, E.H.3028, fols 88v–90r.

83 The eighteen title deeds are dated between 1571 and 1584; TSA, E.7948.

84 Ibid., the deeds dated N. 992 (nos. 15–18) are signed by 'davud beg b. ʿabdullāh [or ʿabdülmennān] çavuş, miʿmārān.' A house endowed for the imam of the masjid of the Begcügez quarter was demolished with the sultan's permission in 1584; among the committee of experts sent to survey that house was the royal architect Üstad Cafer (ḫāṣṣa miʿmārlardan üstād caʿfer); ibid., deed no. 13, dated 14 Ca. 992. Witnesses who signed the deed include Üstād Sinan b. İbrahim.

85 I have slightly modified the translation in Ayvansarayi, 2000, p. 218–19; also cited in Ayvansarayi, 1985, p. 120. The couplet about the architect reads: 'Oldı miʿmār-ı kāmili Davud, / Yapdı cānıyle derc idüb şanʿat.'

86 For Davud's constructions at the harem of the Topkapı Palace, see Necipoğlu, 1991, pp. 172, 175–76.

87 The house endowed for the shaykh is mentioned in the waqfiyya and in Hulvi, 1993, p. 606.

88 TM in Meriç, 1965, p. 26.

89 Ayvansarayi, 2000, pp. 218–19.

90 TSK, E.H.3028, fol. 78r, the 'zāviye' had a shaykh receiving fifteen aspers and twelve dervishes paid two aspers each. The preacher of the mosque was paid as much as the shaykh.

91 Ayvansarayi, 2000, p. 219; Hulvi, 1993, p. 606.

92 Hulvi, 1993, pp. 606–7.

93 Ibid., p. 607.

94 Kuran, 1987, pp. 228–30; Müller-Wiener, 1977, pp. 436–37.

95 See Chapter 10.

CHAPTER 15

1 For the Takkeci mosque, see Ayvansarayi, 2000, p. 257.

2 Examples in the capital include the complexes of Shahsultan (Eyüp and outside Yenikapı), Sinan Pasha in Beşiktaş, Nişancı Mehmed Pasha in Karagümrük, Mehmed Agha in Çarşamba, Dragoman Yunus Beg in Draman, and Ferruh Kethüda in Balat.

3 Ayvansarayi, 2000, p. 96; Kuran, 1986, p. 278, no. 25; Konyalı, 1950, pp. 89–90; M. Baha Tanman, 'Hacı Evhad Külliyesi', ISTA, 3:473–75; Semavi Eyice, 'Hacı Evhad Camii', VIA, 14:472–74.

4 Tanman, 'Hacı Evhad Külliyesi', p. 475.

5 Konyalı, 1950, p. 91; Saatçi, 1988, p. 123, no. 46.

6 Konyalı, 1950, p. 90; Saatçi, 1988, p. 122, no. 45.

7 For the repairs of Sultan Abdülmecid in 1267 (1850), recorded in an inscription, and more recent renovations in 1945, see Tanman, 'Hacı Evhad Küliyesi', pp. 473–75. The repair inscription dated 1267 is recorded in Saatçi, 1988, pp. 124–25, no. 47.

8 The convent had fourteen dervishes; see M. Kılıç, 1997, p. 269, no. 9. For its shaykhs, see Zakir Şükri Efendi, 1980, pp. 35–36.

9 Ayvansarayi, 2000, p. 96.

10 Kuran, 1986, p. 281, no. 34; Konyalı, 1950, pp. 198–99; M. Baha Tanman, 'Ramazan Efendi Camii ve Tekkesi', ISTA, 6:301–3.

11 I have modified the translation in Ayvansayi, 2000, pp. 74–75; also see Ayvansarayi, 1864–65, 1:66–67; Ayvansarayi, 1985, p. 376; Saatçi, 1988, pp. 131–33, no. 50.

12 See Chapter 6.

13 Hulvi, 1993, pp. 596–97.

14 VGM, Defter 1592, dated the beginning of M. 1002, pp. 1–15: ' … ḳoca muṣṭafā pāşā cāmiʿ-i şerīfi ḳurbinde yazıcızāde bāġçesi dimekle maʿrūf olan mülk menzilimde izn-i sulṭānī ve ḥükm-i ḫāḳānī ile … bir cāmiʿ-i şerīf … ve cāmiʿ-i merḳūmuñ cānib-i şimālīsinde ṣūfīler işneyn ve ḫāmis gicelerinde cemiʿet ve tevḥīd ve ḥaṣret-i rabb-i mecīde taḥmīd itmek içün on ḥücre bir ḫānḳāh-ı dilgüşā binā ve inşā idüb …'.

15 Ibid., pp. 16, 22: 've ḫānḳāh-i merḳūmuñ ḥücrelerinde sākin olan ṣūfīler işneyn ve ḫamsīn gicelerinde ḫānḳāh-i mezbūrda cemiʿet idüb, ẕikrullāh ve tevḥīd ve duʿā ve taḥmīd idüb yevmi birer akçe vaẓīfe ve ṭaʿāmiyeye mutaṣarrıf olalar'.

16 See Chapter 13.

17 VGM, Defter 1592, pp. 16–22. The shaykh of the convent (*ḫānḳāh şeyḫi*) would recite the Ikhlas sura each day after the dawn prayers for the souls of the Prophet and the ulema for an additional two aspers. The imam would recite the Ya-Sin sura for the Prophet Muhammad's soul, the al-Nisa sura for the Prophet Abraham's soul, and the al-Mulk sura for the Prophet's daughter Fatima. The preacher (*ḫaṭīb*) would receive five aspers.

18 For a schematic plan of the complex, see Tanman, 'Ramazan Efendi Camii ve Tekkesi', p. 302.

19 Goodwin, 1971, p. 291.

20 For its simpler original canopy, see the old photograph in Aslanapa, 1986, pp. 304–5.

21 Tanman, 'Ramazan Efendi Camii ve Tekkesi', p. 302.

22 Hulvi, 1993, pp. 596–97.

23 Zilfi, 1988, pp. 168–69.

24 See the foundation inscription, and Hulvi, 1993, p. 596.

EPILOGUE

1 Āli, Nuruosmaniye Library, Ms. 3409, fol. 132v; Peçevi, 1864–67, 2:16–17.

2 Franz Babinger [Geza Dávid], 'Sinan Pasha, Khodja', EI(2), 9:631–32; Selaniki, 1989, 1:304–5.

3 Hasanbeyzade, 1980, p. 86.

4 TM in Meriç, 1965, p. 41; TE in ibid., p. 120.

5 A list of Sinan Pasha's monuments and a summary of his waqfiyyas is given in Bayram, 1999.

6 J. Schmidt, 'Siyāwush Pasha', EI(2), 9:697; Peçevi, 1864–67, 2:17.

7 The demolished complex in Harmanlı had a mosque with a triple-domed portico, madrasa, caravansaray, and bath-house. Only its bridge, dated by an inscription of Mustafa Sai to 993 (1585) is extant. An imperial decree dated 1587, which orders kadis in Bulgarian towns to send lead for the grand vizier Siyavuş Pasha's buildings in Harmanlı and Sofia, suggests that its construction had neared completion during Sinan's lifetime (BA. MD. 62, #281, p. 126, dated L. 995). The building in Sofia was a church the pasha converted into a mosque. A decree sent in 1583 to various kadis in Bulgaria orders lead for the grand vizier Siyavuş Pasha's constructions in Sofia when his man Ferruh Çavuş arrives there (BA. MD. 52, #342, p. 135, dated 5 Za. 991).

8 Kuran, 1986, p. 329, no. 189; p. 382, nos. 379–81. The kadi of Haslar (Eyüp) was sent a decree in 1581 permitting the construction of a mausoleum for the vizier Siyavuş Pasha's dead son across the *türbe* of Sokollu Mehmed Pasha in Eyüp (BA, MD, 42, #801, p. 258; dated 5 Ra. 989). For the fountain of the mausoleum, dated 1011 (1602), the year of the pasha's death, see Egemen, 1993, p. 756.

9 Mülayim, 1996.

10 Zeynep Ahunbay, 'Siyavuş Paşa Medresesi', ISTA, 7:20–21. The construction of the late princess's madrasa next to the their palace is mentioned in Selaniki, 1989, 1:222.

11 Her Turkish waqfiyya of 1590 which mentions her will is in VGM, Defter 732, dated the beginning of C. 998, pp. 290–95. A document attached to the waqfiyya (pp. 295–96) shows that the pasha constructed a madrasa on her behalf and assigned Koran readers for her soul.

12 Yusuf Halaçoğlu, 'Cerrah Mehmed Paşa', VIA, 7:415.

13 Müller-Wiener, 1977, pp. 392–93.

14 For her waqfs see Piyale Pasha in Chapter 11. She became the overseer of Cerrah Pasha's waqf when he passed away in 1604. A copy of his waqfiyya is in Süleymaniye Kütüphanesi, Yazma Bağışlar no. 150, dated Ca. 1013, fols 6r–33r.

15 Selaniki, 1989, 1:366. The mosque was built before Mehmed Pasha became grand vizier in 1598–99.

16 'Of the three mosques often grouped together, that of Cerrah Mehmed Pasha is less finely proportioned than the Nişancı and less interesting than Mesih Paşa Camii'; Goodwin, 1971, p. 337.

17 Ibid., p. 376.

18 For the works of these architects, see Nayır, 1975, pp. 39–44, 138–41.

19 Ibid., pp. 170–91. Examples include the complexes of Ekmekçizade and Kuyucu Murad Pasha (1607–19), Kemankeş Mustafa Pasha (1641), Köprülü Mehmed Pasha (1661), Merzifonlu Kara Mustafa Pasha (1681–91), Amcazade Köprülü Hüseyin Pasha (1690s), Çorlulu Ali Pasha (1708), Nevşehirli Damad İbrahim Pasha (1720), and Seyyid Hasan Pasha (1740).

20 See Mehmed Agha's patronage in Chapter 14.

21 Selaniki, 1989, 2:581, 584–85. An account book of the mausoleum and water dispenser, dated 1001 (1593), is in TSA. S.P.79.

22 The mosque's incription is discussed in Chapter 14. For the Pearl Kiosk's signed fountain; see Necipoğlu, 1991, p. 226.

23 Nayır, 1975, p. 24; Doğan Yavaş, 'Sinan Paşa Külliyesi', ISTA, 7:4; Egemen, 1993, pp. 750, 753.

24 TSA, E.9297, dated end of N. 1001. For Gazanfer Agha's Venetian origin and his family connections, see Pedani, 2000.

25 VGM, Defter 571, no. 8, p. 11, dated Ca. 1004 (copied in Defter 2225, pp. 10–25).

26 Nayır, 1975, pp. 24–25.

27 For the early modern ethos, see Kafadar, 1994.

28 Zilfi, 1996, p. 205.

29 Ibid., pp. 129–81. Between 1621–85, of the forty-eight appointments made for Friday preacher posts at sultanic mosques, at least nineteen were Halvetis; ibid., p. 165.

30 Āli, 1997, pp. 177–78.

31 These changes are noted in Selaniki, 1989, 1:427–28.

32 Lokman, TSK, H.1524, fol. 284v. He says the Süleymaniye mosque cost 500,000 florins (30,000,000 aspers) now equal to 1,000,000 gold coins. He makes the same observation for the costs of the Kırkçeşme water system that would have been doubled at the time he was writing, fols 286v–87v.

33 Faroqhi, 1994, p. 98; Barkan, 1972–79, 2:276–90.

34 The construction started in 1071 (1660–61) and ended in 1075 (1664–65) comprising a mosque, mausoleum, elementary school, hadith college, shops and water channels that cost '1540 yük akçe (3,080 kise)' according to a history dedicated to Turhan Sultan; see Kürd Hatib Mustafa, TSK, E.H.1400, pp. 22–23.

35 Ahmed Refik, 1977, pp. 139–52.

36 Watenpaugh, 1999, pp. 161, 191.

37 Examples include the Şerefettin mosque in Konya (1636) and the Ömer Pasha mosque in Elmalı (1610);

see Goodwin, 1971, pp. 310, 351–53. Viziers continued to build mosque complexes in provincial towns during the eighteenth century, such as the Köprülü mosque at Safranbolu, the Kara Mustafa Pasha mosque at Merzifon, and Nevşehirli İ brahim Pasha mosque at Nevşehir; ibid., pp 361–62, 370–71.

38 Goffman, 1990.

39 For Safiye, see Skilliter, 1965; Pedani, 2000.

40 Selaniki, 1989, 2:723. Among planned dependencies of the 'New Mosque' at the 'Emīn-i Gümrük İskelesi', a hospital is also listed in Topçular Katibi Abdülkadir, Süleymaniye Kütüphanesi, Esad Efendi, Ms. 2151, fols 44v, 53r.

41 Selaniki, 1989, 2:733–36.

42 Ibid., 2:761, 763–64.

43 Ibid., 2:849–51.

44 Evliya, 1896–1938, 1:302. For her exile, also see Ottaviano Bon's report in Barozzi and Berchet, eds, 1871–72, 1:102.

45 Barozzi and Berchet, eds, 1871–72, p. 39.

46 Skilliter, 1965, p. 146; Selaniki, 1989, 2:854–57.

47 For the money she donated to the campaign, see Selaniki, 1989, 2:790–91.

48 Kürd Hatib Mustafa, TSK, E.H.1400, p. 20. This source contrasts the late mother of Mehmed III, the conqueror of Eger, whose legitimacy was shaken by her association with Esther Kira who caused much oppression (*ẓulm*), with the impeccable morals and piety of the new queen mother; see p. 18.

49 Silahdar Fındıklılı Mehmed Ağa, 1928, 1:218.

50 The inscription is recorded in Ayvansarayi, 1985, pp. 296–97. The inscription, pavilion and mosque complex are interpreted in Thys-Şenocak, 1994, 1998 and 2000. Also see Nayır, 1975, pp. 135–68.

51 For those buried in her tomb, see Ayvansarayi, 2000, p. 23; Önkal, 1992, pp. 203–10. The successors of Mehmed IV; namely, his brothers Süleyman II (r. 1687–91) and Ahmed II (r. 1691–95) are buried in Süleyman I's tomb.

52 For Nurbanu's complex, see Chapter 7.

53 The queen mother's waqfiyya explains how the mosque built by her deputy and manumited slave, the late chief black eunuch Osman Agha (d. 1603), legally reverted to her along with his waqf; see Williams, 1969, pp. 459, 462–63. The mosque in Cairo is described in Behrens-Abouseif, 1994, pp. 253–57.

54 Simone Contarini left Istanbul in 1612; see Barozzi and Berchet, eds, 1871–72, 1:129, 180–82, 193.

55 Avcıoğlu, 2001. This interpretation was further developed in a seminar paper on the mosque by Emine Fetvacı.

56 Barozzi and Berchet, eds, 1871–72, 1:284, 289–90.

57 For the complex, see Nayır, 1975, pp. 35–133; idem., 'Sultan Ahmed Külliyesi', ISTA, 7:55–61. The sultan's Turkish waqfiyya recorded in the beginning of 1022 (1613) mentions these structures; TSK, E.H.3036, fol. 26r.

58 For the palace in Mahmudpaşa and the two Hippodrome palaces, see the patronage of these couples in Chapter 8. Nayır, 1975, p. 36; Safi, TSK, R.1304, fols 19v–20r; Topçular Katibi Abdülkadir, Süleymaniye Kütüphanesi, Esad Efendi, Ms. 2151, fol. 153r.

59 Cafer Efendi, 1987, p. 66.

60 Dismantled buildings included the royal menagerie and painter's workshop, as well as imperial warehouses; see Safi, TSK, R.1304, fol. 20v; Barkan 1972–79, 2:276–90; and Topçular Katibi Abdülkadir, Süleymaniye Kütüphanesi, Esad Efendi, Ms. 2151, fol. 186r.

61 Safi, TSK, R.1304, fol. 20r.

62 Āli, 1979–82, 1:54, 146, cited in Chapter 2.

63 Courmenin, 1632, p. 107.

64 Grelot, 1683, p. 212.

65 Nayır, 'Sultan Ahmed Külliyesi', p. 56.

66 Evliya, TSK, B.304, 2:273v–75v.

67 Gontaut-Biron, 1888–89, 2:312, 349, 372.

68 The pavilion was extensively renovated after a fire in 1949. For the cost of tile revetments, see TSA, D.101146/2, fol. 2v.

69 Topçular Katibi Abdülkadir, Süleymaniye Kütüphanesi, Esad Efendi, Ms. 2151, fol. 177v.

70 Ibid., fols 184v–85v; Naima, 1865–68, 2:150–51.

71 Barkan, 1972–79, 2:288.

72 TSK, E.H.3036, dated the beginning of 1022, fols 67v–68r. For the ceremonial rules of the *mevlud* ritual held at the Sultan Ahmed mosque, see Esad Efendi, 1979, pp. 24–26.

73 Selaniki, 1989, 2:826.

74 For the role of coffee and coffee-houses in the expansion of the public sphere, see Kafadar, 1994.

75 Topçular Katibi Abdülkadir, Süleymaniye Kütüphanesi, Esad Efendi, Ms. 2151, fol. 186v.

76 Zilfi, 1996, pp. 131–36; Necdet Sakaoğlu, 'Kadızadeliler-Sivasīler', ISTA, 4:367–69.

77 For Vani Mehmed Efendi, see Zilfi, 1996, pp. 146–58, 191–92.

78 For the four water dispensers, see Nayır, 1975, p. 88; Egemen, 1993, p. 73.

79 The dome of the Yeni Valide in Eminönü is 17.5 metres wide and 36 metres high. It comes close to the Şehzade Mehmed mosque's dome (19 metres wide, 37 metres high), but is proportionally higher relative to its base and has a more pronounced pyramidal aspect articulated by stepped buttresses with domical turrets.

80 Before laying the foundations of his own mosque, Sultan Ahmed renovated between 1607–9 the Hagia Sophia, some of whose figural mosaics were covered up; see Necipoğlu, 1992a, pp. 210–18.

81 Peirce, 1993, pp. 97–103.

82 For the inscription and a description of the mausoleum, see Önkal, 1992, pp. 194–98.

83 Cantemir, 1979–80, 2:148, 322.

84 Goodwin, 1971, pp. 344, 349.

85 Grelot, 1683, pp. 211–12. For drawings he discussed with Colbert, see ibid., p. 210.

86 Evliya, 1896–1938, 1:216: 'Bu cāmiʿ İslāmboldaki selāṭīn cāmiʿlerininñ eñ güzelidür;' 1:218: 'Ama bunuñ ṭarz-ı miʿmārisinde olan şīrīnkārlıḳ hiç bir diyārıñ cevāmiʿinde görülmemişdür.'

87 Cafer Efendi, 1987, pp. 67, 75.

88 I have slightly modified the translation, ibid., p. 74.

89 The number of galleries is also equated with Ahmed I's lineage in Hasanbeyzade, 1980, 2:323; Naima, 1865–68, 2:79–80; and Evliya, 1896–1938, 1:219 (who specifically mentions sixteen galleries).

90 Goodwin, 1971, p. 349.

91 For the evolution of royal suites, see Kuran, 1990–91.

92 Provincial mosques with the quatrefoil plan type are discussed in Kiel, 2003.

93 For neo-Ottoman mosques and modernist exceptions in Turkey, see Holod and Khan, 1997, especially pp. 99–105.

APPENDICES

APPENDIX 1

Chronological Catalogue of Friday Mosques and their Dependencies listed in Sinan's Autobiographies, *Tuḥfetü'l-mi'mārīn* (TM), and most copies of the *Teẕkiretü'l-ebniye* (TE).

DATE	LOCATION	NAME	RANK OF PATRON	ORIGIN OF PATRON	AUTOBIOGRAPHY CITATION	CITED DEPENDENCIES	DOME DIAMETER
c. 1537 (1555–56, conversion to Friday mosque)	Istanbul, Eyüp	Shahsultan (d. 1572)	daughter of Selim I, widow of Lutfi Pasha	royal-born	extant (TM, TE)	dervish convent (non-extant: TM)	hipped roof
1538/39–1540 (1550–51, hospital)	Istanbul, Avratpazarı (now Haseki)	Hürrem Sultan (d. 1558) [Haseki Sultan Mosque]	wife of Süleyman I, mother of princes (Haseki)	Christian-born, Polish or Ukranian	extant (TM, TE)	madrasa, hospital (TM, TE); elementary school (TM)	11.3 m
c. 1538–39	Istanbul, Sütlüce (outside Galata)	Çavuşbaşı Mahmud Agha (d. 1550) [Sütlüce Mosque]	chief court messenger	Christian-born	extensively rebuilt (TM, TE)	none	hipped roof
1541–42	Istanbul, Balat (now Draman)	Dragoman (Tercüman) Yunus Beg (d. 1551)	chief court interpreter	Greek from Modone	extensively rebuilt (TM, TE)	madrasa (TM, TE)	hipped roof
c. 1541–44	Diyarbakır	Hadım Ali Pasha (d. 1560)	governor-general	Christian-born from Ioanina in Albania	extant (TM)	madrasa (TM)	14.4m
c. 1542–47	Istanbul, Tophane (outside Galata, now Çukurcuma)	Muhyiddin Mehmed Çelebi (Fenarizade, d. 1548) [Çukurcuma Mosque]	shaykh al-islam	Muslim-born	completely rebuilt (TM, TE)	none	hipped roof
c. 1543	Istanbul, Eyüp	Nişancı Mustafa Çelebi (Celalzade, d. 1567)	chief chancellor	Muslim-born	completely rebuilt (TM, TE)	bath-house (non-extant: TM, TE)	probably hipped roof
1543–44, posthumous	Istanbul, Aksaray	Osmanshah's mother (d. 1538)	daughter of Selim I, wife of İskender Pasha	royal-born	non-extant (TM, TE)	madrasa (non-extant: TM, TE)	hipped roof
c. 1543/44–1548	Istanbul, Üsküdar	Mihrümah Sultan (d. 1578), [İskele Mosque]	daughter of Süleyman I and Hürrem Sultan, wife of Rüstem Pasha	royal-born	extant (TM, TE)	madrasa (TM, TE); hospice (non-extant: TM, TE)	11.4m
1543–48, posthumous	Istanbul, Eski Odalar (now Şehzadebaşı)	Şehzade Mehmed (d. 1543)	heir apparent, son of Süleyman I and Hürrem Sultan	royal-born	extant (TM, TE)	mausoleum, madrasa, hospice (TM, TE); elementary school, caravansaray (TM)	19m
c. 1546–47, posthumous	Aleppo	Divane [Deli] Hüsrev Pasha (d. 1544–45) [Khusrawiyya Mosque]	governor-general and vizier	Serbian from Bosnia	extant (TM, TE)	madrasa (TM)	approx. 18m
1547–48	Sofia	Sofu [Bosnalı, Hacı] Mehmed Pasha (d. 1551)	vizier and governor-general	Christian-born from Bosnia	remodeled as a church (TM, TE)	none	18.3m
1548–59 (1557, inauguration of mosque)	Istanbul, Eski Saray (now Süleymaniye)	Süleyman I (r. 1520–66) [Süleymaniye Mosque]	sultan, son of Selim I and Hafsa Sultan	royal-born	extant (TM, TE)	four madrasas, hadith college, medical college, Koran recitation school, hospital, hospice, caravansaray, bath-house (TM, TE); elementary school (TM)	26.5m
c. 1550–52/53	Rodoscuk (now Tekirdağ)	Rüstem Pasha (d. 1561)	grand vizier, husband of Mihrümah Sultan	Croatian from Bosnia	extant (TM, TE)	hospice, caravansaray (non-extant: TM, TE); madrasa (TM)	13.28m
c. 1550–57	Jerusalem	Hürrem Sultan (d. 1558), [Takiyya al-Khassaki Sultan]	wife of Süleyman I, mother of princes (Haseki)	Christian-born, Polish or Ukranian	partially extant complex (TM)	madrasa (non-extant: TM); hospice (TM)	probably hipped roof
1551	Istanbul, Silivrikapı	Hadım İbrahim Pasha (d. 1562)	vizier	Christian-born from Bosnia	extant (TM, TE)	mausoleum (TM), bath-house (non-extant: TM)	12m

DATE	LOCATION	NAME	RANK OF PATRON	ORIGIN OF PATRON	AUTOBIOGRAPHY CITATION	CITED DEPENDENCIES	DOME DIAMETER
c. 1551–65	Diyarbakır	Çerkes İskender Pasha (d. 1571)	governor-general	Muslim-born, Circassian	extant (TM)	none	approx. 15m
c. 1552–57	Sapanca	Rüstem Pasha (d. 1561)	grand vizier, husband of Mihrümah Sultan	Croatian from Bosnia	completely rebuilt (TM, TE)	hospice, caravansaray (non-extant: TM, TE); bath-house (TE)	hipped roof
c. 1552	Istanbul, outside Yenikapı (now Merkezefendi)	Shahsultan (d. 1572) [Merkez Efendi Mosque]	daughter of Selim I, widow of Lutfi Pasha	royal-born	completely rebuilt (TM, TE)	bath-house (TM, TE)	hipped roof
c. 1552	Gözleve (now Yevpatoria)	Devlet Giray Khan I (r. 1551–57) [Tatar Khan Mosque]	vassal ruler of the Crimean Khanate	Muslim-born	extant (TM, TE)	mausoleum (non-extant: TM)	6m
1553–54 (1574–75, conversion to Friday mosque)	Istanbul, Ahırkapı	Kapıağası Mahmud Agha	chief white eunuch	Christian-born	extensively rebuilt (TM, TE)	madrasa (non-extant: TM, TE); mausoleum (non-extant: TM)	probably hipped roof
1553–54	Istanbul, Tophane (outside Galata)	Defterdar Ebulfazl Mehmed Efendi (d. 1574)	retired chief finance minister	Muslim-born	completely rebuilt (TM, TE)	mausoleum (non-extant: TM)	hipped roof
1554–58/59 (1566–67, madrasa)	Damascus	Süleyman I (r. 1520–66) [Takiyya al-Sulaymaniyya]	sultan, son of Selim I and Hafsa Sultan	royal-born	extant (TM, TE)	hospice (TM, TE); madrasa (TM)	10m
1554–55	Istanbul, Yenibahçe (now Çapa)	Kazasker [Amasyalı, Kızıl] Abdurrahman Çelebi	army judge	Muslim-born	non-extant (TM, TE)	mausoleum (non-extant: TM)	hipped roof
1554–55/56, posthumous	Istanbul, Beşiktaş (outside Galata)	Sinan Pasha (d. 1554) [Beşiktaş Mosque]	grand admiral, brother of Rüstem Pasha	Croatian from Bosnia	extant (TM, TE)	madrasa (TM, TE); bath-house (non-extant: TM, TE)	12.6m
1555 (planned), *c.* 1565–71/72, posthumous	Istanbul, Topkapı	Kara Ahmed Pasha (d. 1555) [Topkapı Mosque]	grand vizier, husband of Fatma Sultan	Christian-born from Albania	extant (TM, TE)	madrasa, mausoleum (TM, TE)	12m
1556–65/66, posthumous	Aleppo	Dukakinzade Mehmed Pasha (d. 1557) [ʿAdiliyya Mosque]	governor-general, son of an Ottoman princess and Dukakinzade Ahmed Pasha	royal-born	extant (TM)	none	unknown
c. 1557–60	Samanlı (now Yalova)	Rüstem Pasha (d. 1561)	grand vizier, husband of Mihrümah Sultan	Croatian from Bosnia	non-extant (TM, TE)	caravansaray (non-extant: TM, TE)	probably hipped roof
c. 1557–60	Dibek (Bolu)	Rüstem Pasha (d. 1561)	same as above	same as above	non-extant (TM, misidentified in TE as mosque of Mustafa Pasha in Bolu)	double caravansaray (non-extant: TM)	probably hipped roof
1557–58	Hercegovina (Mostar)	Sofu (Hacı, Karagöz) Mehmed Beg	fiefholder and brother of a vizier, supervisor of the Mostar bridge	Christian-born from Herzegovina	extant (TM, TE)	none	10.65m
1559–60, posthumous	Mustafa Pasha bridge, near Edirne (now Svilengrad)	Hürrem Sultan (d. 1588) (Haseki Sultan mosque)	wife of Süleyman I, mother of princes (Haseki)	Christian-born, Polish or Ukranian	non-extant (TE)	hospice (non-extant: TE)	hipped roof
1559–60, posthumous	Istanbul, Tophane (outside Galata, now Cihangir)	Şehzade Cihangir (d. 1553) (Cihangir mosque)	son of Süleyman I and Hürrem Sultan	royal-born	completely rebuilt (TM, TE)	none	hipped roof
1559–60	Istanbul, Kanlıca (Bosphorus)	Bostancıbaşı İskender Pasha (d. 1571)	former chief gardener, retired governor-general	Christian-born	extensively rebuilt (TM, TE)	madrasa (non-extant: TM, TE); bath-house (non-extant: TE); mausoleum (TM)	hipped roof
1559–60	Kastamonu	Ferhad Pasha (d. 1575)	vizier, husband of Humashah Hatun	Christian-born from Hungary	extensively rebuilt (TM, TE)	none	hipped roof
c. 1560/61–1562/63	Istanbul, Yenibahçe (Karagümrük)	Hürrem Çavuş (d. 1560–61)	court messenger	Christian-born	extant (TM, TE)	none	hipped roof
1560–63/64 (1569–70, water channel)	Karapınar (Sultaniye)	Şehzade Selim (d. 1574) (Sultaniya mosque)	heir apparent, son of Süleyman I and Hürrem Sultan	royal-born	extant (TM, TE)	hospice, bath-house (TM, TE); caravansaray (TM)	14.8m
c. 1561–65	Marmara Ereğlisi (now Tekirdağ)	Semiz Ali Pasha (d. 1565)	grand vizier	Muslim-born from Hercegovina	extensively rebuilt (TM, TE)	none	hipped roof
c. 1561, posthumous	Bolvadin (Afyon)	Rüstem Pasha (d. 1561)	grand vizier, husband of Mihrümah Sultan	Croatian from Bosnia	extensively renovated (TM, TE)	none	13.87m
c. 1561–63, posthumous	Istanbul, Tahtakale	Rüstem Pasha (d. 1561)	same as above	same as above	extant (TM, TE)	none	15.2m

DATE	LOCATION	NAME	RANK OF PATRON	ORIGIN OF PATRON	AUTOBIOGRAPHY CITATION	CITED DEPENDENCIES	DOME DIAMETER
c. 1563–70	Istanbul, Edirnekapı	Mihrümah Sultan (d. 1568) [Edirnekapı Mosque]	daughter of Süleyman I and Hürrem Sultan, widow of Rüstem Pasha	royal-born	extant (TM, TE)	madrasa, bath-house (TM, TE)	20.25m
1562–63	Istanbul, Balat	Ferruh Kethüda [Balat Mosque]	steward of Semiz Ali Pasha	Christian-born	extant (TM, TE)	none	hipped roof
1562–63	Istanbul, Yenikapı (now Şehremini)	Odabaşı Behruz Agha (d. 1562–63)	chief of the privy chamber	Christian-born	extensively rebuilt (TM, TE)	bath-house (non-extant: TM, TE)	hipped roof
c. 1562–63 (waqfiya dated 1563)	Istanbul, Yenibahçe (now Kadıçeşmesi, Fatih)	Binaemini Sinan Agha	freed slave of grand vizier İbrahim Pasha, building supervisor of the Süleymaniye in 1553–59	Christian-born	extant (TM, TE)	none	hipped roof
1562–63	Erzurum	Lala Mustafa Pasha (d. 1580)	former tutor of prince Selim, governor-general	Serbian from Bosnia	extant (TM, TE)	none	10.56m
1565–69/70	Lüleburgaz	Sokollu Mehmed Pasha (d. 1579)	grand vizier, husband of İsmihan Sultan	Serbian from Bosnia	extant (TM, TE)	hospice (non-extant: TM, TE); caravansaray (non-extant: TE); madrasa (TM)	12.5m
c. 1565–73	Istanbul, Kasımpaşa (outside Galata)	Piyale Mehmed Pasha (d. 1578) [Tersane Mosque]	grand admiral and vizier, husband of Gevherhan Sultan	Croatian from Hungary	extant (TM)	none	each dome 8.9m
1565–66	Ankara	Cenabi Ahmed Pasha (d. 1561?) [Kurşunlu Mosque]	governor-general	Muslim-born	extant: (TM, TE)	none	14.4m
c. 1565–69/70	Isparta	Firdevs Beg (d. 1571)	sanjak governor	Muslim-born	extant: (TM, TE)	none	12.38m
c. 1564/65–1572/73	Diyarbakır	Behram Pasha (d. 1585)	governor-general	Muslim-born	extant (TM)	none	15.9m
c. 1566–70	Kütahya	Lala [Tütünsüz] Hüseyin Pasha (d. 1572–73)	former tutor of prince Selim, governor-general	Christian-born from Albania	extant: (TM, TE)	none	12.46m
c. 1566–78	Buda (now Budapest)	Sokollu [Maktul] Mustafa Pasha (d. 1578)	nephew of Sokollu Mehmed Pasha, governor-general	Serbian from Bosnia	non-extant: (TM, TE)	mausoleum (non-extant: TM)	unknown
c. 1566/67–1570	Trikkala	Osmanshah Beg (d. 1569)	sanjak governor, son of an Ottoman princess and İskender Pasha, nephew of Süleyman I	royal-born	extant: (TM, TE)	none	17.98m
1567–68 (1587–88, mausoleum)	Van	Köse Hüsrev Pasha (d. 1587) [Kurşunlu Mosque]	governor-general	Christian-born	extant (TM	madrasa (non-extant: TM)	14.84m
c. 1567–68, posthumous	Istanbul, Üsküdar	Mevlana Ensari Ahmed Efendi (d. 1567–68) [Mevlana Efendi Mosque]	army judge	Muslim-born	completely rebuilt (TM)	none	hipped roof
c. 1567/68–1571/72 (1574, dervish convent)	Istanbul, Kadırgalimanı (Kadırga)	İsmihan Sultan (d. 1585), [Sokollu Mehmed Pasha Mosque]	daughter of Selim II and Nurbanu Sultan; wife of grand vizier Sokollu Mehmed Pasha	royal-born princess, mosque dependencies by her Serbian husband from Bosnia	extant (TM, TE)	madrasa of Sokollu (TM, TE), dervish convent of Sokollu (TM)	13m
c. 1567–74	Payas (near Aleppo)	Sokollu Mehmed Pasha (d. 1579)	grand vizier, husband of İsmihan Sultan	Serbian from Bosnia	extant (TM)	hospice, caravansaray (TM)	approx. 8m
1568–74	Edirne	Selim II (r. 1566–74) [Selimiye Mosque]	sultan, son of Süleyman I and Hürrem Sultan	royal-born	extant (TM, TE)	madrasa, hadith college (TM, TE), Koran recitation school (TM)	31.22m
c. 1569–74	Edirne	Defterdar Mustafa Çelebi	finance minister	unknown	extant (TM, TE)	none	rebuilt dome, approximately 12m
c. 1569–75, posthumous (1585–86, portico and courtyard)	Babaeski	Semiz Ali Pasha (d. 1565)	grand vizier	Muslim-born from Hercegovina	extant (TM, TE)	madrasa (non-extant: TM, TE)	14m
1571–83 (1584–85/86, posthumous expansion of mosque)	Istanbul, Üsküdar	Nurbanu Sultan (d. 1583) [Atik Valide Mosque]	wife of Selim II, mother of Murad III	Venetian, probably from Corfu	extant (TM, TE)	madrasa, Koran recitation school, hospice, hospital (TM, TE); dervish convent, caravansaray (TM); bath-house (TM, TE)	12.7m
c. 1570–84	Istanbul, Fındıklı (outside Galata)	Molla Çelebi (d. 1590, Mehmed Vusuli Efendi) [Fındıklı Mosque]	retired army judge	Muslim-born	extant (TM, TE)	bath-house (non-extant: TM, TE)	11.8m

DATE	LOCATION	NAME	RANK OF PATRON	ORIGIN OF PATRON	AUTOBIOGRAPHY CITATION	CITED DEPENDENCIES	DOME DIAMETER
1570–71	Baghdad	Murad Pasha	governor-general	unknown	extensively renovated (TM)	none	unknown
1572–79/80, posthumous	İzmit	Pertev Mehmed Pasha (d. 1572) [Yenicuma Mosque]	retired vizier	Christian-born from Albania	extant (TM, TE)	none	16.39m
1573–77, posthumous	Havsa (formerly Hafsa)	Sokollu Kasım Beg [Pasha] (d. 1572)	sanjak governor, formerly governor-general, son of Sokollu Mehmed Pasha	Muslim-born	extant without its portico (TM, TE)	hospice, caravansaray (non-extant: TM, TE); bath-house (TM, TE)	approx. 13m
c. 1573–77/78	Istanbul, Azapkapı (outside Galata)	Sokollu Mehmed Pasha (d. 1579) [Azapkapı Mosque]	grand vizier, husband of İsmihan Sultan	Serbian from Bosnia	extant (TM, TE)	bath-house (TM, TE)	11.8m
c. 1575–88, posthumous	Çatalca	Ferhad Pasha (d. 1575)	retired vizier, husband of Humashah Hatun	Christian-born from Hungary	extant (TM, TE)	none	9.2m
c. 1576–85/86	Kayseri	Hacı (Doğancı) Ahmed Pasha (d. 1587–88) [Kurşunlu Mosque]	royal companion and retired governor-general	Muslim born, descendant of the Kızıl Ahmedli (İsfendiyaroğlu) dynasty	extant (TM, TE)	none	12.3m
1577–90, posthumous	Istanbul, Eyüp	Shahsultan (d. 1577) and Zal Mahmud Pasha (d. 1577) [Zal Pasha Mosque]	daughter of Selim II and Nurbanu Sultan, and her vizier husband	royal-born princess, and her Christian-born husband from Bosnia	extant (TM, TE)	mausoleum (TM, TE), twin madrasas (TM)	12.4m
1578–80/81	Istanbul, Tophane (outside Galata)	Kılıç Ali Pasha (d. 1587) [Tophane Mosque]	grand admiral	Christian-born from Calabria in Italy	extant (TM, TE)	mausoleum, bath-house (TM, TE)	12.7m
1580–81	Istanbul, Üsküdar	Şemsi Ahmed Pasha (d. 1580–81)	royal companion, retired governor-general	royal-born, son of an Ottoman princess and Kızıl Ahmedli Mirza Mehmed Beg	extant (TM, TE)	mausoleum, madrasa (TM, TE); dervish convent (non-extant: TM)	8.2m
1583–86/87 (1590, completion of complex)	Manisa	Murad III (r. 1574–95) [Muradiye Mosque]	sultan, son of Selim II and Nurbanu Sultan	royal-born	extant (TM, TE)	hospice (TM, TE)	10.6m
1584–85	Istanbul, Çarşamba	Mehmed Agha (d. 1590)	chief black eunuch	Ethiopian from Abyssynia	extant (TM)	mausoleum (TM)	11.8m
1584-85/86 (1587, mausoleum)	Istanbul, Yenibahçe	Mesih Mehmed Pasha (d. 1589)	vizier and grand vizier	Christian-born from Bosnia	extant (TM)	mausoleum (TM)	12.8m
1584/85–1588/89	Istanbul, Karagümrük	Nişancı Mehmed Pasha (d. 1594)	vizier and chief chancellor	Muslim-born	extant (TM)	mausoleum (TM)	14.2m
1585	Istanbul, Yedikule	Kasap Ustası Hacı Evhad (d. 1585)	chief butcher	unknown	extant (TE)	none	hipped roof
1585–86	Istanbul, Kocamustafapaşa	Bezirganbaşı Hacı Hüsrev [Ramazan Efendi Mosque]	steward of the Old Bazaar	unknown	extant (TM, TE)	none	hipped roof
c. 1587–91	Diyarbakır	Melek (Melik) Ahmed Pasha (d. 1591)	tax farmer and retired governor-general	Muslim-born	extant (TM)	none	11.49m

FRIDAY MOSQUES DATING BEFORE SİNAN'S TENURE AS CHIEF ARCHITECT (1539)

Mosque of Sultan Selim I (r. 1512–20), Istanbul, posthumously built by Süleyman I (1520/21–1527/28), extant (TM)

Mosque of the vizier Çoban Mustafa Pasha, Gebze, 1523-24, extant (TM, TE)

Mosque of Emir Bukhari, outside Edirnekapı (now Otakçılar) in Istanbul, built by Süleyman I for the Nakshbandi shaykh Emir Ahmed Bukhari's son-in-law, Shaykh Mahmud Çelebi (d. 1531–32), waqfiyya dated 1530, non-extant (TM, TE)

Mosque of Shaykh Abd al-Kadir al-Gilani, Baghdad, built by Süleyman I in 1534–35, completely rebuilt (TM)

Mosque of Abu Hanifa, Baghdad, built by Süleyman I in 1534–35, completely rebuilt (TM)

Mosque of the vizier Güzelce Kasım Pasha, Kasımpaşa in Istanbul, 1533–34, completely rebuilt (TM, TE)

FRIDAY MOSQUES CROSSED OUT IN TM, UNIDENTIFIED OR UNDATED MOSQUES, FRIDAY MOSQUES LISTED UNDER MASJIDS

Mosque of the Van castle, renovated by Süleyman I, c. 1534, extant (crossed-out in TM)

Mosque of the Gulanbar (Shahrizor) castle, built by Süleyman I, c. 1561/62–1563/64, non-extant (crossed out in TM)

Mosque of Bayezid II's daughter, Yenibahçe in Istanbul, date unknown, unidentified (TM, TE)

Mosque of Çerkes Osman Pasha (d. 1553), Kayseri, date unknown, unidentified (TM, TE)

Mosque of Sofu Mehmed Pasha, Diyarbakır, date unknown, unidentified (TM)

Mosque of Dukakinzade Mehmed Pasha, Konya Ereğlisi, date unknown, unidentified (TM)

Mosque of Memi Kethüda (chief merchant of the Old Palace), Ulaş near Sivas, date unknown, unidentified (TM, TE)

Mosque of (Maktul) Ayas Pasha (d. 1559–60), Basra, probably built in 1545–46 to commemorate his campaign to Basra as governor-general of Baghdad, unidentified (TM)

Mosque of Mehmed Beg (Rüstem Pasha's steward), İzmit, date unknown, completely rebuilt (now Fevziye Mosque) (TM, TE)

Mosque of Mehmed Beg (Rüstem Pasha's steward), Trikkala, date unknown, unidentified (probably a scribal error, only cited in a few composite TE/TB manuscripts)

Mosque of Mustafa Pasha, Bolu, date unknown, unidentified (probably a scribal error in TE, referring to Rüstem Pasha's mosque in Dibek near Bolu)

Mosque of Defterdar Abdüsselam Çelebi (d. 1526-27), İzmit, transformed from a masjid into a Friday mosque, date unknown, completely rebuilt (TM, TE)

Mosque of Defterdar Süleyman Çelebi (retired finance minister), near the Üsküblü fountain (now Cibali) in Istanbul, transformed into a Friday mosque from the fifteenth-century

masjid of Çakırağa, date unknown, completely rebuilt (TM, TE)
Mosque of Turşucuzade Hüseyin Çelebi, Kiremitciler or Değirmenciler (Hasköy) in Istanbul, date unknown, rebuilt by Sinan, completely rebuilt (TM, TE)
Mosque of Dökmeciler or Düğmeciler (built by Dökmecizade or Düğmecizade Mehmed Bakır Efendi, d. 1589–90), Eyüp in Istanbul, date unknown, extensively rebuilt (TM, cited among masjids in TE)
Mosque of Mevlana Hacegizade (Hocazade Mustafa Efendi, d. 1589–90), Fatih in Istanbul, date unknown, completely rebuilt (TM, cited among masjids in TE)
Mosque of Hacı Hatun or Hamami Hatun (d. 1540–41, Mihrishah Hatun, daughter of İskender Pasha), Samatya (Sulumanastır) in Istanbul, dated *c.* 1527 and listed in Istanbul's waqf register of 1546 as a masjid, probably converted into a Friday mosque at an unknown date, non-extant (TM, TE)

RENOVATED FRIDAY MOSQUES
Mosque of Bali Pasha and Hüma Hatun (daughter of the vizier İskender Pasha), Yenibahçe in Istanbul, dated by its foundation inscription to 1504-5 and listed in the Istanbul waqf register of 1546, endowments added by Bali Pasha in 1566 and Hüma Hatun in 1563 and 1572, probably rebuilt or completed by Sinan, extant (TM, TE)
Mosque of Bayezid II, Istanbul, strengthened with a new arch in 981 (1573–74), extant (TM)
Mosque of Ahi Çelebi (d. 1524), Yemiş (İzmir) İskelesi in Istanbul, renovated after a fire in 1539, extant (TM, TE)
Mosque of Süleyman Subaşı, Unkapanı in Istanbul, rebuilt in 1571 after a fire in 1569, non-extant (TM, TE)
Old Mosque of İznik (Hagia Sophia), renovated by Süleyman I after a fire, dilapidated (TM, TE)
Mosque of Mahmud Pasha (d. 1473–74), Taşlık in Edirne, renovated with surplus endowment funds during the construction of the Selimiye, *c.* 1569–74, non-extant (TM, TE)
Mosque of Orhan I (Ulu Cami), Kütahya, renovated at an unknown date, extensively rebuilt (TM, TE)
Mosque of the Seljukid Sultan Alaeddin (Ulu Cami), Çorum, renovated under Murad III, *c.* 1574–88, extensively rebuilt (TM, TE)
Ka'ba in Mecca, renewal of its golden rain spout and wooden roof for Süleyman I in 958 (1551) by the chief architect of Cairo, Kara Mustafa (TM); construction of domical arcades around the Haram, begun under Selim II and completed under Murad III, 1571–76, extant (TM, TE)

APPENDIX 2

2.1 Costs of some mosque complexes in aspers

SELİM I, ISTANBUL (1520/21–1527/28)
12,000,000+ more than 200,000 florins (Lokman, TSK, H.1524, fol. 280v)

SÜLEYMANİYE, ISTANBUL (1548–59)
54,096,000 costs of the complex (TSK, H.1425, fol. 100r)
53,760,180 costs of the complex (Sai, 1989, pp. 162–63)
53,760,000 costs of the complex (Saatçi, 1990, p. 58)
53,782,900 costs of the complex (Āli, Nuruosmaniye, Ms. 3409, fol. 118r)
30,000,000 cost of the mosque (Lokman, TSK, H.1524, fol. 284v)
30,360,960 cost of the mosque (TSK, H.1425, fol. 100r)

SELİMİYE, EDİRNE (1568–74)
21,930,000+ money periodically given from the sultan's private inner treasury (TSA, D.2336) (not including posthumous expenses of the outer courtyard and commercial structures, paid from the surplus of the endowment)

ŞEHZADE MEHMED, ISTANBUL (1543–48)
15,100,000 (Sai, 1989, p. 146)
15,000,000 (Āli, Nuruosmaniye, Ms. 3409, fol. 4r)
20,000,000+ (Lokman, TSK, H.1524, fol. 283v)

ŞEHZADE CİHANGİR, TOPHANE (1559–60)
733,851 total costs (TSA, D.9435)
Breakdown of costs:
687,240 the mosque (399,830 materials, 287,410 wages)
46,611 elementary school and rooms (17,310 materials, 29,301 wages)

SİNAN PASHA, BEŞİKTAŞ (1554–55/56)
3,273,800 total costs (VGM, Defter 2113, Kasa 110, dated 1557)
Breakdown of costs:
1,841,398 mosque, madrasa, school, 50 shops, 41 rooms, 1 bakery, and 1 butcher's shop in Beşiktaş
24,246 a masjid in Beşiktaş
263,667 a bath-house and 3 adjacent shops in Beşiktaş
15,862 7 shops and 8 rooms in Beşiktaş
28,430 a dervish convent in Beşiktaş
16,385 4 adjacent rooms and a mill drawn by a mule in Tophane
23,470 3 shops with 5 upper rooms in Galata
23,850 1 bakery, 3 upper-story rooms, 1 mill drawn by a mule near the Great Mosque of Galata
19,849 13 shops at the Kasımpaşa arsenal outside Galata
94,530 a bakery, a mill drawn by a horse, 6 rooms, 10 other rooms, 3 shops and their plot of land at Hasköy outside Galata
75,509 a masjid at Yenibahçe in Istanbul (built to substitute the masjid demolished on the site of Sinan Pasha's Friday mosque in Beşiktaş)
215,201 16 rooms and their plot of land at the Karakadı quarter in Istanbul
117,378 50 rooms and 5 shops at the Ali Pasha quarter in Istanbul
514,025 endowed sum for repairs and the wages of personnel

SHAHSULTAN AND ZAL MAHMUD PASHA, EYÜP (1577–90)
7,828,382 total costs (BA, Evkaf 20/25)
Breakdown of costs:
5,976,819 the mosque, 2 madrasas, 24 rental rooms for married couples, 6 shops, 1 candle factory with 6 rooms, and a water channel
600,000 cost of the mausoleum
1,251,563 costs of an endowed caravansaray and mills in Filibe

ALİ PASHA, SARAJEVO (1558–61)
432,997 total costs (TSA. D.5481, D.3902)
Breakdown of costs:
217,932 the mosque (materials and unskilled laborers)
176,000 debts to individuals (including wages of builders and artisans)
21,347 a bath-house built in the town of Mladina (Mladenovac?)
13,424 wages of the mosque's staff and Koran reciters between 1558–61
625 costs of writing and binding sections of the Koran
3,669 carpets, straw mats, other objects, candles, olive oil for lamps, and the wages of staff

2.2 Costs of other building types in aspers

WATER CHANNEL OF THE BAYEZİD II MOSQUE COMPLEX, EDİRNE (1490–91)
116,267 (Barkan, 1972–79, 2:219–22, no. 548a)

KIRKÇEŞME WATER DISTRIBUTION SYSTEM, ISTANBUL (1561–65, renovated after a flood in 1563)
40,263,063 pre-flood costs (Sai, 1989, p. 152; Saatçi, 1990, p. 58)
9,791,144 post-flood rebuilding of the Mağlova aqueduct (Sai, 1989, p. 152; Saatçi, 1990, p. 152)
331,325 cost of the Turunçluk water channel (Saatçi, 1990, p. 152)
40,203,060 pre-flood costs (Āli, Nuruosmaniye, Ms. 3409, fol. 118v)
50,054,207 total costs including post-flood repairs (ibid., fol. 118v)
41,460,000 pre-flood costs (Lokman, TSK, H.1524, fol. 286v)
48,096,000 total costs including repairs (ibid., fol. 286v)

BÜYÜKÇEKMECE BRIDGE (1565–67, with dependencies added in 1567–68)
11,450,000 cost of the bridge (Āli, Nuruosmaniye, Ms. 3409, fol. 118v)
11,967,331 cost of the bridge with dependencies (Saatçi, 1990, p. 92)
Breakdown of costs:
10,923,852 costs of the bridge, excluding reused scaffolding timbers removed from the Süleymaniye mosque
500,000+ post-flood rebuilding of one stone leg and stone buttresses
427,197 cost of the neighbouring caravansaray built between 1562–68, excluding timbers and lead
116,749 costs of the masjid (endowed by Sokollu Mehmed Pasha), two guest-houses, eight shops, and a bakery

HOSPICE (İMARET) OF HÜRREM SULTAN AT AVRATPAZARI, ISTANBUL (1540)
1,579,085 total costs of the hospice comprising a kitchen, pantry, bakery, storehouse, and a water channel to Aksaray (TSA, D.3904)
Breakdown of costs:
1,377,485 costs of the hospice
201,600 miscellaneous costs including the plot of land, endowed houses and shops

MADRASA OF SÜLEYMAN I AT THE HARAM IN MECCA (1564–65)
3,000,000 total cost of the four-partite madrasa dedicated to the four Sunni schools of law, each with sixteen rooms and a classroom (BA, MAD. 7, p. 314, no. 899, dated 975/1567–68)

BATH-HOUSE OF THE BAYEZİD II MOSQUE COMPLEX IN EDİRNE (1491–92)
448,000 (Barkan, 1972–79, 2:215–19, no. 548)

BATH-HOUSE OF KOCA SİNAN PASHA IN LARENDE (1575)
220,000 (TSA, E.SP.153B)

A ROYAL KIOSK OF BAYEZİD II AT THE TOPKAPI PALACE (1488)
58,836 excluding costs of lead, copper, curtains, gold, and lapis lazuli given from the imperial storehouse and the palace's inner treasury, and the wages of salaried court painters estimated as 4000 aspers (TSA, D.10587)

THREE COST ESTIMATES FOR REBUILDING THE COLLAPSED KIOSK OF BAYEZİD II IN THE EDİRNE PALACE (1573)
70,000 with timber framed mixed masonry walls and plain ceiling
80,000 with stone masonry walls and plain ceiling
100,000 with stone masonry walls and a ceiling with painted decoration (BA, KK.67, fol. 508v)

A ROYAL KIOSK WITH İZNİK TILES AT HARMANKAYA ON THE ASIAN COAST OF ISTANBUL (1562–63)
276,830 (TSA, D.6464)

A ROYAL KIOSK WITH İZNİK TILES AT THE FORMER GARDEN OF İSKENDER PASHA NEAR YEŞİLKÖY, ISTANBUL (1564–65)
327,420 total costs (TSA, D.10131)
Breakdown of costs:
220,549 the kiosk itself (106,841 materials, 113,708 wages)
106,871 the garden, waterworks, and dependencies

THE SHORE (YALI) KIOSK WITH İZNİK TILES AT THE TOPKAPI PALACE (1591–92)
3,624,583+ (not including the costs of İznik tiles bought in 1593 which raised the kiosk's costs to approximately 3,700,000 aspers) (BA, MAD. 750; published in Barkan, 1972–79, 2:266–75; additional costs of İznik tiles recorded in TSA, SP.77)

APPENDIX 3

Building types classified in Sinan's autobiographies

I. *Untitled Treatise* and *Risāletü'l-mi'māriyye*:
1.Friday mosques (*cāmi' ler*), 2.masjids (*mesācidler*), 3.madrasas (*medārisler*), 4.hospices (*'imāretler*); 5.hospitals (*dārü'ş-şifā'*); 6.aqueducts (*ṣuyolı kemerleri*); 7.bridges (*cisrler*); 8.palaces (*sarāylar*); 9.caravansarays (*karbānsarāylar*); 10.storehouses (*maḫāzinler*); 11.bath-houses (*ḥammāmlar*).

II. *Tuḥfetü'l-mi' mārīn* (Added building type: garden kiosks and pavilions):
1.Friday mosques (*cevāmi'*); 2.masjids and sanctuaries (*mesācid ve ma' ābid*); 3.madrasas, hadith colleges, and Koran recitation schools (*medāris ve dārü'l-ḥadīs̱* and *dārü'l-ḳurrā'*); 4.hospices (*' imārāt*); 5.hospitals (*dārü'ş-şifā'*); 6.palaces (*sarāylar*); 7.aqueducts (*ṣuyolı kemerleri*); 8.bridges (*cisrler*); 9.garden kiosks and pavilions (*bāğçelerdeki ḳaṣr ve ḳöşk*); 10.bath-houses (*ḥammāmlar*); 11.storehouses (*maḫzenler*); 12.caravansarays, cisterns, and stables (*kervānsarāylar ve bürkeler ve ribāṭü'l-ḫayl*).

III. *Tezkiretü'l-ebniye* (Added building type: Koran recitation schools and mausoleums. Omitted: garden kiosks and pavilions. Some TE manuscripts list mausoleums as a separate category and hence include thirteen building types):
1.Noble Friday mosques (*cevāmi'-i şerīfe*); 2.masjids and sanctuaries (*mesācid ve ma' ābid*); 3.madrasas (*medāris*); 4.Koran recitation schools and mausoleums (*dārü'l-ḳurrā' ve türbeler*); 5.hospices (*' imāretler*); 6.hospitals (*dārü'ş-şifālar*); 7.aqueducts (*ṣuyolları kemerleri*); 8.bridges (*cisrler*); 9.caravansarays (*kārbānsarāylar*); 10.palaces (*sarāylar*); 11.storehouses (*maḫzenler*); 12.bath-houses (*ḥammāmlar*).

APPENDIX 4

4.1: ROYAL ARCHITECTS REWARDED BY BAYEZİD II (1503–12, Meriç, 1958).
Yakubshah b. Sultanshah, mimar
(His son) Hüdaverdi b. Yakubshah, mimar
Yusuf b. Papas, mimar
Ali b. Abdullah, mimar
(His son) Hamza
Hızır Bali b. Murad Halife, mimar
Mahmud, mimar
Derviş Ali, mimar
İlyas Sinan, mimar
Şeyhi, mimar

4.2: DAILY WAGES OF THE CORPS OF ROYAL ARCHITECTS UNDER THE CHIEF ARCHITECT ALAÜDDİN, NICKNAMED ACEM ALİ Sİ
(X indicates names mentioned in the archival documents listed above the chart)

	TSA, D. 10141 1523–25/26	TSA, D. 9706/2 1525–26	TSA, D. 7843 1526–28	BA, DKRZ.33118 1534	BA, MAD. 559 1536	BA, MAD. 559 1536–37
Alaüddin ser-mimaran 45 aspers	X	X	X	55 aspers	X	X
Mahmud mimar 22 aspers	X	X				
Bali mimar 21 aspers	X	X				
Hüdaverdi mimar, 18 aspers	X	X				
Şeyhi mimar, 13 aspers	X	X				
Derviş Ali mimar, 11 aspers	X	X	X			
İbrahim b. Murad Halife, 8 aspers	X	X	X			
Mustafa b. Şüca, 7 aspers	X	X	X			

	TSA, D. 10141 1523–25/26	TSA, D. 9706/2 1525–26	TSA, D. 7843 1526–28	BA, DKRZ.33118 1534	BA, MAD. 559 1536	BA, MAD. 559 1536–37
Hızır mimar, 7 aspers	X	X	X	X		
Seydi mimar, 7 aspers	X	X	X	X		
Yusuf mimar, 9 aspers	X	X	X	X		
Ali Eflak, 9 aspers	X	X	X	X		
Ali b. Süleyman mimar, 8 aspers	X	X	X	X		
İshak kiremidī, 8 aspers	X	X	X	X		
Süleyman mimar, 13 aspers	X	X	X	X	X	
Alaüddin [Balatī] mimar, 12 aspers	X	X	X	X	13 aspers	X
Ali neccar, 23 aspers	X	X	X	X	X	X
Ali Kuçek, 8 aspers	X	X	X	X	X	X
Yusuf Bosna mimar, 14 aspers			X	X	X	X
Dimitri veled-i Todoros, 20 aspers				X	X	X
Fraçesko kapudan-ı portukal, 50 aspers				X	X	60 aspers
Anton zimmi mimar, 12 aspers						X
Hayrüddin mermerī, mimar 13 aspers						X

4.3: DAILY WAGES OF THE CORPS OF ROYAL ARCHITECTS UNDER THE CHIEF ARCHITECT SİNAN IN 1548–49 (BA, MAD.7118)

Sinan ser-mimaran, 55 aspers
Hayrüddin mermerī [marble cutter], 15 aspers
Kasım mermerī [marble cutter], 8 aspers
Rüstem mimar, 12 aspers
Emin mimar, 33 aspers
Hidayet mimar, 23 aspers
Anton zimmi [non-Muslim] mimar, 18 aspers
Simo zimmi [non-Muslim] mimar, 10 aspers
Yorgi zimmi [non-Muslim] mimar, 8 aspers

4.4: SOME OF THE ROYAL ARCHITECTS WORKING UNDER SİNAN

1. ROYAL ARCHITECTS WHO SIGNED SİNAN'S ENDOWMENT DEED (*c.* 1583–85)

Mimar Mehmed Subaşı: prepared the cost estimate of a new conduit for the water channel of the Süleymaniye complex in 1552–53;[1] supervised the repair of Istanbul's pavements in 1573;[2] ordered to replace the wooden minaret of Hagia Sophia with one in brick and to strengthen its buttresses in 1573;[3] participated in a committee headed by Sinan in 1582 that prepared a survey for a canal connecting the Sakarya river to the bay of İzmit;[4] was selected as lieutenant by Sinan during his trip to Mecca in 1584;[5] upon the death of Mimar Mahmud in 1586 was sent to complete the Muradiye mosque at Manisa.[6]

Mimar Mahmud Halife (d. 1586): repaired after an earthquake the Zağanos Pasha and Yıldırım Bayezid mosques at Balıkesir in 1577; built the Muradiye mosque in Manisa according to a plan designed by Sinan from 1583 until his death in 1586.[7]

Mimar İsmail b. Abdullah: served as water channel superintendent between 1582 and 1588;[8] hydraulic engineer and royal architect in the 1590s;[9] was appointed by the chief architect Davud as the head of masons, carpenters, and hydraulic engineers sent to the Hungarian campaign of 1595.[10]

Mimar Süleyman b. Abdullah: as the 'architect of the imperial complex' he removed columns and marble panels for the Süleymaniye mosque from the church of St Irene in 1552,[11] participated in a committee headed by Sinan in 1582 that prepared a survey for a canal connecting the Sakarya river to the bay of İzmit;[12] was appointed the steward of masons and carpenters sent with a group of royal architects to accompany Ferhad Pasha's Safavid campaign in 1584.[13]

Mimar Mustafa b. Abdullah (d. 1586): a marble cutter receiving three aspers whose wage was increased with Sinan's recommendation first to six then to ten aspers when the 'campaign architect Rüstem' died in 1556;[14] his wage was increased by eight aspers upon the death of the architect Kasım in 1561;[15] he prepared an estimate of repairs at the Zeyrek mosque and Kalenderhane (Eski İmaret) in 1573.[16]

Mimar Hızır b. Abdullah: hydraulic engineer around 1579–92, captain of the corps of water channel experts in 1592.[17]

Mimar Ahmed b. Abdullah: perhaps the architect-restorer of the Hagia Sophia mosque mentioned in 1572;[18] it is unclear whether he is the same person as Dalgıç Ahmed Çavuş who served as water channel superintendent in 1595–98 and became chief architect in 1598–1606.[19]

Mimar Mehmed b. Abdullah: one of several Mehmeds enrolled in the corps of architects, hence difficult to identify; he might be Mimar Mehmed Çavuş listed below.
Mimar Ferruh b. Adbullah: activities unknown.
Mimar Mehmed b. Veys: activities unknown, a resident of the chief architect's quarter in Yenibahçe.

II. ROYAL ARCHITECTS MENTIONED IN SOME ARCHIVAL DOCUMENTS
Mimar Rüstem (d. 1556, listed above in 4:3): passed away after being appointed military campaign architect for the Safavid war in 1555.[20]
Mimar Usta Hidayet (listed above in 4:3): mentioned in a wage register dated 1553; sent to Edirne to supervise the construction of new pavements in 1557.[21]
Mimar Kasım b. Abdullah (d. 1561, listed above as marble cutter in 4:3):[22] sent to repair and prepare cost estimates for several castles in Morea during 1544–45;[23] supervised the cutting of marbles for the Süleymaniye mosque at Aydıncık (Cyzicus) in 1550 according to Sinan's specifications;[24] repaired the Kilidü'l-Bahr castle (Dardanelles) in 1552; and prepared cost estimates for flood damaged bridges in Babaeski and Silivri in 1557–58.[25]
Mimar Hayrüddin (listed above as marble cutter in 4:2–3): built an undated bath-house for an agha of the imperial palace at Ayaş near Ankara;[26] architect of the Mostar bridge built between 1557 and 1566; subsequently appointed to construct the Makarska castle at Hercegovina in 1568;[27] the 'elderly royal architect Hayrüddin' inspected with a committee in 1564 a church in Istanbul which was demolished when he determined that only one of its walls was old.[28]
Mimar Ferhad b. Abdullah: built the monumental north portal at the forecourt of the Süleymaniye mosque;[29] sent to Sarajevo in 1559 to construct the posthumous mosque of the late governor-general Ali Pasha whose foundation inscription is dated 1560–61;[30] his salary was augmented with Sinan's recommendation in 1561.[31]
Mimar Ali: sent to Alanya in 1550 to find columns for the Süleymaniye;[32] dispatched to Edirne in 1552 to supervise the rebuilding of burnt wooden shops in brick according to new construction codes introduced in Istanbul;[33] he prepared in 1552 the cost estimate for building a new house in Istanbul and demolishing the old house on its site on behalf of the chief architect Sinan;[34] he was sent in 1553 to transport from Baalbek to the nearest port the delayed colossal red granite columns urgently needed for the Süleymaniye.[35]
Mimar Müslihüddin: supervised a group of novices at the construction site of the Süleymaniye;[36] travelled to Damascus in 1553 probably to supervise the planning of sultan Süleyman's mosque complex in that city;[37] he surveyed with a group of experts Dar al-Khayzuran at Mecca in 1570 to prepare cost estimates for endowed shops and houses;[38] he inspected the city wall of Istanbul in 1574 and recommended the widening of a water outlet that caused flooding.[39]
Mimar Kiriz Nikola: supervised the stone quarry in İzmit during the Süleymaniye's construction;[40] assisted Sinan in 1561 in preparing a survey for the Kırkçeşme water distribution system of the capital;[41] he must be 'Üstad Nikola', the architect of the crown prince Murad's [III] princely mosque in Manisa who was recommended for a salary raise by his royal patron in 1572.[42]
Mimar Şaban: worked at the construction of a bridge at Silivri in 1568;[43] built the castle of Navarino in 1573 together with the grand admiral Kılıç Ali Pasha's unnamed foreign architect who designed its plan in the 'European manner'.[44]
Mimar Mehmed Çavuş: appointed by Sultan Süleyman in 1552 to build a caravansaray for Rüstem Pasha in Sapanca; appointed in 1571 by Selim II for the construction of his brother Mustafa's (d. 1553) mausoleum in Bursa upon the recommendation of the chief architect Sinan; the mausoleum was completed in 1573 according to its foundation inscription;[45] between 1573 and 1576 he supervised the construction of the ʿArafat water channel and domical arcades around the Kaʿba's precinct;[46] served as water channel superintendent twice in 1577 and 1588–95;[47] sent to Edirne in 1583 to oversee the sale to Muslims of houses Jews bought near seven masjids.[48]
Mimar Hüseyin Çavuş: sent to Edirne in 1584 to repair the minaret of the Selimiye mosque damaged by lightning;[49] he built that mosque's income-producing dependencies between 1588 and 1593 under the chief architect Davud.[50]
Mimar Davud b. Abdullah Çavuş: chief of water channels in 1563-65 before the establishment of the new post of water channel superintendent in 1566;[51] appointed water channel superintendent three times (1575–77, 1577–82, 1588);[52] built a water dispenser with an upper-storey elementary school at Divanyolu for the chief black eunuch Mehmed Agha in 1579–81;[53] participated in a committee headed by Sinan that prepared a survey in 1582 for a canal connecting the Sakarya river to the bay of İzmit;[54] the 'former water channel superintendent' was ordered in 1583 to lead royal architects and masons sent to the east with Ferhad Pasha's Safavid campaign;[55] he supervised the construction of Istanbul's pavements in 1584;[56] assessed the expenses of the Süleymaniye water channels after their repair in 1585;[57] built a bath and royal hall at the imperial harem of the Topkapı Palace in 1585;[58] constructed the chief black eunuch Mehmed Agha's mosque complex at Çarşamba in 1584–85;[59] finally, he succeeded Sinan as chief architect in 1588–98.

4.5: WATER CHANNEL SUPERINTENDENTS AND CHIEF ROYAL ARCHITECTS
Müteferrika Hasan (1566–75)
Davud Çavuş (1575–77), first tenure
Mehmed Çavuş (1577), first tenure
Davud Çavuş (1577–82) second tenure
İsmail Çavuş [Müteferrika] (1582–88)
Davud Çavuş [Müteferrika] (1588) third tenure (Chief Royal Architect, 1588–98)
Mehmed Çavuş (1588–95) second tenure
Dalgıç Ahmed Çavuş (1595–98) (Chief Royal Architect, 1598–1606)
Mimar Mehmed Agha (1598–1606) (Chief Royal Architect, 1606 to *c.* 1622)

REFERENCES

1 BA, MAD. 55, dated 960.
2 BA, MD. 21, #304, p. 126, dated 20 L. 980; decree concerning the repair of Istanbul's pavements under the supervision of the royal architect Mehmed (*ḫāṣṣa miʿmārlardan miʿmār meḥmed*). Also see BA, MD. 21, #318, p. 131, dated 20 L. 980; decree concerning the repair of pavements in front of endowed shops by the royal architect Mehmed Subaşı (*ḫāṣṣa miʿmārlarımdan meḥmed ṣubaşı*).
3 BA, MD. 21, #615 and #654, pp. 258 and 276, dated 16 Z. 980; decrees sent to the waqf administrator of Hagia Sophia and 'ḫāṣṣa miʿmārlardan miʿmār üstād meḥmed'.
4 Akmandor, 1968, p. 3.
5 BA, MD. 52, #714, p. 269, dated 16 S. 992; decree addressed to 'ḫāṣṣa miʿmārlarımdan meḥmed ṣubaşı'.
6 See Muradiye in Chapter 6.
7 BA, MD. 31, #621, p. 280, dated 8 B. 985. For Mahmud's appointment to the Muradiye and his death, see Chapter 6.
8 Referred to as İsmail Çavuş; see Martal, 1989, p. 1635.
9 TSA, E.7953, dated beginning of L. 1000 (1592); decree concerning the water channel of Canfeda Hatun's mosque in Karagümrük, mentioning the royal architect (*ḫāṣṣa miʿmār*) İsmail from the *müteferrika* corps and the water channel superintendent Mehmed Çavuş.
10 Ahmed Refik, 1977, pp. 150–51, no. 19.
11 Document cited in Barkan, 1972–79, 2:24, no. 46, where he is referred to as 'ʿimāret-i ʿāmire miʿmārı olan süleymān'.
12 Akmandor, 1968, p. 3.
13 BA, MD. 44, #474, p. 224, 8 Ra. 992, cited in Ahmed Refik, 1977, p. 128, no. 39.
14 Cited in Turan, 1963, p. 184 (BA, MD. 2, #1037, p. 101, dated 20 Ş. 963).
15 BA, MD. 4, #2109, p. 202, dated 16 B. 968, concerning Sinan's recommendation to increase the wage of 'Mermerci Muṣṭafā' with eight aspers from the ten-asper wage of the late 'Ḳāsım bin ʿAbdullāh'.
16 For his death in 26 Ra. 994, see Afyoncu, 1999, p. 215, no. VI. The estimate of repairs in Za. 980 is mentioned in BA, MD. 21, #462, pp. 191–92, where he is referred to as *'ḫāṣṣa miʿmārlardan muṣṭafā'*.
17 Mentioned in Ra. 988 (1580), TSA, E.7830/3 as 'ṣuyolcılarından üstād ḫızır b. ʿabdullāh'. Also mentioned in TSA, E.7830/2, dated 22 L. 987 (1579). For the endowment made to the Bali Pasha mosque at Yenibahçe in 1592 by Hızır b. Abdullah, the captain (bölükbaşı) of the corps of water channel experts, see Kreiser, 1982, p. 200.
18 Referred to as 'ayaṣofya miʿmārı aḥmed' in BA, MD. 16, #375, p. 194, dated Za. 979.
19 See Appendix 4.5.
20 For the death of 'sefer miʿmārı rüstem' receiving a wage of ten aspers, see BA, MD. 2, #1037, p. 101, dated 20 B. 963; published in Turan, 1963, p. 184.
21 BA, D.BRZ no. 20617, beginning of B. 960: 'Hidāyet miʿmār, 23 [aspers]'. For 'miʿmār usta hidāyet's' repair of Edirne pavements in 965, see BA, MAD. 55, p. 422.
22 Upon Kasım b. Abdullah's death, Sinan recommended portions of his ten-asper salary to be distributed to other architects, see BA, MD. 4, #2109, p. 202, dated 16 B. 968.
23 For the castles, see Chapter 5(I–II) (BA, KK. 62, decrees dated 25 M. 951, p. 79; 18 R. 951, p. 345; end of Za. 951, p. 841).
24 Barkan, 1972–79, 2:37.
25 'Ḳāsım el-miʿmār' received eight aspers a day while repairing the Dardanelles castle in 959; see BA, MAD. 55, fol. 85v. For his repair of bridges in Za. 964 and R. 965, see ibid., fols 398r–v, 400r, 418v.
26 TSA, D. 5991, fol. 1v, mentions the fifteen-asper wage of Mimar Hayrüddin.
27 See Chapter 5(I–II), and decrees cited in Adrejević, 1990.
28 Cited in Ahmed Refik, 1988, pp. 45–46, no. 4.
29 Saatçi, 1990, pp. 58–59, 'Ve şadırvan haremine açılan kapu[-i] lenduha Ferhād nām üstādın işidir'.
30 For the inscription, see Mujezinović, 1998, 1:400–2. See Appendix 2 for the mosque's costs. An account book dated 966 (1559) TSA, D.3902 lists on fol. 1v: 'miʿmār ferhād fī yevm 12'. After fol. 3r, Mimar Ferhad's salary became fourteen

aspers per day, and after fol. 5r, it was raised to fifteen aspers. According to another account book (TSA, D. 5481) the surplus stones of Ali Pasha's mosque were transported to the construction site of Ferhad Beg's mosque in the same city, which carries a foundation inscription dated 1561–62. This second mosque, too, may have been the architect Ferhad's work.

31 BA, MD. 4, #2109, p. 202, dated 16 B. 968: '... ve bāḳī ḳalan iki akçe ḫāṣṣa mi'mārlardan [yedi akçesi olan] Ferhād bin 'Abdullāh ola'.

32 Barkan, 1972–78, 2:19, no. 32.

33 TSK, Koğuşlar 888, decree dated 6 N. 959, fol. 425 v.

34 BA, MAD. 55, dated 5 L. 959, fol. 355 v: 'Defter-i taḫmīn-i ḫāne-i imām ḳulı nāyzen der ḫāne-i merhūm muṣṭafā pāṣā binā kerde būd be-ma'rifet-i üstād 'ali ve üstād (empty) ḫalīfe 'an cānib-i sinān ağa ser-mi'mārān-ı ḫāṣṣa.'

35 Barkan, 1972–79, 2:20–21, nos. 36, 27, 39.

36 Ibid., 2:9, no. 15.

37 Ibid., 1:38; see Chapter 6 for the complex in Damascus.

38 This house of a companion of the Prophet (also known as Dar al-Arqam) was used for clandestine meetings by the first Muslims; it became a visitation site and masjid. BA, MD. 14, #667, p. 472, dated 2 R. 978, concerns the survey prepared by 'Mi'mār Müṣliḥüddin' and other experts.

39 BA, MD. 26, #125, p. 47, dated 3 Ra. 982.

40 See Chapter 5(I).

41 See Chapter 4(II).

42 BA, KK. Ruus no. 225, p. 48, 12 M. 980; cited in Emecen, 1989, p. 102.

43 BA, MD. 7, #1159, p. 404, dated 28 N. 975, ibid., #1160, p. 404.

44 See Chapters 5 and 11.

45 The appointment of 'Mehmed Çavuş' to Sapanca is mentioned in TSK, H. 1425, dated B. 959, fol. 301r. For the decree dated S. 979 appointing 'Mehmed Çavuş' as architect of the mausoleum and the foundation inscription, see Önkal, 1992, pp. 159–63.

46 See Chapter 5(I–II).

47 See Appendix 4:5.

48 BA, MD. 51, #25, p. 8, dated 7 Ş. 991.

49 BA, MD. 52, #707, p. 267, dated 16 S. 992.

50 See the Selimiye in Chapter 6.

51 The rebuilding of the Kırkçeşme water distribution system after a flood between 1563 and 1565 was supervised by the janissary agha Ali [Müezzinzade], and Davud Çavuş was the chief of water channels then ('mīrāb davud çavuş būd'); see Lokman's *Tārīkh-i Sulṭān Sulaymān*, Chester Beatty Library, Dublin, Ms. T.413, fols 22v–23r.

52 See Appendix 4:5. A memorandum of the waqf administrator of Mesih Mehmed Pasha's mosque addresses Davud Agha as the water channel superintendent on 9 February 1588, TSA, E. 3778/2, dated 8 Ra. 996.

53 See Mehmed Agha's patronage in Chapter 14.

54 Cited in Akmandor, 1968, p. 3.

55 Decree cited in Ahmed Refik, 1977, p. 128, no. 38; p. 144, no. 7.

56 Ibid., p. 145, no. 9.

57 Ibid., p. 146, no. 10.

58 Necipoğlu, 1991, p. 172.

59 See Chapter 14.

SELECT BIBLIOGRAPHY

Encyclopædia entries, unpublished archival sources, waqfiyyas, and infrequently cited historical manuscripts are included only in the References. For a more detailed bibliography on Sinan, see Ekmeleddin İhsanoğlu, ed., *Mimar Sinan ve Yapılarıyla İlgili Eserler Bibliyografyası* (Ankara, 1988).

MANUSCRIPTS

Āli, Mustafa Gelibolulu, *Künhü'l-aḫbār*, Nuruosmaniye Library, Ms. 3409; and IÜ, T. 5959.

—, *Nādir el-meḥārib*, TSK, R.1290.

—, *Nuṣretnāme*, TSK, H.1365.

Anonymous, *Cevāhir el-menāḳıb*, IÜ, T.2578.

Ebussuud Efendi, *Fetavā-i Ebū's-Suʿūd*, TSK, A.786.

Evliya Çelebi, *Seyāḥatnāme*, TSK, B.304 (vols 1–2); B.305 (vols. 3–4); B.307 (vol. 5); R.1457 (vol. 6); B.308 (vols 7–8); B.306 (vol. 9).

Feridun Ahmed Beg, *Nüzhet el-esrār der sefer-i zigetvār*, TSK, H. 1339.

Hibri Abdurrahman, *Enīsü'l-müsāmirīn*, ÖNB, Codex Vindobonensis Palatinus, Mxt. 21.

İntizami, *Sūrnāme-i Hümāyūn*, TSK, H.1344.

Kürd Hatib Mustafa, *Risāle-i Kürd Ḫaṭīb*, TSK, E.H.1400.

Lokman b. Seyyid Hüseyin, *Hünernāme*, 2 vols, TSK, H.1523, and H.1524.

—, *Shahanshāhnāma*, 2 vols, IÜ, F.1404, and TSK, B.200.

—, *Shāhnāma-i Salīm Khān*, TSK, A.3595.

—, *Zübdetü't-tevārīḫ*, TSK, H.1321.

—, *Tārīkh-i Sulṭān Sulaymān*, Dublin, Chester Beatty Library, Ms. T.413.

Mehmed (Aşık) b. Hafız Ömer b. Bayezid, *Menāẓırü'l-ʿavālīm*, TSK, R.1667; and TSK, E.H.1446.

Mehmed Zaim (Zaim Mir Mehmed Katib), *Cāmiʿü't-tevārīḫ*. Süleymaniye Library, Hafid Efendi, Ms. 237.

Nadiri, *Dīvān-ı Nādirī*, TSK, H.899.

Piri, *Fetḥ-i cezīre-i ḳıbrīs*, TSK, R.1294.

Ruhi Edrenevi, *Tārīḫ-i āl-i ʿoṣmān*, Berlin, Staatsbibliothek, Or. Quart. 821.

Rüstem Paşa (attrib.), *Kitāb-ı tārīḫ-i āl-i ʿoṣmān*, ÖNB, Codex Vindobonensis Palatinus, Mxt. 339; and IÜ, T.2438.

Safi, Mustafa b. İbrahim, *Zübdetü't-tevārīḫ*, TSK, R.1304.

Sai Mustafa Çelebi, *Adsız risāle*, TSA, D.1461/3.

—, *Risāletü'l-miʿmāriyye*, TSA, D.1461/4.

—, *Tuḥfetü'l-miʿmārīn*, TSA, D.1461/4.

Şemsi Ahmed Pasha, *Şehnāme-i Sulṭān Murād*, BN, Supplement Turc 1144.

Şemsüddin Karamani Derviş, *Tercüme-i tārīḫ-i cāmiʿ-i ayaṣofya*, IÜ, T.259.

Talikizade, *Şehnāme*, TSK, A.3592.

—, *Tebrīzīye*, TSK, R.1299.

Topçular Katibi Abdülkadir, *Tevārīḫ-i āl-i ʿoṣmān*, Süleymaniye Kütüphanesi, Esad Efendi, Ms. 2151.

Vusuli (Molla Çelebi), *Selīmnāme*, Fatih Millet Kütüphanesi, Ali Emiri, T.321.

Wyts, Lambert, *Voyages de Lambert Wyts en Turquie*, ÖNB. Codex Vindobonensis Palatinus, 3325*

PUBLISHED PRIMARY AND SECONDARY SOURCES

Ackerman, James S., 1986, *The Architecture of Michelangelo*, Chicago.

Afyoncu, Erhan, 1999, 'XVI. Yüzyılda Hassa Mimarları', in *İsmail Aka Armağanı*, pp. 207–16, İzmir.

Afyoncu, Fatma, 2001, *XVII. Yüzyılda Hassa Mimarları Ocağı*, Ankara.

Ağaoğlu, Mehmet, 1926, 'Herkunft und Tod Sinans', *Orientalische Literaturzeitung* 29, pp. 858–65.

Ahmed Refik (Altınay), 1988a, *Onaltıncı Asırda İstanbul Hayatı (1553–1591)*, Istanbul.

—, 1988b, *Hicrī On Birinci Asırda İstanbul Hayatı (1000–1100)*, Istanbul.

—, 1977, *Türk Mimarları*, ed. Zeki Sönmez, Istanbul.

—, 1931, *Mimar Sinan*, Istanbul.

—, 1924, *Soḳollı*, Constantinople.

Ahmed Resmi Efendi, 2000, *Ḫamīletü'l-Küberā*, ed. Ahmet Nezihi Turan, Istanbul.

Akalın, Şehabeddin, 1958, 'Mi'mar Dalgıç Ahmed Paşa', *Tarih Dergisi* 9:13, pp. 71–80.

Akgündüz, Ahmed, ed., 1990, *Osmanlı Kanunnameleri ve Hukuki Tahlilleri : Osmanlı Hukukuna Giriş ve Fatih Kanunnameleri*, vol. 1, Istanbul.

Akın, Günkut, 1995, 'The Müezzin Mahfili and Pool of the Selimiye Mosque in Edirne', *Muqarnas* 12, pp. 63–83.

Akkaya, Mehmet, 1995, *Şemsi Paşa: Hayatı-sanatı ve Dīvānı'ndan Seçmeler*, Balıkesir.

Akmandor, Neşet, 1968, 'Koca Sinan'ın Plāncılığı, Eserleri ve Mühendisliği', *Türkiye Mühendislik Haberleri* 14:157, pp. 1–6.

Akozan, Feridun, 1988, 'Ölümünün 400. Yılında Mimar Sinan'ın Hayatı ve Kişiliği', *Türkiyemiz* 18:54, pp. 38–54.

Aktaş-Yasa, Azize, ed., 1996, *Uluslararası Mimar Sinan Sempozyumu Bildirileri*, Ankara.

Aktuğ, İlknur, 1990, *İzmit Pertev Paşa (Yeni Cuma) Camii*, Ankara.

Albèri, Eugenio, ed. 1840–55, *Le relazioni degli ambasciatori veneti al Senato durante il secolo XVI*, Serie III, 3 vols, Florence.

Alberti, Leon Battista, 1989, *On the Art of Building in Ten Books*, ed. Joseph Rykwert, Neil Leach, Robert Tavenor, Cambridge MA, London.

Āli, Mustafa Gelibolulu, 1997, *Mevā'idü'n-nefāis fī-ḳavāʿidi'l-mecālis*, ed. Mehmed Şeker, Ankara.

—, 1996, *Cāmiʿu'l-buḥūr der mecālis-i sūr*, ed. Ali Öztekin, Ankara.

—, 1979–82, *Muṣṭafā ʿĀlī's Counsel for Sultans of 1581*, ed. and trans. Andreas Tietze, 2 vols, Vienna.

Allom, Thomas, 1938, *Constantinople and the Scenery of the Seven Churches of Asia Minor*, vol. 1, London.

Altun, Ara, 1981–82, 'Kütahya'nın Türk Devri Mimarisi "bir deneme"', in *Atatürk'ün Doğumunun 100. Yılına Armağan*, pp. 171–700, Istanbul.

Andrejevic, Andrej, 1990, 'Neimar Hajreddin i Njegov Rad u Hercegovini', *Hercegovina* 7–8, pp. 39–51.

—, 1983, 'Sokollu Mehmet Pasha's Contribution to the Building of the City of Belgrade', in VIII. *Türk Tarih Kongresi, Bildiriler*, vol. 3, pp. 1627–36, Ankara.

Angiolello, Giovanni Maria, 1909, *Historia Turchesca*, 1. Ursu, Bucarest.

Araz, Nezihi, 1954, 'Selimiye Efsaneleri', *İstanbul* 4, pp. 20–22.

Arbel, Benjamin, 1992, 'Nūr Bānū (*c.* 1530-1583): A Venetian Sultana?', *Turcica* 24, pp. 241-59.

Arıkan, Zeki, 1988, XV.–XVI. *Yüzyıllarda Hamit Sancağı*, İzmir.

Artan, Tülay, 1994, 'The Kadırga Palace Shrouded by the Mists of Time', *Turcica* 26, pp. 55–124.

—, 1993, 'The Kadırga Palace: An Architectural Reconstruction', *Muqarnas* 10, pp. 201–11.

Aşık Çelebi, 1971, *Meşāʿiru'ş-şuʿarā or Tezkere of ʿAşıḳ Çelebi*, ed. G. M. Meredith-Owens, London.

Aslanapa, Oktay, 1986, *Osmanlı Devri Mimarisi*, Istanbul.

Atai, Nevizade, 1989, 'Hadāikü'l-hakāik f ī tekmileti'ş-şakaik', in *Şakaik-i Nu'maniye ve Zeyilleri*, ed. Abdülkadir Özcan, vol. 2. Istanbul.

Atallah, Mahmud, 2000, 'Architects in Jerusalem in the 10th–11th/16th–17th Centuries:

The Documentary Evidence', in *Ottoman Jerusalem: The Living City, 1517–1917*, ed. Sylvia Auld and Robert Hillenbrand, vol. I, pp. 159–90, London.
Atasoy, Nurhan, 1997, *1582 Surname-i Hümayun, Düğün Kitabı*, Istanbul.
Ateş, İbrahim, ed. 1990, *Mimar Sinan Vakfı*, Istanbul.
—, ed. 1987, *Kanuni Sultan Süleyman'ın Su Vakfiyesi*, Ankara.
Avcıoğlu, Nebahat, 2001, 'Ahmed I and the Allegories of Tyranny in the Frontispiece to George Sandys's *Relation of a Journey*', *Muqarnas* 18, pp. 203–26.
Aydemir, Abdullah, 1968, *Büyük Türk Bilgini Ebussuud Efendi ve Tefsirdeki Metodu*, Ankara.
Ayn Ali Efendi, 1979, *Kavānīn-i Āl-i Osman der Hülāsa-i Mezāmin-i Defter-i Dīvān*, ed. M. Tayyib Gökbilgin, Istanbul.
Aykut, Nezihi, et al., eds, 1993, *Mühimme Defteri, 3 Numaralı Mühimme Defteri (966–968) / 1558–1560*, Ankara.
Ayvansarayi, Hafız Hüseyin, 2000, *The Garden of the Mosques: Hafiz Hüseyin al-Ayvansarayī's Guide to the Muslim Monuments of Ottoman Istanbul*, trans. and annotated Howard Crane, Leiden, Boston, Köln.
—, 1985, *Mecmuā-i tevārih*, ed. Fahri Ç. Derin and Vahid Çabuk, Istanbul.
—, 1281 (1864–65), *Hadīkatü'l-cevāmi'*, 2 vols, Istanbul.
Ayverdi, Ekrem Hakkı, 1977, 1981–82, *Avrupa'da Osmanlı Mimāri Eserleri*, 4 vols, Istanbul.
—, 1973–74, *Osmanlı Mi'marisinde Fātih Devri 855–886 (1451–1481)*, 2 vols, Istanbul.
—, 1972, *Osmanlı Mi'marisinde Çelebi ve II. Sultan Murad Devri 806–855 (1403–1451)*, Istanbul.
—, 1969, 'Yıldırım Bāyezid' in Bursa Vakfiyesi ve Bir İstibdalnāmesi, *Vakıflar Dergisi* 8, pp. 37–46.
—, 1966, *İstanbul Mi'mārī Çağının Menşe'i Osmanlı Mi'marisinin İlk Devri 630–805 (1230–1402)*, Istanbul.
—, 1958, 19, *Yüzyılda İstanbul Haritası*, Istanbul.
Babayan, Kathryn, 1996, 'Sufis, Dervishes and Mullas: The Controversy over Spiritual and Temporal Dominion in Seventeenth-Century Iran', in *Safavid Persia*, ed. Charles Melville, pp. 117–38, London, New York.
Babinger, Franz, 1978, *Mehmed the Conqueror and His Time*, ed. William H. Hickman, trans. Ralph Mannheim, Princeton.
—, 1959, 'Drei Stadtansichten von Konstantinopel, Galata (Pera) und Skutari aus dem ende des 16. Jahrhunderts', *Österreichische Akademie der Wissenschaften, Philologisch-Historische Klasse, Denkshriften* 77, Band 3 Abhandlung, Vienna.
—, 1924, 'Moschee und Grabmal des Osmān-Schāh zu Trikkala. Ein Werk des Baumeisters Sinān', *Praktika tes Akademias Athenon* 4, pp. 15–18.
—, 1914, 'Die Türkische renaissance, bemerkungen zum schaffen des grossen Türkischen Baumeisters Sinan', *Beiträge zur Kenntnis des Orients* 2, pp. 67–88.
—, and Ludwig H. Heydenreich, 1952, 'Vier Bauvorschläge Linardo da Vincis an Sultan Bajazed II (1502/3)', in *Nachrichten der Akademie der Wissenschaften in Göttingen, I. Philologisch-Historische Klasse*, no. 1, pp. 1–13, Göttingen.
Bacqué-Grammont, Jean-Louis, Hans-Peter Laqueur and Nicolas Vatin, 1990, *Stelae Turcicae II, Cimetières de la mosquée Sokollu Mehmed Paşa à Kadırga Limanı, de Bostancı Ali et du türbe de Sokollu Mehmed Paşa à Eyüp* (Istanbuler Mitteilungen Beiheft 36), Tübingen.
Baltacı, Cahit, 1976, *XV.–XVI. Asırlarda Osmanlı Medreseleri*, Istanbul.
Barkan, Ömer Lütfi, 1972–79, *Süleymaniye Cami ve İmareti İnşaatı (1550–1557)*, 2 vols, Ankara.
—, 1971, 'Süleymaniye Cami ve İmareti Tesislerine Ait Yıllık bir Muhasebe Bilançosu 993/994 (1585/1586)', *Vakıflar Dergisi* 9, pp. 109–61.
—, 1963, 'Osmanlı İmparatorluğunda imāret sitelerinin kuruluş ve işleyiş tarzına ait araştırmalar', *İktisat Fakültesi Mecmuası* 23, pp. 239–96.
—, 1957–58, 'H. 974–75 (M. 1567–68) Malī Yılına āit bir Osmanlı Bütçesi', *Iktisat Fakültesi Mecmuası* 19:1–4, pp. 277–332.
—, 1943. *XV. ve XVI. ıncı Asırda Osmanlı Imparatorluğunda Zirai Ekonominin Hukuki ve Mali Esasları: I Kanunlar*, Istanbul.
—, 1942, 'Osmanlı Imparatorluğunda bir Iskān ve Kolonizasyon Metodu Olarak Vakıflar ve Temlikler', *Vakıflar Dergisi* 2, 279–386.
Barkan, Ömer Lütfi and Ekrem Hakkı Ayverdi, eds, 1970, *Istanbul Vakıfları Tahrir Defteri, 953 (1546) Tarihli*, Istanbul.
Barozzi, Nicolo, and Guglielmo, Berchet, eds, 1871–72, *Le relazioni degli stati europei lette al Senato dagli ambasciatori veneziani nel secolo decimosettimo, Turchia*, 2 vols, Venice.
Bartoli, Lando, et al., 1992, *Mimar Sinan: Architettura tra oriente e occidente*, ed. Luigi Zangheri, Florence.
Başkan, Seyfi, 1993, *Ankara Cenabi Ahmed Paşa Camii*, Ankara.
Bates, Ülkü, 1993, 'The Architectural Patronage of Ottoman Women', *Asian Art* 4:2, pp. 51–65.
—, 1991, 'Façades in Ottoman Cairo', in *The Ottoman City and its Parts*, ed. Irene Bierman, Rifat Abou-El-Haj and Donald Preziosi, pp. 129–72, New Rochelle, New York.
—, 1985, 'Two Ottoman Documents on Architects in Egypt', *Muqarnas* 3, pp. 121–27.
—, 1978a, 'Women as Patrons of Architecture in Turkey', in *Women in the Muslim World*, ed. Lois Beck and Nikki Keddie, pp. 243–60. Cambridge, MA.
—, 1978b, 'The Patronage of Sultan Süleyman: The Süleymaniye Complex in Istanbul', *Memoriam A. L. Gabriel, Edebiyat Fakültesi Araştırma Dergisi Özel Sayısı* 9, pp. 67–76.
Batur, Selçuk, 1968, 'Osmanlı Camilerinde Sekizgen Ayak Sisteminin Gelişmesi Üzerine', *Anadolu Sanatı Araştırmaları* 1, pp. 139–66.
Bayrakal, Sedat, 2001, *Edirnede'ki Tek Kubbeli Camiler*, Ankara.
Bayraktar, Nimet, 1980–81, 'Şemsi Ahmed Paşa: Hayatı, Eserleri', *Tarih Dergisi* 33, pp. 99–114.
Bayram, Sadi, 1999, 'Yemen Fatihi Gazi Sinan Paşa Vakfiyeleri ve Tezyinatı ve Türk Süsleme Sanatındaki Yeri', in *Art Turc / Turkish Art: 10e Congrès international d'art turc*, pp. 163–76, Geneva.
—, ed., 1988, *Mimar Koca Sinan, Yaşadığı Çağ ve Eserleri*, 2 vols, Istanbul.
Beckingham, C. F., 1987, 'A Jewish Fransiscan in the Ottoman Empire', *Asian Affairs: Journal of the Royal Society for Asian Affairs* 18:3, pp. 257–68.
Behrens-Abouseif, Doris, 1994, *Egypt's Adjustment to Ottoman Rule, Institutions, Waqf and Architecture in Cairo (16th & 17th Centuries)*, Leiden and New York.
Berchem, Max van, 1925, *Matériaux pour un Corpus Inscriptionum Arabicarum, Deuxième partie, Syrie du Sud, Jérusalem 'Haram'*, Cairo.
Bernardo, Lorenzo, 1886, *Viaggio a Costantinopoli*, ed. Federico Stefani, Venice.
Beşir Çelebi, 1946, 'Tārih-i Edirne, Hikāyet-i Beşir Çelebi', in *Türk Edebiyatı Örnekleri III*, ed. İ. H. Ertaylan, Istanbul.
Betzek, Jacob von, 1979, *Gesandtschaftsreise nach Ungarn und die Türkei in Jahre 1564–65*, ed. K. Nehring, Munich.
Beysanoğlu, Şevket, 1987, *Anıtları ve Kitabeleri ile Diyarbakır Tarihi*, 2 vols, Diyarbakır.
Bierman, Irene A., 1998, *Writing Signs: The Fatimid Public Text*, Berkeley.
—, Rifat A. Abou-El-Haj and Donald Preziosi, eds, 1991, *The Ottoman City and its Parts: Urban Structure and Social Order*, New Rochelle, New York.
Bilge, Aygen, 1972–73, 'Mimar Sinan Hakkında Araştırmalar II', *İstanbul Üniversitesi Edebiyat Fakültesi Sanat Tarihi Yıllığı* 5, pp. 141–73.
—, 1969, 'Mimar Sinan Hakkında Araştırmalar', *Mimarlık* 7:67, pp. 18–34.
Blair, Sheila S., and Jonathan Bloom, 1994, *The Art and Architecture of Islam, 1250–1800*, New Haven.
Böcüzade, Süleyman Sami, 1983, *Kuruluşundan Bugüne Kadar Isparta Tarihi*, ed. Suat Seren, 2 vols, Istanbul.
Bostan, İ dris, 1992, *Osmanlı Bahriye Teşkilatı: XVII. Yüzyılda Tersane-i Amire*, Ankara.
Bosworth, Clifford Edmund, 1967, *The Islamic Dynasties*, Edinburgh.
Bourdieu, Pierre, 1984, *Distinction: A Social Critique of the Judgement of Taste*, trans. Richard Nice, Cambridge, MA.
Bozdoğan, Sibel, 2001, *Modernism and Nation Building: Turkish Architectural Culture in the Early Republic*, Seattle and London.
—, 1997, 'Against style: Bruno Taut's Pedagogical Program in Turkey, 1936–38', in *The Education of the Architect*, ed. M. Pollak, Cambridge, MA.
Braun, Georg, and Franz Hogenberg, 1572–1618, *Civitates orbis terrarum*, 6 vols, Cologne.
Bredekamp, Horst, 2000, *Bau und Abbau von Bramante bis Bernini: Sankt Peter in Rom und das Prinzip der productiven Zerstörung*, Berlin.
Bruschi, Arnaldo, 1994, 'Religious Architecture in Renaissance Italy from Brunelleschi to Michelangelo', in *The Renaissance from Brunelleschi to Michelangelo*, ed. Henry Millon and V. Lampugnani, pp. 123–81, Milan.
Bumin, Kürşat et al., 1993, photographs by Sami Güner and Sami Pekşirin, *Edirne*, Ankara.
Burelli, Augusto Romano, 1988, *La Moschea di Sinan*, Venice.
Burgoyne, Michael Hamilton, 1987, *Mamluk Jerusalem: An Architectural Study*, London.
Burns, Howard, 1991, 'Building and Construction in Palladio's Vicenza', in *Les Chantiers de la renaissance*, ed. A. Chastel and J. Guillaume, pp. 191–226, Paris.
Busbecq, O. G. de., 1927, *The Turkish Letters of Ogier Ghiselin de Busbecq, Imperial Ambassador at Constantinople, 1554–1562*, trans. Edward S. Forster, Oxford.
Cafer Efendi, 1987, *Risāle-i Mi'māriyye: An Early-Seventeenth-Century Ottoman Treatise on Architecture*, trans. and annotated Howard Crane, Leiden, New York.
Camocio, Giovanni Francesco, 1571, *Isole famose, porti, fortezze, e terre maritime della Republica di Venetia et altri principali cristiani*, Venice.
Cantemir, Demetrius, 1734, *The History of the Growth and Decay of the Ottoman Empire*, trans. N. Tindal, London.
—, 1979–80, *Osmanlı İmparatorluğunun Yükselişi ve Çöküşü*, trans. Özdemir Çobanoğlu, 3 vols, Ankara.
Carboni, Stefano, 1989, 'Oggeti decorati a smalto di influsso Islamico nella vetraria Muranese: Tecnica e forma', in *Arte Veneziana e Arte Islamica*, ed. Ernst Grube, pp. 147–58, Venice.
Carlier de Pinon, 1909–11, 'Relation du voyage en Orient de Carlier de Pinon (1579)', *Revue de L'Orient Latin* 12, pp. 112–421.
Carne, John, 1836–38, *Syria, the Holy Land, Asia Minor &c., illustrated*, London.
Cavalli, Marino, 1914, 'Eine unbekannte venezianische Relazion über die Türkei (1567)', *Sitzungsberichte der Heidelberger Akademie der Wissenschaften, Stiftung Heinrich Lanz, Philosophisch-historische Klasse*, Jahrgang 1914, 5. Abhandlung, Heidelberg.
Çayırdağ, Mehmet, 1981, 'Kayseri'de Kitabelerinden XV. ve XVI. Yüzyıllarda Yapıldığı Anlaşılan İlk Osmanlı Yapıları', *Vakıflar Dergisi* 13, pp. 531–81.
Çeçen, Kazım, 1991a, *İstanbul'un Vakıf Sularından Halkalı Suları*, Istanbul.
—, 1991b, *İstanbul'un Vakıf Sularından Üsküdar Suları*, Istanbul.

—, 1988, *Mimar Sinan ve Kırkçeşme Tesisleri*, Istanbul.
Celalzade Mustafa, 1990 and 1997, *Selīmnāme*, ed. Ahmet Uğur and Mustafa Çuhadar, Ankara.
—, 1981, *Geschichte Sultan Süleymān Ḳānūnīs von 1520 bis 1557, oder Tabakāt ül-Memālik ve Derecāt ül-Mesālik*, ed. Petra Kappert, Wiesbaden.
Cezar, Mustafa, 1988, 'Mimar Sinan'ın Klasik İmar Sistemi Açısından Analizi', in *Mimarlığı ve Sanati*, ed. Zeki Sönmez, pp. 59–72, Istanbul.
—, 1983, *Typical Commercial Buildings of the Ottoman Classical Period and the Ottoman Construction System*, Istanbul.
Chastel, André, 1965, *Renaissance Méridionale: Italie 1460–1500*, Paris.
Chesneau, Jean, 1887, *Le voyage de Monsieur d'Aramon, ambassadeur pour le Roy au Levant (1547)*, ed. Charles Schefer, Paris.
Choiseul-Gouffier, Marie-Gabriel-Florent, comte de, 1782, *Voyage pittoresque de la Grèce*, vol. 2, Paris.
Choisy, Auguste, 1883, *L'Art de bâtir chez les Byzantins*, Paris.
Çifci, Fazıl, 1995, *Kastamonu Camileri, Türbeleri ve Diğer Tarihi Eserler*, Ankara.
Clayer, Nathalie, 1994, *Mystiques, État & Société: Les Halvetis dans l'aire balkanique de la fin du XVe siècle à nos jours*, Leiden, New York, Köln.
Cohen, Amnon, 1989, 'The Walls of Jerusalem', in *Essays in Honor of Bernard Lewis*, ed. C. E. Bosworth, C. Issawi, R. Savory, A. L. Udovitch, pp. 467–77. Princeton, New Jersey.
Concina, Ennio, 1994, *Dell'arabico: A Venezia tra Rinascimento e Oriente*, Venice.
Condivi, Ascanio, 1999, *The Life of Michelangelo*, trans. Alice Sedwick Wohl, ed. Hellmut Wohl, Pennsylvania.
Connors, Joseph, 1996, 'Borromini, Hagia Sophia, and S. Vitale', in *Architectural Studies in Memory of Richard Krautheimer*, ed. Cecil Striker, pp. 43–48, Mainz.
Contarini, Paolo, 1856, *Diario del viaggio da Venezia a Costantinopoli* (1580), Venice.
Courmenin, Louis Deshayes de, 1632, *Voiage de Levant fait per le Commandement du Roy en l'année 1621*, Paris.
Çulpan, Cevdet, 1975, *Türk Taş Köprüleri*, Ankara.
—, 1966, *İstanbul Süleymaniye Camii Kitabesi*, Istanbul.
Ćurčić, Slobodan, 1988, 'Byzantine Legacy in Ecclesiastical Architecture of the Balkans after 1453', in *The Byzantine Legacy in Eastern Europe*, ed. Lowell Clucas, pp. 59–81, Boulder, New York.
Dağlıoğlu, Hikmet T., 1942, 'Ankara'da Cenabī Ahmed Paşa Camii ve Cenabī Ahmed Paşa', *Vakıflar Dergisi* 2, pp. 213–19.
Dagron, Gilbert, 1984, *Constantinople imaginaire: Études sur le recueil des Patria*, Paris.
Denny, Walter B., 1998, photographs by Ahmet Ertuğ, *Gardens of Paradise: 16th-Century Turkish Ceramic Tile Decoration*, Istanbul.
—, 1983, 'Sinan the Great as Architectural Historian: The Kılıç Ali Pasha Mosque in Istanbul', *Turcica* 15, pp. 104–26.
—, 1977, *The Ceramics of the Mosque of Rüstem Pasha and the Environment of Change*, New York.
De Maio, Romeo, 1978, *Michelangelo e la controriforma*, Rome.
De Osa, Veronica, 1982, *Sinan: The Turkish Michelangelo (a biographical novel)*, New York.
Derman, Uğur, 1989, 'Mimar Sinan'ın Eserlerinde Hat San'atı', in *Vakıf Haftası, Türk Vakıf Medeniyeti Çerçevesinde Mimar Sinan ve Dönemi Sempozyumu*, pp. 287–92, Istanbul.
Dernschwam, Hans, 1923, *Hans Dernschwam's Tagebuch einer Reise nach Konstantinopel und Kleinasien (1553–1555)*, ed. Franz Babinger, Munich and Leipzig. (Translated into Turkish by Yaşar Öner, Ankara, 1992.)
De Vos, Lambert, 1991, *Das Kostümbuch des Lambert de Vos, Vollsändige Faksimile-Ausgabe im originalformat des Codex Ms. or, 9. aus dem besitz der Staats-und Universitätsbibliothek Bremen*, ed. Hans-Albrecht Koch, Graz, Austria.
Dibner, Bern, 1950, *Moving the Obelisks*, New York.
Dijkema F. Th., ed., 1997, *The Ottoman Historical Monumental Inscriptions in Edirne*, Leiden.
Dodds, D. Jerrilynn, 1992, 'The Great Mosque of Córdoba', in *Al-Andalus: The Arts of Islamic Spain*, ed. J. D. Dodds, pp. 11–25, New York.
Du Fresne-Canaye, Philippe, 1897, *Le voyage du Levant de Philippe du Fresne-Canaye (1573)*, ed. M. H. Hauser, Paris.
Dündar, Abdülkadir, forthcoming, 'Osmanlı Mimarisinde Vilayet (Eyalet) Mimarları', in *11th International Congress of Turkish Art*, Utrecht.
—, 2001, 'Karapınar Sultan Selim Camii'nin Mimarı Hakkında Yeni bir Kayıt ve Bazı Mülahazalar', in *Karapınar Sempozyumu*, ed. Yusuf Küçükdağ, pp. 165–74, Konya.
—, 2000, 'Osmanlı Mimarisinde Yapıların İnşa Süreci Üzerine bir Araştırma', *KÖK Araştırmalar Dergisi* (Osmanlı Özel Sayısı), pp. 155–84.
Düzdağ, Ertuğrul M., 1972, *Şeyhülislām Ebussuūd Efendi Fetvaları Işığında 16. Asır Türk Hayatı*, Istanbul.
Dzaja, M. Srecko, and Günter Weiss, eds, 1995, *Austro-Turcica 1541–1552: diplomatische Akten des habsburgischen Gesandtschaftsverkehrs mit der Hohen Pforte, im Zeitalter Süleymans des Prächtigen (*Südosteuropäische Arbeiten 95*)*, Munich.
Eaton, W., 1799, *A Survey of the Turkish Empire*, London.
Eberhard, Elke, 1970, *Osmanische Polemik gegen die Safawiden im 16. Jahrhundert nach arabischen Hanschriften*, Freiburg.
Edhem Paşa and Marie de Launay, 1873, *Uṣūl-i miʿmāri-i ʿosmāni, (L'Architecture Ottomane; Die Ottomanische Baukunst)*, Istanbul.
Egemen, Affan, 1993, *İstanbul Çeşme ve Sebilleri*, Istanbul.
Egli, Ernst, 1954, *Sinan: Der Baumeister Osmanischer Glanzzeit*, Zurich.
Egli, Hans, 1997, *Sinan: An Interpretation*, Istanbul.
Eldem, Sedad Hakkı, 1984–87, *Türk Evi*, 3 vols, Istanbul.
—, 1969–74, *Köşk ve Kasırlar*, 2 vols, Istanbul.
—, 1939, 'Milli Mimarī Meselesi', *Arkitekt* 9:10, pp. 220–23.
Emecen, Feridun M., 1989, *XV. Asırda Manisa Kazası*, Ankara.
—, 1983–87, 'Manisa Murādiye Cāmii İnşāsına Dāir', *İstanbul Üniversitesi Edebiyat Fakültesi Tarih Enstitüsü Dergisi* 13, pp. 177–87.
Emir Sedat, 1994, *Erken Osmanlı Mimarlığında Çok-İşlevli Yapılar: Kentsel Kolonizasyon Yapıları Olarak Zaviyeler*, 2 vols, İzmir.
Erdoğan, Abdülkadir, 1942, 'Kanuni Süleyman Devri Vezirlerinden Pertev Paşa'nın Hayatı ve Eserleri', *Vakıflar Dergisi* 2, pp. 233–40.
—, 1938, 'Silivrikapı'da Hadım İbrahim Paşa Camii', *Vakıflar Dergisi* 1, pp. 29–33.
Erdoğan, Muzaffer, 1955, 'Mimar Davud Ağa'nın Hayatı ve Eserleri', *Türkiyat Mecmuası* 12, pp. 179–204.
Eren, İsmail, 1968, 'Mimar Sinan'ın Sofya'da Bilinmeyen Eseri', *Belgelerle Türk Tarihi Dergisi* 8, pp. 66–70.
Eremya Çelebi, Kömürcüyan, 1988, *İstanbul Tarihi: XVII. Asırda İstanbul*, trans. Hrand D. Andreasyan, Istanbul.
Ergenç, Özer, 1995, *Osmanlı Klasik Dönem Kent Tarihçiliğine Katkı : XVI. Yüzyılda Ankara ve Konya*, Ankara.
—, 1981, 'Osmanlı Şehirlerindeki Yönetim Kurumlarının Niteliği Üzerinde bazı Düşünceler', in *VIII. Türk Tarih Kurumu Kongresi, Bildiriler*, vol. 2, pp. 1265–74, Ankara.
Ergin, Osman, 1939, *Türk Şehirlerinde İmaret Sistemi*, Istanbul.
Erzen, Jale, 1996, *Mimar Sinan: Estetik Bir Analiz*, Ankara.
—, 1991a, 'Aesthetics and Aisthesis in Ottoman Art and Architecture', *Journal of Islamic Studies* 2:1, pp. 1–24.
—, 1991b, *Mimar Sinan Cami ve Külliyeleri: Tasarım Süreci Üzerine bir İnceleme*, Ankara.
—, 1988, 'Sinan as Anti-Classicist', *Muqarnas* 5, pp. 70-86.
—, 1981, *Mimar Sinan Dönemi Cami Cepheleri*, Ankara.
Esin, Emel, 1985, 'The Renovations effected in the Kaʿbah Mosque by the Ottoman Sultan Selim II (H. 974–82/1566–74)', *Revue d'histoire maghrebine* 39–40, pp. 225–32.
—, 1977–79. 'Merkez Efendi (H.870/1465–959/1551) ile Şāh Sultan Hakkında bir Hāşiye', *Türkiyat Mecmuası* 19, pp. 65–85.
—, 1974, *Mecca The Blessed, Medina the Radiant*, London.
Esad Efendi, 1979, *Osmanlılarda Töre ve Törenler*, ed. Yavuz Ercan, Istanbul.
Ettinghausen, Richard, Oleg Grabar and Marilyn Jenkins-Madina, 2001, *Islamic Art and Architecture 650–1250*, New Haven, London.
Evliya Çelebi, 1896–1938, *Seyāḥatnāme*, 10 vols, Istanbul.
—, 1999, *Evliya Çelebi's Book of Travels*, ed. Klaus Kreiser, vol. 4: *Manisa nach Evliyā Çelebi, Aus dem Neunten Band des Seyāḥat-nāme*, trans. Nuran Tezcan, Leiden, Boston, Köln.
Eyice, Semavi, 1991, 'İstanbul'da Bālī Paşa Camii ve Mimar Sinan', in *Prof. Dr. Bekir Kütükoğlu'na Armağan*, pp. 507–24, Istanbul.
—, 1965, 'Sultaniye-Karapınar'a Dair', *Tarih Dergisi* 15, pp. 117-40.
—, 1964, 'Svilengrad'da Mustafa Paşa Köprüsü', *Belleten* 28:112, pp. 729-59.
—, 1963, 'İlk Osmanlı Devrinin Dīnī-İçtimai bir Müessesi: Zāviyeler ve Zāviyeli-Camiler', *İktisat Fakültesi Mecmuası* 23, pp. 1–80.
Eyyubi, 1991, *Menākıb-ı Sultan Süleyman*, ed. Mehmet Akkuş, Ankara.
Farago, Claire, ed., 1995, *Reframing the Renaissance: Visual Culture in Europe and Latin America 1450–1650*, New Haven, London.
Faroqhi, Suraiya, 2000, *Subjects of the Sultan: Culture and Daily Life in the Ottoman Empire*, London.
—, 1994, *Pilgrims and Sultans: The Hajj under the Ottomans 1517–1683*, London, New York.
—, 1987, *Men of Modest Substance, House Owners and House Property in Seventeenth-Century Ankara and Kayseri*, Cambridge.
—, 1984, *Towns and Townsmen of Anatolia, Trade, Crafts, and Food Production in an Urban Setting, 1520–1650*, Cambridge.
Feridun Ahmed Beg, 1264–65 (1848–49), *Münşeʿātü's-selāṭīn*, 2 vols, Istanbul.
Filarete, Antonio Averlino, 1972, *Trattato di architettura*, ed. A. M. Finoli and L. Grassi, 2 vols, Milan.
Fischer, Erik, 1990, *Melchior Lorck i Tyrkiet*, Copenhagen.
Flachat, Jean-Claude, 1766, *Observations sur le commerce et les arts d'une partie de l'Europe, de l'Asie, de l'Afrique, et même des Indes orientales (1740–1758)*, 2 vols, Lyons.
Fleischer, Cornell, 1992, 'The Lawgiver as Messiah: The Making of the Imperial Image in the Reign of Süleymān', in *Soliman le Magnifique et son temps*, ed. Gilles Veinstein, pp. 159–77, Paris.
—, 1986, *Bureaucrat and Intellectual in the Ottoman Empire: The Historian Mustafa Āli (1541–1600)*, Princeton.
Fodor, Pál., 1994, 'Sultan, Imperial Council, Grand Vizier: Changes in the Ottoman Ruling Elite and the Formation of the Grand Vizieral Telḫīṣ', *Acta Orientalia Academiae Scientiarum Hungaricae* 47:1–2, pp. 67–85.
Foschi, Silvia, 2002, 'Santa Sofia di Costantinopoli: immagini dall'Occidente', *Annali di architettura; Rivista del Centro Internazionale di Studi di Architettura*

Andrea Palladio 14, 7–33.
—, 1998, 'Santa Sofia di Costantinopoli. Immagini del XV secolo', PhD thesis, Istituto Universitario di Architettura di Venezia.
Fotić, Aleksandr, 1994, 'The Official Explanations for the Confiscation and Sale of Monasteries (Churches) and their Estates at the time of Selim II', *Turcica* 26, pp. 33–54.
Frankfurt 1985, *Türkische Kunst und Kultur aus osmanischer Zeit*, 2 vols, exhibition catalogue, Museum für Kunsthandwerk, Frankfurt am Main.
Freely, John and Augusto Romano Burelli, 1992, photographs by Ara Güler, *Sinan: Architect of Süleyman the Magnificent and the Ottoman Golden Age*, London.
Frishman Martin and Hasan-Uddin Khan, eds, 1994, *The Mosque: History, Architectural Development and Regional Diversity*, London.
Gabriel, Albert, 1940, *Voyages archéologiques dans la Turquie orientale*, Paris.
—, 1936, 'Le Maitre Architecte Sinan', *La Turquie Kemaliste* 16, pp. 2–13.
—, 1926, 'Les Mosquées de Constantinople', *Revue Syria* 7, pp. 359–419.
Gallotta, Aldo, ed., 1983, *Il 'Gazavāt-ı Ḫayreddin Paşa' di Seyyid Murād*, Naples.
Gaube, Heinz, 1978, *Arabische Inschriften aus Syrien*, Wiesbaden.
—, and Eugen Wirth, 1984, *Aleppo: Historische und geographische Beiträge zur baulichen Gestaltung, zur sozialen Organisation und zur wirtschaftlichen Dynamik einer vorderasiatischen Fernhandelsmetropole*, 2 vols, Wiesbaden.
Gaulmier, Jean, 1942–43, 'Note sur l'état présent de l'enseignement traditionnel à Alep', *Bulletin d'Études Orientales* 9, pp. 1–33.
Gerlach, Stephan, 1674, *Stephan Gerlachs dess Aeltern Tage-buch (1573–1578)*, ed. Samuel Gerlach, Frankfurt.
Gévay, Anton von, 1841, 'Versuch eines chronologischen Verzeichnisses türkischen Statthalter von Ofen', *Der Österreische Geschichtsforcher* 2, pp. 61ff.
Gibb, Hamilton A. R., 1962, 'Luṭfī Paşa on the Ottoman Caliphate', *Oriens* 15, pp. 287–95.
Gilles, Pierre, 1988, *The Antiquities of Constantinople*, trans. John Ball, New York.
Goffman, Daniel, 2002, *The Ottoman Empire and Early Modern Europe*, Cambridge.
—, 1990, *İzmir and the Levantine World 1550–1650*, Seattle, WA.
Gökbilgin, Tayyib, ed., 1973, *Tārīḫ-i Ṣāḥib Giray Ḫān*, Ankara.
—, 1955, 'Rüstem Paşa Hakkındaki İthamlar', *İstanbul Üniversitesi Edebiyat Fakültesi Tarih Dergisi* 8:11–12, pp. 11–50.
—, 1952, *XV.–XVI. Asırlarda Edirne ve Paşa Livası: Vakıflar-Mülkler-Mukataalar*, Istanbul.
Goldthwaite, Richard A., 1993, *Wealth and the Demand for Art in Italy 1300–1600*, Baltimore, London.
—, 1980, *The Building of Renaissance Florence*, Baltimore, London.
Golombek, Lisa, and Donald Wilber, 1988, *The Timurid Architecture of Iran and Turan*, 2 vols, Princeton.
Gontaut-Biron, Jean de (Baron de Salignac), 1888–89, *Ambassade en Turquie de Jean de Gontaut-Biron, Baron de Salignac, (1605 à 1610)*, ed. Comte Théodore de Gontaut, 2 vols, Paris.
Goodwin, Godfrey, 1993, *Sinan: Ottoman Architecture and Its Values Today*, London.
—, 1971, *A History of Ottoman Architecture*, London.
Göyünç, Nejat, 1985, 'Mimar Sinan'ın Aslı Hakkında', *Tarih ve Toplum* 4:19, pp. 38–40.
Grabar, Oleg, 1996, *The Shape of the Holy: Early Islamic Jerusalem*, Princeton.
Grelot, Guillaume-Joseph, 1683, *A Late Voyage to Constantinople*, trans. J. Philips, London.
Grosvenor, Edwin A., 1895, *Constantinople*, 2 vols, Boston.
Günay, Reha, 1998, *Sinan: the Architect and His Works*, Istanbul.
—, 1987, *Sinan'ın İstanbul'u – Sinan's Istanbul*, Istanbul.
Gündoğdu, Hamza, 1992, *Erzurum Lala Paşa Külliyesi*, Ankara.
Gurlitt, Cornelius, 1907–12, *Die Baukunst Konstantinopels*, 2 vols, Berlin.
Hadidi, 1991, *Tevārih-i Āl-i Osman (1299–1523)*, ed. Necdet Öztürk, Istanbul.
Haider, S. Gulzar, 1986, 'Sinan – A Presence in Time Eternal', *Afkar Inquiry* 3:2, pp. 38–44.
—, and Hatice Yazar, 1986, 'Implicit Intentions and Explicit Order in Sinan's Work', in *II. International Congress on the History of Turkish and Islamic Science and Technology*, 3 vols, 2:29–42, Istanbul.
Hajnóczi, Gábor, 1991, 'Vitrius, De Architectura (MS Lat. 32) in the University Library, Budapest, and the Milanese Court of Humanists', *Arte Lombarda* 97–98, pp. 98–104.
al-Halabi, Burhan al-Din İbrahim b. Muhammad (d. 1549), 1990, *Multaḳa'l-abḥur* (completed in 1517), adapted by Ahmed Davudoğlu from Turkish translation and commentary of Mehmed Mevkūfātī (*c*. 1640), 2 vols, Istanbul.
Halbswachs, Maurice, 1980, *The Collective Memory*, trans. F. L. Ditter Jr. and V. Y. Ditter, New York.
Han, Verena, 1973, 'Fifteenth and Sixteenth Century Trade in Glass between Dubrovnik and Turkey', *Balcanica* 4, pp. 163–78.
Harff, Arnold von, 1860, *Die Pilgerfahrt des Ritters Arnold von Harff von Coln (1496–99)*, ed. Eberhard von Groote, Köln.
Hasanbeyzade, 1980, *Hasan-Beyzāde Tārīhi*, ed. Nezihi Aykut, PhD thesis, Istanbul University.
Haskan, Mehmet Nermi, 1993, *Eyüp Tarihi*, 2 vols, Istanbul.
Herzfeld, Ernst, 1956, *Matériaux pour un Corpus Inscriptionum Arabicarum, Deuxième partie: Syrie du Nord, Inscriptions et monuments d'Alep*, 2 vols, Cairo.
Hezarfen Hüseyin Efendi, 1998, *Telhīsü'l-Beyān fī Kavānīn-i Āl-i Osmān*, ed. Sevim Ilgürel, Ankara.
Hierosolimitano, Domenico, 2001, 'Relatione della gran città di Costantinopoli (1611)', in *Domenico's Istanbul*, trans. Michael Austin, ed. Geoffrey Lewis, Warminster, Wiltshire.
Hillenbrand, Robert, 2002, *The Architecture of Ottoman Jerusalem: An Introduction*, London.
—, 1994, *Islamic Architecture: Form, Function, Meaning*, New York.
Hilmi, 1995, *Bahrü'l-kemāl*, ed. Cihan Okuyucu, Kayseri.
Hobsbawm, Eric, 1990, *Nations and Nationalism since 1780*, Cambridge.
Holod, Renata and Hasan-Uddin Khan, 1997, *The Contemporary Mosque: Architects, Clients and Designs since the 1950s*, New York.
Howard, Deborah, 2003, 'Venice between East and West: Marc' Antonio Barbaro and Palladio's Church of the Redentore', *Journal of the Society of Architectural Historians* 62:3, pp. 306–25
—, 2000, *Venice and the East: The Impact of the Islamic World on Venetian Architecture 1100–1500*, New Haven.
Huelsen, Cristiano, ed., 1910, *Il Libro di Giuliano da Sangallo*, Leipzig.
Hulvi, Mahmud Cemaleddin, 1993, *Lemezāt-ı Hulviyye*, ed. Mehmet S. Tayşi, Istanbul.
Humphreys, Stephen, 1972, 'Expressive Intent of the Mamluk Architecture of Cairo: A Preliminary Essay', *Studia Islamica* 35, pp. 69–120.
Ibn Battuta, 1983, *İbn-i Batūta Seyahatnāmesi*, trans. Mümin Çevik, Istanbul.
Ibn Khaldun, 1967, *The Muqaddimah: An Introduction to History*, trans. Franz Rosenthal, 3 vols, Princeton.
Imber, Collin, 1997, *Ebu's-su'ud: The Islamic Legal Tradition*, Edinburgh.
—, 1992, 'Süleyman as Caliph of the Muslims: Ebū's-Suʿūd's Formulation of Ottoman Dynastic Ideology', in *Soliman le Magnifique et son temps*, ed. Gilles Veinstein, pp. 179–84, Paris.
İnalcık, Halil, 1998, 'Istanbul: An Islamic City', and 'Ottoman Galata, 1453–1553', in *Essays in Ottoman History*, pp. 249–71 and 275–376, Istanbul.
—, 1993, 'State and Ideology under Sultan Süleyman I', in *The Middle East and the Balkans under the Ottoman Empire: Essays on Economy and Society*, pp. 70-94, Indiana.
—, 1973, *The Ottoman Empire: The Classical Age 1300–1600*, London.
—, and Donald Quataert, eds, 1994, *An Economic and Social History of the Ottoman Empire 1300–1914*, Cambridge.
İnan, Afet A., 1956, *Mimar Koca Sinan*, Ankara.
—, 1937, *Sinan Hayatı ve Eserleri*, Istanbul.
İnciciyan, P. G., 1976, *18. Asırda İstanbul*, trans. Hrand D. Andreasyan, Istanbul.
İpşirli, Mehmet, 1994, 'Osmanlı Devlet Teşkilātına dair bir Eser: Kavānīn-i Osmānī ve Rābıta-i Āsitāne', *Tarih Enstitüsü Dergisi* 14, pp. 9–35.
İskenderoğlu, Reşid, 1989, *Beğlerbeyi Gazi İskender Paşa*, Ankara.
Istanbul, 1995, *İstanbul Topkapı Müzesi Koleksiyonlarından Yüzyıllar Boyunca Venedik ve İstanbul Görünümleri*, exhibition catalogue, Topkapı Palace Museum, Istanbul.
Istanbul, 2000, *The Sultan's Portrait: Picturing the House of Osman*, exhibition catalogue, Topkapı Palace Museum, Istanbul.
İzgi, Cevat, 1997, *Osmanlı Medreselerinde İlim*, 2 vols, Istanbul.
Jardine, Lisa, 2002, *On a Grander Scale: The Outstanding Life of Sir Christopher Wren*, New York.
—, 1996, *Worldly Goods: A New History of the Renaissance*, London, New York.
—, and Jerry Brotton, 2000, *Global Interests: Renaissance Art Between East and West*, Ithaca, NY.
Johansen, Baber, 1981–82, 'The All-Embracing Town and Its Mosques: al-miṣr al-jāmiʿ', *Revue de l'Occident Musulman et de la Méditerranée* 32, pp. 139–61.
Kafadar, Cemal, 1995, *Between Two Worlds: The Construction of the Ottoman State*, Berkeley, Los Angeles, London.
—, 1994, 'The Ottomans in Europe', in *Handbook of European History 1400-1600: Late Middle Ages, Renaissance and Reformation*, ed. T. Brady, H. A. Oberman and J. D. Tracy, pp. 589–635, Leiden, New York, Köln.
—, 1993, 'The Myth of the Golden Age: Ottoman Historical Consciousness in the Post Süleymānic Era', in *Süleymān the Second and His Time*, ed. Halil İnalcık and Cemal Kafadar, pp. 37–48, Istanbul.
—, 1991a, 'Les troubles monétaires de la fin du XVIe siècle et la prise de conscience ottomane du déclin', *Annales Économies, Societes, Civilisations*, pp. 381–400.
—, 1991b, 'On the Purity and Corruption of the Janissaries', *Turkish Studies Association Bulletin* 15, pp. 273–80.
—, 1986, 'When coins turned into drops of dew and bankers became robbers of shadows: the boundaries of Ottoman economic imagination at the end of the sixteenth century', PhD thesis, McGill University.
Kafescioğlu, Çiğdem, 1999a, 'Heavenly and Unblessed, Splendid and Artless: Mehmed II's Mosque Complex in Istanbul in the Eyes of its Contemporaries', in *Essays in Honor of Aptullah Kuran*, ed. Çiğdem Kafescioğlu and Lucienne Thys-Şenocak, pp. 211–22, Istanbul.
—, 1999b, '"In the Image of Rum": Ottoman Architectural Patronage in Sixteenth-Century Aleppo and Damascus', *Muqarnas* 16, pp. 70–96.
—, 1996, 'The Ottoman Capital in the Making: The Reconstruction of Constantinople in

the Fifteenth Century', PhD thesis, Harvard University.

Káldy-Nagy, Gyula, 1972, 'Macht und Immobiliarvermögen eines türkischen Beglerbegs im 16. Jahrhundert', *Acta Orientalia Academiae Scientarum Hungaricae* 25, pp. 441–51.

Kamil, Ekrem, 1937, 'Hicrī onuncu-milādī on altıncı-asırda yurdumuzu dolaşan Arab seyyahlarından Gazzi-Mekki Seyahatnamesi', *Tarih Semineri Dergisi* 1:2, pp. 3–90.

Katip Çelebi, 1973, *Tuhfetü'l-kibar fī esfari'l bihar*, ed. Orhan Şaik Gökyay, Istanbul.

Kayoko, Hayashi, 1992, 'The Vakıf Institution in 16th-Century Istanbul: An Analysis of the Vakıf Survey Register of 1546', *The Memoirs of the Tokyo Bank* 50, pp. 93–113.

Kiechel, Samuel, 1987, *Die Reisen des Samuel Kiechel 1585–89*, ed. Hartmut Prottung, Munich.

Kiel, Machiel, 2003, 'The Quatrefoil Plan in Ottoman Architecture: The "Fethiye Mosque" of Athens', *Muqarnas* 19, pp. 109–22.

—, 1990, 'Some Reflections on the Origins of Provincial Tendencies in the Ottoman Architecture of the Balkans', in *Studies on the Ottoman Architecture of the Balkans*, Great Yarmouth, Norfolk.

Kılıç, Mahmud Erol, 1997, 'Yedi Tepeli Şehrin Tekkeleri ve Muhyiddin Efendi'nin "Tomar-ı Tekayası", in *İstanbul Armağanı*, ed. Mustafa Armağan, vol. 3, pp. 259–74, Istanbul.

Kılıç, Orhan, 1997, *XVI. ve XVII. Yüzyıllarda Van (1548–1648)*, Van.

Kınalızade Hasan Çelebi, 1989, *Tezkiretü'ş-şuarā*, 2 vols, Ankara.

Kocainan, Ziya, 1939, *Mimar Sinan ve XX inci Asır Mimarisi*, Istanbul.

Koçi Beg, 1998, *Risale*, ed. Yılmaz Kurt, Ankara.

Konyalı, İbrahim Hakkı, 1997, *Ābideleri ve Kitābeler ile Konya Tarihi*, Ankara.

—, 1976–77, *Ābideleri ve Kitābeleriyle Üsküdar Tarihi*, 2 vols, Istanbul.

—, 1960, *Ābideleri ve Kitābeleriyle Erzurum Tarihi*, Istanbul.

—, 1953, *Fatih'in Mimarlarından Azadlı Sinan (Sinan-ı Atīk) Vakfiyeleri, Eserleri, Hayatı, ve Mezarı*, Istanbul.

—, 1951, 'Mimar Sinan Türktür, Bizdendir', *Tarih Hazinesi* 6, pp. 289–93.

—, 1950, *Mimar Koca Sinan'ın Eserleri*, Istanbul.

—, 1948, *Mimar Koca Sinan, Vakfiyyeleri, Hayır Eserleri, Hayatı, Padişaha Vekaleti, Azatlık Kağıdı, Alım Satım Hüccetleri*, Istanbul.

Koran, 1953, *The Meaning of the Glorious Koran*, trans. Mohammed Marmaduke Pickthall, New York.

Kostof, Spiro, 1985, *A History of Architecture: Settings and Rituals*, New York, Oxford.

Kreiser, Klaus, 1985, 'Zur Kulturgeschichte der Osmanischen Moschee', in *Türkische Kunst aus Osmanischer Zeit*, 2 vols, 1:75–86, Frankfurt am Main.

—, 1982, 'Archivalisch überlieferte Inschriften aus Istanbul', *Istanbuler Mitteilungen* 32, pp. 258–78.

Kritovoulos of Imbros, 1954, *History of Mehmed the Conqueror by Kritovoulos (1451–1467)*, trans. Charles T. Riggs, Princeton.

Kuban, Doğan, 1999, photographs by Ahmet Ertuğ, *Sinan: An Architectural Genius*, Bern.

—, 1997, *Sinan's Art and Selimiye*, Istanbul.

—, 1996, *Istanbul: An Urban History*, Istanbul.

—, 1987, 'The Style of Sinan's Domed Structures', *Muqarnas* 4, pp. 72–97.

—, 1958, *Osmanlı Dini Mimarisinde İç Mekan Teşekkülü: Rönesansla Bir Mukayese*, Istanbul.

Küçükdağ, Yusuf, 1997, *Karapınar Sultan Selim Külliyesi*, Konya.

Küçükkaya, Gülçin, 1990, 'Mimar Sinan Dönemi İstanbul-Belgrad Arası Menzil Yapıları Hakkında bir Deneme', *Vakıflar Dergisi* 21, pp. 183–253.

Kunt, Metin, 1983, *The Sultan's Servants: The Transformation of Ottoman Provincial Government 1550–1650*, New York.

Kunt, Metin, and Christine Woodhead, eds, 1995, *Süleyman the Magnificent and His Age: The Ottoman Empire in the Early Modern World*, London and New York.

Kunter, Halim Baki, 1960, 'Mimar Ali Bey'in Bilinmeyen İki Vakfiyesi', in *I. Türk Tarih Kongresi, III. Seksiyon*, pp. 438–42, Ankara.

Kuran, Aptullah, 1994, 'Eyüp Külliyesi', in *Eyüp: Dün-Bugün*, ed. Tülay Artan, pp. 129–35, Istanbul.

—, 1990–91, 'The Evolution of the Sultan's Pavilion in Ottoman Imperial Mosques', *Islamic Art* 4, pp. 281–300.

—, 1987, *Sinan: The Grand Old Master of Ottoman Architecture*, Washington DC, Istanbul.

—, 1986, *Mimar Sinan*, Istanbul.

—, 1975, 'Çatalca'daki Ferhad Paşa Camii', *Boğaziçi Üniversitesi Dergisi* 3, pp. 73–90.

—, 1973, 'Mimar Sinan Yapısı Karapınar II. Selim Camisinin Proporsiyon Sistemi üzerine Bir Deneme', in *VII. Türk Tarih Kongresi, Bildiriler*, vol. 2, pp. 711–16.

—, 1968, *The Mosque in Early Ottoman Architecture*, Chicago and London.

Kürkçüoğlu, Kemal Edib, 1962, *Süleymaniye Vakfiyesi*, Ankara.

Kuruyazıcı, Hasan, 1986, 'Edirne Selimiye Külliyesi'ndeki Arastanın Bir Bölümünün Mimar Sinan'ın Yapıtı Olduğu Konusunda Kanıtlar', in *II. International Congress on the History of Turkish and Islamic Science and Technology*, 3 vols, 2:155–68, Istanbul.

Kütükoğlu, Mübahat S., 1983, *Osmanlılarda Narh Müessesi ve 1640 Tarihli Narh Defteri*, Istanbul.

Laguna, Andrés (attrib.), 1983, *Avventure di uno schiavo dei turchi*, trans. Cesare Acutis, Milan. (Same as Cristóbal de Villalón, 'Viaje de Turquía')

Laoust, Henri, 1952, *Les gouverneurs de Damas*, Damascus.

Le Corbusier, 1989, *Journey to the East*, ed. and trans. Ivan Zaknić, Cambridge, MA.

Lefebvre, Henri, 1991, *The Production of Space*, trans. D. Nicholson-Smith, Oxford.

Lescalopier, Pierre, 1921, 'Le voyage de Pierre Lescalopier, parisien', *Revue d'Histoire diplomatique* 35:1, pp. 21–55.

Lokman b. Seyyid Hüseyin, 1987, *Kıyāfetü'l-insāniyye fī şemāil el-ʿosmāniyye*, Istanbul.

Lubenau, Reinhold, 1912–30, *Beschreibung der Reisen des Reinhold Lubenau*, ed. W. Sahm, 5 vols, Königsberg.

Lutfi Paşa, 2001, *Tevārih-i Āl-i Osman*, ed. Kayhan Atik, Ankara.

—, 1991, 'Lütfi Paşa Āsafnāmesi', in *Prof. Dr. Bekir Kütükoğlu'na Armağan*, pp. 49–99. Istanbul.

Mack, Rosamund, 2001, *Bazaar to Piazza: Islamic Trade and Italian Art 1300–1600*, Berkeley.

Mainstone, Rowland J., 1988, *Hagia Sophia: Architecture, Structure and Liturgy of Justinian's Great Church*, London.

Manetti, A. di Tuccio, 1970, *The Life of Brunelleschi by Antonio di Tuccio Manetti*, trans. Howard Saalman, Philadelphia, London.

Mango, Cyril, 1993, *Studies on Constantinople*, London.

—, 1992, 'Byzantine Writers on the Fabric of Hagia Sophia', in *Hagia Sophia: From the Age of Justinian to the Present*, ed. Ahmet Çakmak and Robert Mark, pp. 41–56, Cambridge.

—, 1986, *Sources and Documents: The Art of the Byzantine Empire 312–1453*, Toronto, Buffalo, London.

Manners, Ian R., 1997, 'Constructing the Image of a City: The Representation of Constantinople in Christopher Buondelmonti's Liber Insularum Archipelagi', *Annals of the Association of American Geographers* 87:1, pp. 72–102.

Marsili, Luigi Fernando, 1732, *Stato militare dell'Impèrio Ottomano*, Amsterdam.

Martal, Abdullah, 1989, 'XVI. Yüzyılda Osmanlı İmparatorluğunda Su-Yolculuk', *Belleten* 52:205, pp. 1585–1653.

Martiny, Günter, 1936, 'Die Piyale Pascha Moschee', *Ars Islamica* 3, pp. 13–171.

Matrakçı Nasuh, 1976, *Beyān-ı Menāzil-i Sefer-i ʿIrāḳeyn-i Sulṭān Süleymān Ḫān*, ed. Hüseyin Yurdaydın, Ankara.

Matthews, Henry, 2002, 'Concepts of Ideal Form in Istanbul and Rome: The Sacred Architecture of Sinan and His Italian Contemporaries', in *Myth to Modernity*, ed. Nezih Başgelen and Brian Johnson, pp. 59–70. Istanbul.

—, 2000, 'Bringing Ottoman Architecture into the Mainstream', *The Art Book: Issues, News, and Reviews* 7:4, pp. 15–17.

Maurand, Jérôme, 1901, *Itinéraire de Jérôme Murand d'Antibes à Constantinople (1544)*, ed. and trans. Léon Dorez, Paris.

Mayer, Luigi, 1801, *Views in Turkey in Europe and Asia*, London.

McQuillan, James, 2001, 'The Aesthetics of Ottoman Architecture in the Twenty-First Century', in *Oriental-Occidental: Geography, Identity, Space*, ed. Michelle A. Rinehart, pp. 117–22, Washington, DC.

Mehmed Süreyya, 1996, *Sicill-i Osmanī: Osmanlı Ünlüleri*, ed. N. Akbayar and S. A. Kahraman, 6 vols, Istanbul.

Meinecke, Michael, 1992, *Die mamlukische Architektur in Ägypten und Syrien*, 2 vols, Glückstadt.

—, 1988, 'Die Erneurung von al-Quds/Jerusalem durch den Osmanensultan Sulaimān Qānūnī', in *Studies in the History and Archaeology of Palestine*, ed. Shawqi Shaath, 3 vols, 3:257–83, 338–60, Aleppo.

—, 1978, 'Die Osmanische architektur des 16. Jahrhunderts in Damaskus', in *Fifth International Congress of Turkish Art*, pp. 575–95, Budapest.

Meriç, Rıfkı Melül, 1965, *Mimar Sinan Hayatı, Eseri, Eserlerine Dair Metinler*, Ankara.

—, 1963, 'Edirne'de Meyva Kapanı İnşaatı ve S. Selim Camii Tamiratı için Lüzumlu Kurşun vesaire Hakkında Mevcut Vesikalar', *Türk Sanatı Tarihi Araştırma ve İncelemeleri* 1, pp. 745–63.

—, 1958, *Bayezid Camii Mimarı*, Ankara.

—, 1938, 'Mimar Sinan'ın Hayatı', *Ülkü Halkevleri Dergisi* 11, pp. 195–206.

Mesarites, Nikolaos, 1957, 'Description of the Church of the Holy Apostles in Constantinople', G. Downey, ed., *Transactions of the American Philosophical Society* 47, pp. 855–923.

Millon, Henry A. and Craig Hugh Smyth, 1988, *Michelangelo Architect: the Facade of San Lorenzo and the Drum of the Dome of St. Peter's*, Milan.

Millon, Henry A., and V. Lampugnani, eds, 1994, *The Renaissance from Brunelleschi to Michelangelo: The Representation of Architecture*, Milan.

Moryson, Fynes, 1907, *An Itinerary Containing his Ten Yeeres Travell*, vol. 2, Glasgow.

Müderrisoğlu, Fatih, 1995, 'Osmanlı İmparatorluğu'nun Doğu Akdeniz'deki İskelesi Payas ve Sokollu Mehmed Paşa Menzil Külliyesi', in *9th International Congress of Turkish Art*, 3 vols, 2:513–24, Ankara.

—, 1993. '16. Yüzyılda Osmanlı İmparatorluğu'nda İnşa Edilen Menzil Külliyeleri', PhD thesis, Hacettepe Üniversitesi.

Mujezinović, Mehmed, 1998, *Islamska epigrafika Bosne i Hercegovine*, 3 vols, Sarajevo.

Mülayim, Selçuk, 1996, 'Mimar Sinan ve Halefi', in *Uluslararası Sempozyumu Bildirileri*, ed. A. Aktaş-Yasa, pp. 347–51.

—, 1989, *Sinan ve Çağı*, Istanbul.

Müller-Wiener, Wolfgang, 1994, *Die Häfen von Byzantion Konstantinopolis Istanbul*, Tübingen.

—, 1977, *Bildlexikon zur Topographie Istanbuls: Byzantion, Konstantinopolis, Istanbul bis zum*

Beginn des 17. Jahrhundert, Tübingen.
Murray, Peter, 1971, *Architecture of the Renaissance*, New York.
Mustakimzade Süleyman Sadeddin Efendi, 1928, *Tuhfe-i ḫaṭṭāṭīn*, ed. İbnülemin Mahmud Kemal, Istanbul.
Myres, David, 2000, 'Al-ʿImara al-ʿAmira: The Charitable Foundation of Khassaki Sultan (959/1552)', in *Ottoman Jerusalem: The Living City, 1517–1917*, ed. Sylvia Auld and Robert Hillenbrand, 2 vols, 1:539–81, London.
Naima Mustafa, 1281–83, (1865–68), *Tārīḫ-i Naʿīmā*, 6 vols, Istanbul.
Nayır, Zeynep, 1975, *Osmanlı Mimarlığında Sultan Ahmet Külliyesi ve Sonrası: 1609–90*, Istanbul.
Necipoğlu, Gülru, 2007a, 'Qur'anic Inscriptions on Sinan's Imperial Mosques: A Comparison with their Safavid and Mughal Counterparts', in *Word of God – Art of Man: The Qur'an and its Creative Expressions*, ed. Fahmida Suleman, Oxford, pp. 69–104.
—, 2007, 'Creation of a National Genius: Sinan and the Historiography of "Classical" Architecture,' *Muqarnas* 24, pp. 141–83.
—, 2006, 'Preface: Sources, Themes, and Cultural Implications of Sinan's Autobiographies', in Sai Mustafa Çelebi, *Sinan's Autobiographies: Five Sixteenth-Century Texts*, introduction, critical edition and trans. by Howard Crane and Esra Akın, ed. with a preface by Gülru Necipoğlu, Leiden, pp. vii–xvi.
—, 2000, 'The Serial Portraits of Ottoman Sultans in Comparative Perspective', in *The Sultan's Portrait: Picturing the House of Osman*, pp. 22–61, Istanbul.
—, 1997, 'The Suburban Landscape of Sixteenth-Century Istanbul as a Mirror of Classical Ottoman Garden Culture', in *Gardens in the Time of the Great Muslim Empires: Theory and Design*, ed. Attilio Petruccioli, pp. 32–71, Leiden, New York, Köln.
—, 1996, 'Dynastic Imprints on the Cityscape: The Collective Message of Imperial Funerary Mosque Complexes in Istanbul', in *Cimetières et traditions funéraires dans le monde Islamique*, ed. Jean-Louis Bacqué-Grammont and Aksel Tibet, 2 vols, 2:23–36, Ankara.
—, 1995, *Topkapı Scroll – Geometry and Ornament in Islamic Architecture*, Santa Monica, CA.
—, 1993, 'Challenging the Past: Sinan and the Competitive Discourse of Early Modern Islamic Architecture', *Muqarnas* 10, pp. 169–80.
—, 1992a, 'Life on an Imperial Monument: Hagia Sophia after Byzantium', in *Hagia Sophia: From the Age of Justinian to the Present*, ed. Robert Mark and Ahmet Ş. Çakmak, pp. 195–225, Cambridge.
—, 1992b, 'A Kānūn for the State, a Canon for the Arts: Conceptualizing the Classical Synthesis of Ottoman Arts and Architecture', in *Soliman le Magnifique et son temps*, ed. Gilles Veinstein, pp. 195–216, Paris.
—, 1991, *Architecture, Ceremonial and Power: The Topkapı Palace in the Fifteenth and Sixteenth Centuries*, Cambridge, MA, London.
—, 1990, 'From International Timurid to Ottoman: A Change of Taste in Sixteenth-Century Ceramic Tiles', *Muqarnas* 7, pp. 136–170.
—, 1989, 'Süleyman the Magnificent and the Representation of Power in a Context of Ottoman-Hapsburg-Papal Rivalry', *Art Bulletin* 71:3, pp. 401–27.
—, 1986, 'Plans and Models in Fifteenth- and Sixteenth-Century Ottoman Architectural Practice', *Journal of the Society of Architectural Historians* 45:3, pp. 224–43.
—, 1985, 'The Süleymaniye Complex in Istanbul: An Interpretation', *Muqarnas* 3, pp. 92–117.
Newman, Andrew J., 2001, 'Fayd al-Kashani and the Rejection of the Clergy/State Alliance: Friday Prayer as Politics in the Safavid Period', in *The Most Learned of the Shiʿa: The Institution of Marjaʿ Taqlid*, ed. Linda S. Walbridge, pp. 34–52, Oxford, New York.
Nicolas de Nicolay, 1576, *Les navigations peregrinations et voyages, faicts en la Turquie*, Antwerp.
Nora, Pierre, ed., 1984, *Les lieux de mémoire*, 3 vols, Paris.
Nutku, Özdemir, 1987, *IV. Mehmet'in Edirne Şenliği* (1675), Ankara.
Oberhummer, Eugen, 1902, *Konstantinopel unter Sultan Süleiman dem Grossen aufgenommen im Jahre 1559 durch Melchior Lorich aus Flensburg*, Munich.
Ocak, Ahmet Yaşar, 1992, *Osmanlı İmparatorluğunda Marjinal Sûfîlik: Kalenderiler (XIV.–XVII. Yüzyıllar)*, Ankara.
—, 1991, 'Kanūnī Sultan Süleyman Devrinde bir Osmanlı Heretiği: Şeyh Muhyiddin-i Karamanī', in *Prof. Dr Bekir Kütükoğlu'na Armağan*, pp. 475–83, Istanbul.
Ohsson, Mouradgea d', 1788–1824, *Tableau général de l'empire othoman*, 7 vols, Paris.
O'Kane, Bernard, 1996, 'Monumentality in Mamluk and Mongol Art and Architecture', *Art History* 19:4, pp. 499–522.
—, 1987, *Timurid Architecture in Khorasan*, Costa Mesa, CA.
Önder, Mehmed, 1986, 'Piyale Paşa Camiinin Avrupa'nın Dört Büyük Müzesinde Bulunan Çini Panosu', *Antika* 10, pp. 4–6.
Önkal, Hakkı, 1992, *Osmanlı Hanedan Türbeleri*, Ankara.
Orgun, M. Zarif, 1938, 'Hassa Mimarları', *Arkitekt* 8:10, pp. 333–42.
Orhonlu, Cengiz, 1990, *Osmanlı İmparatorluğu'nda Derbent Teşkilâtı*, Istanbul.
—, 1984, *Osmanlı İmparatorluğunda Şehircilik ve Ulaşım Üzerine Araştırmalar*, ed. Salih Özbaran, İzmir.
—, 1981, 'Şehir Mimarları', *Osmanlı Araştırmaları* 2, pp. 1–30.
Orlandos, Anastos K., 1929, 'I Architektoniki tou tzamiou Osman Sach ton Trikkalon', *Praktikatis Akademias Athenon* 4, pp. 319–25.
Ortaylı, İlber, 1996, 'Rodosto (extension en Marmara de la Via Egnatia) au xvie siècle', in *Via Egnatia under Ottoman Rule 1380–1699*, ed. Elizabeth Zachariadou, pp. 193–202, Rethymnon.
Otto-Dorn, Katharina, 1937, 'Sinan', in *Allgemeines Lexikon der bildenden Künstler von der Antike bis zur Gegenwart*, 31, pp. 83–5, Leipzig.
Ousterhout, Robert, 2000, *Master Builders of Byzantium*, Princeton.
—, 1995, 'Ethnic Identity and Cultural Appropriation in Early Ottoman Architecture', *Muqarnas* 12, pp. 48–62.
Öz, Tahsin, 1962–65, *İstanbul Camileri*, 2 vols, Ankara.
Özcan, Abdülkadir, ed., 1994, *Eyyubi Efendi Kanunnamesi*, Istanbul.
Özergin, Kemal M., 1973–74, 'Eski bir Rūznāme'ye göre İstanbul ve Rumeli Medreseleri', *Tarih Enstitüsü Dergisi* 4–5, pp. 262–90.
Öziş, Ünal and Yalçın Arısoy, 1986, 'Edirne Water Conveyance System Constructed by the Great Mimar Sinan', in *II. International Congress on the History of Turkish and Islamic Science and Technology*, 3 vols, 2:135–44, Istanbul.
Palerne, Jean, 1991, *D'Alexandrie à Istanbul: Pérégrinations dans l'Empire Ottoman 1581–83*, ed. Yvelise Bernard, Paris.
Palladio, Andrea, 1965, *The Four Books of Architecture*, New York.
Parvilée, Léon, 1874, *Architecture et décoration turques au XVe siècle*, with a preface by Eugène-Emmanuel Viollet-le-Duc, Paris.
Pašic, Amir, 1994, *Islamic Architecture in Bosnia and Hercegovina*, Istanbul.
Paspates, A. G., 1877, *Byzantinai meletai*, Konstantinoupolis.
Patrinelis, Christos, 1969, 'The Exact Time of the First Attempt of the Turks to Seize the Churches and Convert the Christian People of Constantinople to Islam', in *Actes du premier congrès international des études balkaniques et sud-est européennes*, 3, pp. 567–72, Sofia.
Payne, Alina A., 1999, *The Architectural Treatise in the Italian Renaissance: Architectural Invention, Ornament, and Literary Culture*, Cambridge.
—, 1994, 'Rudolf Wittkower and Architectural Principles in the Age of Modernism', *Journal of the Society of Architectural Historians* 53, pp. 322–44.
Peçevi, İbrahim, 1281–83 (1864–67), *Tārīḫ*, 2 vols, Istanbul.
Pedani, Maria Pia, 2000, 'Safiye's Household and Venetian Diplomacy', *Turcica* 32, pp. 9–32.
—, 1994, *In Nome del Gran Signore: Inviati Ottomani a Venezia dalla Caduta di Costantinopoli alla Guerra di Candia*, Venice.
Peirce, Leslie P., 2000, 'Gender and Sexual Propriety in Ottoman Royal Women's Patronage', in *Women, Patronage, and Self-Representation in Islamic Societies*, ed. D. Fairchild Ruggles, pp. 53–68, New York.
—, 1993, *The Imperial Harem: Women and Sovereignty in the Ottoman Empire*, New York and Oxford.
Pervititch, Jacques, 2000, *Istanbul in the Insurance Maps of Jacques Pervititch*, Istanbul.
Petrosiyan, Y .E., ed., 1987, *Mebde-i kanun-ı yeniçeri ocağı tarikhi (Kawānīn- i Yeñiçeriyān (1015/1606))*, Moscow.
Petruccioli, Attilio, ed., 1987, *Mimar Sinan: The Urban Vision* (*Environmental Design* nos. 1–2), Rome.
Phillipides, Marios, 1990, *Emperors, Patriarchs and Sultans of Constantinople, 1373–1513: An Anonymous Greek Chronicle of the Sixteenth Century*, Brookline, MA.
Pigafetta, Marcantonio, 1890, 'Itinerario', in P. Matkovic, 'Putopis Marka Antuna Pigafetta u carigrad od god 1567', *Starine* 22, pp. 68–194.
Pinon, Pierre, 1987, 'Sinan's Külliyes: Inscriptions into the Urban Fabric', in *Mimar Sinan: The Urban Vision* (*Environmental Design* nos. 1–2) ed. A. Petruccioli, pp. 106–11.
Plyviou, M., 1994, 'Design and Construction in Eighteenth-Century Building: The Case of the Monastery Xeropotamou Katholikon', *Mnemeio & Perivallon* 2, pp. 83–90.
Popovic, Toma, 1966–67, 'Spisak Hercegovackih Namesnika u xvi veku', *Prilozi za Orijentalnu Filologiju* 16–17, pp. 93–99.
Prochàzka-Eisl, Gisela Maria, 1992, 'Die Wiener Handschrift des Sūrnāme-i Hümāyūn', PhD thesis, Universität Wien.
Raby, Julian, 1983, 'Mehmed the Conqueror's Greek Scriptorium', *Dumbarton Oaks Papers* 37, pp. 15–34.
—, 1982, 'A Sultan of Paradox: Mehmed the Conqueror as a Patron of the Arts', *The Oxford Art Journal* 5/1, pp. 3–8.
—, 1980, 'El Gran Turco: Mehmed the Conqueror as a Patron of the Arts of Christendom', PhD thesis, Oxford University.
—, 1977–78, 'Diyarbakır: A Rival to Iznik', *Istanbuler Mitteilungen* 27–28, pp. 429–59.
—, and Jeremy Johns, eds, 1992, *Bayt al-Maqdis: ʿAbd al-Malik's Jerusalem, Part One*, *Oxford Studies in Islamic Art*, vol 9.
—, and Zeren Tanındı, 1993, *Turkish Bookbinding in the 15th Century: The Foundation of an Ottoman Court Style*, London.
Ramazanzade Mehmed (Küçük Nişancı), 1279 (1862), *Tārīḫ-i Nişāncı Meḥmed Paşa*, Istanbul.
Raymond, André, 1979, 'Les grands waqfs et l'organization de l'espace urbain à Alep et au Caire à l'epoque ottomane (xvie–xviiie siècles)', *Bulletin d'Etudes Orientales* 31, pp. 113–28.

Repp, R.C., 1986, *The Müfti of Istanbul: A Study in the Development of the Ottoman Learned Hierarchy*, Oxford.
Restle, Marcell, 1981, 'Bauplannung und Baugesinnung unter Mehmed II Fātih', *Pantheon* 39, pp. 361–67.
Reyhanlı, Tülay and Ara Altun, 1974–75, 'Edirne-Havsa'da Sokollu (veya Kasım Paşa) Külliyesi', *İstanbul Üniversitesi Edebiyat Fakültesi Sanat Tarihi Yıllığı* 6, pp. 67–88.
Reyhanlı, Tülay, 1977–79, 'Havsa'daki Sokollu veya Kasım Paşa Külliyesi Hakkında Tamamlayıcı Notlar', *Türkiyat Mecmuası* 19, pp. 241–47.
Riefstahl, Rudolf M., 1931, *Turkish Architecture in Southwestern Anatolia*, Cambridge, MA.
—, 1930. 'The Selimieh in Konia: A Replica of the Old Mosque of Fatih in Constantinople', *Art Bulletin* 12:4, pp. 311–18.
Rifat Osman, 1999, *Edirne Evkāf-ı İslāmiyye Tarihi: Camiler ve Mescitler*, ed. Ülkü Özsoy, Ankara.
—, 1927, 'İrtihalinin 339'uncu sene-i devriyesi münāsebetiyle büyük Türklerden Mimar Koca Sinan b. Abdülmennān', *Milli Mecmua* 7:83, pp. 1335–48.
Al-Rihawi, ʿAbd Al-Qadir & Émilie E. Ouéchek, 1975, 'Les deux Takiyya de Damas: la Takiyya et la Madrasa Sulāymaniyya du Marg et la Takiyya as-Salīmiyya de Ṣāliḥiyya', *Bulletin d'Études Orientales* 28, pp. 217–25.
Rosedale, H. G., ed., 1904, *Queen Elizabeth and the Levant Company*, London.
Rogers, J. Michael, 1999, 'Ottoman religious ceremonial in two late 16th century *meremmāt defters* for Süleymaniye, Başbakanlık Arşivi MM/MAD 513 and 5832', in *Acta Viennensia Ottomanica*, ed. Markus Köhbach and Gisela Procházka-Eisl, Claudia Römer, pp. 303–9, Vienna.
—, 1982, 'The State and the Arts in Ottoman Turkey, Part I: The Stones of Süleymaniye'; 'Part II: The Furniture and Decoration of Süleymaniye', *International Journal of Middle Eastern Studies* 14:1, pp. 71–86; 14:3, pp. 283–313.
Rossi, Aldo, 1982, *The Architecture of the City*, Cambridge, MA.
Saatçi, Suphi, 1990, 'Tezkiret-ül Bünyan'ın Topkapı Sarayı Revan Kitaplığı'ndaki Yazma Nüshası', *Topkapı Sarayı Müzesi Yıllık* 4, pp. 55–101.
—, 1988, *Mimar Sinan'ın Yapılarındaki Kitabeler*, Istanbul.
Sadeddin Efendi (Hoca), 1992, *Tācü't-tevārīḫ*, ed. İsmet Parmaksızoğlu, 5 vols, Ankara.
Sahillioğlu, Halil, ed. 2002, *Topkapı Sarayı Arşivi H. 951–52 Tarihli ve E. 12321 Numaralı Mühimme Defteri*, Istanbul.
Sai Mustafa Çelebi, 2006, *Sinan's Autobiographies: Five Sixteenth-Century Texts*, introduction, critical edition and trans. Howard Crane and Esra Akın, ed. with a preface by Gülru Necipoğlu, Leiden.
—, 2000, *Yapılar Kitabı: Tezkiretü'l-Bünyan ve Tezkiretü'l-Ebniye*, ed. and trans. Hayati Develi, with an introduction by Doğan Kuban, Istanbul.
—, 1989, *Mimar Sinan and Tezkiret-ül Bünyan*, trans. Suphi Saatçi, with an introduction by Metin Sözen, Istanbul.
—, 1315 (1897), *Tezkiretü'l-bünyān*, with a biographical introduction by Ahmed Cevdet, Istanbul.
Samardzic, Radovan, 1994, *Mehmed Sokolovitch, Le destin d'un grand vizir*, trans. M. Begic, Paris.
—, 1995, *Sokollu Mehmed Paşa*, trans. Meral Gaspıralı, Istanbul.
Sanderson, John, 1931, *The Travels of John Sanderson in the Levant 1584–1602*, ed. William Foster, London.
Sandys, George, 1621, *A Relation of a Journey begun An. Dom. 1610*, London.
Sarre, F., 1909, 'Michelangelo und der Türkische Hof', *Repertorium für Kunstwissenschaft* 32, pp. 61–6.
Sauvaget, Jean, 1941, *Alep, essai sur le développement d'une grande ville syrienne, des origines au milieu du XIXe siècle*, 2 vols, Paris.
—, 1937, 'Les caravansérails syriens du Hadjdj de Constantinople', *Ars Islamica* 4, pp. 98–121.
Sauvaire, H., 1896, 'Description de Damas', *Journal Asiatique*, pp. 252–58.
Schepper, Corneille Duplicius de (Scepperus), 1857, 'Missions diplomatiques de Corneille Duplicius de Schepper (1533–34)', *Mémoires de l'Académie Royale de Belgique* 30, pp. 21–224.
Schweigger, Salomon, 1964, *Ein newe Reyssbeschreibung aus Teutschland nach Constantinopel und Jerusalem*, Nuremberg, 1606, reprinted in Graz.
Selaniki Mustafa Efendi, 1989, *Tarih-i Selānikī*, ed. Mehmet İpşirli, 2 vols, Istanbul.
Şeşen, Ramazan, 1986, 'Sinan Hakkında Kaynaklar', in *II. International Congress on the History of Turkish and Islamic Science and Technology*, 3 vols, 2:1–11, Istanbul.
Silahdar Fındıklılı Mehmed Ağa, 1928, *Silāḥdār Tārīhi*, 2 vols, Istanbul.
Singer, Amy, 2002, *Constructing Ottoman Beneficence: An Imperial Soup Kitchen in Jerusalem*, Albany, NY.
Sıvaslıyan, Hagop, 1985, 'Mimar Sinan'ın Kökeni Neden Tartışılır?', *Tarih ve Toplum* 4:19, pp. 41–43.
Skilliter, Susan A., 1965, 'Three Letters from the Ottoman "Sultana" Sāfiye to Queen Elizabeth I', *Oriental Studies* 3, pp. 119–57.
—, 1982, 'The Letters of the Venetian "Sultana" Nūr Bānū and Her Kira to Venice', in *Studia turcologica memoriae Alexii Bombaci dicata*, ed. Aldo Galotta and Ugo Marazzi, pp. 515–36, Naples.
Smith, Christine, 1992, *Architecture in the Culture of Early Humanism: Ethics, Aesthetics, and Eloquence 1400–1470*, New York, Oxford.
—, 1989, 'Originality and Cultural Progress in the Quattrocento: Brunelleschi's Dome and a Letter by Alberti', *Rinascimento* 28, pp. 291–318.
—, 1987, 'Ciriaco d'Ancona's Seven Drawings of Santa Sofia', *Art Bulletin* 70, pp. 16–32.
Solakzade Mehmed, 1297 (1879), *Tārīḫ-i āl-i ʿosmān*, Istanbul.
Sönmez, Zeki, 1989, *Başlangıcından 16.Yüzyıla Kadar Anadolu Türk-İslam Mimarisinde Sanatçılar*, Ankara.
—, 1988a, *Mimar Sinan ile İlgili Tarihi Yazmalar-Belgeler*, Istanbul.
—, ed., 1988b, *Mimar Sinan Dönemi Türk Mimarlığı ve Sanatı*, Istanbul.
Soranzo, Jacopo, 1856, *Diario del Viaggio da Venezia a Costantinopoli*, Venice.
Sözen, Metin, 1992, photographs by Sami Güner, *Arts in the Age of Sinan*, Ankara.
—, ed., 1975, *Türk Mimarisinin Gelişimi ve Mimar Sinan*, Istanbul.
—, 1971, *Diyarbakır'da Türk Mimarisi*, Istanbul.
Steinach, Wolf Andreas von, 1881, 'Wolf Andreas von Steinach Edelknabenfahrt nach Constantinopel (1583)', in *Steiermärkische Geschichtsblätter*, Jahr II, no. 4, pp. 193–234.
Stephan, St. H., 1944, 'An Endowment Deed of Khāṣṣeki Sulṭān, Dated the 24th May 1552', *Quarterly of the Department of Antiquities in Palestine* 10, pp. 170–94.
Stichel, Rudolf H.W., 1996, 'Der Istanbuler Palast des osmanischen Grossvezirs Sokollu Mehmet Pascha (gest. 1579) in zeitgenössischen Abbildungen', *Architectura. Zeitschrift für Geschichte der Baukunst. Journal of the History of Architecture*, pp. 197–213.
Stierlin, Henri, 1985, *Soliman et l'architecture ottomane*, Fribourg.
Stirling-Maxwell, William, 1877, *Solyman the Magnificent Going to Mosque: From a Series of Engravings on Wood Published by Domenico De'Franceschi at Venice in MDLXIII*, Florence, Edinburgh.
—, 1873, *The Turks in MDXXXIII: A Series of Drawings made in that year at Constantinople by Peter Coeck of Aelst*, London, Edinburgh.
—, 1872, *Examples of Engraved Portraits of the Sixteenth Century*, London, Edinburgh.
Straton, Arthur, 1972, *Sinan*, London.
Su, Kamil, 1940, *Mimar Sinan'ın Eserlerinden Muradiye Camii*, Istanbul.
Sümer, Faruk, 1991, 'Yavuz Selim s'est-il proclamé calife?', *Turcica* 21–3, pp. 343–54.
Suzuki, Tadashi, 1990, 'Kanuni Sultan Süleyman'ın Veziriazamları ve Vezirleri', in *V. Milletlerası Türkiye Sosyal ve İktisat Tarihi Kongresi*, pp. 885–88, Ankara.
Talikizade, 1983, *Taʿlīkī-zāde's Şehnāme-i Hümāyūn: A History of the Ottoman Campaign into Hungary 1593–94*, ed. Christine Woodhead, Berlin.
al-Tamgruti, Abu'l Hasan, 1929, *En-nafhat el-miskiya fi-s-sifarat et-tourkiya: Relation d'une ambassade marocaine en Turquie (1589–1591)*, ed. and trans. H. de Castries, Paris.
Tanman, Baha M., 2001, 'Edirne Selimiye Camii'nin Hünkār Mahfilindeki bazı Ayrıntılardan II. Selim'in ve Mimar Sinan'ın "Dünyalarına"', in *Arkeoloji ve Sanat Tarihi Araştırmaları, Yıldız Demiriz'e Armağan*, ed. M. B. Tanman and U. Tükel, pp. 151–61, 239–45, Istanbul.
—, 1999, 'Erken Dönem Osmanlı Mimarisinde Memluk Etkileri', in *Osmanlı Mimarlığının 7 Yüzyılı "Uluslarüstü Bir Miras"*, ed. Nur Akın et al., pp. 82–91, Istanbul.
—, 1989, 'İstanbul Kasımpaşa'daki Piyale Paşa Külliyesi'nin Medresesi ve Tekkesi için bir Restitüsyon Denemesi', in *Sanat Tarihinde Doğudan Batıya : Ünsal Yücel Anısına Sempozyum Bildirileri*, pp. 87–94, Istanbul.
—, 1988a, 'Atik Valide Külliyesi', *Sanat Tarihi Araştırmaları Dergisi* 1:2, pp. 3–19.
—, 1988b, 'Sinan'ın Mimarisi: Tekkeler', in *Mimar Koca Sinan, Yaşadığı Çağ ve Eserleri*, ed. Sadi Bayram, 2 vols, 1:311–32, Istanbul.
Tanpınar, Ahmet Hamdi, 1996, 'İstanbul'un mevsimleri ve san'atlarımız', in *Yaşadığım Gibi*, pp. 141–57, Istanbul.
Tanyeli, Gülsün, 1996, 'Bir Osmanlı Kale-Kentinin Yapımı: Anavarin Örneği', in *Prof. Doğan Kuban'a Armağan*, ed. Zeynep Ahunbay, Deniz Mazlum and Kutgün Eyüpgiller, pp. 85–97, Istanbul.
Tanyeli, Gülsün and Uğur Tanyeli, 1993, '16. Yüzyıl Osmanlı Mimarlık Teknolojisi', in *Türk Kültüründe Sanat ve Mimari*, ed. Mehmet Saçlıoğlu and Gülsün Tanyeli, pp. 125–49, Istanbul.
Taşkıran, Nimet, 1972, *Hasekinin Kitabı*, Istanbul.
Tauer, Felix, 1953, 'Notice sur les versions persanes de la légende de l'édification d'Ayasofya', in *Fuat Köprülü Armağanı*, pp. 487–94, Istanbul.
Taut, Bruno, 1938, *Mimari Bilgisi*, Istanbul.
Tayfel, Johann Christoph, 1598, *Il Viaggio del Molto illustre signor Giovanni Christoforo Taifel, Barone in Gunderstoff Austriaco, fatto di Costantinopoli verso Levante*, Vienna.
Taylor, Rabun, 2003, *Roman Builders, A Study in Architectural Process*, Cambridge.
Tevkiʿi Abdurrahman Paşa, 1912–13, 'Kanunname', *Milli Tetebbular Mecmuası* 3, pp. 497–544.
Thys-Şenocak, Lucienne, 2000, 'The Yeni Valide Mosque Complex of Eminönü, Istanbul (1597-1665): Gender and Vision in Ottoman Architecture', in *Women, Patronage and Self-Representation in Islamic Societies*, ed. D. Fairchild Ruggles, pp. 69–89, New York.
—, 1998, 'The Yeni Valide Mosque Complex at Eminönü', *Muqarnas* 15, pp. 58–70.
—, 1994, 'The Yeni Valide Complex in Eminönü, Istanbul (1597–1665)', PhD thesis, University of Pennsylvania.
Tietze, Andreas, 1982, 'Muṣṭafā ʿĀlī on luxury and the Status Symbols of Ottoman Gentlemen', in *Studia turcologica memoriae Alexii Bombaci dicata*, ed. Aldo Galotta and Ugo Marazzi, pp. 577–90, Naples.

Trachtenberg, Marvin, 1997, *Dominion of the Eye: Urbanism, Art and Power in Early Modern Florence*, Cambridge.
Tüfekçioğlu, Abdülhamit, 2001, *Erken Dönem Osmanlı Mimarīsinde Yazı*, Ankara.
Tuncay, Rauf, 1969, 'Edirne'de Selimiye Camii', *Belgelerle Türk Tarih Dergisi* 23, pp. 3–12.
Tuncel, Mehmet, 1974, *Babaeski, Kırklareli ve Tekirdağ Camileri*, Ankara.
Tuncer, Cezmi Orhan, 1996, *Diyarbakır Camileri: Mukarnas, Geometri, Orantı*, Diyarbakır.
Turan, Şerafettin, 1965, 'Gli architetti imperiali (Hassa mimarları) nell'impero Ottomano', in *Atti del secondo congresso internazionale di arte turca*, pp. 259–63, Naples.
—, 1963, 'Osmanlı Teşkilātında Hassa Mimarları', *Tarih Araştırmaları Dergisi* 1:1, pp. 157–202.
—, 1961, *Kanunī'nin oğlu Şehzāde Bayezid Vak'ası*, Ankara.
—, 1958. 'Lala Mustafa Paşa hakkında Notlar ve Vesikalar', *Belleten* 88, pp. 551–93.
Tursun Beg, 1978, *The History of Mehmed the Conqueror by Tursun Beg*, ed. Halil İnalcık and Rhoads Murphey, Minneapolis, Chicago.
Uçtum, Nejat R., 1980, 'Hürrem ve Mihrümah Sultanların Polonya Kıralı II. Zigismund'a Yazdıkları Mektuplar', *Belleten* 44, pp. 697–715.
Ülgen, Ali Saim, 1989, *Mimar Sinan Yapıları*, 2 vols, Ankara.
Uluçam, Abdüsselam, 2000, *Ortaçağ ve Sonrasında Van Gölü Çevresi Mimarlığı: Van*, vol. 1, Ankara.
—, 1989, *Irak'taki Türk Mimari Eserleri*, Ankara.
Uluçay, Çağatay, 1980, *Padişahların Kadınları ve Kızları*, Ankara.
—, 1956, *Harem'den Mektuplar*, Istanbul.
Ünal, Mehmet Ali, ed., 1995, *Mühimme Defteri* 44, İzmir.
Ünsal, Behçet, 1963, 'Topkapı Sarayı Arşivinde Bulunan Mimari Planlar Üzerine', *Türk Sanat Tarihi Araştırma ve İncelemeleri* 1, pp. 168–97.
Ürekli, Muzaffer, 1989, *Kırım Hanlığının Kuruluşu ve Osmanli Himayesinde Yükselişi (1441–1569)*, Ankara.
Uzunçarşılı, İsmail Hakkı, 1984–88, *Osmanlı Devleti Teşkilatından Kapıkulu Ocakları*, 2 vols, Ankara.
—, 1976, 'Yavuz Sultan Selim'in Kızı Hanım Sultan ve Torunu Kara Osman Şah Bey Vakfiyeleri', *Türk Tarih Kurumu Belleten* 159, pp. 467–78.
—, 1945, *Osmanlı Devletinin Saray Teşkilatı*, Ankara.
—, 1932, *Kütahya Şehri*, Istanbul.
Vanmour, Jean Baptiste, 1714, *Recueil de cent estampes représentant différents nations du Levant gravées sur les tableaux peints d'après nature en 1707 & 1708 par les ordres de M. de Ferriol, et mis au jour en 1712 & 1713 par les soins de M. Le Hay*, Paris.
Vasari, Giorgio, 1963, *The Lives of Painters, Sculptors and Architects*, ed. William Gaunt, 4 vols, New York.
Vatin, Nicolas, 1995, 'Aux origines de pèlerinage à Eyüp des sultans ottomans', *Turcica* 27, pp. 91–99.
Vatin, Nicolas and Stéphane Yerasimos, 1994, 'Documents sur les cimetières ottomans II. Status, police et pratiques quotidiennes (1565-1585)', *Turcica* 26, pp. 169–210.
—, 2001, *Les Cimetières dans la ville: Statut, choix et organisation des lieux d'inhumation dans Istanbul intra-muros (*Varia Turcica 35*)*, Istanbul, Paris.
Vogt-Göknil, Ulya, 1993, *Sinan*, Tübingen, Berlin.
—, 1986, 'Sinan und seine zeitgenossen im Westen', in *II. International Congress on the History of Turkish and Islamic Science and Technology*, 3 vols, 2:169–79, Istanbul.
Watenpaugh, Heghnar, 1999, 'The Image of An Ottoman City: Imperial Architecture and the Representation of Urban Life in Aleppo in the Sixteenth and Seventeenth Centuries', PhD thesis, University of Los Angeles.
Weber, Stefan, 1997–98, 'The Creation of Ottoman Damascus: Architecture and Urban Development of Damascus in the 16th and 17th centuries', *Aram* 9–10, pp. 431–70.
Wilber, Donald M., 1955, *Architecture of Islamic Iran: The Il-Khanid Period*, Princeton.
Williams, John A., 1969, 'The Monuments of Ottoman Cairo', in *Colloque international sur l'histoire du Caire*, pp. 453–63, Cairo.
Winkelhane, Gerd, and Klaus Schwarz, 1985, *Der osmanische Statthalter İskender Pascha (gest. 1571) und seine Stiftungen in Ägypten und am Bosphorus*, Bamberg.
Wittkower, Rudolf, 1949, *Architectural Principles in the Age of Humanism*, London, New York.
Wratislaw von Mitrowitz (Baron Wenceslas), 1862, *Adventures of Baron Wenceslas Wratislaw of Mitrowitz*, trans. A. H. Wratilaw, London.
Yaltkaya, Şerafettin, 1942, 'Kara Ahmet Paşa Vakfiyesi', *Vakıflar Dergisi* 2, pp. 43–167.
Yemşel, D. Samuel, 1956, '1641–42 de bir Karayit'in Türkiye Seyahatnāmesi', *Vakıflar Dergisi* 3, pp. 97–106 (trans. F. Selçuk).
Yenişehirlioğlu, Filiz, 1982, 'XVI. yy. Osmanlı Dönemi Yapılarında Görülen Mimari Süsleme Programlarında Mimar Sinan'ın Katkısı Var mıdır?', *Mimarlık* 5–6, pp. 29–35.
—, 1985, 'Les Grandes Lignes de l'evolution du programme décoratif en céramique des monuments ottomans au cours du XVIe siècle', *Erdem* 1:2, pp. 453–76.
—, 1980, 'Şehzade Mehmet Türbesi Çinileri Üzerine Gözlemler', in *Bedrettin Cömert'e Armağan*, pp. 449–56, Ankara.
Yerasimos, Stéphane, 2002, *Süleymaniye*, trans. Alp Tümertekin, Istanbul (*La Mosquée de Soliman*, Paris, 1997).
—, 2000, *Constantinople, Capitale d'empires: De Byzance à Istanbul*, Paris.
—, 1991, *Les Voyageurs dans l'Empire ottoman (XIVe-XVIe siècles)*, Ankara.
—, 1990, *La fondation de Constantinople et de Sainte-Sophie dans les traditions turques*, Paris.
—, 1987. 'Sinan and his Patrons: Programme and Location', in *Mimar Sinan: The Urban Vision* (*Environmental Design* nos. 1–2), ed. A Petruccioli, pp. 124–31, Rome.
Yörüklüoğlu, Nihat, 1984, *Hafsa Sultan ve Külliyesi*, Ankara.
Yücel, Yaşar, and Selami Pulaha, eds, 1995, *I. Selim Kānūnnāmesi (Tirana ve Leningrad nüshaları, 1512-1520)*, Ankara.
Yüksel, I. Aydın, 2004, *Osmanlı Mimârîsinde Kānûnî Sultan Süleyman Devri (926–974/1520–1566): İstanbul*, Istanbul.
—, 1995, 'Sadrāzam Rüstem Paşa'nın Vakıfları', in *Ekrem Hakkı Ayverdi Hātıra Kitabı*, pp. 219–81, Istanbul.
—, 1993, *Bolu Yıldırım Bayezid Külliyesi, Hamamlar ve İmaret Camii*, Ankara.
—, 1983, *Osmanlı Mimârisînde II. Bāyezid ve Yavuz Selim Devri (886–926/1481–1520)*, Istanbul.
Yusuf bin Abdullah, 1997, *Tarih-i Āl-i Osman*, ed. Efdal Sevinçli, İzmir.
Zakir Şükri Efendi, 1980, *Die Istanbuler Derwisch-Konvente und ihre Scheiche (Mecmu'a-i Tekaya)*, ed. Mehmet Serhan Tayşi and Klaus Kreiser, Freiburg im Breisgau.
Zen, Catharin, 1878, 'Descrizione del viazo di Costantinopoli [1550] de ser Catharina Zen, ambassador straordinario a Sultan Soliman e suo ritorno', in Petar Matkovic, ed., *Dva Talijanska Putopisa Po Balkanskom Poluotoku iz XVI. Vieka*, Zagreb.
Zilfi, Madeline C., ed., 1996, *Women in the Ottoman Empire: Middle Eastern Women in the Early Modern Era*, Leiden.
—, 1988, *The Politics of Piety: The Ottoman Ulema in the Postclassical Age (1600–1800)*, Minneapolis.

MAPS

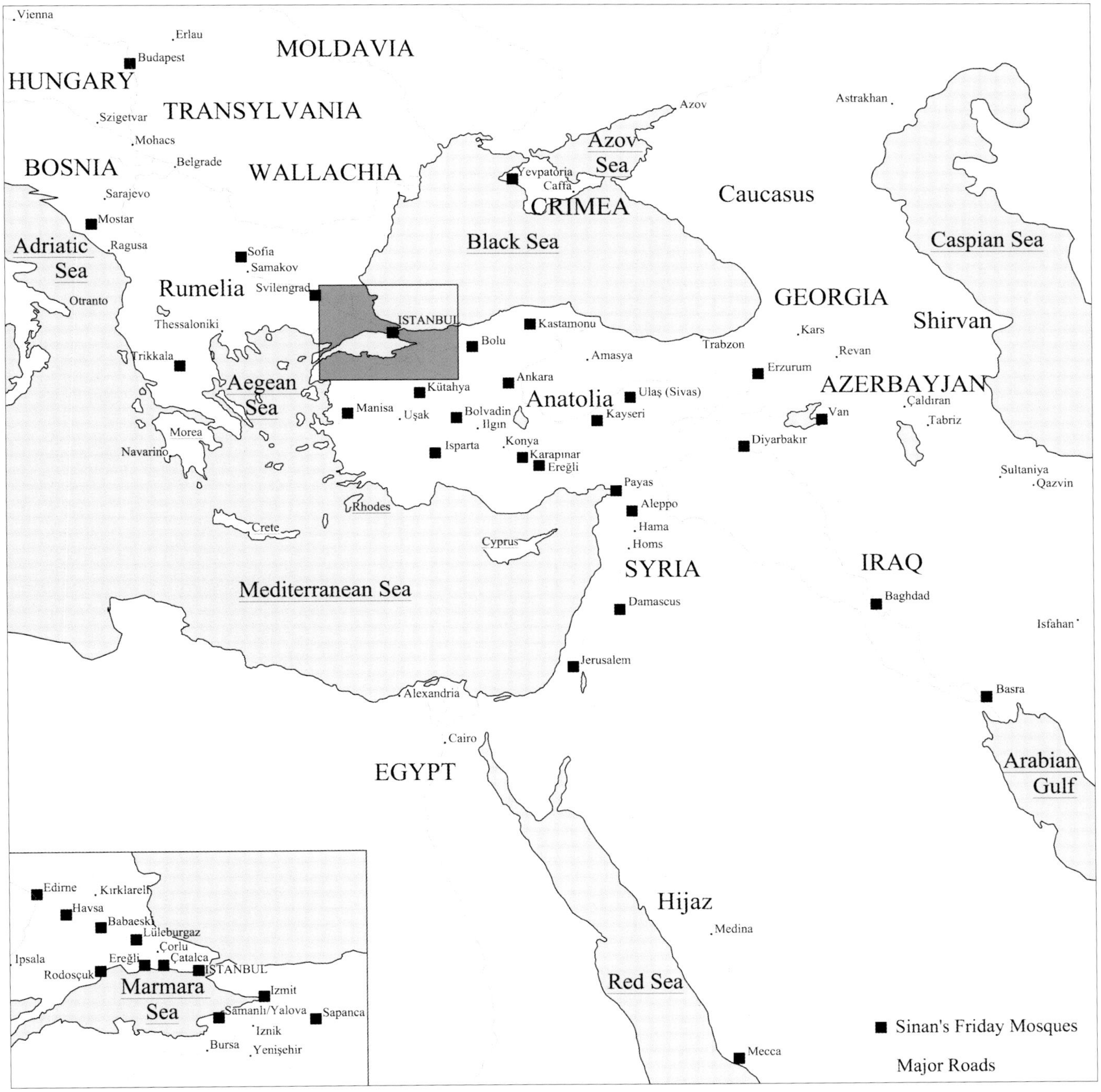

1. Geographical Distribution of Sinan's Mosques.

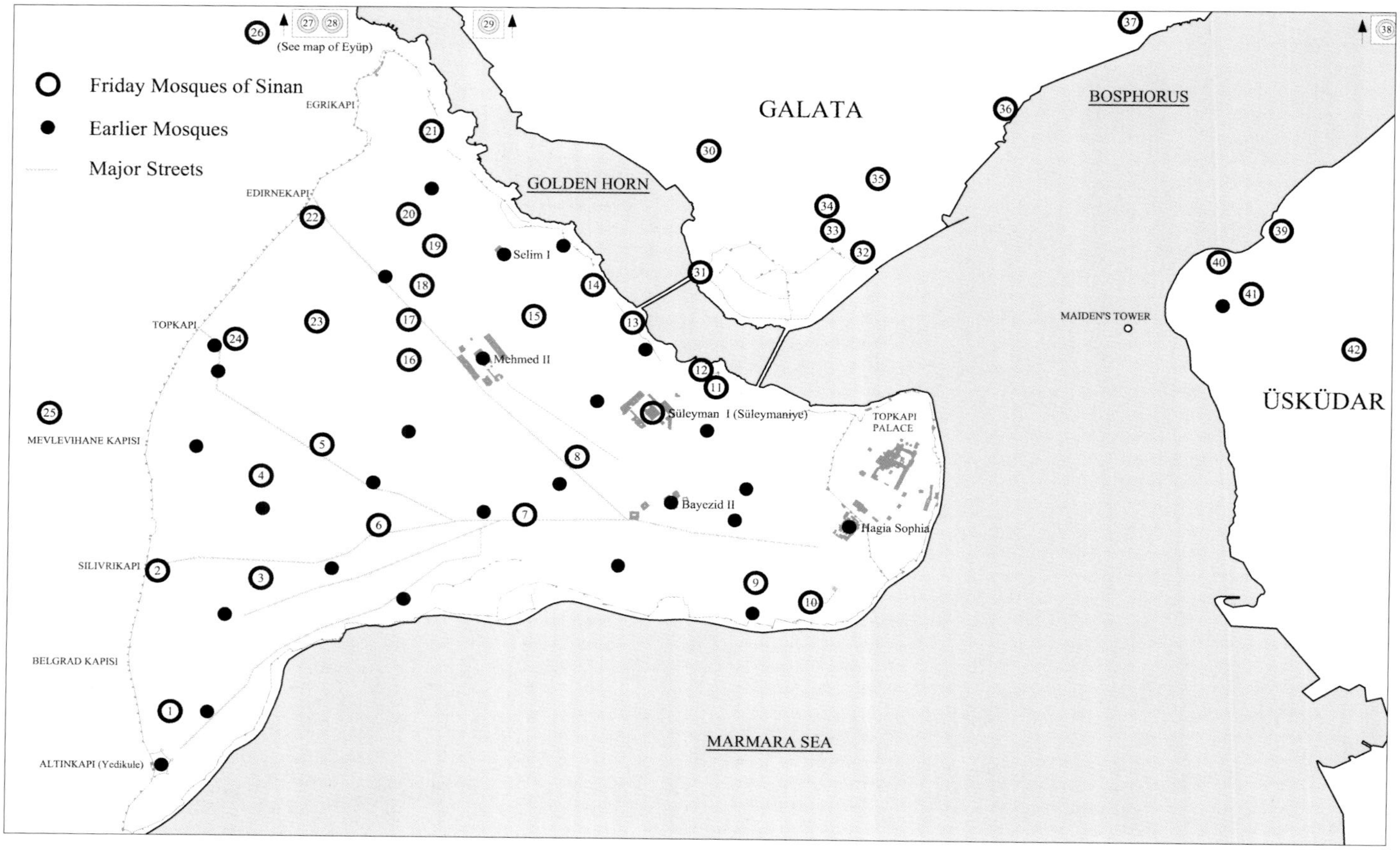

2. Istanbul: Friday Mosques.

LOCATION	PATRON / NAME OF MOSQUE
1. Yedikule	Kasap Ustası Hacı Evhad
2. Silivrikapı	Hadim İbrahim Pasha
3. Kocamustafapaşa	Bezirganbaşı Hüsrev Çelebi (Ramazan Efendi Mosque)
4. Şehremini (Yenibahçe)	Odabaşı Behruz Agha
5. Çapa (Yenibahçe)	Kasasker Abdurrahman Çelebi
6. Haseki (Avratpazarı)	Hürrem Sultan (Haseki Sultan Mosque)
7. Aksaray	Osmanshah's mother
8. Şehzadebaşı	Şehzade Mehmed
9. Kadırgalimanı	İsmihan Sultan and Sokollu Mehmed Pasha (Mehmed Pasha Mosque)
10. Ahırkapı	Kapıağası Mahmud Agha
11. Tahtakale	Rüstem Pasha
12. Yemişiskelesi	Ahi Çelebi
13. Unkapanı	Süleyman Subaşı (Unkapanı Mosque)
14. Cibali	Defterdar Süleyman Çelebi (Üsküblü Mosque)
15. Fatih (Kadıçeşmesi)	Bina Emini Sinan Agha
16. Yenibahçe	Bali Pasha (Hüma Hatun Mosque)
17. Yenibahçe	Mesih Mehmed Pasha
18. Karagümrük	Nişancı Mehmed Pasha
19. Çarşamba	Mehmed Agha
20. Draman	Dragoman (Tercüman) Yunus Beg
21. Balat	Ferruh Kethüda (Balat Mosque)
22. Edirnekapı	Mihrümah Sultan (Edirnekapı Mosque)
23. Karagümrük (Yenibahçe)	Hürrem Çavuş
24. Topkapı	Kara Ahmed Pasha (Topkapı Mosque)
25. Merkezefendi (outside Yenikapı)	Shahsultan (Merkez Efendi Mosque)
26. Eyüp	Nişancı Mustafa Çelebi
27. Eyüp	Shahsultan and Zal Mahmud Pasha (Zal Pasha Mosque)
28. Eyüp	Shahsultan
29. Sütlüce	Çavuşbaşı Mahmud Agha (Sütlüce Mosque)
30. Kasımpaşa	Piyale Pasha (Tersane Mosque)
31. Azapkapı	Sokollu Mehmed Pasha (Azapkapı Mosque)
32. Tophane	Kılıç Ali Pasha (Tophane Mosque)
33. Tophane	Defterdar Ebulfazl Mehmed Efendi
34. Tophane (Çukurcuma)	Muhyiddin Mehmed Çelebi (Çukurcuma Mosque)
35. Cihangir (Tophane)	Şehzade Cihangir
36. Fındıklı	Molla Çelebi (Fındıklı Mosque)
37. Beşiktaş	Sinan Pasha (Beşiktaş Mosque)
38. Kanlıca (Bosphorus)	Bostancıbaşı İskender Pasha
39. Üsküdar	Mihrümah Sultan (İskele Mosque)
40. Üsküdar	Şemsi Ahmed Pasha
41. Üsküdar	Mevlana Ensari Ahmed Efendi (Mevlana Efendi Mosque)
42. Üsküdar	Nurbanu Sultan (Atik Valide Mosque)

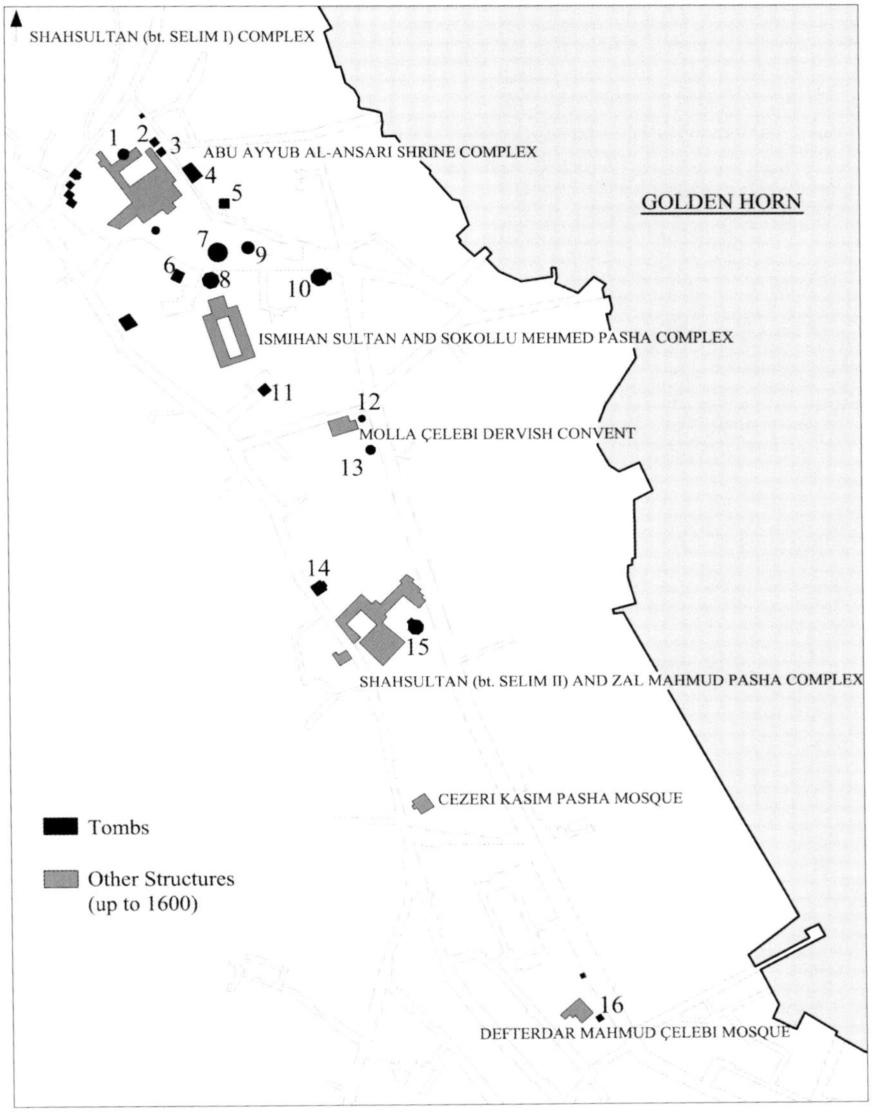

3. Eyüp: Tombs of Grandees and Complexes.

1. Abu Ayyub al-Ansari
2. Ayas Mehmed Pasha
3. Lala Mustafa Pasha
4. Pertev Mehmed Pasha
5. Feridun Ahmed Beg
6. Ebussuud Efendi
7. Siyavus Pasha
8. Sokollu Mehmed Pasha
9. Mirmiran Mehmed Agha
10. Ferhad Pasha
11. Cafer Pasha
12. Hubbi Hatun
13. Molla Çelebi
14. Nakkaş Hasan Pasha
15. Shahsultan and Zal Mahmud Pasha
16. Defterdar Mahmud Çelebi

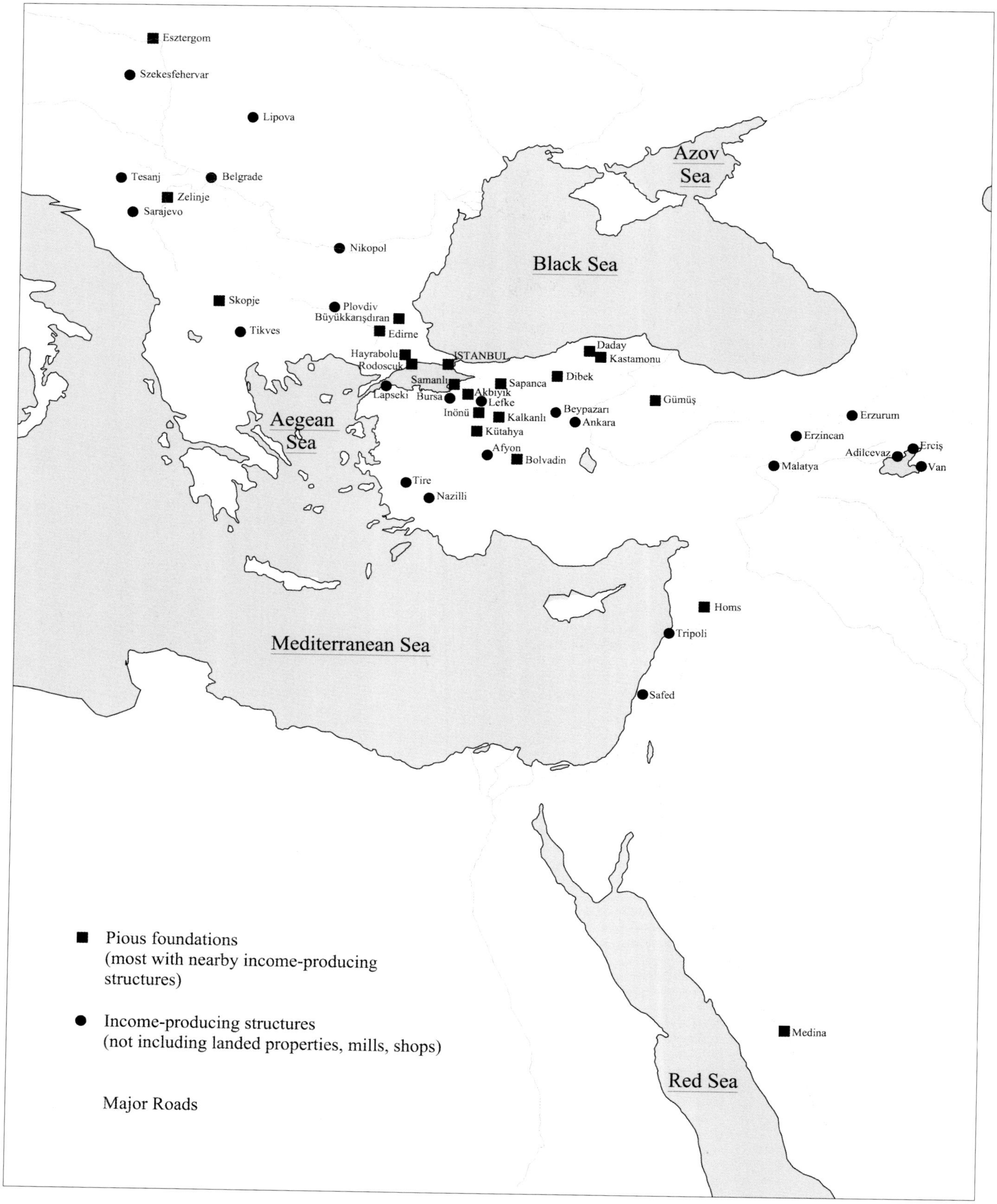

Esztergom
Szekesfehervar
Lipova
Tesanj
Belgrade
Zelinje
Sarajevo
Nikopol
Azov Sea
Black Sea
Skopje
Plovdiv
Büyükkarışdıran
Tikves
Edirne
Hayrabolu
Rodoscuk
ISTANBUL
Daday
Kastamonu
Samanlı
Dibek
Sapanca
Lapseki
Bursa
Akbıyık
Lefke
Gümüş
Inönü
Kalkanlı
Beypazarı
Ankara
Erzurum
Aegean Sea
Kütahya
Erzincan
Afyon
Bolvadin
Adilcevaz
Erciş
Malatya
Van
Tire
Nazilli
Homs
Tripoli
Mediterranean Sea
Safed
Pious foundations
(most with nearby income-producing structures)
Income-producing structures
(not including landed properties, mills, shops)
Major Roads
Medina
Red Sea

4. The Waqfs of Rüstem Pasha.

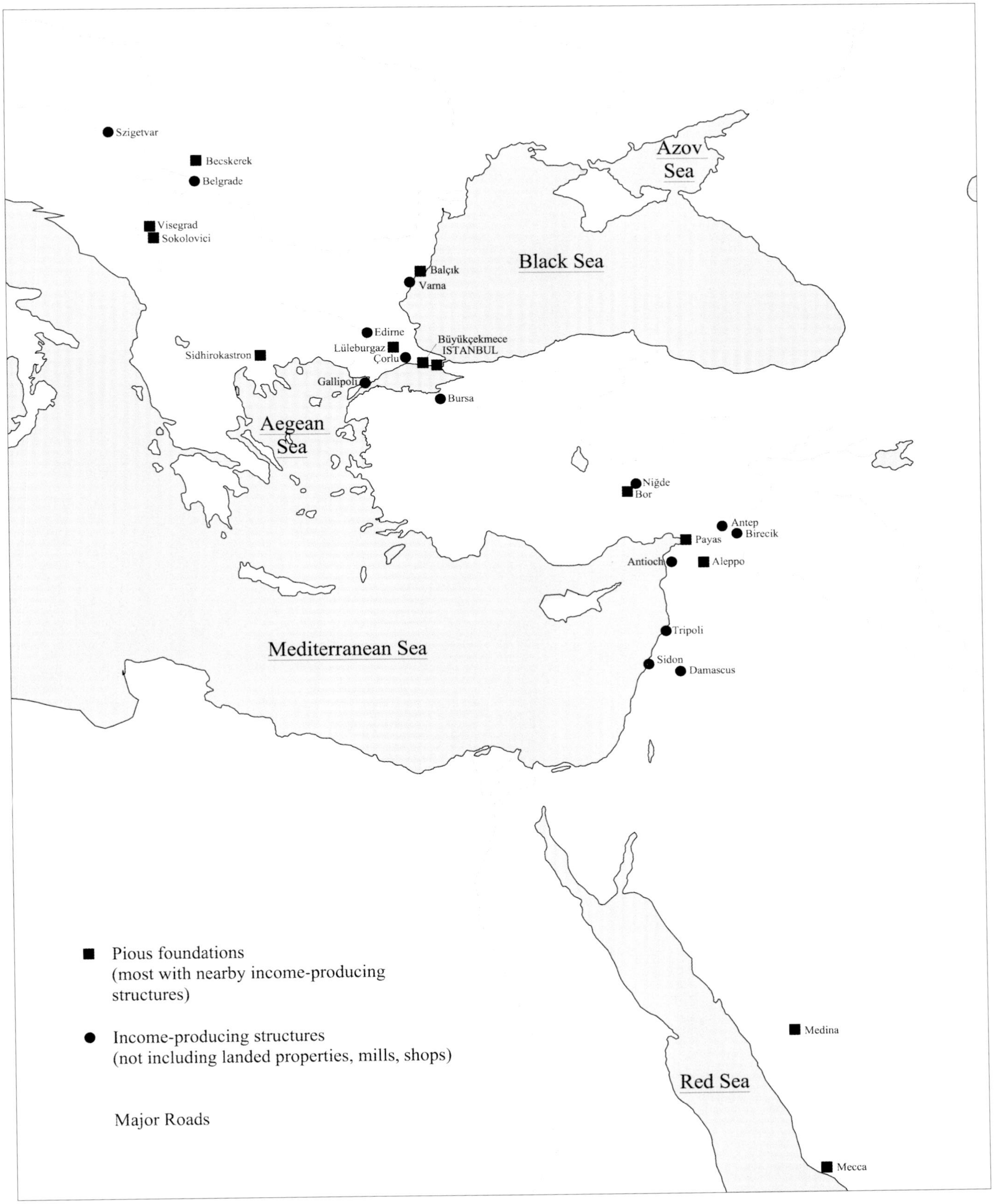
Szigetvar
Becskerek
Belgrade
Visegrad
Sokolovici
Azov Sea
Black Sea
Balçık
Varna
Edirne
Lüleburgaz
Çorlu
Büyükçekmece
ISTANBUL
Sidhirokastron
Gallipoli
Bursa
Aegean Sea
Niğde
Bor
Antep
Birecik
Payas
Antioch
Aleppo
Tripoli
Sidon
Damascus
Mediterranean Sea
Pious foundations
(most with nearby income-producing structures)
Income-producing structures
(not including landed properties, mills, shops)
Major Roads
Medina
Red Sea
Mecca

5. The Waqfs of Sokollu Mehmed Pasha.

PHOTOGRAPHIC ACKNOWLEDGEMENTS

The author and publishers wish to express their thanks to the following sources of illustrative material and/or permission to reproduce it. Donor or collection details are in some cases also given below; for credits for material reproduced with kind permission from books, please consult the Select Bibliography for fuller information.

Reproduced with permission from the copyright holder Altajir World of Islam Trust from Hillenbrand [2002]: 258 (numerals added by the author); American Academy in Rome: 74 (inv. no. 23); drawings by Arben N. Arapi: 3, 4, 5, 27, 28, 78, 85, 87, 154, 155, 167, 168, 190, 191, 203, 204, 209, 210, 236, 237, 245, 251, 252, 261, 262, 265, 274, 276, 279, 280, 286, 287, 296, 297, 301, 302, 318, 320, 321, 335 (after F. Müderrisoglu), 336, 344 (after F. Müderrisoglu), 345, 351, 353, 361, 362, 370, 371, 380, 388, 389, 391, 395, 396, 401, 402, 404, 405, 409, 413, 414, 420, 421, 422, 424 (reconstruction of madrasa and convent cells after B. Tanman), 425, 431, 432, 445, 447 (after a hypothetical reconstruction by M. Kiel), 449, 452, 454, 461 463, 468, 472, 475, 479, 482, 488, 491, 496, 501, 502, 505, 506, 509, 510, 511, 512, 513, 517, 518, 521, 522, 526, 527, 532, 534, 536, 540, 542, 543; drawings by Arben N. Arapi and N. Semiz: 381, 515, 516; photos by the author: 21, 113, 141, 183, 192, 193, 194, 195, 196, 197, 205, 207, 232, 233, 246, 247, 248, 249, 298, 398, 410, 450, 453, 455, 462, 465, 498, 500, 507, 528; Bayerische Staatsgemäldesammlungen, Munich (Alte Pinakotek): 8 (2239), 9 (2248); Biblioteca Apostolica Vaticana, Vatican City, Rome: 70 (Barberini Codex lat. 4424, fol. 28r [from Huelsen, 1910]), 71 (as 70, fol. 44r); photos Bibliothèque Nationale de France, Paris: 295 (Cabinet des Estampes, Res. B. 10), 531 (Estampes et Photographie, no. 2309564); Bildarchiv Preussischer Kulturbesitz, Berlin: 104, 278, 352; courtesy of the Bodleian Library, University of Oxford (Ms. Bodl. Or. 430, fol. 2r): 101, 166; print courtesy of the Boston Athenaeum [from Grelot, 1683]: 541; from Braun and Hogenberg [1572–1618 (vol. 5, p. 60)]: 93; British Library, London: 50 (Add. Ms. 22011, fol. 198v); British Museum, London: 250 (Department of Prints and Drawings, 1878. 4166); from Bumin et al. [1993]: 53, 211, 212, 221; from Burgoyne, 1987: 259; from Camocio [1571]: 32; Castello Sforzesco, Milan: 69 (Civiche Raccolte Archeologiche e Numismatiche), 75, 76, 77 (all Civica Raccolte delle Stampe 'Achille Bertarelli'); The Chester Beatty Library, Dublin (Ms. T. 413, photos reproduced by kind permission of the Trustees of the Chester Beatty Library): frontispiece (fol. 115v), 1 (fol. 115v), 48 (fol. 12v), 118 (fols. 115v–116r), 119 (fols. 22v–23r); photos courtesy of W. Denny: 38, 175, 176, 225, 240, 241, 242, 244, 311, 312, 342; Denizcilik Müzesi, Istanbul: 127 (66. 65, photo courtesy of F. Çagman); Divan Edebiyati Müzesi, Istanbul: 149 (no. 300); from Esin [1974]: 138; Fatih Millet Kütüphanesi, Istanbul: 143 (Ms. 930); from Filarete [1972, vol. II]: 65 (details from fols. 82v, 83v); Galleria degli Uffizi, Florence: 68 (Gabinetto dei Disegni e Stampe Uff. 1A); from Gaube and Wirth [1984]; 490, 495; Germanisches Nationalmuseum, Nürnberg: 58; photos from Gurlitt [1907-12]: 323, 426, 437; photos by Reha Günay: 22, 24, 37, 63, 64, 67, 79, 81, 83, 84, 97, 98, 99, 110, 121, 122, 125, 126, 156, 158, 159, 160, 161, 162, 163, 164, 169, 170, 172, 173, 174, 177, 178, 179, 180, 181, 184, 185, 186, 187, 201, 202, 206, 208, 213, 214, 215, 216, 218, 219, 220, 222, 223, 224, 226, 227, 228, 229, 230, 231, 234, 239, 243, 256, 257, 266, 267, 270, 271, 272, 273, 275, 282, 283, 284, 285, 288, 289, 290, 291, 292, 293, 299, 300, 303, 304, 305, 306, 307, 308, 309, 310, 313, 314, 315, 319, 322, 325, 326, 327, 328, 329, 330, 331, 332, 333, 334, 339, 340, 341, 343, 346, 347, 348, 349, 350, 355, 356, 357, 358, 359, 360, 363, 364, 365, 366, 367, 368, 369, 372, 373, 374, 375, 376, 377, 378, 379, 382, 383, 384, 385, 390, 392, 393, 394, 399, 403, 407, 408, 411, 412, 415, 416, 417, 418, 419, 423, 427, 428, 429, 430, 435, 436, 438, 439, 440, 441, 442, 443, 446, 451, 456, 457, 458, 460, 464, 466, 469, 470, 471, 473, 476, 477, 478, 480, 481, 483, 484, 485, 486, 487, 503, 504, 514, 519, 520, 524, 525, 529, 535, 537, 544, 546; photo courtesy of the Fine Arts Library, Fogg Art Museum, Harvard University: 57, 182, 497; with permission from the Fondation Le Corbusier: 294 [FLC 2385, from Le Corbusier, 1989]; photos courtesy of the Houghton Library, Harvard University: 6 [from Stirling-Maxwell, 1872], 10 [from Stirling-Maxwell, 1873], 11 [from Stirling-Maxwell, 1877], 14 [from Marsili, 1732], 73 [from Serlio, *Libro d'architettura*, Antwerp, 1546, vol. III, fol. 64v], 112 [from de Nicolay, Antwerp, 1576, fol. 128], 114 [from de Nicolay, Antwerp, 1576, fol. 137], 189 [from Carne, 1836–8], 199, 337 [from Mayer, 1801], 338 [from Mayer, 1801], 354, [from Allom, 1938, vol. I], 434 [from Choiseul-Gouffier, 1782, vol. II, plate 95], 545 [from D'Ohsson, 1788, vol. I]; IRCICA (The Research Centre for Islamic History, Art and Culture), Istanbul, Photo Archive: 260 (Abdülhamid Album, no. 9041), Istanbul Technical University Archive: 217; Istanbul University Library: 34 (T. 5964, fol. 105r, after Yurdaydin [1976]), 51 (T. 5964, fols. 31v–32r, after Yurdaydin [1976]), 102 (T. 5964, fols. 8v–9r, after Yurdaydin [1976]), 123 (F. 1404, fols. 56v–57r), 264 (F. 1404, fol. 58r), 489 (F. 1404, fols. 105v–106r); photo courtesy of M. Kiel: 448; from Kuban [1997]: 96; photo courtesy of D. Kuban: 255; Kunsthistorisches Museum, Vienna: 91 (Gemäldegalerie G. G. 29), 235 (Ambras series, no. 5181), 316 (Ambras series, no. 5192, E. 19), 317 (Ambras series, no. 5193, E. 20); Los Angeles County Museum of Art: 30 right (The Edwin Binney 3rd Collection of Turkish Art, M. 85. 237. 20); Museo Civico Correr, Venice: 25, 26 (Ms. Cicogna 1971, fol. 29r), 92, 254 (Ms. Cicogna 1971); Muzeum Mazowieckie w Plocku, Plock: 277 (MMP/S/2); Österreichische Nationalbibliothek, Vienna [ÖNB] (Cod. 8615, Löwenklau album): 13 (fols. 137r–139v), 17 (fol. 116r), 89 (fol. 151r), 90 (fol. 152r), 109 (fol. 129r), 406, 433, 444 (fol. 155r), 467; ÖNB (Cod. 8626*, after Babinger [1959]): 100 top (fols. 159v–160r), 165 (159v–160r); ÖNB (Cod. 8626, after Babinger [1959]): 100 middle, 100 bottom, 171; ÖNB (Cod. 8627): 61; from Plyviou [1994]: 147, 148; Prince and Princess Sadruddin Aga Khan Collection, Geneva: 30 left (TM. 5); photo courtesy of Günsel Renda: 127; from Riefstahl [1930]: 39; Rijksmuseum, Amsterdam: 94 (Rijksprentenkabinett), 459 (SK-A-2055); Sächsische Landesbibliothek, Dresden: 19 (Mscr. J 2a); from G. Sandys, 1621: 253; from Sauvaget, 1941, vol. II: 492, 493; from J. Schrenk von Notzing, *Augustissimorum Imperatorum… imagines…* [Innsbruck, 1601]: 16; from Schweigger [1606]: 31, 41; drawings by N. Semiz: 400, 508; Staats-und-Universitätsbibliothek, Bremen: 18 (Lambert de Vos album, Ms. or. 9, no 71 [from De Vos, 1991]); Staatsbibliothek zu Berlin: 104, 278, 352 (all Orientabteilung, Diez A fol. 57, fols. 28r–v); Statens Museum for Kunst, Copenhagen (Koneglige Kobberstiksamling): 7, 105, 153, 188; Topkapi Sarayi Müzesi Arsivi, Istanbul: 62 (E. 9495/8), 111 (D. 1461), 139 (E. 9495/11), 144 (E. 9495/12), 145 (E. 6342), 146 (E. 12307/2), 474 (E. 9487); Topkapi Sarayi Müzesi Kütüphanesi, Istanbul: 12 (A. 3595, fol. 11v), 15 (H. 1517, fol. 31v), 29 (H. 2134, fol. 8r), 35 (H. 1524, fol. 283r), 40 (H. 1365, fol. 36r), 42 (H. 1523, fols. 146v–47r), 43 (A. 3595, fol. 56v), 44 (H. 1524, fol. 288v), 46 (H. 1524, fol. 290r), 47 (H. 1524, fol. 291r), 49 (H. 1365, fols 195v-196r), 95 (H. 1344, fols. 58v–59r), 103 (H. 1523, fols. 158v–59r), 115 (H. 1365, fol. 113r), 116 (B. 200, fol. 107r), 117 (B. 200, fol. 152r), 120 (A. 3595, fol. 55v), 129 (A. 3593, fols 161r–160v), 130 (A. 1344, fols. 190v–91r), 131 (A. 1344, fols. 128v–29r), 132 (A. 1344, fols. 172v–73r), 133 (A. 1344, fol. 402r), 134 (A. 1344, fol. 325r), 135 (A. 1344, fol. 345r), 136 (A. 1344, fol. 349r), 137 (A. 5395, fol. 95v), 142 (H. 1815), 151 (A. 3593, fol. 162v), 152 (A. 3594, fol. 5v), 198 (H. 2134, fol. 3r), 200 (A. 3595, fol. 156r), 238 (A. 3592, fols. 10v–11r), 263 (B. 200, fol. 146r), 397 (A. 3595, fol. 28r, photo courtesy of Barry Wood), 538 (H. 889, fol. 22r), 539 (H. 1609, fols. 68v–69r); Trinity College Library, Cambridge (Ms. o. 17. 2, the Freshfield album): 107 (fol. 20), 108 (fol. 21); Türk Islam Eserleri Müzesi, Istanbul (photo courtesy of F. Çagman): 150; Türk ve Islam Sanatlari Müzesi, Istanbul: 157 (Tarih no. 3339 [from Çeçen, 1991a]), 523 (Ms. 1973, fol. 88v); reproduced by permission of the Universitäts- und Landesbibliothek, Düsseldorf: 72 (Ms. G. 13, *Liber Insularum Archipelagi*, fol. 54r); Universiteits Bibliotheek, Leiden (Cod. 1758): 33, 106; from Ünsal [1963]: 140; Uppsala Universitetsbibliotek: 530 (Ms. Celcius, 1, fols. 1v–2r [from Frankfurt, 1985, vol. II]); from Vanmour [1714]: 128; Wallraf-Richartz-Museum, Köln (Graphische Sammlung, Rheinisches Bildarchiv, Hittorff-Nachlass): 268 (Je. 97), 269 (Je. 93), 281 (Je. 99), 533 (Je. 88); photo J. Wayman Williams (Princeton University exhibition of 1990): 56; photos courtesy of Steven Wolf: 494 (top and bottom), 499; from *Yedigün*, 11 [1938]: 2; drawings by Z. Yürekli: 20 (after A. Gabriel), 23 (after G. Goodwin), 36, 45 (after F. Müderrisoglu), 52, 54 (after Müller-Wiener), 55, 59, 60, 66, 80, 82, 86, 88, 124 (after Aygen Bilge), 324, 386 (after Stainova).

INDEX

Numbers in *italics* refer to pages on which illustrations can be found; the locations of monuments are shown in brackets after the name, e.g. Abdal Ata convent (Çorum).